P9-DBI-992

ENCYCLOPEDIA OF PSYCHOLOGY

ENCYCLOPEDIA OF PSYCHOLOGY

Alan E. Kazdin

Editor in Chief

VOLUME 1

AMERICAN
PSYCHOLOGICAL
ASSOCIATION

OXFORD
UNIVERSITY PRESS

2000

AMERICAN
PSYCHOLOGICAL
ASSOCIATION

Washington, D.C.

OXFORD
UNIVERSITY PRESS

Oxford   New York

Athens   Auckland   Bangkok   Bogotá   Buenos Aires   Calcutta
Cape Town   Chennai   Dar es Salaam   Delhi   Florence   Hong Kong   Istanbul
Karachi   Kuala Lumpur   Madrid   Melbourne   Mexico City   Mumbai
Nairobi   Paris   São Paulo   Singapore   Taipei   Tokyo   Toronto   Warsaw

and associated companies in
Berlin   Ibadan

Copyright © 2000 by American Psychological Association and Oxford University Press, Inc.

Published by American Psychological Association
750 First Street, NE, Washington, D.C. 20002-4242
www.apa.org
and
Oxford University Press, Inc.
198 Madison Avenue, New York, New York 10016
www.oup.com

Oxford is a registered trademark of Oxford University Press.

Library of Congress Cataloging-in-Publication Data
Encyclopedia of psychology / Alan E. Kazdin, editor in chief
p.   cm.
Includes bibliographical references and index.
1. Psychology—Encyclopedias.   I. Kazdin, Alan E.
BF31 .E52   2000   150'.3—dc21   99-055239
ISBN 1-55798-187-6 (set); ISBN 1-55798-650-9 (vol. 1)

AMERICAN PSYCHOLOGICAL ASSOCIATION STAFF

Gary R. VandenBos, Ph.D., *Publisher*
Julia Frank-McNeil, *Commissioning Editor*
Theodore J. Baroody, *Senior Development Editor*
Adrian Harris Forman, *Project Editor*

OXFORD UNIVERSITY PRESS STAFF

Karen Casey, *Publisher*
Claude Conyers, *Commissioning Editor*
Marion Osmun, *Senior Development Editor*
Matthew Giarratano, *Managing Editor*
Peri Zeenkov and Norina Frabotta, *Project Editors*
Nancy Hoagland, *Production Manager*
Jessica Ryan and Will Moore, *Production Editors*
AEIOU, Inc., *Index Editor*
AEIOU, Inc., Linda Berman, Denise McIntyre,
Space Coast Indexers, Inc., Linda Webster, *Indexers*
Suzanne Holt, *Book Design*
Joan Greenfield, *Cover Design*

1 3 5 7 9 8 6 4 2

Printed in the United States of America
on acid-free paper

CONTENTS

EDITORIAL BOARD

PREFACE

Psychology is a field of scientific study that is diverse in its foci, content, and methods. Core topics in psychology include learning and memory, motivation, perception, cognition, language, communication, interpersonal relations, and development, to name only a few. Psychology encompasses multidisciplinary and interdisciplinary areas of research, as it connects with other disciplines such as biology, medicine, law, political science, anthropology, literature, linguistics, philosophy, computer science, and engineering. Many areas of study and specialization have emerged to reflect psychology's expanded role: for example, cognitive neuroscience, health psychology, and environmental psychology. The diversity, specialization, and manifold topics of psychology could easily be misconstrued as indications of fragmentation or lack of coherence. However, even as the field has advanced and expanded, there remain overarching themes, a historical lineage, and firm foundations that retain the field's identity. A useful reference work on psychology should merge into one source the topics, methods, findings, advances, and applications that characterize the broad field of study. The American Psychological Association and Oxford University Press united with a commitment to publish such a work. The *Encyclopedia of Psychology* is the product of that commitment.

With these two major forces at the heart of development, an effort was begun to produce an encyclopedia that would be unmatched in terms of scope, scholarship, and expertise. The American Psychological Association, the largest organization of psychologists in the world, contributed its vast resources to mobilize the international group of scholars and professionals required to develop and complete the project. Oxford University Press, a publisher with distinguished experience in producing large-scale, scholarly reference works, was well suited to coordinate the development and production needs of an eight-volume encyclopedia.

DEVELOPMENT OF THE PROJECT

The enormous undertaking began with a vision to represent both the history of psychology and the areas that have developed in the years since the field emerged formally as a scientific discipline. An obvious danger exists if one person with a vision or model of psychology dictates the structure, priorities, and scope of the project. At the same time, a vision of the field is essential to coordinate the entries. Without a framework, there is a great risk of diffuse entries, inclusion of entries by lobbying, and no clear themes representing the thrust of the content.

We obtained the active involvement of a diverse and internationally renowned group of Senior Editors, Consulting Editors, and International Advisers to identify essential areas, tributaries, and key issues of the field and to discuss the best way to present them. During the deliberations and development of the content and scope, which spanned a period of four years, the editors, consultants, and advisers participated in numerous meetings, sometimes sequestered in rooms for extended periods to work out key issues. Following this was the creation of an outline of the structure of the encyclopedia, which would be amenable to further input and development as the project proceeded. Although we followed a schedule to complete each stage of the project, the substantive tasks of ensuring comprehensive coverage and scholarship were always the priority. The goal was to understand the manifold branches that would be important to document in the encyclopedia. Consequently, there was never a constraint in contacting a leading authority anywhere in the world to comment on some facet of theory, research, or application.

Psychology is a discipline that knows no geographical or international boundaries; however, conceptual views and frames of reference often have characteristics that vary by country and culture. From the inception of the project, we relied on members of the International Advisory Board to review and expand the coverage as necessary. The purpose was to ensure that the scope of the project was international and that multiple cultural and national traditions, lines of research, issues, and topics were woven into the conceptual fabric and then represented concretely in the entries themselves.

The formal structure of the board of editors provided the mechanisms during development to evaluate and revise the content and scope. Once the project was officially announced, informal mechanisms contributed to the work as well. Many scholars throughout the world wrote to me to ask whether and how a topic was to be treated; several provided advice about how the field ought to be shaped and represented. Although the merit of advice is sometimes mistakenly judged by whether it is solicited or unsolicited, in this project, unsolicited advice proved to be very valuable and greatly complemented the more formal input that was solicited from the editors, consultants, and advisers. I am grateful to all those who wrote with suggestions and who engaged in dialogue with me about the project and its thrust.

Developing an encyclopedia is, of course, much more than merely devising a list of topics or headwords. Once a topic is determined (e.g., attitudes, motivation, statistical significance), the challenge continues. What are the scope of the topic (i.e., the core features), the historical and theoretical background, the areas of psychology and connections with other disciplines, and the current themes and major findings? For each topic, descriptions of the scope, thrust, and focus were compiled to serve as a guide for the contributor.

Although coverage of topics is obviously essential, how the topics are treated is also important. Within psychology, many differing views, debates, and issues prevail. The vitality of science derives not only from the ongoing advances in theory and research but also from the diversity of conceptual models, methods, and interpretations. Indeed, this diversity drives the advances in empirical findings in fundamental ways. The challenge is to represent diverse issues, views, and debates without attempting to resolve them or to go beyond clarification of the issues, their significance, and implications.

The next stage of the project involved commissioning contributors to write the entries in the areas defined during the earlier development stages. Associate Editors with expertise in the various content areas were selected to provide oversight responsibility for the entries and to review and edit the manuscripts. The contributors then wrote their entries; some individuals contributed multiple entries. Not enough can be said in praise of the contributors who provided the rich offerings reflected in the entries.

We were extremely fortunate to recruit key figures at each stage of the project and the most widely recognized authorities in the world on the individual topics that comprise the field. Participants in the project uniformly recognized its importance from the outset. Several persons who served in one role (e.g., Senior Editor, International Adviser) readily agreed to serve in another role (e.g., Associate Editor, contributor) when called upon to do so.

From concept to bound volumes, the *Encyclopedia of Psychology* was created over a period of eight years. The majority of this time was devoted to development and conceptualization of the project. The encyclopedia includes in eight volumes more than 1,500 entries, with nearly 400 biographies of key figures. Over 1,400 scholars and professionals in psychology and related disciplines served as contributors.

SCOPE OF PSYCHOLOGY

The scope of psychology is broad and cannot be captured simply by enumerating the range of concepts and phenomena that psychologists are wont to study. In producing this encyclopedia, every effort was made to represent the field by considering not only the content areas but also the manifold dimensions and perspectives from which they are examined. Several themes organized and shaped the contents of the *Encyclopedia of Psychology*:

- Psychology as a discipline, including its historical development, key areas and subareas of study, major theories and conceptual models, professional issues (e.g., training, employment, and ethics), international psychology, and professional associations and organizations.
- Methods of scientific study, research design, and statistics, including the ways in which research is conducted, the goals, and methods of data evaluation and analyses.
- Psychological testing and assessment, including types of measures, models, and methods of measurement development, as well as many specific assessment instruments and procedures.
- Biological and cognitive processes, including basic biological systems, sensory processes and percep-

tion, learning, memory, states of consciousness, cognition, language, communication, and emotion.

- Personal, interpersonal, and social processes, including personality, self, identity, social cognition and interpersonal perception, intelligence, sex and gender, attitudes and attitude change, attraction and close relationships, and group and intergroup processes.
- Interactive systems and contexts, including the family, school, work and employment, community and neighborhood, and person-machine and person-environment interactions.
- Development across the life span, including key biological and psychosocial processes and development from infancy through late adulthood.
- Cultural and cross-cultural psychology, including key theories, issues, and areas of research; and ethnocultural groups and traditions.
- Adjustment and clinical dysfunction, including behavioral and mental disorders, health and physical illness, and social problems.
- Interventions, including psychosocial and biological treatment, prevention, and institutional care.
- Psychology in relation to other disciplines and areas of study, including law, religion, politics, the military, sports, arts, and the media.

These domains provided a framework to structure key topics, theories, issues, and findings. However, other dimensions of psychology were integrated with this structure to capture the field and the interrelations among the topics. First, the *history of psychology* is a critical perspective encompassed by this work. History is not only an account of the past but also reflects broader themes leading to the development of scientific research and methods and the emergence of psychology as a formal discipline. The *Encyclopedia of Psychology* charts where the field has been, where it currently is, and where it is going, and it illustrates the intellectual, interdisciplinary, and historical factors that influenced this development.

Second, because theory, research, and application pervade many of the topics of psychology, these facets are represented within those topics, and contributors show us the connections among them. *Theory* involves conceptual models and efforts to understand the development, underlying bases, and processes fundamental to a given topic. *Research* involves the substantive findings as well as the methods used to study phenomena of interest. *Application* involves extensions to interventions, nonlaboratory settings, and social policy.

Third, topics within the field are viewed from the standpoint of development and change. Although research takes high-resolution snapshots of basic pro-

cesses of emotion, cognition, and behavior at a given point in development, these processes reflect a moving picture of change as organisms adapt and mature. Psychology focuses on and charts these processes and change and seeks to explain the nature of development more generally. For the *Encyclopedia of Psychology*, this means that topics must be viewed from a developmental perspective. That is, maturation, brain functioning, self-perception, interpersonal relations, and health and illness are constantly changing. The processes that govern or interrupt these changes are central to psychology.

Finally, the subject matter had to be considered from different levels of analysis. These included the study of processes and characteristics of (1) the individual (e.g., brain development and self-esteem), (2) the individual in relation to others (e.g., personal perception and group processes), and (3) individuals and groups in relation to broader contexts (e.g., family, neighborhood, and culture). Relation to others can be conceived quite broadly and includes how persons interact with machines and the physical environment more generally. The different levels of analysis are a useful way to consider both how many psychological processes are studied and the influences that impinge on these processes. Exciting developments within the field alert us to the interrelations among these dimensions. Development of the individual entails dynamic, reciprocal, and bi-directional processes. Relationships and contexts greatly contribute to processes (e.g., biological processes, perceptions) within the individual, and these, in turn, influence relationships and contexts (e.g., how subsequent events are perceived, what subsequent contexts may be sought or pursued). The purpose of identifying processes of individuals in relation to others and to contexts is not to structure the field rigidly but rather to permit elaboration of the richness of the subject matter and the interrelations among areas. Indeed, within many areas, levels of analyses can be more fine-grained than beginning with the individual and moving to culture. The study of basic psychological processes such as learning, perception, and cognition can move from refined evaluation of neural pathways to performance on laboratory tasks or tests.

EDITORIAL PRACTICES

Entries in the encyclopedia are alphabetically arranged, strictly letter by letter. In order to make use of the specialized expertise of individual scholars while ensuring that all aspects of larger topics are fully covered, "composite entries" group together several articles under one headword. For example, the entry "Animal Learning and Behavior" includes three articles, one on the history of the field, another on theoretical issues, and another on methods of study.

To guide readers from one article to related discussions elsewhere in the work, there is an extensive system of cross-references within the articles. In addition, "blind entries" of alternate spellings and synonyms occur throughout the alphabetical range of headwords, providing cross-references to the articles readers seek. For example, the reader looking up "Pavlovian Conditioning" will be directed to the entry "Classical Conditioning." A comprehensive index is a further resource, especially for topics that are not headwords themselves. Readers interested in finding all the articles on a particular subject (e.g., emotion, intelligence) are encouraged to consult the Synoptic Outline of Contents in Volume 8.

ACKNOWLEDGMENTS

I am grateful to have had the opportunity to collaborate with many individuals to bring this project to fruition. To acknowledge appropriately the dedication, efforts, and commitment of these people would require at least one more volume. Permit me to highlight several key persons. At Oxford University Press, Claude Conyers provided critical direction to the project, particularly in the early stages with his vision and vast experience with projects of this scope. In the developmental stages of the project, Marion Osmun at Oxford University Press and Theodore Baroody at the American Psycho-logical Association were pivotal in organizing, synthesizing, and challenging the structure and scope of the entries. Peri C. Zeenkov and Norina Frabotta, at Oxford University Press, served as Project Editors and assisted in the final stages of the project.

At the American Psychological Association, Gary VandenBos and Julia Frank-McNeil played a central role in initiating the project, envisioning its importance and unique features, keeping it on track and schedule, and serving as available resources throughout. Adrian Harris Forman supervised the recruitment of contributors and acquisition of manuscripts and managed scores of unanticipated events and issues that washed on us like an endless series of waves at sea or, perhaps, crashing on the shore.

Most of those involved in the project were committed to it well beyond the confines of their role. Consequently, there was input throughout through informal mechanisms that affected the shape, emphases, and scholarship of the final product. One of the joys of participating in the project as the Editor in Chief was the chance to work with so many gifted scholars and professionals. The task often felt like serving as a conductor in an orchestra composed of the most talented musicians. It has been a privilege and delight to hear and to participate in the marvelous symphony they produced.

—Alan E. Kazdin, Ph.D.
New Haven, Connecticut
November 1999

ENCYCLOPEDIA OF PSYCHOLOGY

A

ABORTION. The medical or surgical termination of a pregnancy, abortion is one of the oldest, most commonly practiced, and most controversial medical procedures currently performed in the United States. It has been a legal procedure in all states since *Roe v. Wade* (1973), when the Supreme Court ruled that the abortion decision was protected by a woman's right to privacy. The Court also noted that the state has legitimate interests in protecting both the pregnant woman's health and potential human life, interests that grow and reach a compelling point at later states of gestation. Subsequent Supreme Court decisions have eroded the broad abortion rights articulated in Roe, while at the same time upholding the general principle of that decision. For example, in *Webster v. Reproductive Health Services* (1989), and *Planned Parenthood of Southeastern Pennsylvania v. Casey* (1992), the Court significantly expanded the states' ability to place restrictions on access to abortion, so long as these restrictions do not impose an "undue burden" on women seeking abortions.

Approximately 1.5 million legal abortions have been performed each year in the United States since *Roe v. Wade*, resulting in the annual termination of about 25% of known pregnancies. Most abortions (more than 90%) are performed in the first trimester of pregnancy; less than 1% are performed at more than 20 weeks. The abortion rate in the United States has been gradually declining since the early 1980s. This decline may be due to a variety of factors. They include the decreased availability of abortion services; increased harassment by antiabortion activists; the increased cost of obtaining an abortion; reluctance of providers to perform abortions at more than 13 weeks gestation; changing attitudes toward abortion and unwed motherhood; exclusion of abortion from Medicaid coverage; and legislative barriers such as the implementation of waiting periods and parental consent rules.

Role of Psychologists

The American Psychological Association (APA) and individual psychologists have had a long history of involvement in matters related to psychological factors associated with abortion and in disseminating results of research on abortion-related issues. In 1969, the APA Council of Representatives adopted a resolution that identified termination of unwanted pregnancies as a mental health and child welfare issue, resolving that termination of pregnancy be considered a civil right of the pregnant woman. In 1980, APA passed a resolution supporting the right to conduct scientific research on abortion. In 1989, APA passed a resolution to initiate a public awareness effort to correct the record on the scientific findings of abortion research, and appointed a panel of experts to review the best scientific studies of abortion outcomes. The report of this panel was published in 1990 in *Science*.

Individual psychologists conduct crisis pregnancy counseling, help women and girls decide how to resolve an unwanted pregnancy, and counsel women who have had an abortion and who report associated distress. Psychological researchers conduct and disseminate research on attitudes toward abortion, psychological responses to abortion, and predictors of those responses. Psychologists also serve as expert witnesses in court cases dealing with abortion-related issues.

Characteristics of Abortion Patients

Demographic characteristics of women obtaining abortions are derived from national surveys of abortion providers. According to the Alan Guttmacher Institute, the majority of women obtaining abortions are young (55% are younger than 25) and never married (66%). The majority have had one or more children (55%), but no prior abortions (53%). Based on total numbers, more White women (61%) than African American or Hispanic women obtain abortions. However, the abortion rate for White women is lower than it is for minority women. Black women are approximately three times as likely to have an abortion as White women and Hispanic women are roughly two times as likely to do so. Abortion rates are also disproportionately higher among women who are disadvantaged economically because of poverty or lack of education. Many of these demographic factors are intercorrelated, making it difficult to attribute differences in abortion rates to any single variable.

The most common reasons women report for obtaining an abortion are concern that having a baby at that point would interfere with work, school, or other responsibilities; the inability to afford a baby financially; and partner-related reasons. Motivations to have an abortion differ substantially among different subgroups of women. Adult mothers, for example, are more likely than nonmothers to cite as reasons for obtaining an abortion, completion of childbearing along with responsibilities to others, including other children.

Controversy over Psychological Consequences of Abortion

Contemporary debates over abortion often focus on psychological issues. One controversy centers on whether abortion is psychologically damaging to women. This controversy became a public policy debate in 1987, when President Ronald Reagan directed Surgeon-General C. Everett Koop to prepare a report on the psychological and physical health effects of abortion. After reviewing the evidence, Koop declined to issue such a report. Rather, in a letter to President Reagan, the surgeon-general concluded that "the scientific studies do not provide conclusive data on the health effects of abortion on women."

Individuals on both sides of the abortion debate disagree with Koop's conclusion. Prolife advocates argue that over time, many or most women who have an abortion suffer psychological damage as a result. Advocates of this view have lobbied the American Psychiatric Association to recognize postabortion syndrome as a psychiatric diagnostic category. Support for this position is based on clinical case studies that derive from two separate sources: (1) women who have sought professional help for psychological problems following their abortions; (2) women who were specifically solicited as participants because they identified themselves in advance as having suffered psychological trauma following abortion. In addition to relying on samples of women who identified themselves as experiencing postabortion adjustment problems, many of these studies fail to distinguish between whether the abortion was performed legally or illegally and whether it was performed in the first or second trimester of pregnancy. Because of these methodological issues, this group of studies is likely to be biased in the direction of overestimating the prevalence of postabortion problems among women who obtain legal, first trimester abortions.

Psychological experts, including the panel convened by the APA, argue in contrast that the very best scientific studies show that freely chosen abortion, particularly in the first trimester of pregnancy, does not pose a significant mental health risk for most women. This conclusion is derived from studies based on random samples of women who have arrived at a doctor's office, clinic, or hospital for an abortion. They are asked to participate in a study and are then interviewed on the day of their abortion and/or some time afterward. These studies generally find that most women do not report psychological distress after an abortion and that the highest rates of distress are generally reported prior to the abortion. The conclusion that abortion does not pose a mental health risk for most women is also derived from epidemiological studies of large populations of women whose prior abortion history is known. These studies generally find no higher incidence of psychological problems among women who have had an abortion than among women who have not. Although these studies also have methodological limitations, they are generally much sounder scientifically than those used to support the argument that severe negative reactions to abortion are common.

Part of the difficulty in drawing firm conclusions about the psychological effects of abortion results from the fact it is impossible to separate the effects of abortion from the effects of experiencing an unwanted pregnancy. Both of these are potentially stressful events. Ultimately, the mental health risks of abortion must be compared to the mental health risks of its alternatives—motherhood or adoption. However, no well-controlled studies are available that compare all three groups, perhaps because relatively few women choose the adoption alternative. In contrast, a number of well-designed studies have compared the psychological well-being of women who have had abortions to the well-being of women who have carried an unintended pregnancy to term and kept the child. The measures of well-being that were used in these studies include self-esteem, anxiety, incidence of psychiatric disorder, progress in school, and economic status. All of these studies have reached the same conclusion—that the well-being of women who have abortions is generally either better than, or not significantly different from, that of women who carry an unplanned pregnancy to term and keep the baby.

Although most women do not experience significant psychological distress following an abortion, some do. The reactions of these women should not be dismissed as inconsequential and deserve attention from psychologists. It is important to remember, however, that distress that occurs after an abortion is not necessarily caused by the abortion, even though it may be attributed to this event. Furthermore, it is important to distinguish between feelings such as sadness and regret that can be experienced after any difficult life choice, and significant mental health outcomes, such as depression or psychosis. Women who feel a sense of sadness, loss, or regret over an abortion may not necessarily experience a psychological disorder following an abortion.

Predictors of Psychological Responses to Abortion

Adjustment to abortion can best be conceptualized within a stress and coping framework. From this perspective, the discovery of an unintended pregnancy can be a stressful life event, and abortion may be used as one means of coping with this stress. However, the abortion procedure may represent an additional source of stress that also requires coping efforts. Just as there is variation in how individuals react to other types of life stressors, so too is there variation in how women react to abortion. Research indicates that many of the same personal and social resources and liabilities that predict adaptation to other types of life stressors also predict adaptation to unwanted pregnancy and abortion.

Personal Factors. Women's general personality characteristics and their specific attitudes and feelings about pregnancy and abortion are important predictors of their mental health following abortion. Especially important in this regard is a woman's mental health before she discovered that she was pregnant. Women who are already experiencing psychological problems before they discover a pregnancy are far more likely than others to experience psychological problems at a later time, regardless of whether they choose to have an abortion. Hence, it is often inappropriate to conclude that psychological problems present after an abortion were caused by the abortion.

Women who have high expectations (or self-efficacy) concerning their own ability to cope with an abortion, or who initially appraise the abortion as less stressful, show higher postabortion adaptation than do women who have lower expectations. Women's personality characteristics also predict adaptation to abortion. Women with personality characteristics such as high self-esteem, an optimistic outlook, and an internal locus of control initially appraise their abortions as less stressful, have higher coping expectations, use more adaptive postabortion coping strategies, are more satisfied with their abortion decision, and have better mental health postabortion than do women who lack these personality resources. Women who have difficulty reaching the decision to have the abortion, or who report that the abortion conflicts with their personal or

religious beliefs, report more postabortion adaptation problems. This is also true of women who report high levels of commitment to the pregnancy and those who report that the pregnancy was meaningful and intended.

The strategies that women use to cope after having an abortion can also affect their postabortion adaptation. Coping refers to the cognitive and behavioral efforts that people engage in to manage stressful events and/or the emotions related to those events. Coping strategies that are associated with better postabortion mental health include trying to accept the abortion, grow from it, and/or reframe it in a more positive light. Coping strategies associated with decreases in postabortion mental health include trying to cope with abortion-related emotions by avoiding thoughts of the abortion, denying it or dwelling on it.

Social and Cultural Factors. Unwanted pregnancy and abortion occur in a social context and this context can also exert an important influence on adaptation to abortion. One important aspect of the social context is how others close to the woman react to her abortion decision. Women who perceive high levels of social support from their conception partner, parents, and/or friends for their abortion decision are more satisfied with their decision and have better mental health postabortion than women who lack perceived social support from close others. Social conflict with close others, in contrast, can be a significant source of additional stress and can result in poorer postabortion mental health.

The larger cultural context within which abortion occurs can also affect women's adaptation to abortion. Publicized opposition to abortion may cause women who obtain abortions to feel vulnerable to being stigmatized and shamed by others. Feelings of stigma may lead women to avoid talking with others about their experience. Exposure to antiabortion picketing at abortion clinics can also negatively affect women's adjustment. Women who are exposed to aggressive antiabortion picketing or who are blocked as they enter a clinic to obtain an abortion are more upset by the picketers and are more vulnerable to depression immediately postabortion than are women not exposed to these encounters.

Legal Controversies Surrounding Abortion

Opponents and supporters of the right to abortion have frequently clashed in the courts on a variety of issues since the historic *Roe v. Wade* decision. One controversy centers on so-called partial-birth abortions, or abortions that take place after the fetus is viable. Although such abortions are extremely rare, as of 1998 many states have adopted bans on them. Another controversy centers on "informed consent." Many states have passed legislation mandating that prior to the procedure women be informed of the physical and/or psychological risks of obtaining an abortion. The nature of these risks, however, is controversial, as noted above. Furthermore, true informed consent cannot be obtained without also informing women of the risks associated with childbearing.

Some of the most contentious legal issues surrounding abortion focus on minors. In 1976 the Supreme Court of the United States decided in *Planned Parenthood of Central Missouri v. Danforth* that minors have a constitutional right to privacy in obtaining an abortion, but that minors' rights to privacy may not be as compelling as those of adults, and accordingly, that states may infringe on those rights given a "significant state interest" in doing so. By 1997, a majority of the U.S. states had enacted statutes requiring minors to either involve parents in abortion decisions (by notifying them of the abortion or by obtaining their consent) or to petition a judge for permission to obtain the abortion without parental notification (commonly referred to as a judicial bypass).

In making these decisions to constrain the ability of minors to obtain an abortion, the Supreme Court made several assumptions. First, the Court assumed that minors would be especially at risk for severe, negative, postabortion sequelae and that such sequelae are not an issue in carrying a pregnancy to term. There is no evidence, however, to support these assumptions. Second, the Court voiced concern that minors would be too immature to make a sound, well-reasoned decision without the benefit of input from an adult. Psychological research on cognitive development and decision-making skills, however, suggests that by about the age of 14, most young people are similar to adults in their ability to reason abstractly about and make decisions concerning relatively complex hypothetical scenarios.

Finally, at the heart of the parental consent laws is the idea that parental consultation is desirable and in the best interests of the minor and her family. Even when no law exists that mandates parental involvement, the majority of minors do consult with at least one parent prior to making an abortion decision. Factors that make it less likely that a minor will consult with parents include (1) the fear that parents will be hurt, unsympathetic, or even violent in response; (2) the minor lives independently or already has children; (3) she has experienced a chaotic home environment characterized by substance abuse, violence, or sexual abuse; or (4) she suspects that her parents will force her into making a specific, undesired decision regarding resolution of the pregnancy.

Critics of consent laws argue that minors who come from supportive family backgrounds will consult with parents without such consultation being legally man-

dated, and that girls who come from unsupportive, dysfunctional, or violent homes will not benefit from the forced disclosure of their pregnancy. Research is consistent with this view. Women who disclose to others who do not support or who oppose their abortion decision are more distressed postabortion than women who do not disclose or who disclose to others who are supportive. Critics of consent laws further argue that these laws create delays in seeking care among a group of women who are already unlikely to seek prompt medical care, thereby increasing the rate of later-term abortions and the rate of teen parenthood.

Another legal controversy surrounding abortion focuses on laws and injunctions against antiabortion demonstrators. Prolife demonstrators in the United States frequently picket abortion clinics and attempt to dissuade women from entering. They sometimes engage in more violent activities such as clinic blockades, bomb threats, stalking of clinic personnel, and murder. Abortion rights activists have sought through legal means to restrict the scope and impact of antiabortion demonstrators at facilities where abortions are performed. Many communities have enacted injunctions mandating that demonstrators remain a specified distance from women entering clinics. In 1994, President Clinton signed into law a bill that makes it a federal crime to use force, the threat of force, or physical obstruction to intimidate abortion clinic workers or clients of clinics.

[*See also* Women's Health Issues.]

Bibliography

Comprehensive Sources

Beckman, L. J., & Harvey, S. M. (Eds.). (1998). *The new civil war: The psychology, culture, and politics of abortion.* Washington, DC: American Psychological Association. A broad overview of the sociopolitical, cultural, and interpersonal contexts in which abortion currently occurs in the United States. Also includes information on issues involved in counseling women who have had abortions.

Wilmoth, G. (Ed.). (1992). Psychological perspectives on abortion and its alternatives. *Journal of Social Issues, 48*(3), 1–216. This special issue of JSI presents ten articles, mostly written by psychological experts on abortion. The articles discuss research, policy, and judicial issues related to abortion and present evidence about many aspects of the debate about the consequences of abortion. This is an excellent source of information about psychological perspectives on abortion.

Abortion Rates and Characteristics of Abortion Patients

Henshaw, S. K. (1995). Factors hindering access to abortion services. *Family Planning Perspectives, 27,* 54–59.

Henshaw, S. K., & Kost, K. (1996). Abortion patients in 1994–1995: Characteristics and contraceptive use. *Fam-*

ily Planning Perspectives, 28, 140–147. Describes characteristics of U.S. abortion patients, using data collected by the Allan Guttmacher Institute.

Torres, A., & Forrest, J. D. (1988). Why do women have abortions? *Family Planning Perspectives, 20,* 169–176.

Psychological Responses to Abortion

Adler, N. E., David, H. P., Major, B. N., Roth, S. H., Russo, N. F., & Wyatt, G. E. (1990). Psychological responses after abortion. *Science, 248,* 41–43. Presents conclusions of the APA panel convened to review the scientific evidence on the psychological consequences of abortion.

Gilchrist, A. C., Hannaford, P. C., Frank, P., & Kay, C. R. (1995). Termination of pregnancy and psychiatric morbidity. *British Journal of Psychiatry, 167,* 243–248. Report of a prospective cohort study of 13,261 women with unplanned pregnancy recruited by their family doctors in the United Kingdom. Compares the rate of psychiatric disorder following childbirth versus termination of the pregnancy.

Russo, N. F., & Zierk, K. L. (1992). Abortion, childbearing, and women's well-being. *Professional Psychology: Research and Practice, 23*(4), 269–280. Report of an empirical study examining the relationship of the experience of abortion to self-esteem in a national sample of 5,295 U.S. women who were followed from 1979 to 1987.

Zabin, L. S., Hirsch, M. B., & Emerson, M. R. (1989). When urban adolescents choose abortion: Effects on education, psychological status, and subsequent pregnancy. *Family Planning Perspectives, 21,* 248–255. Report of an empirical study in which low-income African American adolescents were followed from the day they came to a clinic for a pregnancy test until two years later. Compared the psychological outcomes, educational outcomes, and subsequent pregnancy of girls who were initially pregnant and had an abortion, with those of girls who were pregnant and kept the child, and girls who were not initially pregnant.

Postabortion Self-Help

De Puy, C., & Dovitch, D. (1997). *The healing choice: Your guide to emotional recovery after an abortion.* New York: Fireside Books. This is a nonjudgmental self-help guide for women who have experienced abortion and who are experiencing distress. It is written by two psychotherapists and is based on their interviews with forty women who had experienced one or more abortions and five men.

Predictors of Psychological Responses to Abortion

Adler, N. E., David, H. P., Major, B. N., Roth, S. H., Russo, N. F., & Wyatt, G. E. (1992). Psychological factors in abortion: A review. *American Psychologist, 47,* 1194–1204. Overview of the predictors of psychological responses to abortion written by members of the APA panel appointed to review the scientific literature.

Major, B., Richards, C., Cooper, M. L., Cozzarelli, C., & Zubek, J. (1998). Personal resilience, cognitive appraisals, and coping: An integrative model of adjustment to abortion. *Journal of Personality and Social Psychology, 74,* 735–752. Report of an empirical study which examined the impact of personality, appraisals, and postabortion coping strategies on postabortion mental health among 442 women who had first trimester abortions.

Adolescents and Abortion

Ambuel, B. (1995). Adolescents, unintended pregnancy and abortion: The struggle for a compassionate social policy. *Current Directions in Psychological Science, 4,* 1–5. A recent review of psychological research addressing whether adolescents are capable of giving informed consent for an abortion. The author also discusses the pros and cons of mandating parental involvement in minors' abortion decisions.

Henshaw, S. K., & Kost, K. (1992). Parental involvement in minors' abortion decisions. *Family Planning Perspectives, 24,* 196–213. Based on a nationally representative sample of unmarried minors having an abortion, the authors present statistics regarding the number who told family members about the intended abortion, their reasons for disclosure or nondisclosure, and the reactions of family members who were told or found out about the minors' decision to abort the pregnancy.

Antiabortion Picketing

Cozzarelli, C., & Major, B. (1998). The impact of antiabortion activities on women seeking abortions. In L. J. Beckman & S. M. Harvey (Eds.), *The new civil war: The psychology, culture, and politics of abortion* (pp. 81–104) Washington, DC: American Psychological Association. Reviews research on antiabortion activities and on the relationship between exposure to antiabortion picketing and women's postabortion mental health.

Brenda Major and Catherine Cozzarelli

ABREACTION refers to a clinical phenomenon in which experiences of traumas are recollected, often after a period in which they have not occupied conscious attention. During recollection, the experience is one of reliving the memory. Intense emotions are often felt and expressed.

Sigmund Freud and Josef Breuer used this term in their book, *Studies on Hysteria* (1893–1895/1955). They reported that abreaction might be brought about by the therapist's hypnotic suggestion that a patient remember what instigated the onset of a symptom. These techniques were part of a method aimed at evoking repressed memories. Catharsis, the discharge of emotional potentials by speaking of the related ideas and feelings, was believed to be a curative process.

Freud later modified these early psychoanalytic concepts. He reported that reduction of defensiveness against recollection, and working through topics, was a central part of an overall process of change from a more symptomatic to a less symptomatic state. In other words, abreaction alone did not produce lasting change.

In contemporary psychotherapeutic practices, abreaction is no longer a central goal of technique. Even in posttraumatic stress syndromes, recollection of what happened is only a first step in a larger scope of work. When a person suffers from intrusive and avoidant symptoms as part of a posttraumatic stress disorder (PTSD), the goals are (1) to differentiate reality from fantasy; (2) to increase the individual's sense of personal relationship to what has really happened; (3) to modify pathological defensiveness against acknowledging implications to the self; and (4) to work through closely connected issues of identity, relationships, and future life plans.

In the contemporary setting, abreaction refers to a phenomenon in which the patient may be startled by the intensity of his or her emotional reaction upon recollection and review of episodes of the past. The patient may enter a state in which he or she feels a loss of self-control due to the magnitude of emotion. It is important in such instances to increase control. This can be done by expanding concepts into coherent stories about what happened, and by translating images and somatic sensations into words. The working-through process, then, is an aspect of social communication plus an internal connection of ideas that had been previously dissociated or inhibited from contemplation.

After the intense emotional experiences of an abreaction, even one with expression of negative and distressing emotions, a person may feel exhilarated. Because of such reactions, abreaction may seem like a "breakthrough," a decisively curative moment, and thus it may be overvalued. While such experiences may be one step in a working through and a progressive coping with past traumas, it is important not to overestimate the therapeutic value of abreactive phenomena.

[*See also* Catharsis; Consciousness and Unconsciousness; Memory; *and* Psychotherapy.]

Bibliography

Bibring, E. (1954). Psychoanalysis and the dynamic psychotherapies. *Journal of the American Psychoanalytic Association, 2,* 745–770.

Breuer, J., & Freud, S. (1955) Studies on hysteria. In J. Strachey (Ed. and Trans.), *The standard edition of the complete psychological works of Sigmund Freud* (Vol. 2). London: Hogarth Press. (Original works published 1893–1895)

Freud, S. (1958) Remembering, repeating and working-through. In J. Strachey (Ed. and Trans.), *The standard edition of the complete psychological works of Sigmund Freud* (Vol. 12, pp. 146–156). London: Hogarth Press. (Original work published 1914)

Horowitz, M. (1997). *Stress response syndromes* (3rd ed.) Northvale, NJ: Aronson.

Horowitz, M., Marmar, C., Weiss, D., et al. (1984). Brief psychotherapy of bereavement reactions: The relationship of process to outcome. *Archives of General Psychiatry, 41,* 438–448.

Mardi Horowitz

ACADEMIA EUROPAEA. Founded in 1988 to promote learning, education, and research, the Academia Europaea is an international, nongovernmental association of individual scientists and scholars involved in a wide range of disciplines, including the physical sciences and technology, the biological sciences and medicine, mathematics, the humanities, the social and cognitive sciences, economics, and law. As of September 1999, the organization included some 1,800 members from 33 European and 5 non-European countries.

The purposes and objectives of the Academia Europaea are (1) to promote and support excellence in European scholarship, research, and education; (2) to promote the development of a European identity in scholarship and research and to conduct analyses of issues relevant to Europe; (3) to provide independent advice on matters of scholarly interest or concern to legislatures, governments, universities, the communications media, and to professional, industrial, and commercial organizations in Europe; (4) to encourage interdisciplinary and international studies and research, with particular reference to European issues; (5) to encourage and assist collaboration between scholars and centers of scholarship in Europe and to promote collaboration in education and training; and (6) to encourage and assist the mobility of scholars and students in Europe.

The Academia has three membership categories: Ordinary, Honorary, and Foreign. The great majority of the Academia's membership is in the Ordinary category. There are about 50 foreign members. The election of new members is based on nominations from the existing membership.

The Academia Europaea is governed by a council of 12 members elected at the annual meeting, and by a president, three vice presidents, and a treasurer who form a board. Each member of the Academia is placed in one of 12 interdisciplinary sections, which themselves have a chair and committee.

As an independent body, the Academia Europaea receives financial support from its members and from other sources, including government ministries and research funding councils in several European countries, the European Commission, private foundations, charities, banks, and industries. The Academia is established as a charity under United Kingdom law.

Psychology is well represented in the membership of the Academia Europaea, which includes Paul Baltes, Alan Baddeley, Pieter Drenth, Uta Frith, Willem Levelt, David Magnusson, Lea Pulkkinen, Michael Rutter, Klaus Scherer, Hans Spada, and many others. Initially, psychology formed a subject group within the Academia, but, as a result of a reorganization into more interdisciplinary sections, psychology is now included within the behavioral sciences section.

A three-day scientific meeting is held each year, centered upon a series of interdisciplinary symposia on a wide range of subjects. Among the many issues which have been addressed are the following: the responsibility of the individual scholar to society; human origins; European linguistic diversity and unity; brain and cognition; climatic change in recent millennia; the classical heritage; and nonlinearity and chaotic behavior. Many of the papers have subsequently been published.

The Erasmus Lecture and Medal were introduced in 1992 to provide an opportunity for Academia members and others to hear a renowned scholar. The Erasmus lecturers to date have been Janos Kornai, Ernst Mestmäcker, Lawrence Freedman, Alain Touraine, Hubert Markl, Paul Crutzen, Peter Burke, and Raoul van Caenegen.

The Academia Europaea organizes special working groups and workshops to address topics of scientific or academic interest. Two major themes have been education and the impact of information technology on society. Workshops have included Psychosocial Problems Among Young People; Higher Education in the Twenty-First Century; The Idea of Progress; Teaching Science to Children; The Quality of Life in Old Age; The Impact of Electronic Publishing; and Interdisciplinarity and the Organization of Knowledge. External sponsorship is sought to conduct these workshops, and usually the results are published. *Psychosocial Disorders in Young People: Time Trends and Their Causes*, edited by M. Rutter and D. Smith, is one such publication.

Since 1993 the Academia has organized a system for giving prize awards to young scientists from the republics of the Commonwealth of Independent States, on the basis of open competitions assessed by international experts. In addition, since 1995 prizes have been provided for young scientists from the Baltic republics.

The Academia issues a semiannual newsletter, *The Tree*, and a quarterly journal, the *European Review*, which is distributed to all members and is also available on subscription from Cambridge University Press. The *European Review* includes high-quality papers, frequently of an interdisciplinary character, and articles related to other Academia activities.

One of the principles underlying the foundation of the Academia was the need for independent advice to public and private bodies. With its membership approaching 2,000 eminent scientists and scholars from many disciplines, able to offer independent comment free from any national or organizational bias, the Academia is well placed to offer advice on scientific or academic matters in Europe.

The following are examples of policy advice provided by the Academia Europaea:

In 1990 and 1991 the Academia was invited by the Conference of European Science Ministers to advise on research on the human genome in Europe. The Academia created an international expert group that prepared a report and presented it to European ministers. This study took place at a time when many of the implications of genome research, and the scale of the task, were poorly understood. The Academia's report helped to clarify some of these issues at a high level.

The European Science and Technology Assembly (ESTA) advises the European Commission on matters related to its scientific programs. About forty of the one hundred members of ESTA are also members of the Academia.

In 1996 the Academia was invited by the Netherlands Research Organisation (NWO) to organize a workshop on current developments in the management of higher education and to advise on policy implications for the Netherlands.

Also in 1996 the State Committee of the Ukraine for Science and Technology invited the Academia to conduct an evaluation of the quality of science in the Ukraine, and to participate in an advisory committee on the reorganization of the country's science and research.

Bibliography

Academia Europaea. (1998). *Directory*. London: Author. The Academia Europaea *Directory* is reissued periodically with current information about the Academia.

Peter J. Colyer

ACADEMIC ACHIEVEMENT. *See* Academic Assessment of Performance; *and* Exceptional Students.

ACADEMIC ASSESSMENT–INTERVENTION LINK. The benefits of linking assessment to instruction are that students' motivation for and involvement in learning may increase through enhanced performance feedback. Teachers are informed of their students' progress and difficulties; they are able to evaluate the effectiveness of their instruction accurately; and they may be more responsive to students and improve the quality of their instructional programs.

In considering alternative assessment approaches to maximize the assessment-intervention link, educators should use the following seven criteria. Assessment methods (1) must provide teachers with information about whether skills and learning strategies have been acquired; (2) must provide teachers with information about whether students can apply and integrate skills and strategies in novel, authentic contexts; (3) must provide teachers with information about student growth to help teachers formatively evaluate the effectiveness of instructional programs and determine when adjustments are necessary; (4) must produce detailed analyses of student performance, which are linked to specific instructional actions; (5) must be feasible for routine administration, scoring, and interpretation; (6) should communicate to teachers and students what is important to learn; and (7) should produce information that meets well-agreed-on standards for accuracy and meaningfulness.

Curriculum-Based Measurement

The purpose of curriculum-based measurement (CBM) is to provide teachers with reliable, valid, and efficient procedures for obtaining student performance data to evaluate instructional programs and to answer broad questions about the effectiveness of an instructional program in producing growth over time and in comparison to other instructional approaches.

Curriculum-based measurement incorporates three key features: (1) the measurement methods are standardized (i.e., the behaviors and procedures for measuring those behaviors are prescribed); (2) the focus of measurement is long term, so that the testing methods, difficulty level, and constructs are constant across long time periods, such as one school year; and (3) the measurement methods are used to index student growth over time.

In using CBM, teachers establish broad, long-term outcomes for students, such as performing mathematics competently at the third-grade level. In assessment systems that are based on mastery learning, a skills hierarchy comprising the third-grade curriculum is specified and student performance is measured one skill at a time. By contrast, in CBM the teacher relies on established methods for measuring student proficiency across multiple skills embedded in the entire third-grade curriculum. Specifically, the teacher creates a pool of equivalent assessment tasks, each of which samples key problem types from the third-grade curriculum in the same proportion. Each week, students complete one or two assessments. At the beginning of

the year, students might answer a few problems correctly; as the year progresses and the curriculum is taught, however, performance should gradually improve.

Because each assessment task is of equivalent difficulty and incorporates all types of problems to be learned that year, CBM produces two types of information. First, a total score is graphed over time to represent global progress; the purpose of the graphed presentation of total scores is to allow teachers and students to evaluate growth formatively. Second, an analysis of the student's performance on the curriculum skills is conducted to allow teachers to engage in problem solving to determine how to improve instruction.

Strengths and Limitations

Because CBM incorporates standard measurement techniques, which demonstrate reliability and validity, it provides an accurate and meaningful database. In addition, because of regular administration of assessments that tap long-term goals, the graphed information summarizes overall progress on the year's curriculum. The information can be used to evaluate progress formatively and to determine when an instructional change is warranted. In addition, the performance analysis offers detailed information about student performance on specific skills and can be used to determine how to improve instruction.

Research has also documented that CBM can be linked to instruction in ways that enhance teacher planning. The measurement framework is not tied to any particular instructional paradigm. Curriculum-based measurement does not dictate any particular sequence with which to introduce skills; it does not commit students to mastery of any skills before addressing subsequent material; and it allows teachers to use different methods with the same child to determine which approach is most beneficial.

In addition, the scoring criteria are open and clear so that students know how they are evaluated and can set personal learning goals. Furthermore, the structure of assessments can help teachers identify instructional content. The assessment demands are also relatively manageable for teachers in typical classroom settings, for three reasons: (1) the assessments are brief; (2) the assessment focus remains constant across long periods of time, so that teachers do not shift assessments for different students at different times; (3) computer programs have been developed to administer assessments and to analyze the information automatically, thus freeing teachers from administration, scoring, and management tasks.

Despite these strengths, there is controversy about the extent to which CBM indexes skill application and integration. On the one hand, CBM is designed to assess a grade-level curriculum broadly, with multiple skills represented on every assessment task. It therefore avoids isolated testing of skills and requires a significant degree of skill transfer. On the other hand, especially in mathematics, curriculum-based measurement fails to embed the assessment in complex, real-life situations.

Performance Assessment

Performance assessment is characterized by three key features: (1) the tasks require students to construct, rather than select, responses; (2) the formats create opportunities for teachers to observe student performance on tasks reflecting real-world requirements; and (3) the scoring methods reveal patterns in students' learning and thinking. The major purposes of performance assessment are to direct teachers and students toward well-integrated learning outcomes and to enhance teachers' capacity to design superior instructional plans that lead better student learning.

Varieties of performance assessment are described in the literature, and a wide range of methods are implemented in classrooms. Because performance assessment is relatively new, underdeveloped, and yet to be studied, however, practitioners must operationalize vague design features into specific assessment methods on their own. These operationalizations, understandably, take on various forms, some of which better approximate the conceptual and theoretical underpinnings of performance assessment.

Strengths and Limitations

Performance assessment is not a clearly defined, readily usable technology. And although rhetoric suggests performance assessment's potential contribution to instructional planning, research examining that contribution is not yet available. What follows, therefore, is an analysis of performance assessment's potential strengths and limitations.

A major advantage of performance assessment is its deliberate focus on authentic performance that requires students to integrate many skills in age-appropriate, real-world situations. A second advantage of performance assessment is that what teachers and students see on assessment tasks corresponds closely to desired instructional goals. Teachers are able to use performance-assessment information to direct instruction. To the extent that scoring rubrics are clear, concrete, and visible to students, pupils use assessment information to establish and achieve personal learning goals.

Providing insights into students' strategies is a major goal of performance assessment. Teachers should also be able to formulate useful diagnostic decisions on the basis of the assessment information. Performance assessment permits teachers to identify the strategies students use with complicated problems. This focus on strategies yields rich descriptions with clear connections to instructional ideas. As with any assessment method, however, teachers' capacities vary considerably in noting information about students' strategic behavior and relating those descriptions to instructional techniques. Teachers often experience difficulty in diagnostic planning, even when the assessment method and the conceptual framework for learning are simple. Consequently, despite the potential for performance assessment to yield rich, detailed analyses of student performance that connect to instructional methods, work is required to identify the means by which this will be achieved.

Despite these strengths, major concerns about performance assessment exist. When a child fails to demonstrate skill application and integration in the context of a complex performance task, for example, it is not possible to identify whether failure is a function of poor strategies for generalizing learned skills or whether the child has not mastered the skill in isolation.

Moreover, the methods by which formative evaluation decisions are derived from performance assessment are unclear. Such decisions require scoring methods for describing progress and procedures for designing alternate forms. Initial work suggests there is difficulty in achieving comparability among performance assessments.

In addition, performance assessment requires large amounts of teacher time for designing and administering assessment tasks and for scrutinizing performance to identify learning patterns and connect patterns to teaching strategies. Therefore, constraints on teacher time need to be considered, especially in light of increasing diversity of student skills.

Finally, some have suggested that it may be necessary to rethink the technical standards by which the quality of performance assessments is judged. One proposal for evaluating the accuracy and meaningfulness of performance-assessment information includes the following outcome criteria: (1) intended and unintended effects on the ways teachers and students spend time and think about goals; (2) fairness for different populations of learners; (3) accuracy of generalizations to broader achievement domains; (4) consistency of assessment content with key features of the knowledge domain; (5) comprehensiveness of content coverage; and (6) costs and efficiency.

[*See also* Academic Assessment of Performance; Academic Intervention; *and* Intervention.]

Bibliography

Archbald, D. A., & Newmann, F. M. (1988). *Beyond standardized testing: Assessing academic achievement in the secondary school*. Reston, VA: National Association of Secondary School Principals.

Baker, E. L. (1991, April). *Expectations and evidence for alternative assessment.* Paper presented at the annual meeting of the American Educational Research Association, Chicago.

Baker, E. L., O'Neil, H. F., & Linn, R. L. (1993). Policy and validity prospects for performance-based assessment. *American Psychologist, 48,* 1210–1218.

Baxter, G. P., Shavelson, R. J., Goldman, S. R., & Pine, J. (1992). Evaluation of procedure-based scoring for hands-on science assessment. *Journal of Educational Measurement, 29,* 1–17.

Brewer, R. (1991, April). *Authentic assessment: The rhetoric and the reality.* Paper presented at the annual meeting of the American Educational Research Association, Chicago.

Elliott, S. N. (1995). *Performance assessment of students' achievement: Research and practice.* Paper prepared for the Board on Testing and Assessment, National Research Council, National Academy of Sciences.

Fuchs, L. S. (1994). *Connecting performance assessment to instruction.* Reston, VA: Council for Exceptional Children.

Fuchs, L. S., & Deno, S. L. (1991). Paradigmatic distinctions between instructionally relevant measurement models. *Exceptional Children, 57,* 488–501.

Fuchs, L. S., Fuchs, D., Hamlett, C. L., Phillips, N. R., & Bentz, J. (1995). Classwide curriculum-based measurement: Helping general educators meet the challenge of student diversity. *Exceptional Children, 61,* 440–451.

Fuchs, L. S., Fuchs, D., Hamlett, C. L., & Stecker, P. M. (1990). The role of skills analysis in curriculum-based measurement in math. *School Psychology Review, 19,* 6–22.

Fuchs, L. S., Fuchs, D., Hamlett, C. L., & Stecker, P. M. (1991). Effects of curriculum-based measurement and consultation on teacher planning and student achievement in mathematics operations. *American Educational Research Journal, 28,* 617–641.

Linn, R. L. (1991). Dimensions of thinking: Implications for testing. In B. F. Jones & L. Idol (Eds.), *Educational values and cognitive instruction: Implications for reform* (pp. 179–208). Hillsdale, NJ: Erlbaum.

Linn, R. L., Baker, E. L., & Dunbar, S. B. (1991). Complex, performance-based assessment: Expectations and validation criteria. *Educational Researcher, 3,* 15–21.

Marston, D. (1989). A curriculum-based measurement approach to assessing academic performance: What is it and why do it. *Curriculum-based measurement: Assessing special children.* New York: Guilford Press.

Research for Better Schools. (1988). *Special education in America's cities: A descriptive study.* Philadelphia: Author.

Sammons, K. B., Kobett, B., Heiss, J., & Fennell, F. S. (1992). Linking instruction and assessment in the mathematics classroom. *Arithmetic Teacher, February,* 11–15.

Shavelson, R. J., Baxter, G. P., & Pine, J. (1992). Performance assessments: Political rhetoric and measurement reality. *Educational Researcher, 21,* 22–27.

Shepard, L. A. (1989). Why we need better assessments. *Educational Leadership, 46,* 7–12.

Stiggins, R. J., Griswald, M., & Green, K. R. (1988, April). *Measuring thinking skills through classroom assessment.* Paper presented at the 1988 annual meeting of the National Council on Measurement in Education, New Orleans.

U.S. Congress, Office of Technology Assessment (1992, February). *Testing in American schools: Asking the right questions* (OTA-SET-519). Washington, DC: U.S. Government Printing Office. (ED 340 770)

Wiggins, G. (1989). A true test: Toward more authentic and equitable assessment. *Phi Delta Kappan, 70,* 703–713.

Lynn S. Fuchs

ACADEMIC ASSESSMENT OF PERFORMANCE. The assessment of academic performance has long been a routine part of all educational processes. Defined as "the process of collecting data for the purpose of (1) specifying and verifying problems and (2) making decisions about students" (Salvia & Ysseldyke, 1995, p. 5), assessment of academic performance aims to assist professionals in making decisions about referral, screening, classification, instructional planning, and student progress. Typically, the most common method of academic performance assessment is through teacher-designed tests. These informal metrics identify specific objectives that have previously been taught, and evaluate the degree to which students have mastered these objectives.

Beyond these routine, everyday classroom-based assessment procedures, schools have commonly relied on larger scale evaluation of student performance. Evaluation procedures can be focused on specific individuals or entire groups of students. When focused on individuals, the assessment methods are designed to make decisions about an individual student's performance, typically determining the actual acquisition, retention, and progress of skill development against expected levels of performance. When focused on groups, the decisions are more related to the outcomes of program evaluation, examining the degree to which schools or school districts as a whole are meeting wide-scale, district-defined objectives.

Methods of assessing academic performance can be categorized into one of four types: standardized norm-referenced tests, criterion-referenced tests, performance-based assessment, and curriculum-based assessment. Norm-referenced tests are designed to determine a student's standing relative to similar age/grade peers. The results of the measure are usually reported in some form of standard scores and can be helpful in establishing a student's performance against a sample drawn from a target population. Criterion-referenced tests are designed to determine the acquisition of specific skills against a preestablished standard. Teacher-made tests are some of the best examples of these types of measures. Scores on these measures are usually reported in the percentage of skills mastered. Performance-based assessment measures are designed to provide indications of a student's learned skills as demonstrated through material that is produced under conditions that simulate events occurring in the environment where the skill needs to be produced. Included among these measures would be lab demonstrations, artistic performances, writing samples, job evaluation systems, and other types of skills that demonstrate learning through the integration and application of the knowledge. Curriculum-based assessment represents attempts to assess a student's performance using expected curriculum objectives as the data for evaluation. There are multiple models of curriculum-based assessment (e.g., Fuchs & Deno, 1991; Shapiro, 1996; Shapiro & Elliott, 1999), but all models are focused on evaluating student progress in an ongoing manner directly from a curriculum.

Standardized Norm-Referenced Tests

Each assessment method brings different issues related to psychometric properties. Of all measures, standardized norm-referenced tests possess probably the strongest reliability and validity. These measures often contain well-developed and representative norms that provide opportunities to compare student performance on the measure against a sample that represents similar age/grade peers across the country. If a measure is well developed, it usually contains a sample that is representative of the U.S. distribution by race, socioeconomic level, and other personal characteristics that are known to have correlated influence on the skills being assessed. Test publishers in developing and marketing these measures are careful to establish that the measures have high levels of test-retest reliability (usually correlations >.90), as well as demonstrating excellent concurrent validity. For example, the Woodcock–Johnson Psychoeducational Battery (Woodcock & Johnson, 1989) provides norm-referenced assessment data in areas that include skills ranging from letter-word identification through science, social studies, and humanities. The Wechsler Individual Achievement Test (1992) provides assessment of basic areas of reading, mathematics, and spelling. These types of measures contain numerous subtest scores as well as overall global achievement scores, allowing the user to obtain data on specific subskill development as well as more generally developed areas such as basic reading or math.

Although standardized norm-referenced tests tend to have some of the best and well-documented psychometric properties of all academic assessment measures, these tests have frequently been the subject of substantial criticism. Among the many criticisms of the tests is whether what is tested in published norm-referenced measures overlaps with what is being taught within the curriculum. Several studies have shown that the degree of overlap between the test content and the curriculum for some individual norm-referenced achievement tests is questionable (e.g., Bell, Lentz, & Graden, 1992; Good & Salvia, 1988; Martens, Steele, Massey, & Diskin, 1995; Shapiro & Derr, 1987; Shriner & Salvia, 1988). There is another substantive concern regarding the limited links between norm-referenced tests and instructional design. Given the range of skills and ages which these measures assess, it is difficult to derive clear directions for instructional targets from the results. Clearly, norm-referenced measures were never designed with instructional development in mind, and using these measures in this way is at cross-purposes with the tests' intention. Norm-referenced tests are also potentially influenced by practice effects. As a result, repeated use of the measures over short periods of time can confound real improvement in the learning of skills with simple practice effects. For these and other reasons, educators have sought alternative measures that, while possibly not measuring up to the psychometric properties of norm-referenced tests, try to address some of the criticisms.

Criterion-Referenced Tests

These measures are designed to determine whether or not students are mastering identified instructional objectives. As such, when a teacher gives a test that is based on the teaching of a unit on, for example, "Precursors to the Civil War," he or she is using a criterion-referenced approach to evaluation. When assessing overall student achievement, these measures are used less often than norm-referenced achievement tests. However, there are a few excellent, well-developed criterion-referenced measures such as the KeyMath-Revised (Connolly, 1988) and the Brigance Diagnostic Inventories (Brigance, 1976). For example, the Brigance Diagnostic Inventories are a multiple skill battery of tests that examine a very large number of skill sequences. Measures at the preschool ages are arranged in a developmental hierarchy and those for school-aged children are presented in a grade-level fashion. This approach provides a normative reference for performance; however, the measures are not designed as norm-referenced tests. Psychometrically, no data on reliability or validity are provided; however, the content validity of the measure appears very strong. Other individually administered criterion-referenced achievement tests, such as the Basic Achievement Skills Individual Screener (BASIS; Sonnenschein, 1983), provide stronger indications of the measure's reliability and validity. However, the primary value of these measures lies in their use in the selection of appropriate targets for intervention development.

Performance-Based Assessment

One of the significant criticisms of standardized measures is their failure to evaluate the depth of one's thinking. Additionally, these measures are viewed as artificial and not representative of the types of activities that acquisition of the skills would require. Performance-based assessments are defined as, "testing methods that require students to create an answer or product that demonstrates their knowledge or skills" (U.S. Congress, Office of Technology Assessment, 1992, p. 16). The measures are designed to be authentic analogues of real-life problems. Data obtained through these measures involve examining how students construct their responses. The idea is to determine the strength and depth of the students' learning and thinking processes. Although the primary purpose of performance-based assessment has been to drive instructional intervention, it has increasingly been adopted as a general method for large-scale, schoolwide assessment.

Performance-based assessment has a long history in the workplace and the military. In schools, performance assessment is a natural extension of attempts to develop measures that truly assess the student's capability to demonstrate the application and integration of acquired knowledge. The measures are designed to select tasks that are aligned with curriculum objectives; allow students to know the scoring criteria before they begin work on the task; and provide clear examples of exemplary performance on the task. They are also designed to encourage self-assessment and provide scoring mechanisms that are linked to the standards expected according to the student's age as well as comparisons to others completing the same task.

Psychometrically, performance-assessment methods present important challenges. Typically, the measurement tools of performance assessment require individuals, trained as "experts" in the domain being evaluated, to read or observe the student's performance and rate their product or behavior on an established scale or rubric. For example, if the performance measure asked a student to describe the steps to be taken in designing a science experiment, a typical scoring rubric might have the rater score the student's performance on a numerical scale. Each point of the scale would be anchored to specific behaviors. The development of the scale requires very careful attention to issues of content and discriminant validity. The interrater agreement properties of the rubric must be carefully considered. Attempts to minimize error due to subjective impressions are considered the highest priority in the use of these measures.

Curriculum-Based Assessment

Another alternative approach to assessing academic performance that has been developing since the mid-1980s, is curriculum-based assessment (CBA). Defined as "a procedure for determining the instructional needs of a student based on the student's ongoing performance within existing course content" (Tucker, 1985, p. 200), CBA attempts to determine the degree to which a student is succeeding in the school instruction. Two general approaches to CBA have been identified (Fuchs & Deno, 1992). Specific subskill mastery methods of CBA are similar to other criterion-referenced assessments and examine the degree to which students are mastering identified curriculum skill objectives. These methods use nonstandardized, teacher-developed metrics and are quite useful for developing effective intervention strategies. Those methods described by Gickling and Rosenfield (1995), and Howell, Fox, and Morehead (1993) are good illustrations of this methodology.

General outcome measurement approaches to CBA use standardized measurements across skill areas. Measures are selected from curriculum materials that are linked to identified, long-term curriculum objectives. For example, students might be asked to complete twice each week a sheet of math problems that are derived from all objectives of that grade. As instruction progresses, a student's increase in acquired skills is reflected in a gradually improved performance over time. By repeating these measures frequently and graphically displaying the results, student performance that ceases to progress can be identified. These data then cue the teacher that changes in the instructional processes are needed.

The best example of this approach to CBA is curriculum-based measurement (CBM). Described by Deno and his colleagues (e.g., Deno, Marston, & Mirkin, 1982; Deno, Mirkin, & Chiang, 1982), CBM has been found to have strong psychometric properties. Correlations with standardized norm-referenced assessment measures range from .70 to .95 (Shinn, 1989), and have been shown to be very sensitive to student performance over time (Fuchs, Fuchs, Hamlett, Walz, & Germann, 1993). Additionally, CBM measures have been shown to be useful for instructional planning as well as evaluation (e.g., Fuchs, Fuchs, Phillips, Hamlett, & Karns, 1995).

Students with Disabilities

Recently, concerns have been raised about how students with disabilities are considered in district-wide evaluations of academic achievement. For example, Jayanthi, Havekost, Bursuck, Epstein, and Polloway (1994), in a national survey of district policies concerning standardized and nonstandardized testing, found that between 55 and 60% of the responding districts required some type of accommodations for students with disabilities. In a related national survey, Jayanthi, Epstein, Polloway, and Bursuck (1996) examined the perceptions of general education teachers regarding adaptations for testing commonly used for students with disabilities. These adaptations included among others (1) giving individual help with directions; (2) reading test questions to students; (3) simplifying wording of test questions; and (4) providing extra space on tests for answering. A total of 66.6% of the teachers sampled indicated that it was not fair to make testing adaptations only for students with disabilities.

These and other issues related to the evaluation of academic outcomes for students with disabilities have been examined by the National Center on Educational Outcomes. Exclusion of students with disabilities in large-scale district-wide assessment projects places the consideration of these students in school reform efforts in jeopardy (Ysseldyke & Thurlow, 1993). A large number of recommendations for strategies to include these students in such assessment projects are made by the center. Included among these recommendations are the types, level, and methods for adaptations as well as alterative assessment strategies to better measure outcomes for students who cannot participate in general large-scale assessments.

[*See also* Academic Assessment–Intervention Link; *and* Academic Intervention.]

Bibliography

Bell, P. F., Lentz, F. E., & Graden, J. L. (1992). Effects of curriculum-test overlap on standardized test scores: Identifying systematic confounds in educational decision making. *School Psychology Review, 21,* 644–655.

Brigance, A. H. (1976). *Diagnostic inventory of basic skills.* North Billerica, MA: Curriculum Associates.

Connolly, A. (1988). *KeyMath Diagnostic Arithmetic Test–Revised.* Circle Pines, MN: American Guidance Service.

Deno, S. L., Marston, D., & Mirkin, P. K. (1982). Valid measurement procedures for continuous evaluation of written expression. *Exceptional Children, 48,* 368–371.

Deno, S. L., Mirkin, P. K., & Chiang, B. (1982). Identifying valid measures of reading. *Exceptional Children, 49,* 36–47.

Fuchs, L. S., & Deno, S. L. (1991). Paradigmatic distinctions between instructionally relevant measurement models. *Exceptional Children, 57,* 488–500.

Fuchs, L. S., & Deno, S. L. (1992). Effects of curriculum within curriculum-based measurement. *Exceptional Children, 58,* 232–243.

Fuchs, L. S., Fuchs, D., Hamlett, C. L., Walz, L., & Germann, G. (1993). Formative evaluation of academic progress: How much growth can we expect? *School Psychology Review, 22,* 27–48.

Fuchs, L. S., Fuchs, D., Phillips, N. B., Hamlett, C. L., & Karns, K. (1995). Acquisition and transfer effects of claswide peer-asssted learning strategies in mathematics for students with varying learning histories. *School Psychology Review, 24,* 604–630.

Gickling, E. E., & Rosenfield, S. (1995). Best practices in curriculum-based assessment. In A. Thomas & J. Grimes (Eds.), *Best practices in school psychology* (Vol. 3, pp. 587–595). Washington, DC: National Association of School Psychologists.

Good, R. H., III, & Salvia, J. (1988). Curriculum bias in published, norm-referenced reading tests: Demonstrable effects. *School Psychology Review, 17,* 51–60.

Howell, K. W., Fox, S. L., Morehead, M. K. (1993). *Curriculum-based evaluation: Teaching and decision making* (2nd ed.). Pacific Grove, CA: Brooks/Cole.

Jayanthi, M., Bursuck, W., Havekost, D. M., Epstein, M. H., & Polloway, E. A. (1994). School district testing policies and students with disabilities: A national survey. *School Psychology Review, 23,* 694–703.

Jayanthi, M., Epstein, M. H., Polloway, E. A., & Bursuck, W. D. (1996). A national survey of general education teachers' perceptions of testing adaptations. *Journal of Special Education, 30,* 99–115.

Martens, B. K., Steele, E. S., Massie, D. R., & Diskin, M. J. (1995). Curriculum bias in standardized tests of reading recoding. *Journal of School Psychology, 33,* 287–296.

Salvia, J., & Ysseldyke, J. E. (1995). *Assessment in special and remedial education.* Boston: Houghton Mifflin.

Shapiro, E. S. (1996). *Academic skills problems: Direct assessment and intervention* (2nd ed.). New York: Guilford Press.

Shapiro, E. S., & Derr, T. F. (1987). An examination of overlap between reading curricula and standardized achievement tests. *Journal of Special Education, 21,* 59–67.

Shapiro, E. S., & Elliott, S. N. (1999). Curriculum-based assessment and other performance based assessment strategies. In T. Gutkin & C. Reynolds (Eds.), *Handbook of school psychology* (3rd ed., pp. 383–400). New York: Wiley.

Shinn, M. R. (Ed.). (1989). *Curriculum-based measurement: Assessing special children.* New York: Guilford Press.

Shriner, J., & Salvia, J. (1988). Chronic noncorrespondence between elementary math curricula and arithmetic tests. *Exceptional Children, 55,* 240–248.

Sonnenschein, J. L. (1983). *Basic achievement skills individual screener.* San Antonio: Psychological Corp.

Tucker, J. (1985). Curriculum-based assessment: An introduction. *Exceptional Children, 32,* 199–204.

U.S. Congress, Office of Technology Assessment (1992, February). *Testing in American schools: Asking the right questions (OTA-SET-519).* Washington, DC: U.S. Government Printing Office.

Wechsler, D. (1992). *Wechsler Individual Achievement Test.* San Antonio: The Psychological Corporation.

Woodcock, R. W., & Johnson, M. B. (1989). *Woodcock-Johnson Tests of Achievement-Revised.* Allen, TX: DLM.

Ysseldyke, J. E., & Thurlow, M. L. (1993). *Views on inclusion and testing accommodations for students with disabilities*

(Synthesis Report 7). Minneapolis: University of Minnesota, National Center on Educational Outcomes.

Edward S. Shapiro

ACADEMIC INTERVENTION. [*This entry discusses interventions aimed at social, emotional, and behavioral functioning and profiles the history, development, and purpose of academic intervention.*]

Recent data on the incidence of a variety of disruptive and problem behaviors, including aggressiveness, impulsivity, hyperactivity, antisocial behavior, and violence, suggest that the behavioral and emotional needs of school-aged children are increasing, and they are becoming more complex. Estimates suggest that approximately 5% of children are "seriously maladjusted" and an additional 16% are at risk for significant emotional and mental disorders. At the same time, socializing influences on children are rapidly changing. Twenty-five percent of children live with only one parent, and 50% will live in a single-parent home at some time during their childhood. Surveys indicate that 70 to 80% of these afflicted youth do not receive the necessary interventions. In addition, the interrelatedness of problems such as child abuse, violence, delinquency, substance use, and school difficulty is becoming increasingly apparent. The challenge to mental health professionals is to develop effective approaches to prevention and intervention that can be applied systematically and efficiently.

Changes in psychosocial, family, and health issues faced by children and adolescents provide a basis for changes in the way intervention services are conceptualized and delivered. Historically, psychotherapy services were designed based on the assumption that only a few children would require therapeutic intervention and that children in therapy would be supported in a two-parent family living within a stable community. The current psychosocial realities surrounding children, however, have led to a reconceptualization of the role of schools as an organizing framework for preventing and intervening in problem behavior. Traditional school approaches were based on the view that problem behaviors are due to "within" child deficits. Over the years, attempts to remedy problem behavior by focusing on specific skill deficits have been shown to lack the potency or breadth necessary for long-lasting changes in behavior. Hence, a problem-solving approach based on a broad social-ecological model provides the theoretical framework for many prevention and intervention strategies within schools.

A diverse range of disruptive or problem behavior constitutes the focus of prevention and intervention work. Strategies are both preventative (i.e., aim to alter student outcomes so that problem or disruptive behavior does not begin) and intervention focused (i.e., aim to change or remedy a persistent problem or disruptive behavior pattern). An attempt has been made to review well-established and empirically supported prevention and intervention tactics. Preventative approaches and interventions for youth with serious emotional and behavioral disorders need to be sufficiently intensive yet flexibly responsive to unique and changing characteristics, involve comprehensive individualized care, and incorporate nondiscriminatory practices (Quinn & McDougal, 1998). Students respond best to a preventive curriculum that integrates social skill development, conflict resolution, self-control training, and stress management. Adelman and Taylor (1998) provide some basic guidelines for interventions: (1) Balance an emphasis on discrete or target problems with a focus on similar underlying commonalities across problem behavior. (2) Personalize or individualize intervention based on underlying need, intent, or function. (3) Use the most normalized, least restrictive intervention (e.g., most natural environment, school-based, "best fit"). (4) Incorporate comprehensive, integrative approaches. (5) Prioritize based on consumer needs, not service provider dispositions or preferences.

Fueled by demands to address increasing social and behavioral problems among youth, prevention programs are being advocated to provide more solutions for more children. Recent literature stresses the critical combination of modifying teacher behavior, classroom environment, and school climate, as well as actively teaching prosocial, alternative behaviors across the curriculum. To develop school-based prevention programs, a task force that takes leadership in conducting a needs analysis and resource mapping is suggested. The task force also might examine environments such as the lunchroom and playground to determine general problem behavior concerns. Another task is to examine discipline incidents, including frequency, and reasons related to visits to the principal's office, peer conflicts, suspensions, and expulsions. In addition, it is useful for the task force to consider what schoolwide social discipline procedures exist and whether they match the characteristics of students attending the school and promote desired student outcomes. A schoolwide prevention plan aimed at improving the school climate should be designed to enhance social and behavioral functioning among all students and modified based on outcome or effect data.

Because aggressive and disruptive behaviors place many day-to-day demands on teachers, collaborative teams are viewed as an essential problem-solving mechanism. Collaborative teams consist of school psychologists, teachers, administrators, social workers, and other support service personnel who determine the focus of intervention; generate prevention and intervention strategies; assist in implementing, monitoring, and ensuring the integrity of interventions; provide follow-up activities; and evaluate the effectiveness of preventive or intervention approaches. For collaborative teams to function effectively, they need to establish a shared vision, be goal directed, and, most importantly, provide an engaging forum for problem solving and communication.

Effective prevention programs also require a focus on the teacher and the classroom ecology (Keller & Tapasak, 1997). Students who exhibit aggressive behaviors are more prone to outbursts when frustrated by disorganized or inconsistent teachers, difficulty in learning, boredom, irrelevant curriculum, misunderstanding directions and task expectations, too rapid instruction, and a mismatch between instruction and the student's current level of functioning. Effective teaching strategies are crucial preventative mechanisms for two reasons. First, they prevent the triggering of frustration with learning, a fear of failure, or other academically induced factors that provoke aggression and violence. Second, effective teaching promotes academic engagement, which is incompatible with aggressive behavior (Gettinger & Stoiber, 1999). In addition, getting students to be academically engaged leads to other engagement behaviors, such as coming to school and class on time, being prepared for and participating in class work, putting in the work needed to complete assignments, and not being disruptive in class.

Teacher characteristics that have been shown to lead to more caring classroom communities include (1) demonstrating and communicating respect and caring to students; (2) establishing a positive relationship, trust, and rapport; (3) being able to deescalate tension in the classroom; (4) respecting students' dignity by not resorting to threats or confrontations during stressful situations; (5) applying cooperative learning strategies; (6) displaying enthusiasm and positive expectations; (7) being aware of students' individual needs, interests, and talents; and (8) being able to create a positive classroom environment. Evidence supports the importance of classroom rules that are few in number, brief, concise, and clear for the prevention of disruptive behavior. Providing students with an opportunity to coconstruct classroom rules for behavior is effective because students take ownership for them. Classroom expectations or rules should be posted and reviewed regularly.

Child-focused prevention and intervention programs can be implemented within classrooms or within small groups. Early generations of child-focused approaches were derived from social skills training models and had a behavioral or cognitive-behavioral orientation. Social skills interventions are based on the assumption that children fail to perform social skills in specific situations due to inappropriate arrangement of antecedents and/or consequences. A comprehensive social skills training program that has application at the preschool, elementary, and adolescent level is the "skill-streaming" system of Goldstein and his associates (Goldstein, 1988). Various social skills, such as making friends, dealing with stress, and self-control, are taught directly to students via four basic strategies: modeling, role playing, performance feedback, and transfer and maintenance of training. Unfortunately, evaluation research on the skill-streaming program suggests that generalizability is the exception rather than the rule (DuPaul & Eckert, 1994). There is evidence, however, that skill streaming may be more effective when combined with other interventions, such as anger-control programs that address cognitive-behavioral connections, and when both teachers and parents are involved in implementing the program.

Social problem-solving (SPS) approaches derived from the cognitive-behavioral tradition have emerged as a "second generation" of social competence programs. Theoretically, social problem-solving programs address the problems of transfer and maintenance through an ongoing, long-term program that is integrated into the classroom structure and builds on skill continuity. Elias and Tobias's (1996) SPS program emphasizes three central skills of calming oneself down when upset, approaching and interacting with others in an interpersonally acceptable way, and using social decision-making strategies. Each strategy includes a series of steps that students are taught. In addition, guidelines for using the SPS program are suggested, including: (1) preparing the students by describing relevant situations, describing the skills, and eliciting or sharing a rationale for the skill; (2) breaking the skill into its components and teaching components through modeling; (3) providing hypothetical situations (via stories, books, games, videos) for guided practice and behavioral rehearsal with feedback; and (4) encouraging use of the skill throughout the curriculum.

A meta-analysis by Stage and Quiroz (1997) indicated that group contingencies, self-management (include modeling, correspondence training, self-monitoring, self-reinforcement, and self-recording), and differential reinforcement were effective strategies, resulting in a reduction of disruptive behavior in 85% of students. Other research has suggested the usefulness of differential reinforcement of incompatible behaviors (DRI) for modifying student aggression and promoting prosocial behavior. In using DRI, teachers must carefully monitor and reward or reinforce positive behaviors considered to be incompatible with aggression. In general, research has shown considerable variance among students' responses to group contingencies, self-management, and DRI, with aggressive and conduct-disordered children demonstrating the most resistance to intervention.

Effective interventions for students with attention-deficit/hyperactivity disorder (ADHD) usually incorporate three broad components: altering the beliefs and attitudes of individuals (both peers and adults) who interact with the child; altering the environments in which they live and learn; and altering the behavior of the student. The first step in designing interventions for ADHD is to educate teachers, parents, and peers about the nature, course, outcome, and causes of ADHD. The goal is to address attitudes and beliefs that have a negative effect on the way individuals interpret, interact, and respond to attentional and behavioral difficulties.

Environmental modifications are directed at examining practices that may exacerbate ADHD. For example, the amount of time that a child is expected to wait in line when leaving or returning from recess might be reduced. Other suggested classroom modifications include seating students preferentially, calling on students frequently during discussions, providing a daily check sheet of assignments to help students organize tasks, and providing low-structured, open-ended activities. Children with ADHD generally do not respond to natural, less overt incentives and simple reinforcement procedures that work effectively with other students. Experts in ADHD suggest that several types of classroom-based behavioral systems should be considered for altering the child's functioning, including incentive systems, token economies, response cost, home-school notes, and time-out procedures.

Cognitive-behavioral interventions suggested for children with ADHD aim to improve self-regulation. Recommended procedures are self-monitoring (helping students to become aware of their own attending behavior), self-instruction (teaching students to use self-talk as they work, asking questions such as, "What is my problem?" "How can I do it?" "Am I using my plan?"), and self-evaluation (teaching students to evaluate their progress on academic or behavioral goals). Although more powerful strategies are recommended for modifying the behaviors of students with ADHD, punishment approaches remain controversial and should only be considered as a last resort (Larrivee, 1992) and after ensuring that the rights of students will not be violated and that the procedures will not produce psychological or emotional harm. Punishment strategies, such as response cost, time-out, and overcorrection, may be effective in suppressing unacceptable behavior. Unfortunately, punishment is limited to behavior reduction and does not teach appropriate or desirable behavior.

The development and maintenance of aggressive and antisocial behavior has been linked to complex, interactional processes that require multimodal interventions. Students with aggressive tendencies have trouble controlling their impulses, their moods can change rapidly, and they are easily frustrated or feel "trapped."

These youth also may misinterpret routine experiences as threatening, distort social information, and have a hostile attribution bias. Traditional behavioral approaches have been criticized for not counteracting the intense emotional arousal that may accompany impulsive and explosive outbursts and/or addressing aggressive youth's cognitive-mediational deficiencies. The movement toward comprehensive intervention approaches is based on two phenomena linked to aggression: (1) cognitive processes, such as attributions, decision making, consequential thinking, and self-statements, that influence the development of anger and aggressive responses; and (2) social and interpersonal problem-solving deficiencies. Intervention goals for youth with violence and aggression problems focus on increasing their capacity for empathy and perspective taking and helping them experience affective responses (both positive and negative) without acting out.

Several interrelated anger-control intervention components are necessary for responding effectively to aggressive youth, including arousal management, cognitive restructuring, and prosocial skill development. Feindler and Scalley (1998) point out the advantage of using group anger-management interventions because they permit multiple models and sources of feedback, practice opportunities for appropriate peer interaction, demonstration of appropriate responses to spontaneous and naturalistic provocations, and increased opportunities for cueing and reinforcing prosocial behavior. Through the use of modeling, in-class practice, role-playing, and homework assignments, group members learn to identify anger-provoking incidents, use cognitive strategies and conflict-resolution strategies to control their impulses and manage their arousal, and replace their former aggressive or passive/submissive behaviors with appropriate communication and assertiveness.

Effective prevention of early sexual activity, drug and alcohol use, and other risk-taking behaviors focus on developing assertive responses to peer pressure, provide information about outcomes associated with risk taking, incorporate communication and decision-making activities, and facilitate self-management and problem solving. Considerable evidence suggests that narrow-focused, information-only programs may not alter youthful dispositions toward risk-taking behavior (Stoiber, Anderson, & Schowalter, 1998). Comprehensive risk-taking reduction and health-promotion programs that target multiple issues and are integrated into the school curriculum are effective for at-risk youth due to the interrelated occurrence of problem behaviors.

A problem-solving framework has been suggested to treat the problems of depressed youth (Stark et al., 1998). Children are taught problem-solving steps, using a small therapeutic group, through education, modeling, coaching, rehearsal, and feedback. The steps are problem definition, getting motivated to face the problem, generating alternative solutions, predicting outcomes for solutions, enacting a plan of action, and evaluating progress toward goals. The focus of interventions for depressed youth is to improve their affect or mood, help them develop motivation to cope, and alter their depressive cognitions.

In summary, there is strong support for proactive, multicomponent, problem-solving approaches for preventing and reducing various aggressive, disruptive, and other problem behaviors. Although reactive strategies such as suspension, expulsion, and time-out may provide immediate relief to a problematic situation, they do not provide long-term benefits. Preventive and intervention strategies that are planned and implemented within a broader, ecological context appear to be optimal.

[*See also* Academic Assessment–Intervention Link; Academic Assessment of Performance; *and* Intervention.]

Bibliography

Adelman, H. S., & Taylor, L. (1998). Mental health in schools: Moving forward. *School Psychology Review, 27,* 175–190.

DuPaul, G. J., & Eckert, T. L. (1994). The effects of social skills curricula: Now you see them, now you don't. *School Psychology Quarterly, 9,* 113–132.

Elias, M. J., & Tobias, S. E. (1996). *Social problem solving: Interventions in the schools.* New York: Guilford Press.

Feindler, E. L., & Scalley, M. (1998). Adolescent anger-management groups for violence reduction. In K. C. Stoiber & T. R. Kratochwill (Eds.), *Handbook of group intervention for children and families* (pp. 100–119). Boston: Allyn & Bacon.

Gettinger, M., & Stoiber, K. C. (1999). Excellence in teaching: Review of instructional and environmental variables. In C. R. Reynolds & T. B. Gutkin (Eds.), *The handbook of school psychology* (pp. 933–958). New York: Wiley.

Goldstein, A. P. (Ed.). (1988). *The prepare curriculum.* Champaign, IL: Research Press.

Keller, H. R., & Tapasak, R. C. (1997). Classroom management. In A. P. Goldstein & J. C. Conoley (Eds.), *School violence intervention: A practical handbook* (pp. 107–126). New York: Guilford Press.

Larrivee, B. (1992). *Strategies for effective classroom management: Creating a collaborative climate: Leader's guide to facilitate learning experiences.* Boston: Allyn & Bacon.

Quinn, K. P., & McDougal, J. L. (1998). A mile wide and a mile deep: Comprehensive interventions for children and youth with emotional and behavioral disorders and their families. *School Psychology Review, 27,* 191–203.

Stage, S. A., & Quiroz, D. R. (1997). A meta-analysis of interventions to decrease disruptive classroom behavior in public education settings. *School Psychology Review, 26,* 333–368.

Stark, K. D., Swearer, S., Sommer, D., Hickey, B. B., Napolitano, S., Kurowski, C., & Dempsey, M. (1998). School-based group treatment for depressive disorders in children. In K. C. Stoiber & T. R. Kratochwill (Eds.), *Handbook of group intervention for children and families* (pp. 68–99). Boston: Allyn & Bacon.

Stoiber, K. C., Anderson, A. J., Schowalter, D. S. (1998). Group prevention and intervention with pregnant and parenting adolescents. In K. C. Stoiber & T. R. Kratochwill (Eds.), *Handbook of group intervention for children and families* (pp. 280–306). Boston: Allyn & Bacon.

Karen Callan Stoiber

ACCESSIBLE ENVIRONMENTS. *See* Environmental Research Design.

ACCIDENTS. The one-year prevalence of accidents is about 15 to 20% in most societies in the Western world; about 80% are motor vehicle accidents (MVAs) or occur during sports, at work, or at home. Most accidents occur during working hours, but accidents involving young people, in particular MVAs and accidents involving persons with significant psychological problems, occur more often during evening hours and at night, especially on weekends.

The peak ages for accidents are among the younger age groups. This is only partly explained by lack of driving experience. Males have higher accident rates than females for both fatal and nonfatal accidents—for almost all types of accidents—the ratio being about 2:1. This gender difference in accident rates has been explained in part by differential socialization of males and females, but also in part by hormonal effects (see Gochman, 1997, Vol. 1). The gender difference disappears among people over age 60.

Accidental Injury

About 80% of accidents cause personal injury. In the United States, accidents causing personal injury are estimated to affect more than 28 million individuals annually. In general, 30 to 50% of accidental injuries require medical attention, and about one tenth of such victims require hospitalization. In the United Kingdom (population 58 million), more than 13,000 hospital beds are occupied by accident victims each day. High impact accidents, such as MVAs, more frequently result in significant clinical injuries requiring inpatient hospital treatment (about 40% of hospitalized) than low energy accidents (e.g., sport).

Accidents are also an important cause of premature

death, in particular among the younger age groups. About 5% of annual deaths in Western societies are violent, the majority (95%) being caused primarily by transport accidents (i.e., MVA).

There are several different ways of classifying injuries. The anatomical approach, Abbreviated Injury Scale (AIS), gives a number (0–6) to each body region (general, head, neck, chest, abdomen, pelvis, extremities) where 0 is no injury and 5 is the highest score for injuries not causing immediate death. The Injury Severity Score (ISS) is the sum of the squares of the three highest AIS ratings. While less than 1% of the total population sustaining injuries will have an ISS score higher than 10, at least 25% of hospitalized subjects will have such high scores. In trauma centers admitting the more severely injured, the percentage of high ISS scores is even higher. There is a statistically significant association between ISS score and prevalence of long-term behavioral problems, but neither ISS nor other injury severity classification systems in themselves can predict individual patients who are at risk for short- or long-term behavioral problems.

Differential Accident Involvement

The concept of accident proneness, or what is probably better termed differential accident involvement (McKenna, 1983), has been heavily debated since the term was coined, originally as a result of studies on work injuries after World War I (Greenwood & Woods, 1919). The Incidence of Industrial Accidents upon Individuals with Special Reference to Multiple accidents. (HM Stationery Office, London, 1919). They observed that work injuries did not follow the laws of chance (Poisson distribution). There was an unequal initial liability to accident involvement (negative binomial distribution). This finding, and the fact that 65 to 80% of accidents are caused by human factors, has been replicated consistently ever since.

Individual Variables Predicting Accident Occurrence

The main findings summarized by Shaw and Sichel in their comprehensive review of this topic (1971) was still valid in the late 1990s. Attitudes and personality variables consistently associated with increased likelihood of involvement in an accident are: mild antisocial tendencies (e.g., willingness to break the law and violate rules of safe driving); aggressiveness, hostility, impulsiveness, thrill and adventure seeking, and type-A behavior. Personality assessments demonstrate high extroversion-neuroticism (Eysenck Personality Questionnaire); low harm avoidance (Cloninger's Tridimensional Personality Questionnaire); low conscientiousness (Costa-McCraes's Five Factor model). The repeaters are dependent on external factors and have weak inner control with poor ability to delay action. The majority

of accident repeaters are under 30 years of age. However, actual exposure to risk (e.g., annual mileage driving) is also important. Perceptual and cognitive defects may play a substantial role in a high-risk environment and in many of the MVAs that involve older subjects (e.g., pedestrians).

Longitudinal studies of birth cohort suggest that accident-risk behavior has developmental origins in childhood (Caspi et al., 1997). In the 1988 U.S. National Health Interview Survey, the odds of unintentional injury in children with severe behavioral problems was 1.65 times greater than in children without behavioral problems, after controlling for relevant sociodemographic characteristics. Adolescents and adults with significant psychological problems (psychopathology including substance abuse) are more often involved in accidents. They also sustain more severe injuries. Among adults, patients with schizophrenia and affective illness have more accidental *deaths* compared to the general population.

Nevertheless, psychiatric disorders contribute little to the overall prevalence of accidents, with the notable exception of drug and alcohol abuse. Approximately 15 to 25% of people brought to hospital emergency rooms due to accidental injury have clinically significant blood concentrations of alcohol. Substance abuse problems and severe personality disorders also increase the prevalence of accident repeaters. Some of these subjects may mature, however, explaining why, for some subjects, accident repeating may be a phenomenon of passing duration.

Acute physical illness is a rather infrequent cause of accidents (1–2/1000). Chronic physical illness is not an important cause of accidents, but associated symptoms like sleep problems and fatigue may increase the risk of accidents among those with chronic illnesses.

In conclusion, individual factors are important for being involved in an accident. Considering the high incidence of accidents in the population, however, the positive predictive power of individual psychological variables is too low to be useful in the general prevention of accidents in the population.

Family and Sociological Factors

Those involved in accidents more often have a lower socioeconomic background, with lower elementary and secondary school marks and lower educational attainment overall. The difference is less pronounced for females than males. In children and adolescents, even when controlling for demographic risk, lower family support, more psychological and social problems in the family, and more frequent accident involvement by the parents, contribute to accident risk.

The work environment, morale, and attitudes of work colleagues, social group (gang), friends, or family members are important contributors to the incidence of accidents because of their effect on safety attitudes and behavior. In the classic U.S. Navy study by Pugh and Gunderson (1979) of the accident rates among enlisted crew members aboard 18 destroyers during 6 to 8 months overseas deployment, the highest trauma rate occurred in divisions with low-quality personnel (as expected). However, the level of work-group friendliness was important. Low or very high group friendliness clearly interfered with morale and safety attitudes (low if there was low group friendliness; "goofing off" if there was very high group friendliness), and increased the accident risk in the low-quality personnel but not in the high-quality personnel. Similarly, among teenagers, the MVA involvement rates have been found to be approximately twice as high with passengers as without, and more at-fault fatal crashes are associated with passenger presence for younger drivers.

Environmental Factors

The intensity and amount of occupational exposure to dangerous situations are important predictors of accident involvement. Situational factors like stress and harsh weather conditions may also influence accident risk, primarily by creating difficult conditions for decision (stress) and task execution (situational variables like fog, rain, icy roads). Furthermore, high demands (e.g., complicated technology; poor decision support from equipment; heavy traffic) combined with low control (e.g., large workload, time pressure, less training, impaired cognitive and psychomotor function) increase the risk of accidents.

Accident Prediction in High-Risk Environments

Whatever the cause, environmental factors put the perceptual and performance abilities of the person at stake. Those with lesser cognitive (e.g., attention, perception) and psychomotor abilities, including training and experience, will be at higher risk. For example, impaired ability to sustain attention under stress (high workload; time pressure) followed by less good involuntary control of motor function, are risk factors. Field dependent persons are at risk. Impaired perceptual abilities (e.g., measured by the Defense Mechanism test, a tachistoscopic method for quantification of perceptual ability) also predict accident risk in aviators and motor vehicle drivers. Accordingly, the use of functional cognitive and psychomotor tests are increasingly used to select subjects for exceptionally dangerous occupations.

The Psychology of the Immediate Response

There are several potential sources of distress inherent in an accident. The most important accident related variables include actual severity of the accident (e.g., real degree of threat to life of oneself and others), de-

gree of helplessness, duration of the stressor, the presence of actual physical injury, and exposure to dead and mutilated bodies. The accident may represent a blow to the person's feelings of invulnerability (narcissistic loss) or it may provoke conflictual feelings (e.g., self-blame, survivor guilt) or shame (e.g., own actions or fantasies prior to the situation (see Table 1).

If an injury occurs, the injury may threaten self-esteem and body image, or represent a loss of function, or the injury may even in some instances serve primary gains in a psychodynamic sense. The immediate responses will also be influenced by psychological issues, like fear of losing control. Conflicts related to secondary gains may also influence the clinical response observed by others.

Individual factors play a significant role, however, including the presence of premorbid mental health problems and personality traits (e.g., neuroticism) and a previous history of exposure to accidents. There is variation in the relative contribution of "objective" accident-related variables compared to "subjective" appraisal-related variables in shaping the acute response. A rule of thumb is that the less severe the accident, the more important are variables not directly related to the accident per se (i.e., the personal meaning of the accident and its consequences for the individual).

Clinical Features of the Acute Psychological Response to Accidents

The *immediate* behavioral responses (i.e., within seconds) to subjective significant accidents involve phylogenetic responses common to all mammals: flight (i.e., anxiety, fear; in extreme cases panic [<1%]); fight (i.e., irritability, aggression, anger), or freeze (i.e., halting in surprise, in more extreme cases emotional numbness including marked parasympathic [vagus] responses, "emotional shock"). The latter response may hamper life-saving actions, but occurs less than 10% of the time. Brief periods of derealization ("unreal," "like a dream," "slow movie") are rather common, even in relatively minor accidents, while symptoms of depersonalization (e.g., "out-of-body experiences") are less common and usually signal a more severe psychological response. The majority of accident victims appear reasonably calm from a behavioral point of view; however, most have some degree of inner turmoil. Clinically significant difficulties with concentration and resulting impaired ability to receive, retrieve, and handle information, are rather infrequent (<20%).

Associated psychophysiological symptoms that are frequently reported include (in decreasing frequency) increased heartbeat, tremor, dry mouth, restlessness, shaking/trembling, weakness in the legs, and sweating. Marked or prolonged psychophysiological symptoms predict long-term behavioral problems. If a warning period occurs (i.e., the time between the person con-

ACCIDENTS. Table 1. Sources of acute and long-term psychological distress in accident victims

	Threat	Loss	Conflict
Accident situation	Actual severity of the accident (death risk; death toll); degree of helplessness; duration	Personal sense of invulnerability	Guilt (e.g. sex, aggression) or blame related to accident circumstances
Injury related	Self-esteem and body-image; exposure to mutilated and dead bodies	True (or imagined) injury, loss of own function or being crippled	Primary gain
Response related	Fear of losing emotional control	Loss of "face," i.e., demonstrating abnormal behavior	Secondary gain; showing "weakness" to others
Effect on significant others	Losing others	Death of significant others (bereavement)	Aggression toward injured or dead significant others
Treatment related	Painful procedures	Necessary surgical procedures causing scars or loss of body parts	Dependence-independence
Secondary events	Media, police	Relatives' and friends' responses	Litigation, insurance

sciously detecting the impending danger and the actual impact), some of the symptoms listed here (e.g., derealization) may be present already prior to impact.

Subacute Responses

In the majority of accident victims, the immediate symptoms gradually fade away. As the victim starts the process of working through the accident and its implications (Table 1), a characteristic cluster of emotions, cognitions, and physiological symptoms may be seen (Horowitz et al., 1976; Horowitz, 1997). *Intrusion* is characterized by reexperiencing the accident situation and is more pronounced among victims exposed to severe accidents. Typical intrusive symptoms reported by subjects involved in accidents are having images of the accident popping into their minds; waves of strong feelings about the accident; thoughts about the accident when they did not mean to think about it, and any reminder bringing back feelings about the accident.

Avoidant symptoms include responses, within coping theory often called emotion focused (Richard Lazarus), for example, wishing to banish memories about the accident; avoiding emotional feelings when thinking about the accident or being reminded of it; keeping unresolved feelings under wraps and trying not to talk about the accident. Avoidance also may include derealizationlike responses (e.g., feelings about the accident being somewhat numb; feeling unrealistic about

the accident, as if the accident hadn't happened or as if it wasn't real). While the mean load of intrusive symptoms is related to the severity of the accident, avoidance is more strongly related also to accident-independent variables (i.e., preaccident psychological traits).

Psychophysiological symptoms (hyperarousal) are less frequent during the subacute phase, with the exception of sleep difficulty (reported by about 40% of noninjured subjects exposed to frightening accidents). Other symptoms of hyperarousal, like exaggerated startle response, irritability, difficulty concentrating, and hypervigilance, are rather infrequent in randomly selected accidentally injured subjects (less than 10%). The prevalence of hyperarousal symptoms (e.g., difficulty concentrating; exaggerated startle response; increased heart rate), is somewhat increased among injured compared to noninjured accident victims, however.

Some injuries may also imply biological dysfunctions, which increase the risk of postaccident deviant behavioral responses; for example, impaired cognitive functions due to head injuries and internal bleeding or significant burn injuries that cause confusion involving psychotic features. The risk of delirium (acute confusion with or without behavioral disruption) due to brain dysfunction after injury is associated with age, preexisting cognitive impairment, and severe physical injury (ISS-score higher than 15).

Acute Stress Reaction

Marked responses to the accident characterized by strong anxiety, confusion, or dissociative symptoms during the first minutes to hours after the accident is called Acute Stress Reaction (ASR). There are significant differences in the definitions of ASR in *ICD–10* and Acute Stress Disorder (ASD) in the *Diagnostic and Statistical Manual of Mental Disorders* of the American Psychiatric Association (Washington, D.C., 1994). These differences affect prevalence rates. *ICD–10* limits the definition of ASR to transient shock symptoms, as already outlined. Prolonged responses are called acute posttraumatic stress disorder. In contrast, *DSM–IV* requires the full criteria of posttraumatic stress disorder to be met for a minimum of 2 days; in addition, dissociative phenomena need to be present. Thus severe but transient responses escape *DSM–IV* classification.

Long-Term Consequences

There may be biological, social, and functional effects as a result of accidents.

Biological, Social, and Functional Effects. Most studies have a 3- to 12-month perspective, but some long-term outcome studies exist. Accidents causing hospitalization may cause changes in perceived health (30–50%); decreased capacity to work (children: play) (10–20%), and decreased social contact and leisure pleasure (5–15%). Family members may be significantly affected by the psychological distress and burden caused by an accident (5–15%). If an injury is present, additional problems related to physical sequelae (present in 40–60%) and impaired physical function (20–40%) may occur. The majority of problems are modest, and improvement over time is the rule.

In large accident victim cohorts, worse psychological health correlates strongly (about 0.5) with worse subjective physical health. Scandinavian studies have demonstrated that these findings are valid even among accident victims who were not injured themselves, like bus- or train drivers.

Psychological Outcome

There is considerable variation in the literature in the prevalence of psychological morbidity after accidents, depending on level of sampling (e.g., random, health-care seekers, hospital cases, special treatment centers, MVAs) or method. Self-reports provide higher estimates than clinical interviews, and the better control for attribution of preaccident mental distress to the current accident, the lower the estimates. Samples of accident victims seeking medical or psychological attention suggest an incidence of nonorganic mental disorders of about 15 to 20% after one year and about 10% after 2 years. In MVA samples (more severe injuries and more frighten-

ing accidents), the prevalence has been estimated at about 25%. Anxiety, mood, and somatoform ("psychosomatic") disorders are most frequently reported.

Driving phobia has been reported in up to 30% of MVA victims. The one-year prevalence of posttraumatic stress disorder (PTSD) after accidents is probably not more than 1%. Among MVA survivors brought to medical attention, estimates vary from 4 to 16% (e.g., Blanchard & Hickling, 1997; Mayou, Tyndel, & Bryant, 1997). During the first months following an accident, the prevalence is higher (15–40%). In comparison, the 6-month prevalence of PTSD found in epidemiological studies is about 1%; and the lifetime incidence about 5% in males and 10% in females. PTSD prevalence rates are partly dependent on differences in criteria (higher rates in *DSM–IV* compared to *ICD–10*) and on method of assessment (higher for self-reports than for interviews). The role of minor brain injury for the prevalence of PTSD is unclear.

Depressive Disorders and Symptoms. The prevalence of depressive disorders and symptoms is similar to or even higher than that reported for PTSD. Somatoform disorders, in particular somatoform pain disorders, frequently occur after accidental injury. The prevalence of other psychological problems is less well studied. There is also an ongoing debate whether, and to what extent, mild brain injury sustained during accidents may explain some of the cognitive deficits, behavioral complaints, and emotional symptoms and disability reported by some subjects after accidents. The current evidence does not favor a neurological explanation in the majority of patients claiming such deficits and behavioral symptoms (Binder, 1997). There is no empirical evidence of increased rate of psychotic disorders after civilian accidents except as a result of severe brain injuries.

Comorbidity. The behavioral comorbidity is considerable, particularly among PTSD patients and those seeking treatment. The larger the comorbidity, the larger the functional impairment. In patient samples of PTSD after accidents, the comorbidity rates for significant depressive symptoms have been estimated at from 50 to 100%. The more severe the PTSD, the more depressive symptoms are reported; and those with marked depression report more intrusive symptoms. Increased intake of alcohol or other substances to relieve emotional pain and suffering may occur after major accidents.

Behavior and Attitudes. Accidents may also have long-term effects on behavior and attitudes without causing psychiatric disorders. After severe accidents, survivors may change their attitude toward life (become less "happy-go-lucky," more contemplative, and take life more seriously). A few may respond by being more aggressive and even neglecting danger ("I don't care"). Follow-up of adolescents surviving bus-train collisions demonstrated higher rates of help-seeking behavior during compulsory military service 7 years later. Observed changes in driving behavior after an MVA may be of passing duration, except for some professional drivers, and often are limited to the circumstances and situations that led to the accident.

Predictors of Long-Term Psychological Problems. There is a strong association between the severity of exposure and actual injury (life threat, horrifying visual images; injury, loss of loved ones and friends, property damage; degree of helplessness; and the duration of the accident situation (Table 1) and negative psychological consequences. Marked acute symptoms of arousal (psychophysiological symptoms) also predict later negative outcomes. These findings are quite robust across studies and do not depend solely on the individual's perception of the impact.

Nevertheless, despite the association between behavioral dysfunction and the severity of the accident, independent research groups have consistently observed that the more complex the clinical picture is, and the longer the follow-up period, the more important are variables not directly related to the accident for the well-being and level of function (see Table 1). Furthermore, variables such as preaccident social and emotional adjustment problems are risk factors for postaccident behavioral problems and maladjustment (e.g., Blanchard & Hickling, 1997; Horowitz, 1997; Mayou et al., 1997).

Current evidence suggests that women are at higher risk for anxiety and depression and men are more at risk for substance abuse and antisocial behavior. With regard to age, some studies suggest that middle-aged subjects are most at risk for psychological problems. Only a few studies have adequately examined and controlled for preexisting conditions and the injury severity score in the analyses, however.

Litigation may hamper adjustment, and major clinical improvement does not occur in most cases after compensation settlement. Malingering is an unlikely explanation in most cases of chronic behavioral disturbances after accidents.

Treatment

The concept of primary prevention refers to accident prevention. Social epidemiology findings clearly demonstrate that when people become more empowered socially and economically, they also become healthier and suffer fewer illnesses and injuries. There is also ample evidence that laws (e.g., speed limits, daylight running car lights, gun control) and risk exposure reduction (e.g., separation of motor vehicles from pedestrians and bicycles, restrictions in access to drugs and alcohol) significantly reduce accident rates.

The psychologist plays a key role in promoting

safety. The principles for safety promotion are the same as those used to promote health in general (health psychology). This includes designing and executing public campaigns (e.g., "Stay Alive, Drive 55" signs on highways) and campaigns aimed at specific target groups (e.g., teenagers, young drivers) as well. Key issues are safety cognitions (e.g., perceived vulnerability to accidents, safety attitudes, values); risk behaviors (e.g., alcohol and drug use, handling cellular phones while driving); and life style. Interactive, perceptual tests may be used to select personnel for high-risk tasks, and have larger predictive power than questionnaire approaches.

The concept of secondary prevention is used for any action aimed at reducing the negative consequences of accidents when they occur. Secondary preventive measures include teaching coping skills like decision making and behavior aimed at keeping any injury to a minimum. Applying health psychology principles to increase the use of protective clothing, seat belts, and work site safety equipment are also important secondary preventive measures. Environmental approaches to secondary prevention include laws to ensure minimum safety standards for cars and improved emergency care of trauma victims.

Debriefing

This has become an increasingly popular method aimed at the prevention of the acute and long-term behavioral morbidity that may arise after exposure to trauma. It is now routinely offered in a number of countries. The key elements in debriefing include promoting some form of emotional processing or ventilation (catharsis) by encouraging recollection, ventilation, and reworking of the traumatic event. Several procedures have been operationalized (Wessely et al., 1999). Another variation, known as multiple stressor debriefing, has a similar model, but with more emphasis on discussion of previous experience of trauma and coping.

A systematic Cochrane review by Wessely et al. (1999) assessed the empirical evidence of brief psychological debriefing for the management of psychological distress after trauma and the prevention of posttraumatic disorder. The authors included all randomized debriefing studies (one single session only, which focused on persons recently exposed to a traumatic event (from several days post accident to 4 weeks.) The Cochrane review clearly demonstrated that single-session debriefing did not reduce psychological distress or prevent the onset of PTSD or depression. On the contrary, those who received the intervention had a nonsignificant short-term (3 to 5 months) increase in risk. In conclusion, there is no current evidence that one-session psychological debriefing is a useful treatment for the prevention of behavioral problems after accidents.

Tertiary Prevention. The aim of tertiary prevention is to reduce the severity of behavioral consequences when they occur. In this task, psychologists play a key role. Despite the prevalence of behavioral consequences of accidents and injuries, there are very few randomized controlled trials (RCT). Most studies have a limited focus, mostly on anxiety (Shalev et al., 1996). Psychotropic drugs may be of help in some cases if the patient suffers from a major psychiatric disorder, but drug treatment alone is seldom sufficient to restore well-being and preaccident functioning. Furthermore, there are almost no RCTs conducted to assess the relative efficacy of the different treatment approaches, and there is currently insufficient evidence to decide when to initiate treatment and which treatment should be preferred for various trauma populations (Foa & Meadows, 1997).

Conclusion

Accidents and accidental injury are major causes of human suffering and poor health. Behavioral factors are crucial, not only to understand and prevent their occurrence, but also to predict and improve the outcome. Thus, psychologists are key players in the prevention and rehabilitation process. Despite this fact, there is a clear imbalance among all the studies about psychological and behavioral processes in the course of accidents, and the few randomized treatment or intervention studies designed for the treatment of accident victims with or without physical injury. Such studies are clearly needed for a more science-driven psychological practice in the twenty-first century.

[See also Machine Design; System Error Analysis; and Work Conditions.]

Bibliography

American Psychiatric Association. (1994). The diagnostic and statistical manual of mental disorders (4th ed.). Washington, DC: Author.

Binder, L. M. (1997). A review of mild head trauma. Part II: Clinical implications. Journal of Clinical and Experimental Neuropsychology, 19, 432–457. Reviews the current evidence for an association between mild head trauma and cognitive deficits, symptoms, and disability.

Blanchard, E. B., & Hickling, E. J. (1997). After the crash: Assessment and treatment of motor vehicle accident survivors. Washington, DC: American Psychological Association. This book describes the details of one of the most comprehensive long-term studies ever conducted of MVA survivors and discusses MVA-related PTSD.

Bussing, R., Menvielle, E., & Zima, B. (1996). Relationship between behavioral problems and unintentional injuries in U.S. children. Archives of Pediatrics and Adolescent Medicine, 150, 50–56. Findings of the 1988 National Health Interview Survey reporting the incidence of un-

intentional injuries among children with and without behavioral problems, and the role of ethnicity.

Caspi, A., Begg, D., Dickson, N., Harrington, H., Langley, J., Moffitt, T. E., & Silva, P. A. (1997). Personality differences predict health-risk behaviors in young adulthood: Evidence from a longitudinal study. Journal of Personality & Social Psychology, 73, 1052–1063. In a longitudinal study, the authors classified children into distinct temperament groups at age 3 and looked at four different health-risk behaviors at age 21 (alcohol, violent crime, unsafe sex, and dangerous driving).

Dadds, M. R., Bovbjerg, D. H., Redd, W. H., & Cutmore, T. R. (1997). Imagery in human classical conditioning. Psychological Bulletin, 122, 89–103. Discusses the possible underlying role of imagery of relevant stimuli as a maintainer for conditioned behavior after trauma and the potential therapeutic implications.

Foa, E. B., & Meadows, E. A. (1997). Psychosocial treatments for post-traumatic stress disorder: A critical review. Annual Review of Psychology, 48, 449–480. Has 105 references and includes PTSD research for all types of trauma; discusses issues specific to various trauma populations and factors that may influence treatment efficacy across types of trauma.

Gochman, D. S. (Ed.). (1997). Handbook of health behavior research (Vols. 1–4). New York: Plenum Press. Includes chapters about accident and accident-related behavior including developmental determinants and important chapters about prevention (safety), including safety campaigns, occupational education, health policy, and injury prevention.

Green, B. L. (1996). Traumatic stress and disaster: Mental health effects and factors influencing adaptation. International Review of Psychiatry, 2, 177–210. A comprehensive review of the mental health effects of exposure to a variety of accidents and disasters events, both natural and human caused.

Hickling, E. J., & Blanchard, E. B. (1997). The private practice psychologist and manual-based treatments: Post-traumatic stress disorder secondary to motor vehicle accidents. Behavior Research & Therapy, 35, 191–203. A manual-based brief treatment (9–12 sessions) for post-traumatic stress disorder following a motor vehicle accident.

Horowitz, M. J. (1997). Stress response syndromes: PTSD, grief, and adjustment disorders (3rd ed). Northvale, NJ: Aronson. (Original work published 1976.) A revised version of the classic 1976 text, presenting theory and research on accident and other trauma-related stress response syndromes. Includes information about personality ("neurotic styles") and specific stress responses and the principles for brief treatment for stress-induced symptoms and signs.

Jonah, B. A. (1997). Sensation seeking and risky driving: A review and synthesis of the literature. Accident Analysis & Prevention, 29, 651–665. A review of 40 studies about sensation seeking and driving from 1970–1995.

Littrell J. (1998). Is the experience of painful emotion therapeutic? Clinical Psychology Review 18, 71–102. Reviews the literature (154 references) and points to the dangers of encouraging emotional experience in the absence of acquisition of a new response to the emotion-evoking material. The paper supplements the discussion by the Cochrane group (Wessely et al., 1999) about the reasons for ineffectiveness of one-session psychological debriefing after accidents.

Malt, U. F., & Olafsen, O. M. (1992). Psychological appraisal and emotional response to physical injury: A clinical phenomenological study of 109 adults. *Psychiatric Medicine, 10,* 117–134. A clinical and psychometric in-depth study of the acute psychological response to accidental injury conducted 8 to 96 hours after the accident, with reference to Richard Lazarus's coping theory.

Marks, I., Lovell, K., Noshirvani, H., Livanou, M., & Thrasher, S. (1998). Treatment of posttraumatic stress disorder by exposure and/or cognitive restructuring: A controlled study. *Archives of General Psychiatry, 55,* 317–325.

Mayou, R., Tyndel, S., & Bryant, B. (1997). Long-term outcome of motor vehicle accident injury. *Psychosomatic Medicine, 59,* 578–584. Results from a British study of the psychological outcome at 5 years of a sample of non-head-injured motor vehicle accident victims and identified baseline predictors.

McKenna, F. P. (1983). Accident proneness: A conceptual analysis. *Accident Analysis and Prevention, 15,* 65–71. Discusses the controversy about accident proneness and its reasons.

Rothengatter, T., & Vaya, E. C. (Eds.). (1997). *Traffic and transport psychology: Theory and application.* Oxford: Pergamon/Elsevier. Provides an overview of the developments in the field of traffic and transport psychology, intended for psychologists, ergonomists, engineers, and policymakers interested in the application of psychology to traffic and transport and for applied psychologists in general.

Shalev, A. Y., Bonne, O., & Eth, S. (1996). Treatment of post-traumatic stress disorder: A review. *Psychosomatic Medicine, 58,* 165–82. Reviews 81 articles about treatment of PTSD after trauma in general, not including eye movement desensitization techniques.

Shapiro, F. (1996). Eye movement desensitization and reprocessing (EMDR): Evaluation of controlled PTSD research. *Journal of Behavior Therapy and Experimental Psychiatry, 27,* 209–18. Reviews the literature and points out misconceptions about the method.

Shaw, L., & Sichel, H. (1971). *Accident proneness.* Oxford: Pergamon Press. A comprehensive review of the literature on accident proneness from 1919 until the late 1960s.

Simonet, S., & Wilde, G. J. S. (1997). Risk: perception, acceptance and homeostasis. *Applied Psychology: An International Review, 46,* 235–52. Presents the basic features of risk homeostasis theory and explains how this theory may help to understand the causation of the accident rate and how it may be used to develop an effective accident prevention strategy.

Ursano, R. J., McCaughey, G. B., & Fullerton, C. S., (Eds.). (1994). *Individual and community responses to trauma and disaster.* Cambridge, UK: Cambridge University Press. A compilation of review articles with a clinical focus about small and large-scale accidents with reference to individual, group, and community responses.

Wessely, S., Rose, S., & Bisson, J. (1999). *A systematic review of brief psychological interventions ("debriefing") for the treatment of immediate trauma related symptoms and the prevention of post traumatic stress disorder. (Cochrane Review),* In *Cochrane Library,* issue 2. Oxford: Update Software. A continuously updated review of randomized clinical trials of debriefing for accidents. Contains important consideration about methodology of debriefing studies; discussion about the short-comings in the evidence base for psychological interventions after accidents; and a huge reference list to controlled and uncontrolled treatment studies.

Wisner, D. H. (1992). History and current status of trauma scoring systems. *Archives of Surgery, 127,* 111–117.

Ulrik F. Malt

ACCULTURATION. *See* Culture; Cultural Disintegration; Ethnic and Racial Identity, *article on* Ethnic Identity; *and* Marginalization.

ACH, NARZISS (1871–1946), German psychologist. As a member of Oswald Külpe's Würzburg School, Ach became recognized for his introspective experiments on mental processes including concept formation, determining tendency, volition, and awareness. Ach's experiments were conceived in opposition to associationism, as he did not believe that mental processes could be conceptualized adequately in terms of connections among sensations, and also in contrast to the work of Wilhelm Wundt, as Ach emphasized the notion of imageless thought.

From a methodological point of view, Ach (1935) advocated *systematic experimental introspection*, which should take place during the time immediately following the completion of an experimental task. Ach argued that in order to achieve a complete picture of a subject's experiences, introspection must be systematic, with replicable results, and accompanied by interviews that supplement the subject's report and explore the subject's experiences. To control and assess the power of suggestion in the interview process, protocols must be taken and included in their entirety in publications (Ach, 1935).

Ach coined the term *determining tendency* to denote the idea that mental processes tend to be determined consciously or unconsciously by intended ends and not by associations. For example, a subject may be asked to add two numbers (Ach, 1935). If an experimenter shows the subject a card with the numbers 6 and 2, the number 8, referring to the intended end of addition, enters the subject's awareness. Yet, if a subject is shown the same card after being told to subtract, the number 4 comes into awareness. The same stimulus leads to different thoughts as intended ends determine what the mind does with two numbers. Ach (1921, 1935) performed a variety of experiments to demonstrate the power of this concept and worked with hypnotic suggestion (Ach, 1905/1951) in order to study the unconscious dimensions of the determining tendency.

In his psychology of volition (*Wille*), Ach (1935) argued that the determining tendency is a necessary but not sufficient condition of volition. Will refers to a specific psychological dimension that cannot be reduced to other forms of human experience. To assess volition Ach developed sophisticated experiments. For example, subjects had to learn nonsense pairs of syllables. After associations were learned, and the first syllable automatically elicited the second syllable of the pair, Ach asked the subject to no longer produce the learned second syllable but a syllable that rhymes with the first syllable. Depending on the number of learning trials, it took more or less volition or willfulness (*Vorsatz*) for the subject to suppress the associated syllable and produce the rhymed syllable. Thus Ach was able to compare experimentally and through introspection the effect of volition against the power of learned habit (association).

Ach (1935) also introduced the idea of *determining emotions*, an effect found more strongly in extraverts than in introverts. Late in his career, Ach also supported National Socialism, and his ideological usage of the psychology of volition (Geuter, 1984/1992) raised questions about the relationship between political beliefs and psychological research.

Bibliography

Ach, N. (1921). *Über die Begriffsbildung: Eine experimentelle Untersuchung* [On concept formation: An experimental study]. Bamberg: Buchner.

Ach, N. (1935). *Analyse des Willens* [Analysis of volitions]. Berlin: Urban & Schwarzenberg.

Ach, N. (1951). Determining tendencies: Awareness. In D. Rapaport (Ed.), *Organization and pathology of thought* (pp. 15–38). New York: Columbia University Press. (Original work published 1905)

Geuter, U. (1992). *The professionalization of psychology in Nazi Germany* (R. J. Holmes, Trans.). New York: Cambridge University Press. (Original work published 1984)

Thomas Teo

ACHIEVEMENT MOTIVATION. The achievement motive, a desire to perform well and attain success, clearly plays an important role in individual and societal accomplishments. Henry Alexander Murray, Jr. introduced the term into personality psychology, as one of 20 fundamental human "needs" or motives. Although many personality tests contain a scale designed to measure achievement motivation, the term was popularized in personality psychology by the Thematic Apperception Test (TAT) content analysis scoring system developed by McClelland, Atkinson, Clark, and Lowell (1953; see also Smith, 1992, chaps. 9–10). Based on the effects on TAT stories of several different kinds of experimental arousal of achievement motivation, McClelland and colleagues defined the achievement motive as involving a concern for excellence—specifically, images of positive and negative anticipations, instrumental activity, explicitly stated desire or need, and goal satisfaction. The TAT measure of achievement motivation can also be applied to other verbal material, such as interviews, speeches, or literature.

In fact, the thematic apperceptive (or implicit) and questionnaire (direct or conscious) measures of achievement motivation do not correlate; moreover, they show different patterns of associated actions and life outcomes. Spangler's (1992) analysis suggests that the TAT achievement motivation measure involves sensitivity to intrinsic, task-related achievement incentives; whereas the questionnaire measures reflect a sensitivity to social incentives associated with achievement. These considerations suggest that implicit and conscious achievement motives are embedded in two fundamentally different motivational systems (McClelland, Koestner, & Weinberger, 1989).

People who score high in TAT achievement motivation prefer and work hardest under conditions of moderate and realistic (versus extremely high or low) risk, especially when they have some control over results. They are restless and innovative. They seek and use new information, advice from experts (versus friends), and feedback about their previous performance. They can delay gratification, perhaps because they experience time as moving fast, and display a subdued, somber personal style. They bargain rationally and cooperatively, and get along well with other people. Nevertheless, they are prone to cheat and use illegal (or even revolutionary) tactics when necessary (McClelland, 1985, chap. 7; Smith, 1992, chap. 9; Winter, 1996, chap. 5). They show a facilitating attributional pattern in the domain of achievement tasks, such that they explain their success as due to ability or effort but view their failures as the result of external circumstances or luck (Weiner, 1985). Not surprisingly, therefore, such people tend to be successful in business, especially in small "entrepreneurial" businesses, in sales, or in larger companies that are "open" and achievement oriented. They also show upward occupational mobility.

In a landmark interdisciplinary study, McClelland

(1961) argued that the achievement motive was a psychological operationalization of Max Weber's "Protestant ethic." He used data from laboratory personality research, multination field studies of managers and entrepreneurs, and cross-national archival and social indicator data to document the role of achievement motivation in promoting economic development.

Defined in this way, the achievement motive is not associated with every kind of "achievement." For example, TAT achievement motivation does not predict academic performance, and is therefore quite distinct from the concept of "academic achievement motivation" as used by educational and school psychologists. It is not associated with scientific creativity. In very large, bureaucratic corporations, power motivation plays a greater role in success. And in politics, high achievement motivation (by itself) often leads to frustration, as illustrated by the cases of U.S. presidents Hoover, Nixon, and Carter (see Smith, 1992, chap. 7).

Atkinson and Feather (1966) developed a multivariate model in which achievement motivation interacts with expectation (probability of success) and incentive to explain the characteristic risk preferences, persistence, and other correlates of achievement motivation. Such a model made it possible to use the achievement motivation concept in the multivariate prediction of longitudinal pathways and outcomes. Atkinson later elaborated this model into a general theory of the flow of motivated behavior over time. McClelland (1985, chap. 13) has also suggested a model of how motivation interacts with values and skills in predicting behavior.

The studies collected by Atkinson and Feather also suggest that the achievement motive has separate approach (hope of success) and avoidance (fear of failure) components (see also Heckhausen, 1991, pp. 204–206 on the distinction between these two components). Other TAT measures of achievement-related motives include hostile press and the motive to avoid success, or fear of success (Smith, 1992, chap. 11)—the latter thought to be related to traditional gender-role expectations, especially in the United States during the post–World War II period.

Originally, many researchers believed that there were major sex differences in the ways that achievement motivation was aroused and expressed; however, a comprehensive review by Stewart and Chester (1982) showed no such pattern. In fact, U.S. national surveys documented a substantial increase in women's achievement motivation between 1957 and 1976 (Smith, 1992, chap. 6), doubtless related to the Women's Movement. Explorations with the TAT measure in other cultures have generally confirmed the results obtained in the United States, although there is considerable cross-cultural variation in what constitutes an "achievement" (McClelland, 1961).

Available evidence suggests that achievement motivation develops in children out of high parental expectations, warmth and encouragement, and low control—in short, training for independence (McClelland, 1985, chap. 7). A longitudinal study of children whose mothers had been intensively interviewed further pinpoints the role of scheduled feedings, severity of toilet training (though not overall strictness), and (especially for boys) standards of neatness as correlates of later achievement motivation. These results suggest that establishing voluntary control of one's own autonomic nervous system processes may be an important early precursor of achievement motivation. McClelland further linked arousal of achievement motivation to possible higher levels of the hormone arginine vasopressin, which further supports such a link at the physiological level.

Yet even if achievement motivation has roots in early childhood, it is also affected by later experience. Thus McClelland and Winter (1969) showed that training courses designed to increase achievement motivation through cognitive training, self-study, and other principles of applied behavior change led to improved economic performance.

[*See also* Goals; *and* Motivation.]

Bibliography

Atkinson, J. W., & Feather, N. T. (1966). *A theory of achievement motivation.* New York: Wiley.

Heckhausen, H. (1991). *Motivation and action.* Berlin: Springer-Verlag.

McClelland, D. C. (1961). *The achieving society.* Princeton, NJ: Van Nostrand.

McClelland, D. C. (1985). *Human motivation.* Glenview, IL: Scott, Foresman.

McClelland, D. C., Atkinson, J. W., Clark, R. A., & Lowell, E. L. (1953). *The achievement motive.* New York: Appleton-Century-Crofts.

McClelland, D. C., Koestner, R., & Weinberger, J. (1989). How do self-attributed and implicit motives differ? *Psychological Review, 96,* 690–702.

McClelland, D. C., & Winter, D. G. (1969). *Motivating economic achievement.* New York: Free Press.

Smith, C. P. (Ed.). (1992). *Motivation and personality: Handbook of thematic content analysis.* New York: Cambridge University Press.

Spangler, W. D. (1992). Validity of questionnaire and TAT measures of need for achievement: Two meta-analyses. *Psychological Bulletin, 112,* 140–154.

Stewart, A. J., & Chester, N. L. (1982). Sex differences in human social motives: Achievement, affiliation, and power. In A. J. Stewart (Ed.), *Motivation and society* (pp. 172–218). San Francisco: Jossey-Bass.

Weiner, B. (1985). An attributional theory of achievement and emotion. *Psychological Review, 92,* 548–573.

Winter, D. G. (1996). *Personality: Analysis and interpretation of lives.* New York: McGraw-Hill.

David G. Winter

ACHIEVEMENT TESTS. *See* Academic Assessment of Performance; *and* Testing.

ACQUAINTANCE RAPE. *See* Rape.

ACQUIRED IMMUNE DEFICIENCY SYNDROME. (AIDS) is caused by the human immunodeficiency virus (HIV), which is found in the infected person's blood, semen, vaginal secretions, or breast milk. The virus is spread by unprotected sexual intercourse with an infected person, by needle sharing among injecting drug users, or through transfusions of infected blood or blood clotting factor. Babies born to HIV-infected women may also become infected before or during birth, or shortly after birth through breast-feeding. AIDS itself is a clinical syndrome associated with HIV infection, and is diagnosed when there is evidence of severe immunosuppression in an HIV-infected person (defined by a CD4 T-lymphocyte count of less than 200 cells/ml or less than 14% of total lymphocytes) or the presence of pulmonary tuberculosis, recurrent pneumonia, or invasive cervical cancer.

Incidence and Prevalence of HIV and AIDS

The total numbers of AIDS cases reported worldwide as of 30 June 1997 was 1,644,183, with 576,972 cases in Africa and 797,227 cases in the Americas. In the United States, as of 30 June 1997, the cumulative number of AIDS cases reported to the Centers for Disease Control and Prevention (CDC) was 612,078, with 72,868 incident cases in the previous year. Adult and adolescent AIDS cases totaled 604,176, with 511,934 cases in males and 92,242 cases in females; 7,902 AIDS cases were reported in children (defined as persons under age 13 at the time of diagnosis). Total cumulative deaths of persons reported with AIDS were 379,258 by June of 1997, including 374,656 adults and adolescents, and 4,602 children. All of these numbers of cases reported probably underestimate the actual number of cases because some cases are never reported to agencies such as the World Health Organization (WHO) and CDC. In addition, these numbers do not reflect the number of *HIV infections* because it takes several years for someone with HIV to develop AIDS. The actual number of HIV infections has, for example, been estimated to be 1 million in the United States alone.

According to the CDC, most (49.4%) of the total reported U.S. adult and adolescent AIDS diagnoses have been among "men who have sex with men" (i.e., men who identify themselves as gay or bisexual or who are homosexually active). The second largest group has been injection drug users, who represent 25.6% of all adolescent and adult cases of AIDS. An additional 6.4% of cases are accounted for by men who have sex with men and also inject drugs. Thus, over 80% of cases are accounted for by men who have sex with men and injection drug users. AIDS has also been disproportionately distributed among U.S. racial/ethnic groups: 35.2% of adolescent and adult cases have been among African Americans; 17.8% have been among Hispanics; and 46% have been among Whites. Among women, these rates are especially unevenly distributed, with 55.7% of cases represented by African Americans, 20.2% by Hispanics, and 23.1% by Whites.

Why Psychology?

Psychological research is essential for many aspects of HIV disease including (1) prevention of infection (including studies of determinants of HIV risk and evaluations of intervention strategies to reduce HIV risk); (2) coping with the disease and its burdens; (3) social, neuropsychological, and neuropsychiatric consequences of infection; and (4) adherence and other psychological issues in the treatment of HIV disease. The Office of AIDS Research at the National Institute of Mental Health (NIMH) issued comprehensive research priorities for each of these areas in 1997. As the NIMH report demonstrates, both the completed and prioritized research in these areas is quite voluminous; thus, we discuss a selection of these, and discuss them in a framework of HIV/AIDS prevention. Our discussion is not comprehensive, but rather is intended to demonstrate how psychology has contributed to HIV and AIDS prevention. We will first, however, briefly describe some contributions psychologists have made to studying other psychological phenomena related to AIDS.

HIV and AIDS carry with them a diverse array of psychological processes that can be studied. Among these are prejudice; loss, grieving, and associated sequelae; stress and coping; and empowerment, volunteerism, and community organizing. Because of the populations most affected by HIV/AIDS (i.e., gay and bisexual men and injection drug users) as well as the nature of diseases themselves, a great deal of stigma is encountered by those affected by AIDS, leading many psychologists (especially social psychologists) to examine AIDS-related prejudice. The epidemiological facts of AIDS have had a profound impact on the manner in which AIDS has been received by both the American public and researchers. When the diseases first came into public awareness, it was labeled "gay cancer," and eventually called Gay Related Immune Deficiency (GRID) by medical doctors and scientists. Research into AIDS-related prejudice has found that gay men are more likely than heterosexuals to be blamed for having

HIV (Herek & Glunt, 1988). In addition, because HIV infection has come to be understood, with some exceptions, as being a result of individuals' behaviors, blame has been placed on HIV-infected individuals who are viewed as having responsibility for the acquisition of their illness.

The burden of loss has been enormous as hundreds of thousands of people have died of AIDS. The terror of HIV and AIDS has shed light on the many coping strategies that people have used to deal not only with their own disease, but also that of their loved ones. The loved ones of those who are dying or who have died often experience psychological problems such as depression or anxiety during the grieving process. In addition, gay caregivers must also deal with stress associated with homophobia and the lack of legal recognition of their relationship to their partners. As Folkman has pointed out, however, the primary caregivers of people with AIDS may also experience positive psychological states because of their ability to survive in the face of difficult circumstances and search for and find positive meaning in them. Meaning is created by finding value in loss, not only through the caregiving process but also through engaging in processes such as volunteerism and advocacy in response to losing loved ones to the disease.

HIV/AIDS Prevention

AIDS is *acquired*, raising questions about, how, when, and why a person became HIV-infected. HIV infection occurs as a result of human behavior, making it a logical focus for the science of psychology. AIDS continues to take thousands of lives each year, but a cure or vaccine has eluded medical researchers. Moreover, it is unlikely that any vaccine in the foreseeable future could eradicate AIDS on its own, and a vaccine would be of little use to those already infected with HIV or for whom a vaccine was unavailable or ineffective. Even though medical therapies for persons with AIDS (particularly combination therapies) have shown promise in recent years, they do not work for everyone, and whether they have lasting positive effects is unknown. Furthermore, access to these treatments is limited because of their substantial cost. Thus, HIV disease *prevention* through behavior change is perhaps the best weapon in the fight against AIDS and merits the attention of psychologists and other behavioral scientists.

Remarkable behavioral changes have been observed during the history of AIDS. Although approximately 40,000 new HIV infections occur each year in the United States, this number would be higher were it not for successful HIV prevention efforts. For example, the total number of incident HIV infections in San Francisco in 1982 and 1983 was estimated to be between 6,000 and 8,000, whereas the same estimate was 500 in 1994. Page-Shafer and colleagues have further documented behavioral changes by examining two cohorts of young gay and bisexual men. They found that men surveyed in 1984 reported significantly more sexual partners than those in surveyed in 1992. In addition, only 2% of men surveyed in 1984 reported condom use for receptive anal intercourse, compared to over 57% in 1992. Even though 57% is still a low figure, it certainly is a substantial improvement from 2% and may be sufficient to keep disease incidence at less than 1% even in a high prevalence area. Moreover, sex is a pleasurable activity and it is unrealistic to expect prevention efforts to yield a 100% condom use rate. Indeed, no other health promotion efforts (e.g., those for diet, smoking, or seat-belt use) are held to such a high standard. There is, however, some concern because sexual risk behavior has increased in recent years in vulnerable populations such as young gay men (Ekstrand et al., 1999), suggesting that HIV prevention efforts may need to be re-energized.

Two forms of HIV prevention can be recognized: *primary prevention* refers to preventing individuals from becoming infected with HIV, and *secondary prevention* refers to the prevention of disease progression in those already infected with HIV. The majority of psychological research has focused on the former, with the latter typically viewed as the province of medical scientists. We will present some examples of behavioral research for both kinds of prevention science to highlight the important contributions that have been made in this area. With respect to interventions, our view is that those that are most effective contain a rigorous evaluation component and target the most at-risk populations (particularly gay and bisexual men and injection drug users). Targeting interventions to those most at risk for infection is especially important because of the lack of resources dedicated to HIV prevention. Thus, most of the intervention studies we discuss contain these elements.

Theory in HIV Prevention

Many of the studies we will discuss have employed psychological theories in forming their content. The theory of reasoned action has been widely employed to conceptualize how individuals make decisions regarding HIV risk behaviors. Other psychological and health theories that have been applied to HIV prevention include the stages of change model, diffusion of innovations theory, the common sense model of illness danger, the health belief model, empowerment theory, and social learning theory. In addition, models specific to HIV prevention such as the AIDS risk reduction model have been developed and implemented.

An example of the incorporation of theory into HIV primary preventive research is found in Project Respect, a large longitudinal study of STD clinic patients. The intervention incorporated elements of social learning theory, the theory of reasoned action, and the health belief model in a randomized controlled trial of HIV testing and counseling. Kamb and collaborators reported the results of the intervention with 5,758 HIV-negative heterosexual patients at a clinic for sexually transmitted diseases. The study involved three face-to-face intervention conditions: (1) two brief informational educational messages; (2) HIV prevention counseling with two client-centered sessions based on CDC guidelines; and (3) enhanced counseling with four sessions based on the aforementioned theories. Results indicated that those in both conditions (2) and (3) were significantly more likely than those in condition (1) to use condoms 100% of the time at three-month follow-up and significantly less likely than those in condition (1) to have another STD at six-month follow-up. At 12-month follow-up, participants in conditions (2) and (3) continued to demonstrate reduced risk for acquiring new STDs.

Primary Prevention. Successful primary preventive interventions have been implemented and evaluated by researchers, leaving little doubt that behavioral change can lead to a reduction in new HIV infections. Choi and Coates have reviewed HIV preventive interventions, and found that, although most interventions do not contain rigorous scientific evaluation components, those that do, provide strong evidence for their efficacy. Most such interventions are targeted at individuals and employ HIV testing and counseling or skills training that is intended to change individuals' knowledge, attitudes, and beliefs. In addition, most of these interventions promote condom usage or use of clean needles to inject drugs as the primary behavioral outcomes. They found that effective interventions designed to increase individuals' knowledge about HIV transmission and build their skills have been performed with a variety of populations at risk for HIV (e.g., men who have sex with men, injection drug users, commercial sex workers, and STD patients).

A good example of an effective primary prevention intervention was conducted by Peterson and colleagues (1996), who evaluated a randomized controlled HIV risk reduction intervention with 318 African-American gay and bisexual men. Two intervention groups, one involving a single three-hour session and the other having three three-hour sessions, were compared to a wait-list control group before and after the interventions. Both the three-session and one-session interventions were designed to be culturally appropriate and involved education about HIV transmission, cognitive-behavioral self-management training, assertion training, and efforts to develop personal identity and social support. Results of the study indicated that the prevalence of unprotected anal intercourse (based on the six months previous to assessment) among those receiving the three-session intervention was reduced one year fol-

lowing the intervention (46% baseline decreased to 20%) and that this change was maintained at eighteen-month follow-up (18%). In contrast, those in the wait-list control group did not demonstrate any such behavior change at either the 12- or 18-month follow-ups, and the prevalence of unprotected anal intercourse among those receiving the single-session intervention was reduced only modestly (from 47% baseline to 38% at both 1-year and 18-month follow-ups). Importantly, this study targeted African American gay and bisexual men, who have been underrepresented in research on HIV preventive interventions even though they are at higher risk than other groups for HIV infection.

Community-level interventions have also been highly successful with gay and bisexual men. Kegeles and colleagues implemented a community-wide HIV primary prevention program for young gay and bisexual men in a multiple baseline design. The peer-led intervention consisted of community outreach, small groups, community organizing, and a publicity campaign, and was successful in reducing the amount of unprotected anal intercourse with both primary and nonprimary sexual partners. The intervention was based largely on empowerment theory, and involved the men in important aspects of the intervention implementation. The results of the study showed a decrease in prevalence of reported unprotected anal intercourse from a baseline of 41 to 30% after the intervention, including a decrease from 20 to 11% with nonprimary sexual partners. In contrast, a comparison community that did not receive the intervention demonstrated no such change. Given that gay bars are often the most typical gay community settings and that there is an association between substance use and HIV sexual risk taking, it is worth noting that this intervention may have decreased risk taking not simply because it promoted safer sex and condom use, but also because it provided an alcohol-free community space for gay men called the Mpowerment Center. In addition, the intervention had the advantage of reaching a large number of people because it was implemented community wide rather than to individuals or small groups.

In a series of community studies, Kelly and his colleagues (1997) developed community-level interventions that employed diffusion theory. This primary preventive intervention involved recruiting popular opinion leaders from gay bars and training them in communication of safer-sex messages to their gay peers through active encouragement of safer-sex behaviors in community bars. In a multiple baseline design comparing four small Southern U.S. cities, with four control cities, significant and substantial decreases in HIV-risk sexual behavior were observed following the interventions.

Community-based interventions have been particularly successful in reducing HIV risk behaviors among injection drug users. Lurie and Drucker reviewed the studies to date on needle-exchange programs, the most widely implemented community-based prevention strategy, and concluded that not only are these programs highly effective in reducing HIV risk behaviors, but they also do not lead to an increase in drug use, an outcome that many fear. A study of a successful needle-exchange program was conducted on 5,644 injection drug users in San Francisco (Watters et al., 1994). This study found that 61% of the drug users had obtained syringes from needle-exchange sites in the previous year and that 45% had "usually" used the program to obtain syringes. The number of syringes exchanged in the program increased from 7,821 in the spring of 1989 to 343,883 during the spring of 1992 as the program was implemented more widely in the community. In addition, it was found that those who had used the needle-exchange program frequently were significantly less likely to report having shared syringes than those who had used the program infrequently or not at all.

Secondary Prevention. Until recently, a strong dichotomy existed in the approach to the prevention of AIDS: Prevention of HIV infection was the province of behavioral scientists, and treatment of people with AIDS was the province of physicians and other medical clinicians. The work of prevention educators and scientists was largely confined to primary prevention of infection in HIV-negative people. Once people tested HIV-positive, it was believed that only medical therapies were of use to them. As new medical therapies and innovative behavioral treatments for HIV-infected people became more available, however, psychologists and other behavioral scientists became more engaged in what has come to be known as secondary prevention. Three areas, in particular, in which psychologists have been engaged are psychoneuroimmunology, neuropsychological sequelae of HIV disease, and adherence to medical treatments.

Psychoneuroimmunology is the study of the effects of psychological and environmental stress factors on immune responses and the immune system. With respect to AIDS, those who conduct research in this area are interested in examining how psychosocial variables such as stress and depression influence disease progression and immune system response. To date, little research has been conducted in this area, and results of studies have yielded mixed results. For example, one study examined the association between experiences of stressful life events and biomedical outcomes in a cohort of HIV-positive gay men. The results of the study, however, indicated that self-reported experiences of stress did not appear to exert an impact on disease progression. In contrast, another study found that depression predicted a more rapid decline in CD4 T-lymphocyte counts in a large study of HIV-infected gay

men. In another study, it was found that depressive symptoms were associated with increased mortality in a prospective cohort study of gay and bisexual men (Mayne et al., 1996). Although these studies did not provide evidence for a direct causal relationship between depression and disease progression and mortality, the associations that were documented supported the possibility that prevention and treatment of depression in those living with HIV may be a form of secondary HIV/AIDS prevention.

HIV disease is related to declines in brain function. Two main types of neurobehavioral disorders have been documented in HIV-infected people. These include dementia, which is characterized by a profound impact on daily living, and a milder disorder that is identified by neuropsychological testing. Dementia was observed among HIV-infected persons even before HIV was determined to be the AIDS virus. Other neuropsychological problems have only recently been documented. For example, Heaton and colleagues (1995) performed an eight-hour series of neuropsychological tests (including the Wechsler Adult Intelligence Scale-Revised and the Halstead-Reitan Battery) with a large group of HIV-infected men who were not suffering from dementia and in an HIV-negative control group. They found that HIV disease progression was associated with increased neuropsychological impairments such as attention deficits, slowed information processing, and decreased learning efficiency. These findings were unrelated to mood disturbance or recreational alcohol or drug use, and results of magnetic resonance imagery testing supported the results. Studies such as these provide the formative basis for secondary prevention research to prevent the onset of neuropsychological sequelae of HIV disease.

The importance of medication adherence becomes crucial as medical treatments for HIV disease become more effective. Although new medical therapies have been ineffective for some people, they have undoubtedly slowed HIV disease progression as well as increased the longevity of the lives of many people with AIDS. Data on the incidence of AIDS support this conclusion because the number of estimated U.S. AIDS cases declined for the first time to 57,200 in 1996 from 61,300 in 1995. Thus, the number of HIV-infected persons has not declined, but the number of people who are progressing to AIDS has decreased for the first time in the history of the epidemic, a trend that coincides with the more widespread availability of protease inhibitor combination therapies. Preliminary research indicates that adherence to these drugs may profoundly influence disease progression. HIV-infected people who miss even a few doses of drugs may show sharp increases in the amount of HIV in their plasma (i.e., "viral load"). Similar results have been found with other anti-AIDS drugs.

Adherence to these medical therapies is an area of secondary prevention in which behavioral scientists are becoming active. Given the potential importance of adherence to new medical treatments, behavioral interventions designed to increase adherence need to be evaluated, and the best strategies for enhancing compliance need to be implemented. It will be especially important to study this issue among populations believed to be nonadherent. Research on adherence is underway in the AIDS Clinical Trials Group, but these studies are not yet complete. It is advisable to increase adherence in clinical drug trials so that lack of adherence does not mask the potential positive effects of drug treatments. Thus, psychologists and other behavioral scientists will be called upon not only to monitor adherence in drug trials, but also to design interventions to increase adherence in these studies. In the absence of behavioral compliance, new drug therapies, even if biomedically efficacious, may not prevent HIV disease progression.

Concluding Remarks

Psychologists have clearly had an impact on the field of HIV/AIDS prevention as well as other areas of AIDS research. Prevention still remains the most powerful tool in efforts to stop the AIDS epidemic, and behavioral scientists are the best equipped to study the most effective method of intervention. Randomized controlled trials with discrete endpoints, generally viewed as the gold standard in evaluating interventions, are still rare, however, in HIV prevention research. Although we believe that more studies should attempt to employ this rigorous methodology, we also think that behavioral researchers should broaden their approaches and consider innovative primary prevention strategies such as those at the organizational, community, and policy levels where such methodology is difficult to employ. The main advantage of these interventions is that they have the potential to affect a larger number of people. HIV/AIDS prevention needs to target individuals, but it must also be mindful of other approaches.

AIDS will unfortunately be with us for some time to come, and the possibility of an effective vaccine or cure is remote. Until such time that this possibility becomes reality, psychologists and other behavioral scientists need to contribute their best efforts to both primary and secondary prevention strategies to halt the spread of this deadly disease that continues to take the lives of thousands.

[*See also* Sexually Transmitted Diseases.]

Bibliography

Chesney, M. A., & Folkman, S. (1994). Psychological impact of HIV disease and implications for intervention. *The Psychiatric Clinics of North America: Psychiatric Manifestations of HIV Disease, 17,* 163–182.

Coates, T. J. (1990). Strategies for modifying sexual behavior for primary and secondary prevention of HIV disease. *Journal of Consulting and Clinical Psychology, 58,* 57–69.

Cochran, S. D., Mays, V. M., Ciarletta, J., Caruso, C., & Mallon, D. (1992). Efficacy of the theory of reasoned action in predicting AIDS-related sexual risk reduction among gay men. *Journal of Applied Social Psychology, 22,* 1481–1501.

Ekstrand, M. L., & Coates, T. J. (1990). Maintenance of safer sexual behaviors and predictors of risky sex: The San Francisco Men's Health Study. *American Journal of Public Health, 80,* 973–977.

Ekstrand, M. L., Stall, R. D., Paul, J., Osmond, D., & Coates, T. J. (1999). Gay men report high rates of unprotected anal sex with partners of unknown or discordant HIV status. *AIDS, 13,* 1523–1533.

Fisher, W. A., Fisher, J. D., & Rye, B. J. (1995). Understanding and promoting AIDS-preventive behavior: Insights from the theory of reasoned action. *Health Psychology, 14,* 255–264.

Grant, I., Heaton, R. K., Atkinson, J. H., & the HNRC Group. (1995) Neurocognitive disorders in HIV 1 infection. In M.B.A. Oldstone & L. Vitkovic (Eds.), *Current topics in microbiology and immunology. HIV and dementia, 202,* 11–32. New York: Springer.

Herek, G. M., & Glunt, E. (1988). The epidemic of stigma: Public reaction to AIDS. *American Psychologist, 43,* 886–891.

Ickovics, J. R., & Meisler, A. W. (1997). Adherence in AIDS clinical trials: A framework for clinical research and clinical care. *Journal of Clinical Epidemiology, 50,* 385–391.

Kamb, M. L., Dillon, B., Fishbein, M., & Willis, K. L. (1996). Quality assurance of HIV prevention counseling in a multi-center randomized controlled trial. *Public Health Reports, 111* (Suppl. 1), 99–107.

Kegeles, S. M., Hays, R. B., & Coates, T. J. (1996). The Mpowerment Project: A community-level HIV prevention intervention for gay men. *American Journal of Public Health, 86,* 1129–1136.

Kelly, J. A., Murphy, D. A., Sikkema, K. J., McAuliffe, T. L., Roffman, R. A., Solomon, L. J., Winett, R. A., Kalichman, S. C., & the Community HIV Prevention Research Collaborative (1997). Randomized, controlled, community-level HIV prevention intervention for sexual-risk behavior among homosexual men in three U.S. cities. *Lancet, 350,* 1500–1505.

Kelly, J. A., St. Lawrence, J. S., Brasfield, T. L., Stevenson, Y., Diaz, Y., & Hauth, A. C. (1990). AIDS risk behavior patterns among gay men in small southern cities. *American Journal of Public Health, 80,* 416–418.

Leigh, B. C., & Stall, R. (1993). Substance use and risky sexual behavior for exposure to HIV: Issues in methodology, interpretation, and prevention. *American Psychologist, 48,* 1035–1045.

Lurie, P., & Drucker, E. (1997). An opportunity lost: HIV infections associated with lack of a national needle-exchange programme in the USA. *Lancet, 349,* 604–608.

Mayne, T. J., Vittinghoff, E., Chesney, M. A., Barrett, D. C., & Coates, T. J. (1996). Depressive affect and survival among gay and bisexual men infected with HIV. *Archives of Internal Medicine, 156,* 2233–2238.

Page-Shafer, K., McFarland, W., & Katz, M. H. (1997, December). *1997 Consensus report on HIV prevalence and incidence in San Francisco.* San Francisco, CA: San Francisco Department of Public Health.

Peterson, J. L., Coates, T. J., Catania, J., Hauck, W., Acree, M., Daigle, D., Hillard, B., Middleton, L., & Hearst, N. (1996). Evaluation of an HIV risk reduction intervention among African-American homosexual and bisexual men. *AIDS, 10,* 319–325.

Stryker, J., Coates, T. J., DeCarlo, P., Haynes-Sanstad, K., Shriver, M., & Makadon, H. J. (1995). Prevention of HIV infection: Looking back: Looking ahead. *Journal of the American Medical Association, 273,* 1143–1148.

Sweat, M. D., & Denison, J. A. (1995). Reducing HIV incidence in developing countries with structural and environmental interventions. *AIDS, 9* (Suppl.), S251–S257.

Valdiserri, R. O., Lyter, D., Leviton, L., Callahan, C. N., Kingsley, L. A., & Rinaldo, C. R. (1989). AIDS prevention in homosexual and bisexual men: Results of a randomized trial evaluating two risk reduction interventions. *AIDS, 3,* 21–26.

Vanhove, G. F., Schapiro, J. M., Winters, M. A., Merigan, T. C., & Blaschke, T. F. (1996). Patient compliance and drug failure in protease inhibitor monotherapy. *Journal of the American Medical Association, 276,* 1955–1956.

Watters, J. K., Estilo, M. J., Clark, G. L., & Lorvick, J. (1994). Syringe and needle exchange as HIV/AIDS prevention for injection drug users. *JAMA, 271* (2), 115–120.

Craig R. Waldo and Thomas J. Coates

ACTION RESEARCH is socially useful and theoretically meaningful research developed and carried out in response to a social issue or problem, results of which are used to improve the situation. The term is used primarily in the social and environmental sciences, education, social work, rural and urban studies, and community development. It is also known in the biological and physical sciences, as well as in computer science and medicine. The term designates research in the service of social change, typically associated with a progressive agenda. Within psychology, it is most commonly practiced in social, health, and community psychology, organizational behavior, and in some approaches to program evaluation.

An additional criterion for action research stresses enhanced roles for intended beneficiaries who may identify the research need; conceptualize, design, or carry out the research in collaboration with the researchers; and be involved in developing and implementing subsequent recommendations for change. Thus, current hallmarks of action research include its primary goal of understanding and solving social problems, its collaborative character, and the dissemination of results to various stakeholders for their use.

As a type of applied research, action research may employ one or more of a variety of methods, including experimental, quasi-experimental, environmental-ecological, and ethnographic techniques. Qualitative methods are often used in conjunction with quantitative analyses. While field settings are predominately used, laboratory research is not precluded. Its purposes may vary from exploratory to hypothesis testing. Although action research is, by definition, more problem oriented than theory driven, a grounding in theory is viewed as conferring a distinct advantage.

Within U.S. psychology, action research has a long tradition. The social psychologist Kurt Lewin (*Resolving Social Conflicts: Selected Papers on Group Dynamics,* New York, 1948) is believed to have originated the term to characterize theory-based empirical research wedded to social action, particularly in the areas of leadership studies, group dynamics, prejudice reduction, and the management of organizations. Major psychological journals publishing action research include the *Journal of Social Issues* and the *American Journal of Community Psychology.*

Participatory Action Research (PAR) is a term credited to Orlando Fals-Borda, known for community development research in Latin America. It is commonly used with reference to research in which the roles of researcher and subject are blended or converge. To promote mutual learning and the empowerment of disadvantaged groups, participatory action researchers are engaged as participant-observers (or *accompanimientos*) and the intended beneficiaries are involved as full partners in the research process. PAR proponents contend that, while traditional action research has tended to ally itself with organizational authority and promote "top-down" social change strategies, PAR explicitly allies itself with its intended beneficiaries and employs a "bottom-up" approach in which the researcher provides support to the participants in their analysis and problem solving.

In sum, PAR emphasizes partnership and power sharing. It deemphasizes the distinction between expert and ordinary knowledge, replacing it with a model of reciprocal knowledge between the researcher and those for and with whom the research is done.

Action research and PAR proponents view the blurring of the expert/ordinary knowledge distinction and the resulting power sharing as advantageous. First, to the extent that the research focuses on empowerment and social change, these processes may be better understood by the researcher who is engaged in a collaborative effort with those seeking to improve their situation. Second, the validity of the research is likely to be enhanced when participants with diverse perspectives and experiences bring their knowledge to bear. Third, to the extent that the research incorporates the insights and values of its constituents, it is more likely to be used by them to create structural change.

The most important potential limitations of action research entail negative consequences of combining research and advocacy. The kind of knowledge acquired by involvement in action research is often considered suspect by mainstream social scientists because of the difficulty of simultaneously advocating the truth of a claim and critically examining its validity. A contending view is that the scholarly and activist roles are not contradictory, but are related dialectically. According to this perspective, the knowledge-seeking aspects of research combine with the social change goals of advocacy and intervention, resulting in information that is both descriptive of "what is" and oriented toward change.

The Society for Participatory Research in Asia, located in New Delhi, is perhaps the world's premier institution doing research and publishing in the field of participatory research and evaluation.

[See also Industrial and Organizational Psychology; and Social Psychology.]

Bibliography

Argyris, C., Putnam, R., & Smith, D. M. (1985). *Action science*. San Francisco: Jossey-Bass. Describes a method of action research for analyzing interpersonal interaction and explains how threats to validity are dealt with.

Deutsch, M., & Hornstein, H. A. (Eds.). (1975). *Applying social psychology: Implications for research, practice, and training*. Hillsdale, NJ: Erlbaum. Includes a frequently cited chapter by Hornstein which provides a framework for examining approaches of social psychologists to applications.

Fals-Borda, O. F., & Rahman, M. A. (Eds.). (1991). *Action and knowledge: Breaking the monopoly with participatory action research*. New York: Apex.

Freire, P. (1985). *The politics of education: Culture, power, and liberation*. South Hadley, MA: Bergin & Garvey.

Oskamp, S., & Schultz, P. W. (1998). *Applied social psychology* (2nd ed.). Upper Saddle River, NJ: Prentice Hall. Provides summaries of a variety of action research projects within social psychology and devotes a chapter to the theory, methods, and types of action research, as well as training for action.

Patton, M. Q. (1997). *Utilization-focused evaluation: The new century text* (3rd ed.). Thousand Oaks, CA: Sage.

Rappaport, J. (1977). *Community psychology: Values, research, and action*. New York: Holt.

Rodin, J. (1985). The application of social psychology. In G. Lindsey & E. Aronson (Eds.), *Handbook of social psychology* (3rd ed., Vol. 2, pp. 805–881). New York: Random House. A well-referenced review of the application of social psychological principles to a variety of

content areas, each representing an aspect of action research.

Sommer, B. B., & Sommer, R. (1997). *A practical guide to behavioral research: Tools and techniques* (4th ed.) New York: Oxford University Press.

Whyte, W. F. (1990). *Social theory for action*. Newbury Park, CA: Sage. Develops a framework for action research contributions in industrial/organizational psychology (and agriculture).

Michele Andrisin Wittig

ACTIVITY/DISENGAGEMENT THEORY. *See* Social Gerontological Theories.

ACTUARIAL PREDICTION, in its narrow sense, refers to a certain class of formal procedures for making predictions, constructed on the model of an insurance company's actuarial table. (Demographic and other relevant data, for example, gender and health-related habits such as tobacco smoking, are entered into a table which yields an estimated risk for some event such as death. Such tables are used to set insurance premiums.) In its broader and more common sense, *actuarial prediction* (and the cognate term *statistical prediction*) refers to all forms of mechanical prediction collectively. The broad sense is the one defined here.

The defining characteristic of actuarial prediction is its mechanical nature. Once predictor variables are measured, a clerk or a computer can use the variable scores to make a prediction. No human decisions about how to combine variables influence actuarial predictions, although expert human judgments may be needed to measure the predictors. Because they are mechanical, actuarial predictions are perfectly reproducible. By contrast, even very careful judges' predictions are generally subject to fluctuation over time, even with the same input data.

Another (nondefining) feature of actuarial prediction is that variables may be combined so as to yield the most accurate predictions. For example, it may be that one variable should optimally receive greater weight in making a prediction than another variable which also enters into the prediction, even though both contribute to predictive accuracy.

Actuarial prediction in psychology was first studied by Sarbin (1942), who claimed that what human judges do, when they combine multiple cues to arrive at predictions, is in principle no different from what a clerk can do using a calculator with a formula to combine the cues. Sarbin predicted, given this hypothesis, that the perfect reliability of actuarial prediction methods (along with optimal weighting of predictors) would enable actuarial predictions to outperform human judges, in terms of aggregate absolute accuracy levels. Sarbin found that the predictions of college grades were more accurately made by a linear combination of high-school class rank and college entrance test scores than by trained counselors. Meehl, in his famous 1954 book, *Clinical vs. Statistical Prediction*, disagreed with Sarbin's theoretical claim, arguing instead that in principle a human judge can perform operations (e.g., novel theory generation) which a calculator cannot. However, after reviewing the available empirical evidence (about twenty-two studies), he concluded that the evidence more or less universally favored actuarial prediction over human judgment (generally referred to as clinical prediction, though a clinician need not be the person combining the cue data).

There have been several subsequent reviews of this area (Grove, Zald, Lebow, Snitz, & Nelson, submitted; Sawyer, 1966; Sines, 1971). Grove et al. found 136 studies involving the prediction of human behavior and health, only six of which demonstrated clinical predictions to be notably better than actuarial predictions.

One objection to actuarial prediction, alluded to above, is that humans can develop ad hoc novel theories about how a given organism's behavior is controlled. Statistical formulas and computer programs cannot develop such theories (though future computer programs may gain this capacity). Hence, it ought to be possible in principle for an applied psychologist to develop a theory of the behavior of a single organism, and then use this theory to make highly accurate predictions. However, this capacity awaits empirical demonstration in a practical prediction problem.

Another objection is that clinicians seek to understand, and not predict, behavior. Inasmuch as actuarial predictions do not offer such understanding, they are claimed to be less useful than clinical judgment. However, this objection is faulty. It rests on the false assertion that psychologists seldom try to prognosticate.

Actuarial prediction schemes, despite their many successful applications in research studies, are seldom used in applied psychology. It is not clear why this is so. Meehl and others have offered many possible explanations for this, including nonrational factors such as fear of technological obsolescence.

Actuarial predictions have been used to predict treatment response to psychotherapy, violence and suicide, divorce, criminal recidivism, and occupational choice, among other criteria. Variables used in actuarial predictions rules have included demographic variables such as gender and age, Minnesota Multiphasic Personality Inventory (MMPI) scale scores, coded variables from the Thematic Apperception Test, measures of cognitive functioning and interest, directly observed behaviors, and physiological measurements, to name a few. Data combination methods have included actuarial tables, simple sums of predictors, optimally weighted regression equations, and linear discriminant functions, among other schemes.

Goldberg (1965) published a famous actuarial formula for the broad diagnostic category into which a client's major psychopathology falls (neurosis vs. psychosis) from MMPI scores. Goldberg showed that a wide variety of actuarial prediction schemes outperformed expert clinical judges on this task. Predictions were checked by examining the clients' medical charts. Reasonably accurate predictions could be obtained from a simple sum MMPI scale T-scores. The average clinician did not do as well, and the rule in fact outperformed almost all individual clinicians.

Another actuarial formula, Reitan, Warren, and Akert's 1964 impairment index, combines scores from neuropsychological tests in the Halstead-Reitan Battery to decide whether or not a client has brain damage. In 1970 Stephens, a psychiatrist, applied the Elgin Prognostic scale (which combined demographic and behavioral data) to predict response to electroconvulsive therapy. In this study Stephens blindly predicted response to treatment better, on the average, than did a symptom-based scale. As noted above, this is a rather unusual outcome for such studies.

A final category of actuarial prediction is computerized artificial intelligence. This is represented by the Minnesota Report, which combines MMPI-2 scores in a fashion that draws on the actuarial literature on this test, and also on expert clinical opinion. The latter is introduced by writing the computer program in such a way that it mimics the opinions of a carefully studied human expert. Computerized predictions have been increasingly studied since the advent of inexpensive but powerful computers.

Bibliography

Goldberg, L. R. (1965). Diagnosticians vs. diagnostic signs: The diagnosis of psychosis vs. neurosis from the MMPI. *Psychological Monographs, 79* (Whole No. 602).

Grove, W. M., Zald, D. H., Lebow, B. S., Snitz, B. E., & Nelson, C. (submitted). *Clinical vs. mechanical prediction: A meta-analysis.*

Meehl, P. E. (1954). *Clinical vs. statistical prediction: A theoretical analysis and a review of the evidence.* Minneapolis, MN: University of Minnesota Press.

Reitan, R. M., Warren, J. M., & Akert, K. (1964). Psychological deficits resulting from cerebral lesions in man. In J. M. Warren & K. Akert (Eds.), *The frontal granular cortex and behavior* (Vol. 14, pp. 295–312). New York: McGraw-Hill.

Sarbin, T. R. (1942). A contribution to the study of actuarial and individual methods of predictions. *American Journal of Sociology, 48,* 593–602.

Sawyer, J. (1966). Measurement *and* prediction, clinical *and* statistical. *Psychological Bulletin, 66,* 178–200.

Sines, J. O. (1971). Actuarial versus clinical prediction in psychopathology. *British Journal of Psychiatry, 116,* 129–144.

Stephens, J. H. (1970). Long-term course and prognosis in schizophrenia. *Seminars in Psychiatry, 2,* 464–485.

William M. Grove

ACUPUNCTURE. *See* Non-Western Therapies.

ADD. *See* Attention-Deficit/Hyperactivity Disorder.

ADDICTION. *See* Addictive Personality; Alcoholism; Compulsive Gambling; Drug Abuse; *and* Smoking. *Also, many illicit drugs are the subjects of independent entries.*

ADDICTIVE PERSONALITY. An addictive behavior pattern can represent an addictive disorder (i.e., a syndrome that satisfies diagnostic criteria), such as substance use disorders or pathological gambling. Addictive behaviors also can reflect patterns of activity that are subclinical (i.e., behavior patterns that fail to meet diagnostic criteria), such as intermittently excessive shopping or heavy gambling. Common among all of these patterns is that people prone to addictive behaviors tend to relapse often (Brownell, Marlatt, Lichtenstein, & Wilson, 1986; Marlatt & Gordon, 1985; Tims & Leukefeld, 1986). This repetitive cycle raises the question of whether an underlying cluster of personality traits or an "addictive personality" causes the problem of intemperate behaviors. When people behave excessively and intend otherwise, they often refer to themselves as having an "addictive personality."

Is there a personality that tends toward addiction? For almost 40 years, from the 1930s to the early 1970s, researchers searched for the addictive personality (Shaffer & Burglass, 1981). These investigators used psychological tests to measure and describe the personality attributes of people suffering from narcotic addiction. Clinical investigations gradually revealed an apparent personality type: an angry, impulsive individual who often was also socially deviant. These core traits are only some of the features that distinguished the addictive personality from other typologies during this early research.

Often clinicians report seeing people with other traits that lead them to infer the presence of an addic-tive personality. For example, people with narcotics addiction frequently are disheveled and in poor health. People with addiction tend not to take good care of themselves (Khantzian & Mack, 1983). People dependent on narcotics in particular express a low threshold of pain and a high frequency of medical incidents. They are often in crisis. Their social lives are in conflict, and their families frequently separate from them. People struggling with addictive behavior patterns often express the feeling that they are victims. To the onlooker, people with addictive patterns sometimes appear as if they lack anxiety and do not learn from bad experiences (Vaillant, 1975, 1983a). People with addictive disorders also seem as if they care far less about others than they do about themselves. They seem unmotivated and even resistant to change in spite of their problems (Miller & Rollnick, 1991). People with addictions usually have a very difficult time coping with their emotions. They tend to distrust others and behave defensively; others can easily threaten them. Consequently, people struggling with addiction have difficulty with intimacy. Finally, research often reveals that people with addictive disorders have a very poor self-image.

Given the relative consistency of these observations among both researchers and clinicians, many investigators have thought and continue to think that these are the personality characteristics that lead to drug abuse and addiction. Now, for example, it is popular to think that a specific drug preference corresponds to a personality defect. Khantzian (1975) has suggested that when there is a particular personality problem, an intoxicant-using individual will select a specific drug to feel normal. This notion suggests that people use drugs to self-medicate deficits in their capacity to manage painful feelings and impulses (Hartford, 1978; Khantzian, 1985; Rado, 1933). In short, people with addiction may simply be trying to get normal rather than high.

Clinical experience and research show that while some people do indeed self-medicate, others may use drugs for more varied reasons. During the early 1970s, two Canadian researchers recast the notion of addictive personality. Instead of studying the personalities of people struggling with addiction, they studied personality profiles of individuals to see if these people also abused drugs. Gendreau and Gendreau (1971) identified prison inmates who had the personality profiles that previous research had identified as addictive, asked them about their drug use, but learned eventually that these personality traits do not predict drug abuse.

When researchers study the personalities of drug abusers, they often appear quite similar. However, if scientists first identify the same personalities and then inquire about drug abuse, the apparent relationship disappears. There is an explanation. Investigators have found there is a life style that emerges from drug abuse.

This context subtly influences the personality. Over time, personality changes result from a career of drug seeking and using. People with addiction often withdraw from a wide array of social contacts and retreat to associate with others who suffer similarly with excessive behaviors (Zinberg, 1975). Since the pursuit of addiction is very similar regardless of the particular activity, people with addiction begin to appear as if they share common characteristics.

This point of view is not new. People within groups who share a comparable trauma often have similar experiences. Soldiers who have fought on the front line, concentration camp survivors, and serious accident victims represent groups who have experienced overwhelming trauma. Members of these groups often describe similar changes in personality as a result of their intense experience. Chronic intoxicant abuse is also a trauma that can produce changes in personality (e.g., Vaillant, 1983b). As a result of this new perspective, it is inaccurate to think simply of a predisposing addictive personality. There are some exceptions, but these personalities are likely to represent the minority. Therefore, many experts agree there is no such thing as an addictive personality. The personality similarities among people who experience addiction are most probably the result, not the original cause, of their addiction.

This view has some interesting implications. For example, when people stop their addictive behaviors, do their personalities change again? The answer is yes. Some alcohol studies indicate that it takes about 5 years of sobriety before an addict's personality returns to normal (e.g., Vaillant, 1983b). After this time, psychological tests reveal that the person recovering from alcohol dependence has personality characteristics that are indistinguishable from those who never struggled with alcohol dependence.

Bibliography

Brownell, K. D., Marlatt, G. A., Lichtenstein, E., & Wilson, G. T. (1986). Understanding and preventing relapse. *American Psychologist, 41*, 765–782.

Gendreau, P., & Gendreau, L. P. (1971). Research design and narcotic addiction proneness. *Canadian Psychiatric Association Journal, 16*, 265–267.

Hartford, R. J. (1978). Drug preferences of multiple drug abusers. *Journal of Consulting and Clinical Psychology, 46*, 908–912.

Khantzian, E. J. (1975). Self-selection and progression in drug dependence. *Psychiatry Digest, 36*, 19–22.

Khantzian, E. J. (1985). The self-medication hypothesis of addictive disorders: Focus on heroin and cocaine dependence. *American Journal of Psychiatry, 142*, 1259–1264.

Khantzian, E. J., & Mack, J. E. (1983). Self-preservation and the care of the self: Ego instincts reconsidered. *Psychoanalytic Study of the Child, 38*, 209–232.

Marlatt, G. A., Baer, J. S., Donovan, D. M., & Kivlahan, D. R. (1988). Addictive behaviors: Etiology and treatment. *Annual Review of Psychology, 39*, 223–252.

Marlatt, G. A., & Gordon, J. R. (Eds.). (1985). *Relapse prevention: Maintenance strategies in the treatment of addictive behaviors.* New York: Guilford Press.

Miller, W. R., & Rollnick, S. (Eds.). (1991). *Motivational interviewing: Preparing people to change addictive behavior.* New York: Guilford Press.

Rado, S. (1933). The psychoanalysis of pharmacothymia (drug addiction). *Psychoanalytic Quarterly, 2*, 1–23.

Robins, L. N., Davis, D. H., & Goodwin, D. W. (1973). Drug use by U.S. Army enlisted men in Vietnam: A follow-up on their return home. *American Journal of Epidemiology, 99*, 235–249.

Shaffer, H. J., & Burglass, M. E. (Eds.). (1981). *Classic contributions in the addictions.* New York: Brunner/Mazel.

Tims, F. M., & Leukefeld, C. G. (1986). Relapse and recovery in drug abuse: An introduction. In F. M. Tims & C. G. Leukefeld (Eds.), *Relapse and recovery in drug abuse* (National Institute of Drug Abuse Research Monograph 72, pp. 1–4). Washington, DC: U.S. Government Printing Office.

Vaillant, G. E. (1975) Sociopathy as a human process. A viewpoint. *Archives of General Psychiatry, 32*, 178–183.

Vaillant, G. E. (1983a). Natural history of male alcoholism. V. Is alcoholism the cart or the horse to sociopathy? *British Journal of Addiction, 78*(3), 317–326.

Vaillant, G. E. (1983b). *The natural history of alcoholism: Causes, patterns, and paths to recovery.* Cambridge, MA: Harvard University Press.

Zinberg, N. E. (1975). Addiction and ego function. *Psychoanalytic Study of the Child, 30*, 567–588.

Zinberg, N. E. (1981). High states. In H. J. Shaffer & M. E. Burglass (Eds.), *Classic contributions in the addictions.* New York: Brunner/Mazel. (Original work published 1974)

Zinberg, N. E. (1984). *Drug, set, and setting: The basis for controlled intoxicant use.* New Haven, CT: Yale University Press.

Howard J. Shaffer

ADHD. *See* Attention-Deficit/Hyperactivity Disorder.

ADJECTIVE CHECKLIST. Selected so as to sample broadly from the adjectives used throughout the personality sphere, 300 items make up the Adjective Checklist (ACL). The ACL may be used to obtain descriptions of, for example, the self, an ideal or recollected self, others, historical personages, commercial products, geographical places, movies and television shows, medical and psychiatric pathologies, effects of alcohol and other drugs, religious sects, political leaders, occupational groups, architectural constructions, paintings, sculpture, music, books, spouses' views of each other and of what they want each other to be, and even of abstract concepts such as venality, wisdom, personal soundness, and old age.

The basic postulate of the ACL is that every language has an adjectival class of words, used to characterize the self, experience, and the objects of experience. The ACL is a systematized and structured technique for capitalizing on these universals of natural language. A first 279-item ACL was assembled in 1949, drawing on (1) R. B. Cattell's designation of 171 primary trait continua (1946); (2) personality descriptors taken from the writings of Freud, Jung, and H. A. Murray; (3) experimental use of the adjectival method by H. Hartshorne and M. A. May on honesty, persistence, service, and inhibition in children (1930), and K. H. Mueller on the esthetics of music and poetry (1935, 1937); (4) post–World War II studies of psychiatric nosology by S. R. Hathaway and P. E. Meehl (1951). Provisional use of this first list led to a 284-item list in 1951 and to the current ACL in 1952.

The first manual for the ACL was published in 1965, and the most recent in 1983. The ACL has been translated into more than 35 languages, and used in large-scale studies of topics such as conceptions of femininity and masculinity, aging, and national stereotypes. Examples of other recent applications include studies of creativity, leadership, prejudice, consistency and change of personality over the life span, the effects of debilitating disease, differences in personality among American presidents, feelings of efficacy among women, academic performance in college, and self-views of effective managers. The complete ACL bibliography as of 1999 contains more than 1,000 entries.

Self-descriptions on the ACL are scored for thirty-seven scales, classified under five rubrics: (1) mode of dealing with the task; for example, the total number of adjectives checked; (2) expressed needs, such as for achievement, autonomy, dominance, and order; (3) specific attributes such as self-confidence, self-control, and creative temperament; (4) scales for the five ego states of transactional psychology; and (5) scales for the four quadrants in Welsh's theory of origence and intellect as basic motivators of human behavior. When computer scoring is used, each scale is adjusted for the total number of adjectives checked before being standardized and registered on the profile sheet. Two computerized interpretational narratives are available from the publisher. These focus on tendencies toward productiveness, assertiveness, sociability, individuality, well-being, and submissiveness. *The Counselor's Report* can be obtained by users with relevant psychometric training, and the *Clinical Report* by persons with an advanced degree in psychology or a related field.

Bibliography

Cattell, R. B. (1946). *Description and measurement of personality.* Yonkers, NY: World Book.

Collins, D. R., & Adair, F. L. (1990). *User's guide to the Adjective Check List interpretive reports.* Palo Alto, CA: Consulting Psychologists Press.

Gough, H. G. (1960). The Adjective Check List as a personality assessment research technique. *Psychological Reports, 6,* 107–122.

Gough, H. G., & Heilbrun, A. B., Jr. (1983). *The adjective check list manual* (Rev. ed.). Palo Alto, CA: Consulting Psychologists Press.

Hartshorne, H., & May, M. A. (1930). Honesty, persistence, service and inhibition in children. In *Studies in the nature of character. Vol. 3.* New York: Macmillan.

Hathaway, S. R., & Meehl, P. E. (1951). The MMPI. In *Military Clinical Psychology.* Washington, DC: U.S. Army Technical Manual TM 8-242.

Mueller, K. H. (1935). The affective character of the major and minor modes in music. *American Journal of Psychology, 47,* 103–118.

Mueller, K. H. (1937). The affective value of sound in poetry. *American Journal of Psychology, 47,* 621–630.

Welsh, G. S. (1975). *Creativity and intelligence: A personality approach.* Chapel Hill, NC: Institute for Research in Social Science, University of North Carolina.

Williams, J. E., & Best, D. L. (1990). *Measuring sex stereotypes: A multinational study* (Rev. ed.). Newbury Park, CA: Sage.

Harrison G. Gough

ADLER, ALFRED (1870–1937), Austrian physician. Adler developed a theory of personality and a psychotherapeutic approach known together as *individual psychology.* Adler believed that each person has unique ways of striving for a sense of mastery, completeness, and belonging with others throughout life. When the goals of these strivings are not met or if they are blocked in some way, problems in living or even psychopathology may result. Adler's psychotherapeutic approach was intended to help people to recognize and to change their self-defeating behaviors.

Adler's Life

Adler was born to Jewish parents in Vienna, Austria, and was the second of seven children. His near death from pneumonia at age 5 along with the death of his infant brother contributed to his desire to become a physician. Adler completed his training at the University of Vienna Medical School in 1895 and was married in 1897. The Adlers had four children, the middle two of whom, Kurt and Alexandra, became psychiatrists.

As a young physician in Vienna with an interest in psychology, Adler was invited by Sigmund Freud to participate in a weekly group to discuss nervous and mental disorders (this later became the Vienna Psychoanalytic Society). Although Adler was an active participant in this growing organization for nearly 9 years, he remained ideologically independent of Freud and published his germinal ideas in his first book, *A Study of Organ Inferiority* in 1907. Adler severed his relationship with Freud and the Vienna Psychoanalytic Society in 1911. On a professional level Adler disagreed with Freud that sexual instincts were the primary motivators of behavior. Adler and Freud also were deeply divided on a range of personal and political issues almost from the time that they first met. Historical research suggests that, contrary to popular belief, Adler was not a disciple of Freud and did not receive formal psychoanalytic training from him. After parting with Freud, Adler founded the Society for Free Psychoanalysis, which became the Society for Individual Psychology in 1913.

The destruction and suffering Adler observed during his work as a physician in the Austrian army in World War I helped him to realize the importance of cultivating a sense of social and community feeling (now referred to as social interest) among all persons. Adler believed the best opportunities for a peaceful and harmonious existence among adults could be realized through providing preventive treatment and growth-engendering experiences for children and their parents. In this regard, Adler and colleagues such as Viennese educator Carl Fürtmuller spent nearly 10 years in postwar Austria setting up guidance clinics where childhood behavioral and emotional problems could be treated. These clinics also provided education for parents and teachers on how to manage children's behavior and family relationships in a way that left children feeling encouraged. Adler's emphasis on parent training and child guidance became a hallmark of individual psychology that continues to thrive in the United States and Europe as evidenced by the widespread popularity of programs such as Systematic Training for Effective Parenting (STEP) (D. C. Dinkmeyer & G. D. McKay, *A Parent's Handbook: STEP: Systematic Training for Effective Parenting*, Circle Pines, Minnesota, 1989).

Shortly after the publication of his very popular book, *Understanding Human Nature* (1927), Adler made the first of numerous visits to the United States and obtained U.S. citizenship in 1933 to escape the escalating political tensions heralding World War II. During this time Adler lectured extensively to many American audiences, providing demonstrations of his therapeutic methods, and popularizing his approach. Adler remained an active teacher and therapist throughout his later years, publishing nearly 20 books and a multitude of articles in both popular and scholarly periodicals. He died suddenly of a heart attack while on a lecture tour in Aberdeen, Scotland.

The Legacy of Adler's Work

In stressing that psychological processes are affected more by the person's construction of current and past realities rather than by the actual events themselves, Adler's theory was somewhat ahead of its time. For instance, through valuing a person's subjective perspective and emphasizing the therapeutic value of supportive, encouraging relationships, Adler anticipated the humanistic psychologies of Carl Rogers and Abraham Maslow, the latter of whom worked briefly with Adler in the 1930s. Regarding the ways Adler believed people projected their current goals and desires onto past experiences to construct meaningful life narratives, individual psychology appears particularly consistent with the burgeoning constructivist perspectives on psychotherapy (see J. A. Singer & P. Solovey's *The Remembered Self*, New York, 1993).

Adler's contributions to psychology can be evaluated according to the attention his theories and methods continue to garner among contemporary psychologists. Growing interest in Adler's original work has led researchers at the Alfred Adler Institute of San Francisco to begin translating all of his journal articles and some of his books from German. Regarding ongoing scholarship, between 1986 and 1996 over 20 books and book chapters on diverse topics such as physical disability, antisocial behavior, vocational counseling, and addictions, among others, have been discussed from the perspective of Adler's individual psychology.

There are five journals devoted to various aspects of individual psychology (Mozdzierz & Mozdzierz, 1997) *Zeitschrift für Individualpsychologie* was the original journal for individual psychology established by Adler in 1914. *Individual Psychology: The Journal of Adlerian Theory, Research and Practice* was established in the United States in 1935 and was originally published under the title, *International Journal of Individual Psychology*. These two journals together publish 60 to 70 articles per year on average. Other European journals that include *Bieträge zur Individualpsychologie* (Germany), *Rivista di Psicologia Individuale* (Italy), and *Le Bulletin Psychologie D'Individuale* (France) were all established in the 1970s. Most of these journals disseminate articles on traditional Adlerian topics such as social interest, life style (the long-term ways in which people seek to reach their life goals), psychotherapy, parenting, family relationships, and early recollections (memories of childhood experiences that reveal the nature of current life goals), among others. By far the most widely investigated Adlerian topic concerns how a person's birth order is related to life goals, ability to cope, career interests, among many other personality constructs. Over 30 birth order studies per year, on average, appear in a wide variety of psychology journals.

Adler's contributions to contemporary psychology also are evidenced by the continuing vitality and growth of Adlerian professional organizations and training centers. The North American Society for Adlerian Psychology (NASAP) has a membership of over 1,200 education and mental health professionals. NASAP organizes a national convention once a year to conduct training seminars and disseminate research findings. Regional divisions of NASAP also meet on a yearly basis. Regarding education, there are over 10 regional training institutes in the United States and Canada through which to receive instruction in the theory and practice of individual psychology. Adlerian training centers also exist in Germany, Switzerland, Greece, and Israel, with centers planned for the Czech Republic, Russia, and Japan. The Adler School of Professional Psychology in Chicago (formerly the Alfred Adler Institute), was the first such school established in America and was founded by Adler's student, Rudolf Dreikurs in 1953.

Although Adler died in 1937, professional and popular interest in his ideas about parenting, family relationships, and finding a way to meaningfully belong in one's family and community continues. The ongoing elaboration of his theories by contemporary psychologists and the growth of Adlerian professional and training organizations provide a powerful testimony to the significance and timelessness of Alfred Adler's work.

Bibliography

Works by Adler

Adler, A. (1917a). *A study of organ inferiority and its psychical compensations: A contribution to clinical medicine* (S. E. Jellife, Trans.). New York: Nervous Mental Diseases. (Original work published 1907.) This was Adler's first book and described how feelings of inferiority may be based upon a person's physical weaknesses and limitations.

Adler, A. (1917b). *The neurotic constitution: Outline of a comparative individualistic psychology and psychotherapy.* (B. Blueck & J. E. Lind, Trans.). New York: Moffat, Yard. (Original work published 1912)

Adler, A. (1927). *Understanding human nature* (W. B. Wolfe, Trans.). New York: Greenberg. (Original work published 1927.) This book is a rather complete representation of Adler's thinking up to 1927. It is easy to read and was Adler's most popular book among American audiences.

Adler, A. (1931). *What life should mean to you* (A. Porter, Ed.). Boston: Little, Brown.

Adler, A. (1956). *The individual psychology of Alfred Adler: A systematic presentation from his writings* (H. L. Ansbacher & R. R. Ansbacher, Eds.). New York: Basic Books.

Adler, A. (1964). *Superiority and social interest: A collection of later writings* (H. L. Ansbacher & R. R. Ansbacher, Eds.). Evanston, IL: Northwestern University. The Ansbachers' compilations of Adler's writings are both thorough and understandable by general audiences. They are essential reading for those interested in individual psychology.

Works about Adler

Bottome, P. (1957). *Alfred Adler: A portrait from life.* New York: Vanguard. This was the second biography of Adler, but the first one to appear in English.

Fiebert, M. (1997). In and out of Freud's shadow: A chronology of Adler's relationship with Freud. *Individual Psychology, 53*, 241–269. This article provides a chronology of the relationship between Adler and Freud between 1902 and 1911 based upon letters, notes, and other historical documents.

Hoffman, E. (1994). *The drive for self: Alfred Adler and the founding of individual psychology.* New York: Addison-Wesley. Hoffman's biography represents the most recent and perhaps the definitive study of Adler's life. Relative to other biographical works, Hoffman's book provides detailed information about Adler's life and work in the United States before his death in 1937.

Manaster, G. (Ed.). (1977). *Alfred Adler as we remember him.* Chicago: North American Society for Adlerian Psychology. This short work presents recollections of Adler and his work by persons who knew or worked with him.

Stepansky, P. E. (1983). *In Freud's shadow: Adler in context.* Hillsdale, NJ: Analytic Press.

Alan E. Stewart

ADOLESCENCE. [*This entry provides a general survey of the theories, research, and findings that have informed our knowledge about adolescence. It comprises three articles:*
Puberty and Biological Maturation
Social Patterns, Achievements, and Problems
Adolescent Thought Process
For discussions dealing with other stages of development, see Infancy; Early Childhood; Middle Childhood; *and* Adulthood and Aging.]

Puberty and Biological Maturation

Puberty is the period during which children reach biological maturity. The changes of puberty include physical growth to adult height and weight, as well as the biological growth of internal and external organs related to reproductive functioning. Large increases in sex hormones and changes in physical appearance characterize pubertal maturation. The individual's body shifts from childhood appearance and functioning to that of adulthood.

Puberty as a Biological Process

Pubertal maturation is controlled by the gonadal endocrine system which involves complex interactions among the pituitary gland (which controls hormonal levels), the hypothalamus (the part of the brain that controls the pituitary gland), and the gonads (testes in males and ovaries in females). The gonads release sex hormones (androgens and estrogens). The interactions involve a feedback system to maintain particular levels of sex hormones. The hypothalamus responds to the levels of sex hormones in the body. When these hormone levels drop below the set points, the hypothalamus stops its inhibition of the pituitary, and the release of sex hormones is stimulated (Brooks-Gunn & Reiter, 1990; Grumbach & Styne, 1992).

Hormonal Changes. Despite the dramatic changes in appearance that occur during puberty, the actual underlying hormonal process is based on a system established prenatally (Petersen & Taylor, 1980). After maintaining low levels of hormones during childhood, with puberty the hypothalamus appears to lose some sensitivity to sex hormones, requiring increasingly higher levels of these substances to signal the hypothalamus to inhibit the pituitary gland. Levels of sex hormones rise, and the onset of puberty occurs (Grumbach & Styne, 1992). The specific mechanism called the "neuroendocrine hallmark" of pubertal onset (Grumbach & Styne, 1992) involves maturation of the central nervous system (CNS) centers which decrease neural restraint and permit pulsatile secretion of gonadotropin-releasing hormone by the hypothalamus during sleep in childhood. Consequently, puberty is not an abrupt event, but rather a lengthy process. Other hormone systems (e.g., adrenal) interact with those involved with puberty and play a role in the pubertal process (e.g., adrenarche).

Physical Changes. The five major internal and external changes of puberty identified by Marshall and Tanner are as follows: (1) an acceleration of skeletal growth followed by a deceleration of skeletal growth, which results in dramatic increases in height and weight (i.e., growth spurt); (2) a change in body composition and distribution of fat and muscle; (3) the development of the circulatory and respiratory systems, resulting in greater strength and endurance; (4) maturation of the reproductive organs and secondary sexual characteristics; and (5) changes in the nervous and endocrine systems, which regulate and coordinate pubertal events (Graber, Petersen, & Brooks-Gunn, 1996).

One of the most obvious and striking changes in physical appearance at puberty is the rapid increase in height and weight, referred to as the *adolescent growth spurt*. Growth velocity during puberty occurs at a greater rate than at any time since infancy. Skeletal changes at puberty result in bones becoming harder, more dense, and brittle. By midpuberty, the ends of the long bones in the body begin to close, ultimately resulting in the termination of growth as it relates to height.

Along with the increase in height, the adolescent experiences weight gain during puberty, due to increases in both muscle and fat. However, boys and girls differ in the development of fat versus muscle. Girls develop more body fat at a faster rate than do boys. Conversely, muscle tissue grows faster in boys than in girls.

The adolescent's gains in muscle and weight are accompanied by increased strength. The sex differences in muscle-to-fat ratios are thought to contribute to sex differences in strength and athletic ability that emerge in adolescence. Petersen and Taylor (1980) summarized that in comparison to girls, boys develop larger hearts and lungs relative to their size, higher systolic blood pressure, lower resting heart rate, and greater capacity for carrying oxygen in the blood and for neutralizing the chemical products of exercise (e.g., lactic acid), all differences probably related to the increased physical exercise and activity of boys at that time.

In considering sexual maturation, the physical changes occurring at puberty have been divided into stages. For girls, both breast and pubic hair development have been divided into five stages, with beginning breast development typically occurring first, at an average of 10.5 years of age. The development of pubic hair occurs soon after this, although pubic hair appears prior to breast buds in one fifth of girls. On average, the time interval between the appearance of breast budding and adult breast size is about 4.5 years. Menarche (the first menstruation) is a later event in the pubertal sequence, occurring on average at 12.5 years of age in the United States, just after the peak growth spurt (Brooks-Gunn & Reiter, 1990).

For boys, genital and pubic hair development also are divided into five stages. The onset of testicular growth occurs on average at 11 to 11.5 years of age. The average time interval between the first signs of genital growth and the development of adult male genitalia is three years; however, an interval of five years is within the normal range. Pubic hair growth lags approximately one stage behind genital development. Spermarche, the onset of the release of spermatozoa, occurs between 12 and 14 years of age.

To summarize, the major physical changes of puberty include a dramatic growth in height and weight, the growth of pubic and axillary (underarm) hair, the growth of facial hair in boys, breast development in girls, and genital development in both boys and girls. Voice deepening, acne, and other skin eruptions and the development of sebaceous (oily) and apocrine (sweat) glands are other major pubertal changes (Petersen & Taylor, 1980).

Variations in the Pubertal Process. Although the progression of development on each pubertal indicator is relatively stable, the timing of the onset of development and the rate of progression through the various stages (tempo) varies among indicators for different adolescents. Within any group of 13-year-olds, some individuals will have completed the entire pubertal process while others have not yet begun it, with boys about two years later than girls. Acceleration of growth begins at approximately 9.6 years of age for girls and 11.7 years of age for boys (Brooks-Gunn & Reiter, 1990). Peak height velocity occurs at approximately age 11 in girls and age 13 in boys. Growth in height ends at approximately age 17 in females and age 20 in males.

Pubertal Status and Pubertal Timing. Pubertal status refers to the level of physical development attained by an individual in terms of the indicators of puberty described earlier (Alsaker, 1995). Pubertal status may be measured by medical exams assessing changes in secondary sexual characteristics (e.g., genital, breast, and pubic hair development) utilizing Tanner criteria. Alternative assessments include parents' reports and self-reports of items assessing pubertal stage.

Pubertal timing refers to an individual's level of pubertal development compared to the level of pubertal maturation that it is expected at a particular age or within some reference group (Alsaker, 1995). An individual's pubertal development may be characterized as occurring earlier, later, or at about the same time as most adolescents. Pubertal timing may be assessed using criteria such as the occurrence of some indicator(s) of pubertal development (e.g., menarche, age at peak height velocity) in comparison to reference norms (e.g., national norms, or the norms of the larger sample). Self-perceptions of pubertal timing also have been used. The adolescent indicates whether he or she feels the physical changes are happening at a rate earlier than, the same as, or later than a reference group.

Some boys and girls experience the physical changes of puberty very early (i.e., precocious puberty) or very late (i.e., delayed puberty). According to Grumbach and Styne (1992), precocious puberty may be defined as the appearance of any indicator of secondary sexual maturation at an age more than 2.0 standard deviations below the mean. The lack of any sign of sexual maturation at an age that is two standard deviations above the mean age of onset may be defined as delayed puberty. Precocious puberty is less common in boys than in girls. For males, evidence of increased testicular growth or growth on any other pubertal characteristic prior to age 9 is viewed as precocious. In girls, pubertal development is considered precocious if the onset of breast budding begins prior to age 8, or if the pubertal growth spurt occurs prior to age 7. Delayed puberty is characterized by the absence of pubertal changes after age 13 in girls and age 14 in boys (Brooks-Gunn & Reiter, 1990).

Genetic and Environmental Links to Pubertal Timing. Genetic and environmental factors contribute to differences in the timing and rate of pubertal maturation. Genetic contributions to pubertal timing are evident in research demonstrating significant correlations between mother and daughter menarchal age. Key environmental influences are nutrition, exercise, and health. Restriction of nutritional intake (but not to the point of starvation) in combination with high physical demands on the body via exercise results in delayed pubertal onset. Gymnasts, figure skaters, dancers, and runners may report delays of one to two years in the onset of menarche.

Nutrition and weight during the early years of life (fetal and infancy) and nutrition and weight at the age of puberty may influence the onset of puberty (Brooks-Gunn & Reiter, 1990). For example, the timing of puberty for adolescent girls (especially menarche) has been found to be closely linked to an average critical body weight. Some physical and health conditions during childhood and adolescence may influence maturational timing. For example, hypothyroidism, blindness, and retardation have been linked to advanced menarche. Cystic fibrosis, juvenile onset diabetes, Crohn's disease, and sickle-cell anemia may delay menarche.

A recent body of research suggests that social factors in the adolescent's environment may influence pubertal timing, with two different hypotheses. Belsky, Steinberg, and Draper (1991) posited an evolutionary hypothesis, suggesting that—under conditions of contextual stress—insensitive, inconsistent, and affectively negative parental care is more likely. They proposed that young children in these family contexts are more likely to develop insecure attachments to parents and an opportunistic style of interacting with others. These children are viewed as being more likely to develop behavioral problems prepubertally, such as externalizing problems (e.g., aggression, impulsivity, and noncompliance with adults), or internalizing problems (e.g., high levels of sadness, depression, and social withdrawal). These stressful environmental conditions and behavioral problems likely lead to early pubertal development, early onset of sexual activity, and a risky and opportunistic approach to interpersonal interactions.

Support for the evolutionary hypothesis has been found in research linking early maturation to less positive family relations, suggesting that family stress accelerates pubertal development. Although the mechanisms linking family relationships to pubertal development have not yet been identified, the presumption is that the hormonal pathways controlling puberty are responsible. Stressful family circumstances may produce physiological stress responses leading to hormonal activity that accelerates development.

There is also evidence to suggest that the experience of prepubertal sexual abuse may stimulate an earlier onset of puberty (Trickett & Putnam, 1993). Two possible explanations offered by Trickett and Putnam for how sexual abuse may affect pubertal onset are that sexual abuse may stimulate the endocrine system, activating the onset of puberty, or that exposure to pheromones as the result of repeated abuse may trigger pubertal onset.

Alternatively, research that has looked at the hormonal correlates of social adjustment during puberty suggests that stressful environments may delay pubertal onset rather than accelerate it. Specifically, it is suggested that environmental stress increases the level of stress-related hormones from the adrenal axis, and this in turn inhibits sex steroid levels, which leads to a delayed onset of puberty. Consistent with this hypothesis, Malo and Tremblay (1997) reported that paternal alcoholism contributed to a delay in the onset of puberty in their sample of adolescent males. They suggested that the stress in the family environment stemming from paternal alcoholism activates the hypothalamic-pituitary-adrenal axis, and inhibits the hypothalamic-pituitary-gonadal axis. Furthermore, other research has found a link between negative emotions and delayed pubertal maturation in boys. The available evidence for delayed pubertal development suggests that negative emotions such as depression, anxiety, and hostility increase the level of stress-related hormones from the adrenal axis, which in turn has an inhibitor effect on the gonadal axis (Malo & Tremblay, 1997).

It should be emphasized that the body of research examining the link between stress and pubertal onset is still relatively new, and as noted above, both accelerating and decelerating effects on maturation have been observed. Furthermore, other research has found no link between stress and pubertal onset.

Historical Trends, Race, and Ethnicity. Over the past century, a secular trend in the average age of onset of puberty has been observed, with a trend toward earlier occurrence. This trend cuts across geographic and ethnic lines (Brooks-Gunn & Reiter, 1990). Improvements in socioeconomic conditions, increase in food and nutrition, decrease of infection through immunizations and improved sanitation, and more widespread medical and health care are factors that have contributed to this secular trend, which has slowed or stopped in recent decades (Eveleth & Tanner, 1990). Herman-Giddens et al. (1997) suggested that girls in the United States are developing pubertal characteristics at younger ages than the norms currently used. In

their investigation of a large sample of young girls ages 3 to 12 who were pediatricians' patients in practices across the United States, they found that 1% of Whites and 3% of Blacks already showed signs of pubic hair and/or breast development by age 3. By age 8, 14.7% of Whites and 48.3% of Blacks showed development on these indicators.

Herman-Giddens et al. (1997) also point out racial differences in pubertal development. Specifically, at every age for each indicator, African American girls showed more advanced development than did White girls. Other recent research suggests that African American girls on average begin puberty earlier than White girls. In addition, it should be noted that earlier research reported more advanced development of secondary sex characteristics in African American girls as compared to White girls. However, the Herman-Giddens et al. data are noteworthy because they included children as young as 3 years.

Herman-Giddens et al. (1997) suggested that if the age of menarche for African American girls has decreased, as indicated by their data, it may be due to improved nutritional and health status, as age at menarche may be more sensitive to nutrition and health than the development of secondary sex characteristics. The use of hair products containing estrogen or placenta and the increasing use of certain plastics and insecticides that degrade into substances that have estrogen-related physiological effects also may be contributing to the earlier onset of puberty, and Herman-Giddens et al. (1997) suggest that the potential role of these substances warrants further research attention. Also, the impact of weight may play a role in earlier pubertal onset, as girls are heavier now than in the past.

Although it is widely believed that puberty occurs later among Asians than Whites, this is an erroneous assumption. For example, in China, in urban areas with good nutrition and extensive health statistics, menarche occurs on average at the same age as it does for the population at large in the United States (Brooks-Gunn & Reiter, 1990). Generally speaking, the average age at menarche is lower in those countries where individuals are less likely to be malnourished or suffer from chronic disease. In considering ethnic variation within the United States, there is some evidence to suggest that pubertal events in Mexican-American adolescents are moderately delayed in comparison to other populations (Eveleth & Tanner, 1990). However, these findings are based on research drawing from a sample of participants who were disproportionately from poor socioeconomic backgrounds, and there is a lack of appropriate comparative data.

Puberty as a Psychosocial Process

It also is important to recognize puberty as a psychosocial process. The physical changes of puberty have implications for the adolescent's development in other domains.

Hormones and Behavior at Puberty. Whereas theorists and researchers have long assumed that hormones are important to consider in adolescent behavior and development, research that has specifically addressed the role of hormones in behavior has only been conducted since around 1980 (Susman, 1997). Susman (1997) presented four models for linking hormones and behavior at adolescence. In model I, hormones are viewed as causes of behavior. Increases in gonadal hormones are assumed to lead to changes in adolescent behavior. In contrast, model II views behavior to be a cause of hormone change. Model III posits that hormones and behavior interact. The premise of this model is that change in one domain (either hormones or behavior) influence changes in a second domain. Finally, model IV considers the interconnections among hormones, behavior, and context. It is suggested that the context of development can influence the secretion of adrenal, gonadal, and thyroid hormones that may interact with genes and alter gene expression. Contextual factors that may play a role in this process include psychological processes (e.g., perception), experiences (e.g., abuse), and the individual's environment (e.g., violence).

Research evidence provides support for the hypothesized links between hormones and behavior. For example, adrenal androgens and cortisol have consistently been linked to behavior problems. However, inconsistent associations have been found between gonadal steroids (testosterone in particular) and antisocial behavior in young adolescents. Furthermore, the hormonal changes of puberty may be implicated in the development of depressive affect.

Models Linking Pubertal Status and Timing to Psychosocial Outcomes. In contrast to the smaller body of research that has examined levels of pubertal hormones on behavioral outcomes, a larger body of research has examined the links between pubertal status and/or pubertal timing and various psychosocial outcomes. In particular, the timing of pubertal maturation is an important factor to consider when examining puberty as a psychosocial process.

Models of pubertal maturation and psychosocial adjustment tend to be interactional in nature (Alsaker, 1995). That is, the effect of puberty is not viewed as a direct consequence of the biological changes of puberty, but rather of individual psychological factors (e.g., how the individual interprets his or her pubertal development), the social context (e.g., reactions of parents and peers), and cultural values (e.g., factors related to ethnicity or social class) shape the process.

Specifically, three hypotheses typically are used to describe the possible process by which pubertal development exerts an effect on psychosocial development.

According to the stage termination hypothesis (Petersen & Taylor, 1980), the developmental tasks associated with each developmental stage need time for adequate resolution; consequently, early pubertal maturation may interrupt the ego development that is in process prior to puberty. Negative effects of early puberty may stem from this early termination of the prepubertal developmental process.

According to the deviance hypothesis, negative effects of early or late maturation are the result of off-time maturation (Petersen & Taylor, 1980). That is, either early or late maturation places young adolescents in a socially deviant category. In contrast, the goodness of fit hypothesis offered by Lerner suggests that psychological well-being is influenced by the extent to which there is a good fit between characteristics of the adolescent and characteristics of the context (Alsaker, 1995). Consequently, this hypothesis emphasizes the importance of the fit between the adolescent's pubertal timing and the adolescent's social context. For example, on-time maturers may be at risk in a social context that emphasizes a prepubertal body build, a finding that has been observed in research on adolescent female dancers.

Puberty and Psychological Adjustment. A considerable body of research has examined the links between pubertal development and various indicators of psychological adjustment. In this section the connections between puberty and body image, internalizing behaviors (e.g., depression) and externalizing behaviors (e.g., behavior disorders) are considered. It should be noted that most of the research that has found an effect of puberty on psychological adjustment has found pubertal timing to be a key factor in the process, with pubertal timing effects more pervasive than pubertal status effects.

Body Image. The dramatic physical transformations of puberty have implications for how adolescents perceive their physical selves in terms of body image. In their summary of studies examining body image and pubertal timing, Graber et al. (1996) concluded that when pubertal timing effects on body image were found for girls, they tended to occur after the peak pubertal years rather than during periods of pubertal change. For example, in data from the Adolescent Mental Health Study early maturing girls showed a marked decline in body image scores across adolescence (from grades 6 to 12), with increasing divergence in body image as compared to the late and on-time girls (Graber et al., 1996). Persisting effects for poor body image in early maturing girls are found into young adulthood. For boys, early pubertal timing has been found to be associated with positive body image during early adolescence; however, positive effects of early maturation for boys have not been found to persist into midadolescence.

Dissatisfaction with one's body during adolescence

is strongly related to height in boys (short height perceived negatively) and weight in girls (heavier weight perceived negatively). Whereas early pubertal maturation brings culturally valued muscular development among males, for females, the increased weight associated with pubertal maturation contrasts with the Western cultural ideal of thinness. This dissatisfaction with the physical changes of puberty also has implications for other body image-related outcomes, and earlier pubertal maturation has been associated with the development of eating problems.

Internalizing Behaviors. With regard to internalizing behaviors, the most persistent finding in the literature points to the greater vulnerability of girls with earlier pubertal maturation as assessed by a range of mental health indicators. A prospective study of sixth-, seventh-, and eighth-grade adolescent girls found that girls who showed an onset of internalizing symptoms (e.g., depression, phobic disorders, and subclinical bulimia) were on average five months earlier in pubertal development than were those who were asymptomatic (Hayward et al., 1997). In a subsample followed into high school, early maturing girls were at marginally higher risk for developing internalizing disorders by the study's end.

The research of Graber, Lewinsohn, Seeley, and Brooks-Gunn (1997) similarly found that psychopathology was linked to pubertal timing. They examined whether pubertal timing was associated with present and lifetime history of mental disorders, psychological symptoms, and psychosocial functioning in a community sample of high school students. Early maturing girls and late maturing boys showed more evidence of psychopathology than other same-gender adolescents. With regard to internalizing problems, they found that early maturing girls had significantly elevated lifetime rates of major depression. Late maturing girls also had a significantly elevated lifetime rate of major depression compared to on-time girls. Graber et al. (1997) found that late maturing males as compared to on-time males reported higher depression, more internalizing behavior problems, more negative cognitions, and a more depressotypic attributional style. Early maturing boys as compared to on-time boys also reported a higher level of depression.

Graber et al. (1997) concluded that early maturing girls had the poorest current and lifetime history of adjustment problems, indicating that early maturing girls in particular warrant attention of mental health providers and researchers. The risks of early puberty may be magnified when they occur together with other changes in the adolescent's life. For example, Petersen, Sarigiani, and Kennedy (1991) reported that the experience of synchronous school and pubertal change during early adolescence (more likely in girls due to their earlier maturation) contributed to the development of gender differences in depressive disorders evident in midadolescence. In contrast to research on pubertal timing, the majority of studies have showed no significant association between pubertal status and depressed affect (Connolly, Paikoff, & Buchanan, 1996).

Externalizing Behaviors. Externalizing behaviors may be described as delinquent, deviant, or norm-breaking behaviors. Aggressive behaviors, school-related behavioral problems, and alcohol consumption are examples of externalizing behaviors. Connolly et al. (1996) summarized that research also links pubertal timing to externalizing behaviors. Early maturing girls show more deviant behavior and more contact with deviant peers than do late maturing or on-time girls. Adolescent women who begin puberty early are more likely to smoke cigarettes and use alcohol. Early maturing girls are more likely to have older friends than are on-time and late maturing girls, and their older peers are perceived to be more tolerant of norm-breaking behavior. Consequently, the effect of early pubertal maturation on norm-breaking behavior is mediated by social variables. Graber et al. (1997) found that compared to on-time girls, early maturing girls had significantly elevated lifetime rates of substance abuse/dependence, and disruptive behavior disorders. The longer-term effects of pubertal maturation also are important to consider. By adulthood, early maturing women have been found to have less education and lower prestige jobs.

Among males, more externalizing behaviors as indicated by behavior problems tend to be found in early maturing boys (Connolly et al., 1996). Off-time maturation (early and late) has been related to drinking behavior in adolescent males, and late maturing males may be at greater risk for developing later alcohol problems. However, in the Graber et al. (1997) study, late maturing boys were found to have significantly lower rates of lifetime substance abuse/dependence as compared to on-time boys. Early maturing boys were found to have a higher current rate of tobacco use than were on-time boys (Graber et al., 1997).

Puberty and Sexuality. It is commonly believed that the biological changes of puberty initiate a sexual awakening at adolescence. Biological perspectives on adolescent development suggest that the increases in testosterone which occur at puberty are responsible for increases in sexual interest and motivation at that time. Within the 1990s, conclusions regarding the links between biological indicators and puberty and adolescent sexuality have undergone revision. Research suggests that the links between puberty, hormones, and adolescent sexuality are complex, and biosocial models provide a better fit for the existing data.

A longitudinal study of adolescent males by Halpern, Udry, and colleagues revealed that neither sexual interest nor sexual behavior of adolescent males changed as a function of changes in testosterone levels over a 3-year period. However, significant, positive associations were found between measures of testosterone collected early in adolescence and both concurrent and later measures of sexual activity. The investigators hypothesized that early high testosterone may be considered to be a marker for a growth trajectory identifiable prior to puberty. Therefore, high levels of testosterone in adolescent boys may be more appropriately viewed as a marker for earlier pubertal development, and it is this earlier pubertal development that places these adolescent males on a growth trajectory for earlier sexual behavior.

Similarly, longitudinal research on adolescent girls results in a revision of earlier conclusions. Halpern, Udry, and Suchindran (1997) reported that testosterone levels in adolescent girls predict the initiation of coitus. They found that the transition to coitus was more likely in those girls who had higher testosterone levels. Pubertal development was not significant in these models, which suggested that the testosterone effects did not appear to be the result of indirect effects stemming from the social stimulus value of pubertal development.

It is important to emphasize the social processes involved in the links between puberty, hormones, and adolescent sexuality. Indeed, the start of sexual activity is closely linked to peer group norms (Brooks-Gunn & Reiter, 1990). Halpern and colleagues emphasize the importance of considering biosocial interactions in their research considering the role of attendance at religious services and adolescent sexual attitudes and behaviors. In their study of adolescent males, they found that boys who had higher levels of testosterone upon study entry and who never or infrequently attended religious services were the most sexually active and had the most permissive attitudes about sexual behavior. In contrast, boys with lower levels of free testosterone who attended religious services once a week or more were the least sexually active and held the least permissive attitudes. Similarly, in their study of adolescent girls, Halpern and colleagues found that for White girls, but not for African American girls, church attendance appeared to function as a social control in the initiation of sexual activity.

The salience of pubertal timing for understanding sexual behavior for adolescent girls is important to emphasize. Adolescent women who begin puberty early are more likely to engage in sexual intercourse. The potentially negative consequences in terms of risk for unwanted sexual activity, sexually transmitted diseases, and unplanned pregnancies are important to consider.

Puberty and Parent-Child Relationships. In their comprehensive review, Paikoff and Brooks-Gunn (1991) indicate that during puberty, parent-child relationships experience increases in conflict and less warm interactions. It should be noted, however, that parent-child conflict during adolescence typically is not intense, nor does it indicate a decrease in a strong affective bond. Parent-child conflict is characterized by interactions such as mild bickering and disagreements on everyday issues such as rules and regulations, dating, and clothing.

Whereas most of the research finding effects of puberty on psychosocial development have found effects for pubertal timing, research on puberty and family relations is different in that where effects are found, they are as likely or more likely to be linked to the adolescent's pubertal status rather than to pubertal timing (Connolly et al., 1996). For example, more problems between adolescent girls and their families have been found at menarche (Connolly et al. 1996), and the midpubertal period has been found to be a time of change in parent-child relationships for boys (Paikoff & Brooks-Gunn, 1991).

Research supports a trend toward increased conflicts and difficulties in family relations during puberty for girls and boys. However, this period of conflict is relatively short-lived, and it peaks during puberty and declines postpubertally (Connolly et al., 1996). With regard to pubertal timing and family relationships, there is a weak trend toward increased or longer-lasting conflicts in early maturing girls, but mixed results are found for boys. Paikoff and Brooks-Gunn (1991) conclude that research suggests there is a consistent effect of puberty on parent-child relationships; however, the effect is probably small in magnitude.

Summary and Conclusions

Puberty ushers in a complex array of physical changes which transform the appearance and experience of the adolescent. The biological changes of puberty intricately interact with other aspects of the adolescent's development, including his or her psychological wellbeing, body image, family relationships, and sexuality. Although all adolescents traverse the same biological process, it is clear from the research that there are variations in the experience of puberty due to variations in timing, tempo, and individual psychological variables such as perceptions of the experience, or context features such as the culture or subculture.

The significance of variations in the pubertal process are perhaps clearest in the research examining the implications of pubertal timing. The most recent research presents a case for the potential vulnerability of experience for early maturing girls. Greater risk for internalizing and externalizing disorders, and lower educational and occupational attainment are evident for these girls, and prompt the need for further intervention and prevention efforts. For example, recognizing that early maturing girls may be a group at risk suggests targeting them in prevention efforts to educate them about their physical changes as a normal part of growing up. There would as well be an attempt to divert them away from risky behaviors that may have long-term implications for their development far beyond their adolescent years.

Furthermore, evidence for historical change in the pubertal process is intriguing. Findings of very early signs of pubertal maturation in girls in the Herman-Giddens et al. work illustrate how the standards of pubertal development in terms of timing may warrant revision. The implications of an early pubertal experience are even further underscored, as this research suggests that this is an experience that will be encountered by even more girls, and perhaps especially among African American girls.

Although an impressive body of research has been devoted to understanding both the biological and psychosocial aspects of the pubertal period, it is clear from the available research that new findings are illuminating our understanding of the pubertal process. For example, the research linking stress to pubertal development is intriguing, and represents a clear illustration of the interface between the adolescent's psychosocial and biological milieu. This research area is a relatively new pursuit, and further disentangling the processes involved remains. Similarly, the study of direct hormonal links to behavior and development during adolescence is relatively new, and as methodologies become more sophisticated, previous conclusions have been revised. What is clear is that hormonal links to behavior are complex, and biopsychosocial frameworks clearly provide the best representation of the process.

Bibliography

Alsaker, F. D. (1995). Timing of puberty and reactions to pubertal changes. In M. Rutter (Ed.), *Psychosocial disturbances in young people: Challenges for prevention* (pp. 37–81). New York: Cambridge University Press.

Belsky, J., Steinberg, L., & Draper, P. (1991). Childhood experience, interpersonal development, and reproductive strategy: An evolutionary theory of socialization. *Child Development, 62,* 647–670.

Brooks-Gunn, J., & Reiter, E. O. (1990). The role of pubertal processes in the early adolescent transition. In S. Feldman & G. Elliott (Eds.), *At the threshold: The developing adolescent* (pp. 16–53). Cambridge, MA: Harvard University Press.

Connolly, S. D., Paikoff, R. L., & Buchanan, C. M. (1996). Puberty: The interplay of biological and psychosocial processes in adolescence. In G. R. Adams, R. Montemayor, & T. P. Gullotta (Eds.), *Psychosocial development during adolescence* (pp. 259–299). Thousand Oaks, CA: Sage.

Eveleth, P. B., & Tanner, J. M. (1990). *Worldwide variation in human growth* (2nd ed.). New York: Cambridge University Press.

Graber, J. A., Lewinsohn, P. M., Seeley, J. R., & Brooks-Gunn, J. (1997). Is psychopathology associated with the timing of pubertal development? *Journal of the American Academy of Child and Adolescent Psychiatry, 36,* 1768 1776.

Graber, J. A., Petersen, A. C., & Brooks-Gunn, J. (1996). Pubertal processes: Methods, measures, and models. In J. A. Graber, J. Brooks-Gunn, & A. C. Petersen (Eds.), *Transitions through adolescence: Interpersonal domains and context* (pp. 23–53). Mahwah, NJ: Erlbaum.

Grumbach, M. M., & Styne, D. (1992). Puberty: Ontogeny, neuroendocrinology, physiology, and disorders. In J. D. Wilson & D. W. Foster (Eds.), *Williams textbook of endocrinology* (8th ed., pp. 1139–1221). Philadelphia: Saunders.

Halpern, C. T., Udry, J. R., & Suchindran, C. (1997). Testosterone predicts initiation of coitus in adolescent females. *Psychosomatic Medicine, 59,* 161–171.

Hayward, C., Killen, J. D., Wilson, D. M., Hammer, L. D., Litt, I. F., Kraemer, H. C., Haydel, F., Varady, A., & Taylor, C. B. (1997). Psychiatric risk associated with early puberty in adolescent girls. *Journal of the American Academy of Adolescent Psychiatry, 36,* 255–262.

Herman-Giddens, M. E., Slora, E. J., Wasserman, R. C., Bourdony, C. J., Bhapkar, M. V., Koch, G. G., & Hasemeier, C. M. (1997). Secondary sexual characteristics and menses in young girls seen in office practice: A study from the Pediatric Research in Office Settings Network. *Pediatrics, 99,* 505–512.

Malo, J., & Tremblay, R. E. (1997). The impact of paternal alcoholism and maternal social position on boys' school adjustment, pubertal maturation and sexual behavior: A test of two competing hypotheses. *Journal of Child Psychology and Psychiatry, 38,* 187–197.

Paikoff, R. L., & Brooks-Gunn (1991). Do parent-child relationships change during puberty? *Psychological Bulletin, 110,* 47–66.

Petersen, A. C., Sarigiani, P. A., & Kennedy, R. E. (1991). Adolescent depression: Why more girls? *Journal of Youth and Adolescence, 20,* 247–271.

Petersen, A. C., & Taylor, B. (1980). The biological approach to adolescence: Biological change and psychological adaptation. In J. Adelson (Ed.), *Handbook of adolescent psychology* (pp. 117–155). New York: Wiley.

Susman, E. J. (1997). Modeling developmental complexity in adolescence: Hormones and behavior in context. *Journal of Research on Adolescence, 7,* 283–306.

Trickett, P. K., & Putnam, F. W. (1993). Impact of child sexual abuse on females: Toward a developmental, psychobiological integration. *Psychological Science, 4,* 81–87.

Pamela A. Sarigiani and Anne C. Petersen

Social Patterns, Achievements, and Problems

Adolescence is a period of many changes ranging from the biological changes associated with puberty, to the social/educational changes associated with the transitions from elementary to secondary school, and to the social and psychological changes associated with the emergence of sexuality. With such diverse and rapid change comes a heightened potential for both positive and negative outcomes. And, although most individuals pass through this developmental period without excessively high levels of "storm and stress," a substantial number of individuals do experience difficulty. For example, between 15 and 30% of students (depending on ethnic group) drop out of high school; further, adolescents have the highest arrest rate of any age group; and many consume alcohol and other drugs on a regular basis (Office of Educational Research and Improvement, 1988). In contrast, many adolescents do quite well during this period of life: they acquire the skills to move successfully into meaningful adult roles, they develop lasting friendships, and they form healthy, productive identities.

Biological Changes Associated with Puberty

As a result of the activation of hormones controlling physical development, most children undergo a growth spurt, develop primary and secondary sex characteristics, become fertile, and experience increased sexual libido during early adolescence (Buchanan, Eccles, & Becker, 1992). Because girls experience these pubertal changes approximately 18 months earlier than boys, girls and boys of the same chronological age are likely to be at quite different points in physical and social development during early adolescence. Although early maturation tends to be advantageous for boys, particularly with respect to their participation in sports activities and social standing in school, early maturation is often problematic for European American girls because the kinds of physical changes girls experience (such as weight gain) are not highly valued among many White American groups who value the slim, androgynous female body characteristic of European American fashion models (Simmons & Blyth, 1987). African American females do not evidence this same pattern perhaps because African American culture places higher value on the secondary sex characteristics associated with female maturation.

Stattin and Magnusson (1990) traced the long-term consequences of early maturation in females: Their early maturing girls obtained less education and married earlier than their later maturing peers despite the lack of any differences in achievement levels prior to the onset of puberty. These researchers attributed this difference to the fact that the early maturing females were more likely to join older peer groups and to begin dating older males; in turn, the early maturing girls in these peer groups were more likely to drop out of school and get married, perhaps because school achievement was not valued by their peer social network while early entry into the job market and early marriage was.

Researchers have also studied how the hormonal changes associated with pubertal development relate to changes in children's behavior during the early adolescent years. There are direct effects of hormones on behaviors, such as aggression, sexuality, and mood swings. Hormones also affect behavior indirectly through their impact on secondary sex characteristics, which, in turn, influence social experiences and psychological well-being. For example, when breast development is associated with increases in girls' body image, it is also related to better psychological adjustment, more positive peer relations, and better school achievement (Brooks-Gunn & Warren, 1988).

Changes in Cognition

Cognitive changes during this developmental period involve increases in adolescents' ability to think abstractly, consider the hypothetical as well as the real, engage in more sophisticated and elaborate information processing strategies, consider multiple dimensions of a problem at once, and reflect on oneself and on complicated problems. Such cognitive changes are the hallmark of Piaget's formal operations stage, which he assumed began during adolescence (e.g., Piaget & Inhelder, 1973). Although there is still considerable debate about exactly when these kinds of cognitive processes emerge and whether their emergence reflects global stagelike changes in cognitive skills, as described by Piaget, most theorists agree that these kinds of thought processes are more characteristic of adolescents' cognition than that of younger children.

Cognitive theorists have also investigated more specific information processing skills, cognitive learning strategies, and metacognitive skills (Keating, 1992). They find a steady increase during adolescence in information processing skills and learning strategies, in knowledge of a variety of different topics and subject areas, in ability to apply knowledge to new learning situations, and in awareness of one's strengths and weaknesses as learners. However, in order for these new skills to allow adolescents to become more efficient, sophisticated learners, ready to cope with relatively advanced topics in many different subject areas, they need lots of opportunities to practice using them.

These kinds of cognitive changes can affect individuals' self-concepts, thoughts about their future, and understanding of others. Theorists from Erikson (1963) to Harter (1998) have suggested that the adolescent years are a time of change in children's self-concepts, as they try both to figure out what possibilities are available to them and to develop a deeper understanding of themselves. Such self-reflection requires higher-order cognitive processes. During adolescence, individuals also become much more interested in understanding others' internal psychological characteristics, and friendships become based more on perceived similarity in these characteristics. Again, these types of changes reflect the broader changes in cognition that occur at this time.

Friendships and Peer Groups

Probably the most often discussed changes during adolescence are the increases in peer focus and involvement in peer-related social, sports, and other extracurricular activities. Many adolescents attach great importance to these types of activities—substantially more importance than they attach to academic activities (Wigfield, Eccles, MacIver, Reuman, & Midgley, 1991). Indeed, often to the chagrin of parents and teachers, activities with peers, peer acceptance, and appearance can take precedence over school activities, particularly during early adolescence. Further, European American adolescents' confidence in their physical appearance and social acceptance is often a more important predictor of self-esteem than confidence in their cognitive/academic competence (Harter, 1998). The extent to which this is true in other ethnic groups has yet to be adequately assessed.

In part because of the importance of social acceptance during adolescence, friendship networks during this period often are organized into relatively rigid cliques that differ in social status within the school setting (Brown, 1990). The existence of these cliques seems to reflect adolescents' need to establish a sense of identity; belonging to a group is one way to solve the problem of "who am I."

Also, in part because of the importance of social acceptance, children's conformity to their peers peaks during early adolescence. Most policy concern has focused on how this peer conformity can create problems for adolescents, and about how "good" children can be corrupted by the negative influences of peers, particularly by adolescent gangs—and indeed gangs do pose serious social problems in many cities. However, although pressure from peers to engage in misconduct does increase during adolescence, most researchers do not accept the simplistic view that peer groups are mostly a bad influence during this period. More often than not, adolescents agree more with their parents' views on "major" issues such as morality, the importance of education, politics, and religion. Peers have more influence on things such as dress and clothing styles, music, and activity choice. In addition, adolescents usually seek out peers whose interests are compatible with their own; this means that those who are involved in sports will have other athletes as friends; those who are serious about school will seek friends who are similarly inclined. Finally, adolescents usually select peers who share their parents' fundamental values. In most cases, the peer group acts more to reinforce existing strengths and weakness than to change adolescents' characteristics.

Finally, the quality of children's friendships undergoes some important changes during adolescence (Berndt & Perry, 1990). As suggested by Sullivan (1953), adolescents' friendships are more focused on fulfilling intimacy needs than younger children's friendships. This is particularly true for girls.

Changes in Family Relations

Although the extent of actual disruption in parent-adolescent relations is still debated, there is no doubt that parent-child relations change during adolescence (e.g., Collins, 1990). As adolescents become physically mature they often seek more independence and autonomy, and may begin to question family rules and roles, leading to conflicts, particularly around issues like dress and appearance, chores, and dating. However, despite these conflicts over day-to-day issues, parents and adolescents agree more than they disagree regarding core values linked to education, politics, and spirituality.

Parents and adolescents also have fewer interactions and do fewer things together outside the home than they did at an earlier period—as illustrated by the horror many adolescents express at seeing their parents at places like shopping malls. Both Collins (1990) and Steinberg (1990) argued that this "distancing" in the relations between adolescents and parents is a natural part of pubertal development that has great functional value for adolescents precisely because it fosters their individuation from their parents, allows them to try more things on their own, and develops their own competencies and efficacy. When parents respond to this distancing in a developmentally supportive fashion, while at the same time providing ample guidance and control, their adolescent children exercise their increasing autonomy in a mature, responsible fashion and maintain positive relationships with their parents.

School and Adolescent Development

For some children, the early adolescent years mark the beginning of a downward spiral leading to academic failure and school dropout.

The Junior High/Middle School Transition. Simmons and Blyth (1987) found a marked decline in some early adolescents' school grades as they moved into junior high school, a decline that was predictive of subsequent school failure and dropout. Similar declines have been documented for such motivational constructs as interest in school, intrinsic motivation, self-concepts/self-perceptions, and confidence in one's intellectual abilities, especially following failure. Finally, there are also increases during early adolescence in such negative motivational and behavioral characteristics as test anxiety, learned helpless responses to failure, focus on self-evaluation rather than task mastery, and both truancy and school dropout (see Eccles & Midgley, 1989). Although these changes are not extreme for most adolescents, there is sufficient evidence of gradual decline in various indicators of academic motivation, behavior, and self-perception over the early adolescent years to make one wonder what is happening. And although few studies have gathered information on ethnic or social class differences in these declines, we know that academic failure and dropping out is especially problematic among some ethnic groups and among youth from low socioeconomic communities and families; thus, it is likely that these groups are particularly likely to show these declines in academic motivation and self-perception as they move into, and through, the secondary school years.

A variety of explanations have been offered to explain these "negative" changes: Some have suggested that declines such as these result from the intraspsychic upheaval assumed to be associated with early adolescent development. Others have suggested that these declines are due to coincidental timing of multiple life changes (e.g., Simmons & Blyth, 1987). Still others have suggested that it is the nature of the junior high school environment itself that is important. Drawing upon person-environment fit theory, Eccles and Midgley (1989) proposed that the negative motivational and behavioral changes associated with early adolescence could result from the fact that traditional junior high schools are not providing appropriate educational environments for early adolescents. According to person-environment theory, behavior, motivation, and mental health are influenced by the fit between the characteristics individuals bring to their social environments and the characteristics of these social environments. Individuals are not likely to do very well, or be very motivated, if they are in social environments that do not fit their psychological needs. If the school social environments in the typical middle grades do not fit well with the psychological needs of adolescents, then person-environment fit theory predicts a decline in the adolescents' motivation, interest, performance, and behavior as they move into this environment. There is some evidence for each of these perspectives.

The Relation of Changes in School Environments to Motivational Changes During Early Adolescence. Work in a variety of areas has documented the impact of classroom and school environmental characteristics on motivation. For example, the big school/small school literature has demonstrated the motivational advantages of small secondary schools especially for marginal students (Barker & Gump, 1964). Similarly, the teacher efficacy literature has documented the positive student motivational consequences of high teacher efficacy (Ashton, 1985). Finally, organizational psychology has demonstrated the importance of participatory work structures on worker motivation (Lawler, 1976). The list of such influences could, of course, go on. The point is that there may be systematic differences between the academic environments in typical elementary schools and those in typical junior high and middle schools; if so, these differences could account for some of the motivational changes seen among early adolescents as they make the transition into junior high school or middle school.

Eccles and her colleagues have called this kind of phenomenon "Stage-Environment Fit." At the most basic level, this perspective suggests the importance of looking at the fit between the needs of early adolescents and the opportunities afforded them in their middle school environment. A poor fit would help explain the declines in motivation associated with the transition to either junior high or middle school. More specifically, these researchers suggested that different types of educational environments may be needed for different age groups in order to meet the individual's developmental needs and to foster continued developmental growth. Exposure to the developmentally appropriate environment would facilitate both motivation and continued growth; in contrast, exposure to a developmentally inappropriate environment, especially a developmentally regressive environment would create a particularly poor person-environment fit, which, in turn, would lead to declines in motivation as well as in the attachment to the goals of the institution.

Eccles and Midgley (1989) further argued that many early adolescents experience developmentally inappropriate changes in a cluster of classroom organizational, instructional, and climate variables, including task structure, task complexity, grouping practices, evaluation techniques, motivational strategies, locus of responsibility for learning, and quality of teacher-student and student-student relationships as they move into either middle school or junior high school. They argued, in turn, that these experiences contribute to the negative change in students' motivation and achievement-related beliefs assumed to coincide with the transition into junior high school. Recent research supports these suggestions. For example, Simmons and Blyth (1987) point out that most junior high schools are substantially larger than elementary schools and instruction is also more likely to be organized and taught departmentally. As a result of both of these differences, junior high school teachers typically teach several different groups of students each day and are unlikely to teach any particular student for more than one year. In addition, students typically have several teachers each day with little opportunity to interact with any one teacher on any dimension except the academic content of what is being taught and disciplinary issues. Thus, the opportunity for forming close relationships between students and teachers is effectively eliminated at precisely the point in the students' development when they have a great need for guidance and support from nonfamilial adults (Carnegie Council on Adolescent Development, 1989). Such changes in student-teacher relationships, in turn, are likely to undermine the sense of community and trust between students and teachers. This in turn leads to a lowered sense of efficacy and an increased reliance on authoritarian control practices by teachers, and an increased sense of alienation among students. Such changes are also likely to decrease the probability that any particular student's difficulties will be noticed early enough to get the student necessary help. This in turn increases the likelihood that students on the edge will be allowed to slip onto negative trajectories leading to increased school failure and dropout.

There is also consistent evidence of counterproductive changes in the authority relations between students and teaches. For example, despite the increasing maturity of students, junior high school classrooms, compared to elementary school classrooms, are characterized by a greater emphasis on teacher control and discipline, and fewer opportunities for student decision making, choice, and self-management. Such a mismatch between young adolescents' desires for autonomy and control and their perception of the opportunities in their environments should result in a decline in the adolescents' intrinsic motivation and interest in school; and this is exactly what happens (Eccles et al., 1993).

Finally, junior high school teachers appear to use a higher standard in judging students' competence and in grading their performance than do elementary school teachers. There is no stronger predictor of students' self-confidence and efficacy than the grades they receive. If grades change, then we would expect to see a concomitant shift in the adolescents' self-perceptions and academic motivation. There is evidence that junior high school teachers use stricter and more social comparison–based standards than elementary school teachers to assess student competency and to evaluate student performance, leading to a drop in grades for many early adolescents as they make the junior high school transition (e.g., Simmons & Blyth, 1987).

Eccles and Midgley argued that these types of school environmental changes are particularly harmful at early adolescence given what is known about psychological development during this stage of life. Early adolescent development is characterized by increases in desire for autonomy, peer orientation, self-focus and self-consciousness, salience of identity issues, concern over heterosexual relationships, and capacity for abstract cognitive activity (Simmons & Blyth, 1987). Simmons and Blyth argued that adolescents need a reasonably safe, as well as an intellectually challenging, environment to adapt to these shifts—an environment that provides a "zone of comfort" as well as challenging new opportunities for growth. In light of these needs, the environmental changes often associated with transition to middle grade schools are likely to be particularly harmful in that they emphasize competition, social comparison, and ability self-assessment at a time of heightened self-focus; they decrease decision making and choice at a time when the desire for control is growing; they emphasize lower-level cognitive strategies at a time when the ability to use higher-level strategies is increasing; and they disrupt social networks at a time when adolescents are especially concerned with peer relationships and may be in special need of close adult relationships outside of the home. The nature of these environmental changes, coupled with the normal course of individual development, is likely to result in a developmental mismatch so that the "fit" between the early adolescent and the classroom environment is particularly poor, increasing the risk of negative motivational outcomes, especially for adolescents who are having difficulty succeeding in school academically.

The High School Transition. Although there is less work on the transition to high school, the existing work is suggestive of similar problems. For example, high schools are typically even larger and more bureaucratic than junior high schools and middle schools. Bryk, Lee, and Holland (1994) provide numerous examples of how the sense of community among teachers and students is undermined by the size and bureaucratic structure of most high schools. There is little opportunity for students and teachers to get to know each other and, as a consequence, there is likely to be distrust between them and little attachment to a common set of goals and values. There is also little opportunity for the students to form mentorlike relationships with a nonfamilial adult and little effort is made to make instruction relevant to the students. Such environments are likely to further undermine the motivation and involvement of many students, especially those not doing particularly well academically, those not enrolled in the favored classes, and those who are alienated from the values of the adults in the high school. These hypotheses need to be tested.

Most large public high schools also organize instruction around curricular tracks that sort students into different groups (Lee & Bryk, 1989). As a result, there is even greater diversity in the educational experiences of high school students than of middle grade students; unfortunately, this diversity is often associated more with the students' social class and ethnic group than with differences in the students' talents and interests. As a result, curricular tracking has served to reinforce social stratification rather than foster optimal education for all students, particularly in large schools. Evidence comparing Catholic high schools with public high schools suggests that average school achievement levels are increased when all students are required to take the same challenging curriculum. This conclusion is true even after one has controlled for student selectivity factors. A more thorough examination is needed of how the organization and structure of our high schools influences cognitive, motivational, and achievement outcomes.

On the More Positive Side. Difficulties with secondary school transitions, however, are by no means universal. Hirsch and Rapkin (1987), for example, found no change in self-esteem in students making the transition from sixth grade into a junior high school. These authors did report, however, an increase in depressive symptomatology in girls making the transition as compared to boys. Although some of these differences across studies undoubtedly reflect variations across studies in populations, school environments, and varying methodological techniques, it is likely that individual differences in young adolescents' responses to school transitions also play a role. In support of this hypothesis, several studies have found negative changes for some youth and not for others. For example, Simmons and Blyth (1987) found that girls already involved in dating and showing the most advanced pubertal development were most at risk for negative changes in their self-esteem in conjunction with the transition to junior high school. Similarly, Midgley, Feldlaufer, and Eccles (1989) found more extreme negative effects of the junior high school transition on low achieving students. Finally, Lord, Eccles, and McCarthy (1994) found that adolescents who did well in school during their elementary school years and who have confidence in their academic and social abilities adapt quite well to the junior high school transition.

Bibliography

Ashton, P. (1985). Motivation and the teacher's sense of efficacy. In C. Ames & R. Ames (Eds.), *Research on motivation in education* (Vol. 2, pp. 141–171). Orlando, FL: Academic Press.

Barker, R., & Gump, P. (1964). *Big school, small school: High school size and student behavior.* Stanford, CA: Stanford University Press.

Berndt, T. J., & Perry, T. B. (1990). Distinctive features of early adolescent friendships. In R. Montemayor, G. R. Adams, & T. P. Gullotta (Eds.), *From childhood to adolescence: A transitional period?* (pp. 269–287). Newbury Park, CA: Sage.

Brooks-Gunn, J., & Warren, M. P. (1988). The psychological significance of secondary sexual characteristics in 9- to 11-year-old girls. *Child Development, 59,* 161–169.

Brown, B. B. (1990). Peer groups and peer cultures. In S. S. Feldman & G. R. Elliott (Eds.), *At the threshold: The de-veloping adolescent* (pp. 171–196). Cambridge, MA: Harvard University Press.

Bryk, A. S., Lee, V. E., & Holland, P. B. (1993). *Catholic schools and the common good.* Cambridge, MA: Harvard University Press.

Buchanan, C. M., Eccles, J. S., & Becker, J. B. (1992). Are adolescents the victims of raging hormones? *Psychological Bulletin, 111,* 62–107.

Carnegie Council on Adolescent Development (1989). *Turning points: Preparing American youth for the 21st century.* New York: Carnegie Corporation.

Collins, W. A. (1990). Parent-child relationships in the transition to adolescence: Continuity and change in interaction, affect, and cognition. In R. Montemayor, G. R. Adams, & T. P. Gullotta (Eds.), *From childhood to adolescence: A transitional period?* (pp. 85–106). Beverly Hills, CA: Sage.

Eccles, J. S., & Midgley, C. (1989). Stage-environment fit: Developmentally appropriate classrooms for young adolescents. In C. Ames & R. Ames (Eds.), *Research on motivation in education* (Vol. 3, pp. 139–186). New York: Academic Press.

Eccles, J. S., Midgley, C., Buchanan, C. M., Wigfield, A., Reuman, D., & MacIver, D. (1993). Development during adolescence: The impact of stage/environment fit. *American Psychologist, 48,* 90–101.

Eccles, J. S., Wigfield, A., & Schiefele, U. (1998). Motivation. In N. Eisenberg (Ed.), *Handbook of child psychology* (Vol. 3, 5th ed., pp. 1017–1095). New York: Wiley.

Erikson, E. H. (1963). *Childhood and society.* New York: Norton.

Harter, S. (1998). The development of self representations. In W. Damon & N. Eisenberg (Eds.), *Handbook of child psychology,* (Vol. 3, 5th ed., pp. 553–618). New York: Wiley.

Hirsch, B., & Rapkin, B. (1987). The transition to junior high school: A longitudinal study of self-esteem, psychological symptomatology, school life, and social support. *Child Development, 58,* 1235–1243.

Keating, D. P. (1990). Adolescent thinking. In S. S. Feldman & G. R. Elliott (Eds.) *At the threshold: The developing adolescent* (pp. 54–89). Cambridge, MA: Harvard University Press.

Lawler, E. E. (1976). Control systems in organizations. In M. D. Dunnette (Ed.), *Handbook of industrial and organizational psychology.* Chicago: Rand-McNally.

Lee, V. E., & Bryk, A. S. (1989). A multilevel model of the social distribution of high school achievement. *Sociology of Education, 62,* 172–192.

Lord, S., Eccles, J. S., & McCarthy, K. (1994). Risk and protective factors in the transition to junior high school. *Journal of Early Adolescence, 14,* 162–199.

Midgley, C. M., Feldlaufer, H., & Eccles, J. S. (1989). Changes in teacher efficacy and student self- and task-related beliefs during the transition to junior high school. *Journal of Educational Psychology, 81,* 247–258.

Office of Educational Research and Improvement (1988). *Youth indicators 1988.* Washington, DC: U.S. Government Printing Office.

Piaget, J., & Inhelder, B. (1973). *Memory and intelligence.* London: Routledge & Kegan Paul.

Rosenholtz, S. J., & Simpson, C. (1984). The formation of ability conceptions: Developmental trend or social construction? *Review of Educational Research, 54,* 301–325.

Simmons, R. G., & Blyth, D. A. (1987). *Moving into adolescence: The impact of pubertal change and school context.* Hawthorne, NY: Aldine de Gruyter.

Stattin, H., & Magnusson, D. (1990). *Pubertal maturation in female development.* Hillsdale, NJ: Erlbaum.

Steinberg, L. (1990). Autonomy, conflict, and harmony in the family relationship. In S. Feldman & G. Elliott (Eds.), *At the threshold: The developing adolescent* (pp. 255–276). Cambridge, MA: Harvard University Press.

Sullivan, H. S. (1953). *The interpersonal theory of psychiatry.* New York: Norton.

Wigfield, A., Eccles, J., Mac Iver, D., Reuman, D., & Midgley, C. (1991). Transitions at early adolescence: Changes in children's domain-specific self-perceptions and general self-esteem across the transition to junior high school. *Developmental Psychology, 27,* 552–565.

Jacquelynne S. Eccles and Allan Wigfield

Adolescent Thought Processes

Our adolescents today are exposed to a constantly changing expanse of information from a multitude of sources. Some, like cruising the Internet, were unknown to earlier generations. To stay "in the know" vis-à-vis their peers, adolescents need continuing access to the latest word their culture has to offer. They also must sort through a rapid-fire and often conflicting barrage of input from peers, parents, teachers, and media, to decide what to believe, what to ignore, and what warrants their sustained interest. Moreover, the information processing and judgment demands that today's teens face are central to their survival. Decisions about drug use, sexual activity, and social-group membership can have life-or-death implications.

To meet these challenges, we might ask whether adolescents are equipped with cognitive skills that surpass those they possessed as children. The question of the cognitive competencies of adolescents, relative to those of either the children they so recently were or the adults they are soon to become, is one of particular interest to developmental psychologists. To paraphrase the title of an influential article by Carey (1985), we can ask, "Are adolescents fundamentally different kinds of thinkers and learners from children?"

Is Adolescence Marked by a New Stage of Cognitive Development?

Even casual conversations with adolescents confirm that they know more about a wider variety of topics than do school-age children. But is this knowledge base organized any differently from the less extensive knowledge base of the child, or does it include principles or entities that the child's does not? One long-standing assumption is that with adolescence comes the ability to understand abstract concepts, such as justice or democracy. Of greatest interest to psychologists, however, has been the possibility that adolescents are capable of particular cognitive strategies that were not available to them earlier, enabling them to succeed in new kinds of intellectual tasks.

For several decades the dominant influence in this respect has been Piaget's theory of formal operations. Indeed, his remains the only comprehensive theory specifying a transformation in thinking capacities with the transition from childhood to adolescence. Formal operations, according to Piaget, constitute the final stage in a developmental sequence of major reorganizations of cognitive structure that take place during infancy and childhood. With the attainment of this stage, thought becomes able to take itself as its own object—adolescents are able to think about their own thinking. Formal operations in fact are defined as "operations on operations," that is, mental operations on the elementary operations of classification and relation that define the preceding stage of concrete operations. The adolescent becomes able, for example, not only to categorize animals according to physical characteristics and habitats but also to operate on these categorizations—to put them into categories and on this basis to draw inferences regarding relations that hold among animals' physical characteristics and habitats. The adolescent thus reasons at the level of *propositions* that specify relations between one category (or relation) and another. Associated with this second-order operatory structure, according to the theory, are several other important cognitive strategies—analogy (constructing relations between relations, e.g., subjects: monarchy::citizens:democracy), systematic combination (e.g., of all possible pizza types creatable with four kinds of toppings), conditional reasoning (about if-then statements), and the "scientific method" of controlled experiments in which one factor is varied systematically to assess its effect while all others are held constant to remove their influence.

Much subsequent research has upheld Inhelder and Piaget's (1958) findings that adolescents on average perform better than children in tasks designed to assess these cognitive strategies. Piaget, however, regarded these various acquisitions as tightly linked manifestations of the formal operational thought structure hypothesized to emerge at adolescence. In this respect, subsequent research has been less supportive, yielding little evidence for a singular or abrupt transition from the childhood stage of concrete operations to the adolescent stage of formal operations (Moshman, 1998). Instead, substantial variability has been observed, both within and across individuals, in the age of attainment of the cognitive strategies associated with formal operations, with attainment in some cases still absent at adulthood. Furthermore, modest practice can improve performance (in the absence of any direct teaching). Both of these findings cast doubt on the unity of these attainments as products of a single underlying thought structure unavailable before adolescence.

In this respect, Piaget's developmental claims appear to have been too strong. Still, there is a deep sense in which Piaget understood cognitive development. The ability to think about one's own thought has sweeping implications that extend far beyond the context of scientific inquiry about physical phenomena on which Inhelder and Piaget's (1958) investigations focused. Indeed, "thinking about thinking" may be a key to understanding much about what it is important that adolescents achieve in cognitive growth. Before pursuing this theme, it is necessary to examine four further respects in which research conducted subsequent to Inhelder and Piaget's work complicates a simple stage model.

Complications for a Stage Model of Adolescent Thought

Complications include task variability, strategy variability, interactions between knowledge and thinking, and cognition as socially situated.

Task Variability. The first of these complications has to do with the exact form in which the researcher presents a task, which turns out to make a great deal of difference. A striking example is found in the much studied "four card" problem, assumed to require formal operations. The individual's task is to identify which of four cards need to be turned over to verify the rule, "If a card has a vowel on one side, it has an even number on the other side." The upturned sides of the four cards show an E, K, 4, and 7, respectively. Although improvement occurs during the adolescent years, even adults often fail to construct the correct solution: The two cards that must be turned over to verify the rule are E (to confirm it has an even number on the other side) and 7 (to confirm that it does not have a vowel on the other side). Consider, however, this structurally equivalent problem: If you've turned in your assignment, there should be a check (rather than a zero) in my gradebook. Adolescents (and adults) are much more likely to be able to answer correctly that verifying this type of rule requires checking the pile of turned-in assignments (to confirm each has a check in the gradebook) and each of the zeros in the gradebook (to confirm none is by the name of a person who has turned in the assignment). What psychologists now call "context" makes the difference. The second version of the task connects to the adolescent's everyday experience with obligations that must be fulfilled. As this example illustrates, context often matters more than the formal logical structure of a problem in determining how a person will perform.

Similar findings exist for other forms of reasoning thought to develop at adolescence. In each case, the phenomenon is one of early competence coupled with mature weaknesses in competence—a serious complication for a developmental theory. In other words, very simple problems have been identified in which even young children are successful (in the case of analogy, for example, simple analogies involving familiar terms, such as glove: hand::sock:——?). Other versions of the same form of problem, however, remain difficult even for adults.

Strategy Variability. In addition to the complication of variability in performance across different versions of a task, a second complication arises from the surprising discovery that even when the task stays exactly the same, an individual's performance may vary with repeated engagement with the task. The increasingly popular microgenetic method, which follows an individual engaged with the same task over multiple sessions, reveals that a single individual typically has not just one preferred mode of approaching the task (as traditional stage theory would predict) but a repertory of strategies of varying power and adequacy that the individual applies variably in the course of repeated encounters with a task (Kuhn, Garcia-Mila, Zohar, & Andersen, 1995). Better strategies typically win out over time, but the implications are, first, that abandoning less adequate strategies is at least as formidable a developmental challenge as mastering new ones, and second, that the increases and decreases in frequency of usage of multiple strategies over time are what the researcher must track (rather than a simple stage transition from A to B).

Still another implication, however, is most important: The burden of explanation shifts from strategy performance to strategy selection. If the strategies an individual chooses to apply shift over time, this is the change that needs to be explained in a model of the change process. The shift of focus to strategy selection is significant, since strategy selection entails managing, or operating on, one's own thinking—thinking about thinking, or "meta-knowing" (Kuhn, in press). The question to be asked, then, becomes this: How do adolescents select the strategies they will apply to a problem and do they exhibit different or better control over this process than they did as children? It is an important question, since strategy selection determines what someone actually does, of all the things they might do.

Interactions Between Knowledge and Thinking. A third complicating factor is the greater appreciation we now have of how the adolescent's expanding knowledge base may interact with thinking strategies that are themselves in the process of development. A certain level of knowledge is necessary to reason effectively about a particular topic. Moreover, it has now been shown that exceptional knowledge within a specific problem domain, such as chess, can boost a child's or adolescent's strategic effectiveness beyond that typical for their age (Chi, 1978). At the same time, however, more effective knowledge acquisition strategies enhance acquisition of a knowledge base (Kuhn et al., 1995). The relationship between knowledge expansion and cognitive growth is thus not a simple one, and in particular, the fact of rapid knowledge expansion during the adolescent years does not answer the question of what qualitative changes in an adolescent's thought may be occurring during this time.

Cognition as Socially Situated. Finally, a fourth complication in understanding adolescent thought is the fact that psychologists no longer regard thinking as a private affair that takes place exclusively inside people's heads—the dominant conception in Piaget's day. Instead, thinking, and hence its development over time, have increasingly come to be regarded as "distributed" among multiple minds in social settings. A study by Moshman and Geil (in press), involving the same four-card problem discussed earlier, nicely illustrates the need for this revised conception. Of the college students they asked to solve the original version of the problem, only three of 32 gave the correct answer. Another group of students, however, were asked to discuss the problem in small groups and come up with a solution. In 15 of 20 such groups, the solution the group ultimately agreed on was correct. In many of these groups, moreover, this solution had not been the initial choice of any of the individual members. In another recent study (Kuhn, Shaw, & Felton, 1997), adolescents' arguments for or against capital punishment improved in quality following dialogues on the topic with a series of their peers. Socially distributed cognition is thus likely to be superior to individual cognition and to have a positive effect on it—a claim that, not insignificantly, provides the rationale for a jury system of justice.

Understanding cognition as socially distributed also helps to explain the significant individual and group variation that has been observed in the use of various higher-order thinking skills. Many adolescents show reasoning at the same level as third-grade children, while others outperform average adults (Kuhn, Amsel, & O'Loughlin, 1988). Specific practices in adolescents' schools, homes, and social communities to a large degree shape the kinds of experiences they participate in, and this experience, rather than chronological age, is the most important determinant of the intellectual skills they have available and are likely to use. Indeed, effects of the subcultural variation in intellectual experience and practices already evident in childhood have become enormous by adolescence. This variation, which we return to, may be the single most important fact to be recognized about adolescent thought.

Process Conceptions of Adolescent Thought

The kinds of research described in the preceding section have made it increasingly difficult to claim that there exist a set of abstractly defined thought operations that are absent during childhood and emerge with the onset of adolescence. Still, it is unlikely anyone (including the researchers who have produced these findings) would endorse the view that no important cognitive development occurs during the years between childhood and adulthood—that children are the intellectual equals of adults. It is simply less clear exactly what develops and when (not to mention how). At this point, models that specify dimensions or processes in terms of which change occurs are regarded as more promising than stage models. It would be a mistake to reject Piaget's recognition of the developing ability to think about one's own thought as an important dimension of change in adolescent thought. How can this development be conceptualized in a way that respects the specificities described in the previous section?

Today, thinking about thought is most often studied under the heading of metacognition, or "metaknowing," with the major departure from Piaget's stage conception being the recognition that even very young children are capable of some forms of thinking about thinking (as reflected in the new area of research known as "theory of mind"), while, at the same time, even adults show limited metaknowing skills in important respects. [*See* Theory of Mind.] The other major revision of Piaget's view required by modern research is the one noted above—that experience, rather than chronological age, is the more important determiner of progress.

How, then, might the developing ability to think about one's own thought be best conceptualized? One useful distinction derives from the long-standing one originating in cognitive psychology between procedural knowing (knowing how) and declarative knowing (knowing that). Metaknowing is likely to differ, depending on its object, creating a distinction between what will be referred to here as metastrategic knowing (knowing about the strategies or processes by which one knows) and metacognitive knowing (knowing about the resulting products—what one knows). Both kinds of metaknowing figure importantly, it turns out, when adolescents are observed in the process of acquiring new knowledge—arguably the most fundamental and important intellectual activity that adolescents engage in.

Originally studied as a content-neutral process of learning and then neglected for many years in favor of studies of performance, knowledge acquisition is now understood by cognitive psychologists as a process involving the integration of new information with existing understandings the individual brings to the situation—existing beliefs are the starting point of any new learning. This coordination process (between existing beliefs and new evidence) is enhanced by metaknowing skills of both the metacognitive and metastrategic variety. Metacognitive awareness of these beliefs facilitates the process since one can then think *about* them and hence how evidence bears on them (rather than only *with* them, as an unconscious sieve through which new information is filtered). Metastrategic awareness of one's strategies of investigation and inference is beneficial, since more effective strategies can be selected and applied consistently. Increasing metacognitive and metastrategic control of the processes of belief revision and knowledge acquisition that are basic to human thought may thus be an important dimension in terms of which we can see change in thought processes during the adolescent years.

This claim receives support from microgenetic studies in which adolescents are observed over time acquiring new knowledge. In one set of studies, for example, children just prior to adolescence and young adults were observed over several months (Kuhn et al., 1995). In one problem they investigated a database on children's ratings of TV programs to determine which features of the programs influence their popularity. Adults on average showed greater skill in coordinating their prior theories with the new information they accessed, and by the end of the period voiced more correct conclusions about the effects of the features. However, the kinds of weaknesses observed at both age levels were similar. Rather than seeing their initial theories about the features' effects as theories subject to disconfirmation and representing theory and evidence as distinct entities to be reconciled with one another, many adolescents (as well as adults) merged the two into a single representation of "the way things are," with little apparent metaknowing awareness of the sources of their beliefs.

Theories did sometimes change as conflicting evidence accumulated over time, but often with little awareness or control of the process by the person involved. Many continued to regard the data as supportive of their theories after weeks of investigation of a database that in fact provided no support for them. A common pattern was the use of an effective inference strategy to interpret theory-compatible evidence with respect to one feature and an ineffective or invalid inference strategy to interpret theory-discrepant evidence with respect to another feature, even though the available evidence with respect to the two features was identical. A feature, for example, might be excluded as playing a causal role because the same outcome occurred in its presence and absence (e.g., "They liked long shows as much as short ones"), whereas another feature might be judged causal based on a single instance in which its presence cooccurred with a positive outcome (e.g., "Music makes a difference because this show had music and they liked it"). Weak metacognitive awareness of the basis for one's beliefs and metastrategic inconsistency in the application of infer-

ence strategies thus reinforce one another. Similar findings using somewhat different methods have been reported by Klaczynski and Gordon (1996) among adolescents and Stanovich and West (1997) among college students.

The investigation and interpretation of evidence as a means of knowledge acquisition invokes scientific thinking—a form of thought that, again influenced by Piaget's work, has traditionally been regarded as beyond the capabilities of preadolescents. As by now has been widely noted, however, even quite young children are able to engage productively in very simple forms of scientific investigation. Still, adolescents and adults show characteristic kinds of errors in strategies of scientific investigation and inference (Klahr, Fay, & Dunbar, 1993), creating the same paradoxical developmental course of early competence and late lack of competence noted earlier. At the broadest level, professional scientists engage in the process of coordinating theories and evidence, just as do intuitive scientific thinkers in the knowledge acquisition studies described above. Researchers studying scientific thinking have tended to conceptualize this process in a similar way. Klahr et al. (1993), for example, casting their formulation in explicitly information-processing terms, characterize scientific reasoning as a problem-solving process involving the coordination of search in two spaces, a space of experiments and a space of hypotheses.

In contrast to the intuitive scientist, the professional scientist exercises a high degree of conscious control over this coordination process; for example, designing conditions to produce evidence that will be maximally informative in relation to one or more theories. Yet while this skilled coordination is *central* to scientific thinking, it is not *particular* to it (Kuhn, 1996). In other words, these are features we would like all good thinking to reflect. If so, a high degree of awareness and control of one's own thinking can be regarded as a general feature of skilled thinking that is observable in a number of more traditional categories of higher-order thinking, including scientific thinking, argumentive thinking (Kuhn, 1991; Perkins, 1985), and what has traditionally been called critical thinking (Olson & Astington, 1993). Put in the broadest terms, then, adolescents develop the potential to become effective managers of their own thinking. We return later to factors that affect whether they are likely to realize this potential.

A dimension of this potential, one noted in Piaget's original work, that warrants highlighting, is an enhanced focus on possibility. In contrast to thinking about things in a world that actually exists, thinking about thinking is to think about—to mentally manipulate—propositions, which need not depict what exists in the external world. The ability to represent and reason about states of affairs irrespective of their truth value significantly enhances one's cognitive powers. In conditional (if-then) reasoning, for example, it enables one to reason about the validity of an inference, independent of the truth of its claims, a capacity that shows marked increase during adolescence (Moshman & Franks, 1986). Preadolescents, for example, find it difficult to judge reasoning such as this to be correct: If a motorcycle is faster than a car and a bike is faster than a motorcycle, then a bike is faster than a car.

In scientific and argumentive reasoning, reasoning about possibility enables one to think in a framework of alternatives to one's own or others' claims, and of the evidence bearing on each of them. In this respect, adults do only slightly better than teens (Kuhn, 1991), in responding, for example, to such questions as, What might someone else who had a different view of this say? When asked to make a verdict decision following presentation of legal testimony, teens as well as adults often consider only one verdict and generate evidence to support it, without considering alternative verdicts and the degree to which they may be consistent with the evidence (Kuhn, Weinstock & Flaton, 1994).

In these cases, we are seeing thinking potential that has not been realized even by adulthood. What determines whether development toward more explicit and controlled management of one's thought is likely to develop through and beyond the teen years? This question brings us to one further, often overlooked dimension of this development that deserves emphasis, for it has much to do with whether teens exercise (and hence strengthen) their intellectual skills: namely, what they see as their meaning and purpose. Developing epistemological understanding is a fundamental part of metaknowing and cognitive development. In adolescence, it may become particularly influential. By early adolescence, children, as members of social communities, have acquired fairly firm beliefs about their own and others' intellectual activities and competencies, beliefs that can have a decisive influence on the future course of their lives.

Epistemological Understanding as an Underpinning of Adolescent Thought

Although progress in epistemological understanding is not tightly linked to chronological age, its evolution follows a sequence of three broad positions, with adolescence a characteristic period of change (Hofer & Pintrich, 1997). The initial *absolutist* stance is the norm in childhood and may extend into adolescence and sometimes even adulthood (Chandler, Boyes, & Ball, 1990; King & Kitchener, 1994; Kuhn, 1991; Perry, 1970). The initial progression to absolutism, from a preepistemological acceptance of beliefs as faithful reflections of reality, is a profound one. It is a transition from simply knowing something is true to evaluating whether it

might be. To carry out such evaluation, absolutists rely on the concept of a certain truth, one that is known or potentially knowable through either direct apprehension or the authority of experts, and serves as a standard against which belief states can be judged and claims under dispute can be resolved.

In the modern world, however, it is hard to avoid exposure to conflicting assertions not readily reconcilable by direct observation or appeal to authority. As a result, most people progress beyond absolutism, venturing onto the slippery slope that will carry them to a *multiplist* epistemological stance, which becomes common at adolescence. A critical event leading to the first step down the slope toward multiplism is likely to be exposure to the fact that even experts disagree about important issues. If experts cannot be counted on to provide certain answers, one resolution is to relinquish the idea of certainty itself, and this is exactly the path the multiplist takes. As the next inductive leap along this path, if experts with all of their knowledge and authority disagree with one another, why should their views be accepted as any more valid than anyone else's? A better assumption is that anyone's opinion has the same status and deserves the same treatment as anyone else's. Beliefs or opinions are the possessions of their owners, freely chosen according to the owner's tastes and wishes, and accordingly not subject to criticism. In the words of one adolescent, "You can't prove an opinion to be wrong because an opinion is something somebody holds for themselves" (Kuhn, 1991). Hence—in a conceptual sleight of hand that represents the final step down the slippery slope—because all people have a right to their opinions, all opinions are equally right.

Absolutist and multiplist epistemologies are not always observed in their pure forms—many adolescents (and adults) show a mixture of these types of thinking across varying content (Kuhn, 1991). In the minority, however, are those who progress to an *evaluative* epistemology—one in which all opinions are not equal and knowing is understood as a process that entails judgment, evaluation, and argument. Evaluative epistemologists have reconciled the idea that people have a right to their views with the understanding that some views can nonetheless be more right than others. They see the weighing of alternative claims in a process of reasoned debate as the path to informed opinion, and they understand that arguments can be evaluated and compared based on their merit.

The core dimension underlying and driving the progression in epistemological understanding is the coordination of the subjective and objective components of knowing. The absolutist sees knowledge in largely objective terms, as located in the external world and knowable with certainty. The multiplist becomes aware of the subjective component of knowing, but to such an extent that it overpowers and obliterates any objective standard that would provide a basis for comparison or evaluation of opinions. Only the evaluativist is successful in integrating and coordinating the two, by acknowledging uncertainty without forsaking evaluation.

Concepts of Self as Knower and Learner

Research on the development of epistemological understanding focuses on belief about knowing and thinking at the impersonal, abstract level. While this understanding is influential in how an adolescent approaches intellectual tasks, adolescents are likely to devote more explicit thought to the more personal dimensions of epistemological understanding—concepts of the self as a knower and learner.

By early adolescence, children have developed concepts of themselves that are relatively stable, well-articulated, and integrate isolated behaviors into more abstract generalizations about the self (Damon & Hart, 1998). Among the most significant of the dimensions in terms of which this generalization occurs is competence, particularly intellectual competence. Adolescents' conceptions of themselves as intellectually able or helpless have the power to become self-fulfilling prophecies—a particularly disturbing fact given the increasing tendency for self-concept to vary along gender lines, with girls more likely to view their competence in negative terms.

A further important difference between children's and adolescents' self-conceptions, one congruent with the focus on possibility discussed earlier, is the adolescent's increased concern with the *possible self*—an ideal (or a feared) self, against which the actual self can be compared (Cross & Markus, 1991). Possible selves have an important role to play as adolescents engage in the experimentation that leads to the formation of a more stable, permanent personal identity. Identity formation, however, rather than an exclusively intrapsychic process, is in fact a highly social process, deriving from one's relations to and with others. To a large extent, I am who others take me to be. Moreover, during adolescence, imagined social reactions to the self become as important as real ones. During the years prior to adolescence, children achieve the realization that just as they make judgments and inferences regarding others, others are likely to be making the same kinds of inferences about them. With adolescents' increased focus on possibility, the recognition that they are the object of others' cognition is likely to become magnified and overgeneralized—on the basis of scant evidence, the self is seen as the constant object of others' attention. Adolescent egocentrism (Elkind, 1967) has been widely noted anecdotally, although it is the subject of little systematic research. It is most likely connected, however, to the cognitive challenges adolescents face in coordinating their own ideas and perspectives with those of others—a foundation for mature political thinking. Even young children are capable of political thought, for example in justifying civil liberties such as freedom of speech, but not until they are well into adolescence is the endorsement of individual freedoms likely to be coordinated with concerns for social welfare and potential harm (Helwig, 1995).

The Role of Schools and Communities in the Development of Adolescent Thought

Becoming increasingly able to reflect on one's own thought and take charge of it, it has been suggested, is the most significant intellectual accomplishment that may take place during the teen years. It is an achievement in metacognition, rather than cognition, and is a powerful determinant of whether and when particular cognitive skills will be applied. Knowing what you know and how you know it provides an essential foundation for determining how new information should be interpreted and reconciled with existing beliefs, and for updating those beliefs as seems warranted. Exercise of these metacognitive skills rests at least in part on the growing epistemological understanding emphasized here as an important dimension of adolescent cognitive development. If any opinion is as good as any other, the intellectual effort entailed in examining, evaluating, and judging conflicting claims is not warranted. In one adolescent's words, "It's not worth it to argue because everyone has their opinion." Among the epistemological beliefs that provide a foundation for intellectual self-regulation and management are what Resnick and Nelson-LeGall (1997) describe as "believing that problems can be analyzed and that solutions often come from such analysis, and believing that you are capable of that analysis" (p. 149). Such beliefs go a long way in determining how adolescents use the thinking processes of which they may be capable.

These capacities and dispositions are as relevant in the personal and interpersonal as in the purely intellectual domains. An increased ability to contemplate possibilities and examine choices in the framework of alternatives is basic not only to skilled argumentive reasoning (Kuhn, 1991) but also to personal decision making (Janis & Mann, 1977). What are the options I must choose among, adolescents need to ask themselves, and what are the advantages and disadvantages associated with each? Efforts to teach decision-making skills to adolescents report some success, but more research is needed to isolate the cognitive components of such programs (Beyth-Maron, Fischoff, Jacobs, & Furby, 1989). Related to the systematic contemplation of possibilities that decision making entails is a skill that may be of particular value to the adolescent—what psychologists have termed *counterfactual thinking* (Roese, 1997). This cognitive skill has important implications for future planning and decision making, reflected, for example, in the counterfactual inference: If I hadn't gone along with the other kids, this wouldn't have happened.

Perhaps the most important fact to emphasize is that these intellectual competencies are potential, rather than routine, achievements of adolescence. On a variety of dimensions, relevant data have failed to show substantial differences between the thinking competencies of adolescents and adults (Moshman, 1993, 1998), especially relative to the sizable variation *among* adolescents. But one can interpret this finding as a cup half full or half empty. Are adolescents as intellectually competent as adults, or adults as lacking in intellectual competence as adolescents?

This question is a relative one of perspective, of course, but even those most committed to an emphasis on adolescents' intellectual strengths would agree that few teens fully realize their intellectual potential. The substantial variation in intellectual performance among adolescents points to the significance of the activities and practices (and values that accompany them) that distinguish families, schools, and communities. Schools have a unifying role to play in this respect, and adolescence may be the most fertile time for this influence to be exercised. The adolescent years are the final ones of universal schooling; toward the end of adolescence individual paths diverge even more sharply than they have during the high-school years.

And yet the indications are that schools generally have not lived up to their potential in fostering the intellectual development of adolescents. As Olson and Astington (1993) note, while most adolescents have become competent to comprehend and extract the gist of the texts they read, "their conspicuous failure is in criticizing and otherwise evaluating [them]" (p. 17). Doing so requires that students regard the assertions in their textbooks as reasoned expressions of someone's beliefs, rather than as disembodied facts. The author "must come to be seen (or imagined) as holding those beliefs for some reasons" (p. 18). Even simple manipulations like making an author visible in the text enhance high-school students' evaluations of their textbooks (Paxton, 1997). Such findings point again to the importance of epistemological understanding as an underpinning of adolescent intellectual development. They also place an ever-escalating burden on schools and other educational organizations in a culture to provide environments that will support adolescents' realization of their intellectual potential.

Bibliography

Beyth-Maron, R., Fischoff, B., Jacobs, M., & Furby, L. (1989). *Teaching decision making to adolescents: A critical review.* Carnegie Council on Adolescent Development working paper series. Washington, DC.

Carey, S. (1985). Are children fundamentally different kinds of thinkers and learners than adults? In S. Chipman, J. Segal, & R. Glaser (Eds.), *Thinking and learning skills* (Vol. 2). Hillsdale, NJ: Erlbaum.

Chandler, M., Boyes, M., & Ball, L. (1990). Relativism and stations of epistemic doubt. *Journal of Experimental Child Psychology, 50,* 370–395.

Chi, M. (1978). Knowledge structures and memory development. In R. Siegler (Ed.), *Children's thinking: What develops?* Hillsdale, NJ: Erlbaum.

Cross, S., & Markus, H. (1991). Possible selves across the life span. *Human Development, 34,* 230–255.

Damon, W., & Hart, D. (1988). *Self-understanding in childhood and adolescence.* New York: Cambridge University Press.

Elkind, D. (1967). Egocentrism in adolescence. *Child Development, 38,* 1025–1034. A now classic article speculating on the implications of the focus on self in adolescent thinking.

Helwig, C. (1995). Adolescents' and young adults' conceptions of civil liberties: Freedom of speech and religion. *Child Development, 66,* 152–166.

Hofer, B., & Pintrich, P. (1997). The development of epistemological theories: Beliefs about knowledge and knowing and their relation to learning. *Review of Educational Research, 67* (1), 88–140. A systematic review of the current state of knowledge regarding the development of epistemological understanding.

Inhelder, B., & Piaget, J. (1958). *The growth of logical thinking from childhood to adolescence.* New York: Basic Books. A classic work on adolescent thought processes that has served as a point of departure for much subsequent work.

Janis, I., & Mann, L. (1977). *Decision-making: A psychological analysis of conflict, choice, and commitment.* New York: Free Press.

King, P., & Kitchener, K. (1994). *Developing reflective judgment: Understanding and promoting intellectual growth and critical thinking in adolescents and adults.* San Francisco: Jossey-Bass.

Klaczynski, P., & Gordon, D. (1996). Self-serving influences on adolescents' evaluations of belief relevant evidence. *Journal of Experimental Child Psychology, 62,* 317–339.

Klahr, D., Fay, A., & Dunbar, K. (1993). Heuristics for scientific experimentation: A developmental study. *Cognitive Psychology, 25,* 111–146.

Kuhn, D. (1991). *The skills of argument.* New York: Cambridge University Press.

Kuhn, D. (1996). Is good thinking scientific thinking? In D. Olson & N. Torrance (Eds.), *Modes of thought: Explorations in culture and cognition.* Cambridge, UK: Cambridge University Press.

Kuhn, D. (in press). Metacognitive development. In C. Tamis-LeMonda (Ed.), *Child psychology: A handbook of contemporary issues.*

Kuhn, D., Amsel, E., & O'Loughlin, M. (1988). *The development of scientific thinking skills.* Orlando, FL: Academic Press.

Kuhn, D., Garcia-Mila, M., Zohar, A., & Andersen, C. (1995). Strategies of knowledge acquisition. *Society for*

Research in Child Development Monographs, 60 (4), Serial no. 245. A comparative study of young adolescents and young adults engaged in the processes of examining evidence and acquiring knowledge.

Kuhn, D., Shaw, V., & Felton, M. (1997). Effects of dyadic interaction on argumentative reasoning. *Cognition and Instruction, 15,* 287–315.

Kuhn, D., Weinstock, M., & Flaton, R. (1994). How well do jurors reason? Competence dimensions of individual variation in a juror reasoning task. *Psychological Science, 5,* 289–296.

Moshman, D., (1993). Adolescent reasoning and adolescent rights. *Human Development, 36,* 27–40. An analysis of inconsistencies in societal perspectives on adolescent thinking capabilities, with adolescents in some cases regarded as children and in others as adults.

Moshman, D. (1998). Cognitive development beyond childhood. In W. Damon (Series Ed.) & D. Kuhn & R. Siegler (Vol. Eds.), *Handbook of child psychology: Vol 2. Cognition, language, and perception.* (5th ed., pp. 851–898). New York: Wiley. A comprehensive survey of developments in cognition during the adolescent and early adult years.

Moshman, D. (in press). *Adolescent psychological development: Rationality, morality, and identity.* Mahwah, NJ: Erlbaum. An advanced level text on adolescence, focused on the adolescent's developing awareness in the areas of rationality, morality, and self-understanding.

Moshman, D., & Franks, B. (1986). Development of the concept of inferential validity. *Child Development, 57,* 153–165.

Moshman, D., & Geil, M. (1998). Collaborative reasoning: Evidence for collective rationality. *Thinking and Reasoning, 4,* 231–248.

Olson, D., & Astington, J. (1993). Thinking about thinking: Learning how to take statements and hold beliefs. *Educational Psychologist, 28,* 7–23.

Paxton, R. (1997). "Someone with like a life wrote it": The effects of a visible author on high school history students. *Journal of Educational Psychology, 89,* 235–250.

Perkins, D. (1985). Postprimary education has little impact on informal reasoning. *Journal of Educational Psychology, 77,* 562–571.

Perry, W. (1970). *Forms of intellectual and ethical development in the college years.* New York: Holt, Rinehart & Winston. The pioneering work in the study of the development of epistemological understanding, tracing a cohort of Harvard University young men during their college years.

Resnick, L., & Nelson-LeGall, S. (1997). Socializing intelligence. In L. Smith, J. Dockrell, & P. Tomlinson (Eds.), *Piaget, Vygotsky, and beyond* (pp. 145–158). London: Routledge.

Roese, N. (1997). Counterfactual thinking. *Psychological Bulletin, 121,* 133–148.

Stanovich, K., & West, R. (1997). Reasoning independently of prior belief and individual differences in actively open-minded thinking. *Journal of Educational Psychology 89,* 342–357.

Deanna Kuhn

ADOPTION. Adoption establishes the legal status of parent and child between individuals who are not biologically related. Each year approximately 120,000 adoptions are finalized through a legalization process in state court systems. More than 5 million adults and children living in the United States have been adopted.

Historically in American society, conceiving a child out of wedlock, being unable to bear children, and being an illegitimate child all carried significant social stigma. Partly in an effort to mitigate the shame associated with these experiences, adoption evolved into a confidential process in the early part of the twentieth century. In this model, known as "closed" adoption, little or no information about the birthparent(s) and adoptive parent(s) was shared between the parties. Adoption records were sealed by the courts and no contact between birth and adoptive families was anticipated except under extraordinary circumstances. Hollinger (1988) provides an overview of the legal and social history of adoption in America.

Changes in society over the last 25 years have resulted in alternative models for adoption placements and relationships between the birth and adoptive families. These models include sharing information and varying degrees of pre- and postplacement contact between the birth and adoptive families. These approaches to adoption are often called "open" adoptions.

Types of Adoption

In the latter part of the twentieth century two worlds of adoption exist. In the first, couples and individuals who typically are unable to have children as a result of infertility adopt infants domestically (in-country) or children internationally. This is the world of private adoption, facilitated through agencies, attorneys, doctors, and other intermediaries. In the second, typically older children who have been removed from their families of origin as a result of abuse, neglect, and abandonment are placed for adoption. This is the world of public adoption, facilitated under the auspices of state and federally funded public child welfare agencies.

Within these two worlds, the role of the birth parent(s), or biological parent(s), is quite different. In infant adoption, the birth mother, and often the birth father, make a voluntary plan for the child's adoptive placement with the adoptive parent(s). In international adoption, the children available for placement have typically been voluntarily placed in the care of the state by their birth parent(s) or removed from their birth parent(s) by the state. In public adoption, children have been removed from their birth parent(s)' care by the state as a result of abuse or neglect. These children are most often placed in state-sponsored foster care. Initial efforts of public child welfare agencies are focused on reunifying children with their biological family. Adoption is considered when such efforts prove unsuccessful.

Statistics

No comprehensive national data on adoption are collected in the United States. Since 1983, the primary source of data is the American Public Welfare Association (AWPA), which has collected limited data about children who have been involved in the public child welfare system through the Voluntary Cooperative Information Service (VCIS). This source provides statistics about children who are involved with the public child welfare system. The public system handles only 19% of total domestic adoptions. Private agency adoptions are only occasionally reported by states, and independent adoptions are not reported.

The following data are reported by Stolley (1993). It is estimated that 2 to 4% of American families include an adopted child, 50% of all adoptions occur between relatives, and 50% involve nonrelative adoptions. In addition, 26.5% of all unrelated domestic adoptions are special needs adoptions, 8% of all adoptions are transracial adoptions, and 16% of all unrelated adoptions are foreign adoptions.

Adoption Research

Research studies in adoption have focused on two major areas. The first line of inquiry has examined the incidence and prevalence of adoptees in clinical settings and their psychological problems. The second line of research uses adoption as a context for examining general questions regarding the interaction of nature and nurture; attachment; identity formation; family functioning; and factors that may increase psychological vulnerability.

Clinical Samples. Although the vast majority of adopted children are not referred to psychological counseling, adopted children are overrepresented in clinical populations. There are both anecdotal stories and reports from clinical settings indicating that adopted children have a higher than expected incidence of psychological problems. Clinical research shows that specific disorders are found more commonly among adopted children than nonadopted children and that there is a unique pattern of presenting symptoms in adopted children, which include higher than expected rates of "externalizing behaviors" including aggression, oppositional and defiant behaviors, antisocial behavior, and attention-deficit/hyperactivity disorder.

Psychological Functioning in Nonclinical Samples. Studies examining the psychological adjustment of adopted children in nonclinical samples show mixed results. Some studies find no differences in psychological adjustment between adopted children and nonadopted children; other studies find that adopted chil-

dren have more adjustment problems than nonadopted children.

Attachment. Infants adopted within the first few months of their lives are as securely attached to their adoptive mothers as are nonadopted infants to their biological mothers. In adoption, the quality of attachment appears to be less affected by the separation from the birth parent(s), the child's age, or the adoption placement itself than by the cumulative effects of previous experiences of abuse and neglect, number of temporary placements, institutionalization, and quality of relationships prior to adoption.

Identity. One of the essential tasks in life is the development of a secure and well-defined sense of self. Adoption has been perceived as adding complications to this task. There is much anecdotal literature about how children understand and interpret the facts of their adoption and when and how to tell children about adoption. Yet contrary to claims that adopted children and adolescents are likely to experience difficulties and disturbances in the process of identity formation, most research shows that adolescent adoptees, who were placed as infants, do not experience more difficulties in identity formation than nonadopted adolescents. However, key questions remain unanswered about how adoptees integrate the fact of being adopted into their identity at different stages of their lives.

The significance of genetic heritage to personality characteristics and identity has been well documented in medical literature. Adoptive families often lack information about the birth family such as stories and connections that may support identity formation in adopted children. As a result, adopted children may face a greater challenge in creating an integrated and complete sense of identity.

Family Dynamics and Parenting Style. Parenting style, parental emotional adjustment, and parental expectations in relation to the child and the adoption placement itself have a significant impact on adoptive experience. As noted earlier, acceptance of the unique status of adoptive parenthood combined with an accepting attitude toward the child result in more positive adoption adjustment. It also appears that adopted children, like nonadopted children, are more likely to manifest problems when there are emotional problems in one or both of their parents and/or when there is a history of death or divorce within the adoptive family.

Adoption Disruption. Failure of adoptive placements, called disruptions or dissolutions, has been an issue of great concern because of the dramatic negative impact on the life prospects for the children involved. The children at greatest risk for disruption are those who are older; have experienced multiple losses and temporary placements; have experienced abuse; and have special medical and psychological needs. These children are identified as having *special needs*. Realistic parental expectations and the availability of appropriate services and supports are crucial factors in reducing the risk of disruption.

Theoretical Frameworks for Understanding Adoption

A wide range of theoretical frameworks have been proposed to explain the psychological functioning of adoptees as well as the apparent vulnerability of adopted children and adolescents. In Brodzinsky and Schecter's book, *The Psychology of Adoption* (1990), many of these theoretical frameworks are addressed, including those discussed below.

Kirk (1981), whose seminal studies helped to define the field of adoption research, addresses adoption in terms of social role theory. Kirk identifies that the social context of adoption is different from nonadoptive experience. His research indicates that adoptees may display a variety of vulnerabilities when parents do not acknowledge the unique aspects of adoptive status. He suggests that a more open style of communication about adoption, which includes acknowledging the different circumstances in adoption, facilitates healthier adjustment in adoptees than a style that ignores or rejects those differences.

Brinich (1990) in *The Psychology of Adoption* outlines the psychodynamic view of adoption which focuses on the dynamic relationship within adoptive families, experiences of loss, and the adopted child's fantasies about the birth parent(s). The fact that the child was surrendered for adoption creates the burden of understanding the reasons for the adoption, while the loss of connection to the biological mother creates a challenge to identity formation. Additional factors relevant to older child adoption include: age and circumstances at time of separation from birth parent(s); quality of relationship with birth parent(s); and experience of abuse, neglect, or other trauma. Depending on the ability of the child to cope with these events and experiences, he or she may be vulnerable to problems in attachment and adjustment.

Bowlby (1969, 1971, 1980), in his seminal volumes on attachment theory, predicts that separations from biological caregivers will have a negative, long-term effect on a child's socioemotional development, particularly if the separation takes place at a time when the biological parents have already become the child's primary attachment figures. Repeated losses of caregivers such as might occur through a series of foster care placements or discontinuity of caregivers in institutionalized care facilities, make it less likely that the child will be able to establish a secure attachment to any caregiver.

Brodzinsky (1990) proposes a cognitive-emotional model that emphasizes changes in the child's conceptualization of the adoption process. As children go through stages of development, they become more aware of their status as adopted children and develop cognitive capacities that enable them to understand the fact of adoption in new and different ways. This model implies that adoption complicates the task of identity formation adding a cognitive emotional burden to the child's development, which is normal in the context of adoptive family experience.

Cadoret (1990) outlines a biological model in which genetic factors as well as prenatal and postnatal experiences may result in a range of vulnerabilities in the child. Adverse prenatal experiences, such as heightened maternal stress, poor maternal nutrition, and inadequate medical care, as well as fetal exposure to alcohol, drugs, and other teratogenic agents, are linked to increased developmental problems in childhood.

Though each model makes important contributions to the understanding of the adoption experience, none of them individually can encompass this complex lifelong process and they are all still open to systematic empirical verification. In addition, when considering the view that adopted children are at greater risk for psychological problems, the many reasons that children may be referred to clinical services must also be taken into account. Factors to be considered include issues relating to infertility in the adoptive parent(s) and how these issues impact their perceptions and concerns about their children; the notion that adoptive parent(s) may be more likely to seek professional help for questions or concerns than the general population; and the idea that problems may be attributed to adoptees as a result of the social stigma attached to adoption.

One of the most important elements of adoptive experience that needs further consideration is the role of loss. Adopted children lose connection to their birth families, birth parents lose connection to their children, and adoptive parents often experience the loss of the birth child they could not have due to infertility. Many problems have been attributed to this experience yet the actual relationship of loss to psychological functioning is still unclear.

Controversial Issues in Adoption

International adoption, transracial adoption, open adoption, and the search for relatives have been contentious issues in adoption practice. Adoption research faces the challenge of examining these issues and providing assessments regarding which practices are in the best interest of children.

International Adoption. As interest in international adoption has grown, adoption opportunities have expanded to include a wide variety of countries including Central and South America, Central Europe, Russia, Africa, India, Southeast Asia, and China. Children from many different cultures and circumstances are joining families in America.

Generally, internationally adopted children appear to be well adjusted with regard to family life and psychological functioning. Yet issues of preplacement experience including abuse and neglect, medical history, and transcultural adjustment, are considered critical factors that have impact on attachment, adjustment, and psychological functioning.

Transracial Adoption. Children of color represent nearly 40% of the children in the public foster care system. An ongoing shortage of permanent homes available for these children has led to an increase in transracial adoption. In 1996 the Multiethnic Placement Act (MEPA) was enacted, which requires that race not be the determining factor in placing a child in a permanent home.

Transracial adoption raises several challenging social questions and even more differences of opinion. Hollingsworth's (1997) analysis of research indicates that transracially adopted children do not differ from intraracially adopted children in terms of self-esteem, but they show more identity problems. Yet many questions remain about the nature of racial identity, the impact of parenting style, and the importance of including the child's racial and ethnic culture as part of adoptive family life.

Open Adoption. Currently there is a heated debate regarding the pros and cons of open adoption. Open adoption can include possibilities for a minimal contact between birth and adoptive families at one end of the continuum, to significant ongoing relationships on the other. Some fear that open adoption will result in a lack of entitlement for adoptive parent(s), lack of closure for birth parent(s), and confusion for children regarding the identity and role of parents. On the other hand, some believe it may reduce grief for birth parent(s), result in an increased sense of security for adoptive parent(s), make more critical information available, and be less confusing for the child. With such divergent views, research on open adoption is particularly important.

Grotevant and McRoy (1997), have examined open adoptions in private infant placements. They report in *Openness in Adoption: Exploring Family Connections*, that children's adjustment in open adoption is comparable to the nonadopted population. Adoptive parent(s) in open adoption had higher degrees of empathy about adopted child and birth mother, more open communication, and felt as secure as adoptive parent(s) in confidential and less open adoption.

Open arrangements are being widely used in adoptions involving older children. This practice raises questions regarding the ongoing significance of an older child's relationship with his or her birth parent(s) and its impact on an adoptive placement.

Search. The issue of search has raised significant questions about adoption practices. The search for information about birth relatives and reunions with birth family members may be understood when viewed in relation to the unique challenges that adoption poses to identity development. Although no one knows the actual numbers of adoptees who search for their birth parent(s), search activity has increased significantly over the last 25 years. The motivation for search may relate to concerns about identity or significant life events such as marriage or the birth of a child. Dissatisfaction with adoptive family relationships is not typically associated with the desire to search. In fact, many adopted people who conduct searches report having good relationships with their adoptive parent(s). They are not seeking to replace their adoptive parents with their birth parents.

Reunions between people who were adopted and birth parent(s) raise a number of challenging issues. They create new kinds of relationships that have no standard social models. The prospect of a reunion has been cause for much uncertainty among adoptive and birth families and controversy in clinical practice. Information currently available about the outcomes of search indicate that from the adopted person's point of view, it has a positive impact on their sense of identity and relationships with their adoptive parents. However, little is currently known about what type of relationship birth parent(s) and people who were adopted develop or about the long-term effect of the reunion.

Methodological Challenges in Adoption Research

There are a number of methodological problems in conducting research on adoption that make it difficult to draw firm conclusions about psychological adjustment of adopted children and adolescents. These problems are evident in the following: the recruitment of samples for research, the use of control groups, the use of research measures, and problems in making critical distinctions between adoptees with different preplacement experiences. Further, most adoption research has employed cross-sectional research designs, and only a few studies employed longitudinal designs. Cross-sectional designs limit the ability to draw conclusions about developmental changes in adjustment, make it difficult to examine relationships between early risk factors and later adjustment outcomes, and are subject to generational effects.

Adoption: An Evolving Picture

Although there are three parties in an adoption, the majority of research has focused only on the adopted child. Ultimately appreciating the complexities of adoption requires examining both the experience of children and their families and the social context in which adoption occurs.

For much of this century, confidentiality and secrecy in adoption practice made it impossible to examine the real impact of adoptive experience. It also made it easy to attribute a wide range of psychological risks and problems to adoption. Changes in society have decreased the degree of secrecy and shame associated with adoption, and knowledge based on research has been advancing alongside these changes.

[*See also* Fathering; Parent-Child Relationship; *and* Sibling Relationships.]

Bibliography

Bowlby, J. (1969). *Attachment and loss, Vol. 1: Attachment.* New York: Basic Books.

Bowlby, J. (1971). *Attachment and loss, Vol. 2: Separation.* New York: Basic Books.

Bowlby, J. (1980). *Attachment and loss, Vol. 3: Loss.* New York: Basic Books.

Brinich, P. M. (1990). Adoption from the inside out: A psychoanalytic perspective. In D. M. Brodzinsky & D. E. Schechter (Eds.), *The psychology of adoption* (pp. 42–63). New York: Oxford University Press.

Brodzinsky, D. M. (1990). A stress and coping model of adoption adjustment. In D. M. Brodzinsky & D. E. Schechter (Eds.), *The psychology of adoption* (pp. 3–24). New York: Oxford University Press.

Cadoret, R. J. (1990). Biologic perspectives on adoptive adjustment. In D. M. Brodzinsky & D. E. Schechter (Eds.), *The psychology of adoption* (pp. 25–41). New York: Oxford University Press.

Grotevant, H. D., & McRoy, R. G. (1998). *Openness in adoption: Exploring family connections.* Thousand Oaks, CA: Sage.

Hollinger, J. H. (Ed.). (1991). *Adoption law and practice.* New York: West.

Hollingsworth, L. D. (1997). Effect of transracial/transethnic adoption on children's ethnic identity and self-esteem: A meta-analytic review. *Marriage and Family Review, 25,* 99–130.

Kirk, D. (1981). *Adoptive kinship—A modern institution in need of reform.* Toronto: Butterworth.

Stolley, K. S. (1993). Statistics on adoption in the United States. *The Future of Children, 3,* 26–42.

Attachment

Singer, L. N., Brodzinsky, D. M., Steir, M., & Waters, E. (1985). Mother-infant attachment in adoptive families. *Child Development, 56,* 1543–1551. Empirical study of attachment behavior of transracially and intraracially adopted children in the United States.

Identity

Grotevant, H. D. (1997). Coming to terms with adoption: The construction of identity from adolescence into adulthood. *Adoption Quarterly, 1,* 3–27. Outlines a theory of identity development for adopted children that takes the specific situation of adoptive children into account.

Stein, L. M., & Hoopes, J. L. (1985). *Identity formation in the adopted adolescent.* New York: Child Welfare League of America. Reviews different theoretical approaches to identity development in adopted children and includes empirical study of different aspects of identity development in adopted children.

Review of Clinical Studies

Brodzinsky, D. M., Smith, D. W., & Brodzinsky, A. B. (1998). *Children's adjustment to adoption: Development and clinical issues.* Thousand Oaks, CA: Sage. Comprehensive review of research on adjustment and psychological functioning of adoptees.

Haugaard, J. (1998). Is adoption a risk factor for the development of adjustment problems? *Clinical Psychology Review, 18,* 47–69. Comprehensive review of research on the psychological adjustment of adopted children and adolescents in clinical and nonclinical settings.

Ingersoll, B. D. (1997). Psychiatric disorders among adopted children: A review and commentary. *Adoption Quarterly, 1,* 57–73. Reviews research on clinical samples of adopted children and discusses different explanations of the findings.

Wierzbicki, M. (1993). Psychological adjustment of adoptees: A meta-analysis. *Journal of Clinical Child Psychology, 22,* 447–454.

Transracial Adoption

Rushton, A., & Minnis, H. (1997). Annotation: Transracial family placements. *Journal of Child Psychology & Psychiatry, 38,* 147–159. Discussion of historical, political, and policy aspects of transracial adoption in the United States and Great Britain, and review of empirical studies of transracially adopted children.

International Adoption

Altstein, H., & Simon R. J. (Eds.). (1991). *Intercountry adoption: A multinational perspective.* New York: Praeger. Legal aspects, research, and practice of international adoptions are reviewed by authors from different countries.

Tizard, B. (1991). Intercountry adoption: A review of the evidence. *Journal of Child Psychology & Psychiatry, 32,* 734–756.

Adoption Disruption

Barth, R. P., & Berry, M. (1988). *Adoption and disruption: Rates, risks and response.* Hawthorne, NY: Aldine de Gruyter. Includes a review of research on adoption disruption and presents the findings of a study on factors related to adoption disruption.

Search

Modell, J. (1997). "Where do we go next?" Long-term reunion relationships between adoptees and birth parents. *Marriage & Family Review, 25,* 43–66. Discusses the issue of reunification between adopted children and birth parents from a sociological perspective.

Pacheco, F., & Eme, R. (1993). An outcome study of the reunion between adoptees and biological parents. *Child Welfare, 72,* 53–64. Empirical study of the outcome of reunification between adopted children and their birth parents, and of the effects of reunifications on the well-being of adopted children.

Peter Gibbs

ADULTHOOD AND AGING. [*This entry provides a general survey of the theories, research, and findings that have informed our knowledge about adulthood and aging. It comprises four articles*:

Biological Processes and Physical Development
Cognitive Processes and Development
Personality Process and Development
Social Processes and Development

For discussions dealing with other stages of development, see Infancy; Early Childhood; Middle Childhood; *and* Adolescence.]

Biological Processes and Physical Development

Changes in the body associated with the aging process can have many profound effects on the quality of everyday life of the older adult as well as assessments of personal competence and self-esteem. It is important for psychologists to understand what these changes are and also to appreciate the distinction between the course of "normal" aging versus changes due to disease processes more prevalent in later life. Many age-related normal changes can be compensated through behavioral measures taken by the individual, but whether the individual takes advantage of these measures depends heavily on awareness of these preventive and compensatory avenues as well as on the individual's motivation to maintain maximum levels of functioning. Following a brief review of biological theories of aging, major changes in the body will be reviewed here along with implications for psychological functioning of the individual who experiences these changes. Mechanisms of prevention and compensation will also be summarized.

Biological Theories of Aging

There are a number of theoretical approaches developed by biologists to explain the underlying mechanisms of the aging process. These theories range from the "wear and tear" theory, according to which aging occurs as the result of a mechanical deterioration of the body, to programmed aging theories, which are based on the assumption that there is a genetic basis for the aging process. Various approaches that have been popular from time to time focus on specific organ systems such as the endocrine system or on general processes such as caloric restriction or exposure to free radicals. Current research focuses on finding genes that influence longevity and understanding their interaction with environmental influences throughout the life span.

Effects of Age on Skin and Hair

Age changes in the outward appearance of the body are reflected in wrinkling of the skin, changes in muscle tone and fat distribution, and loss of body height. Many of the changes in the skin's appearance and structure can be explained by exposure to the ultraviolet rays of the sun (photoaging). Wrinkling and sagging of the skin throughout the body occurs due to decreases in collagen and increasing brittleness of elastin. The subcutaneous fat on the limbs decreases, and there is a decrease in muscle mass, further adding to the loss of firmness in the skin's appearance. There are also significant changes in the sweat and oil-producing glands that maintain body temperature and lubricate the skin surface. The skin becomes rougher, drier, and more vulnerable to surface damage. Age-related alterations also occur in the coloring of the skin. There are fewer melanocytes, and those that remain develop irregular areas of dark pigmentation. Under the skin surface, capillaries and small arteries become dilated, creating small irregular colored lines.

With increasing age, the hair on the head and body loses pigmentation and takes on a white appearance due to a decrease in melanin production in the hair follicles. The rate at which hair color changes varies from person to person due to variations in the timing of onset and rate of melanin production decrease across the surface of the scalp. Gradual and general thinning of scalp hair also occurs in both sexes over adulthood due to destruction or regression of the germ centers that produce the hair follicles. Men may also experience thinning of the hairs in their whiskers, and a growth of coarse hair on the eyebrows and inside the ear. Patches of coarse terminal hair may develop on the face in women, particularly around the chin.

For many individuals, particularly in middle age, age changes in the skin that lead to wrinkling are very noticeable and can have an impact on the individual's sense of self. In particular, comparisons of present appearance with pictures or memories of early adulthood can cause unhappiness in older people who valued their youthful image. Age-related changes in the skin and supporting tissues alter the skin's protective functions as well as its appearance, and may also cause discomfort.

There are many ways to slow or compensate for aging of the skin. Fair-skinned people should avoid direct exposure to the sun and all can benefit from sunscreens, emollients, and fragrance-free cosmetics. There is some supportive evidence emerging for preventive and restorative treatments, including facial massage and vitamin E. Unlike wrinkles, gray hairs can be returned to virtually their original state through the use of hair dye. Changes in hair thickness, however, are not so easily reversed. The desire to disguise or stop the apparent signs of aging through surgery, chemical treatments, or the wearing of hairpieces is widespread, as is evident in the many advertisements for hair loss replacement therapies.

Effects of Age on Body Build

Over the course of adulthood standing height is reduced, occurring at a greater rate after the 50s and particularly pronounced in women. Total body weight increases from the 20s until the mid-50s, after which it declines. Most of the weight gain in middle adulthood is due to an accumulation of body fat, particularly around the waist and hips. The weight loss that occurs in the later years of adulthood is due to loss of lean body mass consisting of muscle and bone. Consequently, very old adults may have very thin extremities but fatty areas in the chin, waist, and hips.

Fortunately, changes with age in distribution and amount of body fat may be readily compensated. Participation in active sports and exercise can offset the deleterious effects of aging on body fat accumulation. Resistance training can also promote loss of body fat in middle-aged and older adults. As will be seen later, the same activities that middle-aged people might engage in to combat body fat changes can also have positive effects on other bodily systems.

Effects of Age on Mobility

Mobility changes in important ways over the course of the adult years such that movement becomes more difficult, more painful, and less effective. Between ages 40 and 70, there is a loss of muscle strength amounting to approximately 10 to 20% with more severe losses of 30 to 40% after ages 70 to 80; losses are more pronounced in the muscles of the lower extremities. However, the extent to which aging affects loss of muscle strength depends in part on the general level of activity in which the individual has typically engaged, the particular muscle group being tested, and whether the type of muscle strength being assessed is isometric or dynamic.

The overall course of bone development in adulthood is also toward loss of bone strength, resulting in diminished ability of the bones to withstand mechanical pressure and to show greater vulnerability to fracture. The decrease in various measures of bone strength ranges from 5 to 12% per decade from the 20s through the 90s.

Body weight is positively related to bone mineral content, meaning that heavier individuals lose less bone mineral content and that less bone loss occurs in weight-bearing limbs. Genetic factors also play a role as does life style, including factors such as physical activity, smoking, alcohol use, and diet which can account for up to 50 to 60% of the variation in bone density. African American women have higher bone mineral density than do White women. Bone mineral loss in women proceeds at a higher rate in postmenopausal women who are no longer producing estrogen in monthly cycles. In men, testosterone levels are positively related to several measures of bone mineral formation.

Declines in joint functioning throughout adulthood can be accounted for by age losses in virtually every structural component of the joint. Starting in the twenties and thirties, the arterial cartilage begins to thin, fray, shred, and crack so that the underlying bone eventually begins to wear away. At the same time, outgrowths of cartilage develop and these interfere with the smooth movement of the joint. Age-related weakening of the muscles further contributes to restrictions in range of movement.

Changes in the structures that support movement have many pervasive effects, resulting in pain and restrictions in activity. One of the most serious outcomes is heightened susceptibility to falls, particularly for women. After a fall, individuals may develop a lowered sense of self-efficacy regarding the ability to avoid a fall. As a result, they become less stable on their feet and avoid physical activities that might benefit their strength and stability leading to a downward spiral of functioning.

There are many interventions individuals can take in response to changes in mobility, primarily involving exercise. A regular program of exercise can help compensate for the loss of muscle fibers even in persons as old as ninety years. Older individuals can also benefit from resistance training exercises, that, within limits, increase the stress placed upon the bone. Older women can supplement their diets with vitamin D, which can retard bone loss. Balance and flexibility training can be an effective intervention to minimize the risk of falls in older women, as can t'ai Chi. Within recent years a great deal of attention has been focused on supplementation with growth hormone as a "treatment" for various age-related changes in muscle and bone. Unfortunately, consumers are misled by the exaggerated claims of advertisers into believing that growth hormones will reverse or retard the aging process. The research on which the original claims for the effectiveness of hormone therapy are based was conducted on individuals (not necessarily elderly) with growth hormone deficiency. Some positive effects of growth hormone therapy on muscle and bone have been demonstrated in studies on normal aging. However, the majority of findings fail to support the advertised benefits of this form of intervention and in fact there are indications that such treatments may have harmful side effects (Lamberts, van den Beld, & van der Lely, 1997).

Effects of Age on the Cardiovascular System

The aging process results in serious limitations of the heart's ability to pump blood through the circulatory system at a rate that adequately perfuses the body's cells. Effects of aging on the arteries further compromise the system's ability to distribute blood to the body's cells. The effects of aging of the circulatory system are most apparent while the individual is engaging in aerobic exercise, when there is a reduction both in maximum oxygen consumption (aerobic capacity) and the maximum attainable heart rate. Aerobic capacity decreases in a linear fashion throughout the adult years, so that the average 65-year-old individual has 30 to 40% of the aerobic capacity of the young adult. This decrease is significantly lower, however, in very active individuals, amounting to 5 to 7% per decade (Trappe, Costill, Vukovich, Jones, & Melham, 1996).

Because the efficient functioning of the cardiovascular system is essential to life, threats to the integrity of this system are perceived as highly dangerous. Thus, the quality of functioning has an important influence on the individual's feelings of well-being or otherwise. Awareness of reduced cardiovascular efficiency can therefore serve as reminders of one's own personal mortality.

On the positive side, there is a wealth of research pointing to the effectiveness of exercise in slowing or reversing the effects of the aging process. The results of this research consistently reveal improved functioning in long-term endurance athletes, master athletes, exercisers, and previously sedentary adults. Even moderate or low-intensity exercise can have beneficial effects on healthy, previously sedentary elderly people. Other benefits of exercise training are improvements in the peripheral vasculature, lipid metabolism, and blood pressure during or immediately after exertion. A word of caution, however, as noted above, even individuals who maintain a high level of physical fitness nevertheless lose aerobic capacity by the time they reach their sixties.

Effects of Age on the Respiratory System

Aging reduces the quality of gas exchange in the lungs, vital capacity, the amount of air that is moved into and out of the lungs at maximal levels of exertion, and forced expiratory volume, the amount of air that can be breathed out during a short amount of time. These reductions result from changes in pulmonary structures such that the airways, and particularly lung tissue, lose the elastic ability to resist expansion they fill with air. These changes mean that less than the maximal amount of air can be brought into and out of the lungs, particularly under conditions of exertion. Age changes in respiration can lead to unpleasant feelings of dyspnea and fatigue which in turn may lead the individual to avoid strenuous activities, a consequence that further impairs the individual's cardiovascular and respiratory efficiency.

The effects of exercise on respiratory functioning are not as dramatic as are the effects on the cardiovascular system. Equally, if not more beneficial to the respiratory function is the avoidance of cigarette smoking.

Effects of Age on Renal and Urinary Systems

There are significant and widespread changes in the structure of the kidneys, changes that are reflected in cross-sectional studies in impaired efficiency across adulthood on every measure of renal functioning studied. There are also independent losses in mechanism within the kidney responsible for concentrating urine. Particularly challenging to the aging kidney is aerobic exercise because it diverts blood to the working skeletal muscles, and thereby causes a further reduction in the blood flow through the kidneys. Equally important, the urine concentrating mechanism begins to fail during exercise or under extreme conditions of heat when the individual begins to perspire. Fatigue, changes in body chemistry, and potentially harmful changes in bodily fluid levels occur more rapidly in the older adult who cannot adequately conserve sodium and water under these conditions.

Adults past the age of 65 years experience a reduction in the total amount of urine they can store before feeling a need to void, and more urine is retained in the bladder after the individual has attempted to empty it. Furthermore, recognition of the need to void may not occur until the individual's bladder is almost or even completely filled. This means that the individual has less or perhaps no time to reach a lavatory before leakage or spillage occurs.

Urinary incontinence is the most significant effect of age changes in the bladder, with a prevalence among the population 60 years and older estimated to be 19% for women and 8% for men. Women are more likely to suffer from stress incontinence—loss of urine at times of exertion. Urge incontinence, which is more prevalent in men, involves urine loss following an urge to void or lack of control over voiding with little or no warning. Each of these conditions is reversible and may disappear within a year or two of its initial development. Incontinence can also be managed through behavioral strategies, sometimes involving only very simple Kegel exercises.

Age effects on renal functioning significantly reduce the older person's ability to excrete medications, a fact that can be of great importance in a therapeutic context. Unless the dosage is adjusted to take into account this lower rate of tubular transport, drugs may have an adverse impact instead of their intended benefits.

Effects of Age on Digestion

Although documented age changes in digestive organs are relatively minor, there are important ramifications of age changes in patterns of nutrition that may lead to symptoms mimicking those of psychological or cognitive impairment disorders. Unchecked, a vicious cycle may be created, as depression can lead to loss of interest in food and food preparation. Conversely, the establishment of healthy dietary patterns can serve to compensate for declines in other areas of physiological functioning.

Another issue related to digestion concerns fecal incontinence. Although, at least for women, there are changes in the anal sphincters that can eventually lead to incontinence, this condition does not affect the majority of the aged population. However, older adults may associate irregularities in defecation with feared diseases and the prospects of institutionalization in later life. The anxiety created by this concern may contribute further to gastrointestinal problems so that what originates as a temporary problem comes to have a more prolonged course. Interventions by professionals that involve sensitive discussion of this very personal and potentially frightening area of daily life can be extremely beneficial.

Effects of Age on the Immune System

There is mixed evidence regarding the quality of the aging immune system but some changes appear to occur that lower its ability to protect the body's cells against infections and the development of abnormal cells. T-cells, which destroy antigens (foreign substances that enter the body), lose effectiveness over the adult years. Other immune system cells, including NK cells, K cells, and macrophage indicates appear to retain their functioning into old age, and there is some evidence that the remaining T-cells are able to produce an enhanced response despite their smaller numbers.

Increasing evidence is accumulating in the field of psychoneuroimmunology, in which the intricate connections are examined between affective states such as stress and depression, nervous system functioning, and the immune system (Kiecolt Glaser & Glaser, 1995). For example, elderly individuals with high levels of life stress experience lower T-cell functioning. Conversely, social support, at least among women, was found to be positively related to immune system competence measured in terms of lymphocyte numbers and response to mitogens (Thomas, Goodwin, & Goodwin, 1985).

Apart from changes in the immune system that interact with psychological functioning, the lowered effectiveness of the immune system in older adults has important implications for health. The aging immune system has been linked to increased vulnerability to influenza, infections, cancer, and certain age-associated autoimmune disorders such as diabetes and possibly atherosclerosis and Alzheimer's disease. A less competent immune system can put the elderly individual at higher risk at least for developing certain forms of cancer and other illnesses that are more frequent in later life.

Effects of Age on the Reproductive System and Sexuality

Throughout the 40s and 50s, men and women experience altered hormonal functioning, resulting for women in the menopause, and for men in a reduction in the number of viable sperm. Men and women also undergo changes in the anatomical structures of the genitals and sex organs that alter their experience of sexual relations. In both sexes, there is a general slowing down in the progression through the human sexual response cycle.

Age changes in patterns of sexual responsiveness in and of themselves do not impair the older individual's ability to enjoy sexual relations, but these changes may present a problem if the partners are unfamiliar with the fact that sexual responsivity naturally becomes altered in later adulthood. The woman may worry that she has lost her orgasmic capacity because it takes her longer to become aroused, excited, and stimulated. The aging male may be at high risk for developing symptoms of secondary (nonphysiological) impotence. It is crucial for aging individuals to be aware of normal sexual changes to prevent such unfortunate occurrences. Furthermore, interventions are becoming increasingly available such as estrogen replacement therapy for women and, if necessary, treatments for erectile dysfunction in men.

Effects of Age on the Central Nervous System

In the central nervous system (CNS), as in the other major organ systems, changes that are due to aging alone are difficult to separate from changes that are the result of disease. For example, neurofibrillary tangles and amyloid plaques are deleterious changes that occur in Alzheimer's disease, but are also found to a lesser extent in normal aging brains.

Apart from this distinction between normal aging and disease, there is considerable interindividual variability in patterns of brain changes. Some of this variability may be accounted for by health status. There also may be significant gender variations with greater reductions in both the frontal and temporal lobes in men but more in the hippocampus and parietal lobes of women (Murphy et al., 1996). In studies of the frontal lobes using both magnetic resonance imaging (MRI) and positron emission tomography (PET) scans, age reductions appear to be more conclusively demonstrated than in studies of other cortical areas amounting to 1% per decade (De Santi et al., 1995). Such findings, in conjunction with alterations in the limbic system with age, are interpreted as providing a neurological basis for the behavioral observations of memory changes in older adults (Nielsen Bohlman & Knight, 1995).

Effects of Age on Vision

The normal aging process affects a number of visual functions, including acuity, dark adaptation, sensitivity to glare, and the ability to focus on near objects, a condition known as presbyopia. These changes in functioning are due to age-related alterations in the pupil, retina, and lens capsule. Even though many of the ensuing visual problems can be corrected, there are residual symptoms that may remain in special circumstances such as after overwork or when reading small print.

Visual problems have many effects on everyday life, including heightened vulnerability to falls, increased dependence on others, and interference with the ability to complete basic tasks of living such as driving, housekeeping, grocery shopping, and food preparation.

Effects of Age on Hearing

Presbycusis, the general term used to refer to age-related hearing loss, includes several specific subtypes reflecting different changes in the auditory structures. The most common form of hearing loss reduces sensitivity to high-frequency tones earlier and more severely than sensitivity to low-frequency tones, a loss that is particularly pronounced in men. Speech perception is affected both by the various forms of presbycusis operating at the sensory level and by changes in the central processing of auditory information at the level of the brain stem and above.

Hearing deficits greatly interfere with interpersonal communication, leading to strained relationships and greater caution by the elder in an attempt to avoid making inappropriate responses to uncertain auditory signals. Furthermore, hearing deficits can indirectly affect cognitive processes. Listening is more effortful for the older adult with hearing loss and consequently, is more draining of cognitive resources. There is evidence linking hearing loss to impaired physical functioning and psychological difficulties including loneliness and depression.

Those who interact with hearing-impaired elders can benefit from learning ways to communicate that lessen the impact of age-related changes. Modulating one's tone of voice, particularly for women, so that it is not too high, and avoiding distractions or interference can be important aids to communicating clearly with older adults.

Effects of Age on Taste and Smell

Although there are general decreases in taste sensitivity across age groups of older adults, there is nevertheless wide variability across individuals and within the same individual among the four primary tastes. Similarly, although there are general cross-sectional decreases in the ability to recognize and detect odors, there are wide individual variations in part due to differences within the older population in health status. Different odors also show differential sensitivity to age effects. Contributing to the observed age differences in sensitivity to taste and smell are apparent cognitive differences in the ability to identify odors and food tastes (Corwin, 1992). Age effects in these higher-order cognitive and perceptual processes may lead to a distorted picture of the effects of aging on the sensory processes involved in taste and smell.

Conclusions

A number of age-related changes have been described that occur throughout the body's organ systems and sensory processes. It has been postulated that an individual's reactions to these changes varies according to how central the area of functioning is to identity as well as how the individual approaches the age change (Whitbourne, 1996). Older adults who overreact to physical changes may experience an unnecessary and potentially harmful sense of discouragement or despair. Conversely, those who deny or minimize the presence of age-related limitations in physical functioning may place themselves at risk due to overexertion or failure to take preventative actions.

In any case, it is crucial for psychologists to recognize the independence, autonomy, and vitality of spirit seen in many elders, even those with severe losses or age-related limitations. They are coping daily with physical changes that would daunt the younger professional or specialist. Professionals who condescend to the elderly or patronize them (perhaps as a result of their own fears of aging) are missing important treatment opportunities as well as important opportunities to learn from the wisdom of their elders.

Bibliography

Corwin, J. (1992). Assessing olfaction: Cognitive and measurement issues. In M. J. Serby & K. L. Chobor (Eds.), *Science of olfaction* (pp. 335–354). Berlin: Springer-Verlag.

De Santi, S., de Leon, M. J., Convit, A., Tarshish, C., et al. (1995). Age-related changes in brain: II. Positron emission tomography of frontal and temporal lobe glucose metabolism in normal subjects. *Psychiatric Quarterly, 66,* 357–370.

Kiecolt Glaser, J. K., & Glaser, R. (1995). Psychoneuroimmunology and health consequences: Data and shared mechanisms. *Psychosomatic Medicine, 57,* 269–274.

Lamberts, S. W. J., van den Beld, A. W., & van der Lely, A.-J. (1997). The endocrinology of aging. *Science, 278,* 419–424.

Murphy, D. G., DeCarli, C., McIntosh, A. R., Daly, E., Mentis, M. J., Pietrini, P., Szczepanik, J., Schapiro, M. B., Grady, C. L., Horwitz, B., & Rapoport, S. I. (1996). Sex differences in human brain morphometry and metabolism: An in vivo quantitative magnetic resonance imaging and positron emission tomography study on the effect of aging. *Archives of General Psychiatry, 53,* 585–594.

Nielsen Bohlman, L., & Knight, R. T. (1995). Prefrontal alterations during memory processing in aging. *Cerebral Cortex, 5,* 541–549.

Thomas, P. D., Goodwin, J. M., & Goodwin, J. W. (1985). Effect of social support on stress-related changes in cholesterol, uric acid level, and immune function in an elderly sample. *American Journal of Psychiatry, 142,* 735–737.

Trappe, S. W., Costill, D. L., Vukovich, M. D., Jones, J., & Melham, T. (1996). Aging among elite distance runners: A 22-yr longitudinal study. *Journal of Applied Physiology, 80,* 285–290.

Whitbourne, S. K. (1996) *The aging individual: Physical and psychological perspectives.* New York: Springer.

Susan Krauss Whitbourne

Cognitive Processes and Development

The first large dataset with results relevant to aging and cognitive abilities was based on the administration of the Army Alpha test to over 1.7 million enlisted men and officers in World War I. Later analyses of these data revealed substantial age trends, even before the age of 50, in many of the subtests of this cognitive test battery. The initial report of these data, and reports of other early studies by Foster and Taylor (1920) and by Jones and Conrad (1933), also had two additional noteworthy aspects. One was the discovery that different types of cognitive tests had different relations with age. That is, measures of knowledge and acquired information were found to be fairly stable across the adult years, but measures assessing flexible or novel thinking exhibited moderate to large age-related declines. These two types of cognition were later labeled *crystallized* and *fluid* intelligence, respectively, by Raymond Cattell.

A second interesting feature of the Army Alpha report and the reports of the other early studies was the discussion of several possible interpretations of age-related cognitive declines, such as differential represen-

tativeness, disuse, lack of motivation, and biological change. Many of these hypotheses proposed in the 1920s and 1930s to account for age-related declines in fluid cognition are still being debated.

Some of the best evidence concerning the relations between age and various cognitive measures is based on data from large representative samples used to provide the norms for standardized tests. For example, the WAIS III cognitive abilities test was recently normed with data from 2,450 adults ranging from 17 to over 85 years of age. Figure 1 portrays the scores from four of the subtests in this test battery as a function of age. In order to facilitate comparison across different variables, the means at each age have been converted to scores scaled relative to the distribution in a reference group between 20 and 34 years of age. The mean of the reference group distribution is 10 and the standard deviation is 3. Notice that the measures of acquired knowledge, information, and vocabulary, increase slightly during middle adulthood and then appear to decline in later adulthood. However, the other two measures, matrix reasoning representing the ability to detect and apply abstract relations, and letter-number sequence, reflecting the ability to simultaneously remember and reorganize information, both declined fairly steadily from about age forty on. Similar patterns have been found in other studies with large samples, although there is some controversy with respect to whether the age relations in cognitive variables are smaller in longitudinal comparisons than in cross-sectional ones (e.g., Laursen, 1997; Salthouse, 1991; Schaie, 1996; Zelinski & Burnight, 1997).

There are at least two ways in which the magnitude of age effects on cognitive abilities can be considered. One is in terms of the average performance at each age relative to the distribution of scores at earlier ages, which in the case of fluid measures frequently corresponds to a difference in means of approximately 1 standard deviation between ages 25 and 65. To illustrate, the means at age 65 for the matrix reasoning and letter-number sequence variables are about 7, which is 1 standard deviation below the mean for the reference group whose age range was 20 to 34 years. Differences of this magnitude indicate that even though there is overlap in the distributions, the average 65-year-old would perform at approximately the sixteenth percentile of the distribution from a sample of 20- to 34-year-old adults.

A second manner in which age-related effects can be expressed is with respect to the proportion of total interindividual variance in the measure that is associated with age. Because proportions of variance correspond to the square of the relevant correlation coefficient, estimates of the proportion of total between person variability that is associated with age can be derived from correlations between age and various cognitive measures. Verhaeghen and Salthouse (1997) reported a meta-analysis on age-cognition relations in which the weighted estimates of the age correlations were −.40 for measures of reasoning, and −.38 for measures of spatial ability. Squaring these values reveals that approximately 15% of the total interindividual variability in certain cognitive measures is associated with the age of the individual. Although most of the variation across people is not related to age, both of these estimation methods nevertheless indicate that the age-related effects on some measures of cognitive functioning are moderately large. There is clearly considerable variability at each age, but at least for the fluid cognitive measures, fairly substantial age-related declines are typically evident in cross-sectional samples of adults.

Normal Versus Abnormal Aging

Because increased age is associated with lower scores in many cognitive variables, and because dementia and certain other types of pathological aging are characterized by extremely low levels of cognition, it is meaningful to ask whether dementia, and in particular Alzheimer's dementia, is merely an end point on a single quantitative continuum. This is an important question because if the answer turns out to be yes, then it might imply that virtually everyone will experience dementia if he or she lives long enough. However, this issue has been very controversial, in part because it is not clear exactly what type of evidence would be most relevant to its resolution. The discovery of a qualitative difference in cognitive functioning between individuals with dementia and healthy adults of the same age would seem to be convincing, but it has been difficult to achieve consensus among researchers from different perspectives about what constitutes a true qualitative difference (see Nebes, 1992, for a review).

Although there is controversy with respect to whether dementia is qualitatively distinct from normal aging, there is much more agreement about how to detect pathology. David Wechsler, who developed one of the most successful adult intelligence tests, argued that certain age-related cognitive declines are normal, and consequently that this normative trend should be taken into account by evaluating the individual with respect to his or her own age peers. Despite little understanding of the reasons for the negative age relations in measures of cognitive functioning, this idea has generally been accepted. That is, for clinical and other evaluative purposes it is often asserted that the most meaningful information about an individual is not his or her level relative to adults of all ages, but rather to adults of the same age. (Because life expectancy has increased and negative relations between age and cog-

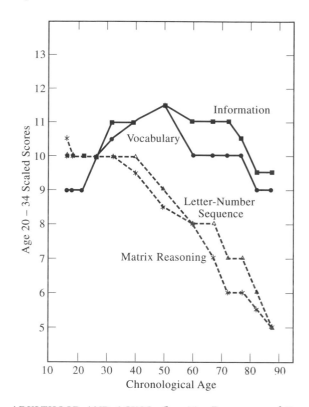

ADULTHOOD AND AGING: Cognitive Processes and Development. Figure 1. Performance on four WAIS-III subtests as a function of age. Data from the WAIS-III normative sample with the mean at each age expressed in scaled scores relative to the distribution of a reference group between 20 and 34 years of age.

nitive functioning continue beyond age seventy, this position has led to a need for norms for very old adults that are only now starting to become available.)

Two major criteria used for the diagnosis of pathology are that performance is at a low level (e.g., two standard deviations below the mean, or at approximately the bottom 5% of one's age group) on several different cognitive tests, and that this level reflects a relatively rapid change from an earlier higher state. The former criterion provides an objective basis for documenting that the level of functioning is low, and the latter criterion establishes that this condition has not always existed. A variety of different cognitive tests has been used for diagnosis of cognitive impairments, but most include assessments of comprehension, memory, orientation, and judgment. For example, some of the most frequently used general screening tests ask the examinee to perform several relatively simple activities requiring comprehension and memory, to answer biographical questions, and questions about time and location.

Gender and Ethnic Differences

Significant differences related to gender and to ethnic or racial group have been documented on a number of cognitive measures, but there is little evidence of interactions with age that would indicate that the magnitude of the age-related effects on cognition vary as a function of gender or race. Some of the most convincing evidence with respect to race is from analyses of data reported by Avolio and Waldman (1994) on over 16,000 Whites, 7,000 Blacks, and 1,700 Hispanics. These researchers found that the functions relating age to measures of several cognitive abilities were remarkably parallel across the three racial groups. A meta-analysis of age and gender effects by Meinz and Salthouse (1998) also found little evidence of larger age-related effects for one gender than for the other on a variety of cognitive measures. As an example, although males tend to perform somewhat higher than females on many tests of spatial ability, the weighted estimates of the age correlations for measures of spatial ability from a total of 2,585 adults were −0.35 for males, and −0.36 for females. At least on the basis of the available data, therefore, it appears that the relations of age to cognitive measures are similar across major ethnic or racial groups, and between males and females.

Specific Cognitive Abilities

There are two general approaches to investigating the relations between age and cognitive functioning in adulthood; the psychometric perspective which focuses on the quantity or quality of cognitive products, and the cognitive perspective which focuses on the processes used to achieve those products. The two perspectives are often considered separately because they are associated with different traditions and different types of analytical methods. However, the two approaches actually complement one another, and because they are becoming integrated in recent research the distinctions will be ignored in the following review.

Creativity. There are many anecdotal reports of remarkable individuals exhibiting creativity at very advanced ages, but relatively little systematic data has been reported on age and creativity. Work by Simonton (1996) is a notable exception, but most of his research has focused at the relatively gross level of overall achievements instead of the cognitive processes that might be responsible for those achievements. For example, many of the analyses he has reported concern the relation of age to the quantity or quality of products by authors, artists, composers, inventors, etc., with little attention devoted to the mechanisms by which those products were produced.

Laboratory assessments of creativity have often involved measures of divergent thinking such as generating unusual usages for a familiar object (e.g., McCrae, Arenberg, & Costa, 1987), or arranging blocks in as many different patterns as possible. Age-related declines have been reported in both types of measures, but even if assessments of this kind are valid as measures of creativity, they almost certainly reflect only a narrow aspect of creativity. At the present time it must be admitted that not much is yet known about the cognitive processes involved in creativity, and even less is known about the relation of age to those processes.

Wisdom. Several types of cognition, such as good judgment and sagacity, are postulated to improve with increased age and experience. Wisdom is perhaps the most frequently mentioned cognitive ability of this type, but it has been difficult to investigate because there are no generally accepted definitions of wisdom that are amenable to objective measurements. Several researchers have been active in investigating a variety of different operational definitions of wisdom, but there is not yet convincing evidence that increased age is associated with increases in the available measures of wisdom (see Baltes & Staudinger, 1993, for a review).

Problem Solving and Decision Making. Relatively little age-comparative research has been reported on higher-order cognitive processes such as problem solving and decision making. There have been a few studies of age-related differences in decision-making styles (Birren, 1969) and strategies (Streufert, Pogash, Piasecki, & Post, 1990), but the quality of the resulting decisions or problem solutions has seldom been assessed in these types of studies. Research in this area has been difficult because many complex problems are ill-defined in that there may be no single correct answer, and because solution quality in complex problems is likely to interact with the amount of knowledge and experience in the relevant domain. However, recently there have been a number of studies specifically focusing on the relations of age to effectiveness in naturalistic or everyday problem solving. The age trends in this area are not easily summarized, but the literature and major issues have been thoroughly described in a review (Berg & Klaczynski, 1996).

Reasoning. Several different types of reasoning have been investigated in age-comparative studies. For example, deductive reasoning has been studied with tasks requiring the evaluation of syllogisms, or the integration of premises to verify a deduction. Inductive reasoning has been studied with tasks that require extrapolation on the basis of the presented information to make an inference. Assessments of inductive reasoning are represented in many standardized cognitive ability batteries with tests such as series completion, analogies, and matrix completions. Concept formation tasks are another type of inductive reasoning task in which the goal is to determine which attribute or combination of attributes is the basis for classifying stimuli into categories or attributes. Versions of this task have been used in many experimental studies, and in neuropsychological tests such as the Wisconsin Card Sorting Test and the Category Test.

Proverb interpretation tests have also been administered to adults of different ages in a number of studies. These tests are hypothesized to reflect abstract reasoning, and possibly even characteristics of wisdom, because proverbs are sometimes assumed to capture fundamental aspects of human experience. All of these types of reasoning have been found to have moderate to large negative age relations (see Salthouse, 1992, for a review). As an example, the WAIS III matrix reasoning test provides a measure of inductive reasoning, and the data in Figure 1 illustrate that there are nearly monotonic cross-sectional age-related declines in this measure in the normative sample for the WAIS III.

Spatial Abilities. The efficiency and effectiveness of manipulating or transforming spatial information is important in certain occupations (e.g., pilots and architects), and is related to other cognitive abilities such as numeric ability and some types of reasoning.

A variety of spatial ability tests have been administered to adults of different ages. For example, spatial visualization tests such as cube comparison, cube assembly, paper folding, and form boards require the individual to imagine an object in a different arrangement or perspective. Tests of spatial relations such as mental rotation and figural relations require rapid decisions about the identity of a stimulus in different orientations, and tests of perceptual closure assess the speed and accuracy of identifying distorted or incomplete stimuli. Moderate to large age differences similar to those found with reasoning measures have been found in both standardized psychometric tests and in specially devised experimental tasks of spatial ability (see Salthouse, 1992, for a review).

Language. Some of the most common tests of language and verbal ability are those that assess vocabulary. Vocabulary is a type of knowledge often thought to increase with age, but the age trends are actually somewhat mixed, and are possibly related to the manner in which word knowledge is assessed. For example, in the conventional word-to-definition format in which the respondent is required to provide a definition of the word, performance often increases across the middle adult years, and sometimes decreases in late life. The data in Figure 1 for the vocabulary test from the WAIS III are an example of this pattern. However, negative age trends are more pronounced when a definition is supplied and the respondent has to provide the target word. This pattern suggests that the age differences are greater when the individual needs to converge on a single target item, and there is no opportunity for cir-

cumlocutions. Consistent with this interpretation is the existence of sizable age differences in the tip-of-the-tongue phenomenon in which the individual has difficulty retrieving the name of a target item despite the availability of other information about the item.

Another aspect of language that often exhibits age-related differences is fluency, as reflected in the rapidity of access to stored information. Commonly used tests of verbal fluency require the individual to produce as many items as possible within a specified time interval either beginning with a particular letter, or belonging to a particular semantic category. The relations between age and measures of fluency appear to depend on level of vocabulary, which is reasonable if fluency performance is a function of both speed of search and retrieval, and of the size of the knowledge base being searched.

Age-related differences have also been found in other aspects of language such as comprehension and generation of syntactically complex utterances, efficiency of communication, maintenance of conversational topic, and inhibition of off-target verbosity (see Kemper, 1992, for a review).

Memory. A great many distinctions have been made among types of memory, but only three will be mentioned here. Semantic memory refers to the contents of an individual's general knowledge, and it is often assessed with general information questions such as "Who was the president of the United States during the Civil War?" and "What is the current name of the country formerly known as Persia?" It was noted earlier that this type of knowledge tends to be preserved through most of the adult years, and this is evident in the function for the information variable in Figure 1.

Episodic memory refers to encoding, storage, and retrieval of previously presented information. It is referred to as episodic because unlike the contents of semantic memory, the individual is usually aware of when and where information in episodic memory was acquired, as though the spatial and temporal properties of the acquisition episode were preserved. Most assessments reveal fairly large negative age differences in measures of episodic memory.

Working memory is probably the most relevant type of memory for cognitive functioning because it is sometimes considered to be memory in service of, or working for, cognition. An example of a test of working memory is the WAIS III letter-number sequence test in which the individual hears a mixed list of letters and numbers, and is then required to repeat the items back first with numbers in ascending order and then with letters in alphabetic order. Because successful performance in this task requires the individual to remember items while also carrying out transformations on those items, the task satisfies the definition of working memory as involving simultaneous storage and processing. Figure ı reveals that there are moderate to strong negative age relations on measures of this type.

Attention. One classification scheme for attention distinguishes among sustained, divided, and focused categories of attention. Sustained attention refers to the ability to maintain a high level of awareness for extended periods, as is required in vigilance situations. The results have been rather mixed with respect to age differences in sustained attention, but if there are age-related effects in this type of attention they are probably fairly small. Divided attention is involved when multiple activities are performed simultaneously. Large negative age effects are often found with measures of divided attention, but it is still unclear whether the effects are greater than what one would expect on the basis of single-task performance. That is, because young and old adults typically differ in the performance on each task when performed in isolation, at least some of the differences in dual-task performance may be attributable to differences in single-task performance. Among the ways in which this possibility has been investigated are by adjusting the conditions to equate people of different ages in single-task performance before administering the dual-task conditions and by statistical control of single-task performance when examining dual-task performance. Unfortunately, only a limited number of studies have been reported with these procedures, and the available results have been somewhat inconsistent.

Focused or selective attention refers to the ability to ignore distraction or irrelevant information and concentrate on the target. Measures of focused attention frequently yield moderate to large age effects, with some variation depending on the nature of the non-target distractors, and the type and amount of practice with the task (see Hartley, 1992, for a review).

Major Issues

As is evident in the preceding sections, adult age differences have been documented in a wide range of variables reflecting different types of cognitive abilities. The primary theoretical questions at this time include how many distinct age-related influences are contributing to these differences, and what are the mechanisms responsible for those influences?

An issue relevant to the first question is whether the age-related effects on different cognitive measures are independent of one another, as though many separate causal determinants are operating to produce age differences, or whether there are shared or common age-related influences on different variables. Some progress has been made in resolving this question with multivariate analytical procedures. These methods are only feasible when several variables are available from all of the individuals in moderately large samples, but a number of recent analyses have revealed that a substantial proportion of the age-related effects on different cog-

nitive variables is shared, rather than being specific to a particular variable. Results of this type suggest that fewer causal mechanisms may be needed to account for age-related cognitive differences than is sometimes assumed. It is still not known which cognitive variables have the largest proportions of age-related variance shared with other cognitive variables, and why, but the discovery that many of the age-related effects are not independent of one another seems likely to have important implications for the eventual interpretation of age-cognition relations.

A second major theoretical issue concerns the causes for the observed age-related differences in cognition; that is, why and how do they occur? Several different approaches to answering this question have been employed. One way of classifying the approaches is according to the primary focus or level of analysis, which can be either proximal or distal.

The proximal level of analysis emphasizes characteristics of processing at the time of assessment. The goal of this approach is to seek correlates of the observed differences in cognitive performance either in terms of more fundamental cognitive attributes, or in terms of neuroanatomical characteristics. At the cognitive level the basic correlates may correspond to efficiency of hypothesized components, effectiveness of specific or general strategies, or to the quantity of relatively general resources related to controlled attention, working memory, or rapid processing (see Salthouse, 1991, for a review). Correlates at the neuroanatomical level may correspond to the size of particular neuroanatomical structures or regions, efficiency of neural circuits, density of synapses, quantity of neurotransmitters, etc. (see Raz, in press, for a review). The major advantage of the proximal focus is that it has the potential to describe the mechanisms by which observed behavior is related to more primitive or fundamental constructs. A possible disadvantage is that even when the proximal approach is successful at linking performance on cognitive tasks to these more detailed characteristics, there is still a need to determine how and why the age-related changes originated.

It is in this latter respect that the distal level of analysis may be most useful. The distal approach emphasizes factors operating at earlier periods in one's life that may be responsible for the characteristics observed at the time of assessment. Among the possibilities that could be involved at this level are experiential factors such as quality or quantity of education or patterns of experience with certain activities. There are also biological factors involved such as early nutrition or physical stimulation, and cumulative exposure to various kinds of toxins. Although there is still considerable uncertainty about these aspects and their implications for the interpretation of developmental relations, convincing evidence now exists that more recently born people perform at higher levels in a variety of different cognitive tests (e.g., Flynn, 1987; Schaie, 1996). Genetic influences could also be involved in age-related cognitive differences in the form of the late-life release of a genetic program. In fact, it has recently been reported that genetic influences on cognition are as strong among adults in their 70s and 80s as among adults in their 20s and 30s, which is surprising because it has sometimes been assumed that experiential factors increase in importance as people age and accumulate unique sets of experiences.

Most distal factors have been difficult to investigate because the relevant information is typically not available across a span of 50 years or more. Furthermore, to the extent that distal factors interact with one another, it may be unrealistic to expect simple relationships involving a single type of distal variable on current cognitive performance.

Conclusion

Although age-related differences in several different types of cognitive functioning have been well documented, the causes of age declines in cognitive measures are still not well understood. Furthermore, there is still relatively little information available about positive aspects of cognitive aging, such as the influence of specific knowledge that is almost certainly acquired as a function of experience within a domain. Nevertheless, this is currently a very active area of research and both the quality of the researchers, and the breadth of approaches being employed, suggest that optimism is warranted concerning further advances in knowledge.

Bibliography

Avolio, B. J., & Waldman, D. A. (1994). Variations in cognitive, perceptual, and psychomotor abilities across the working life span: Examining the effects of race, sex, experience, education, and occupational type. *Psychology and Aging, 9,* 430–442.

Baltes, P. B., & Staudinger, U. (1993). The search for a psychology of wisdom. *Current Directions in Psychological Science, 2,* 75–80.

Berg, C. A., & Klaczynski, P. A. (1996). Practical intelligence and problem solving: Searching for perspectives. In F. Blanchard-Fields & T. M. Hess (Eds.), *Perspectives on cognitive change in adulthood and aging* (pp. 323–357). New York: McGraw-Hill.

Birren, J. E. (1969). Age and decision strategies. *Interdisciplinary Topics in Gerontology, 4,* 23–36.

Flynn, J. R. (1987). Massive IQ gains in 14 nations: What IQ tests really measure. *Psychological Bulletin, 101,* 171–191.

Foster, J. C., & Taylor, G. A. (1920). The applicability of mental tests to persons over fifty years of age. *Journal of Applied Psychology, 4,* 39–58.

Hartley, A. A. (1992). Attention. In F. I. M. Craik & T. A. Salthouse (Eds.), *The handbook of aging and cognition* (pp. 3–49). Hillsdale, NJ: Erlbaum.

Jones, H. E., & Conrad, H. S. (1933). The growth and decline of intelligence: A study of a homogeneous group between the ages of ten and sixty. *Genetic Psychology Monographs, 13.*

Kemper, S. (1992). Language and aging. In F. I. M. Craik & T. A. Salthouse (Eds.), *The handbook of aging and cognition* (pp. 213–270). Hillsdale, NJ: Erlbaum.

Laursen, P. (1997). The impact of aging on cognitive functions: An 11-year follow-up study of four age cohorts. *Acta Neurologica Scandinavica Supplementum, 96,* No. 172.

McCrae, R. R., Arenberg, D., & Costa, P. T. (1987). Declines in divergent thinking with age: Cross-sectional, longitudinal, and cross-sequential analyses. *Psychology and Aging, 2,* 130–137.

Meinz, E. J., & Salthouse, T. A. (1998). Is age kinder to females than to males? *Psychonomic Bulletin & Review, 5,* 56–70.

Nebes, R. D. (1992). Cognitive dysfunction in Alzheimer's Disease. In F. I. M. Craik & T. A. Salthouse (Eds.), *The handbook of aging and cognition* (pp. 373–446). Hillsdale, NJ: Erlbaum.

Raz, N. (in press). Aging of the brain and its impact on cognitive performance: Integration of structural and functional findings. In F. I. M. Craik & T. A. Salthouse (Eds.) *Handbook of aging and cognition* (2nd ed.). Mahwah, NJ: Erlbaum.

Salthouse, T. A. (1991). *Theoretical perspectives in cognitive aging.* Hillsdale, NJ: Erlbaum.

Salthouse, T. A. (1992). Reasoning and spatial abilities. In F. I. M. Craik & T. A. Salthouse (Eds.), *The handbook of aging and cognition* (pp. 167–211). Hillsdale, NJ: Erlbaum.

Schaie, K. W. (1996). *Intellectual development in adulthood: The Seattle Longitudinal Study.* New York: Cambridge University Press.

Simonton, D. K. (1996). Creative expertise: A life-span developmental perspective. In K. A. Ericsson (Ed.), *The road to excellence: The acquisition of expert performance* (pp. 227–253). Mahwah, NJ: Erlbaum.

Streufert, S., Pogash, R., Piaseki, M., & Post, G. M. (1990). Age and management team performance. *Psychology and Aging, 5,* 551–559.

Verhaeghen, P., & Salthouse, T. A. (1997). Meta-analyses of age-cognition relations in adulthood: Estimates of linear and nonlinear age effects and structural models. *Psychological Bulletin, 122,* 231–249.

Zelinski, E. M., & Burnight, K. P. (1997). Sixteen-year longitudinal and time lag changes in memory and cognition in older adults. *Psychology and Aging, 12,* 503–513.

Timothy A. Salthouse

Personality Processes and Development

A classic question that has intrigued and preoccupied researchers interested in the psychological aspects of the aging process is whether the physical, cognitive, and social changes associated with development prompt alterations in the organization and structure of personality. Some theorists have proposed stage models that postulate a series of qualitative reorganizations throughout adulthood in the structure and content of personality. Other theorists have promoted stability in personality throughout adulthood due to the existence of enduring dispositions whose structure and levels are set very early in life. A third viewpoint is based on a process model in which change is predicted to occur continuously and cumulatively throughout adulthood and old age without radical shifts or alterations. These three perspectives will be explored.

An introductory note recognizes the role of a pivotal early study on personality changes in relationship to well-being and adaptation in old age. The Kansas City Study conducted by Neugarten and her associates in the late 1950s and early 1960s laid the groundwork for the "disengagement theory," arguing that old age brings with it a mutual withdrawal of the individual from society and vice versa. According to this theory, those happiest in old age have turned their attention inward toward the self and away from involvement in the outside world. The ensuing disengagement-activity theory debate was resolved by the end of the 1970s in favor of the "continuity theory," the notion that older people are happiest when they are enabled to maintain their preferred level of social involvement. Throughout this debate, various researchers attempted to delineate patterns or personality types and relate these to patterns of well-being. Although current research has moved away from attempts to form typologies, attempts to understand the factors that influence well-being in later life has remained a central issue (Harlow & Cantor, 1996).

Stage Theories of Personality

The best known stage theory of personality is that proposed by Erik Erikson (1963) who described a psychosocial crisis model of the life cycle divided into eight stages. Although Erikson's theory emphasizes social factors and development throughout life, it is nevertheless strongly grounded in Freudian psychoanalytic theory. Erikson's stages of development are intended to represent the growth of the ego, a structure postulated by Freud to control the rational, executive functions of personality.

According to Erikson, each of the eight crisis stages is a critical period during which the individual experiences heightened vulnerability to two opposing forces. These two polarities are represented within the theory as the positive ego quality "versus" the negative ego quality, as in generativity (a positive quality) versus stagnation (the polar opposite). The outcome of the crisis is the addition (or lack thereof) of a new strength or facet to the ego, such as "fidelity" or "wisdom."

Erikson's stage theory is based on an epigenetic prin-ciple, according to which each stage emerges through a ground plan that is part of the individual's genetic inheritance. The stages are linked to each other in that the favorable resolution of an earlier stage is critical for the positive resolution of later stages. Despite the fact that the stages are linked in theory with specific age periods, it is also true that any psychosocial crisis can emerge at any given age. The usual sequence of age-stage progressions is thought to reflect vulnerability to certain psychosocial issues at particular ages due to the confluence of biological, cognitive, emotional, and social forces. Personality growth in adulthood and old age according to Erikson focuses on the establishment of close interpersonal relationships (intimacy versus isolation), and the passing on to the future of one's creative products (generativity versus stagnation). In the final stage (ego integrity versus despair), the individual must resolve conflicted feelings about the past, adapt to the changes associated with the aging process, and come to grips with the inevitability of death.

Erikson's ideas, although difficult to operationalize, have provided a major intellectual inspiration to workers in the field of adult personality development. The writings of midlife theorists (Gould, 1978; Levinson, Darrow, Klein, Levinson, & McKee, 1978; Vaillant, 1977) are based on the fundamental proposal that personality continues to develop in important ways throughout life. Although the concept of the midlife crisis that developed as a result of these writings has been discounted in psychological gerontology (Whitbourne, 1996), the notion of personality change in adulthood continues to receive empirical support (VanManen & Whitbourne, 1997; Whitbourne, Zuschlag, Elliot, & Waterman, 1992).

Expanding on Erikson's theory, Loevinger (1976) proposed a stage model of ego development, with five of the eight stages or levels covering the years of adulthood: the conformist level, the conscientious-conformist level, the individualistic level, the autonomous level, and the integrated level. The components of the ego that develop through these stages are character, interpersonal style, and cognitive style. The conscientious-conformist level is occupied by the majority of adults, and indicates that individuals are able to think independently rather than blindly subscribing to group norms. In the integrated stage, which is very much like Erikson's concept of ego integrity, the individual is able to recognize and resolve inner conflicts and feels a sense of acceptance. This stage also brings with it an open approach to new situations and experiences and a continuing commitment to fulfilling one's inner potential. According to Loevinger, not all individuals progress through all stages; in fact, the last stage is achieved only by very few older adults. There is some evidence in support of Loevinger's theory relating ego level to age and maturity of personality processes in adulthood

(Blanchard-Fields, 1986; Helson & Roberts, 1994; Labouvie-Vief, DeVoe, & Bulka, 1989).

Stability Theories of Personality in Adulthood

In contrast to the stage models is the position that personality remains stable across the adult years and into old age. Traditionally, trait theorists such as Eysenck and Cattell regarded personality structure as invariant from a very early age onward, reflecting the influence of genetic and constitutional factors on enduring personal dispositions. More recently, the five-factor model or "Big Five" model of personality has been proposed by McCrae and Costa (1990). This model updates the trait position with substantial amounts of supporting evidence from large cross-sectional and longitudinal studies to indicate consistency of underlying personality dimensions well into the later years of adulthood. The five factors assumed to form the core of personality are neuroticism, extraversion, openness to experience, agreeableness, and conscientiousness.

McCrae and Costa have applied the five-factor model to many areas of functioning, including psychopathology, occupational development, and physical health. Data from their research and that of others on the stability of these dimensions over adulthood support the propositions of the trait model that individuals show little change in mean scores from the 30s through middle adulthood and even into old age (Conley, 1985; Field & Millsap, 1991). These findings are consistent with those of other researchers working from different models in suggesting that there may be a constitutional or genetic basis for personality that endures throughout life, as in Cloninger's theory of temperament and character (Cloninger, Svrakic, & Przybeck, 1994). However, it should be kept in mind that the stability of personality traits demonstrated in these studies does not imply that the individual's identity remains static throughout the adult years. Personality traits may remain stable, but the individual's awareness of these traits and ability to adapt behaviors accordingly may shift over time.

Process Theories of Personality

In contrast to the view that personality develops through a series of qualitatively distinct stages is the position that the evolution of personality occurs gradually throughout the adult years. These models emphasize quantitative increments and decrements and regard as continuous development in early, middle, and later adulthood.

Cognitive Theories. Cognitive theories of adult personality emphasize the individual's thoughts about the self and world as the primary organizers of experience. Developmental changes over adulthood are hypothesized to occur as the individual seeks to resolve discrepancies between the self-constructions and the data gathered from life experiences. Implicit is the assumption that individuals attempt to maintain a consistent sense of the self over time, but are able to modify their self-concepts in response to experiences that challenge this view.

The roots of adult personality development theories that emphasize cognitive processes can be traced to the personal construct theory of Kelly who regarded the individual's desire to predict and control experiences as the fundamental component of personality. The humanistic theory of Rogers also emphasized the individual's desire to seek congruence between the self and experiences as a major driving force in personality. Both theoretical perspectives take a phenomenological point of view, emphasizing the individual's interpretation of experiences. Thus, it is how experiences are perceived, rather than what they are "in reality" that determines the impact those experiences will have on the self. The desirable state of optimal adjustment is one of maximal congruence between the self and the "true" nature of experiences. People who regard themselves as great successes but in reality are dismal failures would be considered maladapted according to these theories.

More recently, social psychologists have emphasized that even presumably "normal" individuals may have self-concepts that are considerably distorted in comparison to the objective nature of their experiences. For example, Baumeister has proposed that people interpret experiences in a way that allows them to maintain a consistent, positively biased view of the self (Baumeister, 1996, 1997). They prefer to think of themselves as being competent and as having desirable personality traits, and distort their perceptions of others to bolster this image (Newman, Duff, & Baumeister, 1997).

Whitbourne's (1996) identity development model proposes that the maintenance of a positive identity over the years of adulthood occurs through continuing interactions between the individual and environment. Identity is regarded as a schema through which the individual interprets and reacts to life events through processes of assimilation and accommodation akin to those proposed by Piaget. Through identity assimilation, the individual interprets new events in terms of existing cognitive and affective schemas. When experiences cannot be assimilated, the process of identity accommodation involves changing identity in response to experiences. Thus, as in Baumeister's theory, it is assumed that an event that reflects unfavorably on one's identity is likely to be processed first through assimilation. Only after such efforts prove unsatisfactory will identity accommodation follow. As in the theories of Kelly and Rogers, a healthy state of emotional adaptation involves a balance or equilibrium between assimilation and accommodation. The individual maintains a sense of consistency over time but is able to change when there are large or continuous discrepancies between the self and experiences.

Several theorists have proposed mechanisms that promote such balance or equilibrium as people adapt to changing circumstances in life, proposing that individuals develop a narrative or story about their lives and organize the events in the past, present, and future in terms of this narrative. The organizing framework for this narrative, according to Whitbourne (1985), is identity and according to Baumeister, is the motivation to make sense out of experience (Baumeister & Newman, 1994). In the process of constructing such a narrative, the individual's interpretation of past experiences and projections regarding future experiences are heavily influenced by current views of the self and the desire to maintain consistency with this view.

Motivational Theories. Cognitive theories of the self regard the driving force of personality as being fed through the interaction of the individual and experiences. By contrast, motivational theories of personality development regard the thrust of personality as being oriented toward the striving for and attainment of self actualization or self-realization. The roots of these theories can be traced to motivational theories of Maslow and Murray. A more recent example is Emmon's (1996) motivational theory. According to Emmons, individuals hold "personal strivings" that are expressed in a variety of situations and ultimately affect their well-being through their impact on self-evaluations. Conflict between personal strivings (such as between goals for intimacy and career goals) is inevitable, but individuals can maintain their well-being through creative integration of these goals or "personal projects." Ultimately, subjective well-being is related more to the development of an overarching and coherent philosophy of life that integrates the many subgoals rather than simply the achievement of specific individual goals (Emmons, 1996).

The ability to adapt one's goals to the constraints of the situation is the focus of theories of motivation developed specifically with regard to aging. According to these theories, the central theme of motivation in adulthood is the need to adjust to changing physical and cognitive capacities and an altered physical and social environment. The goals themselves do not change with age, but the individual's methods of achieving these goals are seen as becoming modified along with changing circumstances.

In the primary and secondary control model of Heckhausen and Schulz (1995), changes are proposed in the way that adults attempt to control the outcome of their interchanges with the environment. Primary control refers to behaviors directed at changing the actual environment and secondary control is targeted at altering the self to fit the environment. Control is seen as the driving force behind personality throughout life. The theory is based on the assumption that in moving from adulthood to old age, individuals must adapt their methods for achieving goals. The proposed developmental trajectory is toward decreased primary and increased secondary control as individuals lose the ability to effect changes in the world. Instead, they must content themselves with changing their perceptions of themselves in the world.

Similarly, Brandtstädter and Rothermund (1994) have argued that with increasing age adult individuals gain in flexibility regarding the achievement of their goals. They use the term *accommodation* to apply to the notion of flexible pursuit of goals. In contrast, *assimilation* involves tenacious goal pursuit, or sticking to the original goal despite changes in circumstances and abilities with age. According to Brandtstädter, successful aging involves the shift from assimilative to accommodative strategies.

Cognitive-Motivational Theory. Cognitive-motivational theories integrate the focus of cognitive theories on the self with the pursuit of goals of the motivational theories. Individuals seek to gain goals that are congruent with the individual's self-concept, as motives derived from the self serve to instigate goal-oriented behaviors. Developmental versions of these theories stress changes in both self and goals as occurring over the adult years. In Cantor's life task theory, specific goals relevant to the individual's position in the life course guide decisions and appraisals of life events (Cantor, Norem, Niedenthal, & Langston, 1987). Life tasks are the vehicle that individuals use to give personal meaning to the whole of their lives. These direct specific behaviors that organize personal effort in specific activities (Zirkel & Cantor, 1990). Individuals attempt to make sense of their experiences in view of their own goals and needs as these interact with the characteristics of the environment. Cantor and her colleagues have studied the interaction of appraisals with decisions about "life tasks," or experiences on the life choices that individuals make specific to their point in the life course (Cantor & Fleeson, 1994).

The notion that a self-schema guides future endeavors is at the basis of the "possible selves" model of Markus (Markus & Nurius, 1986), a framework that has proved highly testable in research on aging and the self. Possible selves are theorized to serve as psychological resources that can both motivate the individual toward future behavior and serve as a defense of the self in the present. To the extent that the individual is successful in this process, it is theorized that positive feelings of life satisfaction emerge. When the individual is unable to realize a hoped for self or is unable to avoid the dreaded self, negative self-evaluations and affect will follow. However, here the defensive function of the possible self-construct comes into play. Assuming that most psychologically healthy adults attempt to preserve a positive self-concept, the realization that one is approaching a state of unfulfillment will lead the individual to revise the possible self so that it is more consistent with current experiences.

Applications of the possible selves construct to middle-aged and older adults have revealed that the possible selves are accessible to conscious awareness, can be objectively rated into content-based categories, and relate in predicted ways to life satisfaction and self-reports of behavior (Cross & Markus, 1991). There is a growing body of literature on the possible selves construct, and it has proven to be fruitful in identifying the ways that individuals anticipate and adapt to their own aging processes (Hooker & Kaus, 1994).

Coping Theory. Rather than developing broad theoretical models of adult personality, coping theories attempt to relate specified personality processes to life events and, ultimately, to adaptation and mental health. One approach within this tradition with tremendous heuristic value is the cognitive model of stress and coping proposed by Lazarus and Folkman (1984). According to this view, and as elaborated in a larger model on emotions in general (Lazarus, 1991), the individual's psychological well-being is a function of the way he or she appraises situations. If a situation is perceived as threatening, this will trigger an appraisal of the situation as stressful; the appraisal of a situation as a challenge stimulates a more positive emotional response. This stress appraisal model was developed in part on community middle-aged samples and has been applied over the past two decades to a wide range of studies on adaptation in the later years of adulthood (Aldwin, Sutton, Chiara, & Spiro, 1996).

In addition to proposing a model of stress, the appraisal model suggests that there are systematic variations in the processes that individuals use to reduce stress through coping. Two major categories of coping mechanisms are proposed: emotion-focused and problem-focused coping. Examples of problem-focused coping include confrontational coping or "facing up" to the situation and planful problem solving in which the problem is broken down into manageable units. An example of an emotion-focused coping strategy is the individual's attempts to find something worthwhile or beneficial about a situation that is essentially negative, such as "finding new faith" after suffering a serious illness. Other coping strategies involve a combination of problem- and emotion-focused coping, such as seeking social support in which the individual attempts to feel better about a situation by taking the action of talking to others or asking for their help.

Investigations linking coping with adaptation to stress associated with the aging process have revealed a general advantage for the more active problem-focused coping methods in contrast to the more passive emotion-focused coping. Emotion-focused coping is regarded as having negative effects on psychological and physical health outcomes (Aldwin & Revenson, 1987; Smith, Patterson, & Grant, 1990). However, emotion-focused coping can have positive adaptive value if the situation is out of one's control. As Lazarus points out, when faced with an uncontrollable stressor, direct confrontation is not always necessary for successful coping. In fact, in some cases denial may actually be adaptive.

The study of coping has yet to be successfully integrated into personality theories of adult development. The role that coping plays in the cognitive construction of the self or the adjustment of goals in response to aging, has not been directly investigated. Such intersections would provide a useful integration of what appear to be highly related theoretical systems and constructs.

Summary

The field of personality and aging has received varying attention during the past several decades, with much of the controversy revolving around specific theoretical propositions such as the existence of a "midlife crisis" or the varying implications of disengagement versus activity theories of well-being. Broad theoretical issues have remained less of a focus and theoretical models of the aging personality tend to develop separately from the mainstream of personality theories and research. However, interest in the concept of the self, in motivational aspects of personality, and in adaptation to stressful life events in later life has stimulated several significant lines of research. Valuable insights have been made into the dynamic and evolving nature of personality processes and their relation to the physical and social challenges associated with the aging process. It is also clear that the field will increasingly be incorporating contextual issues relating to the sociocultural influences on personality (Cantor & Zirkel, 1990; Kitayama & Markus, 1995). This emphasis is consistent with the increasing emphasis in developmental science on multidimensional influences on life-span processes.

Bibliography

Aldwin, C. M., & Revenson, T. A. (1987). Does coping help? A reexamination of the relation between coping and mental health. *Journal of Personality and Social Psychology, 53,* 337–348.

Aldwin, C. M., Sutton, K. J., Chiara, G., & Spiro, A. R. (1996). Age differences in stress, coping, and appraisal: Findings from the Normative Aging Study. *Journals of Gerontology: Psychological and Social Sciences, 51,* 179–188.

Baumeister, R. F. (1996). Self-regulation and ego threat:

Motivated cognition, self-deception, and destructive goal setting. In P. M. Gollwitzer & J. A. Bargh (Eds.), *The psychology of action: Linking cognition and motivation to behavior* (pp. 27–47). New York: Guilford Press.

Baumeister, R. F. (1997). Identity, self-concept, and self-esteem: The self lost and found. In R. Hogan, J. A. Johnson, & S. R. Briggs (Eds.), *Handbook of personality psychology* (pp. 681–710). San Diego, CA: Academic Press.

Baumeister, R. F., & Newman, L. S. (1994). How stories make sense of personal experiences: Motives that shape autobiographical narratives. *Personality and Social Psychology Bulletin, 20,* 676–690.

Blanchard-Fields, F. (1986). Reasoning on social dilemmas varying in emotional saliency: An adult developmental perspective. *Psychology and Aging, 1,* 325–333.

Brandtstädter, J., & Rothermund, K. (1994). Self-percepts of control in middle and later adulthood: Buffering losses by rescaling goals. *Psychology and Aging, 9,* 265–273.

Cantor, N., & Fleeson, W. (1994). Social intelligence and intelligent goal pursuit: A cognitive slice of motivation. In D. S. William (Ed.), *Integrative views of motivation, cognition, and emotion. Nebraska symposium on motivation* (Vol. 41, pp. 125–179). Lincoln, NE: University of Nebraska Press.

Cantor, N., Norem, J. K., Niedenthal, P. M., & Langston, C. A. (1987). Life tasks, self-concept ideals, and cognitive strategies in a life transition. *Journal of Personality and Social Psychology, 53,* 1178–1191.

Cantor, N., & Zirkel, S. (1990). Personality, cognition, and purposive behavior. In A. P. Lawrence (Ed.), *Handbook of personality: Theory and research* (pp. 135–164). New York: Guilford Press.

Cloninger, C. R., Svrakic, D. M., & Przybeck, T. R. (1994). A psychobiological model of temperament and character. *Archives of General Psychiatry, 50,* 975–990.

Conley, J. J. (1985). Longitudinal stability of personality traits: A multitrait-multimethod-multioccasion analysis. *Journal of Personality and Social Psychology, 49,* 1266–1282.

Cross, S., & Markus, H. (1991). Possible selves across the lifespan. *Human Development, 34,* 230–255.

Emmons, R. A. (1996). Striving and feeling: Personal goals and subjective well-being. In P. M. Gollwitzer & J. A. Bargh (Eds.), *The psychology of action: Linking cognition and motivation to behavior* (pp. 313–337). New York: Guilford Press.

Erikson, E. H. (1963). *Childhood and society* (2nd ed.). New York: Norton.

Field, D., & Millsap, R. E. (1991). Personality in advanced old age: Continuity or change? *Journal of Gerontology: Psychological Sciences, 46,* 299–308.

Gould, R. L. (1978). *Transformations: Growth and change in adult life.* New York: Simon & Schuster.

Harlow, R. E., & Cantor, N. (1996). Still participating after all these years: A study of life task participation in later life. *Journal of Personality and Social Psychology, 71,* 1235–1249.

Heckhausen, J., & Schulz, R. (1995). A life-span theory of control. *Psychological Review, 102,* 284–304.

Helson, R., & Roberts, B. W. (1994). Ego development and personality change in adulthood. *Journal of Personality and Social Psychology, 66,* 911–920.

Hooker, K., & Kaus, C. R. (1994). Health-related possible selves in young and middle adulthood. *Psychology and Aging, 9,* 126–133.

Kitayama, S., & Markus, H. R. (1995). Culture and self: Implications for internationalizing psychology. In N. R. Goldberger & J. B. Veroff (Eds.), *The culture and psychology reader* (pp. 366–383). New York: New York University Press.

Labouvie-Vief, G., DeVoe, M., & Bulka, D. (1989). Speaking about feelings: Conceptions of emotion across the life span. *Psychology and Aging, 4,* 425–437.

Lazarus, R. S. (1991). *Emotion and adaptation.* New York: Oxford University Press.

Lazarus, R. S., & Folkman, S. (1984). *Stress, appraisal, and coping.* New York: Springer.

Levinson, D. J., Darrow, C. N., Klein, E. B., Levinson, M. H., & McKee, B. (1978). *The seasons of a man's life.* New York: Knopf.

Loevinger, J. (1976). *Ego development.* San Francisco: Jossey-Bass.

Markus, H., & Nurius, P. (1986). Possible selves. *American Psychologist, 41,* 954–969.

McCrae, R. R., & Costa, P. T. J. (1990). *Personality in adulthood.* New York: Guilford Press.

Newman, L. S., Duff, K. J., & Baumeister, R. F. (1997). A new look at defensive projection: Thought suppression, accessibility, and biased person perception. *Journal of Personality & Social Psychology, 72,* 980–1001.

Smith, L. W., Patterson, T. L., & Grant, I. (1990). Avoidant coping predicts psychological disturbance in the elderly. *Journal of Nervous and Mental Disease, 178,* 525–530.

Vaillant, G. E. (1977). *Adaptation to life.* Boston: Little, Brown.

VanManen, K. J., & Whitbourne, S. K. (1997). Psychosocial development and life experiences in adulthood: A 22-year sequential study. *Psychology and Aging, 12,* 239–246.

Whitbourne, S. K. (1985). The psychological construction of the life span. In J. E. Birren & K. W. Schaie (Eds.), *Handbook of the psychology of aging* (2nd ed., pp. 594–618). New York: Van Nostrand Reinhold.

Whitbourne, S. K. (1996). *The aging individual: Physical and psychological perspectives.* New York: Springer.

Whitbourne, S. K., Zuschlag, M. K., Elliot, L. B., & Waterman, A. S. (1992). Psychosocial development in adulthood: A 22-year sequential study. *Journal of Personality and Social Psychology, 63,* 260–271.

Zirkel, S., & Cantor, N. (1990). Personal construal of life tasks: Those who struggle for independence. *Journal of Personality & Social Psychology, 58,* 172–185.

Susan Krauss Whitbourne

Social Processes and Development

Since the late 1960s, there has been marked progress in the health and life expectancy of Americans. In 1900, the typical newborn in the United States had a life expectancy of 47 years. By contrast, the average newborn in the United States today can expect to live about 75 years. In part because of this increase in longevity, the U.S. population in the future will have a higher percentage of older people than ever before—a demographic change popularly referred to as "the graying of America." Because life expectancy has increased so dramatically, most people today can expect to live at least ten years beyond retirement age. The fastest growing proportion of the aging population is the oldest old (those 80 and older).

At the same time, there have been dramatic changes in the structure of U.S. families. Today's families are strikingly diverse. Only 6% of Americans live in two-parent, single-earner, two-child families. In addition, the birthrate steadily decreased over the course of the twentieth century, which, along with the increase in life expectancy, brought about the changes in American families. Where family structure was once a "pyramid" with very few elders at the top and many younger individuals at the bottom, it has become a "beanpole" structure, with more generations represented in one family, and roughly equivalent numbers of individuals in each generation. The prevalence of two-earner families and the beanpole family structure suggests that grandparents can play a more active role in the lives of their grandchildren.

In the same historical period, the American economy has undergone significant changes. In the second half of the twentieth century the economic base in the United States shifted away from industry and manufacturing toward a more service-based economy built upon increasing levels of technological innovation. This change led to widespread economic restructuring, resulting in significant changes in the amount of education and training needed by workers, the types of jobs available, as well as in corporate culture and attitudes toward workers. For example, people no longer expect to work for a single company throughout their career, the importance of corporate fidelity to workers (and vice versa) having decreased significantly. Additionally, most jobs no longer pay a "family wage" (i.e., enough money for a single-wage earner to support a family).

Research Perspectives on Adulthood and Aging

The demographic, family, and economic transformations described above have altered the fabric of American life and the contexts in which we age. In response to these changes, the field of adulthood and aging has developed in significant ways over the last several decades. With the vast increase in life expectancy over the course of the twentieth century, adulthood and aging are now thought of as continuous and evolving periods that last well into the seventies, eighties, and beyond. Most recently, the study of social processes and

development throughout adulthood has been influenced by theoretical perspectives which recognize continuities and discontinuities in life-course development; the role of the family within and across generations; and the interrelatedness of various societal and familial contexts influencing individual development. We will discuss current conceptual, theoretical, and empirical assertions to provide a broad overview of social processes and development considered crucial for an understanding of adulthood and aging.

Developmental research has evolved from the study of specific age groups (e.g., children, adults, the elderly) to a more inclusive framework which recognizes the importance of incorporating a life-span perspective in the study of individuals over time. Thus, in the last quarter of the twentieth century, it became increasingly clear that understanding older adults requires an examination of individual experiences across the life course. It is now widely accepted that we become more differentiated as we age because individual life experiences accumulate in specific ways to produce increasingly unique adults. Similarly, the importance of understanding the societal and familial contexts in which an individual develops is now acknowledged. This dual conceptualization—which includes individual experiences and the external contexts in which they occur—is especially critical to the study of adult development and aging, and recognizes the importance of diverse experiences (e.g., individual, familial, and societal) on the emergent adult.

The multigenerational longitudinal survey design described by Jackson and Antonucci (1994) illustrates a conceptual framework for encompassing these multiple perspectives. In this design, age provides a guideline for documenting organismic growth and change. The word *period* specifies the influence of historical and cultural influences on the individual. The word *cohort* specifies the broader temporal dimension with respect to institutional and environmental characteristics. Essentially, this design allows researchers to study several generations of the same family, enabling the researcher to understand individual change over time, representative samples of family lineages, and age, period, and cohort effects on individual development.

Others have proposed research designs with similar aims. For example, Schaie and Hertzog (1982) describe the cohort sequential design which combines features of cross-sectional and longitudinal designs by following cross-sectional samples over time. Bengtson is known for his attention to multiple generations within families, and he describes how perceptions of family relationships may differ by generation (e.g., Bengtson, Cutler, Mangen, & Marshall, 1985).

Classic Theories of Adult Development

Major theoretical attempts at explaining the course of development in adulthood are typified in the writings of Erikson (1982), Levinson (1978), Valliant (1977), and Neugarten (1968). The basic postulates of these theories have generated an enormous body of theoretical and empirical literature. Essentially, the aim of these theories has been to elucidate how healthy or optimal adult development occurs. Generally, they have focused on explaining the development of (1) a sense of *well-being*, or the gradual gaining of a sense of wholeness, self-acceptance, and fulfillment; and (2) one's *personality*, or the characteristics, values, attitudes, and concerns which compose the individual's internal experience (e.g., Neugarten, 1968; Valliant, 1977; Gould, 1978; Levinson, 1978; Erikson, 1982). These theorists generally posited that the ability to make commitments to social roles builds on resources of personality developed earlier in life. In turn, personality develops in roles and contributes to further personality growth, which leads to happiness and well-being in later adulthood.

The basic elements of adult life which influence the development of these psychological products comprise the central components of most adult developmental theories. Generally, these elements include (1) pressures and/or demands of the external world (such as cultural norms or societal values) which influence and shape developmental trajectories; (2) internal developmental pressures, such as struggling with a sense of self (e.g., who one is and who one is not); and (3) major developmental tasks, such as negotiating major life transitions (e.g., the transition from adolescent to adult; transitions to marriage or parenting, etc.). Overall, these theories posit that successful negotiation or completion of developmental tasks over the course of adulthood will aid individuals in acquiring a sense of well-being and self-concept.

Erikson (1982), for example, described development as a progression in which later developmental achievements are built on the foundation of successful negotiation of earlier developmental tasks. In Erikson's scheme of adult development, in youth and adolescence individuals develop a sense of identity (a commitment to the self and one's place in the world); in early adulthood they develop a sense of intimacy (closeness and connection with one heterosexual partner); in midlife they develop a sense of generativity (a commitment to the world and future generations); and finally, in later life, individuals come to a sense of integrity, of having lived a worthy life.

Neugarten (1968) proposed the notion of "social clock projects," stemming from her observation that for every cohort there are normative times in the life course for specific life events (such as going to school, going to work, getting married, having children, retiring). Neugarten wrote of the negative developmental consequences of being "off-time" with regard to particular social clock projects. In particular, Neugarten believed that transitions that were anticipated and viewed as being on time in the life course were received with little stress, but that changes that were unexpected or came either too early or too late were highly stressful.

Finally, Levinson (1978), borrowing much from both Erikson and Neugarten, proposed a developmental sequence in which individuals continually build up and then tear down life structures appropriate for different stages of adult life (e.g., building a career, entering retirement). According to Levinson, adults alternate between stable and transitional stages of life. Stress associated with solving developmental tasks characterizes the transitional phases, which occur at predictable ages. For example, in Levinson's theory, between the ages of 22 and 28 years individuals are entering the adult world. Their primary task in this stage is to build their first adult life structure. Then, between the ages of 28 and 33, they enter the "age 30" transition in which the first adult life structure is modified so that it is more appropriate for later stages. Between the ages of 33 and 40 there is a settling down period. It is during that settling down period that the individual "becomes one's own man" and begins to build a second structure more appropriate for the midlife period he or she is now entering. Levinson's original work focused exclusively on men, although his later work has attempted to apply to women's lives the ideas generated from studying men.

Valliant's (1977) work also was consistent with Erikson's theory. Valliant, however, proposed two additional stages—a stage of career consolidation between the stages of intimacy and generativity and a stage related to "keeping the meaning" (i.e., questioning what is important and reorganizing priorities) between generativity and integrity. He argued that identity formation and reformation characterize development across the life span.

The basic ideas and postulates in these theories have been widely influential because they have genuinely illuminated many of the basic struggles and issues of development in American society. Yet, regardless of their impressive qualities, these developmental theories (with the exception of Neugarten) also share one fundamental and problematic assumption—they tacitly assume that all people, regardless of social position or group membership, experience the same basic socialization processes and have equal access to the highest levels of education, career, and overall life quality. For example, Erikson focused on college as a place where individuals explore different identities and discussed intimacy as occurring only in the context of relationships between men and women. Does this mean that individuals who do not attend college will never develop identities or that heterosexuality is a prerequisite for intimacy? The assumption of universal applicability is characteristic of "grand theories" of psychology (which represent most of the "classic" theories across psychological subdisciplines).

This assumption, however, is highly problematic because socialization pressures and processes vary tremendously according to social position and group membership (e.g., race, class, gender, and sexual orientation). With the increasing diversity in the American population (e.g., with respect to ethnicity, race, family life experience, etc.), this is more true today than ever before. Another important problem with the "classic" adult development theories is that they were describing developmental trajectories of cohorts of people living before the demographic, family structure, and economic changes that have taken place in America since the 1960s. It has become increasingly inappropriate to apply these theories to current cohorts of adults in mid- and later life.

More Recent Theories of Adult Social Development

The lack of theories addressing the changes in America has not gone unnoticed. Riley's structural lag theory (Riley, Kahn, & Foner, 1994), for example, proposes that structures and norms in work, family, and other social institutions have failed to adjust to changes in people's lives, and this results in strains on individuals and society. As noted earlier, because life expectancy has increased so dramatically, most people today can expect to live at least ten years beyond retirement age, and the fastest growing proportion of the aging population is the oldest old (those 80 and older). However, there are few productive and meaningful roles available to people in later life because social structures have lagged behind and are designed to meet the needs of a younger population. For example, places of employment do not make room for aging workers who continue to be capable and are not yet ready to retire. According to Riley, broad structural changes are needed because those currently in place are no longer adequate to address the needs of adults today. Changing lives and changing social structures must be considered jointly. Riley calls for an age-integrated society in which role opportunities in education, work, and leisure are open to people of every age. The question which lies before us is how best to provide social structural and role opportunities for these healthy and vibrant elders so that they may maintain high levels of productivity and psychological well-being.

In contrast to the emphasis on broad social structures taken by structural lag theory, family systems theories have emerged in recognition of bidirectional influences that family members have on one another. According to a family systems perspective, each individual in the family has an impact on how each other family member functions. The family functions as a system because a change in the functioning of one member is accompanied by compensatory changes in other family members. Family systems theories emphasize the emergent nature of family processes which cannot be predicted from characteristics of a single member without reference to others. Systems theories are concerned with functional as well as structural aspects of family relationships.

In their convoy model of social relations, Kahn and Antonucci (1980) also provide a life-span perspective on social development. According to the convoy model, individuals go through life surrounded by a "convoy" or personal network of individuals from whom they receive and to whom they give social support. Social support has been shown to be an important resource in adaptation to life circumstances, moderating the effects of stress on individuals, and especially important as a buffer during times of role transitions, particularly if these changes are unwanted or unpredicted. Thus, the influence of personal and situational factors on well-being throughout the life cycle is moderated by convoy properties and the adequacy of the support they provide, contributing to life-span continuity in development.

Evidence suggests that social support affects how people feel about themselves, which in turn affects their overall feelings of integration in the community and affects their ability to cope with specific life circumstances. The support/efficacy model (Antonucci & Jackson, 1987) holds that one important role of social support is to reinforce feelings of self-efficacy in specific situations and over the life course. This concept may be central to an understanding of productive and successful aging and has been supported in current research.

Carstensen's socioemotional selectivity theory (1993) also takes a life-span approach and explains age-related changes in social behavior in terms of emotion conservation and goals for interpersonal interactions. According to this theory, as individuals age they deliberately withdraw from social contact in peripheral relationships, while maintaining or increasing involvement in their relationships with close friends and family. As a result of the growing preference for interactions with close friends and family members, there is a gradual decrease in the *total* number of social interactions over the life course. Socioemotional selectivity theory is able to account for research findings that as individuals age, they report having fewer people in their social networks but report being emotionally close to and satisfied with members who are in their networks. Specifically, Carstensen posits that this selective narrowing of social interactions functions adaptively to maximize gains and minimize risks in social and emotional domains as individuals age.

Socioemotional selectivity theory challenges long-held beliefs that the majority of older people are in despair due to their social isolation. Traditionally, decreases in social interaction with age were assumed to be both unwanted (e.g., as family, peers, and/or friends begin to die and as interactions with grown children gradually decrease, etc.) and detrimental to the well-being of older adults. However, socioemotional selectivity theory suggests that decreases in the number of social relationships as people age mainly result from a deliberate decision to spend one's remaining time with close friends and family.

Myths of Adult Social Development

Although announced with some fanfare, certain stages of adult social development thought to be normative actually occur in the lives of very few people. Thus, the notion that children leaving home (or the "empty nest") is a time of parental sadness, that most people experience a midlife crisis, that women experience regret during menopause, and that old age is a period of isolation and uniform decline are all myths. Research indicates that most people, men and women alike, do not suffer from depression or despair when their last child leaves home. On the contrary, parents generally feel privileged and proud to see their children "successfully launched," and most couples experience a sharp increase in marital satisfaction after their children have gone.

Similarly, the much touted "midlife crisis" is, in fact, fairly rare—the vast majority of individuals negotiate the midlife period with relative ease. Rather, midlife crises tend to occur among individuals who have had early life crises and to represent a continuity in life experience rather than a change. Instead of feeling a sense of loss or regret during menopause, most women report feelings of empowerment and satisfaction. Finally, many studies indicate that most older people are embedded within family and friendship networks that are important but different sources of well-being for the older adult. Thus, the stereotype of older people as despondent due to social isolation and/or abandonment is incorrect. Furthermore, because of advances in medical care, nutrition, and life style, adults enter later life in good physical and mental health with many years of productive and independent functioning, as well as active leisure activities before them.

Changing Family Roles

With historical shifts in women's roles in the workforce, new theories have been proposed to account for multiple roles of both men and women. Generally, these have focused on three main roles of adulthood—spouse, parent, and worker. The number of women in the paid workforce has increased steadily since the early 1900s, but the increase has been especially dramatic since the 1950s. Men have not increased their work in the home in proportion to women's work outside the home. This has led women to be burdened by

a "second shift," in Hochschild's (1989) terms, of having a full set of role responsibilities both in and out of the home. Research has shown that if hours spent in nonpaid productive activities (childcare, homemaking, chores) are included, women work 342 more hours per year than men. Women's extra responsibilities help account for the leisure gap between men and women, with men having more time for leisure activities. In addition to caring for children, many women are now also caring for aging parents. This new family form has led to the labeling of the "sandwich generation" of men and women who are simultaneously caring for both their children and their parents.

Some scholars have argued that multiple role occupancy is beneficial while others argue that conflicts among roles are stressful. Early theorists often focused on the negative effects of multiple roles. Goode (1960) proposed a theory of "role strain," according to which well-being is impaired by the overload and conflict inherent in filling numerous, often incompatible, roles. This hypothesis has also been termed the *scarcity hypothesis* because it assumes that human energy is limited. In direct contrast to the scarcity hypothesis, the "enhancement hypothesis" (Marks, 1977) emphasizes the benefits rather than the costs of multiple role involvements; these include status, privileges, multiple bases for self-esteem, and the ability to trade off undesirable components of roles.

Findings for both women and men tend to show positive relationships between the number of roles a person occupies and various indices of psychological well-being. It seems that multiple role involvements enhance well-being because positive experiences in one role can compensate for negative experiences in another. Research shows, however, that there is one important exception to this—positive experiences in other roles are not able to compensate for stress in the marital role. Perhaps this is because marital partners, particularly men, tend to rely on their spouse to help process troubling events and act as a source of comfort in the face of external stressors. In addition to being a spouse, many men also name their wife as being their best friend.

Developmental Challenges Facing Adults

Despite generally positive aspects of adult social development it should be noted that there are also negative aspects of social development that are represented within the life span, multigenerational perspective. Thus, people who were as youths disconnected from normal social relationships may, indeed, continue in this vein and become disconnected, alienated middle-aged and older adults. People who witness or experience domestic violence, spouse or child abuse, may in turn become the perpetuators of child, spouse, or elder abuse. These are clearly abnormal developments but should be recognized for the important and far-reaching impact they have on the lives of individuals and those around them.

In this consideration of changes in family structure and functioning it is important to recognize that social relationships can have both positive and negative characteristics. Through relationships with family members and friends, adults find companionship, acceptance, support, and affection. On the other hand (and sometimes simultaneously) social relationships can also involve abuse, unsolicited (and bad) advice, invasion of privacy, or overuse/abuse of resources. It has been suggested that negative features of relationships can detract from well-being more than positive features increase well-being. Thus, it is important to be aware that relationships can have harmful as well as supportive aspects.

It is a myth that most older adults are unhealthy and unable to care for themselves. However, some of the individuals in the coming senior cohort will need assistance in a variety of areas—financial, medical, mental health, and simple daily activities. It is commonly acknowledged that our social and health care institutions (e.g., social security, Medicare) will be unable to accommodate the needs of the vast numbers of aging people (who live longer than ever) requiring such assistance. Because of this, much of the responsibility of caring for older generations will rest within the family itself. The increase in life expectancy means that more and more generations of family members are alive at the same time; it is no longer unusual for a child to know his or her great grandparents. Families caring for three generations at once need both social support and practical assistance to manage the multiple demands on their time and emotional energy.

Intergenerational family relationships are important throughout adulthood, but relationships within generations are also important. Divorce is now much more common than it was several decades ago, and marital transitions affect the development of many American adults and their families. Most younger adults who divorce remarry within 5 years. In later life, because women have longer life expectancies than do men, women are more likely to become widowed and are much less likely to remarry than older men who are widowed. Thus, issues surrounding the establishment of intimacy may arise repeatedly throughout adulthood.

Conclusions and Future Directions

In summary, demographic and economic changes have transformed the context of American life during the last several decades. Americans are living longer than ever before and are living in increasingly diverse family structures. Classic theories of adult development such as those of Erikson and Levinson described major de-velopmental tasks to be achieved during adulthood, but these theories do not acknowledge the tremendous variability in development that can be a reflection of different social backgrounds and positions in society. There is increasing recognition that access to societal resources and opportunities differs tremendously according to the social structural positions of different groups. Moreover, access to these opportunities has important consequences for people's adult development.

Recent theories of adult social development have been more sensitive to current demographic transformations in American society, and new research has helped to dispel myths which characterize midlife as a time of crisis and later life as a time of bleakness and isolation. Developmental challenges facing adults today are in part a result of changes in family roles and structure. Optimally, the inclusion of these elements in future theoretical and empirical examinations of adult development will serve to further our understanding of people's social development over the course of their adult lives. Including an analysis of the influences of the social structure on individuals' development should help to make the basic postulates of current major theories of adult development more widely meaningful and applicable than they are at present.

Developmental scholars almost uniformly recognize that a life-span developmental perspective is critical to understanding the aging individual. An individual's childhood and early adult experiences (e.g., as economically privileged or disadvantaged, as a member of the minority or majority culture) shape the emergent adult. Similarly, being part of a loving, caring family or an abusing, rejecting family as a child influences the kind of adult one becomes, and no doubt, the kind of family one forms as an adult. An individual, family, and life-span developmental focus is critical to understanding the influence of multiple social processes shaping experiences in adulthood as the individual is confronted with the changing, and often challenging, personal circumstances associated with aging.

Bibliography

Antonucci, T. C., & Jackson, J. S. (1987). Social support, interpersonal efficacy, and health. In L. L. Carstensen & B. A. Edelstein (Eds.), *Handbook of clinical gerontology* (pp. 291–311). New York: Pergamon.

Bengtson, V. L., Cutler, N. E., Mangen, D. J., & Marshall, V. W. (1985). Generations, cohorts, and relations between age groups. In R. H. Binstock & E. Shanas (Eds.), *Handbook of aging and the social sciences* (2nd ed., pp. 304–338). New York: Van Nostrand Reinhold.

Carstensen, L. L. (1993). Motivation for social contact across the life span: A theory of socioemotional selectivity. In J. E. Jacobs (Ed.), *Nebraska Symposium on Mo-*

tivation (Vol. 40, pp. 209–254). Lincoln, NE: University of Nebraska Press.

Erikson, E. (1982). *The life cycle completed.* New York: Norton.

Goode, R. (1960). A theory of role strain. *American Sociological Review, 25,* 483–496.

Gould, R. L. (1978). *Transformations: Growth and change in adult life.* New York: Simon & Schuster.

Hochschild, A. (1989). *The second shift.* New York: Avon Books.

Jackson, J. S., & Antonucci, T. C. (1994). Survey methodology in life-span human development research. In S. Cohen & H. Reese (Eds.), *Life-span developmental psychology: Methodological contributions.* Hillsdale, NJ: Erlbaum.

Kahn, R., & Antonucci, T. C. (1980). Convoys over the life course: Attachment, roles, and social support. In P. B. Baltes & O. Brim (Eds.), *Life-span development and behavior* (Vol. 3, pp. 253–286). New York: Academic Press.

Levinson, D. J. (1978). *The seasons of a man's life.* New York: Ballantine Books.

Marks, S. R. (1977). Multiple roles and role strain: Some notes on human energy, time and commitment. *American Sociological Review, 42,* 921–936.

Neugarten, B. L. (Ed.). (1968). *Middle age and aging: A reader in social psychology.* Chicago: University of Chicago Press.

Riley, M. W., Kahn, R., & Foner, A. (Eds.). (1994). *Age and structural lag: Need for change in work, family and leisure for people of all ages.* New York: Wiley.

Schaie, K. W., & Hertzog, C. (1982). Longitudinal methods. In B. B. Wolman (Ed.), *Handbook of developmental psychology* (pp. 91–115). Englewood Cliffs, NJ: Prentice Hall.

Valliant, G. (1977). *Adaptation to life.* Boston: Little, Brown.

Toni C. Antonucci, Elizabeth A. Vandewater,
and Jennifer E. Lansford

ADVERTISING. *See* Consumerism of Psychological Services; Consumer Psychology; *and* Media Effects.

AEROSPACE SYSTEMS. Problems of protecting astronauts in the inhospitable environment of space were central in the early manned space flight program. Possibly the most important of these factors were the then unknown and multiple effects of weightlessness in both physiological and psychological terms. How would the human body react to the prolonged weightlessness of space flight? How would human cognitive capabilities be influenced, and how could astronauts perform physical work in a weightless environment? Psychological and physiological concerns included how well astronauts could adapt to moving and working under conditions of zero gravity (g) in the complex and confined environment of a space vehicle. Weightlessness would mean that unless astronauts were restrained they would float away from their work stations. When a lever was moved, weightlessness would cause the astronaut to turn instead of the lever. This particular problem was solved by designing hand and foot restraints so that the lever, not the astronaut, would move.

The bulky space suit that had to be worn to provide life support and protection reduced the ability to move and inhibited fine motor ability, for example, finger movement. Anthropometric models of the human body were developed so that suits could be designed to provide maximal protection with the widest range of movement and comfort possible. Early vehicle and suit dimensions placed restrictions on the size of astronauts. In order to keep the vehicle payload as small as possible, weight restrictions had to be met. A large number of suits were designed, manufactured, and tested. As a result, the suits evolved a great deal over time so that mobility and limb movement were gradually improved (in later space vehicles the suits were designed so that they could be taken off and put on in space). In turn, space vehicles had to be designed to accommodate astronauts wearing space suits. So first the suits were designed, and then the vehicles were designed so that the astronauts could perform their tasks wearing the suits. For example, hand rails and holds had to be placed in appropriate places to enable astronauts to move about in the vehicle. Knobs and levers had to be designed so that they could be correctly manipulated while wearing the space suit. Tools and special fasteners were developed for use in the weightless environment. It had to be considered in designing the vehicle and the tasks to be performed that any task in a weightless environment would take 100% or more time than the same task performed on Earth.

Scientists and engineers had to devise methods of simulating less-than-1-g environments, not an easy task on Earth. Specially modified aircraft flying parabolas could provide 0 g conditions for up to 30 seconds. This was the only technique that could provide true 0 g conditions. The short duration of the 0 g and the preceding and succeeding loads of up to 2 g were problems. However, various control panel designs were evaluated for use in space using the 0 g aircraft.

Underwater experiments were carried out using neutral buoyancy techniques that also simulated 0 g. While not producing true 0 g effects, these techniques permitted astronauts to experience long-term exposure to environments similar to 0 g. An underwater environment was also used to test panel, tool, and hatch designs, provide data on entry and exit requirements, and gain information about the use of restraints when working and sleeping in space. The underwater environment was also a very useful training device for astronauts, particularly in establishing how long particular tasks would take to complete in space. In addition, special mechanical devices that used counterweights and low friction bearings were developed to simulate 0 g. These devices were especially useful in simulating locomotion and lunar landings.

Early in the space program there were concerns about how the restricted sensory environment in space would affect astronauts. The detrimental effects of sensory deprivation on psychological well-being were well known. Research had shown that psychological problems such as performance decrements and even hallucinations could result from the lack of normal sensory stimulation.

Before longer term space missions were undertaken, laboratory research was carried out to study the effects of long-term isolation. Subjects showed decrements in performance and psychological changes, in both individual and group isolation. Boredom was found to be the major cause of complaints in the isolation experiments. However, boredom and sensory deprivation did not turn out to be a problem during actual space flights, at least in part because the astronauts had a constant flow of tasks to perform.

Astronaut selection was clearly very important. Astronauts live in a very hostile environment in a highly complex vehicle containing many different systems. If one or more of the systems were to fail, the astronauts could be stranded in space. Astronauts must be able to determine the nature of a problem with a system and repair it themselves with the help of ground control. Clearly, if serious problems are not corrected at once, this could lead to death for all on board. In addition to being able to withstand the many dangers of flight in space, astronauts had to be able to live in a confined space where they worked and lived with other crew members. The first astronauts were former test pilots and therefore homogeneous in terms of professional background. On later missions, astronauts were selected from science and medicine and obviously had no prior training as test pilots, so new selection issues were raised.

On longer missions, contact with people other than mission control is especially important to diminish any effects of isolation, so arrangements are made for astronauts to talk to family members, friends, and celebrities.

Time perception was thought to be an area of possible trouble, especially on longer missions. Because astronauts circle the Earth several times each day, there was concern that they would lose track of Earth time. Sunrise and sunset, which we use as markers of the time of day, occur on each circuit. Would time distortion lead to performance errors by disorienting astro-

nauts? This didn't happen because of the regular time checks relating to tasks completed. There was also a concern that space flight would disrupt the astronauts' circadian rhythms based on the 24-hour cycle of light and dark, which would cause astronauts to suffer from a kind of jet lag, with accompanying psychological and physiological difficulties, resulting in deteriorating performance. Indeed, astronauts on longer missions have reported fatigue, which is probably a combined effect of disruptions in their circadian rhythms and difficulty sleeping.

Bibliography

Baker, D. (1981). *The history of manned space flight*. New York: Crown. A comprehensive discussion of manned space flight.

Engle, E., & Lott, A. (1979). *Man in flight: Biomedical achievements in aerospace*. Annapolis, MD: Leeward. Covers human flight in general with an emphasis on manned space flight.

Nicogossian, A. E., Huntoon, C. L., & Pool, S. L. (1989). *Space physiology and medicine* (2nd ed.). Philadelphia: Lea & Febiger. Medically and physiologically oriented with interesting chapters on performance in space and astronaut training.

Ryan, C. (1995). *The Pre-astronauts: Manned ballooning on the threshold of space*. Annapolis, MD: Naval Institute Press. Covers the pioneers of high altitude balloon flights that preceded the manned space program.

Glenn F. Wilson

AESTHETICS. Psychological aesthetics began with the 1876 publication of Gustav Theodor Fechner's *Vorschule der Aesthetik* (The elements of aesthetics). Fechner's approach to aesthetics was based on empiricism as opposed to speculation or deduction. He opposed the philosophical approach, which he viewed as coming *von oben* (from above); that is, philosophical aesthetics' attempts to deduce aesthetic principles from abstract generalities. Fechner argued for an inductive approach *von unten* (from below)—that is, gathering basic data empirically and attempting to infer general principles from them.

Fechner proposed three methods that are still the basic ones used in psychological aesthetics. With the method of *choice*, people are asked to indicate their preference for objects either by choosing one over another (paired comparisons) or by indicating their degree of preference for a single object (single stimuli). With the method of *production*, people are asked to create a maximally pleasing object. The method of *use* involves examination of everyday objects, the notion being that the proportions, colors, etc., that are the most pleasing should be most used.

The structuralist psychologists such as Wundt and Külpe saw aesthetics as an important subdivision of psychology. Early work on empirical aesthetics, mainly concerned with simple stimuli such as shapes and colors, is carefully surveyed by Beebe-Center (1932). With the rise of behaviorism, interest in aesthetics essentially collapsed among experimental psychologists. Work on the topic, though usually not of an experimental nature, did continue among Gestalt psychologists and their followers such as Rudolf Arnheim (1954) and Ernst Gombrich (1956).

With the collapse of the behaviorist paradigm in the 1960s came a renewed interest in psychological aesthetics. D. E. Berlyne's *Aesthetics and Psychobiology* in 1971 ushered in the modern era. Berlyne proposed an elegant and general theory of aesthetic preference. The theory is based upon the well-established fact that organisms prefer a moderate level of overall arousal or tension, whereas both high and low levels of arousal are unpleasurable. Any stimulus has arousal potential—the capability to induce arousal. The arousal potential of a stimulus comes from psychophysical properties (properties of the stimulus itself such as loudness, size, or brightness), ecological properties (meaning or signal value), and collative properties (which derive from comparing or collating different parts of a stimulus [e.g., incongruity] or from comparing the stimulus with expectations [e.g., novelty, surprise]). Preference for a stimulus is hypothetically a function of its arousal potential, with stimuli having moderate arousal potential being maximally preferred.

Berlyne and others gathered evidence supportive of his theory. However, for both logical and empirical reasons, the theory has had to be considerably revised (Martindale, 1988). The most important problem with the original theory is that it draws one into an isohedonic trap: Any stimuli that elicit equal amounts of arousal must be equally pleasing. However, this cannot be the case. If we determine how much arousal a beautiful painting elicits, we can produce exactly the same amount of arousal with, say, a mild electric shock. Clearly the painting and the electric shock will not be equally pleasing. An empirical problem is that Berlyne vastly overrated the importance of collative variables. In general, meaning has been found to be a far more important determinant of aesthetic preference than are collative variables.

The current consensus among cognitive psychologists is that natural categories are defined not by lists of features but by prototypes. The prototype may be thought of as a best example or "average" of the category. Given the dominance of meaning in determining aesthetic preference, a good deal of recent work has focused upon the relationship between prototypicality and preference. It has been known for a century that prototypes formed by taking composite photographs of a group of faces are more attractive than faces of individual members of the group. For purely perceptual categories such as colors, there is a strong positive relationship between prototypicality and preference (Martindale, 1988). For more conceptual categories, the relationship is often U-shaped, with preference being shown for both prototypical and exotic or extremely atypical category members.

In 1965, Berlyne—along with Robert Francès, Albert Wellek, and Carmelo Genovese—founded the International Association of Empirical Aesthetics. The biannual congresses of the association have, since that time, provided an international forum for researchers on all aspects of psychological aesthetics as well as allied disciplines such as the psychology of creativity. The meetings of Division 10 (Psychology and the Arts) at the annual American Psychological Association conventions are the main North American forums for presentation of work on these topics. The main general journal in the field is *Empirical Studies of the Arts*. Specialized journals include *Music Perception*, *Psychology of Music*, and *Visual Arts Research*. Allesch (1987) provides a comprehensive bibliography of research on psychological aesthetics; Beebe-Center (1932) reviews early work; reviews of later work may be found in Berlyne (1971), Kreitler and Kreitler (1972), and Martindale (1988).

[*See also* Creativity.]

Bibliography

Allesch, C. G. (1987). *Geschichte der psychologischen Aesthetik: Untersuchungen zur historischen Entwicklung eines psychologischen Verstandnisses aestheticher Phanomene* [A history of the psychology of aesthetics: An examination of the historical development of a psychological understanding of aesthetic phenomena]. Göttingen: C. J. Hogrefe.

Arnheim, R. (1954). *Art and visual perception: A psychology of the creative eye*. Berkeley: University of California Press.

Beebe-Center, J. G. (1932). *The psychology of pleasantness and unpleasantness*. New York: Van Nostrand.

Berlyne, D. E. (1971). *Aesthetics and psychobiology*. New York: Appleton-Century-Crofts.

Fechner, G. T. (1876). *Vorschule der Aesthetik* [The elements of aesthetics]. Leipzig: Breitkopf und Härtel.

Gombrich, E. H. (1956). *Art and illusion*. Princeton, NJ: Princeton University Press.

Kreitler, H., & Kreitler, S. (1972). *Psychology of the arts*. Durham, NC: Duke University Press.

Martindale, C. (1988). Aesthetics, psychobiology, and cognition. In F. Farley & R. Neperud (Eds.), *The foundations of aesthetics, art, and art education* (pp. 7–42). New York: Praeger.

Colin Martindale

AFFECT. Like many words in the vocabulary of psychology, *affect* comes from the common language. In everyday English, *affect* is both transitive verb and noun. The meanings of the verb that are closest to the psychological term are: (1) to act upon or have an effect upon, to impress or influence; and (2) to touch or move emotionally. The meanings of the noun *affect* that are shared with psychology are: (1) that which arouses emotion rather than cognition or thought and the resulting diffuse mental condition; and (2) the fundamental controlling element in an emotional state.

In common usage the term *affect* can describe either a stimulus or a response, i.e., a cause or an effect. In psychology affect is most frequently used as a description of a response—a mental or emotional state. Yet, psychologists generally recognize that affect is causal and that it influences perception, cognition, and behavioral action. Psychology adopted the adjectival form, *affective*, to denote the feeling or mental condition that arises from affect or emotion.

As suggested by the last phrase, many psychologists use the terms *affect* and *emotion* interchangeably. Some psychologists, however, use *affect* to describe any motivational condition, whether an emotion or a drive state like sexual urge, hunger, thirst, the need to eliminate, and physical pain. Note that these drive states are associated with localized sensations, and that except for pain, their activation is cyclical. Furthermore, these drive states are quite specific in regard to activating stimuli and their requirements for satisfaction. For example, the sights and smells of desirable foods stimulate or intensify hunger, and only foods will satisfy the drive state effectively. In contrast, any emotion can be activated by an array of mental and physical stimuli, and it can be regulated—attenuated, amplified—by an equally diverse set of events or processes ranging from the almost purely sensory to the cognitive. Thus drives are quite special-purpose motivational states, whereas emotions are much more general-purpose motivational conditions. Some psychologists believe that emotions are distinguished from drive states by these differing characteristics. Nevertheless, because the term *affect* can encompass all the emotions, and because some emotion is virtually always present in consciousness at least as a low intensity mood state, much of what is said here about affect could be said of emotion as well.

In common language, *affect* describes a diffuse mental state. In psychology, *affect* may refer either to a diffuse mental state or to a specific mental state. The choice between these meanings is a matter of theoretical orientation. Some psychologists believe that an affective state is inherently diffuse and gains specificity only through cognitive evaluation of the event that caused the affect and the cognition that flows from the affective arousal. Others believe that an affective arousal may consist of a specific feeling such as joy or sadness. The disagreement is difficult to settle. Affective states or feelings cannot be measured objectively but only through subjective self-report.

Bibliography

Clark, D. A. (1986). Cognitive-affective interaction: A test of the "specificity" and "generality" hypotheses. *Cognitive Therapy and Research, 10,* 607–623.

Isen, A. (1984). Toward understanding the role of affect in cognition. In R. Wyer & T. Srull (Eds.), *Handbook of social cognition* (Vol. 3, pp. 179–236). Hillsdale, NJ: Erlbaum.

Izard, C. E. (1993). Four systems for emotion activation: Cognitive and noncognitive processes. *Psychological Review, 100,* 68–90.

Panksepp, J. (1996). Affective neuroscience: A paradigm to study the animate circuits for human emotions. In R. D. Kavanagh, B. Zimmerberg, & S. Fein (Eds.), *Emotion: Interdisciplinary perspectives* (pp. 29–60). Mahwah, NJ: Erlbaum.

Weiner, B., & Graham, S. (1989). Understanding the motivational role of affect: Life-span research from an attributional perspective *Cognition and Emotion 3,* 401–419.

Zajonc, R. B. (1984). On the primacy of affect. *American Psychologist, 39,* 117–123.

Carroll Izard

AFFECTIVE DISORDERS. *See* Mood Disorders; *and* Seasonal Affective Disorder.

AFFECTIVE UNIVERSALS reflect the tendency of people in all parts of the world to see stimuli as having an evaluative, potency, and activity aspect. These terms are related to emotions (affect). For example, Schlosberg's (1954) theory of emotion had three dimensions: pleasant-unpleasant, rejection-attention, and arousal (tension-sleep).

Charles E. Osgood, who developed the perspectives on affective universals, argued that humans in primitive environments are frequently placed in situations where a stimulus must be evaluated: Is it good or bad (so I can approach it or avoid it? Is it powerful or weak (had I better run away, or can I relax)? Is it active (e.g., alive, so I'd better act right away) or not active (e.g., dead, so I can forget about it)? These psychological processes have corresponding emotions. Behavior must reflect the universal tendency to see stimuli along these three dimensions. The three dimensions measure the connotative meaning of stimuli (Osgood, 1952).

In other words, stimuli can be pleasant (e.g., love) or unpleasant (e.g., hate), powerful (e.g., threatening stimulus, say a lion attacking an unarmed man) or weak (e.g., an ant approaching an elephant), and active (e.g., moving quickly) or passive (e.g., stationary, slow moving). In many cases potency and activity are highly correlated; this correlation is called dynamism.

Osgood, May, and Miron (1975) published a study that was consistent with the argument that these dimensions of affective meaning are universal. The study was done with 28 samples from the following countries: Afghanistan, Belgium, Costa Rica, Finland, France, Germany, Greece, Hong Kong, Hungary, India (three samples from Calcutta, Delhi, Mysore), Iran, Italy, Japan, Lebanon, Malaysia, Mexico (three samples: Mexico City, Chiapas, Yucatan), the Netherlands, Poland, Sweden, Thailand, Turkey, Yugoslavia, and the United States (Illinois, Hawaii).

The study began by identifying 100 culture-fair nouns. A culture-fair noun is translatable from English to another language, and when another bilingual translates it back into English the original term is retrieved relatively intact. Next, the 100 culture-fair nouns were placed into sentence completion tasks such as "My mother is   ," "The ——— mother." In each sample, 100 high-school males carried out this task. Thus a sample of "qualifiers" was obtained in each of the local dialects.

The 10,000 qualifiers that were obtained (100 people giving 100 qualifiers) in each language were ordered according to their frequency across the 100 participants and the probability of occurrence in the set of qualifiers in that language. A measure of entropy was used to select qualifiers that were minimally similar to one another.

Next, each qualifier was presented to 10 independent informants in each community. The informants were asked to provide antonyms. If two antonyms were available, they were asked to select the most frequent. Thus, scales like good-bad, strong-weak, and active-passive were generated in each culture, in the local language.

In the next step, in each sample, 100 male high school students rated, on a seven-point scale, each of the 100 culture-fair nouns on the 60 most diverse scales consisting of a qualifier and its opposite. For example:

FIRE

GOOD __'__'__'__'__'__'__ BAD

Since 6,000 judgments were required (100 culture-fair nouns on 60 scales) the task was divided randomly.

Each participant rated only 10 nouns on all the scales. In each sample 200 participants rated 10 concepts, half in one order and the other half in the counterbalanced order.

The matrix of correlations of 60 by 60 scales (with 100 observations per scale) was computed. The matrix was factor analyzed by the principal components method, with a Varimax rotation. Thus, in each sample, a different factor analysis was done.

The resulting factor structure in most cases had evaluative, potency, and activity scales. For example, the top three scales of the first factor in English were nice-awful, sweet-sour, and heavenly-hellish. In Afghan Dari they were good-bad, safe-dangerous, and necessary-unnecessary; in Afghan Pashtu, good-bad, attractive-unattractive, tasty-tasteless. In Hong Kong Cantonese they were good-poor, respectable-despicable, and lovable-hateful, and in Turkish the result was beautiful-ugly, sweet-bitter, and pleasant-unpleasant.

The book contains many other analyses. For example, one analysis was based on 10,000 observations per scale—100 nouns rated by 100 participants on each scale. In most analyses the evaluative factor was clear. In some analyses a dynamism factor provided a clearer solution. In some countries some of the factors split into two factors. In a pancultural factor analysis, individual differences were ignored. In each culture the average response of all participants to each noun on each scale was computed. These means across all cultures were submitted to factor analyses.

Osgood et al. (1975) also contains the beginnings of an *Atlas of Affective Meaning*, which consisted of 620 nouns, selected to sample as wide a domain as possible of human activities (e.g., time units, kinship terms, colors, food objects, body parts, work, private matters, moral, religious, technological, communication, philosophical concepts, and relationships and concerns), were judged on four evaluation, potency, and activity scales, in most of the samples.

The data have been stored in the Osgood Laboratory of Psycholinguistics (Oliver Tzeng, director) at the University of Indiana-Purdue in Indianapolis and can be used by scholars interested in testing specific hypotheses. An example of a test of such hypotheses is provided by Triandis (1973), who studied the meaning of *work* across cultures. A detailed probe of the Human Relations Area Files suggested the hypothesis that work will be seen as a burden to be avoided in parts of the world that make rewards obtained from work either too easy (e.g., the postindustrial societies, tropical paradises) or too difficult (e.g., inaccessible mountains, the polar region). On the other hand, work will be seen as a challenge and interesting in environments where rewards are probable but uncertain. Thus, the concept *work* should have a positive profile (high in evaluation) in some of the Osgood samples and a negative profile in other samples. An examination of the reactions of the samples to terms such as *work, problem,* and so on supported the hypothesis.

The availability of local semantic differentials in several languages that are measuring constructs equivalently is an important advantage of this work. Thus it is possible to see how specific concepts are rated across the world. For example, *Punishment* is rated as very bad among the Belgium French and as not bad by the Greeks, Afghani, and Hong Kong samples. An explanation can be that in societies that are "tight" (where people are punished for not following the norms of the society), "punishment" is more acceptable than it is in societies that are tolerant of deviation from norms. The *Atlas* was also used to check if Japan is a "tight" society relative to the United States (Chan, Gelfand, Triandis, & Tzeng, 1996).

Bibliography

Chan, D. K-S., Gelfand, M. J., Triandis, H. C., & Tzeng, O. (1996). Tightness-looseness revisited: Some preliminary analyses in Japan and the United States. *International Journal of Psychology, 31,* 1–12.

Osgood, C. E. (1952). The nature and measurement of meaning. *Psychological Bulletin, 49,* 197–237.

Osgood, C. E., May, W. H., & Miron, M. S. (1975). *Cross-cultural universals of affective meaning.* Urbana, IL: University of Illinois Press.

Schlosberg, H. (1954). Three dimensions of emotion. *Psychological Review, 61,* 81–88.

Triandis, H. C. (1973). Intercultural conceptions of work and nonwork. In M. Dunnette (Ed.), *Work and nonwork in the year 2001* (pp. 29–52). Monterey, CA.: Brooks/Cole.

Harry C. Triandis

AFFILIATION has been defined as "the basic human tendency to seek the company of others" (Taylor, Peplau, & Sears, 1997, p. 463). Aristotle showed an early interest in affiliation when he described humans as social animals over 2,300 years ago. In twentieth-century psychology, concern with affiliation can be traced back to Henry Alexander Murray's classic *Explorations in Personality* (1938). Searching the *Psychinfo* bibliographic database from 1887 to September 1998 yielded 1,954 items containing "affiliation" as either a title or subject word. Of these 1,954 articles, 13 were published before 1950, 52 in the 1950s, 152 in the 1960s, 440 in the 1970s, 650 in the 1980s, and 647 in the 1990s. In perhaps 25 to 30% of these entries affiliation is used in a way that is beyond the scope of this review (e.g., religious affiliation, affiliation in animals).

The fundamental focus in the affiliation literature has been on the correlates, including both the antecedents and the consequences, of the extent of affiliation. There have been two prominent traditions for addressing this question: the personality and the social psychological approaches. Psychologists have speculated on the philosophical issue of why humans affiliate, but that question has not been readily amenable to empirical investigation.

Two Traditions for Studying Affiliation

As an individual difference variable, the need for affiliation has been measured via projective methods (Heyns, Veroff, & Atkinson, 1992), self-report questionnaires (e.g., Mehrabian, 1994), and coding of archival materials (Winter, 1992). In the projective approach, participants write stories to a series of four to six pictures similar to those in the Thematic Appreciation Test (TAT). Interrater reliability in scoring stories is high and test-retest reliabilities have varied from 0.66 over 8 months to 0.30 over 10 years (Heyns et al., 1992). Projective and self-report measures are typically not strongly correlated (cf. Koestner & McClelland, 1992, p. 206).

Heyns et al. (1992, p. 212) see affiliation motivation as a concern "over establishing, maintaining, or restoring a positive affective relationship with another person" or group of persons. From this perspective, the affiliative motive energizes and directs behavior, generates sensitivity to cues related to affiliation, and fosters quickly learning what is necessary to reach affiliation goals. Both Boyatzis (1973) and Koestner and McClelland (1992) have reviewed a number of findings consistent with this framework. For instance, people high in n affiliation spend more time interacting with others, visit their friends more frequently, and communicate more via letters and the phone. They belong to more clubs and act in a friendlier manner. If they are asked to adjust their behavior, they are more likely to comply. When they are alone, high n affiliation people are more likely to wish they were with others.

One might expect women to be higher in n affiliation than men and people high in n affiliation to be popular and socially successful. The data on gender differences in n affiliation appears equivocal (Stewart & Chester, 1982). The expectation regarding popularity has not been supported by the available studies involving a projective measure (Koestner & McClelland, 1992). Indeed, some studies show high n affiliation people to be low in popularity. One possible explanation for this is that the need for affiliation scoring taps both a positive drive to be with others and a fear of rejection. To some extent, high n affiliation scores may reflect a failure to have established fulfilling relationships. Dissatisfaction with this fear of rejection theme in affiliation scores was one factor prompting McAdams (1980) to develop a new thematic scoring system for assessing intimacy motivation that emphasizes the peaceful, hopeful aspects of human affiliation.

McClelland and his coworkers examined n affiliation cross-culturally by coding affiliative themes in post–World War II children's readers. Chile, Israel, and Italy were high in n affiliation, the United States was slightly above the mean, and Iran and Iraq were low. Need for affiliation has been connected to collectivism and other direction. Affiliation-motivated societies tend to have lower levels of spouse abuse, lower rates of death from suicide, and more interpersonal helping (Winter, 1992, pp. 115, 124).

Stanley Schachter's 1959 monograph, *The Psychology of Affiliation*, was a seminal publication for the second, social psychological tradition in affiliation research. Schachter observed that people in isolation often experience anxiety. He wondered if the reverse of this was also true: Do people who are anxious want to affiliate? In Schachter's first experiment, he told subjects, as a cover story, that he was interested in the effects of electric shocks on physiological responses. As part of this ruse, he described the shocks as painful to some participants and as a tickle to others. This was his anxiety manipulation. Then he told subjects there would be a delay. He gave subjects the opportunity to wait alone or with other participants during this delay. Their choice was his measure of affiliation. (Participants were never really shocked.) As expected, 63% of the participants in the high anxiety condition wanted to wait with their peers while only 33% of those in the low anxiety condition selected this option. Schachter did additional studies showing these affiliative tendencies were stronger among first born and only children than among later borns.

In search of a theoretical explanation of affiliation, Schachter considered the possibility of "indirect anxiety reduction," the notion that others help us take our minds off our troubles. Schachter reasoned that if this is true, it shouldn't make any difference with whom we can affiliate. He did an experiment showing a stronger tendency to affiliate when the person with whom participants could wait was another person participating in the experiment rather than a student waiting to see her adviser. He concluded this outcome didn't fit with the indirect anxiety reduction explanation. He found more support for a social comparison explanation of affiliation (i.e., that we affiliate with others, especially similar others, so that we can evaluate ourselves and verify our viewpoints via comparison with them).

Recent Developments

Although the early publications by personality psychologists and by Schachter have framed the way many subsequent investigators have approached affiliation, there have been a variety of advances since the early 1970s (e.g., extensions and applications, new methods, and new theoretical frameworks). Illustrative of an extension and application of Schachter's work, Kulik, Mahler, and Moore (1996) examined whether preoperative affiliation (i.e., having a hospital roommate) reduced anxiety and fostered recovery. The overall effect of affiliation on anxiety wasn't significant, but cardiac patients who waited with a postoperative cardiac roommate were less anxious preoperatively, walked more during their postoperative hospital stay, and went home sooner.

In terms of methodological advances there have been several experience sampling (pager) studies in which participants are beeped as they go about their daily activities and asked questions about whether they are alone or with other people. Although not always labeled as affiliation research, these investigations give rich information about participants' patterns of association. For instance, Larson, Csikszentmihalyi, and Graef (1982) found that adolescents were in the presence of others roughly 75% of the times they were paged and that participants' proclivity toward being with others was substantially related to where they were and what they were doing. Thus, when they were at work or at school, adolescents were more likely to be with others than when they were at home.

In a methodological cum conceptual contribution, Hill (1987) developed an Interpersonal Orientation scale. It assesses four dimensions assumed to underlie affiliation motivation: attention, emotional support, positive stimulation, and social comparison. Factor analysis supported the multidimensional nature of affiliative motivations. Furthermore, when participants were asked to role-play their responses to various situations, the most crucial dimension of affiliative motivation depended on the nature of the situation. For instance, positive stimulation was the affiliative subscale most strongly correlated with desiring affiliation in a party setting.

O'Connor and Rosenblood (1996) have offered a social affiliation model (SAM) for conceptualizing affiliation in everyday life. They believe affiliation operates according to a homeostatic principle. Each person tries to maintain an optimal level of contact, although different people may have different optimal levels. If individuals are in their optimal range, they will endeavor to maintain it. When they deviate from their optimal level as in nonelected solitude (or nonelected social contact), or they reach satiation after long periods, they will seek to reestablish their optimal contact level. O'Connor and Rosenblood differentiate their model from somewhat similar dialectic models. According to SAM, people are likely to maintain an elected level of contact for an extended period; according to dialectic views, people should be constantly oscillating between sociability and solitude rather than staying in one state over time. Using a pager methodology, O'Connor and Rosenblood found support for their SAM predictions.

Differences in the personality and social approaches can be seen (e.g., personality theorists are concerned with enduring tendencies toward close relationships whereas social psychologists focus on states of contact). Yet, O'Connor and Rosenblood's model is a nice way of bringing this review full circle. In focusing on both the process aspects of affiliation and on differences in optimal levels of affiliation, they conclude that their model offers an inclusive formulation that can "link social psychological views of affiliation with views from personality psychology" (p. 521).

Bibliography

Boyatzis, R. (1973). Affiliation motivation. In D. C. McClelland & R. S. Steele (Eds.), *Human motivation: A book of readings* (pp. 252–276). Morristown, NJ: General Learning Press.

Heyns, R. W., Veroff, J., & Atkinson, J. W. (1992). A scoring manual for the affiliation motive. In C. P. Smith, J. W. Atkinson, D. C. McClelland, & J. Veroff (Eds.), *Motivation and personality: Handbook of thematic content analysis* (pp. 211–223). New York: Cambridge University Press.

Hill, C. A. (1987). Affiliation motivation: People who need people . . . but in different ways. *Journal of Personality and Social Psychology, 52*, 1008–1018.

Koestner, R., & McClelland, D. C. (1992). The affiliative motive. In C. P. Smith, J. W. Atkinson, D. C. McClelland, & J. Veroff (Eds.), *Motivation and personality: Handbook of thematic content analysis* (pp. 205–210). New York: Cambridge University Press.

Kulik, J. A., Mahler, H. I. M., & Moore, P. J. (1996). Social comparison and affiliation under threat: Effects on recovery from major surgery. *Journal of Personality and Social Psychology, 71*, 967–979.

Larson, R., Csikszentmihalyi, M., & Graef, R. (1982). Time alone in daily experience: Loneliness or renewal? In L. A. Peplau & D. Perlman (Eds.), *Loneliness: A sourcebook of current theory, research, and therapy* (pp. 40–53). New York: Wiley-Interscience.

McAdams, D. P. (1980). A thematic coding system for the intimacy motive. *Journal of Research in Personality, 14*, 413–432.

Mehrabian, A. (1994). Evidence bearing on the Affiliative Tendency (MAFF) and Sensitivity to Rejection (MSR) scales. *Current Psychology: Developmental, Learning, Personality, Social, 13*, 97–117.

Murray, H. A. (1938). *Explorations in personality.* London: Oxford University Press.

O'Connor, S. C., & Rosenblood, L. K. (1996). Affiliation motivation in everyday experience: A theoretical comparison. *Journal of Personality and Social Psychology, 70*, 513–522.

Schachter, S. (1959). *The psychology of affiliation.* Stanford, CA: Stanford University Press.

Stewart, A. J., & Chester, N. L. (1982). Sex differences in human social motives: Achievement, affiliation, and power. In A. J. Stewart (Ed.), *Motivation and society* (pp. 172–218). San Francisco: Jossey-Bass.

Taylor, S. E., Peplau, L. A., & Sears, D. O. (1997). *Social psychology* (9th ed.). Upper Saddle River, NJ: Prentice Hall.

Winter, D. G. (1992). Content analysis of archival materials, personal documents, and everyday verbal productions. In C. P. Smith, J. W. Atkinson, D. C. McClelland, & J. Veroff (Eds.), *Motivation and personality: Handbook of thematic content analysis* (pp. 110–125). New York: Cambridge University Press.

Daniel Perlman

AFRICA. *See* North Africa; South Africa; *and* Sub-Saharan Africa.

AFRICAN AMERICAN PSYCHOLOGY, also known as Black psychology, is both an old and a new discipline. It is old in the sense that many African American psychologists are reclaiming an ancient African heritage in the origins of psychology; it is new in that these developments are occurring at the end of the twentieth century. Just as traditional psychology traces its philosophical underpinnings to the ancient Greek philosophers, African American psychology finds its roots in the philosophies and religions of ancient Africa. These common origins in ancient philosophical traditions produce similarities between African American psychology and the traditional psychology of Western Europe and America. What is much more striking, however, are their dissimilarities.

African American psychology can, in part, be thought of as a *reaction to* traditional psychology (which could also be appropriately labeled White psychology). This reactive stance is due to the fact that psychology, like all other social science disciplines, developed in the Western world in the context of the strong racial dynamics of colonialism, imperialism, slavery, and other forms of racial exploitation. These dynamics, then, were translated into scientific justifications for the social policies of the day: Africans, Native Americans, Asians and East Asians, and Pacific Islanders were viewed as innately *inferior* to White Europeans and Americans, so that their exploitation was actually viewed as beneficent.

In recent years, however, African American psychology has also developed more proactive approaches to the philosophical and scientific study of human behavior. These proactive approaches may be viewed, in part, as the reclamation of ancient traditional theorems of human "Beingness," but may also be appropriately characterized as affirmative actions to more truthfully examine African American personality, health and mental health, and interpersonal relationships.

A Definition

African American psychology is the body of knowledge that is concerned with the understanding of African American life and culture. African American psychology recognizes the commonality of experiences of African people throughout the world, and therefore may be applied with greater or less precision to African people in Africa, Europe, South America, Central America, the Caribbean, and North America. African American psychology focuses on the mental, physical, psychological, and spiritual nature of humanity. It is the collection of works that has been produced by African psychologists in the United States (African Americans) and throughout the world.

African American psychology is distinguished from White psychology by a number of idealistic dialectics, or ideals in opposition. These ideals may be viewed as European American centered versus those that are African centered, and are values and worldviews that are fundamental to European American versus African ways of life. Table 1 provides a summary of these idealistic dialectics.

Overview

African American psychology is presented from two perspectives: the reaction of African American psychology to racist attacks on Black people by White social science ("deconstruction"), and the more proactive work of African and African American psychologists to better understand Black life, culture, and behavior.

African American Psychology: Deconstruction

Many historians of psychology trace the modern origins of psychology to Wilhelm Wundt's psychological laboratory in Leipzig, Germany, established in 1879 (William James established a psychology laboratory at Harvard University in the same year). It is even more important to place psychology's origins in its geohistorical context.

It was in the late fifteenth century and afterward when European explorers "discovered" and made contact with indigenous peoples in Sub-Saharan Africa, Asia, and the Americas. These early contacts were marked by racial theories that dehumanized the newly "discovered" people. Unfortunately, the ensuing 300 years witnessed unprecedented genocide against indigenous peoples, particularly in the Americas and in Western and Southern Africa, and the enslavement of tens of millions of African men, women, and children. The cultural ethos of Europe and White America during these centuries was one of "Manifest Destiny": the White races had a God-ordained mandate to "civilize" the primitive peoples of the world. That this "civilizing" included murder, rape, and enslavement is one of the longest and saddest chapters in modern human history.

In the scientific community, Charles Darwin's *On the Origin of Species*, published in 1859, had a mammoth influence on the emerging social sciences. Just 10 years later, in 1869, Darwin's cousin, Sir Francis Galton, published what was to be a forerunner of scientific racism, *Hereditary Genius*, which is still in print. Thus, it is no surprise that the founders of Western psychology embraced the ideological underpinnings of scientific racism. As a result, the list of avowedly racist social scientists in the early years of European American psychology read like a "Who's Who" of "great men" in psychology: Herbert Spencer, Edward Thorndike, Lewis Terman, William McDougall, G. Stanley Hall, J. Cattell, Carl Jung, Charles Spearman, and many others. More contemporary proponents of these ideas are Arthur Jensen, J. Philippe Rushton, William Shockley, and Richard Herrnstein.

From the earliest years of African American psychology (in the early twentieth-century United States), Black psychologists challenged or "deconstructed" the theories, methods, and conclusions of the scientific racism that was based on intelligence tests (for a review of this early work, see Robert Guthrie's *Even the Rat Was White* [2nd ed.], New York, 1998). These challenges, by people such as Francis Cecil Sumner, who, in 1920, was the first Black American to receive a Ph.D. degree in psychology, illustrated the flawed conceptions of intelligence, the fact that tests of intelligence were inherently grounded in a particular cultural frame of reference (and therefore were culturally biased against Black people), and the more fundamental problems of a lack of controlled observation in making racial comparisons (that is, middle-class Whites, who had lived lives of advantage, were typically compared against lower class Blacks, who were disadvantaged by segregation and the lack of equal educational opportunities).

Contemporary Black psychologists have challenged racism in psychology as fraudulent, with one leading exponent, Asa Hilliard III, calling the work "nonscience" and "nonsense" (see his summary article in *Cultural Diversity & Mental Health*, 1996, 2, 1–20; also see Halford Fairchild, *Journal of Social Issues*, 1991, 47, 101–115). More specifically, race and IQ arguments are flawed on both conceptual and methodological grounds. The first and most important of the conceptual problems has to do with the definition of the key hypothetical constructs: race and IQ. Race is best viewed as a socially constructed concept with little biological meaning—the overlap in genetic code between

AFRICAN AMERICAN PSYCHOLOGY. Table 1. European American–centered vs. African-centered ideals

European American–Centered Ideals	African-Centered Ideals
Individualism: The focus is on the individual—her or his interpretation of events and reaction to changing situations. The individual is the unit of analysis in research	*Collectivism:* The focus is on the collective or the "tribe." One cannot understand an individual's functioning in a way that is divorced from the group. The unit of analysis in research is the group
Materialism: An emphasis is placed on material reality, and the acquisition of material goods. Material reality is that which is observed, manipulated, and quantified	*Spiritualism:* An emphasis is placed on spiritual reality, and the development of spiritual congruence with the Creator. The most important aspects of human existence are unseen, unobservable, and nonquantifiable
Control of nature: An emphasis is placed on controlling nature—through science and development	*Harmony with nature:* An emphasis is placed on harmonizing with nature, through a spiritual connection with the things of the world
Objective: An emphasis is placed on purporting to be "value free" and "unbiased" in fact finding	*Subjective:* An emphasis is placed on acknowledging values and biases and using these to bring about the liberation of African people

races is very close to 100% (indeed, there is often more genetic variation *within* so-called races than there is *between* races). The concept of IQ, too, is conceptually suspicious. Although viewed as a "fixed capacity" to learn or acquire information, the measure of intelligence (the IQ test) necessarily adapts to the changing ages of children, youth, and adults because their acquisition of information is a constantly changing (and growing) dynamic. Finally, by way of conceptual confusion, is the effort to partial out hereditary from environmental influences, as if these influences operate in isolation. In fact, genes and environment always operate together so that disentangling their unique contributions to intellectual functioning is a methodological impossibility (at least among humans).

One of the founders of modern African American psychology was Robert L. Williams of Washington University in St. Louis, Missouri. His work covered a great deal of ground in deconstructing racist theories of intellectual functioning, personality functioning, and language. In the area of intelligence, Williams developed the Black Intelligence Test of Cultural Homogeneity, which was grounded in African American culture. He was able to demonstrate, not surprisingly, that Blacks outperformed Whites on this test, demonstrating that racial comparisons on culturally based instruments were invalid. His work on personality assessment similarly demonstrated the biases inherent in standardized personality measures and led to his creation of more culturally appropriate alternatives. Finally, Williams

coined the term *Ebonics* (ebony plus phonics) to refer to the linguistic patterns of African Americans, and he showed that perjorative views of "Black English" were unwarranted.

Another very proactive approach within African American psychology was the assistance rendered in the legal challenges to the use of intelligence tests for educational placement. In California, this challenge was concretized in the well-known *Larry P. v. Wilson Riles* class action civil trial that alleged that African American schoolchildren were being disproportionately and inappropriately placed in special education classes on the basis of IQ tests. From 1977 to 1980, members of the Association of Black Psychologists, led by Harold Dent and William Pierce, provided expert testimony and guidance in the trial that culminated in a judgment in favor of the plaintiffs. From then through the end of the twentieth century, the use of IQ tests for the purposes of educational placement was banned in California.

Challenges to the Integrity of Black Pupils. Although the idea of innate racial differences in intellectual capacity may be considered adequately debunked, it is the case that racial differences in scholastic achievement are a fairly enduring finding in the social sciences. African American students, by and large, have lower average academic achievement levels than White students. Much of this racial difference in achievement has been improperly tied to differences in intelligence, as noted above. But more "liberal" approaches to the understanding of racial differences—those that may eschew the odious notion of inherent (and therefore immutable) biological differences—have still reached questionable conclusions that challenged the personal integrity of Black students, their peers, or their families. Thus, William Ryan's idea of "blaming the victim" (New York, 1976) has surfaced in the majority of studies that examined racial differences in academic achievement. This line of research is perhaps best symbolized by the largest study of its kind, *Equality of Educational Opportunity*, by James Coleman and his colleagues (Washington, D.C., 1966).

Theory and research by African American psychologists have critiqued the above line of research on both conceptual and methodological grounds. Many of the criticisms directed toward the race and IQ controversy apply to the study of racial differentials in achievement (as they should; IQ tests are, in the main, tests of scholastic achievement). A growing body of research within African American psychology has demonstrated that academic underachievement of Black youth is tied to many factors: teacher attitudes and the "self-fulfilling prophecy"; an alien curriculum (one that extols the cultures of others at the expense of Black cultures); an inappropriate pedagogical praxis (emphasizing sitting, listening, and competitive testing rather than active learning in a more cooperative framework); and structured inequalities in educational opportunities (Black students, on average, attend schools that are underfunded, overcrowded, and have less experienced teaching and administrative staffs). It could be argued that any individual-level explanation for academic underachievement among Blacks should be held in abeyance until the structural inequities are rectified. In the context of systematic racial inequities in educational opportunity, studies that compare racial groups on scholastic achievement violate the criterion of controlled observation in social science research.

Challenges to the Integrity of Black Families. Perhaps due to the virtual absence of African American scholars in the social sciences until the 1950s (with the exception of a handful of pioneers, mentioned previously), research on African American life and culture was almost entirely performed by "outsiders" to the African American community. As with research on race and IQ and scholastic achievement, research on the family life of African Americans has been fraught with conceptual, methodological, and ideological problems. Thus, a long line of research has pathologized the African American family by pointing to its presumed matriarchal structure, father absence, under- or overstimulation of children, and its either permissive or rigidly authoritarian child-rearing styles. This line of research culminated in the highly influential policy paper on the Black family authored by Daniel Patrick Moynihan (*The Negro Family: The Case For National Action*, Washington, D.C., 1965). Popularly known as the "Moynihan Report," this policy document concluded that the African American family was best viewed as a disorganized "tangle of pathology," with little hope of remediation.

The reaction within African American psychology, again, has been to challenge the conceptual, methodological, and ideological biases that have characterized much of the work that focused on family pathology. In addition, Black researchers began to focus more on the strengths of Black families rather than their weaknesses. Throughout the history of systematic family disruption during the centuries of slavery and *de jure* discrimination, the majority of Black families could be described as "nuclear" (two-parent) and egalitarian. Moreover, it is critically important to understand that any examination of family life must take the broader social, political, and economic contexts into account. Thus, the problems found among Black families are more related to these contextual variables than racial ones. Excellent sources for these views may be found in Robert Hill's *Strengths of the Black Family* (New York, 1972) and the edited volume, *Black Families*, by Harriette Pipes McAdoo (Beverly Hills, CA, 1981).

Far from being disorganized, African American families have been shown to exist in a complex kin network that spans space and time. These extended kin networks, operating in conjunction with the Black church, facilitated upward mobility and provided a buffer against the myriad stresses that confronted African American people in the eras of slavery, segregation, and discrimination. Harriette McAdoo, a leading researcher in this area, has called these effects a "kin-insurance" policy.

Challenges to the Integrity of the Black Personality. The primary sets of literature against which African American psychologists have been forced to react—to debunk or deconstruct—had to do with intelligence, achievement, and family functioning. As if these were not enough, a whole host of additional research foci have imperiled the integrity of Black people on a variety of other, more personal, grounds. Thus, lines of research question the personality functioning of Black people (low self-esteem, external locus of control, low impulse control, inability to delay gratification), their psychological functioning (Blacks are overdiagnosed with schizophrenia), or their culture (Blacks have been alleged to have a culture of poverty, a counterculture, no culture, etc.). In each instance, Black psychologists have reacted with criticisms and reanalyses that demonstrated the general lack of validity of the pathology perspectives for conceptual and methodological reasons similar to those already covered.

Constructive Approaches in African American Psychology

A fair case may be made for the perception that African American psychology is dominated by reactions to White psychology, particularly those applications of White psychology that have falsely portrayed African Americans as inferior or pathological. It may also be the case that were it not for the anti-Black biases of White psychology, African American psychology may never have had its genesis.

Robert Guthrie's *Even the Rat Was White* traces both the history of White psychology's fascination with race differences (with its anti-Black biases) as well as the early history of African American psychology. As noted earlier, African American psychology may be traced to the awarding of the Ph.D. degree to Francis Cecil Sumner in 1920. But African American psychology witnessed its rebirth in 1968 with the founding of the Association of Black Psychologists (ABPsi).

At the 1968 Annual Convention of the American Psychological Association (APA) in San Francisco, a group of about 80 Black psychologists, led by Joseph White (Professor Emeritus, University of California, Irvine), coalesced to discuss their frustrations within the nearly all-White APA. This was just 3 years after the publication of the "Moynihan Report" and 2 years after the publication of the *Coleman Report* (both of which were interpreted as disparaging to African Americans). It was 1 year prior to the publication of Arthur Jensen's hotly debated treatise on race and IQ.

The year 1968 was also the peak of the "Black is Beautiful" and Black Power movements that emanated from the Civil Rights struggle of the late 1950s and early 1960s. This year also marked the assassination of Dr. Martin Luther King and was just 3 years after the assassination of Malcolm X. It is not coincidental, then, that ABPsi would coalesce into an autonomous organizational entity at this crucial juncture in American history. Guided by the principle of self-determination, the founders of ABPsi sought to address the professional needs of its members and to begin the development of new models of human behavior that would benefit the broader Black community. At the time of its founding, eight goals were articulated; these goals continue to guide the mission of the Association today:

1. To enhance the psychological well-being of Black people in America and throughout the world.
2. To promote constructive understanding of Black people through positive approaches to research.
3. To develop an approach to psychology that is consistent with the experience of Black people.
4. To define mental health in consonance with newly established psychological concepts and standards regarding Black people.
5. To develop internal support systems for Black psychologists and students of psychology.
6. To develop policies for local, state, and national decision making which affect the mental health of the Black community.
7. To promote values and a lifestyle that supports the survival and well-being as a race.
8. To support established Black organizations and aid in the development of new independent Black institutions to enhance our psychological, educational, cultural, and economic situation.

Now celebrating over 30 years of existence, ABPsi thrives in the United States and has membership in a dozen countries worldwide. ABPsi is governed by a board of directors consisting of a national president, an immediate past president, a president elect, a secretary, a treasurer, four regional representatives, the chair of the general assembly, and the chair of the student division. Appointed members of the board include the chairpersons of the national convention and publications committees, and historian. The board of directors is advised by the Council of Past Presidents and the Council of Elders. At the close of the twentieth century, ABPsi had approximately 30 chapters in cities around the United States, with chapters in the early formation stages in Canada, Britain, and South Africa. ABPsi publishes *The Journal of Black Psychology* and *Psych Discourse: The Monthly News Journal of the Association of Black Psychologists*. Through these publications and texts authored by its members, the proactive scholarship of African American psychology has focused on racial identity, African-centered models of health and mental health (and related research and intervention strategies), and the reclamation of a spirit-centered epistemology.

Racial Identity Research. The cultural movements that contributed to the founding of the ABPsi were associated with a dramatic transformation in the psychological status of African American people. Once considered "colored" and "Negroes," the African American population discarded internalized negative images and embraced signs and symbols that reflected a positive affirmation of self and group. These signs and symbols included changing the group name from *Negro* to *Black*, the adoption of positive slogans that reflected group pride (*Black is Beautiful!* and *I'm Black and I'm Proud!*), the naming of children in African-centered traditions, and the readoption of pride in the African heritage.

Black psychologists gave considerable attention to these psychological and cultural transformations. Perhaps the most influential theorist in this area, William Cross of Cornell University, developed the idea of " 'Nigrescence': The Psychological Transformation of becoming Black." First published in 1971, Cross's model of the "Negro-to-Black Conversion Experience" posited a series of stages that characterized this transformation. [*See* Ethnic and Racial Identity.] This idea of identity transformation, in recent years, has been seen as a model of personality development, that is, the changes that may occur in a person's identity over the life span. It has also been invoked as a model of social-cultural development, or the collective racial identity of the broader African and African American community. Finally, the idea of racial identity has been shown to be important in psychotherapeutic interventions. In this latter regard, the individual's stage or level of racial identity development is implicated as both a process and outcome of psychotherapy. That is, different approaches must be used for individuals in different stages or states of racial identity; and movement toward self-acceptance is a necessary goal of the therapeutic process.

Models of Health and Mental Health

One of the distinguishing features of African American psychology is the emphasis on the historical origins of contemporary reality. Thus, African people, throughout the world, have been characterized as the product of the *Maafa*: the 400-year history of domination, exploitation, genocide, slavery, and psychological inferiorization that is unprecedented in human history. Some Black psychologists view the effects of these historical and contemporary forces as producing various forms of psychopathology among the majority of Africans (and African Americans), thus normalizing pathology within the African American community. Some have gone so far as to develop a "nosology" that classifies psychic diseases within the African American population. Others, however, are pointing to the unique resilience and strengths produced within African populations as a result of these experiences.

These cultural theories of African American functioning point to the enduring African value structures that have sustained African Americans through hundreds of years of slavery and discrimination. These values include an emphasis on the community, cooperative interdependence and sharing, respect for others, and a strong religious orientation.

Contemporary theorists and practitioners in African American psychology have focused a great deal of attention on redefining the African personality and conceptions of health and mental health. These efforts of redefinition have generally focused on African-centered epistemological frameworks or worldviews. What this means, practically, is that functioning is defined holistically and through the individual's connection within a larger collective. Most important is the emphasis on *Spiritness* (as opposed to mere spirituality) as a crucial aspect of human functioning. Here, human existence is explicitly acknowledged to consist of seen and unseen elements that operate together to produce health or illness. Optimal theory, as articulated by Linda James Myers (*Understanding an Afrocentric World View: Introduction to an Optimal Psychology*, [2nd ed.], Dubuque, IA, 1993), introduces the conjunction of spirit and matter in an African-centered cosmology, and is particularly concerned with this reintegration of spiritual elements into human functioning.

An African-centered orientation, then, is literally translated into a "back to Africa" movement in terms of studying and applying the many generations of knowledge that have accumulated through traditional African medicine practices. These practices focus on understanding and applying traditional pharmacology (emphasizing natural herbs, grasses, barks, and the like), utilizing communal human resources in the healing process, and reintegrating the person into spiritual-material wholeness.

The health and mental health challenges that confront African American psychology today include the continuing need to understand and cope with the racial stresses that result from the daily slights and indignities that produce feelings of marginality and threaten self-esteem; and grappling with the "excess deaths" that confront the African American community through human immunodeficiency virus/acquired immunodeficiency syndrome (HIV/AIDS), violence, hypertension, heart disease, cancers, and other behaviorally mediated life-threatening diseases.

Assessment

As noted earlier, much of African American psychology has been concerned with reacting to and correcting racist theory and research. Much of this negative research relied on tests and measures (such as standardized IQ tests) that were alien to African American culture and experience. In the past 30 years, however, a plethora of tests and measures have been developed that have been more culturally congruent with African American cultural experiences. These assessment devices focus on racial identity, informal help giving and receiving (as alternatives to formal psychotherapy), giftedness, spirituality, perceived racial stress and coping styles, cultural mistrust, acculturation, African worldview, parenting attitudes and behaviors, values, African self-consciousness, and family structure and relations (among others). Indeed, the work in this area of assessment has been so extensive that it proved worthy of two edited volumes by Reginald Jones (*Handbook of Tests and Measurements for Black Populations*, Hampton, VA, 1996).

In the latter third of the twentieth century, a plethora of tests and measures have been developed that are grounded within an African-centered point of view. These include Joseph Baldwin's African Self Consciousness Scale, Tonya Armstrong's Measure of Spirituality, and a variety of measures that focus on self-esteem, alienation, life satisfaction, attitudes toward marriage and the family, and personality functioning.

Applications

In addition to the health-related foci and assessment described above, African American psychologists apply their approach to the solution of a variety of problems that are unique to the African American community. These include the problems of psychoeducational assessment; gender, sexuality and male-female relationships; and broader issues attendant on the continuing oppression and exploitation of African people around the world.

A very promising line of research is that stimulated by Harold Dent and his colleagues, known as "dynamic assessment." Here, instead of the static measuring of what children know (as in standardized IQ tests or academic achievement tests), dynamic assessment focuses on the actual learning styles of students. Thus, students are tested, taught, and retested, in order to discern the strengths and weaknesses in their styles of learning.

Similarly, contemporary African American psychologists have eschewed the pathology-laden treatment of Black women and men and have developed more transformative models of female and male functioning and male-female relationships. Leading these revisionist approaches are Na'im Akbar (*Visions for Black Men*, Tallahassee, FL, 1991) and Gail Wyatt (*Stolen Women: Reclaiming Our Sexuality, Taking Back Our Lives*, New York, 1997).

Notable advances in this vein are clinical treatment models for African American clientele. Anna Mitchell Jackson's model emphasizes a community of helping professionals working together in a more holistic approach that provides a "service chain" through multiple systems. This model, then, views treatment as inextricably tied to family functioning, functioning within the Black community, embracing Black cultural values and practices, and embedded within a particular political and economic context.

Fred Phillips's idea of Ntu psychotherapy (Ntu is Bantu for "spirit energy") is also noteworthy. Here, Ntu is reflective of African philosophical traditions that emphasize the linkages between mind and body, object and spirit, and client and healer. The task of therapy is to reconnect a person's mental life to his or her physical, emotional, and spiritual beings. The therapist-healer is viewed as necessarily connected to the client in helping in this transformative process. In addition, the Ntu model focuses on the seven principles of the Nguzo Saba, as developed by Maulana Karenga in connection with the observation of Kwanzaa (the seven-day nonsectarian holiday celebrated by Africans and African Americans—and others—around the world between

Christmas and New Year). These principles are Nia (purpose), Imani (faith), Ujima (collective work and responsibility), Umoja (unity), Kujichagulia (self-determination), Kuumba (creativity), and Ujamaa (cooperative economics).

Finally, through the work of ABPsi, African American psychology is becoming more globally self-conscious in reaching out to African psychologists in Europe, the Caribbean, Central and South America, and throughout the African continent. In this regard, it is explicitly recognized that many parallels exist in the histories and contemporary life circumstances of African people throughout the world. Through it all, the mission of African American psychology remains the illumination and liberation of the African spirit around the world. And in this, it is recognized that one cannot illuminate and liberate the African spirit without also illuminating and liberating the spirit of all of humanity.

[*See also* Minority Psychology.]

Bibliography

Ani, M. (1994). *Yurugu: An African-centered critique of European cultural thought and behavior*. Trenton, NJ: Africa World Press. This theoretical text exposes the historical and contemporary establishment of the ideology of White supremacy.

Bronstein, P., & Kat, N. (Eds.). (1988). *Teaching the psychology of people*. Washington, DC: American Psychological Association. This volume provides guidelines and resources for teachers who wish to integrate cultural, sexual, and gender diversity into the psychology curriculum. Included are several chapters pertinent to African American psychology.

Burlew, A. K. H., Banks, W. C., McAdoo, H. P., & Azibo, D. A. (Eds.). (1992). *African American psychology: Theory, research and practice*. Newbury Park, CA: Sage. This volume examines African American psychology in terms of its theoretical, methodological, and practice distinctions; family life; children; cognitive and measurement issues; and praxis (with an emphasis on the areas of personality, clinical, social, and health psychology). It includes a chapter on the celebrated *Larry P* case.

Cross, W. E. (1971). The Negro-to-Black conversion experience: Toward a psychology of Black liberation. *Black World, 20*, 13–37.

Grills, C., & Rowe, D. (1998). African traditional medicine: Implications for African-centered approaches to healing in R. L. Jones (Ed.), *African American mental health: Theory, research and intervention* (pp. 71–100). Hampton, VA: Cobb & Henry. Provides a comprehensive overview to traditional healing methods in Africa, the Caribbean, and the Americas. Reviews current knowledge and future directions.

Helms, J. E. (Ed.). (1990). *Black and White racial identity: Theory, research and practice*. New York: Greenwood Press. This text, edited by one of the leading researchers in racial identity, examines the theory and measurement of Black and White racial identity, their correlates, and practical applications. The appendices provide the Black Racial Identity Attitude Scale and the White Racial Identity Attitude Scale.

Hilliard, A. G., III (Ed.). (1991). *Testing African-American students*. Morristown, NJ: Aaron Press. This edited volume is a special reissue of the *Negro Educational Review* (Volume 38, Numbers 2–3, April-July 1987). It includes articles that focus on psychological assessment from an African frame of reference, the abuses of standardized testing on African Americans, a critique of IQ tests, and directions for "revolutions" in professional practice.

Jones, R. L. (Ed.). (1988). *Psychoeducational assessment of minority group children: A casebook*. Berkeley, CA: Cobb & Henry. This volume presents a variety of assessment strategies for minority children. The foci include dynamic assessment, adaptive behavior assessment, behavioral assessment, bilingual assessment, group methods, and other methods.

Jones, R. L. (Ed.). (1991). *Black psychology* (3rd ed.). Berkeley, CA: Cobb & Henry. After an overview, this text examines the perspectives of Black psychology, the reactive approaches (known as "deconstruction"), the proactive approaches (known as "reconstruction"), and a variety of applications (fields of inquiry, counseling and psychotherapy, racism, and research).

Jones, R. L. (Ed.). (1998). *African-American identity development*. Hampton, VA: Cobb & Henry. This edited volume is divided into three parts: (1) stage models and perspectives; (2) Symposium on Cross's Stage Model; and (3) other perspectives and models. Taken together, the text provides a comprehensive review of the research and theory in African American identity development. Contributions from the major theorists and empiricists in this area are included.

Jones, R. L. (Ed.). (1998). *African-American mental health: Theory, research and intervention*. Hampton, VA: Cobb & Henry. This edited volume provides a state-of-the-art collection of articles on African American psychology. It is organized in six parts: perspectives and paradigms, spirituality and mental health, self-concept, stress and hypertension, therapeutic interventions, and symposia on psychotherapeutic approaches (which focus on psychoanalytic psychotherapy and "Rootwork and Voodoo").

Kambon, K .K. K. (1998). *African/Black psychology in the American context: An African-centered approach*. Tallahassee, FL: Nubian Nation. This text, from one of the most prolific and original thinkers in African American psychology, provides a comprehensive overview of the field. It covers historical and paradigmatic foundations and contemporary expressions in the field that include personality functioning, mental ability, African-centered vs. non-African-centered models, and training issues.

Wilcox, R. C. (Ed.). (1971). *The psychological consequences of being a Black American: A collection of research by Black psychologists*. New York: Wiley. This edited text presents 49 of the earliest articles in the modern history of African American psychology. The material is presented in seven parts: (1) Cultural disadvantage, minority groups, and exceptional children; (2) Racial integration: Academic and social implications; (3) Intelligence and achievement; (4) Higher education; (5) Educational psychology; (6) Attitude, personality, and emotional characteristics; and (7) Psychology as a study and as a profession.

Halford H. Fairchild

AGEISM. The term *ageism* was introduced in 1968 by the psychiatrist Robert Butler (a former director of the National Council On Aging) to describe a pervasive combination of disparagement and discrimination directed against the elderly in our society. While technically the term could be used to refer to a bias against *any* group primarily on the basis of their chronological age, it has become more commonly used to describe negative stereotypes concerning the character and capabilities of the elderly, as well as discrimination against older persons in the workplace and in other social institutions.

Like race and gender, the age of an individual can exert a significant influence on the attributions made concerning that person's abilities and dispositions. In fact, researchers have found that attributions made about another person are affected as much by age-related stereotypes as by gender-related ones. Psychologists and gerontologists have drawn explicit analogies between ageism and other "isms" extensively researched by social scientists (i.e., racism and sexism), especially in terms of the formation of negative stereotypes and the potentially malignant consequences of age discrimination.

Negative Attributions and Stereotypes

Age-related stereotypes may be as flagrant as the belief that most of the elderly are senile and incompetent to make decisions concerning their own affairs, or as subtle as the idea that ill health and infirmity are natural consequences of aging. When individuals have little contact with older persons, or are relatively uninformed about the actual processes of aging, it is easier for exaggerations and misconceptions such as these to become established.

Stereotypes of "typical" elderly persons have been found to include a variety of negative attributions, at various times ascribing the following traits to the aged: slow, forgetful, withdrawn, rigid, unhappy, tired, poorly coordinated, accident-prone, unproductive, asexual, and incompetent. A national survey commissioned by the National Council On Aging in the mid-1970s found that the majority of Americans identified only two positive traits consistently associated with persons over 65 years of age (warm and wise) while at the same time associating many negative traits with the older age group: incapable, inactive, not being alert, not open-minded, not bright, and others (Harris & Associates, 1975).

These stereotypes have routinely been reinforced in popular media by portrayals of older persons in weak, unproductive, and sometimes unpleasant roles. For example, content analysis of the portrayals of older adults in television programs has found that elderly characters are frequently portrayed as irritable, dependent, and in ill health; portrayals of older female characters are even more negative and stereotypical than those of older male characters. Researchers have also examined depictions of the elderly in media as diverse as children's magazines and books, cartoons, popular literature, greeting cards, magazine advertisements, newspapers, movies, and music. In most of these reviews, negative and stereotyped depictions of the elderly were found to be more prevalent than positive portrayals.

As with other prejudices, negative attitudes regarding the elderly can emerge in subtler ways than in the direct attribution or endorsement of negative traits. The tendency to associate negative traits with older persons may over time become an automatic and even unconscious part of processing information about them, and thus difficult to control. As another example, researchers studying the processes of causal attribution have found that perceivers may tend to *explain* the task performances of young persons in fundamentally different ways than similar performances by older persons. Poor performances or failures by older persons tend to be attributed to internal causes such as a lack of ability, while poor performances by younger persons may be more likely to be explained in terms of external factors such as chance or bad luck. Biases such as these may occur even among observers who would not consciously admit to endorsing stereotyped beliefs about the elderly.

On the other hand, some researchers have suggested that age-related stereotypes might not be as universal or as uniformly negative as was once assumed. For example, a few studies have reported that children and adolescents spontaneously describe older persons using a mixture of both negative and positive characteristics. Children appear to perceive older adults as physically incapable, but as possessing some positive personality traits. As a methodological caveat, Kogan (1979) and others have suggested that evidence for ageist stereotypes is more likely to be found in certain types of research designs, as when individuals are directed to make explicit comparisons between older persons and some other, younger group.

Part of the danger in permitting negative attitudes toward the elderly to proliferate is that they are likely to have consequences for the abilities, self-esteem, and even the mental health of those persons (Levy 1996). If older persons are consistently labeled as tiresome and unattractive by others, they may come to believe that the stereotypes are accurate depictions of themselves. In a kind of self-fulfilling prophecy, they may as a consequence tend to withdraw from activities and social interactions. These negative attitudes may even have more drastic health consequences; the symptoms of potentially treatable illnesses may be disregarded in the elderly because they are dismissed as the "typical" complaints of the aged.

Discrimination

It has been suggested that negative stereotypes may provide a convenient justification for continuing indifference to the problems of the elderly. Characterizing the aged as unemployable, unadaptable, and "inevitably" unhealthy may help some to rationalize discriminatory practices in employment, social support, and health care. Blaming the victims of age discrimination for their unfair treatment may allow some individuals to maintain their beliefs in an equitable social system, or a "just world."

Many employers still endorse negative stereotypes about the reliability and productivity of older workers. Although the federal Age Discrimination in Employment Act (ADEA) prohibits arbitrary age discrimination by most employers, and many states have also passed laws against age discrimination, older workers continue to believe that they are victims of job discrimination based solely on their chronological age and not their ability to perform essential functions of the job. At least 20% of the job discrimination complaints addressed to the Equal Employment Opportunity Commission (EEOC) are age related: that is, they are instances where older workers felt that they had been unfairly denied jobs, passed over for promotions, been fired or subjected to "involuntary" retirement simply because of their age. It is likely that many older employees have been unfairly eliminated from the labor force by the conventional "wisdom" that job performance declines with age, and the misconception that older employees are not flexible enough to cope with changing work environments and technological innovations. In fact, with the exception of a few jobs that require great physical strength or rapid reaction times, industrial-organizational psychologists find that there is no consistent relationship between chronological age and job performance.

Even more disturbing has been the realization that the quality of health care received by individuals may depend in part upon their age. Many studies have found that health care professionals have more negative attitudes toward their elderly patients. These attitudes can be reflected—perhaps unintentionally—in a failure of practitioners to provide an equivalent quality of care for their oldest patients, or to assign a lower priority to treatment of the elderly. Surveys of students in medical schools and social work programs have uncovered a preference for avoiding work with elderly clients, and reviews of the advertisements for prescription drugs in medical and gerontological journals find that the writers of the ads assume older patients will be more "difficult," in the sense that they are more likely to be insecure, hypochondriacal, apathetic, reclusive, and moody (Smith, 1975).

Ageism may do real harm if, for example, a physician fails to aggressively treat a condition such as heart disease or breast cancer in their oldest patients because they are thought to have their "best years" behind them. Similarly, a social worker or case worker who imagines that symptoms of anxiety and depression are "normal" in the elderly may not report the signs of a potentially treatable mental illness.

Modern Ageism

Although there are cultures (such as some Asian societies) which venerate their older members and accord them greater status, ageism appears to be a long-standing problem in Western societies. For example, while youthfulness is considered to be an attractive trait in most cultures, in the United States the pursuit of a youthful appearance (and the abhorrence of physical aging) has been elevated to an extreme degree in the marketing of cosmetics, drugs, clothing, and even surgery intended to disguise the physical signs of aging. It appears that older women experience more societal pressure to obscure the outward signs of aging than do older men.

In recent years, however, there has been some indication that these views may have started to change. Although negative attitudes may still predominate, Americans are more likely to acknowledge the possibility of "successful aging," in which the vigor and health of the individual are preserved into the later years of life.

These changes may be due in part to the "graying" of the U.S. citizenry, as the proportion of older adults in the population increases significantly. Because of the aging cohort of "baby-boomers" born between 1946 and the early 1960s, and the increased longevity provided by advances in health care, we may expect that by the turn of the century almost 35 million Americans will be over 65 years old; by the year 2050 one in five persons in the United States may be over 65 (U.S. Bureau of the Census, 1995). The increasing representation of older individuals in the population may provide a concomitant increase in the numbers of visible, active, and healthy older role models.

While there does seem to have been some progress in reducing the impact of ageism in recent years (primarily through education and legislation), some gerontologists have become concerned about the emergence of a more insidious "new ageism" (Kalish, 1979). It has been argued that when well-meaning partisans of service agencies for the aged attempt to convince others of the need for their programs, they may do so by focusing our attention on the least able and the most unhealthy of the elderly. Ironically, this may contribute to the stereotype of the "helpless" older person who is a drain on societal resources. In the view of those who are concerned with this more subtle ageism, while developing social agencies and institutionalized support programs for the support of the elderly is laudable, it may be a mixed blessing if by doing so we contribute to the stereotype that all older persons are inevitably passively dependent upon those services.

"New ageism" may in some respects be analogous to "modern" racism, a less obvious and thus more "politically correct" expression of prejudices by those who are concerned about managing the impressions that they give to others. Modern racism, for example, may be more likely to be observed in an individual's attitudes on issues such as affirmative action and social welfare policies than in overtly hostile statements concerning minorities. In a similar fashion, individuals who are ostensibly supportive of the elderly may still indirectly express ageist attitudes, such as concerns about the social cost of supporting that age group.

Ultimately, psychologists studying ageism have the same hope as those studying other biases such as racism and sexism: to dispel inaccurate stereotypes and diminish the unfair treatment of these groups in society.

[See also Adulthood and Aging; and Discrimination.]

Bibliography

Aaronson, B. W. (1966). Personality stereotypes of aging. *Journal of Gerontology, 21,* 458–462.

Ansello, E. F. (1977). Age and ageism in children's first literature. *Educational Gerontology, 2,* 255–274.

Avolio, B. J., Waldman, D. A., & McDaniel, M. A. (1990). Age and work performance in nonmanagerial jobs: The effects of experience and occupational type. *Academy of Management Journal, 33,* 407–422.

Barnes-Farrell, J. L., & Piotrowski, M. J. (1989). Workers' perceptions of discrepancies between chronological age and personal age: You're only as old as you feel. *Psychology and Aging, 4,* 376–377.

Bennett, R., & Eckman, J. (1973). Attitudes toward aging: A critical examination of recent literature and implications for future research. In C. Eisdorfer & M. P. Lawton (Eds.), *The psychology of adult development and aging.* Washington, DC: American Psychological Association.

Butler, R. N. (1969). Age-ism: Another form of bigotry. *Gerontologist, 9,* 243–246.

Charles, D. C. (1977). Literary old age: A browse through history. *Educational Gerontology, 2,* 237–254.

Cowgill, D. O., & Holmes, L. D. (1972). *Aging and modernization.* New York: Appleton-Century-Crofts.

Greenberg, B. S., Korzenny, F., & Atkin, C. K. (1979). The portrayal of the aging: Trends on current television. *Research on Aging, 1,* 319–334.

Harris, L., & Associates (1975). *The myth and reality of aging in America.* Washington, DC: National Council on Aging.

Kalish, R. A. (1979). The new ageism and the failure models: A polemic. *Gerontologist, 19,* 85–89.

Kalish, R. A. (1982). *Late adulthood: Perspectives on human development* Monterey, CA: Brooks-Cole.

Kogan, N. (1979). Beliefs, attitudes, and stereotypes about old people: A new look at some old issues. *Research on Aging, 1,* 11–36.

Lachman, M. E., & McArthur, L. Z. (1986). Adulthood age differences in causal attributions for cognitive, physical, and social performance. *Psychology & Aging, 1,* 127–132.

Levin, J., & Levin, W. C. (1980). *Ageism: Prejudice and discrimination against the elderly.* Belmont, CA: Wadsworth.

Levy, B. (1996). Improving memory in old-age through implicit self-stereotyping. *Journal of Personality and Social Psychology, 71,* 1092–1107.

McTavish, D. G. (1971). Perceptions of old people: A review of research methodologies and findings. *Gerontologist, 11,* 90–102.

Nuessel, F. (1992). *The image of older adults in the media: An annotated bibliography.* Westport, CT: Greenwood Press.

Palmore, E. B. (1990). *Ageism: Negative and positive.* New York: Springer.

Perdue, C. W., & Gurtman, M. B. (1990). Evidence for the automaticity of ageism. *Journal of Experimental Social Psychology, 26,* 199–216.

U.S. Bureau of the Census. (1995). *Statistical abstract of the United States, 1995* (115th ed.). Washington, DC: U.S. Government Printing Office.

Ward, R. B. (1977). The impact of subjective age and stigma on older persons. *Journal of Gerontology, 32,* 227–232.

Charles W. Perdue

AGENCY. [*To survey the concept of agency, this entry comprises two articles. The first article presents an overview of the concept of human agency and its relationship to the idea of free will and determinism. The second article focuses on agency and control theory.*]

An Overview

The word *agency* has Latin roots meaning "to act," and it therefore refers in some way to doing something, or having the power and capability of producing an effect. But the particular way in which this action is understood and analyzed differs across disciplines. In the realm of ethics, for example, the concern is over how an agent (a person having agency) will act, whether virtuously or immorally. In the legal profession, on the other hand, an agent is someone who is entrusted with the interests of others, who acts instrumentally to carry out the intentions of a client. There are two aspects to agency: (1) the framing of an intention, as in freely deciding to behave morally or seeking a just outcome from the court, and (2) carrying out the intention as planned. It is one thing to decide to behave morally and quite another to actually do so. It is one thing to seek justice and quite another to arrange the legal steps that will accomplish this end. In psychology, the concept of agency takes us into even more fundamental terminological issues having to do with what causes actions in human behavior. What do we mean by an agent acting or behaving? What causes agency?

We usually begin a discussion of causation with Aristotle (384–332 BCE). The Greek word he used for cause was *aitiá*, which means assigning the responsibility for why something exists or takes place. Aristotle showed how philosophers before him had been assigning four different kinds of responsibility in their explanations. There was the *material cause* or substance of which things are made. We make the cushions on a pool table of rubber and not straw, for we want the balls to bank off them in a lively manner. There is the *efficient cause*, or the impetus that moves things along, as when one rolling pool ball collides with another, causing the latter to bounce off a cushion or possibly roll into a pocket. There is the *formal cause*, which is to be seen in the shape of the pool table, a rectangular layout with six pockets and so forth. The rules of the game which position the balls and stipulate in what order they are to be struck are also manifestations of formal causation, conveying the very essence of what it means to "play" pool. Finally, there is the *final cause*, which involves "that (reason, goal, end) for the sake of which" the game is being played in the first place, such as to compete, prove a skill, socialize, or "just for the fun of it."

Using these four causal meanings as abstract predicates we can explain literally everything in our experience. Aristotle believed that the more types of causes we bring to bear in our explanation of anything the richer our account. Thus, he used all four causes to explain natural events, giving special emphasis to the final cause. He believed that nature operated purposefully (Aristotle, 1952, pp. 276–277), so that leaves on trees existed "for the sake of" shading the fruit on their limbs. A purpose is like a goal or an intended "end" that is being carried out. The Greek word for end is *telos*, so any explanation using final causation to explain things is called a *teleology* (the study of "ends"). Teleologies were widely used in ancient and medieval science, but in the sixteenth and seventeenth centuries (for reasons that need not concern us here) they were rejected as inappropriate in the rise of Newtonian "natural" science. When psychology was introduced as an academic discipline in the closing decades of the nineteenth century, it followed Newtonian precepts—which meant it avoided final causation in the explanation of human behavior.

This Newtonian limitation has led to many problems in psychological theorizing, especially when we consider agency. As envisioned by Aristotle and many scholars over the centuries since his time, each of the causes brings about a distinctive form of determinism. The word *determine* takes its roots from the Latin, meaning to set a limit on something. Continuing with the game of pool as our example, we can say that a material-cause determinism can be seen in the fact that the weight of a marble pool ball limits what takes place on the table when compared to one made of rubber, which can roll and bounce in every direction—including off the table. Efficient-cause determinism is to be seen in the fact that the thrust of a cue stick impels the ball to roll in strictly one direction, thereby limiting the many other directions that it might have taken on the pool table. Formal-cause determinism is reflected in the fact that the rules of the game limit what a player must do to play the game, forcing uniformity on what takes place. And a final-cause determinism is to be found in the fact that the person playing the game has purposely decided to do so, and is therefore carrying out an intentional action, limiting the many other things that he or she might be doing (like seeing a movie, going biking, and so forth).

And it is right here that the problem of agency in psychological explanation enters. If, as good Newtonians, we presume that it is improper to explain behavior using final causes then we are unable to assign such characteristics as choice, purpose, and intention to the acting person. All such concepts are based on final causation. What would we substitute for these teleological conceptions? We would probably follow the same course psychology has followed by going to material and especially efficient causation. Biological explanations are material-causal in nature, so we might say the person plays pool due to a drive of some sort, a biological need to compete with others based on a "survival of the fittest" remnant of organic evolution. The efficient-cause determinism might now be brought in to suggest that the selection of pool as a way to manifest the drive to compete is due to social conditioning, modeled or shaped by others and then carried out by the person in a way that is not truly intentional, but rather is mechanistic or automatic.

This somewhat oversimplified example is the predominant view of agency in psychology today. It has been furthered by the conviction of many psychologists that they have proven empirically that people are manipulated organisms. In an experiment the so-called independent variable (IV) is what we measure and manipulate in some way. Let us say that we are assessing something we call ego strength. Using a test which supposedly measures ego strength, we identify two groups of people, one high in ego strength and one low. We then have both groups take a challenging task of some sort, like assembling mechanical parts. We measure the speed of their assembling in terms of seconds. This measurement is our dependent variable (DV). We find that, as predicted in our experimental hypothesis, the high ego-strength participants do such assembly work faster than low ego-strength participants. Since we have made certain that nothing else in our experimental groups could account for this difference we draw certain conclusions.

Actually, two conclusions are likely to be drawn, one formal and one informal. The formal conclusion is that the experimental hypothesis has been supported—high ego strength goes along with good performance. But an informal decision that is invariably drawn is that, since we were able to use our IV to align two groups and predict beforehand what the outcome would be on the DV performance, the participants were themselves mechanically manipulated and not acting freely as agents. Because the nature of an experimental design has the IV and DV aligned in a way suggesting efficient causality (we do, after all, manipulate our two groups to contrast in a certain way), a mechanistic theorist is likely to believe that he or she is actually "seeing" behavior under causation without a final-cause determination being involved.

In contrast, the agential theorist would argue that in taking the test of ego strength at the outset, the participants are giving us their self-assessments, or, as we might call it, the attitude "for the sake of which" they expect to behave—confidently or with uncertainty. This interpretation of ego strength would, of course, draw on a final-cause determination. As agents, the participants in the experiment were predicating their expected performance from the outset. And they achieved their intended "ends," thereby fulfilling the experimental hypothesis. There is ample evidence that people in experiments contribute significantly to what takes place (Brewer, 1974). Some psychologists maintain that there is comparable evidence supporting agency in human behavior. There are also psychologists who rely on mechanism to explain agency (see Bandura, 1992, versus Rychlak, 1994, for a mechanistic versus teleological interpretation of the same empirical evidence).

Of course, as with many problem areas in psychology, this question of agency is far from settled. Some psychologists speak of a difference between reasons and causes in explaining behavior. In doing so, they fail to appreciate that a "reason" is a formal cause pattern which is employed in final causation as the "that [reason] for the sake of which" some action takes place. On the Aristotelian scheme, a reason *is* a cause! The reason we leave a room is to do something or other;

conversely, we can negate our reasons or change our mind and *not* leave the room.

The fact that it is possible for individuals to negate their intentions is very important and, to this point in psychological theorizing and experimentation, it has been relatively overlooked. Unlike computing machines, human beings can and do reason oppositionally like this. They can twist what was said into its contrary implication, or draw meaningful hunches from what was never stated or done. This human capacity to reason oppositionally was called "dialectical" reasoning by the Greek philosophers. Aristotle said that people were intentional, purposive organisms because he believed that they could reason dialectically. People could set a course of action in contradiction to what their biology or their social shaping was impelling them to do. This takes us to a definition of agency:

Agency is the capacity that certain organisms have to behave or believe in conformance with, in contradiction of, in addition to, or without regard for what is perceived to be environmental or biological determinants.

Agency has good and bad outcomes. Thus, a person (agent) can deny physical symptoms and risk severe illness or even death rather than confront the immediate threat by seeing a physician. Agents can contradict their moral instructions ("shapings") and behave badly. Or, on the other hand, agents can behave morally, with a sense of personal responsibility. They can reject social pressures which are put on them by others (such as using drugs), but they can also go along with such social influences. Agency and the teleology to which it is tied is what we mean by *free will*. If a person could have behaved otherwise in a situation (contradictorily), all circumstances remaining the same, then we say this person has free will. A freely willing agent sets the grounds "for the sake of which" he or she will be determined (via final-cause determination!). An agent is never an efficiently caused instrumentality. An agent is always the executive identity, affirming assumptive premises leading to decisions and choices, even though the resulting intentions and purposes may be misguided or flatly incorrect. Social pressures can and often do influence persons, but thanks to their oppositional reasoning capacities this never turns them into permanent robots. Agents ultimately make a difference in the line of action we call their "behavior."

[*See also* Metaphysics; Moral Discourse; *and* Philosophy, *articles on* Philosophy of Mind *and* Philosophy of Science.]

Bibliography

Aristotle (1952). Physics. In R. M. Hutchins (Ed.), *Great books of the western world* (Vol. 8, pp. 257–355). Chicago: Encyclopedia Britannica.

Bandura, A. (1992). Exercise of personal agency through the self-efficacy mechanism. In R. Schwarzer (Ed.), *Self-efficacy: Thought control of action* (pp. 3–38). Washington, DC: Hemisphere Press.

Brewer, W. F. (1974). There is no convincing evidence for operant or classical conditioning in adult humans. In W. B. Weimer & D. S. Palermo (Eds.), *Cognition and the symbolic processes* (pp. 1–42). Hillsdale, NJ: Erlbaum.

Rychlak, J. F. (1994). *Logical learning theory: A human teleology and its empirical support.* Lincoln: University of Nebraska Press.

Joseph F. Rychlak

Agency and Control Theory

One of the challenges of middle and later adulthood is to maintain a sense of control in the face of aging-related declines. To the extent that adults feel control over key areas of their lives, they have an important psychological resource (Lachman, Ziff, & Spiro, 1994; Rodin, Timko, & Harris, 1985). Control beliefs, along with other factors, seem to play a protective role in the face of decrements and loss (Baltes & Baltes, 1986). On the one hand, a sense of control may facilitate adaptive responses to declines associated with the aging process (Lachman et al., 1994). At the same time, maintaining a sense of control may help one to prevent or minimize decrements via behavioral (e.g., life style) or physiological factors (e.g., immune function, stress hormones) (Rodin et al., 1985).

Definitions

The control construct appears in many forms and its application is widespread within psychology (e.g., social, developmental, personality, organizational, clinical) and in related fields such as medicine, public health, and education. There are numerous terms used somewhat interchangeably, including *locus of control, personal mastery, self-efficacy,* and *sense of control* (Skinner, 1996). To represent the general themes of theory and research in this heterogeneous area, the terms *agency* and *control* are used here. Agency refers to the perceived abilities of the self to perform actions, to reach desired outcomes, and to avoid or cope with undesired events. Control focuses on the responsiveness of the environment, and deals with the degree to which one believes outcomes are contingent on one's own actions. These two aspects of the self, agency and control, are distinct, but they are often positively related. Nevertheless, there are circumstances wherein one may believe that one has the requisite skills for a goal (agency), yet realizes that outcomes are not attainable due to circumstances beyond one's control.

Origins

An early conceptual forerunner of agency and control is the desire to master the environment called *effectance motivation* by Robert White (1959). In this motivational view, the desire to demonstrate mastery and competence was considered an innate basic human drive.

More recent work on control has been developed within a cognitive social learning framework, wherein control is conceived as a set of beliefs. The earliest formulation focused on the internal-external locus of control, which was conceived as a generalized, unidimensional, individual difference variable (Rotter, 1966). Over the past few decades, there have been a number of refinements to the construct including acknowledgment of its multidimensionality and domain specificity. A multidimensional approach distinguishes among different sources of control such as internal, external, and powerful others (Lefcourt, 1981). Domain-specific approaches to control enable assessment of variations in control beliefs across different sectors of life.

The focus on beliefs emphasizes perceptions of control with the assumption that beliefs influence behavior irrespective of their veridicality. In fact, the actual contingency or degree of control is often not known unless it is directly manipulated in the laboratory. Nevertheless, the perception that one has control is adaptive in most circumstances.

Assessment/Measurement

Control beliefs are typically measured with self-report instruments assessing degree of agreement with statements about the means to achieve outcomes and whether one is capable of attaining them (Skinner, 1996). There are numerous instruments available including Rotter's (1966) internal-external locus of control scale (Lefcourt, 1981) as well as multidimensional and domain-specific instruments for assessing control over aging-relevant areas such as memory (Lachman et al., 1994) or health (Lefcourt, 1981).

Correlates

Beliefs in agency and control are related to a host of other variables (Rodin et al., 1985). A greater sense of control is found among those with higher levels of education and income. Differences by age, gender, race, and cultural groups have been reported, but the findings are somewhat inconsistent. In adulthood and old age, a sense of control is related to psychological well-being, good health, engaging in health-promoting behaviors, and better cognitive functioning. Much of the research has been correlational, although there is some experimental work showing that increasing levels of control has positive consequences for health and well-being (Langer & Rodin, 1976).

Age Differences/Changes

Control beliefs have been shown to be less stable than other aspects of the self such as personality traits. Research shows that beliefs about personal control gradually increase from childhood to adulthood and then decline in later life (Skinner, 1996). The findings from cross-sectional and longitudinal studies are fairly consistent. Decline in control beliefs associated with aging is less pronounced for generalized beliefs than for domain-specific beliefs, especially for the domains in which there are aging-related declines such as health and cognitive functioning (Lachman, 1986). Agency beliefs remain relatively stable with aging, whereas beliefs about the influence of external factors such as powerful others show significant increases. This may reflect the increased probability of constraints due to retirement, illness, and loss of significant others with aging (Lachman, 1986; Rodin et al., 1985). Under circumstances where goals are seen as difficult or unattainable, a sense of control may be maintained by using primary or secondary control strategies (Heckhausen & Schulz, 1995).

Mechanisms

Much effort is currently being devoted to establishing the mechanisms that link control with desirable outcomes such as health and and well-being. A reciprocal relationship in which beliefs affect outcomes as well as outcomes affect beliefs has been postulated (Lachman et al., 1994). Motivational, behavioral, and physiological factors have been identified as some of the possible mechanisms. Believing one is in control of outcomes leads to greater investment of effort. For example, if one believes that heart disease is something that can be controlled one is more likely to engage in health-promoting behaviors such as exercising and eating a low fat diet. There is also evidence that a sense of control is associated with better immune functioning and less reactivity to stress, which could in turn affect health. As more information is obtained about the mechanisms through which control beliefs influence health and other outcomes, this will enrich the potential for developing adaptive interventions.

Interventions

Given that control beliefs appear to decline in later life, there is interest in developing strategies to enhance control beliefs using cognitive restructuring or environmental supports. There is some evidence for success in changing beliefs about control. For example, beliefs about memory efficacy and controllability were enhanced using cognitive restructuring in conjunction with memory training (Lachman et al., 1994). Langer and Rodin (1976) gave older adults in a nursing home opportunities to control their environment and found positive effects on health and mortality. Further research is needed to examine whether modifying control beliefs has long-term positive consequences for successful aging (Baltes & Baltes, 1986).

[*See also* Adulthood and Aging.]

Bibliography

Baltes, M. M., & Baltes, P. B. (Eds.). (1986). *The psychology of control and aging* (pp. 207–236). Hillsdale, NJ: Erlbaum.

Heckhausen, J., & Schulz, R. (1995). A life-span theory of control. *Psychological Review, 102*, 284–304.

Lachman, M. E. (1986). Locus of control in aging research: A case for multidimensional and domain-specific assessment. *Psychology and Aging, 1*, 34–40.

Lachman, M. E., Ziff, M. A., & Spiro, A. (1994). Maintaining a sense of control in later life. In R. Abeles, H. Gift, & M. Ory (Eds.), *Aging and quality of life* (pp. 116–132). New York: Sage.

Langer, E. J., & Rodin, J. (1976). The effects of choice and enhanced personal responsibility for the aged: A field experiment in an institutional setting. *Journal of Personality and Social Psychology, 34*, 191–198.

Lefcourt, H. M. (Ed.). (1981). *Research with the locus of control construct: Assessment methods (Vol. 1).* New York: Academic Press.

Rodin, J., Timko, C., & Harris, S. (1985). The construct of control: Biological and psychosocial correlates. In C. Eisdorfer, M. P. Lawton, & G. L. Maddox (Eds.), *Annual review of gerontology and geriatrics* (pp. 3–55). New York: Springer.

Rotter, J. B. (1966). Generalized expectancies for internal versus external control of reinforcement. *Psychological Monographs, 80* (1, Whole No. 609).

Skinner, E. A. (1996). A guide to constructs of control. *Journal of Personality and Social Psychology, 71*, 549–570.

White, R. W. (1959). Motivation reconsidered: The concept of competence. *Psychological Review, 66*, 297–333.

Margie E. Lachman

AGGRESSION. *See* Violence and Aggression; *and* Violence Risk Assessment.

AGNOSIAS. The term *agnosia* comes from the Greek for "not knowing," and covers a broad array of neuropsychological disorders in which the patient does not recognize an object or person despite seemingly adequate perceptual and mnemonic abilities. Visual agnosias are the most common and best understood agnosias, probably because much of the posterior half of the human brain is devoted to visual processing.

The Visual Agnosias

Information from the eyes is transmitted to a number of different subcortical and cortical brain structures. Damage to any part of this complex system results in impaired visual perception. In some cases, the damage does not affect brain mechanisms that process light or color perception, acuity, or other elementary visual abilities and is confined to brain regions specific to visual recognition. This results in visual agnosia. Patients with visual agnosia cannot recognize many objects by vision alone, despite their good or at least adequate elementary visual abilities. Their problem appears to be specific to visual object recognition, as they have no difficulty identifying objects that they can hear or touch.

The Apperceptive Associative Distinction. As far back as the nineteenth century, neuropsychologists have distinguished between two broad categories of visual agnosia: "apperceptive" and "associative" (Lissauer, 1890). Originally, the underlying impairment in apperceptive agnosia was thought to be perceptual in nature. Although not blind, such patients seemed unable to perceive normally, and their object recognition impairment appeared to be secondary to this perceptual impairment. In contrast, Lissauer suggested that perception in associative agnosia was normal, and the problem must therefore lie downstream in the process of associating a perceptual representation with more general knowledge. Teuber (1968) noted that associative visual agnosics were believed to see "a normal percept stripped of its meaning."

The apperceptive-associative dichotomy is useful insofar as it distinguishes between two broad but fairly distinct classes of patients: those with obvious perceptual impairments and those without. However, the underlying theoretical assumption that perception is at fault only in agnosics in the apperceptive group is no longer held. Indeed, the study of so-called associative agnosia has taught us much about the nature of higher-level visual perception. It is to this class of agnosias that we now turn.

Associative Visual Agnosia. The criteria for associative visual agnosia include an inability to identify visually presented objects by verbal or nonverbal means, coupled with good or at least adequate memory and attention, and the ability to see objects clearly enough to draw them. Hence perception in the associative agnosic is not just preserved at an elementary level, as in apperceptive agnosics, but seems impressively good. Figure 1 shows examples of copies made by a typical associative agnosic of drawings, the content of which he could not label. The preservation of the ability to copy seems to demonstrate that perception is not at fault in associative agnosia, but this conclusion is probably not correct. By its very nature, copying requires piecemeal processing (lines can only be drawn one at a time), whereas normal object recognition requires seeing the whole object simultaneously. When tested directly, the ability of associative visual agnosics to apprehend the whole of an object is impaired, and the errors of agnosics often reflect their reliance on local features (e.g., calling a fork a "comb" on the basis of the tines) or an impoverished overall view of the object (e.g., calling a salt shaker a "barrel"). The functional locus of damage in associative visual agnosia is therefore presumed to be high-level visual perceptual representations of object shape, analogous to the representations found in monkey inferotemporal cortex.

Dissociations within Associative Visual Agnosia. Associative visual agnosics vary in the scope of their recognition impairment, with some encountering difficulty primarily with faces, others with printed words, and others showing little comprehension of these categories of stimuli. The dissociations among visual stimulus categories are of theoretical interest for what they tell us about the organization of normal visual recognition processes.

Prosopagnosia. Prosopagnosics cannot recognize familiar people by their faces alone, and must rely on other cues for recognition such as a person's voice, or distinctive clothing or hairstyles. The disorder can be so severe that even close friends and family members will not be recognized. Although many prosopagnosics have some degree of difficulty recognizing objects other than faces, in some cases the deficit appears strikingly selective for faces. Some writers have suggested that prosopagnosia is simply a mild agnosia, and that faces are simply the most difficult type of object to recognize. Evidence is accumulating against this position. Prosopagnosics have been found to be disproportionately impaired with faces, when normal subjects' recognition difficulty has been taken into account relative to a variety of comparison stimuli including sheep faces, eyeglass frames, and inverted faces. Further evidence that prosopagnosia represents damage to a distinct system for face recognition comes from agnosic patients who show relative preservation of face recognition.

Pure Alexia. The impairment of visual word recognition, in the context of intact auditory word recognition and writing ability, is known as *pure alexia* and may be found alone or in association with visual object agnosia. The early and influential theory of Geshwind (1965) that pure alexia results from an anatomical disconnection between visual and verbal areas of the brain is no longer widely held, although disconnection does appear to play a role in some cases. Instead, pure alexia is now generally viewed as a type of visual agnosia, most severe for letter and word representations. As with prosopagnosia, the opposite dissociation also exists, namely spare word recognition with impaired object and face recognition.

Neuropathology of Associative Visual Agnosia. By examining the lesion locations in cases of visual agnosia, we can infer the parts of the human brain that are critical for visual recognition. Almost invariably the lesions are posterior and inferior, affecting ventral, temporal, and occipital regions. Damage is frequently bilateral, although in some cases only the left or right

AGNOSIAS. Figure 1. Copies made by an associative agnosic patient of drawings he could not recognize. (From Rubens & Benson, 1971, Associative visual agnosia, *Archives of Neurology, 24*, pp. 305–316, copyright 1971 by the American Medical Association.)

hemisphere is affected. The precise location of damage appears to correlate with the scope of the agnosic impairment. In patients who are agnosic for objects, faces, and printed words, damage is bilateral. If the impairment mainly affects faces, damage may be bilateral or confined to the right hemisphere. When reading alone is impaired or when reading and object recognition are impaired but face recognition is spared, the damage is generally confined to the left hemisphere.

Related Syndromes. The term *associative agnosia* has been applied to a number of distinct but related syndromes. Two that merit discussion here are semantic memory impairments and optic aphasia. In the former, patients lose general knowledge about the world (termed *semantic memory* by cognitive psychologists), resulting in an inability to name, or otherwise indicate recognition of, visually presented objects. The impairment may affect all types of stimuli, as in Alzheimer's disease or in the selective loss of semantic memory known as *semantic dementia*, or it may disproportionately affect knowledge from specific categories such as living things. Because the functional locus of damage is postperceptual, in semantic memory, these patients also perform poorly in entirely nonvisual tasks; for example, answering verbal questions about objects.

Optic aphasics encounter difficulty when naming visually presented objects. They can convey their recognition of a visual stimulus by pantomime (e.g., a drinking motion when shown a cup) or sorting semantically related stimuli together, and can name stimuli in modalities other than vision. Most authors currently distinguish between associative agnosia and optic aphasia, although patients suffering the latter have sometimes been called *associative agnosics*. The underlying impairment in optic aphasia is unclear. To the extent that optic aphasics are able to derive semantic understanding of visual stimuli, it seems strange that they should be unable to name them.

Nonvisual Agnosias

The nonvisual agnosias are primarily auditory and tactile.

Auditory Agnosias. As with visual recognition, auditory recognition may break down in a number of different ways. What the auditory agnosias have in common is a failure of recognition of verbal or nonverbal sounds, in the context of roughly normal audiometric test performance. The auditory agnosia that seems most analogous to visual associative agnosia is *nonverbal auditory agnosia*, also known as *environmental sound agnosia*. The patient with this condition fails to recognize common objects and events by their sounds such as a dog barking, keys jingling, or the slamming of a door.

The impairment of environmental sound recognition described here is usually found in conjunction with impaired recognition of speech sounds, although selective nonverbal auditory agnosias have been reported. Auditory agnosias also exist for spoken words, analogous to pure alexia, for voices, analogous to prosopagnosia, and for music.

Tactile Agnosia. Tactile agnosia refers to a disorder of object recognition through touch that cannot be attributed to a more basic somatasensory impairment. As with vision and hearing, tactile perception can break down at a number of different stages. Disorders of tactile object recognition can be distinguished from basic and intermediate somesthetic dysfunction on anatomical grounds. A particularly pure tactile agnosic was shown to have adequate perception of light touch, vibration, joint position, superficial pain and temperature, and good two-point discrimination, as well as weight and texture discrimination and simple form discrimination such as being able to distinguish between flat and curved surfaces and edges. Nevertheless, she was impaired at complex shape discrimination and the recognition of common objects such as a key, a tape cassette, and a bottle. Thus, tactile agnosia, like visual and auditory, represents a disruption of the highest level perceptual processes, necessary for recognition.

Bibliography

Bauer, R. M., & Zawacki, T. (1997). Auditory agnosia and amusia. In T. E. Feinberg & M. J. Farah (Eds.), *Behavioral neurology and neuropsychology* (pp. 267–276). New York: McGraw-Hill. A comprehensive review of disorders of auditory recognition affecting verbal and nonverbal sounds, including music.

Farah, M. J. (1990). *Visual agnosia: Disorders of object recognition and what they tell us about normal vision.* Cambridge, MA: MIT Press. A book-length review of apperceptive and associative visual agnosias, including prosopagnosia and optic aphasia.

Geschwind, (1965). *Brain, 88,* 584–644.

Klein, R. M., & McMullen, P. A. (Eds.). (in press). *Converging methods for understanding reading and dyslexia.* Cambridge, MA: MIT Press. Contains a number of chapters on acquired disorders of visual word recognition.

Lissauer (1890). *Archiv fur Psychiatrie und Nerven Krankheiten, 21,* 222–270.

Reed, C. L., Caselli, R., & Farah, M. J. (1996). Tactile agnosia: Underlying impairment and implications for normal tactile object recognition. *Brain, 119,* 875–888. A brief review of the relatively small literature on tactile agnosia and a detailed case presentation.

Teuber, H.-L. (1968). *Analysis of behavioral change,* L. Weiskrantz (Ed.). New York.

Martha J. Farah

AIDS. *See* Acquired Immune Deficiency Syndrome.

ALCOHOLICS ANONYMOUS (AA) is the largest self-help organization in the world, having approximately 2 million members in over 50 countries. AA members are alcoholics who are committed to helping each other stay "sober." In AA, sobriety involves not only abstaining from alcohol (termed being *dry*), but also undergoing psychological and spiritual changes that result in greater honesty, humility, patience, and compassion for others. To support this change process, AA members meet regularly in small self-help groups and learn a philosophy known as the 12 steps.

Although AA is now an influential worldwide organization, its origins were humble. In 1935, William Griffith Wilson and Dr. Robert Holbrook Smith met each other at a friend's house in Akron, Ohio. Both men had struggled with alcoholism for many years and had undergone multiple unsuccessful treatments. In the eyes of 1930s medicine, including psychoanalysis, alcoholics were often viewed as hopeless cases. However, in a 5-hour discussion, Wilson and Smith found that their identification with each other's stories and their ability to help each other had a profoundly positive effect. Over time, they decided to bring their mutual helping method to other alcoholics by forming the organization that is today called Alcoholics Anonymous. This name captures two critical components of the AA program: its focus on alcoholics helping alcoholics and its desire "to put principles above personalities" in conducting its business. In the service of the latter tradition, Wilson and Smith became known as Bill W. and Dr. Bob within the AA fellowship.

Over the next several years, a few AA groups were formed, and AA members began more fully developing their approach. One of their critical early decisions was to establish a tradition of AA cooperating with treatment professionals yet always remaining an independent, self-supporting organization operated entirely by alcoholics. Further, rather than restricting membership based on professional credentials or ability to pay, membership in AA would be open and free of charge (save for small, voluntary, "pass the hat" contributions) to anyone who had a desire to stop drinking.

AA also made an innovative decision regarding members' alcohol consumption. As surprising as it may sound today, in the 1930s, psychotherapists did not always consider the drinking of alcoholic patients as a serious problem. In the psychoanalytic framework dominant at the time, alcohol consumption was viewed merely as a symptom of a deeper disturbance in personality, rather than as a problem in itself. Hence, instead of addressing alcohol consumption directly, psychoanalysts focused on their patients' personality problems, in the hopes that alcohol consumption would abate as soon as the personality conflict was resolved. Although AA members accepted the premise that alcoholics had characterological problems that would ultimately require attention, their personal experience told them that the first order of business in helping alcoholics was to insist on abstinence. This approach was formulated in simple advice for AA newcomers: "Don't drink. Go to AA meetings." Treating alcohol consumption as a central problem rather than merely as a symptom is now a well-established principle in professional treatments for alcoholism, just as it has always been in AA.

Another important aspect of AA's approach is making storytelling a central part of the recovery process. Honest recounting of stories about alcoholism and recovery serves as a way for AA members to further the process of accepting their alcoholism and owning up to past mistakes. Further, when experienced members describe the process through which they descended into alcoholism and then began their recovery in AA (this occurs at what are known in AA as "speaker's meetings"), newer members can identify similarities with their own experience, and therefore see how AA could benefit them. Reflecting this belief in the power of stories, the primary text of AA *Alcoholics Anonymous* (1939/1976), is composed almost entirely of members' stories of how alcoholism affected their lives and how their lives have changed since their involvement in AA.

An additional key component of AA's developing philosophy was that alcoholism was caused by moral and spiritual defects, particularly self-centeredness and grandiosity. In order to minimize these negative character flaws, AA members are asked to admit their alcoholism and their character flaws to themselves and to their group; for example, by always introducing their contributions at meetings with "My name is X, and I am an alcoholic." In addition, AA members are asked to engage in less selfish behavior, most notably listening to and helping other alcoholics. AA conceptualizes this change as a spiritual process culminating in a state of serenity. In understanding alcoholism in this way, early AA members were drawing both on their personal experiences with alcoholism and their contact with a quasi-religious movement of the period known as the Oxford Group. They were also influenced by the ideas of the American psychologist/philosopher William James and, to a lesser degree, the Swiss psychiatrist Carl Jung.

Jung had treated an alcoholic member of the Oxford Group who also was in contact with early AA members. Jung told his patient that curing alcoholism was hopeless from the point of view of medicine, but that a spiritual transformation might hold the key to recovery. Bill W. experienced such a spiritual transformation during a hospitalization in 1934, and he interpreted its meaning in light of William James's *Varieties of Religious Experience* (1902/1985), so James's pragmatism was also absorbed into AA. For example James's concept that acting and behaving in a new way could produce corresponding feelings and views of the self is also endorsed in AA, as reflected in organizational slogans such as "Bring the body and the mind will follow" and "Fake it until you make it."

With the publication of their book in 1939 and very favorable mass media coverage in the 1940s, AA membership skyrocketed. The organization has continued to grow at an astonishing rate since then, both in the United States and around the world. According to AA's 1996 membership survey (AA World Services 1997), AA now has 96,997 groups worldwide.

Who Attends AA?

Bill W. and Dr. Bob, like most of AA's early members, were White, middle-class, middle-aged men. However, AA's membership has changed markedly since its early days. The proportion of women among AA members in different countries today ranges from 10% (in Mexico) to more than a third (in the United States, Canada, Austria, and Switzerland). Further, significant proportions of AA members are under 30 years old in most countries. AA has also become more racially and ethnically diverse since its founding. In the United States and Canada, respondents to AA's 1996 membership survey were 86% Caucasian, 5% African American, 4% Hispanic, 4% Native American, and 1% of other backgrounds. Although reliable data on the race of AA members outside of the United States and Canada is not available, diversity is suggested simply by the number and variety of regions that have AA meetings. Internationally, AA has spread throughout Europe, South America, Oceania, and parts of Asia and Africa. However, AA has yet to gain a foothold in a socialist or Islamic country.

Research has had little success at identifying personal characteristics that consistently and powerfully predict AA participation. A meta-analytic review by Emrick, Tonigan, Montgomery, and Little (1993) suggested that there is a modest relationship between AA attendance and more severe alcohol problems. This may be because individuals with more severe alcohol problems can more easily identify with AA members' stories, many of which describe severe life problems (e.g., divorce, family violence, imprisonment) and symptoms of high alcohol dependence (e.g., delirium tremens, blackouts). At the same time, the presence of individuals with more severe alcohol problems within AA may merely reflect the well-established relationship between greater distress and greater help-seeking from outside sources, of which AA is only one. Because AA is a diverse organization even within single countries, it is unlikely that a consistent profile of AA attenders will ever be established.

The Impact of AA

One way to evaluate the impact of AA is to examine how its members are affected by participating in it. Whether or not AA helps members reduce alcohol consumption and related problems continues to be debated. This debate has been fueled by two problems. One is bias: that of some professionals toward assuming that professional help is inherently better than help provided by nonprofessionals and that of some AA members toward assuming that AA is appropriate for every alcoholic. The other is the lack, until quite recently, of well-designed longitudinal outcome studies of AA participants.

Recent studies with stronger designs support AA's effectiveness. For example, a 10-year followup of 158 alcoholic patients found that AA involvement was the only variable predicting abstinence from alcohol out of a set of predictors that included demographic variables and problem severity (1990). Similar results have been reported in other long-term outcome studies.

AA may also reduce alcohol-related health care costs. Humphreys and Moos (1996) compared individuals who sought out AA or an outpatient service provider for help with an alcohol problem. At baseline, the two groups were similar on demographic and problem severity measures. At 1- and 3-year follow-up, both groups improved significantly, with no differences in improvement between groups. However, alcohol-related health care costs were 45% lower in the AA group over the course of the study (almost $2,000 per person), indicating that in addition to promoting positive outcomes in its members, AA may take a significant burden off the formal health care system.

As mentioned earlier, the AA program is not just about abstaining from alcohol, but also about learning a new way to live and be in the world. The studies already mentioned provide evidence that such changes do occur in AA members. For example, AA participation has been shown to predict decreased depression and higher quality relationships with friends and spouse. Qualitative studies of AA members have also shown that, for at least some members, change in AA involves more than cessation of alcohol use. Over time, committed AA members undergo changes in identity; for example, coming to think of themselves as alcoholics. Many also develop a rich spiritual life. However, how common these experiences are in AA is unknown. Clearly, some members attend the organization for many years and manage only to modify their drinking behavior, and others drop out after experiencing little or no benefit from participation.

In sum, research on the effects of AA participation shows positive effects, particularly for highly involved members. However, because much of the research is cross-sectional and does not include comparison groups, this conclusion must remain tentative. It is hoped that longitudinal studies of AA will become more common, allowing a more definitive examination of AA's effects on members, as well as information on whether AA is more helpful to some alcoholics than to others.

If one thinks of AA as a treatment for alcoholism, assessing AA's impact would end with a review of the data on how AA members are changed as a result of their participation. However, this is too narrow a conception of AA, because the organization is in many ways more like an international social movement than a clinical intervention for alcohol problems. Indeed, because of its size and scope, AA has influenced not only its members, but also the structure of the professional alcoholism treatment system and the formation of many other self-help groups.

As an organization, AA takes no public stands on issues nor does it attempts to influence the outside world (e.g., the health care system). However, individual AA members have been quite successful at influencing the shape of the U.S. alcoholism treatment system. AA members (e.g., Marty Mann and Senator

Harold Hughes) were instrumental in the establishment of the National Institute on Alcohol Abuse and Alcoholism and the National Council on Alcoholism. Other AA members started treatment programs on their own. AA members are often employed on staff as counselors, even in treatment programs not founded by AA members, or hold meetings for patients at treatment programs. In fact, the majority of alcoholism treatment programs in the United States adopt some part of AA's program. AA has also influenced the nature of professional treatment in other countries, although to a lesser extent than in the United States.

AA has also been an inspiration to many other self-help organizations. At least 100 other self-help organizations for various problems have adapted the 12-step approach developed in AA. Further, many non-12-step programs also adopt some AA principles, for example storytelling and having more experienced members sponsor new members and help them through the recovery process.

All available data indicates that AA will continue to grow in the coming years, both in the United States and abroad. Because of its size and influence, an understanding of AA (whether one believes it to be effective or not) is a prerequisite to understanding how substance dependence is conceptualized and addressed in the United States. Individuals interested in understanding addiction, as well as those interested in social movements and grassroots organizations, would benefit from educating themselves about AA. The AA World Services Office in New York can provide interested persons with literature on AA, and local AA hotlines may be contacted for the location of AA meetings.

[See also Alcoholism; and Twelve-Step Programs.]

Acknowledgments. The author acknowledges the support of the Rotterdam Addiction Research Institute and the Veterans Affairs Mental Health Strategic Health Group.

Bibliography

Alcoholics Anonymous. (1939/1976). *Alcoholics Anonymous: The story of how many thousands of men and women have recovered from alcoholism.* New York: AA World Services. AA's primary text presents stories of its members, and provides insight into the organization's philosophy and approach.

Cross, G. M., Morgan, C. W., Martin, C. A., & Rafter, J. A. (1990). Alcoholic treatment: A ten-year follow-up study. *Alcoholism: Clinical and Experimental Research, 14,* 169–173.

Denzin, N. K. (1987). *The recovering alcoholic.* Newbury Park, CA: Sage. A participant-observer study of twelve-step-influenced alcoholism treatment and of AA.

Emrick, C. D., Tonigan, J. S., Montgomery, H., & Little, L. (1993). Alcoholics Anonymous: What is currently known? In B. S. McCrady & W. R. Miller (Eds.), *Research on Alcoholics Anonymous: Opportunities and alternatives.* New Brunswick, NJ: Rutgers Center of Alcohol Studies.

Humphreys, K., & Moose, R. (1996). Reduced substance abuse–related health care costs among voluntary participants in Alcoholics Anonymous. *Psychiatric Services, 47,* 709–713.

James, W. (1985). *The varieties of religious experience.* Cambridge, MA: Harvard University Press. (Original work published 1902)

Kurtz, E. (1979). *Not God: A history of Alcoholics Anonymous.* Center City, MN: Hazelden Educational Services. Widely regarded as the definitive history of the AA organization.

Mäkelä, K., Arminen, I., Bloomfield, K., Eisenbach-Stangl, I., Helmersson Bergmark, K., Kurube, N., Mariolini, N., Ólafsdottir, H., Peterson, J. H. Phillips, M., Rehm, J., Room, R., Rosenqvist, P., Rosovsky, H., Stenius, K., Swiatkiewitz, G., Woronowicz, B., & Zielinski, A. (1996). *Alcoholics Anonymous as a mutual help movement: A study in eight societies.* Madison: University of Wisconsin Press. The first comprehensive cross-cultural study of AA.

McCrady, B. S., & Miller, W. R. (Eds.). (1993). *Alcoholics Anonymous: Opportunities and alternatives.* New Brunswick, NJ: Rutgers Center of Alcohol Studies. Edited book that reports research results on AA—including a meta-analysis of effectiveness research by Emrick and colleagues—as well as methods for researching AA in the future.

Project Match Research Group (1997). Matching alcoholism treatments to client heterogeneity: Project MATCH posttreatment drinking outcomes. *Journal of Studies on Alcohol, 58,* 7–29. Randomized clinical trial demonstrating the effectiveness of "twelve-step facilitation" counseling, which is intended to introduce AA concepts in a psychotherapy setting and encourage attendance at AA meetings.

Tournier, R. E. (1979). Alcoholics Anonymous as treatment and as ideology. *Journal of Studies on Alcohol, 40,* 230–239. A widely cited critique of AA's influence on the alcoholism treatment system.

Keith Humphreys

ALCOHOLISM. In 1785, the American physician Benjamin Rush described the problem of "drunkenness" as a progressive disease characterized by excessive drinking and increased tolerance to the effects of alcohol. The disease model of alcoholism is now widely accepted, though there is also widespread agreement that both its etiology and its clinical features are highly heterogeneous. Traditional definitions of alcoholism have been based upon assessment of the consequences of the use of alcohol, the circularity of which has been well demonstrated. Recent standardized classification systems have now attempted to separate the actual alcohol-seeking behavior and its physiological concomitants from the social, psychological, and physical consequences of such behavior.

The major classification systems have been developed by the World Health Organization (WHO)—which produces the *International Classification of Diseases* (*ICD*), currently in its tenth version—and the American Psychiatric Association (APA)—which provides the *Diagnostic and Statistical Manual of Mental Disorders* (*DSM*), currently in its fourth iteration. The codes and terms of the most recent versions of these classification schemes, the *ICD–10* and the *DSM–IV*, are highly compatible and serve to improve the reliability and validity of clinical and research work on alcoholism. The development and consistent use of reliable and valid classification systems and diagnostic procedures is vital to the understanding of the etiology of alcohol-related disorders and the creation of effective treatment and prevention strategies. [*See* Diagnostic and Statistical Manual of Mental Disorders, International Classification of Diseases; *and* World Health Organization.]

The two major forms of problematic drinking that have been widely accepted as standard diagnostic nomenclatures include alcohol abuse and alcohol dependence. *Alcohol abuse* involves a pattern of alcohol consumption that persists despite recurrent significant adverse consequences resulting directly from alcohol use, including neglect of important personal, financial, social, occupational, or recreational activities; absenteeism from work or school; repeated run-ins with the police; and the use of alcohol in situations in which drinking is hazardous (e.g., driving while intoxicated). *Alcohol dependence*, the disorder most commonly likened to alcoholism, is a pattern of repeated or compulsive use of alcohol despite significant behavioral, physiological, and psychosocial problems, plus indications of physical and psychological dependence—tolerance, withdrawal—resulting in impaired control. Alcohol dependence is further differentiated from alcohol abuse by the preoccupation with obtaining alcohol or recovering from its effects, and the overwhelming desire for experiencing alcohol's intoxicating result (i.e., craving). *Tolerance* refers to the marked diminished response to alcohol that results from the continuous use of the same amount of alcohol, or the need to ingest increasingly large amounts of alcohol in order to experience the desired degree of intoxication. *Withdrawal* constitutes the group of physical symptoms that arise when abstaining from repeated and prolonged heavy alcohol use. Withdrawal symptoms include nervousness, irritability, nausea, sweating, and, in some cases, hallucinations, seizures, and delirium tremens. Alcoholics experiencing withdrawal symptoms typically turn to drinking alcohol as a way to alleviate their discomfort.

Impaired control is characterized by the inability to moderate drinking behavior, reduce drinking, or abstain from drinking altogether.

Prevalence of Alcoholism

The results of recent large-scale epidemiological studies have revealed that alcoholism is highly prevalent in the U.S. population. Estimates of the prevalence of alcohol abuse and dependence in the United States come from several such surveys. The Epidemiologic Catchment Area (ECA) study was conducted at five sites throughout the United States between 1980 and 1984 (Robins, Locke, & Regier, 1991; Regier et al., 1990). According to diagnostic criteria from the *DSM–III*, alcoholism is the second most prevalent psychiatric syndrome in the adult population, with lifetime and past-year rates of 13.8% and 6.3%, respectively. More recently, the National Comorbidity Survey (NCS) assessed the prevalence of major psychiatric disorders in a national probability survey of the United States (Kessler et al., 1997). The NCS estimated that 14% of U.S. adults have a lifetime history of alcohol abuse, whereas 9% have a history of alcohol dependence (Kessler et al., 1997). Rates very similar to the NCS come from the National Longitudinal Alcohol Epidemiologic Survey (NLAES), designed to gather updated estimates of alcohol-related disorders among a representative sample of nearly 43,000 United States adults. Relying on *DSM–IV* classification, the prevalence rates of lifetime and past-year alcohol dependence were estimated at 13.3% and 4.4%, respectively.

Risk Factors and Correlates of Alcoholism

The following several sections will examine the effects that age, sex, ethnicity, family and genetic factors, and comorbid psychiatric disorders have on alcoholism.

Age, Sex, and Ethnicity. Patterns of alcoholism tend to differ by gender, age, and ethnicity. The results of recent large-scale community-based studies in the United States reveal that alcoholism is far more frequent in males than in females. In the ECA study, the lifetime prevalence of alcohol abuse or dependence in males was sixfold greater than in females (i.e., 23.8% versus 4%). At the time of the survey, 9% of males and 2% of adult females had met criteria for alcohol abuse or dependence during the past six months, and 5% of men and 0.9% of women met criteria during the past 30 days. There is a particularly disturbing increase in alcohol and drug problems among adolescents, and the age of onset is steadily decreasing.

There are also major cultural and religious differences in rates of alcoholism. In terms of ethnic differences, estimates of alcoholism by the ECA study reveal that past-month rates of alcoholism were highest among Hispanics (3.6%), intermediate for African

Americans (3.4%), and lowest for whites (2.7%). The patterns of age also varied by ethnicity. In the ECA study, lifetime prevalence rates for alcoholism tended to peak between ages 30 and 44 for whites and Hispanic males, and between 18 and 29 for white and Hispanic females. In contrast to whites and Hispanics, whose rates decreased between ages 45 and 64, especially for females, the prevalence of alcoholism among African Americans reached a peak during this age range.

Family and Genetic Factors. A defining feature of alcoholism that has been recognized for centuries is its tendency to run in families. Aristotle, Plato, and Plutarch each observed that the drinking behavior of children often resembled that of their parents. More recently, scientific inquiries into the etiology of alcoholism indicate that the strongest risk factor for the development of alcohol-related disorders is a family history of alcoholism. Controlled family studies with direct interviews with probands (index cases) and their relatives show an average sevenfold increase in the risk of alcoholism among the first-degree relatives of probands as compared to controls. The relative risk is consistently greater in male than in female relatives, in proportions of the same magnitude as those reported in epidemiological studies. A strategy that identifies those at high risk by investigating the offspring of parents with alcoholism, usually prospectively, has been widely employed in investigating premorbid risk factors for the development of alcoholism. Most of the resulting studies confirm the familial aggregation of alcoholism and show that offspring of alcoholics have less subjective reaction to alcohol than their low risk counterparts (Schuckit & Smith, 1996). These studies have also examined the role of preexisting psychopathology in enhancing the risk for the development of alcoholism (Merikangas, Dierker, & Szatmari, 1998).

Twin and adoption studies provide evidence that genetic factors may underlie some of the familial aggregation of a disorder. Among the handful of twin studies that have assessed alcohol-related behavior, the average correlation between monozygotic twins is significantly greater (0.54, range 0.37–0.56) than that among dizygotic twins (0.23, range 0–0.50), with heritability estimates for females exceeding those for males (Pickens et al., 1990; Heath et al., 1997).

Results from adoption studies examining severe behavioral and medical consequences of alcohol use constitute the major evidence to date favoring the role of transmissible genes in the etiology of alcoholism. The average relative risk of alcoholism in adoptees with a family history of alcoholism is 2.4 for males and 2.8 for females. An adoptee is 2.5 times more likely to develop alcoholism if a biological parent has alcoholism, irrespective of exposure to the alcoholic parent. In contrast to the family studies, there is some evidence for sex-specific transmission in some of the adoption studies of alcoholism (Bohman, Sigvardsson, & Cloninger, 1981).

Thus, the majority of the family, twin, and adoption studies have implicated genetic factors in the development of alcoholism, although genes explain less than half of the variability in alcoholism. Despite large expenditure of effort on identifying genes for alcoholism, there are still no confirmed findings of either specific vulnerability markers or genes for alcoholism. This is likely attributable to the complexity of alcoholism that results from heterogeneous etiologic pathways with varying degrees of environmental and genetic contributions (Merikangas, 1990).

In addition to possible genetic explanations for the strong degree of familial aggregation of alcoholism, alternative explanations need to be further evaluated, particularly because not all children of alcoholics develop alcoholism. These include the possible changes in the susceptibility to alcohol of the fetus as a result of in utero maternal ingestion of alcohol, negligent rearing manifested in dietary deficiency, exposure to toxic substances, brain trauma, and damage to paternal germ cells from alcohol. The development of alcoholism has also been associated with numerous psychosocial factors including parental conflict or rejection, abuse, personality characteristics, coping styles, attitudes toward drunkenness, exposure to stress, as well as broad sociological factors such as culture and socioeconomic conditions.

Comorbid Psychiatric Disorders. Clinical and epidemiologic studies have revealed that alcoholism and depression are inextricably linked (Regier et al., 1990; Kessler et al., 1997). Whereas 32% of the general population meets criteria for an additional diagnosis, 47% of alcoholics meet criteria for a second diagnosis. Alcoholism is specifically associated with antisocial personality, drug abuse/dependence, nicotine dependence, mania, schizophrenia, anxiety states such as panic disorder and social phobia, and major depression. Recent international collaborative studies have revealed that despite large variation in the magnitude of alcoholism, patterns of comorbidity are virtually identical across the world (Merikangas, Dierker, & Szatmari, 1998a).

The link between alcoholism and depression has been the most widely studied form of comorbidity. Depression may be either primary to or a consequence of alcoholism. In the former case, alcohol may be used to self-medicate dysphoric or irritable affective states, whereas in the latter, it may be a secondary manifestation of alcohol. Longitudinal research shows that the onset of the bipolar subtype of alcoholism tends to predate that of alcoholism; individuals with bipolar illness (or manic depression) tend to use alcohol to reduce agitation during the manic phase of the illness rather than during depressive episodes (Merikangas & Gelernter, 1990). The results of a recent study reporting the efficacy of lithium treatment in the reduction of both depression and alcohol problems among adolescents with bipolar disorder with secondary alcohol abuse has been extremely promising (Geller et al., 1998). The results of this and several other studies are beginning to provide a model for treatment and prevention early in the course of the development of these problems.

Likewise, clinical and epidemiologic studies have shown that anxiety states and substance disorders are strongly associated (Regier et al., 1990; Kessler et al., 1997). Social phobia, the fear of public scrutiny, is severely distressing and often leads people to drink or use anxiety-reducing drugs in order to function in social contexts in which others feel comfortable (Merikangas et al., 1998c).

A third major pathway to substance abuse, though less specific, is conduct disorder (severe behavior problems beginning in childhood) and its adult form, antisocial behavior (Rohde, Lewinsohn, & Szeley, 1996). This condition primarily affects males and has received by far the most clinical attention because affected individuals tend to cause trouble at school and at home. The association between conduct problems and substance abuse is not specific to alcohol, since most of these individuals tend to use multiple drugs and develop problems in many different spheres.

Treatment, Intervention, and Prevention of Alcoholism

Despite the high rates of alcoholism in the general population, very few alcoholics receive treatment for their drinking problems. Among participants in the ECA with a lifetime diagnosis of alcohol abuse or dependence, only 15% reported ever mentioning their alcoholism to a doctor, and less than 10% reported seeking treatment specifically for alcoholism. Nonetheless, there are a multitude of options available to individuals seeking treatment for alcohol abuse and alcoholism.

Treatment for alcohol abusers often involves interventions aimed at moderating alcohol consumption, such as behavioral self-control training. The major goals of alcoholism treatment include short-term management of alcohol withdrawal, long-term management of alcohol dependence, prevention of relapse and, ultimately, abstinence. Treatment approaches include detoxification followed by inpatient rehabilitation, individual or group psychotherapy, family system therapy, pastoral counseling, pharmacologic interventions, and behavioral therapy. Treatment settings vary from public facilities (as with Alcoholics Anonymous meetings) and private therapy offices to public and private outpatient clinics and inpatient facilities. Some evidence suggests that long-term group and individual supportive therapies are more effective in sustaining alcohol cessation,

but the current health care management environment no longer allows economic support for continued lifelong supportive treatment. The effectiveness of various treatment approaches, which has generally been disappointing, remains controversial due to the paucity of scientific evidence, the tendency for many recovering alcoholics to drop out of treatment or choose not to participate in outcome research, the broad heterogeneity of alcoholics, and the custom among specialists to provide treatment that is individualized for each patient. Furthermore, subjects in most existing treatment studies of alcoholism, who have been obtained from treatment studies, represent the "tip of the iceberg" of alcoholism in the population. Because only a small proportion of persons seek treatment or come to the attention of the authorities for alcohol-related behavior, the generalizability of the results of studies in which the sampling source is comprised of treatment or temperance board registries may be limited and subject to unknown biases. [See Alcoholics Anonymous; and Twelve-Step Programs.]

For the prevention of alcohol-related disorders, the available evidence strongly supports the critical importance of family-based programs for prevention (Kumpfer & Hopkins, 1993). Targeted prevention should be geared toward offspring of substance abusers, even those who have not been identified in treatment settings. Primary prevention programs should seek to evaluate risk factors for the development of substance abuse, including both parental and family factors and any individual characteristics of the children that may be associated with elevation in the risk of substance abuse, particularly such psychopathologies as conduct problems and depression/anxiety (Kessler & Price, 1993). Comprehension of the complex interrelationships among individual, familial, and broader social environment is critical to reduce continued substance abuse in both adults and children. This suggests that a combination of individual and family treatment in conjunction with broader efforts toward education and prevention at the community level will provide the optimal approach in reducing substance abuse problems. [See Community Prevention and Intervention; Family Therapy; Intervention; and Prevention.]

Recent findings regarding the lack of effectiveness of universal-based prevention programs for substance use in youth have generated substantial publicity. The failure of the bulk of school-based programs in long-term reduction of substance problems has led to a shift in emphasis of prevention efforts toward programs that apply more intensive prevention and intervention efforts to those at high risk of substance disorders. New evidence indicates that the risk of developing substance disorders due to familial factors is greater than 60% (i.e., 60% of those in the general population with drug and alcohol disorders have a family history of substance disorders (Merikangas, Dierker, & Szatmari, 1998a). Hence, prevention programs that include both families and children, particularly those with emotional or behavior problems, would appear to be extremely promising in ultimately reducing the incidence of substance disorders.

Social Impact of Alcoholism. Alcoholism constitutes a major public health problem in many parts of the world. [*See* Public Health.] While the abuse of illegal drugs tends to attract greater public concern and resources, alcohol is the most abused substance throughout the world. Alcoholism has a dramatic impact on the family, particularly among children; on the economy, in terms of decreased productivity; and on public health, with its role in morbidity and mortality stemming from accidents, homicide, and suicide. The effects of alcoholism on morbidity and mortality have been grossly underestimated in world health statistics. Approximately 20 to 60% of all hospital admissions in the United States are related to consequences of alcohol (Institute of Medicine, 1987). Moreover, if its secondary role in deaths due to homicide, suicide, accidents, and alcohol-related cancers are considered, it is the fourth leading cause of death in the United States, according to a comprehensive review of research on alcohol-related problems conducted by the Institute of Medicine in 1987. Alcohol is also believed to play a significant role among nonlethal accidents, including falls, burns, and drownings. Crime, too, has long been thought to be associated with alcohol. A substantial proportion of criminals report histories of having alcohol-related problems, and many appear to have been under the influence of alcohol when committing crimes, particularly violent crimes such as homicide and assault. Alcohol consumption has also been linked to violent victimization. For example, persons visiting hospital emergency rooms for treatment of violence-related injuries, compared to other-related injuries, are more likely to be intoxicated at the time of admission, to be drinking prior to the violent event, and to have alcohol-related problems. Despite these findings, however, a causal relation between alcohol and crime and violence has not yet been demonstrated. Alcohol abuse and dependence also takes an enormous toll on medical resources, as excessive alcohol consumption has been known to result in damage to the liver, gastrointestinal tract, pancreas, heart, and neurological systems.

Given the many serious consequences of alcohol abuse and alcohol-related disorders, future research, prevention, and intervention strategies should seek an understanding of the biological and environmental mechanisms associated with the development of substance abuse problems.

[*See also* Addictive Personality; *and* Drug Abuse.]

Bibliography

Bohman, M., Sigvardsson, S., & Cloninger, C. R. (1981). Maternal inheritance of alcohol abuse: Cross fostering analysis of adopted women. *Archives of General Psychiatry, 38,* 965–969.

Botvin, G. J., & Botvin, E. (1992). Adolescent tobacco, alcohol, and drug abuse: Prevention strategies, empirical findings, and assessment issues. *Journal of Developmental and Behavioral Pediatrics, 13,* 291–301.

Edwards, G. (1986). The alcohol dependence syndrome: A concept as stimulus to enquiry. *British Journal of Addiction, 81,* 171–183.

Geller, B., Cooper, T. B., Sun, K., Zimerman, B., Frazier, J., Williams, M., & Heath, J. (1998). Double-blind and placebo-controlled study of lithium for adolescent bipolar disorders with secondary substance dependency. *Journal of the American Academy of Child & Adolescent Psychiatry, 37,* 171–178.

Heath, A. C., Bucholz, K. K., Madden, P. A. F., Dinwiddie, S. H., Slutske, W. S., Bierut, L. J., Statham, D. J., Dunne, M. P., Whitfield, J. B., & Martin, N. G. (1997). Genetic and environmental contributions to alcohol dependence risk in a national twin sample: Consistency of findings in women and men. *Psychological Medicine, 27,* 1381–1396.

Institute of Medicine. (1987). *Causes and consequences of alcohol problems.* Washington, DC: National Academy Press.

Kessler, R., Crum, R., Warner, L., Nelson, C., Schulenberg, J., & Anthony, J. (1997). Lifetime co-occurrence of *DSM-III-R* alcohol abuse and dependence with other psychiatric disorders in the National Comorbidity Survey. *Archives of General Psychiatry, 54,* 313–321.

Kessler, R., & Price, R. (1993). Primary prevention of secondary disorders: A proposal and agenda. *American Journal of Community Psychology, 21,* 607–633.

Kumpfer, K. L., & Hopkins, R. (1993). Recent advances in addictive disorders—Prevention: Current research and trends. *Psychiatric Clinics of North America, 16,* 11–20.

McCord, J. (1988). Alcoholism: Toward understanding genetic and social factors. *Psychiatry, 51,* 131–141.

McCord, J. (1995). Relationship between alcoholism and crime of the life course. In H. B. Kaplan (Ed.), *Drugs, crime, and other deviant adaptations: Longitudinal studies* (pp. 129–141). New York: Plenum Press.

Merikangas, K. R. (1990). The genetic epidemiology of alcoholism. *Psychological Medicine, 20,* 1–22.

Merikangas, K. R., Dierker, L., & Szatmari, P. (1998a). Psychopathology among offspring of parents with substance abuse and/or anxiety: A high risk study. *Journal of Child Psychology and Psychiatry, 39,* 711–720.

Merikangas, K. R., & Gelernter, C. S. (1990). Comorbidity for alcoholism and depression. *Psychiatric Clinics of North America, 13,* 613–632.

Merikangas, K. R., Mehta, R., Molnar, B. E., Walters, E. E., Swendsen, J. D., Aguilar-Gaziola, S., Bijl, R. V., Borges, G., Caraveo-Anduaga, J. J., DeWit, D. J., Kolody, B., Vega, W. A., Wittchen, H. U., & Kessler, R. C. (1998b). Comorbidity of substance use disorders with mood and anxiety disorders: Results of the International Consortium in Psychiatric Epidemiology. *Addictive Behaviors*, 23, 893–907.

Merikangas, K. R., Stevens, D. E., Fenton, B., O'Malley. S., Woods, S., Stolar, M., & Risch, N. (1998c). Co-morbidity and familial aggregation of alcoholism and anxiety disorders. *Psychological Medicine*, 28, 773–788.

Meyers, J. K., Weissman, M. M., Tischler, G. L., Holzer, C. E., Leaf, P. J., Orvaschel, H., Anthony, J. C., Boyd, H. J., Burke, J. D., Kramer, M., & Stoltzman, R. (1984). Six-month prevalence of psychiatric disorders in three communities. *Archives of General Psychiatry*, 41, 959–967.

Pickens, R. W., Svikis, D. S., McGue, M., Lykken, D. T., Heston, L. L., & Clayton, P. J. (1991). Heterogeneity in the inheritance of alcoholism: A study of male and female twins. *Archives of General Psychology*, 48, 19–28.

Regier, D. A., Farmer, M. E., Rae, D. S., Locke, B. Z., Keith, S. J., Judd, L. L., & Goodwin, F. K. (1990). Comorbidity of mental disorders with alcohol and other drug abuse: Results from the epidemiologic catchment area (ECA) study. *Journal of the American Medical Association*, 264(19), 2511–2518.

Robins, L. N., Locke, B. Z., & Regier, D. A. (1991). An overview of psychiatric disorders in America. In Robins, L. N., & Regier, D. A. (Eds.), *Psychiatric disorders in America: The Epidemiologic Catchment Area Study* (pp. 53–81). New York: Free Press.

Rohde, P., Lewinsohn, P., & Seeley, J. (1996). Psychiatric comorbidity with problematic alcohol use in high school students. *Journal of the American Academy of Child and Adolescent Psychiatry*, 35, 101–109.

Searles, J. S. (1988). The role of genetics in the pathogenesis of alcoholism. *Journal of Abnormal Psychology*, 97, 153–167.

Shapiro, S., Skinner, E. A., Kessler, L. G., Von Korff, M., German, P. S., Tischler, G. L., Leaf, P. J., Benham, L. B., Cottler, L., & Regier, D. A. (1984). Utilization of health and mental health services. *Archives of General Psychiatry*, 41, 971–982.

Schuckit, M. A., & Smith, T. L. (1996). An 8-year follow-up of 450 sons of alcoholic and control subjects. *Archives of General Psychiatry*, 53, 202–210.

U.S. Department of Health and Human Services. (1990). *Seventh special report to the U.S. Congress on alcohol and health from the Secretary of Health and Human Services*. (1990). Washington, DC: U.S. Government Printing Office.

Williams, G. C., & DeBakey, S. F. (1992). Changes in levels of alcohol consumption: United States, 1983–1988. *British Journal of Addictions*, 87, 643–648.

Kathleen R. Merikangas and Kevin Conway

ALIENATION. In one sense, sociologists explain alienation, a deep-seated sense of dissatisfaction with one's personal existence, as an estrangement from one's social group (e.g., family, workplace, community, or bureaucratic institution such as a government agency, school, or church). The individual believes he or she does not count and lacks the power to influence the social group. In another sense, alienation is rooted in a deeply personal human experience driven by subconscious motivations, biological drives, and social development. In each case alienation is a source of lack of trust in one's social or physical environment or oneself.

It is in the personal experience with the world that the individual learns, as Erik Erikson points out, to trust or mistrust the stimuli that he or she constantly experiences. It is this personal experience of the world where lack of trust leads to the alienated person's deep sense of self-dissatisfaction, which is manifested externally through a variety of symptoms. This sense of personal dissatisfaction, according to the Menninger Foundation (*Menninger Perspective*, 1997, 28 [1]), is influenced biopsychosocially where the biology of the brain, the psychological composition of the individual, and the various social groups of which each individual is a member, contribute to his or her personal construction of the world. The dynamic interaction of these three areas determines, to a great degree, the depth of one's sense of alienation.

To some extent, all human beings are alienated. It is as if we realize at some point in our existence that we have been left all alone on a planet in the cosmos and challenged to make meaning from a potentially meaningless accident. The conscious struggle to overcome this sense of alienation is the mark of a healthy person. Conversely, the inability to face this challenge inherent within the subconscious leads to a deepening sense of alienation. As Carl Jung said (*Modern Man in Search of a Soul*, New York, 1933), "When we must deal with a problem, we instinctively refuse to try the way that leads through darkness and obscurity" (p. 97).

At one level we view this phenomenon from the perspective that the alienation of the individual is expressed in a mood, thought, and appearance resulting in a malaise toward self and life. Want of material goods, social status, or professional position does not cause the alienation felt by the individual. It is more a sense that things are not exactly as they should be and that life should be better. This is especially true in first world countries where constant activity is used as a temporary sedative for the symptoms caused by alienation. In this environment, technological advances separate workers from their work and create conditions where the worker cannot relate a personal contribution to the end product or its impact on the consumer.

Alienation is also an expression of the fragmentation of one's personality, where the self wears different masks each day, never claiming a unique identity. David Bohm (*Fragmentation and Wholeness*, The Van Leer Jerusalem Foundation, 1976) speaks of fragmentation as "causing one to lose awareness of what they are doing and thus extend the process of division beyond the limits within which it works properly" (p. 2). The alienated or fragmented self becomes what the context desires so that the self is a response to the stimuli that exist in its immediate environment. One day the self is the lover, the next the warrior, and the next the caring nurse. Never sure of its identity, the self, unable to trust its real being, continues to seek answers from multiple environments. The fragmentation of the self contributes to the feeling of alienation. Consequently, alienation is the result of this search for one's true identity in a world where answers cannot be trusted.

Individuals wander through life searching for a personal identity since their true selves are long since hidden through socialization and nurturing. This "diffusion of identity" (Erikson, 1980), creates a strong sense of separation between the individual's external and inner worlds. We can relate this sense of separation to the angst the individual feels from not being able to reach a level of fulfillment consistent with that defined by the ego. This angst, Karen Horney suggested (1945/1992), is caused by conflicts originating in false standards set up by the individual that can never be achieved. "In contrast to authentic ideals, the idealized image has a static quality. It is not a goal toward whose attainment he/she strives but a fixed idea which he/she worships" (p. 98). These illusory standards set up a myth that the person can never grasp yet, at times, seems very close. The identification of the self with this idealized image leads to consistent failure and personal dissatisfaction. The identification with the idealized self becomes the root of personal alienation. This idealized self is what the individual was taught to become in order to satisfy the needs of a parent, teacher, priest, minister, or other significant person in his or her life. Keen (*Faces of the Enemy*, New York, 1986) says:

> The good people send out armies as the symbolic representatives to act out their repressed shadows, denied hostilities, unspoken cruelties, unacceptable greed, unimagined lust for revenge against punitive parents and authorities, uncivil sexual sadism, denied animality, in a purifying blood ritual that confirms their claim to goodness before the approving eyes of history or God. (pp. 91–92)

This idealized self has no defects in the eyes of its owner. Since the idealized self is not attainable, the quest always ends in failure. Each time the quest ends in failure, the individual deepens the sense of estrangement with the true self. The individual continues to reject this self as long as the idealized self is considered the ultimate identity. This search to become like the idealized self becomes the source of inner conflict and alienation.

The failure to attain the idealized image leads the individual either to face the pain of discovering the real self or to assume the journey is impossible. Unwilling to examine the real self and to integrate those parts that one accepts with those one rejects, the person becomes alienated. Such individuals believe that separation from people, institutions, and objects is an appropriate response to their state. The greater the desire to identify with the idealized image, the greater the sense of failure and the greater the sense of separation from those whom the individual perceives as encouraging frustrating attempts to become like the idealized self.

The alienated individual feels a deep frustration from not being able to connect to this illusory ideal. The separateness from the self is manifested in a separateness from the world. The sense of separation felt by the alienated person is manifested in a variety of symptoms or characteristics. Understanding the link between these characteristics and alienation provides insight into the alienated individual's struggle. These characteristics may be associated with personality types. Horney suggested three types of personalities: the compliant, aggressive, and detached types. The compliant type asks, "Will I be liked?" The aggressive type asks, "Will I get hurt?" The detached type asks, "Will I be left alone?" To the extent that each of these types is not able to answer these questions favorably, the individual becomes alienated. Inherent in these types are expressions of alienation such as *isolation* with the detached type, *emptiness* with the compliant type, and *estrangement* with the aggressive type.

When alienation is described as isolation, a state of loneliness is created that is different from aloneness. The person experiences a separation from others, a sense of being different. The person believes that others are not like him or her. This person feels misunderstood. This creates a widening gulf of separateness that forces the isolated person to move to greater levels of isolation and away from the connectedness that serves as a healing source. No other option seems open but to move away from those who would ultimately be the source of healing.

When alienation is described as emptiness, one cannot trust oneself. Viktor Frankl believed (1984) that the innate capacity of the healthy person is to seek meaning or purpose in life. Those who are empty no longer have a purpose and simply exist. Each moment becomes a dreary replication of past moments with the future holding little, if any, hope. This sense of emptiness leaves little that is worth saving. The world is empty because the individual is empty. There is nothing inside or outside this individual to fill this void. Although this sense of emptiness can be eradicated through engagement in pursuit of a productive goal, this pursuit is often forsaken as the alienated individual asks, "What is the use?" Unlike the isolated-alienated person, the empty-alienated person moves toward social contacts to escape from his or her personal emptiness. However, personal social contacts in this case are a way of forgetting rather than becoming engaged.

When alienation is described as estrangement, the person displays anger toward the self, social institutions, and authority. The individual is estranged because he or she cannot trust people or institutions. The estranged person frames his or her environment to see a world filled with enemies and sinister plots that are designed to harm. In this context, the estranged individual wants to be loved and accepted, but his or her actions suggest the opposite. As the estranged individual moves into the world and challenges authority, others move away. This movement toward others by the estranged person and the movement away by those in the estranged person's environment confirm the person's lack of trust. As the person moves to protect himself or herself, the person buries more deeply the basic need to be unconditionally accepted.

These characteristics are not all-inclusive. They provide a view of the depth of the struggle the alienated person experiences. This struggle is manifested in these individuals' relationships with social groups—never belonging or feeling that they can trust the group. In many larger societies, there is the experience of not being able to trust the government, so there is a sense of alienation with the ruling forces within the governing structure. However, it is not the government that causes the alienation, since the government is no more than a mirror of the people who support the government's existence.

This sense of alienation is deepened for traditionally disenfranchised groups who have sought integration into first world countries. In the United States, African Americans have historically been disenfranchised. Latinos, Mexicans, women, and immigrants from Caribbean countries are also part of the disenfranchised groups. Members of these groups trust neither the government nor the majority population. Their deep sense of alienation is often expressed in creative endeavors such as music and writing. It often gives rise to people, both men and women, who seem to carry all of the alienation felt by members of their group and challenge the *status quo* of the existing structure. For example, Martin Luther King, Jr., spoke of the need to challenge the establishment as a means of healing the oppressor.

The resolution of a personal or collective sense of alienation requires the liberating of ghosts, both living and dead, who reinforce the idealized images that hold the alienated person or group prisoner. These ghosts speak from the grave and across centuries to control the behavior of the present moment. The shackles of these ghosts are manifested in the ego, which constantly demands that the person's real image match that of the idealized image. By becoming aware of the pain caused by the ego and its alienating effects, the person may become liberated from the influence of alienation.

Bibliography

Erikson, E. H. (1980). *Identity and the life cycle.* New York: Norton.

Frankl, V. (1984). *Man's search for meaning.* New York: Touchstone Press. (Original work published 1959)

Fromm, E. (1981). *On disobedience and other essays.* New York: Seabury Press.

Hammond, G. (1965). *Man in estrangement: A comparison of the thought of Paul Tillich and Erich Fromm.* Nashville, TN: Vanderbilt University Press.

Horney, K. (1937). *The collected works of Karen Horney.* New York: Norton.

Horney, K. (1992). *Our inner conflicts.* New York: Norton. (Original work published 1945)

Montagu, A., & Matson, F. (1983). *The dehumanization of man.* New York: McGraw-Hill.

Raymond L. Calabrese

ALLOCENTRISM-IDIOCENTRISM. Allocentrism is a personality attribute that is found among those who believe, feel, and act like people do in collectivist cultures (Triandis, 1995). That is, they tend to define their self as interdependent (Markus & Kitayama, 1991) with and feel close to members of their ingroups (family, co-workers, tribe, nation, or whatever group or collectivity is important in a specific culture). They give priority to ingroup goals over personal goals, emphasizing duties and obligations toward the ingroup more than attitudes as predictors of their social behavior. During social interactions they pay much attention to the needs of the other person. They tend to feel similar to other ingroup members, giving considerable weight to the desires of ingroup members, and they are willing to share resources with and to help ingroup members. They feel honored when ingroup members are honored and often feel that they have contributed to honors received by ingroup members.

Idiocentrism is a personality attribute that is found among those who believe, feel, and act as people do in individualistic cultures (Triandis, 1995). That is, they define themselves as autonomous entities, unrelated to groups; they give priority to their personal goals over the goals of ingroups; their social behavior is determined almost completely by their own attitudes, and thus norms play a minor role. They regulate their social behavior according to exchange theory, and are strongly motivated by their own preferences, needs, and rights.

The evidence shows that in collectivist cultures, such as in East Asia, there are more allocentrics than idiocentrics; in individualistic cultures, such as in Europe and North America, there are more idiocentrics than allocentrics. But the upper classes in all cultures are more idiocentric than the lower classes. Allocentrics in individualistic cultures are more likely to participate in communes, gangs, and other collectives. Idiocentrics in collectivist cultures are likely to try to escape the "oppression" of their ingroups. Idiocentrics in collectivist cultures are likely to emphasize human rights and the importance of the individual in relation to the state.

The terms were coined by Triandis, Leung, Villareal, and Clack (1985), from the Greek, *allos* = other, *idios* = self. They are commonly used together as endpoints on a continuum, much like terms such as *extraversion* and *introversion*. Allocentrics center their behavior in relation to others; idiocentrics are self-centered, at least to some extent.

The 1985 paper reported empirical evidence that allocentrics show more subordination of personal goals to ingroup goals, they define the self as an aspect of a group, and they submerge their personal identity into group identity. Idiocentrics use equity rather than equality or need to distribute resources; allocentrics use equality or need more often than equity. Allocentrics emphasize cooperation, self-sacrifice, and honesty, while idiocentrics emphasize self-reliance, a comfortable life, competition, pleasure, and social recognition. Allocentrics report receiving more and a better quality of social support than idiocentrics; idiocentrics report being lonely more frequently than allocentrics. Idiocentrics report more emphasis on achievement than allocentrics, but they also feel more alienated from their social environment. Idiocentrics are skilled in entering new groups and developing friendly but superficial conversations. Allocentrics are often shy and have difficulties in starting new relationships, but when they do develop a relationship they become more intimate than is typical among idiocentrics.

Hui and Villareal (1989) found that allocentrics were high in affiliation and idiocentrics were high in dominance.

Subsequent research has found the following:

1. Uncertainty in person perception is reduced in the case of allocentrics when they are given information about the social group membership of the stimulus person, and in the case of idiocentrics when they are given information about the accomplishments of the stimulus person.

2. Allocentrics with high self-esteem see themselves as high in their ability to have good social relations, while idiocentrics with high self-esteem see themselves as high in their competence in sports, creativity, and academics.

3. In both collectivist and individualist cultures allocentrics were more concerned with rewards and punishments received from ingroups than were idiocentrics. Allocentrics also had stronger affiliating tendencies than idiocentrics, along with higher sensitivity to rejection, and a lower need for uniqueness (Yamaguchi, Kuhlman, & Sugimori, 1995).

The antecedents of allocentrism include limited resources, ingroups that are perceived as a means of survival, and stability of residence in a homogeneous cultural environment. The antecedents of idiocentrism include affluence, exposure to a culturally heterogeneous environment, migration, social mobility, and large exposure to U.S. television programs.

The consequences of allocentrism include childrearing patterns that emphasize obedience, duty, and responsibility. Allocentrics have been found to have happy marriages more often than idiocentrics (Antill, 1983). The consequences of idiocentrism include childrearing patterns that emphasize self-reliance, independence, achievement, and creativity.

[*See also* Cross-Cultural Psychology, *article on* Theories and Methods of Study; *and* Personality.]

Bibliography

Antill, J. K. (1983). Sex role complementarity versus similarity in married couples. *Journal of Personality and Social Psychology, 45,* 145–155.

Hui, C. H., & Villareal, M. (1989). Individualism-collectivism and psychological needs: Their relationship in two cultures. *Journal of Cross Cultural Psychology, 20,* 310–323.

Markus, H., & Kitayama, S. (1991). Culture and self: Implications for cognition, emotion, and motivation. *Psychological Review, 98,* 224–253.

Triandis, H. C. (1995). *Individualism and collectivism.* Boulder, CO: Westview Press.

Triandis, H. C., Leung, K., Villareal, M., & Clack, F. L. (1985). Allocentric versus idiocentric tendencies: Convergent and discriminant validation. *Journal of Research in Personality, 19,* 395–415.

Yamaguchi, S., Kuhlman, D. M., & Sugimori, S. (1995). Personality correlates of allocentric tendencies in individualist and collectivist cultures. *Journal of Cross-Cultural Psychology, 26,* 658–672.

Harry C. Triandis

ALLPORT, FLOYD HENRY. Often heralded as the "founder of modern experimental social psychology" (Post, 1980, p. 369), Allport, who was born in Milwaukee, Wisconsin, was the second child in a talented family of four sons that included psychologist Gordon Allport.

Floyd Allport's interest in psychology first developed at Harvard University where he earned a bachelor's degree in 1914 and a doctorate in 1919. In graduate school, he worked with Hugo Münsterberg on a dissertation in social psychology, a field then dominated by the notions of group mind and instinct. In his dissertation, entitled *The Social Influence: An Experimental Study of the Effect of the Group upon Individual Mental Processes* (1919), Allport proposed to take the field of social psychology in a new conceptual and methodological direction. This project culminated in *Social Psychology* (1924), a book published shortly after Allport moved to Syracuse University, and one widely hailed as a landmark text in the field.

The significance of *Social Psychology* lies in its focus, methodological orientation, and theoretical rationale. In the book, Allport broke with the prevailing norms of social psychology by emphasizing the individual over the group. He dismissed previous work on the group mind and suggested that everything of psychological importance was to be found within the individual. "There is no psychology of groups," Allport maintained "which is not essentially and entirely a psychology of individuals" (p. 4). Concurrent with this shift in focus, Allport called for a change in the field's method. He abandoned earlier techniques of historical, cultural, and philosophical analysis in favor of the experimental method. Finally, Allport provided a behavioristic framework for social psychology. The result was a social psychology defined largely in terms of stimuli and reactions; the former consisting of the behavior of other individuals while the latter consisted of the adjustments of the individual under study. Although sociologists resisted Allport's formulations, his perspective was highly influential in psychology, and it helped establish a tradition of experimental social psychology that continues into the present day (Danziger, 1992).

The remainder of Allport's career was devoted largely to developing the themes he had mapped out in *Social Psychology*. In *Institutional Behavior*, published in 1933, he renewed his attack on imprecision in social science. The following year he proposed an elaborate program of empirical research on conformity. In the postwar period, Allport's work took an increasingly theoretical turn. His goal was to develop a scientific framework for explaining the "basic realities" of social psychological life. Known as "enestruence theory" this ambitious project attempted to explain the nature of social reality through an analysis of the psychobiological processes within the individual and between interacting individuals.

Allport retired in 1957. For his many theoretical and empirical contributions, he received the Distinguished Scientific Contribution Award from the American Psychological Association and the Gold Medal Award from the American Psychological Association Foundation. A dedicated and at times controversial figure, Allport helped define modern social psychology, and his stress on objectivity, experimentation, and conceptual rigor remain at the heart of the field.

Bibliography

Allport, F. (1919). *The social influence: An experimental study of the effect of the group upon individual mental processes*. Unpublished doctoral dissertation, Harvard University.

Allport, F. (1924). *Social psychology*. Boston: Houghton Mifflin.

Allport, F. (1933). *Institutional behavior: Essays toward a reinterpreting of contemporary social organization*. Chapel Hill, NC: University of North Carolina Press.

Allport, F. (1934). The J-curve hypothesis of conforming behavior. *Journal of Social Psychology, 5,* 141–183.

Allport, F. (1974). Floyd H. Allport. In G. Lindzey (Ed.), *A history of psychology in autobiography* (Vol. 6, pp. 3–29). Englewood Cliffs, NJ: Prentice Hall.

Danziger, K. (1992). The project of an experimental social psychology: Historical perspectives. *Science in Context, 5,* 309–328.

Graumann, C. (1986). The individualization of the social and the desocialization of the individual: Floyd H. Allport's contribution to social psychology. In C. Graumann & S. Moscovici (Eds.), *Changing conceptions of a crowd mind and behavior* (pp. 97–116). New York: Springer-Verlag.

Katz, D. (1979). Floyd H. Allport. *American Psychologist, 34,* 351–353.

Post, D. (1980). Floyd H. Allport and the launching of modern social psychology. *Journal of the History of the Behavioral Sciences, 16,* 369–376.

Ian A. M. Nicholson

ALLPORT, GORDON WILLARD (1897–1967), American psychologist. Gordon Allport played a major role in shaping the fields of both personality and social psychology in the first half of the twentieth century. His undergraduate and doctoral degrees were both from Harvard, where he studied with Hugo Münsterberg, and later Herbert Langfeld and William McDougall. Through college teaching in Turkey and postgraduate study at the Universities of Berlin, Hamburg, and Cambridge during the years immediately after World War I, he became familiar with the Gestalt movement and other important developments in German psychology. These intellectual experiences and personal contacts had an enduring impact on his own later work and his contributions to American psychology. Apart from a few years at Dartmouth, his entire academic career was spent at Harvard.

Allport wrote one of the first dissertations and taught one of the first courses on "personality." His classic early text (Allport, 1937; revised version, 1961), along with several key earlier papers (e.g., Allport, 1927, 1931) laid out the basic conceptual framework of the field, identified key issues, and established *trait* as the key concept and class of variable for the description of personality. Allport's conception of trait, however, led to some later confusion of terminology, since he used the same word to refer to stylistic or expressive traits and motivational or "dynamic traits," a very different class of variables that other psychologists, such as Henry Alexander Murray, Jr., preferred to label as "needs" or motives; (see Winter, John, Stewart, Klohnen, & Duncan, 1998).

Allport also introduced or promoted several other key personality concepts. He emphasized the central role of the *self* in the organization of personality, along with the related notion of *propriate striving* (i.e., ego involvement). He stressed the importance of *values* and developed, with Philip Vernon, the *Study of Values* (Allport, Vernon, & Lindzey, 1960), which became one of the most widely used personality tests between 1930 and 1970. Allport introduced the concept of the *functional autonomy of motives* to suggest that behaviors originally (e.g., in childhood) based on one motive may later come to acquire a quite different motivational base in the mature adult personality. While Allport's notion of functional autonomy remains controversial, it did prefigure more widely accepted later concepts such as intrinsic motivation, "life tasks" or goals derived from age-graded roles (Cantor & Zirkel, 1990), actualization as a motivational force, and even the concept of developmental "stages" (i.e., nonlinear reorganizations of motivation, cognition, and behavior).

Throughout his career, Allport emphasized the *idiographic approach* (later termed "morphogenic") to personality—that is, the study of how traits and other personality variables become integrated into the unique structures of individual persons, in contrast to the *nomothetic* (later "dimensional") approach of studying one or more variables across a large sample of different persons. (The idiographic-nomothetic distinction was especially emphasized by the nineteenth-century German theorists Windelband and Dilthey, as well as the psychologist William Stern, with whom Allport studied in Germany.) Allport's position was not exclusively idiographic, however; he argued that nomothetic research and idiographic methods were necessary complements (Allport, 1962). Consistent with this emphasis, Allport argued for the importance of case studies in personality psychology—though he himself only carried out a few, most notably that of "Jenny" (Allport, 1965), the widowed mother of his college roommate (Winter, 1997).

In the end, however, Allport's most enduring contribution to personality was probably his intellectual stance of eclectic humanism, maintained in polite but determined opposition to the more doctrinaire approaches of both psychoanalysis and behaviorism. While the questions he asked and the criticisms he raised sometimes seemed out-of-date to his contemporaries, they often reemerged in later developments (e.g., the impact of the "cognitive revolution" on personality, or the reemergence of interest in case studies and idiographic methods).

Allport was also a major figure in social psychology during the first half of the twentieth century. He proposed *attitude* as the central organizing concept of the field. He defined attitude as a "mental and neural state

of readiness . . . exerting a directive or dynamic influence upon the individual's response to all objects and situations with which it is related" (1935, p. 810). Allport's psychological analysis of prejudice (1954) was a definitive theoretical statement that established the main lines of much subsequent research.

Overall, Allport's contributions reflected an older, broad-based style of doing social psychology; thus the rise to prominence of laboratory experimentation and a microcognitive perspective in the 1960s may have obscured his influence. In fact, he made important and enduring contributions to a wide variety of other social psychological and personality topics. In the psychology of religion, his distinction between intrinsic and extrinsic religiosity remains widely used (Allport & Ross, 1967). His research on radio, as the first systematic study of the psychological impact of radio on individuals and groups, exerted an important influence on later experimental research in communications (Cantril & Allport, 1935). Other landmark studies included the patterning of expressive behavior (Allport & Vernon, 1933), the psychology of rumor (Allport & Postman, 1947), and the use of personal documents in psychological analysis (Allport, 1942).

Allport played an important administrative and editorial role in twentieth-century American psychology. He served a long term as editor of the *Journal of Abnormal and Social Psychology*. He was a founder of the Society for the Psychological Study of Social Issues. At a distance as well as directly, he was a mentor to many twentieth-century psychologists. From his experience in Europe, for example, he brought a broad, interdisciplinary, and historical perspective to American psychology, most explicitly in his personality texts (1937, 1961) and his handbook chapter on the historical background of social psychology (1969).

In the years after World War I, he was a major channel for the spread of European concepts and approaches; in the years before World War II, he helped to establish refugee psychologists fleeing Hitler's Germany. During the war, he participated in an interdisciplinary workshop at Harvard on "morale"; after the war, he was a member of the key interdisciplinary group that founded Harvard's Department of Social Relations, which during its 24 years of existence combined psychology, sociology, and anthropology. At his death, he was Harvard's first Cabot Professor of Social Ethics, thereby helping to unite psychological knowledge and ethical concerns, the two interests of his undergraduate years.

Bibliography

Allport, G. W. (1927). Concepts of trait and personality. *Psychological Bulletin, 24,* 284–293. Allport's early survey of important personality concepts.

Allport, G. W. (1931). What is a trait of personality? *Journal of Abnormal and Social Psychology, 25,* 368–372. The first systematic analysis of the concept of trait as used in personality.

Allport, G. W. (1935). Attitudes. In C. Murchison (Ed.), *A handbook of social psychology* (pp. 798–844). Worcester, MA: Clark University Press. Allport's early systematic statement of the concept of attitude.

Allport, G. W. (1937). *Personality: A psychological interpretation.* New York: Holt. As one of the first personality texts, it helped to define the major concepts and issues in the field.

Allport, G. W. (1950). *The nature of personality: Selected papers.* Cambridge, MA: Addison-Wesley.

Allport, G. W. (1954). *The nature of prejudice.* Reading, MA: Addison-Wesley. Classic statement of the concepts and issues in the psychological study of prejudice.

Allport, G. W. (1960). *Personality and social encounter: Selected essays.* Boston: Beacon Press.

Allport, G. W. (1961). *Pattern and growth in personality.* New York: Rinehart, & Winston. A substantial revision and elaboration of Allport's 1937 textbook.

Allport, G. W. (1962). The general and the unique in psychological science. *Journal of Personality, 30,* 405–422. Allport's late discussion of the idiographic approach and associated methods.

Allport, G. W. (1965). *Letters from Jenny.* New York: Harcourt Brace.

Allport, G. W. (1968). *The person in psychology.* Boston: Beacon Press. Contains twenty of Allport's later papers on topics such as the concept of trait, idiographic methods, prejudice, intrinsic-extrinsic religious orientation, and evaluations of William James, William Stern, Kurt Lewin, and others. Concludes with an autobiography.

Allport, G. W. (1969). The historical background of modern social psychology. In G. Lindzey & E. Aronson (Eds.), *Handbook of social psychology* (Vol. 1, 2nd ed. pp. 1–80). Reading, MA: Addison-Wesley.

Allport, G. W., & Postman, L. J. (1947). *The psychology of rumor.* New York: Holt. Analysis of the concept of rumor, based on World War II research.

Allport, G. W., & Ross, J. M. (1967). Personal religious orientation and prejudice. *Journal of Personality and Social Psychology, 5,* 432–443.

Allport, G. W., & Vernon, P. E. (1933). *Studies in expressive movement.* New York: Macmillan.

Allport, G. W., Vernon, P. E., & Lindzey, G. (1960). *A study of values* (3rd ed.). Boston: Houghton Mifflin.

Cantor, N., & Zirkel, S. (1990). Personality, cognition, and purposive behavior. In L. Pervin (Ed.), *Handbook of personality theory and research* (pp. 135–164). New York: Guilford Press.

Cantril, H., & Allport, G. W. (1935). *The psychology of radio.* New York: Harper.

Craik, K. H., Hogan, R., & Wolfe, R. N. (Eds.). (1993). *Fifty years of personality psychology.* New York: Plenum Press. Collection of papers about Allport and the current status of issues and concepts related to his perspective on personality.

Winter, D. G. (1997). Allport's life and Allport's psychology. *Journal of Personality, 65,* 723–731. Relates aspects and experiences of Allport's life to his concepts and theories of personality psychology.

Winter, D. G., John, O. P., Stewart, A. J., Klohnen, E., & Duncan, L. E. (1998). Traits and motives: Toward an integration of two traditions in personality research. *Psychological Review, 105,* 230–250.

David G. Winter

ALTERED STATES OF CONSCIOUSNESS. Currently, the notion of altered states of consciousness (ASCs) is used in psychology in rather general terms. It denotes states in which the content, form, or quality of experiences is significantly different from ordinary states of consciousness and it depicts states that are not symptoms of any mental disorders. Due to the lack of a commonly accepted view on ordinary states of consciousness, this definition remains imprecise. It is a general concept uniting studies and knowledge of a variety of states differentiated from the most common, ordinary waking states of consciousness. It includes states experienced in not too well understood conditions, such as sleep, hypnosis, activity under psychoactive drugs, meditation, and biofeedback, as well as unique states described as mystical ecstasy or union, samadhi in yoga, satori in Zen, or trans states. This term is also applied in transpersonal psychology to studies of transpersonal states and in parapsychology to research on extrasensory perception and psychokinesis (PSI Phenomena).

The concept became commonly applied in the meaning proposed by Arnold Ludwig in 1966 (*Archives of General Psychiatry, 15,* 225–234) and popularized by Tart (1969), where Ludwig's paper was reprinted. He defined altered state(s) of consciousness as follows:

[A]ny mental state(s) induced by various physiological, psychological, or pharmacological maneuvers or agents, which can be recognized subjectively by the individual himself (or by an objective observer of the individual) as representing a sufficient deviation in subjective experience or psychological functioning from certain general norms for that individual during alert, waking consciousness. This sufficient deviation may be represented by a greater preoccupation than usual with internal sensations or mental processes, changes in the formal characteristics of thought, and impairment of reality testing to various degrees. (Ludwig 1966, p. 225)

The author acknowledged that such a general definition poses certain difficulties, but it is compensated by including a wide range of related phenomena.

Along with the development of knowledge about altered states of consciousness, some more specific concepts have been offered: discrete altered states of consciousness (Tart, 1975), alternate state of consciousness (Zinberg, 1977), ultraconsciousness (Dean, *American Journal of Psychiatry*, 1973, *130*, 1036–1038). However, none of these terms has become widely applied.

After a period of domination by behaviorism and psychoanalysis, studies on ASCs brought issues of consciousness and subjective experiences into the mainstream of psychology, in the 1970s. Behaviorism did not consider consciousness at all; psychoanalysis focused on unconscious rather than conscious problems. The common occurrence of ASCs was documented by reexamination of phenomenological descriptions gathered in a variety of writings and by questionnaire surveys. Altered states of consciousness were studied in experiments with meditation, sensory deprivation (and restricted environmental stimulation techniques), hypnosis, and consciousness-altering drugs and were taken into consideration in other research, including sleep and daydreaming. Results of a meaningful number of questionnaire surveys indicated that some ASCs are occasionally experienced by most of the population. The results of research suggested that human beings have the potential to achieve a specific psychophysiological state of rest, described originally as a "fourth state of consciousness" (besides ordinary waking, REM, and NREM sleep; R. K. Wallace, H. Benson, and A. F. Wilson, *American Journal of Physiology*, 1971, *221*, 795–799). It was later elaborated and popularized as "the relaxation response" by Benson (1975). Unfortunately, similar psychophysiological reactions were also described during rest (D. S. Holmes, *American Psychologist*, 1984, *39*, 1–10). Electroencephalographic studies did not bring unequivocal results; however, alterations in states of consciousness are often considered in terms of changes in brain hemisphere activity.

The Phenomenology of ASCs

Ludwig presented the following characteristics of ASCs: (1) alterations in thinking; (2) disturbed time sense; (3) loss of control; (4) change in emotional expression; (5) body image change; (6) perceptual distortions; (7) change in meaning or significance; (8) sense of the ineffable; (9) feelings of rejuvenation; and (10) hypersuggestibility.

Various lists of characteristics of more specific ASCs, based on theoretical analyses, were incorporated in a questionnaire survey (Kokoszka, 1992–1993) that differentiated profoundly ASCs, which encompass unusual states considered as mystical or ultraconsciousness states from more common superficially ASCs, occurring in relaxation or in hypnoticlike states or during common everyday trans states. It was found that profoundly ASCs (a feeling of being one with the universe, the experience of contact with God, and the impression of understanding "everything") were accompanied, in more than 15% of reports, by such experiences as a feeling of happiness, peace, and joy; a feeling of devo-

tion to God; an intellectual illumination, understanding of an essence of the Universe, God, and so on; and a feeling of total love for all living creatures.

In contrast, superficial ASCs—experiences of sitting staring off into space; being engrossed in a book or a movie; or a lack of awareness of surroundings during a monotonous activity—were most frequently (more than 20% of reports) accompanied by the following experiences; a disturbed sense of time; a loss of the sense of reality; a constriction of perception; a feeling of absolute peace and silence; and a feeling of being sunk in pleasant positive feelings.

Theories and Hypotheses

Of the many theories and hypotheses explaining ASCs, only some of the most important will be mentioned here. Altered states of consciousness are considered in terms of deautomatization of psychological structures that organize, limit, select, and interpret perceptual stimuli (A. J. Deikman, *Psychiatry*, 1966, *29*, 324–338); influences that interfere with the normal inflow of sensory stimuli or the normal outflow of motor impulses (included in Ludwig's 1966 article already mentioned); temporary reorganizations of brain functioning (Tart, 1985); breakdown of the bicameral mind (Jaynes, 1976); factors triggering a natural drive to ASCs (A. T. Weil, *The Natural Mind*, Boston, 1972); positions on two natural continua of potentially attainable states of consciousness, that is, perception-hallucination and perception-meditation (Fischer, *Science*, 1971, *174*, 897–904); common everyday trans—a daytime manifestation of the ultradian rhythm causing the REM-NREM cycle during sleep (Rossi, in B. B. Wolman and M. Ullman, Eds., *Handbook of States of Consciousness*, New York, 1986); temporal simultaneous fluctuations of the current state of consciousness along the developmental levels of personality (vertical dimension) and among the four main states of consciousness on a horizontal plane: REM sleep, NREM sleep, ordinary waking states of consciousness, and differentiated waking states of consciousness (a daytime equivalent of NREM and REM, respectively) (Kokoszka, 1993). Altered states of consciousness have also been interpreted as higher states of consciousness according to Eastern philosophy and transpersonal psychology and as regressive phenomena according to psychoanalysis.

[*See also* Consciousness and Unconsciousness; *and* Dreams.]

Bibliography

Benson, H. (1975). *The relaxation response.* New York: Morrow. A very popular book on the psychophysiological concept of ASCs and method of relaxation.
Farthing, G. W. (1992). *The psychology of consciousness.* En-

glewood Cliffs: Prentice Hall. This book includes a comprehensive review of literature covering altered states of consciousness.

James, W. (1902). *The varieties of religious experience.* Cambridge, MA: Harvard University Press. Classical descriptions of the variety of ASCs. Published in numbered editions.

Jaynes, J. (1976). *The origin of consciousness in the breakdown of the bicameral mind.* Boston: Houghton Mifflin. Controversial theory based on historical analysis of human development, which received a lot of attention from scientists and the wider public, published in numbered editions.

Kokoszka, A. (1993). A rationale for psychology of consciousness. In J. Brzeziński, S. Di Nuovo, T. Marek, & T. Maruszewski (Eds.), *Creativity and consciousness. Philosophical and psychological dimensions* (pp. 313–322). Poznań Studies in the Philosophy of the Sciences and the Humanities, Vol. 31. Amsterdam: Rodopi, 1993. The recapitulation of a series of papers on models of consciousness aimed at integration of existing theories of ASCs.

Kokoszka, A. (1992–1993). Occurrence of altered states of consciousness among students: Profoundly and superficially altered states in wakefulness. *Imagination Cognition and Personality, 12,* 231–247. An analysis of phenomenology of ASCs based on the results of a questionnaire survey.

Ornstein, R. (1996). *The psychology of consciousness.* New York: Penguin Books. (Original work published 1986.) A classical, popular study of consciousness states, enriched by excerpts from the most meaningful texts dealing with consciousness and its altered states.

Pope, K., & Singer J. (Eds.). (1978). *The stream of consciousness.* New York: Plenum Press. The philosophical and psychological roots of the psychology of states presented in a comprehensive, understandable way.

Tart, C. T. (Ed.). (1990). *Altered states of consciousness* (3rd ed. rev.). New York: Psychological Processes. (Original work published 1969.) A classical book of readings including fundamental concepts of ASCs.

Tart, C. T. (1975). *States of mind.* New York: Dutton. Theory explaining a variety of natural states of consciousness, including discrete ASCs.

Wallace, B., & Fisher, L. E. (1999). *Consciousness and behavior* (4th ed.). Boston: Allyn & Bacon. A comprehensive review of knowledge about consciousness and its altered states, based on understanding of consciousness as a multileveled phenomena.

Ward, C. A. (Ed.). (1989). *Altered states of consciousness and mental health. A cross-cultural perspective.* Newbury Park: Sage. Cross-cultural descriptions and analyses of a variety of ASCs.

Walsh, R. N., & Vaughan, F. (Eds.). (1993). *Paths beyond ego. The transpersonal vision.* Los Angeles: Tarcher. Excerpts from the most meaningful texts of transpersonal studies on ASCs.

Zinberg, N. E. (Ed.). (1977). *Alternate states of consciousness.* New York: Free Press. Some influential theories of ASCs briefly presented by their authors.

Andrzej Kokoszka

ALTERNATIVE DISPUTE RESOLUTION (ADR) is the use of nonadjudicative third-party procedures to resolve disputes. ADR was so named because it is an "alternative" to adjudication. In practice, it is also an alternative, or sometimes a preliminary, to negotiated settlement. ADR services were originally provided by the private sector and by not-for-profit agencies, and such services have greatly proliferated. In addition, since the late 1970s, there has been rapid development of court-administered ("court-annexed") dispute resolution services.

Most cases that go to ADR involve civil disputes; for example, disagreements about visitation rights in divorce or controversies initiated by dissatisfied customers, injured motorists, violated patent holders, or businesses suffering from construction flaws in their buildings. Many contracts provide for ADR hearings if a dispute develops. ADR is also sometimes used as a substitute for minor criminal proceedings or as an adjunct to sentencing in more serious criminal cases.

The most common ADR procedures involve either mediation, in which a third party (or sometimes a team of third parties) tries to help disputants reach their own agreement, or arbitration, in which a third party listens to both sides of a case and then renders a judgment. Arbitration judgments may either be binding on or advisory to the disputants. If the latter, they tend to structure subsequent negotiation between the disputants, providing an alternative to wishful thinking that might otherwise block agreement. Another common procedure involves a combination of mediation and arbitration called "med-arb," in which the third party first tries to mediate the dispute and then, if the disputants do not reach agreement, turns to binding arbitration. Fact finding, in which an expert such as an accountant renders a judgment on a difficult technical issue, is sometimes also classified as ADR. There are a number of more esoteric ADR procedures, including nonbinding ("summary") jury trials and victim-offender confrontations.

The literature on ADR consists mainly of practitioner manuals, commentary on the field of practice, case studies, and evaluation studies. Theory-driven research on such topics as negotiation, conflict resolution, and procedural justice is highly relevant to ADR but has not greatly influenced the field.

According to MacCoun, Lind, and Tyler (1992), ADR programs are usually adopted in the hope of achieving one or more of the following outcomes:

> [T]o save money and time, to decrease court backlogs, to enhance litigant satisfaction and perceptions of fairness, to generate outcomes that are better fitted to the particular situation in the dispute, to facilitate continuing interaction among the disputants, and to increase the legitimacy and acceptance of the decision and the legal process. (p. 96)

These outcomes are the main criteria against which ADR programs have been evaluated.

Evaluation studies reveal that court-annexed ADR has not made a significant inroad into court backlogs. This may well be because ADR hearings are only held in a small percentage of the entire court caseload. In addition, court-annexed programs do not appear to have produced much cost reduction for the disputants or the court. This may be because some cases that would otherwise be settled by out-of-court negotiation are being sent to the court for mediation or arbitration. The findings on time saved are mixed, presumably because some ADR programs are speedier than others.

The most persistent pro-ADR finding is a high level of disputant satisfaction and sense of fairness concerning these procedures. For example, Roehl and Cook (1989) report that "80 to 89 percent of disputants in diverse criminal and civil disputes were satisfied with the mediator, the terms of agreement, and the mediation process" (p. 33); and E. Allan Lind et al. (1990) report that disputants were more satisfied with the process and outcome of court-annexed arbitration hearings than with negotiated settlements. A possible explanation for such positive evaluations is that ADR hearings usually get the disputants (rather than their lawyers) heavily involved in the proceedings and cover the issues that the disputants feel are most important.

McEwen and Maiman (1984) have found considerably greater compliance with settlements in small claims mediation than in small-claims adjudication; and Pearson and Thoennes (1989) report somewhat less striking results in the same direction for divorce agreements. The latter study also found that there was a better relationship between the disputants after mediation than after adjudication, though the authors properly make no claim for mediation as a cure for distressed relationships. Perhaps the most compelling argument for ADR is that it provides third-party assistance with many disputes that would otherwise not be settled because the legal issues are too cloudy or the disputants too impecunious to employ adjudication.

Most of the evaluation research on ADR has looked at the impact of one or another type of program, ignoring more detailed questions about the kinds of programs that work best with different types of disputes or the third-party tactics that are most effective in each kind of program. It will be hard to provide definitive answers about the value of ADR until research about these and similar questions is done. Such research will need to rely much more heavily on theory in related fields, such as social psychology and conflict resolution, than has most of the research on ADR to date.

Bibliography

Duffy, K. G., Grosch, W. W., & Olczak, P. V. (Eds.). (1991). *Community mediation: A handbook for practitioners and researchers.* New York: Guilford Press. Behaviorally oriented chapters on most ADR techniques.

Goldberg, S. B., Green, E., & Sander, F. (1985). *Dispute resolution.* Boston: Little, Brown. Classic textbook surveying ADR as a field of practice.

Kressel, K., Pruitt, D. G., & Associates. (1989). *Mediation research: The process and effectiveness of third-party intervention.* San Francisco, CA: Jossey-Bass. The directors of seventeen research projects on mediation, summarize their research.

Lind, E. A. (1990). *Law & Society Review, 24,* 953–996.

MacCoun, R. J., Lind, E. A., & Tyler, T. R. (1992). Alternative dispute resolution in trial and appellate courts. In D. K. Kagehiro & W. S. Laufer (Eds.), *Handbook of psychology and law* (pp. 95–118). New York: Springer-Verlag. Theoretically informed overview of evaluation research in court-annexed ADR programs.

McEwen, C. A., & Maiman, R. J. (1984). *Law & Society Review, 18,* 11–49.

Pearson, J., & Thoennes, N. (1989). In K. Kressel, D. G. Pruitt et al. (Eds.), *Mediation research.* San Francisco: Jossey-Bass.

Roehl, J. A., & Cook, R. F. (1989). In K. Kressel, D. G. Pruitt et al. (Eds.), *Mediation research.* San Francisco: Jossey-Bass.

Rolph, E., Moller, E., & Petersen, L. (1994). *Escaping the courthouse: Private alternative dispute resolution in Los Angeles.* Santa Monica, CA: Rand. Overview of the fast-growing private-sector branch of ADR services.

Dean G. Pruitt

ALTERNATIVE FAMILIES. *See* Family Psychology, *article on* Theories of Family Dynamics.

ALTERNATIVE SCHOOLS. The standard practice of school assignment in the United States has been to designate attendance areas based upon neighborhoods from which students are drawn. Parents may believe the assigned school is not consonant with the values, political views, social milieu, or academic content they want for their children and may seek alternative institutions for the education of their children. In the broad sense this is what is meant by alternative schools.

Public schooling is situated at the intersection of two distinct rights which may come into conflict. On the one hand, parents have the right to rear their children in the manner and with the values to which they are committed. On the other hand, society has the right to establish a common schooling experience to prepare the population for continued social reproduction of a common set of economic, linguistic, cultural, and political institutions. To meet this social goal, public schooling is guaranteed by state constitutions with the details of their operations ensconced in legislation designed to promote the public interest. These obligations are discharged by local educational authorities with compulsory attendance required by the young. Even when the latter arrangements are determined through elected legislatures and school boards, the outcomes may violate the views and preferences of families. Under these conditions, families may seek alternatives. After decades of indeterminacy, the United States Supreme Court ruled in 1923 that private schools subject to state regulations can serve as alternatives for meeting compulsory attendance laws.

Historically, religious beliefs were the most important basis for seeking alternative schools. For example, nineteenth-century public schools were based upon religious values and practices that were alien to Catholics. In response, Catholics started their own alternative system of education in the form of parish or parochial schools, highly subsidized through contributions and the poverty vows of their religious teachers. Other religious groups also sought alternatives to existing public schools, as did those who desired more exclusive or elite academic institutions of privilege for their children.

There are a number of theoretical frameworks for understanding the phenomenon of alternative schools. Hirschman (1970), emphasized two mechanisms by which clients of an institution seek satisfaction, *voice* and *exit*. Voice refers to the use of democratic processes such as discourse, debate, protest, and other forms of governance and participation to change an institution. Exit refers to the act of leaving one institution in favor of a better alternative rather than struggling for change. When the effort required to use voice is perceived to be high and the probability of change is low, clients are likely to consider exit. Alternative schools exemplify the exit option in which parents seek a schooling option for their child which matches more closely their values and beliefs about what will benefit their child. With either the income to pay for private alternatives or the mobility to move to another neighborhood or community, families can take advantage of alternative schools.

In the 1960s, the alternative school concept began to take on new life. The generally rebellious spirit of youth that accompanied the escalation of the Vietnam War created substantial resistance to traditional schooling among parents and students. Many schools responded by providing more variety in the curriculum, as well as credit for engaging in community-based activities. In other cases, public alternative schools were established that were responsive to student concerns. At the same time, a large number of independent alternative schools were established that put aside conventional rules and curriculum and empowered students with considerable freedom to design their own

studies, a movement documented by Graudbard (1972). These schools were premised on the view that it was futile to try to alter the culture of the public school. Instead, parents set up their own institutions, classic examples of social learning and collective efficacy fitting the analysis of Bandura (1986).

A more traditional theme from learning psychology that lies at the heart of alternative schools is that of "aptitude-treatment interaction," a field developed by Cronbach and Snow (1981). Students are characterized by different learning aptitudes for which the same instructional treatment may have different consequences. For example, some students have learning aptitudes that thrive on structure and memorization, whereas others benefit from open and creative learning situations stressing individual initiative and personal interpretation. Direct instruction reinforced with associative learning exercises may benefit the first group, but have negative consequences on learning for the second. Self-directed activities based upon constructivist assumptions as elaborated by Brooks and Brooks (1993) may favor learning in the second group, but have discouraging effects on learning in the first. In theory, each school and teacher should create classrooms which provide individualized instructional treatments that match the specific learning aptitudes of students. This may not be possible when different treatments are incompatible in the same entity or when a large number of aptitudes are represented. Classrooms and schools tend to provide instructional approaches that support some types of aptitudes rather than others. Thus, parents may seek a different type of school which more closely matches the instructional treatments they believe will maximize their children's learning.

In the past, these alternatives could only be obtained by moving to a different neighborhood or community or by sending a child to a private school. Both of these are costly. Since the 1970s, there have been major thrusts to create alternative schools in the public sector. Many districts and some states now permit public choice among their schools, if space is available. Of particular importance has been the establishment of magnet schools that specialize in particular subjects (e.g., science, technology, the arts, multicultural, or international studies) or different instructional strategies (e.g., computers, independent projects, traditional lectures) to attract students with different interests and learning aptitudes. Such schools have been used as an instrument for desegregating neighborhood schools by attracting students throughout a school district around common themes, rather than assigning students according to their residential location. In the 1990s, the alternative school movement has extended to "charter" schools which are proposed and implemented by parent groups or teachers with public funding, but with quasi-autonomy from many state and district restrictions. A more extensive initiative is to permit parents to choose any school that meets minimal standards established by the state whether sponsored under public or private auspices. These schools would be funded by public vouchers that could be used at any "approved" school, even those sponsored by religious authorities. Under a voucher plan, all schools would become alternative schools. Such an approach to schooling would maximize family choice, but at the potential expense of sacrificing common educational experiences required to prepare the young for democratic life with shared values, language, institutions of political participation, and economic tenets.

Bibliography

Bandura, A. (1986). *Social foundations of thought and action.* Englewood Cliffs, NJ: Prentice Hall.

Brooks, J, & Brooks, M. (1993) *In search of understanding: The case for constructivist classrooms.* Alexandria, VA: Association for Supervision and Curriculum Development.

Clune, W., & Witte, J. (Eds.). (1990). *The theory of choice and control in education* (Vols. 1 & 2). London & New York: Falmer Press. The best comprehensive work on educational choice and its implications for alternative schools with essays on the different forms of educational choice including vouchers and magnet schools.

Cronbach, L. J., & Snow, R. E. (1981). *Aptitudes and instructional methods: A handbook for research on interactions.* New York: Irvington.

Friedman, M. (1962). The role of government in education. In *Capitalism and Freedom.* Chicago: University of Chicago Press. Provides the classic rationale for vouchers and alternative schools that are largely financed by the government, but operated by private entities.

Graubard, A. (1972). *Free the children: Radical reform and the free school movement.* New York: Pantheon Books. The best source on the origins of alternative schools as an outcome of the decade of the sixties and the reaction of youth to the Vietnam War.

Hirschman A. (1970). *Exit, voice and loyalty.* Cambridge, MA: Harvard University Press.

Levin, H. M. (1991) The economics of educational choice. *Economics of Education Review, 10,* 137–158. Addresses the consequences of alternative schools under a market system.

Nathan, J. (1996). *Charter schools.* San Francisco: Jossey-Bass.

Sarason, S. (1982). *The culture of the school and the problem of change* (2nd ed.). Boston: Allyn & Bacon. Sets out a picture of why school culture is resistant to change.

Henry M. Levin

ALTRUISM. Questions of when, to what extent, and why people help one another have long been of interest to psychologists, and from the early 1970s to the present such research has flourished. [*See* Prosocial Behavior.] Most explanations for altruistic behavior rely on the assumption that people help (or avoid helping) to maximize personal rewards and to minimize personal costs. For instance, researchers have asserted, and found evidence for, such things as people helping others in order to maintain their own good mood or to alleviate their guilt, and people avoiding helping those with aversive characteristics to avoid their own distress.

Only a small, but a very determined, number of scientists have asked whether helping is ever truly altruistic, with some using the term *altruistic* to refer to helping that entails more costs than benefits to the donor, and a few using it to refer to helping that is solely motivated by concern for others' welfare.

These scientists have discussed at least five antecedents of altruistic helping: inclusive fitness, reciprocal benefits, the docility of humans, spontaneous communication of motives and emotions, and empathy. Discussions of the first four arise from evolutionary theory. Although empirical evidence consistent with these arguments is available, the arguments are difficult to prove. Discussions of empathy motivating helping have come out of mainstream psychology and, although still difficult to prove, have been subjected to empirical tests.

Inclusive Fitness

Evolutionary theory is based on the notion of the fittest or best adapted individuals being most likely to pass their genes on to future generations. Theorists who argue that "inclusive fitness" can explain altruism point out that although it might seem detrimental to the survival of a person's genes for that person to incur more costs than benefits in helping others, this is not necessarily the case. For humans to survive long enough to pass their genetic characteristics on to their offspring, these theorists point out, it is advantageous for them to belong to a group which protects all its members. The genes of people who act not just in their own self-interests but who help other, closely related, members of their group will be more likely to survive. This is because both the altruistic person and his or her relatives share genes that are more likely to survive and reproduce if the group takes care of its members. Thus, unselfish helping may have been selected for through evolution (e.g., Hamilton, 1964).

Consistent with these arguments are findings reported by Burnstein, Crandall, and Kitayama (1994). Research participants imagined their home on fire and themselves having time to save just one of three people who differed in genetic closeness. Participants preferred saving those with close genetic ties (e.g., siblings) to those with more distant genetic ties (cousins), as well as younger (more fertile) relatives to older relatives. Moreover, the bias in favor of helping close to distant relatives was evident only when helping might make the difference between life and death, not in choosing to provide more mundane, everyday sorts of helping.

Reciprocity of Helping

Other evolutionary theorists have argued that motives to help even nonrelated individuals could have evolved if such are reciprocal (Trivers, 1971). If members of a group need one another's help often, live close together, and can punish members who do not reciprocate (by denying those members future help), all members of the group may enhance their chances of survival by helping one another. Thus, what Trivers calls "reciprocal altruism" may have evolved.

Others question the idea that a very specific tendency to help has evolved (as the inclusive fitness and reciprocal helping theorists posit). They suggest instead that something more general may have evolved that can still account for altruism. For instance, a tendency to adopt culturally transmitted norms or the capacity for empathic emotion may have evolved. Either (or both) might lead to altruistic motivation (Hoffman, 1981). Consider each possibility in turn.

Docility—Receptivity to Social Influence

Simon (1990) has argued that an evolved trait of docility (i.e., being predisposed to accept teaching) can account for the existence of altruistic motivation. He starts his argument by pointing out that human infants require years of nurture to survive and that even adults require the assistance and forbearance of other adults to survive. Second, aided greatly by language, humans can and do easily transfer skills, goals, values, and attitudes to one another and such learning enhances fitness in an evolutionary sense. Third, and important, being disposed to accept teaching without having to verify everything, or, in Simon's terms, being docile, greatly contributes to fitness in an evolutionary sense and presumably has been selected for through evolution.

What does this have to do with altruism? Simon argues that *overall* what is learned from others is personally advantageous. Included in what we are taught from others and are inclined to accept are some individually costly behaviors—helping even at a personal cost being one such behavior. As long as the costs of individual acts of altruism do not exceed the long-term, overall, benefits of docility, that docility enhances survival. Thus, from Simon's perspective, it is not altruism *per se* that has been selected in the process of evolution, but rather docility. Altruism falls out of the process as an individual cost of behaving in a manner that, overall, is profitable.

Spontaneous Communication

Buck and Ginsburg (1991, 1997) provide still another evolutionary explanation for altruism. Using evidence from ants, slime mold, dogs, wolves, and monkeys, they argue that genes for spontaneous communication have been selected. As examples, they describe chemical signals by which even individual slime mold cells communicate when food is inadequate. They use this information to merge into multicelled sluglike creatures capable of moving through the soil until sufficient nutrients are located.

Spontaneous communication in humans presumably includes nonintentional, noneffortful leakage of emotion from one person to another through the first person's facial, bodily, and vocal cues. This communication is direct, not intended by the sender nor thought about in depth by the receiver. It happens because it is wired into people. At the bottom line, both sending and receiving abilities are essential for good social coordination and, ultimately, survival.

Buck and Ginsburg consider spontaneous communication a likely candidate for a biological characteristic that promotes helping within social groups. People help each other at least in part because they become aroused by other group members' arousal. Because the sender and receiver of spontaneous communication both experience arousal, both are motivated to end the arousal, and the result is that the receiver helps the sender.

Consistent with these ideas is Hoffman's (1981) evidence that, in very early infancy, when one infant cries out in distress, nearby infants cry as well, even though nothing in their own situations has changed. Young infants have also been shown to mimic the facial expressions of adults, and when adults see another person in distress, their facial expressions, postures, and states of arousal reveal that they too become distressed.

Interestingly, and also fitting with the theory, empathic arousal is greater when the distressed person is a member of the perceiver's own group than when the person is an outgroup member (Feshback & Roe, 1968; Stotland, 1969). This fits with the idea that communication developed to allow members of a particular group to coordinate their efforts in the interest of their own survival. It also fits well with the inclusive fitness position described above.

Batson's Arguments for Altruism

Quite independently of the various evolutionary theorists, but also quite compatibly with Buck and Ginsburg's ideas in particular, Batson, a social psychologist, has devoted much of his career to demonstrating that true altruism exists (i.e., helping without selfish motivation). Batson believes that the precursor of altruism is empathy. He, along with many other researchers, has conducted experiments showing that feeling empathy with a person in need of help enhances the amount of help that person will receive (Batson, 1991). What distinguishes his work on the linkage of empathy to helping from that of others is that he has taken up the task of answering many challengers who have pointed out that observing an empathy-helping link does not necessarily prove that helping is unselfishly motivated. These challengers have made various arguments that empathy-induced helping could be egotistically motivated.

It is impossible to describe here all of Batson's studies, his challengers' studies, his responses to them, and their responses to him (but see Batson, 1991, 1998). However, a description of one of his studies should convey the sort of experimental approach he utilizes to argue for empathy producing true altruism and against various alternative explanations.

One challenge to his claim that empathy leads to altruism is that taking another's perspective gives rise not only to concern for the other but personal feelings of distress and revulsion. Thus, a person who takes another's perspective may help not primarily to benefit the other but rather primarily to terminate his or her own personal distress. To rule this out, Batson, Duncan, Ackerman, Buckley, and Birch (1981) undertook an elegant study. Students were recruited for a study supposedly designed to investigate task performance under unpleasant conditions. Another student (Elaine, a confederate) performed a task during which she received electric shocks. The true participant observed. Empathy was manipulated by telling half the participants that Elaine was similar to them (high empathy) and half that she was not similar (low empathy)—a procedure previously established as effective in manipulating empathy. During the task Elaine expresses considerable distress at receiving the shocks and stops to explain that she had been thrown from a horse as a child and had landed on an electric fence. She is, however, reluctantly willing to go on.

The experimenter expresses concern and comes up with an idea—perhaps the participant and Elaine can switch places. At this point the experimenter varies how easy it is for the participant to avoid taking Elaine's place. In an easy-to-escape condition, the participant is allowed to leave after witnessing just two of ten trials during which Elaine is shocked. In the difficult-to-escape condition, the participant has to stay for all ten trials.

What happens? When empathic concern is low, the majority of participants in the difficult-to-escape condition do help, *but* the majority in the easy-to-escape condition choose to leave instead. In other words, it appears that they are primarily concerned with alleviating their own distress. If they can leave they do. If the only way they can lower their distress is by helping, they will. In contrast, when empathic concern is high, the majority of the people in *both* the difficult and easy escape condition help. Why? Presumably they do so because *only* by providing help can they alleviate their

true, *altruistic*, feelings of concern for Elaine. A desire to alleviate distress cannot explain the results in the high-empathy condition, Batson argues. True altruism exists.

Over the years Batson has faced many other alternative explanations for the empathy-helping link. Perhaps the person feeling empathy who helps is helping out of a selfish desire to feel good about the self, a desire to receive accolades from others, or a sense that the other's outcomes and one's own self-interests are the same. Although not denying the existence of such selfish motivations, Batson has performed a great number of studies in which he has worked systematically at eliminating these various other explanations and still has come up with evidence for the empathy-helping link. Others have also designed elegant experiments and have provided their own experimental results supporting egoistic interpretations of the empathy-helping link.

What is the bottom-line answer? It is not yet available. Many researchers (e.g., Cialdini, Brown, Lewis, Luce, & Neuberg, 1997) remain unconvinced that true altruism exists, and the debate continues. However, at least two recent reviewers of the evidence have concluded that "the preponderance of evidence from the twenty or so years of experimentation on this question strongly suggests that true altruistic motivation may exist and all helping is not necessarily egoistically motivated" (Dovidio & Penner, in press).

[*See also* Prosocial Behavior.]

Bibliography

Batson, C. D. (1998). Altruism and prosocial behavior. In D. Gilbert, S. Fiske, & G. Lindzey (Eds.), *The handbook of social psychology* (4th ed., Vol. 2, pp. 282–316). New York: McGraw-Hill.

Batson, C. D., Duncan, B. D., Ackerman, P., Buckley, T., & Birch, K. (1981). Is empathic emotion a source of altruistic motivation? *Journal of Personality and Social Psychology, 40,* 290–302.

Buck, R., & Ginsburg, B. (1991). Spontaneous communication and altruism: The spontaneous gene hypothesis. In M. S. Clark (Ed.), The spontaneous gene hypothesis. In M. S. Clark (Ed.), *Prosocial behavior* (pp. 149–175). Newbury Park, CA: Sage.

Buck, R., & Ginsburg, B. (1997). Communicative genes and the evolution of empathy. In W. Ickes (Ed.), *Empathic accuracy* (pp. 17–43). New York: Guilford Press.

Burnstein, E., Crandall, C., & Kitayama, S. (1994). Some neo-Darwinian decision rules for altruism: Weighing cues for inclusive fitness as a function of the biological importance of the decision. *Journal of Personality and Social Psychology, 67,* 773–789.

Cialdini, R. B., Brown, S. L., Lewis, B. P., Luce, C., & Neuberg, S. L. (1997). Reinterpreting the empathy-altruism relationship: When one into one equals oneness. *Journal of Personality and Social Psychology, 73,* 481–494.

Dovidio, J. F., & Penner, L. A. (in press). Helping and altruism. In G. Fletcher & M. S. Clark (Eds.), *Handbook of social psychology: Interpersonal processes*. London: Blackwell.

Feshback, N. D., & Roe, K. (1968). Empathy in six- and seven-year-olds. *Child Development, 39,* 133–45.

Hamilton, W. D. (1964). The genetical theory of social behavior (I, II). *Journal of Theoretical Biology, 7,* 1–52.

Hoffman, M. L. (1981). Is altruism part of human nature? *Journal of Personality and Social Psychology, 40,* 211–225.

Simon, H. (1990). A mechanism for social selection and successful altruism. *Science, 250,* 1665–1668.

Stotland, E. (1969). Exploratory investigations of empathy. In L. Berkowitz (Ed.), *Advances in experimental social psychology* (Vol. 4). New York: Academic Press.

Trivers, R. (1971). The evolution of reciprocal altruism. *Quarterly Review of Biology, 46,* 35–57.

Margaret S. Clark

ALZHEIMER'S DISEASE is a progressive dementia syndrome of insidious onset that is brought about by a degenerative brain disease first described by the German neuropathologist Alois Alzheimer in 1907. The disease that now bears Alzheimer's name is characterized by neocortical atrophy, neuronal death, synapse loss, and accumulation of neuritic plaques and neurofibrillary tangles in temporal lobe limbic structures (e.g., hippocampus, entorhinal cortex) and the association cortices of the frontal, temporal, and parietal lobes. Primary motor and sensory cortices and most subcortical brain structures are relatively spared. Significant neuron loss does occur, however, in subcortical nuclei that constitute two of the major ascending projection systems of the brain, the nucleus basalis of Meynert and the locus ceruleus, resulting in an extensive reduction in neocortical levels of the neurotransmitters acetylcholine and norepinephrine, respectively. The neurotransmitter peptide somatostatin is also significantly diminished in association with a reduction in neurons that provide corticocortical connectivity.

The primary clinical manifestation of Alzheimer's disease is a profound global dementia characterized by severe amnesia with additional deficits in language, "executive" functions, attention, and visuospatial and constructional abilities. Although the course of the disorder may be quite variable, an inability to learn and retain new information is usually the most prominent feature during the initial stage, consistent with evidence suggesting that neuropathological changes in the hippocampus and entorhinal cortex are the first and most severe to occur in the disease. This anterograde amnesia appears to reflect ineffective consolidation (i.e., storage) of new information as patients show little improvement in acquiring information over repeated learning trials, and rapid forgetting of information over time. There is a tendency to recall only the most recently presented information (i.e., a heightened recency effect) in free recall tasks, an inability to benefit normally from effortful or elaborative encoding at the time of acquisition, and equally impaired performance when memory is tested with a recognition or free recall format.

While memory impairment is the most prominent early feature of the dementia syndrome of Alzheimer's disease, a deficit in executive functions is often observed relatively early in the course, particularly on set shifting, sequencing, or self-monitoring tasks that require the concurrent manipulation of information. Early language deficits also occur in the form of mild anomia and word-finding difficulties in spontaneous speech. Some evidence suggests that this language deficit is indicative of a loss of semantic knowledge and a breakdown in the organization of semantic memory. Consistent with this view, patients with Alzheimer's disease are disproportionately impaired on verbal fluency tasks when they must generate exemplars from a semantic category compared to when they must generate words that begin with a particular letter. They perform poorly on tests of confrontation naming and their errors often reflect semantic confusions. They consistently miss the same item across language tests that use different methods and modes of access. A general deficiency in the ability to effortfully retrieve semantic information may also contribute to their language deficit, as patients with Alzheimer's disease perform relatively well on some priming tasks that allow semantic knowledge to be assessed in an automatic, noneffortful fashion. Linguistic abilities at the phonemic or syntactic level typically remain unimpaired in the early stages of the disorder. There is little evidence that mildly demented patients exhibit agrammatism, repetition deficits, phonological disturbance, or problems with processing prosodic aspects of speech.

As the disease progresses beyond the early stages, patients with Alzheimer's disease often develop deficits in higher order visuospatial, visuoperceptual, and constructional abilities. These deficits are most evident on tasks that require spatial orientation, drawing or copying of complex figures, or the demonstration of skilled movement (i.e., praxis). Aspects of selective attention are also adversely affected, with the ability to disengage, shift, and divide attention most prominently impaired. Memory abilities worsen and a pronounced retrograde amnesia (i.e., loss of memory for information that was acquired prior to the onset of dementia) often develops. In its initial manifestation, this retrograde amnesia may be temporally graded with memories from the distant past (i.e., childhood and early adulthood) better remembered than memories from the more recent past (i.e., middle and late adulthood). Executive dysfunction also worsens and deficits in judgment, problem solving, and concept formation ability become apparent. A paucity of speech, paraphasic errors, and comprehension deficits become evident as language abilities further deteriorate. A number of behavioral disturbances may occur, including agitation, sleep disorders, mood disorders, delusions, and hallucinations. Despite the pervasive and profound dementia that is evident in the middle stages of Alzheimer's disease, neurologic function remains essentially intact.

In the more advanced stages of Alzheimer's disease virtually all cognitive abilities are severely impaired, and verbal output is fragmentary, and may consist only of repetition of words or phrases. Basic activities of daily living such as grooming, dressing, toileting, and eating cannot be performed without extensive assistance. The patient with advanced Alzheimer's disease may become bedridden, incontinent, and develop neurologic dysfunction that includes extrapyramidal features (e.g., rigidity, Parkinsonian gait, postural instability), myoclonus, and abnormal reflexes (e.g., suck, snout, glabellar, and grasp reflexes). In some cases, a persistent vegetative state may ensue. The duration of Alzheimer's disease, from the time of diagnosis until death, can vary from 2 to more than 20 years, but in the usual case is between 7 and 10 years.

It is widely recognized that the clinical presentation of Alzheimer's disease is quite heterogeneous; however, the source of this heterogeneity is largely unknown. A biological basis for some of the variability in presentation may reside in the recently identified Lewy body variant of Alzheimer's disease, which is a condition characterized by the typical neuropathological changes of Alzheimer's disease along with Lewy bodies (i.e., abnormal neuronal inclusion bodies that are the hallmark of Parkinson's disease) in the brain stem nucleus substantia nigra and diffusely distributed throughout the neocortex. The condition is not rare, occurring in from 15 to 35% of all individuals with autopsy-verified Alzheimer's disease. Although the clinical manifestation of the Lewy body variant (LBV) of Alzheimer's disease is similar to that of Alzheimer's disease in many respects, retrospective studies indicate that LBV is characterized in the early stages by an increased prevalence of mild extrapyramidal motor findings (e.g., bradykinesia, rigidity, masked facies) and visual hallucinations, fluctuation in consciousness, and possibly a more rapid course. In addition, disproportionately severe deficits in psychomotor speed, verbal fluency, and visuospatial and constructional abilities are evident in conjunction with the typical cognitive changes associated with Alzheimer's disease. The recognition and clinical characterization of this disease has led to the development by the International Workgroup on Dementia with Lewy bodies of a set of working, standardized criteria for its neuropathological and clinical diagnosis.

Because dementia is associated with more than 50 different causes of brain dysfunction, and there are no known peripheral biological markers for Alzheimer's disease, it can only be definitively diagnosed by histopathological verification of the presence of characteristic neurodegenerative abnormalities (i.e., neuritic plaques and neurofibrillary tangles) in the brain. However, documentation of the presence of dementia and the exclusion of all other known potential causes allows Alzheimer's disease to be clinically diagnosed during life with some certainty. To aid in this process, and to standardize the diagnosis to some degree, criteria for the clinical diagnosis of probable and possible Alzheimer's disease were developed by the Work Group on the Diagnosis of Alzheimer's Disease established by the National Institute of Neurological and Communicative Disorders and Stroke and the Alzheimer's Disease and Related Disorders Association (NINCDS-ADRDA). Probable Alzheimer's disease is indicated when dementia is documented, other causes are excluded, and the disorder aligns with the typical presentation and course. Possible Alzheimer's disease refers to those cases of documented dementia in which Alzheimer's disease is suspected but the disorder has an atypical onset, presentation, or clinical course, or a second disorder capable of producing dementia (e.g., alcohol abuse) is present, although it is not thought to be the primary source of cognitive dysfunction.

When tested against autopsy verification of Alzheimer's disease or one of its variants (i.e., the Lewy body variant of Alzheimer's disease, mixed Alzheimer's disease, and vascular disease), the accuracy of clinical diagnoses made using the NINCDS-ADRDA criteria ranges from 85 to 100%, even when the clinical diagnosis is made in the early stages of the disease. In one large retrospective study, for example, 103 of 111 patients diagnosed with probable Alzheimer's disease (93%), and 20 of 26 patients diagnosed with possible Alzheimer's disease (77%), met neuropathological criteria for definite Alzheimer's disease at autopsy, for an overall accuracy rate of 90%.

Although the cause of Alzheimer's disease remains unknown, a number of risk factors have been identified. Age is considered to be the single most important risk factor given that the prevalence of the disease rises in an approximately exponential fashion between the ages of 65 and 85. Estimates of the prevalence of Alzheimer's disease suggest that 5 to 15% of people between the ages of 65 and 85, and 30 to 47% of those 85 years of age and older, are affected. The prevalence of Alzheimer's disease doubles approximately every 5 years between the ages of 65 and 85. A similar relationship has been shown between the incidence of Alzheimer's disease and age. It is estimated that new cases of Alzheimer's disease will be diagnosed each year in approximately 0.5% of individuals between the ages of 65 and 69, 0.75% of those between the ages of 70 and 74, 1.5% of those between the ages of 75 and 79, 2.5% of those between the ages of 80 and 84, and 4.5% of those age 85 and over.

The risk of developing Alzheimer's disease is increased approximately fourfold by a family history of the disease in a first-degree relative, and there is little question that this familial association is genetically based. Mutations on three genes have been identified in large families that display an autosomal dominant inheritance pattern of an early-onset form of the disease (i.e., onset generally before the age of 60): the amyloid precursor protein gene on chromosome 21, the presenilin 1 gene on chromosome 14, and the presenilin 2 gene on chromosome 1. These forms of familial Alzheimer's disease are rare and account for only about 1 to 2% of all cases of the disease. A far more common genetic risk factor for sporadic, late-onset Alzheimer's disease is the type ε4 allele of the gene for apolipoprotein E (APOE), a low density lipoprotein cholesterol carrier. Located on chromosome 19, the APOE ε4 allele has been found to be present in 50 to 60% of patients with Alzheimer's disease (compared to 20 to 25% of healthy older adults), regardless of whether or not they have a family history of dementia. Unlike the genes associated with early-onset familial Alzheimer's disease, the APOE ε4 allele is not deterministic, but confers an approximately threefold risk of developing Alzheimer's disease if one copy of the ε4 allele is present, and an eightfold risk if two copies are present.

A number of other risk factors for Alzheimer's disease have been identified, but have only a weak association with the disease (generally a twofold risk or less). Women appear to have a slightly greater risk for Alzheimer's disease than men; however, this may be attributable, in part, to differential survival after the onset of dementia due to their longer life expectancy. A previous head injury that led to loss of consciousness or hospitalization has been identified as a risk factor for Alzheimer's disease, particularly (and perhaps exclusively) in conjunction with the presence of the ε4 allele of the gene for APOE. Several epidemiological studies have shown that lack of education and/or low occupational attainment may be an important risk factor for Alzheimer's disease, perhaps because these variables are a surrogate for a brain or cognitive reserve that helps to delay the onset of the usual clinical manifestations of the disorder.

There is currently no known cure for Alzheimer's disease, but the development of potential treatments is burgeoning as new insights into the mechanisms underlying the disease occur. The best-developed strategy for treating the disease is to counteract the profound reduction of the neurotransmitter acetylcholine by administering a pharmacological agent that prolongs its action by inhibiting its breakdown by acetylcholinesterase. Two such agents, tacrine hydrochloride and donepezil (Aricept), have recently been shown in placebo-controlled, double-blind studies to modestly reduce cognitive decline over a 12- to 30-week period in about 25 to 50% of the patients with Alzheimer's disease who were treated. These two agents are currently the only drugs approved by the U.S. Food and Drug Administration specifically for the treatment of Alzheimer's disease. A number of additional acetylcholinesterase inhibitors, as well as direct agonist of both nicotinic and muscarinic acetylcholine receptors, are currently under development or in clinical trial.

In addition to these symptomatic approaches to the treatment of Alzheimer's disease, compounds that target mechanisms of neuronal death in the disease are being developed and tested. Among these are agents that may reduce the production or aggregation of the neurotoxic beta-amyloid protein that is the core of the neuritic plaque, and those that might prevent the hyperphosphorylation of the tau protein, which leads to disruption of the neuronal cytoskeleton and the formation of neurofibrillary tangles. Other potential treatments include anti-inflammatory agents, estrogen replacement therapy, neurotrophic agents that promote the growth and survival of neurons, and antioxidants such as vitamin E and idebenone that reduce the formation or enhance the clearance of free radicals.

Bibliography

Albert, M. S., & Moss, M. B. (1988). *Geriatric neuropsychology*. New York: Guilford Press. A comprehensive review of the neuropsychological aspects of normal aging, Alzheimer's disease, and other neurodegenerative disorders.

Alzheimer, A. (1907). Uber eine eigenartige Erkrankung der Hirnrinde [On a singular disease of the Cortex]. *Allgemeine Zeitschrift fur Psychiatrie und Psychisch-Gerichtliche Medizin, 64*, 146–148. The first description of the neuritic plaques and neurofibrillary tangles in the brain of a woman who died at age 55 with progressive dementia. These neuropathological features have become the hallmark of Alzheimer's disease.

Blessed, G., Tomlinson, B. E., & Roth, M. (1968). The association between quantitative measures of dementia and of senile change in the cerebral grey matter of elderly subjects. *British Journal of Psychiatry, 114*, 797–811. The first prospective demonstration of the relationship between dementia and the neuropathological abnormalities of Alzheimer's disease.

Evans, D. A., Funkenstein, H. H., Albert, M. S., Scherr, P. A., Cook, N. R., Chown, M. J., Herbert, L. E., Hennekens, C. H., & Taylor, J. O. (1989). Prevalence of Alzheimer's disease in a community population of older persons: Higher than previously reported. *Journal of the American Medical Association, 262*, 2551–2556. A large, well-controlled epidemiological study of dementia and Alzheimer's disease that provided reliable estimates of the prevalence and incidence of the disease.

Galasko, D., Hansen, L. A., Katzman, R., Wiederholt, W.,

Masliah, E., Terry, R., Hill, L. R., Lessin, P., & Thal, L. J. (1994). Clinical-neuropathological correlations in Alzheimer's disease and related dementias. *Archives of Neurology, 51*, 888–895. A relatively large study that assessed the accuracy of the clinical diagnosis of probable and possible Alzheimer's disease made using the NINCDS-ADRDA criteria against autopsy verification of the disease.

Katzman, R. (1986). Alzheimer's disease. *New England Journal of Medicine, 314*, 964–973.

Levy-Lahad, E., & Bird, T. D. (1996). Genetic factors in Alzheimer's disease: A review of recent advances. *Annals of Neurology, 40*, 829–840. A comprehensive review of the major developments concerning the genetic aspects of Alzheimer's disease.

McKhann, G., Drachman, D., Folstein, M., Katzman, R., Price, D., & Stadlan, E. M. (1984). Clinical diagnosis of Alzheimer's disease: Report of the NINCDS-ADRDA Work Group under the auspices of Department of Health and Human Services Task Force on Alzheimer's disease. *Neurology, 34*, 939–944. The widely accepted standard criteria for the clinical diagnosis of probable and possible Alzheimer's disease.

Nebes, R. D. (1992). Cognitive dysfunction in Alzheimer's disease. In F. I. M. Craik & T. Salthouse (Eds.), *Handbook of cognitive aging* (pp. 373–446). Hillsdale, NJ: Erlbaum.

Perry, R., McKeith, I., & Perry, E. (1996). *Dementia with Lewy bodies: Clinical, pathological, and treatment issues.* Cambridge, UK: Cambridge University Press. A comprehensive review and proposed clinical criteria for the newly identified neuropathologic condition of diffusely distributed cortical Lewy bodies with or without concomitant Alzheimer's disease.

Salmon, D. P. (1997). Neuropsychological features of Alzheimer's disease. In J. D. Brioni & M. W. Decker (Eds.), *Pharmacological treatment of Alzheimer's disease: Molecular and neurobiological foundations* (pp. 129–147). New York: Wiley.

Strittmatter, W. J., Saunders, A. M., Schmechel, D., Perlcak-Vance, M., Enghild, J., Salvesen, G. S., & Roses, A. D. (1993). Apolipoprotein E-high-avidity binding to B-amyloid and increased frequency of type 4 allele in late-onset familial Alzheimer disease. *Proceedings of the National Academy of Science, 90*, 9649–9653. The first demonstration of a genetic risk factor for late-onset, sporadic Alzheimer's disease.

Terry, R. D., Katzman, R., & Bick, K. L. (1994). *Alzheimer's disease.* New York: Raven Press.

David P. Salmon

AMBIENT ENVIRONMENT. *See* Environment Research Design; *and* Human Performance Theory.

AMERICAN ASSOCIATION FOR THE ADVANCEMENT OF SCIENCE. In 1848, when officers of the Association of American Geologists and Naturalists invited other leaders of science to join them in fulfilling their plan to extend their organization into a comprehensive association of scientists, the American Association for the Advancement of Science (AAAS) was born. Then, and in later revisions of its constitution, AAAS has adopted three broad objectives. The first is internal to science: "to further the work of scientists, to facilitate cooperation among them . . . to improve the effectiveness of science in the promotion of human welfare." The other two look outward: "to advance education in science, and to increase public understanding and appreciation of the importance and promise of the methods of science in human progress."

To aid in achieving these objectives and to broaden their scope, the association has elected many of the more specialized scientific societies as AAAS affiliates. Each affiliate is attached to one or more of the 24 AAAS sections, such as astronomy, engineering, history and philosophy of science, or psychology. The psychology section includes such affiliates as the American Psychological Association, regional psychological associations, the American Psychological Society, and the Society for Neuroscience. Representatives of those affiliates help govern the sections and sometimes join them in arranging sessions at AAAS meetings, or in other activities.

Advancement of Science

The first method of working toward the advancement of science and the work of scientists was the holding of annual meetings. These have been peripatetic meetings, this year in one city and next year in another. Meeting once a year has been the norm but some years there have been two meetings. These meetings have included sessions ranging over the whole scope of science. The AAAS has also sponsored more specialized meetings, such as the first International Congress on Oceanography, which was planned and managed by AAAS, cosponsored by UNESCO, and held in 1959; or the now annual Symposia on Science and Technology Policy.

The second method of advancing science has been through publications. Initially, *Proceedings* volumes gave accounts of AAAS meetings and activities. Later, the weekly journal *Science* became the primary publication. *Science* was started by Thomas Edison in 1880, but his support lasted only one year. Tired of meeting weekly deficits, he gave the magazine to its editor, John Michels. Michels published a few scattered issues and then a group of scientists in Cambridge, Massachusetts, took over for a while. *Science* did not become a permanent organ until 1894 when James McKeen Cattell, Professor of Psychology at Columbia University, bought it. As owner, editor, and publisher, and with the help of Mrs. Cattell and their sons, Cattell made *Science* into a valued weekly contributor to scientific literature and a regular reporter of AAAS meetings and activities.

In 1900 Professor Cattell and AAAS entered into a mutually beneficial arrangement. AAAS agreed to give Cattell $2.00 from the $3.00 annual dues of each member and, in return, Cattell gave each member a subscription to *Science*. *Science* became the official journal of AAAS, and AAAS membership became more attractive and grew. For his part, by selling subscriptions at $2.00 a year instead of the normal charge of $5.00, Cattell increased circulation substantially and reduced the per-copy cost of production. This arrangement continued until 1944 when Cattell died. In accordance with an earlier agreement, AAAS then purchased *Science* from the Cattell estate.

The years after World War II were a time of change for the Association. Willard Lee Valentine, Treasurer of the American Psychological Association, came to Washington to become the editor of *Science* and the AAAS, previously housed in the Smithsonian Institution building, was looking for a new location. Dael Wolfle, the American Psychological Association's first full-time Executive Secretary, was looking for a place to establish the APA's central office. The APA and AAAS shared a building when AAAS leased a large house at 1515 Massachusetts Avenue NW and sublet the third floor to the APA.

Valentine died unexpectedly a year later, but under his leadership and under a succession of later editors, *Science* flourished. In the 1950s the section of news items was transformed into the popular "News and Comment" section written by reporters who had experience in newspaper writing, in government service, or some other relevant area. At the same time, a true editorial page was started.

As a nonprofit organization, AAAS was barred from devoting more than a minor part of its activities to efforts to influence federal legislation, but it could and did answer congressional requests for information, for appropriate witnesses for hearings on matters related to science or technology, or give other help. Occasionally AAAS took the initiative: The most effective example resulted from the failure of Congress to enact National Science Foundation legislation when it was first proposed in 1945 and 1946. James Conant, then President of both Harvard University and AAAS, took the initiative in organizing a new Inter-Society Committee for a National Science Foundation, to which some 75 affiliated societies each named two members. From then until 1950, that committee informed Congress of scientists' wishes and worked with Congress to get National Science Foundation legislation enacted.

Science Education

From its earliest years, AAAS has been involved in efforts to improve science education, not only at the collegiate level but also in elementary and secondary schools. Such means as the association's Traveling Science Libraries; provision of speakers brought from Europe to address summer institutes for science or mathematics teachers supported by the National Science Foundation, or by distribution of *Science Books and Films* were all used to aid school science programs.

In the 1950s AAAS developed a program for teaching science in the elementary grades. Called "Science, a Process Approach," it stressed not the usual names and dates approach, but gave many thousands of children experience in using some of the basic processes of science: observation, measurement, comparison, making and testing predictions, and drawing inferences and conclusions.

In 1985, AAAS started its largest and strongest program on science education, "Project 2061." Two reports, *Science For All Americans* in 1988 and *Benchmarks for Science Literacy* in 1993 provided teaching materials and set standards for what all children at several selected grade levels should be able to understand and do. Those benchmarks have been adopted by science education programs developed by several other organizations. In 1996 SRI International concluded that Project 2061 was having a broad positive influence on science education and that over 90% of the educational leaders consulted were using *Benchmarks* in their day-to-day work.

Public Understanding of Science

In 1957 AAAS began providing the content for a series of TV programs comparable to the later *Nova* programs. The earlier program, called *Conquest*, drew audiences of around 15 million and received several awards for excellence and for contributing to public understanding. They came to an end after three years when a new advertising manager at Monsanto, which had financed the programs, preferred to use his funds for more specific advertisement of Monsanto products.

Other methods of enhancing public understanding have been more permanent. One of the first was to invite the general public to some of the evening addresses at AAAS meetings. Material for brief radio programs has been widely distributed. Seminars for members of Congress and for congressional staff members; some special publications; and cooperative relationships with a wide variety of organizations have all helped improve public understanding. In 1973, the Association inaugurated its Science and Technology Fellows program, supporting scientists for one-year congressional office appointments. The model for the Congressional

Science Fellowships has since been expanded to include Diplomacy Fellowships, Environmental Fellowships, and Executive Branch Fellowships.

Conclusion

Since 1848 there have been many changes in science, technology, educational institutions, and in the socio-economic climate encompassing science and technology. Over the years AAAS membership has grown from the original 461 to nearly 150,000, and "headquarters" has changed from the office of whoever was serving as Secretary, to the Association's building in Washington, D.C. Adjusting to these changes and the methods used by AAAS in pursuit of its three major objectives have been primary themes in the history of the American Association for the Advancement of Science.

Bibliography

Kohlstedt, S. G. (1976). *The formation of the American scientific community: The American Association for the Advancement of Science, 1848–1860.* Urbana, IL: University of Illinois Press.

Wolfle, D. (1989). *Renewing a scientific society: The American Association for the Advancement of Science from World War II to 1970.* Washington, DC: American Association for the Advancement of Science.

Dael Wolfle

AMERICAN BOARD OF PROFESSIONAL PSYCHOLOGY. Founded and incorporated in 1947 with the broad support of the American Psychological Association (APA) and the profession, the American Board of Examiners in Professional Psychology—now the American Board of Professional Psychology (ABPP)—is the oldest credentialing organization in professional psychology. The ABPP has been committed to fostering excellence in the specialty practice of psychology and the identification of psychologists who meet rigorous standards for the preparation and practice of a specialty in professional psychology. The organization is a credentialing body, not a membership body. It is guided by the precept that the clearest and most responsible way for a psychologist to represent herself or himself to the public, third parties, and the profession as a specialist in professional psychology is to be certified through a voluntary, organized peer review process as meeting the standards and demonstrating the competencies required in a specialty.

The ABPP emerged from an APA committee that had been formed to consider the formation of a credentialing body for individual psychologists in a particular specialty. The board recognized that state psychological association and state legislative licensure was either nonexistent or recognized only general proficiency and that membership in a division of the APA cannot serve both as a means of expressing interest and as a certification of proficiency. As a specialty recognition and certification body, ABPP was considered one of several features essential for the establishment of a profession. The other features included education and training standards, a process of accreditation, a code of ethics, and improved communication through such vehicles as journals and APA divisions.

The ABPP was initially supported by a $7,500 allocation from the APA Council of Representatives for its founding corporation and subsequent financial support through the 1950s. The founding Board Members were Carlyle Jacobson (President), George A. Kelly (Vice President), John G. Darley (Secretary-Treasurer), John G. Jenkins, Marion A. Bills, David Wechsler, Carroll L. Shartle, Frederick Lyman Wells, and David Shakow.

Recognizing that many psychologists were already working in applied settings, the ABPP established a system of "grandfathering" such psychologists without examination who met experience and training standards. This proved to be a ponderous task with 1,086 out of 1,557 candidates "grandfathered" after 26 meetings. In 1949 a requirement was introduced for written and oral examinations in the specialties now known as *clinical, counseling,* and *industrial/organizational* psychology.

The early organizational structure of the ABPP consisted of a Board of Trustees (BOT) whose membership was approved by the APA. Each of the original three specialties was represented, plus a member representing general psychology. In 1968, school psychology was recognized as a specialty to be certified by the board, and a school psychologist representative was then added.

The practice of psychology became increasingly complex over the years, particularly in the independent practice sector. Several new specialties emerged through public and professional needs; some specialties organized independently incorporated boards. Although the ABPP has resisted recognizing new specialties since 1968, compelling reasons to recognize new specialties in the absence of APA action led to the recognition of clinical neuropsychology, forensic psychology, family psychology, and health psychology in the 1980s. Behavioral psychology, psychoanalysis, rehabilitation psychology, and group psychology were recognized in the 1990s.

The ABPP established rigorous application standards for emerging specialties desiring affiliation with the organization. These standards include operational, competency-based definition; education, training, and experience requirements of both generic and specialty preparation; and good standing with the legal and professional community. There are standards for the recognition of the specialty board itself which must demonstrate compliance with the ABPP's standards, especially the capacity to administer specialty examinations nationally on a regular basis.

The addition of new specialties and their incorporated boards led ABPP to require that all specialty boards be independently incorporated. The ABPP board continues its oversight responsibility at the central office, provides a forum for resolving problems between boards, formulates policies and standards for the organization, appoints and supports committees, and acts as a spokesperson to the public and the profession. An ethics committee was established independent of the BOT and serves as a consultant to the board on ethical matters concerning diplomates. Additionally, the ABPP promoted the development of membership organizations called specialty academies in each of its affiliated specialties to involve diplomates in the election of specialty boards, continuing educational delivery, advocacy, and other member services.

Each specialty board, such as the American Board of Forensic Psychology, is responsible for developing and administering examinations at national sites. To qualify as a candidate to be admitted to the examination the applicant must meet common eligibility requirements. These include a doctoral degree from a recognized program in professional psychology, licensure in good standing in the state in which the psychologist practices, and postdoctoral training. The latter requires at least 2 years of supervised practice in the specialty or 1 year of predoctoral and 1 year of postdoctoral supervision or the successful completion of a recognized postdoctoral program in the applicant's specialty. Each specialty requires appropriate doctoral education and training as a foundation for the specialty, as well as the specific requirements characteristic of the specialty.

Having met the eligibility requirements, a candidate must pass an examination administered by the specialty board. The ABPP originally had a two-day written examination, in vivo practice samples, and an oral examination. The written examination was eventually eliminated, with the exception of the clinical neuropsychology specialty. The examination has focused more upon competencies characteristic of the specialty and is about 4 to 5 hours in length following a preparatory submission of practice samples representative of the candidate's work. The format of the examination is typically that of a professional conversation, based upon the candidate's practice samples, fundamental knowledge and skills expected in the specialty, situational content, professional issues, and ethical problem-solving capacity.

There are over 3,500 diplomates distributed among the various specialties. Clinical psychology has the largest number of diplomates; however, the granting of diplomas in the 1980s and 1990s among the new specialties, as a group, led by clinical neuropsychology, has surpassed clinical psychology.

The number of diplomates conferred each year over the early decades of the organization approached 100, with the average number increasing to about 150 in recent years. Although candidates still are more senior in status, ABPP encourages newly trained specialists to apply for certification. The emphasis upon certification as a specialist following and continuous with specialty training is similar to the medical profession.

The organization publishes brochures and information packages related to its affiliate specialty boards. A *Directory of Diplomates* is periodically published, providing an extensive description of each specialist together with locator information. The ABPP publishes a newsletter, *The Diplomate*, twice yearly, which reports the activities of the BOT, each specialty board's activity, and information relevant to the mission of the organization. Special reports, standards, and requirements for affiliation are periodically published as manuals.

Each year a convocation is held during the APA annual meeting at which time newly certified specialists are awarded the diploma, a presidential report summarizes activities of the organization, the ABPP Distinguished Service Award is announced, and an address by the previous convocation awardee is delivered. A few past Distinguished Service Awardees were Roy Schafer (1984), Leona Tyler (1985), Arthur Benton (1986), Joseph Matarazzo (1987), Paul Meehl (1989), Nelson A. Butters (1993), and Florence W. Kaslow (1994).

The organization has been the only organization with multiple peer reviewed specialty designation and credentialing activities in professional psychology. As such, government, third party payors of services, the public, and the professional community has recognized and often incorporated the definitions and standards of the ABPP into their procedures and activities. The diploma has been widely recognized as a mark of a quality, specialized, service provider.

The ABPP has participated in dozens of conferences over the years and sponsored a number of important professional initiatives. Most recently the organization's proposal to initiate a national organization to coordinate policy and development among credentialing organizations in psychology has resulted in the Council of Credentialing Organizations in Professional Psychology (C-COPP). Responding to the need for a coherent development of specialization, particularly through postdoctoral specialty training, the ABPP initiated the establishment of the Interorganizational Council for the

Accreditation of Postdoctoral Residency Programs in Professional Psychology, referred to as the IOC. This council has developed guidelines for the accreditation of postdoctoral training programs from an interorganizational perspective. The APA Committee on Accreditation has incorporated the extensive work of the IOC into its newly established postdoctoral accreditation requirements. The ABPP has formal liaison relationships to the National Register of Health Service Providers in Psychology and the Association of State and Provincial Psychology Boards. Together with the newly established specialty academies and the involvement of the 11 individual affiliated specialty boards, the BOT has been a major force in the development of specialization in professional psychology.

The central office of the organization's early years was managed by Noble H. Kelly, secretary-treasurer and executive officer for two decades. The central office is currently located in Jefferson City, Missouri.

Bibliography

American Board of Professional Psychology. (1992, July). 45th ABPP anniversary issue. *The Diplomate, 12(1)*.

American Board of Professional Psychology. (1997, July). 50th ABPP Anniversary Issue. *The Diplomate, 17(1)*.

American Psychological Association. (1946). *Report of the policy and planning board on certification of professional psychologists*. Washington, DC: Author.

Bent, R. J., Packard, R. E., & Goldberg, R. W. (1999). The American Board of Professional Psychology, 1947 to 1997: A historical perspective. *Professional Psychology: Research and Practice, 29*, 65–73.

Russell J. Bent

AMERICAN EDUCATIONAL RESEARCH ASSOCIATION. Believed to be the largest membership organization in the world established solely for the advancement of research into the nature, policies, practices, and contexts of education, the American Educational Research Association's (AERA) publications include a monthly journal *Educational Researcher*, the quarterly *American Educational Research Journal (AERJ)* and *Educational Evaluation and Policy Analysis*, and the annual *Review of Educational Research* (*RER*, established in 1931). The AERA Annual Meeting, held in the United States or Canada, attracted 11,000 participants by the mid-1990s, fully half of its U.S. and international membership.

AERA originated in 1915 when eight men formed the National Association of Directors of Educational Research at a meeting of the Department of Superintendence, National Education Association of the United States (NEA). Notable among them were Albert Shiels from New York, Frank Ballou from Boston (later Superintendent in Washington, D.C.), S. A. Courtis from Detroit, and Leonard P. Ayers, representing the Russell Sage Foundation.

Educational research at that time was defined by two dominant schools of thought. One was the educational psychology of measurement and assessment, as championed by Edward L. Thorndike, a psychologist from Teachers College, Columbia University. The other was the movement for "scientific management" in public education: a set of theories and practices for school-district growth, consolidation, and bureaucratization that fed the development of a cadre of local and state school administrators and university professors of educational administration.

Those two movements shared the common historical context of that period's massive immigration and urbanization, plus three forces—unionization, the rise of progressive social thought, and ultimately the Great Depression—that ended legalized industrial labor for children and mushroomed enrollment in public schools. Educational research, accordingly, proceeded along two parallel tracks: first, the standardized testing, sorting, and categorizing of children by perceived academic promise; and second, the promulgation of what Raymond Callahan called a "cult of efficiency" in administrative practices affecting the curriculum, teaching methods, the supervision of teachers, and all aspects of school finance and management. The 1930s brought one round of assaults on the hegemony of these movements, and the 1960s another, eroding their share of the association's and the field's priorities.

After an intermediate name change, AERA adopted its current title in 1928 and became a department within the NEA structure in 1930, where it remained until 1968, when it was established as an independent association. From 1922 to 1968, the association existed alongside NEA's separate research division which concerned itself principally with gathering and charting data about school districts and teaching conditions. For the developing cadre of AERA members, reporting school data did not constitute a "scientific" approach to research. The AERA members' orientation tended to drive a wedge between themselves and K-12 practitioners. This problem developed despite the fact that much of their work, as reflected in the first three decades of the *Review of Educational Research*, addressed practical organizational and curricular issues in relatively nontechnical language.

Ellen Lagemann (1997, December) has analyzed AERA's early decades as a period in which educational research emerged

[A]s an identifiable field of study . . . paralleled by the emergence of a research community in education . . . mostly white, male, Protestant . . . faculty . . . at places like Chicago, Harvard, Michigan, Stanford, Teachers College, Wisconsin, or Yale . . . summoned to diagnose and prescribe solutions for local school problems. [They] were increasingly isolated from both their non-educationist colleagues in the university and their school-based colleagues in education. (p. 7)

Until 1951, AERA maintained a restrictive membership policy, requiring an invitation and an involved application process, which favored its two traditional strands of research and its close collegial ties. However, internal financial stresses, coupled with the field's growth and the democratization and expansion of higher education, gradually pushed the doors open. Nevertheless, the twenty-fifth anniversary edition of *Review of Educational Research* (1956) chronicled only cautious growth in what AERA considered legitimate research areas: school administration, curriculum, educational psychology, educational measurement, "counseling and adjustment," and a brief nod to emerging work in the history, philosophy, and sociology of education. Launched in 1964, the journal *AERJ* headlined educational psychology and measurement and did not create planned space for "social and institutional analysis" for another 26 years. Survey design, quantitative assessment instruments, school finance, and behavioral psychology continued to hold sway in the 1971 *RER*, alongside the "Negro inferiority" research of psychologist William Shockley. White men continued to dominate the association and the field.

By the 1982 volume, however, other methodological and political breakthroughs were evident. These included "Problems of Reliability and Validity in Ethnographic Research"; a discussion of values education and children's conceptual development; and a critically conceived "Toward a Political Economy of Educational Innovation." The 1987 volume featured an exploration of "Qualitative Research Traditions," as well as "Teacher Receptivity to System-Wide Change," an early example of AERA's emerging interest in learning from the voices of teachers.

Between 1964 and 1968, AERA decentralized its authority structure by creating divisions—both a reaction to and a catalyst for what became a 30-year period of unprecedented expansion for the organization. Today its twelve divisions include history/historiography, social context of education, and teaching/teacher education. Its standing committees include groups on the role and status of women and minorities in educational research and development. Its more than 100 special interest groups (SIGs) embrace a variety of modern and postmodern themes.

Membership and annual meeting participation have grown among teachers and teacher-educators who are not affiliated with research institutions. Governing and editorial board positions, both elected and appointed, however, predominantly represent major research universities, including those cited by Lagemann from decades ago. The SIGs include fledgling groups of K-12 teachers and their allies who conduct action research and other inquiries, and who attend and present at annual meetings.

Debates continue within the organization over its roles in the practitioner community and in public policy, particularly with regard to whether AERA should be a purely academic or also an advocacy organization. Two current trends generate particular debate and discussion: the expansion of qualitative research generally, and the particular role of classroom-based, teacher-conducted action research. Also prominent among emerging research traditions are postmodern, multicultural, and feminist scholars, who allege, from varying perspectives, that the field has produced overly linear, prescriptive, and generalized work that is not responsive to local and cultural knowledge, context, or voice. These strands became increasingly prominent in AERA annual meeting sessions of the 1980s and 1990s.

Persons elected AERA president since the 1980s help to illustrate continuity and change within the Association and the field. With their research specialties indicated, notable presidents have included Maxine Greene, 1981 to 1982 (philosophy); Lauren Resnick, 1986 to 1987 (cognitive psychology); Nancy Cole, 1988 to 1989 (president of the Educational Testing Service); Philip Jackson, 1989 to 1990 (sociology of teaching); Larry Cuban, 1990 to 1991 (history of the curriculum and school reform); Ann Lieberman, 1991 to 1992 (school leadership and change); Penelope Peterson, 1996 to 1997 (effective teaching), and James Banks, 1997 to 1998 (multicultural education).

AERA's headquarters are in Washington, D.C. Its archives are divided, located principally in Special Collections at the University of Washington Library and in the Paul Hanna Collection at the Hoover Institution, Stanford University, California.

Bibliography

Berliner, D. C., Resnick, L. B., Cuban L., Cole, N., Popham, W. J., & Goodlad, J. I. (1997, June/July). "The vision thing": Educational research and AERA in the 21st century, Part 2—Competing visions for enhancing the impact of educational research. *Educational Researcher, 26,* 12–18, 27.

Bloom, B. (1966). Twenty-five years of educational research. *American Educational Research Journal, 33,* 211–221.

Buckingham, B. R. (1941). Our first twenty-five years. *NEA Proceedings 79*, 347–363. Washington, DC: National Education Association of the United States.

Callahan, R. (1962). *Education and the cult of efficiency*. Chicago: University of Chicago Press.

Hollingsworth, S., & Sockett, H. (1994). Teacher research and educational reform. *Ninety-third Yearbook of the National Society for the Study of Education, Part I*. Chicago: NSSE. (Distributed by the University of Chicago Press)

Kaestle, C. F. (1992). *Everybody's been to fourth grade: An oral history of federal R&D in education*. Research Report No. 92-1. Madison, WI: Wisconsin Center for Education Research. A complete set of audiotapes containing Dr. Kaestle's interviews is housed at AERA Archives, Paul Hanna Collection, Hoover Institution, Stanford University.

Kaestle, C. F. (1993, January). The awful reputation of educational research. *Educational Researcher 22*, 23–31.

Kennedy, M. M. (1997, October). The connection between research and practice. *Educational Researcher 26*, 4–12.

Lagemann, E. C. (1989). The plural worlds of educational research. *History of Education Quarterly, 29*, 185–214.

Lagemann, E. C. (1997, December). Contested terrain: A history of education research in the United States, 1890–1990, *Educational Researcher, 26*, 5–17.

Lather, P. (1996). Troubling clarity: The politics of accessible language. *Harvard Educational Review, 66*, 525–545.

Mershon, S., with Narasimhan, T. (1990). *The development of the American Educational Research Association, 1915–1970*. Unpublished manuscript, Department of History, Carnegie Mellon University.

Neumann, A., & Peterson P. L. (Eds.). (1997). *Learning from our lives: Women, research, and autobiography in education*. New York: Teachers College Press.

Popkewitz, T. S. (1997, December), A changing terrain of knowledge and power: A social epistemology of educational research. *Educational Researcher, 26*, 18–29.

Urban, W. J. (1998). *More than the facts: The research division of the National Education Association, 1922–1997*. Lanham, MD: University Press of America.

Warren, D. (Ed.). (1989). *American teachers: Histories of a profession at work*. New York: Macmillan.

Robert A. Levin

AMERICAN INDIAN PSYCHOLOGY refers to the indigenous people of North America and their descendants. The term does not imply that there is a unique American Indian and Alaska Native collective psychological style or modal personality profile; that is, there is no common psychological character or set of personality characteristics that can be uniformly applied to all of those who identify themselves as being American Indian and Alaska Native. American Indian psychology also represents a field of inquiry involving a number of academic disciplines other than psychology. These include anthropology, education, history, literature, philosophy, political science, psychiatry, sociology, and social work. Each discipline may approach the joint inquiry in different ways using stylized levels of analysis; however, the locus of interest is psychological. Often investigators from different academic disciplines convene and collaborate on some psychological problem occurring among American Indians and Alaska Natives, such as alcoholism, in an effort to explore and isolate factors that influence it. In these joint and collaborative efforts, each discipline adds a unique perspective that can expand the understanding of factors that are associated with or caused by psychological structures and processes.

The term, *American Indian*, is an "ethnic gloss" used to refer to the indigenous, aboriginal peoples of North America (Trimble, 1990–1991). In the United States the terms *Native American* or *Native American Indian* sometimes are used interchangeably with *American Indian* and *Alaska Native*. It is important to note that the two terms are not preferred by most American Indians and Alaska Natives as they are not considered to be an accurate description of the indigenous people of the United States. Moreover, American Indian organizations such as the National Congress of American Indians, the National Indian Education Association, and the Society of Indian Psychologists among many others consider the term *Native American* to be too broad a term for the indigenous ethnic groups in the United States. Many groups such as Native Hawaiians may consider themselves "Native" but in fact they are not of American Indian background. The term *Native American* therefore blurs the meaning and definition of what it means to be an American Indian and Alaska Native. In general, American Indians and Alaska Natives actually prefer to be referred by their tribal names such as Dine for Navajo, Lakota (or Dakota and Nakota) for Sioux, Tohono O'odham for Papago, etc. Many of the tribal names, such as Navajo, Apache, Papago, and Sioux, were imposed on the people by Europeans or were terms used by some tribes and adopted by Europeans; some of the terms are considered derogatory and offensive. Changes in tribal designation reflect a need on the part of many tribes to be referred to as they actually refer to themselves in their respective tribal languages.

Other descriptors are used to refer to the indigenous peoples of Central and South America to set them apart from North American Indians. Such terms include *Mexican Indians, Mayan* or *Yucatecan Indians, Central American Indians, Brazilian Indians, Peruvian Indians*, etc. As a term, *American Indian* is often used to include Alaska Natives (Aleut, Athabascan, Eskimo, or Inuit) where the intent is to refer inclusively to the indigenous peoples of the United States. The American Indian "gloss" is an imposed fabrication and category that is arbitrary and inconsistent in its usage (Trimble, 1990–1991). In the United States, for example, the term refers to close to 2 million people representing over 300 federally recognized tribes, an additional 200 or so non-federally recognized tribes, and residents of about 220 Alaska Native villages (Snipp, 1996). The extraordinary diversity contributed by tribal background and linguistic preferences compounds any attempt to advocate or develop a modal American Indian psychology or personality.

Over the decades behavioral and social scientists, especially anthropologists, attempted to capture modal personality styles of particular tribes such as the Navajo, Zuni, Teton Sioux, Kwakiutl, and Tlingit among others. Often referred to as the culture and personality school of anthropology, researchers such as Ruth Benedict, Margaret Mead, and John Honigmann researched tribes as collective units and presumed that members embodied some universal personality style that could be differentiated from members of other tribes and ethnic groups. Yet efforts to advance a tribal-specific psychology can be criticized on grounds that such an endeavor has not or could not truly capture the within-tribe variations that exist today among its members.

The field of American Indian psychology has a varied history. It is derived in part from the historical and contemporary experiences of the tribal people, and those who have worked to place those experiences in a psychological context. To understand the context of those who work with and conduct psychological research with American Indians it is best to use some basic background information that follows in the next sections. After presenting the background information, additional material is included describing some of the psychologists and the activities in which they have been involved. These include major studies and publications, major figures, and current professional organizations devoted to the topic.

American Indian Characteristics

In the nineteenth century, for historical, political, and legal reasons, the United States government found it necessary to formulate and implement a legal definition of American Indians. The concept of using a legal definition was first set forth by the U.S. Congress through the Curtis Act of 1898 when the then Bureau of Indian Affairs had to authorize land settlement allotments to members of the Five Civilized Tribes of Oklahoma. Although the definition has undergone several changes since the policy was first introduced, the Bureau of Indian Affairs, a federal agency, defines an American Indian as one who is an enrolled or registered member of the current 317 federally recognized tribes or whose blood quantum is one fourth and can legally demonstrate that fact to the Bureau of Indian Affairs. Indi-

vidual tribes, however, have the constitutional right to establish their own criteria for membership. About 7% of the tribes require that one have more than one-fourth blood quantum and about 32% have no set blood quantum criteria. Whatever the criteria, an individual must be able to establish his or her claim by providing documentation showing that one or more of their relatives or ancestors are on some version of a tribe's role or census (Thornton, 1996).

Some tribes are recognized by individual states but do not have federal recognition. About 125 or more tribes are seeking federal recognition, however, and many of them are those who hold state recognition. Members of state-recognized tribes are considered to be American Indians but not by the federal government. Additionally, there are some tribes that have no state or federal recognition, yet for historical reasons lay claim to their American Indian heritage; some of these tribes have applied for federal recognition, too.

The U.S. Bureau of the Census currently uses a self-identification procedure to establish American Indian identity. Their definition is a departure from those developed by tribes, states, and the Bureau of Indian Affairs in that there is no requirement for supporting documentation. The Bureau of the Census data therefore is at odds with the data maintained by the U.S. Bureau of Indian Affairs and data monitored by state agencies. In 1990, the U.S. Bureau of the Census declared that 1,959,000 citizens were American Indians and Alaska Natives. In 1960, the U.S. Bureau of the Census noted that 552,000 reported they were American Indian. Thus between 1960 and 1990 the American Indian population had grown by about 255%. The rapid 30-year population increase is somewhat hard to believe, but suggest, that many more citizens in 1990 chose to identify with their American Indian heritage than did in 1960—such population increases are almost unheard of in the field of demography.

The Census Bureau's use of self-identification criteria indeed had some effect on this growth in numbers because individuals probably declared an ancestral identification without necessarily having legal ties to a tribe. Some of these individuals are those who claim multiple tribal backgrounds, yet their blood quantum for any one of them is insufficient for them to become officially registered or enrolled. For example, such individuals may have a combined "Indian" blood quantum of one half but no one tribal quantum is acceptable by each of the tribes represented in their ancestral background. They may have all of the facial features demonstrative of American Indians (that is, they look "Indian") but are not qualified to be recognized by either state or federally recognized tribes.

Many Americans of American Indian mixed ethnic ancestry choose to identify as Indian or Alaska Native because it creates a new identity for them that brings with it pride along with the desire to learn tribal customs, traditions, and language. Additionally, there are some people who, regardless of their degree of blood quantum, are obligated by family traditions to continue their identities as Indian or Native. Typically, they are descended through matrilineal or patrilineal lines that are part of a highly complex clan or moiety system. To sever the ties by refusing to identify, or by ignoring their ancestry, often brings about banishment from the clan and hence the tribe, casting a shadow of foreboding on the entire extended family.

In 1990, slightly over half of the American Indian population lived in urban areas. The demographer Matthew Snipp maintains that "roughly half of the all urban American Indians can be found in as few as 16 cities including Tulsa, Oklahoma City, Los Angeles-Long Beach, Phoenix, Seattle-Tacoma, Riverside-San Bernardino, New York City, and Minneapolis-St. Paul" (p. 38). According to the sociologist Russell Thorton, urban Indians are less likely to speak or understand their tribal language, participate in tribal cultural activities, report tribal affiliation, and marry Indians than those who live in rural communities, villages, or reservation communities. "If these trends continue," Thorton argues, "both the genetic and tribal distinctiveness of the total Native American population will be greatly lessened" (Thornton, 1996, p. 110). He adds that "urbanization is likely not only to result in increased intermarriage as more and more Native Americans come in contact with non-Native peoples, but also to diminish further the identity of Native Americans as distinctive tribal peoples tied to specific geographical areas" (p. 111).

Organizations and Societies

In the late 1960s, active and concerted interest began in conducting research and advancing mental health and substance use topics among American Indians from a psychological perspective. At that time, the nation's four major ethnic minority groups (Asian American, African American, American Indian, and Hispanic American), women, and economically disadvantaged groups rallied, demonstrated, and protested demanding recognition, respect, equality, and an affirmation of their civil rights. Coincident with the demonstrations and protests, students and faculty from underrepresented groups and their supporters called for reform in admissions, hiring, curriculum, and research themes in higher education. In psychology, for example, women and ethnic minorities were woefully underrepresented in faculty ranks, federally sponsored research review programs and committees, graduate programs, and the infrastructure of professional associations and societies. Furthermore, curriculum and research themes in psychology were nearly devoid of content dealing with gender, cultural, and ethnic topics. To fill the gaps and make the concerns and problems of

American Indians known, small interest groups emerged and formed from the heated debates and turbulent controversy of the late 1960s and early 1970s.

In the late 1960s there were probably fewer then 10 doctoral-level psychologists of American Indian background living in the United States. The actual count was elusive and therefore could have been larger since there were no known procedures available to derive the real numbers. At that time, two seminal organizational attempts occurred to identify American Indian psychologists and form small working groups to bring the attention of the social and psychological needs and concerns to the community of psychologists. In the spring of 1971 Joseph Trimble, then at Oklahoma City University, created an American Indian Interest Group through cooperation and support from the Society for the Psychological Study of Social Issues (SPSSI), a division of the American Psychological Association. About the same time, Carolyn Attneave, working from her home in the Boston, Massachusetts area began identifying psychologists of American Indian background by contacting psychologists from around North America. As her small list of names increased, she formed a group initially called the Network of Indian Psychologists. Four years later Attneave changed the name to the Society of Indian Psychologists (SIP). In 1973, Trimble shared his few findings and accomplishments with Attneave, terminated his SPSSI sponsored interest group, and aligned his venture and activities with SIP.

SIP eventually grew to have a mailing list of more than 100, consisting of non-Indian and American Indian and Alaska Native psychologists and graduate students. A newsletter is distributed, usually about twice annually, to members and organizations interested in American Indian psychology. SIP typically convenes its annual meetings in conjunction with the Conference of American Indian Psychologists and Graduate Students in Logan, Utah around the third week of June and at the annual meeting of the American Psychological Association usually held in August.

A number of psychologists interested in American Indian psychology are members of the American Psychological Association's (APA) Division 45, the Society for the Psychological Study of Ethnic Minority Issues (SPSEMI). In the division's short history American Indians have been heavily involved in its governance structure and instrumental in its formation. Each year at the APA's annual convention one is likely to find several presentations dealing with American Indian psychology on the program sponsored by the SPSEMI.

Over the years SIP activities contributed to increases in the number of Indians who chose psychology as a career; a good deal of the influence occurred through the active mentoring that many SIP members provided for Indian students interested in the profession. The

"Indians into Psychology Doctoral Education" program, initiated by Arthur L. McDonald in the mid-1980s, has also contributed significantly to the growth in numbers.

Working with a team of public policy specialists from the American Psychological Association and congressional aides, McDonald was able to influence the support of the U.S. Senate to include a provision for INDPSYDE in the 1992 Indian Health Care Improvement Act. A permanent INDPSYDE program exists at the University of North Dakota. Initially established at the University of North Dakota, the program has expanded to include students from colleges and universities in Montana, South Dakota, Utah, and Colorado.

Arthur L. McDonald also was responsible for developing a Rural Minority Mental Health Training program in 1991. The intent of the program is to provide academic training to psychology students interested in providing clinical and counseling services in rural settings, especially American Indian reservations; most of the students are of American Indian and Alaska Native background. Training consists of teaching classes, working in the college clinic, and providing community services through Dull Knife Memorial College in Lame Deer, Montana. Students take a full course load that includes courses in the foundation of oral history, tribal healing systems, and rural mental health practice issues.

In 1994, the American Psychological Association (APA) reported that 109 members of the APA identified themselves as American Indian or Alaska Native; about 63% of the total were male. Yet not all psychologists of American Indian background are members of the APA, so the actual number is unknown. The promising training and recruitment efforts of many institutions and organizations such as SIP have contributed to increases in the number of American Indian psychologists in the past thirty years and the numbers appear to be increasing.

Significant Publications

An extensive number of books, journal articles, and monographs have been written about American Indians and Alaska Natives in the field of anthropology. From early ethnographic accounts at the turn of the nineteenth century to detailed descriptions of lifestyle patterns, developmental stages, kinship relationships, rituals, and traditions, anthropologists have been almost on the doorstep of Indian communities documenting nearly all facets of tribal life. Until recently, however, psychologists have contributed little to the literature on Indians.

During the 1920s and 1930s a few articles appeared in journals describing intelligence test score patterns among small samples of Indians. Not much else of importance and substance on American Indian psychological topics appeared in the scientific literature until the 1960s. In 1965, Alonzo T. Spang published what perhaps was the first article on the subject of counseling American Indians. Two years later Father John Francis Bryde released an interesting small monograph entitled *Acculturation or Modern Indian Psychology*. The monograph was written under a contract from the Bureau of Indian Affairs and focused almost exclusively on American Indians in South Dakota and, in particular, those on the Pine Ridge Indian Reservation. The tone and contents of the monograph were heavily influenced by psychoanalytic theory. In 1971, Bryde published a revised and expanded version of his monograph and entitled it *Modern Indian Psychology* (Bryde, 1971). Bryde's revised text included expanded material on Indians in general, departed from a reliance on psychoanalysis, and dealt with topics such as "Indian personality," Indian self-concept, Indian values, and value conflicts with non-Indians, and "dealing with cultural conflicts." John Bryde's works were intended for use as textbooks by American Indians in school settings.

A flurry of articles on Indians and psychology began to appear toward the end of the 1960s and the rate has accelerated since then. Most articles and books dealt with mental health and alcohol and drug use topics. Two literature summaries have been published that reflect the extensive nature of the writing on American Indian psychology. In 1981, Dianne R. Kelso and Carolyn L. Attneave compiled and published an extensive bibliography of 1,363 citations dating back to 1930 on North American Indian mental health (Kelso & Attneave, 1981); the citations, however, include articles covering many academic disciplines and not just psychology. In 1994, Joseph E. Trimble and Weldon M. Bagwell edited a bibliography of psychological and behavioral articles on North American Indians and Alaska Natives published from 1967 to 1994; most of the 2,328 citations are presented in abstract or summary form (Trimble & Bagwell, 1994).

From 1967 to 1994 close to 3,000 behavioral and social scientists, psychiatrists, physicians, social workers, and those from related academic professions were involved in publishing psychologically oriented articles, book chapters, monographs, and books about North American Indians and Alaska Natives (Trimble & Bagwell, 1994). However, it is difficult to identify how many of the authors were psychologists, since an author's actual professional affiliation is often not included as part of a publication.

In the past decade or so a few significant and frequently cited articles and texts on American Indian psychology have been written by psychologists, and reflect the major themes and topics of interest to those in the field. Counseling and psychotherapy services for American Indian clients and communities are the subject of publications by Teresa D. La Fromboise (La Fromboise, Trimble, & Mohatt, 1990), and Joseph E. Trimble (Trimble, Fleming, Beauvais, & Thurman, 1996), and most often appear in the literature and in literature citations. In the American Indian alcohol and drug use field a few psychologists have contributed important and significant findings to the literature including Eugene R. Oetting, Ruth Edwards, and Fred Beauvais (Oetting, Edwards, & Beauvais, 1988).

In other psychological topics a number of psychologists have contributed interesting and often-cited articles in areas such as stereotypes and prejudice (Trimble, 1988), self-concept (Trimble, 1987), life skills development and biculturalism (La Fromboise, 1996), American Indian women and psychology (La Fromboise, Berman, & Sohi, 1994), and acculturation of American Indians (Choney, Berryhill-Paapke, & Robbins, 1995). It is noteworthy that in recent decades, many psychologists have contributed heavily to the literature on American Indian psychology in a multitude of areas. Eduardo and Bonnie Duran (1995) present an interesting theoretical discussion of contemporary Indian problems and issues from the perspective of American Indians; their thought-provoking work is one of a few full-length books focusing on contemporary American Indian experiences from a psychological perspective. The psychologically trained husband and wife team argue that it is imperative to understand the underlying trauma and internalized oppression of American Indians to fully understand the issues American Indians and Alaska Natives experience in today's world.

The journal of the National Center for American Indian and Alaska Native Mental Health Research, edited by the medical and cultural anthropologist, Spero M. Manson, publishes a number of scholarly articles annually dealing with American Indian psychological topics. The journal is now known as *American Indian and Alaska Native Mental Health Research*. Often referred to as the "Journal of the National Center" or the "Journal of American Indian and Alaska Native Mental Health Research," the journal has its origins at the former White Cloud Center in Portland, Oregon where the first issue was published in the spring of 1978. Robert A. Ryan was the founding and inaugural editor as well as the center director. Initial volumes were referred to as the *White Cloud Journal of American Indian/Alaska Native Mental Health*. However, the journal name was changed when the National Center moved several years later from the Oregon Health Sciences University in Portland and the University of South Dakota, to its present location at the University of Colorado Health Sciences Center in Denver, Colorado.

[*See also* Minority Psychology.]

Bibliography

Bryde, J. (1971). *Modern Indian psychology.* (Revised ed.). Vermillion, SD: Dakota Press, University of South Da-

kota. (Original work published 1967.) Based on Indian oral accounts collected from older Indians over a 23-year span, this revised edition incorporates suggestions from Indian students and their teachers, Indian and non-Indian social studies experts, and other Indian people.

Choney, S. Berryhill-Paapke, E., & Robbins, R. (1995). The acculturation of American Indians: Developing frameworks for research and practice. In J. Ponterotto, J. M. Casas, L. Suzaki, & C. Alexander (Eds.), *Handbook of multicultural counseling* (pp. 73–92). Thousand Oaks, CA: Sage.

Duran, E., & Duran, B. (1995). *Native American postcolonial psychology.* Albany, NY: State University of New York Press. Presents a theoretical discussion of problems and issues encountered in the Native American community from a perspective that accepts Native knowledge as legitimate.

Kelso, D., & Attneave, C. (Eds.). (1981). *Bibliography of North American Indian mental health.* Westport, CT: Greenwood Press.

La Fromboise, T. (1996). *American Indian skills development curriculum.* Madison, WI: University of Wisconsin Press. The curriculum described in this workbook addresses key issues in American Indian adolescents' lives and teaches such life skills as communication and problem solving, and depression and stress management, anger resolution, and goal setting.

La Fromboise, T., Berman, J., & Sohi, B. (1994). American Indian women. In L. Comas-Diaz & B. Greene (Eds.), *Women of color: Integrating ethnic and gender identities in psychotherapy* (pp. 30–71). New York: Guilford Press.

La Fromboise, T. D., Trimble, J. E., & Mohatt, G. (1990). Counseling intervention and the American Indian tradition: An integrative approach. *The Counseling Psychologist, 18,* 628–654.

Oetting, E., Edwards, R., & Beauvais, F. (1988). Drugs and Native-American youth. *Drugs & Society, 3*(1–2), 1–34.

Snipp, C. M. (1996). The size and distribution of the American Indian population: Fertility, mortality, residence, and migration. In G. Sandefur, R. Rindfuss, & B. Cohen (Eds.), *Changing numbers, changing needs: American Indian demography and public health* (pp. 17–52). Washington, DC: National Academy Press.

Spang, A. (1965). Counseling the Indian. *Journal of American Indian Education, 5,* 10–15.

Thornton, R. (1996). Tribal membership requirements and the demography of "old" and "new" Native Americans. In G. Sandefur, R. Rindfuss, & B. Cohen (Eds.), *Changing numbers, changing needs: American Indian demography and public health* (pp. 103–112). Washington, DC: National Academy Press.

Trimble, J. E. (1987). Self-understanding and perceived alienation among American Indians. *Journal of Community Psychology, 15,* 316–333.

Trimble, J. E. (1988). Stereotypic images, American Indians and prejudice. In P. Katz & D. Taylor (Eds.), *Toward the elimination of racism: Profiles in controversy* (pp. 181–202). New York: Pergamon.

Trimble, J. E. (1990–1991). Ethnic specification, validation prospects and the future of drug abuse research. *International Journal of the Addictions, 25,* 149–169.

Trimble, J., & Bagwell, W. (Eds.). (1995). *North American Indians and Alaska Natives: Abstracts of psychological and behavioral literature, 1967–1995 (No. 15. Bibliographies in Psychology).* Washington, DC: American Psychological Association.

Trimble, J., Fleming, C., Beauvais, F., & Thurman, P. (1995). Essential cultural and social strategies for counseling Native American Indians. In P. Pedersen, J. Draguns, W. Lonner, & J. Trimble (Eds.), *Counseling across cultures* (4th ed., pp. 177–209). Thousand Oaks, CA: Sage.

Joseph E. Trimble

AMERICAN INSTITUTES FOR RESEARCH IN THE BEHAVIORAL SCIENCES. An independent not-for-profit corporation, the American Institutes for Research in the Behavioral Sciences (AIR) conducts basic and applied research, performs policy analysis, and provides technical assistance in the behavioral and social sciences. Its clients include federal and state governmental agencies, the military services, foundations, and private corporations. AIR's research program currently encompasses ten program areas: human performance, education, child development, health, program planning and implementation, employment equity, program evaluation, statistical methods, usability engineering, and information design.

AIR's primary goal is to apply the behavioral and social sciences to the solution of important social problems. Since its founding, AIR's distinguishing features have remained remarkably constant: a focus on the enhancement of human performance, broadly conceived, and an emphasis on measurement and quantitative analysis. Over the years AIR has continually applied its expertise in new areas, and has always been concerned that the results of its work make a difference in the quality of people's lives.

AIR was founded in Pittsburgh, in 1946, for the purpose of studying human resources and their effective use. John C. Flanagan, AIR's founder, derived his inspiration for AIR from his successful leadership of the U.S. Army Air Force's Aviation Psychology Program during World War II.

During its early days, AIR attracted as board members, staff, and consultants, many of Dr. Flanagan's illustrious colleagues. Early members of the board of directors included Truman Lee Kelley, Walter R. Miles, Phillip J. Rulon, Robert L. Thorndike, Frederick B. Davis, Paul Horst, and S. Rains Wallace.

During the first year of AIR's existence, John Flanagan joined B. F. Skinner, Robert Sears, Carl Rogers, Rensis Likert, and others in a symposium on current trends in psychology. Dr. Flanagan presented a 20-year program for AIR, focusing on the scientific study of human resources with the goal of developing the individual and increasing his or her satisfactions. In the next two decades, AIR made important research contributions to these topics.

The organization grew rapidly from a staff of 17 in 1949 to 74 in 1955. Consistent with that growth, AIR opened a second office, located in Washington, D.C., to facilitate contact and coordination with an array of clients in the federal government. After the twenty-year plan was completed, John Flanagan moved to AIR's new office in Palo Alto, remaining as chairman of the board but turning over the presidency to S. Rains Wallace, who served in that capacity from 1967 to 1970 when he joined the faculty of Ohio State University. Today, AIR has a staff of 500 who carry on a diverse program of research and analysis at four research centers in the Washington, D.C. area, one in Concord, Massachusetts, and another in Palo Alto, California.

The growth and diversification in staff has been accompanied by other organizational changes. During its first decade, AIR's research program was primarily concerned with the definition of key personnel requirements for successful performance in a broad array of jobs, ranging from airline pilots to police officers. In its first project, a commercial airline asked AIR to screen pilots based on their predicted performance. Using tests adapted from World War II, AIR developed a selection process that raised the quality of pilots and has been applied over the years by many airlines around the world. Other early projects included preparing new procedures for reporting Air Force officers' performance, developing tests of the leadership abilities of noncommissioned officers, and improving highway safety through development of explicit rationales for driver training, changed regulations, and improved road designs. During this same period, human engineering and systems design became increasingly central to AIR's work, leading to improvements in the interface between users and equipment.

Fundamental to much of this work was development and application of the Critical Incident Technique (Flanagan, 1954), a procedure for systematically collecting information about individual difference constructs contributing to job performance. This methodology is still widely used today and Flanagan's 1954 article has been designated as the article most frequently cited by industrial and organizational psychologists (Sackett, 1994). An allied technique, known as the method of rationales (Flanagan, 1951), has been widely adopted for use in specification of test items and training content, and has served as the conceptual underpinning of program evaluation.

As AIR grew, the organization's focus expanded to include the resolution of problems in education, both at home and abroad. The first major project in this arena, Project TALENT, measured the aptitudes and interests of 400,000 students in a stratified random sample of 1,000 secondary schools. Follow-ups occurred after 1, 5, and 11 years. AIR also turned its attention overseas. For example, it developed tests to help Nigerians classify students for entry into secondary, technical, or alternative schools so that more students would satisfactorily complete courses. Similar aptitude tests were constructed for other countries in Africa and other parts of the world. Educational research and policy analysis, both here and abroad, continue to constitute one of AIR's largest program areas.

In the early 1970s, AIR's program was further broadened. Under the leadership of its board and Paul A. Schwarz, who served as president from 1973 to 1987, the organization added major new initiatives in health care research, usability engineering, and information design. Social program evaluation became a major emphasis. For example, AIR was asked to evaluate the effectiveness of Push for Excellence (PUSH-EXCEL), a program designed to aid the performance of minority children in schools, as well as assess other inner-city programs related to crime prevention, jobs, and support for teenage mothers.

Under the stewardship of AIR's fourth president, David A. Goslin, the Pelavin Research Institute and the Institute for International Research joined AIR to increase the organization's capabilities to conduct educational policy analysis and research. Work in other traditional areas has continued apace. AIR conducted a study for the National Collegiate Athletic Association of the effects of participation in intercollegiate athletics from the perspective of student-athletes. The organization recently has headed a consortium of research organizations working with the Department of Labor to replace the *Dictionary of Occupational Titles* with a new database system (known as the Occupational Network or O*NET) for the description and classification of jobs in the U.S. economy. AIR remains committed to providing leadership in applying the behavioral and social sciences to improve the quality of people's lives.

Bibliography

American Institutes for Research. Available Web site: URL http://www.air.org

Flanagan, J. C. (1951). The use of comprehensive rationales in test development. *Educational and Psychological Measurement, 11,* 151–155.

Flanagan, J. C. (1954) The critical incident technique. *Psychological Bulletin, 51,* 327–358.

Flanagan, J. C. (1984) The American Institutes for Research. *American Psychologist, 39,* 1272–1276. A detailed history of AIR for further reading.

Sackett, P. R. (1994). *The content and process of the research enterprise within industrial and organizational psychology.* Presidential address delivered at the Society for Industrial and Organizational Psychology Convention, Nashville, TN.

George R. Wheaton and W. J. McKeachie

AMERICAN PSYCHIATRIC ASSOCIATION. The oldest national medical society in the United States, the American Psychiatric Association (APA) was founded in Philadelphia in 1844 by 13 distinguished physicians who administered the mental hospitals of their day. Through its members, the Association seeks to advance its objectives to improve the treatment, rehabilitation, and care of individuals with mental disorders; to promote research and professional education in psychiatry and allied fields, and the prevention of psychiatric disabilities; to advance the standards of psychiatric services and facilities; to foster cooperation of all who are concerned with the medical, psychological, social, and legal aspects of mental health and illness; to make psychiatric knowledge available to other medical practitioners, to scientists in other fields of knowledge, and to the public; and to promote the best interests of patients and those utilizing mental health services.

The association, initially the Association of Medical Superintendents of American Institutions for the Insane, began as a small organization of hospital superintendents and grew rather slowly during its first 50 years of existence. By 1890, membership was less than 200. It was the triumph of these early leaders that they presided over the transfer of the mentally ill from jails and almshouses to medical institutions, and that they inaugurated a program of moral treatment that embodied the rudiments of modern community psychiatry.

Toward the end of the century, members sought a new name for the association, one that would reflect the broadening scope of their interests and practice. Although the word *psychiatric* had come into professional use, members rejected its use out of concern that its meaning could not readily be conveyed to laypeople. In 1892 they settled on the name American Medico-Psychological Association.

By 1910 the membership had grown to about 500. The next decade saw the membership approximately double. By this time American psychiatry had produced such leaders as Adolf Meyer, William A. White, Elmer Southard, and Thomas W. Salmon, all of whom became presidents of the association. The intellectual currents they set in motion combined with European influences to precipitate the rapid growth of twentieth-century psychiatry.

In 1921 the name American Psychiatric Association was adopted. Beginning in the 1930s the membership grew dramatically, doubling each decade—from 1,300 in 1930, up to 11,500 in 1960. This strong growth has continued, with nearly 39,000 members as of January 1994.

The association is governed by an elected board of trustees, which formulates and approves policies and positions of the association. In addition to the officers of the association, members of the board include nationally and regionally elected trustees as well as a trustee who is a member in training.

To facilitate the democratic process, the Association is divided geographically into 76 local psychiatric societies called *distinct branches*. These distinct branches are constituent parts of the association and work locally to foster the science of psychiatry, promote its progress as a healing profession, and maintain high professional standards. The requirements for membership in a district branch are the same as for membership in the association. Since 1963, with rare exceptions, APA members must belong to a district branch. The district branches are grouped into seven geographic areas called *councils*. The district branches form the basis of the assembly, the representative legislative component of the APA. Beginning in the late 1980s, the board of trustees and the assembly became extensively involved in trying to cope with major economic constraints on the practice of psychiatry.

The APA offers a wide range of benefits, from competitive liability insurance to excellent continuing education programs. Through participation in seminars and workshops, members can learn how to establish a practice, understand the law as it applies to the profession, and become informed about new approaches to care. Members receive the most up-to-date information about research and events affecting psychiatry via APA journals, newspapers, and newsletters. The principal periodicals of the association are the *American Journal of Psychiatry* and *Psychiatric Services*, both monthly journals, and *Psychiatric News*, a biweekly newspaper.

The APA Office of Research conducts activities related to science policy, scientific assessment, the conduct of research studies, and residency training. These include the development of the *Diagnostic and Statistical Manual of Mental Disorders* (*DSM*), which is regularly revised, the APA Practice Guidelines program, and the APA Practice Research Network. Public affairs efforts serve to diminish stigma associated with mental illness, and government relations activities ensure that psychiatry has a voice in setting policy for mental health care. The Office of Economic Affairs serves as an information resource for APA members on health insurance, reimbursement, and economic questions concerning psychiatric care. The Office of Education assists members with obtaining high-quality continuing medical edu-

cation and produces such materials as the Psychiatric Knowledge and Skills Self-Assessment Program. The Division of Government Relations serves as the APA's link with the U.S. Congress, advocating on behalf of psychiatry on a wide variety of issues, including funding for research and training, equitable insurance coverage for mental illness, and other service delivery issues for individuals with mental illness.

The APA library and archives, established in 1961, provides members with access to over 10,000 volumes, 4,000 autographed copies of books written by members of the association, and 300 journal titles, as well as audiovisual materials selected to fulfill the continuing education needs of psychiatrists. The library staff can assist with literature searches, photocopying of articles, locating material in other repositories, and checking references. The library also prepares bibliographies on topics of interest to the membership.

These are only a few examples of the vast resources and services the American Psychiatric Association provides to its members and the general public. Those studying the history of the APA and the development of mental health policy and care will find many resources in the APA Archives, which contains the official records of the APA dating from the 1940s, the papers of individuals significant in the history of psychiatry, and oral history interviews. The massive growth of the Association over the past decade reflects the APA's efforts to provide national leadership in dealing more effectively with all aspects of mental illness.

[*See also* Psychiatry.]

Bibliography

American Psychiatric Association. (1994). *The diagnostic and statistical manual of mental disorders* (4th ed.). Washington, DC: Author.

Andreasen, N. C. (Ed.). (1997). Festschrift in honor of Melvin Sabshin, M.D. *American Journal of Psychiatry, 154* (Suppl. 6).

Deborah A. Zarin and Melvin Sabshin

AMERICAN PSYCHOLOGICAL ASSOCIATION. [*This entry comprises two articles. The first article provides an overview of the history, nature, and purpose of the association. The second article focuses on the structural organization of the association. For discussions about various regional psychological associations, see* Regional Psychological Associations.]

History

The world's largest psychological organization, the American Psychological Association (APA), headquartered in Washington, D.C., was founded as a learned society late in the nineteenth century. Initially, its stated purpose was "the advancement of psychology as a science," and membership was invited exclusively from those "who are engaged in this work." By 1917, its purpose was broadened to the advancement of psychology as both a science and a profession, and in the mid-1940s the promotion of human welfare was added as an explicit goal. Its membership grew slowly during the first decades of its existence from 26 in 1892 to about 300 in the early 1930s, then escalated to 3,000 by the early 1940s. By mid-century the number of members approached 10,000, by the early 1980s it exceeded 50,000, and in the late 1990s the total number of members and affiliates had surpassed 150,000. From a small academic organization at a time when experimental psychology as a scientific discipline was struggling to establish its identity as an academic endeavor separate from philosophy, the APA grew into an enormous, diverse organization with much broader purposes, attempting to serve the needs of professional practicing psychologists and academic research psychologists, as well as facilitating the application of psychological knowledge and lore to the alleviation of individual and social problems.

The Founding of the APA

The APA began at a "preliminary" meeting convened by the president of Clark University, G. Stanley Hall, in his study in Worcester, Massachusetts, on 8 July 1892. The first regular meeting of the association, at the invitation of George S. Fullerton, occurred on 27 December 1892 at the University of Pennsylvania. Late in the nineteenth century, psychology was changing from "moral philosophy" to an experimental science, several prominent institutions of higher education had begun to emphasize graduate training rather than solely undergraduate instruction, and a number of academic disciplines had institutionalized themselves by founding specialized societies (e.g., the American Association for the Advancement of Science, the American Social Science Association, the American Chemical Society, the Modern Language Association, and the American Historical Association). The American Physiological Society was founded in the late 1880s by several of Hall's colleagues at Johns Hopkins University, where Hall had established a psychological laboratory earlier that decade. It became a model for Hall's vision of the new psychological association. The time may have been ripe for the founding of the organization, but the ambition of Hall to be the leader of American psychology also played a role in the events that led to the formal establishment of the APA.

Convened in the summer of 1892 in Hall's study at Clark were some of the most illustrious figures of the day in psychology, as well as representatives of neigh-boring disciplines such as psychiatry, philosophy, and pedagogy. Reported to have been there, for example, were psychologists William James of Harvard University, James Mark Baldwin of the University of Toronto, Joseph Jastrow of the University of Wisconsin, George Trumbull Ladd of Yale University, and James McKeen Cattell of Columbia University. Also present were philosophers John Dewey of the University of Michigan, George S. Fullerton of the University of Pennsylvania, James H. Hyslop of Columbia University, and Josiah Royce of Harvard University; psychiatrists Edward Cowles and William Noyes of McLean Hospital near Boston; and educators William H. Burnham and Benjamin I. Gilman of Clark University. Reliable sources, however, indicate that James was in Europe at the time, and that neither Cattell nor Jastrow attended the meeting; the actual participants at the historic "preliminary" meeting can no longer be determined with certainty.

The first regular meeting of the APA, at the University of Pennsylvania in late December 1892, was attended by 18 of the 31 individuals who had become members by that time. The dozen papers presented there covered a broad range, from a critique of classical psychophysics by James McKeen Cattell to Joseph Jastrow's description of the experimental psychology exhibit planned for the following summer's World's Fair and William L. Bryan's report on the use of psychological tests in the schools of Springfield, Indiana, to Lightner Witmer's presentation on chronoscopic measurements of simple reactions. Some, such as Cattell's and one by Hugo Münsterberg (deploring the work of some of his colleagues as "rich in decimals but poor in ideas"), show that intellectual controversy was present at annual APA meetings from the start. Hall was formally elected president of the APA, and delivered the first presidential address, on "History and Prospects of Experimental Psychology in America."

APA's First Half-Century

At its 1894 meeting at Princeton University, APA adopted a formal constitution. William James of Harvard University was president, and James McKeen Cattell, APA's secretary-treasurer, reported that expenses for the year had totaled $63.93, leaving a balance in APA's treasury of $127.17. Annual dues were set at $3.00 per member but were reduced in 1905 to $1.00 as the Association's coffers grew, and were not raised again (to $2.00) until 1919. During APA's first decade, no national philosophical organization had yet been founded, and presentations on purely philosophical topics were common at the association's annual conventions. With the establishment in 1900 of the Western Philosophical Association and then the American Philosophical Association in 1901, philosophers finally had their own national forum and the proportion of papers on philosophical topics at annual APA conventions dropped significantly. As early as 1896 complaints had been voiced about APA's support of philosophy. This concern, together with the desire for meetings that concentrated specifically on experimental psychology, not on practical or applied issues, led Edward B. Titchener in 1904 to establish by invitation "The Experimentalists," later renamed the Society of Experimental Psychologists.

Between 1910 and 1920 applied psychology emerged as a specific focus of identity for a significant number of psychologists, an identity which the APA initially was reluctant to endorse. In 1917 a group of frustrated clinical psychologists formed the American Association of Clinical Psychologists, and so the APA decided to establish a clinical section within its own table of organization. This resulted in the members of the AACP becoming members of the APA, and the AACP, its purpose having been achieved, dissolved.

In 1922, the APA embarked on its journal publication program by offering to purchase five journals (*Psychological Review, Psychological Bulletin, Journal of Experimental Psychology, Psychological Monographs,* and *Psychological Index*) from Howard C. Warren. The APA began publication of *Psychological Abstracts* in 1927, first complementing, then replacing, other indexes of psychological literature. Applied psychologists continued to believe that the APA, even though it was now both a learned and a professional society, did not adequately fulfill their needs, and by 1937 founded the American Association for Applied Psychology. The conflict between "basic" and "applied" psychology, between "academic" and "professional" psychology, came to a head early in 1941, when Karl M. Dallenbach, chair of the Emergency Committee on Psychology established by the National Research Council to mobilize psychology for World War II, appointed Robert M. Yerkes to head a Subcommittee on Survey and Planning for Psychology. Yerkes asked six prominent psychologists, five of them strongly identified with APA's image as a society for experimental psychology, to join him on this committee: Edwin G. Boring, Alice Bryan, Edgar Doll, Richard Eliot, Ernest R. Hilgard, and Calvin Stone.

The Reorganization of the APA

The charge to Yerkes's committee was dual: to consider how psychology could be used for the war effort, and to recommend how psychology should develop as both a science and a profession after the war. The second charge led to a major change in the APA's structure in the mid-1940s. The committee met in 1942, and recommended an Intersociety Constitutional Convention of Psychologists. That convention, attended by 26 representatives from nine national psychology associations, met in New York in 1943, and appointed a Continuation Committee, headed by Hilgard, to develop detailed bylaws for a new organization that would be responsive to the needs and interests of all psychologists. These bylaws were ratified by the constituent organizations in 1944, and the reorganized APA came officially into existence in 1945. The AAAP, having fulfilled its mission, ceased to exist.

The new APA consisted of 18 "divisions," each identified with a major endeavor, activity, or research focus within psychology. Several were successors to previously existing sections of the AAAP. The divisions were thus a hodgepodge of organizations ranging from those representing the teaching of psychology, experimental psychology, and military psychology through social, developmental, and comparative psychology to clinical, industrial, and consulting psychology. The new structure reflected the broadly diversified state of the field in the middle of the twentieth century; it sought to bring all psychologists together into a single overarching society. Provisions were made for the establishment of additional divisions as specialties in the field continued to proliferate, and indeed the number of divisions climbed to 50 by late in the twentieth century.

APA's Second Fifty Years

Since APA's reorganization, the new divisions that were established were primarily practice oriented. The APA became less an academic learned society and more an organization devoted to practitioner and professional issues. It became a major publisher of 29 highly respected technical journals and, especially later in the twentieth century, of books and monographs. Its conventions sponsored thousands of annual presentations, and convention attendance soared to between ten and twenty thousand. Its annual budget climbed above $70 million by the late 1990s, and its central office had over 500 employees.

Initially the APA had been administered by its officers at their own academic institutions, often with resources supplied in part by those colleges and universities. After the reorganization, a professional staff in Washington, D.C., performed administrative duties, and the *American Psychologist,* a monthly journal of scholarly articles and association news, began publication. Dael Wolfle was the association's first executive secretary and editor of the *American Psychologist.* Later the APA purchased, and then even constructed, its own facilities. In 1992 it built and occupied a large new building next to Union Station in Washington, D.C., and by late in that decade constructed another massive building nearby. By late in the twentieth century, the APA had become a vast, diverse organization and a major business establishment.

The APA became increasingly responsive both to the needs of its ever more diverse membership and to developments in the society and culture within which it exists. Its central office staff was reorganized into major "directorates:" practice, science, education, and public interest. During its earliest years the APA recognized the contribution of women to the field: Two APA presidents were women during the organization's first few decades. That responsiveness declined between 1921 and 1972, when none of the presidents were women—but five women were elected to the APA presidency between 1972 and 1997.

The APA has sponsored many annual awards. The first, for scientific contributions, was first awarded in 1956, to Wolfgang Köhler, Carl R. Rogers, and Kenneth W. Spence. Other awards, and their first winners, are for contributions to applications of psychology (Conrad Kraft, 1973), professional contributions (Carl R. Rogers, 1972), contributions to the public interest (Kenneth B. Clark, 1978), contributions to education and training (Wilbert J. McKeachie and Florence L. Denmark, 1987), research in public policy (Sandra Scarr, 1988), international advancement of psychology (Otto Klineberg, 1991), and early career contributions (Norman Adler, John Neale, and Michael Turvey, 1974). A special award for lifetime contributions to psychology was inaugurated in 1990, when it was presented to B. F. Skinner.

Founded as a scientific organization, the APA became progressively more identified with practitioner concerns during the latter half of the twentieth century. Academic and research psychologists, believing that the APA no longer sufficiently spoke to their interests, founded the rival Psychonomic Society in 1960. Pointedly, the requirements for membership in that society included publication of at least two refereed research articles beyond the doctoral dissertation. During the 1980s major efforts were mounted to make the APA more relevant to the perceived needs and interests of academic and research psychologists, but the APA's center of gravity had swung far toward the professional practice side of the field. Proposals to change the APA so as to continue to make it the primary organization for scientific psychologists failed to be endorsed by the membership. The rival American Psychological Society (APS) was, as a result, founded in 1988, but many members of the new APS, as well as many of the Psychonomic Society's members, continued to maintain their membership in the APA as well. Specialized behavioral science research organizations, such as the Society for Neuroscience and the Society for Research in Child Development, also compete with the APA for members.

[*See also* American Psychological Association of Graduate Students.]

Bibliography

Benjamin, L. T., Jr. (Ed.). (1992). The history of American psychology [Special issue]. *American Psychologist, 47*

(2). This special issue, published on the occasion of the 100th anniversary of the APA, includes 25 articles on the history of American psychology.

Evans, R. B., Sexton, V. S., & Cadwallader, T. S. (1992). *100 years: The American Psychological Association: A historical perspective.* Washington, DC: American Psychological Association. The definitive work on the history of the APA.

Fernberger, S. W. (1932). The American Psychological Association: A historical summary, 1892–1930. *Psychological Bulletin, 29,* 1–89.

Fernberger, S. W. (1943). The American Psychological Association, 1892–1942. *Psychological Review, 50,* 33–60.

Pate, J. L. (Ed.) (1997). History of psychology: 50th anniversary of divisions [Special section]. *American Psychologist, 52,* 721–741. Three articles on the reorganization of the APA and the history of its divisions.

Sokal, M. M. (1992). Origins and early years of the American Psychological Association, 1890–1906. *American Psychologist, 47,* 111–122.

Michael Wertheimer

Structure

The American Psychological Association (APA) is a scientific and professional membership association incorporated in the District of Columbia. Founded in 1892, APA was the world's first national psychological association, and it remains the largest. APA was a relatively small academic society until after World War II when an increasing interest in applied psychology, especially clinical psychology, brought thousands of veterans and others into psychology. In 1945, APA was reorganized to encompass several smaller psychological groups, becoming, in effect, a new organization with a broader mission, but retaining the APA name for historical reasons.

The mission of the new APA was expanded to include professional as well as scientific issues, and a concern for psychology's contributions to the public interest. A new, multifaceted structure that included divisions and state psychological associations was developed to reflect the diversity of APA's membership and its expanded size and mission.

The reorganization, the broadened mission, and the rapidly increasing size and complexity of the association led to a decision to establish, for the first time, a central office with an executive officer and a staff to provide services to the membership.

Governing Documents

APA is chartered as a corporation in the District of Columbia, and the certificate of incorporation determines, within broad limits, the nature of the association, and takes precedent over all of the association's internal documents. The APA bylaws, which take precedence over all other internal governing documents, have remained fundamentally unchanged since they were ratified by the members a half-century ago. The bylaws establish the major structural units of APA: the Council of Representatives, the Board of Directors, the officers, the standing boards and committees, and the central office, as well as the relationships of APA to its members, divisions, state and provincial psychological associations, and external organizations. Changes in the bylaws require approval by a two-thirds vote of the members voting. The association rules, which can be changed by the Council of Representatives, specify operational procedures within the framework of the bylaws.

Membership

The members of APA exercise their authority over the affairs of the association through direct vote for bylaw changes and for the APA president, and through the election of members to serve on the Council of Representatives. The membership consists of several classes: members, fellows, associate members, and affiliates. The standard for election to member status is receipt of a doctoral degree from a regionally accredited institution of higher learning; fellows are members recognized as having made outstanding contributions to the field of psychology. The standard for associate member status is 2 years of graduate work in psychology or a master's degree plus a year of professional work. Affiliates, who are not members of the association, include international, student, and high school teacher affiliates.

In 1997, the membership of APA reached a total of 151,000 members and affiliates, making it the world's largest behavioral science association and the second largest among all scientific organizations. Of its total membership, there were 79,000 members and fellows, 8,000 associate members, and 64,000 affiliates.

Council of Representatives

The members of the Council of Representatives are elected by the members of the two primary constituencies: the divisions, which are an integral part of the association's structure, and the state and provincial psychological associations (SPPA), which are affiliates of APA. The number of representatives to which each unit (division or SPPA) is entitled is determined by an apportionment ballot on which members allocate votes among the units according to their own priorities and preferences. A division or SPPA may have one, more than one, or no representative at all, depending upon the number of votes assigned to them by the members.

The Council of Representatives has broad authority to develop the internal and external policies of the association, within the framework of the charter and the bylaws. It has full authority over the affairs and funds of the association. The council elects the members of all standing boards and committees created by the bylaws. The council also elects the recording secretary and the treasurer, and confirms the appointment of the chief staff officer, the chief executive officer.

Board of Directors

The council elects six of its members to serve, along with the elected officers (president, past-president, president-elect, treasurer, recording secretary, and chief executive officer), as members-at-large of the 12-person board of directors, which manages the affairs of the association subject to the general oversight of the council. In its corporate role, the board oversees the business of the association. With the advice and assistance of the Finance Committee, which is elected by the council, the board presents an annual budget for the approval of the council and monitors any deviations from the budget during the year. The board acts for the council between the council's twice yearly meetings. The president, who is elected by the membership at large, chairs both the council and the board of directors.

Boards and Committees

Much of the work of the association is done on a volunteer basis by the members serving on boards and committees, which carry out a wide variety of tasks as indicated by some of their titles: ethics, membership, accreditation, scientific affairs, continuing education, etc. Some boards and committees have broad responsibility for monitoring major programs such as the directorates, the journals, and international affairs. Others have more specific responsibilities such as membership, ethics, or animal care. In the course of their work, committees often generate proposals for new policies or new activities for the association. Ordinarily, these proposals are submitted for review by the Board of Directors and referred by the board to the council for final determination.

Divisions

In its first half-century, APA had a relatively homogeneous membership consisting mostly of college and university faculty members, but with its reorganization to include a more diverse membership, 19 divisions were established to reflect the special interests of the members. By 1997, APA had 50 divisions, representing areas of specialization (e.g., clinical, counseling, developmental), areas of special interest (international affairs, women's issues, psychology and the law), and areas of employment (public service, independent practice, military). Divisions are formed when the Council approves a petition signed by 1% or more of the voting members for a new division. Divisions range in size from 300 to 7,500. Even the smallest divisions have officers and bylaws, a newsletter, and an annual business meeting. Some divisions have, in addition, divisional journals and other publications, staff, administrative offices, and other characteristics of independent professional organizations. Some divisions are separately incorporated, but all are integral parts of the APA structure and have the same rights in and obligations to the association. The APA divisions are as follows:

1. Society for General Psychology
2. Society for the Teaching of Psychology
3. Experimental Psychology
5. Evaluation, Measurement and Statistics
6. Behavioral Neuroscience and Comparative Psychology
7. Developmental Psychology
8. Society for Personality and Social Psychology
9. Society for the Psychological Study of Social Issues—SPSSI
10. Psychology and the Arts
12. Society of Clinical Psychology
13. Consulting Psychology
14. Society for Industrial and Organizational Psychology
15. Educational Psychology
16. School Psychology
17. Counseling Psychology
18. Psychologists in Public Service
19. Military Psychology
20. Adult Development and Aging
21. Applied Experimental and Engineering Psychology
22. Rehabilitation Psychology
23. Society for Consumer Psychology
24. Theoretical and Philosophical Psychology
25. Experimental Analysis of Behavior
26. History of Psychology
27. Society for Community Research and Action: Division of Community Psychology
28. Psychopharmacology and Substance Abuse
29. Psychotherapy
30. Psychological Hypnosis
31. State Psychological Association Affairs
32. Humanistic Psychology
33. Mental Retardation and Developmental Disabilities
34. Population and Environmental Psychology
35. Psychology of Women
36. Psychology of Religion
37. Child, Youth, and Family Services
38. Health Psychology
39. Psychoanalysis
40. Clinical Neuropsychology
41. American Psychology-Law Society
42. Psychologists in Independent Practice
43. Family Psychology
44. Society for the Psychological Study of Lesbian, Gay and Bisexual Issues
45. Society for the Psychological Study of Ethnic Minority Issues
46. Media Psychology
47. Exercise and Sport Psychology
48. Peace Psychology
49. Group Psychology and Group Psychotherapy
50. Addictions
51. Society for the Psychological Study of Men and Masculinity
52. International Psychology
53. Clinical Child Psychology
54. Society of Pediatric Psychology

State and Provincial Associations (SPPA)

Each state, three U.S. territories, and five Canadian provinces have psychological associations that are affiliated with APA and are entitled to seek representation on the Council of Representatives. SPPAs range in size from 25 to 6,000, and in complexity from small groups that only meet occasionally to large organizations with substantial personnel and operations. Most SPPAs have offices, a paid executive director, newsletters, annual meetings, and officers.

Central Office

With nearly 500 employees, the central office provides staff for all of the boards and committees, operates a large publishing house, invests in stocks, manages real estate, and interacts with private, state, and federal agencies and organizations. In addition to collecting roughly $12 million in member dues and fees each year and $11 million from publications, the central office generates additional income of almost $15 million to expand the activities and services of APA. General dues represent only 18% of the revenues needed to run APA.

The executive vice-president and chief executive officer (CEO), as the chief administrative officer of the association, is responsible for the management and staffing of the central office and for running the business aspects of APA. The Board of Directors oversees the work of the CEO and evaluates the CEO's performance on an annual basis.

Directorates

The activities of the central office are organized into seven units referred to as directorates and offices. The professional concerns of the membership are reflected in the four directorates: science, practice, education, and public interest. Each directorate is headed by an executive director who is responsible for staff and programs and a budget of several million dollars. The directorates provide staff for the boards and committees and other governance groups assigned to them, and conduct programs mandated by the board and the council of representatives. Each directorate has a standing board or committee that provides general oversight for the activities of the directorate. The executive directors, and, through them, the staff, report to the CEO.

Those activities that do not fit easily into one of the four directorates are managed by one of four major offices: central programs, financial affairs, publications and communications, and the executive office.

Central programs manages those offices and programs that serve the organization as a whole, such as membership, convention, research, boards and committees, APA graduate students, international affairs, public communication, and the *APA Monitor*.

The office of communications is responsible for the publication of APA's journals and books, PsycInfo, APA's database of the world's psychology literature, and PsycNet, APA's Website.

The office of financial affairs maintains all financial records, receives and disburses all funds, and oversees APA's business affairs, administrative services, and management information services.

The executive office provides coordination among the APA offices and directorates, oversees all central office operations, maintains contact with other national and international organizations, provides support to the officers, Board of Directors, Council of Representatives, and the APA governance, and conducts all association elections.

APA Graduate Students

For many years, the APA has had a student affiliate category that provides psychology students with the *APA Monitor*, the *American Psychologist*, and access to APA publications and services. The APA Graduate Student organization (APAGS) permits psychology graduate students to participate more actively in APA, to elect their own officers, and to carry out projects of interest to them. By the late 1990s, there were approximately 59,000 student affiliates of whom 33,000 were APAGS members.

Annual Convention

The first APA convention was held in December 1892, just a few months after the founding meeting, and the convention has always been a major APA activity. The convention is held annually in different parts of the country, usually in August, and it regularly attracts 12,000 to 20,000 participants. The program is primarily organized by the divisions, each of which has an assigned number of hours depending on the size of the division and the participation of its members in prior conventions. In addition to the scientific and professional program, many divisions and other psychological organizations have their annual business meetings at the convention.

Federal Advocacy

Because of the importance of congressional actions and the activities of many federal agencies to psychology, APA employs a number of staff members who specialize in advocacy and are trained and experienced in working with congressional and agency personnel. These staff members review proposed legislation, iden-

tify areas relevant to psychology's agenda, and advocate on behalf of psychologists. They also work actively with federal agencies to assure that psychology participates in appropriate programs.

Interorganizational Activities

APA maintains contact and communication with a large number of psychology and psychology-related organizations throughout the world. The office of international affairs publishes a newsletter for several thousand APA international affiliates, maintains contact with virtually all other national psychological societies, and participates actively in international congresses, including sponsoring and organizing such events as the International Congress of Applied Psychology. Each of the directorates maintains contact with the U.S. psychological organizations that relate to their domain, and APA participates in many interdisciplinary coalitions for advocacy and information exchange.

Bibliography

American Psychological Association. Available Web site (PsycNet): http://www.apa.org. PsycNet is a rich source of updated information about the APA and the science and practice of psychology.

American Psychologist archival issues. APA news, important notices to members, and the proceedings of the annual business meetings have been published in the *American Psychologist* since it began publication in 1946. In recent years, the August issue has been entirely devoted to association business. Prior to 1946, these matters were published in *Psychological Bulletin*.

Raymond D. Fowler

AMERICAN PSYCHOLOGICAL ASSOCIATION OF GRADUATE STUDENTS. Prior to the founding of the American Psychological Association of Graduate Students (APAGS), a number of attempts had been made to organize and establish a formal association of psychology students within the American Psychological Association (APA). All of these previous attempts ultimately failed for one reason or another. As with many organizations, the initial impetus for the APAGS came from the ranks, from the students themselves. Two graduate students, Scott Mesh from St. John's University, New York, and David Pilon from the University of Waterloo, Ontario, began developing independent ideas regarding the role and status of graduate students within APA. In 1987, they were brought together by Ellin Bloch, Chair of Division 29's (Independent Practice) Student Development Committee. Together they became convinced that APA had yet to establish a method or structure that responded to the unique concerns of psychology students.

With the additional assistance of Pierre Ritchie, who at that time was president of the Ontario Psychological Association, Mesh and Pilon contacted various APA organizations and individuals. Dr. Ritchie was able to enlist the support of Dr. Raymond D. Fowler, then the president-elect of APA, which led to a number of contacts with various staff and governance individuals within the APA hierarchy. Early interactions with Ira Cohen and Jan Woodring of APA's Office of Educational Affairs led to proposals that began the formal process of developing an official student organization within APA. The Office of Educational Affairs arranged for an open forum at the 1988 APA Annual Convention in Atlanta to discuss the needs of APA student affiliates. In addition, a survey was conducted to ascertain current student activities within all APA divisions. Finally, Mesh and Pilon spoke at the annual APA Division Leadership Conference where they consolidated support for the development of a national student organization within APA.

During the 1988 APA Convention, a number of activities converged that were instrumental in the creation of APAGS. The open forum was extremely well attended: several hundred students participated in developing ideas and demonstrating support for such an organization. In addition, there were a growing number of individual and organizational advocates for the student movement, including the APA Board of Directors. The energy from these sources culminated in the APA Council of Representatives unanimously approving a motion to establish a national student organization within APA.

For the next several years, the new organization was extremely active. While the Council of Representatives had created a new organization and provided a financial base by increasing the student fee by $5.00, no direction was given as to how the new organization might be structured. As the fledgling association was addressing issues of organization and structure, it was also beginning to address substantive issues facing psychology students. An initial APAGS Executive Board was identified and included Scott Mesh and David Pilon as co-chairs, Dawn Royall as chair-elect, Sam McFarland Jr. as treasurer, Judy Plaisance as secretary, and James Campbell and Cynthia Erickson as members-at-large. A number of initial decisions needed to be made quickly, including such aspects as an organizational name, membership requirements, a governing structure, election procedures, bylaws development, and methods of communication.

Initially, APAGS membership was composed of all APA student affiliates. However, as APAGS primarily focuses on issues facing graduate students, the leadership within APAGS, as well as the broader APA organization, decided that automatic membership in APAGS would be limited to graduate student affiliates. Undergraduate student affiliates would be allowed to join but would hold a different membership status. In 1988, the membership in APAGS began at approximately 15,000 and over the next nine years grew to more than 41,000.

A sample of APAGS's early achievements includes publishing a quarterly newsletter; developing convention programs; establishing an enhanced membership plan for student affiliates; and instituting reduced rates on APA journals and books. Access to a health care insurance program for students was negotiated, and the Raymond D. Fowler Award was initiated in recognition of a psychologist who advances student development. Four committees (Advocacy, Convention Affairs, Newsletter, and Professional Development) were established, and a network of campus representatives was created. A liaison structure with other psychology governance bodies was developed.

An early controversy developed over how APAGS would fit into the APA governance structure. Because APAGS is a unique entity and since there were no similar components of APA, a new category of organizational structure needed to be developed which would not only accommodate the particular needs of APAGS, but also incorporate the accountability needs of APA. The resulting structure established APAGS as a Task Force of the Board of Directors which provides a balance between suitable autonomy from unwarranted interference and appropriate oversight by APA officers.

Since its beginnings in 1988, APAGS has continued to mature and grow, modifying its structure and focus as needs change. It constitutes the major organization dedicated to promoting the highest standards in teaching, training, and practice of psychology in order to further the education and development of all psychology students. It has established a presence on the APA Council of Representatives and has a voting member on APA's Committee on Accreditation. In addition, it has initiated three scholarships of up to $2,200 each to be awarded yearly to students in the areas of science, practice, and public interest, and it has established the annual Kenneth and Mamie Clark Award to honor a psychologist who has made an outstanding contribution to the professional development of ethnic minority students.

The growth and vibrancy that APAGS displays speaks volumes to the continuing need for such an organization. Its energy and enduring influence provides confidence for its future impact on the lives of both graduate students and those who work with them. Past leaders of APAGS have gone on to take leadership roles within APA.

[*See also* American Psychological Association.]

James L. Campbell and Elizabeth L. Nelson

AMERICAN PSYCHOLOGICAL FOUNDATION. Established by the American Psychological Association (APA), the American Psychological Foundation (APF) was created as an instrument for psychologists to contribute financially to the continuing development of psychology. Ernest Hilgard, J. McVicker Hunt, Donald G. Marquis, and Laurance F. Shaffer convened the first meeting of the APF in 1953 at the Hotel Cleveland in Cleveland, Ohio. Dr. Hunt became the foundation's first president and Donald Marquis, the first vice-president. A board of trustees of no fewer than seven past APA presidents was instituted to manage the foundation, a practice that continues to this day.

APF began with total assets of $550. In the first 10 years of its existence, the trustees grappled with the sort of programming they could support with their limited resources, as well as with ways to generate revenue. The trustees believed they were not likely to raise the funds necessary for scholarships or research support, and funding monographs did not have broad-based appeal. When President J. P. Guilford convened the APF's third meeting in 1955 in San Francisco, the trustees decided to support an annual Gold Medal Award to a psychologist with a "distinguished and protracted history of scientific and scholarly accomplishment." The first recipient of the Gold Medal Award was Robert S. Woodworth in 1956.

In 1957 the foundation inaugurated an annual Science Writer's prize to encourage the sound and accurate reporting of psychological information in the public media: the public press, periodicals, books, radio, and television. Mr. Ernest Haneman won APF's first Science Writer's prize for his series of articles in *Life* magazine.

In the 1960s and 1970s, APF continued to give the Gold Medal Award and expanded its support of promoting psychology in the media with awards in six categories: television, radio, books, film, magazine, and newspapers. APF also instituted the Distinguished Teaching Award in 1970. The first winners of the award were Freda Gould Rebelsky and Fred S. Keller.

During the first 10 years, APF used foundation funds to make small contributions to foreign journals, and provide American journals and review volumes to libraries of foreign universities. In the 1970s, APF added support for research grants to foreign psychologists trained in the United States and journal subscriptions to foreign universities.

In 1974, APF received $406,099 from Esther Katz Rosen, a psychologist from Philadelphia, Pennsylvania, for the advancement and application of knowledge about gifted children. The Esther Katz Rosen Fund has generated research, publications, youth programs, and symposia on gifted children for the last 20 years and has grown to more than $1 million.

In the 1980s, APF expanded the Gold Medal Award to include medals for science, application, and public interest, and provided support for recording psychological journals for the blind. Fundraising revenue did not keep pace with APF's activities, and the trustees were forced to phase out the recorded journals for the blind and media awards toward the end of the 1980s. The trustees initiated the Esther Katz Rosen Symposium on the Gifted and Talented, a series of symposia that would take place at the University of Kansas for three years. At the end of 1989, APF's assets had increased to $848,000.

In 1991, the trustees hired a full-time staff person to manage APF. Since that time, APF has shown considerable growth. In addition to the Gold Medal and Teaching awards, the trustees identified three programmatic support areas: education, public policy, and research. In 1996, APF gave more than $20,000 toward education, which included approximately $17,000 in scholarships. In public policy, APF funded two Congressional Fellows. In research, APF funded several awards and grants, sponsored five lectures at the APA convention, and the continuation of the Esther Katz Rosen symposia. APF's most recent area of growth was made possible through a bequest from Wayne F. Placek, who gave more than $550,000 to Evelyn Hooker for research to increase the public's understanding of gay men and lesbians. Dr. Hooker and a committee of three others gave this fund to APF in 1992, and the fund has grown to more than $900,000 while supporting two $15,000 grants per year.

The APF Board has expanded to include individuals with expertise in gifted children, gay and lesbian issues, and fundraising. APF also supports a full-time staff. The foundation's assets have increased to more than $6 million by the end of the twentieth century. APA members have become increasingly interested in the idea of "giving back" to psychology, and have made the original purpose of the foundation a reality.

Elisabeth R. Straus

AMERICAN PSYCHOLOGICAL SOCIETY. Founded to advance scientific psychology in research and application and to promote psychology in the public interest, the American Psychological Society (APS) was 15,000 members strong at the end of the twentieth century. Since its creation in 1988, APS has become a clear, strong, and steady advocate for psychological science at the national level. It also promotes international exchange and cooperation among psychological scientists.

APS members are a diverse group of psychological scientists and academics, working across the broad span of knowledge encompassed by basic and applied psychological science. Through highly respected publications, members learn of the latest research developments. APS also educates those in key policy-making positions about the pivotal role human behavior plays in societal problems, and of the necessity for scientific research to find solutions. APS meetings and conventions offer opportunities not only to engage in colloquy with leading researchers but also to experience the camaraderie of human-scale gatherings. APS advances the science of psychology through research advocacy, supports the teaching of psychology, and contributes to the general welfare by freely disseminating scientific knowledge.

The society's mission is to promote, protect, and advance the interests of scientifically oriented psychology in research, application, teaching, and the improvement of human welfare. APS meets the demands of this mission through its strong and committed leadership, a minimal bureaucracy, and a sense of urgency in the scientific community about adequate representation of psychological science in policy making and public discourse.

APS was founded on 12 August 1988 to carry out this mission. During the preceding decade, demographic changes within the American Psychological Association (APA), coupled with declining emphasis on scientific interests and participation, led to widespread dissatisfaction about the APA within the scientific community. Many reorganization plans had been proposed for the APA, only to be shelved and then abandoned. In May 1987, the Assembly for Scientific and Applied Psychology (ASAP) was founded by a coalition of APA Division leaders, as a means of promoting scientific goals within the APA. ASAP's existence provided a rallying point, and within a year a comprehensive reorganization plan was put to a vote of the full APA membership. Although only 42% of APA's voters favored the plan, its rejection triggered an ASAP referendum on incorporation. By a vote of 419 in favor to 13 against, ASAP adopted bylaws to transform itself into APS. Within 6 months, APS membership surpassed the 5,000-member mark.

The impetus for creating APS came from widespread recognition that (1) the needs and interests of scientific, applied, and academic psychologists are distinct from those of psychologists whose sole or primary interest is clinical therapy, and (2) psychological science needs a clear, strong, steady voice at the national level, a role that neither specialized organizations nor coalitions can easily play. Within the first year, APS hosted its first

Summit meeting, held its first convention, and established the journal *Psychological Science*.

APS Publications

The APS has been very active in the field of publication. *Psychological Science*, APS's flagship journal, presents refereed, authoritative articles of interest across all of scientific psychology's subdisciplines, summarizes new research developments, reviews new publications, and discusses public issues of immediate relevance to psychologists.

Current Directions in Psychological Science provides concise, informative reviews on emerging trends, controversies, and important issues across the entire spectrum of scientific psychology and its applications. This bimonthly journal identifies current topics of concern, invites contributions from experts in those areas, and presents peer-reviewed papers of high-quality scholarship in a brief, readable format.

A bimonthly newsletter, *The APS Observer* keeps members up to date on current activities of the society, national and international events, and the latest news for scientific psychologists in both the research and political arenas. Profiles on other psychological societies and the Student Caucus sections also appear regularly. The *APS Employment Bulletin*, a monthly indexed listing of employment opportunities for scientific psychologists, is published as part of *The APS Observer* and also issued separately in months when *The APS Observer* is not published. Electronic access is also available on the Internet, providing flexible and powerful capability for searching or browsing.

The *APS Membership Directory* is a listing of all APS members that includes postal and e-mail addresses, affiliations, and brief biographical information. It contains geographic and affiliation indexes, a directory of psychology departments, and is updated regularly.

The APS World Wide Web site contains abstracts from the most recent APS convention, information about APS, job ads from *The APS Observer*, other *Observer* articles, other APS documents, and links to psychology departments and other psychology sites.

Meetings

A three-day annual convention features the latest scientific research and theory, presented for an educated but nonspecialist audience: typical attendance is 2,000 people. Invited addresses and symposia explore major issues in psychological science from multiple perspectives; poster presentations highlight specific research questions and findings; and exhibits offer the latest in publications, teaching, research equipment, and technology. The convention has begun to attract specialized satellite meetings of other, related organizations, such as the Society for Personality and Social Psychology, the American Association for Applied and Preventive

Psychology, the Society for Text Processing, and the Society for Chaos Theory in Psychology.

The APS Teaching Institute precedes the annual APS convention and features leaders in psychological science who showcase the latest in methods and substantive content for effective teaching to a gathering of 400 teachers of psychology. In addition, APS is a cosponsor of the annual winter meeting of the National Institute for the Teaching of Psychology.

Membership

Total membership grew extremely rapidly during APS's first five years, and has grown steadily but more slowly since then, now topping 16,000 fellows, members, and affiliates. The criterion for voting membership (fellow or member) is a doctoral degree in psychology or evidence of sustained and significant contributions to scientific psychology. The typical renewal rate for voting members is 92%.

The APS Student Caucus (APSSC), the Society's active student organization, provides many professional growth activities for both graduate and undergraduate students of psychology. With the assistance of APSSC, nearly 50 local student chapters across the country have been established offering APS student affiliates opportunities to hear invited guest speakers, host regional conferences, and attend career development workshops. APSSC awards travel grants for the annual convention, manages a mentorship program, and operates an electronic bulletin board (APSSCNET) for discussion of student concerns, including timely posting of job and research opportunities. APSSC elects its own officers and advocates who advise the board of directors on student member recruitment and retention, their conversion to full membership, program accreditation, and employment concerns.

Organizations may affiliate with APS over issues of common cause. In 1999, 22 organizations held this nonvoting membership status, enabling the rapid exchange of information in support of the psychological science community. The list of organizational affiliates includes both autonomous societies and divisions of the APA.

Awards

APS recognizes exceptional contributions to scientific psychology with the William James Fellow and James McKeen Cattell Fellow awards. The James award recognizes outstanding contributions to the advancement of psychological science, and the Cattell award recognizes outstanding applications of psychological science. As of 1999, 94 psychologists had been honored as William James Fellows, and 27 had been honored as James McKeen Cattell Fellows.

Advocacy Activities

One of the primary reasons APS was founded was to provide a strong and distinct "presence" for scientific psychology in Washington, D.C. Although still relatively new, APS has established itself as an influential force in Washington, D.C., as it represents the interests of its members and strengthens the ties of research-oriented psychologists with such institutions as the National Science Foundation (NSF), the National Institutes of Health (NIH), the National Institute of Mental Health, and the U.S. Congress. For example, the national science press credited APS's advocacy as instrumental in the establishment of the behavioral science directorate at NSF and also the separate office for behavioral and social science at the NIH. Congress has directed several federal research agencies to give greater priority to behavioral science research funding. APS is a member of many coalitions. It collaborates widely with other organizations in pursuit of its mission.

APS's initial science leadership activity was to convene a Summit of Scientific Psychological Societies, which was held in January 1989, at the University of Oklahoma. Attendees representing more than 40 psychological organizations discussed how to strengthen psychology's research base: the role of science advocacy at the national level, enhancing the identity of psychology as a coherent scientific discipline, protecting scientific values in education and training, using science in the public interest, and scientific values in psychological practice. Two subsequent summits (Tucson, 1990; Houston, 1991) led to the Human Capital Initiative.

Participants representing 70 organizations at the Tucson summit debated whether scientific psychologists should attempt to create a national research agenda. They authorized the creation of a steering committee to try to draft one. A year later in Houston, they reviewed that committee's work and authorized publication and distribution of *The Human Capital Initiative*, a research agenda which brings attention to six major national problems (productivity, education, health, substance abuse, violence, and aging), each examined from the perspectives of four broad research themes (brain, mind, and behavior; human development and families; human relations and organization; and education, training, and performance). The Houston summit participants also authorized a coordinating committee to handle the continuing development of the initiative. To date, five additional publications have been distributed to members of Congress and their staffs, members of the executive branch, including all managers with policy or budgetary responsibility for psychological research, and research-oriented psychologists: *The Changing Nature of Work, Vitality for Life: Psychological*

Research for Productive Aging, Doing the Right Thing: A Research Plan for Healthy Living, Reducing Mental Disorders, and *Reducing Violence: A Research Agenda.*

Accreditation

Although the accreditation system applies only to doctoral training for clinical, counseling, or school psychologists, the process of accreditation affects all of graduate education in psychology through its direct influence on the content and curricula of programs. Accreditation requirements affect the distribution of financial resources across different programs, the use of faculty time, and the priorities of graduate students within those programs. A summit meeting on accreditation was held in Chicago in April 1992 to discuss these issues. The summit played a key role in the creation of the Academy of Clinical Psychological Science, an association of research-oriented clinical training programs.

Governance

The drafters of the APS bylaws created a streamlined organizational structure. The membership, finance, publications, convention, and election committees report to the elected officers (the president, past president, president-elect, and six directors), and ad hoc committees may be created as needed. The elected officers are responsible for carrying out the mission and overseeing the work of the executive director and the headquarters office. Elections are held annually. The bylaws have been amended twice, but still fill only two printed pages.

The APS headquarters office consists of a small staff, fulfilling a goal of the founders to keep bureaucracy at a minimum. Further, less than 2% of the annual budget goes to pay the expenses of committees. This permits the society to put the major portion of its resources into advocacy for psychological science.

APS has refrained from creating an internal substructure of divisions or special interest groups. Thus, internal political representation issues are moot—governance is strictly one person, one vote. This strategy runs counter to the trend of differentiation of interests and identities, but it is consistent with the APS's goal of bringing together the common interests of all psychological researchers.

The elected officers of APS constitute a who's who of psychological research. The list of presidents begins with Janet Spence (although Charles Kiesler was awarded the first status of past-president because of his leadership of ASAP), and continues with James McGaugh, Gordon Bower, Richard Thompson, Marilynn Brewer, Sandra Scarr, Kay Deaux, and Elizabeth Loftus. The members of the Board of Directors are equally well known.

Milton D. Hakel and Lee Herring

AMNESIA, the pathological loss of memory, can result from a wide variety of causes and can take several distinct forms. The most extensively studied form of amnesia is the classical amnesic syndrome, in which damage to specific brain regions leads to a severe and permanent memory deficit. Insights gained from the study of the amnesic syndrome have had a major influence on the development of current views of the function, organization, and neurological basis of human memory, and the study of human amnesia continues to shape our conceptions of the nature of human memory.

Historical Background

The clinical study of patients with amnesia has a long history. As early as 1889, Sergei Korsakoff, a Russian psychiatrist, in a landmark report provided an accurate description of amnesia resulting from long-term alcoholism, now referred to as Korsakoff's syndrome. Following a brief period of psychosis, patients with this disorder had a severe, enduring difficulty in learning new information and were frequently unable to recall memories of events from the years preceding their illness. In contrast, their memories of early life, general intelligence, and language ability appeared normal. Other early clinical reports described similar amnesic syndromes resulting from other etiologies, such as carbon monoxide poisoning and damage to the temporal lobe of the brain. Although these clinical descriptions of amnesia have been reported since the 1800s, the identification of the brain structures critically involved in amnesia and the elucidation of their functions has been a relatively recent development. The modern era in the study of amnesia is often considered to have begun with the case of H. M., a young man who in 1953 underwent bilateral surgical removal of large parts of his medial temporal lobes to relieve intractable epilepsy. Although it alleviated his epilepsy, the operation caused bilateral damage to H. M.'s hippocampus, parts of the cortex surrounding his hippocampus, and his amygdala.

After his surgery, H. M. exhibited what are now considered the hallmarks of the amnesic syndrome in humans. His most striking symptom was a profound and permanent memory impairment. In essence, any information that passed out of his immediate consciousness was completely forgotten. His amnesia also extended into the past: he forgot virtually all the autobiographical events that had occurred during a period of a few years immediately preceding his surgery.

Though the operation decimated his long-term memory, H. M.'s intelligence, perception, and general knowledge about the world, including the meaning and use of words and concepts, were unaffected. In addition, his short-term memory, as assessed by having him repeat short series of numbers, was normal. H. M.'s case illustrates that brain damage can result in a selective, severe, and permanent impairment of a specific ability, long-term memory, while leaving completely intact other higher mental abilities such as perception and intellectual functions. His deficit serves as the prototype of the modern definition of amnesic syndrome: a severe and stable impairment in acquiring new long-term memories resulting from brain injury, frequently accompanied by a variable degree of amnesia for recent life periods, in the presence of preserved short-term memory and preserved higher mental functions including intelligence, language, and perception.

Retrograde and Anterograde Amnesia

Memory deficits in amnesia can be broadly classified into two types based on the time period involved. *Anterograde amnesia* refers to deficits in encoding and storing new memories acquired after the onset of amnesia. For example, a patient with anterograde amnesia would have difficulty learning about new events, persons, or concepts. Anterograde amnesia is thought to reflect the inability of the brain to execute its normal encoding and storage functions as a result of specific brain damage, rather than a deficit in memory retrieval processes.

The term *retrograde amnesia* refers to loss of memories which were encoded and stored prior to the onset of amnesia. Retrograde amnesia often shows a temporal gradient in which memories acquired earlier in life are more likely to be remembered than those acquired later in life. This pattern is strikingly different from the normal pattern in which more recent events are typically better remembered than more remote ones. This preservation of remote memories in retrograde amnesia is captured in Ribot's law (after Théodule-Armand Ribot, the French psychologist) which states that the vulnerability of a memory to loss following brain damage (as occurs in amnesia) is inversely related to the age of the memory.

A leading explanation of why temporal gradients occur in retrograde amnesia is that new memories must undergo a time-limited consolidation process, in which they are converted into a more stable form which is resistant to forgetting and disruption. Memories of the distant past are more resistant to retrograde amnesia because they have already been consolidated, whereas recent memories are less likely to have been consolidated and are thus more vulnerable to disruption. The degree of anterograde amnesia and the degree of retrograde amnesia are not always correlated in individual amnesic patients. This lack of a strong correspondence between anterograde and retrograde amnesia has led to speculation that these two manifestations of amnesia

may depend at least in part on different brain mechanisms.

Etiologies of Amnesia

What causes amnesia? Several different explanations of the memory deficits in amnesia have been proposed. One complication that must be dealt with is the fact that organic amnesia (amnesia resulting from brain injury rather than some other cause) can result from a wide variety of conditions. For example, amnesia can result from long-term alcoholism in conjunction with thiamine deficiency (Korsakoff's syndrome), closed-head injury, stroke, lack of oxygen to the brain, penetrating brain injury, surgical lesions, tumors, viral encephalitis, as well as several less common etiologies. From this diversity of etiologies, two primary regions in the brain have been identified as critical to producing amnesia: the hippocampus (a small structure deep in the temporal lobe) and its surrounding cortical areas, and the thalamus and mamillary bodies in the diencephalon (a major structural division of the brain). These two regions are thought to form an interconnected circuit of processing structures important for long-term memory. One might expect different kinds of amnesia to result from damage to either of these two very different brain areas, but no major differences of this kind have been found, perhaps because these regions are linked in such a way that damage to one of these two regions is sufficient to disrupt processing in the other.

Other differences in etiology do result in qualitatively different types of memory deficit, however. For example, amnesia following left-sided brain damage typically results in a more severe memory deficit for verbal material, whereas right-sided brain damage results in a more severe nonverbal memory deficit. An excellent example is the case of patient N. A., a soldier who was stabbed through the nostril with a miniature fencing foil, damaging his left diencephalon and left temporal lobe. N. A. has a severe impairment in learning new verbal material, but his memory is almost normal for nonverbal material. Another important factor is the degree of damage sustained outside of the hippocampal and diencephalic regions. For example, damage to the frontal lobe does not itself cause amnesia, but if it occurs together with amnesia the nature of the amnesic deficit is substantially altered, a condition termed *frontal amnesia*. The characteristics of frontal amnesia can include an increase in interference from past learning in tasks where a new response must be learned to an old cue; difficulty in discriminating the order in which events occurred or how recently they occurred; source amnesia (forgetting where or when something was encountered); and confabulation, the fabrication of recollection to fill a gap in memory. Infrequently, this fabrication is wildly implausible, a phenomenon referred to as *fantastic confabulation*.

The memory deficits characteristic of the amnesic syndrome can also occur as part of other, more global disorders. For example, memory problems are frequently the earliest and most severe symptoms of Alzheimer's disease. Because other cognitive impairments accompany these disorders in areas such as attention, language, and thought, however, these disorders are categorized separately from the amnesic syndrome, since the amnesic syndrome is defined as circumscribed impairment of memory in the absence of other significant intellectual impairment. Also distinct from the amnesic syndrome is the normal age-related memory loss experienced by the elderly, which is typically much milder than the severe memory deficits encountered in amnesia.

Theories of Human Amnesia

One of the central questions in the study of amnesia is how best to characterize and explain the memory deficits exhibited by amnesic patients. This question is part of a larger, ongoing debate over how best to characterize the function and organization of human memory in general. Theories of amnesia are thus in actuality general theories of memory applied to the specific domain of amnesia.

The memory deficit in amnesia was for many years considered to be global, encompassing virtually all aspects of human memory (with minor exceptions, such as short-term memory and the learning of motor skills). However, in the late 1990s a variety of different types of memory was discovered to be normal in amnesia. So many spared memory abilities have been identified, in fact, that amnesia is now defined as a selective impairment of memory rather than a global one. Here we will consider briefly the major theories of human amnesia and how they explain the pattern of spared and impaired memory abilities in amnesia.

Preserved Memory Function in Amnesia

As noted earlier, short-term memory is unaffected in amnesia, as well as the learning of motor skills. However, the type of preserved memory ability that has most influenced theories of amnesia has been priming, which is shown when there is improvement or bias in perceiving, producing, or identifying a word or object resulting from a prior experience. A critical difference between priming and more traditional forms of memory is that it does not involve conscious recollection. Memory tasks that require conscious recollection are termed *explicit* tasks, whereas priming and other types of memory that do not require conscious recollection are termed *implicit* tasks. For example, reading the word

elephant increases the probability that a person will later respond *elephant* (rather than another alternative such as *elegant*) when asked to produce the first word that comes to mind that completes the cue *ele-*. Priming can also occur for conceptually related items; reading "cry" will increase the probability of giving that word when later free-associating to the word *baby*. Importantly, these memory effects have been shown to occur regardless of whether one can consciously remember the prior occurrence of the word, and they have also been demonstrated to be normal in amnesia. Historically, it was early findings of intact memory performance on priming tests that galvanized interest into the question of what other hidden memory abilities lay untapped in amnesic patients. Priming was exciting in part because it involved retrieving words, the same complex entities that amnesic patients otherwise found so hard to retrieve in conventional memory tests.

A variety of other memory abilities are also intact in amnesia. Amnesic patients can develop increased preference for stimuli to which they are exposed, preferring music, words, or pictures to which they have been previously exposed to novel ones. They also show intact fear conditioning, in which previously neutral stimuli such as tones become associated with responses to aversive stimuli such as electric shocks. More complex forms of preserved learning in amnesia include learning to discriminate stimuli generated by a complex rule, learning to make simple perceptual category judgments, learning a sequence of moves in a reaction time task, and learning about probabilistic relationships between events.

Multiple Memory Systems and Processing Views

Theories of amnesia must account for why some types of memory such as recall and recognition are impaired in amnesia whereas other types of memory such as priming are normal. Two broad classes of theories of amnesia can be identified: multiple memory systems views and the processing views.

Under the multiple systems views, amnesia reflects damage to a specific memory system that handles performance on memory tasks such as recall and recognition but which is separate from the memory systems that handle other types of memory such as short-term memory and priming. Each of these multiple memory systems is proposed to have a specific neural basis of brain structures and connections which carry out its functions.

There are differing views regarding which memory functions are associated with different systems. One influential framework proposed by Endel Tulving distinguishes between episodic memory (specific event and autobiographical), semantic memory (generic knowledge), procedural memory (motor skills and habits), priming, and short-term memory. It postulates that the deficit in amnesia is primarily or wholly concentrated in the episodic system. This view gains support from the fact that amnesic patients with retrograde memory impairment perform much better on tests assessing their general knowledge (semantic memory) than their recollection of specific events (episodic memory). However, it has been suggested that the relative sparing of semantic memory might reflect differences in the tests used to assess episodic and semantic memory. For example, tests of semantic information typically assess information that was acquired well before the onset of amnesia, whereas tests of episodic memory typically assess learning of new information.

A different but related approach, proposed by Larry Squire, groups episodic and semantic memory together under the term *declarative memory*. This approach maintains that amnesia is best characterized by an impairment in memory for both facts (semantic memory) and events (episodic memory). This impairment results from damage to a brain system comprised of the interconnected medial temporal lobe and diencephalic brain regions that are involved in amnesia, referred to as the medial temporal lobe memory system. Declarative memory is defined as information that can be voluntarily brought to mind by conscious recollection. By this view, the spared memory abilities of amnesic patients are handled by a heterogeneous variety of other specific forms of memory, collectively termed *nondeclarative memory*, which have their neural basis outside of the medial temporal lobe system.

Squire has suggested a way to reconcile this view with the view that episodic and semantic memory are handled by separate systems. As noted above, damage to the frontal lobes can result in source memory deficits, in which it is difficult to retrieve the spatial and temporal context of an event. Such a deficit would be expected to affect the retrieval of episodic memories (with their rich associated context) to a much greater extent than semantic memories. Thus, the distinction between episodic and semantic memory could be explained if episodic memory is proposed to be more dependent on the frontal lobes than semantic memory.

Processing views of amnesia concentrate on identifying the important differences between the cognitive processes required to perform different memory functions and on specifying which processes are impaired in amnesia. This contrasts with the multiple memory systems views, which concentrate on identifying the functional neuroanatomical systems underlying different major functions of memory which are impaired in amnesia. There are a variety of processing views of the amnesic syndrome, each focusing on a different cognitive process hypothesized to be impaired. For example, one view, based on a framework proposed by Henry Roediger, distinguishes between conceptual (semantic

and associative) and perceptual memory processes. This view holds that amnesic patients are impaired on memory tasks that require the use of conceptual information (such as recall) but are normal on memory tasks that require only perceptual information (such as perceptual priming). Another view distinguishes between familiarity (knowing that something has been experienced previously) and recollection (the additional ability to recall the context of the previous experience). This view maintains that the memory deficit in amnesia reflects a loss of the recollection process with a sparing of the familiarity process.

Clearly, no single theory of amnesia has emerged yet which has won universal acceptance. It is important to note that processing and multiple systems views are not necessarily mutually exclusive accounts of amnesia. For example, recollection deficits in amnesia specified by the processing views can be mapped onto the memory functions attributed to the frontal lobes in multiple systems views. Ultimately, some combination of the insights achieved by each approach will inform future theories of the nature of human amnesia.

Transient Amnesia

A benign, temporary condition, transient global amnesia (TGA) closely resembles the classical amnesic syndrome. The exact cause of TGA is unknown, and it usually occurs only in older adults, with incidence rising after the age of 50. It has been speculated that TGA may result from temporary interference with the normal functioning of the medial temporal lobe or diencephalon, on the basis of the regions implicated in the amnesic syndrome, but there is no direct evidence supporting this hypothesis. Curiously, TGA is not associated with any detectable abnormalities in laboratory tests or brain scans. TGA typically has an abrupt onset and a short duration, often lasting only a few hours and resolving in the course of a day. As in the classical amnesic syndrome, both anterograde and retrograde memory deficits are observed in TGA, whereas general intellectual, perceptual, and language functions are unaffected.

Psychogenic Amnesia

Forms of amnesia can result from psychiatric conditions such as hysterical or dissociative disorders rather than from specific brain damage as in the amnesic syndrome. These are termed *psychogenic amnesias* because of their psychological rather than organic origin. *Selective amnesia* is a form of psychogenic amnesia involving a loss of memory from a specific time period, typically centered around a traumatic experience such as a natural disaster or war. The specific features of selective amnesia are highly variable and its specific cause is unclear, although it has been linked to dissociative mechanisms and the need to escape from highly distressing thoughts and feelings. Severe cases of selective amnesia can take the form of *fugue states* in which persons may claim to have lost all knowledge of their past, even including their own identity, and may adopt a new identity. Finally, multiple personality disorder has been conceptualized as a form of psychogenic amnesia in which the personal memories of a patient appear to be divided among more than one distinct personality. Each personality may be unaware of the memories possessed by the others. Multiple personality disorder is thought to reflect an extreme state of dissociation.

[*See also* Dissociative Disorders.]

Bibliography

Baddeley, A. D., Wilson, B. A, & Watts, F. N. (Eds.). (1995). *Handbook of memory disorders.* Chichester, U.K.: Wiley. An up-to-date collection of articles relating to amnesia, with a clinical emphasis and coverage of rehabilitation issues. Contains an excellent article on psychogenic (functional) amnesia.

Gabrieli, J. D. E. (1995). A systematic view of human memory processes. *Journal of the International Neuropsychological Society, 1,* 115–118. A cogent discussion of the relative merits of the multiple memory systems and processing frameworks of memory in the context of amnesia, by a leading amnesia researcher.

Hodges, J. R. (1991). *Transient amnesia: Clinical and neuropsychological aspects.* London: Saunders. An extensive treatment of the transient amnesia syndrome.

Johnson, M. K., Kim, J. K., & Risse, G. (1985). Do alcoholic Korsakoff's syndrome patients acquire affective reactions? *Journal of Experimental Psychology: Learning, Memory, & Cognition, 11,* 22–36. Experimental report describing the intact ability of amnesic patients to demonstrate the mere-exposure effect (increased liking for stimuli to which they have been previously exposed).

Milner, B., Corkin, S., & Teuber, H. L. (1968). Further analysis of the hippocampal amnesic syndrome: 14-year follow-up study of H. M. *Neuropsychologia, 6,* 215–234. Describes in detail the case of patient H. M., the most influential case in the history of the study of the amnesic syndrome.

Parkin, A. J. (1997). *Memory and amnesia: An introduction* (2nd ed.). Oxford, UK: Blackwell. An accessible introduction to further topics in amnesia, written by a leading British amnesia researcher.

Roediger, H. L. III, Weldon, M. S., & Challis, B. H. (1989). Explaining dissociations between implicit and explicit measures of retention: A processing account. In H. L. Roediger, III & F. I. M. Craik (Eds.), *Varieties of memory and consciousness: Essays in honour of Endel Tulving* (pp. 3–41). Hillsdale, NJ: Erlbaum. Contains an excellent description of the processing view of memory and amnesia.

Schacter, D. L., & Tulving, E. (Eds.). (1994). *Memory systems 1994.* Cambridge, MA: MIT Press. A collection of chapters from experts in memory and amnesia that gives an excellent overview of contemporary multiple memory systems views. The initial chapter proposes specific criteria for postulating memory systems and gives an up-to-date account of Tulving's view.

Squire, L. R. (1987). *Memory and brain.* New York: Oxford University Press. A classic work by a leading memory researcher that integrates insights from the neuroscience, neuropsychology, and cognitive psychology approaches to memory and amnesia.

Squire, L. R. & Butters, N. (1992). *Neuropsychology of memory* (2nd ed.). New York: Guilford Press. A collection of articles on a wide variety of topics relating to amnesia and other memory disorders. Both clinical and experimental topics are well covered.

Squire, L. R., Knowlton, B., & Musen, G. (1993). The structure and organization of memory. *Annual Review of Psychology, 44,* 453–495. A comprehensive review of the human and nonhuman memory literature, from the perspective of Squire's declarative/nondeclarative memory view. The discussion of mechanisms of retrograde amnesia is particularly notable.

Squire, L. R., & Zola-Morgan, S. (1991). The medial temporal lobe memory system. *Science, 253* (5026), 1380–1386. Integrates the existing experimental data regarding the neuroanatomical basis for declarative memory in humans and nonhuman primates into a view which has subsequently become highly influential.

Victor, M., & Yakovlev, P. I. (Trans.). (1955). S. S. Korsakoff's psychic disorder in conjunction with peripheral neuritis, *Neurology, 5,* 394–406. (Original work published 1889.) English translation of Korsakoff's landmark report on the amnesic syndrome resulting from chronic alcoholism. Original report: Korsakoff, S. S. (1889). Uber eine besondere Form psychischer Storung, Kombiniert mit multiplen Neuritis. *Archiv fur Psychiatrie und Nervenkrankheiten, 21,* 669–704.

Stephan B. Hamann

ANAL STAGE. *See* Psychosexual Stages.

ANALYSIS OF COUNTS. A categorical variable is one for which the measurement scale is a set of categories. For instance, mental impairment might be measured with categories (none, slight, moderate, severe). For categorical variables, the data are the counts in the categories.

For count data, the binomial distribution plays the central role that the normal does for continuous variables. Denote the probability of classification in a particular category by p and the sample size by n. The binomial refers to the sample proportion $\hat{p}$ of subjects falling in that category. One can use it to test whether p takes some value p_0 (such as .5); for large samples, the approximately normal test statistic is

$$z = \frac{\hat{p} - p_o}{[p_o(1 - p_o) / n]^{1/2}}$$

More informatively, a confidence interval contains the p_o values deemed plausible by this test; for instance, a 95% confidence interval consists of those p_o values for which the P-value exceeds .05, or equivalently $|z| \leq 1.96$.

Contingency Tables

For studies having two or more categorical variables, a *contingency table* displays the counts for their cross-classification of categories. For instance, the contingency table relating a binary response with categories (positive, negative) to type of treatment (standard, new) has counts in four cells, for the combinations (standard, positive), (standard, negative), (new, positive), (new, negative).

Two categorical variables are *independent* if the probability of response in any particular category of one variable is the same for each category of the other variable. Test statistics for the hypothesis of independence compare the observed counts in the table to those expected under the hypothesis. The expected counts are numbers that have the same marginal totals as the observed data but perfectly satisfy the hypothesis. For instance, if one hundred subjects receive the standard treatment and one hundred subjects receive the new treatment, and if 60% of the overall sample has a positive response, then the expected frequencies are 60 in the positive category and 40 in the negative category for each treatment; these expected counts, totaling 100 for each treatment, satisfy independence in the sense that the percentage of successes (and of failures) is the same for each treatment.

The most commonly used test statistics are

$$\text{Pearson statistic} = \sum \frac{(\text{observed} - \text{expected})^2}{\text{expected}}$$

Likelihood − ratio statistic

$$= 2 \sum \text{observed} \log \left(\frac{\text{observed}}{\text{expected}}\right).$$

These both have large-sample chi-squared distributions, when most expected frequencies exceed roughly 5. For r rows and c columns, $df = (r - 1)(c - 1)$, and the P-value is the right-tail probability above the observed statistic value. These chi-squared statistics also apply for comparing observed frequencies to expected frequencies for more complex hypotheses than independence, though the df formula depends on the form of the hypothesis. When a contingency table has ordered row or column categories (ordinal variables), specialized methods can take advantage of that ordering (Agresti, 1996, sections 2.5, 7.2, 8.2, 8.3, 9.4).

Multidimensional contingency tables result from cross-classifying more than two categorical variables, such as a treatment variable, a binary response, and control variables such as race, gender, or educational level. The hypothesis of *conditional independence* states that two categorical variables are independent at each level of a third. The Cochran-Mantel-Haenszel test is a large-sample chi-squared test of this hypothesis. Originally formulated for stratified 2-by-2 tables, generalizations exist for stratified r-by-c tables with ordered or unordered categories.

Small-sample tests of independence and conditional independence are also available. Fisher's exact test applies to 2-by-2 tables (i.e., $r = 2$, $c = 2$). Exact tests for larger tables or under stratification are computationally complex but available in statistical software.

Tests of significance have limited use, and it is more informative to study the nature and the strength of the association. Goodman and Kruskal (1979) discussed a variety of summary measures. Measures for ordinal variables, such as their *gamma* measure, are correlationlike indices that fall between -1 and $+1$. For nominal variables, it is usually more helpful to study the difference of proportions or odds ratio for 2-by-2 subtables.

Logistic Regression

For multidimensional contingency tables, modeling approaches are vital for investigating association and interaction structure. *Logistic regression* is an analog of ordinary regression for binary response variables (Agresti 1996; Hosmer & Lemeshow 1989). The predictor variables can be qualitative or quantitative, with qualitative ones handled by dummy variables.

Let p denote the probability of outcome in a particular response category. For a set of predictors X_1, X_2, ..., X_p, the logistic regression model is

$$\log\left(\frac{p}{1 - p}\right) = \alpha + \beta_1 X_1 + \beta_2 X_2 + \cdots + \beta_p X_p$$

The ratio $p/(1 - p)$ is called the *odds*, and the logarithm of the odds appearing on the left-hand side is called the *logit*. The main reason for using the logit instead of p itself is to constrain predicted probabilities to fall between 0 and 1. The antilogs of $\{\beta_k\}$ represent odds ratios, which are multiplicative effects of a 1-unit change in X_k on the odds. Simpler interpretations result from linear approximations. When p equals approximately .5, for instance, $\beta_k/4$ is the approximate change in p for a one-unit change in X_k, controlling for the other predictors.

To test the effect of a term in the model, the ratio of the estimate of β_k to its standard error has an approximate standard normal distribution, under the hypothesis of no effect ($H_o: \beta_k = 0$). One can also estimate the probability p at various settings of the predictors. When all predictors are qualitative, chi-squared tests analyze the adequacy of the model fit by comparing the observed cell counts to values expected under the model.

Generalizations of logistic regression exist for categorical responses having more than two categories. A multicategory extension of the binomial distribution, called the *multinomial*, applies to the response counts at each setting of the predictors. For nominal responses, a generalized model forms logits by pairing each response category with a baseline category. For ordinal responses, a cumulative logit model describes the effects of predictors on the odds of response below any given level instead of above it (i.e., the model refers to an odds for the cumulative probability).

Loglinear Models

Logistic regression resembles ordinary regression, in distinguishing between a response variable and a set of predictors. *Loglinear models*, by contrast, are relevant for analyses analogous to correlation analyses, studying the association structure among a set of categorical response variables (Agresti 1996; Fienberg 1980; Wickens, 1989).

For multidimensional tables, a variety of models are available, varying in terms of the complexity of the association structure. For three variables, for instance, models include ones for which (1) the variables are mutually independent; (2) two of the variables are associated but are jointly independent of the third; (3) two of the variables are conditionally independent, given the third variable, but may both be associated with the third; (4) each pair of variables is associated, but the association between each pair has the same strength at each level of the third variable.

We will not present loglinear model formulas here, but basically the log of each cell expected frequency is predicted by a formula that resembles ones for analysis of variance. Dummy variables represent levels of the qualitative responses, and their interaction terms represent associations. The associations are described by odds ratios. Logit models with qualitative predictors are equivalent to certain loglinear models, having identical estimates of odds ratios and identical goodness-of-fit statistics. For ordinal variables, specialized loglinear models have parameters describing trends in associations.

Repeated Measurement Data

Specialized methods exist for handling repeated measurement on categorical responses (Agresti, 1990, 1996). Repeated measurement is common with longitudinal studies in which subjects respond at various times, such as when a (success, fail) response is observed before and after subjects undergo a certain treatment.

McNemar's test is a binary-data analog of the matched-pairs t test for continuous responses. The null hypothesis states that the proportion of "success" responses is identical for the two populations. The relevant data are the count n_{sf} of subjects responding success for the first measurement and failure for the second and the count n_{fs} of subjects responding failure for the first and success for the second. Under the null hypothesis, the $(n_{fs} + n_{sf})$ observations of these two types have a binomial distribution with chance ½ of each type. The test statistic $z = [(n_{fs} - n_{sf}) / (n_{fs} + n_{sf})^{1/2}]$ has an approximate standard normal null distribution, and its square is approximately chi-squared with $df = 1$.

Cochran's Q statistic extends McNemar's test to t repeated measurements, that statistic having $df = t - 1$. With explanatory variables, recently developed methods enable one to model how the logit of the probability of success depends on the occasion of measurement and the predictors.

Sampling Design and Method of Analysis

The analysis of categorical data, like that of any type of data, requires assumptions about the sampling mechanism that generated the data. In many cases, such as in most surveys, the overall sample size is fixed and the multinomial applies as the probability distribution for the counts in a contingency table. In many other cases, certain marginal totals are also fixed, such as in experimental designs in which the number of subjects receiving each treatment is fixed. In addition, in regression-type models such as logistic regression, it is common to treat the counts at the combinations of levels of the predictor variables as fixed even if they are not fixed in the sampling design. In these cases, at each such combination, the response is usually assumed to have a binomial distribution when the response is binary and a multinomial distribution when the response is multicategory; this replaces the usual normal response assumption for regression models for continuous responses. Other sampling possibilities, less common in practice, are that the sample size is itself random (i.e., no counts are fixed, such as in observing categorical outcome measures for all subjects who visit some clinic over a future time period) or, at the other extreme, all marginal totals are fixed.

Although some methods depend on the sampling assumption, estimates and test statistics for most of the standard models and analyses are identical for the common sampling designs. For instance, for two-way contingency tables, the chi-squared statistic, its degrees of freedom, and its large-sample P-value are the same when only the total sample size is fixed, when the row totals are fixed, when the column totals are fixed, or when both row and column totals are fixed.

Software

The method of maximum likelihood is the standard way of estimating parameters in models for count data. Except in a few simple cases, no closed-form solutions exist for the estimates, and numerical methods are used to obtain the estimates and their standard errors. Software for basic description and inference and for fitting standard models is reasonably well developed in the major statistical packages. Agresti (1996) surveyed SAS and SPSS for these methods, and Stokes, Davis, and Koch (1995) provided a more detailed discussion for SAS. StatXact (Cytel Software, Cambridge, MA) can perform small-sample analyses, and many of these analyses are available in the SPSS Exact Tests module and in PROC FREQ in SAS (Release 6.12).

Historical Notes

The early development of methods for count data took place in England. In 1900, Karl Pearson introduced his chi-squared statistic (though the correct formula for *df* was not given until 1922, by R. A. Fisher) and G. Udny Yule presented the odds ratio and related measures of association. Much of the early literature consisted of debates about appropriate measures of association for contingency tables. Goodman and Kruskal (1979) surveyed this literature and made significant contributions of their own.

In the 1950s and early 1960s, analyses of multidimensional contingency tables were advanced by several authors. These articles were the genesis of substantial research on logit and loglinear models between about 1965 and 1975. Much of the work in that decade took place at the universities of Chicago, Harvard, and North Carolina. At Chicago, Leo Goodman wrote a series of groundbreaking articles for statistics and sociology journals that popularized the methods for social science applications. Simultaneously, related research at Harvard by students of Frederick Mosteller (such as Stephen Fienberg) and William Cochran, and at North Carolina by Gary Koch and several students and co-workers was highly influential in the biomedical sciences.

In the last quarter of the twentieth century, further advances included specialized models for ordinal data, the development of exact small-sample methods, and methodology for longitudinal and multivariate categorical responses. Perhaps the most far-reaching contribution was the introduction by British statisticians John Nelder and R. W. M. Wedderburn in 1972 of the concept of *generalized linear models*. This unified the primary categorical modeling procedures—logistic regression models and loglinear models—with long-established regression and analysis of variance methods for normal-response data (see Agresti, 1996, ch. 4 for an introduction to this topic and ch. 10 of that text for a more detailed historical survey; that text also contains details about methods discussed in this article).

[*See also* Analysis of Variance.]

Bibliography

Agresti, A. (1990). *Categorical data analysis.* New York: Wiley. Advanced-level discussions of theory and methods, with emphasis on logistic regression and loglinear models.

Agresti, A. (1996). *An introduction to categorical data analysis.* New York: Wiley. Similar subject matter as Agresti (1990) but shorter and at a much lower technical level.

Agresti, A., & Finlay, B. (1997). *Statistical methods for the social sciences* (3rd ed.). Englewood Cliffs, NJ: Prentice Hall. Text for two-semester statistics sequence, with greater emphasis than usual on methods for categorical data; chapters on contingency tables, handling multiway tables, and logistic regression and loglinear models.

Andersen, E. B. (1980). *Discrete statistical models with social science applications.* Amsterdam: North Holland. A psychometric approach covering advanced methods not discussed in this article, such as item response models.

Bishop, Y. M. M., Fienberg, S. E., & Holland P. W. (1975). *Discrete multivariate analysis.* Cambridge, MA: MIT Press. Groundbreaking text on loglinear models; technically rather advanced.

Clogg, C. C., & Shihadeh, E. S. (1994). *Statistical models for ordinal variables.* Thousand Oaks, CA: Sage. Surveys recently proposed models for ordinal variables.

DeMaris, A. (1992). *Logit modeling: Practical applications.* Beverly Hills, CA: Sage. Introduction to logit models, with emphasis on qualitative predictors.

Fienberg, S. E. (1980). *The analysis of cross-classified categorical data* (2nd ed.). Cambridge, MA: MIT Press. Emphasizes loglinear models, more elementary than Bishop et al. 1975.

Goodman, L. A., & Kruskal, W. H. (1979). *Measures of association for cross classifications.* New York: Springer-Verlag. Compendium of articles appearing in *Journal of the American Statistical Association* in 1954, 1959, 1963, 1972.

Hosmer, D. W., & Lemeshow, S. (1989). *Applied logistic regression.* New York: Wiley. Detailed discussion of logistic regression modeling.

Stokes, M. E., Davis, C. S., & Koch, G. G. (1995). *Categorical data analysis using the SAS system.* Cary, NC: SAS Institute.

Wickens, T. D. (1989). *Multiway contingency table analysis for the social sciences.* Hillsdale, NJ: Erlbaum. Emphasizes loglinear models, more elementary than Bishop et al., 1975.

Alan Agresti

ANALYSIS OF VARIANCE (ANOVA) is a collection of techniques for examining differences among two or more means and testing hypotheses about the means of the populations from which they were sampled. It is called analysis of *variance* (rather than analysis of *means*) because the basic operation in testing the overall null hypothesis ($H_{0,\ ov}$) that k population means are identical is a comparison of the variance of the sample means to the variance we would expect those means to display if the underlying population means were identical. $H_{0,\ ov}$ is tested by comparing the ratio of these two variance estimates—the overall *F*-ratio (F_{ov})—to its *critical value*, which is determined by α (the highest probability the researcher is willing to accept that he or she might falsely reject a true H_0), and by two *degree-of-freedom* parameters: the degrees of freedom for the variance estimate that appears in the numerator of F_{ov} (which is always based on differences among your sample means) and the degrees of freedom on which the variance estimate that appears in its denominator was based.

Multiple Comparisons

When F_{ov} exceeds its critical value, $H_{0,\ ov}$ is rejected, and the researcher concludes that not all of the populations from which the means were sampled have identical population means. If there are only two means involved in the design, the only additional step required is to examine the sample means so that the researcher can specify whether μ_1 (the mean of the population from which the group-1 observations were sampled) $> \mu_2$ or vice versa. When, however, there are three or more means being compared, rejection of $H_{0,ov}$ tells us nothing about *which* means differ from which other means in *what direction(s)*.

Any specific pattern of differences can be represented as a *contrast* among the means. A contrast among a set of k means is a test of the H_0 that $\Sigma c_j \mu_j = 0$, with the only restriction on the c_j's (the *contrast coefficients*) being that they sum to zero. Thus, for instance, a contrast between groups one and three of a four-group design would employ contrast coefficients of ½, 0, − ½, and 0, respectively; and a test of the difference between the average of means 1 and 3 versus the average of means 2 and 4 would use c_j's of ¼, − ¼, ¼, and − ¼. More generally, any hypothesis about the pattern of the population means can be tested by generating a set of k numbers that represent that pattern, subtracting from each the mean of all k, and employing the resulting k numbers as contrast coefficients.

The H_0 that $\Sigma c_j \mu_j = 0$ is tested by computing an F for contrast (F_{contr}), whose numerator is a function of how closely the sample means fit the hypothesized pattern of means and whose denominator estimates the variance of the sample estimate of $\Sigma c_j \mu_j$. If the researcher's interest (and that of her audience) is limited to a single contrast *specified in advance of examining the data*, F_{contr} for this single a priori contrast is compared to an F critical value with a single denominator degree of freedom. If, however, two or more contrasts are of

interest, some adjustment for *familywise alpha* (the probability that one or more of the comparisons yields statistical significance even though $H_{0,ov}$ is true) should be made. The most flexible approach is to employ *Bonferroni adjustment* of the critical values for the individual tests—i.e., to compute an F ratio for each comparison of interest, but to use a lower alpha (α_t) in determining the critical value for that comparison, with the sum of the α_ts adding to whatever familywise alpha is preferred. (For example, to keep familywise alpha to at most 0.05 when testing four pairwise comparisons, you could set α_t for each of the four tests to 0.0125, or you could test one of them at the 0.02 level and the other three at the 0.01 level.) It is important to keep in mind that familywise alpha must be distributed among all the comparisons that are of possible interest *before* examining the data—*not* just among the tests that are actually carried out, once the data are in hand.

Although Bonferroni adjustment is always available for controlling familywise alpha, several tests tailored to the detailed structure of particular families of comparisons have been developed, each yielding lower critical values than would Bonferroni adjustment. Examples include Tukey's HSD (Honestly Significant Difference) test for examining all $k(k-1)/2$ pairwise comparisons among the k means and by Dunnett's test for examining the k-1 comparisons between a single control group and each of the k-1 experimental conditions.

Finally, if all possible contrasts are of potential interest, each F_{contr} computed should be tested against the Scheffé critical value, which equals the critical value used in testing F_{ov} multiplied by the numerator degrees of freedom for that overall test. F_{ov} reaches statistical significance if and only if there is at least one contrast whose F_{contr} is statistically significant by the Scheffé critical value, whereas it is not uncommon to find that F_{ov} is statistically significant but that no pairwise comparison achieves significance, even by the Tukey HSD critical value. Conversely, F_{ov} may fail to reach statistical significance even though one or more pairwise comparisons would be statistically significant by the Tukey HSD critical value. Therefore investigators who are interested only in pairwise comparisons might wish to begin their analysis by testing the difference between their largest and smallest sample means against the Tukey HSD critical value, continuing on to tests of additional pairwise differences if and only if this initial test reaches statistical significance.

Complex Designs

Since its initial formulation by R. A. Fisher (*Statistical Methods for Research Workers*, Edinburgh, 1925) ANOVA has become one of the most ubiquitous of statistical tools. ANOVA has proven itself particularly useful as a tool for organizing examination of the results of studies that can be conceptualized as involving more than just a single independent variable (a "factor" in ANOVA terminology). In a *complete factorial* design data are collected on every possible combination of the levels of the various factors. Thus, for example, a factorial study of the effects of Gender (two levels), Anxiety (three levels: low versus moderate versus high), and Task Difficulty (three levels: not, moderate, and very difficult) would require examining $2 \times 3 \times 3 = 18$ means. Usually one examines only (1) the *main effects* of each of the three factors (e.g., for Anxiety, the differences among the mean level of performance at each of the three levels of anxiety, averaging across gender and task difficulty); (2) the three *two-way interactions* between pairs of factors (e.g., for the Gender × Anxiety interaction, the differences between male and female participants in the way in which anxiety affects their performance); and (3) the single *three-way interaction* (examining the way in which any of the two-way interactions "looks different," depending on which level of the third factor you examine). Examination of each family of contrasts usually begins with an overall test specific to that family of contrasts; if this F_{uv} is statistically nonsignificant then no contrast within that family will be statistically significant by a fully *post hoc*, Scheffe' critical value, and there is thus no reason to test specific contrasts—unless there are specific *a priori* predictions of the direction of particular contrasts.

Selection of error terms (denominators of F ratios) for the various overall tests and specific contrasts depends on the nature of the factor(s) involved. One crucial distinction is between factors that involve *between-subjects* comparisons (i.e., in which each subject receives or appears at a single level of the factor—e.g., gender) and those that involve *within-subjects* comparisons (i.e., in which each subject is exposed to all levels of that factor—e.g., successive trial blocks in a learning study). There is considerable disagreement as to whether the *univariate* or the *multivariate approach* should be employed in analyzing repeated-measures designs. Harris (1994) and Maxwell and Delaney (1989) provide relatively up-to-date assessments of the state of that debate.

A second crucial distinction is between *random* factors (those for which the levels employed in any given study are a random sample from a much larger number of possible levels—e.g., the particular towns in which a field study is conducted) and *fixed* factors, the levels of which are the same every time that factor is used in a study.

Finally (with respect to complete factorial designs), we must distinguish between *balanced* designs (of which equal-group-size designs are a special case) and *unbalanced* designs (in which the proportion of individuals at a given level of one factor differs from one level to the next of the other factors).

ANOVA can also be applied to *incomplete factorial* designs, which are studies involving muliple factors but which do not include all combinations of the levels of those factors. There are three main classes of such incomplete designs. In a *nested* design in which factor A is nested within levels of factor B, only a subset of the levels of A appears in combination with any given level of factor B. For instance, if we wish to study differences in the effects on mood of aerobic versus anaerobic exercise, each particular exercise we consider (walking, running, tennis, biking, etc.) will be either an aerobic or an anaerobic exercise; thus "particular exercise" will be nested within the "aerobic vs. anaerobic" type-of-exercise factor. In a *deliberately incomplete factorial design* (of which Latin Square, Graeco-Latin Square, and Fractional Replication designs are examples), the researcher employs a systematic algorithm (often involving modular arithmetic) to select only a small subset of all the cells (combinations of factor levels) that a complete factorial design would require. This is done in such a way that main effects (and possibly low-order interactions) will be confounded only with high-order interactions. Finally, *haphazardly incomplete factorial designs* are those that are planned as complete factorials but (usually because of low population proportions of some of the levels of participant-characteristic factors such as ethnicity or choice of major field) yield no data on some of the combinations of factor levels (e.g., there may be no members of a particular group who received the low anxiety, moderate difficulty combination). Procedures for analyzing nested designs are discussed in all of the ANOVA textbooks in the bibliography. Roger Kirk's (1995) text devotes several chapters to deliberately incomplete factorial designs; and Harris's (1994) text deals more extensively than most with haphazardly incomplete factorials.

When Assumptions Are Suspect

While ANOVA tests are generally robust (have type I error rates that are relatively insensitive to violations of the assumptions used to derive them), they are inappropriate in some situations. The most obvious violation of distributional assumptions comes when the dependent variable of interest is a discrete variable with a small number of possible values (e.g., which of three different candidates each voter favors). Techniques for analyzing the data from such studies (e.g., chi-square and loglinear analyses) are discussed in much more detail in the entry on *Analysis of Counts* in this encyclopedia.

Where extreme heterogeneity of variance is present (e.g., a ratio of largest to smallest within-group variance of 10/1 or worse in the equal-n case, with a somewhat lower "danger threshold" if sample sizes are themselves quite heterogenous), one can seek a variance-equalizing transformation. As an alternative, many nonparametric analogs to ANOVA are discussed in the entry on *Nonparametric Statistics* in this encyclopedia.

Experimental Design

The design considerations that are most likely to arise in studies that are candidates for analysis via ANOVA techniques are (1) whether a given factor should be manipulated between or within subjects; (2) whether each factor should be considered fixed or random; (3) whether the possibly confounding effects of a continuous covariate should be controlled for by recoding it into discrete categories and making it another factor in the ANOVA (*blocking* on the covariate) or by keeping it as a continuous covariate in an *analysis of covariance* (ANCOVA); (4) how to express the precision of the estimates of various contrasts among the means; and (5) what sample size is necessary to be sure that the precision of the effect-size estimates will be adequate and/or that the power of design will be adequate. These issues are discussed (with varying emphases) in Maxwell and Delaney (1989), Harris (1994), and Kirk (1995).

Bibliography

Harris, R. J. (1994). *An analysis of variance primer.* Itasca, Il.: F. E. Peacock. Unique features include consistent use of Henry Kaiser's three-valued logic for hypothesis testing (Directional statistical decisions, *Psychological Review*, 1960, 67, 160–167), which avoids the unscientific implications for research practice entailed in traditional, two-valued logic; emphasis on selection of one's overall test (e.g. F_{ov} versus the Studentized Range) to be consistent with the set of contrasts of possible interest to the researcher; presentation of the Minimally Important Difference Significant (MIDS) criterion for selecting sample size (R. J. Harris and D. Quade, The minimally important difference significant criterion for sample size, *Journal of Educational Statistics*, 1992, 17, 27–49); and strong advocacy of the multivariate approach to repeated measures designs, rather than attempting to "patch up" the univariate approach.

Kirk, R. E., (1995). *Experimental design: Procedures for the behavioral sciences* (3rd ed.) Pacific Grove, CA: Brooks/Cole. Employs a unique system of notation for ANOVA designs that takes some getting used to, but rewards the reader with, among other features, an unusually comprehensive discussion of the very strange contrasts one is actually testing when employing hierarchical models for unbalanced factorial designs (A × B corrected for confounds with A and B but not A × B × C, etc.), and several chapters devoted to incomplete factorial designs.

Maxwell, S. E., & Delaney, H. D. (1989). *Designing experiments and analyzing data: A model comparison perspective.* Belmont, CA: Wadsworth. Comprehensive, scholarly, 900-page tome that pushes the general linear model (multiple regression) framework for ANOVA to its limit (which is reached when it becomes necessary to employ more than one error term for various effects). Very conscientious about presenting all sides of each controversial issue.

Richard J. Harris

ANALYTIC PSYCHOLOGY. *See the biography of Jung.*

ANASTASI, ANNE (1908–), American psychologist. During a career spanning more than 60 years, Anne Anastasi established an international reputation based on contributions in research, writing, and organizational leadership. She is best known for her work in psychological testing, which has included research on trait formation, individual differences, test construction, the misuse of tests, and statistical test issues. She has also written on more conceptual subjects, including the nature/nurture issue. Her books are well known in the psychological community and are read throughout the world.

The daughter of Anthony and Theresa Gaudiosi Anastasi, Anne Anastasi was born on 19 December 1908, in New York City. Her father died when she was a year old, and she was raised in a family consisting of her mother, her grandmother, and her mother's brother. At first, she was educated at home by her grandmother. She entered the public school system at age nine, was accelerated by several classes, and was graduated with a gold medal for general excellence. She dropped out of high school after 2 months. However, following special preparatory school study, she entered Barnard College in 1924 at age 15.

Anastasi originally chose mathematics as a major, but was drawn to psychology by a stimulating teacher, Harry Hollingworth, later a president of the American Psychological Association. She was also impressed by an article written by the English psychologist Charles Spearman on correlation coefficients that convinced her she could select psychology as a major and still remain true to mathematics.

In 1928, she graduated from Barnard at the age of 19, having been elected to Phi Beta Kappa and awarded a graduate fellowship. That fall, she entered Columbia University to study for a doctorate in general experimental psychology. In her first year, she took courses from Henry E. Garrett, Robert Woodworth,

Carl Warden, and Gardner Murphy. Her dissertation, mentored by Garrett, used the tetrad technique and identified a group factor in immediate memory for rote material.

While at Columbia, Anastasi met John Porter Foley, Jr., who had just begun working for a doctorate in psychology. They were married on 26 July 1933. Foley's interests, which included animal learning and anthropology, were somewhat different from those of Anastasi, but she learned from them. She has said that her marriage gave her the benefit of two Ph.Ds.

A year after her marriage, she was diagnosed with cervical cancer. The radium and X-ray treatments which followed left her unable to have children. She has described this illness as one of two critical factors in her life (the other was the premature death of her father). The cancer treatments allowed her to remain childless without guilt or conflict, and she believes they were, however inadvertently, at least partially responsible for her success.

The early years of marriage were marked by geographic separation, with Anastasi teaching at Barnard and Foley teaching at George Washington University in Washington, D.C. His interests turned increasingly to industrial psychology and he eventually joined the Psychological Corporation in New York City. They remained in New York for the rest of their lives. Foley died in 1994.

Anastasi began her academic career as an instructor in psychology at Barnard in the fall of 1930, at an annual salary of $2,400. In 1939 she became assistant professor, "chairman," and sole faculty member of the new Department of Psychology at Queens College, City University of New York. Eight years later she was appointed associate professor of psychology in the Graduate School of Arts and Sciences at Fordham University and, in 1951, professor.

She remained at Fordham until her retirement in 1979 when she became professor emeritus and was awarded an honorary doctor of science degree. She continued to be active in writing and other professional activities into the 1990s. The seventh edition of her testing book (Psychological Testing, Upper Saddle River, NJ, 1997) with Susana Urbina was her last major publication.

A major focus of Anastasi's research has been on the nature and measurement of psychological traits, with particular emphasis on the role of experience in trait formation. Related topics include her research on language development among Black and Puerto Rican children, sex differences in psychological traits, intelligence and family size, and changes in adult test performance over time.

Another interest area has been test construction, evaluation, and interpretation, which includes topics ranging from the purely conceptual to problems of test bias, item selection, and coaching. She and her husband also produced several articles on various psychological aspects of art. The information they gathered on cultural differences in art led her to question the appropriateness of projective drawing tests in clinical assessment.

Anastasi's textbooks have had an enormous impact among students and scholars. Her major works (Differential Psychology, New York, 1958; Fields of Applied Psychology, New York, 1979; Psychological Testing, Upper Saddle River, NJ, 1997) are all considered classics and have appeared in multiple translations throughout the world. Her books have been called models of clarity, comprehensiveness, and synthesis.

In one of Anastasi's most reprinted articles (Psychological Review, 1958, 65, 197–208) she examined the nature/nurture issue, which many consider to be one of the most fundamental in all of psychology. She argued that psychologists too frequently have been asking the wrong question. Nature and nurture never exist independently; they are always inextricably linked in any behavior. The only appropriate nature/nurture question to ask is "How do they interact?"

In 1972, Anastasi was elected the first female president of the American Psychological Association in 50 years. She has also served as president of the Eastern Psychological Association (1946–1947), the APA Division of General Psychology (1956–1957), the APA Division of Evaluation and Measurement (1965–1966), and the American Psychological Foundation (1965–1967).

She has been awarded honorary degrees from five colleges and universities: University of Windsor (1967), Villanova University (1971), Cedar Crest College (1971), La Salle College (1979), and Fordham University (1979). Among her other honors are awards from the Educational Testing Service Award (1977), the American Psychological Association (1981), the American Educational Research Association (1983), and the American Psychological Foundation (1984). In the summer of 1987 she was presented with the National Medal of Science by President Ronald Reagan. In a survey conducted by Gavin, her peers rated her the most prominent living woman in psychology in the English-speaking world (Psychotherapy in Private Practice, 1987, 5, 53–68).

Bibliography

Anastasi, A. (1972). Reminiscences of a differential psychologist. In T. S. Krawiec (Ed.), The psychologists (pp. 3–37). New York: Oxford University Press.

Anastasi, A. (1980). Autobiography. In G. Lindzey (Ed.), History of psychology in autobiography (Vol. 7, pp. 1–37). New York: Freeman.

Sexton, V. S., & Hogan, J. D. (1990). Anne Anastasi. In

A. N. O'Connell & N. F. Russo (Eds.), *Women in psychology: A biobibliographic sourcebook* (pp. 13–22). New York: Greenwood Press.

John D. Hogan

ANDROCENTRISM. *See* Sexism.

ANDROGYNY. *See* Gender Identity.

ANGELL, JAMES ROWLAND (1869–1949), American psychologist. Angell graduated in 1890 from the University of Michigan where his first contact with psychology was in courses with John Dewey. With encouragement from Dewey, he stayed on at Michigan to complete his master's degree in 1891. During that year he read William James's *Principles of Psychology* with great enthusiasm, and decided, on Dewey's recommendation, to continue his studies under James and Josiah Royce at Harvard. While there, he conducted experimental studies in the laboratory that had been established by James. He also assisted James in the collection of documentary material for the American Society for Psychical Research. In 1892 he decided he "would more wisely go abroad for further study" (Carl Murchison, Ed., *A History of Psychology in Autobiography*, Vol. 3, Worcester, MA, 1936, p. 7). On finding that Wilhelm Wundt's laboratory in Leipzig could accommodate no more students, he went to Berlin to attend lectures in philosophy from Friedrich Paulsen and Wilhelm Dilthey, and in psychology from Hermann Ebbinghaus. In the spring of 1893, he moved on to Halle to study philosophy with Hans Vaihinger and psychology with Benno Erdmann. Under Vaihinger he wrote a dissertation on Kant's conception of freedom, but in the fall of 1893, before it was finally accepted, he was drawn by an offer from the University of Minnesota to teach philosophy and psychology.

Angell's stay at the University of Minnesota was brief. John Dewey had moved to the University of Chicago as head of the department of philosophy and invited Angell to join him. Angell accepted and went there in 1894 to assume charge of the laboratory and courses in psychology. He was made chair of psychology when it became a department separate from philosophy in 1904. This marked the beginning of a gradual shift in Angell's career toward administration. He became dean of the Senior College in 1908, dean of the faculties in 1911, and acting president of the university from 1918 to 1919.

Outside the university, Angell worked with the wartime Adjutant General's Committee on Classification of Personnel from 1917 to 1918, developing means of integrating military and civilian training programs. This work led to the establishment of the Student Army Training Corps. Angell was granted a leave of absence from the university from 1919 to 1920 to become chairman of the National Research Council. In 1920 he received an invitation to become president of the Carnegie Corporation, the acceptance of which marked his final departure from the University of Chicago.

A return to university life came in 1921 with an offer of the presidency of Yale University. Angell accepted and remained in that position until his retirement in 1937. In 1924 he was instrumental in establishing an Institute of Psychology dedicated to the integration of research in psychology, biology, and anthropology. Subsequently, the school of medicine was strengthened in the field of psychiatry. This included the appointment of Arnold Gesell and the establishment of the Child Development Clinic. In 1931, under Angell's leadership and after years of planning, the institute and the clinic were brought together under an enlarged Institute of Human Relations devoted to research in psychology, primate biology, clinical psychiatry, child development, and social science.

Angell was elected to the National Academy of Sciences in 1920, to the American Philosophical Society in 1932, and to the American Academy of Arts and Sciences in 1932. He served on the Council of the American Psychological Association from 1903 to 1906, and was elected president of the association in 1906. From 1912 to 1922 he served, as his former student Walter S. Hunter described it in the *American Journal of Psychology* (1949, 62, p. 450), "with great wisdom and distinction" as editor of the *Psychological Monographs*.

Edward B. Titchener had introduced the distinction between structural and functional psychologies in 1898 and defended the former as the only type to possess the promise of becoming a truly scientific psychology. It was Angell who took up this challenge, defending and urging a functional psychology in his APA presidential address of 1906 (*Psychological Review*, 1907, 14, 61–91). This became the founding document and manifesto for what came to be known as American functionalism, a general theoretical position that some maintain has characterized most American psychology since that time (cf. D. A. Owens and M. Wagner, Eds., *Progress in Modern Psychology: The Legacy of American Functionalism*, Westport, CT, 1992). Although William James and John Dewey had not themselves made a sharp distinction between structure and function, Angell found inspiration in their work to support his program. In his presidential address, Angell described three conceptions of functional psychology that converged to form the broader functionalism that he advocated. The first was a psychology of mental operations in contrast to a psychology of mental elements. The second was a psychology that conceived of the mind as principally mediating between the external world and the needs of the organism. The third was a psychophysical psychology that insisted on the essential significance of the mind-body relationship for understanding mental life. Angell saw these conceptions as converging in the fundamental problem of just how the mind participates in accommodatory reactions. Functional psychology's stress on the utilities of consciousness marked it off sharply from the structural psychology of Titchener that was concerned with the identification of elemental features of the mind through the use of systematic introspection.

Angell's functional psychology, with its emphasis on adaptive behavior and the biological context, was strongly identified with Darwinian evolution theory. Angell's theory of habit formation, for instance, represented an adaptation to individual experience of Darwin's doctrines of natural selection and "lapsed intelligence." According to the former, early stages of habit formation were characterized by excessive reactions from which useless movements were gradually eliminated and successful movements selected. According to the latter doctrine, consciousness was needed most in early stages in which behavioral coordinations were most insecure and least organized. As perfection was achieved, consciousness, having fulfilled its function, was thought to drop out, leaving a fully automated reaction.

Walter Hunter described Angell as one of "the great figures who shaped the development of American psychology during the formative years" (*American Journal of Psychology*, 1949, *62*, p. 439) The extent of his influence is indicated by the large number of his students who went on to very distinguished careers in psychology, including five presidents of the American Psychological Association.

Bibliography

Angell, J. R. (1907). The province of functional psychology. *Psychological Review, 14*, 61–91. Angell's APA presidential address of 1906. Generally regarded as the definitive statement on functional psychology.

Angell, J. R. (1908). *Psychology. An introductory study of the structure and function of human consciousness* (4th ed.). New York: Henry Holt. (Original work published 1904.) The final edition of Angell's immensely successful and influential textbook.

Angell, J. R. (1909). The influence of Darwin on psychology. *Psychological Review, 16*, 152–169. Angell assigns to Darwinism a "larger part of the responsibility for the change which has brought into prominence functional and genetic psychology (including animal psychology), in distinction from the older and more conventional analytic psychology."

Angell, J. R. (1922). The evolution of intelligence. In G. A. Baitsell (Ed.), *The evolution of man* (pp. 103–125). New Haven, CT: Yale University Press. For its time, a characteristic and uncontroversial account of the evolution of animal and human intelligence, thoroughly compatible with Angell's functional psychology.

Angell, J. R. (1970). *American education.* New York: Books for Libraries Press. (Original work published 1937.) A collection of articles and addresses on higher education, written between 1921 and 1937. It reveals more of the man and his general outlook on life than any of his scientific works.

Charles W. Tolman

ANGER is a negatively toned emotion, subjectively experienced as an aroused state of antagonism toward someone or something perceived to be the source of an aversive event. It is triggered or provoked situationally by events that are perceived to constitute deliberate harm doing by an instigator toward oneself or toward those to whom one is endeared. Provocations usually take the form of insults, unfair treatments, or intended thwartings. Anger is prototypically experienced as a justified response to some "wrong" that has been done. Although anger is situationally triggered by acute, proximal occurrences, it is shaped and facilitated contextually by conditions affecting the cognitive, arousal, and behavioral systems that comprise anger reactions. Anger activation is centrally linked to threat perceptions and survival responding.

As a normal human emotion, anger has considerable adaptive value, although there are sociocultural variations in the acceptability of its expression and the form that such expression takes. In the face of adversity, it can mobilize psychological resources, energize behaviors for corrective action, and facilitate perseverance. Anger serves as a guardian to self-esteem, operates as a means of communicating negative sentiment, potentiates the ability to redress grievances, and boosts determination to overcome obstacles to our happiness and aspirations. Akin to aggressive behavior, anger has functional value for survival.

Despite having multiple adaptive functions, anger also has maladaptive effects on personal and social well-being. Generally, strong physiological arousal impairs the processing of information and lessens cognitive control of behavior. Because heightened physiological arousal is a core component of anger, people are not as cognitively proficient when they become angry. Also, because the activation of anger is accompanied by aggressive impulses, anger can motivate behavior that does harm to others, which in turn can produce undesirable consequences for the angered person, either from direct retaliation, loss of supportive relationships, or social censure. An angry person is not optimally alert, thoughtful, empathic, prudent, or physically healthy.

In parallel to these counterpoised functions of anger is the duality of psychosocial images associated with anger experience and anger expression. The emotional state is depicted as eruptive, destructive, unbridled, savage, venomous, burning, and consuming but also as energizing, empowering, justifying, signifying, rectifying, and relieving. The metaphors, on the one hand, connote something pressing for expression and utilization, and, alternatively, they imply something requiring containment and control. This duality in psychosocial imagery reflects conflicting intuitions about anger, its expression, and its consequences that abound in ordinary language and are reflected in both scholarly literature and artistic works from the classical period to contemporary times. This Janus-faced character of anger foils attempts to understand it and to intervene therapeutically with recurrently angry individuals.

The Experience of Anger

The facial and skeletal musculature are strongly affected by anger. The face becomes flushed, and the brow muscles move inward and downward, fixing a hard stare on the target. The nostrils flare, and the jaw tends toward clenching. This is an innate pattern of facial expression that can be observed in toddlers. Tension in the skeletal musculature, including raising of the arms and adopting a squared-off stance, are preparatory actions for attack and defense. The muscle tension provides a sense of strength and self-assurance. An impulse to strike out accompanies this subjective feeling of potency.

When people report anger experiences, they most typically give accounts of things that have "happened to them." For the most part, they describe events physically and temporally proximate to their anger arousal. As a rule, they provide accounts of provocations ascribed to events in the immediate situation of the anger experience. This fosters the illusion that anger has a discrete external cause. The provocation sources are ordinarily identified as the aversive and deliberate behavior of others; thus, anger is portrayed in the telling as being something about which anger is quite fitting. People are very much inclined to attribute the causes of their anger to the personal, stable, and controllable aspects of another person's behavior.

However, the response to the question, "What has made you angry?" hinges on self-observational proficiencies and is often based on intuitions. Precisely because getting angry involves a loss in self-monitoring capacity, people are neither good nor objective observers when they are angry. Inspecting any particular episode, the immediate "causes" of the anger are readily identifiable. Far less commonly do people disaggregate their anger experiences into multicausal origins, some of which may be prior, remote events and ambient circumstances, rather than acute, proximal events. Anger experiences are embedded or nested within an environmental-temporal context. Disturbances that may not have involved anger at the outset leave residues that are not readily recognized but that operate as a lingering backdrop for focal provocations.

Anger and Aggression

The emotion of anger must be sharply distinguished from aggression, which is behavior intended to cause psychological or physical harm to someone or to a surrogate target. Aggressive behavior may be verbal or physical, direct or indirect. The relationship of anger to aggressive behavior is that anger is a significant activator of aggression and has a mutually influenced relationship with it, but anger is neither necessary nor sufficient for aggression to occur. The activation of anger does not guarantee aggression, and the occurrence of aggression does not necessitate anger as an antecedent.

Anger is inherently a disposition to respond aggressively, but aggression is not an automatic consequence of anger because aggressive behavior is regulated by inhibitory control mechanisms, engaged by internal and external cues. In this regard, physical constraints, expectations of punishment or retaliation, empathy, consideration of consequences, and prosocial values operate as regulatory controls on aggression. Although the experience of anger creates a readiness to respond with aggression, that disposition may be otherwise directed, suppressed, or reconstituted. Thus, the expression of anger is differentiated from its experience.

One aspect of anger that influences the probability of aggression is its degree of intensity. The higher the level of arousal, the stronger the motivation for aggression, and the greater the likelihood that inhibitory controls will be overridden. Strong arousal not only impels action, it impairs cognitive processing of aggression-mitigating information. A person in a state of high anger arousal is perceptually biased toward the confirmation of threat, is less able to attend to threat-discounting elements of the situation, and is not so capable of reappraising provocation cues as benign. Because anger and aggression occur in a dynamic interactional context, the occurrence of aggression will, in turn, influence the level of anger.

Important forms of the dynamic interrelation of anger and aggression are the escalation of provocation and the "cathartic effect." Escalation involves increases away from equilibrium, whereby succeeding events intensify their own precursors. In the case of anger and aggression, escalation refers to incremental change in their respective probabilities, occurring as reciprocally heightened antagonism in an interpersonal exchange. Anger-elicited aggression may evoke further anger in response, progressively generating justification for retaliation. In contrast, when physical aggression is deployed by an angry person against the anger instigator, and there is no retaliation, anger arousal and further aggression are diminished. This is called the *cathartic effect*, and its conditions should not be confused with those involving aggression by nonangry people, vicarious or observed aggression, or aggression not received by the anger instigator. However, the arousal-reducing effect of aggression carried out by angry people against those who have made them angry increases the likelihood of aggressive behavior when anger is reinstated.

Anger Physiology

A defining condition of anger is physiological arousal, the activation of which has evolutionary roots. For our prehistoric ancestors, when a threat to survival or survival resources was detected, it was advantageous to be mobilized to response energetically and to sustain effort. The fight/flight response refers to this hard-wired physiological mechanism that gets instantaneously triggered to engage survival behavior, to focus attention on the survival threat, and to enable the organism not to succumb to pain. Anger is the emotional complement of the organismic preparation for attack, which also entails the orchestration of signals of attack readiness so as to ward off opponents or to coerce compliance.

The arousal of anger is marked by physiological activation in the cardiovascular, endocrine, and limbic systems, as well as other autonomic and central nervous system areas, and by tension in the skeletal musculature. In an abundance of laboratory studies and self-report surveys, autonomic arousal has been identified as a concomitant of anger. It is noteworthy that autonomic arousal, especially cardiovascular changes, have been commonly observed in conjunction with anger, by scholars from the classical age (especially Seneca, Aristotle, and Plutarch), and the early behavioral scientists of the nineteenth and twentieth centuries (especially Charles Darwin, William James, G. Stanley Hall, and Walter B. Cannon). Laboratory research has reliably found anger arousal to entail increases in both systolic and diastolic blood pressure, and, to a somewhat lesser extent, heart rate. Associated with this cardiovascular activation is facial flushing, which is often reported by people reflecting on their anger experience. Indeed, in terms of psychosocial imagery, there is no better metaphor for anger than hot fluid in a container.

Autonomic arousal is primarily engaged through adrenomedullary and adrenocortical hormonal activity. The secretion by the andrenal medulla of the catecho-

lamines, epinephrine, and norepinephrine, and by the andrenal cortex of glucocorticoids provides a sympathetic system effect that mobilizes the body for immediate action (e.g., the release of glucose, stored in the liver and muscles as glycogen). In anger, the catecholamine activation is more strongly norepinephrine than epinephrine (the reverse being the case for fear). The adrenocortical effects, which have longer duration than the adrenomedullary ones, are mediated by secretions of the pituitary gland, which also influences testosterone levels. The pituitary-adrenocortical and pituitary-gonadal systems are thought to affect readiness or potentiation for anger responding.

The central nervous system structure that has been identified in anger activation is the amygdala, the almond-shaped, limbic system component located deep in the temporal lobe. Activation in the corticomedial amygdala is associated with anger and attack priming. The central nervous system neurotransmitter serotonin, which is also present in blood platelets, affects anger potentiation, as low levels of this hormone are associated with irritable mood. Serotonin imbalances are related to deficits in the modulation of emotion.

These various physiological mechanisms thus pertain not only to the intensity of anger arousal but also its duration. Arousal activation eventually decays to baseline levels, but recovery time may be prolonged by exposure to new arousal sources or by rumination. The potency of a provocation may be heightened by the carryover of undissipated excitation from a prior arousal source, which may not have been anger-specific (i.e., an otherwise stressful circumstance, such as exposure to bad news, work pressure, or traffic congestion). This "excitation transfer" of arousal residues facilitates anger, augments its intensity, and raises the probability of aggression.

Cognition and Anger

To get angry about something one must pay attention to it. Anger is often the result of selective attention to cues having high provocation value. A principal function of cognitive systems is to guide behavior, and attention itself is guided by integrated cognitive structures, known as schemas, which incorporate rules about environment-behavior relationships. What receives attention is a product of the cognitive network that assigns meaning to events and the complex stimuli that configure them. Expectations guide attentional search for cues relevant to particular needs or goals. Once a repertoire of anger schemas has been developed, events (e.g., being asked a question by someone) and their characteristics (e.g., the *way* the question was asked, *when* it was asked, or *who* asked it) are encoded or interpreted as having meaning in accord with the preexisting schema. Because of their survival function, the threat-sensing aspect of anger schemas carries urgent priority and can preempt other information processing.

Since the writings of the Stoic philosophers of the classical period, anger has been understood to be strongly determined by personal interpretations of events. The concept of appraisal is that of interpretation, judgment, or meaning embedded in the perception of something—not as a cognitive event occurring after that something has happened. The appraisal of provocation is *in* the seeing or hearing. Appraisal, though, is an ongoing process, so various reappraisals of experience will occur and will correspondingly affect whether or not the probability of aggression is lessened, maintained, or intensified. Rumination about provoking circumstances will of course extend or revivify anger reactions. The occurrence of certain thoughts can also prime semantically related ideas that are part of an anger schema.

Perceived malevolence is one of the most common forms of anger-inducing appraisal. When another person's behavior is interpreted as intending to be harmful to oneself, anger and aggression schemas are activated. In turn, receiving information about mitigating circumstances (e.g., learning that the person was fatigued and working overtime) can defuse the appraisal of personal attack and promote a benign reappraisal. Perceiving malevolence pulls for anger by involving the important theme of justification, which includes the externalization of blame. When harm or injustice have been done, social norms of retaliation and retribution are engaged. Indeed, one view of anger is that it is a socially constituted syndrome or a transitory social role governed by social rules. Thus, its meaning and function would be determined by the social systems in which it occurs and of which it is an integral part.

Justification is a core theme with regard to the activation of anger and aggression, being rooted in ancient religious texts, such as the Bible and the Koran, as well as classical mythologies about deities and historical accounts of the behavior of ancient rulers. Correspondingly, anger and physical aggression are often viewed as applying a legitimate punitive response for transgression or as ways of correcting unjustice. Frequently, however, an embellished justification serves the exoneration of blame for destructive outcomes of expressed anger.

Anger Dyscontrol and Regulation

Anger is a highly functional human emotion, and it is one to be appreciated as a rich part of cultural life, but the survival value of the aggression-enabling function of anger is an archaic remnant with rare contemporary necessity. The challenges presented by civilized society are predominantly psychological, rather than physical, thus attenuating anger's adaptive worth. Effective coping with the demands of modern life requires understanding complex information, problem solving, and prudent action, not energized rapid responding. Even in emergency situations, anger requires regulation. Contrary to intuitions, anger can be detrimental to survival in a physical threat crisis. It is counterproductive for energy conservation in a prolonged fight, for monitoring additional threat elements and hazards, and for effective strategy selection in circumstances where survival threat lingers and/or remains obscure. The regulation of the intensity and duration of anger arousal is pivotal to its merit or utility.

Unregulated anger has been found to be associated with physical and psychological health impairments. In the realm of physical health, chronic anger has been established as having detrimental effects most centrally on the cardiovascular system, which are related to mortality. Persons high in generalized hostility who are reactively angry are at considerable risk for coronary heart disease. When such persons are confronted with a stressful demand, they have strong cardiovascular responses in blood pressure, neurohormonal secretions, and cholesterol. A hostile, cynical, and distrusting outlook also necessitates high vigilance for thwarting and malevolence, resulting in prolonged neurohormonal activation conducive to atherosclerosis. In addition to these pathogenic effects for a personality style that is overly expressive of anger, the coronary system is also impaired by recurrently suppressed anger, long identified as a causal variable in the etiology of essential hypertension. People who have difficulties expressing anger tend to be at risk for chronically elevated blood pressure, as mediated by high plasma renin activity and norepinephrine.

With regard to psychological well-being, anger occurs in conjunction with a wide range of psychiatrically classified disorders, including a variety of impulse control dysfunctions, mood disorders, personality disorders, and forms of schizophrenia, especially paranoid schizophrenia. In addition, the activation of anger has long been recognized as a feature of clinical disorders that result from trauma, such as dissociative disorders, brain damage syndromes, and, especially, posttraumatic stress disorder. Anger also appears in mental state disturbances produced by general medical conditions, such as dementia, substance abuse disorders, and neurological dysfunctions resulting from perinatal difficulties.

Among hospitalized psychiatric patients in long-term care in both civil commitment and forensic institutions, anger is a salient problem, as identified by both clinical staff and by the patients themselves. Importantly, it is linked to assaultive behavior by psychiatric patients both inside and outside such facilities. Such patients typically have traumatic life histories, replete with experiences of abandonment and rejection, as well as economic and psychological impoverishment. For them, anger becomes entrenched as a mode of reactance to stressful or aversive experiences, and it is a significant aspect of their resistance to treatment. Chronically angry people are reluctant to surrender the anger-aggression system that they have found useful to engage and because they discount the costs of its engagement.

In the treatment of anger disorders, cognitive-behavioral approaches have been found to be effective with a wide range of clinical populations. These psychotherapeutic approaches incorporate many elements of behavior therapy, such as training in self-monitoring, relaxation, and social skills. Cognitive-behavioral treatments centrally seek to modify cognitive structures and the way in which a person processes information about social situations. They strongly emphasize self-regulation, cognitive flexibility in appraising situations, arousal control, and the learning of prosocial values and scripts. Making extensive use of therapist modeling and client rehearsal, anger proneness is modified by first motivating client engagement and then by restructuring cognitive schemas, increasing capacity to regulate arousal, and facilitating the use of constructive coping behaviors.

Bibliography

Averill, J. R. (1982). *Anger and aggression: An essay on emotion.* New York: Springer-Verlag.

Berkowitz, L. (1993). *Aggression: Its causes, consequences, and control.* New York: McGraw-Hill.

Kemp, S., & Strongman, K. T. (1995). Anger theory and management: A historical analysis. *American Journal of Psychology, 108,* 397–417.

Konecni, V. J. (1975). The mediation of aggressive behavior: Arousal level versus anger and cognitive labeling. *Journal of Personality and Social Psychology, 32,* 706–712.

Konecni, V. J. (1991). Psychological aspects of the expression of anger and violence on the stage. *Comparative Drama, 25,* 215–241.

Lakoff, G., & Kovecses, Z. (1987). The cognitive model of anger inherent in American English. In D. Holland & N. Quinn (Eds.), *Cultural models of language and thought* (pp. 195–221). Cambridge, UK: Cambridge University Press.

Novaco, R. W. (1985). Anger as a clinical and social problem. In R. Blanchard & C. Blanchard (Eds.), *Advances in the study of aggression* (Vol 2.) New York: Academic Press.

Novaco, R. W. (1994). Anger as a risk factor for violence among the mentally disordered. In J. Monahan & H. J. Steadman (Eds.), *Violence and mental disorder: Developments in risk assessment.* Chicago: University of Chicago Press.

Potegal, M. & Knutson, J. F. (1994). *The dynamics of aggression: Biological and social processes in dyads and groups.* Hillsdale, NJ: Erlbaum.

Schimmel, S. (1979). Anger in Graeco-Roman and modern psychiatry. *Psychiatry, 42,* 321–337.

Siegman, A. W., & Smith, T. W. (Eds.). (1994). *Anger, hostility, and the heart.* Hillsdale, NJ: Erlbaum.

Zillmann, D. (1979). *Hostility and aggression.* Hillsdale, NJ: Erlbaum.

Raymond W. Novaco

ANHEDONIA. The French physician T. H. Ribot coined the term *anhedonia* in 1897, introducing it as a counterpoint to analgesia, and using it first to describe a young female patient experiencing loss of pleasure secondary to liver damage. The physician Abraham Myerson commented on the nature of the pleasure deficit in anhedonia in works published from the 1920s to the 1940s. In his early writings, Myerson (1923) described anhedonia as an innate characteristic manifested as a progressive decline in the capacity for sensual pleasures. Later, he argued that anhedonia included the diminished capacity to derive pleasure from social interactions (1944). Sándor Rádo (1953) extended Myerson's idea of an anhedonic constitution, postulating that the compromised capacity for pleasure in anhedonia affects social and sexual functioning and ultimately leads to withdrawal. The American psychologist Paul Meehl depicted anhedonia as a heritable, individual differences variable, much like temperament (1975). According to Meehl, deficient hedonic capacity results in increased sensitivity to life stress and vulnerability to psychological distress. Based on the theoretical work of Rádo and Meehl, Jean and Loren Chapman and colleagues developed the Scales for Physical and Social Anhedonia, which remain the standard self-report measures of anhedonia (Chapman, Chapman, & Raulin, 1976).

Anhedonia is a prominent feature of many psychological disorders, including depression and schizophrenia. However, some research suggests that anhedonia in schizophrenia is an enduring state, while anhedonia in depression varies with depressed mood. Nevertheless, anhedonia in both of these disorders has been linked with a pervasive decrease in the experience of positive emotions such as joy, happiness, and serenity. Additionally, anhedonia in schizophrenia has been associated with diminished reports of positive experience to positive stimuli, such as amusing film clips.

Important gains in understanding hedonic deficit have been made by the development of animal models of anhedonia. Animal behavior in relation to pleasurable or rewarding stimuli can be divided into two categories: appetitive behaviors and consummatory behaviors. Appetitive behaviors represent an anticipatory response following cues of forthcoming pleasurable stimuli. This anticipation of pleasure is typically followed by the approach of the stimulus and subsequent consummatory behavior, such as eating or sexual activity. Some research using "anhedonic" rats suggests that it is the appetitive and approach behaviors, such as entering a feeding niche when a food cue is presented, which are deficient in anhedonia, whereas consummatory behaviors, such as eating the food that is presented, appear intact.

A number of studies of anhedonia in human subjects support the hypothesis that anhedonia involves a deficit in the *anticipation* of the experience of pleasure. For example, an anhedonic individual might not anticipate experiencing pleasure eating a tasty cookie, thus engendering no motivation to buy and eat the cookie. In separate studies in France and the United States, researchers have found that anhedonic individuals do not show the same pattern of brain activity as nonanhedonic individuals in anticipation of responding to a pleasurable stimulus. In addition, other research has found that anhedonia is associated with diminished motivation to approach and obtain pleasurable objects and experiences in the environment.

[*See also* Depression; *and* Emotion, *article on* Theories.]

Bibliography

Bernstein, A. S., & Riedel J. A. (1987). Psychophysiological response patterns in college students with high physical anhedonia: Scores appear to reflect schizotypy rather than depression. *Biological Psychiatry, 22*, 829–847. Study suggesting anhedonia is traitlike in schizophrenia but reflects a depressed mood state in depression.

Blackburn, J. R., Phillips, A. G., & Fibiger, H. C. (1987). Dopamine and preparatory behavior: I. Effects of pimozide. *Behavioral Neuroscience, 101*, 352–360. Study of anhedonia in rats showing drug induced appetitive pleasure deficit.

Blanchard, J. J., Bellack, A. S., & Mueser, K. T. (1994). Affective and social-behavioral correlates of physical and social anhedonia in schizophrenia. *Journal of Abnormal Psychology, 103*, 719–728. Study showing that anhedonia in schizophrenia is related to reports of positive emotion following the presentation of emotional films.

Blanchard, J. J., Mueser, K. T., & Bellack, A. S. (1999). Anhedonia, positive and negative affect, and social functioning in schizophrenia. *Schizophrenia Bulletin.* Study showing the stability of anhedonia in schizophrenia and its relationships to other measures of positive emotion.

Chapman, L. J., Chapman, J. P., & Raulin, M. L. (1976). Scales for physical and social anhedonia. *Journal of Abnormal Psychology, 85*, 374–382. Contains information about the most commonly used paper-and-pencil measures of anhedonia.

Germans, M. K., & Kring, A. M. (in press). Hedonic deficit in anhedonia: Support for the role of approach motivation. *Personality and Individual Differences.* Study showing self-report of anhedonia is related to measures of approach motivation.

Loas, G., & Boyer, P. (1996). Anhedonia in endogenomorphic depression. *Psychiatry Research, 60*, 57–65. Study of anhedonia in depression.

Meehl, P. E. (1975). Hedonic capacity: Some conjectures. *Bulletin of the Menninger Clinic, 39*, 295–307. Theoretical account of anhedonia as a heritable characteristic.

Myerson, A. (1923). Anhedonia. *American Journal of Psychiatry, 2*, 87–103.

Myerson, A. (1944). Constitutional anhedonia and the social neurosis. *Journal of Nervous and Mental Disease, 99*, 309–312. Theoretical account of anhedonia as a disposition.

Pierson, A., Ragot, R., Ripoche, A., & Lesèvre, N. (1987). Electrophysiological changes elicited by auditory stimuli given a positive or negative value: A study comparing anhedonic with nonanhedonic subjects. *International Journal of Psychophysiology, 5*, 107–123. Study showing psychophysiological differences between anhedonic and nonanhedonic individuals.

Rádo, S. (1953). Dynamics and classification of disordered behavior. *American Journal of Psychiatry, 110*, 406–416. Theoretical account of anhedonia and its relation to interpersonal functioning.

Ribot, T. H. (1897). *The psychology of emotions.* London: Scott.

Simons, R. F., MacMillan, F. W., & Ireland, F. B. (1982). Anticipatory pleasure deficit in subjects reporting physical anhedonia: Slow cortical evidence. *Biological Psychology, 14*, 297–310. Study showing brain electrical potential differences between anhedonic and nonanhedonic individuals in response to pleasurable stimuli.

Ann M. Kring and Marja K. Germans

ANIMAL INTELLIGENCE. See Nonhuman Intelligence.

ANIMAL LEARNING AND BEHAVIOR. [*This entry comprises three articles, which discuss the history of the field, the theoretical issues, and the methods of study of animal learning and behavior. For related discussions, see* Learning, *article on* Cognitive Approach for Animals; *and* Learning and Memory, *article on* Learning and Memory in Animals.]

History of the Field

Animal learning lies at the crossroads of some of the most important human issues that have arisen historically in religion, philosophy, psychology, and science, particularly biological science. These ancient issues, which are capable of arousing controversy even today, are not merely academic; they have long been recognized as concerned with the personal and spiritual relations of human beings to each other and to our conception of our place in the universe. An example of one of the more important of these issues is concerned with the psychological similarities and differences between people and animals (animal learning theorists would say people and other animals). Are people and animals fundamentally different in that the former are rational while the latter are not? This claim has been and continues to be made by some of the world's great religions and philosophers.

A variety of important implications flow from the substantive issue considered above, only a few of which are considered here. On the one hand, it matters enormously to those who see rationality as the hallmark of our species, and as a capacity directly conferred upon us by the creator, whether or not rationality is a capacity unique to humans. Rationality, according to this view, distinguishes us from the beasts in a particular sense: it allows us but not animals to tell right from wrong, and so we, but not animals, may be held responsible for our acts. On the other hand, it matters much less to evolutionary theory in general and animal learning in particular whether rationality is or is not unique to people. From an evolutionary standpoint, rationality, whatever that may be, is an adaptation, like any other adaptation—a claw, a hoof, gills—which, if it exists, arose as a result of environmental adjustment.

It is safe to say that most animal learning theorists are of the opinion that continuity or overlap exists between the learning processes of people and other animals. Learning has been defined by Domjan (1998) as follows: "Learning is an enduring change in the mechanisms of behavior involving specific stimuli and responses that result from prior experience with those stimuli and responses" (p. 13). Studies of animal learning are concerned with isolating and identifying the mechanisms of behavior which explain performance. Such studies tend to employ a few species, most notably rat and pigeon, which are investigated in depth. Thus, determining the extent to which people and other animals are similar and different in the mechanisms of learning is an issue to which the data and theory of animal learning are clearly relevant.

Three major assumptions or rationales lie at the heart of the justification for the discipline of animal learning. Each of these rationales arose from a variety of historical forces. One rationale is that there are certain important problems that can be investigated and justified ethically when employing animals but not people. For example, the effects of certain drugs on learning, memory, and problem solving might be investigated in animals prior to employing them in research

with people. This approach, which is considered ethically dubious by some, has been defended at length by Neal Miller (1985).

A second major justification for animal learning as a discipline is in terms of the increased experimental control it allows relative to similar research on people. As one example, we know that an animal's performance in some current learning task may be influenced, sometimes enormously, by its experience in some other learning task, particularly a similar learning task. Better control over some aspects of prior experience is possible in some cases with animals than with people. For example, in some rare cases, investigators have resorted to raising animals in isolation.

The third major justification for animal learning assumes that important relationships, such as laws, can be more easily isolated in simpler systems, e.g., with rats, than in more complicated systems, e.g., with people. Having isolated these relationships in the simpler system, so the argument goes, it will be easier to determine their function in the more complicated system. Obviously this rationale assumes that there is at least some continuity between the learning processes of animals and people.

The Historical Background of Animal Learning

The view that studying learning in animals should prove useful for understanding learning in general, and more specifically in people, is not one peculiar to our age, nor is it one that has necessarily achieved greater acceptance in our age. For example, in ancient times, Aristotle attributed a high level of intelligence to certain animals (snakes are crafty, elephants are wise) but considered the ability to reason confined to our species. Roberts (1998) has indicated that the Roman philosopher Plotinus held that animals had souls and thus should not be either killed or eaten, a view also held by Celsus, a Christian heretic. Celsus suggested also that animals were capable of reasoning. Cheney and Seyfarth (1990) note the following:

> [In the Middle Ages in Europe,] animals ranging from insects to horses were commonly brought to trial, provided with defense lawyers, and charged with crimes such as the willful destruction of crops, murder, and sodomy. People in the Middle Ages were not careless anthropomorphizers; they clearly recognized that animals were not people. Nevertheless, the behavior of their animals often led people to believe that animals could be aware of what they did and held accountable for their acts. (p. 1)

However, within the Christian tradition, generally speaking, animals were seen as lacking an immortal soul and thus the ability to reason and to tell right from wrong. Among philosophers René Descartes (1596–

1650) was the most influential in suggesting that a fundamental difference exists, psychologically speaking, between people and animals. According to Descartes's view, called Cartesian dualism, there are two types of human behavior, voluntary and involuntary. Actions which are involuntary and occur in response to external stimuli were called reflexes. Voluntary actions may occur in humans as a result of conscious choice. According to Descartes, animals are capable only of involuntary actions or reflexes. In agreement with the Christian tradition in Europe, Descartes believed that only humans have souls and thus only humans possessed free will and the ability to reason. In 1859, with the publication of *The Origin of Species*, Darwin provided a great challenge to Descartes's view and provided the basis for a scientific study of the psychological similarities and differences which exist between different species.

According to Darwin, the evolution of humans from some earlier animal form involved not only physical features but mental ones as well. As a result of Darwin's theory, as Darwin himself recognized, it was not only desirable but inevitable that the behavior of animals would be studied both for its own value and for its relevance to human behavior. In Darwin's view, expressed most clearly in *The Descent of Man, and Selection in Relation to Sex* (1871), while much mental functioning in people is more sophisticated than in animals, many prized psychological capacities of people are not unique. Rather, he suggested, many intellectual capacities of people were gradually improved through natural selection. Darwin suggested that nonhuman animals possessed a moral sense, spirituality, a sense of property, memory, an ability to reason, and other psychological capacities thought by some to be unique to our species. While Darwin's theory is one of the greatest of scientific accomplishments, reading *The Descent of Man* with modern eyes, one is struck by his psychological naiveté, according to modern standards of evaluating evidence. Darwin often reached a conclusion concerning an animal's particular mental capacity of one on the basis of evidence that is totally unacceptable by modern standards. Much of the so-called evidence provided by Darwin in support of his conclusions was anecdotal in character. Despite this, we should not overlook Darwin's great contributions in putting the study of animal psychology on a scientific path.

Darwin's close friend George T. Romanes, in his book *Animal Intelligence* (1882), presented a case for continuity of intelligence throughout the animal kingdom, and he did so, like Darwin himself, by resorting frequently to anecdotes. Romanes seriously reported stories suggesting considerable animal intelligence that were told to him by some single individual. Sometimes the report relayed to Romanes might be a second- or third-hand account witnessed in the first instance (if at all) by a naive and credulous observer. In defense of Romanes, it should be indicated that he was aware of the limitations of the anecdotal method, employing it because there was no better evidence at his disposal. This recognition began the process which still marks the study of animal behavior today, of attempting to provide the best methodological basis available for any conclusions reached concerning the learning or cognitive abilities of animals.

C. Lloyd Morgan was among the first to travel the road to methodological sophistication in the scientific study of animal learning cognition. In his book, *An Introduction to Comparative Psychology* (1903; reprinted in 1993), Morgan was critical of the use of anecdotes by Darwin and Romanes. He offered a by now famous principle for the interpretation of animal behavior which is now known as Morgan's canon. According to Morgan's canon, in no case may we interpret an action as the outcome of the exercise of a higher psychological faculty, if it can be interpreted as the outcome of the exercise of one which stands lower in the psychological scale (Morgan, 1906, p. 53). This principle has come to mean that simpler explanations of behavior should be tried before more complex ones are invoked.

With C. Lloyd Morgan we begin a period in which many of the sophisticated methodological procedures that are employed today to study animal learning and intelligence began to be introduced. Two extremely influential individuals in this regard were Edward L. Thorndike and Ivan P. Pavlov.

Thorndike (1911), like C. Lloyd Morgan, was highly critical of the use of anecdotes as a means of establishing animal intelligence. Thorndike is particularly notable for two things: he brought the study of animal learning into the laboratory, and he devised a theory of learning, known as connectionism, which postulated continuity in animal intelligence. According to this view, associations between stimuli and responses are at the basis of all learning in all species. Different species differ in the type and complexity of the associations formed. A famous apparatus employed by Thorndike to study animal learning is known as the puzzle box. Essentially, animals were put in a box from which they could be released to obtain food. Release was possible by performing some response such as pulling a string which opened a door, thus providing access to food. Thorndike observed that over trials the time required by an animal (cat, dog, chick) to obtain release from the box declined systematically in a negatively accelerated fashion. That is, the time dropped sharply in the early trials and more slowly in the later trials. Thorndike's theory of learning was very influential in its day.

Before moving on to Pavlov it should be noted that another major theorist who, like Thorndike, brought learning into the laboratory and promoted associations was Herrman Ebbinghaus (1885). Ebbinghaus did not study animals but rather employed himself as the participant in his investigations. But because Ebbinghaus promoted the use of careful methodological procedures, which he himself devised, as well as a sophisticated associationism, he may be regarded as representing an ethos common to great figures of his period.

Thorndike employed what has come to be known as instrumental learning. In an instrumental learning task a response in the presence of a discriminative stimulus produces a reward. For example, a hungry rat might obtain food by pressing a bar when a light flashes. Pavlov, in his monumental investigations, employed another procedure called either classical or Pavlovian conditioning. Under this procedure, stimuli are presented regardless of the animal's behavior. For example, after the offset of a 5 s tone, food may be provided regardless of the animal's behavior. With training, the animal might come to salivate to the tone. Pavlov, a Russian physiologist, who won the Nobel Prize in 1904, contributed to the study of learning not only a method of very considerable usefulness, but also much in the way of empirical data and theory that remains influential to this day. It would be difficult to overvalue Pavlov's methodological, empirical, and theoretical contribution.

As experimental data of the sort provided by instrumental and Pavlovian conditioning accumulated, the tendency grew to focus on behavior observed under highly controlled conditions. This tendency was formalized, as it were, in a very famous paper published in 1913 by J. B. Watson entitled, "Psychology as the Behaviorist Views It." Watson argued that the only proper subject matter of psychology is behavior. Behaviorism became a dominant movement in psychology and was all but totally ascendant in animal learning. From about 1930 to roughly 1960, animal learning was a dominant area of psychology. A variety of behaviorisms were offered, three of which are identified here. Radical behaviorism, which is identified with B. F Skinner, eschews all mentalistic concepts, suggests that the causes of behavior are to be found in the environment, and seeks to identify functional relations between variables (Skinner, 1938). Methodological behaviorism, which is identified with Clark Hull (1943), allows that overt behavior could be controlled by internal events which themselves were implicit behaviors. From about 1930 to 1952, Hull developed a most sophisticated version of stimulus-response (S-R) theory, the view that stimuli come to elicit responses. Cognitive behaviorism is identified with E. C. Tolman (1932), who suggested that purpose is evident in molar behaviors. Today, while many would describe themselves as Skinnerians, few could call themselves Hullians or Tolmanians. This does not mean, for example, that Hullian theory is dead. Hull's general approach, if not some of his specific the-

oretical assumptions, may be found in various contemporary theories such as the Rescorla-Wagner model.

In the period roughly 1930 to 1960, debate raged in learning between S-R theory and cognitive theory. While much in the way of what may be called cognitive data were reported (latent learning, a concern with cognitive maps, place vs. response learning, to name a few) the S-R approach was clearly dominant. Dissatisfaction with behaviorism in general and S-R psychology in particular began to be expressed around 1960, ushering in what is often called the cognitive revolution. This approach characterized behaviorism in general and S-R psychology in particular as inadequate, in the process shifting attention away from animal learning and toward the examination of complex processes in humans such as attention, problem solving, information processing, and the like. It may be argued that the so-called cognitive revolution was more of a palace revolt than an entirely new way of doing business. Leahey (1992) notes many similarities between behaviorism and cognitive psychology.

Whether or not a revolution occurred circa 1960, it is the case that since then research and theorizing in animal learning has become broader. However, interest did not wane in the traditional theoretical issues of concern, nor were classical and instrumental conditioning abandoned. In fairness, it should be indicated that much of the broadening had antecedents in earlier work. As merely one example, the ability of animals to count, or more broadly to use numerical information, which began to be heavily studied in the 1990s, had attracted much attention as early as 1900 (Roberts, 1998). It would be rash to attribute the relative absence of an overt interest in numerical processing in animals from roughly 1940 to 1980 entirely to either behaviorism or to S-R psychology. For example, it is the case that theories dating from the 1940s and 1950s began to mature in the 1980s to the point where they were able to be used to encompass numerical processing in animals. Theoretical progress of that sort also had an influence in broadening the scope of animal learning to include animal cognition and comparative cognition.

Memory in animals became a much more active area of investigation from about 1960 on, as did attention, rehearsal, concept learning, examining serial processing and timing, and revisiting that ancient concern, reasoning in animals. Language acquisition in animals, particularly apes, continues to receive much attention. But each of these areas of investigation had received some attention either prior to and/or during the behaviorist period.

Traditionally, animal learning has been concerned with three broad issues: what is learned (e.g., associations, cognitions); under what conditions learning occurs (e.g., is temporal continuity between stimuli sufficient to establish an association between them); and how learning is transformed into performance. Much progress along these lines has occurred in the past 25 years or so. For example, in addition to the traditional rivalry between S-R associations and cognitive psychology, stimulus-stimulus (S-S) and response-stimulus (R-S) associations have come under fruitful examination. Many new theories have been offered that look beyond the traditional continuity and reinforcement principle. It has been suggested, for example, that association formation may require surprisingness because animals may only process or attend to surprising events.

Two other relatively recent developments in animal learning are worthy of mention. The practical application of learning principles, so-called behavioral modification (or behavior therapy), has become widely employed and is now an established area in its own right. Behavior modification is concerned with behaviors that can be acquired via learning, from how to drive a car to how fears may be established and extinguished. How the biological makeup of animals influences learning and performance is another issue of much concern. For example, do all species learn according to the same laws? Within a given species, are different things learned according to different laws? General process learning theory suggests that all learning in mammals, for instance, is accomplished according to the same principles. Others suggest that the acquisition of some things (phobias, imprinting, aversion to poisonous foods) is accomplished by means of specialized laws different from those governing tasks like maze learning.

Psychologists who study animal learning are academic psychologists with Ph.D.s employed primarily in universities and colleges. This is because the field requires access to animal laboratories. The main professional organizations for animal learning are the Psychonomic Society and the Association of Behavior Analysts, although practitioners also participate in the APA, APS, the regional psychological associations, and many related associations where practitioners employ animal subjects (e.g., Society for Neuroscience). Expertise in the methods of animal learning is very valuable as a tool in many other disciplines.

Bibliography

Cheney, D. L., & Seyfarth, R. M. (1990). *How monkeys see the world: Inside the mind of another species*. Chicago: University of Chicago Press.

Darwin, C. (1859). *The origin of species*. London: John Murray.

Darwin, C. (1871). *The descent of man, and selection in relation to sex*. London: John Murray.

Domjan, M. (1998). *The principles of learning and behavior* (4th ed.) Pacific Grove, CA: Brooks/Cole.

Ebbinghaus, H. (1885). *Memory: A contribution to experimental psychology* (H. A. Ruger & C. E. Bussenius, Trans.). New York: Dover.

Hull, C. L. (1943). *Principles of behavior*. New York: Appleton-Century-Crofts.

Leahey, T. H. (1992). *A history of psychology: Main currents in psychological thought*. Englewood Cliffs, NJ: Prentice Hall.

Miller, N. E. (1985). The value of behavioral research on animals. *American Psychologist, 40*, 423–440.

Morgan, C. L. (1903; reprinted in 1993). *An introduction to comparative psychology*. London: Walter Scott.

Roberts, W. A. (1998). *Principles of animal cognition*. Boston, MA: McGraw-Hill.

Romanes, G. J. (1882). *Animal intelligence*. London: Kegan Paul, Trench.

Skinner, B. F. (1938). *The behavior of organisms: An experimental analysis*. New York: Appleton-Century-Crofts.

Thorndike, E. L. (1911). *Animal intelligence: Experimental studies*. New York: Macmillan.

Tolman, E. C. (1932). *Purposive behavior in animals and men*. New York: Appleton-Century-Crofts.

Watson, J. B. (1913). Psychology as the behaviorist views it. *Psychological Review, 20*, 158–177.

E. John Capaldi

Theoretical Issues

The field of animal learning and behavior is concerned with what various species of animals (including humans) learn and how they learn it. No one theoretical approach dominates studies of animal learning and behavior. The various approaches differ in (1) whether they emphasize species differences or similarities; (2) whether they allow cognitive mechanisms, and the kinds of cognitive mechanisms they invoke; (3) whether they describe behavior at a molar or molecular level of analysis; and (4) whether they are concerned with the functions or mechanisms of learning.

General Process Versus Comparative Approaches

Since the field of animal learning and behavior deals with how learning occurs in various species, a fundamental conceptual issue concerns how to deal with species differences. Comparisons invariably reveal both similarities and differences, and one can elect to focus on one or the other. The general process approach to the study of learning focuses on similarities in how learning occurs in various species and situations. Comparative approaches focus on species differences.

The general process approach is rooted in the assumption of the physical and biological sciences that a limited number of elements interacting according to a few basic laws can explain the diversity of all physical and biological events. This approach was imported into studies of physiology in the development of the isolated physiological preparation. The assumption was that basic physiological processes occur in much the same way wherever they are found. For example, neural activation of muscle contractions is assumed to occur in much the same way at all neuromuscular junctions. Therefore, one can study the mechanisms of neuromuscular junctions in general by carefully examining one particular example. Given these assumptions, the particular example can be chosen on the basis of convenience and ease of access.

The Russian physiologist Ivan Petrovich Pavlov was naturally familiar with isolated physiological preparations and adopted this approach in his studies of associative learning. Pavlov became well known for his studies of the conditioning of salivation in dogs. However, he was not especially interested in salivation. Rather, he studied conditioned salivation as a way to discover general rules of learning and general principles of neural plasticity that presumably operate in all situations involving associative learning.

The general process approach was subsequently adopted by B. F. Skinner and other American behaviorists, who were also intent on identifying universal rules of learning or behavior modification. Skinner was especially interested in developing experimental preparations that would reveal general rather than species-typical features of behavior. However, as has been pointed by Timberlake (1990), in doing so Skinner was unable to ignore the genetically based behavioral predispositions of his experimental subjects.

In contrast to the general process approach, the comparative approach begins with the assumption that evolution has created adaptive specializations in learning (Rozin & Schull, 1988). These specializations may be evident in species differences or differences in how learning takes place in different situations. Early comparative approaches emphasized differences in learning related to evolutionary grade (Bitterman, 1975). More recently, comparative psychologists have tried to integrate species differences with ecological and functional considerations (Dewsbury, 1990).

Species differences in learning have turned out to be rather difficult to demonstrate because learning tasks given to different species often also differ in terms of the stimuli, responses, or reinforcers involved. The general process approach has been challenged more successfully by studies showing that animals learn in different ways about different stimuli and/or responses. Garcia, Hankins, and Rusiniak (1974), for example, showed that animals learn differently about their external and internal environment, and Domjan (1997) has shown that different mechanisms are involved in learning about appetitive and consummatory components of sexual behavior.

Cognitive Versus Behavioral Approaches

A second conceptual issue that has dominated the field of animal learning and behavior is the distinction between cognitive and behavioral approaches. Behavioral approaches are limited to descriptions of quantitative relationships between behavior and environmental events or procedures. Cognitive approaches, in contrast, make reference to internal mediational variables as determinants of behavior.

The behavioral approach originated in the behaviorism of J. B. Watson, who argued that only behavior can provide valid data for a science of psychology—not thoughts or conscious experience. Although behaviorism was short-lived in many areas of psychology, it remained an enduring influence in animal learning as a result of the work of B. F. Skinner and the development of what has come to be known as the experimental analysis of behavior. Skinner argued that theories invoking intervening variables do not advance knowledge (Skinner, 1950), and that a science of behavior can be based entirely on quantitative empirical generalizations that relate behavioral and procedural variables.

A major contemporary example of the behavioral approach is Herrnstein's matching law (Herrnstein, 1997). According to the matching law, when an organism has two response alternatives available, and each response is reinforced according to its own independent schedule of reinforcement, the relative rate of responding between the alternatives will match the relative rate of reinforcement for the two response alternatives. The matching law specifies a quantitative relationship between rates of responding and rates of reinforcement, with no reference to any internal states or cognitive variables.

Interest in cognitive interpretations and animal cognition was stimulated by the writings of Charles Darwin, although cognition in animals had been entertained by various philosophers as far back as Aristotle (Roberts, 1998). [See Animal Learning and Behavior, article on History of the Field.] Darwin contended that evolutionary theory applies to the phylogenetic development of intelligence and other mental faculties, just as it applies to the phylogenetic development of physical traits. Early comparative psychologists focused on behavioral plasticity and learning in their efforts to study animal intelligence. Watson's behaviorism then eclipsed studies of animal cognition. However, interest in cognitive mechanisms reemerged with the work of neobehavioral theorists like Hull and Tolman and subsequent advances in experimental methods for the study of cognition. Cognitive approaches range from limited intervening variables that are tied closely to observable events, to complex representations, mental states, and cognitions such as "intentionality" that are entertained by cognitive ethologists.

Theoretical analyses of what is learned as a result of instrumental conditioning procedures illustrate some of the range of intervening or cognitive variables that have been used in explanations of animal learning. The first proposal was Thorndike's law of effect, which states that the delivery of a reinforcer after an instrumental response R serves to establish an association between that response and the stimuli S that were experienced when the response was performed. [*See* Law of Effect.] The only intervening variable in the law of effect is the concept of an S-R association. Subsequent theorists suggested that instrumental conditioning also results in the learning of various expectancies. The most obvious of these is the expectancy of reward. Reward expectancy is neither a measurable stimulus nor a measurable response. Rather, it is an intervening variable or mental state that is presumed to be activated by stimuli and in turn helps to generate the instrumental response.

Reward expectancy has been operationalized in various ways over the years. An early conceptualization was provided by the fractional anticipatory goal response mechanism of the neobehaviorists Hull and Spence. In the fractional anticipatory goal response mechanism, reward comes to be expected based on exposure to the cues that are present when the instrumental response is reinforced. Subsequent theorists argued that reward expectancy also comes to be stimulated by the instrumental response itself.

Molar Versus Molecular Approaches

Another important conceptual dimension for studies of animal learning and behavior concerns the level of analysis at which the investigation is conducted. Molar analyses focus aggregates of responses or measures that characterize occurrences of a response over a fairly long period, such as an entire experimental session. In contrast, molecular analyses focus on the determinants of individual responses. The matching law is a good example of the molar approach because it is stated in terms of rates of responding and rates of reinforcement averaged over entire experimental sessions. Another area of research in which the molar approach has predominated is the study of optimal foraging behavior (Kamil, Krebs, & Pulliam, 1987). In contrast, analyses of the associative structure of instrumental behavior (e.g., Colwill, 1994) are conducted at a molecular level because they are stated in terms of individual stimuli and responses. The molecular approach has also predominated in studies of classical or Pavlovian conditioning, which involve characterizing how individual stimuli become associated with one another.

The molar versus molecular distinction also has been important in conceptualizations of stimuli by learning psychologists. According to the molecular approach, a stimulus consists of a number of distinct features or elements. For example, a triangle consists of three line segments. The molar approach, in contrast, emphasizes holistic features of a stimulus that depend on its total integrity—features that emerge from how the elements are organized. According to the molar approach, the essence of a triangle is not three line segments but how those line segments are arranged. Line segments do not make a triangle unless they are arranged so they form a closed figure. The molar approach emphasizes configural properties of stimuli, whereas the molecular approach emphasizes elemental features.

The molecular approach to stimuli has been dominant in studies of animal learning. A prominent early example was stimulus sampling theory proposed by W. K. Estes. According to this theory, stimuli consist of numerous elements, a random subset of which are detected on a particular trial. Only the elements that have been sampled on a trial enter into associations and control behavior on that trial. However, with repeated trials, eventually all of the elements of a stimulus will become sampled and learned about. The molar or configural approach was emphasized by Gestalt psychologists early in the twentieth century and has been applied since then in certain limited domains of learning. A recent example is Pearce's configural theory of discrimination learning (Pearce, 1994).

Function Versus Mechanism

Approaches to the study of animal learning and behavior also differ in the extent to which they are concerned with the functions or mechanisms of learning. Functional aspects of learning refer to the ways in which learning contributes to the solution of various challenges of living. Mechanisms of learning refer to the factors that mediate learning or the internal machinery that is responsible for the changes that are brought about by learning.

The ultimate function of a biological or behavioral system is to enhance reproductive success. However, with few exceptions, investigators have not measured directly whether learning increases the number of offspring that animals produce. Rather, functional studies have focused on how learning facilitates achieving various proximate goals such as digestion, food selection, mate selection, and territorial defense (e.g., Hollis, 1997).

The mechanisms of learning also may be investigated in various ways. Learning inevitably involves neurophysiological changes. Those changes may be described in terms of events that take place within neurons, at neural synapses, or at the level of neural systems. The mechanisms of learning also may be described at the level of stimuli and responses using theoretical concepts such as associations, response strength, or conditioned excitation and inhibition.

Learning gained center stage in psychology during the twentieth century because of its functional importance. In fact, the functional significance of learning was considered to be so obvious that it required little discussion. This strong presumption of utility led investigators to ignore functional issues and focus instead on the mechanisms of learning. Performance factors, or the behavioral manifestations of learning, became relegated to secondary status. Investigators could not ignore behavior altogether, but many of them came to regard behavior as just a methodological necessity in their quest to uncover the mechanisms of learning.

Systematic consideration of functional issues in learning reemerged with discoveries of adaptive specializations and biological constraints on learning, such as long-delayed food aversion learning (see Hinde & Stevenson-Hinde, 1973; Seligman & Hager, 1972). [*See* Taste Aversion Learning.] These data suggested that how animals learn a task may be related to the biological functions served by that task. The function of food aversion learning, for example, is to minimize the intake of poisonous foods. However, this function cannot be achieved unless an animal is able to associate the taste of poisonous food with the usually delayed toxic consequences. Such functional considerations help us understand why animals (mammals in particular) have the ability to learn to associate the taste of a novel food with illness that occurs several hours after ingestion.

Bibliography

Bitterman, M. E. (1975). The comparative analysis of learning. *Science, 188,* 699–709. Describes comparative studies of learning organized in terms of evolutionary grade.

Colwill, R. M. (1994). Associative representations of instrumental contingencies. *The psychology of learning and motivation* (Vol. 31, pp. 1–72). San Diego, CA: Academic Press. Describes research on molecular analyses of instrumental conditioning.

Dewsbury, D. A. (Ed.). (1990). *Contemporary issues in comparative psychology.* Sunderland, MA: Sinauer. Describes research in comparative psychology conducted within a functional/ecological framework.

Domjan, M. (1997). Behavior systems and the demise of equipotentiality: Historical antecedents and evidence from sexual conditioning. In M. E. Bouton & M. S. Fanselow (Eds.), *Learning, motivation, and cognition* (pp. 31–51). Washington, DC: American Psychological Association. Describes differences in how animals learn about appetitive and consummatory sexual behavior.

Garcia, J., Hankins, W. G., & Rusiniak, K. W. (1974). Behavioral regulation of the milieu interne in man and rat. *Science, 185,* 824–831. Describes differences in how animals learn about internal versus external events.

Herrnstein, R. J. (1997). *The matching law* (H. Rachlin & D. I. Laibson, Eds.). Cambridge, MA: Harvard University Press. Describes Herrnstein's research on the matching law.

Hinde, R. A., & Stevenson-Hinde, J. (Eds.). (1973). *Constraints on learning.* New York: Academic Press. Describes early research on biological constraints and adaptive specializations in learning.

Hollis, K. L. (1997). Contemporary research on Pavlovian conditioning: A "new" functional analysis. *American Psychologist, 52,* 956–965. Reviews functional aspects of classical conditioning.

Kamil, A. C., Krebs, J. R., & Pulliam, H. R. (Eds.). (1987). *Foraging behavior.* New York: Plenum Press. Describes research on foraging behavior, illustrating molar levels of analysis of instrumental behavior.

Pearce, J. M. (1994). Similarity and discrimination: A selective review and a connectionist model. *Psychological Review, 101,* 587–607. Provides an example of a molar or configural approach to stimulus analysis in learning.

Ristau, C. A. (Ed.) (1991). *Cognitive ethology.* Hillsdale, NJ: Erlbaum. Describes recent research and theory on mind and cognition in nonhuman animals.

Roberts, W. A. (1998). *Principles of animal cognition.* Boston: McGraw-Hill. Summarizes contemporary research in animal cognition.

Rozin, P., & Schull, J. (1988). The adaptive-evolutionary point of view in experimental psychology. In R. C. Atkinson. R. J. Herrnstein, G. Lindzey, & R. D. Luce (Eds.), *Stevens' handbook of experimental psychology* (2nd ed., Vol. 1, pp. 503–546). New York: Wiley. Discusses evolutionary issues in learning and other areas of experimental psychology.

Seligman, M. E. P., & Hager, J. L. (Eds.). (1972). *Biological boundaries of learning.* New York: Appleton-Century-Crofts. Describes early research on biological constraints and adaptive specializations in learning.

Skinner, B. F. (1950). Are theories of learning necessary? *Psychological Review, 57,* 193–216. A historically important paper in which Skinner argues against the use of intervening variables in explanations of behavior.

Timberlake, W. (1990). Natural learning in laboratory paradigms. In D. A. Dewsbury (Ed.), *Contemporary issues in comparative psychology* (pp. 31–54). Sunderland, MA: Sinauer. Describes how evolutionary considerations were taken into account in the design of experimental preparations for the study of general learning processes.

Michael Domjan

Methods of Study

To a significant extent the history of animal learning may be illuminated by examining the methods it has embraced or rejected at particular times in its development. Understanding why this is so produces a better appreciation of methodology in general, a topic often considered (unfairly) to be dry and uninteresting. Methodology is less appreciated than is warranted because often the rationale for employing particular methods is either unstated or is simply incorrect. It is unstated in many of the methods texts written for undergraduates which simply introduce particular methods, e.g., experimentation, in the absence of any justification, the implication being that none is needed so wonderful is the method. Incorrect rationales for employing methods have been advanced by philosophers of science such as Karl Popper who have suggested that methods are conventions. A convention is something which is accepted rather than justified, as, for example, whether to place the salad fork to the left or the right of the dinner fork.

Another more correct view, one which may be more implicit than explicit in the practice of scientists, is that methods are employed to the extent that they are useful for providing information that might be sought at a particular time. A method is useful to the extent that it provides better information than could be obtained in its absence or by employing some other method. Thus, a heavily employed method may be discarded as soon as a better one comes along. As new issues have come to the fore in animal learning, new methods have been devised to deal with them. It may be expected that animal learning methods (as in any scientific area), will continue to come and go as they have in the past.

A method may be defined as a way of achieving some end according to a definite plan. The earliest attempts to understand the intellectual capabilities of animals (or the lack thereof) were those of philosophers and theologians. The method employed by them may be characterized as armchair speculation in the service of preconceived ideas. While the armchair method produced a variety of views, the most popular and generally accepted of these was that humans possess a quality completely lacking in animals: rationality. The best known exponent of this view was the philosopher René Descartes. The rationality idea, which preceded Descartes by centuries, is still accepted in some circles today.

The Armchair Method and the Anecdotal Method

The armchair method and the idea that people and animals differ qualitatively in some psychological respects, began to be abandoned, at least in science, with the appearance of Darwin's theory of evolution. Evolution strongly implied that psychologically, people and animals may differ in degree rather than kind. To test this newer conception, Darwin and his close friend George T. Romanes employed the anecdotal method, one hardly better than that of armchair speculation. That is, they accepted as useful information verbal reports, of some particular feat of some particular animal. For example, Darwin, in his book *The Descent of Man, and Selection in Relation to Sex* (1871), theorized on hearing from a zookeeper that a monkey retained a stone which it used to crack nuts, that monkeys, and other animals including birds, had a sense of property. Whether or not either the zookeeper's story or Darwin's speculation is correct is not the point. The point is that the zookeeper's report allows many other possible interpretations that cannot be evaluated or tested by the anecdotal method.

Both C. Lloyd Morgan (1906) and E. L. Thorndike heavily criticized the use of anecdotes, and it was Thorndike and Pavlov who did much to bring animal learning into the laboratory where experimental methods might be employed. While experimental methods are of the greatest usefulness in animal learning, less rigorous methods have a place. For example, filial imprinting which involves the learned attachment between parent and offspring, was initially discovered by employing observation in the field. Later, imprinting was examined under more highly controlled laboratory conditions.

Laboratory Studies

Highly controlled laboratory studies tend to be employed in animal learning because that approach provides the best means available for answering two of the issues of major interest in the field: the issue of what is learned and under what conditions learning occurs. Consider how the sort of question one might ask might determine the sort of methodology one might employ. For example, on the assumption that learning involves an association between stimuli, that is, an increase in the capacity of one stimulus to give rise to a representation of another stimulus, it would be appropriate to employ Pavlovian conditioning. This involves a procedure in which a tone, say (stimulus 1) is followed by food, say (stimulus 2). Then the observer determines whether with training the animal responds to the tone in some manner (say by salivating) which indicates that it anticipates the food. Moreover, to test the idea that learning occurs only if two stimuli are contiguous, i.e., occur together in time, the tone could be terminated for some period of time before onset of the food. If the association between tone and food were formed despite the lack of temporal contiguity between them one might posit that memory of the tone bridged the temporal gap between them, so to speak, which would lead one to run additional experiments employing yet other variations of the Pavlovian procedure or, indeed, other non-Pavlovian procedures useful for examining the role of memory in association formation. Such procedures are considered below. Each of the procedures described below has been employed for (usually) a variety of reasons. Unfortunately, these reasons cannot always be indicated in the space available here: the interested reader may find the rational for these methods in several recent excellent texts (Domjan, 1998; Tarpy, 1997).

Classification of Methods

Any classification of methods is bound to be arbitrary to some extent. The plan followed here is as follows. First, major divisions among commonly employed methods in animal learning are noted, these methods being habituation-sensitization, Pavlovian conditioning, and instrumental conditioning. Some procedures which apply equally to both Pavlovian and instrumental conditioning are then described. Subsequently, procedures which are characteristic of Pavlovian and instrumental conditioning are described separately. Sometimes instrumental procedures are modified in order to study some complex process such as concept formation or concept utilization. Space permits us to supply only two examples of this use of instrumental methods.

Habituation-Sensitization, Pavlovian or Classical Conditioning, and Instrumental or Operant Conditioning. These three methods together constitute the major divisions among methods employed in animal learning. Habituation is concerned with a decline in responding with repeated presentation of a stimulus. For example, a startle response might decline with repeated presentation of a loud noise. Increased responding to a repeated stimulus is called sensitization. Pavlovian conditioning involves the presentation of stimuli without regard to the behavior of the animal. In the example given earlier, the tone would be presented in the same temporal relation to the food whether or not the animal responds to the tone. In instrumental conditioning, a response in the presence of a discriminative stimulus produces a reinforcer. For example, pressing a bar when a light comes on might produce food. In instrumental conditioning, then, a response is required to secure reinforcement.

The reinforcer employed in any of the above methods might be either appetitive, e.g., food, or aversive, e.g., shock. A given investigation might involve discrimination learning. In discrimination learning, different reward outcomes are associated with different stimuli; in Pavlovian conditioning, for example, food might be given following a bright light but not a dim one. In instrumental conditioning, pressing the left bar but not the right one might produce food. A reinforcement schedule describes a rule for presenting reinforcers. Some reinforcement schedules common to Pavlovian and instrumental conditioning include consistent reward and partial reward. Under a schedule of consistent reinforcement, for example, reinforcement occurs on every trial. Under a schedule of partial reinforcement only some trials terminate in reinforcement. The size of magnitude of the reinforcer may be large or small. Reinforcement may be discontinued under either Pavlovian or instrumental conditioning, a procedure called extinction. Extinction is widely employed in animal learning. The interval elapsing between trials, the intertrial interval, may be varied either in the acquisition phase or the extinction phase or both.

Pavlovian Conditioning. The following definitions are important for understanding Pavlovian conditioning. A conditioned stimulus (CS) is one which does not elicit a particular response initially but comes to do so as a result of being paired with a stimulus that does, the unconditioned stimulus (US). The response that comes to be made to the conditioned stimulus is called the conditioned response (CR). The response elicited by the unconditioned stimulus at the outset of training is called the unconditioned response (UR). There are four general acquisition procedures in Pavlovian conditioning. The CS and the US may be presented at the same time (simultaneous conditioning), the CS may begin some time before the US is presented (delayed conditioning), the CS may begin and terminate before the US is presented (trace conditioning), and the CS may be presented after the US (backward conditioning).

Some Pavlovian procedures have become so widespread they merit separate mention. In the explicitly unpaired procedure, the CS and US are scheduled such that they do not occur close together and the CS does not occur either prior to or just after the US but rather occurs in between US presentations. In overshadowing investigations, two CSs such as a light and a tone, may be presented simultaneously prior to the US. In blocking investigations, after an association has been established between one CS and the US (say between light and shock), a second CS is added, the compound (say light and tone) now preceding shock US. In higher order conditioning (also called second-order conditioning) after a first CS (CS_1) has been associated with some US, a second CS (CS_2) may be paired with CS_1, i.e., CS_2 may be followed by CS_1. In sensory preconditioning, two CSs may be paired (CS_1 and CS_2). CS_2 may then be associated with a US. Subsequently CS_1 may elicit the CR in the absence of having been paired with the US. A CS may inhibit a CR, i.e., reduce or prevent its occurrence. A popular inhibitory procedure is as follows. Whereas CS_1 is fallowed by the US, the compound CS_1 and CS_2 is not, and so CS_2 acquires the capacity to inhibit responding. Two procedures often employed to determine if CS_2 is an inhibitor are summation and retardation. In summation, the suspected inhibitor is presented in compound with an excitatory CS; if responding which would otherwise occur to the excitatory CS is reduced, the added CS is considered to be an inhibitory. A retardation test involves attempting to convert an inhibitory CS into an excitatory one by now pairing it with a US. If the suspected CS is an inhibitor, acquisition of excitation should be retarded.

Two quite important procedures involve presenting the CS (CS preexposure procedure) or the US (US preexposure procedure) prior to presenting CS-US pairings. Both preexposure procedures may retard subsequent conditioning. In taste aversion learning, animals may be given a flavored solution to drink prior to being made sick by administering either a drug or X-radiation. As a result, ingestion of the flavored solution is either reduced or eliminated. In counterconditioning, a CS which has been paired with one US, say shock, may subsequently be paired with another US, say food, which elicits an opposite type CR. In modulation experiments a stimulus (the modulator) signals the type of relationship to occur between two other events. For example, the US may follow a tone CS if the tone is preceded by a light modulator, but the US may not follow the tone in the absence of the light modulator. In sign-tracking investigations (also called autoshaping) animals are allowed to approach and contact stimuli that signal the availability of food.

Instrumental Conditioning. This method is identified with Thorndike. In his early investigations, hungry animals could obtain food and release from a box by performing some response such as pulling a string. Subsequently, a variety of procedures were employed in which some simple response was required. In a runway an animal is required only to run from a start box to a goal box in order to obtain reinforcement. In a Skinner box, a rat might be required to press a bar to obtain food and a pigeon might be required to peck an illuminated disc for food. In the discrete trial procedure, the animal is removed from the apparatus after each trial. In the free trial procedure, animals remain in the apparatus and can repeat the response (e.g., peck the disk) freely.

Four types of instrumental situations are usually distinguished. In reward training, responding terminates in an appetitive event either a primary reinforcer such as food or water, or a secondary or learned reinforcer, a stimulus which was previously paired with a primary reinforcer. In punishment training, a response produces an aversive event such as shock. In escape training, a response terminates an aversive event. In avoidance training, a response prevents the occurrence of an aversive event.

Numerous types of reinforcement schedules have been employed in instrumental learning. In ratio schedules, reinforcement depends upon making a specified number of responses. Reinforcement follows a fixed number of responses in fixed ratio schedules and a variable number of responses in variable ratio schedules. In interval schedules, reinforcement is given for a response which occurs after a given period of time has elapsed. In fixed interval schedules the animal is reinforced for responding after a fixed period of time has elapsed. In variable ratio schedule the animal is reinforced for responding after varying periods of time have elapsed. Many other types of reinforcement schedules have been employed, unfortunately too many to be described here (but see Domjan, 1998; Tarpy, 1997).

Mazes are a form of discrimination learning, which were more widely employed in the past. The radial maze, however, is very widely used today. In the radial maze a number of paths (arms) diverge from a central platform. Each arm is baited with a single reinforcer.

The animal (usually a rat) is placed on the central platform and is allowed to traverse the arm freely. Even when many paths are involved, say 16, the rat may readily learn to traverse each path only once. A much used discrimination learning procedure to study memory is matching to sample. In this procedure, three keys which a pigeon may peck may be involved. A stimulus which appears on the center key (say horizontal lines) indicates which of two different stimuli that appear on the side keys will be reinforced (say horizontal and vertical lines). In the example given a response to the horizontal lines would be reinforced. If vertical lines had appeared in the center key, a response to the vertical lines on the side key would be reinforced. If the stimulus on the center key is removed sometimes before the stimuli on the side keys are presented, the procedure is called delayed matching to sample.

A popular theory, two-process theory, suggests that instrumental performance is regulated by Pavlovian processes which necessarily occur in instrumental situations. A variety of procedures have been employed to test this view. In concurrent measurement investigations, both Pavlovian and instrumental reactions are measured, i.e., salivation (the Pavlovian) and bar pressing for food (the instrumental) may be measured simultaneously. A most popular technique for measuring fear is the conditioned emotional response or conditioned suppression procedure. Rats may first be trained to press a bar for food (instrumental phase). Subsequently, a CS may be presented for say one or two minutes followed by shock (Pavlovian phase). Decreased bar pressing when the tone is present rather than absent indicates that the rat fears the tone.

Many instrumental procedures may be modified to study higher level or cognitive processes. One example is matching to sample. After an animal has mastered a first matching problem it may then be given an entirely new one. If the animal learned only specific associations in the first problem (peck green on the side key if the center key was green, and blue if it was blue) it should not show lots of transfer on the second different problem. However, if the animal learned some general principle in the first problem (peck the stimulus on the side key which matches that which occurred on the center key) it should show lots of transfer on the new problem.

Another example of modifying an instrumental procedure to study a complex process is supplied by concept learning. Concept learning investigations are actually fairly complicated discriminated learning investigations. In one procedure a pigeon may be trained to peck a key when a photograph is presented. If the photograph is that of, say, a flower, the pigeon may be reinforced with food for pecking. Pecks to other photographs are not reinforced. With training the pigeon may come to peck at a high rate when a photograph of a flower is presented but at a low rate whenever some other photograph is presented. Of course, even though many photographs are presented in such investigations, it is possible that the pigeon solves the problem by memorizing which photographs lead to reinforcement and which do not. A finding which renders that interpretation unlikely is that pigeons are able to respond correctly to novel photographs. Employing the general procedure described above, animal concept learning investigations have tested many of the same hypotheses in human concept learning investigations.

Bibliography

Darwin, C. (1871). *The descent of man, and selection in relation to sex.* London: John Murray.

Domjan, M. (1998). *The principles of learning and behavior* (4th ed.) Pacific Grove, CA: Brooks/Cole.

Morgan, C. L. (1906). *An introduction to comparative psychology.* London: Walter Scott.

Tarpy, R. M. (1997). *Contemporary learning theory and research.* New York: McGraw-Hill.

E. John Capaldi

ANIMAL SUBJECTS. *See* Ethics, *article on* Ethics in Research.

ANOREXIA. Descriptions of what is now termed *anorexia nervosa* can be found in the literature of Western civilization over the centuries. One of the most notable descriptions of the disorder was of Saint Catherine of Siena, who restricted her eating and became severely emaciated. She used a reed to induce vomiting following a binge, and also made use of herbal cathartics for purging. Anorexia nervosa is characterized by an intense fear of gaining weight, marked restriction of dietary intake, excessive exercise, and weight loss often to the point of emaciation. Technically, anorexia nervosa is diagnosed when an individual is 15% or more below ideal body weight and meets the remaining criteria for diagnosis. The disorder is accompanied by a distorted perception regarding body weight and shape with individuals feeling fat, or that specific parts of their bodies are fat, despite evidence to the contrary. In females, amenorrhea may occur relatively early in the disorder before large amounts of weight have been lost. These patients usually develop obsessional thinking about food, may have irrational food rules, e.g., only eating certain types of food, usually vegetables and fruits, and may also develop rituals around eating: They may chew food a certain number of times before swallowing or cut food into small pieces before eating. Patients may also surreptitiously throw away food, giving the impression that they are eating more than they actually are. Denial of the severity of their illness is common, as is refusal to seek treatment. Two subtypes of the disorder are recognized: a restricting type in which the individual does not engage in binge eating or purging, and a binge eating/purging type in which the individual regularly engages in binge eating and purging such as inducing vomiting, or misusing laxatives or diuretics. About half of all patients with anorexia nervosa are pure restrictors, while the remaining half are purgers, although some studies suggest that the proportion of purging anorexics is increasing. Only about 5% of patients with anorexia nervosa are male.

It is not uncommon for anorexia to begin following a period of mild weight gain, which has provoked critical comments from a parent, teacher, or coach, and results in the onset of dieting. In other cases, a stressful event may be the precipitant. Populations at particular risk of developing the disorder include: athletes, ballet dancers, and those from the higher social classes. These populations share a demand for high performance coupled with a high demand to maintain a thin body shape. However, the disorder is now seen in all social classes and in all ethnic groups.

From a physiologic viewpoint, the body reacts to the starvation induced by anorexia nervosa by conserving many functions. Hence, the abnormal physical findings associated with starvation are also found in cases of anorexia nervosa and most of these findings normalize when patients regain their ideal body weight. In addition to marked emaciation, physical examination reveals dry skin that may be covered with fine body hair, (lanugo), cold and blue hands and feet, a slow pulse rate, and low blood pressure. Hair tends to be thin and patients often complain that their hair is falling out. Stomach emptying is slow, leading to complaints of gastric distress following eating. Because of the poor nutrition, bone density is reduced and fractures of long bones or of the vertebrae may occur as a result of the osteoporosis. Thinking may be impaired, with difficulty in concentrating, poor memory, and poor judgment.

Both anemia (too few red blood cells) and leukopenia (too few white blood cells) are common, and cholesterol levels are often elevated. A variety of hormonal measures are abnormal suggesting hypothalamic dysfunction in response to starvation. Among the more serious medical complications seen in anorexia nervosa are those affecting the cardiovascular system. Cardiac arrhythmias may occur secondary to both the starvation and low levels of potassium consequent on purging, and these abnormalities may lead to the sudden deaths occasionally seen in the low-weight bulimic anorexic.

From a psychosocial viewpoint individuals with anorexia nervosa are often high achievers who are markedly perfectionistic. The disorder is accompanied by social withdrawal, restricted interpersonal relationships, and often an avoidance of heterosocial relationships. It has been suggested that the disorder is a faulty way of coping, by avoidance, with the new and anxiety provoking interpersonal demands that emerge in adolescence. The emaciation to some extent protects the individual against the anxiety engendered by heterosocial relationships by returning the young woman to a more asexual form. From a developmental viewpoint, the illness if long lasting will deprive individuals of the normal learning that occurs in adolescence about the handling of interpersonal relationships, leading to deficits in interpersonal behavior that may be long lasting, hence impeding full recovery from the disorder. Moreover, formal education is often impaired by the illness, lowering the opportunities for career advancement. Anorexia nervosa is also associated with much psychological comorbidity. Persons with this disorder have higher rates of major depression, anxiety disorders including obsessive-compulsive disorder and social phobia, and personality disorder, than are found in the general population.

Since there are no disorders with a similar symptom pattern to anorexia nervosa diagnosis of the fully developed syndrome is highly reliable. In the early stages of the disorder, before marked weight loss has occurred, diagnosis is more difficult since the various causes for weight loss will often need to be investigated, particularly if the patient denies concerns about body shape and weight. The subclassification into restrictor and purger types also appears reasonable. Studies have shown that certain characteristics differ between the two types. For example, patients classified as nonrestrictor types tend to be more impulsive, have more experience with sexual relationships, and use alcohol and drugs more frequently than the pure restrictors.

Frequency and Course of the Disorder

Anorexia nervosa is a relatively rare disorder with an incidence of about 5 cases per 100,000 population, and because it is a chronic disorder, a much higher prevalence rate of between 250 and 500 per 100,000 (0.25 to 0.5%). There is evidence from a number of studies in several countries that both the incidence and prevalence of this disorder among young women is increasing, possibly doubling during the last 30 years. However, the results of these studies must be viewed with some caution because of the varying definitions of anorexia nervosa used between studies and over time, and differing methods of case finding.

Anorexia nervosa usually begins in adolescence with the greatest number of cases presenting in two peaks at 14 and 18 years of age. Less commonly, the disorder may begin in childhood or early adult life. It is likely that a proportion of cases are relatively mild and such individuals may recover without treatment. For cases receiving treatment, long-term follow-up studies reveal that anorexia nervosa is usually a chronic disorder with death rates between 5 and 15% depending on the length of follow-up. About half the deaths are due to suicide, presumably due to the association between depression and anorexia nervosa, while the remainder are due to medical complications associated with malnutrition. Follow-up studies suggest that between 40 and 50% of cases will completely recover over a 10-year period. The remaining individuals continue to have an eating disorder, most frequently low-weight clinical or subclinical bulimia nervosa.

Treatment

The relative rarity of new cases, combined with the reluctance of anorexics to seek treatment, has retarded research into the treatment of anorexia nervosa, as compared for example, with the more commonly occurring eating disorder bulimia nervosa. Cases involving considerable weight loss and/or medical complications require hospitalization. The usual inpatient approach to treatment has been to remediate any physiologic problems and focus on weight gain, preferably a gain up to 90% or more of ideal body weight. Such treatment may span many weeks since the average weight gain for inpatient treatment is about 1.5 kg per week. Factors demonstrated effective in controlled studies include serving large meals, providing feedback on caloric intake and weight gain, and using simple reinforcement procedures to motivate weight gain such as making access to certain desirable activities contingent on a certain rate of weight gain. In the later phases of treatment, family therapy is often used to prepare the patient and family for return to home. Despite a relatively large number of controlled studies of different medications, there is no evidence that pharmacologic approaches are useful in the inpatient phase of treatment, except to treat comorbid psychopathology such as an anxiety disorder or severe depression. Although the majority of patients regain weight within such inpatient treatment programs, relapse rates are high. There is some evidence that anorexics may require a larger number of calories to maintain their weight than would be predicted for their body size, a factor that may lead to relapse. Predictors of poor outcome from treatment include a late onset of the disorder, longer duration of illness, and disturbed relationships between the anorexic and their family.

The advent of managed care has resulted in a considerable reduction of inpatient services to the patient with anorexia nervosa in many parts of the United States, often only providing for physiologic stabilization of the patient in a relatively brief hospital stay. This has put increased emphasis upon partial hospitalization programs and outpatient care. Partial hospitalization, sometimes termed day-care, usually involves treating the patient for a whole day, five days a week. Group therapy is usually the primary mode of treatment together with nutritional counseling and the serving of adequate meals in the day-care setting. Anorexics usually gain to within the lower limits of the population norms of weight at about one-fifth the cost of inpatient care.

Unfortunately, few controlled studies of the outpatient management of anorexia nervosa have appeared to date. One study suggested that outpatient psychotherapy, either individual or group, may be as effective as inpatient care for the anorexic. Another set of studies suggested that a particular form of family therapy was more effective than individual therapy, but only for patients with an early onset and short duration of the disorder. Preliminary studies also suggest that fluoxetine (Prozac), a serotonin reuptake inhibitor, may be useful in helping patients maintain their weight gains.

Continued research on the biological and psychological determinants of anorexia nervosa is essential both to our increased understanding of this disorder and to enhance the effectiveness of current treatments. One factor retarding controlled treatment studies is the relative rarity of the disorder, and the ambivalence of the anorexia nervosa patient about treatment, leading to high dropout rates from treatment studies, making assessment of the efficacy of treatment difficult.

Social Impact

Anorexia nervosa is a chronic disabling disorder with usual onset in adolescence. Although affecting a relatively small number of individuals, as compared with the other eating disorders, it can be severely disabling, affecting physical and emotional health, as well as lifespan. Reproductive potential is also lessened in the young women who suffer from this disorder. Moreover, education may be deleteriously affected by the disorder and work potential may be reduced, so for a small minority of women the social impact of this disorder is high.

[*See also* Eating Disorders.]

Bibliography

Bell, R. (1985). *Holy anorexia.* Chicago: University of Chicago Press. An interesting account of medieval cases of anorexia nervosa in convents.

Bruch, H. (1978). *The golden cage: The enigma of anorexia nervosa.* Cambridge, MA. Harvard University Press. A classic account of the psychological features of anorexia nervosa.

Brownell, K. D., & Fairburn, C. G. (Eds.). (1995). *Eating disorders and obesity: A comprehensive handbook.* New York: Guildford Press. Excellent short chapters reviewing the etiology, symptoms, complications, and treatment of the eating disorders.

Halmi, K. A. (1994). Eating disorders: Anorexia nervosa, bulimia nervosa, and obesity. In Hales, R. E., Yudofsky, S. C., & Talbott, J. A. *Textbook of psychiatry* (2nd ed.). Washington, DC: American Psychiatric Press. An excellent description of the syndrome of anorexia nervosa.

Hsu, L. K. G. (1988). The outcome of anorexia nervosa: A reappraisal. *Psychological Medicine, 18,* 807–812. A review of long-term outcome studies of anorexia nervosa.

Jones, D., Fox, M. M., & Babigian, H. M. (1980). Epidemiology of anorexia nervosa in Monroe County, NY, 1960–1976. *Psychosomatic Medicine, 42,* 551–558. Evidence for the increase in incidence of anorexia nervosa.

Szmukler, G. I., & Dare, C. (1991) The Maudsley study of family therapy in anorexia nervosa. In D. B. Woodside, & N. Shekter-Wolfson (Eds.), *Family approaches in the treatment of eating disorders.* Washington, DC: American Psychiatric Press. A detailed account of research using family therapy in anorexia nervosa.

Weltzin, T. E., Fernstrom, M. H., Hansen, D., McConaha, C., & Kaye, W. H. (1991). Abnormal caloric requirements for weight maintenance in patients with anorexia nervosa and bulimia nervosa. *American Journal of Psychiatry, 148,* 1675–1682. A study suggesting that restrictor anorexics require a larger caloric intake to maintain weight than bulimic anorexics.

W. Stewart Agras

ANTHROPOLOGY. As a discipline, anthropology is concerned with the varied spatiotemporal manifestations of the human species. Four subdisciplines of the field are conventionally recognized: biological anthropology, archaeology, linguistic anthropology, and sociocultural anthropology.

Biological anthropology focuses primarily on two types of questions, those relating to human paleontology and the emergence in the fossil record of prehumans, humans, and their near relatives; and those relating to the study of primates. This subfield, like most others within anthropology, converges in several places with the interests and goals of psychologists, especially those who are working within a Darwinian or neo-Darwinian paradigm. Compatible research agendas can be found in such areas as evolutionary psychology, the evolution of language, primate cognition, language learning in chimpanzees, and developmental comparisons between chimpanzees and young children.

The study of race, until the 1950s a third leg of biological anthropology, essentially disappeared within the subdiscipline as ongoing analyses revealed greater variation within than between breeding populations, significant intermixing of many breeding groups, and overlapping distributions of gene frequencies among groups so-named as the macroraces, *Caucasoid, Mongoloid*, and *Negroid*. But within psychology, the category of race tends to be used unquestioningly (see *Publication Manual of the American Psychological Association*, 4th ed., Washington, D.C., 1994), and nearly half of a sample of 600 specialists in intelligence testing expressed the belief that the Black-White IQ differential was attributable, at least in part, to genetic factors (Mark Snyderman and Stanley Rothman, "Survey of expert opinion on intelligence and aptitude testing," *American Psychologist*, 1987, 42, 137–144).

In archaeology, focus on reconstruction of the customs of past peoples is supplemented by an interest in the processes involved in cultural change. Some of these processes appear to be related to organizational requirements; for example, the tendency for early city-states to exert political and military control over broad areas, with accompanying trade benefits, technological specialization, and social stability and stratification. But along with this adaptational emphasis, there has been a recent attempt to understand some of the characteristics of early Mexican civilization as a consequence of individual actions of forceful, charismatic leaders (Joyce Marcus and Kent V. Flannery, *How Urban Society Evolved in Mexico's Oaxaca Valley*, New York, 1996). In this interpretation, the self-serving behavior of certain leaders, in trying to advance their positions, created changes ranging from the material to political power to ideologies that attributed a supernatural ancestry to them and subsequently to their descendants. Periods of relative stability would typically follow on the rapid changes instigated by these leaders. The similarity of stage sequences among ancient civilizations, and the possible contributions to that similarity by individual motivational and cognitive factors, would seem to offer a challenge in which psychologists can usefully aid the efforts of archaeologists.

Linguistic anthropology and psychology are both closely allied with the discipline of linguistics, but at different points of contact. It is in the use of comparative language data that anthropology meets linguistics, and in neuroscience and related areas that psychology and linguistics find common ground. The arena of study for linguistic anthropology is natural languages—their phonological and grammatical structures, semantic systems, and contexts and uses. In psychology, occasional use of cross-language data is only found in the field of human development. Differences in approach between anthropology and psychology are seen in topics treated by both disciplines. In studies of language acquisition, anthropologists attend to the interaction between linguistic factors and the cultural context, whereas psychologists more often investigate the effects of intralinguistic factors like prosodic and phonological information. In studies of language use, anthropological questions revolve around issues such as linguistic relativity, language and ethnic/national borders, and religious or legal language, while those in psychology deal with problems like verbal learning and memory, comprehension of the sentence, and understanding of the written text. As the examples indicate, a molar-molecular distinction characterizes the differences in approach between the two fields.

Anthropology's molar-level emphasis, reflecting its macro-order analyses and main concern with natural communities (or groups) rather than individuals, is all the more salient in the largest of the subdisciplines, sociocultural anthropology. Thus the typical themes and topics are institutional; for example, cities, consumption and commodities, colonialism, nongovernmental organizations (NGOs), and refugees and exile. Also included in this category are specialties like anthropology of education, economic anthropology, kinship, and medical anthropology. Despite long-term goals of comparison and generalization, the norm continues to be the case study—of a culture group, community, or subgroup. In recent decades, as remote sites have begun exhibiting the effects of significant contact with the urban-industrial world, and as research authorization has become problematic in many areas, sociocultural anthropologists have turned increasingly to the investigation of plural societies and complex urban groups, and to the study of businesspeople, physicists, street children, urban witches, and National Science Foundation panels. The preferred methodological stance remains that of the single investigator pursuing a problem by means of intensive fieldwork, but archival materials are widely used as well, and some researchers now employ systematic observations, tests, and instrumentation (e.g., assessment of energy expenditure with calorimeters, and of internal responses to social stimuli with measures of cardiovascular reactivity and salivary cortisol).

A schism exists between sociocultural anthropology's positivist scientific branch, which tends to be generalizing and comparative, and its other major sections, which may be characterized as interpretive (usually particularistic, with emphasis on the cultural-historical context and the contingent status of knowledge) and advocative (emphasis on furthering of political agendas). Studies within a specialty like medical anthropology might produce the following varied angles of attack in the study of, say, nursing homes: for the scientific, how socioeconomic status (SES) and education may affect adaptation to a nursing-home regimen or how cultural values may affect the organization of nursing homes in different societies; for the interpretive, how patients' personal narratives might yield rich raw materials for analysis, how the definition of the interviewer's role might affect patients' responses to questions, or how variables beyond SES and education might be brought to bear in understanding patients' adjustments; for *advocacy*, how the treatment of those in nursing homes exemplifies our modern practice of everyday violence, of "small wars" against the powerless, and how we must be sensitive to these capacities in ourselves and fight against them. These differing perspectives employ varied methodologies, and their viewpoints and outcomes, though not in principle incommensurable, are seldom synthesized.

Psychological Anthropology

Constructs like "identity," "self-representation," and "personhood" abound within sociocultural anthropology generally, but such terms are typically applied to culture groups rather than to individuals. More familiar to psychologists would be the concepts and analyses used in the specialty labeled psychological anthropology, which in broadest form explores the relationships between psychological phenomena and their social and cultural contexts. Some of the primary theoretical orientations in psychological anthropology follow more or less closely on traditional perspectives in psychology, but others diverge radically and claim a central and essential place for cultural content and process in trying to account for psychological functioning. Among the former are general behavioral theory (including many standard conceptualizations from developmental and social psychology and personality theory), cognitive anthropology, evolutionary thought, and psychoanalytic approaches; and among the latter are cultural psychology, the closely related activity theory, and ethnopsychology.

General behavioral theory research in psychological anthropology has primarily involved attempts to refine and extend hypotheses and formulations established in the European American tradition. This type of research marks the one orientation often devoted to sets of programmatic studies or to studies with multiple society samples. In socialization and child development, for example, comparative inquiries have assessed the variability of ecocultural niches and parents' cultural belief systems, and have endeavored to measure their effects on child health and developmental outcomes. Others have looked for and found regularities mirroring results from Western research, such as the more frequent expression of aggression among boys than girls, or the behavioral and psychological effects on males of early father absence. In social-psychological inquiry, the consistent and pervasive in-group favoritism discovered in Western samples has been confirmed cross-culturally, and the frequently found two-dimensional structure of social behavior labeled "status/solidarity" has been shown cross-culturally in parallel form among personality trait descriptors. Cognitive approaches also have often meshed with Western psychological research, as in the finding that on a worldwide basis, difficult-to-

learn "disjunctive" kin terminologies for siblings occur in only 2% of societies.

Psychological-Evolutionary. The evolutionary and psychoanalytic ideas pursued by psychological anthropologists (and by some psychologists) are largely outside the mainstream of psychological thought. A fundamental assumption in much psychological-evolutionary thinking is that specific traits and abilities reflect past not present adaptiveness, but that testable hypotheses can be constructed based on suppositions about early human adaptive problems. The resulting research questions relate to survival and reproduction issues, including genetic relatedness and preferential treatment, and differential male-female reproductive strategies. Although this research is usually well designed, and the findings consistent with hypotheses, often the same predictions could have been derived from other theoretical sources. A related area, biocultural inquiry, is interested in integration of physical and cultural dimensions, as in the consequences for child health of inevitable trade-offs between adult mating effort and parenting effort.

Psychoanalytic Anthropology. Psychoanalytic anthropology is wide ranging in its concerns: methodologically, in an argument for adoption of the "empathic method" in fieldwork, much as used in the clinical psychoanalytic interview; epistemically, in the claim that the anthropological material of description and interpretation is *mutually* constructed by psychoanalytic anthropologists and the people with whom they work; substantively, in the analysis of what are termed *psychosocial adaptations* (as in resolution of individual conflict by means of cultural institutions), or of Oedipal-type folktales, which are ubiquitous cross-culturally, yet appear in more disguised or repressed form in stratified societies than in simpler ones (Allen W. Johnson and Douglass Price-Williams, *Oedipus Ubiquitous*, Stanford, Calif., 1996).

Cultural Psychology

A more radical orientation like cultural psychology argues that mind is content driven, that mind is variable across cultures because cultural forms are variable, and that mind cannot be separated from its specific culture-historical determinants. Activity theory likewise rejects the notion of the psychic unity of humankind, but places less emphasis on analysis of "mental representations" as revealed in language and discourse, and more on the grounding of concepts, both psychological and cultural, in socially organized activities. Both cultural psychology and activity theory are built upon early theorizing by Lev Vygotsky, Alexander Luria, and other European psychologists who took as fundamental the proposition that mental activity is inspired by practical social activity. This approach has been used to study decision making and problem solving in natural settings and to analyze cognitive processes like memory.

Ethnopsychology

The study of indigenous models of persons, selves, and experiences, ethnopsychology takes as problematic the Western psychology-based conceptions of these terms. It asserts, for example, that the concept of personality, so central to Western and social-scientific thought, is a culture-bound concept based in individual-centered theorizing, and that in some other societies the person descriptions refer almost entirely to *inter*personal behavior. Similar arguments are made with respect to phenomena like emotions, the self, mental illness, and altered states of consciousness. Against these claims, there exists within psychological anthropology a set of counterpositions usually based upon the existence of human commonalities, that is, species-wide biopsychological regularities.

The Profession of Anthropology

As a profession, anthropology is relatively small, with the total number of active anthropologists worldwide at about 20,000, and more than half of them in the United States. During the second half of the twentieth century the profession grew markedly from tiny beginnings, and American academic programs in anthropology now turn out more than 400 Ph.D.s and 8,000 B.A. degrees annually compared with 22 and 352, respectively, in 1950. As with psychology, the majority of U.S. doctorates are now awarded to females (versus one third in the early 1970s). Besides the gender shift, another important change in the profession is a movement away from the academic setting for employment. In the late 1990s, approximately one third of new U.S. Ph.D.s in anthropology took nonacademic jobs (in the private sector, government, museums, and research institutes), while in the 1970s only one eighth had done so.

[See also Cross-Cultural Psychology; *and* Cultural Psychology.]

Bibliography

Bock, P. K. (Ed.). (1994). *Handbook of psychological anthropology*. Westport, CT: Greenwood Press. Overview of the major research traditions in psychological anthropology (for example, cognitive anthropology, culture and personality), and of lines of evidence and methodological approaches.

Coe, M. D. (1992). *Breaking the Maya code*. New York: Thames & Hudson. An account of the 50-year-long decipherment of Classic Maya texts, which were earlier thought to be linguistically impenetrable.

Duranti, A. (1997). *Linguistic anthropology*. Cambridge, U.K.: Cambridge University Press.

Ember, C. R., & Ember, M. (1996). *Anthropology* (8th ed.). Upper Saddle River, NJ: Prentice Hall. A standard textbook, with more coverage of biological anthropology, archaeology, and sociocultural anthropology than of linguistic anthropology.

Farmer, P. (1992). *Aids and accusation: Haiti and the geography of blame*. Berkeley: University of California Press. Analyzes AIDS in Haiti in terms of social conditions and political aspects.

Geertz, C. (1973). *The interpretation of cultures*. New York: Basic Books. *Locus classicus* of the interpretive social-science alternative to the positivistic social sciences.

Hutchins, E. (1995). *Cognition in the wild*. Cambridge, MA: MIT Press. Analysis of shipboard navigation. Focuses on the ways human cognition (outside the laboratory) is socially distributed and shaped by culturally constituted activities.

Levinson, D., & Ember, M. (Eds.). (1996). *Encyclopedia of cultural anthropology* (4 vols.). New York: Holt.

Schwartz, T., White, G. M., & Lutz, C. A. (Eds.). (1992). *New directions in psychological anthropology*. Cambridge, UK: Cambridge University Press. Covers cognition, learning, psychiatry, psychoanalysis, and biosocial approaches from the vantage points of psychological anthropology.

Shore, B. (1996). *Culture in mind*. New York: Oxford University Press. Argues that culture must be considered an intrinsic component of the human mind, that an "ethnographic" conception of the mind is necessary.

Suárez-Orozco, M. M., Spindler, G., & Spindler, L. (Eds.). (1994). *The making of psychological anthropology II*. Ft. Worth, TX: Harcourt Brace. Provides a format for leading figures in psychological anthropology to discuss their intellectual careers, including relevant personal background.

Wolf, E. R. (1982). *Europe and the people without history*. Berkeley: University of California Press. Makes the case that the tribal peoples of the world cannot be understood in isolation but only in relation to emerging (European) capitalist production over the past four hundred years.

Wrangham, R., & Peterson, D. (1996). *Demonic males. Apes and the origins of human violence*. Boston: Houghton Mifflin. Treats aggression from the perspectives of evolutionary biology and primatology.

Robert L. Munroe

ANTHROPOMETRY is the measurement of human morphology, a set of quantitative techniques to characterize body form and structure. Traditional anthropometric data include measurements such as height, length, breadth, depth, and circumference that describe the size and proportions of the body and its parts. In contemporary usage, anthropometry may also include functional measurements such as muscle forces, range of motion in joints, body surface areas, volume, and mass distribution properties.

Anthropometric techniques, while inherently descriptive, are widely applied in the biological, medical, forensic, and engineering sciences. Human biologists, nutritionists, and epidemiologists use anthropometry to assess growth and development, nutritional status, and general health of individuals and populations. Medical geneticists, physicians, and surgeons use anthropometry to classify and diagnose developmental abnormalities, and to create plans for surgical repair and reconstruction of both developmental anomalies and traumatic injuries. Forensic specialists in the medical, engineering, and law enforcement communities utilize anthropometric data to help identify unknown persons, to develop age progression drawings of missing children, and in accident reconstructions. In the exercise sciences, anthropometry is used to assess individual fitness and athletic potential, to guide the physical training of amateur and professional athletes, and to measure the results obtained from various training regimens.

Anthropometry is also used extensively by ergonomists, engineering psychologists, and engineers in the automobile, aerospace, industrial hygiene, apparel, and recreational equipment industries to ensure that products fit their intended users in a safe, comfortable, and efficient manner. Anthropometric data influence design concepts, sizing, and adjustability decisions at the outset of the engineering process; they ensure the biofidelity of computerized human models used in computer-aided design and virtual prototype testing; and they inform the selection of human test subjects and/or specifications for instrumented manikins used in system validations. Engineering anthropometry plays a particularly important role in the design and sizing of military matériel such as uniforms, protective clothing, body armor, helmets, armored vehicles, and aircraft. Unlike commercial manufacturers, whose products by design often fit a narrowly defined market segment, the military must equip 90% or more of its personnel with little or no customized fitting. In the U.S. military, this means designing systems that fit the body shapes and sizes of both genders and a virtual melting pot of ethnic origins.

Anthropometric variables are defined, measured, and analyzed in different ways depending upon their intended application. Biacromial breadth and bideltoid breadth, for example, are both shoulder widths. However, the anatomical locations of the measurements differ such that biacromial breadth measures skeletal frame size for growth and fitness studies, and bideltoid breadth measures maximum clearance for engineering

applications. Anthropometric measuring devices range from simple tools such as calipers and tape measures that measure the body directly, to complex systems such as laser scanners and magnetic resonance imaging that electronically digitize hundreds of thousands of points from which measurements can later be calculated. Regardless of application or data acquisition technique, however, all anthropometric measurements share a need to be carefully defined (standardized) in relation to anatomical landmarks, subject clothing and body positions, and instrumentation so that measurement differences among subjects reflect actual morphological variation rather than artifacts of technique differences.

Anthropometric data are generally analyzed with one of several purposes in mind: describing morphological variation in a population of interest; comparing individuals against some reference standard or classification scheme; predicting the most likely value of one dimension from another; and predicting the anthropometry of individuals or populations at some future period. Cross-sectional studies (standardized measurements made at one particular point in time on different subjects) are often conducted on national populations, schoolchildren, occupational groups, or individuals with a particular medical condition or physical disability in order to establish the ranges of size and shape variability characteristic of the group. Univariate statistics that indicate the range (minimum, maximum), central tendency (mean, median, or mode), and distribution (e.g., 5th and 95th percentiles) of each measurement are usually reported in cross-sectional studies. Most applications, however, require the simultaneous consideration of several body measurements or indices, so multivariate statistical analyses are also commonly conducted on cross-sectional data: principal components analysis to identify the primary sources of variation in a group; regression and linear models to characterize the quantitative relationships between body parts for predictive purposes, and cluster analysis and discriminate functions to identify subgroups with common size and shape and to create anthropometric algorithms for classifying individuals.

Longitudinal studies (standardized measurements on the same subjects at different points in time) are used to quantify individual and group body size and shape changes due to the growth, aging, secular trends, medical interventions, and physical training. Linear models that quantify the relationships between body measurements and age, for example, are used to establish normative standards for growth. Statistical models that relate age-specific body measurements to year of birth are a special case of cross-sectional data analyzed longitudinally in order to quantify secular trends in body size and predict future body size distributions.

Bibliography

Beunen, G., & Borms, J. (1990). Kinanthropometry: Roots, developments, and future. *Journal of Sports Sciences, 8,* 1–15.

Gordon, C. C., Bradtmiller, B., Churchill, T., Clauser, C. E., McConville, J. T., Tebbetts, I., & Walker, R. A. (1989). *1988 anthropometric survey of U.S. army personnel: Methods and summary statistics.* NATICK/TR-89/044. Natick, MA: U.S. Army Natick Research, Development, & Engineering Center. (AD A209 600). Includes protocols, illustrations, and statistics for two hundred and sixty body dimensions; appendices address observer error, applications, and comparability to other surveys.

Himes, J. A. (Ed.). (1991). *Anthropometric assessment of nutritional status.* New York: Wiley-Liss. Twenty-four chapters cover theory and research methods, maternal/fetal outcomes, malnutrition, growth monitoring, national nutritional surveys, and management of the obese, elderly, and ill.

Kolar, J. C., & Salter, E. M. (1996). *Craniofacial anthropometry: Practical measurement of the head and face for clinical, surgical and research use.* Springfield, IL: Charles C. Thomas.

Kroemer, K. H. E. (1989). Engineering anthropometry. *Ergonomics, 32,* 767–784. A comprehensive and concise review, authored by a leading expert in the field.

Lohman, T. G., Roche, A. F., & Martorell, R. (1988). *Anthropometric standardization reference manual.* Champaign, IL: Human Kinetics Books. Detailed protocols are given for forty body dimensions, including their purposes, reliability, and sources of comparative data. Brief overviews of anthropometry in physical anthropology, growth, body composition, obesity, cardiovascular disease, cancer, and sports medicine are also included.

Malina, R. M., & Bouchard, C. (1991). *Growth, maturation, and physical activity.* Champaign, IL: Human Kinetics Books. Written at the graduate level, this excellent textbook is noteworthy for its extensive bibliographic references and suggested readings.

Pheasant, S. (1996). *Bodyspace: Anthropometry, ergonomics, and the design of work* (2nd ed.). Bristol, UK: Taylor & Francis. A leading graduate textbook with practical discussion of anthropometric methods, work and living space design, and accident and injury prevention. Comparative data on adults from eleven nations and extensive comparative data on British children are included.

Rathbun, T. A. & Buikstra, J. E. (Eds.). (1984). *Human identification: Case studies in forensic anthropology.* Springfield, IL: Charles C. Thomas. Thirty case studies provide a particularly broad overview of how anthropometry is used in forensic studies and courtrooms. For more recent case studies, consult the *Journal of Forensic Sciences.*

Roebuck, J. A. (1995). *Anthropometric methods: Designing to fit the human body.* Santa Monica, CA: Human Factors and Ergonomics Society. Intended for use by practitioners and graduate students of human factors/human engineering, this monograph addresses engineering anthropometry for workstations and clothing design.

Ulijaszek, S. J., & Mascie-Taylor, C. G. N. (Eds.). (1994). *Anthropometry: The individual and the population.* Cambridge, UK: Cambridge University Press. Twelve invited chapters by leading scholars address statistical issues and research methods for growth monitoring and health surveillance, physical performance, strength and fitness, and military applications.

Claire C. Gordon

ANTIANXIETY MEDICATION. The pharmacopoeia for anxiety disorders includes agents traditionally used as antidepressants—tricyclic antidepressants, serotonin selective reuptake inhibitors (SSRIs), and monoamine oxidase inhibitors (MAOIs)—as well as benzodiazepines, buspirone, and beta-blockers. Although the antidepressants and benzodiazepines tend to be broadly effective for a range of anxiety disorders, assessment of their relative efficacy and appropriateness in clinical practice is specific to the anxiety disorder under treatment, associated comorbid conditions, and medication-related side effects.

Treatment Overview

For *panic disorder*, treatment is often initiated with SSRIs, benzodiazepines, or a combination. Tricyclic antidepressants and MAOIs are also effective for panic disorder, but are not usually considered to be first-line agents because of their less favorable side-effect profiles. For *social phobia*, MAOIs have long been the treatment of choice, but the efficacy of the SSRIs, and the positive performance of benzodiazepines in recent trials, may well eclipse the use of the less tolerable MAOIs. *Generalized anxiety disorder* (GAD) has long been the domain of benzodiazepine treatment, but controlled trials also support the efficacy of tricyclic antidepressants and buspirone, and clinical experience suggests that the SSRIs also may be effective, although there is little controlled data at present. Newer antidepressants, such as venlafaxine, nefazadone, and mirtazapine are also likely to be applied to any of the above anxiety disorders.

For *obsessive-compulsive disorder* (OCD), serotonin selective antidepressants (including clomipramine and the SSRIs) have consistently received empirical support, and are considered first-line agents. At times, benzodiazepines may be combined with these agents to provide additional control of anxiety symptoms. Studies of *posttraumatic stress disorder* (PTSD) have lagged behind those for other anxiety disorders, and case reports of pharmacotherapy for PTSD have often targeted individual and sometimes comorbid symptoms. Recent findings support the efficacy of antidepressants, particularly more serotonergic agents, for treating the core symptoms of PTSD, and further application of these agents can be expected in the future. Treatment of *specific phobias* is traditionally viewed as the domain of behavior therapy, although benzodiazepines are frequently applied to aid coping with occasionally encountered phobic events.

Although effective for a range of anxiety disorders, treatment benefit from pharmacotherapy tends to be maintained only when medication use is continued. Because cessation of pharmacotherapy is associated with relapse unless alternative treatment is instituted, at least as much care needs to be taken in planning medication discontinuation as medication initiation. For any of the anxiety disorders, the prescribing clinician may choose to combine agents (commonly, antidepressants and benzodiazepines) in an attempt to boost efficacy. In addition, there is evidence that exposure-based interventions (e.g., stepwise exposure assignments for patients with agoraphobia) or full cognitive-behavior therapy (CBT) packages can improve outcome and extend treatment gains for pharmacotherapy. Characteristics of each class of agents are discussed below.

Serotonergic Antidepressants

Serotonergic selective agents have received particular attention in the treatment of panic disorder and obsessive-compulsive disorder. In panic disorder, the serotonin selective reuptake inhibitors (SSRIs), including fluoxetine, sertraline, paroxetine, and fluvoxamine emerged in the 1990s as first-line agents, in part because of their favorable side-effect profile, broad spectrum of efficacy, and lack of a specific potential for abuse or dependence. The use of SSRIs for panic disorder preceded the emergence of the supportive data from controlled clinical trials; these data are now available. The favorable side-effect profile and emerging evidence of efficacy encouraged the application of SSRIs for social phobia as well.

Typical target doses for panic disorder range from 10 to 40 mg/day for fluoxetine, 20 to 60 mg/day for paroxetine, and 50 to 200 mg/day for sertraline. Initiation of treatment with antidepressants may be associated with jitteriness and increased anxiety, which can be minimized by initiating treatment with SSRI doses less than half of target doses (e.g., 5–10 mg/day for fluoxetine or 10 mg/day for paroxetine). Minimization of this side effect is especially important in the treatment of panic disorder, a disorder characterized by marked fears of the somatic sensations of anxiety. In general, antidepressants may take at least two to three weeks to start demonstrating efficacy. In clinical practice, SSRIs are frequently combined with benzodiazepines, as part of a strategy to provide earlier relief from symptoms and minimize the anxiogenic side effects of the SSRIs. SSRIs are generally better tolerated than the older agents, e.g., tricyclics, but are associated with nausea or other gastrointestinal symptoms, sexual dysfunction, headaches, and apathy. SSRIs are frequently prescribed for morning use, because of occasional associated sleep disturbance, but nighttime dosing is not unusual.

Serotonin selective agents, also including the tricyclic, clomipramine, have received particular attention in OCD where they are considered to have antianxiety, antiphobic, and antiobsessional actions. Compared to panic disorder, higher doses of medications are frequently applied in OCD, although there is limited controlled data supporting this practice. Clomipramine may be given in dosages up to 250 mg/day, fluoxetine, up to 80 mg/day; fluvoxamine, up to 300 mg/day; paroxetine, up to 60 mg/day; and sertraline, up to 200 mg/day.

The SSRIs have been applied only recently to the treatment of PTSD. Data from initial studies have examined primarily fluoxetine, and supports the efficacy of this agent. There is some evidence that higher doses (e.g., 60 mg/day of fluoxetine) may be more effective.

Tricyclic Antidepressants

Perhaps the best established agent for the treatment of panic disorder is the tricyclic antidepressant, imipramine. The typical target dose of tricyclic medications is approximately 2.25 mg/kg/day (100–200 mg/day). Treatment should be initiated with low doses, on the order of 10 mg/day of imipramine or its equivalent. Although effective, use of the tricyclic antidepressants is associated with a variety of side effects, including anticholinergic effects (e.g., dry mouth, constipation, weight gain, blurred vision), orthostatic hypotension (producing a feeling of faintness upon standing up rapidly), cardiac conduction defects, and fatality in overdose. There is also evidence that a significant proportion of patients with panic disorder eventually discontinue treatment with antidepressants because of side effects, particularly weight gain. Tricyclic antidepressants have also been applied successfully to the treatment of GAD, but are generally considered to be less effective for the treatment of social phobia than the MAOIs or the SSRIs, and with the exception of clomipramine, are typically not used for OCD. However, the side-effect profile of these medications limits their acceptability for chronic use for anxiety disorders, and the SSRIs and benzodiazepines are frequently considered as more first-line agents.

MAO Inhibitors

Many clinicians consider MAOIs (phenelzine 60–90 mg/day, tranylcypromine 30–60 mg/day) to be the most comprehensively effective agents for treating anxiety disorders, particularly social phobia and panic disorder. However, this optimism is countered by the need for careful dietary monitoring and avoidance of sympathomimetic amines (particularly tyramine containing foods, e.g., aged cheeses, yeast extracts, red wine, aged meats) and certain medications (e.g., cough, cold, or diet preparations containing pseudoephedrine), which when ingested by patients taking MAOIs may induce a potentially fatal hypertensive crisis. Side effects for the MAOIs include insomnia, weight gain, edema, sexual dysfunction, and myoclonus. As a result of the potential adverse effects associated with MAOI therapy, these agents are usually applied only after more tolerable pharmacologic interventions (e.g., SSRIs and/or benzodiazepines) have failed. Reversible inhibitors of (MAOA) (e.g., moclobemine) require less stringent dietary restrictions, but data from well-controlled studies have provided inconsistent evidence for their efficacy.

Other Antidepressants

Newer antidepressants, such as venlafaxine and nefazodone, have been used clinically for the treatment of anxiety disorders, but there is relatively little systematic data documenting their efficacy. As with other antidepressants, treatment initiation may be associated with the "antidepressant jitteriness syndrome." Consequently, dosing is started in the range of 18.75 mg/day for venlafaxine and 50 mg/day for nefazodone, with target doses in the range of 75 to 300 mg/day for venlafaxine and 300 to 500 mg/day for nefazodone.

Benzodiazepines

Long the mainstay of pharmacologic treatment of GAD as well as sleep difficulties, in the last decade, benzodiazepines have also been shown to be effective for panic disorder and social phobia, with relatively greater empirical attention on higher potency agents (e.g., alprazolam, prescribed at dosages of 2–8 mg/day; and clonazepam, prescribed at dosages of 1–4 mg/day). These agents have the advantage of a relatively rapid emergence of treatment effects, and tend to be well tolerated. Short half-life agents (e.g., alprazolam) offer the potential for both fast onset of action and rapid clearing but bringing with them the need for more frequent dosing (e.g., 4/day) and the possibility of the return of anxiety between doses. Clonazepam is a longer acting benzodiazepine, and can be given on a twice-a-day basis with less risk of interdose return of anxiety.

Common side-effects of the benzodiazepines include sedation (minimized by initiation with low doses), memory impairment, and the potential for abuse in individuals predisposed toward drug or alcohol abuse. Although relatively safe in overdose by themselves, benzodiazepines react synergistically with other central nervous system depressants, and may cause fatal respiratory depression if ingested concomitantly with high doses of barbiturates, narcotics, or alcohol.

Discontinuation of benzodiazepines is often difficult, particularly for patients with panic disorder. Benzodiazepine discontinuation may expose patients to anxiety symptoms that can be as bad or worse than pretreatment levels, making attempts to discontinue these agents problematic. At the present time, adjunctive cognitive-behavioral treatment appears to be the best strategy for helping patients achieve successful benzodiazepine discontinuation and maintain control over anxiety and panic symptoms thereafter.

Buspirone

Buspirone is a nonbenzodiazepine anxiolytic which lacks significant sedative or anticonvulsant properties or abuse potential. These characteristics have encouraged the application of buspirone to comorbid anxiety and substance use conditions. Empirical evaluation of buspirone primarily supports its use in GAD. Treatment can be initiated at 10 to 20 mg/day, with a target dose in the range of 45 to 60 mg/day. Like the antidepressants, therapeutic benefit may only begin to emerge following three to four weeks of treatment. Buspirone is also considered as a potential adjunctive strategy to be used when anxiety patients do not respond to monotherapy with an antidepressant.

Beta-Blockers

The role of beta-blockers for the amelioration of anxiety is generally confined to the treatment of performance anxiety (i.e., propranolol 20–80 mg/day, and atenolol 50–150 mg/day), although they may also be useful, in some cases, as adjunctive treatment for GAD. These medications reduce the somatic symptoms of anxiety, including tremor and tachycardia. They are generally administered 1.5 to 2 hours before a performance situation (e.g., public speaking, musical recital). Beta-blockers are not generally considered to be effective for the treatment of generalized social phobia or the affective symptoms of anxiety.

Comparison With Other Empirically Supported Treatment

Pharmacotherapy is one of the two treatment modalities that have been the focus of extensive empirical investigation in the anxiety disorders literature; cognitive-behavioral therapy is the other. Both treatment modalities are associated with clear benefit, are acceptable to patients, and offer roughly similar outcome in short-term treatment trials, but tend to be different in the longer-term requirements of treatment. Cognitive-behavioral treatments are more effortful than pharmacotherapy during the acute treatment phase (frequently 12 to 16 sessions), although this effort offers patients a means to avoid the possible side effects, regular office visits, chronic dosing, and the monetary cost of pharmacotherapy over the long term. Pharmacotherapy has the additional characteristic of being widely available, with many patients initiating treatment with their primary care physicians. Nonetheless, patients choosing pharmacotherapy for anxiety disorders should consider the long-term requirements and costs of such treatment.

Bibliography

Ballenger, J. C. (1994). Overview of the pharmacotherapy of panic disorder. In B. E. Wolfe & J. D. Maser (Eds.), *Treatment of panic disorder: A consensus development conference* (pp. 59–72). Washington, DC: American Psychiatric Press.

Goodman, W. K., McDougle, C. J., & Price, L. H. (1992). Pharmacotherapy of obsessive compulsive disorder. *Journal of Clinical Psychiatry, 53*(Suppl.), 29–37.

Gould, R. A., Buckminster, S., Pollack, M. H., Otto, M. W., & Yap, L. (1997). Cognitive-behavioral and pharmacological treatment for social phobia: A meta-analysis. *Clinical Psychology: Science and Practice, 4,* 291–306.

Gould, R. A., Otto, M. W., & Pollack, M. H. (1995). A meta-analysis of treatment outcome for panic disorder. *Clinical Psychology Review, 15,* 819–844.

Gould, R. A., Otto, M. W., Pollack, M. P., & Yap, L. (1997). Cognitive-behavioral and pharmacological treatment of generalized anxiety disorder: A preliminary meta-analysis. *Behavior Therapy, 28,* 285–305.

Greist, J. H., Jefferson, J. W., Kobak, K. A., Katzelnick, D. J., & Serlin, R. C. (1995). Efficacy and tolerability of serotonin transport inhibitors in obsessive-compulsive disorder. *Archives of General Psychiatry, 52,* 53–60.

Lydiard, R. B., Brawman-Mintzer, O., & Ballenger, J. C. (1996). Recent developments in the psychopharmacology of anxiety disorders. *Journal of Consulting and Clinical Psychology, 64,* 660–668.

Penava, S. J., Otto, M. W., Pollack, M. H., & Rosenbaum, J. F. (1996/1997). Current status of pharmacotherapy for PTSD: An effect size analysis of controlled studies. *Depression and Anxiety, 4,* 240–242.

Pollack, M. H., & Smoller, J. W. (1996). Pharmacologic approaches to treatment-resistant panic disorder. In M. H. Pollack, M. W. Otto, & J. F. Rosenbaum (Eds.), *Challenges in clinical practice: Pharmacologic and psychosocial strategies* (pp. 89–112). New York: Guilford Press.

Perel, J. M. (1996). Pharmacology for anxiety disorders. In M. R. Mavissakalian & R. F. Prien (Eds.), *Long-term treatments of anxiety disorders* (pp. 71–107). Washington, DC: American Psychiatric Press.

Rosenbaum, J. F., Pollack, M. H., Otto, M. W., & Bernstein, J. G. (1997). Anxiety patients. In N. H. Cassem, T. A. Stern, J. F., Rosenbaum, & M. S. Jellinek (Eds.), *Massachusetts General Hospital handbook of general hospital psychiatry* (4th ed. pp. 173–210). St Louis, MO: Mosby.

Schweizer, E. (1995). Generalized anxiety disorder, Longitudinal course and pharmacologic treatment. *Psychiatric Clinics of North America, 18,* 843–858.

Smoller, J. W., & Pollack, M. H. (1996). Pharmacologic approaches to treatment-resistant social phobia and generalized anxiety disorder. In M. H. Pollack, M. W. Otto, & J. F. Rosenbaum (Eds.), *Challenges in clinical practice: Pharmacologic and psychosocial strategies* (pp. 141–170). New York: Guilford Press.

Michael W. Otto and Mark H. Pollack

ANTIDEPRESSANTS. Following the accidental discovery in the mid-1950s that certain drugs (e.g., iproniazid) used to treat tuberculosis both induced mania and relieved symptoms of depression, monoamine oxidase inhibitors (MAOIs) rapidly came into widespread use for the management of depression. Certain of these agents, including tranylcypromine (Parnate) and phenelzine (Parnate), remain in use today. However, by the mid-1960s the tricyclic antidepressants (TCAs), such as imipramine (Tofranil) and amitriptyline (Elavil) became available and largely supplanted the MAOIs because of an improved safety profile. The TCAs dominated the field until the introduction of the serotonin selective reuptake inhibitors (SSRIs) and newer heterocyclics in the late 1980s. Again, largely because of an improved safety and side effect profile, these agents have come to be preferred as first-line medications in the treatment of depression. Table 1 lists the major types of antidepressants and the specific medications currently approved for use in the US.

Mechanisms of Action

Most antidepressant drugs share the common feature of increasing the synaptic availability of monoamine neurotransmitters such as norepinephrine, serotonin, or dopamine, although they do so via different routes. The MAOIs work by inhibiting monoamine oxidase, one of the principal enzymes that metabolize these neurotransmitters. Most of the other antidepressants, including the TCAs and SSRIs, inhibit the reuptake of serotonin or norepinephrine (and to a much lesser degree dopamine) into the presynaptic neuron. Either process leaves more of the neurotransmitter free to bind with postsynaptic receptors, initiating a series of events in the postsynaptic neuron that is thought to produce the actual therapeutic effect. Until recently, antidepressants have been thought to exert their action via down-regulation of postsynaptic receptors. However, there has been increasing attention to the indirect effects of antidepressants on postsynaptic transductional mechanisms, genes, and gene products. Similarly, even those medications that are specific to a single neurotransmitter system appear to produce comparable antidepressant effects. This suggests that the drugs may differ in their initial mechanisms of action, but still work

ANTIDEPRESSANTS. Table 1. Chemical and trade names of commonly used antidepressants by class of drug.

Class	Chemical Name	Trade Name
Monoamine oxidase inhibitors	Phenelzine	Nardil
	Tranylcypromine	Parnate
Tricyclics	Amitriptyline	Elavil
	Nortriptyline	Aventyl, Pamelor
	Imipramine	Tofranil
	Desipramine	Norpramin
	Protriptylene	Vivactil
	Doxepin	Sinequan
	Trimipramine	Surmontil
	Clomipramine	Anafranil
Heterocyclics	Maprotiline	Ludiomil
	Amoxipine	Asendin
	Trazodone	Desyrel
	Bupropion	Wellbutrin
	Venlafaxine	Effexor
	Nefazodone	Serzone
	Mirtazepine	Remeron
Serotonin selective reuptake inhibitors	Citalopram	Celexa
	Fluoxetine	Prozac
	Fluvoxamine	Luvox
	Paroxetine	Paxil
	Sertraline	Zoloft

through a common set of biological processes to produce their antidepressant effects.

Clinical Indications

Unipolar and bipolar depression and dysthymia are often treated successfully with antidepressants.

Unipolar Major Depression. The antidepressants have been shown to be superior to pill-placebo controls in literally hundreds of trials with patients with major depressive disorder (MDD). Drug-placebo differences are typically more pronounced among more severely depressed patients. About 60 to 75% of unipolar patients with MDD will show significant improvement with any effective antidepressant drug. It is not clear that adding psychotherapy necessarily improves upon this rate of response, although it is often done in clinical practice. Although these rates of improvement are impressive, response is usually defined as a 50% improvement on some clinician-rated instrument. Many patients who do respond to treatment fail to show a full clinical remission.

In the practice arena, a number of factors contribute to a less than robust response. These factors can include issues like including concurrent medical conditions (e.g., hypothyroidism, Cushing's disease, or Parkinsonism), misdiagnosis, inadequate dosing or duration of treatment, and noncompliance. The latter problem can be contributed to by both the side effect problems associated with antidepressants, and the am-

bivalence that many persons (or their families) have about taking psychotropic drugs. The latter concerns are amplified by the incorrect notions about the nature of antidepressant drug therapy (such as believing the drug is addictive) and by inadequate patient preparation by the treatment provider.

Most antidepressant drugs require initiation at low dose and titration over a period of several weeks. Alternately, some SSRIs can be initiated at a dose that will be effective for a majority of patients: 20 mg per day for fluoxetine (Prozac) or paroxetine (Paxil) or 50 mg per day for sertraline (Zoloft). However, for all antidepressants, dosage adjustment to a higher or lower dose is required often to maximize the beneficial effect and minimize side effects.

Major depression can be separated into melancholic and atypical subtypes. Melancholic depression is characterized by classic symptoms of depression, including anhedonia, initial insomnia, loss of appetite, and loss of interest in sex. Some clinicians believe that melancholic depression responds better to TCAs than to other types of antidepressants; however, this belief remains controversial and has not been well substantiated empirically. Conversely, atypical depression is characterized by the so-called reverse vegetative features, such as mood reactivity, hypersomnia, and increased appetite. There is some evidence that this subtype may be particularly responsive to drugs that affect serotonin, like the SSRIs and MAOIs.

Recently remitted patients appear to be at elevated risk for relapse (the return of symptoms associated with the treated episode) for several months, that is, although no longer symptomatic, they have not yet fully recovered from the underlying episode. For this reason, drug treatment is usually continued for up to a year after the patient first remits and longer for patients with a history of chronic illness. Moreover, rates of recurrence (the onset of a wholly new episode) are sufficiently high even after recovery that many physicians now recommend extending maintenance treatment indefinitely for patients with a history of multiple prior episodes. There are indications that combining drugs and psychotherapy may enhance both the stability and breadth of response to medications alone, although that remains controversial.

Bipolar Depression. Special management problems arise when treating bipolar depression with antidepressant drugs. For example, antidepressants can precipitate episodes of mania and may accelerate the frequency of cycles. The latter problem appears to be more common with the TCAs than with other types of antidepressants; therefore, these drugs should be avoided in bipolar disorder. However, in virtually all bipolar patients, a mood-stabilizing agent such as lithium carbonate, carabamazepine (Tegretol), or valproic acid (Depekene and Depakote) will be required in long-term management.

Dysthymia. Until recently, clinical lore held that persons with chronic depressive disorders, especially dysthymia, were unresponsive to antidepressants and such patients were typically treated with psychotherapy alone. However, recent trials indicate that this condition is amenable to antidepressant therapy, including the tricyclics and the SSRIs. Few studies have systematically compared drugs versus psychotherapy in this population, but even chronic dysthymic patients do appear to show a "true" drug effect.

Other Indications. There are a number of other conditions that respond to antidepressant drugs. For example, obsessive-compulsive disorder (OCD) has been shown to respond, in part, to certain antidepressants, particularly those that enhance serotonin transmission. This would include the SSRIs and clomipramine (Anafranil). Currently, clomipramine, fluvoxamine (Luvox), paroxetine (Paxil), and sertraline (Zoloft) are approved by the U.S. food and Drug Administration (FDA) for the treatment of OCD. Although these drugs appear to be beneficial for the treatment of OCD, most persons continue to have significant residual symptoms after extended treatment. Therefore, concomitant treatment with behavioral therapy or cognitive-behavioral psychotherapy is usually indicated in a comprehensive treatment approach.

Panic disorder (PD) also is amenable to treatment with antidepressant drugs. The frequency and intensity of panic attacks is reduced with a wide variety of drugs, including TCAs, MAOIs, and SSRIs. However, many persons with PD will require lower doses of drug and longer periods of dosage titration than usually used in MDD. In addition, residual anticipatory anxiety and phobic avoidance is seen commonly and requires behavioral or cognitive-behavioral management.

Some research evidence supports the effectiveness of antidepressants in the management of other anxiety disorders, including generalized anxiety disorder, social phobia, and posttraumatic stress disorder, although the widespread use of these drugs is seen only in the latter condition. Eating disorders, particularly bulimia, may be amenable to treatment with antidepressants. However, anorexia nervosa, except when accompanied by MDD, is probably not improved with antidepressants. Finally, there are a wide variety of other conditions for which antidepressants are commonly used, including chronic pain, headache (especially migraine), fibromyalgia syndrome, neuropathies, attention deficit disorder, sleep disorders, narcolepsy, sleep apnea, and enuresis, although controlled research is limited.

Adverse Effects

These medications can produce a wide assortment of side effect problems. However, there is a general division between the older antidepressants, like the TCAs and MAOIs, which tend to produce very high rates of side effect and discontinuation problems, and newer drugs, like the SSRIs, in which such problems are reduced. The TCAs and MAOIs for example, commonly cause problems like dry mouth, blurred vision, constipation, urinary hesitancy and retention, orthostatic hypotension, drowsiness or insomnia, anxiety, memory problems and confusion, impotence and anorgasmia, nausea, and increased appetite with weight gain. It's obvious why compliance rates are relatively low with these drugs.

These drugs also may cause more serious reactions. The TCAs can cause cardiac conduction abnormalities which may induce heart rhythm disturbances. The MAOIs can be particularly risky because of potential interactions with certain foods or drugs. Foods containing high amounts of tyramine (e.g., cheese, sauerkraut, and other fermented foods, some alcoholic beverages like red wine, broad bean pods, and liver) can interact with MAOIs to induce marked increases in blood pressure, which can lead to myocardial infarction, stroke, or other problems. These drugs also interact with a wide variety of drugs and yield serious adverse events. These include stimulant drugs, including those in decongestants, cold and allergy preparations, and diet products as well as methylphenidate [Ritalin™] and amphetamine; meperidine [Demerol™]; certain asthma inhalants; and other antidepressants. Both the TCAs and the MAOIs are highly lethal in overdosage. Given the more benign nature of newer antidepressants, the TCAs and MAOIs are now usually reserved as "second-line" medications for treatment-refractory patients.

Although the SSRIs (as well as other drugs that potently effect serotonin availability like venlafaxine [Effexor]) produce a much more benign profile of side effects, some problems remain. Certain effects like nausea and diarrhea (and much less commonly vomiting), anxiety, tremor, insomnia (or occasionally fatigue or hypersomnia), and headache are common, although usually relatively mild and limited in duration. Sexual dysfunction, including loss of sexual interest and anorgasmia can occur, and may result in noncompliance. These problems often improve with time, but persistent dysfunction may require switching to an alternative antidepressant with a lower profile of associated sexual problems (e.g., bupropion [Wellbutrin], nefazodone [Serzone], or mirtazapine [Remeron]). Nonetheless, these drugs are better tolerated than the TCAs and MAOIs, and are much safer if taken in overdose.

Treatment Failure

Even given the liberal definition of response, at least 25% of persons with MDD fail to respond to any single medication, and a larger proportion experience significant residual symptoms. Factors that predict nonresponse include a prior history of nonresponse, the presence of psychotic symptoms, and an underlying personality disorder. Chronicity and an earlier age of onset may also predict nonresponse. Patients free of any of these factors are quite likely to respond to any reasonable pharmacological intervention, whereas patients with multiple factors tend to show a very poor response. This indicates that there are clinical predictors of treatment failure, and that combinations of factors exert a more powerful negative effect.

Prior to determining that a given person has experienced a true treatment failure, the adequacy of the therapeutic trial should first be addressed. Many patients are undermedicated or do not fully comply with the treatment regime. Further, no patient should be considered refractory until an alternative antidepressant of a different therapeutic class has been tried. However, there are a number of alternative strategies available for the management of true failure of antidepressant response. Augmentation, that is, the addition of a second drug to an antidepressant to enhance therapeutic responsiveness, represents the maneuver that has been most often studied. A variety of agents have been used successfully, including lithium addition to TCAs or SSRIs, triiodothyronine (Cytomel) addition to TCAs, the combination of TCAs and SSRIs (e.g., desipramine [Norpramine] and fluoxetine [Prozac]) or TCAs and MAOIs.

A final resort in many refractory patients is the use of electroconvulsive therapy (ECT). Although a significant proportion of refractory major depressives will respond initially to ECT, many do not and a sizable number will show rapid relapse. Therefore, ECT is generally reserved for use when multiple alternative strategies have failed.

Conclusions

The antidepressants are quite effective in the treatment of depression and a number of other disorders. The SSRIs and newer heterocyclics have largely supplanted the TCAs and the MAOIs as the first-line medications of choice because they are safer and easier to tolerate. Patients who do not respond to one family of antidepressants will often respond to another and augmentation often enhances response in refractory patients. Clinical practice is increasingly moving toward long-term maintenance strategies in an effort to reduce risk for relapse and recurrence, especially among patients with histories of chronic or recurrent depression. Although their precise mechanisms of action remain unclear, the antidepressants' clinical effects may be mediated by a series of postsynaptic events triggered by a range of different direct effects at the synapse.

Bibliography

American Psychiatric Association (1993). Practice guidelines for major depressive disorder in adults. *American Journal of Psychiatry, 150*(4), 1–26. Practice guidelines for the treatment of major depressive disorder, with particularly reference to pharmacotherapy.

American Psychiatric Association. (1994) Practice guidelines for treatment of patients with bipolar disorder. *American Journal of Psychiatry, 151*(12), 1–35. Practice guidelines for the treatment of bipolar disorder, with particular reference to pharmacotherapy.

Cusack, B., Nelson, A., & Richelson, E. (1994). Binding of antidepressants to human brain receptors: focus on newer generation compounds. *Psychopharmacology, 114*, 559–565. This is a review of the basic pharmacology of newer antidepressants in contrast to older tricyclics and MAOI's.

Dolberg, O. T., Iancu, I., Sasson, Y., & Zohar J. (1996). The pathogenesis and treatment of obsessive-compulsive disorder. *Clinical Neuropharmacology, 19*(2), 129–147. This is a fairly comprehensive review of pharmacological treatments of obsessive-compulsive disorder.

Greden, J. F. (1993). Antidepressant maintenance medications: when to discontinue and how to stop. *Journal of Clinical Psychiatry, 54*(8), 39–43. Knowing when to discontinue and when to continue antidepressant drugs is a vexing clinical problem. This article reviews the results of the NIMH collaborative projects and makes recommendations regarding continuation treatment.

Knight, D. J., Frank, E., Perel, J. M., Cornes, C., Mallinger, A. G., Thase, M. E. McEachran, A. B., & Grochocinski, V. J. (1992). Five-year outcome for maintenance therapies in recurrent depression. *Archives of General Psychi-*

atry, 49, 769–773. This article deals with the issue of the effectiveness of long-term treatments for depression.

Liebowitz, M. R., Quitkin, F. M., Stewart, J. W., McGrath, P. J., Harrison, W., Rabkin, J., Tricamo, E., Markowitz, J. S., & Klein, D. F. (1984). Phenelzine and imipramine in atypical depression. A preliminary report. *Archives of General Psychiatry, 41,* 669–677. An early but important study suggesting that MAOIs may be more effective than tricyclics in the treatment of atypical depression.

Phillips, K. A, & Nierenberg, A. A. (1994). The assessment and treatment of refractory depression. *Journal of Clinical Psychiatry, 55*(2), 20–26. A very thorough review of refractory major depression.

Rosenbaum, J. F., Pollock, R. A., Jordan, S. K., & Pollack, M. H. (1996). The pharmacotherapy of panic disorder. *Bulletin of the Menninger Clinic, 60*(2A), A54–75. Very complete review of drug treatments for panic disorder.

Thase M. E., Fava, M., Halbreich, U., Kocsis, J. H., Koran, L., Davidson, J., Rosenbaum, J., & Harrison, W. (1996). A placebo-controlled, randomized clinical trial comparing sertraline and imipramine for the treatment of dysthymia. *Archives of General Psychiatry, 53,* 777–784. This represents the largest controlled study of pharmacotherapies for dysthymia. This study indicates that imipramine and sertraline are more effective than placebo for this condition.

Thase, M. E., & Kupfer, D. J. (1996). Recent developments in the pharmacotherapy of mood disorders. *Journal of Consulting and Clinical Psychology, 64*(4), 646–659. A comprehensive overview of the major types of antidepressant medications that discusses their clinical indications, side-effect profiles, and mechanisms of action in language that is targeted for a nonmedical audience.

Warrington, S. J. (1992). Clinical implications of the pharmacology of serotonin reuptake inhibitors. *International Clinical Psychopharmacology, 7*(2), 13–19. A reasonably complete review of SSRIs.

Richard C. Shelton and Steven D. Hollon

ANTINEUROTIC MEDICATION. *See* Antianxiety Medication.

ANTI-PSYCHIATRY. *See* Critical Psychiatry.

ANTIPSYCHOTIC MEDICATION. The modern era of the treatment of schizophrenia began with the serendipitous discovery of the antipsychotic properties of chlorpromazine in 1952. At that time "therapy" for schizophrenia consisted mainly of cold packs, restraints, sedatives, electric and chemical shock treatments, and frontal lobotomy. Most patients spent most of their lives receiving custodial care in large mental hospitals. The introduction of chlorpromazine (Thorazine) produced a remarkable change, allowing most patients to be treated as outpatients and permitting a massive exodus of patients from state hospitals. The ensuing years saw the development of many chlorpromazinelike drugs, known as neuroleptics because of their neurological side effects. Because neuroleptics have fairly specific effects on psychotic symptoms independent of sedation, the older term *tranquilizers* is inappropriate. Despite these advances, schizophrenia remains a major public health problem, and promising new drugs with different modes of action have been and are being developed. Although no one drug to date provides a cure for schizophrenia, drugs do provide varying degrees of control over its symptoms.

Conventional Neuroleptics

The chlorpromazine like drugs include trifluoperazine (Stelazine), thioridazine (Mellaril), fluphenazine (Prolixin), and haloperidol (Haldol), none of which has shown unequivocal superiority to the others. The latter two are available in depot (long-lasting) form.

Usage and Limitations

Many cases of schizophrenia follow an episodic course. Periods of remission are punctuated by episodes of acute psychosis in which positive symptoms (e.g., delusions, hallucinations, thought disorder, agitation, and/or aggressiveness) are exacerbated. Initiating neuroleptics or increasing their dose are well established as effective treatments in these situations. Neuroleptics are also used to treat acute episodes of psychotic depression, mania, and organic psychoses.

Most patients with schizophrenia require chronic neuroleptic treatment. Although the efficacy of neuroleptics over placebo has been documented extensively, there is great heterogeneity in their effectiveness both in relieving symptoms and in side effects; not all patients respond to neuroleptics, and the majority achieve incomplete remission of symptoms. Neuroleptics are much more effective in treating positive than negative symptoms (symptoms reflecting a loss of normal function such as a lack of interest, anhedonia, motor retardation, affective flattening, and sociality). Moreover, the effects on negative symptoms may be due to improvement in positive symptoms because some negative symptoms may be secondary to positive symptoms.

Side Effects. The most common early-onset side effect involving the extrapyramidal motor system is akinesia: reductions in facial expression, motor retardation, apathy, and slow and unexpressive speech. In its severe form it resembles Parkinsonism with increased rigidity of face and limbs, tremor, and severe poverty of movement. Acute dyskinesias and akathisia may also occur. Many of these symptoms resemble negative symptoms. Depressed mood may be secondary to the neurological side effects or be independent of those. Autonomic side effects include dry mouth, blurred vision, constipation, urinary retention, and postural hypotension. Because of these side effects drug noncompliance in outpatients can be a significant problem. The side effects may be alleviated by reducing the dosage, but this risks lessened control over psychotic symptoms. Some, but incomplete, improvement in extrapyramidal side effects may occur with treatment with anticholinergic drugs.

The primary long-term side effect of neuroleptics is tardive dyskinesia, a potentially irreversible syndrome characterized by hyperkinetic movements, such as choreiform movements of the mouth, tongue, lips, and limbs. Its incidence is 40 to 50% in patients undergoing continuous treatment for two years or more. Both the incidence and severity of the disorder increase with longer treatment. It is not clear if drug holidays can prevent this syndrome. Tardive dyskinesia may be temporarily exacerbated by discontinuation of treatment. Symptoms disappear only very gradually, if at all, over months and years after drug discontinuation. There is no effective treatment for tardive dyskinesia.

Mode of Action. The antipsychotic properties (and side effects) of neuroleptics have been shown to be due primarily to their action in blocking the dopamine D2 receptor. The evidence for this is partly a close correspondence of the antipsychotic efficacy of the various neuroleptics and their affinity for the D2 receptor, a finding which is a cornerstone of the dopamine theory of schizophrenia. Although neuroleptics differ in their effects on other neurotransmitters such as acetylcholine and serotonin, these effects seem uncorrelated with either their intended or side effects.

Atypical Antipsychotic Drugs

Chlorpromazinelike neuroleptic drugs are of great benefit in treating psychoses in most cases, but they do not provide an optimal treatment profile as indicated above. The clinical efficacy of clozapine, a drug with a quite different mode of action, has produced a search for modes of treatment that do not depend entirely on blockade of the D2 receptor.

Clozapine (Clozaril). Clozapine was first used in the treatment of schizophrenia in the 1960s. Because it causes the potentially fatal blood disease of agranulocytosis in 1 to 2% of cases its use might have been discontinued had it not been uniquely effective in many treatment-resistant patients. This has been confirmed by studies which show clinically significant improvement in 40 to 60% of patients who failed trials of conventional neuroleptics. Clozapine has also been shown to be superior to haloperidol in stabilizing and preventing relapse in moderately symptomatic outpatients.

Like conventional neuroleptics, clozapine is most effective on positive symptoms. Improvement in negative symptoms has been reported as well, but this may have been due primarily to a reduction in secondary rather than in primary negative symptoms. While clinical improvement can occur in the first 1 to 2 weeks, a trial of at least 4 months may be necessary to demonstrate improvement in almost all potential responders. Marked improvement from clozapine in both psychosis and mania in treatment-resistant bipolar affective disorder has been shown. Clozapine may also be useful in treating psychosis engendered by dopamine-enhancing drugs used to treat Parkinson's disease.

The possibility of agranulocytosis requires a weekly white blood cell count, adding considerable expense to the treatment. Discontinuation of treatment after a positive test prevents serious disease. Importantly, extrapyramidal symptoms and tardive dyskinesia are virtually absent during clozapine treatment. Side effects include transient sedation at treatment onset, tachycardia, salivation, weight gain, and increased probability of generalized seizures, most of which can be treated by other medications. Clozapine is generally well tolerated; compliance is not a problem.

Clozapine has a relatively weak affinity for D2 receptors but a much stronger relative affinity for other dopamine receptors, and for receptors for serotonin, norepinephrine, and acetylcholine than conventional neuroleptics. Which of these characteristics is responsible for its antipsychotic properties is not known at present.

Risperidone (Risperdal). This is the other major new drug that has been approved for the treatment of schizophrenia in the United States. Clinical trials have shown risperidone to be superior to placebo and to haloperidol in controlling both positive and negative symptoms in schizophrenia and psychosis in general. However, it is not clear if this superiority applies to a wider spectrum of patients or mainly to treatment-resistant patients. As with clozapine, the improvement in negative symptoms may be just in *secondary* negative symptoms.

Risperidone has fewer extrapyramidal side effects than conventional neuroleptics. Optimal clinical improvement, on the average, occurs at lower doses than that which produces extrapyramidal symptoms. The incidence of tardive dyskinesia has not been determined, but would be predicted to be low. Other side effects include transient sedation, orthostatic dizziness, palpitations and tachycardia, diminished libido, and erectile dysfunction. No hematological effects have been reported.

Risperidone has about half the affinity for the D2 receptor as haloperidol but much more than for clozapine. Like clozapine it binds to serotonergic and noradrenergic receptors, but even more strongly, and has some but lower affinity for cholinergic receptors.

Other Antipsychotic Drugs. The success of clozapine and risperidone in treating schizophrenia, along with advances in basic knowledge in neurobiology, has led to the development of several new drugs, based on more sophisticated hypotheses about the biological bases of schizophrenia. These are in various stages of testing at this time.

A number of other drugs are frequently added to conventional neuroleptics to attempt to augment their efficiency or to reduce side effects. These include benzodiazapines, anticonvulsants, beta blockers and other drugs which act on the noradrenergic system, antidepressants, and serotonin receptor antagonists. Studies have shown wide individual differences in response to these treatments.

Drugs for Bipolar Affective Disorder

The preceding sections concerned drugs used to control the symptoms of schizophrenia, although their usefulness in other psychotic states was also pointed out. This section covers drugs used primarily in psychotic states occurring in affective disorders.

Lithium. The discovery in 1949 that lithium salts were effective mood stabilizers in manic-depressive disorders began one of the major success stories in psychopharmacology. Lithium is the treatment of choice for long-term prevention of both manic and depressive episodes in patients with bipolar illness, 70 to 80% of whom achieve at least a partial response to the treatment. It is also used to treat acute episodes, but neuroleptics and/or benzodiazepines may be useful as adjuncts for faster clinical response. Whether lithium is as effective for acute depressive episodes as it is for mania is controversial, but in bipolar patients this may be the case. It is not as effective for either short- or long-term control of unipolar depression as it is in controlling depression in bipolar patients. Conversely, tricyclic antidepressants may produce manic episodes in bipolar patients. Lithium is an effective treatment for schizoaffective conditions and is occasionally used for other forms of schizophrenia.

Unfortunately, in a small number of patients chronic lithium treatment produces serious renal insufficiency and cannot be used. Other side effects include excessive thirst, polyuria, cognitive and memory problems, tremor, weight gain, and drowsiness and tiredness. The cognitive, obesity, and tremor side effects are the most serious reasons for noncompliance.

It is not known how lithium produces its clinical efficacy. It promotes serotonin neurotransmission by increasing its synthesis and enhancing its release. Its effects on other neurotransmitters include the inhibition of postsynaptic dopamine receptor supersensitivity, which could be involved in mood stabilization. Current research is evaluating lithium's effects on second messenger systems, especially those involving g-proteins.

Anticonvulsants. Two drugs which were developed to control seizures are useful for patients with bipolar illness who cannot tolerate or do not respond to lithium: carbamazapine (Tegretol) and valproate or valproic acid (Depakote). There is evidence that valproate may be as effective as lithium for both acute mania and prophylaxis. It may have fewer side effects and be less toxic to the kidneys, but may cause hepatitis in some patients. Anticonvulsants may also control episodic bursts of anger and aggression. The benzodiazapine clonazapam is also sometimes used for mania, but it is highly sedative.

Relationships of Drug Treatments to Psychosocial Treatments

The conditions for which antipsychotic drugs are useful are largely unresponsive to psychodynamic insight-oriented psychotherapy. Persons in acutely psychotic states are unlikely to respond to any psychosocial intervention. Therefore, one benefit of antipsychotic drugs is to make patients more receptive to whatever healing forces exist in their environments, including psychosocial treatments. Some interventions may enhance the effectiveness of maintenance drug treatment. For example, a hostile and overcontrolling home environment increases the risk of relapse in outpatients with schizophrenia. Counseling family members may improve the effectiveness of both maintenance drugs and psychosocial treatments in preventing relapse. Conversely, social skills training and other rehabilitative procedures in schizophrenia and the preferred mode of therapy in affective disorders will be aided to the extent that psychotic symptoms and side effects are controlled. The reduced extrapyramidal side effects of the atypical antipsychotics and consequent increased patient compliance should be especially beneficial for psychosocial approaches. Thus pharmacotherapy is usually a necessary, but may not be a sufficient condition for optimal outcomes in the psychoses. Continuing research on how best to effectively combine these two modes of treatment should pay large dividends.

Bibliography

Bloom, F. E., & Kupfer, D. J. (Eds.). (1995). *Psychopharmacology: The fourth generation of progress*. New York: Raven Press. A gigantic tome written by the foremost experts on a comprehensive selection of basic and clinical topics which impact the field of psychopharmacology.

Breier, A. (Ed.). (1996). *The new pharmacotherapy of schizophrenia*. Washington, DC: American Psychiatric Press. A survey of theory and practice emphasizing newer developments in atypical and conventional neuroleptics, drugs under development, use of adjunct drugs, and treatment of side effects.

Coyle, J. T., & Enna, S. J. (Eds.). (1983). *Neuroleptics: Neurochemical, behavioral, and clinical perspectives.* New York: Raven Press. A compendium of basic and clinical research on conventional neuroleptics which has stood the test of time.

Gitlin, M. J. (1996). *The psychotherapist's guide to psychopharmacology* (2nd ed.). New York: Free Press. Very clinically oriented with only minor coverage of the biological bases of the disorders and of their treatment.

Goodwin, F. K., & Jamison, K. R. (1990). *Manic-depressive illness.* New York: Oxford University Press. The most comprehensive and authoritative treatise available on the biological, psychological, and social aspects of bipolar affective disorder with excellent sections on treatment.

Hogarty, G. E., Kornblith, S. J., Greenwald, D., DiBarry, L., Cooley, S., Flesher, S., Reiss, D., Carter, M., & Ulrich, R. (1995). Personal therapy: A disorder-relevant psychotherapy for schizophrenia. *Schizophrenia Bulletin, 21,* 379–393. A description of a multifaceted, three-stage psychosocial treatment program, the success of which depends on adequate control of psychosis and neuroleptic side effects by astute management of dose levels.

Schatzberg, A. F., & Nemeroff, C. B. (Eds.). (1995). *The American Psychiatric Press textbook of psychopharmacology.* Washington, DC: American Psychiatric Press. This comprehensive survey explores thoroughly the biological bases of the disorders and of their treatment as well as the clinical uses of the drugs.

Schatzberg, A. F., Cole, J. O., & DeBattista, C. (1997). *Manual of clinical psychopharmacology.* Washington, DC: American Psychiatric Press. A short outline of the indications and doses for a wide variety of therapeutic drugs which covers virtually all psychiatric disorders.

Schooler, N. R., & Hogarty, G. E. (1987). Medication and psychosocial strategies in the treatment of schizophrenia. In H. Y. Meltzer (Ed.) *Psychopharmacology: The third generation of progress* (pp. 1111–1119). New York: Raven Press. A critical review of studies which combine pharmacological management with various forms of psychosocial treatment.

Theodore P. Zahn

ANTISOCIAL BEHAVIOR. Although the term *antisocial behavior* is widely employed in psychology and psychology and psychiatry (but not in sociology), most discussions of this type of conduct do not clearly indicate just what is involved in antisocial actions. This lack of specificity can be illustrated by the exceedingly general descriptions of conduct disorder and antisocial personality disorder given in the American Psychiatric Association's *Diagnostic and Statistical Manual of Mental Disorders* (DSM–III–R, DSM–IV) Both *DSM–III–R* (1987) and its successor, *DSM–IV* (1994), generally speak of a behavior as antisocial if it deviates from the social norms appropriate for one's age and violates others'

rights. In many instances, moreover, the act is grounds for arrest.

However, any number of actions can satisfy such a wide-ranging conception. There must be more than just a listing of possible counternormative and/or illegal behaviors if the construct is to be maximally useful as a guide to research and an aid in the development of intervention programs. In particular, since much of the psychological/psychiatric interest in antisocial behavior grows out of a concern with individual differences, it is important to determine if there is some commonality among the various ways in which social norms can be violated and laws broken, at least in the case of some persons, and whether a certain kind of behavior is especially indicative of a general readiness to engage in antisocial conduct.

The best known research findings that bear on these matters will be reviewed, and in doing so, several of the most significant attempts to develop an empirically based construct of antisocial behavior will be summarized. Although wrongs obviously are committed by children or adults of both genders, I will concentrate on the results of studies with male youths, mostly but not only in the United States, since the concept of antisocial behavior has been used most frequently in connection with this particular population.

Determining Degrees of Antisociality

A major problem with the conception of antisocial behavior as counternormative or even illegal conduct is that many of the actions given this label are exceedingly common, particularly in adolescence. Kazdin (1987) noted that more than half of the teenagers in some U.S. surveys admitted to theft and 60% acknowledged having performed antisocial behaviors such as arson, vandalism, and drug use. After reviewing a number of studies in which teenagers were asked to report any illegal actions they had committed, Moffitt (1993) has concluded that rates of law violations "soar so high during adolescence that participation in delinquency appears to be a normal part of teen life" (p. 675).

Nonetheless, an index of the degree of antisociality, or seriousness, of each of these different forms of illegal behavior could conceivably be useful for some purposes, much as a number of investigators have believed it would be helpful to have scales of the seriousness of different crimes. These latter attempts to devise crime seriousness measures point to some of the problems that could be encountered by efforts at developing indices of the antisociality of the separate behaviors. In general, as Gottfredson, Warner, and Taylor (1988) have shown, independent raters tend to have little agreement about where they place any one offense along a single dimension of seriousness, although it is possible to obtain reliable ratings of the characteristics of the different crimes. The Gottfredson team also found that how serious any one type of offense is thought to be varies with the judge's degree of familiarity with crime; by and large, those who are more familiar with law violations in general tend to regard all offenses as less serious.

If it is undoubtedly difficult to judge the antisocial nature of any one kind of counternormative behavior, it is apparently much easier to order those persons who engage in antisocial actions along one or more relevant dimensions. Such an ordering can be established, particularly for teenagers, based on a pattern of counternormative and illegal actions. In the well-known West and Farrington (1977) investigation of over 400 working-class youths in London, the researchers found that many of the adolescents who deviated from conventional norms in one way, for example by being highly aggressive, also tended to reject social rules in other ways, such as by drinking excessively, using drugs, driving recklessly, and engaging in vandalism. And similarly, Huesmann, Eron, Lefkowitz, and Walder (1984) observed that the adult men in their 22-year longitudinal study who committed fairly serious criminal acts were also apt to have driven while intoxicated and also have abused their wives.

Farrington (e.g., 1991) has devised a series of antisocial personality scales on the basis of the London findings. For the 14-year-old sample his internally consistent antisociality measure included such behavioral characteristics as being frequently disobedient, lying, stealing outside the home, and being truant from school. The comparable index for the sample at approximately 32 years of age embraced such actions as being involved in fights, drinking heavily, taking drugs, and having been convicted of a crime.

Is Contemporaneous Antisociality Uni- or Multidimensional?

Farrington's measures were generally contemporaneous in that they were based on actions within a relatively narrow time period. If we confine ourselves now to such relatively contemporaneous behaviors, one might ask whether there are somewhat different clusters of antisocial behavior. More particularly, since much of the best evidence comes from research with children, our question here is whether youngsters specialize to some extent in the ways they violate accepted social rules even though they may occasionally engage in any of a broad spectrum of counternormative actions.

Several investigators have sought to answer such a question empirically with multivariate analyses of youthful antisocial behavior (see Achenbach, 1985; Kazdin, 1987; Quay, 1987). For Quay (1987), a number of these investigations have isolated four dimen-

sions: socialized aggression (which generally seems to "reflect gang delinquency") (p. 122); undersocialized aggression (including, among other things, boisterous, destructive, and assaultive behavior); attention deficit (showing such qualities as a short attention span and impulsivity); and anxiety-withdrawal (being hypersensitive and shy). These findings are somewhat ambiguous, however, as Quay (1987, p. 123) has commented, because the dimensions tend to be statistically interrelated.

Patterson offered another well-known multicluster proposal in 1982 on the basis of his early research into troublesome children in Oregon who had been referred for treatment. He suggested that some of the youths were pure "stealers," others were highly aggressive, and a third group was a mixed type who both stole and fought. A later analysis of adolescents in the Oregon samples by Loeber and Schmaling indicated that the mixed type teenagers were the ones most likely to have contact with the police (see Patterson, Reid, & Dishion, 1992, pp. 30–31). However, additional research has now led Patterson to propose that these different types of youths are best located along a single dimension. Consistent with such a notion, Loeber and Schmaling (1985) analyzed the findings from 22 different studies of school-age children, and concluded that many of the youngsters' antisocial actions could be ordered along a "covert-overt" continuum. The covert end of this dimension consisted of such actions as stealing, fire setting, gang membership, and alcohol and drug use, whereas the other end was composed of more overt behaviors such as hyperactivity, attacking others, and fighting. Disobedience was located between these extremes. Other findings from the Oregon research (Patterson et al., 1992, p. 31) generally corroborate the Loeber-Schmaling analysis and add further details. What is especially important here is that a high level of aggressiveness seems to be characteristic of those at the extremely antisocial end of this dimension, so much so that the Patterson and his colleagues think of the antisocial trait as a stable disposition to employ coercive (i.e., largely aggressive) behaviors contingently "to shape and manipulate their social environment" (Patterson et al., 1992, p. 22). More will be said later about this last mentioned notion of aggression as instrumental behavior.

Patterson and his associates (1992) not only envision children's antisociality as a single bipolar dimension but they also contend that problem children with the right environment and temperament are at risk of "progressing" along this dimension as they get older.

First the child learns to be very noncompliant and have frequent temper tantrums backed up with hitting. This sets the stage for learning to steal and lie at high rates, followed by truancy and dropping out of school. We are not suggesting that every child moves through all the prior steps in the progression, but we do believe that the progression describes three out of four cases. It has also been shown that the further the youth moves into the progression, the greater the risk for later delinquency. (p. 29)

Consistent with the developmental hypothesis advanced by Robins and Wish (1977), the Oregon investigators also proposed that the more frequently children engage in antisocial behavior, the greater is the likelihood that they will perform extremely counternormative actions. Moreover, according to this formulation, the progression is transitive, for boys at least. Those youths who carry out the most serious, low base rate acts will also engage in the more common, less serious behaviors as well, whereas those who only engage in trivial misdeeds do not necessarily move on to more serious offenses (Patterson et al., 1992).

Does Longitudinal Research Reveal Multiple Dimensions?

The seemingly different kinds of antisocial youths identified in longitudinal research cast some doubt on the contention that antisocial actions are best understood as lying along a single continuum. Studies have consistently found that the frequent display of illegal and counternormative actions in childhood is a good predictor of adult antisocial conduct (see Farrington, 1995; Huesmann et al., 1984; Moffitt, 1993; Robins, 1978). Some persons evidently have a disposition to engage in socially disapproved behavior that continues from their formative years into adulthood, although the exact way in which this inclination is manifested varies with time and place. And yet, as Moffitt (1993) has noted, offense statistics have also consistently shown that crime rates for the different age groups show a rise as children get older, reach a peak in late adolescence, and then decline steadily with increasing maturity. This decrease in crimes rates after adolescence appears to be due much more to a drop in the number of people who commit illegal acts rather than to a decline in the number of offenses by any one person, as if many individuals lose their strong antisocial tendencies when they become adults.

To reconcile the seeming contradiction between these two sets of observations, Moffitt (1993) argued that there are two distinct categories of delinquents, one that displays "life-course-persistent" antisocial behavior and the other whose counternormative and illegal actions are "adolescent limited." It is the former, a small group presumably consisting of approximately 5% of all teenagers, that continues its youthful antisocial conduct into adulthood. Moffitt (1993, p. 680) also suggested that the men in this category are apt to maintain their aggressiveness as they get older, at least in the form of domestic violence. The second and much larger category, as its name implies, is comprised of

adolescents who change their modes of conduct as they mature and especially when they leave high school. According to Moffitt:

> [A]dolescence-limited delinquents are likely to engage in antisocial behavior in situations where such responses seem profitable to them, but they are also able to abandon antisocial behavior when prosocial styles are more rewarding. They maintain control over their antisocial responses and use antisocial behavior only in situations where it may serve an instrumental function. (p. 686)

Our question now is whether there are behavioral differences between the two types of delinquents identified by Moffitt. She suggested that "measures of the frequency or seriousness of adolescent offending will not discriminate very well between life-course-persistent and adolescence-limited delinquents" and that a person's "developmental history is needed for confident classification" (p. 678). Nonetheless, she also raised the possibility that the "life-course-persistent" teenagers are more overtly aggressive than their "adolescence-limited" counterparts. This high level of aggressiveness, if it is indeed characteristic of the "life-course-persistents," may contribute to the continuity of their antisocial disposition over the years. One of the studies Moffitt cited (by Vitaro et al., see Moffitt, 1993, p. 683) indicated that strong aggressive inclinations that are not countered by prosocial tendencies may help maintain one's antisocial proclivities.

Can the Various Analyses Be Integrated?

We cannot say for sure at this time just how Moffitt's analysis of delinquents can be integrated with the formulations proposed by other investigators such as Quay (1987) and with Patterson's (1992) thesis of a single bipolar antisociality continuum. One obvious possibility is that Moffitt's two categories overlap to a considerable extent with two of Quay's types, and that the actions most characteristic of each of these groups can be located at the extreme ends of Patterson's bipolar antisociality dimension. Thus, Patterson (1992, p. 31) described the behaviors at the overt aggression pole of his conjectured dimension as including stubbornness, irritability, and temper tantrums. Since Moffitt's discussion indicates that her life-course-persistents as children were often difficult to control and had frequent temper tantrums (pp. 682–683), and Quay has characterized the undersocialized aggressors as frequently disruptive, disobedient, and difficult to control, it would appear that many of their antisocial behaviors match those at the overtly aggressive pole of the antisociality continuum.

Similarly, Moffitt's other category, the adolescent-limited delinquents, seems to have much in common with Quay's socialized aggression group, and at least some of their most typical actions are easily located at the covert (or clandestine) end of Patterson's (1992) dimension. Thus, all three of these formulations hold that the children of this type are socially competent and that their illegal, counternormative actions are greatly influenced by the behavior of their peers.

Motives for Antisocial Behavior

Most discussions of adolescent antisocial behavior devote little attention to the motivations behind the counternormative actions. However, Patterson's (1992) analysis of antisocial conduct emphasizes the instrumental role of these acts, and in accord with his formulation, it is quite likely that many of these behaviors are instrumentally oriented in the sense that they are performed in order to achieve some extrinsic benefit. Farrington (1995) has listed some of the gains that delinquents might anticipate when they contemplate a transgression. When the persons in his London sample who reported having violated the law were queried as to why they had acted as they did, "The most common reasons given ... were utilitarian, rational or economic: offences were committed for material gain .... The next most common category of reasons were for excitement, for enjoyment, or to relieve boredom ..." (p. 935).

We do not know at present whether each of the different types of delinquents postulated by Moffitt or by other investigators such as Quay would give the same kinds of reasons for many of their offenses. Moffitt (1993) held, however, that much of the counternormative conduct displayed by her adolescent-limiteds grows out of the tension these youths feel because of the discrepancy between their physiological maturity and their socially defined immaturity. As a result, they presumably are especially determined to gain "mature status, with its consequent power and privilege" (p. 686) and thus want to demonstrate their independence. In general, although we would expect life-course-persistent delinquents to be at least somewhat responsive to anticipated rewards and punishments, Moffitt's conception seems to imply that adolescent-limited offenders are much more sensitive to shifting reinforcement contingencies. As was mentioned earlier, "they maintain control over their antisocial responses and use antisocial behavior only in situations where it may serve an instrumental function" (p. 686).

Whether or not the adolescent-limiteds (and/or the socialized aggressors) are characteristically more responsive to changing reinforcement contingencies than the life-course-persistents (and/or the undersocialized aggressors), many of the aggressive actions carried out by the latter group apparently are not entirely instrumental in nature. Moffitt's discussion of the life-course-persistents certainly suggests that these persons are

subject to periodic outbursts of temper during which they may assault those they believe have affronted them. Assuming that they are at the extreme overt aggression pole of Patterson's antisociality continuum, these outbursts might be an older version of the temper tantrums they are likely to have exhibited as younger children. It is also possible that these people are similar to the reactive aggressors described by Dodge and Coie (1897). In the research conducted by these latter investigators, children identified by their teachers as easily angered and assaultive were typically quick to attribute hostility to others around them and also to say they had to strike back at those who had wronged them. We can also see this pattern in the individual (rather than group) fights engaged in by a number of Farrington's highly antisocial youngsters. According to Farrington (1995), those who fought in groups often did so to help a friend or to defend themselves; but in "individual fights, the boy was usually provoked, became angry, and hit out to hurt his opponent" (p. 935).

[*See also* Antisocial Personality Disorder; *and* Prosocial Behavior.]

Bibliography

Achenbach, T. M. (1985). *Assessment and taxonomy of child and adolescent psychopathology.* Newbury Park, CA: Sage.

American Psychiatric Association. (1987). *Diagnostic and statistical manual of mental disorders* (3rd ed. rev.). Washington, DC: Author.

American Psychiatric Association. (1994). *Diagnostic and statistical manual of mental disorders* (4th ed.). Washington, DC: Author.

Dodge, K. A., & Cole, J. D. (1987). Social-information-processing factors in reactive and proactive aggression in children's peer groups. *Journal of Personality and Social Psychology, 53,* 1146–1158.

Farrington, D. P. (1991). Antisocial personality from childhood to adulthood. *The Psychologist, 4,* 389–394.

Farrington, D. P. (1995). The development of offending and antisocial behaviour from childhood: Key findings from the Cambridge Study in Delinquent Development. *Journal of Child Psychology and Psychiatry, 36,* 929–964.

Gottfredson, S. D., Warner, B. D., & Taylor, R. B. (1988). Conflict and consensus about criminal justice in Maryland. In N. Walker & M. Hough (Eds.), *Public attitudes to sentencing: Surveys from 5 countries* (pp. 16–55). Aldershot, UK/Brookfield, VT: Gower.

Huesmann, L. R., Eron, L. D., Lefkowitz, M. M., & Walder, L. O. (1984). Stability of aggression over time and generations. *Developmental Psychology, 20,* 1120–1134.

Kazdin, A. E. (1987). *Conduct disorders in childhood and adolescence.* Newbury Park, CA: Sage.

Loeber, R., & Schmaling, K. B. (1985). Empirical evidence for overt and covert patterns of antisocial conduct problems: A metaanalysis. *Journal of Abnormal Child Psychology, 13,* 337–353.

Moffitt, T. E. (1993). Adolescent-limited and life-course-persistent antisocial behavior: A developmental taxonomy. *Psychological Review, 100*, 674–701.

Patterson, G. R., Reid, J. B., & Dishion, T. J. (1992). *Antisocial boys: A social interactional approach.* Eugene, OR: Castalia.

Quay, H. C. (1987). Patterns of delinquent behavior. In H. C. Quay (Ed.), *Handbook of juvenile delinquency* (pp. 118–138). New York: Wiley.

Robins, L. N. (1978). Sturdy childhood predictors of adult antisocial behaviour: Replications from longitudinal studies. *Psychological Medicine, 8*, 611–622.

Robins, L. N., & Wish, E. (1977). Childhood deviance as a developmental process: A study of 223 urban Black men from birth to 18. *Social Forces, 56*, 448–473.

West, D. J., & Farrington, D. P. (1977). *The delinquent way of life.* London: Heinemann.

Leonard Berkowitz

ANTISOCIAL PERSONALITY DISORDER is the presence of a chronic and pervasive disposition to disregard and violate the rights of others (Widiger & Hicklin, 1995). Persons with this disorder have a pervasive disregard for others (e.g., lack of empathy, conscience, guilt, or remorse) that is typically and characteristically expressed through a violation of the rights of others (e.g., through criminal, exploitative, abusive, or other comparable behaviors). The disorder is diagnosed by the presence of repeated failures to conform to social norms with respect to lawful behavior, exploitation of others, deceitfulness, lack of remorse, impulsivity, aggressiveness, reckless disregard for the safety of self and others, and irresponsibility (American Psychiatric Association, 1994).

Antisocial personality disorder is one of the most harmful and destructive mental disorders. The disorder is of substantial concern to clinicians because its presence will invariably undermine the treatment of other mental disorders, and of tremendous concern to the general public because they are victimized by the disorder as much, if not more, than the persons with the disorder. It is not surprising then that it has been the most heavily researched personality disorder.

Antisocial personality disorder has gone by many names throughout its history, including *psychopathy, sociopathy,* and *dyssocial personality disorder* (Widiger & Hicklin, 1995). Clinicians throughout history have described persons who were impulsive, rageful, and immoral without any obvious impairment in reasoning. These persons lacked the apparent signs of a mental disorder, such as depression, anxiety, or hallucinations, yet they also appeared to be incapable of feelings of remorse, empathy, or morality. One of the more influential formulations of the disorder was provided by Cleckley (1941). He emphasized such features as a failure to learn from experience, lack of remorse or shame, superficial charm, deceitfulness, lack of empathy, callousness, egocentricity, arrogance, and absence of anxiety. The American Psychiatric Association's (1994) diagnostic criteria in the *Diagnostic and Statistical Manual of Mental Disorders* (*DSM–IV*) relate closely to this original description, but place relatively more emphasis on overt, behavioral indicators (e.g., repeated history of arrests, failure to honor financial obligations, and physical assaults) in order to ensure a reliability in clinical assessment. A more faithful and equally influential reproduction of the original Cleckley diagnostic criteria for psychopathy has been developed for research purposes (Hart & Hare, 1997), but it is unclear whether these criteria could be used reliably within general clinical practice (Widiger & Corbitt, 1995).

Approximately 1% of females and 3% of males within the general community will have the disorder, although substantially more males than this may have clinically significant antisocial personality traits (Robins, Tipp, & Przybeck, 1991). There do not appear to be any differences between ethnic groups in the rate of the disorder when socioeconomic differences are considered. The disorder does occur more often within lower socioeconomic populations and urban settings, which may be both an effect and a cause. Persons with this disorder are likely to drift toward a lower socioeconomic level, and a tough, harsh, impoverished, and crime-ridden environment will facilitate its development. As many as 50% of male inmates will meet the *DSM–IV* criteria for the disorder, but the emphasis within the *DSM–IV* on overt acts of criminality, irresponsibility, impulsivity, aggression, and deliquency may contribute to an overdiagnosis within prison settings (as well as an underdiagnosis within more legitimate professions). A more conservative estimate is that 20% of male inmates have the disorder (Hart & Hare, 1997; Widiger & Corbitt, 1995).

Antisocial personality disorder does not develop and cannot be diagnosed until the age of 18, as many adolescents who display delinquent, violent, and other criminal behaviors do not in fact have the disorder. However, the premorbid symptoms of the disorder are present within a childhood conduct disorder (Lynam, 1996), and evidence of a conduct disorder is required for the diagnosis in adulthood (*DSM–IV*). A prototypic developmental course for the disorder is the occurrence of irritability and negativism during infancy; harshly defiant and argumentative behavior during preschool; fighting, deceit, and petty theft during grade school; assault, destruction of property, and sexual precocity during preadolescence; robbery and substance abuse during adolescence; and callous, brutally exploitative relationships and repeated criminal activity as an adult (Caspi & Moffitt, 1995).

There does not appear to be a specific etiology for the development of an antisocial personality disorder.

There appear instead to be a multitude of contributing factors (biological, psychological, and social) that interact over time in different ways across different individuals. There is support from twin, family, and adoption studies for a genetic disposition toward antisocial behaviors (Carey & Goldman, 1997). A variety of pathologies have also been proposed, including low baseline levels of arousal, deficits in the processing of emotional cues, impairment in passive avoidance learning, neuropsychological deficits in executive functions, and/or deficits in behavioral inhibition (Caspi & Moffitt, 1995; Newman, 1997). It should be emphasized, however, that the research does not suggest that antisocial personality disorder is itself inherited. The phenotypic traits that are correlated with the transmitted genotypes are unclear. These may include tendencies toward impulsivity (low constraint or self-regulation), antagonism (aggressiveness), and/or low anxiety. For example, normal levels of anxiety will facilitate the internalization of a moral conscience by associating distress and anxiety with the social mores modeled and reinforced by parents, and the temperament of self-regulation (constraint) may be necessary to modulate impulses into a socially acceptable manner (Kochanska, 1991).

The interaction of genetic dispositions with a variety of additional, important environmental experiences may develop the behavior pattern diagnosed as antisocial personality disorder. Many studies have indicated the contribution of family, peer, cultural, and other environmental factors, such as (1) modeling by parental figures and peers; (2) excessively cruel, lenient, or erratic parental discipline; and (3) a tough, harsh environment in which feelings of empathy and warmth are often discouraged (if not punished), and tough-mindedness, aggression, and exploitation are rewarded. Antisocial personality disorder may, in some cases, be the cumulative result of early experiences of physical and sexual abuse, aggressive parental models, and erratic discipline, which are further reinforced over time through the encouragement of peers, the immediate benefits of exploitation, and a selective attention for cues of antagonism and hostility (Dishion, French, & Patterson, 1995).

A concern regarding the validity of the diagnosis is whether it is simply a moral judgment masquerading as a clinical diagnosis. Persons with this disorder rarely seek treatment, and their motivation for change is often provided by an external source, such as a court order or an ultimatum by an employer or relative. However, those with the disorder will often fail to appreciate that it was not really their choice to be irresponsible, exploitative, impulsive, callous, and hedonistic, and they rarely recognize the maladaptive nature of their lifestyle (Widiger & Hicklin, 1995). An antisocial lifestyle is at times romanticized within literature and media, but the benefits and pleasures are usually fleeting and often illusory. The material success depends on a failure of society to find and punish them. They are hunters of victims, but they are also themselves the focus and concern of various agencies of law enforcement. Antisocial personality disorder is associated with an increased risk for premature and violent death, accidents, incarceration, unemployment, and impoverishment (Robins et al., 1991). Persons with this disorder will often develop other conditions, particularly substance abuse and dependency, depression, pathological gambling, and other disorders of impulse dyscontrol. Even those who succeed in avoiding these outcomes will usually experience other costs, such as failed relationships. Persons with this disorder will lack substantial feelings of guilt, remorse, and empathy. They may find this to be advantageous in their exploitation of others, but these deficits will be equally problematic in developing meaningful and sustained relationships. Their relationships and their lives will often be shallow and superficial.

Antisocial personality disorder is the most difficult of the personality disorders to treat. There is no pharmacotherapy for psychopathy, and individual psychotherapy is rarely successful. A prognostic indicator is the ability to establish a meaningful rapport and a sincere motivation for change. Residential treatment programs that remove the person from his or her criminal environment and provide a firm structure with daily and intense confrontation by peers have at times provided positive results, but it is unclear if the improvements are sustained. Preventive interventions during childhood may be the most effective approach, but the prevention and treatment of conduct disorder is itself expensive, problematic, and uncertain (Reid & Eddy, 1997).

[*See also* Antisocial Behavior; *and* Personality Disorders.]

Bibliography

American Psychiatric Association. (1994). *Diagnostic and statistical manual of mental disorders* (4th ed.). Washington, DC: Author.

Carey, G., & Goldman, D. (1997). The genetics of antisocial behavior. In D. M. Stoff, J. Breiling, & J. D. Maser (Eds.), *Handbook of antisocial behavior* (pp. 243–254). New York: Wiley. Review of scientific research on heritability of antisocial behavior.

Caspi, A., & Moffitt, T. E. (1995). The continuity of maladaptive behavior: From description to understanding in the study of antisocial behavior. In D. Cicchetti & D. J. Cohen (Eds.), *Developmental psychopathology* (Vol. 2, pp. 472–511). New York: Wiley. Review of longitudinal development and course of antisocial behavior.

Cleckley, H. (1941). *The mask of sanity*. St. Louis, MO: Mosby. Historically influential description of antisocial personality disorder.

Dishion, T. J., French, D. C., & Patterson, G. R. (1995). The development and ecology of antisocial behavior. In D. Cicchetti & D. J. Cohen (Eds.), *Developmental psychopathology* (Vol. 2, pp. 421–471). New York: Wiley. Scientific overview of childhood development of antisocial behavior.

Hart, S. D., & Hare, R. D. (1997). Psychopathy: Assessment and association with criminal conduct. In D. M. Stoff, J. Breiling, & J. D. Maser (Eds.), *Handbook of antisocial behavior* (pp. 22–35). New York: Wiley. Influential alternative diagnostic formulation of antisocial personality disorder.

Kochanska, G. (1991). Socialization and temperament in the development of guilt and conscience. *Child Development, 62,* 1379–1392. Integrative, scientific model of biological dispositions and environmental experiences for the development of a moral conscience.

Lynam, D. R. (1996). Early identification of chronic offenders: Who is the fledgling psychopath? *Psychological Bulletin, 120,* 209–234. Scientific overview of premorbid (childhood) indicators of antisocial personality disorder.

Newman, J. P. (1997). Conceptual models of the nervous system: Implications for antisocial behavior. In D. M. Stoff, J. Breiling, & J. D. Maser (Eds.), *Handbook of antisocial behavior* (pp. 324–355). New York: Wiley. Scientific overview of neurochemical models for antisocial personality disorder.

Reid, J. B., & Eddy, J. M. (1997). The prevention of antisocial behavior: Some considerations in the search for effective interventions. In D. M. Stoff, J. Breiling, & J. D. Maser (Eds.), *Handbook of antisocial behavior* (pp. 343–356). New York: Wiley. Scientific overview of alternative approaches to the prevention of antisocial behavior.

Robins, L. N., Tipp, J., & Przybeck, T. (1991). Antisocial personality. In L. N. Robins & D. A. Regier (Eds.). *Psychiatric disorders in America* (pp. 258–290). New York: Free Press. Epidemiology of antisocial personality disorder.

Widiger, T. A., & Corbitt, E. M. (1995). Antisocial personality disorder in DSM-IV. In W. J. Livesley (Ed.), *The DSM-IV personality disorders* (pp. 103–126). New York: Guilford Press. Description, rationale, and controversies concerning the DSM-IV diagnosis of antisocial personality disorder.

Widiger, T. A., & Hicklin, J. (1995). Antisocial personality disorder. In P. Wilner (Ed.), *Psychiatry* (pp. 1–13). Philadelphia: Lippincott-Raven. Overview of etiology, pathology, diagnosis, and treatment of antisocial personality disorder.

Thomas A. Widiger

ANXIETY is an emotion characterized by heightened autonomic system activity, specifically activation of the sympathetic nervous system (i.e., increased heart rate, blood pressure, respiration, and muscle tone), subjective feelings of tension, and cognitions that involve apprehension and worry. Although the subjective experience of anxiety is not necessarily accompanied by particular behaviors, behavioral indicators are often present, such as speech dysfluencies, avoidance of the focal object or event, immobilization, or observable tremor.

Several subtypes of anxiety, such as test anxiety, social anxiety, performance anxiety, appearance anxiety, sexual anxiety, and speech anxiety, have been identified. These subtypes share certain features in common, and any one of them could be characterized with terms such as *apprehension, dread, panic, tension,* and *worry.* The *Diagnostic and Statistical Manual of Mental Disorders (DSM–IV,* 1994) lists no fewer than a dozen different diagnostic categories of anxiety disorders, including panic attacks, specific phobias, social phobias, posttraumatic stress disorder, and generalized anxiety disorder.

Two constructs to which anxiety is related are fear and phobia. Although the terms are frequently used interchangeably, *fear* is often defined as a response to a clearly identifiable danger, whereas *anxiety* is conceptualized as a response to an unidentifiable threat or an anticipated danger. In addition, whereas the fear response is proportionate to the objective danger, anxiety responses are often more intense than is warranted by the perceived threat. However, not all theorists agree with these distinctions between fear and anxiety.

Phobia is defined as excessive anxiety or fear that occurs in response to a particular stimulus. The magnitude of the person's response to the feared stimulus clearly exceeds the objective threat, and phobias usually have a debilitating effect on the person's life. Phobias are typically divided into three categories: specific phobias, social phobia, and agoraphobia. As the name implies, specific phobias are fears of specific objects or situations, such as heights, flying, and animals. Social phobia represents a person's fear of social or performance situations in which he or she might be embarrassed or humiliated. People with agoraphobia fear being in situations from which they would have difficulty escaping, such as crowds, buses, or airplanes.

As anyone who has experienced anxiety can attest, anxiety can have a detrimental effect on behavior and cognitions. Students who anticipate performing poorly on a test may experience anxiety to such a degree that they have difficulty recalling relevant information. However, like most emotions, anxiety is inherently adaptive. The performance-enhancing effects of moderate levels of arousal have long been known. In addition, anxiety acts as an interrupt mechanism drawing attention away from secondary concerns to the problem at hand, thereby leading the individual to stop behavior that may be dangerous or threatening. For example, a person who experiences social anxiety may stop behaviors that are potentially embarrassing and might lead to interpersonal rejection.

One way of distinguishing adaptive from maladaptive anxiety is by viewing the "reasonableness" of the anxiety. For example, a person who is afraid of heights is, in fact, in little danger of falling. However, a person who is socially anxious may be rightfully concerned with being evaluated by others in undesired ways.

State Versus Trait Anxiety

People differ markedly in their tendency to experience anxiety. Whereas some people experience anxiety quite often, others feel anxious only rarely. Many of the early difficulties in defining anxiety stemmed from the failure to distinguish between state and trait anxiety. As defined by Charles Spielberger in *Anxiety and Behavior* (New York, 1966), state anxiety refers to transient feelings of anxiety at a given moment in time (i.e., "I feel anxious"). Trait anxiety, on the other hand, reflects individual differences in anxiety proneness or people's tendency to appraise situations as threatening and to respond to those situations with state anxiety behaviors (i.e., "I am an anxious person"). Trait anxiety does not imply that the person is chronically anxious but rather that he or she has a higher tendency than low trait anxious people to experience anxiety.

Low and high trait anxious people do not differ in their responses to nonthreatening situations or to situations that nearly everyone would appraise as stressful. Rather, the state anxiety reactions of trait anxious individuals exceed those of low trait anxious people only in situations that trait anxious people appraise as more threatening than low trait anxious people.

Theoretical Perspectives on Anxiety

A complete understanding of the etiology of anxiety has remained elusive, due in large part to the myriad of factors that may precipitate and maintain anxiety. Generally speaking, however, the diverse theoretical perspectives on anxiety can be divided into four general approaches: psychodynamic, expressive-behavioral, biological, and cognitive. Each of these theories explains aspects of anxiety, and all are needed to understand the phenomenon fully.

Psychodynamic. Tracing their origins back to Freud, psychodynamic theories of anxiety view anxiety as an unpleasant affective state originating in the unconscious. The anxiety is a signal or a symptom of an unconscious conflict, usually stemming from childhood, that remains unresolved. To deal with their feelings of anxiety, people develop psychological defenses that may be either adaptive (i.e., realistic anxiety) or maladaptive (i.e., neurotic anxiety).

Expressive-Behavioral Theories. Expressive-behavioral theories view anxiety as an innate response that has evolved because of its adaptive value. In an extension of Darwin's original formulation, Izard, in his book *Human Emotions* (New York, 1977), conceptualized anxiety as a composite of a number of discrete emotions, the most notable of which is fear. Other emotions that most frequently combine with fear to create anxiety include anger, guilt, shame, and interest. Which of these emotions combines with fear to create anxiety depends on the situation in which the anxiety is experienced. Discrete emotion theorists focus on the affective or feeling component of anxiety, deemphasizing cognitive elements of anxiety.

Biological Theories. Building on Harvard physiologist Walter Cannon's assertion earlier in the century that emotions are linked to brain function, biological theorists suggest that different emotions result from activation of specific parts of the brain. An influential biological theory of anxiety was proposed in *The Neuropsychology of Anxiety* (New York, 1982) by Jeffrey Gray, who stated that anxiety stems from activation of the behavioral inhibition system (BIS). As its name implies, the BIS inhibits behavior in response to threatening stimuli. People who are high in trait anxiety have very reactive behavioral inhibition systems.

Support for a biological basis of anxiety has also been found in studies showing that heredity plays a role in the experience of trait anxiety. Genetic factors create a biological vulnerability to anxiety, the manifestation of which is determined by environmental factors. Thus, individuals who are genetically predisposed to experience anxiety will be more likely than those with a low vulnerability to anxiety to interpret internal and external stimuli as threatening.

Cognitive Theories. All of the prominent cognitive theories of anxiety are appraisal theories. The appraisal process involves two stages, a primary appraisal in which an individual determines the threat posed by the environment, and, following a threatening primary appraisal, a secondary appraisal where the individual evaluates his or her ability to cope with the demands imposed by the environment. In their book *Anxiety Disorders and Phobias: A Cognitive Perspective*, Beck, Emery, and Greenberg (New York, 1985) suggest that maladaptive anxiety results from distortions in this appraisal process. People who suffer from chronic anxiety are those who misperceive benign situations as threatening.

In an extension of the cognitive approach, David Barlow suggests that anxiety is a cognitive-affective phenomenon, at the core of which lies negative affect. Perceptions of threat are influenced by early experiences with uncontrollability that create a psychological vulnerability to anxiety and by a biological predisposition to experience anxiety in the face of negative life events. Specifically, negative life events activate the biological vulnerability to stress, leading trait anxious individuals to perceive the environment as threatening even in the absence of an identifiable stressor. If the person then perceives that the event is uncontrollable and unpredictable (i.e., it could happen again) and perceives that he or she lacks the necessary coping resources, anxiety will be experienced.

Summary. Because of the multifaceted nature of anxiety, no one of these theories adequately describes all of the factors related to its onset and maintenance. Genetic predispositions, early childhood experiences with uncontrollable events, certain kinds of cognitions and information processing, all contribute to creating anxiety.

The Measurement of Anxiety

Self-report measures have been used in the measurement of anxiety, along with physiological measures (e.g., heart rate, blood pressure, respiration), and behavioral observations (e.g., speech dysfluencies, self-manipulation, bodily movement, hand-wringing). One problem, however, is that the correlations among the three types of measures are often low. Thus, an individual who is experiencing heightened physiological arousal and who reports feeling anxious may display few, if any, behaviors indicating anxiety.

Self-Report Measures. Self-report measures can be divided into three categories: measures of trait anxiety, state anxiety, or situation-specific anxiety (e.g., social anxiety, test anxiety, etc.). One of the most commonly used self-report measures of anxiety is the State-Trait Anxiety Inventory (STAI) developed by Spielberger, Gorsuch, and Lushene (*Test Manual for the State-Trait Anxiety Inventory*, Palo Alto, CA, 1970). Participants respond to each of the 20 state anxiety items using a four-point Likert scale to indicate the intensity with which they experience anxiety at a particular point. Representative items include "I feel tense," "I feel high-strung," and "I feel anxious." The 20-trait anxiety items examine the frequency with which respondents generally experience anxiety through items such as "I feel nervous and restless," "I feel like crying," and "I take things hard."

In spite of the wide use of the STAI as a measure of anxiety, researchers have tended to study specific manifestations of anxiety, such as performance anxiety, social anxiety, test anxiety, and speech anxiety, rather than anxiety more generally. Thus, they use situation specific measures that are tailored to the specific type of anxiety being researched. For example, to study social anxiety, a researcher might use the Interaction Anxiousness Scale, the Social Avoidance and Distress Scale, or the Fear of Negative Evaluation Scale.

Physiological Measures. Because anxiety involves activation of the sympathetic nervous system, physiological measures of anxiety include assessments of heart rate, blood pressure, muscle tone, and respiration. Unlike self-report and behavioral assessments of anxiety, physiological measures are less easily regulated by the respondent, thereby providing a potentially more accurate assessment of anxiety.

Behavioral Measures. Ideally, direct observations of behavior would occur in a naturalistic environment. However, due to the infrequent nature of many behaviors, the lack of experimental control, and the potential biasing effects of the presence of an observer, naturalistic observations of anxious behaviors have not always proved viable. Thus, most behavioral assessments of anxiety have occurred within a laboratory setting. However, laboratory studies that induce anxiety in humans have themselves been problematic, primarily for ethical reasons. Nevertheless, depending on the type of anxiety under investigation, any number of behavioral observations can be made including speech dysfluencies, performance during role plays, and avoidance of anxiety producing stimuli.

Cultural Variations

Although anxiety is a universal emotion, the experience, expression, and interpretation of anxiety vary across cultures. Thus, not surprisingly, the prevalence rates of particular types of anxiety vary across cultures. Societies that emphasize conformity and interpersonal evaluation show higher proportions of social anxiety, for example, than societies that place less importance on the evaluations of others. Depending on the standards of a particular culture, what is considered normal in one culture might be considered pathological anxiety in another.

In spite of some cross-cultural variability in the experience of anxiety, facial expressions of fear and anxiety are universally recognized, as discussed by Ekman and Friesen in *Unmasking the Face* (Englewood Cliffs, NJ, 1975). Moreover, some fears, such as the fear of snakes and children's fear of strangers, are believed to be uniformly experienced across cultures, lending support to theories concerned with the genetic basis of some types of anxiety.

[*See also* Anxiety Disorders.]

Bibliography

American Psychiatric Association. (1994). *Diagnostic and statistical manual of mental disorders* (4th ed.). Washington, DC: Author.

Barlow, D. H. (1988). *Anxiety and its disorders.* New York: Guilford Press. One of the most readable and comprehensive sources for information related to anxiety.

Barlow, D. H. (1991). The nature of anxiety: Anxiety, depression, and emotional disorders. In R. M. Rapee & D. H. Barlow (Eds.), *Chronic anxiety: Generalized anxiety disorder and mixed anxiety-depression* (pp. 1–28). New York: Guilford Press. This chapter is best viewed as a summary of information contained in Barlow's *Anxiety and its disorders* book. The entire edited volume by Rapee and Barlow contains very interesting information related to anxiety, its antecedents, and anxiety disorders.

Baumeister, R. F., & Tice, D. M. (1990). Anxiety and social exclusion. *Journal of Social and Clinical Psychology, 9,* 165–195. Suggests that anxiety serves as an interrupt mechanism alerting individuals to threats to their social inclusion. Anxiety stops ongoing behavior that might jeopardize the degree to which one was included.

Bellack, A. S., & Lombardo, T. W. (1984). Measurement of anxiety. In S. M. Turner (Ed.), *Behavioral theories and treatment of anxiety* (pp. 51–89). New York: Plenum Press.

Edelmann, R. J. (1992). *Anxiety: Theory, research, and intervention in clinical and health psychology.* New York: Wiley. Provides a good overview of anxiety as well as looking at specific anxiety disorders.

Goodwin, D. W. (1986). *Anxiety.* New York: Oxford University Press. Readable overview of anxiety along with coverage of anxiety disorders.

Spielberger, C. D. (1976). The nature and measurement of anxiety. In C. D. Spielberger & R. Diaz-Guerrero (Eds.), *Cross-cultural anxiety* (pp. 3–12). New York: Wiley.

Taylor, C. B., & Arnow, B. (1988). *The nature and treatment of anxiety disorders.* New York: Free Press. Scholarly and comprehensive examination of anxiety and its disorders.

Robin M. Kowalski

ANXIETY DISORDERS. The term *anxiety disorders* refers to a group of 12 disorders that have as their central organizing theme, the emotional state of fear, worry, or anxious apprehension. Anxiety disorders usually are conceptualized as having three distinct components (Lang, 1977). The somatic component refers to the presence of physical sensations. Common somatic symptoms include heart palpitations, sweating, trembling or shaking, shortness of breath, choking, chest pain, nausea or abdominal distress, dizziness or lightheadedness, derealization, numbness or tingling, and chills or hot flashes. These physical symptoms may occur alone or in various combinations. When four or more symptoms occur together (or fewer physical symptoms in combination with a fear of dying or a fear of losing control or going crazy) the result is termed a *panic attack*. Panic attacks can occur in the context of any of the anxiety disorders, although they are most common in panic disorder, where they are often considered to occur "out of the blue." However, they also can be triggered by the occurrence or in anticipation of a specific feared situation or event.

The second component of anxiety disorders (subjective distress), sometimes termed the *cognitive component*, usually consists of recurrent and unwanted intrusive thoughts, images, or worries. The form of the cognitions can include (1) a sudden flashback: (2) a fearful or catastrophic thought associated with a particular object or event: or (3) recurrent and hard to eliminate thoughts, images, or impulses, as in obsessions or worries. Content of the cognitions ranges from excessive concern about a specific event such as dying in a plane crash or being contaminated by germs, or about a myriad of everyday events such as family matters, personal finances, or personal health. Like physical symptoms, cognitive phenomena can be triggered by the occurrence of a specific event such as boarding an airplane. At other times, they occur spontaneously or are described as "ever present."

The third component of anxiety disorders is behavioral avoidance, wherein the individual avoids situations or events that create subjective and physiological distress. If thrust into such a situation (e.g., a person who fears public speaking is asked to speak extemporaneously), the individual might attempt to escape. A special form of behavioral avoidance are rituals, which are repetitive, specific acts designed to prevent or undo the effects of certain stimuli, events, or situations. Examples of rituals include repetitive washing or cleaning behaviors.

All of the anxiety disorders have characteristic physical, cognitive, and behavioral components. By far the most common disorders in the general population are phobias. The category of *specific phobia* includes conditions characterized by excessive distress elicited by the presence or in anticipation of certain objects, situations, or events. The most common subtypes of specific phobias include the animal type (e.g., dogs, insects), the natural environment type (e.g., water), the blood-injection-injury type (e.g., needles, blood tests), and the situational type (e.g., heights, darkness). Approximately 11% of the general population will suffer from a specific phobia during their lifetime (Kessler et al., 1994).

Social phobia is excessive fear that one will do or say something in front of others that will be considered embarrassing or humiliating. Examples include fear of speaking, eating, drinking, or writing in front of others. In addition, those with this disorder often fear general social interactions such as informal conversations, business meetings, or meeting new people. Some individuals with social phobia fear only a few specific situations such as reading or speaking in front of an audience. For others, fear is much more pervasive, encompassing a broad range of social situations. Approximately 13% of the general population suffers from social phobia during their lifetime (Kessler et al., 1994).

There are three disorders (panic disorder without agoraphobia, panic disorder with agoraphobia, and agoraphobia without history of panic disorder) that represent various combinations of (1) avoidance of places from which escape might be difficult (i.e., the individual might feel trapped and unable to leave the situation) and (2) the presence-absence of panic attacks. In panic disorder without agoraphobia, the individual has recurrent and unexpected panic attacks but does not avoid situations from which it might be difficult to escape (i.e., due to emotional distress). Panic disorder with agoraphobia includes recurrent and unexpected panic attacks plus avoidance of places and situations from which escape might be difficult. In agoraphobia without history of panic disorder, behavioral avoidance is present but the person has never experienced panic attacks. Approximately 9% of the general population has one of these disorders during their lifetime (Kessler et al., 1994).

Individuals with obsessive-compulsive disorder (OCD) experience recurrent, intrusive, and unwanted thoughts. The content includes worries about contamination, harm to oneself or others, or thoughts that a catastrophic event might happen. The thoughts usually are accompanied by ritualistic behaviors designed to prevent or undo feared events. Rituals might include repeated washing or cleaning, repeatedly checking door locks or oven jets, or collecting (and refusing to throw away) useless items such as old newspapers or magazines. OCD affects about 2% of the general population.

Post-traumatic stress disorder (PTSD) is somewhat different from the other anxiety disorders because it begins with experiencing or witnessing an actual event that involves death or serious physical injury, or threat to the physical integrity of self or others (i.e., a traumatic event). The event is then recurrently reexperienced (primarily in the form of flashbacks) and is accompanied by behavioral avoidance, emotional numbing, and increased physiological arousal. *Acute stress disorder*, like PTSD, also involves initial exposure to a traumatic event and has the same symptoms as PTSD, but the symptomatology does not last longer than four weeks.

Excessive anxiety about various events or activities (such as one's financial or employment status, physical health of self or family) coupled with physical symptoms such as restlessness, inability to concentrate, irritability, and sleep disturbance are the clinical features of *generalized anxiety disorder*, which affects about 5% of the general population (Kessler et al., 1994). Finally, there are three less frequently discussed anxiety disorders, anxiety disorder due to a medical condition, substance-induced anxiety disorder and anxiety disorder not otherwise specified. In anxiety disorder due to a medical condition, the anxiety symptoms are the direct physiological consequence of a general medical state (e.g., hyperthyroidism). Similarly, a diagnosis of substance-induced anxiety disorder indicates that the symptoms result from substance intoxication, withdrawal, or medication use. Finally, the term *anxiety disorders not otherwise specified* is used for those cases where anxiety is a prominent feature but the symptoms do not fit the criteria for any of the disorders listed above. These latter three conditions rarely have been the focus of research and little is known about them.

Developmental Considerations

Anxiety disorders can occur at any age and children as well as adults can suffer from any of the conditions. However, panic disorder (with or without agoraphobia) is rare in young children but more common in adolescents. The core features of anxiety disorders in children are similar to those seen in adults who suffer from the same disorder, but children often do not discuss their experience in the same fashion. Thus, developmental stage affects certain aspects of the clinical presentation. One difference relates to physical symptoms experienced by children and adults. Although any of the previously mentioned physical symptoms may occur in children, the most common physical complaints in this age group are stomachaches and headaches. A second difference is that younger children are less able to report specific negative cognitions or worries. Rather, they often describe a general sense of unease or nonspecific distress.

In addition to the range of disorders listed above, children also may be diagnosed with separation anxiety disorder which is excessive and developmentally inappropriate anxiety when separated from home or a primary caretaker. This disorder, rarely seen in adults, can be seriously impairing. Children may refuse to go to school, sleep over at a friend's house, or otherwise separate from a major attachment figure. Until recently, children sometimes received a diagnosis of school phobia when they expressed reluctance or refusal to attend school. However, the term *school phobia* is a misnomer. Children who refuse to go to school rarely are afraid of the school itself. Rather, their refusal is a behavioral expression of an underlying disorder such as an anxiety disorder, an affective disorder, or perhaps a conduct disorder. Due to the recognition that school refusal may result from various disorders, the term *school phobia* is no longer used.

In general, the exact relationship between childhood and adult anxiety disorders is unclear. Some adults with anxiety disorders report that they experienced anxiety "all their lives." Other studies have reported that children sometimes "outgrow" their fears. However, the specific characteristics of those who outgrow their fears versus those who do not are currently unknown.

Etiology of Anxiety Disorders

Both biological and psychological theories have been offered as explanations for the etiology of anxiety disorders. Twin studies and family studies are cited commonly as evidence of biological causation. For example, the probability of both twins having an anxiety disorder is higher for monozygotic (identical) twins than dizygotic (fraternal) twins. Similarly, family studies (Beidel & Turner, 1997) indicate that overall, about 5 to 15% of relatives of an individual with an anxiety disorder also have anxiety disorders. The rate is much lower among normal individuals, with only 1 to 5% having an anxiety disorder. Overall, rates for affected relatives are higher for specific phobia, but the relationship remains the same. That is, among those with a specific phobia, 31% of family members also had a specific phobia whereas only 11% of the relatives of someone without a disorder had specific phobia (Fyer et al., 1990). However, the available evidence does not support a strict genetic interpretation of etiology. For example, even though identical twins were both more likely to have an anxiety disorder, it was not the same disorder; i.e., one twin might have panic disorder and the other a specific phobia. Similarly for family studies, although the presence of an anxiety disorder was higher among the relatives of an individual with an anxiety disorder, most relatives did not develop disorders. In summary, these results suggest that what might be inherited is a tendency to develop maladaptive anxiety but not a specific anxiety disorder (Turner, Beidel, & Wolff, 1996).

The construct of behavioral inhibition (BI) has been suggested as the constitutional or biological basis for anxiety disorders. Identified in approximately 10 to 20% of Caucasian toddlers, BI is defined as reluctance to interact with unfamiliar people, objects, or situations (Kagan, Reznick, & Snidman, 1987). Precursors to BI have been identified as early as four months of age, but it is not stable among all the children who exhibit it at an early age. That is, some children appear to "outgrow" their inhibition. Although children who are behaviorally inhibited in early childhood are more likely to develop an anxiety disorder than other children, not all behaviorally inhibited children develop anxiety disorders, again leading to the conclusion that biology probably provides only part of the etiological explanation.

Pathways to Fear Development

Behavioral theories of etiology usually invoke one of three pathways to the development of fear: direct conditioning, observational learning, or information transfer. Direct conditioning is the method laypeople usually invoke when attempting to understand the etiology of fears and phobias. A direct conditioning model of fear acquisition was first demonstrated in 1920 when Watson and Rayner (1920) reported on the conditioning of fear in Little Albert. Mowrer's (1947) two-factory theory is sometimes invoked to explain fear acquisition and maintenance. Initially, fear is acquired through classical conditioning (i.e., a neutral event is paired with an aversive stimulus, in this case, one that elicits fear).

Once the fear is acquired, it is maintained through operant conditioning (i.e., fear motivates the individual to avoid or escape from the fear-producing stimulus and via negative reinforcement, these avoidant responses become strengthened). Direct conditioning explains the etiology of some, but not all, anxiety disorders and may be particularly relevant for PTSD. However, it does not address other aspects of fear acquisition, such as why some individuals exposed to traumatic events do not develop an anxiety disorder (e.g., Stemberger, Turner, Beidel, & Calhoun, 1995)

A second method of fear acquisition is through vicarious conditioning, also known as social learning or modeling. In this method, fear is acquired vicariously by watching another behave fearfully. By watching the model, the observer acquires the same fear. Mineka and colleagues (e.g., Cook & Mineka, 1989) reported that fear of snakes was acquired vicariously by rhesus monkeys after as little as 8 minutes of observation. Finally, a third behavioral explanation of fear acquisition is information transfer, whereby an individual is instructed that a particular object, situation, or event is dangerous or should be avoided. Both modeling and information transfer can be powerful methods of fear acquisition and provide an alternative hypothesis for the higher prevalence of anxiety disorders among family members. That is, observation of another family member behaving fearfully or being told, particularly by a parent, that something is dangerous may explain higher rates of anxiety disorders in particular families.

Studies examining behavioral acquisition of phobias indicate that direct conditioning is the most commonly reported method, followed by observational learning and then information transfer (e.g., Ost & Hugdahl, 1984). However, there are a number of individuals who deny the acquisition of anxiety through any of these methods or who cannot recall a specific method. Furthermore, as noted, not every individual who suffers a traumatic event develops an anxiety disorder. In summary, the etiology of anxiety disorders is a complex issue, defying a simple explanation. Most researchers believe that the development of anxiety disorders includes both biological and environmental factors. Furthermore, there probably is not one single pathway. That is, different individuals may develop the same disorder through different means.

Clinical Course of Anxiety Disorders

Anxiety disorders, unlike affective disorders, are considered to have a chronic course, albeit waxing and waning in intensity. Overall, symptom exacerbation appears correlated with the occurrence of significant life stressors. Some individuals probably do overcome anxiety disorders without professional intervention, but the characteristics of those who are successful on their own are unknown. Some individuals may so successfully avoid the feared event, object, or situation that the disorder may appear to be in remission or to have disappeared entirely. Thus, behavioral avoidance may reduce symptoms. However, avoidance can result in substantial functional impairment. For example, an individual with panic disorder with agoraphobia may become "housebound" (i.e., avoid going out into the community in order to avoid panic attacks and thereby becoming unable to leave the house). Furthermore, if the person were forced to leave the house, the symptoms often return. Therefore, avoidance can reduce anxious symptomatology but rarely eliminates it. Finally, with respect to children, parents may play an important role in the maintenance of a child's anxiety disorder. Data suggest that parents of children with anxiety disorders are more likely to reinforce children's avoidance behaviors. This parental behavior may be a factor in maintaining the disorder and attenuating treatment outcome (e.g., Barrett et al., 1996).

Overlap in Symptomatology

One important recent change in the conceptualization of anxiety disorders has been the recognition that panic attacks are not unique to any one particular disorder. Previously, panic attacks were assumed to have a distinct biological etiology and considered to occur only in the context of panic disorder. However, closer examination revealed that panic attacks occurred in many, if not all, of the anxiety disorders (except agoraphobia without history of panic), as well as in other disorders (e.g., depression) and among those with no disorder at all. This acknowledgment of the pervasive nature of panic attacks is one of the clearest examples of the overlapping symptomatology among these disorders.

In addition to the overlapping physical symptoms, anxiety disorders often co-occur. Early studies suggested that over 50% of anxiety patients seeking treatment in a specialty anxiety clinic were diagnosed with more than one anxiety disorder (Sanderson, Rapee, & Barlow, 1987). Generalized anxiety disorder was one of the commonly co-occurring disorders in both adults and children. In fact, this disorder rarely occurs in isolation. Furthermore, overlap among anxiety disorders is even more prominent in children than in adults. In one sample, 69% of children had more than one anxiety disorder (Costello & Angold, 1995)

Anxiety and affective disorders also often co-occur. Due to overlap in specific symptomatology, it sometimes is difficult to determine if the patient has an anxiety disorder, an affective disorder, or both. For example, somatic complaints such as difficulty falling asleep, loss of appetite, and difficulty concentrating can be associated with either class of disorders. In addition, second-ary depression (i.e., depression that occurs after the onset of the anxiety disorder) is common among anxiety patients, with estimates ranging from 17.54 to 60% of all anxiety patients (Beidel & Turner, 1997).

The current diagnostic system differentiates Axis I disorders (clinical syndromes such as anxiety disorders and affective disorders) from Axis II (personality) disorders. However, despite this distinction, anxiety often is the chief presenting complaint among individuals with personality disorders. Those with paranoid personality disorder, for example, may describe feeling anxious when in the company of strangers. Similarly, those with obsessive-compulsive personality disorder may become anxious if they are unable to maintain control of their physical or interpersonal environment. Thus, even in cases where the individual is suffering from an Axis II personality disorder, anxiety symptoms may be an important part of the clinical presentation.

Summary

Except for substance abuse, the anxiety disorders are the most common mental health problem in the United States, affecting approximately 25% of the general population (Kessler et al., 1994). They occur at any age and can be associated with substantial functional impairment. Without treatment, they tend to be chronic. However, effective pharmacological and psychological interventions exist and offer a good long-term prognosis. Finally, anxiety may be part of the clinical picture of many different conditions and may result from, or be associated with various medical conditions.

[*See also* Anxiety; Obsessive-Compulsive Disorder; Panic Disorder; Posttraumatic Stress Disorder; *and* Specific Phobia.]

Bibliography

Barrett, P. M., Dadds, M. R., Rapee, R. M., & Ryan, S. M. (1996). Family intervention for childhood anxiety: A controlled trial. *Journal of Consulting and Clinical Psychology, 64,* 333–342.

Beidel, D. C., & Turner, S. M. (1997). Anxiety disorders. In S. M. Turner & M. Hersen (Eds.), *Adult psychopathology and diagnosis* (3rd ed., pp. 282–332). New York: Wiley.

Cook, M., & Mineka, S. (1989). Observational condition of fear to fear-relevant versus fear-irrelevant stimuli in rhesus monkeys. *Journal of Abnormal Psychology, 98,* 448–459.

Costello, E. J., & Angold, A. (1995). Epidemiology. In J. S. March (Ed.), *Anxiety disorders in children and adolescents* (pp. 109–124). New York: Guilford Press.

Fyer, A. J., Manuzza, S., Gallops, M. S., Martin, L. Y., Aaronson, C., Gorman, J. M., Liebowitz, M. R., & Klein, D. F. (1990). Familial transmission of simple phobias and fears: A preliminary report. *Archives of General Psychiatry, 47,* 252–256.

Kagan, J., Reznick, J. S., & Snidman, N. (1987). The physiology and psychology of behavioral inhibition in children. *Child Development, 58,* 1459–1473.

Kessler, R. C., McGonagle, K. A., Zhao, S., Nelson, C. B., Hughes, M., Eshelman, S., Wittchen, H., & Kendler, K. S. (1994). Lifetime and 12-month prevalence of DSM-III-R psychiatric disorders in the United States. *Archives of General Psychiatry, 51,* 8–19.

Lang, P. J. (1977). Physiological assessment of anxiety and fear. In J. D. Cone & R. P. Hawkins (Eds.), *Behavioral assessment: New directions in clinical psychology* (pp. 178–195). New York: Brunner/Mazel.

Mowrer, O. H. (1947). On the dual nature of learning: A re-interpretation of "conditioning" and "problem-solving." *Harvard Educational Review 17,* 102–148.

Ost, L. G., & Hugdahl, K. (1987). Acquisition of phobias and anxiety response patterns in clinical patients. *Behaviour Research and Therapy, 21,* 623–631.

Sanderson, W. C., Rapee, R. M., & Barlow, D. H. (1987, November). *The DSM-III-R revised anxiety disorder categories: Descriptors and patterns of comorbidity.* Paper presented at the 21st Annual Association for Advancement of Behavior Therapy Annual Convention, November, Chicago, IL.

Stemberger, R. T., Turner, S. M., Beidel, D. C., & Calhoun, K. S. (1995). Social phobia: An analysis of possible developmental factors. *Journal of Abnormal Psychology, 104,* 526–531.

Turner, S. M., Beidel, D. C., & Wolff, P. L. (1996). Is behavioral inhibition related to the anxiety disorders? *Clinical Psychology Review, 16,* 157–172.

Watson, J. B., & Rayner, R. (1920). Conditional emotional reactions. *Journal of Experimental Psychology, 3,* 1–14.

Deborah C. Beidel

APHASIA refers to disorders of language due to neurological disease. Aphasia is unfortunately not an uncommon consequence of neurological disease. Stroke is the disease that is most commonly thought of as the cause of aphasia. A recent study estimates that there are about 700,000 new stroke cases annually in the United States (Broderick et al., 1998), a large number of which lead to aphasia. Aphasic language disorders also occur as part of cementing diseases like Alzheimer's disease, after head trauma, as a consequence of brain tumors, and after many other neurological diseases. It is estimated that approximately 80,000 individuals acquire aphasia each year and that about 1 million persons in the United States currently have aphasia (National Institute on Deafness and Other Communication Disorders).

Aphasia can take a wide variety of forms. Language is a complex system, with many different structures, such as words, words derived from other words, sentences, discourse, etc. Disorders of language can affect any of these parts of language, and can do so in one or more of the tasks of speaking, understanding spoken language, reading or writing (Caplan, 1992). The classification of aphasic disorders has tried to capture these various manifestations of this condition. Early approaches to aphasia divided aphasic patients into groups in which one or more of the major production and comprehension channels for language—speech, auditory comprehension, reading, and writing—and repetition were relatively intact compared to the others when examined clinically (Goodglass & Kaplan, 1983). These clinical classifications are commonly used to describe patients, but they are subject to many limitations, including the fact that patients with the same syndrome can have widely different symptoms, that patients with different syndromes can have many of the same symptoms, that interobserver reliability with respect to classification is low, and that therapy cannot be developed on the basis of these syndromes alone but requires a more specific description of the nature of the language disorder in an individual patient.

In recent years, more detailed descriptions of aphasic impairments have emerged from the work of psychologists and linguists. These studies have identified aphasic disorders that are highly selective in their effects. For instance, patients have been described who have difficulty reading irregularly spelled words but not regularly spelled words and nonsense words (Patterson, Coltheart, & Marshall, 1985), and others have been described who have difficulty reading nonsense words aloud but are able to read even low frequency irregularly spelled words (Marshall, Patterson, & Coltheart, 1980). Patients have been described who have difficulty naming certain classes of objects, such as fruits and vegetables but not others, such as man-made tools (Hart, Berndt, & Caramazza, 1985). There are those who have difficulty producing certain grammatical classes of words (nouns) in speech but not in writing, and others who have the opposite pattern of production impairments in writing (Caramazza & Hillis, 1991). There are those who can understand sentences in which the meaning can be inferred from the meaning of the words and knowledge of events in the world (e.g., "The cake the man is eating is delicious") but not sentences in which it is necessary to assign syntactic structure to determine who is accomplishing an action and who receiving it (e.g., "The boy the girl is chasing is tall") (Caramazza & Zurif, 1976). These highly selective language deficits are not common, but they have become the focus of much research because they have considerable theoretical importance.

Aphasic symptoms depend to a large extent upon the nature and location of the damage to the brain that is responsible for the impairments. The left hemisphere of the brain has long been thought to be specialized for processing language (Caplan, 1987). It is now better appreciated that this specialization is for certain aspects of language—the sounds of words, word formation processes, the syntax of sentences, certain aspects of intonation, etc. Other aspects of language, such as aspects of discourse (how ideas are related to each other in a conversation or a presentation) are more likely to be processed in the right hemisphere (Brownell, Potter, Birhle, & Gardner, 1986), and some aspects of language such as the meanings of words are likely to be represented in both (Chiarello, 1990). These general patterns are only tendencies, and these tendencies mainly apply to right-handed people; individuals who are left-handed or ambidextrous are much more likely than right-handers to have language supported by the right hemisphere or both (Goodglass & Quadfasel, 1954). Therefore two important factors in determining the nature of a language disorder is which brain hemisphere is affected by the disease and whether the patient is right- or left-handed. Sex differences, educational level, literacy, and the language that one speaks play much less of a role, if any, in determining the likelihood of a brain disease leading to aphasia (Caplan, 1987).

For over a century, neurologists and psychologists have tried to be more specific about the relation between aphasic symptoms and the brain. It is clear that a moderate-sized region centered around the sylvian fissure is the major language area of whatever hemisphere processes language, but the boundaries of this region are still under investigation, and recent studies implicate other brain regions in some language functions. There are many studies that localize aspects of language processing to relatively small parts of the language zone. These relations are fairly specific for motoric aspects of speech (Naeser, Palumbo, Helm-Estabrooks, Stiassny-Eder, & Albert, 1989). Disorders affecting pronunciation are closely associated with lesions anterior in the brain, near the brain's motor region. For processing of more abstract parts of language, including most aspects of auditory comprehension, studies of localization tend to be somewhat imprecise and/or contradictory (Caplan, 1994). If there is a narrow localization of specific language operations in the brain, the details of this localization have yet to be firmly established.

To some extent, the nature of aphasic impairments is also correlated with the type of central nervous system (CNS) disease that is present. Strokes and other acute lesions in language areas can affect virtually any aspect of language processing. Degenerative diseases are of course slower to cause aphasia, and some may be associated with specific impairments. Alzheimer's disease, for instance, tends to show up first as a disorder affecting meaning, not form (Chertkow & Bub, 1990; Chertkow, Bud, & Seidenberg, 1989; Hodges, Patterson, Oxbury, & Funnell, 1992). For instance, patients with Alzheimer's disease are sometimes able to read aloud well—even low frequency irregularly spelled words like *yacht*—at a time when they do not understand what these words mean.

Selective impairments provide insights into the nature of normal language processing. The fact that some patients can read only regularly spelled words and nonsense words while others can read all real words but not sound out nonsense words suggest that there are two partially separate cognitive mechanisms that are used in normal reading—one that associates a pronunciation with a word as a whole (damaged in the first kind of patient) and one that assembles a pronunciation from letters and graphemes (damaged in the second kind of patient). The existence of patients with category-specific naming impairments suggest that items are coded for their category membership; the existence of grammatical-category-specific deficits in speech and writing suggest that a considerable amount of abstract planning of speech and writing is accomplished quite late. This may take place as part of the set of mechanisms that guide specific motor movements in language production. The existence of patients with impairments affecting syntactic processing but not inferencing in sentence comprehension suggest that these are separate processes. These selective impairments only *suggest* these features of normal human cognition; they have to be confirmed by experimentation in normal subjects, simulation of deficits in computer models, and additional investigation of patients.

The natural history of aphasia is dependent upon the pathology that causes it. Patients tend to recover spontaneously to some extent from acquired monophasic neurological illnesses such as stroke, head injury, treated infections, etc., and to deteriorate with progressive illnesses such as Alzheimer's disease. Discerning the effect of therapy as opposed to natural improvement, or of specific types of therapy as opposed to others, is a difficult task because of the wide range of functional outcomes and the large number of factors that may affect the natural history of aphasia and the response to therapy (e.g., age; education; handedness; sex; location, size, and nature of brain injury, etc.). Most therapy in the United States is provided by licensed speech and language pathologists. Studies have documented the value of such therapy for many aphasic patients with strokes (Wertz, 1985; Wertz et al., 1986). Intervention and language stimulation can also be beneficial when provided by nonprofessionals, such as family members, who can be guided in their work by professionals. More focused approaches have been tried in controlled studies. Some of these trials have shown benefits (Schwartz, Saffran, Fink, Myers, & Martin, 1994), although the extent to which training generalizes to new forms seems in most studies to be limited. Augmentative communication training is available for some patients in whom the speech and writing output channels are not likely to become operative. Aphasia therapy is making greater use of computer training programs, which can be used by patients when they wish, and are able, to take some of the burden of training off professionals and caregivers. The combination of pharmacological therapy designed to enhance patients' attention and therapeutic intervention has shown some promise. Therapy for aphasia is an area in which new approaches are being rapidly developed.

Bibliography

Broderick, J., Brott, T., Kothari, R., Miller, R., Khoury, J., Pancioli, A., Gebel, J., Mills, D., Minneci, L., and Shukla, R. (1998). The Greater Cincinnati/Northern Kentucky stroke study: Preliminary first-ever and total incidence rates of stroke among Blacks. *Stroke, 29,* 415–421.

Brownell, H. H., Potter, H. H., Bihrle, A. M., & Gardner, H. (1986). Inference deficits in right brain-damaged patients. *Brain and Language, 27,* 312–321.

Caplan, D. (1987). *Neurolinguistics and linguistic aphasiology.* Cambridge UK: Cambridge University Press.

Caplan D. (1992). *Language: Structure, processing, and disorders.* Cambridge, MA: MIT Press.

Caplan, D. (1994). Language and the brain. In M. A. Gernsbacher (Ed.), *Handbook of psycholinguistics* (pp. 1023–1074). New York: Academic Press.

Caramazza, A., & Hillis, A. E. (1991). Lexical organization of nouns and verbs in the brain. *Nature, 349,* 788–790.

Caramazza, A., & Zurif, E. B. (1976). Dissociation of algorithmic and heuristic processes in language comprehension: Evidence from aphasia. *Brain Language, 3,* 572–582.

Chertkow, H., & Bub, D. (1990). Semantic memory loss in Alzheimer's disease: What do indirect measures measure? *Brain, 113,* 397–417.

Chertkow, H., Bub, D., & Seidenberg, M. S. (1989). Priming and semantic memory loss in Alzheimer's disease. *Brain and Language, 36,* 420–446.

Chiarello, C. (1990). Interpretation of word meanings by the cerebral hemispheres: One is not enough. In P. J. Schwanenflugel (Ed.), *The psychology of word meanings* (pp. 2–37). Hillsdale, NJ: Erlbaum.

Goodglass, H., & Kaplan, E. (1983). *The Boston diagnostic aphasia examination* (2nd ed.). Boston: Little, Brown.

Goodglass, H., & Quadfasel, F. A. (1954). Language laterality in left-handed aphasics. *Brain, 77,* 521–548.

Hart, J., Berndt, R. S., & Caramazza, A. (1985). Category-specific naming deficit following cerebral infarction. *Nature, 316,* 439–440.

Hodges, J., Patterson, K., Oxbury, S., & Funnell, E. (1992). Semantic dementia. Progressive fluent aphasia with temporal lobe atrophy. *Brain, 115,* 1783–1806.

Marshall, J. C., Patterson, K., & Coltheart, M. (1980). *Deep dyslexia.* London: Routledge.

Naeser, M. A., Palumbo, C. L., Helm-Estabrooks, N., Stiassny-Eder, D., & Albert, M. L. (1989). Severe nonfluency in aphasia: Role of the medical subcallosal fasciculus and other white matter pathology in recovery of spontaneous speech. *Brain, 112,* 1–38.

National Institute on Deafness and Other Communication Disorders. (1998, June). Available Web site: http://www.nih.gov/nidcd/

Patterson, K., Coltheart, M., & Marshall, J. C. (1985). *Surface dyslexia.* London: Erlbaum.

Schwartz, M., Saffran, E., Fink, R., Myers, J., & Martin, N. (1994). Mapping therapy: A treatment programme for agrammatism. *Aphasiology, 8,* 19–54.

Wertz, R. T. (1985). Neuropaths of speech and language: An introduction to patient management. In D. F. Johns (Ed.), *Clinical management of neurogenic communicative disorders* (pp. 58–65). Boston: Little, Brown.

Wertz, R., Weiss, D., Aten, J., Brookshire, R., Garcia-Bunuel, L., Holland, A., Kurtzke, J., Lapointe, L., Milianti, F., Brannegan, R., Greenbaum, H., Marshall, R., Vogel, D., Carter, J., Barbes, N., & Goodman, R. (1986). Comparison of clinic, home and deferred language treatment for aphasia: A Veteran's Administration cooperative study. *Archives of Neurology, 43,* 653–658.

David Caplan

APPLIED BEHAVIOR ANALYSIS is a comprehensive approach to behavior change based on principles derived from the experimental analysis of behavior. Together these applied and basic areas are known as behavior analysis. The experimental analysis of behavior discovers and elaborates fundamental principles of behavior viewed as the interaction of a whole organism in and with its environment, considered both historically and situationally. Applied behavior analysis uses these principles to predict, influence, and thereby understand socially important human behaviors, and to achieve large and clinically significant changes in these behaviors. Applied behavior analytic research seeks interventions that are technologically precise, conceptually systematic, effective, and broad in scope and generality (Baer, Wolf, & Risley, 1968).

History

Although traditional behaviorism was defined by John B. Watson as early as 1913 ("Psychology as the behaviorist views it," *The Psychological Review, 20,* 158–177), the science of behavior analysis traces its more immediate beginnings to *The Behavior of Organisms* (1938), in which B. F. Skinner described the application of respondent and operant conditioning principles to nonhuman animals. The science was further elaborated in Keller and Schoenfeld's *Principles of Psychology* (1950), which combined Skinner's concepts with earlier methods of experimental psychology and presented it to a wider audience, and Skinner's own *Science and Human Behavior* (1953), in which he extrapolated laboratory findings with nonhuman animals to a wide variety of human experiences. Beginning in the 1950s with the application of operant conditioning to the developmentally disabled, by 1968 the use of behavioral principles to solve human problems was common enough to necessitate the founding of a new scientific forum: the *Journal of Applied Behavior Analysis*.

Unit of Analysis

While the unit of analysis for other behaviorisms is the stimulus-response (S-R) relationship, in which the stimulus is held to cause the response, the unit of analysis for behavior analysis is three-term contingency: the dynamic relationship between an antecedent stimulus, response, and consequent stimulus. The "establishing operation" is commonly accepted as a fourth term. It refers to motivational variables, such as deprivation and satiation, which can temporarily alter the effectiveness of a three-term contingency (Michael, 1993). The hallmark of contingency thinking is to focus on the consequences of behavior that alter the future probability of responding under given circumstances. Behavior analysts also focus on classical conditioning principles, and on the importance of genetic and epigenetic influences on behavior.

Philosophical Basis

Radical behaviorism is the much misunderstood philosophy of science which underlies behavior analysis. What is "radical" about radical behaviorism is not that it is extreme but that it applies behavioral reasoning to scientists themselves and thus to the epistemological basis of the field. Radical behaviorism rejects traditional dividing lines between what is scientific and what is not (e.g., it rejects the idea that scientific observations must be publicly agreed upon) in favor of contingency analysis (does the scientist have a history that brings observations under appropriate stimulus control). This produces several important differences from traditional (i.e., John B. Watson) and methodological (i.e., Clark L. Hull) behaviorism. For example, private events such as thinking, remembering, or feeling, are viewed as appropriate for scientific analysis, and verbal reports of private events are not automatically eschewed. Similarly, just as behavioral principles focus on the function of behavior given the history and current situation of the organism, scientific concepts in behavior analysis must be functional for the scientist in both predicting *and* influencing behavior as a pragmatic truth criterion. This contextualistic, pragmatic approach produces a characteristic and unusual psychology. For example, unlike most other approaches to psychology, behavior analysts do not point to thoughts, feelings, or any other form of action as causes of other forms of action. This is not because thoughts or feelings are unimportant, but because all behavioral events must ultimately be tied to manipulable, contextual features for the pragmatic purposes of behavior analysis (both prediction *and* influence) to be achieved. The pragmatic goals of behavior analysts also lead them to reject the hypotheticodeductive style of theory that "appeals to events taking place somewhere else, at some other level of observation, described in different terms, and measured, if at all, in different dimensions" (Skinner, "Are theories of learning necessary?" *Psychological Review*, 1950, 57, 193–216), while embracing analytic-abstractive forms of theorizing that allow prediction and influence of behavior to be accomplished with precision and scope.

Methods

The methods and concepts utilized by applied behavior analysis are distinctive. In contrast to most scientific researchers, who use group experimental designs and analyze their results with inferential statistics, applied behavior analysts tend to use single-subject designs and analyze their results using descriptive statistics and visual inspection of graphically displayed data. The rationale behind these differences includes a concern that the unit of analysis described above will be lost when averaged into large groups and that statistical significance is not necessarily helpful when one's goal is to accomplish meaningful behavioral change. Research designs often used by applied behavior analysts include multiple-baseline, alternating treatments, A/B/A, and similar intensive designs (Hayes, Barlow, & Nelson, 1984, in press; Sidman, 1960).

Principles and Techniques

When the rate of a response in a given situation is increased by the contingent presentation of a consequence, reinforcement has occurred. If responding decreased due to contingent consequences, punishment has occurred. What will function as a reinforcer or punisher depends on the person's biological endowment, learning history, and the current situation. A conditioned reinforcer is any event having a reinforcing effect due to its relation to another reinforcer (e.g., money). Shaping is the process by which a new response is created through the reinforcement of successive approximations of that new response. Behavior analysts use these direct contingency principles, and many more like them, in such techniques as token economies. Contingency management procedures are particularly common with children, the chronically mentally ill, or institutionalized populations where direct contingency manipulation is practical. More recently, basic experimental work on stimulus equivalence, relational frames, and other indirect verbal behavioral processes has led to several forms of behavior analytic psychotherapy. The scope of applied behavior analysis now covers the entire range of problems with which applied psychologists might work.

Controversies

One controversy within applied behavior analysis involves the use of punishment and aversive stimulation.

As early as 1953, Skinner cautioned against the use of aversive procedures. Although punishment is an important principle within the science, and can produce behavior change in applied settings, especially with severely disturbed clients, some behavior analysts argue that punishment procedures should almost never be used. While the evidence documenting undesirable side effects is limited, punishment procedures increasingly seem to be falling into disfavor.

Another controversy involves the negative connotations surrounding the language of "behavior control." This issue is the result of philosophical differences between the determinism and radical pragmatism of behavior analysis and the tradition of mentalism and prescientific thinking within our society.

[*See also* Association for Behavior Analysis; Behavior Analysis; *and* Behavior Therapy.]

Bibliography

Baer, D. M., Wolf, M. M., & Risley, T. R. (1968). Some current dimensions of applied behavior analysis. *Journal of Applied Behavior Analysis, 1*, 91–97. A classic article laying out the basic aspects and purposes of applied behavior analysis.

Hayes, S. C., Barlow, D. H., & Nelson-Gray, R. O. (1999). *The scientist practitioner: Research and accountability in the age of managed care* (2nd ed.). New York: Allyn & Bacon. (Original work published 1984.) A well-known modern within-subject methodology text.

Kazdin, A. E. (1994). *Behavior modification in applied settings* (5th ed.). Pacific Grove, CA: Brooks/Cole. A well-written text covering applied behavior analysis techniques.

Keller, F. S., & Schoenfeld, W. N. (1950). *Principles of psychology*. New York: Appleton-Century-Crofts. Through its readability as an introductory psychology text, this book helped to popularize the science of behavior analysis.

Michael, J. L. (1993). *Concepts and principles of behavior analysis*. Kalamazoo, MI: Society for the Advancement of Behavior Analysis. A short summary of behavioral principles.

Sidman, M. (1960). *Tactics of scientific research: Evaluating experimental data in psychology*. Boston: Authors Cooperative. This is a classic work in within-subject experimental design and behavioral methodology.

Skinner, B. F. (1938). *The behavior of organisms*. New York: Appleton-Century-Crofts. Lays out for the first time the core concepts of the science of behavior analysis and its philosophy, radical behaviorism.

Skinner, B. F. (1953). *Science and human behavior*. New York: Macmillan. Takes the work in *The behavior of organisms* and, in the context of an introduction to the natural sciences, applies behavior analytic concepts to complex human behavior.

Steven C. Hayes and David Sayrs

APPRENTICESHIP. From ancient times, apprenticeship has been a persistent educational approach apart from formal schooling. Apprentices learned a craft or trade working under the direction of a skilled master. In ancient Rome, for example, especially in jurisprudence, diplomacy, or war, it was customary for young citizens to attend statesmen or military leaders for observation and practical experience that would prepare them for careers in law or statesmanship. In this type of apprenticeship, novices learned physical skills by observing experts, practicing parts of the task under the guidance of mentors, and gradually assuming responsibility for completing such tasks independently. This type of apprenticeship persisted through the Middle Ages to Colonial America and continues today in vocational education apprenticeships.

One early but significant contribution to the study of apprenticeship as an educational-psychological construct has been advanced by Jean Lave (1977) who conducted ethnographic research among apprentice tailors in Liberia. Lave administered a set of hypothetical tailoring problems whose solutions required elementary arithmetic to a sample of 63 tailors with varying degrees of formal schooling. She concluded that the unfamiliar problem-solving ability of these apprentice-trained tailors was enhanced by formal schooling but did not depend on it. Lave's groundbreaking study demonstrated the potential of apprenticeship as an inductive method of skill learning, a process of inductive generalization evidenced by the tailors' high performance on unfamiliar arithmetic problems. Previous work had characterized apprenticeship as task specific and unlikely to produce transfer.

In addition to craft learning, novices have been learning from experts in intellectual tasks since the time of the Greek philosopher Socrates whose disciples learned to debate philosophical issues with him. Recently, attention has been given in academic psychology to the construct of cognitive apprenticeship, which attempts to uncover and transmit covert thinking processes embedded in specific tasks. Collins, Brown, and Newman (1989) developed a model of "cognitive apprenticeship" based on four aspects of traditional apprenticeship: *modeling*, in which apprentices observe masters demonstrating how to perform tasks; *scaffolding*, in which masters support apprentices in carrying out tasks; *coaching*, in which masters coach apprentices through a wide range of activities; and *fading*, in which masters gradually remove support, increasing apprentices' responsibility. In school settings, cognitive apprenticeship is a challenging goal to achieve: teachers' thinking must be made visible; they are challenged to situate abstract tasks of school curricula in more authentic contexts, and, they must present a range of tasks in varying contexts to help students generalize and transfer skills to novel situations (Collins, Brown, & Newman, 1989).

There have been numerous embodiments of cognitive apprenticeship in school settings designed to simulate work situations. In *Toward the Thinking Curriculum* (1989), Resnick and Klopfer focused attention on the cultivation of students' intellectual competencies, calling for a "thinking curriculum" incorporating features of traditional apprenticeship. These included authentic tasks like those confronted in daily life, contextualized practice, and opportunities for students to observe others doing work they were ultimately expected to do themselves. Although not always identified by name, cognitive apprenticeship approaches have been studied across disciplines: in reading (Palincsar & Brown, 1984), mathematics (Schoenfeld, 1985), writing (Hayes & Flower, 1980), and foreign language (Hosenfeld, Cavour, & Bonk, 1996).

Another embodiment of the apprenticeship construct in schooling is the school to career movement. A U.S. Labor Department report (Secretary's Commission on Achieving Necessary Skills [SCANS], 1991), identified workplace competencies, personal qualities, and basic academic and thinking skills essential for work. The School to Work Opportunities Act of 1994 then authorized funding to establish workplace learning opportunities, including mentorships.

Mentors and Apprentices

Mentoring has a long history tracing back to Homer's *Odyssey*. Odysseus entrusted the care and education of his son to Mentor, a wise and learned friend. In its present application, mentoring has been used to ease initiation into a number of fields, including nursing, psychology, teaching, sociology, and business. In education, for example, peer coaching (Showers, 1996) has been used to facilitate induction of beginning teachers, improve teaching, and provide leadership opportunities for experienced teachers. But mentoring programs in education may be highly situational; mentors' training and responsibilities vary across sites (Bendixon-Noe & Giebelhaus, 1997).

In the *Mentor Connection*, Zey (1984) defined a mentor as a person who oversees the career development of a junior. Mentors establish trust, offer advice, introduce alternatives, challenge, motivate, and encourage (Galbraith & Cohen, 1996). Studying mentorship of adult students, Daloz (1986) characterized mentors as guides, providing direction, support, and challenge on a metaphorical learning journey. Research has described mentoring as a progression, in which mentors initiate apprentices into a field, providing support until the apprentices become competent and independent. Sometimes, depending on how separation is negotiated, the relationship is redefined as a mutually supportive friendship (Kram, 1985).

Psychological Theory and Research

Influenced by the English publication in 1978 of Vygotsky's *Mind in Society*, modern sociocognitive theory views learning as collaborative, situated, and distributed (Greeno, Collins, & Resnick, 1996). In this perspective, learning is a social activity and learners participate in thinking and problem solving just beyond their competence or "zone of proximal development" with the assistance of more experienced members of the community (Vygotsky, 1978). In *Social Foundations of Thought and Action* (1986), Albert Bandura also emphasized social aspects of learning through internalization of models. In *Apprenticeship in Thinking*, Barbara Rogoff (1992) extended the work of Vygotsky and Bandura, positing that cognitive processes are integrated with, rather than products of, sociocultural activities. Studies of children and caregivers led Rogoff to conclude that children develop into skilled members of society through observation and guided participation in ongoing cultural activities.

Studies of apprenticeship outside formal schooling contexts have led researchers to call into question what school teaches. In the *Psychology of Literacy* (1981), Scribner and Cole speculated that schools may promote didactic use of language rather than the discourse of practice. Apprenticeship learning, on the other hand, acculturates learners through guided participation in activities and discourse of the community. Thus, cognitive science research has focused attention on transforming schools into learning communities (Brown, 1997).

Bibliography

Bendixon-Noe, M., & Giebelhaus, C. (1997). Mentoring: help or hindrance? *Midwestern Educational Researcher, 10,* 20–23.

Brown, A. (1997). Transforming schools into communities of thinking and learning about serious matters. *American Psychologist, 52* (4), 399–413. Describes a program of research that transforms schools into learning communities and leads children to discover the deep principles of the domain through inquiry and guided participation in authentic activity.

Collins, A., Brown, J. S., & Newman, S. E. (1989). Cognitive apprenticeship: Teaching the crafts of reading, writing and mathematics. In L. Resnick (Ed.), *Knowing, learning and instruction: Essays in honor of Robert Glaser* (pp. 453–494). Hillsdale, NJ: Erlbaum. Differentiates traditional and cognitive apprenticeship; then describes three models of teaching in the domains of writing, reading, and mathematics and how these models embody the principles of cognitive apprenticeship.

Daloz, L. A. (1986). *Effective teaching and mentoring.* San Francisco: Jossey-Bass.

Galbraith, M., & Cohen, N. (1996). The complete mentor role: Understanding the six behavioral functions. *Journal of Adult Education, 24*, 2–11.

Greeno, J. G., Collins, A., & Resnick, L. (1996). Cognition and learning. In R. Calfee (Ed.), *Handbook of educational psychology* (pp. 15–46). New York: Macmillan. Traces three historical perspectives that have influenced research on cognition, learning, and teaching and argues that current advances in cognitive psychology are moving the field toward a more integrated view of individual, social, and environmental factors that influence learning. New understandings of the relationship between theory and practice are embodied in apprenticeship learning.

Hayes, J. R., & Flower, L. S. (1980). Identifying the organization of writing processes. In L. Gregg & E. Steinberg (Eds.), *Cognitive processes in writing* (pp. 3–30). Hillsdale, NJ: Erlbaum.

Hosenfeld, C., Cavour, I., & Bonk, D. (1996). Adapting a cognitive apprenticeship method to foreign language classrooms. *Foreign Language Annals, 29*, 588–596.

Kram, K. (1985). Improving the mentoring process. *Training and Development Journal, 39*, 40, 42–43.

Lave, J. (1977). Cognitive consequences of traditional apprenticeship training in West Africa. *Anthropology and Education Quarterly, 12*, 181–187.

Lave, J. & Wenger, E. (1991) *Situated learning: Legitimate peripheral participation*. Cambridge, UK: Cambridge University Press. Characterizes apprenticeship as legitimate peripheral participation in communities of practice.

Palincsar, A., & Brown, A. L. (1984). Reciprocal teaching of comprehension fostering and comprehension-monitoring activities. *Cognition and Instruction, 1*, 117–175. Reciprocal teaching is a way of conducting reading groups in which beginners learn comprehensions strategies from more experienced readers.

Schoenfeld, A. (1985). *Mathematical problem solving*. New York: Academic Press.

Showers, B. (1996). The evolution of peer coaching. *Educational Leadership, 53*, 12–16.

Judi Randi

APTITUDE TESTS. Tests that purport to measure aptitude, or a potential for acquiring knowledge or skill, have been an integral part of the modern psychmetric repertoire since the early part of this century. While some early theorists from around 1910 into the 1920s equated *intelligence* uniquely with an "ability to learn," intelligence testing became distinct from aptitude testing during the 1920s. While aptitude testing had been a part of the psychometric repertoire since early in the century, its use increased in the 1920s. This increase was connected to the greater use of mental testing in academic and industrial applications that had been sparked by the high visibility of intelligence testing in the U.S. Army during World War I. Broadly speaking, the distinction between aptitude and intelligence tests during this period was that aptitude tests were developed for prediction purposes, whereas intelligence tests could be used for prediction or for other assessment purposes. Aptitude tests could be as broad as the Scholastic Aptitude Test, which began as the Scholastic Aptitude Examinations in 1926 and yielded two scores, a verbal aptitude score and a quantitative aptitude score. Conversely, aptitude tests can be quite narrow: The Seashore Measures of Musical Talent, developed in the 1930s, yields measures of musical pitch and rhythm, among other musical aptitudes.

With L. L. Thurstone's development of techniques for common factor analysis in the 1930s, and the seminal work by L. L. Thurstone and T. G. Thurstone in the 1930s and 1940s in developing multiple ability tests, such as the primary mental abilities battery (PMA), aptitude tests became very popular for both educational and occupational purposes. By identifying an individual's relative strengths and weaknesses on a set of aptitude measures, it was believed that counselors and employers could successfully match individual students or job applicants to the course of study or job that best matched the individual's aptitudes. Such testing was touted highly in both scientific and lay forums—especially in contrast to intelligence assessment, which was seen as only providing unidimensional information (high, average, or low intelligence). That is, a parent or counselor could often find solace in relative peaks in a multiple aptitude profile (an intraindividual analysis), even when an aggregate intelligence score might be low.

Over subsequent decades, the preference for multiple aptitude batteries over broad intelligence tests has been clear among educational selection situations—especially in the adolescent and adult testing domains (in contrast to the historical dominance of intelligence testing for young children). Currently, there are many widely used aptitude test batteries, such as the Differential Aptitude Test battery (published by the Psychological Corporation, and used for scholastic counseling and selection purposes); the General Aptitude Test Battery, used by federal and state government employment agencies; and the Armed Services Vocational Aptitude Battery used by the United States military for both selection and classification purposes. (Classification is a process of assigning particular individuals to jobs that often is based on matching the individual's profile or pattern of aptitude strengths and weaknesses to the job's pattern of requirements.) In these examples, aptitude tests are used to predict an individual's likelihood of success or expected level of performance in some future educational activity or training activity, or used to identify the individual's relative strengths and weaknesses.

During much of the twentieth century, there has been considerable discussion and disagreement about providing a proper definition for the term *aptitude test* in the context of the broad domain of mental measurement. Usually, the focus of controversy is the difficulty in delineating which kinds of tests fall into one of three categories: (1) intelligence, (2) aptitude, or (3) achievement. Controversy lies along several lines, including theoretical, applied, political, and practical.

The theoretical distinction between aptitude tests on the one hand, and intelligence and achievement tests on the other hand, traditionally revolves around the notion of prediction. Aptitude tests are thought of as providing a basis for making predictions for an individual about future success in either an educational or occupational situation. Typical use of aptitude tests is the prediction of grade point average or grade progression in school. Usually, for aptitude testing, there is an explicit or implicit sense that learning or some other adaptation is part of the criterion to be predicted. In contrast to aptitude tests, achievement tests are considered to reflect the amount of learning already obtained, and intelligence tests are considered to represent something further removed from specific learning situations.

Psychologists and others often speak about tests that assess, for example an "aptitude for language acquisition" or "aptitude for spatial skills." Such thinking is consistent with the notion that an aptitude test represents a measure of an individual's *"potential."* The difficulty with this understanding of aptitude was pointed out by Clark Hull (1928), namely, that aptitude tests sample *behavior* (and this is true of intelligence and achievement tests as well). Potential is inferred only by operational means (e.g., one might conclude that a particular examinee has a low likelihood of succeeding in a particular training program on the basis of a test score, and thus has a low "potential" for learning the critical skill). But, like the height potential of seed corn, the actual expression of the quality (e.g., height of the corn stalk) is dependent on external sources (such as water). Indeed, an individual's aptitude (or potential) for language learning may not even be a fixed property during the progression from childhood to adulthood, because of the decreasing neural plasticity with increasing age.

Thus, many theorists have called for a more careful description of aptitude tests, not as measures of potential, but merely mental tests that are used for prediction purposes. Another reason for the difficulty with the concept of aptitude assessment has to do with the popular misconceptions about overachievement and underachievement. For example, an individual may be called an underachiever if he or she has a high aptitude test score but a low achievement test score in the same domain. If aptitude is imbued with a construct of "po-tential," aptitude test scores seem inevitably linked to a comparison with the current status of the individual, to see how well the individual is meeting his or her potential.

From an applied psychology perspective, whether or not a mental test is an "aptitude test" often lies in judgments made about the nature of the items. Conventional wisdom among applied psychologists is that aptitude tests lie *in between* the two other kinds of tests on several dimensions, including (1) breadth of item content (intelligence tests have the broadest content and achievement tests have the narrowest content); (2) response to drill and practice (intelligence tests show the least response, achievement tests the most response); (3) recency of learning sampled by the tests (intelligence tests have the most remote learning, achievement tests the most recent learning). With this characterization, though, a single test may be an aptitude test for some examinees and an achievement test for other examinees (depending on the recency of the initial topic learning). This kind of distinction can be visualized in the college and postcollegiate tests, such as the Scholastic Aptitude Test and the Graduate Record Examination. The quantitative content of these tests is remote, when completed by a college student (and under the above considerations, these are "aptitude tests"), but the same content administered as final exams at the end of high school classes on algebra or geometry would be considered achievement tests.

In recent years, partly due to the continued controversy about race, ethnic group, and gender differences on intelligence and aptitude tests, psychological testing organizations and companies have come under political pressure to deemphasize the notion that psychological tests are legitimate measures of "aptitude" (in the context of aptitude as "potential"). Although group differences in aptitude test scores are historically less controversial than group differences in intelligence scores, some organizations have recast aptitude tests as achievement tests, or dropped the term *aptitude* from the test names (e.g., the Scholastic Aptitude Test was recast as the Scholastic Assessment Test in the 1990s). It is not yet clear what effect, if any, such efforts have on the use and interpretation of test scores by professionals and the lay public. However, it is clear that the lay population has much less trepidation over an individual with a low achievement test score—which is more often attributed to poor schools or lack of student motivation, than it does over an individual with a low aptitude test score—because of the attribution of aptitude as something that is not malleable.

In the final analysis, though, aptitude tests have an uncertain status as uniquely different from intelligence tests and achievement tests. From a practical perspective, standardized tests of intelligence, aptitude, and achievement (when achievement is more broadly stated than a single school course) all tend to correlate so highly with one another as to yield nearly indistinguishable rank orders of individuals. As such, whether a test is formally identified as an aptitude test ultimately depends on the purpose of the test, on the sample of examinees who take the test, and on subjective judgments of the characteristics of the test.

[See also Testing.]

Bibliography

Anastasi, A. (1990). *Psychological testing* (6th ed.). New York: Macmillan. A classic textbook on psychological testing. Includes an extensive listing of current and historically important aptitude tests.

Carroll, J. B. (1982). The measurement of intelligence. In R. J. Sternberg (Ed.), *Handbook of human intelligence* (pp. 29–120). Cambridge, UK: Cambridge University Press. A detailed history of the measurement of intelligence, from the late 1800s. This chapter provides a strong theoretical overview of assessment issues.

Carroll, J. B. (1993). *Human cognitive abilities: A survey of factor-analytic studies.* New York: Cambridge University Press. This book is a review and quantitative reanalysis of 460 significant data sets on ability measurement from 1940 to 1990. Includes a three-stratum hierarchical description of the structure of intelligence and a somewhat less extensive but important discussion of other aptitudes.

Cronbach, L. J. (1990). *Essentials of psychological testing* (5th ed.). New York: Harper & Row. A classic textbook on the tactics of psychological testing. Less oriented toward specific tests than Anastasi (1990), but provides more in-depth statistical and theoretical review of testing issues.

Green, D. R. (Ed.). *The aptitude-achievement distinction. Proceedings of the Second CTB/McGraw-Hill conference on issues in educational measurement.* Carmel, CA: CTB/McGraw-Hill. This is a series of conference presentations and discussions that revolve around the controversy as to whether there are any important differences between aptitude tests and achievement tests.

Hull, C. L. (1928). *Aptitude testing.* New York: World Book.

Thorndike, R. L. (1963). *The concepts of over- and underachievement.* New York: Columbia University, Teachers College Press. This is a concise quantitative and rational treatment of the problems in using terms like *overachievement* and *underachievement*, based on aptitude test and achievement test comparisons.

Phillip L. Ackerman

ARAB STATES. [*This entry provides the history of the field of psychology in Arab countries. It comprises four articles:*

Egypt and the Arab States
Lebanon, Syria, Jordan, and Iraq
Saudi Arabia and Kuwait
Yemen, Oman, and Sudan
Also discussed are the current status and future direction of the field in each of the regions.]

Egypt and the Arab States

The Arab states extend from Morocco and Mauretania on the west coast of North Africa to the Arab Emirates on the Gulf and include the Comoros Islands off the southeast coast of Africa and Sudan and Somalia on the African continent further to the north. There are 21 countries in all, plus the Palestine Authority (until the advent of a Palestinian state), all of which are members of the Arab League. They are: Algeria, Bahrain, Comoros Islands, Djibouti, Egypt, Iraq, Jordan, Kuwait, Lebanon, Libya, Mauretania, Morocco, Oman, Qatar, Saudi Arabia, Somalia, Sudan, Syria, Tunisia, the United Arab Emirates, and Yemen.

The term *Arab* was originally applied to the Semitic peoples of the Arabian Peninsula. Today, the word refers to those whose first language is Arabic, and while it also includes Arabic-speaking Christians, the majority of Arab speakers are Muslims, and Arabic is the language of the Islamic sacred scripture, the Qur'an. The Arab population in the mid-1990s was about 256 million, of whom 63 million were Egyptians, the largest group in the Arab League countries.

The Arab Personality

Islam is not only a religion but a culture too, and it forms the core of the Arab personality. Its teachings regulate the tempo of Arab life, including daily rituals as well as Islamic principles and values which guide and harmonize all behaviors. While Islam remains the key to understanding Arabs, we should differentiate between Islam as a religion and Muslims as human beings. Islam offers clear direction for living one's life, balancing material, psychological, and spiritual needs and motivating human beings toward knowledge and peace. Muslims or Arabs, however, may deviate from these teachings to some extent in some situations.

In general, Arab society is culturally homogeneous, conservative, and is for the most part centered around family or tribal identification. Arabs are religious, fatalistic, generous, humanitarian, emotional, loyal, and they give paramount importance to personal dignity, honor, and reputation.

Arabs and Psychology—The Heritage

Arab scientists have been studying what we regard as modern concepts of psychology for more than a thousand years, taking the Qur'an as their guide and motivator. The Qur'an includes many verses which stress the importance of learning in the life of a devout Muslim. The following are quotations from *The Meaning of the Glorious Koran*, which demonstrate the importance of learning (Pickthall, 1930):

- Read: In the name of the Lord who createth. (Qur'an, Sura 96:1)
- Allah will exalt those who believe among you, and those who have knowledge, to high ranks. (58:11)
- My Lord! Increase me in knowledge. (20:114)
- And (also) in yourselves. Can ye then not see. (51:21)
- Have they not pondered upon themselves. (30:8)

The early Arab scientists discussed below each made important contributions to different scientific fields, but here we are concerned only with their psychological contributions.

Rhazes (854–932 CE). A physician who nonetheless focused on the importance of psychotherapy, Rhazes said that suggestion was more effective in some cases than medicines.

Ibn Sina or Avicenna (980–1037 CE). Ibn Sina is the most famous of the early Islamic physicians, and both he and his major works, *The Canon of Medicine* and *The Book of Healing* are regarded as masterpieces to this day. The latter work, a philosophical discussion of the soul or psyche, stresses the mutual relationship between psyche and body, and the importance of early childhood experiences in shaping the personality. It also discusses the significance of punishment and reward in education.

Ibn Sina illustrated in *The Book of Politics* the necessity for a good psychological match between the individual and the work he or she is to do. He also dealt with such psychological subjects as sensation and perception, imagination and creativity, reminiscence and forgetfulness, and finally, the relationship between dreams and psychological disorders, which he saw as being useful in diagnosis.

Al-Ghazzali (1058–1111 CE). A famous Islamic philosopher who wrote on psychology, Abou-Hamed al-Ghazzali's books were translated into Latin before the year 1150 CE. One of his most important books is *Animation of Sciences of Religion*. It is possible to consider al-Ghazzali as a pioneer of behaviorism. He showed the importance of acknowledging the laws governing psychological life that influenced people's behaviors. He saw human beings as being good by nature, and saw personality as being the outcome of both heredity and environment. He said that the seed, which is the origin of every plant, cannot become an apple or a palm tree without first being planted and then nurtured. But nurturing (education) will never change the nature of the seed so that an apple seed grows up into a palm tree, or vice versa.

Ibn-Khaldun (1332–1406 CE). Born in Tunisia, and living for some time in Morocco, Ibn-Khaldun eventually settled in Egypt, where he is buried. Ibn-Khaldun is well known as the founder of sociology. He identified "selective perception," i.e., that perception is affected by the individual's mentality, subjectivity, and purpose. He also described identification with the aggressor, a concept familiar in modern times, noting that conquered people often imitate the conqueror in ideology, clothing, and customs.

The Arabs and Modern Psychology

Arab psychologists have studied modern psychology at a number of universities in Western countries. As a result, in the Arab states the different branches of psychology generally follow the mainstream of Western psychology in terms of methodology, but are perhaps less progressive. In the first half of the twentieth century, Egyptian psychologists, who were pioneers in the field, obtained doctorates in psychology in British, French, and North American universities, returning to universities in Egypt and other Arab countries to teach psychology and found departments of psychology. Psychology in the Arab states is developing at different levels in different Arab countries, according to the cultural, social, and economic conditions in each country. Each Arab country has one or more local psychological associations, and there are associations that cross national boundaries with the aim of drawing together Arab psychologists from different countries throughout the Arab world. Arab psychologists are increasing in numbers, regularly participating in the annual psychology conferences that are now held in most Arab states. Today there is a trend toward greater participation in the activities of international psychology on the part of Arab psychologists.

Because Egyptian psychology has a longer history than that of some Arab states, we will focus on it here.

Egypt

The founders of modern academic psychology in Egypt are Abdel Aziz Kosy and Ezat Rageh, who obtained doctorates in psychology, respectively, from British and French universities in the 1930s, and Yousuf Murad and Mustafa Zaior, who obtained doctorates in psychology in France in the early 1940s. The first psychology department in Egypt was founded by Abdel Aziz Kosy at the Faculty of Education, Ein-Shams University, in 1934. It included a laboratory, assessment facilities, and a clinic. Psychology programs were subsequently started at the Faculty of Arts, Cairo University, by Yousuf Murad, at Ein-Shams University by Mastafa Zaior, the godfather of Freudian psychology in Egypt, and at Alexandria University by Ezat Rageh. Initially, psychological studies were part of philosophy or sociology departments, but in the 1970s psychology departments became independent.

During the 1950s and 1960s psychology flourished

during the general cultural flowering in Egypt at that time. Many psychologists obtained master's or doctoral degrees from foreign and Egyptian universities, and as a result there was an increase in publications, and more translations were published, thus making non-Arab writing on psychology more widely accessible. There was also an increase in effective research in different branches of psychology.

During the same period, applied psychology became significant at a government level. Batteries of psychological tests were used in the selection of people for jobs and for vocational guidance to match the right person to the right job, particularly in the ministries of management development, industry, education, and defense. Studies and field research in forensic psychology were supported by the National Center for Social and Criminological Research, which issues a quarterly journal, *The National Review of Social Sciences*. A 1956 law defined the requirements for a psychology license that enabled psychologists to qualify as psychotherapists, an occupation hitherto reserved for psychiatrists.

During the 1960s, psychology was viewed very optimistically in Egypt, and this in itself was a reflection of Egyptian society as a whole. It was a self-confident, achievement-oriented society until June 1967 when Israel defeated Egyptian and Syrian military forces. At that point everything changed, and both the Egyptian people, and indeed all the Arab states, entered a period of acute crisis.

The Crisis in Egyptian Psychology. For 30 years, from the late 1960s to the mid-1990s, there was a continuing crisis in Egyptian psychology, the very antithesis of the prior 25 years which had been so fruitful. It was a part of the overall crisis throughout Egyptian society. A deep crack had appeared after the defeat of June 1967; many questions and contrary views arose about the reasons for social discord and ways to overcome them. Although Egypt quickly recovered its military dignity in October 1973, nonetheless the negative effects of June 1967 remained, and called for radical cultural, social, political, and economic change.

Samir Farag wrote two dissertations, one for his master's and one for his doctoral degree. Both discuss the kinds of questions that arose after June 1967. The first, *Loyalty and the Psychology of Personality*, deals with questions regarding loyalty in general and the meaning of loyalty to a country in particular. How do the different loyalties, to family or tribe, to king or president, or to religion, cause social conflicts or wars? The other work, *Psychology of the Egyptian Personality*, investigated the question of whether Egypt has had one identity from the pharaonic periods through the Christian, Islamic, and the modern era, or has there been a "different" Egypt for every age? What are the strengths and weaknesses of modern Egyptian society and how do we deal with them?

In the early 1990s, new managerial problems arose in Egypt because of the pressures of globalization, privatization, and restructuring of the business sector. Samir Farag has made significant contributions to the field of managerial psychology and total quality management (TQM).

There were conflicts at the departmental level as well as among individual psychologists working in different branches of psychology, whether Freudian, behaviorist, or psychometricist, who wanted to keep out those with differing approaches. While there were increases in both research and publication, quality in both areas suffered. More universities and more psychology departments were founded, but they were not always at an acceptable academic level. There were setbacks in applied psychology. The use of psychological tests in selecting workers in government and private business declined. The issuing of psychotherapy licenses for psychologists was frozen. Participation by Egyptian psychologists in international conferences decreased because of shrinking budgets that made travel difficult or impossible.

The Present and Future of Egyptian Psychology. The Egyptian people will rise to the occasion to meet a challenge, something Arnold Toynbee mentioned in *The Study of History* when he spoke about challenge and response. Egypt's victory in the October 1973 war was a response to the defeat of June 1967, and the peace treaty between Egypt and Israel in 1979 was a good solution to the difficulties caused by their mutual hostility. Similarly, the escalation of the psychology crisis in Egypt, the increase in worldwide communication via the Internet, and continuing globalization at all levels were all challenges that demanded a response. Egyptian psychologists moved to overcome the crisis in their discipline in order to be able to share in the international achievements of psychology.

In the early 1990s, an integrative view began to overcome the academic conflicts between the different branches of psychology. For example, mutual support now exists between clinical and psychometric approaches to the same research. Departments of psychology have set higher standards for their graduates, especially those working toward a diploma, a master's degree, or a doctoral degree, with a foreign language requirement, especially in English, and obligatory courses in computer skills.

In the late 1990s psychology in Egypt became more involved in social issues such as substance abuse prevention (G. Abou-el Azayem & M. Saueif), family and social conflict resolution (A. Abou el-Azayem & S. Farag), and human resource development according to modern management criteria for increasing corporate effectiveness. At the same time, the Egyptian Ministry of Health again began to give licences to psychologists with doctoral degrees who have undergone practical training, to enable them to practice psychotherapy, either along with psychiatrists on therapy teams or in private practice. It is clear now that most psychologists in Egypt today want to use methodology that is a cultural match both for the Egyptian personality in particular and Arab culture in general.

The continuing increase in the numbers of psychology associations, journals, and conferences in Egypt is a sign that psychology is indeed making progress. Below are listed some of the most important psychological associations in Egypt and their significant features and activities.

Egyptian Association for Psychological Studies. Founded in 1948, it was one of the founding members of the International Union of Psychological Science (1951). The association holds an annual conference and issues a quarterly journal and a yearbook (in Arabic). Notable presidents included the first president, A. Kosy, S. Fahmy, who was the first woman psychologist in Egypt, and F. Abou-Hatab.

Egyptian Association for Mental Health. Founded in 1948, it was one of the founding members of the World Federation for Mental Health (1948). Its founder and first president was Gamal Abou el-Azayem, M.D., who was president of the World Federation for Mental Health (1985–1989). The association holds a yearly conference and issues a yearbook. It has a psychological service and a free mental health hotline available.

Egyptian Psychologists Association. The association was founded in 1988 by Safwat Farag, Ph.D. It publishes a quarterly journal, *Psychological Studies*, in Arabic but with English-language abstracts. Farag Taha, member of the Institut d'Egypte, was the editorial director.

Egyptian Association for Family and Social Conflict Resolution. The association was founded in 1995 by Ahmed Abou el-Azayem (who became the first president) and Safwat Farag. Dr. Abou el-Azayem was president of the World Federation for Mental Health (1997–1999). The association holds an annual conference and issues a yearbook.

The Arab Federation of Nongovernmental Organizations for Combatting Substance Abuse. Founded in 1995 in Egypt, the federation holds an annual conference and issues a yearbook.

World Islamic Association for Mental Health. Founded in 1983, the association holds an annual conference. It publishes a quarterly journal, *Mental Peace Journal*, in Arabic and English.

In addition to the journals of the psychological associations, there is the psychology journal of the Culture Ministry, edited by K. Abdel Fattah; the psychological counseling journal of the Education Faculty, Ein-Shams University, edited by A. Al-Ashwal;

and a journal published by the Faculty of the Department of Childhood Restraints on Girls, edited by F. Sadek.

Psychology is a part of the comprehensive growth in Egypt today and is an innovative and vital part of the culture. Associations, journals, highly qualified psychologists, and social contributions are all on the increase, and there is also more cooperation with psychologists from other Arab states. The current state of psychology in Egypt bodes well for the twenty-first century.

Bibliography

Abou-el Azayem, A. (1998). *Concepts of the prevention of substance abuse.* Paper presented at the Annual conference of the Arab Federation of NGOs For the Prevention of Substance Abuse. Cairo, Egypt.

Abou-el Azayem, G. (1994). The *Qur'an and mental health.* Cairo, Egypt: Dar-el Helal.

Abou-el Azayem, G. (1996, July). Substance abuse combat. *Mental Peace Journal, The International Journal of World Islamic Association,* Vol. 47.

Abou-Hatab, F. (1984, April). Future of school psychology in Egypt. [Special issue]. *Journal of International School Psychology.*

Farag, S (1977) *Sadat and the peace initiative: A psychosocial analysis.* Cairo, Egypt: The United. A study of the unexpected visit of President Sadat to Israel in 1977, which paved the way for peace between Egypt and Israel

Farag, S. (1986). *Loyalty in war and peace.* Paper presented at the international conference of political psychology, Amsterdam.

Farag, S. (1989). *Loyalty between psychology and the Qur'an.* Cairo, Egypt: The United. It includes an appendix: "Loyalty in Islam, A Psycho-Social Approach," a paper presented at the conference of the International Association of Cross-Cultural Psychology, Istanbul, Turkey, 1986.

Farag, S. (1997). *Family and violence in Egypt: Responses to TAT test.* Paper presented at the second international conference of the Egyptian Association for Family and Social Conflict Resolution, Cairo, Egypt.

Hemdan, G. (1980). *The personality of Egypt.* Cairo, Egypt: World of Books. A Geographical-cultural study.

Milaika, L. (1990). *Readings in social psychology in Arab states.* Cairo, Egypt: Egyptian Public Organization for Books. A collection of psychological studies.

Moones, H. (1989). *Egypt and its mission.* Cairo, Egypt: Egyptian Public Organization for Books, A cultural study.

Nagaty, O. (1982). *The Qur'an and psychology.* Cairo, Egypt: Sharok.

Nydell, M. K. (1987). *Understanding Arabs.* Yarmouth, ME: International Press.

Osman, S. (1985). *Toward developing psychology in Egypt: Yearbook of psychology.* Egyptian Association for Psychological Studies, Cairo, Egypt.

Pickthall, M. M. (1930). *The meaning of the glorious Koran* (1985 ed.) New Delhi: Taj Company.

Shaheen, O., et al. (1994). Study of psychiatric and social aspects in Egyptian children. *Yearbook of Egyptian Association for Mental Health*, Vol. 35, Cairo, Egypt.

Shibl, F. (1971). *The role of Egypt in the foundation of civilization.* Cairo, Egypt: Egyptian Public Organization for Books.

Soueif, M. (1994). *We and the future.* Cairo, Egypt: Dar El-Helal.

Soueif, M. (1996). Drugs and society. *World of Knowledge*, No. 205, Kuwait.

Taha, F. (1998). Industrial and organizational psychology in the Arab world. *Deraa'sat Nafseyah, 8*, pp. 112–135. (Psychological Studies), The Egyptian Psychologists Association.

Samir Farag

Lebanon, Syria, Jordan, and Iraq

The founding of the American University in the mid-1860s (rechartered in the early 1920s) and the French University (1893) were significant influences on the development of psychology in the region, providing the kind of facilities which make possible the study of human and animal thought processes and behavior. The founding of the Mount Carmel Psychiatric Hospital in Haifa in the mid-1930s was also of major importance to the study of psychopathology, while the founding of a psychology department within the Faculty of Education at Ein-Shams University in Egypt in the mid-1930s also gave major support to the idea of psychology as an important academic discipline in the region. From the 1930s to the 1950s, significant work was published by K. Bleument in the late 1930s; in Syria, A. Tarakji and H. Al-Ghali were publishing their work in the 1940s and 1950s; in Lebanon in the 1940s H. K. Sa'adi and A. Bowez made contributions to the field; and in the 1940s and 1950s in Iraq, H. Al-Witry and T. A. Shaby were active. The teaching of psychology began in the 1940s, and took the form of courses within the faculties of philosophy at the American and French universities in Lebanon. Psychology became an independent specialty within those faculties in the late 1950s and early 1960s. By the early 1970s there were independent psychology faculties at the region's universities.

There have been inevitable conflicts within psychology faculties. Many professors were trained at Egyptian, French, and American universities in the region, though in Lebanon, the French school has predominated. In Jordan the Egypt-trained psychologists predominated, while the so-called socialist school of psychologists predominated in Syria and Iraq. This diversity, often with cultural roots outside the region, led to a diminishing focus on local cultures and consequently diminished research relating to the special needs of people within the societies of the region. However, there are cultural issues which are so powerful that at the clinical level they were and are impossible to ignore. Examples of problems having particular significance to the societies of the region include first wife syndrome; brief religious psychotic disorders; mystic (Sufi) doctrine; and such religious rites as fasting, prayer, and the use of amulets and talismans. However, the region's clinics have been finding an increased number of posttraumatic stress disorder (PTSD) cases, particularly in Lebanon and Iraq, where there has been a growing interest in treatment methods, particularly psychoanalysis, as noted elsewhere.

Associations, Institutions, and Leading Figures of the Region

In all four countries under discussion here, psychology associations tend to specialize in particular problems, for example, mental handicaps, child development, women's issues, drug addiction, and aging. The following is a brief selection of the organizations in the region: in Lebanon, the Society for Psychological Studies and the Lebanese Society for Psychiatric, Psychological and Psychosomatic Studies Center; in Syria, the Syrian Society for Psychological Sciences and the Syrian Psychiatric Association; in Jordan, the Jordanian Society for Psychiatry and the Jordanian Society for Rehabilitation; in Iraq, the Iraqi Society of Psychiatry and the Psychological Guidance Center.

Of the leading figures of the region, in Lebanon, N. Zain and M. Chamoun have done significant work in psychology. M. Hajjar and N. Rifai are the central figures in Syrian psychology, while in Jordan, A. Owaidat and I. Obeiwi have done work of major importance. In Iraq, A. Fadhli has been the leading researcher in psychology.

Publications

The Lebanese Center for Psychological and Psychosomatic Studies has been the main publisher of professional books on psychopathology in the region, and their most important author is M. Naboulsi. The Center also publishes the specialized journal, *The Interdisciplinary Psychological Culture.* Publishing companies in Iraq, Syria, and Jordan are general trade publishers who rarely publish academic books on psychology. However, in Syria, the printing department of Damascus University produces academic books for teaching purposes, all of them officially approved by faculties and colleges. The university focuses on general psychology, educational psychology, and the principles of scientific research, F. Akel being the leading author in the latter field, while M. Hajjar is a leading researcher and writer on techniques in behavioral treatment. In Jordan, Abou Amedan and colleagues have written a practical guide to treating behavioral problems in children.

Research

It is impossible to cover all the areas of research since the mid-twentieth century, but the following are of major significance.

The Psychosomatic Field. From the early 1940s to the present time there has been a focus on PTSD and psychosomatic symptoms, and their treatment using psychoanalytic methods. Leading workers in this area include M. H. Hajjar and S. Radwan in Syria; M. Naboulsi and R. H. Chahin in Lebanon; and A. K. Cheikheli in Iraq.

Combined Research. Since the 1950s there has been interdisciplinary research on psychometric, experimental, psychoanalytic, clinical, and applied issues.

Research Specific to the Cultures of the Region. Research has focused on issues relevant to the changes in Arab culture and society in response to the challenges and conflicts encountered in the region. Identification of the multiple aspects of PTSD remains an important area in which M. H. Hajjar, M. Naboulsi, and A. K Cheikheli have done significant work. Other important issues include the use of children's drawings in diagnosis and therapy, women's roles in a changing world, and studies of creativity and personality.

Mohamed Ahmed al-Naboulsi

Saudi Arabia and Kuwait

The people of Saudi Arabia and Kuwait for the most part have Arab tribal origins in common, and follow one religion: Islam. This cultural background influences both Saudi and Kuwaiti attitudes toward psychology throughout the social strata, and there is a cautious view of Western psychological theories regarding mental disturbances, with a preference for parapsychological explanations such as the evil eye, witchcraft, or possession by spirits. The patriarchal and extended family social structure does not encourage the expression of problems in psychological terms, but rather in physical terms, hence the frequency of somatization. (It is interesting to consider this somatization of problems in parallel with the extraordinary levels of emotional experience found in Arab poetry.) However, the enormous influence of Western cultures in the region since the mid-twentieth century has resulted in the development of psychology programs in secondary school, university, and postgraduate education and in health care services.

Saudi Arabia

Psychology was first taught in secondary schools in 1970 as part of the arts program. A typical program consisted of an introduction to psychology, which included the basic principles and main theories, and the role of Muslim psychologists.

The subject was taught at the university level from the 1940s, but until the early 1960s it was a part of education departments. The first independent department of psychology was established in 1963 at Umm Ul-Qura University in Makkah Almukkarammah and in 1972 at King Saud University in Riyadh. Several departments were then established in other universities, colleges for women, and teachers' colleges, all of which awarded a bachelor of arts degree in psychology. In the late 1980s, postgraduate programs were developed, leading to masters' degrees in educational, counseling, industrial, and clinical psychology, but with only a few institutions offering doctoral programs.

At the end of the twentieth century there were psychological health services in most intermediate and secondary schools, and also in mental health hospitals and clinics where counseling and a number of other psychological treatment modalities, along with psychological testing, were provided. Other institutions such as prisons, social welfare services, and institutions for the handicapped provide psychological health services.

Saudi Psychological Institutions and Associations. The Saudi Educational and Psychological Association was established in 1981, but the first meeting for the entire membership was not held until 1988. Since that time, however, regular monthly and annual meetings are scheduled.

There are several institutes where psychology research takes place, such as the Psychology and Education Research Center at Umm Ul-Qura University, Makkah; the Psychology and Education Research Center at King Saud University, Riyadh; and the Crime Research Center and Naif Academy for Security Studies at the Ministry of the Interior.

Publications. There are a number of professional journals on psychology. The *Journal of Psychological and Educational Sciences* and the *Journal of Educational and Islamic Studies* both emanate from King Saud University. Al-Imam University publishes the *Journal of Social Sciences;* there is also the *Journal of Umm Ul-Qura University,* the *Journal of the College of Education* at Al-Madina, and the *Bulletin of Education and Psychology* published by the Saudi Educational and Psychological Association.

While psychology as an academic discipline was first established in the region by non-Saudis, especially Egyptians, Professors Abdullah Al-Nafae, Abdulaziz Al-Dakhil, Mohammed Ismail, and Sulaiman Alshamman were the pioneers in the Saudi Kingdom.

Kuwait

Psychology has been taught at the secondary-school level since the 1960s. At the university level, the psychology department at the Arts College was founded in 1966, and in 1979 the department of educational psychology was established at the College of Education, University of Kuwait. Postgraduate programs in psychology at master's and doctoral levels were founded in the 1970s, but in 1979 they were suspended while the curriculum was reevaluated. In 1997 the first master's program in clinical psychology opened.

Psychology Services. By the 1990s there were psychology services in Kuwait under the aegis of the Ministry of Health, which established a psychology unit, and in 1996, an early intervention center for handicapped children.

Associations and Journals. At the end of the twentieth century there was no psychology association in Kuwait. However, psychology research is effectively supported by several organizations: the Gulf and Arabian Peninsula Studies Center, the Academic Publication Council, University of Kuwait; the Social Development Center, the Prince's Cabinet; and the Science Development Establishment. These organizations publish a number of journals, including the *Social Sciences Journal* and the *Journal of Education,* which are published by the Academic Publication Council at the University of Kuwait, and the *World Literature Journal,* published by the Kuwait Ministry of Information.

As was the case in Saudi Arabia, psychology in Kuwait was initially established by non-Kuwaitis. However, in the early 1980s national pioneers emerged such as Drs. Adnan Al-Shatty, Najmah Al-Kharafy, Jasim Al-Khawajah, and Owaied Al-Mashaan.

Research in Saudi Arabia and Kuwait. Research in both countries has focused on two areas in the main: standardization of several personality, intelligence, and mental illness inventories and tests, and small-scale epidemiology surveys of a variety of psychological disturbances. At the end of the twentieth century research turned toward acculturization by constructing culturally specific scales and tests and also reviewing psychological theories in the light of Islamic literature.

Rules and Regulations for Psychologists. In both Saudi Arabia and Kuwait psychologists must now be registered, and there are a number of rules and regulations governing the professional behavior of practicing psychologists.

Bibliography

al-Harthi, Z. O. (1993). Attitudes of Saudi university students toward psychology. *Egyptian Journal for Psychological Studies, 3,* 53–85. [in Arabic]

Makhawi, B. A. (1997). *Status and future of clinical psychology services in the Ministry of Health: A report on the symposium on psychological services in Kuwait,* 6–8 April 1997. College of Arts, University of Kuwait. [in Arabic]

Ministry of Health. (1996). *Annual health report.* Riyadh, Saudi Arabia: Author. [in Arabic]

Ministry of Higher Education (1995). *Guide for higher education in Saudi Arabia.* Riyadh, Saudi Arabia: Author. [in Arabic]

el-Sendiony, M. F. et al. (1987). School psychology in Saudi Arabia. *Journal of School Psychology, 25,* 267–275.

University of Kuwait. (1997). *Guide for studies (1995–1997).* [in Arabic]

Abdulrazzak M. Alhamad

Yemen, Oman, and Sudan

Most ordinary people in Yemen, Oman, and Sudan have an enduring interest in the workings of the human psyche. It is an interest inspired by the African animist religions and Arab Islamic religious beliefs. Traditional healers continue to practice rituals, perform ceremonies, and often also prescribe herbs for their clients who have problems of the spirit or psyche and who may also suffer from somatic disorders.

Psychology is young both as a science and profession in these countries. It has only existed since the midtwentieth century in Sudan, after the establishment of higher education and the founding of Khartoum University and the Egyptian-sponsored Cairo University in Khartoum. The impact of Egyptian higher education processes earlier in the twentieth century and the development of psychology movements in Egypt in the 1940s and 1950s had a major influence on the development of psychology in Yemen, Oman, and Sudan. In Egypt, psychoanalysis, whose main proponent was Mustafa Zaior, as well as integrative psychology under the leadership of Yousuf Murad, were especially influential.

Egyptian publications in Arabic have been widely distributed throughout the region, and as a result not only research in psychology from the Arab world but from Europe and North America has become available to an Arabic-speaking audience. A high percentage of Arab psychologists are graduates of Egyptian universities.

Sudan began graduating psychologists in the 1950s; the first group of Yemen psychologists graduated in the late 1960s; in Oman, students in psychology began graduating in the 1970s after radical social and economic reforms led by Sultan Qabus. For the most part, these first groups of psychologists were employed in educational psychology. Demands in all three countries for professional psychologists emerged in the 1980s and 1990s when mental health services were organized as part of the national health services. A number of psychologists have joined hospital-based mental health teams along with psychiatrists. However, for years psychologists had no job description, occupied an unofficial niche, and were not subject to professional standards and regulations. Thus, into the 1980s, it was not entirely clear in any of these three countries exactly who practiced psychology, and which branches of psychology they worked in. However, this situation began to change in the 1990s as the number of graduates in psychology increased, and the need for regulation and identification of psychology practice became clear. To meet that need, a regional symposium was organized in Damascus, Syria, in May 1998 by the Syrian Association of Psychological Sciences in coordination with other Arab psychological societies from Yemen, Kuwait, Lebanon, Egypt, Algiers, and other countries. The purpose was to define and describe the scope of professional psychology in the Arab world.

National psychological associations and societies in the Arab world play an important role in social issues that arise in the greater society. No reliable information about nongovernmental organizations (NGOs) or psychological associations in Oman is available. In Sudan a psychological association exists in conjunction with the Department of Psychology at the University of Khartoum. The head of the association is also the head of the department. The association is not active at a national, regional, or international level, perhaps due to economic or political reasons. However, some Sudanese psychologists are key figures in the association and are well known for their scientific contributions to Arab Islamic psychology, amongst whom Drs. Mallek Albadri and Bashir Taha, emeritus professors at universities in Gulf Arab countries, are of particular note.

The number of professional psychologists in Yemen in the early 1990s was over 450. This represents a considerable increase in the number of psychology graduates who studied at Arab and European universities, particularly those in Central Europe and the former Soviet Union. At the end of the twentieth century the majority of psychologists in Yemen hold either bachelor's or master of science degrees. Most have jobs in the Ministry of Health, mental health services, hospitals, the Ministry of Social Welfare, and the Ministry of Education where they are employed as social workers in schools. There are no more than 15 holders of doctoral degrees, and most are employed in university research centers.

This increase in the number of psychologists in Yemen results from an initiative by a group of academic and clinical professionals, led by Professor Hassan Kassim Khan, chair of the Department of Medical and Behavioral Sciences, to take steps to organize a formal psychological body that would govern the work of psychologists in the country. In May 1990, at the first congress, the Yemen Psychological Association (YPA) was established. The association unites and organizes psychologists in Yemen, and at the same time the organization makes contributions to social development. It also advocates and implements research programs and training in the psychological sciences. In addition, the association acts to define the duties and defend the rights of professional psychologists.

Since the YPA's founding, it has organized several psychological programs and congresses. In conjunction with its first congress, a scientific symposium, "The Profession of Psychology in Yemen," was organized. Its purpose was to contribute to the development of psychology in the country and to advocate its importance to socioeconomic development in Yemen. In April 1991 a national conference was organized on juvenile delinquency under the auspices of the Minister of Social Welfare. In 1993, at the second congress of the association, a National Mental Health Symposium was held on "Depression in Yemen." Papers presented at the symposium were published in the *Mental Health Journal*, which is published by the association and edited by a professional committee with representatives from different aspects of psychology. The chief editor of the journal is president of the association.

No psychological journal or newsletter is published in either Oman or Sudan. For the most part, the majority of psychological research in Sudan is conducted by Egyptian scholars and has been published in the Arab world. The department of psychology at Khartoum University has initiated research programs to enable students to obtain postgraduate degrees at the master's level. In Yemen, academic research is part of the psychology department's curriculum leading to bachelor's and master's degrees.

In the 1990s, the YPA has focused on the rights of children, making it a priority in their social and health programs. They conducted national surveys and established research programs to help improve the mental health of juvenile delinquents, children in prison, and children who became victims of posttraumatic stress disorder (PTSD) as a result of the 1994 civil war in Yemen. Moreover the YPA has led a coalition of 45 nongovernmental organizations to defend the rights of Yemenite children in accordance with the United Nations Convention. The association is a member of a number of regional and international organizations in psychology and mental health. It participated actively in the formation of the Eastern Mediterranean Region Council of the World Federation of Mental Health. In November 1997, a Joint Regional Symposium involving the YPA, the World Federation of Mental Health, and Aden University was organized in Aden. It was entitled "Mental Health and Conflict Resolution Programs for Social Peace." Participants from a number of Arab countries representing a variety of federations and associations attended the symposium.

The Future Development of Psychology in Yemen, Oman, and Sudan

While there have been achievements and gains in psychology in all three countries, there have also been problems. Yemen, Oman, and Sudan need to develop an effective network to exchange information and experiences with other psychological associations at the regional and international level. The roles of psychologists in these countries are not well defined, and there are no rules or regulations governing the conduct of psychologists or setting educational standards. Departments of psychology in universities in the three countries need to review their undergraduate and graduate curriculums to meet recent developments and to respond to the needs of local markets for expertise provided by professional psychologists.

The demand for active participation by psychologists in training and research in mental health networks and primary health services is overwhelming in these countries and requires considerable attention.

Bibliography

Naboulsy, M. (1993). Arab psychology associations directory. *Journal of Culture and Psychology*, This is the publication of the Psychosomatic Studies Research Center, Tripoli, Lebanon.

Ramdan, A. (1998, August). Interview with the author of *Psychology in the Arab world*. Dr. Ramdan's book was published in Cairo, Egypt, 1999.

Yemen Psychological Association. (1991). Reports on the first congress. *Mental Health Journal, 3*. The journal is published in Aden, Yemen.

Yemen Psychological Association. (1992). Studies on juvenile delinquency in Yemen. *Mental Health Journal, 5*.

Yemen Psychological Association. (1997). Abstracts of the regional symposium on mental health and conflict resolution. *Mental Health Journal, 14*.

Hassan Kassim Khan

ARBITRATION. *See* Negotiation.

ARCHETYPES. Carl Jung introduced the term *archetype* into the psychological literature in 1919 to explain the corresponding themes he identified among dreams, waking imagery, private ideas, myths, religious symbolism, occult disciplines, and tribal lore. He attributed these apparently universal patterns of human cognition to preexisting psychological motifs—underlying templates that shape subsequent perception, imagination, and understanding. As embryonic forms, archetypes *by definition* transcend culture, race, and time, causing people to apprehend and respond to the world in a distinctly human way. Jung conceived of *archetypes* (a Greek term) as "organs of the psyche" that unfold according to an inborn maturational plan, directing the developmental path and essential forms of consciousness. He understood these preexisting psychological motifs as originating in what he termed the *collective unconscious*, the accumulated experience of humanity that resides in each individual's psyche. For Jung, archetypes carry the heritage of our ancestors' adaptations to the environment, "born anew in the brain structure of every individual" ("The Structure of the Psyche," *Collected Works*, Vol. 8, Princeton, NJ, 1927/1969, p. 158).

Archetypes—such as the Wise Old Man, the Great Mother, the Child, Paradise, the anima (the feminine principle residing within a man), the animus (the masculine principle residing within a woman), and the "shadow" (disowned parts of the personality)—are revealed to awareness through dreams, fantasies, and aesthetic creations. In archetypal psychology, it is through dialogue between the conscious ego and the archetypes that people are able to most meaningfully discover their place and purpose in the universe. Archetypes are oriented, on the one hand, toward natural biological processes, and on the other, toward the world of values and spirit. They govern our quest for food and our quest for meaning.

Difficult to penetrate empirically, this seemingly metaphysical concept has, until recently, been largely discounted in mainstream scientific circles. One area of confusion has been around the critical distinction between fundamental archetypal forms and their various expressions in individuals and societies. The commonalties found in disparate cultures, such as the "Hero's Journey," "The Great Mother," and parallel representations of birth, death, and rebirth have, for example, been explained not as species-wide imagery, but as products of similar neurological structures spontaneously encoding common features of human experience—such as mating, food procurement, and the infant's extended dependence on the mother.

Prototypes of the archetype are, however, clearly evident in instinctive animal behavior, such as the elaborate communication dance of the honeybee, the salmon's upstream return to its spawning ground, and the monogamous bonding of Canadian geese. In humans, clinical evidence for the archetype has been accumulating. Stanislav Grof, for instance, has documented cases where people with no previous knowledge of specific mythological figures from a distant culture were, while in nonordinary states of consciousness, "not only able to *experience* them accurately and with great detail but they were able to draw pictures with details that perfectly matched ancient descriptions of those figures" (*The Holotropic Mind*, San Francisco, 1992, p. 161). Even Freud, based on his observation that individuals in therapy keep producing similar themes, wondered: "How is it to be explained that the same phantasies are always formed with the same content? I have an answer to this which I know will seem to you very daring. I believe that these *primal phantasies* . . . are a phylogenetic possession. In them the individual . . . stretches out to the experiences of the ages" (*A General Introduction to Psychoanalysis*, New York, 1924/ 1953, p. 380).

Evolutionary psychologists have, in fact, come to view the human mind as consisting of evolved information-processing mechanisms within the nervous system, "specialized to produce behavior that solves particular adaptive problems such as mate selection, language acquisition, family relations, and cooperation" (Barkow, Cosmides, & Tooby, *The Adapted Mind: Evolutionary Psychology and the Evolution of Culture*, New York, 1992, p. 24). Since Jung first described archetypes, findings in anthropology, behavioral biology, dream psychology, ethology, linguistics, and sociobiology have also added empirical support for an inherited "deep structure" of the human psyche (Stevens, *The Two Million-Year-Old Self*, College Station, TX, 1993); research in brain lateralization and subcortical structures suggests possible neurological substrates for Jung's formulation of the archetype (Rossi, "The cerebral hemispheres in analytical psychology," *Journal of Analytical Psychology*, 1977, 22, 32–51); and some theorists contend that quantum mechanics will reveal a physical basis for archetypal imagery (Laszlo, *The Interconnected Universe: Conceptual Foundations of Transdisciplinary Unified Theory*, London, 1995).

Quantum properties such as "nonlocality," where one photon influences another photon that is not in its proximity, may govern not only microlevel particles, but also consciousness. Jung anticipated this possibility. In a letter written shortly before his death in 1961, he wrote, "We might have to give up thinking in terms of space and time when we deal with the reality of archetypes." Based on findings from within their respective disciplines, atypical *fields of information* that influence consciousness and behavior have been postulated by anesthesiologists, biologists, engineers, neurologists, physicists, physiologists, psychologists, and systems theorists (summarized in Feinstein's "At play in the fields of the mind: Personal myths as fields of information," *Journal of Humanistic Psychology*, in press). The theory that nonlocal fields of information—where an idea or image may be simultaneously available at distant locations—has been applied to explain such documented anomalies as telepathy, the distant effects of prayer on healing, and the capacity of some people to mentally influence the mood of an experimental subject at another location. Nonlocal fields may also provide the physical basis of such otherwise amorphous phenomena as the archetype and the collective unconscious.

Jung initially believed that archetypes are genetically coded, but he later concluded that genes alone cannot account for the range of universal symbolism he had identified ("Synchronicity: An Acausal Connecting Principle," *Collected Works*, Vol. 8, Princeton, NJ, 1952/ 1969). As was true in Jung's time, the manner by which DNA codes inherited symbolism has not been established, and informational fields may prove a viable alternative explanation. Meanwhile, archetypes offer a dynamic language for systematically thinking about inherited structures in the human psyche.

[*See also* Religious Symbol, Myth, and Ritual; *and the biography of Jung.*]

Bibliography

Edinger, E. F. (1972). *Ego and archetype: Individuation and the religious function of the psyche.* New York: Penguin. A lucid synthesis of Jung's most far-reaching ideas with particular attention to their religious and spiritual implications.

Hillman, J. (1979). *The dream and the underworld.* New York: Harper & Row. A creative extension of Jung's ideas about the archetype and the collective unconscious, applied to the world of dreams.

Jacobi, J. (1959). *Complex/archetype/symbol in the psychology of C. G. Jung* (R. Manheim, Trans.). Princeton, NJ: Princeton University Press. An introduction to the interrelated concepts of the archetype, the complex, and the symbol, written by one of Jung's primary disciples. Jung, himself, provides the Foreword.

Jung, C. G. (1968). The archetypes and the collective unconscious. In *Collected works* (Vol. 9, Part 1; 2nd ed.; R. Hull, Trans.). Princeton, NJ: Princeton University Press A collection of papers written between 1934 and 1955, including "Archetypes of the Collective Unconscious," "A Study in the Process of Individuation," "The Phenomonology of the Spirit in Fairytales," and psychological treatments of the mother archetype, the child archetype, rebirth, the trickster figure, and the mandala.

Jung, C. G. (1968). Aion: Researches into the phenomenology of the self. In *Collected works* (Vol. 9, Part 2; 2nd ed.; R. Hull, Trans.). Princeton, NJ: Princeton University Press. Jung's later thoughts about the archetype, including treatments of the ego, the shadow, the anima and animus, the sign of the fishes, the structure and dynamics of the self, and Christ as a symbol of the self.

Laughlin, C. D. (1996). Archetypes, neurognosis and the Quantum Sea. *Journal of Scientific Exploration*, 10, 375–400. Opening by stating that Jung left a great deal of ambiguity around the ontological status of the archetypes and the collective unconscious because the requisite neurophysiology and physics upon which to ground his understanding were unavailable, this essay speculates on the way Jung might have formulated these concepts today.

Stevens, A. (1983). *Archetypes: A natural history of the self.* New York: Quill. A comprehensive yet accessible synthesis of Jung's archetypes with subsequent findings in biology, ethology, and psychology.

Van Eenwyk, J. R. (1997). *Archetypes and strange attractors: The chaotic world of symbols.* Toronto: Inner City Books.

After demonstrating parallels between the dynamics of chaos in the world of matter and in the world of symbols, this work concludes that dynamic systems theory lends support to Jung's conception of the archetype.

Whitmont, E. C. (1969). *The symbolic quest: Basic concepts of analytical psychology.* Princeton, NJ: Princeton University Press. In this superb survey of the theory and practice of Jung's depth psychology, the author emphasizes the urgency and importance of the human quest for symbolic experience.

Wilber, K. (1995). *Sex, ecology, spirituality.* Boston: Shambhala. A sweeping synthesis of findings from the physical, biological, and human sciences as they apply to the evolution of human consciousness, this book places the archetype into its larger context. Chapter 6, in particular, offers a critical examination of the application and misapplication of an archetypal perspective.

David Feinstein

ARCHIVAL RESEARCH. The raw data of archival research is obtained from a distinctive source: information stored in archives, the most common archival source being the university library, with its store of encyclopedias, biographical dictionaries, histories, anthologies, print collections, and manuscripts. However, many large institutions will often keep archival records of various kinds. Professional and amateur sports organizations preserve athletic records; businesses keep documents regarding economic performance; and governments maintain archives concerning legislation, judicial decisions, and executive actions. Although most archival records focus on individuals and events of historic importance, archives can include much more, including the personal diaries of otherwise anonymous people (e.g., American pioneer women).

Archival data have been used in psychological research ever since the advent of the behavioral sciences. The first published examples are to be found in Alphonse Quetelet's *Treatise on Man* (New York, 1835). Another early figure in the development of archival methods is Francis Galton, whose *Hereditary Genius* (London, 1869) examined the family pedigrees of eminent creators, leaders, and athletes. Since these initial efforts, archival data have been exploited by many different psychologists in highly variable ways. The overwhelming majority of the applications may be grouped into three categories: psychobiographical, comparative, and historiometric.

Psychobiographical studies take advantage of archival information in order to perform a detailed analysis of a particular notable personality of the past. A classic example is Erik Erikson's *Young Man Luther: A Study in Psychoanalysis and History* (New York, 1958). Psychobiographical studies are almost exclusively qualitative and idiographic in approach. In addition, until very recently most psychobiographies had a strong allegiance to psychoanalytic theory.

Comparative studies exploit archival data in order to examine the lives of eminent individuals. Like psychobiography, comparative research is qualitative rather than quantitative in orientation. Unlike psychobiography, however, comparative studies usually aim to make nomothetic statements. It is for this reason that the approach adopts a multiple- rather than single-case strategy; an example would be Gardner's *Creating Minds: An Anatomy of Creativity Seen Through the Lives of Freud, Einstein, Picasso, Stravinsky, Eliot, Graham, and Gandhi* (New York, 1993).

Historiometric research is the archival method that most closely approximates standard psychometric techniques. First, it scrutinizes multiple cases, with sample sizes much larger than those found in comparative studies. Second, this approach is explicitly quantitative, applying standard statistical methods to objective measurements. Third, this archival technique is explicitly nomothetic in design; the goal is to test hypotheses about human thought, feeling, and behavior. One of the most impressive examples is the monograph on *The Early Mental Traits of Three Hundred Geniuses* by Catharine Cox (Stanford, California, 1926).

Despite the differences among these three types of archival analysis, all approaches have certain advantages and disadvantages in common. On the one hand, a persistent drawback of all archival methods is that causal inferences are always more tentative than those provided by laboratory experiments. On the other hand, archival data provide psychologists with unobtrusive (or nonreactive) observations of human activity in natural settings. [*See* Unobtrusive Measures.] In addition, archives permit the study of phenomena that otherwise cannot be easily investigated—such as creative genius, political leadership, and aesthetics.

Bibliography

Elms, A. C. (1994). *Uncovering lives: The uneasy alliance of biography and psychology.* New York: Oxford University Press. A balanced presentation of psychobiographical methods, with many interesting examples drawn from the author's own research on outstanding creators and leaders.

Hill, M. R. (1993). *Archival strategies and techniques.* Newbury Park, CA: Sage. An overview of the diverse approaches to the use of archival data in the social sciences.

Simonton, D. K. (1990). *Psychology, science, and history: An introduction to historiometry.* New Haven, CT: Yale University Press. A detailed discussion of the diverse ways that psychologists can analyze historical data in order to test general hypotheses about human behavior.

Zaitzow, B. H., & Fields, C. B. (1996). Using archival data

sets. In F. T. L. Leong & J. T. Austin (Eds.), *The psychology research handbook: A guide for graduate students and research assistants* (pp. 251–261). Thousand Oaks, CA: Sage. A practical guide for novices in the psychological use of archival data.

Dean Keith Simonton

ARISTOTLE (384–322 BCE), Ancient Greek philosopher. Aristotle's work on human and animal functioning represents the apogee of insight and sophistication produced by the Hellenic era. Born in Stagira, Macedonia, Aristotle was the son of the court physician to the Macedonian king. In 367 he went to Athens and enrolled in Plato's Academy where he remained an active participant until Plato's death 20 years later, though Plato's influence on him waned as his own views matured. After some years of biological research in Asia Minor, he returned to Macedonia and was appointed tutor to the young Alexander the Great. He returned to Athens in 335, shortly after Alexander ascended the throne, and founded a school at the Lyceum where he organized his ideas into lectures, which are the basis for his extant works. Aristotle left Athens again in 323 and died about a year later, but his influence remained enormous throughout the classical era. He was also the most influential philosopher of the Middle Ages. The advent of Newtonian physics diminished his impact on science, but he has remained one of the handful of significant philosophers in other domains to this day.

Although the categories of psychological phenomena discussed by Aristotle and his contemporaries differ from those of modern psychology, the problems that they address are generally very much like our own. Moreover, Aristotle's work not only has been a major influence on psychological theorizing through the intervening centuries, but also seems especially apposite for twenty-first-century inquiry. Part of this relevance has to do with Aristotle's highly naturalistic perspective on human and animal functioning, but it also results from the acuteness, simplicity, and sophistication with which he diagnosed and analyzed psychological problems.

Perhaps the most fundamental contribution Aristotle made to the theory of mind is that his is the first systematic alternative formulation to the two standard ways of understanding mental functioning: as identical with and reducible to physical events, or as qualitatively different from physical events. Aristotle was the first to present the full range of psychological and logical arguments revealing the pitfalls in both these approaches and to offer arguments supporting a "hylomorphic" alternative (or even a generally functionalist alternative as Putnam, 1975, has argued). He proposed that all

events that can be known must be physical events, but these may be *described* in two complementary ways, depending upon one's focus: the "material" and the "formal." The matter describes the physical constituents of the entities involved and the form describes the organization of these constituents into a unitary whole. In the simplest case that Aristotle presents, that of a golden ring, the gold constitutes the material description and the shape of the ring constitutes the formal description. In addition, there is the ring's functional form, so that if it is a wedding band another sense of the ring's form would be its function as a conjugal symbol. The situation naturally gets more complicated in trying to describe and understand living things, because the form of a living thing refers both to the way that it functions as a whole and to the related ways that its parts function. Moreover, as creatures get more complex materially, the classes of functions they can perform also become more complex. The *totality* of a creature's living functions constitutes its *psyche*, or life principle. Human functioning is the most complex because it includes not only the capacity to live, grow, and reproduce (as with plants), nor just perception, desire, memory, imagination, and voluntary motion (as with animals), but also the capacity to reason about and organize one's life according to a plan. This hierarchy of living capacities constitutes the human *psyche* (*De anima* II.1), an inclusive part-whole system, in which events at the physiological level necessarily participate in but do not by themselves constitute psychological events.

Consideration of Aristotle's analysis of the hierarchically organized nature of biological functioning leads directly to an understanding of what is perhaps his most valuable concept: *teleology*. It is precisely because biological systems are so inherently organized that it makes sense to suppose that biological events regularly achieve something: that they are *for* something rather than occurring by chance. As the first systematic philosopher of science, Aristotle was deeply concerned with what it meant to explain events. His analyses revealed four classes of explanation: two, the material and the formal, are alternative descriptions of substances, while the other two, the efficient and the final, are alternative explanations of changes that substances undergo. Efficient explanations refer to those previous events that are necessary and sufficient for a change to occur, whereas final explanations refer to the outcome achieved by the change, its *telos* (*Physics* II.3). These alternative modes of explanation of change must be viewed as complementary rather than conflicting. But teleological explanation was widely rejected as unscientific in biology and psychology until quite recently because, allegedly, it could not be used as a basis for prediction. Such criticism is largely the result of medieval thinkers imposing "God's design" on the concept of *telos*, which led scientists to restrict their models of causality to those in which all events in the natural world are the mechanical consequences of causes that immediately precede them. From such a model, it would make no sense to try, as Aristotle does, to understand events by searching for the relationships between them and the larger organized context in which they function.

Aristotle used teleological explanation for three classes of biological relationships: those in which the functioning of organismic subsystems is explained by the functioning of the whole organism; those in which particular developmental changes in an organism are explained by the nature and functioning of the mature organism; and those in which the voluntary behavior of an animal is explained by the value of the outcome that it normally produces. This third class of explanation may also be a type of part-whole explanation, since the goals achieved by voluntary behavior may be described as broader classes of behavior (e.g., when a bear's going to the river and running its paw through the water produces a fish as an outcome, which can also be described as an instance of food-seeking behavior). Thus, the classes of voluntary action an animal engages in are generally illuminated by relating them to the normal way in which a mature animal of that species functions and flourishes (its form). And that form may he construed as the end or *telos* of such action (Nussbaum, 1978, pp. 76–85). None of this requires any conscious deliberation to take place in nature nor, said Aristotle, does the absence of deliberation rule out such purposive explanation (*Physics* II.8).

It is the explanation of voluntary behavior by its outcome that has the greatest relevance for psychology. Exactly which classes of human and animal action should be grouped together because they are controlled by common classes of outcome, and exactly what laws describe the nature of such control, are empirical questions that investigators of operant behavior, comparative psychology, and child development have studied for generations. And the organization of related human goals (as well as the conflict among incompatible ones) has been studied by cognitive, social, and personality psychologists with equal intensity. While both mechanistic and physiological analyses may reveal *how* a pattern of behavior emerges, it is teleological explanation that reveals *why* it emerges.

Aristotle's analysis of voluntary action shows it to be contingently linked to and necessarily coordinate with sense perception, for without such coordination no animal could survive, let alone flourish (*De anima* III). In addition, he argues that all human knowledge originates with sense perception which, in turn, is based upon the ability to discriminate what *is* from what is *not*, and one object from another (*De anima* II;

De sensu I). Any perception that occurs, however, requires that the sense organ itself be organized in such a way that the information it receives about objects in the world is correlated with those objects' form. This constrains the stimuli that the senses receive and allows us to perceive the world as it is (*De anima* II.12). The potential of the five specialized senses to react in their appropriate ways to relevant stimulation is an active capacity for discrimination rather than a passive subjective state. Data from the specialized senses are integrated by a nonspecialized perceptual capacity into discrimination of the real objects of the world. In addition, Aristotle portrays perceptual capacity at any moment as limited, so that stimuli compete both within and between sense modalities in order to be perceived. Nor are clear perceptions possible when a person is distracted by thought or a strong emotional state (*De sensu* I.447).

Remembering and imagining depend upon the persistence of physical traces of sensation that are reactivated under suitable stimulating circumstances. The revival of such sensorylike actions in the absence of their environmental stimuli is the consequence of the principles of association. For all animals, certain movements naturally produce others with which they are connected, either because they have occurred together in the past or because they are similar to one another. Thus, the retrieval of the associated representations will occur when the stimuli with which they are associated occur (*De memoria* 450–452.) The occurrence of desire in humans and animals depends entirely on such retrieval, for without it no active pursuit of or withdrawal from its objects would be possible.

Aristotle's approach to the question of how we acquire knowledge and reasoning capacities is a determinately developmental one, which provides a clear alternative to both the empiricist and nativist extremists of his era (and ours). How people are changed by any particular experiences depends both on their cumulative, prior experiences and their current, organized state of potentiality, in interaction with the environmental releasers of such potentiality (Silverstein, 1990). Nowhere is this clearer than in his discussion of the acquisition of practical reasoning, both for understanding (*Posterior Analytics* II) and for ethical choice (*Nichomachean Ethics* III, VI). Here he demonstrates how particular types of experiences are needed for reasoning to develop, but also that the individual must be ready to profit from those experiences. Such readiness requires both a certain developed capacity and adequate previous relevant learning; so that in order to understand the effects of particular types of experience at each stage of a child's development, we must integrate information about the current level of that child's potential for understanding these new experiences and the types of change that such experiences typically produce. The developing child's current level of reasoning also can be understood as a set of formal operating rules which set the limits on succeeding transformations that can be achieved.

Aristotle's developmental perspective also manages to capture within a single focus both the uniqueness of the individual and the universal processes that are typical of the species. This unity of focus can be achieved through a concept composed entirely of Aristotelian features, recently labeled a *developmental functional history* (Silverstein, 1988). The material career of every animal, including humans, must function according to the general principles that are proper to and serve the survival functions for its species. Thus, it is a functional history that each animal has which, moreover, will be developmental and cumulative in nature, influencing how it can and cannot change in the future. The developmental functional history (DFH) of any individual animal must be unique, and this uniqueness is a defining (necessary) rule of its functional organization. Because no two DFHs can be exactly alike, it follows that no two individuals can be identical.

Aristotle's arguments concerning the DFH and its constituents make it clear that all animals, and especially all humans, are essentially composed of their developmental functional histories and that each DFH reveals the transactional nature of an animal whose future life is constrained by prior interactions between its essential nature and its circumstances. He also uses that concept to discuss the composition of the state and how its citizens should be educated (*Politics* VII, VIII) and to discuss the nature of the *hexis*, that settled state or condition of character which is proper to each person and plays a crucial role in trying to achieve the Good Life (*Nichomachean Ethics* X). In the latter discussion we find Aristotle's powerful argument that the Good Life requires actualizing the potential encapsulated within one's own DFH.

Bibliography

Ackrill, J. L. (1981). *Aristotle the philosopher*. Oxford: Clarendon Press. A concise and erudite introduction to Aristotle's philosophy by one of the great scholars in the field.

Barnes, J. (Ed.). (1984). *The complete works of Aristotle*. Princeton, NJ: Princeton University Press. This revision of the standard Oxford translation of Aristotle's complete works (Smith & Ross, Eds., 1930) is the most reliable English translation currently available. Of particular interest to psychologists are: *De anima, De sensu, De memoria, De motu animalium, Nichomachean ethics, Politics,* and *Rhetoric*. Reference notations to Aristotle's larger works (e.g., *De anima*) are generally cited first by book (indicated by Roman numerals) and then by chapter (indicated by Arabic numerals); the shorter works (e.g., *De sensu*) are divided only into chapters. Where specific references are made above, the printed numbers referred to are those used cumulatively in Immanuel Becker's 1831 standard edition of the Greek text. References consist of a page number, a column letter, and a line number. This is the standard reference form for all scholars who write about Aristotle.

Journal of Theoretical and Philosophical Psychology. (1990). 10 (1). This issue is devoted entirely to implications for modern psychology of Aristotelian theories.

Kraut, R. (1989). *Aristotle on the human good*. Princeton, NJ: Princeton University Press. An insightful reconstruction of Aristotle's psychology of human happiness.

Nussbaum, M. C. (1978). *Aristotle's de motu animalium*. Princeton, NJ: Princeton University Press. A new translation of and critical essays on a long neglected Aristotelian masterpiece about voluntary motion.

Nussbaum, M. C., & Rorty, A. E. (Eds.). (1992). *Essays on Aristotle's De anima*. Oxford: Clarendon Press. See especially the essays by Nussbaum and Putnam, Richardson, and Sorabji.

Putnam H. (1975). Philosophy and our mental life. In *Mind, language and reality: Philosophical papers*. Cambridge, UK: Cambridge University Press.

Rachlin, H. (1994). *Behavior and mind*. New York: Oxford University Press. An innovative analysis of the roots of scientific psychology, with an emphasis on the amalgamation of Aristotelian functionalism and modern behavior theory.

Robinson D. N. (1989). *Aristotle's psychology*. New York: Columbia University Press. An instructive and scholarly overview of Aristotle's entire psychological corpus, written from a rather intellectualist viewpoint.

Sherman, N. (1989). *The fabric of character*. Oxford: Oxford University Press. An insightful and engaging account of Aristotle's theory of moral reasoning and ethical education. The contemporary implications for psychology and education are perspicuously drawn.

Silverstein, A. (1988). An Aristotelian resolution of the idiographic versus nomothetic tension. *American Psychologist, 43*, 425–430.

Silverstein, A. (1990). The application of Aristotle's philosophy of mind to theories in developmental psychology. *Journal of Theoretical and Philosophical Psychology, 10*.

Albert Silverstein

AROUSAL is an inferred central process, or behavioral state, that involves coordinated, sustained, state-specific alterations in activity in numerous brain regions, producing coherent patterns of behavioral, endocrine, and autonomic output. The principal measure of brain electrophysiological activity that has been used to characterize or quantify arousal is electroencephalographic

(EEG) activity. During intense arousal, the EEG exhibits low-amplitude and high-frequency characteristics in the neocortex and is dominated by theta (4–7 Hz) activity in the hippocampus. In the periphery, increases in muscle tone, heart rate, respiration, release of particular pituitary hormones, and adrenal secretion are typical components of heightened arousal and are often used to operationally define "level of arousal." These peripheral and central measures often shift in a coordinated fashion so that particular clusters of measures constitute well-defined behavioral states (or stages, as in the sleep-wake cycle). In the behavioral dimension, the magnitudes of startle and other reflex responses generally vary systematically with level of arousal as assessed by EEG and other measures. The probability that a sensory stimulus will be detected, discriminated, further analyzed, and remembered varies systematically with the status of these indices of arousal and with the context that "shapes" this arousal.

Is Arousal a State or a Process?

The term *arousal* has been used to refer to either qualitative "state" changes or to incremental "process" changes. For example, it has been used to designate the transition from sleep to waking, implying that arousal is a qualitative change in behavioral state. Alternatively, it has been viewed as involving a unified, reproducible constellation of co-varying values of these measures, implying that arousal is a unidimensional, coherent process that varies along a definable, quantitative scale. Most commonly, this use of the term refers to variations within the waking state along a continuum from drowsy to highly aroused. From this perspective, the waking state is a precondition for other processes related to, but probably distinguishable from, arousal, such as alertness, attention, and vigilance. These latter processes may involve more elaboration, selectivity, and refinement than arousal, perhaps drawing on different or more focused constellations of forebrain structures and activity than the generalized condition of high arousal. Arousal can be viewed as constituting one aspect, perhaps the least differentiated constituent, of complex behaviors such as aggression, reproduction, athletic performance, flight from attack, and others. The "validity," or at least the usefulness, of the concept of arousal is based on the consistency of the signs of arousal that occur during many behaviors and on the reproducibility of the behavioral state that, indeed, serves as the precondition for many essential behaviors. The validity of the concept also depends on the observation that these signs can be produced by stimulation of a circumscribed region of the brain stem without the simultaneous production of a specific, goal-directed, behavioral constellation.

The survival and reproductive value of adjustable levels of arousal seems straightforward. An initial mod-est level of arousal, activation, or responsiveness is essential for the initiation of many behaviors. In addition, each of the wide variety of behaviors necessary for survival would seem to have a different optimal level of arousal for its performance. Also, the available evidence from metabolic studies indicates that, in the brain and some other organs, there is a considerable metabolic cost to arousal, which may explain why the "default" condition is one of modest behavioral activation. Finally, reduced levels of activation are probably necessary for the initiation of sleep, and, to the extent that sleep has physiologically and/or behaviorally mediated survival benefits, this provides additional impetus for the modulation of arousal.

Problems in Characterizing Arousal

Although arousal may be viewed as either a state or a process, both of these perspectives, at least as they are presented above, are ultimately oversimplified. Detailed study of the many central and peripheral physiological indices of behavioral states has revealed that these indices do not co-vary in a simple, linear fashion. Thus, a finer grained typology reveals that there are different types or aspects of arousal (e.g., when emotional behaviors are considered). In certain circumstances, the defining signs of arousal become dissociated or aggregate into other constellations that define additional "normal" or even "abnormal" states. A straightforward example is the issue of how waking arousal compares with the arousal characteristic of rapid eye movement (REM) sleep. In REM sleep, the brain is highly activated in terms of EEG and other electrophysiological measures, and yet this is the brain-behavior state when behavioral responsivity, as measured by sensory stimulation thresholds, is at a minimum. There are also instances of complex relationships among these measures *within* the waking state. Some of these are revealed during close examination of the EEG correlates of particular types of behavior. For example, as just noted, hippocampal theta activity generally indexes arousal in that it occurs during activated waking and during REM sleep, simultaneously with desynchronized neocortical EEG. However, there are certain behaviors, such as grooming and freezing in the rat, during which the neocortical, hippocampal, and behavioral signs of arousal exhibit more complex relations to one another. A final example of the complexities of the relationship between arousal and behavior within the waking state is embodied in the familiar inverted-U relationship between arousal and accuracy of performance on demanding tasks. That is, there are numerous observations that there is an optimal level of arousal for performance of a given task, and arousal either above or below this level impairs such performance. Thus, there are numerous examples of nonlinear relationships among the brain and behavior variables that generally co-vary to define level of arousal.

Neural Substrates of Arousal

A number of observations generated since the 1950s have identified certain brain-stem structures as being crucial for the occurrence of central nervous system (CNS) and behavioral arousal. The classical concept is that there is an ascending reticular activating system whose activation is necessary and sufficient for the electrophysiological activation of forebrain structures and for normal responsiveness to sensory stimulation. This inference is based on the observation that electrical stimulation of certain portions of the reticular core of the brain stem produces an aroused status of the forebrain, while lesions of this reticular zone produce a perpetual somnolent state. It appears that much of the ascending influence of this system is mediated via midline thalamic structures and the nucleus reticularis thalami and by interactions of these two subdivisions of the thalamus with the neocortex. While there is some validity to the idea that overall levels of neuronal activity increase with arousal, decades of electrophysiological studies indicate that changes in arousal are much more a case of altered organization or patterns of neuronal activity than a matter of increases or decreases in mean discharge rates of neuronal populations.

Affect and Arousal

Arousal has been viewed as being an important component of stress, anxiety, and fear, both in their "normal" and in their "pathological" manifestations. These conditions are often viewed as the "negative" aspects of arousal in that most organisms will avoid circumstances that produce these states. Clearly, heightened arousal also accompanies behaviors with a positive affective tone.

In the context of emotional behaviors, a major conceptual dilemma is whether arousal has an independent neural substrate that can be activated in the absence of a specific, affective behavior. In psychological terms, this is the question of whether there can be "contentless" arousal. Perhaps the most likely scenario is that there is a common arousal mechanism that is activated in very much the same way by several distinguishable affective circuitries, such as those putatively embodied in the amygdala, hypothalamus, and central gray. Indeed, the hypothalamus and amygdala may well serve to integrate the intra-CNS aspects of arousal with its autonomic and endocrine aspects. The pathways by which particular stimuli can elicit arousal are not well understood. There is evidence that sensory information arising via brain-stem and thalamic relays can possibly elicit arousal without any processing by "higher," neocortical centers. However, the more elaborate the information (reading a death threat versus sensing a painful somatosensory stimulus), the more elaborate information processing must be before arousal is elicited.

One way in which the putative nonspecificity of arousal might be related to the specificity of emotional circuitry is that arousal systems may further enhance activation of areas that are receiving appropriate sensory input, while simultaneously not activating (or even suppressing) activity in brain circuitry that is not receiving such input. Thus, during times of arousal, the differentiation between activated and nonactivated brain circuitry would be enhanced, permitting more efficient, and less ambiguous, selection of appropriate sensory input for analysis and more appropriate (or stereotyped) motor output. This "motor" output may involve reactivation of brain arousal systems as well as autonomic and skeletal motor systems, and there is a danger of a self-perpetuating (i.e., stimulus → arousal → response → stimulus → . . .) positive feedback loop.

Pathologies of Arousal

Certain psychiatric disorders, such as panic attacks or generalized anxiety disorder, can be viewed as disorders of arousal, in which arousal occurs in inappropriate circumstances, such as without relevant sensory stimulation. Also, certain sleep disturbances have been viewed as pathologies of arousal systems, leading, for example, to sleep disruption. Attention-deficit/hyperactivity disorder has also commonly been viewed as reflecting a dysregulation of attentional systems that are closely intertwined with arousal mechanisms.

Bibliography

Aston-Jones, G., Rajkowski, J., Kubiak, P., Valentino, R. J., & Shipley, M. T. (1996). Role of the locus coeruleus in emotional activation. *Progress in Brain Research, 107,* 379–402. Scholarly consideration of the interrelationships among vigilance, arousal, and emotion circuitry in the context of a transmitter-specific brain stem to forebrain system.

Hobson, J. A. (1989). *Sleep.* New York: Scientific American Library/Freeman. A description, at the nonspecialist level, of the psychological, psychiatric, and neuroscientific phenomenology of sleep.

Hobson, J. A. (1994). *The chemistry of conscious states: How the brain changes its mind.* Boston, MA.: Little, Brown. An exposition for the general reader concerning the brain systems underlying the dramatic shifts in consciousness that occur throughout the sleep-wake cycle.

Hobson, J. A., Lydic, R., & Baghdoyan, L. H. (1986). Evolving concepts of sleep cycle generation: From brain centers to neuronal populations. *Behavioral and Brain Sciences, 9,* 371–448. A conceptual, databased, provocative consideration of the brain mechanisms subserving behavioral state control.

Kahn, D., Pace-Schott, E. F., & Hobson, J. A. (1997). Consciousness in waking and dreaming: The roles of neuronal oscillation and neuromodulation in determining similarities and differences. *Neuroscience, 78,* 13–38. Explores the specific differences between the waking and the sleeping brain that may underly the differences in consciousness that characterize these states.

LeDoux, J. E. (1987). Emotion. In F. Plum (Ed.), *Handbook of physiology, section 1: The nervous system, vol. 5: Higher functions of the brain,* (pp. 419–460). Bethesda, MD: American Physiological Society. A scholarly overview of this immense field.

LeDoux, J. E. (1995). Emotion: Clues from the brain. *Annual Review of Psychology, 46,* 209–235. A review of recent research on emotions and brain circuitry from the perspective of a researcher actively dealing with these issues.

LeDoux, J. E. (1996). *The emotional brain: The mysterious underpinnings of emotional life.* New York: Simon & Schuster. An incisive analysis of how emotions fit into the overall organization of brain, behavior, and conscious experience.

Moruzzi, G., & Magoun, H. W. (1949). Brain stem reticular formation and activation of the EEG. *Electroencephalography and Clinical Neurophysiology, 1,* 455–473. A classic report that was a major impetus to the development of the concept of an ascending reticular activating system.

Steriade, M., & McCarley, R. W. (1990). *Brainstem control of wakefulness and sleep.* New York: Plenum Press. A detailed, systematic, scholarly analysis of the neuronal stubstrates of waking and the stages of sleep.

Stephen L. Foote

ARTHRITIS is not simply about the aches and pains associated with old age. There are a number of rheumatic and musculoskeletal diseases (including systemic lupus erythematosus, osteoarthritis, and ankylosing spondylitis) that share the following characteristics: they are chronic, painful, recurrent, and debilitating, and affect daily functioning and quality of life. The form of arthritis that has received the most study by psychologists is rheumatoid arthritis (RA), in part because it is the most painful and disabling form of arthritis. Thus, we will use adult RA as an exemplar to understand how psychological status affects and is affected by the illness (for information on how arthritis affects children, see the bibliography below).

RA is a chronic systemic disease characterized primarily by joint inflammation, which can result in pain, swelling, stiffness, and deformity. Although not life-threatening, the course of RA is unpredictable and highly variable, and symptoms of pain and stiffness tend to flare and remit. RA affects 1 to 2% of the adult population of the United States, and it affects 2.5 times as many women as men. Despite stereotypes of arthritis as an old person's disease, the average age of RA onset is between 25 and 50, and the prevalence increases with age.

It is difficult to discuss the psychological aspects of arthritis without considering the effects of gender and age. More women than men are affected by arthritis. In fact, arthritis is the most common self-reported chronic condition affecting women. Some studies suggest that women report more arthritis symptoms than do men, but that this is because women actually experience more symptoms, not because they are more likely to overreport symptoms. As women live longer than men, they are more likely to have arthritis (both RA and osteoarthritis) in older age, experiencing the physical losses of normal aging combined with accelerated disease processes.

The symptoms of arthritis are controllable, but the disease is not currently curable. As with other chronic illnesses, the effectiveness of medical treatment is related to the degree to which patients adhere to prescribed medical regimens. Arthritis treatment may require that patients engage in behaviors such as taking medication, maintaining a regular pattern of exercise, scheduling and keeping appointments, wearing splints, and practicing pain self-management. Some factors that have been found to affect RA patients' adherence to their prescribed treatment include open communication between patients and health care providers, patients' expectations about their ability to manage the pain and treatment regimen (what are termed self-efficacy beliefs), and characteristics of the home environment and medical regimen. Complex regimens are more difficult to follow, as are regimens that change frequently. Often patients need to try many different treatments before an effective one is found.

Effects of Arthritis on Well-Being

The effects can include changes in lifestyle and interpersonal relationships, and depression.

Lifestyle Changes. Many of the changes in lifestyle precipitated by RA are a direct result of frequent pain episodes and increasing physical disability. Many RA patients report decreases in social, recreational, and leisure activities. Problems with activities that previously might have been taken for granted require patients to find new ways to perform tasks or to redefine roles at home and at work. RA has a profound effect on employment status, with many people unable to maintain their jobs as the disability worsens. RA has been shown to affect the ability to perform regular activities of daily life, such as childcare, which in turn affects feelings of self-worth. Several studies of women with RA have shown that because of the loss of a valued caregiver/nurturer role, women with RA experience lowered self-worth and perceived competence. This has been shown in both Hispanic and non-Hispanic White populations.

Changes in Interpersonal Relationships. RA affects relationships with friends and family, as those in the person's natural support system try to help him or her cope with RA. Social support from friends and family has been found to buffer RA patients from the negative effects of illness on well-being. Unfortunately, this well-intended support often backfires, as patients do not want the help or comfort that is offered, creating more tension within interpersonal relationships. For patients to benefit, the type of support they need must fit with what providers offer.

Among married couples in which one partner has RA, the illness affects communication, supportiveness, and sexual satisfaction. The degree of disability is a major determinant of the degree to which the marital relationship is affected. Spouses may feel frustrated about a reduction in shared pleasurable activities, helpless in response to seeing a wife or husband in pain, and fearful regarding the future.

Depression. Despite numerous potential stressors caused by arthritis, most individuals with arthritis do not experience clinical depression. However, people with arthritis are more likely to experience depression than people without any serious chronic illness. If depression does occur, it can worsen the pain and disability associated with arthritis. It is important that health care professionals monitor their patients for depressive symptoms and treat them appropriately, rather than overlooking signs of depression or assuming that depression is a normal part of chronic illness.

Factors Affecting Positive Adaptation to Arthritis

Coping, social support, and cognitive factors all affect positive adaptation to RA.

Coping. Research on how individuals cope with arthritis has shown that some strategies work better than others. Strategies such as actively seeking information and trying to view one's situation in a more positive light have been associated with better psychological functioning. Coping strategies such as wishful thinking and self-blame have been associated with poorer psychological functioning among both men and women. However, reports of emotion-focused coping strategies such as self-blame may reflect levels of distress rather than actual coping efforts.

Most of the research on coping with arthritis has focused on individuals' coping efforts despite the fact that a chronic illness such as arthritis affects the entire family. A study of married couples in which one partner had arthritis found that couples in which the husband and wife coped in a similar fashion were not always better off than those with nonsimilar coping styles: what counted was how the husbands' and wives' strategies complemented each other.

Social Support. As described above, social support from friends and family can bolster the coping efforts of people facing arthritis; this is particularly important for those RA patients with severe pain and disability. The type of social support that is most helpful may vary during different points in the illness. For instance, informational support may be most helpful around the time of diagnosis when one has to learn how to follow a treatment regimen and alter one's lifestyle. In contrast, tangible support, or the provision of help and assistance (such as help with chores and errands) may be most effective in later stages of the illness when symptoms and disability have become more severe. Emotional support is likely to be helpful throughout the course of the illness, as emotional support makes patients feel loved, valued, and part of a family or community. Social support can be a doubled-edged sword, however. Types of social support likely to be perceived as unhelpful by arthritis patients include expressions of pity, minimization of the severity of the illness, and pessimistic comments.

Cognitive Factors. The extent to which patients believe that they have control over their illness appears to have a significant impact on their adjustment. For example, research has shown that perception of personal control over RA treatment is related to positive mood and that perceived control over pain generally is related to less daily pain over time. Beliefs about the cause of illness also may affect mood; one study of RA patients found depressed mood among those who perceived little control over their illness *and* attributed the cause of an arthritis flare-up to personal rather than external factors.

Psychological Interventions

In addition to biomedical treatment, participation in psychological interventions can contribute to decreases in physical symptoms as well as increases in quality of life. Cognitive-behavioral therapy (CBT) is a type of psychological intervention that uses education and teaching of specific skills—including relaxation techniques, goal setting and activity pacing, and coping skills training—to help patients control problems such as pain. CBT can occur within either group or individual settings. Controlled studies of RA patients who participated in CBT interventions have found positive effects at the end of treatment, which sometimes are sustained through subsequent follow-up assessments. The Arthritis Self-Management Program (ASMP), conducted by the Arthritis Foundation, is a structured group intervention led by trained laypersons with arthritis. Reported benefits of the program include increased knowledge, self-care behaviors such as exercise and relaxation, and decreased pain.

In sum, arthritis provides a good example of how chronic physical illness affects mental health, while at the same time psychological factors such as perceptions of control, coping, and depression affect management of the disease. The experience of people with arthritis also illustrates that chronic illness does not affect patients in a vacuum. Rather, family members and friends are also affected and may play important roles in patients' adaptation to the illness.

Bibliography

Arthritis Care and Research. Bimonthly, peer-reviewed official journal of the Association of Rheumatology Health Professionals. Presents the best research on the nonmedical aspects of arthritis and musculoskeletal disease. Published by the American College of Rheumatology.

Arthritis Today. Monthly magazine written for people with arthritis and the people who take care of them, featuring articles on many of the issues discussed in this entry. Published by the Arthritis Foundation.

DeVellis, B. M., Revenson, T. A., & Blalock, S. J. (1997). Rheumatic disease and women's health. In S. J. Gallant, G. P. Keita, & R. Royak-Schaler (Eds.), *Health care for women: Psychological, social, and behavioral influences* (pp. 333–347). Washington, DC: American Psychological Association.

Kewman, D. G., Warschausky, S. A., & Engel, L. (1995). Juvenile rheumatoid arthritis and neuromuscular conditions: Scoliosis, spinal cord injury, and muscular dystrophy. In M. C. Roberts (Ed.), *Handbook of pediatric psychology* (2nd ed., pp. 384–402). New York: Guilford Press.

Lorig, K. (1995). *The arthritis helpbook: A tested self-management program for coping with arthritis and fibromyalgia* (4th ed.). Reading, MA: Addison-Wesley.

Manne, S. L., & Zautra, A. J. (1992). Coping with arthritis: Current status and critique. *Arthritis and Rheumatism, 35,* 1273–1280.

Newman, S., Fitzpatrick, R., Revenson, T. A., Skevington, S., & Williams, G. (1996). *Understanding rheumatoid arthritis.* London: Routledge.

Newman, S. P., & Shipley, M. (Eds.).(1993). Psychological aspects of rheumatic disease. *Bailliere's Clinical Rheumatology, 7*(2), 215–420. London: Bailliere Tindall.

Tracey A. Revenson and Sharon Danoff-Burg

ARTIFACT. [*This entry comprises two articles*: Artifact in Research *and* Artifact in Assessment.]

Artifact in Research

An artifact, as viewed in the context of research, is a type of error that occurs systematically rather than randomly and, if ignored or left uncontrolled or uncorrected, can jeopardize the validity of conclusions concerning the research hypothesis. [*See the article on Ar-*tifact in Assessment *in this entry.*] Interestingly, artifacts that are inherent in research with human subjects had been recognized as early as 1885 by Hermann Ebbinghaus, a pioneering German experimental psychologist, but did not attract much attention until three quarters of a century later. [*See the biography of Ebbinghaus.*] Since their rediscovery by Saul Rosenzweig (*Psychological Bulletin,* 1933, *40,* 337–354), and the development of empirical work in the late 1950s and early 1960s, artifacts have been investigated from the perspective of both the experimenter and the research participants (or subjects). The results of these investigations—in an area known as the *social psychology of the experiment*—have led to substantive insights and to procedures for isolating, measuring, assessing, and, sometimes, eliminating these artifacts.

Experimenter Artifacts

The investigator (or experimenter) is not a disinterested, passive participant in the research process but, rather, is an involved participant with all the hopes, interests, and aspirations of any individual in the pursuit of knowledge. Robert Rosenthal's classic work (1966a/1976) defines two broad types of experimenter-related artifacts as noninteractional and interactional and notes a number of subclasses of each type. Noninteractional artifacts are biases that do not influence how the research participants respond to the experimental stimuli, per se, but rather refer to how the investigator observes, interprets, and reports the research results. Three subclasses of this type of artifact are called *observer bias, interpreter bias,* and *intentional bias.* Interactional artifacts receive their name from the fact that they are connected with the interaction between the experimenter and the research participants and actually affect how the participants will respond. Five subclasses of this type of artifact are called biosocial effects, psychosocial effects, situational effects, modeling effects, and the experimenter expectancy effect.

Observer biases imply the over- or underestimation of the variable of interest during the observation and recording phase of the research. For example, unintentional recording errors favoring the researcher's hypothesis would imply that the researcher "saw" what he or she *wanted* to see. Such biases have also been well documented and investigated outside the context of artifact research. [*See Rumors.*] A fascinating case, noted by M. L. Johnson (*New Biology,* 1953, *15,* 60–80), involved a radiologist who mistook a button caught in a patient's throat for a button "on the vest"—where a button *ought* to be present.

Bias in the *interpretation* of results was documented by John J. Sherwood and Mark Nataupsky (*Journal of Personality and Social Psychology,* 1968, *8,* 53–58), who found that the nature/nurture conclusion that experts drew from research on racial differences in intelligence could be predicted from the experts' demographic profiles. In another demonstration study, Allan J. Kimmel (*American Psychologist*, 1991, 46, 786–788) showed that ethical evaluations of the risks and benefits of research studies could be predicted in part from a knowledge of certain biographical characteristics of the evaluators, raising the possibility of specifiable biases in the ethical decision making of institutional review boards (IRBs) as a function of their composition.

Observer and interpreter biases are predicated on the assumption that the researcher unknowingly or unwittingly introduced this systematic error into the experimental situation, whereas *intentional* biases occur when individuals willingly engage in unethical activity by fabricating, unjustifiably manipulating, or suppressing data in order to support a particular conclusion. Dishonesty is devastating to science because it misleads others, wastes valuable resources, and undermines the respect for the literature on which the advancement of science depends. An attitude that abhors dishonesty and that values integrity and honest scholarship is paramount in science, and researchers are held to standards of ethical accountability which touch on virtually all aspects of the research process. [*See* Ethics, *article on* Ethics in Research.]

Among various interactional artifacts, the best known and most widely studied is *experimenter expectancy bias*. [*See* Expectancy Effects.] This type of systematic error results when the experimenter's hypothesis leads unintentionally to behavior toward the participants that increases the likelihood that the hypothesis will be confirmed. A classic case in psychology involved not human subjects but a horse named "Clever Hans." Oscar Pfungst (*Clever Hans: The Horse of Mr. von Osten*, New York, 1911) described the results of a set of experimental trials, undertaken with the collaboration of the eminent psychologist Carl Stumpf, in which they showed that unintentional cues from the horse's questioners led the animal to respond in ways that seemed to imply complex intellectual functioning. The horse was indeed "clever," although not in the way that popular folklore stressed but rather as a creation of the questioners' self-fulfilling prophecies. [*See* Self-Fulfilling Prophecy; *and the biography of Stumpf.*]

Biosocial effects can be attributed to the sex, age, ethnicity, and race of the experimenter, such as when male and female experimenters behave differently toward their subjects. *Psychosocial* effects can be attributed to the experimenter's personality. For example, Rosenthal and coworkers filmed and analyzed the interactions of experimenters and their subjects and found that experimenters who scored high on a scale of need for social approval behaved so as to gain approval from their subjects (psychosocial effect). The experimenters spoke to their subjects in a more enthusiastic and affable tone of voice, smiled more often, and slanted their bodies more toward the subjects than did experimenters who scored lower in the need for social approval.

Situational biases are a function of uncontrolled aspects of the setting or the experimenter's prior experience. For example, experimenters usually become more accurate and faster in their reading of the instructions to their later-contacted subjects, and the experimenter's behavior may also become less tense with more experience. By contrast, *modeling* effects are a function of the example set by the investigator. In survey research, for example, respondents sometimes seek to emulate what they think the interviewer believes rather than disclosing their own personal beliefs.

Subject Artifacts

Awareness of potential subject artifacts is of particular importance in behavioral research because humans are sentient, motivated beings who actively, rather than passively, react to the research stimuli. As a consequence, the research participants might play an active role in the introduction of artifacts into an otherwise well-designed study. In this vein, the methodological *Hawthorne effect* refers to the reactions of research participants to knowingly being observed. Because the participants are aware that their behavior is being observed, they may respond differently to the experimental stimuli than if they were not being observed. To minimize this potential problem of reactivity (i.e., observation or measurement that affects what is being observed or measured), investigators sometimes employ the use of unobtrusive measures of the outcome variable of interest. [*See* Hawthorne Effect *and* Unobtrusive Measures.]

Participants' motivations upon entering the experimental situation also create the potential for subject artifacts. Martin T. Orne (*American Psychologist*, 1962, 17, 776–783) suggested that one powerful motivation that participants may have upon entering an experimental situation is to be a "good subject." This term was defined in an ironic way to imply that the participant may not be passively reacting to stimuli but rather taking an active role in trying to discern the "true" purpose of the experimental investigation. Presumably, by acting in a way that ostensibly supports the perceived experimental hypothesis, the subject introduces artifacts into the research situation. Studies by Rosnow and coworkers found that, consistent with Orne's theory, persons who willingly volunteered for research participation were more sensitive and accommodating to demand characteristics (i.e., task-orienting cues) than were nonvolunteers.

Other role-related motivations of subjects for research participation have also been described and studied. Milton J. Rosenberg argued that the research participant's behavior in an experimental situation is not motivated by attempts to be a "good subject" but rather by the arousal of apprehension when one is knowingly being evaluated (Rosenthal & Rosnow, 1969). Presumably, the goal of the research subject who is experiencing *evaluation apprehension* is to "look good" rather than "be good" in responding to the experimental stimuli. Alternatively, subjects may merely be viewing the investigator as an authority figure whom one must obey. As such, the subjects may not be responding only to the experimental manipulation but to the perceived authority status of the experimenter. There is evidence to suggest that, to some degree, all of these factors tend to be associated in prospective participants' minds with "being a subject in a psychology experiment."

Coping with Artifacts

There are general and specific methods for addressing these potential problems. For example, it is possible to use simple statistical analyses to detect changes in experimenter behavior from the first to the last set of participants, and it is also possible to "correct" for an implied artifact once we find a correlation between the suspected source and the variable of interest. A design strategy for avoiding expectancy biases is based on the idea that, if the experimenter does not know whether the subject is in the experimental or the control condition, the experimenter can have no validly based expectation about how the subject *should* respond. In a *double-blind* experimental design, both the experimenters and the subjects are kept from knowing what treatment has been administered.

To isolate experimenter expectancy bias, one can use an *expectancy control design*. Experimenters are randomly assigned to conditions in which they are led to believe they are administering the experimental treatment or the control treatment, and within these two conditions the experimenters are randomly assigned to administer either the experimental or the control treatment. In this way, it is possible to tease out the experimental effect of interest independently of the effect of experimenter expectancy bias. In experimental designs that use a placebo control, it is possible to evaluate whether the subject's experimental behavior is due to the experimental stimulus or rather to the expectation that one has been exposed to a specific experimental stimulus. [*See* Placebo Effect in Research Design.]

Quasi-control procedures proposed by Orne can be used to detect the contribution of inadvertent task-orienting cues in experiments. Quasi-control subjects are participants who step out of their traditional role as a "subject" and act as a kind of "consultant" to the experimenter. In one variant, the investigator does not actually expose the quasi-control subjects to the experimental stimuli, but rather asks them to reflect on how they might respond if they were exposed to such stimuli. By examining the possible responses as well as the beliefs and perceptions of quasi-control subjects to the experimental stimuli as well as the experimental situation itself, the investigator attempts to gain insights into subject artifacts that are operating in the situation. In another variant, the quasi-control subjects are removed from the experiment at some point and the researcher then interviews them in order to probe the reasoning behind the participants' behavior as well as beliefs about the experimental stimuli up to and including the point at which the quasi-control subjects' participation in the study was terminated. [*See* Demand Characteristics.]

The most critical control for artifacts is woven into the fabric of scientific research by the tradition of replications by independent investigators. However, replicated observations made under very similar conditions of anticipation, instrumentation, and psychological climate might themselves be similarly biased. Therefore, Donald T. Campbell recommended that investigators employ multiple methods—also called *multiple operationalism*—in order to "triangulate" (or zero in) on the phenomenon of interest by aggregating evidence from studies whose methodological strengths and weaknesses will presumably balance out. [*See the biography of Campbell.*]

Bibliography

Campbell, D. T. (1988). *Methodology and epistemology for social science: Selected papers* (E. S. Overman, Ed.). Chicago: University of Chicago Press. An anthology of essays by a major contributor to the methodology of the behavioral and social sciences.

Morawski, J. G. (Ed.). (1988). *The rise of experimentation in American psychology*. New York: Oxford University Press. Essays examining the subjects used in early experiments, the role of debriefing, the history of artifact research, the controversy regarding the Hawthorne studies, and related issues in American psychology.

Rosenthal, R. (1976). *Experimenter effects in behavioral research* (Rev. ed.). New York: Irvington. (Original work published 1966). A detailed discussion of the nature and control of noninteractional and interactional experimenter artifacts, this is an expanded edition of Rosenthal's 1966 classic text, published by Appleton-Century-Crofts, New York.

Rosenthal, R., & Rosnow, R. L. (Eds.). (1969). *Artifact in behavioral research*. New York: Academic Press. A collection of original essays by leading contributors to research on the social psychology of the experiment.

Rosenthal, R., & Rosnow, R. L. (1975). *The volunteer subject*. New York: Wiley. A comprehensive discussion of the characteristics of volunteers for research participation, circumstances conducive to volunteering, the artifacts that can result, and procedures for estimating and reducing volunteer bias.

Rosnow, R. L. (1997). Hedgehogs, foxes, and the evolving social contract in psychological science: Ethical challenges and methodological opportunities. *Psychological Methods, 2,* 345–356. Explores attempts to strike a balance between ethical accountability and the elimination of artifacts.

Rosnow, R. L., & Rosenthal, R. (1997). *People studying people: Artifacts and ethics in behavioral research.* New York: Freeman. Easy-to-read coverage of the problems posed for psychological inquiry by the use of humans as research participants.

Rosnow, R. L., Rotheram-Borus, M. J., Ceci, S. J., Blanck, P. D., & Koocher, G. P. (1993). The institutional review board as a mirror of scientific and ethical standards. *American Psychologist, 48,* 821–826. Discusses the shifting role of institutional review boards (IRBs) as changes have occurred in experimental interventions and protocols, codes of federal regulatory agencies, norms among investigators, and expectations of research participants.

Ralph L. Rosnow, David Strohmetz, and Ram Aditya

Artifact in Assessment

This article considers the production and functioning of artifacts that operate in the measuring of human attributes. An artifact, as the term is used here, is a factor affecting the participants' responses and hence their assessment scores as a function of the social context in which the responses are made. *Assessment* is a general term that usually refers to obtaining a number of scores for each participant, to provide a fairly comprehensive picture of that person.

In all psychological research, the participant is reacting not only to the specific stimuli provided by the experimenter but also to other aspects of the total situation. For example, participants react to the appearance and behavior of the experimenter, if present. If the experiment or measurement is conducted by computer, the computer may very well be seen as animated (especially by those who remember Hal, the evil computer in the movie *2001*).

Artifacts are systematic effects stemming from participants' reactions to stimuli other than those on which the experimenter wants them to focus. Thus artifacts in assessment reflect individual differences in that the responses of some participants will show more influence from a given artifact than those of others. Note that the effects of such artifacts are always positive. They add variance to measurements—in no case do they represent the absence of something. Hence the primary control over them is by the removal from the measuring situation of anything that can cause bias in the measurements obtained.

But where do such artifacts occur? They are found when the measuring situation is somewhat uncontrolled, when the participant is permitted considerable freedom in selecting a response. On job application forms, when the applicants are told to give their address, there is little freedom allowed: The components of an address are well understood. But if the blank asks the question, "If you are hired for this job, what salary will you expect to receive?" the applicant has a lot of things to think about before writing in an answer. If he or she gives a low amount, that might make it more likely that he or she would be offered the job. If a high estimate is made, in keeping with the aspirations of the applicant, the applicant may be ruled out as too ambitious or overconfident. The applicant may wonder what a "good applicant" would say. So artifacts would be no problem regarding the completion of the address question but could enter into determining the response in the salary question.

In the field of assessment, and especially in measuring personality attributes and attitudes, the respondent's basis for selecting a response is multiply determined and there is typically no right answer, as the instructions often state. So it is in this domain that artifacts commonly enter. They provide the respondent with an alternative basis for choosing one of the multiple choices over another. The harder it is for the respondent to choose a response, the more likely it is that an artifact will enter and settle the matter for the respondent. Similarly, the more freedom the respondent has in making a choice between alternative responses, the more likely it is that an artifact will enter.

Artifacts can also come into the choosing of responses in aptitude and ability tests. When in doubt, some respondents will choose the first alternative choice and some will choose the last. Respondents having difficulty with many items in a test of this kind will have more opportunities to pick a choice on the basis of its position, and so will receive a high score on the response set or artifact. Those respondents for whom the test is easy and who have no problems with choosing the right answers will not need to fall back on the artifacts of position as a way to decide which response to choose. Still another artifact is the willingness to take a risk and guess at the answer to a test item.

Respondent Artifacts

Artifacts became a noticeable factor when psychologists first began measuring personality. One of the earliest of the identifications and labelings, around World War I, was the "halo effect," the disposition to rate various traits at about the same level. Mary is smart and pretty. So, although I have little relevant evidence on other matters, I guess she must also be well adjusted and outgoing. Bill is surly, unhappy, and a loner. So he probably is not much of an athlete. Good qualities are perceived as going together, and so are poor ones. Rating scales ask us to rate qualities in ourselves or in others that we haven't thought much about. Thus, when we are not sure how to rate a person, we choose a response like the others that we have chosen for that target. The tendency to rate oneself in an unduly favorable way is very similar to the halo effect, but probably has different motivations.

In the 1930s, many psychologists felt that participants could not be trusted to respond honestly to personality items. There was considerable surprise when it was found that, when participants were asked to present as favorable a picture of themselves as possible, the responses were quite different from those made under standard instructions.

Those developing the Minnesota Multiphasic Personality Inventory (MMPI) felt it was necessary to have scales for lying (L) and falsifying (F), and so developed empirical scales for these in addition to the scales for various pathologies. Later, the scale constructors decided that they needed one more scale, this time to correct for apparent distortions by some types of respondents. So a K scale was developed, to be used in adjusting the several pathology scales appropriately. Note that these correctional scales were developed with minimal conceptualizing. After studying empirical data, the scale constructors simply decided that a new scale was needed and selected the two groups, one presumed to be high on the new variable and one low. Their responses would be compared to determine which items should be included in the new scale. [See Minnesota Multiphasic Personality Inventory.]

At about the same time the MMPI was being refined, Lee J. Cronbach (1946) introduced the concept of response sets, response characteristics that were not relevant to the variable in which the investigator was interested. One such set can be observed and scored when participants making self-descriptive responses are given multiple choices that include yes and no; some will show a preference for giving the yes response (and a few will prefer to make no responses). Similarly, on attitude scales, some participants will tend to answer yes to many items, that is, to be yea-sayers. [See Attitudes, article on Attitude Measurement.] These tendencies can be shown to be reliable, consistent within a particular test, and are often consistent across more than one test. Other such sets include a tendency to pick, and a tendency to avoid, the central response category in a multiple choice test. Another set is the tendency to avoid making extreme responses, when there are four or more possibilities offered. Although some of the latter sets can be shown to have some consistency (reliability), they do not seem to make substantial contributions to the total scores.

One of the first major studies of an artifact was done by Allen L. Edwards (1957). For group data, he showed substantial correlations between frequency of self-ascription of an item and its perceived social desirability. It was later shown, however, that for individuals one at a time, the relationship between perceived social desirability of an item and ascribing it to oneself was much lower. And perhaps socially desirable traits are actually more frequent than less desirable ones.

Social desirability is a motivational variable, part of the participant's reactions to the situation as a whole. Another such variable, identified by Milton J. Rosenberg (1969), is evaluation apprehension. The participant may respond to the feeling of being evaluated by trying to look good in the eyes of the experimenter, an authority figure. Martin T. Orne has proposed the concept of "demand characteristics" (1962). If the experimenter has made a good impression, the participant will try to be a "good subject" and will try to make the experiment come out the way the subject thinks the experimenter expects and hopes. [See Demand Characteristics.]

Almost without exception the participants studied by psychologists are volunteers; they ordinarily do not offer their services on their own initiative, but they enter into the research project of their own free will. Not all agree to participate. Robert Rosenthal and Ralph L. Rosnow (1975) have summarized the findings from studies comparing those who agree to participate with those who do not. To cite a few findings from the dozens of studies that have been conducted: volunteers are in general better educated, more approval motivated, more intelligent, more sociable, and of higher social class. The implications of this self-selection artifact depend of course on the topic of any given research study. In no case do we have a random sample of any population although certain recruitment strategies may induce more "nonvolunteers" to enter the sampling pool. [See Sampling.]

Experimenter Artifacts

As noted elsewhere, the experimenter can also introduce artifacts or biases into the data. [See Artifact, article on Artifact in Research.] For example, the experimenter can unwittingly bias observations toward the kind of results he or she hopes to obtain. Experimenters can also bias the interpreting and reporting of data, persuading themselves that the data or the analyses they leave out are not as dependable as the ones they include. There is also a very small amount of intentional bias, of fabricating or falsifying or otherwise intentionally misinforming the reader of the research report. These different biases do not involve the participant directly and do nothing to influence that person's actual behavior.

Another set of artifacts stems from the interaction of experimenter and participant. The appearance and interactive style of the experimenter (or whoever is conducting the actual interaction with the subject) can influence the responses made. And finally, there are expectancy effects. Insofar as the experimenter or the teacher has certain expectancies about the performance of the participant-subject, those expectancies will, to some degree, influence the subject's behavior. [*See* Expectancy Effects.]

An Evaluation of Artifacts

Why should we be concerned with artifacts? Why can't experimenters fall back on unobtrusive measurement, making measurements without the subjects' knowing that they are producing data? [*See* Unobtrusive Measures.] While data on groups can be obtained this way, under special circumstances and only for some kinds of variables, there is no satisfactory way to use it in the study of individuals.

In general, there seems to be a decline of interest or concern with artifacts in assessment. They have been recognized, but they seem largely inescapable. We take steps to minimize their effects, and then we return to our concerns with more major variables.

It is interesting to consider the fate of the several artifacts considered in this brief article. Some have become independent attributes demanding separate study. Social desirability is perhaps the best example of this group. Some have been encapsulated in the standard procedures for test constructors. Test format variables illustrate this group. We try to have about equal numbers of items keyed for yes and for no. Some are in a mental list consulted by experienced researchers as they plan a project. Finally, some have dropped from sight entirely. They are recognized as existing, but they seem to account for very little of the variance in assessment data. Tendencies to prefer extremes in Likert-type scales, especially ones with five or more ordered answer choices, or to prefer middle, more conservative choices, do exist but seem to have no important correlates. [*See* Likert Scale.]

Artifacts are among the factors that make it so hard to study behavior or to assign scores on attributes to individuals. Behavior is complex. Many factors may affect it at any one point in time. We see this clearly when we watch people interacting, as at a party. In contrast, there are many situations where behavior shows little variation, from moment to moment and from person to person. Consider military personnel being reviewed or people in a church service.

When psychologists assess people, they hope that the people's behavior will be controlled. They want the people to respond exactly as the instructions indicate. Consider a participant in a laboratory study. The instruction may be to push button A if the stimulus on the left is larger and button B if the stimulus on the right is larger. This is similar to the people attending church, except that the psychological respondent is asked to make a response at a particular point. Only a few assessment variables can be studied under such highly controlled conditions. Much more commonly, we have to make assessments within less controlled con-

ditions. We ask questions of a fairly general sort, in our relatively loose and imprecise everyday language. We ask "Which would you rather read—an adventure story or a detective story?" What does the participant do if neither type is appealing? Or: "In a conversation with a friend, who talks more? You or your friend?" How does a participant integrate all recent conversations in order to decide how to answer the question? And note that the response will be determined by the participant's perceptions, not by any real, objective index of relative talking time.

Some participants will answer the question on the basis of a general impression that they form or have formed about themselves. Others will answer on the basis of a few vivid memories of recent conversations, or even just one recent conversation. Are the participants answering on different bases really answering the same question? As noted by Ruth B. Kuncel and Donald W. Fiske (1974), a participant's response to a personality item is less likely to be replicated on a second trial when he or she, in answering an item the first time, had found the item ambiguous or had trouble in applying it.

In much assessment, the participants must interpret some vague general instructions and some words or phrases presented as stimulus items. There is little control as to how the participants will go about their task, and many irrelevant factors can enter into the choice of responses. When these factors are to some degree systematic, they are often identified as artifacts.

There are many potential artifacts, aspects of the interaction between the participants and the conditions under which the measurements are made. These may be attributed to the experimenter, the participant, or their interaction. Fortunately, the effects of any one artifact tend to be small, much smaller than the individual differences on the trait being measured.

These artifacts tend to lower the observed (measured) agreement between measurements made under different conditions. Of course, if the two sets of conditions are essentially the same, as in repeated measurements, common artifacts could increase the observed agreement. But as conditions become more dissimilar, opportunities increase for artifacts to affect one set of measurements and not the other, thereby reducing the degree of observed agreement.

[*See also* Social Desirability.]

Bibliography

Cronbach, L. J. (1946). Response sets and test validity. *Educational and Psychological Measurement, 6* (4), 475–494.

Edwards, A. L. (1957). *The social desirability variable in personality assessment and research.* New York: Dryden.

Kuncel, R. B., & Fiske, D. W. (1974). Stability of response

process and response. *Educational and Psychological Measurement, 34* (4), 743–755.

Orne, M. T. (1962). On the social psychology of the psychological experiments with particular reference to demand characteristics and their implications. *American Psychologist, 17* (4), 776–783.

Rosenberg, M. J. (1969). The conditions and consequences of evaluation apprehension. In R. Rosenthal & R. L. Rosnow (Eds.), *Artifact in behavioral research* (pp. 279–349). New York: Academic Press.

Rosenthal, R., & Rosnow, R. L. (Eds.). (1969). *Artifact in behavioral research.* New York: Academic Press. A compilation of research on six specific topics framed by two chapters emphasizing controls to minimize the effects of artifacts.

Rosenthal, R., & Rosnow, R. L. (1975). *The volunteer subject.* New York: Wiley.

Rosnow, R. L., & Rosenthal, R. (1997). *People studying people: Artifacts and ethics in behavioral research.* New York: Freeman. A readable account of what research on artifacts has taught us.

Donald W. Fiske

ARTIFICIAL INTELLIGENCE (AI) is intelligence exhibited by a system other than a living creature. Humans or other creatures require intelligence to (1) perform tasks calling for attention and thought (i.e., deciding, solving problems, speaking and listening, acting); (2) combine knowledge and use it to observe and understand the outside world; and (3) learn. This article focuses on the significance of artificial intelligence for contemporary psychology.

Intelligence is shown either by *outcomes* (whether behavior reaches its goal), or by *processes* (the steps taken along the way). Outcomes tell us what tasks computers can perform. Processes tell us to what extent a computer's processes resemble those used by people performing the same task. In psychology, artificial intelligence uses computer programs as theories of human thought processes, and tests these theories by comparing the programs' behavior with human behavior.

General and Specialized Intelligences

A system may perform intelligently in one domain, but exhibit no intelligence in others. Although most individual AI systems perform intelligently only over rather specific tasks, the totality of AI systems spans a wide range of tasks—from memorizing nonsense syllables to discovering scientific laws embedded in data, steering a car on a highway, learning algebra, investing in stocks, composing music, or painting a picture.

Human intelligence is also highly specialized: few constitutional lawyers are also professional biologists.

Although most people in a given culture can perform a range of everyday tasks, few city dwellers can perform the everyday tasks of a farmer, or vice versa. Both human and artificial intelligence generally depend upon previous learning and experience. Human beings do exhibit a general ability to learn new skills gradually, whereas current computer learning abilities are less general than those of people.

History of Artificial Intelligence

Early in human history, fascination with the mind produced myths of artificial creatures who could think. Pandora was one such creature, commissioned by Zeus to punish mankind for accepting the gift of fire. Myth begins to become fact with the complex mechanical devices that began to appear in the Middle Ages; for example, the great clock in Strasbourg Cathedral, with human figures that move when the hour is struck. But the modern period really begins with the computing devices of seventeenth-century mathematician and philosopher, Blaise Pascal, which performed arithmetic calculations, and reaches its first climax in the nineteenth century, with Charles Babbage's never completed analytic engine. Pamela McCorduck, in *Machines Who Think* (San Francisco, 1979), provides an excellent account of AI from the earliest times.

The revival of Babbage's dream in Great Britain, Germany, and the United States in the 1930s finally brings us to the modern electronic digital stored-program computer, embodying an organization of serial processes and memory named after John von Neumann, who first described it formally. This architecture, with minor departures, still dominates today.

Very early, Alan Turing, an English logician, recognized the computer's capabilities for processing symbols of all kinds: not just numbers, but words, pictures, and every sort of pattern. In 1943, W. Pitts and W. S. McCulloch showed how to represent the processes of neuronlike elements by logic expressions. Also in 1943, Norbert Wiener and two colleagues showed how the feedback mechanisms used to control machinery (e.g., thermostats) exemplified purposeful, goal-oriented behavior. These and other developments were brought to wide attention by Wiener's book, *Cybernetics: Control and Communication in the Animal and the Machine* (New York, 1948).

The new electronic computers had much stronger claims to intelligence than the earlier desk calculators. Their programs made their behavior depend on their inputs and the information in their memories. Provided with sensory and motor organs, they became robots. Finally, they could be programmed to modify their own programs and data (to learn).

Initial Artificial Intelligence Programs. Among the first tasks that tested the potential for AI in the 1950s were playing games and recognizing patterns.

Feigenbaum and Feldman (*Computers and Thought*, New York, 1963/1995), reprints many "classical" AI papers, including most of those mentioned below. An early program by Selfridge and Dineen recognized hand-printed alphabetic letters; another, by Arthur Samuel, played checkers, storing information from previous games and altering its criteria for evaluating positions in response to feedback about success and failure. With a day's practice, it could raise its own performance from novice to expert level.

The Logic Theorist. In 1956, Newell, Shaw, and Simon implemented the logic theorist (LT), which was capable of discovering proofs of theorems in Whitehead and Russell's classic: *Principia Mathematica*. In addition to performing an intellectually challenging task, LT showed how to solve problems intelligently by selective (*heuristic*) search. The research also produced computer programming languages (the IPLs), especially adapted to such tasks. The languages reassigned computer memory dynamically to meet the demands of each problem, and provided flexible links among symbols, modeled on the associational structure of human memory. The IPLs were later substantially improved by John McCarthy, who incorporated these same list-processing capabilities in the Lisp language.

Electric Motor Design. Also in 1956, engineers at the Westinghouse Electric Corporation wrote programs that automatically designed electric motors, transformers, and generators. The work was published in engineering journals, and as a result it failed to attract the attention of AI scientists, but it illustrates how contact with the new computers stimulated imaginative thinking about expert systems.

From the beginnings of AI, some separation has existed between research aimed at understanding human thinking and research aimed at building powerful, intelligent systems. However, extensive communication and overlap between the two communities has continued, with considerable mutual borrowing of ideas.

Computer Programs as Theories of Cognition

AI research depends mainly on computer software rather than hardware. Although each new generation of computers has used different physical principles from its predecessors (permitting rapidly increasing memory size and speed), each has had the same functional capabilities. Almost all computers used in AI research, whatever their physical basis, incorporate von Neumann architectures and operate serially.

Physical Symbol Systems. A computer can receive and store signals (patterns), modify these patterns, display or print out patterns, and choose among actions by discriminating among the patterns it receives. Thus it senses stimuli (inputs), manipulates memory (learns), chooses, and acts (outputs). As the programs are stored in memory, they can be modified by commands, thereby acquiring new processes and new knowledge. The basic hypothesis underlying computer simulation of cognition is that these are precisely the capabilities a human being uses in thinking and learning, and that consequently, computers, programmed appropriately, can handle any tasks requiring intelligence, handle them in humanoid ways, and increase these capabilities by learning.

Programs as Difference Equations. Programs, as mathematical objects, are systems of *difference equations*, which predict the change of a system in each machine cycle as a function of its previous state and current inputs. AI programs incorporate both general processes (e.g., means-ends analysis for problem solving, sorting nets for recognizing stimuli) and more specific elements that apply to specific tasks (e.g., chess knowledge, medical knowledge for diagnosis). General programs can be specialized to a particular task by providing them, through programming or learning, with task-specific knowledge.

Meaning of "Symbol." Words are not the only kinds of symbols. A symbol is any pattern that is used to point to other patterns in the brain, or in the outside world. Whereas spoken or printed *dog* is a verbal pattern that denotes a particular kind of mammal recognized by its appearance or its barking, the mental signal in our "mind's eye" when we see a dog is also a symbol, denoting that same dog, as is a picture of a dog, and the image of that picture in memory. Hence, AI makes no claim that human thinking is verbal, much less that it is "logical," or wholly conscious. Indeed, much human thinking is pictorial or diagrammatic rather than verbal, and often subconscious.

In the brain, a pattern need not be localized. In parallel systems that are now being investigated as possible theories of thinking (called "connectionist" systems or "neural nets"), a pattern denoting a concept may be distributed over many neurons, intermingled with the patterns of other concepts. Such distributed patterns are symbols, for they can be distinguished from other patterns and can denote.

Problem Solving

Solving problems, a primary focus in the first years of AI research, remains a major research area. The General Problem Solver (GPS) incorporates methods that apply to any task whose *problem space* can be described in terms of goals, objects, relations among objects, and actions upon objects. GPS compares the current situation in problem space with the goal situation, finds a difference between them, selects an operator capable of reducing differences of that kind, and applies the operator to reach a new position in the problem space. It then repeats the process in the new situation, successively removing differences separating it from the goal.

This method (*means-ends analysis*) is general, but each task must be described before GPS can apply it. Like the human problem solver, GPS may be successful or unsuccessful in any given case, and its search may not be efficient. GPS is described by Newell and Simon (1972).

Search by means-ends analysis can be highly selective rather than exhausting the problem space. Selectivity depends on the richness and accuracy of the information in memory that connects conditions (C) in the existing situation with actions (A) to be taken when those conditions are present: $C{\longrightarrow}A$. These connections are called *productions*. For example:

IF your goal is G, and the current situation contains feature B, which is absent from G,
THEN take action A that often removes B.

Asked to solve an equation ($8x + 5 = 3x + 15$, say), GPS notices the unwanted $3x$ on the right-hand side and subtracts it from both sides (leaving $5x + 5 = 15$). It then notices the unwanted 5 on the left-hand side and subtracts it from both sides (leaving $5x = 10$). Finally, it notices the coefficient of x, and divides both sides of the equation by this coefficient, giving the answer, $x = 2$.

Problem solving can be facilitated by planning, which removes inessential features, then seeks to solve the abstracted problem. A solution of the abstract problem serves as a guide to solving the original problem, with greatly curtailed search. Planning was used implicitly in the algebra example above, for we abstracted the step of simplifying expressions by combining terms, saving three search steps.

Memory and Recognition. Simulation of expert performance shows that heuristic search requires substantial information. In medical school, a student learns to recognize many symptoms, and learns how to treat the associated disease. The trained physician's mind is like an indexed encyclopedia: The symptoms ("index") are "differences," and retrieving associated information ("text"), corresponds to "actions." The entries are productions: *If* the patient has the following symptoms . . . , *Then* . . . the cause is probably . . . , and is treated by . . . .

The "indexed encyclopedia" has been modeled in the Elementary Perceiver and Memorizer (EPAM) (Feigenbaum & Feldman, 1995). EPAM acquires from experience a network of tests for discriminating among features, thereby learning to recognize words, medical symptoms, types of chess positions, insects, and so on. At each terminal node of its discrimination net it accumulates information about the kind of object sorted to that node. Experiments with human subjects show that EPAM can account for the main experimentally observed phenomena of verbal learning, expert memory performance, and concept attainment (categorization).

Experts can often solve problems in their domains rapidly and without being able to explain how they found the solution. As intuitive responses look exactly like recognitions (rapidity of response and unconsciousness of details of how it was done), the same EPAM mechanism can explain both. Intuitive thinking simply recognizes what is already familiar and retrieves knowledge about it. Experts can solve problems much more rapidly than novices because paths that have to be searched step by step by novices can be traversed "instantly" by experts through an intuitive act of recognition.

Knowledge-Rich Domains. As experience with simple tasks accumulated, AI research turned to tasks calling for extensive knowledge and special methods to exploit the domain structure. Chess was an early research topic because its structure is rich, but without the regularity that supports formal mathematical analysis. As early chess programs could store only a little chess knowledge, these programs conducted large look-ahead searches, and concentrated their knowledge in a criterion for evaluating positions reached by search. They undertook far more search than did human chess masters to compensate for the limits of their knowledge and the inaccuracy of their evaluations.

With increasing machine speed and memory size, chess programs advanced from novice level to equality with high-level human professionals. Greater speed allowed deeper searches; larger memories permitted storage of more knowledge about opening strategies and about how to evaluation positions. But chess programs continue to rely far more on speed and search than human players do; for the best evidence suggests that top human players seldom examine more than about one hundred branches in the game tree, whereas the best programs look at millions or even billions of branches.

The best human players have knowledge that permits them to search very selectively, and only in the most important directions. However, there do exist programs that while not yet the most powerful or general, find the correct moves in sharp attacking positions with no more search than human players use. For example, the MATER program using strong selective heuristics, has found deep checkmates (one requiring eight moves and seven replies) with look-ahead searches having at most 108 branches.

Another early knowledge-rich AI task was finding derivatives and integrals in calculus using production rules in a divide-and-conquer strategy. For example, to find the derivative of the product of two expressions, find the derivative of the first, then multiply it by the second; next find the derivative of the second and multiply it by the first; and finally add these two components. Slagle's early SAINT system was followed by MACSYMA, and then by a number of powerful systems (e.g., Mathematica) that allow a mathematician to solve problems interactively: the computer finding derivatives and integrals, solving equations, or inverting matrices while the user tells the machine what goal to attempt next.

Another landmark for knowledge-rich domains was DENDRAL, which, from data on the molecular fragments produced by a mass spectrograph, seeks to infer the structure of the original molecule, but without close imitation of human processes. Among systems that were usable in practical terms that followed DENDRAL were MYCIN, a medical diagnosis system for microbial diseases, and The Doctor's Assistant, a diagnosis system for internal medicine that compared favorably with human diagnosticians on test cases. Expert systems that perform hundreds, perhaps thousands, of different tasks are now in practical use.

Neural Nets. The brain can execute many processes in parallel, so there has been strong interest from the beginnings of AI in exploring parallel computation, simulating some of the properties of neural networks.

Paradoxically, most of the research on parallelism has been carried out on serial computers, for a serial machine, if given sufficient time, can simulate a parallel machine. Individual neurons are slow in comparison with electronic circuits, as it takes about one millisecond for a signal to cross a single synapse, whereas comparable electronic operations are performed in microseconds or faster. Programs can simulate the operation of hundreds of thousands of simplified parallel "neurons," if not yet of the tens of billions of neurons the human brain contains.

Most efforts at modeling neural systems use highly abstracted networks of links (each with a numerical level of activation) and nodes (each with a numerical strength). Such modeling is usually termed *parallel distributed processing* (PDP) or connectionist modeling. Its resemblance to neural processing is still a matter of debate and investigation.

As the elementary processes in PDP simulations are simpler and faster than the elementary processes in most serial simulations, the PDP approach is often referred to as bottom-up, and the serial symbolic approach as top-down. The difference between the two resembles the difference between a molecular and a physiological theory of food metabolism; or between a DNA-level and a gene-level genetic theory. In general, we might expect parallelism to be most important for peripheral, especially sensory, processes; and seriality for central processes that must operate within the narrow constraints of human short-term memory capacity.

Only a few direct comparisons have thus far been made between PDP and serial systems on identical tasks, so it is not known where each simulates human processing more closely. Some recent systems combine serial rule-based and connectionist properties; for example, by associating probabilities or other weights with rules, and adjusting these weights through learning processes. John Anderson's ACT* and ACT-R exhibit such hybrid characteristics. Parallel and serial theories are complementary, not competitive, and will eventually require bridging links.

Learning and Discovery

A fine line separates performance from learning; for a program that solves a problem can store the path to the solution and recover it if the same problem arises again. LT, the first heuristic search program, used this learning method. Similarly, a case-based reasoning system can store cases it has handled, so that closer and closer analogues can be found to new problems. These are a few among many mechanisms for learning.

The Role of Learning in Expertise. No person, however talented, attains world-class performance in any domain without at least a decade of intensive training effort. Even Mozart composed no music that is acclaimed as world class until he was at least 17, although he began composing at four years of age. Major effort en route to expertise is devoted to acquiring the "indexed encyclopedia" for the task. A chess program resembling EPAM has stored more than 70,000 patterns of pieces, enabling it, like a chess master, to reproduce nearly flawlessly a position from an unknown game after viewing it for five seconds. This memory was "grown" by exposing the program to collections of chess positions from professional games, from which it extracted recurring patterns of pieces.

There are at least three human learning products: (1) ability to recognize and discriminate among stimuli (the "index"); (2) accumulated knowledge associated with each of the discriminated classes of things (knowledge); (3) new processes and refinements of old ones (skills).

Discrimination Learning and Knowledge Acquisition. EPAM can learn in the first two ways. In learning to discriminate, it gradually builds up a network of paths, with tests at their nodes for stimulus features, separating distinct classes of objects (Figure 1, upper half). When it confuses distinct objects, it searches for a feature test that distinguishes them, inserts it in the net, and creates new paths from that point to separate terminal nodes for the objects. At each terminal it stores information about the objects it sorts there, and also creates association links to other terminals.

PDP systems focus on the first form of learning, but can be combined with other structural elements to encompass the other forms as well. PDP systems connect features of the stimuli to be discriminated to a set of intermediate nodes ("hidden layer"), and the intermediate nodes to the terminal nodes representing the clas-

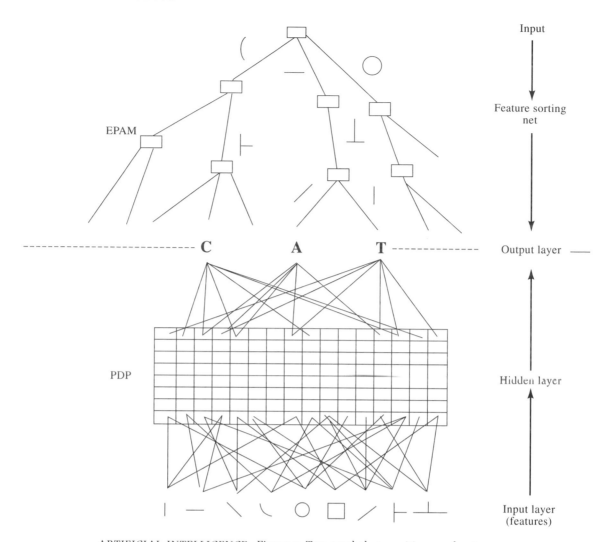

Input

Feature sorting
net

EPAM

- **C**   **A**   **T** - - - - - - - - - - - - - -   Output layer ───

PDP

Hidden layer

Input layer
(features)

ARTIFICIAL INTELLIGENCE. Figure 1. Two symbol recognition mechanisms:
EPAM (top-down), PDP (bottom-up). Each recognizes the word CAT by means of
the features possessed by the letters of the word.

ses to be distinguished (Figure 1, lower half). Each stimulus type is represented by a set of feature weights. Learning gradually adjusts the strengths of the links connecting stimulus nodes to intermediate nodes and the links connecting intermediate nodes to response nodes, so that when a particular stimulus is presented, the correct response node receives the strongest signal along the paths.

Acquisition of New Processes. The *adaptive production system* is a powerful mechanism for learning new processes. It can construct new productions and modify existing ones, adding these new symbol structures to those already present.

New productions can be created (in machine or human learning) by studying worked-out examples. If given the solution steps for the algebra problem shown

earlier, the adaptive production system notes how the differences between the given expression and the desired expression are removed one by one: first the term in x on the right, then the numerical term on the left, then the unwanted coefficient of x. The system now creates productions in each of which the condition is an unwanted difference and the action removes this difference. For example,

IF there is a term in x on the right,
THEN subtract it from both sides and simplify.

With its new productions, the system is now able to solve many kinds of linear equations. Acquiring new productions by studying worked-out examples has been shown to be a general and powerful learning technique, for both people and computers.

Robotics

A major use of intelligence is to interact with the environment through sensory and motor organs, using sensory information and information already in memory to build an internal model of the environment, then using the model to plan actions which are implemented. Much of the internal computation may be subconscious, or implicit. Limits on size and complexity allow the internal model to describe the environment only crudely, so that the system must frequently obtain new sensory information, and revise plans and actions.

The special branch of AI known as robotics deals with sensory pattern recognition (including visual scene, object and word recognition, and auditory sound and speech recognition), model revision and plan updating, and motor action (including language production). Visual scene recognition and motor action have been challenging tasks. Model revision only began to be studied extensively in the 1980s.

At first it was thought that progress in understanding sensory and motor processes would proceed rapidly, while understanding "higher" mental processes would be much more difficult. On the contrary, it has proved easier to simulate processes that we associate with doctors, lawyers, and scientists than processes we associate with tractor drivers or acrobats. Most of the work in robotics, of course, is not concerned with imitating human processes, but with designing practically useful systems; but even without requiring simulation of human processes, the design tasks are formidable.

Interpretation of Scenes and Objects. Enough progress has been made in extracting objects and other patterns from visual displays to automate steering an automobile at high speed on a highway. Even this "simple" task involves such tasks as distinguishing shadows from changes in road surface, recognizing road berms and lane stripes. In recent years, many feature extraction systems have been built with the help of learning schemes, but recognizing human faces is still a difficult task for which wholly satisfactory solutions are not available.

Speech and Word Recognition. Programming computers to understand and speak a natural language, or to learn these skills, has not been an easy task, but substantial progress has been made. Large computers today can recognize human speech at a normal rate of utterance, and can adjust to differences between speakers, but only if vocabulary is limited. Computers can also produce understandable speech, and can analyze (parse) and construct sentences. Language translation schemes are now in practical use, but usually require some human postediting of the translated text. Currently, machines require much more computation to perform these tasks than do humans.

Programs have been constructed that *understand* language sufficiently to perform various tasks. For example, Gordon Novak's ISAAC program can read simple physics textbook problems about forces in equilibrium, and use knowledge of English syntax and vocabulary to draw diagrams of the situations and set up and solve the equations. The UNDERSTAND program, on reading descriptions of simple problems like the Tower of Hanoi puzzle, can set up representations of the problems that are suitable for the General Problem Solver. These programs provide theories of the processes that humans use in these tasks.

Only a little progress has yet been made in machine *learning* of natural languages, although as early as 1968 Laurent Siklóssy built a system that acquired vocabulary and correct syntax in French or Russian by exposure to sets of sentences matched with simple pictures.

Model Revision. Revising a robot's model of its environment as it moves and gains new information is another challenging task. An early effort was the SHAKEY system at Stanford Research Institute, which maintained a changing internal model of the environment in which it was moving. Weimin Shen's LIVE system builds up information about a physical system by observing a succession of states. Whereas it is impossible to infer the genetic makeup of an organism by examining the members of a single generation, LIVE can infer the genes by collecting data from three or more generations.

Creative Activities

Human activities are regarded as creative if they produce interesting or valuable novelty. Creativity is nurtured and celebrated in all fields of serious human endeavor, and there is much curiosity about how it is achieved. To illustrate how AI can cast light on human creativity we draw on examples from the fields of scientific discovery, art, and music.

Scientific Discovery. Scientists discover patterns (laws) in data; construct explanations (theories); design experimental strategies; use theories to make predictions; find new ways of representing phenomena; invent new instruments. When successful, interesting, or valuable, these activities are described as "creative."

Each of these aspects of scientific research has been investigated to some extent by building expert systems to simulate humans performing them. For example, the BACON system, given observations of variables, searches for laws that fit the observed data. BACON also invents and introduces new concepts to make the laws more parsimonious. Tested on data from great scientific discoveries in physics and chemistry, and using only information that was available to the original discoverers, BACON has been able, for example, to rediscover

Kepler's Third Law of planetary motion, Black's law for temperature equilibrium of liquids, Ohm's law of electrical resistance, and many others. BACON uses highly selective search and only modest amounts of computation, and both historical and some experimental data support its claims to parallel human processes in these tasks.

Deepak Kulkarni's KEKADA system simulates the choice of a series of experiments to solve a research problem. Modest progress has been made toward systems that find new problem representations, and systems that look for analogies between phenomena.

Art and Music. Because thought in the fine arts is often believed to be quite different from thought in science or practical affairs, research on computer art and computer music can test the reach of computer simulation of human thought. As early as 1956, Hillier and Isaacson, at the University of Illinois, wrote a computer program that composed a *Computer Cantata* that many listeners (not knowing its authorship) found musically interesting.

The most sustained approach to computer drawing and painting is the Aaron program of the painter Harold Cohen. Beginning with a program that conceived abstract designs, Aaron was progressively modified, to create, for example, landscapes with plants and interacting human figures. The basic mechanisms required by the musical composition programs and Aaron, like those of other expert systems, are a large knowledge base and processes to search and recognize aesthetically satisfying patterns.

Artificial Intelligence and Cognitive Psychology

Obviously, the brain does not use the same physical mechanisms as a computer: the claim for simulation of human thought is that brain and computer, using quite different machinery, can execute the same programs, thereby carrying out the same functions organized in the same way.

We discover how a computer performs a task by printing out a trace of the processes it executes. In discovering how people do the task, two techniques have been of special value: (1) tracking eye movements and (2) asking people to talk aloud while performing the task. For example, a person who is adding a column of figures might say: "3 and 5 is 8, and 7 is 15, and 4 and 6 is 25, and 2 is 27, and 6 is 33." From this *protocol*, we infer that the subject adds successive figures to the total obtained so far, retaining this total in memory while shifting attention to the next figure. It is easy to program a computer to simulate these processes. As it takes about one millisecond for a signal to cross the synapse from one neuron in the brain to another, and as even simple mental processes require signals to be transmitted along dozens of neurons, eye movements and talk-aloud protocols can capture much detail of human thought processes.

Combining such information with data on speed of performance, capacities of memories, brain locations where particular processes are performed, and losses in performance from specific brain damage, we can build computer programs that match human processes. As in any science, similarity of the performance of the program with the human performance tests the theory.

Motivation, Attention, and Emotion. The human brain is not only the seat of thinking, but also of most processes associated with goals, motives, and feeling. Some progress has been made in extending information processing theory from thought to motivation and emotion.

Human Attention. People can generally deal with only one attention-demanding task at a time. By sharing attention between tasks, they can converse when driving a car, but when traffic becomes heavy, the conversation lags. The limits on human attention result from the limited capacity of *short-term memory* (STM).

If brains generally attend to only one thing at a time, some mechanism must shift attention to urgent tasks. Sudden movements or loud sounds attract attention while also arousing emotions that prepare for response. Emotions (e.g., hunger) are also aroused by the autonomic (internal) nervous system. Finally, emotions (e.g., pleasure, fear, sexual desire) are aroused when memories that have acquired emotional associations are evoked. Emotions, then, either intensify attention to the current task, or interrupt it, causing it to shift to the emotion-producing topic.

The computer program PARRY, designed by the psychiatrist Kenneth Colby, uses this idea to simulate a paranoid patient. If the simulated patient reads words that evoke emotions, it may become "fearful" or "angry" and switch its attention to an imagined threat. It may be hard to find a topic that will again interrupt attention and bring PARRY back to more normal conversation. PARRY provides a hypothesis about the mechanisms that underlie the symptoms of paranoia, and evidence for the hypothesis.

Conclusion

The goal of artificial intelligence is to explore intelligence and thought in order to deepen our understanding of human thinking and to build systems that can augment it. This article has described the progress that has been made toward the former goal, and the theory of intelligence that has emerged. While a great deal has been learned, the research task is no more finished than are other fundamental research tasks. We can expect vigorous activity and major continuing progress in AI over many decades to come.

[*See also* Computer Learning; Human-Computer Interface Design; *and* Virtual Reality.]

Bibliography

Anderson, J. R. (1983). *The architecture of cognition*. Cambridge, MA: Harvard University Press. Description and tests of a model of semantic memory and learning.

Ericsson, K. A., & Simon, H. A. (1993). *Verbal reports as data* (Rev. ed.). Cambridge, MA: MIT Press. Theory and methods of analyzing human thinking-aloud protocols.

Feigenbaum, E. A., Barr, A., & Cohen, P. R. (1989). *The handbook of artificial intelligence* (4 vols.). New York: Addison-Wesley. A comprehensive encyclopedia of AI and cognitive science.

Feigenbaum, E. A., & Feldman, J. (1995). *Computers and thought*. Cambridge, MA: MIT Press. (Original work published 1963.) An annotated collection of classical AI papers, and an extensive bibliography of "prehistoric" and early publications in AI.

Langley, P., Simon, H. A., Bradshaw, G. L., & Zytkow, J. M. (1987). *Scientific discovery: Computational explorations of the creative process*. Cambridge, MA: MIT Press. Computer simulation of historic scientific discoveries.

Luger, G. F. (1994). *Cognitive science: The science of intelligent systems*. San Diego, CA: Academic Press.

Luger, G. F. (Ed.). (1995). *Computation and intelligence: Collected readings*. Cambridge, MA: MIT Press. Collection of classical AI papers, from about 1960 to the present.

McCorduck, P. (1979). *Machines who think*. San Francisco, CA: W. H. Freeman. A history of AI based on extensive interviews with the early researchers.

McCorduck, P. (1990). *Aaron's code*. New York: W. H. Freeman. Computer drawings made by the Aaron program.

Newell, A. (1990). *Unified theories of cognition*. Cambridge, MA: Harvard University Press. The Soar system, an approach to unified modeling of an extensive range of human thought processes.

Newell, A., & Simon, H. A. (1972). *Human problem solving*. Englewood Cliffs, NJ: Prentice Hall. A theory of problem solving based on computer models tested by experiment, and using thinking-aloud reports of subjects.

Rumelhart, D. E., & McClelland, J. L. (1986). *Parallel distributed processing* (2 vols.) Cambridge, MA: MIT Press. An introduction to connectionist simulation, with many examples.

Russell, S. J., & Norvig, P. (1995). *Artificial intelligence*. Upper Saddle River, NJ: Prentice Hall. A comprehensive AI textbook giving some attention to human simulation.

Schank, R. C., & Colby, K. M. (Eds.). (1973). *Computer models of thought and language*. San Francisco, CA: W. H. Freeman. Includes chapters on the PARRY system, and other studies of the relation of thinking to emotion.

Simon, H. A. (1996). *The sciences of the artificial* (3rd ed.). Cambridge, MA: MIT Press. Chapters 3 and 4 provide an overview of what has been learned about human thinking with the aid of computer simulation.

Herbert A. Simon

ART THERAPY is an interdisciplinary field, blending art, psychology, and therapy. Although the field of art therapy formally emerged in the 1940s, in the late nineteenth century there was a growing interest in Europe in the art of adults with mental illness. In 1872, Tardieu, a French psychiatrist, published a book on mental illness that included a brief outline of what he thought were the characteristics of art work created by people who had been diagnosed as insane. A few years later, Paul-Max Simon, a psychiatrist, published a more comprehensive series of studies of the drawings of people with mental illness. Simon has been called the "father of art and psychiatry" and has been credited with influencing the diagnostic uses of drawings, based on his belief that symptoms could be related to the content of art works. In the 1920s, Hans Prinzhorn, an art historian turned psychiatrist, began soliciting art created by mental patients from doctors and hospitals throughout Europe, amassing a collection of 5,000 pieces by over 500 patients. This collection drew attention to the notion that art expressions might have both diagnostic value and a role in psychological rehabilitation.

During this time Sigmund Freud wrote of the images presented in dreams and Carl Jung provided a foundation for understanding symbolic meanings of imagery through his theories on archetypes, collective unconscious, and universalities in visual art. Jung was particularly interested in the psychological meanings and clinical applications of art expressions, including his drawings and those of his patients. Freud's and Jung's observations inspired and eventually confirmed the belief that art expression could be a route to understanding the inner world of the human psyche.

Emergence of the Field of Art Therapy

It was not until the 1940s that the field of art therapy emerged simultaneously in both Great Britain and the United States. In Great Britain, the profession of art therapy was formally established in 1946 with the first art therapy post in the National Health Service, and officially recognized in 1981 by the government. Art therapy in Great Britain was influenced by Sir Herbert Read, an art educator; Adrian Hill, an artist who worked in medical settings; Edward Adamson, an artist who worked with patients in a hospital studio; and Viktor Lowenfeld, who coined the term *art education therapy* to define the synthesis of art education and therapy in work with children. Lowenfeld is also credited with establishing developmental stages for the art of normal children which have been used as the baseline for understanding the art of normal individuals as well as those with mental illness or physical disabilities.

Although many individuals were involved in art therapy's beginnings, several people are thought to be primarily responsible for the field's development in the United States. In the 1930s the Menninger Clinic invited artist Mary Huntoon to offer art classes to psychiatric patients. Huntoon used her understanding of the visual arts to help patients use art to express and release emotional problems. She coined the word *art-synthesis* for the process of self-discovery many of her patients experienced after completing a piece of artwork. Huntoon felt that the therapeutic potential of art was in the making of it, rather than in analyzing it for diagnostic or symbolic meaning.

The introduction of the term *art therapy* in the United States is attributed to Margaret Naumburg during the 1940s. Naumburg viewed art expression as a way to manifest unconscious imagery, an observation consistent with the predominate psychoanalytic viewpoint of the early twentieth century. In her view, the primary value of art therapy was in spontaneous expression and in communication; she considered the images produced by clients to be a form of symbolic speech. In the 1950s, Edith Kramer, an artist and art educator, pointed to another important therapeutic component inherent to art making. Kramer believed that the healing potentialities of art therapy resided in the psychological processes that are activated in creative work and stressed creativity, not merely communication of visually symbolic speech, as key. In 1958, Hana Yaxa Kwiatkowska introduced individual and family art therapy at the National Institute of Mental Health. She believed that specific drawing activities were helpful in identifying family members' roles and in providing a positive therapeutic experience. Her work at the NIMH generated some of the earliest research in the field and established art therapy as an adjunct to family treatment.

Art Therapy Today

The American Art Therapy Association (AATA) was formed in 1969 to promote standards of professional practice, research, and procedures for registration of individuals who have met specific educational and postgraduate clinical experiences in art therapy. At the same time graduate programs leading to a master's degree in art therapy were initiated; currently there are approximately 30 training programs throughout the United States. In 1991, a separate certification board, the Art Therapy Credentials Board (ATCB), was established and in 1994, the first national certification examination for art therapists was administered by the ATCB.

Art therapists have generated many definitions of art therapy, but most seem to fall into two general categories. The first is based on the belief that the *creative process* of art making is healing and therapeutic and is referred to as *art as therapy*. Art making is seen as an experience which provides the opportunity to express oneself imaginatively, authentically, and spontaneously, a process which, over time, can lead to personal fulfill-

ment, emotional reparation, and transformation. This definition asserts that the creative process can be a health-enhancing and growth-producing experience, in and of itself.

The second definition of art therapy is based on the idea that art is a means of symbolic communication. This view is often referred to as *art psychotherapy*, emphasizing the *products* made in art therapy—drawings, paintings, and other art expressions—as helpful in communicating issues, emotions, and conflicts. Psychotherapy is essential to this approach and the art image becomes significant in enhancing verbal exchange between the person and therapist and in achieving insight. With therapeutic guidance and support, art can be a way to arrive at new understandings, a vehicle for developing new insights, resolving conflicts, problem solving, and formulating new perceptions which lead to positive changes, growth, and rehabilitation.

In reality, most art therapists integrate both art as therapy and art psychotherapy in varying degrees into their work with people. In other words, both the idea that art making can be a healing *process* and that art *products* communicate information relevant to personality, insight, personal growth, and change are important. Practitioners may emphasize one area over another, depending on their own philosophy and the person's needs and goals in art therapy.

Art therapists utilize art media (such as drawing materials, paints, collage/mixed media, and clay sculpture) and their knowledge of the creative process to help patients explore issues, interests, concerns, conflicts, and potentials through art expression. In order to accomplish this, the images are reviewed throughout the therapeutic relationship, with both patient and therapist responding to the work and dialoguing together about its meaning.

Depending upon their training, experiences, credentials, and licensure, art therapists work in a variety of ways, from many theoretical stances (psychoanalytic, Jungian, humanistic, person-centered, cognitive-behavioral, systems, and other approaches), and with many different patient populations, including children, adults, families, and groups. For example, a therapist in a hospital setting might work from a psychoanalytic perspective with psychiatric patients individually to help them to use art to explore emotional conflicts or within a group to develop interpersonal skills. With a child who has been traumatized, a therapist might use art activities as crisis intervention to help the child explore feelings about the trauma and to reduce feelings of anxiety, fear, or depression. In addition, the therapist might employ family art therapy techniques, using a systems approach with the child's family to assist parents and siblings in expressing their feelings and understanding family dynamics. Some art therapists work as private practitioners, others are employed by schools, hospitals, clinics, correctional facilities, or community agencies, and many serve as part of a treatment team. Many psychologists, mental health counselors, or social workers also incorporate art therapy in their clinical work with children, adults, groups, and families as a form of treatment and as an adjunct to assessment.

Initially, art therapy was mainly used with psychiatric, rehabilitation, and special education populations. However, in the last two decades art therapy has been applied to more diverse settings, including the treatment of physical and sexual abuse, domestic violence, addictions, eating disorders, dementia, hospice/terminal illness, neurological disease, posttraumatic stress disorders, forensics, and physical illness. The field of art therapy has been acknowledged as a "mind-body intervention" by the National Institutes of Health Office of Alternative Medicine, recognizing its importance in mental, physical, and spiritual health and in therapy.

Despite the wide application of art therapy there has been little research on its effectiveness as a treatment. The majority of research, both within the field and from other mental health professionals, has been directed toward increasing understanding of diagnostic uses of art expression, rather than how the process of art therapy works in treatment. The AATA is currently directing efforts to encourage more art therapy research in the area of outcome studies which would demonstrate how the process of art therapy helps various client populations.

More information on the field of art therapy can be obtained from the American Art Therapy Association, Inc., Chicago, IL (http://www.arttherapy.org) and the British Association of Art Therapists, Sussex, England.

[See also Literature; Music Therapy; and Performing Arts.]

Bibliography

Books

Case, C., & Dalley, T. (1992). *The handbook of art therapy*. London: Tavistock. Provides an overview of art therapy theory and practice in Britain.

Junge, M., & Asawa, P. (1994). *A history of art therapy in the United States*. Mundelein, IL: AATA.

Kramer, E. (1994). *Art as therapy with children*. Chicago, IL: Magnolia Street. (Original work published 1971.) Classic volume on work with children.

Landgarden, H. (1981). *Clinical art therapy*. New York: Brunner/Mazel. Comprehensive guide to art psychotherapy with individuals, couples, and families.

Malchiodi, C. A., & Riley, S. (1996). *Supervision and related issues*. Chicago: Magnolia Street. Covers contemporary professional, legal, and ethical issues related to the practice of art therapy.

Malchiodi, C. A. (1997). *Breaking the silence: Art therapy with children from violent homes*. New York: Brunner/Mazel. Introduction to the use of art therapy in crisis intervention and work with children traumatized by abuse and family violence.

Malchiodi, C. A. (1998). *Understanding children's drawings*. New York: Guilford Press. Comprehensive volume on the use of children's drawings in assessment and therapy.

McNiff, S. (1981). *The arts in psychotherapy*. Springfield, IL: Charles C. Thomas. Discusses the origins and connections between various art therapies (art, music, dance, drama) and psychotherapy.

Naumburg, M. (1987). *Dynamically oriented art therapy: Its principles and practice*. Chicago, IL: Magnolia Street. (Original work published 1966.) A classic in the field of art therapy.

Prinzhorn, H. (1972). *The artistry of the mentally ill*. Berlin: Springer-Verlag. Presents Prinzhorn's art collection and his beliefs about art expression and mental illness.

Rubin, J. (1987). *Approaches to art therapy*. New York: Brunner/Mazel. Describes various philosophical approaches to the practice of art therapy with a variety of populations.

Rubin, J. (1998). *Art therapy: An introduction*. Philadelphia: Brunner/Mazel. Comprehensive overview of the history and practice of art therapy.

Wadeson, H. (1980). *Art psychotherapy*. New York: Wiley. Provides a discussion of the theory and practice of art psychotherapy and clinical applications with individuals, groups, couples, and families.

Periodical

Art Therapy: Journal of the American Art Therapy Association, quarterly journal on theory, practice, and research in the field.

Cathy A. Malchiodi and Frederick L. Coolidge

ASCETICISM. *See* Religious Experience, *article on* Religious Experiences and Practices.

ASCH, SOLOMON E. (1907–1996), American social psychologist. The great challenge for social psychology has been to create a felicitous combination of the rigor of natural science with the rich complexity of human social life. Solomon Asch showed the way to this balanced and productive blend of natural and social science. On the one hand, he was a pioneer of the clever and crucial experiment, of disciplined data collection with an eye toward alternative accounts. On the other hand, he insisted on the fundamental role of context and relations, the richness of the human mind, and the importance of being informed by history, culture, the arts, and human common sense. In contrast to the two dominant ideologies in psychology in his time, behaviorism and psychoanalysis, Asch assumed that humans were basically rational and decent, and that the social world and social matrix of human life had a level of organization worthy of attention, in its own right. In his classic text (Asch, 1952/1987), he begins with an extended discussion of views of human nature, and later devotes a whole chapter to the problem of how we know of the existence of other minds.

Asch was a Gestalt psychologist, and studied perception, memory, thinking, and metaphor from this perspective. His social psychology emphasized phenomena, mental events, the importance of context and relationships, and the existence of innate predispositions. As opposed to the behaviorists, Asch held that behavior is not a response to the world as it is, but to the world as perceived. American students avowed different levels of agreement with the statement, "I hold it that a little rebellion, now and then, is a good thing, and as necessary in the political world as storms are in the physical," depending on whether it was attributed to Jefferson or Lenin. Asch showed that although the "stimulus" might be the same in both cases, the meaning (judged by paraphrases) was not.

Asch's Gestalt approach put him at odds with the behaviorist elementism dominant in the 1940s and 1950s. In his experiments on impression formation, he showed that the meaning of a personality trait depended upon the structure and context of other traits attributed to the same person. For example, the intelligence of a person both "intelligent" and "cold" is not the same as the intelligence of a person who is "warm" and "intelligent." The network of inferences from one individual difference characteristic to another that Asch uncovered is still being studied; his technique of comparing impressions generated by descriptions differing in only one characteristic is elegant and is still employed.

Asch's most famous experiments demonstrated the importance of socially defined reality. He had subjects judge physically unambiguous stimuli (lines of different lengths) after a number of supposed other subjects who all gave the same incorrect judgment. Subjects were very upset by the discrepancy between their perceptions and those of others; only 25% of subjects never yielded to the bogus majority. This technique was a powerful means for examining the social construction of reality, and became a focus for investigation for a half-century. Stanley Milgram's studies of obedience to authority were inspired directly by Asch's studies.

Asch's classic textbook, *Social Psychology* (1952/ 1987), offers an eloquent statement of his vision and persuasively presents the human person as complex but researchable, socially situated yet independent. Psychology's substance, he argues, "must center on great and permanent problems, and psychologists should avoid the undignified posture of those whom in another connection Santayana has described as redoubling their

effort when they have forgotten their aim" (p. 31). On method: "If there must be principles of scientific method, then surely the first to claim our attention is that one should describe phenomena faithfully and allow them to guide the choice of problems and procedures" (p. xv). On culture: "Most social acts have to be understood in their setting, and lose meaning if isolated. No error in thinking about social facts is more serious than the failure to see their place and function" (p. 61).

Solomon E. Asch was born in Warsaw, Poland, on 14 September 1907. He came to the United States in 1920, and received a doctorate degree from Columbia University in 1932. His principal mentor was the pioneering Gestalt psychologist Max Wertheimer, and throughout his life, Asch explored perception, association, learning, thinking, social life and metaphor, with a gestalt orientation. He taught for 19 years at Swarthmore College, where he was a part of a group of Gestalt psychologists that included Wolfgang Kohler.

Modern social psychology built on and elaborated the phenomena and experimental approaches that Asch pioneered in his experiments. But to his distress, the context-oriented perspective that he pioneered has too often been overlooked. "We cannot be true to a fragment of man if we are not true, in at least a rudimentary way, to man himself," he argued (1959, p. 368). He further noted: "One would not often suspect that we were talking of an organism capable of keeping or betraying faith with others, in whose history religious beliefs have played quite a part, who can cry out for justice" (1959, p. 367).

Solomon Asch showed us how to construct a meaningful social psychology. After a half-century, his work still offers the right prescription.

Bibliography

Asch, S. E. (1946). Forming impressions of personality. *Journal of Abnormal and Social Psychology, 41*, 258–290.

Asch, S. E. (1948). The doctrine of suggestion, prestige and imitation in social psychology. *Psychological Review, 55*, 250–276.

Asch, S. E. (1951). Effects of group pressure upon the modification and distortion of judgments. In H. Gustzkow (Ed.), *Groups, leadership, and men* (pp. 177–190). Pittsburgh, PA: Carnegie Press.

Asch, S. E. (1987). *Social psychology.* New York: Oxford University Press. (Original work published 1952)

Asch, S. E. (1956). Studies of independence and conformity: I. A minority of one against a unanimous majority. *Psychological Monographs, 70*, 1–70.

Asch, S. E. (1959). A perspective on social psychology. In S. Koch (Ed.), *Psychology: A study of a science* (Vol. 3, pp. 363–383). New York: McGraw-Hill.

Asch, S. E. (1968). A reformation of the problem of associations. *American Psychologist, 24,* 92–103.

Ceraso, J., Rock, I., & Gruber, H. (1990). On Solomon Asch. In I. Rock (Ed.), *The legacy of Solomon Asch: Essays in cognitive and social psychology* (pp. 3–19). Hillsdale, NJ: Erlbaum.

Rock, I. (Ed.) (1990). *The legacy of Solomon Asch: Essays in cognitive and social psychology.* Hillsdale, NJ: Erlbaum.

Paul Rozin and Clark McCauley

ASIAN AMERICAN PSYCHOLOGY. Given the numerous subgroups and the varying political conditions both in the Asian home countries and the United States, the history and immigration experience of Asian Americans is a complex one.

History of Asian Americans

Historically, Asian Americans have faced various forms of discrimination ranging from immigration exclusion acts aimed at the Chinese and passed by Congress, to the unjustified internment of Japanese Americans during World War II. First-generation Asians were denied naturalization privileges until the 1940s to 1950s. The Chinese were the first group of Asians to emigrate to the United States in large numbers—during the California gold rush of 1849. This flow was eventually ended by the Chinese Exclusion Act of 1882 (Uba, 1996). The Japanese first emigrated to Hawaii in large numbers in the 1880s and this was followed by the Filipinos around 1909. Various restrictions were placed on the immigration of Asian Americans throughout the first half of the twentieth century.

Eventually, the Immigrant Act of 1965 resulted in a large influx of Asians into the United States. As a result of this liberal immigration policy, the proportion of immigrants entering the United States who were Asian grew from 9% in 1960 to 25% in 1970 to 44% in 1980 (Min, 1995). The next major influx of Asians into the United States was the arrival of over 130,000 Southeast Asian refugees after the end of the Vietnam War in 1975. This was followed by various immigration programs that sought to arrange the orderly departure of Amerasian children from Vietnam to the United States.

The internment of Japanese Americans during World War II was the pivotal event in the historical experience of this Asian American group. In 1980, the United States Congress created the Commission on Wartime Relocation and Internment of Civilians to investigate the whole process and make appropriate recommendations. Finally, in early 1983, after a long investigation, the commission found that a great injustice had been done to the Japanese American people and it was officially recommended that the federal government formally apologize and each survivor be granted a tax-free onetime payment of $20,000.

Demographics

There are two salient demographic patterns among Asian Americans. First, they are the fastest growing ethnic minority group in the United States. Between 1980 and 1990, the number of Asian Americans, including Pacific Islanders, grew at a rate of 95%, nearly double that of Hispanic Americans, the next fastest growing group; more than triple that of Native American, Eskimo, and Aleuts; and more than seven times the growth rate of African Americans. According to a projection by the U.S. Department of Commerce, the number of Asian Americans will grow from 7 million to over 40 million by the year 2050 (Gall & Gall, 1993). According to the 1990 Census, there were 2 million Asian Americans and Pacific Islanders in the United States.

Second, Asian Americans are comprised of many heterogeneous subgroups that come from all over Asia (e.g., Chinese, Japanese, Filipino, Korean, Vietnamese, etc). According to the 1990 Census, there were 1.6 million Chinese Americans (23% of Asian Americans and Pacific Islanders); 1.4 million Filipino Americans (19% of Asian Americans and Pacific Islanders); 847,562 Japanese Americans (12% of Asian Americans and Pacific Islanders); 815,447 Asian Indians (11% of Asian Americans and Pacific Islanders); 798,849 Korean Americans (11% of Asian Americans and Pacific Islanders); and 614,547 Vietnamese Americans (8% of Asian Americans and Pacific Islanders). The smaller subgroups include Thais, Hmong, Cambodians, and Laotians. The subgroups use different languages and have different cultural backgrounds and immigration histories in the United States (Sue & Morishima, 1982). Relatedly, it should be pointed out that the Pacific Islanders (e.g., Hawaiians, Samoans, etc.) have often been lumped together with the other Asian American groups by the federal government for convenience in statistical accounting despite the major differences between the "East Asia" Asian Americans and the Pacific Islanders. Due to these significant differences, this article will focus on Asian Americans and will not deal with the Pacific Islanders. It should be noted that the Pacific Islanders will be categorized separately from the Asian Americans in the 2000 census.

The Model Minority Myth

Stereotyping of Asian Americans has changed drastically since they first settled in the United States. Throughout their history in the United States, Asian Americans have been stereotyped as exotic, unassimilable, and immoral. More recently, however, the stereotypes have changed. Asian Americans are now stereotyped as law-abiding, quiet, intelligent, and hard-working (Gaw, 1982). Gaw suggests that both kinds of stereotypes are harmful because they ignore individual differences and prevent accurate assessment of mental health needs of Chinese Americans. According to Huang (1991), some social and psychological issues Chinese Americans face have to do with their status in United States society. These include the immigration experience and its stresses (e.g., culture shock, alienation), racism, and discrimination, all of which include anti-immigrant sentiment and harassment. These issues also apply to the other Asian American groups.

In the early 1970s, Kitano and Sue (1973) had introduced the concept of Asian Americans as the "model minority" to the social sciences in the *Journal of Social Issues*. In the introduction to the special issue on Asian Americans, the authors noted that Asian Americans are perceived as a nonoppressed minority, and are therefore overlooked in terms of research attention and aid. Implicit in the view of Asian Americans as "model minorities" who have overcome prejudice and oppression is the idea that the lack of success in other minority groups stems from their own personal shortcomings or lack of hard work, rather than from the shortcomings of society (Leong, Chao, & Hardin, in press).

Kitano and Sue (1973) noted the relative lack of research on Asian Americans, stemming from lack of interest in this group and difficulty in obtaining adequate samples, especially of nonstudent populations. The authors also noted that although Asians have made strides in American society, they continue to face more subtle forms of prejudice and discrimination along with higher expectations for success. In an article in a special issue, Sue and Kitano (1973) traced the historical development of different stereotypes of Asian Americans that eventually ended up in the stereotype of Asian Americans as the model minority. However, as pointed out by many scholars and researchers this notion of Asian Americans being the successful "model minority" is inaccurate and misleading.

This characterization of Asian Americans has come to be referred to as the "model minority myth" where Asian Americans are stereotyped as the minority that has most effectively adapted to life in the United States. This myth ignores the bimodal distribution within many Asian American communities where there are successful Asian Americans as well as Asian Americans living at the poverty level and working in sweat shops. It also overlooks the distribution of severe mental illnesses and major adjustment difficulties among many Asian Americans (Leong et al., in press).

The perpetuation of this model minority myth, as opposed to a realistic portrait of the Asian-American community, creates many additional problems: (1) it pits Asian Americans against other ethnic minority groups; (2) it presents a false and inaccurate picture of the economic and social success of Asian Americans as more pervasive than it really is; (3) it sets up unrealistic expectations and standards for Asian Americans who have to live up to this image of the "Super Minority"; (4) it discourages researchers from studying the problems and adjustment difficulties of Asian Americans since funding agencies are more likely to pay for research on the more disadvantaged minorities; and (5) it encourages policy makers to overlook the special needs and concerns of Asian Americans in terms of funding and distribution of resources. Many scholars continue to struggle against the model minority myth being perpetuated on Asian Americans.

Educational Attainment

One of the most enduring features of the model minority stereotype is the notion that Asian Americans do better academically than other racial and ethnic groups in the United States (Leong et al., in press). According to Leong et al., interviews and empirical data show that more often than other students, Asian American youth are viewed as good students by peers and teachers. Moreover, Asian American youth are aware of being judged by this stereotype. As a group, Asian Americans do indeed have higher grade-point averages, SAT math scores, and higher general achievement scores than all other groups in the United States. Even after accounting for differences due to parents' level of education and socioeconomic status (SES), Asian American adolescents outperform their peers.

Leong et al. observed that during the 1980s popular magazines throughout the United States were portraying Asian American students as "whiz kids," while researchers tended to focus on cultural differences in attempting to explain the differences in achievement. The cultural explanation attributes the academic success of Asian Americans to "Asian" values and characteristics, such as highly valuing education and guilt induced by parental sacrifices. Some researchers have partially attributed Asian American academic success to family structure. For example, children from intact families tend to do better in school, and Asian Americans are more likely to come from intact families.

Theories combining cultural and environmental factors are potentially more explanatory (Leong et al., in press). To account for differences in achievement among minority groups in the United States, Ogbu (1989) distinguished between voluntary and involuntary minorities. Unlike other minorities who historically became part of the United States through slavery (e.g., African Americans) or colonization (e.g., Native Americans), Asian Americans are voluntary minorities because they chose to come to this country, and therefore perceive themselves as guests. Although both types of minorities face discrimination, Obgu argued that voluntary minorities, who perceive themselves as guests, are willing to "play by the rules" of the host society. Since education is a respected avenue to success in White, middle-class society, Asian Americans see education as a way to overcome prejudice and achieve success. On the other hand, involuntary minorities expect discrimination and limited opportunities regardless of their education, perceive the school system as a tool of White middle-class society, and therefore reject education as a route to success. This so-called cultural-ecological theory accounts well for differences in academic achievement between Asian Americans and other minorities, but does not explain as well the superior achievement of Asian Americans compared to Whites (Leong et al., in press).

One explanation is provided by Sue and Okazaki's (1990) theory of relative functionalism. They argue that Asian Americans experience and perceive limited mobility in many areas, especially those in which success does not rely heavily on education, such as sports, politics, and entertainment. Asian Americans thus see education as the only route to success. Consistent with this hypothesis, Asian American students and their parents believe more strongly in the value of education and its importance for getting a good job than do others. Asian American adolescents also tend to hold significantly higher standards for acceptable grades and achievement than their White peers.

Consistent with Sue and Okazaki's relative functionalism hypothesis, Asian Americans are overrepresented in education-dependent math and science occupations as adults. Asian American parents and students, as well as their teachers, reported in interviews that Asian Americans are better suited for jobs that do not emphasize language skills. Since Asian Americans likely perceive school as relatively more functional than other groups, this theory argues, they perform better in school (Leong et al., in press).

Career and Work Adjustment

One consistent pattern in the vocational behavior among Asian Americans is their tendency to be occupationally segregated. According to Leong and Serafica (1995), the occupational distribution for Asian Americans in the 1980 census provides some information about this pattern. Hsia (1988) analyzed the data for nine major occupational groupings and found that Asian Americans were more likely than European Americans to be in three of them: professional (18 vs. 12.8%), technical (5.5 vs. 3.1%), and service (15.6 vs. 11.6%) occupations. Conversely, there were fewer Asian than European Americans in sales (8.4 vs. 10.7%), production/craft (8.4 vs. 13.4%), and operator/laborer (14.2 vs. 17.1%) occupations. Hsia (1988) also provides similar data on specific Asian American subgroups

(Japanese, Chinese, Filipino, Korean, etc.). The greater tendency for Asian Americans to work in the professional and technical occupations and lower tendency to enter sales and laborer occupations are consistent with the pattern of career interests observed earlier by Sue and Kirk (1973, cited in Leong & Serafica, 1995).

Several investigators have demonstrated that Asian Americans are overrepresented in some occupations while being underrepresented in others. Such a skewed distribution of any group in the occupational structure indicates occupational segregation which could be the result of differential, including restricted, access to various occupations. Hsia (1988) provides a good illustration of the overall pattern of occupational segregation among Asian Americans by presenting a table of the representation index (RI) for Asian Americans in various occupations. For Asian Americans, the RI, a single numerical representation of the degree of segregation, is derived by dividing the percentage of Asian Americans in a particular occupation by the percentage of Asian Americans in the total civilian labor force, then multiplying the result by 100. For example, an RI of 100 for Asian Americans in a particular occupation means that they are represented according to their proportion in the general population whereas an RI of 200 means that twice the number of Asian Americans relative to their proportion in the population are in that particular occupation.

Asian Americans in the occupational group, physicians, have the highest RI (537). Representation of Asian Americans in the physician group is five times more than expected given their representation in the general U.S. population. The other occupations in which Asians are highly segregated into include medical scientist (RI = 372), physicist and astronomer (RI = 357), biological and life scientist (RI = 316), engineers (RI = 293), architects (RI = 251), accountants and auditors (RI = 202). The occupational categories in which Asian Americans are underrepresented or segregated out of include lawyers (RI = 41), judges (RI = 35), chief executive officers, and general administrators (RI = 60).

Family influence is another important factor in the career development of Asian Americans. Asian American parents are inclined to provide strong parental guidance, particularly in regard to careers. They are aware that discrimination in the world of work is quite common and that their children would have an easier time if they were in a respected and autonomous profession in which many Asian Americans have already succeeded. Hence, they may be more likely than their European American counterparts to exert direct influence on the career aspirations and choices of their children. Asian American youth would be more apt than their European American peers to defer to parental guidance given the values placed by Asian cultures on respecting authority and submitting to the wisdom of the elderly. For example, when Chinese American parents give advice to their children, they usually preface their remarks with an observation such as, "In my lifetime, I have eaten more salt than you have eaten rice." Loosely translated, the saying implies that the elderly have more experience and by extension much more wisdom than the young on most matters.

There has been a dearth of empirical studies on occupational stress among Asian Americans. One form of job stress is underemployment. There is some evidence that Asian Americans do perceive themselves to be underemployed at work. Brown, Minor, and Jepsen (1991, cited in Leong & Serafica, 1995) found that Asian Pacific Islanders (47%) were less likely than European Americans (54%), African Americans (60%), or Hispanics (63%) to report that their skills were being used very well. More Asian Pacific Islanders also reported experiencing stress on the job than members of other minority groups. African Americans (59%) and Hispanics (61%) were significantly more likely than European Americans (46%) and Asian Pacific Islanders (48%) to report little or no job stress.

Cultural Values and Beliefs

Historically, Chinese conceptions of mental health and mental illness have moved from supernatural beliefs, to emphasis on natural forces, to a somatic focus on the human body as a source of abnormality. Since the nineteenth century, psychological causes for mental illness have been accepted, although the preferred method of treatment is still herbs and medicine.

Huang (1991) suggests the traditional Chinese worldview revolves around interconnections between mind and body, parent and child, and neighbor and neighbor. While Westerners value autonomy and independence, Chinese traditionally value harmony, togetherness, and unity. Chinese culture was traditionally a shame-based culture that emphasized public disgrace as punishment, as opposed to the Western guilt-oriented culture's emphasis on self-blame as punishment. The four primary coping strategies in Chinese culture were: endurance, looking the other way, not thinking too much, and activity.

Modern Asian American values still retain some traditional aspects of Chinese culture. According to Sue and Sue (1971), these values include filial piety, stress on family bonds and unity, importance of roles and status, somatization of mental problems, control over strong emotions, emphasis on academic achievement, and low assertiveness. Huang (1991) pointed out that emotional problems still tend to be expressed in somatic ways. As such, most Chinese Americans do not view "talk therapy" as particularly helpful and seek psychotherapy only as a last resort.

Finally, Chinese American culture values self-control and inhibition of strong emotions, and individuals learn that their behavior is very significant in that it reflects upon the entire family. If one has feelings that might disrupt family harmony, one is expected to restrain those feelings. Lin (1958; cited in Huang, 1991, p. 86) comments, "Chinese worldview emphasizes the interpersonal to such an extent that the Chinese look to their relationships with people instead of to themselves as the cause of their stress." Many of these observations about Chinese Americans also apply to the other Asian American groups, especially those from East Asia.

Ethnic Identity and Acculturation

A common issue for Asian Americans is their acculturation level and ethnic identity status. Since the 1970s different theories have been proposed to explain the acculturation process for Asian Americans. According to Sue and Sue (1971), Chinese Americans may adjust to the conflicting demands of Asian and American cultures in three different ways: traditionalist, marginalist, and Asian American. Traditionalists are individuals who are typically foreign-born or first-generation immigrants who prize the cultural values of their parents and socialize only with members of their ethnic group. A marginalist, on the other hand, rejects Asian values in order to assimilate into American culture. These individuals typically only associate with Whites. The third group, those labeled as "Asian American," have achieved a balance in their identity by feeling pride in their ethnic group while at the same time combining the values of the dominant group.

Atkinson, Morten, and Sue (1983) have developed a model of ethnic identity formation specific to Asian Americans that is based on clinical experience. This model is also a stage theory framework in that there is a sequential progression in which individuals experience specific conflicts that must be resolved in order to move to the next stage. The first stage involves the notion of conformity; the second stage involves dissonance, confusion, and conflict over the dominant culture's system, and an awareness of one's own cultural system. A resistance and immersion period is followed by a period of introspection or questioning of both the minority and majority cultures. Finally, individuals achieve a synergy of articulation and awareness that involves the resolution of conflicts in previous stages and the development of a cultural identity. This complex sequence, based on clinical experience with Asian Americans, emphasizes the many conflicts experienced as the adolescents negotiated the development of their ethnic identity. Clearly, ethnic identity development is not an easy process for many Asian Americans, contrary to the model minority image of Asian Americans as easily adjusted to American society.

The second theoretical framework, acculturation

theory, is similar to Atkinson, Morten, and Sue's (1983) theory in its emphasis on a conflict model of ethnic identity. Both theories assume there will be an apparent conflict for ethnic minorities because of being part of two different cultural systems, the minority group to which they belong and the majority or dominant group. The primary model of acculturation has been proposed by Berry (1980). In Berry's two-dimensional model, two questions are assessed in determining which of four varieties of acculturation characterizes a person. The first question asks to what degree one wishes to remain culturally as one has been (in terms of identity, language, and way of life) as opposed to giving it all up to become part of a "modern" society. The second question asks to what extent one wishes to have day-to-day interactions with those of other groups, as opposed to relating only to those of one's own group. Each question is answered yes or no, yielding four possible varieties of acculturation. An interest in both maintaining one's original culture and engaging in daily interactions with those of other groups ("Yes" to both questions) characterizes integrationists. Assimilationists do not wish to maintain their ethnic identity and seek interaction with the host society. Separationists value holding onto their original culture and wish to avoid interaction with the host culture. Marginalists have little possibility of or interest in cultural maintenance, and little interest in relations with others ("No" to both questions).

Mental Health

One of the negative consequences of the model minority myth is the creation of a parallel myth that all or most Asian Americans are psychologically well adjusted and free from mental health problems since they are so successful in the United States (Leong et al., in press). Research on Asian American adolescents has found that they experience conflict in resolving their ethnic identities and stress from trying to meet academic expectations. They tend to have less pride in their ethnic group than other minority adolescents, and Asian American females have exhibited lower self-esteem than any other group (Leong et al., in press).

Research on adult samples of Asian Americans has already demonstrated that Asian Americans have the same and sometimes higher levels of mental health problems relative to adult White European Americans (e.g., see Sue & Morishima, 1982; Uba, 1994). Unfortunately, many of these studies have been based on "treated prevalence rates" (i.e., patients in hospitals and community mental health centers) which may not provide an accurate estimate of the nature and extent of mental health problems among Asian Americans. In addition, research on counseling and psychotherapy with Asian Americans has found that they tend to underutilize such services and are more likely to prema-

turely terminate from treatment than their White counterparts (Leong, 1986; Sue & Morishima, 1982; Uba, 1995). This pattern of underutilization of mental health services among Asian Americans further exacerbates the problem with treated prevalence studies.

It is important to determine what factors undermine the appropriateness of traditional mental health services delivered to Asian Americans. Unfortunately, and partly due to the difficulty of conducting such studies, there are very few empirical studies of psychotherapeutic services for Asian Americans (Leong, 1986). A few studies have emerged which attempt to address factors that ameliorate psychotherapy persistence and outcomes for Asian Americans. One barrier to treatment persistence that has garnered widespread attention is the lack of accessibility to culturally responsive services. Research by Stanley Sue and his colleagues (Sue, Fujino, Hu, Takeuchi, & Zane, 1991) has demonstrated that a lack of bicultural and bilingual staff may be a very important factor in Asian Americans' underutilization of mental health services. In their study of 60,000 clients in the Los Angeles County mental health system, Sue and colleagues demonstrated that ethnic match between client and therapist was associated with increased utilization of services and decreased likelihood of premature termination among Asian Americans. Moreover, among Asian American clients who did not speak English as their primary language, ethnic and language match were predictors of both length and outcome of treatment. The authors conclude that the ethnic match afforded by bilingual and bicultural staff leads to the provision of more culturally responsive services. More recently, research has been conducted to evaluate the effectiveness of ethnic-specific mental health services (ESS) for Asian Americans. These studies of the effectiveness of ESS compared with traditional or mainstream mental health services have provided reasons to be optimistic about ESS.

[See also Minority Psychology.]

Bibliography

Atkinson, D. R., Morten, G., & Sue, D. (1983). *Counseling American minorities*. Dubuque, IA: W. C. Brown.

Berry, J. W. (1980). Acculturation as varieties of adaptation. In A. M. Padilla (Ed.), *Acculturation: Theory, models and some new findings* (pp. 9–25). Boulder, CO: Westview Press.

Gall, S. B., & Gall, P. L. (Eds.). (1993). *Statistical record of Asian Americans*. Washington DC: Gale Research.

Gaw, A. (1982). Chinese Americans. In A. Gaw (Ed.), *Cross-cultural psychiatry* (pp. 1–29). Littleton, MA: PSG.

Hsia, J. (1988). *Asian Americans in higher education and at work*. Hillsdale, NJ: Erlbaum.

Huang, K. (1991). Chinese Americans. In N. Moknau (Ed.), *Handbook of social services for Asian and Pacific Islanders* (pp. 79–96). New York: Greenwood Press.

Kitano, H. H. L., & Sue, S. (1973). The model minorities. *Journal of Social Issues, 29,* 1–9.

Leong, F. T. L. (1986). Counseling and psychotherapy with Asian-Americans: Review of the literature. *Journal of Counseling Psychology, 33,* 196–206.

Leong. F. T. L., Chao, R. K., & Hardin, E. E. (in press). Asian American adolescents: A research review to dispel the model minority myth. In R. Montemayor, G. R. Adams, & T. P. Gullotta (Eds.), *Advances in adolescent development: Vol. 9. Adolescent experiences: Cultural and economic diversity in adolescent development.* Newbury Park, CA: Sage.

Leong, F. T. L., & Serafica, F. C. (1995). Career development of Asian Americans: A research area in search of a good theory. In F. T. L. Leong (Ed.), *Career development and vocational behavior of racial and ethnic minorities* (pp. 67–102). Hillsdale, NJ: Erlbaum.

Min. P. G. (1995). *Asian Americans: Contemporary trends and issues.* Thousand Oaks, CA: Sage.

Ogbu, J. U. (1989). The individual in collective adaptation: A framework for focusing on academic underperformance and dropping out among involuntary minorities. In L. Weis, E. Farrar, & H. G. Petrie (Eds.), *Dropouts from school: Issues, dilemmas, and solutions* (pp. 181–204). Albany: State University of New York Press.

Sue, S., Fujino, D. C., Hu, L., Takeuchi, D. T., & Zane, N. (1991). Community mental health services for ethnic minority groups: A test of the cultural responsiveness hypothesis. *Journal of Consulting and Clinical Psychology, 59,* 533–540.

Sue, S., & Kitano, H. H. L. (1973). Stereotypes as a measure of success. *Journal of Social Issues, 29,* 83–98.

Sue, S., & Okazaki, S. (1990). Asian-American educational achievements: A phenomenon in search of an explanation. *American Psychologist, 45,* 913–920.

Sue, S., & Morishima, J. (1982). *Mental health of Asian Americans.* San Francisco: Jossey-Bass.

Sue, S., & Sue, D. W. (1971). Chinese-American personality and mental health. *Amerasia Journal, 1,* 52–63.

Uba, L. (1994). *Asian Americans: Personality patterns, identity, and mental health.* New York: Guilford Press.

Frederick T. L. Leong

ASSERTIVENESS TRAINING. *See* Social Skills Training.

ASSESSMENT. Measurement is an inherent characteristic of virtually all human behavior. The very earliest forms of written language dating to about 3300 BCE were apparently tax receipts, and measurement now pervades nearly every aspect of contemporary human life, from love and marriage (e.g., how big is the stone in the engagement ring?) to sports (e.g., he hit 70 home runs), and, of course, to the sciences. Measurement is not only important but also controversial, and it is not just the act of measurement itself that can be a highly emotionally charged issue, but it is also often the consequences of measurement that may arouse controversy. For example, measurements are used daily to make decisions about people's lives, their careers, their education, their children's education, and their elected representatives to Congress.

In the discipline of psychology, semantic distinctions have been made between psychological assessment, and testing and measurement (Matarazzo, 1990). Assessment may be considered the broader of the terms and may be defined as the gathering and integration of data in order to make a psychological evaluation, decision, or recommendation. Psychologists assess diverse psychiatric (e.g., anxiety, substance abuse) and nonpsychiatric concerns (e.g., intelligence, career interests), and assessment can be conducted with individuals, dyads, families, groups, and organizations. Psychological data may be gathered through various methods such as clinical interviews, behavioral observation, psychological tests, physiological or psychophysiological measurement devices, or other specialized test apparatuses. *Psychological testing* is considered to be a narrower term referring to the measurement of psychological characteristics by an apparatus or procedure designed to obtain a behavior sample. Although there is certainly some ambiguity in the differentiation of the two terms, *psychological assessment* may be thought of as having a much older historical precedent, by perhaps thousands of years, while the foundations of modern psychological testing may extend only a century or so.

Historical Overview of Psychological Assessment

Probably the earliest of suspicions for the causal nature for behavior was a supernatural or divine influence.

Ancient History. The earliest of written explanations included the latter causes and started to include more mundane influences on behavior such as air, water, earth, and fire. Early Mesopotamian writings and later Chinese and Greek treatises recognize not only supernatural causes for abnormal behavior but also a kind of interaction between organs of the body, like the heart, spleen, stomach, and lungs, and the environment (Finger, 1994). Ironically, not until about 500 BCE was the brain considered an undeniable cause of human behavior. Before that time, the brain was a nearly incidental organ. The Edwin Smith surgical Egyptian papyrus, which dates to about 1750 BCE (and is itself a copy of a much more ancient text), records the assessment and treatment of many common diseases and injuries. It contains accurate descriptions of the brain (convolutions are likened to molten metal), but the heart was considered the seat of behavior, thinking, and feeling. This same bias was present even in the earliest of Chinese medical documents. It appears as if the strongest suspicions that the brain played a central role in behavior occur in Greece around 500 BCE. Although not the first to make the claim, the Greek physician Hippocrates (460–377 BCE) made his argument clearly:

> Men ought to know that from nothing else but the brain come joys, delights, laughter and sports, and sorrows, griefs, despondency, and lamentations. And by this, in an especial manner, we acquire wisdom and knowledge, and see and hear, and know what are foul and what are fair, what are bad and what are good. . . . And by the same organ we become mad and delirious, and fears and terrors assail us, some by night, and some by day, and dreams and untimely wanderings. And cares that are not suitable. . . . All of these things we endure from the brain, when it is not healthy, but is more hot, more cold, more moist or more dry than natural. . . . And we become mad from its humidity. (1952, p. 336)

It is evident from his writings that Hippocrates believed in the brain's susceptibility to other influences such as external environmental factors. Interestingly, it is thought that this view simply reflected a modification of the earlier ideas that air, water, earth, and fire caused abnormal behavior. Hippocrates apparently viewed the four elements as associated with dryness, warmth, cold, and moisture, respectively. Furthermore, the four elements and their associated features influenced the bodily fluids of yellow and black bile, blood, and phlegm. These four fluids formed Hippocrates' famous humoral theory, that is, differences in individual temperaments could be attributed to excesses or deficiencies in the four body fluids or humors. Hippocrates' descriptions of their actions are vivid:

> As long as the brain is at rest, the man enjoys his reason, but the depravement of the brain arises from phlegm and bile, either of which you may recognize in this manner: Those who are mad from phlegm are quiet, and do not cry out nor make a noise; but those from bile are vociferous, malignant, and will not be quiet, but are always doing something improper. (1952, p. 337)

Hippocrates and his followers had a profound effect upon assessment by fighting the long popular notions of supernatural and divine control upon human behavior, by emphasizing the brain, and not the heart, as the premier instigator of all behavior, and also by his recognition that external forces (like climate) and internal forces (like digestion and diet) exert influence on the brain and play a role in abnormal behavior. However, Hippocrates' beliefs were not universally accepted even by Greek philosophers nearly 100 years later. Indeed, the notion that the heart was the seat of emotion and memory was difficult to dislodge after a 2,000-year

prehistory. Still, the foundations of modern assessment as an evaluative and decision-making process were laid when Hippocrates made these observations and suggested treatments based on his classification, including blood-letting, purging, starving, and cauterizing.

There was a steady decline of interest in medicine and other sciences in Greece after the reign of the first Ptolemies (about 300 BCE). Many of the Greek-trained physicians then turned to Rome and the Roman Empire for further study and support. Galen (130–200 CE), a Greek-born and trained physician, became one of the most famous of the later Roman physicians and remained one of Hippocrates' chief supporters. He defended Hippocrates' theory of body humors against critics who advanced their own theories of humors and vapors in the human body. To Galen's credit, he emphasized that the organ of consciousness was the brain, including imagination, intelligence, and memory, and there were even hints in his writings that the brain might have areas that were localized by their function. Galen's chief legacy may be his classification of people into at least two types, the melancholic and the sanguine. The melancholic type has many modern counterparts including the introvert, dysthymic, and depressive personality. The sanguine type serves as a model for the modern concept of extroversion. Galen recognized, like Hippocrates before him, that human behavior can be affected by diet and climate, and Galen is often credited with the biological influences on human behavior now known as temperaments, that is, biological predispositions to act in consistent ways (Galen, 1952).

However, Galen began an unfortunate line of thought that considered the spaces in the brain, the ventricles, to contain "spirits" that were the essence of brain function and that no brain injury would have consequences unless the ventricles were also penetrated. By about the third or fourth century the "Dark Ages" began in Western Europe and persisted for about a thousand years. There was a further decline in the sciences as the Church's hierarchy played an increasing role in many aspects of day-to-day life. During this time, there was a further decline in the sciences, the belief in supernatural effects on behavior flourished again, and insanity was believed to be caused by demonic possession. One popular "diagnostic manual" of the time was the *Malleus Maleficarum (The Witches' Hammer)* which presented methods for identifying and assessing witches, such as tying the accused woman's hands and feet together and throwing her into a river. If she floated, she was deemed a witch. There were, however, pockets of cultures in the rest of the world that still venerated the works of Hippocrates, Aristotle, and Galen (Cohen, Swerdlik, & Phillips, 1996).

The Middle Ages and the Modern Era. With the onset of the Renaissance, a renewed interest in brain-behavior relationships began, and foremost among these brain scholars was Leonardo Da Vinci (1472–1519). Although the pope had forbidden human autopsies, Leonardo conducted over 300 of them and made over 1,500 drawings of the human body and brain. He conducted experiments with cattle brains in order to make anatomically correct drawings of the ventricles, but, consistent with the thinking of the time, he also ascribed various brain functions to the ventricles. Leonardo, whether intentionally or not, began a rich tradition of anatomical descriptions of the brain that may have reached an ironic zenith about 300 years later in the work of Franz Gall (1758–1828), Austrian anatomist and physician.

At the beginning of Gall's life, psychological assessment meant classifying human behavior based on facial characteristics or physiognomy. Gall, in his own writings, claims that at the age of nine he discovered his theory of brain localization. A friend of his at school was very good at memorization, and he had bulging eyes. Gall decided that his friend's bulging eyes were due to overdeveloped frontal lobes, and thus was born Gall's theory of phrenology (Finger, 1994). In Vienna, Gall began giving popular public lectures, but Church authorities worked to pass legislation prohibiting Gall's orations, and Gall subsequently moved to Paris to continue his work. Although the French Academy of Sciences soundly rejected Gall's notion that skull indentations and bumps reflected human temperaments, Gall was well received within certain circles and was lavishly supported (Finger, 1994).

While phrenology became popular among laypeople, most scientists were vehement in their rejection of the new discipline. Two major ironies may be discerned: one is that Gall was actually correct on the central feature of his thesis that the brain does have some specific localization of function. Although Gall was wrong in his claims that he could measure the localization of function by way of head bumps, and he was wrong in his attributions of functions, he was essentially correct that the brain has particular areas that have neuronal specialization of function. He was also essentially correct when he postulated that particular character traits and mental aberrations might be biologically based and inherited. The second irony is that he made brain localization so scientifically distasteful that some scientists resisted localization theories into the twentieth century, even in the face of compelling evidence. It may even be suggested that the rejection of hereditary forces as an influence on human behavior in the early twentieth century, like the works of American psychologist and preeminent behaviorist John B. Watson, may have gained momentum from the reactions against biological classification as typified in Gall's phrenology.

Charles Darwin's 1859 book, *On the Origin of the Species by Means of Natural Selection*, created the biggest clash between the religious establishment and science since Polish astronomer Copernicus, about 350 years earlier, claimed that the earth revolved around the sun. Copernicus was subsequently excommunicated by the Catholic Church. Darwin's revolutionary ideas sparked an interest in his cousin, Francis Galton (1822–1911). Galton was particularly interested in the social aspects of natural selection, and his experiments led him to believe in the overwhelming effects of inheritance upon intelligence. This led him to suggest that "eminent" people should be encouraged to reproduce whereas less eminent people should be discouraged from reproduction. In order to develop and test his theory of eugenics (enhancing the human race by selective breeding), Galton opened up a booth at a health exhibition in London in 1884. In two years, he tested 9,337 people from ages 5 to 80 years old. He measured most of them on 17 variables, primarily physical characteristics, but also perceptual acuity and memory. Galton's analysis of the data led him to the discovery of the foundations of the correlation coefficient. There was a prevailing view that physical superiority as well as perceptual acuity was a critical basis for intelligence, so Galton's choice of variables actually heralded later measurements of intelligence. As it turned out, there was essentially no relationship between any of his measures and intelligence, but Galton was testing the accepted notions about intelligence during his time (Rogers, 1995; Schultz, 1969).

Interestingly, an underlying presumption of Galton's work was that there are measurable individual differences among people. The German psychologist Wilhelm Wundt (1832–1920) founded the first experimental psychology laboratory in 1879 in Leipzig, Germany. His studies were also focused on assessment, like measuring reaction time, perception, and attention span, but ironically, Wundt was interested in similarities among people. Wundt viewed individual differences as a frustrating source of experimental error that should be eliminated or minimized. Wundt's work may be viewed as an important contribution to modern psychological assessment since he was concerned with the standardization of testing procedures such that extraneous and confounding variables were controlled across participants. Thus, any differences that may arise in an assessment would be due to genuine individual differences and not to chance differences.

Wundt's laboratory and research program at Leipzig later became the most productive in the early history of psychology, particularly in assessment and measurement. Among Wundt's students were James McKean Cattell, Charles Spearman, Emil Kraepelin, G. Stanley Hall, Lightner Witmer, and Victor Henri. Cattell later published measures on the assessment of children's intelligence and coined the term *mental test*. Spearman developed the concept of test reliability and created the rank-order correlation technique. Kraepelin was a major contributor to the first modern diagnostic classification system of psychopathology, and he formalized the word association technique as a psychological test. In 1892, Hall helped to found and became the first president of the American Psychological Association. In 1896, Witmer developed the first psychology clinic in the United States.

Witmer's contribution to psychology's identity cannot be overstated. After completing his doctoral studies with Wundt, Witmer returned to the University of Pennsylvania. When asked by a teacher to help with a problem student, Witmer gave a series of tests and determined that the student was deficient in spelling, reading, and memory. He recommended that the child be tutored in these areas. Under some criticism, he established the first psychological clinic at the university for the purposes of diagnosis, evaluation and testing, and treatment, primarily for school-related problems of children. He also envisioned a multidisciplinary approach to these problems and saw the clinic as an appropriate place for the training of psychology students. Witmer's contribution was criticized by some of his contemporaries because some purists saw psychology as a scientific discipline that should be devoted to the understanding of general psychological principles of behavior and not to the practice of remediation of abnormal or dysfunctional behavior (Cohen et al., 1996).

In 1895, Frenchman Victor Henri began publishing a series of articles with his colleague Alfred Binet, arguing that mental tests could be used successfully to predict higher mental processing. Binet and Henri were critics of the view then current that psychomotor and physical measures were related to success in school. Binet vociferously argued that intelligence would be better measured by the evaluation of comprehension, judgment, and memory. In 1904, Binet was appointed by the Ministry of Public Education in France to develop an assessment program to evaluate school readiness for children entering the school system for the first time. Chief among his tasks was to determine which children would benefit from the traditional education system and which children would benefit from remedial education. In 1905, Binet, in collaboration with Simon, created the 30-item Binet–Simon scale, the first recognized measure of intelligence in the psychological literature. It subsequently underwent many revisions, including a major overhaul, translation, and standardization in 1916 in America by Lewis Terman at Stanford University. The name of the test was changed to the Stanford–Binet Intelligence Test, and the concept of intelligence quotient (IQ) was also first introduced.

Binet and Henri had also been briefly interested in the use of inkblots as determiners of behavior. During the late 1800s and early 1900s, there was a spate of interest, primarily by laypeople, in inkblot tests and games. Swiss psychiatrist Hermann Rorschach took up empirically based research on the usefulness of the blots to distinguish among normal and clinical samples. Unfortunately, Rorschach died soon after the publication in 1921 of his now eponymous inkblot test, although a number of his collaborators began to refine and explore further aspects of the test. With the advent of the Stanford–Binet Intelligence Test and the Rorschach, the discipline of professional psychology had begun its inchoate but highly important early identity: The practice of psychology would involve assessment and testing (e.g., Groth-Marnat, 1997). Even nonclinical areas of psychology like experimental psychology and developmental psychology would be involved with aspects of assessment and testing such as measurement and statistical evaluations related to these activities. By the late 1930s, Buros (1938) listed nearly 4,000 different psychological tests in print (and this impressive collection continues to be updated; see Conoley, Impara, & Murphy, 1995). It may even be argued that a bias had developed that persisted throughout the twentieth century: that psychologists were viewed by people outside the discipline as specialists only in assessment and testing. Only late in the twentieth century were the activities of psychologists perceived more diversely, and psychologists are now involved in a wide range of other activities including psychotherapy, consultation, administration, organizational development, and program evaluation.

Development of the Current Classification System. The specialized role of psychology in assessment, classification, and measurement was strengthened immensely during World War I. With the immediate and sudden burden of large numbers of recruits, the armed services were in dire need of a means of assessing the recruits' capabilities quickly and efficiently, and required a classification system for making determinations for who was mentally fit for service and who was not. The American Psychological Association volunteered its services and developed (with Terman as a committee member) the Army Alpha (verbal) and Army Beta (nonverbal) tests of intelligence for literate and nonliterate recruits, respectively. At the same time, psychologist Robert Woodworth helped to develop a paper-and-pencil test of psychiatric fitness for the armed services, asking such questions as whether a recruit felt others were watching him when he walked down a street (Cohen et al., 1996).

In May 1917, the American Medico-Psychological Association (now the American Psychiatric Association) drew up and adopted the first national diagnostic classification system and took responsibility for its maintenance and publication. Its original purpose was to gather descriptive statistical data from mental hospitals. There were only minor revisions of the classification system in 1933 and 1942. Again, however, with the advent of another world war, the United States military was faced with the need for a more sophisticated psychological diagnostic system. It was estimated that 90% of those unfit for military service did not fit within the diagnostic nomenclature. In the 1940s, the Army, Navy, and Veterans Administration all created their own systems of classification. From about 1948 to 1951, the American Psychiatric Association worked to create a single revised system, and the result of this monumental task was the publication in 1952 of the *Diagnostic and Statistical Manual of Mental Disorders* (*DSM*; APA, 1952). The *DSM* then consisted of only seven major diagnostic categories. It has since been revised several times up to the current and most comprehensive version, *DSM–IV* (APA, 1994), which is indisputably the psychologist's primary diagnostic guide (see Coolidge & Segal, 1998 for a more detailed review of the diagnostic system changes). The *DSM–IV* provides specified criteria for several hundred mental disorders and encourages a full multiaxial diagnosis including information on clinical disorders (Axis I), personality disorders and mental retardation (Axis II), relevant medical conditions (Axis III), psychosocial and environmental stressors (Axis IV), and a global assessment of functioning (Axis V). Indeed, the output of most clinical assessments is a thorough report concluding with a full multiaxial diagnosis according to *DSM–IV* convention.

With the development of a plethora of psychological tests and the creation and refinement of a psychopathological diagnostic system, clinical psychology's identity was firmly set in the broad field of assessment. Psychologists would be called upon to observe, interview, and test those in need of their services. They would evaluate, analyze, and integrate the resulting data. And, finally, and perhaps most importantly, the modern clinical psychologist would provide a context and a summary evaluation of the patient's data, resulting in the patient's diagnosis and classification. Treatment recommendations, and perhaps treatment itself, would be provided.

The preceding review has attempted to establish the roots of modern clinical psychology's identity in assessment. It also seems clear that the role of the clinical psychologist has continued to evolve. With major revisions in health delivery and reimbursement in the 1990s, psychology clinics and private practices had to undergo sweeping reforms themselves in order to remain financially viable. At least one ramification of these reforms was that psychologists had to reinvent themselves. No longer reimbursed as they once were for psychological testing and therapy, psychologists expanded their traditional roles into the areas of industry and organizational management, administration, and other aspects of professional consultation such as per-

formance enhancement, sports psychology, health and medical psychology, and forensic applications. Whether their traditional specialties in assessment, classification, and testing will continue to play a primary role in these new areas remains to be determined. However, it is likely that the psychologist's undeniable role as the expert in assessment will continue to flourish in diverse contexts.

Assessment Methods and Techniques

The primary psychometric concepts relevant to the understanding and evaluation of psychological assessment strategies and instruments include the topics of reliability, validity, and norms.

Psychometric Issues. The term *reliability* refers to the degree to which measurement is consistent and stable over time. For example, a reliable psychological test yields consistent scores when the person takes the test again after an interval. The estimates of reliability most relevant to psychological tests are internal consistency and test-retest reliability. Internal consistency is a measure of the extent to which items in a test are interrelated with each other. Test-retest reliability refers to the extent to which test scores are consistent from one administration to the next. Since reliability is the first requirement for good measurement, tests used by psychologists should show ample evidence of reliability.

The term *validity* refers to the extent to which a test measures what it purports to measure and the extent to which the test can be used to make accurate predictions. Does a depression test truly measure depression? Notably, reliability and validity are closely intertwined, as reliability is a necessary, but not sufficient, condition for validity. An unreliable test cannot possibly be valid, although it is possible for a test to have good reliability but poor validity if the test does not measure anything meaningful. The primary types of validity of psychological tests are content, construct, predictive, and concurrent validity. Only proven and validated tests should be used during psychological assessment.

The term *norms* refers to the provision of standards for interpreting test scores, so that one's responses can be compared to an appropriate reference group. Scores on most psychological tests rarely provide absolute measures of the construct being assessed (e.g., intelligence, anxiety, self-esteem). Rather, tests frequently indicate the relative performance of the respondent when compared to others. Thus, most popular psychological tests are standardized, which means that there are fixed procedures for administration and scoring and that the test has been given to many different people so that statistical norms for age, grade, sex, race, and so on can be established. Without standardization and norms, it would be impossible to determine if a respondent's score is typical, above, or below average compared to the person's peer group, making the assessment worthless.

Notably, assessment tools have been devised for countless specific clinical disorders (e.g., depression, alcohol abuse, PTSD), and relevant clinical constructs (e.g., assertiveness, dysfunctional thinking patterns, social support, dissociation). It should also be noted that specialized assessment instruments have been developed for various distinct populations, such as older adults and children. Examples of specialized scales for older persons include the Geriatric Depression Scale, Geriatric Hopelessness Scale, and Michigan Alcoholism Screening Test-Geriatric Version. Tools specific for children include the Wechsler Intelligence Scale for Children–III, Kaufman Assessment Battery for Children, and Kiddie Schedule for Affective Disorders and Schizophrenia. Consistent with the traditional role of the psychologist as the expert in assessment issues, a tremendous amount of psychological research has been devoted to the evaluation of psychometric properties of most of today's popular assessments instruments. Careful attention to such literature ensures that clinicians and researchers apply tests that are the most suitable for a particular assessment situation.

Primary Methods of Clinical Assessment. In general, psychological assessment techniques are designed to evaluate a person's cognitive, emotional, social, and personality functioning. In clinical settings, the purpose of assessment is to find out what kinds of problems the person is experiencing and what may have caused the problem, to assist in clarification of personality features, to identify and diagnose mental disorders, to develop case conceptualization and intervention plans, and to evaluate effects of treatment. Due to the complex nature of assessment, diverse strategies have been developed. Multiple strategies are often used in combination to elicit the most accurate, comprehensive, and meaningful description of the individual.

The Clinical Interview. One of the hallmark traditions of clinical psychology is the ability of clinicians to effectively interview clients as part of a psychological assessment. The interview is the most widely used assessment tool. The clinical interview is performed by clinicians to gather important information about the person's current problems, situation, and needs and to assess behavior. Clinicians usually start with why the person came in for help (called the presenting problem or current illness), followed by a discussion of the history of that problem. Other topics typically covered include an in-depth personal history, psychiatric treatment history, family history, mental status examination, and current social and occupational functioning. Various basic clinical skills (e.g., empathic listening, reflection of feeling and content, summarization, acceptance) are employed throughout the interview to develop and maintain rapport with the client to allow the client to disclose intensely personal and often troubling information about their current experience.

Interviews can be unstructured or structured. Unstructured interviews have no prescribed course and can vary considerably from interviewer to interviewer based on the theoretical orientation adopted by the interviewer. The course and process of the session can be easily altered to maximize rapport and investigate intriguing areas at the clinician's discretion. In contrast, structured interviews follow a prescribed course and have standardized questions. Many structured interviews are now available to aid in the assessment of most major *DSM–IV* Axis I (clinical disorders) and all Axis II (personality) disorders. Structured interviews have many beneficial features including comprehensive, systematic, and objective coverage of disorders of interest, and improved reliability and validity compared to unstructured interviews. Well-validated interviews for mental state disorders include the Structured Clinical Interview for *DSM–IV* Axis I, the Diagnostic Interview Schedule, and the Schedule for Affective Disorders and Schizophrenia. Popular and psychometrically sound interviews for personality disorders include the Structured Clinical Interview for *DSM–IV* Axis II Personality Disorders, Structured Interview for *DSM–IV* Personality, and the International Personality Disorder Examination (for a more complete description of major issues and instruments, see Segal, 1997; Segal & Falk, 1998). Due to the numerous benefits of structured interviews, they are employed heavily by researchers, and it is widely anticipated that the application of structured interviews will increase markedly in traditional clinical contexts as well in the near future.

Personality Assessment. Personality tests strive to uncover the structure and features of one's personality, or one's characteristic way of thinking, feeling, and behaving. Personality tests can be broadly conceptualized as falling into two distinct types: projective and objective.

Projective personality tests typically present stimuli whose meanings are not immediately obvious and have an open-ended response format, such as a story from the respondent. Projective tests have their origins in psychodynamic theory: the assumption is that, due to the intentional ambiguity of stimuli, the respondent projects his or her unconscious emotions, perceptions, and desires into the test situation. Examples of popular projective tests include the Rorschach Inkblot test, the Thematic Apperception Test (TAT), and Sentence Completion Tests.

During administration of the Rorschach test the respondent provides associations to 10 bilaterally symmetrical inkblots chosen for their prior, specific abilities to elicit certain classes of responses from normal people (e.g., mother responses, authority-figure responses, sexual content). After Hermann Rorschach's death, at least five different major scoring systems were popularized and in widespread use until the late 1960s. In 1969, John Exner devised his revolutionary scoring system which now enjoys virtually unrivaled popularity. Exner's scoring system uses only empirically derived interpretations as well as standardized administration and scoring instructions. Exner's adherence to strict empirical validation has led to a veritable renaissance in the teaching and use of the original Rorschach test. The TAT consists of 31 black-and-white pictures that tend to induce particular themes, such as sexuality and achievement. Some cards are well structured and clear, some are somewhat ambiguous, and others are bizarre. Typically 10 to 20 cards are selected by the clinician and administered, and the respondent is asked to create a story explaining what is happening in the picture currently, what led up to the picture, and what is going to happen. Sentence completion tests have been designed for children, adolescents, adults, and older adults. Tests provide provocative sentence "stems" that are completed by the respondent.

Objective personality tests are typically self-report pencil-and-paper tests based on standardized, specific items and questions. The most widely used and thoroughly researched objective personality instrument is the Minnesota Multiphasic Personality Inventory-2 (MMPI). The original MMPI was developed by Hathaway and McKinley at the University of Minnesota in the early 1940s. It was updated, revised, and named the MMPI-2 (Butcher, Dahlstrom, Graham, Tellegen, & Kaemmer, 1989). The MMPI-2 is not theoretically based, but rather was developed using the criterion keying method in which items for each scale were selected for their ability to discriminate statistically psychiatric patients with distinct mental disorders from healthy individuals. The MMPI-2 has 10 standard clinical scales (hypochondriasis, depression, hysteria, psychopathic deviance, masculinity-femininity, paranoia, psychasthenia, schizophrenia, hypomania, and social introversion) and several validity scales to detect unusual test-taking attitudes such as intentionally presenting oneself in a favorable light, or conversely, exaggerating psychopathology in order to give an unfavorable impression. There is a tremendous body of empirical literature supporting diverse applications and modifications of the MMPI-2. A version specific for adolescents, the MMPI-A, is available and increasingly popular for clinical and research purposes. The main disadvantage of the MMPI-2 is its length: 567 items. Notably, the original version of the MMPI was slowly phased out and was formally withdrawn from use in September 1999, leaving only the MMPI-2 and MMPI-A. While the MMPI-2 focuses primarily on clinical conditions, several self-report inventories have been designed specifically to evaluate *DSM–IV* personality disorders. A popular personality disorder test is the Millon Clinical Multiaxial Inventory-III (Millon, 1994) which has 14 personality pattern scales, 10 clinical syndrome scales, and 3 validity scales.

There are a myriad of popular, objective, brief *self-report questionnaires* designed to assess a wide variety of problems. The assumption underlying these types of tests is that the respondent can accurately report the kinds of psychiatric symptoms and problem behaviors they are experiencing. It is likely that a symptom inventory has been developed for every possible psychological condition or problem of interest. For example, the Beck Depression Inventory is a widely used depression screening scale consisting of 21 items tapping psychological and somatic manifestations of major depression. Two commonly applied self-report checklists of anxiety are the Beck Anxiety Inventory (BAI) and the State-Trait Anxiety Inventory (STAI). The BAI is a 21-item self-rating scale to measure severity of anxiety and to discriminate anxiety from depression. The STAI is a theoretically derived 40-item Likert scale that assesses separate dimensions of "state" anxiety as well as "trait" anxiety. The 53-item Brief Symptom Inventory, a popular multidisorder inventory, taps 10 clinical conditions (e.g., depression, phobic anxiety, hostility, paranoia). The attractions of symptom inventories include their simplicity, and ease of administration and scoring; the main disadvantage is that they are obvious in their intent and therefore easy to fake.

Cognitive Assessment. Evaluation of cognitive functioning has long been a hallmark of psychological practice. Virtually hundreds of tests have been designed to tap various aspects of cognitive functioning. Two specific forms of cognitive assessment will be discussed here: intelligence testing and neuropsychological testing.

Intelligence tests are standardized tests designed to measure a person's mental ability. Despite this seemingly simple definition, there is no area in psychology richer in controversy than the assessment of intelligence. The difficulty of intellectual assessment is exacerbated by its own abstract nature. It can only be inferred from observable behavior, yet the illusory label, *intelligence*, no doubt refers to a complex group of mental processes. Nevertheless, applications of these tests are substantial, including diagnosis of mental retardation and learning disabilities, identification of gifted children, and prediction of progress in school. The most widely employed intelligence tests are the series of Wechsler tests (i.e., Wechsler Preschool and Primary Scale of Intelligence–Revised, Wechsler Intelligence Scale for Children–Third Edition, and the Wechsler Adult Intelligence Scale–Third Edition). As an example, the WAIS-III consists of 14 separate subtests: seven verbal and seven performance. Raw scores for each subtest are converted into scaled scores (mean = 10, SD = 3). Scaled scores are added together separately for the verbal and performance subtests. Based on groupings of the participant's age, scaled score sums are converted into a verbal intelligence quotient, performance intelligence quotient, and a full-scale intelligent quotient. Because of the careful age, gender, race, and geographic stratification in its standardization, the use of the WAIS-III is continually substantiated at least on a psychometric basis. There are, however, potentially as many abuses as uses with the WAIS-III: it largely does not measure motivation, nor does it measure the worth of an individual, or one's creativity, emotional stability, conscientiousness, leadership, or memory. The second most popular intelligence test is the Stanford–Binet Intelligence Test–Fourth Edition.

Neuropsychological testing assesses brain-behavior relationships in multiple domains and helps to quantify and localize brain damage. Typically, a battery of tests designed to assess behavioral disturbances that are caused by brain dysfunctions are administered. The most prominent battery is the Halstead-Reitan Battery, which consists of 10 tests in conjunction with the WAIS-III and MMPI-2. Examples of subtests include the Category Test, Speech-Sounds Perception Test, Trail Making Test, and Modified Halstead-Wepman Aphasia Screening Test. Another popular approach besides the standard battery is for the examiner to carefully choose a variety of different tests to assess particular neuropsychological domains of interest. Numerous individual tests are available to measure diverse aspects of cognitive functioning. Finally, laboratory tests (e.g., electrolyte panel, urinalysis, electroencephalography) and high-tech brain-imaging procedures (e.g., computerized axial tomography, magnetic resonance imaging) are often used to complement traditional neuropsychological assessment.

Behavioral Observation. The strategy of behavioral observation was born out of the recognition of limitations inherent in self-report and interview assessments; namely, respondents may intentionally or unintentionally distort their responses. Rather than focusing on verbal reports, behavioral observation is concerned with direct observation of behaviors that occur in the real world. Behavioral therapists typically are concerned with a functional analysis of behavior, which involves analysis of antecedent events and consequences of the problem behavior. Functional analyses allow therapists to discover environmental factors that impinge on behavior and to develop a case conceptualization. Specific forms of behavioral observation include naturalistic observation (in which clinicians observe clients in their natural environments), self-monitoring (in which one observes and records one's own behavior in an objective manner), and as-

sessment of cognitions (in which one focuses on describing the cognitions or thoughts that underlie one's behavior). Behavioral observation is the first step in a behaviorally oriented intervention plan. Despite the potential quality of data garnered, behavioral observation can be time-consuming, expensive, and ethically problematic in some cases.

Concluding Comments

This article has described the rich tradition of the role of assessment in psychology and has traced the historical development of modern clinical assessment. Notably, the main applied functions of psychologists since the birth of psychology through at least World War II were assessment and measurement. Psychologists have come a long way in their ability to accurately evaluate and measure diverse forms of normal and abnormal behavior, but many areas for improvement remain. In recent years, increased attention (but not enough) has been given to the consideration of cultural factors that may impinge on assessment results and interpretation. The *DSM–IV* now has a section devoted to a description of culturally bound mental syndromes, and a growing body of literature focuses on the explication of cultural factors in the expression and experience of diverse mental disorders. Additionally, expanded reliability and validity studies are warranted as tests are administered to new and unique populations. Finally, assessment strategies and results will likely become more intimately tied to specific validated treatment interventions for psychological problems. Future psychologists will undoubtedly continue to refine existing assessment methods and develop new breakthrough strategies as the future in assessment will hopefully be as bright as past.

[*See also* Violence Risk Assessment. *Also,* many of the people mentioned in this article are the subjects of independent biographical entries.]

Bibliography

American Psychiatric Association. (1952). *Diagnostic and statistical manual of mental disorders*. Washington, DC: Author.

American Psychiatric Association. (1994). *Diagnostic and statistical manual of mental disorders* (4th ed.). Washington, DC: Author.

Buros, O. K. (Ed). (1972). *The 1938 mental measurements yearbook*. New Highland Park, NJ: Gryphon. (Original work published 1938)

Butcher, J. N., Dahlstrom, W. G., Graham, J. R., Tellegen, A., & Kaemmer, B. (1989). *MMPI-2: Manual for administration and scoring*. Minneapolis: University of Minnesota Press.

Cohen, R. J., Swerdlik, M. E., & Phillips, S. M. (1996). *Psychological testing and assessment: An introduction to tests and measurements*. Mountain View, CA: Mayfield.

Conoley, J. C., Impara, J. C., & Murphy, L. L. (Eds.). (1995). *The twelfth mental measurements yearbook.* Lincoln, NE: Buros Institute of Mental Measurements.

Coolidge, F. L., & Segal, D. L. (1998). Evolution of personality disorder diagnosis in the Diagnostic and Statistical Manual of Mental Disorders. *Clinical Psychology Review, 18,* 585–599.

Finger, S. (1994). *Origins of neuroscience: A history of explorations into brain function.* New York: Oxford University Press.

Galen (1952). On the brain. In M. J. Adler (Ed.), *Great books of the western world.* Chicago, IL: Britannica.

Groth-Marnat, G. (1997). *Handbook of psychological assessment.* New York: Wiley.

Hippocrates (1952). On the sacred disease. In M. J. Adler (Ed.), *Great books of the western world.* Chicago, IL: Brittanica.

Matarazzo, J. D. (1990). Psychological assessment versus psychological testing: Validation from Binet to the school, clinic, and courtroom. *American Psychologist, 45,* 999–1017.

Millon, T. (1994). *Millon Clinical Multiaxial Inventory III (MCMI III) manual.* Minneapolis, MN: National Computer Systems.

Rogers, T. B. (1995). *The psychological testing enterprise: An introduction.* Belmont, CA: Brooks/Cole.

Schultz, D. P. (1969). *A history of modern psychology.* New York: Academic Press.

Segal, D. L. (1997). Structured interviewing and DSM classification. In S. M. Turner & M. Hersen (Eds.), *Adult psychopathology and diagnosis* (3rd ed., pp. 25–57). New York: Wiley.

Segal, D. L., & Falk, S. B. (1998). Structured interviews and rating scales. In A. S. Bellack & M. Hersen (Eds.), *Behavioral assessment: A practical handbook* (4th ed., pp. 158–178). New York: Allyn & Bacon.

Daniel L. Segal and Frederick L. Coolidge

ASSOCIATION FOR BEHAVIOR ANALYSIS. The Association for Behavior Analysis (ABA) is an international organization committed to advancing a natural science of behavior, the application of that science to the common good, and related philosophical investigations. It has 2,700 full, associate, and student members in more than 30 countries and is affiliated with 18 state and regional chapters and 15 international associations having another 1,500 members.

The association represents three interrelated subdisciplines within behavior analysis: (1) the experimental analysis of behavior, which entails research on basic behavioral processes (e.g., operant and respondent conditioning, discrimination and generalization, concept formation) and extensions of those processes to the analysis of individual and group behavior (e.g., social development, self-control); (2) applied behavior analysis, which addresses problems of individual, social, and cultural importance (e.g., school failure, developmental disabilities, drug abuse, family violence, workplace hazards), alters standing conditions that produce those problems, or develops techniques, procedures, and programs for preventing or remediating them, and disseminates solutions that are replicable and accountable (cf. behavior therapy and behavior modification); and (3) conceptual analysis, which encompasses philosophical, theoretical, methodological, and ethical issues in the science of behavior and its application (e.g., philosophy of science, behavioral interpretation, units of analysis, social validity). In representing these interests, ABA attracts members from across many disciplines, including psychology, biology, sociology, and regular and special education, as well as philosophy, gerontology, organizational management, nursing, rehabilitation, and social work.

The association began in the early 1970s as a series of sessions organized by Gerald Mertens at the meetings of the Midwestern Psychological Association (MPA). These sessions provided a scientific and professional forum for behavior analysts in the Midwest, especially when the MPA was disinclined toward single-subject research designs and applied behavior analysis. In 1974, Israel Goldiamond and Mertens convened a meeting, independent of MPA, at the University of Chicago, which brought together 90 concerned scientists, educators, and students from universities, colleges, and research institutes throughout the region. An organizational committee was selected and the Midwestern Analysis of Behavior Association (MABA) was founded.

MABA held its first convention the following year in Chicago and adopted official bylaws. The organizational committee elected Nathan H. Azrin and Goldiamond its first and second presidents, and established a governing council with a representative each for the membership-at-large, the experimental analysis of behavior, and nonpsychologists in MABA. In 1978, the council approved a motion by Sidney W. Bijou, the third president, to change MABA's name to the Association for Behavior Analysis, with "International" an optional subtitle. Among the presidents who soon followed were A. Charles Catania, Barbara C. Etzel, Jack Michael, Ogden R. Lindsley, Ellen P. Reese, and Beth Sulzer-Azaroff.

The association has continued to evolve to meet the needs of its members. It now has an executive director and an executive council, with the council having a representative each for the experimental and applied analyses of behavior, two members-at-large, and a student representative. Its structure includes 34 boards and committees, several task forces and ad hoc committees, and 23 special interest groups (SIGs). The boards oversee the association's major functions (e.g., accreditation, membership), the committees carry them out (e.g., legislative affairs, professional development), and the task forces and ad hoc committees address issues needing special attention (e.g., the right to effective education). The SIGs give ABA members means for addressing specific topics, such as animal behavior management, autism, the experimental analysis of human behavior, legal and ethical issues, the teaching of behavior analysis, and social action.

Among the association's major functions is an annual convention that attracts more than 2,000 registrants from around the world. The program is devoted to paper, symposium, panel, and poster sessions, but also includes workshops, continuing education courses, business meetings, and special events. In the early years, banquet programs featuring B. F. Skinner and Fred S. Keller highlighted the special events. More recently, they include invited addresses by speakers from outside the discipline, a "newcomers" session, book exhibits, social hours, and reunions. [See the biographies of Skinner and Keller.]

The outside speakers are only one means by which the association maintains relations with organizations having related disciplinary and professional interests. ABA is also a member of the Federation of Behavioral, Psychological, and Cognitive Sciences and of the Council on Quality and Leadership in Support for People with Disabilities. It is a partner in the American Psychological Society's Human Capital Initiative and its convention meets in conjunction with the Society for the Quantitative Analysis of Behavior. ABA also sponsors an annual meeting for leaders and directors of more closely aligned organizations, such as divisions of the American Psychological Association (e.g., Division 25 for the Experimental Analysis of Behavior, Division 33 for Mental Retardation and Developmental Disabilities), the B. F. Skinner Foundation, and the Cambridge Center for Behavioral Studies.

The ABA Executive Council serves as the Board of Directors for the Society for the Advancement of Behavior Analysis (SABA). Chartered in 1980 as a nonprofit organization, SABA receives donations to support ABA-related activities (e.g., affiliations with other organizations and accrediting bodies) and an annual awards program. Awards are given for Distinguished Service, Enduring Programmatic Contributions, International Dissemination, Public Service, Lifetime Achievement, and the Effective Presentation of Behavior Analysis in the Mass Media.

Finally, the association publishes a newsletter and two journals. The *ABA Newsletter* is its primary means for informing members about current, future, and proposed activities. *The Behavior Analyst* is ABA's house journal, devoted to research reviews, conceptual issues, and disciplinary and professional topics. *The Analysis of Verbal Behavior* publishes reports of empirical research

and theoretical articles on verbal behavior, language, and communication. ABA also prints membership and graduate training directories and task force reports, and distributes texts and tapes pertinent to its mission.

[*See also* Applied Behavior Analysis; *and* Behavior Analysis.]

Bibliography

Association for Behavior Analysis. Available Web site: http://www.wmich.edu/aba/

Lattal, K. A. (1992). Special issue: Reflections on B. F. Skinner and psychology. *American Psychologist, 11,* 1269–1530.

Michael, J. (1985). Behavior analysis: A radical perspective. In B. L. Hammonds (Ed.), *The master lecture series: Vol. 4. Psychology and learning* (pp. 97–121). Washington, DC: American Psychological Association.

Peterson, M. E. (1978). The Midwestern Association for Behavior Analysis: Past, present, future. *The Behavior Analyst, 1,* 3–15.

Edward K. Morris

ASSOCIATION FOR THE ADVANCEMENT OF PSYCHOLOGY. Founded in early 1974 following a very turbulent winter session of the American Psychological Association Council of Representatives, the Association for the Advancement of Psychology (AAP) was psychology's second political action group, preceded in 1972 by the Council for the Advancement of the Psychological Professions and Sciences (CAPPS). For the first 80 years of its existence, American psychology had no organized public policy arm; now it had two. These developments reflected the emergence of professional psychology as a major national force in psychology.

From its inception, American psychology was essentially an academic pursuit concerned primarily with research. When psychological service delivery existed at all, it was provided primarily through psychological "clinics" housed in university settings, typically as an adjunct of research programs.

The onset of World War II brought dramatic changes. The military's needs for classification of individuals on factors such as intelligence and aptitude, and for treatment of the psychological casualties of the war, along with the public's developing awareness and acceptance of the need for psychological services, combined to create support for the emergence of psychological service delivery.

By the late 1950s, the increasing numbers of practitioners delivering psychological services generated widespread concern about issues such as licensing laws for psychologists, federal funding for health service delivery, and funding for training and research. The concurrent emergence of prepaid third-party health insurance, which initially excluded reimbursement for psychological services, began to impose severe restrictions on their delivery. Psychological practitioners quickly became sensitized to the importance of their participation in public policy and political activities.

Initial concern with public policy issues was limited to the "clinical" wing of the APA and became a paramount issue in the organization's developing struggle between applied interests and academic-scientific interests. In the early 1970s APA's Board of Directors, beset with intraorganizational struggles and pressed from within by practitioners, decided that public policy and political advocacy activities should be developed outside the APA. The board endorsed a proposal by a group of nationally visible psychology practitioners to develop an independent advocacy arm for psychology.

Psychology's first "lobbying arm," CAPPS, was founded by Drs. Theodore Blau, Nicholas Cummings, Melvin Gravitz, Ernest Lawrence, Helen Sunikian, Jack Wiggins, and Rogers Wright, chairman. CAPPS quickly became a national force in psychology's professional affairs and was directly responsible for the recognition of psychologists as reimbursable providers under the Federal Government Employees Health Plan, one of the world's largest health delivery systems. Concurrently, CAPPS founders were among the highly visible and articulate leaders of the practitioner movement within APA, attempting to wrest organizational and governance control from the academic and scientific interests which had dominated APA governance throughout its existence. In such a context, it was perhaps inevitable that the competing concerns would have an impact on advocacy as well.

Charging the CAPPS leadership with "lack of balance" and failure to advocate sufficiently for academic and scientific interests, the APA sponsored the founding of its own advocacy group, the Association for the Advancement of Psychology (AAP). AAP was established with a large governing board composed of equal numbers of representatives of APA's major interest groups: practice, public interest, and science.

The resulting "troika," composed of some 23 psychologists, was not only large and unwieldy from its inception, but it was additionally burdened by another founding principle, that its commitments and activities would at all times equally reflect the interests of APA's three major political groups. This well-intended principle overlooked the reality that (1) issues neither arise nor are driven in all three areas simultaneously and (2) that public interest and research-academic psychologists were not as committed to public policy advocacy

as were practitioners. Furthermore, psychology, after years of no active commitment to public policy and advocacy, now had two independent major groups each committed to representing psychology. Recognizing the inherent dangers to the two competing organizations, the CAPPS and AAP leadership merged the two organizations in 1975.

Concurrently, professional interests within APA forced a reorganization, so that the needs of various factions within APA could be more productively addressed and mediated through "directorates" devoted to professional practice, academic-science, and public interest. This functional reorganization within APA allowed public policy issues of concern to one or more of the factions within the association to be addressed by APA through the directorate structure.

Consequently, much of the support for AAP was further diminished, and over a span of several years, AAP's activity level became essentially moribund. Its governance structure was reduced to a six-member board, but maintained the principle of equal representation from psychology's three major interests. There followed an unfortunate spiral of diminished economic support, leading to further limitations of advocacy and such a loss of visibility, credibility, and action options that the organization essentially existed in name only. Subsequent developments nationally and outside psychology, such as continued reductions in support for research and training, the advent of managed health care, and increasing limitations imposed on public policy actions by APA's tax-exempt status, dramatized psychology's urgent need for an effective policy and advocacy organization.

In this context, it became widely apparent that AAP needed to be revitalized or a successor organization established. Consequently, in 1989, at the recommendation of the APA Chief Executive Officer, the AAP Board of Trustees committed itself to revitalizing AAP by rebuilding its support base and by developing an aggressive federal public policy advocacy. As part of the revitalization process, AAP (1) recruited a new staff experienced with political action and fund raising; (2) required its officers to have a history of personal involvement in advocacy; and (3) modified its bylaws so that members of its Board of Trustees would represent AAP's members rather than interest groups within APA. AAP selected Rogers Wright as Executive Officer and charged him with developing an effective advocacy program.

The new program has been extremely successful in establishing national visibility and credibility for the organization. By the late 1990s, the activities of AAP's political action committee, AAP/PLAN, had elevated the political action committee to the eleventh most active nationally among all health care political action committees.

Bibliography

Advance. Association for the Advancement of Psychology: Colorado Springs, CO. The quarterly newsletter of the AAP.

Rogers H. Wright

ASSOCIATIONISM. From an associationist viewpoint, knowledge itself is believed to be acquired mainly through the establishment of associational connections. The evolution of mental abilities, both ontogenically and phylogenically, is regarded as linked to the acquisition of capacities for forming and holding onto more and more complex linkage patterns between bits of information. Even very primitive organisms such as amebas learn to associate chemical stimuli with noxious conditions, as a kind of conditioned learning. The most highly developed mammals in terms of social learning, such as dolphins, whales, elephants, and the higher primates, have brains that can process information about shifting roles of affiliation between self and others. This is believed to be what makes complex status hierarchies and attachments possible.

The theory of associational connections stems from Aristotle and, later, European empiricists. It is still being revised and added to in the modern era, with concepts such as parallel distributive processing. The earliest scientific theories of association emphasized the linkage between two or more mental elements, or bits of information. The history of theory about associations started with studies of the linkage between simple ideas, or between feelings and perceptual stimuli. These linkages could also be between feelings, perceptual stimuli, and behavioral responses; for example, a loud noise could cause pain in a person's ear, leading to fear. Subsequently, a loud noise could lead to fear even if it did not directly cause pain in the ear. The connection in the mind is an association.

From such simple linkages between concepts, a larger and more complex system of meanings could be deduced or inferred. Ideas in the mind were then conceptualized as being arranged in associational hierarchies. If it was round, red, fist sized, with a juicy and tasty white interior with black seeds in the center, it was an apple, a kind of fruit, a kind of food. When a person is hungry, apples are desirable, and when blood sugar falls a person might image a round red fruit or think the word *apple* due to the associational connections. The nesting of round, with red, with fist-sized, and the word *apple* under the concept of apple, and the status of the apple concept as subsidiary to the concept of fruit, conveys a hierarchy: smaller-order concepts are subsumed under an organizing umbrella of larger-order concepts. The overall associational theme is one of a nested hierarchy. The largest domains of associational connections into a network are called supraordinate; the lower and smaller domains are subordinate.

Connections between meanings can explain otherwise strange phenomena. Probes are sometimes needed to find connections. One of the probes developed in the early days of psychotherapy was the use of free association, usually credited to Sigmund Freud and Josef Breuer. Freud replaced hypnotic suggestion with free association. The focus was on neurotic symptoms. The patient was asked to focus on when these symptoms first appeared, but instead of telling a story, was asked to say whatever came to mind. The psychoanalyst listened to the flow of these associations, seeking an interpretation for the cause of the symptoms. By this means, unconscious connections of meanings were sometimes clarified and made accessible to consciousness.

At about the same time, various associational tests were developed. These emphasized quick "free" responses of spoken words to given word stimuli. Such work continued for decades. The context of associating was found to effect the connections made. If an investigator in a word association test asks for a response to a stimulus in a glum tone, the response is more likely to be negative than if an optimistic or buoyant expectancy were conveyed. Moreover, the mental states of two people who are communicating with each other changes associational linkages. The pair creates new "wholes" not previously intrinsic to the subject's mind.

Associationism has been transformed in modern cognitive sciences, including cognitive-psychodynamic integrations, into a theory of parallel, distributive, unconscious mental processing. The flow of associated bits of information is no longer regarded as necessarily linear, from one bit to the next. The basic concepts are that several networkings of associations can be processing simultaneously. A person who speculates on a stimulus unconsciously activates many possible lines of interpretation. A social contextual situation, for example, might be rapidly interpreted according to different internal person schemas (networks of self and other person meanings).

Bibliography

Baars, B. J. (1986) *The cognitive revolution in psychology.* New York: Guilford Press.

Freud, S. (1953). *The interpretation of dreams.* In J. Strachey (Ed. and Trans.), *The standard edition of the complete psychological works of Sigmund Freud* (Vols. 4 & 5). London: Hogarth.

Horowitz, M. (1992). *Person schemas and maladaptive interpersonal patterns.* Chicago: University of Chicago Press.

Horowitz, M. (1998). *Introduction to psychodynamics: A new synthesis.* New York: Basic Books.

Horowitz, M. (1998). *Cognitive psychodynamics: From conflict to character.* New York: Wiley.

Kris, A. O. (1982). *Free association.* New Haven, CT: Yale University Press.

Mandler, G. (1962). From association to structure. *Psychological Review, 69,* 415–427.

Newell, A., & Simon, H. A. (1972). *Human problem solving.* Englewood Cliffs, NJ: Prentice Hall.

Thorndike, E. L. (1931). *Human learning.* New York: Appleton-Century-Crofts.

Mardi Horowitz

ASTHMA. The word *asthma* is derived from the Greek term for panting. Hippocrates provided an early account of asthma, although Aretaeus and Galen in the Christian era contributed the first detailed description of the disorder (McFadden & Stevens, 1983). Many early descriptions proved accurate, particularly in sketching three characteristics: the intermittent, variable, and reversible nature of asthma. These characteristics remain prominent features of the disorder, although they are not as distinct markers of asthma as was thought a few decades ago. The term *intermittent* denotes asthma symptoms or attacks that occur on an episodic basis, although there are patients in whom exacerbations occur on a perennial basis. The term *variable* refers to the fact that asthma symptoms may range from chest tightness and mild wheezing to status asthmaticus, or steadily worsening asthma. Spector and Nicklas (1995) noted that asthma severity is a continuum across the population and often within a given individual. The term *reversible* indicates that attacks are partially reversible, although there are patients in whom complete reversibility of symptoms is unobtainable even with intense medical therapy. While all of the characteristics are of varying significance across patients, they are important in establishing the diagnosis of asthma (Expert Panel Report, 1991, 1997).

Attention has increasingly been focused on three other characteristics of asthma: airway obstruction, airway inflammation, and airway hyperresponsiveness. Airway obstruction is the narrowing of the airways responsible for the clinical manifestations of asthma, such as wheezing, dyspnea, and cough. Airway narrowing may worsen gradually and persist despite therapy, but it can also occur abruptly and produce acute respiratory insufficiency (Expert Panel Report, 1991). Airway obstruction is reversible either spontaneously or with treatment. Airway inflammation refers to the recognition that asthma is a chronic inflammatory disorder of the airways. This process involves epithelial injury, edema, and mast cell infiltration. Airway inflammation contributes to airway hyperresponsiveness, airflow limitation, respiratory symptoms, and asthma chronicity (Expert Panel Report, 1997). Airway hyperresponsiveness is an exaggerated bronchoconstrictor response to many physical, chemical, and pharmacological agents, including allergens, environmental irritants, viral respiratory infections, cold air, and exercise (Expert Panel Report, 1991). Patients with asthma show an increased sensitivity to specific stimuli which produce no effect in other people; specific stimuli are triggers of attacks in specific asthmatic patients.

Prevalence of Asthma

Prevalence rates for asthma are rising. Based on the National Health Interview Survey from 1980 to 1990, the age-adjusted rate of self-reported asthma increased by 38%; this included a 50% increase in females and a 27% increase in males. Among people aged 5 to 34 years—considered the most stable population to study—the rate of asthma increased 52% from 34.6 per 1,000 to 52.6 per 1,000 in the years between 1981 and 1992. The rate of asthma increased by 29% for males and 82% for females (Centers for Disease Control, 1996). Asthma is often diagnosed in early childhood. The prevalence rate of asthma in the pediatric population is estimated at about 7% in the United States, a rate that is increasing more rapidly than for the entire population (Centers for Disease Control, 1996; Evans, 1993). Prevalence rates among children vary according to their age. Stempel and his colleagues (1996) reported prevalence rates were highest for boys between birth and 6 years (6.9%) and for girls aged 13 to 18 years (5.1%).

Racial and gender differences for asthma are notable. Both Black and Hispanic populations in the United States have a higher prevalence of asthma than do Whites (Coultas et al., 1993; Evans, 1993). Coultas and coworkers (1993) derived an odds of asthma occurrence of 2.5 : 1 comparing Black to White children. The Centers for Disease Control (1992) reported the prevalence rate for Black females increased 45% between 1981 and 1988; the annual prevalence rate for White females increased by 63% over the same period.

Management of Asthma

Characteristics of asthma create a template that serves to guide the diagnosis, management, and prevention of the disorder. The result has been a fundamental shift in the way asthma is treated. There has been a movement away from a physician-dominated model toward an interdisciplinary model that blends the expertise of medical and behavioral scientists with that of patients. Several factors have prompted this change, including the need for patients to change their environment to prevent and to manage asthma, the need for greater involvement by patients in recognizing stimuli that trigger their asthma attacks and in reacting quickly to early warning signals of these exacerbations, and in improving patient adherence to medication instructions. The latter, in particular, requires greater self-monitoring and improved decision making on the part of patients. Asthma medications are categorized into two general classes: long-term control drugs used to achieve and maintain control of persistent asthma, and quick-relief medications used to treat acute symptoms of asthma. These drugs are mutually exclusive: while controller medications may prevent attacks, they cannot reduce the symptoms of an acute attack. Quick-relief drugs can help reduce the symptoms of asthma, but they do not prevent attacks.

The expanded role of behavioral scientists in an interdisciplinary model of asthma management was recognized by both Expert Panel Reports (1991, 1997). The Expert Panel Report (1997) recommended self-management training for all asthma patients, beginning with their diagnosis, and emphasized that such training be integrated into every step of clinical asthma care. The report recommends that all members of the health-care team should, at every opportunity, teach and reinforce such self-management skills as developing treatment goals; self-monitoring; deciding when and where to take action; action skills, such as medication compliance and initiating environmental control measures; and reviewing and adjusting treatment as needed. Indeed, a number of asthma self-management programs have demonstrated that achieving an active partnership with their physician can produce significant improvements for patients, including their knowledge about asthma, performance of self-management skills, medication compliance, self-efficacy, and quality of life. These changes have been accompanied by reductions in frequency of attacks, decreases in hospitalizations and ER visits for asthma, increased school and work attendance, improved medication use, and reduced costs for asthma (Wigal, Creer, Kotses, & Lewis, 1990). Evidence that these outcomes may be maintained for five years or longer after self-management training (Creer & Levstek, 1998) suggests an even larger role for behavioral scientists in helping to control asthma in the future.

Bibliography

Centers for Disease Control. (1992). Asthma—United States, 1980–1990. *Morbidity and Mortality Weekly Report, 41,* 733–735.

Centers for Disease Control. (1996). Asthma mortality and hospitalization among children and young adults—United States, 1980–1993. *Morbidity and Mortality Weekly Reports, 45,* 350–353.

Coultas, D. B., Gong, H., Grad, R., Handler, A., McCurdy, S. A., Player, R., Rhoades, E. R., Samet, J. M., Thomas, A., & Westley, M. (1993). Respiratory diseases in minorities of the United States. *American Journal of Respiratory and Critical Care Medicine, 149,* S93–S131.

Creer, T. L., & Levstek, D. A. (1998). Respiratory disorders. In A. Bellack & M. Herson (Eds.), *Comprehensive clinical psychology* (pp. 339–359). Oxford, UK: Elsevier Science.

Evans, R., III (1993). Epidemiology and natural history of asthma, allergic rhinitis, and atopic dermatitis. In E. Middleton, Jr., C. E. Reed, E. F. Ellis, N. F. Adkinson, Jr., J. W. Yunginger, & W. W. Busse (Eds.), *Allergy: Principles and practice* (4th ed., pp. 1109–1136). St. Louis: Mosby.

McFadden, E. R., Jr., & Stevens, J. B. (1983). A history of asthma. In E. Middleton, Jr., C. E. Reed, & E. F. Ellis (Eds.), *Allergy: Principles and practice* (2nd ed, pp. 805–809). St. Louis: C. V. Mosby.

National Asthma Education Program. (1991). *Expert Panel Executive Summary: Guidelines for the diagnosis and management of asthma* (Publication No. 91-3042A). Washington, DC: U.S. Department of Health and Human Services.

National Asthma Education and Prevention Program. (1997). *Highlights of the Expert Panel Report 2: Guidelines for the diagnosis and management of asthma* (Publication No. 97-4051A). Washington, DC: U.S. Department of Health and Human Services.

Spector, S. L., & Nicklas, R. A. (Eds.). (1995). Practice parameters for the diagnosis and treatment of asthma. *Journal of Allergy and Clinical Immunology, 96,* 707–870.

Stempel, D. A., Hedbloom, E. C., Durcanin-Robbins, J F, & Sturm, L. L. (1996). Use of a pharmacy and medical claims database to document cost centers for 1993 annual asthma expenditures. *Archives of Family Medicine, 5,* 36–40.

Wigal, J. K., Creer, T. L., Kotses, H., & Lewis, P. D. (1990). A critique of 19 self-management programs for childhood asthma. Part I. The development and evaluation of the programs. *Pediatric Asthma, Allergy, and Immunology, 4,* 17–39.

Thomas L. Creer

ATHLETES. In early Greek and Roman times, an athlete was a person who competed for prize money. While the term is used more generally today to describe sport participants, it does connote performers possessing superior skills and physical capacities. Concern about mental abilities has placed the study of athletes as a central concern in sport psychology. Researchers interested in understanding the development of exceptional athletes have also followed the main currents of mainstream psychology. Thus, the issues of giftedness, childhood rearing, and pedagogical nurturing, which had earlier been considered in terms of scholastic ability, have been more recently considered in the terms of ability in sport.

Personality

The pioneer research on intelligence testing of Lewis Madison Terman (1877–1956) (*The Gifted Child Grows Up*, Stanford, CA, 1947), predated comparable personality research on athletes by almost 20 years (e.g., Oglivie & Tutko, 1966). [*See the biography of Terman.*] During the 1970s there was extensive study of personality profiles of male athletes versus male nonathletes, and between athletes from different sports. While certain characteristics such as hardiness, competitiveness, emotional stability, and tough mindedness have been shown to differentiate some athletic populations from nonathletes, Vealey (1992) concluded that "there are no consistent research findings showing that athletes possess a general personality type distinct from the personality of nonathletes" (p. 50). Similar research has been conducted on female athletes and nonathletes with no general athletic profiles emerging. However, profiles of female athletes are more similar to those of male athletes than to those of female nonathletes.

Related to the early work on personality profiling of athletes is the research on single constructs such as anxiety and self-confidence. Spielberger (1972) distinguished between two forms of anxiety, trait anxiety, or a general predisposition to experience apprehension in a variety of relatively unthreatening situations, and state anxiety, or feelings of anxiety in specific threatening situations. Martens, Vealey, and Burton (1990) argued that state anxiety was a better predictor of athletic performance, and the Competitive State Anxiety Inventory (CSAI-2) was created with three subscales: cognitive anxiety, somatic anxiety, and self-confidence. Cognitive anxiety referred to worry and fear of failure, while somatic anxiety concerned athletes' perceptions of their physiological reactions to stressful situations. In general, cognitive anxiety and self-confidence were best predicted by athletes' perceived readiness to perform and their years of experience, while the specific nature of certain stressful situations was related to state anxiety. Female athletes' cognitive anxiety was more related to their readiness to perform and to do well on process-centered perceptions or task orientation. Males' cognitive anxiety was related to the relative skill levels of their opponents and the probability of winning ego orientation, or concerning one's self on the outcome of winning (Hardy, Jones, & Gould, 1996). While stable personality traits have not effectively differentiated successful athletes from lesser performers, the profile of mood states has been used to consistently predict successful performances in specific sport situations. Typically, successful performers show the "iceberg profile" of a high level of vigor and low levels of tension, depression, anger, fatigue, and confusion (Weinberg & Gould, 1995).

Athlete Development

The argument of whether athletes are born or made is leaning toward an environmental perspective based on Bloom's ecological research (1985) and Ericsson's cognitive research (1996). Bloom interviewed 120 world experts in science, the arts, and sport, as well as their parents and teachers or coaches. Obviously, these exceptional performers in sport reached the pinnacle of their careers at a much younger age than those in the arts and sciences. He was able to show how a delicate interplay between the athletes, their parents, and coaches existed at three different phases of their athletic careers. As the athletes passed through each stage, their attitudes, activity patterns, and goals delicately interacted in a predictable manner with those of their parents and various coaches.

The Swedish cognitive psychologist K. Anders Ericsson (1996) has pointed out that the acquisition and maintenance of exceptional performance by athletes has paralleled the development of other gifted amateurs in chess, music, medicine, and the arts. Within a developmental framework, Ericsson has shown that successful performers carried out significantly more "deliberate practice," or effortful practice with the intent of improving current performance, than less successful performers, and that musicians and others shared this characteristic with athletes. The fact that these exceptional performers did not excel with laboratory tasks that supposedly measured innate capacities led him to conclude that exceptional performance was driven by environmental rather than innate biological factors. The main constraints which limited deliberate practice were those of effort, motivation, and human and physical resources. Aside from any innate predispositions which athletes may possess, Bloom points out that parents and coaches are central agents in the development of exceptional performance in sport.

American sociologist Jay Coakley (1992), has shown that the sport culture and subcultures have their specific values, beliefs, and attitudes, and that children who successfully internalize these dimensions become socialized into the sport culture, as a precursor to success. One of the most powerful socializing agents is the family, especially the parents, with the fathers having an especially strong influence and siblings less influence. It has been shown that parents play crucial roles with developing athletes during the experimentation, specialization, and investment years of their youth. During the adolescent years, athletes' peers and coaches also act as significant agents for both boys and girls in sport.

The passion, knowledge, and skills of trained coaches have been shown to be major factors in shaping the learning environment of athletes by judiciously establishing a vision, creating and monitoring achievement goals, and facilitating the acquisition and maintenance of exceptional performance in training and competition by removing the constraints which limit deliberate practice (Weinberg & Gould, 1995).

Participation Motives

Despite these powerful external forces acting on athletes, it is clear that the environment must be well matched with athletes' individual aspirations and motivational profiles. Research on athletes' decisions to be involved in sport reveals that there are a number of motives for participating either alone or in combination. Gill, Gross, and Huddleson (1983) have developed a Participation Motivation Inventory in which the dimensions of skill development, team affiliation, fun, achievement-status, friendship, energy release, fitness, and situational factors have been outlined. The presence or absence of these factors is believed to determine whether athletes participate further or drop out of sport.

Both skill development and need for achievement have been shown to be important motives for certain children who wish to improve their skills and reach superior performance levels. Susan Harter's competence motivation theory is especially useful in studying successful athletes. They participate in sports more than nonathletes because success in sport enhances perceived control, positive emotional reactions, and self-worth (Weiss, 1987). Thus, participation in activities in which athletes can demonstrate competence improves their self-image. This is even more pronounced in complex, interactive team sports, while activities which do not require high levels of skill, such as speed walking, also contribute to the fitness motive by providing health benefits, such as weight loss, which, in turn, enhances self-image. The Sport Orientation Questionnaire has been used to assess achievement of athletes in regard to competitiveness, desire to win, and desire to attain goals (Duda, 1993).

The need to be part of a social group, whether formal or informal, has also been shown to be a strong motive for participation, especially during adolescence when the search for identity is paramount. Affiliation is especially strong within local subcultures where membership is readily identified for both males and females since sport participation provides a sense of belonging with significant peers (Coakley, 1992).

The pleasure of engaging is sport is another prime motive for athletes of all ages. While it has been shown that having fun is a central concern for children in sport, this also has been shown to be an important motive for Olympic and professional athletes (Orlick & Partington, 1988). The three most powerful predictors of fun for young competitive athletes were their postgame emotional reactions, perceptions of competence during the game, and the difficulty of the challenge. The Physical Activity Enjoyment scale was designed to assess the level of fun of athletes and nonathletes.

Athletes participate in certain activities since they provide a form of cathartic energy release once the activity is over or a heightened sense of euphoric stress, or eustress, that accompanies participation in exciting or even dangerous activities as witnessed by high risk "extreme" or X-sports such as parachute surfing and skateboarding. A Sensation Seeking scale was developed to assess individuals who are attracted to eustress activities (Weinberg & Gould, 1995).

Mental Skills

Professional athletes in the major sports are often the individuals who come to mind when the word *athlete* is used. Exceptional athletes' mental skills sometimes pay an even greater role than physical prowess in their success (Orlick, 1986). There is also a growing consensus on the fundamental components that athletes must enhance to reach the highest performance levels. A differentiation will be made between the traitlike predispositions discussed earlier under personality, and the learning of various acquired mental skills with sufficient practice and experience. Some elements necessary for optimal preparation of athletes are traitlike and relatively stable, while other mental skills must be learned in the same manner as physical skills. Vealey (1988) referred to the basic attribute of volition, self-awareness, self-esteem, and self-confidence as being foundation skills, and control of attention and physical and mental arousal as being performance skills.

Foundation Skills. Central to the attainment of exceptional athletic performance are a number of fundamental characteristics that relate to an athlete's motivation in pursuing the highest levels of attainment over at least a 10-year period of grueling, deliberate practice.

Motivation. Exceptional performance in sport is culturally linked to the specific values and opportunities provided by each society (e.g., rugby in New Zealand, soccer in Brazil, football in the United States, or ice hockey in Canada). It is believed that these motivational states and goal orientations are more the result of environmental shaping than due to innate characteristics (Ericsson, 1996).

While a variety of factors incite athletes to participate in sport, it is clear that both intrinsic and extrinsic motivation play significant roles for elite athletes at different stages of their careers. Bloom (1985) has shown that intrinsic factors such as fun, discovery, and perceived competence are necessary for young athletes to continue long enough in sport to develop a love of, or to be "hooked" by the game. The intrinsic joy of sport can indeed be undermined when extrinsic rewards are introduced, such as money or trophies, when these extrinsic rewards are perceived by young athletes as bribes rather than rewards. Athletes may subsequently abandon an inherently interesting activity if the rewards are later taken away. In the same manner, it is clear that substantial intrinsic motivation is necessary to carry an individual over the long periods of training for exceptional athletic performance, even when the extrinsic rewards of status and wealth are at the end of the journey.

The work of Deci and Ryan (1985) on cognitive evaluation theory has shown that specific events will predict increases in intrinsic motivation if they lead to improving performers' perceptions of increased personal competence and control. Personal competence is increased by praise and recognition of parents, peers, and coaches, while the personal control, or self-determination, must be felt by athletes in terms of their own personal successes. Thus, process or task-centered goals which relate to the means of achieving long-term outcomes tend to allow athletes to perceive both greater competence and control. Focusing only upon winning, given the inherent instability of competition in sport, can decrease intrinsic motivation (Burton, 1993).

Goals. The work of Joan Duda (1993), a sport psychology researcher, has permitted the measurement of athletes' goal orientation with the Task and Ego Sport Orientation questionnaire in relation to the levels of perceived competence in different athletic populations. It has been shown that individuals who have low self-perceptions and an ego orientation toward the outcome will demonstrate low levels of effort control, low self-efficacy, and high anxiety. However, superior athletes who have high perceived ability would probably benefit from a blend of ego orientation for their long-term goals (i.e., winning the gold) and task orientation (deliberate practice on performance details) to attain exceptional performance.

Ecologically based research on Olympic athletes (Orlick & Partington, 1988) demonstrates that Olympic medal winners have shown the ability to establish dream and long-term ego orientations, as well as daily, specific process goals. A number of researchers in sport psychology have conceptualized the relation of these core or foundation skills as being central to the development of exceptional athletic performance (Hardy et al., 1996; Orlick, 1986; Vealey, 1988). These central constructs have included the overlapping and interactive terms of goal-setting, desire, competitiveness, commitment, belief, and self-confidence. Comprehensive measurement instruments for assessing these core skills as well as peripheral mental skills have been elaborated (Hardy et al., 1996).

Performance Skills. Mental skills important to the development of exceptional athletic performance involve an athlete's ability to control both thoughts and emotions.

William James (1890) wrote: "Everyone knows what attention is. It is taking possession of the mind, in clear and vivid form, of one out of what seem several simultaneously possible objects or trains of thought" (pp. 403–404). In that attention is central to most learning, it is not surprising that attention control, or focusing, is a common attribute associated with exceptional athletic performance. Robert Nideffer (1976), an American psychologist, developed the concept of attentional styles, by which individuals tended to fall within one of four attentional quadrants depending on the locus of attention (internal or external) or its breadth (broad or narrow). Individuals who were broad-external, for example, would be apt at reacting to complex sport environments, such as a quarterback in football, while external-narrow individuals would be more suited to aiming tasks, such as pistol shooting. Skilled performers have been shown to demonstrate the ability to switch their attention to various features, both of the environment and their thought processes. Stress was believed to first decrease attentional flexibility, then progressively narrow and internalize it.

The maintenance of attention has also been studied in activities which take place over extended periods. Successful marathon racers use an associative focus by attending to cues from their bodies during the race, while less successful runners used a dissociative strategy to block out or distract themselves from both the pain and negative thoughts. Orlick (1986) introduced the concept of refocusing, or bringing one's attention back to the relevant cues once distraction had occurred, as being a crucial performance enhancement skill for athletes.

Control of arousal is central to successful athletic performance, not only because of its effects on focusing, but also because of its direct effects on physical performance. Physical arousal, or the elevation of bodily activity, is measured by increases in physiological parameters such as heart rate or muscle tension. Typically, using a unidimensional view of physical arousal, athletes perform best with an optimal level of arousal that is specific for any given sport task. Arousal states that are too low or too high produce inferior results, as is represented in the inverted ∪ hypothesis, which shows a curvilinear relationship between performance and stress by which there is an appropriate level of stress for maximal performance in each activity. Tasks which require high levels of exertion and are relatively simple, for example, shot putting, can be performed at high levels of arousal, while more refined activities, such as archery, require low levels of arousal.

More recently, arousal has also be shown to have a cognitive component or what Vealey (1988) called mental arousal, or feelings of apprehension or worry. Martens, Vealey, and Burton (1990) have shown that levels of state anxiety were preceded by an athlete's expectation of success. Lew Hardy proposed a multidimensional catastrophe model of anxiety and performance in which performers who had low levels of mental anxiety would perform in accordance with the inverted U hypothesis. However, if the levels of mental or cognitive anxiety increased along with increases in physical anxiety, there was a point beyond which performance deteriorated catastrophically (Hardy et al., 1996).

John Kerr (1989) has also demonstrated that an athlete's interpretation of the state of high anxiety could be changed to one of excitement, or boredom could be changed to relaxation, in an adaptation of Apter's (1982) reversal theory. Thus not only do successful athletes modulate their attentional focus, they also develop necessary skills for the reinterpretation of states of anxiety. The final adjustments build upon the athlete's psychological core that has been shaped by a necessary foundation of socialization, coaching, training, and performance skills (Hardy et al., 1996).

[See also Achievement Motivation; Athletic Coaching; Body Image; Cooperation and Competition; Leadership; Self-Concept and Self-Representation; Self-Efficacy; Self-Esteem; and Training.]

Bibliography

Apter, M. J. (1982). The experience of motivation: The theory of psychological reversals. London: Academic Press.

Bloom, B. S. (1985). Developing talent in young people. New York: Ballantine. Provides a holistic overview of exceptional tennis players and swimmers based upon retrospective reports of the athletes, their coaches, and parents.

Burton, D. (1993). Goal-setting in sport. In R. N. Singer, M. Murphy, & L. K. Tennant (Eds.), Handbook of research on sport psychology (pp. 467–491). New York: Macmillan.

Coakley, V. (1992). Sport in society: Issues and controversies (4th ed.). St. Louis: Mosby. Reviews broad issues regarding women and Blacks in sport, aggression, overcompetitiveness, and abuses in professional and youth sport.

Deci, E. L., & Ryan, R. M. (1985). Intrinsic motivation and self-determination in human behavior. New York: Plenum Press.

Duda, J. L. (1993). Goals: A socio-cognitive approach to the study of achievement motivation in sport. In R. N. Singer, M. Murphy, & L. K. Tennant (Eds.), Handbook of research on sport psychology (pp. 421–436). New York: Macmillan.

Ericsson, K. A. (1996). The acquisition of expert performance: An introduction to some of the issues. In K. A. Ericsson (Ed.), The road to excellence: The acquisition of expert performance in the arts and sciences, sports and games (pp. 1–50). Mahwah, NJ: Erlbaum. Takes a somewhat radical stance regarding the role of extensive, effortful practice as being the prime determinant of exceptional performance in any achievement domain, rather than innate abilities or talent.

Gill, D. L., Gross, J. B., & Huddleson, S. (1983). Participation motivation in youth sports. International Journal of Sport Psychology, 14, 1–14.

Hardy, L., Jones, G., & Gould, D. (1996). Understanding psychological preparation for sport: Theory and practice of elite performers. Chichester, UK: Wiley. Provides a sound theoretical and practical guide to the development of psychological skills for sport.

James, W. (1890). Principles of psychology. New York: Holt.

Kerr, J. H. (1989). Anxiety, arousal, and sport performance: An application of reversal theory. In D. Hackfort & C. D. Spielberger (Eds.), Anxiety in sport: An international perspective (pp. 137–151). Washington, DC: Hemisphere.

Martens, R., Vealey, R. S., & Burton, D. (1990). Competitive anxiety in sport. Champaign, IL: Human Kinetics.

Nideffer, R. M. (1976) Test of attentional and interpersonal style. Journal of Personality and Social Psychology, 34, 394–404.

Nideffer, R. N. (1990). Use of test of attentional and interpersonal style in sport. The Sport Psychologist, 4, 285–300.

Ogilvie, B. C., & Tutko, T. A. (1966). Problem athletes and how to handle them, London: Pelham. One of the pioneering books in applied sport psychology with a clinical orientation toward problem athletes.

Orlick, T. (1986). Psyching for sport: Mental training for athletes. Champaign, IL: Human Kinetics

Orlick, T. & Partington, J. (1988). Psyched: Inner views of winning. Ottawa, Canada: Coaching Association of Canada. Provides insights from Olympic medal winners on the preparation strategies and mental skills used at the highest levels of competition.

Singer, R. N., Murphy, M., & Tennant, L. K. (Eds.), Handbook of research on sport psychology. New York: Macmillan. The most comprehensive, research based text in sport psychology which is directed to students at the graduate level and serious academics interested in the study of athletes.

Spielberger, C. D. (1972). Anxiety as an emotional state. In C. D. Spielberger (Ed.), Anxiety: Current trends in theory and research (Vol. 1, pp. 23–49). New York: Academic Press.

Vealey, R. S. (1988). Future directions in psychological skills training. The Sport Psychologist, 2, 318–336.

Vealey, R. S. (1992). Personality in sport: A comprehensive view. In T. S. Horn (Ed.), Advances in sport psychology (pp. 25–59). Champaign, IL: Human Kinetics.

Weinberg, R. S., & Gould, D. (1995). Foundations of sport and exercise psychology. Champaign, IL: Human Kinetics. Provides a very comprehensive but accessible overview of issues related to sport psychology in general, and athletes in particular.

Weiss, M. R. (1987). Self-esteem and achievement in children's sport and physical activity. In D. Gould & M. R.

Weiss (Eds.), *Advances in pediatric sport sciences* (Vol. 2, pp. 87–119). Champaign, IL: Human Kinetics.

John H. Salmela

ATHLETIC COACHING is involved with competitive physical activities. To prepare individuals to compete a coach should attempt to develop the nature (form/technique and scope/repertoire), quality (normally an increase in behavioral effects), and quantity (an increase in volume and consistency) of relevant sporting behaviors. Sporting environments include a diverse range of performance standards (young age-group activities to professional championships) and activity components (Ultraman triathlon to target sports such as prone rifle shooting). Sporting performances involve metabolic, skilled, and mental activities. Metabolic states can be altered through physical conditioning and skill levels through changes in movement economy, usually by employing better mechanical elements in movements. Changes are best achieved under appropriate psychological conditions (e.g., positive feedback, performance progress, athlete self-control). While psychological factors determine effective use of trained skill and physical states in many sports, as fitness components become less important, such as in archery, psychological factors increase in importance.

Problems with conditioning ("overreaching," "overtraining"), skill ("loss of feeling," imprecision), and deterioration in performance are manifested behaviorally ("negative attitudes," "loss of motivation") in athletes. A major difficulty in the psychology of coaching is determining true psychological problems as opposed to expressions of symptoms derived from other performance capacities. To treat all abnormal "sport-psychological" behaviors in athletes without contemplating their causes often results in failures to solve problems and consequently, undermines a coach's credibility.

Rushall and Siedentop (1972) first proposed that coaching effectiveness was governed by the applications of principles of applied behavior analysis. The tenets advocated have since been fully supported by substantive research and represent the most fruitful avenue for investigating and describing athletic coaching.

Behavioral coaching emphasizes specific, detailed, and frequent measurement of athletic performance and/or behaviors and uses those measures as the primary means for evaluating the effectiveness of specific coaching techniques. It recognizes that some already developed behaviors need to be maintained while others need to be developed further or changed. The evaluation of behavior change is usually focused on each athlete's progressive analyses. Athletes and coaches are encouraged to improve on the previous assessment when pursuing change. Behavioral coaching is predominantly limited to using techniques that have been validated as being effective. Effective coaching focuses on the behavior of the coach rather than vague descriptions of "personality traits," "types," or "characteristics" of coaches. It also requires social validation by the athlete and the related family or organization.

Martin and Hrycaiko (1983) provided extensive examples of behavior modification techniques for changing aspects of athletes' performance and behaviors. Techniques included task analysis, positive reinforcement, goal setting, publicly posted feedback, and motivational procedures as well as cognitive techniques for controlling anxiety and self-modifying behavior. Their work demonstrated common techniques that are applicable and successful in sports. It represents an alternative approach to coaching: successful coaching is the adaptation of acknowledged general behavioral techniques associated with behavior change and maintenance to specific sport situations. Martin and Lumsden (1987) then provided the "manual" for behavioral coaching that is structured by tasks and problem classifications of events which occur in athletic settings. Adopting behavioral and cognitive-behavioral techniques for solving particular problems or programs of explicit change or development can increase coaching effectiveness.

Much folklore surrounding coaching has resulted from an absence of definitive studies. The behavioral approach has described what coaches have to do to be effective. Only recently have assessment formats been described that allow reliable and valid observations of coaching behaviors. Rushall's Practice Session Coaching Performance Assessment Form (PSCPAF) is a self-assessment schedule containing activities designed to yield an enjoyable and successful experience for athletes as well as produce obvious changes in performance and behaviors. Effective coaching is also dependent upon athletes' perceptions. The Coach Evaluation Questionnaire (CEQ) allows athletes to rate a coach on 36 items of "good coaching." This valid and reliable instrument provides feedback for coaches about how well they do in important facets of coaching from their athletes' viewpoint. The CEQ is completed anonymously by athletes with a particular coach in mind. To be deemed "effective" it is proposed that a coach's conduct should admirably fulfill as many of the CEQ items as possible. The contents of valid and reliable coaching assessment tools provide a definition of the expectations for what a coach should do and how those expectations are fulfilled in the opinions of clients (athletes).

Attempts have been made to describe "types" of coaches who have distinctive modes of behavior. Gallon

(1989) listed six categories: authoritarian, "nice-guy," intense, easygoing, businesslike, and creative. Daly and Parkin (1991) only classified three: dominating, personable, and casual. Daly and Parkin also listed characteristics of a respected coach: intelligence, drive, persistence, patience, enthusiasm, knowledge, conscientiousness, confidence, emotional stability, decisiveness, character, organization, preparation, and sense of humor. While these classifications might seem impressive they are not usually backed by substantive research to establish their validity. These general labels have little value other than for description and focusing attention on the originators' opinions. Descriptive lists proposing a singular model for coaching are frequently used to introduce texts that serve as the central information source for educating coaches in national accreditation schemes, particularly in the area of "general" coaching theory.

Within coaching there are a number of subcultures. There are sport-specific modes of behavior that are expected of coaches. Swimming coaches are dominantly negative and wary of parental involvement; basketball coaches are intolerant of player errors; and high school coaches wear a cap, uniform, carry a clipboard, and have a whistle close at hand. The incongruity of coaches wearing expensive suits to participate in a game is something generally accepted in the college and professional basketball and ice hockey ranks. These specific features are minor trappings but seem to be expected within a particular sport. Rushall (1985) described the use of the Coach Observation Schedule (COS) to systematically observe convenient samples of coaches in a number of sporting environments. The behaviors of coaches in women's volleyball, men's and women's basketball, ice hockey, swimming, and physical education were compared. It was concluded that "since the behaviors of coaches varied so much between sports, coach education schemes should alter their singular focus of developing all coaches through the same medium and adapt the content and emphases to the needs of those involved in each sport" (p. 299). Attempts to develop a particular type of coach with certain characteristics for all sports seem to be unjustified. Important coaching behaviors and knowledge are specific to each particular sport whereas interpersonal and organization skills may be common to most sports. Within any sport there is a greater diversity of coach and athlete personality types than between sports. Coaches are not discriminated between sports based on personality traits or general characteristics.

Another source of knowledge about coaching consists of detailed personal opinions, for example, Nakamura (1996). Books often contain recollections of valid experiences that were "effective." They are frequently used as the basis for invalid generalization to all coach-

ing situations. Often a useful source of anecdotal suggestions, these types of books and presentations are not substantive scientific data for a disciplined description of athletic coaching.

Some important coaching generalizations have evolved despite there having been a considerable number of factors investigated but many with insufficient depth or replication to form reliable generalizations. Although athletes are not differentiated between sports on the basis of personality there are gender differences that are consistent across sports. Female skiers require different coaching strategies and handling procedures than do males, as do swimmers, rowers, volleyball players, and indeed every sport. That gender differences exist in sport psychology should not be surprising for they also exist in physiology and levels of skill precision. A lack of awareness of this requirement probably stems from an overwhelming majority of studies involving only male coaches and a frequent failure to compare subgroups of athletes based on gender. Little is known about female coaches, particularly whether their behavior is different from that of male coaches in any definitive way.

Individual and team sports have commonly been distinguished in the literature. Results have generally shown neither coaches nor athletes differ between the two classifications. Other social forces, rather than personality or characteristics, direct participation into particular sports.

To date, no sport-specific personalities have been identified among athletes. Environments and gender are better discriminated by psychological tests than is sport participation. Thus, to be successful a coach's interpersonal skills have to be extensive to accommodate diversity among athletes.

Coaching roles and behaviors vary depending upon the group. It is known that the desired experiences of children in their first year of consistent participation are different from those in subsequent sets of years as maturity advances through puberty, early and late adolescence, adulthood, and finally masters' participation. Successful coaches should align program content and handling procedures with the developmental needs of particular athletes. Treating children as "young adults" is a common flaw in unsuccessful coaches and an example of an inappropriate interactional strategy for a particular development level of athlete.

A feature of coaching that is rarely questioned is a coach's knowledge of athletes in a squad. Henn (1996) showed that one of every two coaches could not accurately predict athletes' opinions of them. Among those who could not, the majority of male coaches exaggerated athletes' assessments while females were evenly divided between over- and underestimations. It is the individual nature of each athlete that must be accommodated by a coach. When that is recognized and provided, the possibility of individual athlete improvements in sport participation and performance are possible.

Coaching is subjected to many of the demands and expectations of any profession. Performance is evaluated, organizational and communication skills are essential, and knowledge of athlete performance modifiers other than psychology is required. Stress is part of the conditions of employment. Society at large generally evaluates coaching effectiveness on the basis of win-loss records or the highest achievements of individual athletes. As with most professions, performance is evaluated by the behaviors of clients (athletes). Without direct control in competitive settings, a considerable amount of a coach's accountability is in the hands of athletes and their performances. Sports are particularly public affairs. Athletes' achievements are outcomes that can be known by everyone. Since sports are also competitive, a coach's performance is compared to that of other coaches, an evaluation that does not exist in most other professions. That heightened public awareness and critical evaluation increases job stress in coaching, the severity of criticism increasing with the standard of competition. Syndromes such as burnout, withdrawal, and denial, are frequently witnessed in coaching as consequences of these stresses and stress levels.

Present research is inadequate to explicitly determine what are the necessary and sufficient features of effective athletic coaching. Appropriate techniques of behavior change and maintenance exist and have been shown to be valid for use in sport settings. Although pure "how-to-do-it" prescriptions are useful, they are insufficient to determine goals, philosophies, and standards to be obtained. So a full psychological description of an effective athletic coach does not yet exist. When that definition becomes available it will very likely show that a coach cannot and should not emphasize one area of sport science in program content. Effective athletic coaching will involve an integration of psychological, physiological, and biomechanical principles and their application to the needs of each athlete.

[See also Athletes; Cooperation and Competition; Leadership; and Training.]

Bibliography

Daly, J. A., & Parkin, D. A. (1991). The role of the coach. In F. S. Pyke (Ed.), *Better coaching* (pp. 3–14). Canberra, Australia: Australian Coaching Council. The introductory chapter in the text assigned for the level II coaching accreditation course in the Australian Coaching Council's education program.

Gallon, A. J. (1989). *Coaching ideas and ideals* (2nd ed., pp. 19–22). Prospect Heights, IL: Waveland. One of the more traditional books, it is mainly concerned with organizational factors in coaching.

Henn, J. C. (1996). *A comparison of coach and athlete opinions of coaching.* Unpublished master's thesis, San Diego State University, San Diego, California. A research project assessing athletes' and coaches' perceptions of each other.

Martin, G. L., & Hrycaiko, D. (Eds.). (1983). *Behavior modification and coaching: Principles, procedures, and research.* Springfield, IL: Charles C. Thomas. An edited volume of research articles demonstrating the efficacy of behavioral coaching.

Martin, G. L., & Lumsden, J. A. (1987). *Coaching: An effective behavioral approach.* St. Louis, MO: Times Mirror/ Mosby. A full description of the behavioral concepts, applications, and "how-to-do-its" of effective coaching.

Nakamura, R. A (1996). *The power of positive coaching.* Boston: Jones & Bartlett. A personal view of coaching responsibilities and tactics.

Rushall, B. S. (1985). Coaching styles: A preliminary investigation. In G. L. Marlin & D. Hrycaiko (Eds.), *Behavior modification and coaching* (pp. 299–320). Springfield, IL: Charles C. Thomas.

Rushall, B. S. (1994). *The assessment of coaching effectiveness: A manual for coaches.* (Available from Sports Science Associates, 4225 Orchard Drive, Spring Valley, CA 91977). How to use and score the Practice Session Coaching Performance Assessment Form, the Coach Observation Schedule, and the Coach Evaluation Questionnaire.

Rushall, B. S., & Siedentop, D. (1972). *The development and control of behavior in sport and physical education.* Philadelphia: Lea & Febiger. An in-depth description of the elements of behavior modification and how they could be implemented in sport and physical education settings.

Brent S. Rushall

ATTACHMENT. The development of attachment relationships between children and parents constitutes one of the most important aspects of development. Although most major theories of socioemotional development have contributed to our understanding of parent-child attachment, the most popular explanation of the processes involved was provided by John Bowlby (1969). Bowlby, a psychoanalyst who was much impressed by ethological theories explaining the emotional communication between nonhuman infants and their parents, believed that infants had an innate capacity to emit signals to which adults were biologically predisposed to respond. He began with the assumption that, during the early phases of human evolution, survival depended on the infants' ability to maintain proximity to protective adults. Unlike the young of many other species, however, human infants cannot maintain proximity to adults on their own because they cannot walk or crawl and cannot cling to adults. Instead, human infants rely on signals (like cries and smiles) to entice adults to approach them, and their signals are effective because human adults are predisposed to respond to them. Infants come to focus their bids for attention on a small number of familiar individuals, and the process of attachment formation involves four developmental phases: indiscriminate social responsiveness (first and second months); discriminating sociability (2 to 7 months); maintenance of proximity to a discriminated figure (month seven through the second year); and goal-corrected partnerships (year 3 on).

Phase 1: Indiscriminate Social Responsiveness (First 1 to 2 months)

This phase is marked by the development of a repertoire of signals, of which the cry is most effective. Infant cries have a markedly arousing effect on those who hear them because adults can reliably judge the emotion they convey and are highly motivated to relieve the causes of distress, often by picking up and holding babies when they are distressed. This reaction frequently calms the infants, at least momentarily, and the speed with which adults respond appears to influence the frequency of later crying.

Crying is the first example of a class of behaviors labeled *attachment behaviors* by Bowlby. The defining characteristic of these behaviors is that they provide comfort and security by bringing babies close to protective adults. Smiling is another signal that powerfully affects adult behavior; it enters the baby's repertoire in the second month of life. Smiles encourage adults to stay near the baby in order to prolong rewarding interactions, whereas cries encourage adults to approach in order to terminate signals that they find aversive.

Newborns experience marked, sudden, unpredictable changes in state (levels of arousal and distress) and cannot regulate their states of arousal or coordinate their movements well. Behavior becomes increasingly organized over time as neural control mechanisms develop, however, and the parents' responsiveness plays a major role in helping children gain self regulatory capacities. During the first two months, therefore, caretakers have a major impact on the baby's state of arousal. For example, by picking up distressed infants, parents both soothe them and put them into states of alertness. Because infants can thus feel, smell, hear, and see caretakers who are in close proximity, they learn to associate the presence of their caretakers with alertness and the relief of distress (Lamb & Malkin, 1986).

Distress-relief sequences are not the only contexts in which infants interact with their parents, of course. Parents attempt to capture and maintain their infants' attention in the course of face-to-face play by moving their heads, exaggerating their facial expressions, modulating their vocal intonation, and employing a variety of rhythmic behaviors. Papoušek and Papoušek (1995) have argued that these patterns of behavior and responsiveness constitute biologically "wired" or intuitive parenting practices that are evident the world over. In addition, various caretaking routines, including feeding, provide the context for social interaction. As babies become more vocal, mothers begin to act as if the baby is taking turns, pausing as long as in adult conversations, and listening for an imagined response before they respond (Stern, 1977). This systematic turn-taking alerts the infant to the basic principle of reciprocity, although noted, coordinated reciprocal interaction is not typical.

Frequent interactions between caretakers and alert infants may facilitate the ability to recognize specific individuals. Bowlby suggested that this ability marked the transition to the second phase of attachment development, but later studies showed that infants are able to recognize their parents much earlier than Bowlby believed. For example, young infants appear able to distinguish and prefer their own mother's voice and smell from those of other mothers within the first two weeks of life (Porter, Balogh, & Makin, 1988).

Phase 2: Discriminating Sociability (2 to 7 months)

Presumably because they have been associated with pleasurable experiences and the relief of distress, familiar people like parents become persons with whom babies prefer to interact. Initially, these preferences are evident in fairly subtle ways—certain people are better able than others to soothe the baby or to elicit broad smiles and coos, for example. Parents feel enormously rewarded by this change in the baby's behavior, however, because it signifies the first obvious appreciation of their devoted efforts.

During this phase, behavior becomes increasingly coordinated. There is less variation in levels of arousal, less distress is experienced, more time is spent in alert states, and interactions with adults increasingly involve play. Although face-to-face games with parents initially appear in the first phase, they are most common, at least in Western cultures, between three and six months of age. Although adults assume the major responsibility for keeping interactions going, babies are not simply passive partners in face-to-face games. For example, 2- to 3-month-olds sometimes withdraw when their mothers fail to respond to their signals or bids (Lamb, Morrison, & Malkin, 1987). The infant's behavior in this context appears to reflect "disappointment" or "puzzlement" over the adult's failure to behave appropriately, suggesting that the infant is beginning to comprehend the rules of social interaction. Likewise, the fact that distressed 4-month-old infants protest when adults approach but do not pick them up (Lamb & Malkin, 1986) signals that infants develop clear expectations about the "rules" of these interactions, too. Because instances of well-coordinated reciprocity are actually quite rare, these rules are learned slowly, but babies do appear to learn three things from repeated experiences of distress relief and face-to-face play (Lamb, 1981a). First, they learn the rule of reciprocity—during social interactions, partners take turns acting and reacting. Second, babies learn that they can affect the behavior of others in a consistent and predictable fashion. Third, babies learn trust, because their parents can be counted on to respond when signaled. These lessons signify major transitions in the development of coherent views of the self, of significant others, and of the social world. The degree to which babies feel confident in their predictions regarding the behavior of others (i.e., the degree to which they trust or have faith in the reliability of specific people) may influence the security of their attachment relationships, a topic to which we return later.

Phase 3: Attachments (7 to 24 months)

By 6 or 7 months of age, infants have made great progress in all domains of development. Exploiting their newly acquired mobility, infants begin to take responsibility for attaining proximity to their caretakers instead of waiting for parents to respond to their signals. Because they now understand and respect the rule of reciprocity, intentional social behavior becomes possible. Infants thus play an increasingly active role in interactions with their attachment figures, and initiate an increasing proportion of their social interactions. One sign of this new social sophistication is that 7-month-olds begin to protest more reliably when their parents leave, although they can tolerate growing distances from attachment figures as they grow older and become increasingly adept at interacting with peers and unfamiliar adults. Wariness of strange adults also becomes more prominent around this time, as does the incipient awareness that others have their own "states of mind" (Thompson, 1998).

According to Bowlby (1969) and Ainsworth (1979), infants become attached to those persons who have been associated over time with prompt and appropriate responses to their signals. Most babies in two-parent families may become attached to both of their parents at about the same time, even though they spend much less time with their fathers than with their mothers (Lamb, 1997). Presumably because mothers tend to be the primary care providers, they tend to be the preferred attachment figures of young infants, who seek out their mothers when under stress.

Phase 3 is also marked by a growing awareness that others have their own mental states, and that they can

be useful sources of information. Beginning in this phase, infants use adults' facial and vocal expressions to help evaluate ambiguous events and situations, altering their own emotions and behavior accordingly.

Phase 4: Goal-Corrected Partnerships (24 to 40 months)

The defining feature of this poorly described and little studied phase is the growing ability to recognize that parents have goals and needs independent of the child's. As a result, the child learns to accommodate delays in the adult's responses and alterations in his or her form. These declines in egocentricity are gradual and reflect changes in the child's understanding of both the physical and social world. Joint planning between parents and children becomes increasingly common as children become less egocentric, and thus come to take their parents' feelings, motives, and plans into account, accommodating their parents' plans so as to achieve mutually acceptable compromises. These "partnership" skills may lay the foundation for negotiation in a variety of later relationships. As Thompson (1998) notes, "a new kind of relationship becomes possible that is not merely an extension of the security derived from infant attachment, but broadens to incorporate shared (and potentially conflicting) understandings, attitudes of mutual cooperation and respect, and the growth of new strategies for resolving conflict when it occurs" (p. 73).

Despite these important developments, preschoolers' understanding of the physical and social world remains quite immature (Piaget, 1932/1965), and the tendency to think egocentrically continues to have an important influence on children's sociopersonality development. Young children implicitly assume that others perceive the social world the same way that they do. One implication is that children under about 7 years of age may be limited in the ability to empathize and take the perspectives of others. It is only as children enter the school years that they become fully capable of the metarepresentation that enables them to reflect more competently on their own mental processes, including the thoughts, beliefs, emotions, and other psychological phenomena that influence their behavior (Flavell, Miller, & Miller, 1993).

Individual Differences and Their Implications

Although normative developmental changes characterize the processes of attachment formation, parent-child relationships obviously vary. These individual differences may affect the quality of children's adjustment and later development.

Researchers inspired by the ethological-adaptational theorists have made extensive efforts to explore the origins, characteristics, and consequences of individual differences in infant-parent attachment (e.g., Ainsworth, Blehar, Waters, & Wall, 1978; Thompson, 1998). Instead of focusing on discrete behaviors, these researchers have concentrated on the patterned organization of attachment behavior. Individual differences in attachment behavior are usually assessed using a procedure called the Strange Situation (Ainsworth et al., 1978). This procedure is designed to subject 10- to 24-month-old infants to gradually increasing amounts of stress induced by the strange setting, the entrance of an unfamiliar female, and two brief separations from the parent. According to Ainsworth, stress should increase the infant's desire for proximity to and/or contact with the parent or attachment figure, thus leading to the intensification of attachment behaviors (e.g., crying, approaching, and clinging) which help infants to attain or maintain proximity/contact. As stress increases, infants should reduce their exploration and social interaction (e.g., with strangers) and increasingly organize their behavior around their parents. They should thus exhibit distress when separated from their parents, attempt to search for them, and try to reinitiate interaction when reunited.

When American infants and parents are observed in the Strange Situation, about two thirds behave in the pattern just described, which is termed the secure (or B) pattern because the infant seems to gain security and comfort from the parent to whom it turns in times of stress or alarm. The remainder display one of two types of "insecure" reactions. Typically, around a quarter of them behave in an avoidant (A) fashion—turning away from rather than toward the adult, especially upon reunion, when one would expect proximity-seeking behaviors to be most intense. Another group, the resistant or C group, comprising a little over a tenth of most samples, consists of infants who are unable to use parents as a base for exploration even in the preseparation episodes. These infants behave in an ambivalent fashion upon reunion, both seeking contact and angrily rejecting it when offered. Main and Solomon (1990) have also identified a fourth group of children characterized by disorganized or disoriented (D) behavior in the Strange Situation.

Ainsworth et al. have suggested that these different patterns of behavior in the Strange Situation are the consequences of individual differences in earlier patterns of parent-infant interactions. When parents respond promptly and appropriately, infants develop confidence in their own ability to act upon the environment successfully, and learn that parents will respond to their needs in predictable ways. Adults differ in their sensitivity to infant signals and cues, however, and thus infants should differ in the extent to which they have confidence in their own effectance and in the reliability and predictability of others (Ainsworth et al., 1978). Ainsworth hypothesized that sensitively responsive parents should have babies who behave in the B-type pattern, whereas A- and C-type behaviors would be exhibited by children of insensitively responsive parents.

Many researchers have attempted to replicate Ainsworth's findings, often in naturalistic longitudinal studies like her own. In general, research on the origins of attachment security supports the view that maternal sensitivity in particular, and nurturant, attentive, nonrestrictive parental care in general, foster the development of secure attachments (see de Wolff & van IJzendoorn, 1997; Thompson, 1998, for reviews). Thus, mothers who respond more positively, consistently, and warmly to their infants' signals are more likely to have securely attached infants, whereas major deviations from these behavioral patterns are associated with insecure attachments. However, the reliable associations with parental sensitivity are quite modest (de Wolff & van IJzendoorn, 1997), suggesting that other sources of influence remain to be uncovered. Like many aspects of parental behavior, sensitivity is not always stable over time, furthermore, and appears particularly sensitive to changes in the parents' sociopsychological status and perceptions of stress. In addition, individual differences in the degree of sensitivity manifest in one domain of parenting are often not evident in other domains or contexts.

In an attempt to move beyond the exclusive focus on behavior in the Strange Situation, Waters and Deane (1985) developed a Q-sort procedure for measuring individual differences in the attachment behavior of infants and toddlers. The procedure involved training observers or parents to rate their children's behavior on ninety items which were then combined into a composite assessment of the children's tendencies. Strange Situation- and Q-sort-based classifications are significantly associated (Vaughn & Waters, 1990), and many researchers have been able to explore the origins and consequences of individual differences in attachment security using Q-sort ratings of behavior in the home or day-care center rather than the traditional classifications of Strange Situation behavior (e.g., Waters, Vaughn, Posada, & Kondo-Ikemura 1995).

From an organizational-relational perspective, attachment classifications should predict aspects of children's future behavior and there is some evidence that they do so (Thompson, 1998). Thus, securely attached infants appear to be more cooperatively playful and more sociable when interacting with both their mothers and friendly adult strangers than is the case with avoidant or resistant infants. Strange Situation behavior is also associated with the frequency and quality of interactions with peers such that securely attached infants engage in somewhat more frequent and more mature forms of interaction with their peers, share more, and are better able to initiate and maintain interactions. Other researchers have reported that when kindergarten-aged children are placed in cognitively challenging situations, those who were classified as securely attached in infancy persisted longer and more enthusiastically than did those who behaved insecurely as infants. In addition, securely attached infants were more compliant, exhibited more self-control, and appeared to be more focused on assigned tasks, trying to perform better than insecurely attached infants. Finally, securely attached infants appear more socially competent and independent in preschool, they show fewer behavior problems, and they appear to be more emotionally resilient when stressed or challenged in a variety of situations. Disorganized (D) behavior in the Strange Situation also seems to predict behavior problems later in childhood.

The security of infant-mother and infant-father attachment appears to affect infants' behavior in comparable ways, although the relationship with the primary caretaking parent—typically the mother—appears more important. Children who were securely attached to both parents appear to be more trusting and open with strangers by the time of kindergarten and first grade.

The long-term predictive validity of the Strange Situation classifications is far from perfect, however. First, all of the associations reported in the previous paragraphs appear quite weak and unreliable. Second, researchers have typically failed to demonstrate that the avoidant and resistant patterns of behavior in the Strange Situation have different consequences. Third, the relation between Strange Situation behavior in infancy and subsequent child behavior is found only when there is stability in caretaking arrangements, family circumstances, and patterns of parent-child interaction. This raises a question: Are predictions over time attributable to individual differences in the quality of early parent-child interaction, or is stability in the quality of parent-child interaction more important? Unfortunately, this question has not received much attention, so no definitive conclusion is possible. Nevertheless, it is clear that individual differences in attachment do not single-handedly determine developmental outcomes. Development is multidetermined, and parental sensitivity is but one of the factors affecting Strange Situation behavior, which is in turn one of the factors affecting later functioning.

Internal Working Models

Although most of the research on parent-child attachments has concentrated on relationships between parents and their infants, developmentalists have sought to examine the nature and function of parent-child and parent-adolescent attachment relationships on the assumption that parent-child relationships continue to develop and change in ways that require continued coordination and integration as individuals develop and mature (Greenberg, Cicchetti, & Cummings, 1990; Sroufe, 1988). In much of this research, it has been assumed that, in the course of early interactions, infants and young children construct internal working models which guide their behavior in later relationships. Although internal working models continue to be formed during and after early childhood, maintaining continuity in individual developmental pathways, Bowlby (1973) suggested that there exists wide variation across individuals in the degree to which working models reflect the individual's own experiences, as well as his or her cognitive, linguistic, and behavioral skills.

Internal working models represent children's conceptions of attachment figures as reflected in their interactions and in the feedback they receive from their parents. Working models affect the display of behavior as children grow older, but attachment behavior becomes more subtle with age because older children are more capable of evaluating the intentions, motives, and behaviors of attachment figures.

Main and her colleagues (George, Kaplan, & Main, 1985) have also developed the adult attachment interview (AAI) to assess adults' ability to integrate early memories of their relationships with parents into overarching working models of relationships. According to Main, these working models fall into one of three categories, with adults classified as *autonomous* (free to evaluate their early attachment relationships), *dismissive* of their attachment relationships, or *preoccupied* with their attachment relationships. Autonomous adults appear more sensitively responsive to their infants than are adults in the dismissive and preoccupied groups, and their children are more likely to be securely attached.

Research on the associations between individual internal working models and parent-child relationships suggests that secure children, adolescents, and adults see attachment figures as well as themselves as primarily good, though not perfect, are able to communicate with ease, tend to have flexible interpersonal styles, express empathy for others, and discuss attachment relationships coherently without idealizing them.

[*See also* Attachment Theory.]

Bibliography

Ainsworth, M. D. S. (1979). Attachment as related to mother-infant interaction. In J. S. Rosenblatt, R. A. Hinde, C. Beer, & M. Busnel (Eds.), *Advances in the study of behavior* (Vol. 9, pp. 1–51). New York: Academic Press.

Ainsworth, M. D. S., Blehar, M. C., Waters, E., & Wall, S. (1978). *Patterns of attachment*. Hillsdale, NJ: Erlbaum.

Bowlby, J. (1969). *Attachment and loss: Vol. 1. Attachment.* New York: Basic Books.

Bowlby, J. (1973). *Attachment and loss: Vol. 2. Separation: Anxiety and anger.* New York: Basic Books.

de Wolff, M. S., & Van Ijzendoorn, M. H. (1997). Sensitivity and attachment: A meta-analysis on parental antecedents of infant attachment. *Child Development, 68,* 571–591.

Flavell, J. H., Miller, P. H., & Miller, S. A. (1993). *Cognitive development* (3rd ed.). Engelwood Cliffs, NJ: Prentice Hall.

George, C., Kaplan, N., & Main, M. (1985). *Adult attachment interview.* Unpublished manuscript, University of California, Berkeley.

Greenberg, M. T., Cicchetti, D., & Cummings, E. M. (Eds.) (1990). *Attachment in the preschool years: Theory, research, and intervention.* Chicago, IL: University of Chicago Press.

Lamb, M. E. (1981). Developing trust and perceived effectance in infancy. In L. P. Lipsitt (Ed.), *Advances in infancy research* (Vol. 1, pp. 101–130). Norwood, NJ: Ablex.

Lamb, M. E. (1997). The development of father-infant relationships. In M. E. Lamb (Ed.), *The role of the father in child development* (3rd ed., pp. 104–120). New York: Wiley.

Lamb, M. E., & Malkin, C. M. (1986). The development of social expectations in distress-relief sequences: A longitudinal study. *International Journal of Behavioral Development, 9,* 235–249.

Lamb, M. E., Morrison, D. C., & Malkin, C. M. (1987). The development of infant social experiences in face-to-face interaction. *Merrill-Palmer Quarterly, 33,* 241–254.

Main, M., & Solomon, J. (1990). Procedures for identifying infants as disorganized/disoriented during the Ainsworth Strange Situation. In M. T. Greenberg, D. Cicchetti, & E. M. Cummings (Eds.), *Attachment in the preschool years* (pp. 121–160). Chicago: University of Chicago Press.

Mumme, D., Fernald, A., & Herrera, C. (1996). Infants' responses to facial and vocal emotional signals in a social referencing paradigm. *Child Development, 67,* 3219–3237.

Papoušek, H., & Papoušek, M. (1995). Intuitive parenting. In M. H. Bornstein (Ed.), *Handbook of parenting* (Vol. 2, pp. 117–136). Hillsdale, NJ: Erlbaum.

Piaget, J. (1965). *The moral judgment of the child.* New York: Van Nostrand. (Original work published 1932)

Porter, R. H., Bologh, R. D., & Makin, J. W. (1988). Olfactory influences on mother-infant interactions. In C. Rovee-Collier & L. P. Lipsitt (Eds.), *Advances in infancy research* (Vol. 5, pp. 39–69). Norwood, NJ: Ablex.

Sroufe, L. A. (1988). The role of infant-caregiver attachment in development. In J. Belsky & R. Nezworski (Eds.), *Clinical implications of attachment* (pp. 18–40). Hillsdale, NJ: Erlbaum.

Thompson, R. A. (1998). Early sociopersonality development. In W. Damon & N. Eisenberg (Eds.), *Handbook of child psychology: Vol. 3. Social, emotional, and personality development* (5th ed., pp. 25–104). New York: Wiley.

Vaughn, B. E., & Waters, E. (1990). Attachment behavior at home and in the laboratory: Q-sort observations and Strange Situation classifications of one-year-olds. *Child Development, 61,* 1965–1990.

Waters, E., & Deane, K. E. (1985). Defining and assessing individual differences in attachment relationships: Q-methodology and the organization of behavior in infancy and early childhood. In I. Bretherton & E. Waters (Eds.), Growing points of attachment theory and research. *Monographs of the Society for Research in Child Development, 50* (1/2, Serial No. 209), 41–65.

Waters, E., Vaughn, B. E., Posada, G., & Kondo-Ikemura, K. (Eds.). (1995). Caregiving, cultural, and cognitive perspectives in secure-base behavior and working models. *Monographs of the Society for Research in Child Development, 60* (2–3, Serial No. 244).

Michael E. Lamb

ATTACHMENT THEORY. The developing tendency observed in most 6- to 12-month-old infants to cry when selected important persons depart (especially in unfamiliar settings), to attempt to follow these persons when possible, and to cling to them and otherwise show pleasure upon their return, appears to be relatively universal, and so well known that it is almost taken for granted. It was not until the twentieth century, however, that a number of theories were put forward to attempt to explain these phenomena. Most such theories, at least initially, rested upon the reasonable supposition that the infant's behavior was "learned" or acquired as specific persons became associated with the satisfaction of more basic instincts. Thus, it was assumed that the infant's often highly emotional expression of attachment to parental figures is secondary to a recognition of the parent's role in, feeding, say. These "secondary drive" theories of attachment, popular with learning theorists as well as many analysts, did not consider the infant's survival to be the primary motivational factor in its effort to maintain proximity.

If it were actually the case that early affectional ties are secondary rather than primary, however, the infant should readily accept separation from attachment figures so long as food and other satisfying experiences are appropriately provided by others. Early observations indicated, instead, that caregiving figures are not readily exchangable and that between one and three years of age extended, stressful separations from known persons could have notably unfavorable consequences. As Ainsworth (1969) has noted, these observations were compatible with many later developing "object relations" theories, which often stressed the intrinsic import of the infant's earliest relationships independent of their association with more basic "drives." Object relations theories can, however, still be sharply differentiated from the theory of attachment developed by John Bowlby (below) in that these theories do not consider the infant's concern with maintaining proximity to the parent within the context of natural selection, and hence as tied to safety and survival.

The central formulations of this new approach to understanding the nature of the child's tie to its mother—called "ethological-evolutionary attachment theory"—were developed by the London family psychiatrist and psychoanalyst John Bowlby (1958, 1969, 1973, 1980, 1988) over a period of approximately 30 years. Having already concluded—together with many other clinicians and social workers—that a close, continuous, and mutually satisfying relationship with a mother figure across the first few years of life serves as a foundation to mental health, Bowlby began to search for new explanations of the origin and import of this tie. At this point, his attention was drawn to Konrad Lorenz's work on imprinting, which pointed out that social bond formation need not be tied to feeding. Like the ethologist Robert Hinde, Lorenz, Tinbergen, and other leading ethologists believed that species-wide behavior patterns, like species' morphology, could best be understood as being adapted to selection pressures originating in what Bowlby would later term the *environment of evolutionary adaptedness* (Bowlby, 1969).

Following a review of evolutionary theory and the nonhuman primate literature, Bowlby gradually came to the conclusion that crying, clinging, following, and other primate behavior patterns which become focused upon selected persons are to be attributed to the working of an "attachment behavioral system," a system equal in import to but independent of feeding and reproduction. Like other behavioral systems (formerly known as instinctive behavior patterns) ensuring species survival, the development of the attachment system was attributed to evolutionary selection pressures. Drawing upon the nonhuman primate and anthropological literature, then, Bowlby pointed out that once an attachment figure has been selected (usually but not necessarily the biological mother or even a biological relative) the infant closely monitors her whereabouts, preserving a reasonable degree of proximity even under nonstressful conditions.

Bowlby originally proposed protection from predation as the selection pressure leading to the incorporation of attachment into the behavioral repertoire of ground-living primates. Maintaining proximity to protective older individuals would decrease the likelihood that an individual infant would be targeted for predation, while flight to protective, older conspecifics as a haven of safety when threatened would greatly increase the chance of survival if targeted. In addition to providing protection from predation, however, attachment behavior is currently understood to serve multiple survival functions, including protection from starvation, unfavorable temperature

changes, natural disasters, attacks by conspecifics, and the risk of separation from the group.

For all of these reasons, therefore, attachment behavior represents the primary mechanism for the regulation of infant safety, and maintenance of proximity to attachment figure(s), is the *sine qua non* of primate infant survival. Attachment is therefore especially closely related to fear. The relations between attachment and fear are described by Bowlby with the attachment and "escape" (fear) behavioral systems conceptualized as separable but closely intertwined. Bowlby also makes the critical point that for primate infants— as opposed to other mammals, who may seek the mother for nourishment, but flee to a den or burrow when frightened—the attachment figure is the single location which must be sought in times of alarm. For both human and nonhuman primates, then, the infant's insistent concern with maintenance of relations to the attachment figure represents its primary solution to situations of danger and fright.

While most readily activated in younger individuals, the attachment behavioral system is viewed as remaining influential throughout the lifetime, and accounting throughout the lifetime for central aspects of an individual's emotional reactions and overall mental state. In later life, early attachment figures may become partially supplanted in import by friends or sexual partners, who then become the individual's "primary attachment figure" in times of stress. For most adults, attachment behavior is less readily activated than for young children, and in most well-functioning couples, both partners feel free to either turn to the other as an attachment figure, or alternately, to provide caregiving for the other as necessary. A major field of inquiry is now focused upon adult romantic or "partner" attachments, and their behavioral, psychophysiological, and cognitive correlates. Most work in this field is based upon self-report.

With respect to Bowlby's general theory of attachment, the following further points should be noted:

1. Specific or "focused" attachments appear by the third quarter of the first year of life in most human infants, and are believed to be based upon contingent social interactions. There is no evidence that these interactions need be positive, and infants unquestionably take insensitive and maltreating parents as attachment figures.

2. Attachment behavior is a species-wide characteristic which fails to develop only in extremely anomalous circumstances. Initially, the behavior is organized along relatively simple lines. By the second year of life, however, it comes to be mediated by increasingly sophisticated behavioral systems organized cybernetically and incorporating representational models (sometimes termed *internal working models*) of the attachment figure and the self.

3. Certain conditions provide "natural clues to danger," and are therefore expected to activate attachment behavior. These activating conditions include unfamiliarity, hunger, fatigue, illness, and anything immediately alarming.

4. The conditions most likely to terminate (more recently, the term *modulate* has been used) attachment behavior include sight or sound of the mother figure; in the case of high activation, physical contact with the attachment figure may be required.

5. The attachment behavioral system is not expected to function normally if the individual (a) has not had interaction with a caregiving figure sufficient to form an attachment during the first three years of life or (b) has experienced repeated, stressful, long-term separation from all attachment figures during this same time period.

Ainsworth's Extensions of Attachment Theory: Applications and Consequences for the Observation of Infant-Parent Interactions

Working intensively with relatively small samples of infant-mother dyads first in Uganda and later in Baltimore, Mary Ainsworth (1969) provided several extensions to Bowlby's theorizing regarding infant-mother relations. First, by pointing to the infant's tendency to alternatively explore away from, then return to the attachment figure (the "secure base" concept), she emphasized the import of studying the influence of competing behavioral systems even when infant attachment behavior was the chief object of study. Additionally, she corrected Bowlby's early theorizing, which had referred to the attachment behavioral system as being switched on or off by varying activators and terminators, by pointing out that in order to be sufficiently alert and responsive to the external and internal environment to seek the attachment figure whenever necessary, the system must be continually active.

Early studies conducted by Bowlby, among others, had indicated that, subjected to major, stressful separations from the parent even previously secure toddlers (approximately 18 months to 3 years of age) eventually tended to actively avoid and ignore the parent on reunion. In some cases, a continuing state of "detachment" developed, which Bowlby compared to "repression in the making." Ainsworth, however, developed a 20-minute laboratory procedure which combined several of Bowlby's "natural clues to danger" by exposing the infant (1) to two brief separations from the parent (2) in an unfamiliar environment. This procedure was first employed with 12-month-old infants who had never been subjected to major separations from the parent and remarkably, ultimately indicated that avoidance

of the parent could develop in the absence of traumatic separation, that is, out of repeated experiences of minor rejection during daily interactions. Ultimately, Ainsworth identified three "organized" patterns of 12-month-old attachment to the parent, based on the infant's behavioral response to separation and reunion. These were termed *secure, insecure-avoidant*, and *insecure-ambivalent*, and each was linked to a differing pattern of early infant-mother interaction as observed in the home environment, with the mother's "sensitivity to infant signals and communications" consistently being found linked to the secure Strange Situation response pattern (Ainsworth, Bell, & Stayton, 1971).

Work conducted in many laboratories—including a poverty sample studied by Egeland, Sroufe, and their colleagues in Minnesota (Sroufe, 1997), and a middle-class sample studied by Grossmann and Grossmann (1991) in Germany—later found secure versus insecure infant response to the mother in this situation highly predictive of favorable versus unfavorable social and emotional outcomes, extending to adolescence. Although some workers initially speculated that such remarkable predictability could only be due to continuities in the infant's "temperament," Sroufe has argued persuasively that, at least in infancy, Strange Situation behavior largely reflects the infant's experiences involving the parent with whom it is being observed.

Although Ainsworth had originally identified only three categories of infant attachment, Main and Solomon developed a system for identifying conflict behavior in the parent's presence, and infants showing substantial levels of "disorganized/disoriented" behavior under these conditions are now placed in a fourth Strange Situation category of that title (Main, 1991, 1995). On the basis of Bowlby's theory, which postulates that gaining access to the attachment figure (the infant's "haven of safety") is the infant's primary solution to situations of alarm, Hesse and Main (in press) suggested that disorganized behavior is virtually inevitable when an infant is frightened by the same individual whom it expects to approach in situations of fright. Disorganized infant Strange Situation behavior is currently being found especially predictive of psychopathology, particularly dissociative experiences and conduct disorders.

Representational Models of Attachment in Adulthood: Relations to Caregiving and Clinical Distress

Although originally focused upon attachment and the influence of attachment-related experiences as seen at the behavioral level, Bowlby gradually turned to a consideration of the role which "representational models," "representational states," or "internal working models" concerning the self and the attachment figure might play in controlling behavior and—in the case of "multiple (contradictory) models"—contributing to the development of psychopathology. In this context, Main and colleagues devised a system for assessing a mother's representational models of her own early attachment experiences, using an hour-long Adult Attachment Interview (AAI) (Main, 1991, 1995). Four categories of adult "state of mind with respect to attachment" have been identified from verbatim transcripts of this interview. Each category has been found specifically associated with the theoretically correspondent category of infant attachment to the speaker, so that, for example, a coherent and collaborative interview response on the part of a parent—whether life history appears to have been favorable or unfavorable—has repeatedly been found associated with a secure Strange Situation response to the speaker on the part of the infant.

Bowlby suggested that multiple, contradictory "internal working models" could develop out of unfavorable early experiences, and would be found associated with vulnerability to psychopathology. Main has postulated that speakers unable to maintain coherent, collaborative discourse throughout the Adult Attachment Interview can be seen as having multiple, contradictory models of their early attachment-related experiences. This given, it is especially interesting that, even screening for organic and thought disorders, exceptionally few clinically distressed individuals and criminals have been judged secure-autonomous (coherent-collaborative) in their response to the Adult Attachment Interview. Recent studies of low-risk samples have indicated predictability of AAI response from early Strange Situation response to the mother, but no such relation has been identified in a high-risk sample, stressing again that no "critical period" exists ensuring secure versus insecure mental states with respect to attachment in later life. Indeed, as Bowlby had stressed in his earliest writings, even secure young children are highly vulnerable to attachment-related trauma across the first years of life. Conversely, individuals insecure in infancy and early childhood may well become secure in later life, and as Main and others have argued, the capacity for metacognitive monitoring and for reflections upon others' mental states may play some role in individual differences in resilience.

Biological and Cognitive Aspects of Attachment Theory: Emerging Directions

Other recent extensions and suggested refinements to attachment theory can be found in a handbook on attachment edited by Cassidy and Shaver (in press). These include updated refinements in, for example, the relations among memory systems in the "working models" of attachment figures and the self; speculative proposals taken from sociobiology that some individuals may be less vulnerable than others to early experience, and that some forms of insecure attachment status may be associated with favorable biological (reproductive) outcomes in unfavorable environments; recognition of the role played by separable aspects of early experience with the mother in regulating infant behavior and psychophysiology, including endogenous opioids; and new findings from primate studies indicating not only the long-term deleterious biological and behavioral effects of early maternal deprivation but also interestingly differing outcomes (favorable vs. unfavorable) dependent upon whether a genetically hypersensitive individual is raised by a "sensitive" versus "insensitive" mother.

However, as Hinde and Stevenson-Hinde (1990) have pointed out, it is critical in theorizing regarding attachment to consider that individual, cultural, and biological "desiderata" may differ or even be at cross-purposes. Thus, while a secure attachment and parental caregiving patterns which foster a secure attachment may generally be associated with an increased sense of psychological well-being (individually desirable), the parental or offspring behavior associated with this outcome may or may not be in accordance with locally admired customs (culturally desirable), and may or may not be associated with reproductive success on the part of the individual or their kin (biologically desirable).

[*See also* Attachment; *and* Parent-Child Relationship.]

Bibliography

Ainsworth, M. D. S. (1969). Object relations, dependency and attachment: A theoretical review of the infant-mother relationship. *Child Development, 40*, 969–1025.

Ainsworth, M. D. S., Bell, S. M., & Stayton, D. J. (1971). Individual differences in Strange Situation Behavior of one-year-olds. In H. R. Shaffer (Ed.), *The origins of human social relations* (pp. 17–57). New York: Academic Press.

Bowlby, J. (1958). The nature of the child's tie to his mother. *International Journal of Psycho-Analysis, 39*, 350–373.

Bowlby, J. (1969). *Attachment and loss: Vol. 1. Attachment.* London: Hogarth Press.

Bowlby, J. (1973). *Attachment and loss: Vol. 2. Separation: Anxiety and anger.* New York: Basic Books.

Bowlby, J. (1980). *Attachment and loss: Vol. 3. Loss: Sadness and depression.* New York: Basic Books.

Bowlby, J. (1988). *A secure base: Parent-child attachment and healthy human development.* New York: Basic Books.

Cassidy, J., & Shaver, P. R. (Eds.). (in press). *Handbook of attachment: Theory, research and clinical applications.* New York: Guilford Press.

Grossmann, K. E., & Grossmann, K. (1991). Attachment quality as an organizer of emotional and behavioral responses in a longitudinal perspective. In C. M. Parkes, J. Stevenson-Hinde, & P. Marris (Eds.), *Attachment across the life cycle*. London: Tavistock/Routledge.

Hesse, E., & Main, M. (in press). Frightened behavior in traumatized but non-maltreating parents: Previously unexamined risk factor for offspring. *Psychoanalytic Inquiry*.

Hinde, R. A., & Stevenson-Hinde, J. (1990). Attachment: Biological, cultural and individual desiderata. *Human Development, 33,* 62–72.

Main, M. (1991). Meta-cognitive knowledge, meta-cognitive monitoring, and singular (coherent) vs. multiple (incoherent) models of attachment: Findings and directions for future research. In C. M. Parkes, J. Stevenson-Hinde, & P. Marris (Eds.), *Attachment across the life cycle* (pp. 127–159). London: Routledge.

Main, M. (1995). Attachment: Overview, with implications for clinical work. In S. Goldberg, R. Muir, & J. Kerr (Eds), *Attachment theory: Social, development and clinical perspectives* (pp. 407–474). Hillsdale, NJ: Analytic Press.

Sroufe, A. (1997). Psychopathology as an outcome of development. *Development and Psychopathology, 9,* 251–268.

Mary Main

ATTENTION. [*This entry comprises two articles. The first article provides a broad overview of attention. The second article presents a general survey of models of attention.*]

An Overview

Discussions of attention can be traced back to ancient Greece. However, it was not until the nineteenth century that attention became a focus of scientific inquiry. For the structuralists, such as Edward Bradford Titchener and Wilhelm Wundt, attention was defined in terms of the clearness of sensory processes. In contrast, William James (1890/1950) emphasized the functional significance of attention. He argued that there are many items simultaneously available to the senses that fail to enter into one's conscious experience. They fail to register because they are not of interest to the observer. In short, experience is what one agrees to attend to; without selective interest, experience would be utter chaos.

In the early 1900s attention was an active field of research. However, with the rise of behaviorism in America and Gestalt psychology in Europe, interest in attention declined. Both of these schools of thought were based on the control of behavior by sensory input; on the surface at least, they are not compatible with the observer determining the importance of a particular stimulus. Historical forces have, however, brought attention back to a central role in psychology in the years since World War II. These forces include the decline of the Gestalt and behaviorist schools of psychology, changes in our understanding of how the brain works, and the cybernetic (i.e., computer) revolution. Also crucial in the renaissance of attention was applied work conducted during and immediately after World War II that focused on the practical significance of the fact that humans are quite limited in their ability to process information.

Perceptual Selectivity

In an important early study, Cherry (1953) played two simultaneous auditory messages to subjects, one message to each ear (this is known as *dichotic listening*). Subjects were asked to repeat back one of the messages word-by-word as it was presented (this is known as shadowing). When they were finished, they were then asked to report the other, unattended, message. In these circumstances recall of the unattended message was virtually impossible. At most, subjects could report some conspicuous physical features of that message, such as whether it was spoken by a man or a woman. Based on these and other results, Broadbent (1958) proposed the *filter theory* of selective listening. This theory assumed a large-capacity input mechanism that could briefly (for a fraction of a second) store sensory messages. From this storage system information may be passed by a selective filter for further processing (one consequence of which could be storage in a more permanent memory). The filter selects messages based on physical cues such as voice, spatial location, and the like. These cues specify what Broadbent called *channels* of input. A message arriving on an unattended channel would be stopped by the filter; thus a listener would be unaware of the verbal content of such a message—just as Cherry had found. Because the filter operates before "further processing" occurs, this is known as an *early selection* model.

Subsequent research was soon to call filter theory into question. One striking example is the finding by Moray (1959) that when a message in the unattended ear is preceded by the subject's own name, the likelihood of hearing and reporting the message is increased. It is as if the subject's name captures attention, thus causing a switch to the heretofore ignored message. Obviously, this could not have happened if the unattended message had been entirely excluded from further analysis. Two alternative explanations for such failures of perfect selectivity were proposed. Treisman (1960) modified Broadbent's theory, suggesting that the filter attenuated rather than completely blocked unattended messages. Deutsch and Deutsch (1963) rejected the early selection approach and instead argued that there was no need to postulate a filter mechanism at all. A message receives the same analysis whether it is attended or unattended. This is known as *late selection* because selection is assumed to operate only after perceptual analysis is complete.

There have been many attempts to adjudicate among these models. For example, Francolini and Egeth (1980) asked participants to count the number of red letters in a display, and to ignore the black characters in the display. The time required to initiate the vocal response was measured. In one condition, the black characters were neutral (imagine there were three red Gs, and one black T). In another condition, the irrelevant black characters carried information that was incompatible with the vocal response (imagine three red Gs, and one black 2.) In this case, we might expect the black digit to create a tendency for the participant to say "two," which would be incompatible with the correct response, "three" (this is a variation of the famous Stroop Color-Word test in which the subject must name the color in which an incompatible color name is printed, e.g., the word "red" in green ink, with the correct response being "green"). In fact, there was no interference at all. However, when the incompatible information was carried by the relevant red characters, substantial interference was found. (Imagine three red 2s and one black T. The correct response is "three," but the identity of the red characters prompts the incorrect response "two.")

The fact that there is much more interference from items in the relevant color than in the unattended color suggests either early selection or attenuation. The additional fact that interference from items in the irrelevant color was nonexistent might suggest that subjects had no knowledge of the content of the unattended black items (which would support early selection). However, Driver and Tipper (1989) showed that even though the black digits did not create interference, they did produce identity-specific *negative priming* on the following trial. (For example, if black 2s were presented on trial N, then reaction time was slow if red 2s had to be responded to on trial N+1.) Thus, the black digits were not completely ignored. The attentuation model seems to be consistent with this pattern of results.

Lavie and Tsal (1994) suggested an interesting compromise between early and late selection. They point out that much of the evidence for late selection comes from situations in which only a few stimuli are presented (what they call a light perceptual load). When the available processing capacity is greater than that demanded by the relevant stimuli in the current display, then the excess capacity is used, automatically, to process any irrelevant stimuli that are present. In contrast, evidence for early selection comes from situations in which perceptual load is heavy. When processing capacity is exhausted by the demands of relevant stimuli, irrelevant stimuli will fail to be processed.

Division of Attention

The preceding discussion tells us that, as James thought, observers can selectively attend to inputs of interest. However, it may still be surprising that we seem to be limited to attending to just one event at a time. Is this actually the case? This brings us to the topic of *divided attention*, that is, the ability to do more than one thing at a time. Obviously, we do have some ability to perform two complex tasks at once; for example, we can drive a car and carry on a conversation at the same time. However, the ability to divide attention depends in detail on the nature of the two tasks. For example, it is possible to perform quite well at the dual tasks of shadowing a spoken message and typing a different, visually presented, text. However, if the tasks are simply reversed, so that now one speaks aloud the printed message while typing the auditorily presented message, then performance on both tasks is drastically impaired (Shaffer, 1975).

It is difficult to draw firm scientific conclusions from the study of tasks as complex as driving and talking, because they permit subjects to switch back and forth between tasks, and because the input is highly predictable. More analytic research with tight control of stimulus sequences and careful measurement of behavioral output has attempted to explore the source of dual-task interference. One line of research has investigated how many input channels we can *monitor* at one time. The results are not entirely consistent with one another. For example, if one is set to detect a tone, detection of the tone is as good when it can be presented to either ear as when one knows in advance to which ear it will be presented (Sorkin, Pastore, & Pohlman, 1972). However, more recent studies in vision have obtained clear evidence that foreknowledge of target location improves performance (e.g., Luck, Hillyard, Mouloua, & Hawkins, 1996).

What seems to be the case is that when the perceptual load is light there is a small advantage to being able to focus resources on a single channel. However, when perceptual load is heavier, the advantage can be substantial (see Pashler, 1998, for a review).

In monitoring experiments, a single target signal is presented on each trial, even though the observer may be uncertain as to how it will be delivered. The results are drastically different when to-be-reported targets can appear on two channels simultaneously (e.g., one to each ear), and each has to be responded to separately. A dramatic performance decrement is often observed in such circumstances. Pashler and Johnston (1998) have reviewed experiments of this sort in which the nature of the stimuli and responses was varied systematically.

What the research suggests is that there is a *processing bottleneck* associated with the process of deciding what response to make. In contrast, other cognitive operations such as perception and response execution can often be carried out simultaneously, as long as the tasks are not too demanding and the stimuli not too numerous.

The Consequences of Attention

James argued that unattended stimuli failed to enter one's conscious experience. Do such stimuli have any effect at all on behavior? Mack, Tang, Tuma, Kahn, and Rock (1992) conducted an experiment in which subjects paid careful attention to a central stimulus on two successive trials. On the third trial participants again made a judgment about the central stimulus. Unexpectedly, an additional stimulus was also presented on that trial, and subjects were asked to make a judgment about it. In several experiments subjects demonstrated no knowledge of the unexpected stimulus, an effect the authors referred to as *inattentional blindness*. However, Moore and Egeth (1997) showed that even though the unexpected stimulus could not be reported, it still affected performance, and because of that it must have been perceived. There are many experiments like this that show that performance can be affected in the absence of explicit awareness of the stimulus. Thus, attention does not seem necessary for at least some degree of perceptual processing, but does seem to be necessary for an event to enter consciousness or to be remembered.

Bibliography

Broadbent, D. E. (1958). *Perception and communication.* London: Pergamon Press.

Cherry, E. C. (1953). Some experiments on the recognition of speech, with one and with two ears. *Journal of the Acoustical Society of America, 25,* 975–979.

Deutsch, J. A., & Deutsch, D. (1963). Attention: Some theoretical considerations. *Psychological Review, 70,* 80–90.

Driver, J., & Tipper, S. P. (1989). On the nonselectivity of "selective" seeing: Contrasts between interference and priming in selective attention. *Journal of Experimental Psychology: Human Perception and Performance, 15,* 304–314.

Francolini, D. M., & Egeth, H. E. (1980). On the nonautomaticity of "automatic" activation: Evidence of selective seeing. *Perception & Psychophysics, 27,* 331–342.

James, W. (1950). *The principles of psychology* (Vol. 1). New York: Dover. The chapter on attention in this classic book anticipates many of the important developments in current research on the topic. (Original work published 1890)

Lavie, N., & Tsal, Y. (1994). Perceptual load as a major determinant of the locus of selection in visual attention. *Perception & Psychophysics, 56,* 183–197.

Luck, S. J., Hillyard, S. A., Mouloua, M., & Hawkins, H. L. (1996). Mechanisms of visual-spatial attention—Resource allocation or uncertainty reduction? *Journal of Experimental Psychology: Human Perception and Performance, 22,* 725–737.

Mack, A., Tang, B., Tuma, R., Kahn, S., & Rock, I. (1992). Perceptual organization and attention. *Cognitive Psychology, 24,* 475–501.

Moore, C. M., & Egeth, H. (1997). Perception without attention: Evidence of grouping under conditions of inattention. *Journal of Experimental Psychology: Human Perception and Performance, 23,* 339–352.

Moray, N. (1959). Attention in dichotic listening: Affective cues and the influence of instructions. *Quarterly Journal of Experimental Psychology, 11,* 56–60.

Pashler, H. E. (1998). *The psychology of attention.* Cambridge, MA: MIT Press. A broad survey of the entire topic of attention.

Pashler, H., & Johnston, J. (1998). Attentional limitations in dual task performance. In H. Pashler (Ed.), *Attention* (pp. 155–189), East Sussex, UK: Psychology Press.

Shaffer, L. H. (1975). Multiple attention in continuous verbal tasks. In P. M. A. Rabbitt & S. Dornic (Eds.), *Attention and performance,* (Vol. 5, pp. 157–167). New York: Academic Press.

Sorkin, R. D., Pastore, R. E., & Pohlmann, L. D. (1972). Simultaneous two-channel signal detection: II Correlated and uncorrelated signals. *Journal of the Acoustical Society of America, 51,* 1960–1965.

Treisman, A. (1960). Contextual cues in selective listening. *Quarterly Journal of Experimental Psychology, 12,* 242–248.

Howard Egeth

Models of Attention

The first modern theory of attention was Donald Broadbent's *filter theory* (1958). The theory was summarized in a flow diagram (see Figure 1). Information enters the system through a number of parallel input channels. The input channels lead to a short-term memory store that can hold information for a period of the order of

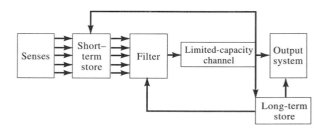

ATTENTION: Models of Attention. Figure 1. Donald Broadbent's filter theory. (Adapted from Broadbent, D. E. (1958). *Perception and communication.* London: Pergamon Press, p. 299.)

seconds. Later in the system there is a *limited-capacity channel*, whose capacity for transmitting information is very much smaller than the total capacity of the parallel input channels. Between the short-term memory and the limited-capacity channel is a selective filter. The filter acts as an all-or-none switch that can select information from just one of the parallel input channels at a time. Switching the filter between channels takes an appreciable time.

In Broadbent's original theory, an input channel was a class of sensory events having some simple physical feature in common (e.g., a position in auditory space). Except for analysis of such features, a stimulus on a nonattended channel should not be perceived. This prediction fitted the results of studies in the early 1950s by Colin Cherry on the ability to listen to, and follow, one speaker in the presence of others (the *cocktail party problem*). In Cherry's studies, subjects were asked to repeat a prose message while they heard it (*shadow* the message), rather than waiting until it finished. A message to be ignored was presented at the same time. Often the two messages were fed into separate ears (*dichotic* presentation). Typically subjects were unable to recall any words from the nonattended message.

Later studies showed that subjectively important words (e.g., the subject's own name) tended to be recognized even if presented on the nonshadowed channel. Such results led Anne Treisman to propose a variation of filter theory in which the filter operates in a graded rather than an all-or-none fashion. In Treisman's theory, nonattended messages are weakened (*attenuated*) rather than blocked from further analyses. Both selected and attenuated messages are transmitted to a pattern recognizer, which contains a large number of word recognition units with variable thresholds. Thresholds of recognition units for important words are lowered, which explains why important words tend to be recognized even if appearing in attenuated messages.

In the filter theories of Broadbent and Treisman, attentional selection occurs before pattern recognition. Such theories are called *early-selection* theories. In *late-selection* theories, attentional selection occurs only after pattern recognition. The first late-selection theory was proposed by J. Anthony Deutsch and Diana Deutsch in 1963. Deutsch and Deutsch built on the same experimental data as Treisman, but found the lower level filter (the early-selection mechanism) in Treisman's theory redundant. They proposed that wanted and unwanted messages receive the same amount of analysis by the pattern recognition system. After an incoming signal has been recognized, the *importance* of the signal is determined. The signal with the greatest importance is selected for further processing, including conscious awareness.

The theories of Broadbent, Treisman, and Deutsch and Deutsch set the stage for the development of more specific, quantitative models of attention. Most of these models drew on experimental data on visual processing: data on our ability to *divide* attention between multiple, simultaneous targets and data on our ability to *focus* attention on targets rather than distractors.

Simple Serial Models

In *whole-report* experiments by George Sperling in the early 1960s, subjects were instructed to report as many letters as possible from a briefly exposed array of unrelated letters terminated by a mask. The number of reported letters increased with the duration of the stimulus exposure. Sperling proposed a simple serial model to account for the results. By this model, the subject encodes one letter at a time, requiring 10 to 15 milliseconds to encode a letter. The serial encoding is interrupted when the stimulus is terminated by the mask or when the number of encoded letters reaches the immediate memory span of the subject, which is about four items.

Simple serial models of *visual search* were developed in the 1960s by William K. Estes, Saul Sternberg, and others. In most experiments on visual search, the subject is instructed to decide "as quickly as possible" whether a predesignated target is present in a display that contains one or no occurrences of the target. Positive (*present*) and negative (*absent*) reaction times are analyzed as functions of the number of items in the display (*display size*).

In a simple serial model, items are scanned one by one. As each item is scanned, it is classified as a target or as a distractor. A negative response is initiated if and when all items have been scanned and classified as distractors. Thus the number of items processed before a negative response is initiated equals the display size, N. If the search process is *self-terminating*, a positive response is initiated as soon as a target is found. Because the order in which items are scanned is independent of their status as targets versus distractors, the number of items processed before a positive response is initiated varies randomly between 1 and N with a mean of $(1 + N)/2$. Thus, as display size N is increased, the rate of increase in mean positive reaction time equals one half of the rate of increase in mean negative reaction time.

Treisman has introduced a widespread distinction between feature and conjunction search. In *feature search*, the target differs from the distractors by possessing a simple physical feature (e.g., a particular color, size, or curvature) not shared by any of the distractors. In *conjunction search*, the target differs from the distractors by showing a predefined conjunction of physical features (say, both a particular color and a particular shape), but the target is not unique in any of the component features of the conjunction (i.e., in color or in shape). For example, the target can be a green *T* among distractors that are brown *T*s and green *X*s.

Many experiments on conjunction search have yielded positive and negative mean reaction times that are approximately linear functions of display size with substantial slopes and a positive-to-negative slope ratio of about 1:2. This pattern conforms to predictions from simple self-terminating serial models, and Treisman and her associates have concluded that conjunction search is performed by scanning items one at a time. However, search for some types of conjunctions has shown very small effects of display size. This finding has suggested that serial processing may be selective.

Selective Serial Models

In selective serial models, items in the stimulus display are attended one at a time, but the serial order in which items are attended depends on their status as targets versus distractors: When a target and a distractor compete for attention, the target is more likely to win.

In 1989, Jeremy Wolfe, Kyle Cave, and Susan Franzel proposed a selective serial model called *guided search*. The model includes elements of the *feature integration theory* of Treisman. As in feature integration theory, simple stimulus features such as color, size, and orientation are registered automatically, without attention, and in parallel across the visual field, but registration of objects (items defined by conjunctions of features) requires a further stage of processing at which attention is directed serially to each object. In guided search, the outcome of the first, parallel stage of processing guides the serial processing at the second stage. The model works as follows.

For each feature dimension (e.g., color, size, or orientation), the parallel stage generates an array of activation values, which forms a map of the visual field. Each activation value is a sum of a bottom-up and a top-down component. The bottom-up component is a measure of differences between the value of the feature at the given location and values of the same feature at other locations. The top-down component is a measure of the similarity between the value of the feature at the given location and the target value for the feature dimension. After activations have been calculated in separate maps for each feature dimension, they are summed across feature dimensions to produce a single overall activation map. In simulations, a certain level of random noise is also added at each location. The final overall activation values represent the evaluation given by the parallel stage of how likely the stimulus at each location is to be the target.

Whereas the parallel stage suggests probable targets, the serial stage classifies each item it processes as a target or as a distractor. Items are processed one by one in order of decreasing activation in the overall activa-

tion map. The serial processing stops when a target is found or when all items with activations above a certain value have been processed.

Guided search accounts for many findings on visual search. The model was motivated by demonstrations of fast conjunction search that seemed to undermine the basis of feature integration theory. Some cases of fast conjunction search are explained by assuming that for some feature dimensions, top-down control is very effective; other cases are explained by assuming that in some subjects, the level of random noise is very low.

Simple Parallel Models

In parallel models of attention, simultaneously presented stimuli are processed at the same time. In simple parallel models, the processing of a stimulus is independent of the number of simultaneously presented stimuli. Simple parallel models of visual whole report and search were developed by Charles Eriksen and others in the 1960s. Eriksen assumed that display items presented to separated foveal areas are processed simultaneously and independently up to and including the level of pattern recognition.

The notion of simple (*unlimited-capacity*) parallel processing has been applied to cases in which visual search is highly efficient (small effects of display size). High efficiency is found in feature search with high target-distractor discriminability. By a theory proposed by Richard Shiffrin and Walter Schneider in 1977, high efficiency is also found in search for more complex targets such as particular alphanumeric characters when subjects have been trained consistently in detecting those particular targets.

In the theory of Shiffrin and Schneider, slow, serial, *controlled search* for particular items can develop into fast, parallel *automatic detection* of the same items. Automatic detection occurs without subject control and without stressing the capacity limitations of the system. The development of automatic detection presupposes that the mapping of stimuli to responses is *consistent* rather than *varied* over trials.

Evidence From Automatic Interference

Suggestive evidence for the assumption of parallel processing has come from demonstrations by Eriksen and others of *Strooplike interference* in processing of multi-item displays. In the original Stroop task, subjects are asked to name the color of the ink used to print a word. The *Stroop effect* is the fact that the task is more difficult when the word itself is the name of a different color (e.g., *red* printed in blue) than when the word does not refer to a color or refers to the color shown by the ink (*blue* printed in blue).

The original Stroop task concerns selective attention to a particular feature of an item (*featural attention*). In the *flankers task* of Eriksen, subjects are asked to focus attention on a target presented in a known spatial location (*spatial attention*). Usually the target is a letter presented at fixation, and the subject is required to make a speeded binary classification of the shape of the letter. The target is flanked by letters in irrelevant display locations. Although the flankers should be ignored, performance is impeded when the flankers are letters of a type associated with a response opposite to that required by the target. Eriksen suggested that the flankers are processed in parallel with the target up to and including the level of pattern recognition.

Recent studies by Nilli Lavie and others have shown that the interference from a distractor in an irrelevant display location can be reduced by increasing the number of items in the relevant display location. Lavie hypothesized that irrelevant distractors are processed whenever target-processing load is low: With a low load in relevant processing, spare capacity automatically spills over to the processing of irrelevant information.

Limited-Capacity Parallel Models

The linear relations between mean reaction time and display size predicted by simple serial models are hard to explain by simple parallel models. However, as shown by James T. Townsend and others in 1969, the linear relations can be explained by parallel models with *limited processing capacity*. In such models, the time taken to process an item is inversely related to the amount of processing capacity allocated to that item.

In a limited-capacity parallel model developed by Eriksen (the *zoom lens* model), the attentional field can vary in size from an area subtending less than one degree of visual angle to the full size of the visual field. Because total processing capacity is limited, the amount of processing capacity allocated to a given attended location decreases as the size of the attentional field increases. However, the attentional field cannot be split among noncontiguous locations. Direct tests of this hypothesis have been attempted, but the issue is still open.

Race Models of Selection

In race models of selection from multi-item displays, display items are processed in parallel, and attentional selection is made of those items that first finish processing (the winners of the race). Thus, selection of targets instead of distractors is based on processing of targets being faster than processing of distractors.

Race models of selection were developed by Claus Bundesen and Hitomi Shibuya in the 1980s. In a limited-capacity race model called FIRM, a stimulus display is processed as follows. First an *attentional weight* is computed for each item in the display. The weight is a measure of the strength of the sensory evidence that the item is a target. Then the available processing capacity is distributed across the items in proportion to their weights. The amount of processing capacity that

is allocated to an item determines how fast the item can be encoded into visual short-term memory (VSTM). Finally the encoding race between the items takes place. The items that are selected (i.e., stored in VSTM) are those items whose encoding processes complete before the stimulus presentation terminates and before VSTM has been filled up.

In a generalization of FIRM called TVA (theory of visual attention), selection depends on the outcome of a race between possible perceptual categorizations. The rate at which a possible categorization ("item x belongs to category i") is processed increases with (1) the strength of the sensory evidence that supports the categorization; (2) the subject's bias for assigning objects to category i; and (3) the attentional weight of item x. When a possible categorization completes processing, the categorization enters VSTM if memory space is available there. The span of VSTM is limited to about four items. Competition between mutually incompatible categorizations of the same item are resolved in favor of the first-completing categorization.

TVA accounts for many findings on single-stimulus recognition, whole report, partial report, search, and detection. The theory was extended by Gordon Logan in the late 1990s to encompass aspects of perception and memory as well as attention.

Connectionist Models

Formal theories like TVA are highly abstract. Connectionist models are attempts to theorize at a level that is closer to neurobiology. In connectionist models, processing is viewed as a flow of activation through a network of neuronlike units, which are linked together by facilitatory and inhibitory connections.

There are many ways of implementing selective attention in a connectionist network. For example, target selection by *integrated competition* (John Duncan) can be realized by arranging the connections so that units representing mutually compatible categorizations of the same item facilitate each other, but units representing incompatible categorizations inhibit each other, and units representing categorizations of different items also inhibit each other. Search, say, for a red target can then be done by preactivating units representing redness. If a red target is present, the preactivation will directly facilitate the correct categorization of the target with respect to color. Indirectly the preactivation will facilitate categorizations of the target with respect to other properties than color, but inhibit categorizations of items other than the target.

Numerous connectionist models of attention have appeared since the mid-1980s. Important examples are the multiple object recognition and attentional selection model (MORSEL) of Michael Mozer; the selective attention model (SLAM) of Hans Phaf, A. H. C. van der Heijden, and Patrick Hudson; the search via recursive rejection model (SERR) of Glyn Humphreys and Hermann Müller; and the FeatureGate model of Cave.

Conclusion

Modern theories of attention have sprung from the theoretical framework developed by Broadbent in the 1950s. Current models include selective serial models and parallel models with differential attentional weighting such as race models of selection. No extant model has accounted for the full range of empirical data, but substantial progress has been made.

Bibliography

Tutorials

Bundesen, C. (1996). Formal models of visual attention: A tutorial review. In A. F. Kramer, M. G. H. Coles, & G. D. Logan (Eds.), *Converging operations in the study of visual selective attention* (pp. 1–43). Washington, DC: American Psychological Association. Elaborates on much of the material in the present article.

Desimone, R., & Duncan, J. (1995). Neural mechanisms of selective visual attention. *Annual Review of Neuroscience, 18*, 193–222.

Moray, N. (1969). *Attention: Selective processes in vision and hearing.* London: Hutchinson. Summarizes the major work up to 1968.

Norman, D. A. (1976). *Memory and attention: An introduction to human information processing* (2nd ed.). New York: Wiley. Reviews work up to 1975. A highly readable introduction.

Posner, M. I., & Petersen, S. E. (1990). The attention system of the human brain. *Annual Review of Neuroscience, 13*, 25–42.

Shiffrin, R. M. (1988). Attention. In R. C. Atkinson, R. J. Herrnstein, G. Lindzey, & R. D. Luce (Eds.), *Stevens' handbook of experimental psychology: Vol. 2. Learning and cognition* (pp. 739–811). New York: Wiley. Provides a broad review of data and theories with emphasis on the distinction between controlled search and automatic detection.

Sperling, G., & Dosher, B. A. (1986). Strategy and optimization in human information processing. In K. Boff, L. Kaufman, & J. Thomas (Eds.), *Handbook of perception and performance* (Vol. 1, pp. 1–65). New York: Wiley. Analyzes strategies in allocation of mental resources. A technically advanced review.

Swets, J. A. (1984). Mathematical models of attention. In R. Parasuraman & D. R. Davies (Eds.), *Varieties of attention* (pp. 183–242). New York: Academic Press. Includes many models based on signal detection theory.

Townsend, J. T., & Ashby, F. G. (1983). *The stochastic modeling of elementary psychological processes.* Cambridge, UK: Cambridge University Press. Analyzes numerous mathematical models of attention. An advanced introduction.

van der Heijden, A. H. C. (1992). *Selective attention in vision.* London: Routledge. Provides a broad review and an original interpretation of the field.

van der Heijden, A. H. C. (1993). The role of position in object selection in vision. *Psychological Research, 56*, 44–58. Reviews data and contrasting theories on the role of spatial position in selective attention.

Primary Sources

Broadbent, D. E. (1958). *Perception and communication.* London: Pergamon Press.

Bundesen, C. (1990). A theory of visual attention. *Psychological Review, 97*, 523–547.

Cherry, E. C. (1953). Some experiments on the recognition of speech, with one and with two ears. *Journal of the Acoustical Society of America, 25*, 975–979.

Deutsch, J. A., & Deutsch, D. (1963). Attention: Some theoretical considerations. *Psychological Review, 70*, 80–90.

Duncan, J., & Humphreys, G. W. (1989). Visual search and stimulus similarity. *Psychological Review, 96*, 433–458.

Logan, G. D. (1996). The CODE theory of visual attention: An integration of space-based and object-based attention. *Psychological Review, 103*, 603–649.

Mozer, M. C. (1991). *The perception of multiple objects: A connectionist approach.* Cambridge, MA: MIT Press.

Treisman, A. M. (1988). Features and objects: The fourteenth Bartlett memorial lecture. *Quarterly Journal of Experimental Psychology, 40A*, 201–237.

Wolfe, J. M. (1994). Guided search 2.0. A revised model of visual search. *Psychonomic Bulletin & Review, 1*, 202–238.

Claus Bundesen

ATTENTION-DEFICIT/HYPERACTIVITY DISORDER. In the realm of childhood behavior problems, attention-deficit/hyperactivity disorder (ADHD) is a distinctive and intriguing syndrome in a number of ways. First, the core difficulties are familiar, differing more in degree than in kind from common everyday behavior patterns. Second, ADHD tends to be both handicapping and chronic, affecting a wide range of behavioral domains and often persisting throughout childhood well into adulthood. Third, ADHD affects not only an individual but also the environment, influencing other people's actions and the overall climate of the home, classroom, or workplace. Fourth, there is a well-known pharmacological treatment, stimulant medication, that is both highly effective and highly controversial. And fifth, ADHD has received the most intensive and sophisticated empirical scrutiny of all childhood behavior problems.

Characteristics and Concomitants

For people with ADHD, common requests and routines can pose uncommon challenges. They have difficulty getting organized, remaining focused on a task over time, formulating workable plans, and thinking before acting. They may be fidgety, restless, noisy, and overtalkative. Problems modulating emotion, energy, and arousal in accord with changing situational demands also surface in day-to-day transactions. Their performance on intellectual and academic tasks is often disappointing. Still unknown is the extent to which this panoply of problems is attributable to specific cognitive deficits or to more general limitations. Over recent decades, theories about the core difficulties have evolved from an emphasis on excessive motor activity, to an interest in attentional deficiencies, to a current focus on disrupted "executive functions" such as effort allocation, strategic problem solving, time management, and the protection of motivation and goal orientation. Contemporary research and theories suggest that people with ADHD may have a basic deficit in behavioral inhibition that delays their development of self-regulation skills and underlies the majority of their performance problems.

The same difficulties with impulsivity, inattention, and response modulation found in the world of tasks emerge in the world of people. With adults, children with ADHD can be oppositional and noncompliant; with peers, they can be disruptive, aggressive, or socially inept. Often inadvertently, they derail the rhythm and routine of social exchange, displaying a style that strikes others as too intense or intrusive. Many individuals with ADHD are socially active and busy, whereas others are more avoidant or withdrawn. Whatever their level of social interest, they tend to be ignored or actively rejected, and reciprocated friendships often elude them. Although they may demonstrate an understanding of social cues and routines, there are problems converting this knowledge to effective action, especially when excited, frustrated, or provoked. There may be differences in social goals or agendas, with people with ADHD orienting more toward fun and excitement than toward appropriateness, accomplishment, and social harmony. Some studies have demonstrated that children with ADHD have social catalytic effects in the sense that other people (parents, teachers, and peers) become more intense, negative, and controlling when interacting with or around them.

Diagnosis and Epidemiology

In *DSM–IV*, the current *Diagnostic and Statistical Manual* of the American Psychiatric Association (1994), three subtypes of ADHD are identified: predominantly inattentive (IA), predominantly hyperactive-impulsive (HI), and the two types of problems combined (C). Children diagnosed with ADHD-IA seem to be in the minority. They are more likely than those in the other two groups to be female, have cognitive deficits, and have concomitant problems with anxiety.

Receiving two or several diagnoses, known as comorbidity, is more the rule than the exception. Many children are diagnosed with ADHD plus conduct disorder or oppositional defiant disorder. A smaller number are diagnosed with ADHD plus learning disabilities, depression, or one or more anxiety disorders. Those experiencing both ADHD and conduct (especially aggression) problems tend to have more severe psychopathology, but researchers are just beginning to learn how comorbid and "pure" disorders differ in terms of etiology, course, or treatment response. The need for clinicians to assess comorbidity is underscored by evidence that the major treatment modality, stimulant medication, may be ineffective or even contraindicated for youngsters with ADHD and severe anxiety.

Although prevalence rates vary widely across samples and methods, the best estimate is that ADHD occurs in approximately 3 to 5% of school-age children. Boys outnumber girls, often by four or five to one. Compared to their male counterparts, girls with ADHD tend to have lower levels of hyperactivity and other externalizing behaviors such as aggression and oppositionality, but may also have greater cognitive impairment. The gender discrepancy is much greater in studies of clinical than community samples, perhaps because the higher levels of disruptive behaviors among males result in higher referral rates. It has been suggested that ADHD in girls may be an underrecognized disorder. Many ADHD studies include only boys, and the degree to which current knowledge about etiology, course, and treatment also applies to girls remains largely unknown.

ADHD does not appear to favor specific cultures or societies; the disorder has emerged in all groups assessed thus far. Prevalence rates vary widely across countries and cultures, however, just as they do from sample to sample within the United States. Variations in cultural norms, parenting practices, and societal expectations undoubtedly contribute to differential prevalence rates, and there are also indications that diagnostic practices differ across professional disciplines as well as geographic regions.

Causes

There is no doubt that ADHD runs in families, but the question is why. The bulk of the evidence from twin and family studies indicates a strong genetic contribution, and research investigators are actively searching for the genes responsible for the overall syndrome as well as for behavioral components such as impulsivity. Evidence of abnormalities in neurotransmitter systems and brain metabolism is emerging as methods for assessing such processes become progressively more sophisticated and less risky. Environmental toxins, especially lead, may also be implicated, if only for a minority of cases. Although sugar, food additives, and food allergies have long been suspected, systematic investigation has failed to produce compelling evidence that diet plays a causal role. Psychosocial adversity (e.g., parental psychopathology, marital conflict, ineffective or coercive parenting) may also contribute, at least to persistence, severity, and long-term outcome if not to initial causation. ADHD is a highly heterogeneous disorder, and it is unlikely that a single causal agent will emerge.

Developmental Course and Long-Term Outcomes

The peak period for diagnosis of ADHD comes during the early school years, ages 7 to 9, when children are expected to be gaining self-control and society is increasing its academic and social demands. Smaller numbers are recognized during the preschool years, and some escape identification until adolescence or adulthood. Early assumptions that ADHD vanished with puberty have been disconfirmed, and it is now recognized that, for many, ADHD is a chronic, and perhaps a lifetime, disorder. Approximately 50% of individuals diagnosed during childhood experience continuing problems with impulsivity, concentration, and restlessness during the adolescent and adult years. The profile of problems shifts in synchrony with developmental maturation: excessive motor activity and fidgetiness may convert to restlessness; academic and adjustment difficulties at school become performance difficulties in the workplace; and childhood disruption and disobedience may develop into frequent job and relationship changes, high rates of traffic tickets and accidents, substance abuse, and even criminal activity. Even when they show no signs of serious dysfunction as adults, many people with ADHD do not reach the educational and occupational levels of other family members. Thus far, the extensive search for reliable predictors of long-term adjustment has been relatively unsuccessful, although there are some indications that the poorest outcomes occur in those with childhood histories of serious aggression or family adversity.

Evidence is growing that there is an adult variant of ADHD that may or may not be detected during childhood. Some studies have uncovered differences between child and adult ADHD, including a more comparable gender ratio and a more variable response to stimulant treatment in adults. But other studies underscore the similarities between child and adult ADHD in terms of symptom constellations, familial patterns, and treatment effects. Adult ADHD remains a controversial notion, because the primary symptoms such as distractibility and impulsivity characterize several psychiatric disorders and are widespread in the general population. There are also concerns that some people may seek this diagnosis as a vehicle for obtaining special services, a reason for occupational or social failure, or even a means of obtaining stimulant drugs.

Treatment

Stimulant pharmacotherapy is the most widely used treatment for both children and adults with ADHD. Drugs such as methylphenidate (Ritalin) and dextroamphetamine (Dexedrine) typically result in rapid but temporary improvements in performance and social interaction. In 60 to 90% of cases, when children with ADHD are given stimulant medication, their approach to schoolwork improves, they become more focused and organized, and they are better able to think before acting. They get along better with adults and peers, they break fewer rules and conventions, and they often seem happier and more self-accepting. There is also evidence that medicating a child with ADHD can improve the behaviors of those who interact with this child, another example of social catalytic effects. Although documentation of long-term improvements is still relatively sketchy, there can be no doubt that the immediate benefits of stimulant pharmacotherapy are typically refreshing and often dramatic.

Despite the welcome results of stimulant pharmacotherapy for ADHD, there are limitations and risks that must be considered. Stimulant effects are highly variable, both within and between individuals. Some behaviors may not improve, others may improve but fail to normalize, and still others may improve in the short term but not in the long run. Dramatic changes in some realms may mask noneffects or even adverse reactions in others. A further complication is that the dosage that works for one problem may be ineffective for another. Serious side effects are quite rare, but there are always risks of untoward consequences in both medical and psychosocial realms. Concerns have been raised about long-term effects on physical growth (height), cardiovascular functioning, and motoric tics. There are also doubts about the message of the medication: Does the very effectiveness of this treatment discourage personal efforts on the part of children and their parents to build their problem-solving repertoire and interpersonal competencies? Does it reinforce society's penchant to seek a pill for every ill? Another concern is that the eligibility criteria are expanding and prescription rates are increasing as stimulant pharmacotherapy is being recommended for a widening array of problems in living, throughout the life span, whether or not the individual meets ADHD diagnostic criteria.

All things considered, however, there is little evidence of harmful effects, and the cost-benefit ratio continues to favor a trial of stimulant treatment in the majority of cases. To date, no psychosocial treatment has achieved a comparable track record. But most specialists agree that pills neither teach skills nor cure ills.

Additional interventions are typically needed, especially in the most intractable domains: academic achievement and interpersonal relations. Parent education, family therapy, and supportive interventions can also be helpful. Whether the beneficial effects of educational and psychosocial interventions extend beyond those of stimulant medication is a question now undergoing ambitious empirical scrutiny.

The complexity, multiplicity, and persistence of the difficulties that define ADHD dictate multimodal therapies and systematic monitoring of a broad range of possible treatment effects, both intended and unintended. But even if maximally efficacious treatments were available, questions would remain about the feasibility as well as the desirability of normalizing the behaviors of people with ADHD. For these individuals, life is full of provocation ecologies that highlight or exacerbate their difficulties. But there are also ecologies in which their energetic action, rapid decision making, risk taking, and imperviousness to consequences could serve adaptive functions. Perhaps one of the greatest challenges for society posed by people with ADHD is to facilitate the process of "niche-picking" so that some of these behavioral differences can function more as assets than as liabilities for the individual as well as the social group.

[*See also* Disruptive Behavior Disorders.]

Bibliography

American Psychiatric Association. (1994). *Diagnostic and statistical manual of mental disorders.* (4th ed.) Washington, DC: Author.

Arnold, L. E., Abikoff, H. B., Cantwell, D. P., Conners, C. K., Elliott, G., Greenhill, L. L., Hechtman, L., Hinshaw, S. P., Hoza, B., Jensen, P. S., Kraemer, H. C., March, J. S., Newcorn, J. H., Pelham, W. E., Richters, J. E., Schiller, E., Severe, J. B., Swanson, J. M., Vereen, D., & Wells, K. C. (1997). National Institute of Mental Health Collaborative Multimodal Treatment Study of children with ADHD (the MTA). *Archives of General Psychiatry, 54,* 865–870. Describes the design, methodology, and challenges of the first National Institute of Mental Health (NIMH) multisite comparative treatment study for childhood disorders. The effects of psychosocial and stimulant medication therapies for ADHD, alone and in combination, are compared over a 14-month treatment and 10-month follow-up period. Strategies are discussed for meeting the dual challenges of scientific control and clinical flexibility.

Barkley, R. A. (1997). *Defiant children. A clinician's manual for assessment and parent training* (2nd ed.). New York: Guilford Press. Details assessment and training procedures designed to enhance parenting skills. Includes training handouts that can be photocopied for use by clinicians, parents, and teachers. Assessment materials and handouts are also available in a Spanish-language translation.

Brown, R. T., & Sawyer, M. G. (1998). *Medications for school-age children: Effects on learning and behavior.* New York: Guilford Press. Overviews fundamental concepts, methods, and practices of pediatric psychopharmacology. Distinguishes between short-term and long-term effects with an emphasis on how medications affect children's learning and behavior. Considers psychosocial as well as pharmacological issues, including treatment evaluation, acceptability, and adherence; research and training; and the ethical, legal, and cultural contexts of pediatric psychopharmacology.

Campbell, S. B., Pierce, E. W., Moore, G., Marakovitz, S., & Newby, K. (1996). Boys' externalizing problems at elementary school age: Pathways from early behavior problems, maternal control, and family stress. *Development and Psychopathology, 8,* 701–719. Describes different developmental pathways from preschool externalizing behaviors to long-term adjustment problems. Focuses on the role of parental socialization practices and family stress in combination with early child behavior patterns.

Hallowell, E. M., & Ratey, J. J. (1994). *Answers to distraction.* New York: Bantam Books. Written in a question-and-answer format for nonprofessional audiences, this book addresses the most common questions asked about ADHD. The authors, both psychiatrists who have been diagnosed with attention deficit disorder, also provide a compendium of tips for the management of ADHD and a list of community, professional, and government resources.

Hinshaw, S. P. (1992). Academic underachievement, attention deficits, and aggression: Comorbidity and implications for intervention. *Journal of Consulting and Clinical Psychology, 60,* 893–903. Summarizes the links between ADHD, aggression, and academic underachievement. Focuses on the pervasiveness, early onset, chronicity, and serious consequences of comorbid ADHD and learning problems. The limitations of standard intervention programs and the need for long-term, combined treatment regimens are highlighted.

Klein, R. G., Abikoff, H., Barkley, R. A., Campbell, M., Leckman, J. F., Ryan, N. D., Solanto, M. V., & Whalen, C. K. (1994). Clinical trials in children and adolescents. In R. F. Prien & D. S. Robinson (Eds.), *Clinical evaluation of psychotropic drugs: principles and guidelines* (pp. 501–546). New York: Raven Press. Overviews approaches to the assessment of childhood disorders, covering general as well as disorder-specific methods and measures for assessing child psychopathology and treatment-related changes. Relevant diagnostic and methodological issues are discussed, after which specific instruments are described and compared. Assessment domains include parent and teacher rating scales, school observations, parent-child interactions, peer relations and interactions, cognitive functions, and child self-assessments.

Quay, H. C., & Hogan, A. E. (Eds.). (1999). *Handbook of disruptive behavior disorders.* New York: Plenum Press. Distinguished contributors analyze contemporary theories and signature research on the three disruptive behavior disorders: ADHD, oppositional defiant disorder, and conduct disorder. They review classification, diagnostic, and assessment issues; precursors and risk factors; epidemiology; cognitive functioning; psychobiology; family, school, and peer factors; prevention and treatment modalities; and long-term outcomes. Salient ethical and legal issues are also considered.

Weiss, G., & Hechtman, L. T. (1993). *Hyperactive children grown up. ADHD in children, adolescents and adults* (2nd ed.). New York: Guilford Press. Summarizes one of the earliest follow-up studies of ADHD and, more generally, reviews symptomatology, neurobiology, developmental changes, predictive factors, and treatment considerations. Case histories and personal retrospective accounts are included.

Whalen, C. K., & Henker, B. (1997). Stimulant pharmacotherapy for attention deficit/hyperactivity disorders: An analysis of progress, problems, and prospects. In S. Fisher & R. Greenberg (Eds.), *From placebo to panacea: Putting psychiatric drugs to the test* (pp. 323–355). New York: Wiley. Critically analyzes stimulant treatment from a transactional, social ecological perspective. Compares pharmacological and behavioral strategies along an array of dimensions that includes accountability, applicability, feasibility, and palatability. Balances findings on the clinical efficacy of stimulant pharmacotherapy against an array of limitations, concerns, and unknowns. Emphasizes the rationale and promise of multimodal treatment packages that include but do not rely on stimulant medication.

Whalen, C. K., & Henker, B. (1998). Attention-deficit/hyperactivity disorders. In T. H. Ollendick & M. Hersen (Eds.), *Handbook of child psychopathology* (3rd ed., pp. 181–211). New York: Plenum Press. Integrates research and theory on the characteristics, concomitants, causes, course, and consequences of ADHD. Describes the problems experienced by the ADHD child as an individual and as a social being. Includes coverage of diagnostic and assessment issues, epidemiological patterns, and research needs and trends.

Carol K. Whalen

ATTITUDE ACCESSIBILITY. *See* Category Accessibility.

ATTITUDES. [*This entry comprises four articles:*

An Overview
Attitude Structure
Attitude Change
Attitude Measurement

The first article provides a broad overview of attitudes. The companion articles discuss the structure, change, and measurement of attitude.]

An Overview

A broad range of subjective constructs including beliefs, feelings, evaluations, and response tendencies have often been referred to as *attitudes*. However, within contemporary psychological research, the term *attitude* is typically used to refer to a relatively general and enduring evaluation of some object, person, group, or concept along a dimension ranging from negative to positive. Thus, attitudes are global evaluations that can be differentiated from specific beliefs and emotions. Attitudes provide summary evaluations of objects and are often assumed to be derived from specific beliefs, emotions, and past behaviors associated with those objects. Additionally, attitudes are relatively enduring evaluations stored in long-term memory rather than transitory psychological states.

The Centrality of Attitudes

Attitudes have long played a central role in social psychology and the construct continues to generate more research in the field than perhaps any other. There are a number of possible reasons for the centrality of the attitude construct (Pratkanis, Breckler, & Greenwald, 1989, ch. 1). One reason is that research suggests that evaluation may be one of the most fundamental and pervasive dimensions used by people in categorizing objects in their environment (Osgood, Suci, & Tannenbaum, 1957). A second reason is that attitudes have been presumed to serve important psychological functions (e.g., Smith, Bruner, & White, 1956). For example, attitudes have been postulated to assist people in obtaining rewards and avoiding punishments, structuring information about their environment, facilitating social interaction, expressing core values, and maintaining self-esteem. Another reason for the centrality of attitudes is that research suggests attitudes can exert substantial influence on the manner in which information is processed and the behaviors people enact. Finally, the attitude construct has proven to be extremely versatile in explaining findings in many domains of social behavior. Indeed, many other popular constructs in social psychology (e.g., self-esteem, prejudice) can be conceptualized as types of attitudes. Furthermore, many areas of social psychology (e.g., person memory, self, intergroup relations) have assumed and obtained evidence consistent with the notion that general evaluations are an important dimension by which information is organized.

Themes in Attitudes Research

In light of these factors, it is not surprising that the attitudes literature is both vast and multifaceted. Nonetheless, most of the research in the area has been guided by one of four major themes. Although each theme can be thought of as addressing a somewhat distinct set of issues, they are interrelated. Thus, many theories and empirical findings can be readily classified as relevant to more than one theme.

Attitude Measurement. Few if any constructs in social psychology have generated as large a measurement literature as attitudes. [See Attitudes, *article on* Attitude Measurement.]. Early research concentrated on the development and validation of formal self-report scaling procedures for assessing attitudes. Such self-report procedures remain the most prevalent approach to assessing attitudes (Summers, 1970).

One important new line of inquiry in attitude measurement has been the exploration of the cognitive processes underlying responses to self-report attitude measures (e.g., Sudman, Bradburn, & Schwarz, 1996). This research has been aimed at understanding the cognitive tasks involved in responding to such questions so as to clarify the nature of response biases and how to minimize them. Another development has been the creation of implicit measures of attitudes (e.g., Greenwald, McGhee, & Schwartz, 1998). These measures rely on procedures such as cognitive priming and do not require a respondent to report his or her evaluation. A third important development has been the emergence of improved physiological measures of attitudes (Cacioppo, Petty, Losch, & Crites, 1994).

Attitude Function. As noted earlier, theorists have long assumed that people form attitudes because basic psychological functions are served by them (e.g., Smith et al., 1956). Likewise, they have postulated that knowing the function an attitude serves can provide insights into its impact on behavior and information processing. Early empirical work was hampered by the lack of methods for measuring or manipulating functions. In recent years, several approaches to determining functions have been used (for a review, see Pratkanis et al., 1989, ch. 12). Some researchers have determined the function an attitude serves based on the nature of the attitude object. Others have assessed functions by measuring personality traits related to particular functions. Still others have assumed that certain types of situations tend to activate particular functions. These approaches have made possible empirical tests of long-standing theoretical assumptions. Most notably, research has suggested that persuasive appeals which target the functional basis of an attitude are more effective than appeals that do not (see Pratkanis et al., 1989, chs. 12, 13; however, for important limiting conditions, see Petty & Wegener, 1998).

Attitude Structure. Another central theme in attitude research is the underlying structure of attitudes and the consequences of variations in structure. [*See* Attitudes, *article on* Attitude Structure.] Early work concentrated on classifying the content of different attitude-relevant knowledge structures and on characterizing the manner in which these structures are associated with one another. Research also examined the maintenance of consistency among these structures. Contemporary theorizing has refined many aspects of this literature. Most notably, knowledge representation models from cognitive psychology (e.g., semantic network models) have been used as a basis for providing greater precision in the specification of attitude structure characteristics (Pratkanis et al., 1989, chs. 4, 5). Methods from cognitive psychology such as the use of response latencies have been used in assessing structural properties (Petty & Krosnick, 1995, ch. 10). Contemporary research also examined the consequences of variations in attitude structure. Much of this work has focused on identifying structural properties that influence the stability and resistance of attitudes, and the impact of attitudes on information processing and behavior (for reviews, see Petty & Krosnick, 1995).

Impact of Attitudes on Behavior and Information Processing. Early research incorrectly suggested that attitudes have a minimal influence on information processing and behavior. Subsequent research, conducted in both field and laboratory settings, has been directed at clarifying when attitudes are consequential. For example, attitudes are more effective in predicting behavior when the attitude and behavior are assessed at comparable levels of specificity (Ajzen & Fishbein, 1980).

Another reason attitudes sometimes fail to influence behavior is that they vary in their underlying strength (Petty & Krosnick, 1995). Some attitudes are enduring and consequential whereas others are less so. Research has identified numerous properties of attitudes related to strength (Krosnick & Petty, 1995, ch. 1). These properties include structural features of the attitude, the process by which the attitude is formed, subjective beliefs about the attitude, and aspects of the attitude itself.

A third important issue that has guided this area of research is the development of theories explaining how attitudes influence behaviors and judgments. The dominant perspectives have been the Theory of Reasoned Action (TORA; Ajzen & Fishbein, 1980) and a related perspective, the Theory of Planned Behavior (Ajzen, 1987). Both theories postulate that behaviors are a result of deliberate decisions to perform behaviors and both specify determinants of these decisions. The theories have been shown to be useful for predicting behaviors in many applied settings. One criticism of them has been that they presume behaviors are performed as a result of deliberative processing, which may not be possible in all contexts. The MODE model has been developed to address this criticism (Fazio, 1990). This model suggests that when a person is motivated and able to deliberate regarding a behavior, the process by which attitudes influence behavior will be similar to that proposed by TORA. However, the model outlines a different set of processes to explain how attitudes influence behaviors when motivation and/or ability to deliberate are low.

Attitude Change. Much of the early work in this area was motivated by cognitive consistency theories and concentrated on how performance of behaviors could produce attitude change. [*See* Attitudes, *article on* Attitude Change.] These perspectives postulated that motivation to maintain consistency among cognitive elements is an important mechanism underlying the impact of behaviors on attitude change. Contemporary research has established limiting conditions for when attitude change occurs as a result of consistency motivations and on more precisely describing the psychological processes underlying these effects (see Harmon-Jones & Mills, 1999). Research has also examined the utility of dissonance theory relative to competing theoretical perspectives (e.g., Bem, 1972; Steele, 1988).

The other major focus of attitude change research has been on understanding the processes by which persuasive messages change attitudes. Systematic research on this topic began with Hovland and his colleagues (e.g., Hovland, Janis, & Kelly, 1953) and contemporary research has continued to investigate many of the key variables they identified. However, newer "dual-process" theories of persuasion such as the Elaboration Likelihood Model (Petty & Cacioppo, 1986) and the Heuristic-Systematic Model (Chaiken, Liberman, & Eagly, 1989) have altered thinking about how these variables influence persuasion. First, rather than postulating a single process underlying change, these theories recognize that change can result from either thoughtful or nonthoughtful processes. Second, these theories suggest that the impact of a variable on attitude change can differ depending on if the attitude change process is thoughtful or nonthoughtful in nature. Third, these theories suggest that the strength of the attitude will vary as a function of the process by which the attitude was changed. Such "dual-process" persuasion theories have done much to resolve inconsistencies in the literature and generate new research.

Acknowledgments. The authors acknowledge the support of a grant from the Social Sciences and Humanities Research Council of Canada to Leandre R. Fabrigar.

Bibliography

Ajzen, I. (1987). Attitudes, traits, and actions: Dispositional prediction of behavior in personality and social psychology. *Advances in Experimental Social Psychology*, 20, 1–63.

Ajzen, I., & Fishbein, M. (1980). *Understanding attitudes and predicting social behavior*. Englewood Cliffs, NJ: Prentice Hall.

Bem, D. J. (1972). Self-perception theory. In L. Berkowitz (Ed.), *Advances in experimental social psychology* (Vol. 6, pp. 1–62). San Diego, CA: Academic Press.

Cacioppo, J. T., Petty, R. E., Losch, M. E., & Crites, S. J. (1994). Psychophysiological approaches to attitudes: Detecting affective dispositions when people won't say, can't say, or don't even know. In S. Shavitt & T. C. Brock (Eds.), *Persuasion: Psychological insights and perspectives*. (pp. 43–69). Boston, MA: Allyn & Bacon.

Chaiken, S., Liberman, A., & Eagly, A. H. (1989). Heuristic and systematic information processing within and beyond the persuasion context. In J. S. Uleman & J. A. Bargh (Eds.), *Unintended thought* (pp. 212–252). New York: Guilford Press.

Fazio, R. H. (1990). Multiple processes by which attitudes guide behavior: The MODE model as an integrative framework. In M. P. Zanna (Ed.), *Advances in experimental social psychology*, (Vol. 23, pp. 75–109). New York: Academic Press.

Greenwald, A. G., McGee, D. E., & Schwartz, J. L. K. (1998). Measuring individual differences in implicit cognition: The implicit association test. *Journal of Personality and Social Psychology*, 74, 1464–1480.

Hovland, C. I., Janis, I. L., & Kelley, H. H. (1953). *Communication and persuasion: Psychological studies of opinion change*. New Haven, CT: Yale University Press.

Osgood, C. E., Suci, G. J., & Tannenbaum, P. H. (1957). *The measurement of meaning*. Urbana, IL: University of Illinois Press.

Pratkanis, A. R., Breckler, S. J., & Greenwald, A. G. (Eds.). (1989). *Attitude structure and function*. Hillsdale, NJ: Erlbaum.

Petty, R. E., & Cacioppo, J. T. (1986). The elaboration likelihood model of persuasion. In L. Berkowitz (Ed.), *Advances in experimental social psychology* (Vol. 19, pp. 123–205). San Diego, CA: Academic.

Petty, R. E., & Krosnick, J. A. (Eds.). (1995). *Attitude strength: Antecedents and consequences*. Mahwah, NJ: Erlbaum.

Petty, R. E., & Wegener, D. T. (1998). Matching versus mismatching attitude functions: Implications for scrutiny of persuasive messages. *Personality and Social Psychology Bulletin*, 24, 227–240.

Smith, M. B., Bruner, J. S., & White, R. W. (1956). *Opinions and personality*. New York: Wiley.

Steele, C. M. (1988). The psychology of self-affirmation: Sustaining the integrity of the self. In L. Berkowitz (Ed.), *Advances in experimental social psychology* (Vol. 21, pp. 261–302). San Diego, CA: Academic Press.

Sudman, S., Bradburn, N. M., & Schwartz, N. (1996). *Thinking about answers: The application of cognitive processes to survey methodology*. San Francisco: Jossey-Bass.

Summers, G. F. (Ed.). (1970). *Attitude measurement*. Chicago: Rand-McNally.

Steven M. Smith and Leandre R. Fabrigar

Attitude Structure

The set of related mental representations associated with an attitude, attitude structure research generally deals with associations among the attitude, the attitude object, and other related knowledge structures. Properties of the set of associations include their number, strength, and organization, as well as the type (content) of the knowledge structures involved. Although these associations have often been discussed in terms of associative network models, they could also be conceptualized within more recent connectionist perspectives (see Eagly & Chaiken, 1998, for a discussion). The properties of *content, number, strength,* and *organization* are often interrelated, but many research questions can be categorized as primarily emphasizing one of these properties.

Content: To What Are Attitudes "Linked"?

For some time, attitudes were defined as predispositions to respond to an "object" in cognitive, affective, and behavioral ways. This *tripartite* view set the stage for current classifications of the content of attitude-related knowledge structures even though the definition of attitude itself has come to focus on evaluation rather than on classes of responding per se (Eagly & Chaiken, 1993; Petty, Wegener, & Fabrigar, 1997). The cognitive component has typically referred to beliefs about the attitude object, the affective component to feelings experienced when encountering or considering the attitude object, and the behavioral component to past behaviors enacted or imagined in conjunction with the attitude object (though unfortunately, some researchers have used the terms *affect* and *attitude* interchangeably; see Eagly & Chaiken, 1998, for discussion).

Much work on attitudes has emphasized associations between beliefs and attitudes. The most popular model for relating beliefs to attitudes has been the expectancy-value model (Fishbein, *Readings in Attitude Theory and Measurement,* New York, 1967; Rosenberg, 1956) which combines subjective assessments of the likelihood that the attitude object possesses certain attributes (the "expectancy" component) with assessments of the extent to which the attributes are desirable (the "value" component; see Eagly & Chaiken, 1998; Petty, Priester, & Wegener, 1994). Of course, attitudes can also be closely related to other components of attitudes (such as feelings associated with the attitude object) or to other structures (such as values—attitudes toward abstract concepts—or attitudes toward other objects), and these associations can have consequences for when and how the attitude can be changed (Eagly & Chaiken, 1998; Petty & Wegener, 1998).

Organization of Associations

One issue in the organization of attitude-relevant knowledge structures is the possible *dimensionality* of those representations. For example, some work has suggested that attitude-relevant knowledge can be organized along the evaluative dimension (i.e., with evalua-

tively consistent, rather than inconsistent, elements more closely associated with one another in memory). Of course, a plethora of additional dimensions also exist, and issues of dimensionality are relevant to organizations of both single attitudes and sets of attitudes (McGuire, 1989; Pratkanis, 1989).

The *complexity* of the attitude structure is a concept related to dimensionality. In work on belief complexity, the term *complexity* has typically referred to the number of dimensions along which attributes of the attitude object differ (i.e., the degree to which the attributes of the object tap multiple dimensions of meaning). The concept of integrative complexity (most prominent in political domains) refers not only to the number of different dimensions, but to interactions of dimensions such that implications for the attitude object of one dimension depend on the level(s) of other dimensions. In general, high levels of integrative complexity have been associated with relatively moderate political positions (Tetlock, 1989; cf. Judd & Lusk, 1984).

Especially during the 1960s, much emphasis was placed on pressures toward evaluative consistency of the components underlying attitudes (Abelson, Aronson, McGuire, Newcomb, Rosenberg, & Tannenbaum, 1968; Hovland & Rosenberg, *Attitude Organization and Change: An Analysis of Consistency among Attitude Components,* New Haven, CT, 1960). Although variation in consistency was acknowledged, it was generally assumed that any inconsistency would be resolved over time, unless the person never became aware of the inconsistency (Abelson & Rosenberg, 1958). To this day, consistency theories of one kind or another also account for much of the work on interattitudinal structure (in which a change in one attitude creates a force toward changing other related attitudes; see Abelson & Rosenberg, 1958; Eagly & Chaiken, 1995; Eagly & Chaiken, 1998; McGuire & McGuire, 1991). A hierarchical type of organization could encourage consistency across attitudes, thus providing a structure in which specific attitudes are aligned with or even deduced from general attitudes or values. Such hierarchical structures are often part of the theorizing in studies of ideology (see Eagly & Chaiken, 1998; McGuire, 1989).

The notion of possible deduction of attitudes from other existing attitudes is quite consistent with the notion that attitudes themselves can have a syllogistic structure. For example, McGuire (1960) and Wyer (*Cognitive Organization and Change: An Information Processing Approach,* Hillsdale, NJ, 1974) proposed mathematical models of belief syllogisms (e.g., in which an attitudinal evaluation is the conclusion that follows from two or more premises; see Petty et al., 1994). McGuire and McGuire (1991) elaborated the syllogistic (probabilogical) model by discussing the origins of perceptions of likelihood and desirability of elements (of syllogisms).

Although much work assumed some level of evaluative consistency among attitude components, a number of research programs developed to address variation of consistency between components underlying the attitudes. For example, evaluative-cognitive consistency (the extent of consistency between measures of an attitude and the evaluative implications of associated beliefs) has been shown to have a number of attitude-strength related consequences (Chaiken, Pomerantz, & Giner-Sorolla, 1995). Although sparsely studied, variations in the extent of evaluative-affective and evaluative-behavioral consistency might also produce differing attitudinal consequences (Eagly & Chaiken, 1998). With the recent development of new measurement procedures for identifying the affective versus cognitive bases of attitudes (e.g., Crites, Fabrigar, & Petty, 1994), evidence bearing on such research questions should be forthcoming.

Since the 1940s, theorists have periodically argued for the importance of considering the existence of evaluatively conflicting reactions within the structure of an attitude (i.e., attitude ambivalence; see Cacioppo & Berntson, 1994; Priester & Petty, 1996, for recent reviews). Studies of attitude ambivalence have proliferated of late (see Eagly & Chaiken, 1998; Petty, Wegener, & Fabrigar, 1997), with attitude ambivalence being shown to produce a variety of strength-related consequences (Eagly & Chaiken, 1998; Erber, Hodges, & Wilson, 1995; Thompson, Zanna, & Griffin, 1995). Importantly, conflicted reactions toward an attitude object might not only reflect inconsistency within the single attitude, but also inconsistency across related attitudes (e.g., when two or more relevant values conflict with one another). Such interattitude (intervalue) conflict might be especially important in accounting for reactions to social groups (e.g., see Katz & Hass, 1988).

Number of Associations

Undoubtedly, many of the effects dealing with organization of attitude-relevant knowledge also depend somewhat on the number of associations involved in that attitude or attitude system. In part, the concept of *embeddedness* of an attitude (Scott, 1968) reflects that an attitude is associated with a large number of (inter) related structures. The amount of knowledge associated with an attitude object has also been investigated in some detail (for a review, see Wood, Rhodes, & Biek, 1995). In such studies, it is unknown whether the effects are due to the number of associations per se. Effects could also be due to other aspects of structure such as the interconnected organization or specific content of such knowledge.

Strength of Associations

Perhaps the most studied structural variable over the past decade has been the extent to which an attitude is *accessible*. This work follows from an approach in which attitude is conceptualized as an evaluation directly linked to an attitude object in memory (and the strength of the attitude is the strength of that object-evaluation association; see Fazio, 1995, for a review). Although this work has focused on the strength of the object-evaluation association, one could also profitably investigate the strength of other associations in the attitude system (e.g., the strength of an association between an attitude and a particular value or between two attitudes; see Judd & Krosnick, 1989).

Links to Attitude Strength

Perhaps the most important reason for researchers to care about issues of attitude structure is that many characteristics of attitude structure carry with them consequences for the attitude related to attitude strength (i.e., the extent to which the attitude persists over time, resists persuasive attempts, and influences judgments and behavior; Petty & Krosnick, 1995). In fact, many of the structural variables noted earlier (accessibility, ambivalence, knowledge, and structural consistency) have been studied as antecedents or indices of attitude strength. Other strength-related variables such as elaboration of attitude relevant information (Petty, Haugtvedt, & Smith, 1995) are hypothesized to create structural changes (see Petty & Krosnick, 1995, for chapters reviewing many aspects of attitude strength).

[See also Attitudes, *articles on* Attitude Change *and* Attitude Measurement.]

Bibliography

Abelson, R. P., Aronson, E., McGuire, W. J., Newcomb, T. M., Rosenberg, M. J., & Tannenbaum, P. H. (Eds.). (1968). *Theories of cognitive consistency: A sourcebook.* Chicago, IL: Rand-McNally. An influential set of chapters presenting viewpoints anchored in the consistency-oriented views characteristic of the attitudes area in the 1960s.

Abelson, R. P., & Rosenberg, M. J. (1958). Symbolic psycho-logic: A model of attitudinal cognition. *Behavioral Science, 3,* 1–13. Presentation of a consistency-based model of interattitudinal structure.

Cacioppo, J. T., & Berntson, G. G. (1994). Relationship between attitudes and evaluative space: A critical review, with emphasis on the separability of positive and negative substrates. *Psychological Bulletin, 115,* 401–423. Review of attitude ambivalence including arguments for differential impact of positive versus negative reactions to attitude objects.

Chaiken, S., Pomerantz, E. M., & Giner-Sorolla, R. (1995). Structural consistency and attitude strength. In R. E. Petty & J. A. Krosnick (Eds.), *Attitude strength: Antecedents and consequences* (pp. 387–412). Mahwah, NJ: Erlbaum. Discussion of the attitude strength consequences of evaluative-cognitive consistency, with secondary attention given to evaluative-affective consistency and the relation between these structural properties and other measures of attitude structure.

Crites, S. L., Jr., Fabrigar, L. R., & Petty, R. E. (1994). Measuring the affective and cognitive properties of attitudes: Conceptual and methodological issues. *Personality and Social Psychology Bulletin, 20,* 619–634. Review of past measures of affective and cognitive bases of attitudes and development and validation of a new procedure.

Eagly, A. H., & Chaiken, S. (1993). *The psychology of attitudes.* Fort Worth, TX: Harcourt Brace Jovanovich. Graduate-level text reviewing theories and empirical studies of attitude measurement, structure, and change.

Eagly, A. H., & Chaiken, S. (1995). Attitude strength, attitude structure, and resistance to change. In R. E. Petty & J. A. Krosnick (Eds.), *Attitude strength: Antecedents and consequences* (pp. 413–432). Mahwah, NJ: Erlbaum. Discussion of attitude strength treating resistance to change as primary among the attitude strength properties and including both intra-attitudinal and inter-attitudinal structures in creating "resistant" attitudes.

Eagly, A. H., & Chaiken, S. (1998). Attitude structure and function. In D. Gilbert, S. Fiske, & G. Lindzey (Eds.), *The handbook of social psychology* (4th ed., pp. 269–322). New York: McGraw-Hill. Review of major theories and studies of attitude structure, from a volume aimed at comprehensive coverage of social psychology.

Erber, M. W., Hodges, S. D., & Wilson, T. D. (1995). Attitude strength, attitude stability, and the effects of analyzing reasons. In R. E. Petty & J. A. Krosnick (Eds.), *Attitude strength: Antecedents and consequences* (pp. 433–454). Mahwah, NJ: Erlbaum. Discusses attitude persistence in the context of an "attitudes-as-constructions" view of evaluation, with special attention given to consistency of the database underlying attitudes.

Judd, C. M., & Krosnick, J. A. (1989). The structural bases of consistency among political attitudes: Effects of political expertise and attitude importance. In A. R. Pratkanis, S. J. Breckler, & A. G. Greenwald (Eds.), *Attitude structure and function* (pp. 99–128). Hillsdale, NJ: Erlbaum. Presentation of theory and data concerning consistency among attitudes, focusing on political expertise and attitude importance as applied to consistency of political attitudes.

Judd, C. M., & Lusk, C. M. (1984). Knowledge structures and evaluative judgments: Effects of structural variables on judgmental extremity. *Journal of Personality and Social Psychology, 46,* 1193–1207. Empirical paper demonstrating that attitude complexity can result in either more moderate or more extreme attitudes, depending on the relations among the dimensions along which the attitude-relevant knowledge structures are organized.

Katz, I., & Hass, R. G. (1988). Racial ambivalence and American value conflict: Correlational and priming studies of dual cognitive structures. *Journal of Personality and Social Psychology, 55,* 893–905. Presents empirical studies guided by a value-conflict view of attitude ambivalence.

McGuire, W. J. (1960). A syllogistic analysis of cognitive relationships. In C. I. Hovland, & M. J. Rosenberg (Eds.), *Attitude organization and change: An analysis of consistency among attitude components* (pp. 65–111). New Haven, CT: Yale University Press. Presentation of a syllogistic view of attitude structure.

McGuire, W. J. (1989). The structure of individual attitudes and attitude systems. In A. R. Pratkanis, S. J. Breckler, & A. G. Greenwald (Eds.), *Attitude structure and function* (pp. 37–69). Hillsdale, NJ: Erlbaum. Review of dimensional views of individual attitude structure and presentation of postulates aimed at conceptualizing the structure of attitude systems.

McGuire, W. J., & McGuire, C. V. (1991). The content, structure, and operation of thought systems. In R. S. Wyer, Jr., & T. K. Srull (Eds.), *Advances in social cognition* (Vol. 4, pp. 1–78). Hillsdale, NJ: Erlbaum. Presents a theory of the structure and operation of thought systems in a volume including commentaries on the thought systems approach.

Petty, R. E., Haugtvedt, C. P., & Smith, S. M. (1995). Elaboration as a determinant of attitude strength: Creating attitudes that are persistent, resistant, and predictive of behavior. In R. E. Petty & J. A. Krosnick (Eds.), *Attitude strength: Antecedents and consequences* (pp. 93–130). Mahwah, NJ: Erlbaum. Review of empirical work regarding the Elaboration Likelihood Model hypothesis that elaboration creates strong attitudes.

Petty, R. E., & Krosnick, J. A. (Eds.). (1995). *Attitude strength: Antecedents and consequences.* Mahwah, NJ: Erlbaum. Collection of chapters reviewing recent research and theories guided by concepts of attitudes strength (i.e., persistence of attitudes over time, resistance to counterpersuasion, and influences on related judgments and behaviors).

Petty, R. E., Priester, J. R., & Wegener, D. T. (1994). Cognitive processes in attitude change. In R. S. Wyer and T. K. Srull (Eds.), *Handbook of social cognition* (2nd ed. Vol. 2, pp. 69–142). Hillsdale, NJ: Erlbaum. Discussion of cognitive processes underlying attitude change, including attitude bases and structure, reception, evaluation, and integration of information from persuasive messages, and consequences of different attitude change processes.

Petty, R. E., & Wegener, D. T. (in press). Attitude change. In D. Gilbert, S. Fiske, & G. Lindzey (Eds.), *The handbook of social psychology* (4th ed., pp. 323–390). New York: McGraw-Hill. Comprehensive review of research and theory on attitude change, from a volume aimed at a comprehensive coverage of social psychology.

Petty, R. E., Wegener, D. T., & Fabrigar, L. R. (1997). Attitudes and attitude change. *Annual Review of Psychology, 48,* 609–647. Review of research and theory on attitudes and attitude change from 1992 to 1995.

Pratkanis, A. R. (1989). The cognitive representation of attitudes. In A. R. Pratkanis, S. J. Breckler, & A. G. Greenwald (Eds.), *Attitude structure and function* (pp. 71–98). Hillsdale, NJ: Erlbaum. Review of definitions of the attitude concept, the heuristic function of attitudes, and the unipolar versus bipolar structure of attitudes.

Priester, J. R., & Petty, R. E. (1996). The gradual threshold model of ambivalence: Relating the positive and negative bases of attitudes to subjective ambivalence. *Journal of Personality and Social Psychology, 71,* 431–449. Comprehensive review of past models of attitude ambivalence and presentation of the gradual threshold model.

Rosenberg, M. J. (1956). Cognitive structure and attitudinal affect. *Journal of Abnormal and Social Psychology, 53,* 367–372. Early research paper that demonstrated the viability of the expectancy-value model of attitude structure.

Scott, W. A. (1968). Attitude measurement. In G. Lindzey & E. Aronson (Eds.), *Handbook of social psychology* (2nd ed., Vol. 2, pp. 204–273). Reading, MA: Addison-Wesley. Discussion of attitude measurement that includes a discussion of properties or dimensions along which attitudes might be differentiated.

Tetlock, P. E. (1989). Structure and function in political belief systems. In A. R. Pratkanis, S. J. Breckler, & A. G. Greenwald (Eds.), *Attitude structure and function* (pp. 129–151). Hillsdale, NJ: Erlbaum. Discussion of attitude structure and function for political attitudes, focusing on issues of integrative complexity and political ideology.

Thompson, M. M., Zanna, M. P., & Griffin, D. W. (1995). Let's not be indifferent about (attitudinal) ambivalence. In R. E. Petty & J. A. Krosnick (Eds.), *Attitude strength: Antecedents and consequences* (pp. 361–386). Mahwah, NJ: Erlbaum. Review of the ambivalence construct in attitude change and presentation of an empirical comparison of formulae for combining positive and negative reactions into measures of ambivalence.

Wood, W., Rhodes, N., & Biek, M. (1995). Working knowledge and attitude strength: An information processing analysis. In R. E. Petty & J. A. Krosnick (Ed.), *Attitude strength: Antecedents and consequences* (pp. 283–313). Mahwah, NJ: Erlbaum. Review and conceptualization of the role of working knowledge in attitude change.

Duane T. Wegener and
Aiden P. Gregg

Attitude Change

Attitudes are formed and changed on the basis of cognitive, affective, and behavioral processes. Research on the cognitive determinants of attitude change has shown that people form beliefs about the characteristics of entities in their environment (known as "attitude objects") and that the evaluative content of these beliefs determines how favorable or unfavorable attitudes are. In addition, affective experiences (i.e., the emotions and feelings that people experience in relation to attitude objects) contribute to attitudes. Behaviors also inform people about their attitudes and therefore may be part of the network of associations that underlies attitudes. Attitudes can be modified by changing the beliefs, affects, or representations of behavior that people hold in relation to an attitude object. By making various as-

sumptions about the cognitive, affective, and behavioral determinants of attitudes, psychologists (and researchers in allied fields) have developed detailed theories about the particular processes that underlie attitude change and tested these theories in a very large number of research programs.

The great majority of psychological research on attitude change is experimental in its methods, although some naturalistic field studies are found in this research literature as well. Typically, in a controlled laboratory setting, research participants receive information that characterizes a particular attitude object, or they engage in behavior that has implications for the attitude object. Generally, this information or behavior challenges participants' prior attitudes, so that attitude change toward the information can be easily assessed, although some research concerns the initial formation of new attitudes. Within this tradition, there are several quite different experimental paradigms (see reviews by Chaiken, Wood, & Eagly, 1996; Eagly & Chaiken, 1993; Petty & Wegener, 1998). The most prominent of these paradigms, often referred to as the study of "message-based persuasion," concerns the effects of exposing people to relatively complex messages emanating from other people. Also important is research on the effects of people's own behaviors and messages on their attitudes, a research area often referred to as the study of "attitudinal advocacy." In this tradition, participants engage in behaviors or deliver messages that counter their own attitudes, and the researchers assess the impact of these behaviors or messages on participants' attitudes. Also relevant are investigations of social influence in group situations. [*See* Conformity.]

Message-Based Persuasion

Persuasion theory, which has a long history in social psychology (Hovland, Janis, & Kelley, 1953), examines psychological processes that serve as mediators of the effects of information on attitudes. Some of these theories have emphasized what can be termed *systematic processing* in the sense that message recipients' detailed processing of a communication's content is assumed to produce acceptance of its conclusions. For example, McGuire's (1972) information-processing paradigm described the impact of persuasive communications as a sequence of processes consisting of attention to the message, comprehension of its content, and acceptance of its conclusions. This paradigm has important links to research on *attitudinal selectivity,* which concerns the ways that attitudes affect the processing of information that is congruent or incongruent with the attitudes (Eagly & Chaiken, 1998). Although psychologists have long assumed that attitudes bias information processing in favor of material that is congruent with one's attitudes (for example, by making it easier to remember), this congeniality principle has often not been substantiated. Instead, attitudes have been shown to have a variety of effects on information processing.

Other approaches to understanding persuasion have emphasized that people construct their attitudes from the thoughts that come to mind as they receive and think about persuasive communications (e.g., Greenwald, 1968; Petty, Ostrom, & Brock, 1981). This tradition reflects the proposition that people's attitudes are a function of the cognitions that they generate about the objects of their attitudes. This general cognitive theme is basic to psychologists' understanding of attitudes and central to many attitude theories. Fishbein and Ajzen's (1975) theory of attitudes' effects on behavior, for example, emphasized that people derive their attitudes toward behaviors from their beliefs about the consequences of these behaviors.

In the contemporary period, persuasion theories have incorporated the principle that people can adopt attitudes on bases other than their understanding and cognitive elaboration of the semantic content of persuasive argumentation. These *dual-process* models of persuasion emphasize contrasting modes of processing and trade at least in part on the depth-of-processing idea that has been popular in cognitive psychology. Among these approaches is the heuristic-systematic model (Chaiken, Liberman, & Eagly, 1989), which postulates that simple decision rules or cognitive heuristics may underlie persuasion, in addition to careful, systematic scrutiny of the content of messages. For example, the decision rule that an "expert's statements can be trusted" might underlie persuasion by an expert communicator. Another dual-process approach, the elaboration likelihood model (e.g., Petty & Cacioppo, 1986), incorporates a peripheral route to persuasion, defined in terms of psychological mechanisms that do not require detailed thinking about the content of the message. For example, adopting someone's attitude merely because she is a friend would constitute persuasion by the peripheral route. This model contrasts the peripheral route to persuasion with the central route, which involves careful, detailed processing of messages' semantic content.

These dual-process models of persuasion represent an advance because their assumption that multiple processes mediate persuasion has enabled them to make sense of a broader range of empirical findings than earlier persuasion theories. The principles of these theories have allowed investigators to cast a much wider net among independent variables and to make more effective predictions about the conditions under which these variables influence persuasion. Classically, the independent variables studied by persuasion researchers were organized into the categories of source, message, channel or medium, recipient, and context variables. These categories are only descriptively useful, however, because variables within a single category do not necessarily impact similarly on persuasion, nor do they necessarily act on attitudes through similar processes. Instead, decades of research have demonstrated that most persuasion variables (e.g., communicator credibility) can have varying kinds of impact on persuasion. Although making sense of these complex relationships remains challenging, dual-process theories have been very helpful in their many demonstrations that particular persuasion variables can exert their influence through more than one type of psychological process (Petty & Wegener, 1998).

A key assumption of dual-process theories is that people process information superficially and minimally unless they are motivated to do otherwise. Thus, these theories emphasize that people must have sufficient motivation to turn to more effortful, systematic forms of processing persuasive messages. They must also have the capacity or ability to engage in this more deliberative processing, which entails careful evaluation of the argumentation contained in messages. Dual-process theories of persuasion suggest that those who desire to be persuasive should consider whether the target audience for their appeal has the capacity and motivation to engage in detailed processing of argumentation that might be placed in the appeal. If most audience members lack the ability or motivation to comprehend, scrutinize, and evaluate the content of a message, communicators do not need to expend a great deal of effort developing thoughtful, detailed argumentation. Instead, they should consider relying on mechanisms that do not depend on argumentation for their effectiveness—for example, heuristic processing of simple cues, the association of attitude objects with positive stimuli (i.e., classical conditioning), or favorable attitude change from repetitive mere exposure to very simple messages that are devoid of argumentation. Simple persuasive devices of these and other types are commonly used in advertising, because members of target audiences are often not motivated to devote much attention to processing messages or may not be able to do so. However, if most people in the target audience are motivated and able to assess the validity of more complex reasoning, it is indeed desirable to present thoughtful argumentation.

As this brief presentation illustrates, persuasion theories' predictions are contingent on conditions such as the ability and motivation of members of the target audience. Because of such complexities, these theories do not provide simple, general-purpose prescriptions for changing attitudes. Therefore, theory-guided design of practical persuasion campaigns that are intended to achieve particular goals in natural settings requires exploratory research in which potentially effective materials are given to samples of people from target audiences whose reactions are carefully studied. With assistance from such exploratory research, theories of persuasion can provide extremely useful guides for the design of information campaigns.

Attitude research has also yielded knowledge about how to protect people from persuasive efforts. Thus, theories of resistance to change have been proposed, although in less abundance than theories of change. For example, at an early point theorists proposed that persuasive messages that are far enough from recipients' own attitudes to fall in what has been labeled their *latitude of rejection* tend to be resisted and negatively evaluated (Sherif, Sherif, & Nebergall, 1965). In contrast, messages that are closer to recipients' own attitudes and that therefore fall in their *latitude of acceptance* or *latitude of noncommitment* are more likely to produce attitude change and are more favorably evaluated. This perspective suggests that effective persuasive messages seldom advocate positions that are extremely distant from recipients' own attitudes. Also important is the principle that recipients who are strongly involved in an issue because the issue implicates their values and important reference groups are especially likely to resist being persuaded by messages that challenge their attitudes. People defend their important attitudes through a variety of mechanisms including active counterarguing of persuasive efforts and more passive avoidance of thinking about argumentation (Johnson & Eagly, 1989).

Other approaches to understanding resistance to change suggest that certain treatments can facilitate resistance. Key among these efforts is McGuire's (1964) inoculation theory, which argues that exposing people to weakened versions of the arguments that will subsequently attack their attitudes allows them to develop arguments that they can use to counter the attack. Using the lessons of this research program, a campaign directed to preventing alcohol or drug abuse among teenagers, for example, might expose them to weak arguments in favor of such substance abuse. Such a treatment should inspire these individuals to develop counterarguments against the weak proabuse arguments; this counterarguing might be enhanced by having them role-play resistant reactions to social pressures to use alcohol and drugs. Interventions that use the principles of inoculation theory have been shown to be effective in reducing tendencies to engage in the targeted behaviors.

Attitudinal Advocacy

Another potentially powerful technique for changing attitudes is to induce people to engage in behavior that has implications for their attitudes. Instead of effecting attitude change by presenting target individuals with a communication, their own behavior provides the feedback that produces change in their attitudes. Systematic investigation of the impact of behavior on attitudes, like systematic research on message-based persuasion, began with the early research program of Hovland et al. (1953), within which the influence of role-playing on attitudes was examined. In Janis and King's (1954) experiment, for example, participants who were assigned to give talks on various topics were more persuaded by talks that they themselves delivered to other students than by talks that these other students delivered to them. Similarly, Janis and Mann (1965) had female participants who were heavy smokers role-play a cancer patient who was told by a physician that she had lung cancer. Role-playing proved more effective in reducing these women's smoking than passive exposure to the same antismoking information, and this difference in effectiveness was maintained over an 18-month period.

Research on the effects of behavior on attitudes has been organized around competing theoretical positions that feature differing assumptions about underlying psychological processes. Important in the early period was Janis's (1968) biased-scanning hypothesis whereby role-players focus their thoughts on role-supportive arguments and suppress thoughts that would be critical of such arguments. Janis reasoned that, in order for attitude change to occur, positive incentives for holding the advocated position must also be present and negative incentives must be absent. In contrast, Festinger's (1957) dissonance theory took the view that holding a position inconsistent with one's attitude created *cognitive dissonance*, an unpleasant state of arousal that motivated attitude change. One of the early insights from dissonance research was that counterattitudinal behavior changes attitudes toward such behaviors, but only when the incentives for the behaviors are kept to a level that is so minimal that the incentive itself is not seen as the main reason for the behavior. Subsequent research showed that dissonance from counterattitudinal advocacy is particularly motivating and attitude change is especially pronounced when an individual accepts personal responsibility for his or her behavior bringing about an unwanted consequence (Cooper & Fazio, 1984). An example of such an unwanted consequence for a person who gives a counterattitudinal speech is effectively persuading audience members to adopt a viewpoint that he or she does not privately endorse. If the inducement to give this speech was small and personal responsibility for this behavior was present as well, the person who gave the speech would be likely to change toward his or her advocacy.

As several theorists have suggested, the reason that arousal ensues in experiments on attitudinal advocacy in the classic dissonance paradigm is that such acts threaten the role-player's self-identity or integrity (Aronson, 1969; Steele, 1988). It is indeed plausible that people would be uncomfortable thinking of themselves as willing to engage in behavior with undesirable consequences. Having others think of oneself in this way should also create discomfort. However, if the role-player adopts the advocated position, it would no longer seem harmful to persuade others to hold this same attitude. Attitude change thereby restores the role-player's self-integrity and produces a favorable self-presentation as well. These self-interpretations of the effects of attitudinal advocacy thus elaborate and clarify dissonance theory by providing a rationale for the generalization that taking responsibility for aversive consequences produces attitude change.

An alternative proposal about the processes that mediate the impact of behavior on attitudes gives priority to attributional processes. According to this "self-perception" account (Bem, 1972), such attitude change is a product, not of the motivationally driven process assumed by dissonance theory, but of a cool interpretive process of explaining why one has engaged in a behavior. Thus, when people engage in counterattitudinal behavior in the presence of a strong inducing force (e.g., the offer of a substantial amount of money), they infer that their behavior reflects the inducing force, not their underlying attitude. When people instead engage in counterattitudinal behavior in the absence of such a force, they manifest attitude change because they infer that their behavior follows from their underlying attitude. This behavior-congruent attitude, which would differ from their initial attitude, would thus be a by-product of an attributional process whereby role-players attempt to explain their own behavior. By this account, in the absence of an external pressure, people make a simple inference that their attitude corresponds to their recent and salient behavior. This theory does not consider the aversiveness of the consequences of behavior, nor the arousal that behavior may produce. In Bem's (1972) view, incentives for engaging in behavior affect attitudes by means of their attributional significance, in contrast to Janis's (1968) assumption that incentives portray consequences of the behavior and Festinger's (1957) assumption that they can justify the behavior.

Bem's attributional account does not now appear to provide a viable explanation of the self-persuasion produced by typical dissonance experiments on attitudinal advocacy. This inadequacy reflects the abundant evidence that an unpleasant state of arousal is a critical determinant of this type of attitude change, as dissonance theorists argued. However, the self-perception process that Bem described does provide a plausible account of people's attitudes under more limited circumstances. Specifically, when people initially form their attitudes, they may indeed use their behavior as a guide to their attitudes, because they lack other information and ordinarily have little reason to experience negative arousal. Similarly, to the extent that people's prior attitudes are weak or ambiguous, they are more likely to make the simple inference that their attitudes are consistent with the attitudinal implications of their recent behavior. Although the motivational processes described by dissonance theory do not necessarily presume that prior attitudes are strong, they do require that the person engaging in the advocacy behavior be upset by the unwanted consequences of this behavior. This arousal may be more likely to ensue when the attitude relevant to the advocacy is strong or at least unambiguous.

In summary, attitudinal advocacy can be a powerful means for changing attitudes and behaviors. The key principle is that bringing people's attitudes and behaviors together in their minds can produce an uncomfortable state of arousal when this conjunction threatens their self-identity or integrity. Attitude change may ensue, but under some circumstances behavior change may ensue as well. For example, if existing behaviors are undesirable (e.g., eating high-fat foods, discriminating against members of minority groups), these behaviors can be portrayed as inconsistent with attitudes and as having undesirable consequences. Illustrating this technique, researchers made participants aware that, despite their proconservation attitudes, their actual behavior needlessly wasted precious water and energy resources (Dickerson, Thibodeau, Aronson, & Miller, 1992). To reduce the ensuing dissonance, participants increased the frequency of behaviors that conserve water and energy.

Conclusion

Research on attitude change has examined a great range of variables: for example, communicator variables such as credibility or likability, message content variables such as level of fear or repetition, and recipient variables such as self-esteem and need for cognition. This research has shown that such variables seldom have simple effects, but can operate to increase or decrease persuasion or under some circumstances can have no effect. Modern theories of attitude change have revealed that the reasons for this empirical complexity lie in the multiple psychological processes that can mediate attitude change. In demonstrating that many processes are important, this research has begun to display the true complexity of attitude change. This complexity is consistent with the fact that a great variety of persuasive appeals appear in advertising, public health announcements, and political campaigns, and that many of these techniques are effective in producing attitude change. Achieving systematic understanding of why differing approaches to persuasion are effective remains a challenging goal, toward which attitude researchers have made considerable progress.

[See also Cognitive Consistency Theories.]

Bibliography

Aronson, E. (1969). The theory of cognitive dissonance: A current perspective. In L. Berkowitz (Ed.), *Advances in experimental social psychology* (Vol. 4, pp. 1–34). New York: Academic Press.

Bem, D. J. (1972). Self-perception theory. In L. Berkowitz (Ed.), *Advances in experimental social psychology* (Vol. 6, pp. 1–62). New York: Academic Press.

Chaiken, S., Liberman, A., & Eagly, A. H. (1989). Heuristic and systematic processing within and beyond the persuasion context. In J. S. Uleman & J. A. Bargh (Eds.), *Unintended thought* (pp. 212–252). New York: Guilford Press.

Chaiken, S., Wood, W., & Eagly, A. H. (1996). Principles of persuasion. In E. T. Higgins & A. W. Kruglanski (Eds.), *Social psychology: Handbook of basic principles* (pp. 702–742). New York: Guilford Press. Includes a review of attitude change research organized into areas of attitudinal advocacy, message-based persuasion, and social influence.

Cooper, J., & Fazio, R. H. (1984). A new look at dissonance theory. In L. Berkowitz (Ed.), *Advances in experimental social psychology* (Vol. 17, pp. 229–266). Orlando, FL: Academic Press.

Dickerson, C. A., Thibodeau, R., Aronson, E., & Miller, D. (1992). Using cognitive dissonance to encourage water conservation. *Journal of Applied Social Psychology, 22,* 841–854.

Eagly, A. H., & Chaiken, S. (1993). *The psychology of attitudes.* Fort Worth, TX: Harcourt Brace Jovanovich. A general book on attitudes that includes detailed consideration of all areas of attitude change research.

Eagly, A. H., & Chaiken, S. (1998). Attitude structure and function. In D. T. Gilbert, S. T. Fiske, & G. Lindzey (Eds.), *The handbook of social psychology* (4th ed., Vol. 1, pp. 269–322). New York: McGraw-Hill.

Festinger, L. (1957). *A theory of cognitive dissonance.* Evanston, IL: Row, Peterson.

Fishbein, M., & Ajzen, I. (1975). *Belief, attitude, intention, and behavior: An introduction to theory and research.* Reading, MA: Addison-Wesley.

Greenwald, A. G. (1968). Cognitive learning, cognitive response to persuasion, and attitude change. In A. G. Greenwald, T. C. Brock, & T. M. Ostrom (Eds.), *Psychological foundations of attitudes* (pp. 147–170). New York: Academic Press.

Hovland, C. I., Janis, I. L., & Kelley, H. H. (1953). *Communication and persuasion: Psychological studies of opinion change.* New Haven, CT: Yale University Press.

Janis, I. L. (1968). Attitude change via role playing. In R. P. Abelson, E. Aronson, W. J. McGuire, T. M. Newcomb, M. J. Rosenberg, & P. H. Tannenbaum (Eds.), *Theories of cognitive consistency: A sourcebook* (pp. 810–818). Chicago: Rand-McNally.

Janis, I. L., & King, B. T. (1954). The influence of role playing on opinion change. *Journal of Abnormal and Social Psychology, 49,* 211–218.

Janis, I. L., & Mann, L. (1965). Effectiveness of emotional role-playing in modifying smoking habits and attitudes. *Journal of Experimental Research in Personality, 1,* 84–90.

Johnson, B. T., & Eagly, A. H. (1989). The effects of involvement on persuasion: A meta-analysis. *Psychological Bulletin, 106,* 290–314.

McGuire, W. J. (1964). Inducing resistance to persuasion: Some contemporary approaches. In L. Berkowitz (Ed.), *Advances in experimental social psychology* (Vol. 1, pp. 191–229). New York: Academic Press.

McGuire, W. J. (1972). Attitude change: The information-processing paradigm. In C. G. McClintock (Ed.), *Experimental social psychology* (pp. 108–141). New York: Holt, Rinehart, & Winston.

Petty, R. E., & Cacioppo, J. T. (1986). *Communication and persuasion: Central and peripheral routes to attitude change.* New York: Springer-Verlag.

Petty, R. E., Ostrom, T. M., & Brock, T. C. (Eds.). (1981). *Cognitive responses in persuasion.* Hillsdale, NJ: Erlbaum.

Petty, R. E., & Wegener, D. T. (1998). Attitude change: Multiple roles for persuasion variables. In D. Gilbert, S. Fiske, & G. Lindzey (Eds.), *The handbook of social psychology* (4th ed., Vol. 1, pp. 323–390). New York: McGraw-Hill. Provides a comprehensive review of persuasion research, organized around various classes of persuasion variables.

Sherif, M., & Hovland, C. I. (1961). *Social judgment: Assimilation and contrast effects in communication and attitude change.* New Haven, CT: Yale University Press.

Sherif, C. W., Sherif, M., & Nebergall, R. E. (1965). *Attitude and attitude change: The social judgment-involvement approach.* Philadelphia: Saunders.

Steele, C. M. (1988). The psychology of self-affirmation: Sustaining the integrity of the self. In L. Berkowitz (Ed.), *Advances in experimental social psychology* (Vol. 21, pp. 261–302). San Diego, CA: Academic Press.

Alice H. Eagly

Attitude Measurement

Theoretically, the term *attitude* refers to a hypothetical construct, namely a predisposition to evaluate some object in a favorable or unfavorable manner. The predisposition cannot be directly observed and is inferred from individuals' responses to the object. These responses can run from overt behavior (such as approaching or avoiding the object) and explicit verbal statements to covert responses, which may be outside of the individual's awareness (such as minute facial expressions or the speed with which a letter string can be recognized as a meaningful word, as explained below). In practice, however, most researchers rely on answers to direct questions, such as, Do you approve or disapprove of how the president is handling his job? Direct questions are the most feasible procedure for assessing the attitudes of the population at large; for example, in representative sample surveys. In laboratory research, direct questions can be supplemented with more indirect procedures. Self-reports of attitudes are highly context dependent and minor changes in question wording, question format, and question order can dramatically alter the obtained results. Accordingly, a discussion of attitude measurement cannot be restricted to making an inventory of the most popular measurement procedures; instead, it needs to address how individuals answer attitude questions, including the psychological processes underlying the emergence of context effects.

Direct Attitude Questions

Answering an attitude question entails several tasks. Respondents (1) need to determine the meaning of the question; (2) need to retrieve relevant information from memory to (3) form an attitude judgment; and (4) usually need to format this judgment to fit the response alternatives provided by the researcher. Moreover, (5) they may want to edit their judgment before they report it, due to reasons of social desirability and self-presentation. Respondents' performance of these tasks is highly context dependent (for a comprehensive review of relevant theorizing and research see Sudman, Bradburn, & Schwarz, 1996, chapters 3–6).

Question Comprehension. The crucial issue at this stage is whether the respondent's understanding of the question matches what the researcher had in mind: Is the attitude object that the respondent identifies as the target of the question the one that the researcher intended? Does the respondent's understanding tap the intended facet of the issue and the intended evaluative dimension? Not surprisingly, researchers are urged to write clear and simple questions and to avoid unfamiliar or ambiguous terms. Sudman and Bradburn's *Asking Questions* (San Francisco, 1983) provides much useful advice in this regard. Even familiar terms, however, are open to interpretation, and minor changes in question wording may result in markedly different answers. Moreover, question comprehension is highly context dependent and preceding questions, as well as the formal response alternatives presented as part of a question, may influence respondents' interpretation.

Suppose, for example, that respondents are asked to report how highly they think of a politician along an 11-point rating scale, ranging from "not so highly" to "very highly." To provide a rating, they need to determine if "not so highly" pertains to absence of positive thoughts or to the presence of negative thoughts. To do so, they may draw on the context of the question, including formal characteristics of the rating scale. When the numeric values of the rating scale run from $0 =$ "not so highly" to $10 =$ "very highly," respondents have been found to interpret "not so highly" as reflecting the absence of positive thoughts; but when the scale runs from $-5 =$ "not so highly" to $+5 =$ "very highly," they have been found to interpret "not so highly" as pertaining to the presence of negative thoughts. Empirically, this shift in the interpretation of the verbal end anchors resulted in dramatic shifts in the obtained ratings. Chapter 3 of Sudman et al. (1996, cited above) discusses the interplay of semantic and pragmatic processes that underlies such changes in question interpretation and reviews relevant findings.

Information Retrieval and Judgment. Once respondents determined what the question refers to, they need to recall relevant information from memory. In some cases, they may have direct access to a previously formed relevant judgment that they can offer as an answer. In most cases, however, they will not find an appropriate answer readily stored in memory and will need to compute a judgment on the spot. To do so, they need to form a mental representation of the attitude object and of a standard, against which the object is evaluated. The resulting judgment depends on which information happens to come to mind at that point in time and on how this information is used.

As a large body of research in social cognition demonstrated, individuals rarely retrieve all information that may bear on an attitude object but truncate the search process as soon as enough information has come to mind to form a judgment with sufficient subjective certainty (see Wyer & Srull, *Memory and Cognition in Its Social Context*, Hillsdale, NJ, 1989, for a review). Hence, the judgment depends on the first few pieces of information that come to mind. Whereas some information may always come to mind when the person thinks of this object (and is therefore called chronically accessible), other information may be only temporarily accessible; for example, because it has been brought to mind by preceding questions. Changes in what is temporarily accessible are at the heart of many context effects in attitude measurement, whereas chronically accessible information contributes some stability to attitude judgments.

How accessible information influences the attitude judgment depends on how it is used. Information that is included in the mental representation formed of the attitude object results in assimilation effects, i.e., the judgment becomes more positive (negative) when information with positive (negative) implications comes to mind. In contrast, information that is used in forming a mental representation of the standard against which the attitude object is evaluated results in contrast effect. In this case, the judgment becomes more negative (positive) when information with positive (negative) implications comes to mind and is used as a positive (negative) standard of comparison. As an example, suppose a preceding question brings a politician to mind who was involved in a scandal (say, Richard Nixon). When a subsequent question pertains to the trustworthiness of American politicians in general, Richard Nixon is likely to be included in the representation formed of "politicians" as a group, resulting in judgments of decreased trustworthiness (an assimilation effect). Suppose, however, that the question pertains to the trustworthiness of Bill Clinton, rather than to politicians in general. In this case, Richard Nixon cannot be included in the representation formed of the attitude object "Bill Clinton"; instead, he is likely to serve as a (rather negative) standard of comparison, relative to which Bill Clinton will be evaluated as more trustworthy than would otherwise be the case (a contrast effect). As this example illustrates, the same context question can have profoundly different effects on superficially similar subsequent questions, resulting in many apparent inconsistencies.

A host of different variables are involved depending on whether a given piece of information is used in constructing a representation of the attitude object (resulting in assimilation effects), or of a standard of comparison (resulting in contrast effects). Chapter 5 of Sudman et al. (1996) reviews these variables and summarizes a theoretical model that predicts the direction, size, and generalization of context effects in attitude measurement.

Response Formatting. Once respondents have formed a judgment, they can only report it in their own words when an *open response format* is used, which requires the researcher to content analyze the answers prior to statistical analysis. In most studies, however, respondents are asked to provide an answer in a *closed response format*, either by rating the attitude object along a scale or by selecting one of several substantive response alternatives presented to them.

Categorical Response Alternatives. When the question offers several distinct opinions and asks the respondent to select the one that is closest to his or her own position, it is important to ensure that the set of response alternatives offered covers the whole range of plausible positions. Any option omitted from the set of response alternatives is unlikely to be reported, even when respondents are offered a general "other" response option, which is rarely used. Similarly, few respondents report not having an opinion on an issue when this option is not explicitly provided—yet, they may be happy to report so when "don't know" is offered as an alternative. Howard Schuman and Stanley Presser review such question constraint effects (and numerous other findings) in *Questions and Answers in Attitude Surveys* (New York, 1981).

Rating Scales. Rating scales are the most commonly used response format in attitude measurement. Typically, a numerical scale with verbally labeled endpoints (e.g., -3 = strongly disagree; $+3$ = strongly agree) is presented and respondents are asked to check the number that best represents their opinion. As noted above, the numeric values may themselves influence the interpretation of the verbal endpoints and a format that presents a continuum from negative to positive numbers emphasizes the bipolar nature of the underlying dimension, whereas a format that presents only

positive numbers is more adequate for a unipolar dimension. Alternatively, each point of the rating scale may be labeled, a format that is common in telephone interviews. In general, the retest-reliability of fully labeled scales is somewhat higher than that of partially labeled scales, and retest reliability decreases as the number of scale points increases beyond seven, reflecting the difficulty of making many fine-grained distinctions. Jon Krosnick and Leandre Fabrigar review the relevant literature in *Handbook of Attitude Questionnaires* (New York, in press).

Respondents' use of rating scales is highly context dependent. As numerous studies demonstrated, respondents use the most extreme stimuli to anchor the endpoints of a rating scale. As a result, a given stimulus will be rated as less extreme if presented in the context of a more extreme one, than if presented in the context of a less extreme one. In addition, if the number of stimuli to be rated is large, respondents attempt to use all categories of the rating scale about equally often to be maximally informative. Accordingly, the specific ratings given also depend on the frequency distribution of the presented stimuli. These processes have been conceptualized in a number of related models of rating scale use, of which Alan Parducci's range-frequency model is the most comprehensive. (For an accessible summary see his article "The Relativism of Absolute Judgment," *Scientific American*, 1968, *219*, 84–90.) As a result, ratings of the same object cannot be directly compared when they were collected in different contexts, rendering comparisons over time or between studies difficult.

Response Editing. Finally, respondents may want to edit their answer before they communicate it, reflecting considerations of social desirability and self-presentation. Not surprisingly, editing on the basis of social desirability is particularly likely when the question is highly threatening and it is more pronounced in face-to-face interviews than in self-administered questionnaires, which provide a higher degree of confidentiality. Attitude researchers have developed a number of techniques to attenuate respondents' self-presentation concerns (Sudman and Bradburn, 1983, for a review).

Some Classic Attitude Scale Formats. In representative sample surveys, as well as most psychological experiments, respondents' attitudes toward an object are typically assessed by asking only one or two questions, despite the usual textbook admonition to use multi-item scales. In fact, the classic textbook examples of multi-item attitude scales are rarely used in practice. [*See* Guttman Scale *and* Likert Scale.] All of these scales require extensive topic-specific item development and pretesting to arrive at a set of items that forms an internally consistent scale, a factor that contributes to their limited use.

In contrast, the Semantic Differential scale (Osgood,

Suci, & Tannenbaum, Urbana, IL, 1957), is a ready-to-use scale that can be applied to any topic without new development work, making it considerably more popular. Respondents are asked to rate the attitude object (e.g., "abortion") on a set of 7-point bipolar adjective scales. The adjectives used as endpoint labels reflect three general factors, namely evaluation (e.g., good-bad; pleasant-unpleasant), potency (e.g., strong-weak; small-large), and activity (e.g., active-passive; fast-slow). Of these factors, evaluation is considered the primary indicator of respondents' attitude toward the object, as reflected in the objects' (relatively global) connotative meaning.

Attitude Accessibility. Finally, attempts to measure attitudes by asking a direct attitude question may be complemented by assessing (in milliseconds) how long it takes a respondent to provide an answer. The assumption is that respondents who have formed a strong object-evaluation link in the past will be faster in answering the question than respondents who form an evaluation for the first time, when thinking about the question. Even when both respondents arrive at the same evaluative answer (and feel equally strongly about the attitude object), the speed with which they can give the answer has been found to provide important additional information. Most importantly, attitudes that are more accessible in memory, as indicated by faster responses, are more likely to guide an individual's behavior than attitudes that are less accessible. Fazio and Roskos-Ewoldson provide an accessible review of relevant research (in Shavitt & Brock, Eds., *Persuasion*, Boston, 1994).

Indirect Measures. Complementing direct attitude questions, researchers have developed a number of indirect measures, often intended to assess attitudes that respondents may not be willing to report or of which they may themselves be unaware. Such measures include projective procedures, such as the Thematic Apperception Test, as well as more recent developments aimed at assessing the connotations of an attitude object or the accessibility of an evaluative response in memory. [*See* Thematic Apperception Test.]

One promising procedure, referred to as the Lexical Decision Task, is based on the observation that a letter string (e.g., "doctor") is more quickly recognized as a meaningful word when preceded by a closely related concept (e.g., "nurse") rather than an unrelated one (e.g., "butter"). In applications of this method, meaningful words as well as meaningless letter strings are presented for a very short time and respondents are asked to say, as quickly as possible, if what they see is a word or a nonword. Of interest is how fast they can recognize a given evaluatively laden word when it is, or is not, preceded by the attitude object. Using this procedure to assess racial attitudes in the United States, researchers observed, for example, that words describing positive personality traits were recognized faster than words describing negative personality traits when preceded by "Whites," whereas the reverse held true when the same traits were preceded by "Blacks." These findings indicate that positive traits are more closely associated with the attitude object "Whites" than negative traits, whereas the reverse holds for the attitude object "Blacks." The results obtained with this indirect procedure are usually unrelated to direct self-reports of racial attitudes. Dovidio and Fazio (in J. M. Tanur, Ed., *Questions about Questions*, New York, 1992) provide a review of this and related techniques.

Observational Measures

There are two basic observational measures: behavior observation and bodily reactions.

Behavioral Observation. In principle, an individual's attitude toward some object may be inferred from his or her behavior toward it. Unfortunately, however, individuals' behavior is influenced by many variables other than their attitudes and the attitude-behavior relationship is typically weak. Hence, direct behavioral observation is rarely used to assess an individual's attitude.

Bodily Reactions. Alternatively, researchers may observe individuals' physiological responses to the attitude object. If an attitude object evokes strong feelings, exposure to it should be associated with increased activation of the sympathetic nervous system. Increased sympathetic activation results in increased sweat glands activity, which can be measured by *electrodermal measurements*: assessing the resistance of the skin to low level electric currents. Unfortunately, these measures do not reflect the direction (favorable or unfavorable) of the evaluative response, which limits their usefulness.

More promising are attempts to assess changes in individuals' facial expression in response to an attitude object. Overt facial expressions (like smiling or frowning) may often be observed in response to attitude objects that elicit strong reactions. But these expressions may be intentionally concealed and many evaluative reactions may be too subtle to evoke overt expressive behaviors. Even subtle evaluative reactions are associated, however, with low-level activation of facial muscles that can be detected by electromyography (EMG). These muscle reactions reflect the direction (favorable vs. unfavorable) as well as the intensity of the evaluative response, yet the obtained measures can be distorted by facial movements that are unrelated to the evaluative reaction, rendering their interpretation somewhat ambiguous in the absence of additional evidence.

Another potentially promising development involves the measurement of brain activity through electroencephalography (EEG), the assessment of small electric signals recorded from the scalp. This procedure, however, does not lend itself to a direct assessment of positive or negative responses. Instead, it capitalizes on the observation that unexpected stimuli evoke brain wave activity that differs from the activity evoked by expected stimuli. Hence, one may detect if a target object is evaluated positively or negatively by embedding its presentation in a long series of other objects with a known evaluation. The brain activity evoked by the target object will then indicate if its evaluation is consistent or inconsistent with the evaluation of the context objects.

An accessible introduction to these and related procedures is provided by Cacioppo, Petty, Losch, and Crites (in Shavitt & Brock, 1994, cited above).

Bibliography

Cacioppo, J. T., Bush, L. K., & Tassinary, L. G. (1992). Microexpressive facial reactions as a function of affective stimuli. *Personality and Social Psychology Bulletin, 18,* 515–526. Illustrates the use of physiological measures of facial reaction in attitude measurement.

Cacioppo, J. T., Crites, S. L., Berntson, G. G., & Coles, M. G. H. (1993). If attitudes affect how stimuli are processed, should they not affect event-related brain potential? *Psychological Science, 4,* 108–112. Illustrates the use of event-related brain potential in attitude measurement.

Clark, H. H., & Schober, M. F. (1992). Asking questions and influencing answers. In J. M. Tanur (Ed.), *Questions about questions* (pp. 15–48). New York: Russell Sage. A comprehensive review of the communicative processes involved in question comprehension.

DeMaio, T. J. (1984). Social desirability and survey measurement: A review. In C. F. Turner & E. Martin (Eds.), *Surveying subjective phenomena* (Vol. 2, pp. 257–281). New York: Russell Sage. Reviews the influence of social desirability and self-presentation concerns on attitude reports.

Eagly, A. H., & Chaiken, S. (1993). *The psychology of attitudes.* Fort Worth, TX: Harcourt Brace Jovanovich. A comprehensive attitudes textbook, including a good treatment of classic approaches to attitude measurement.

Fazio, R. (1995). Attitudes as object-evaluation associations: Determinants, consequences, and correlates of attitude accessibility. In R. Petty & J. A. Krosnick (Eds.), *Attitude strength: Antecedents and consequences* (pp. 247–282). Mahwah, NJ: Erlbaum. A review of attitude accessibility research, based on the speed with which respondents answer attitude questions.

Krosnick, J. A., & Fabrigar, L. (in press). *Handbook of attitude questionnaires.* New York: Oxford University Press. A comprehensive review of research into the design of attitude questionnaires.

Oskamp, S. (1991). *Attitudes and opinions.* Englewood Cliffs, NJ: Prentice-Hall. A general attitudes textbook, including a good treatment of classic approaches to attitude measurement and opinion surveys.

Schwarz, N., & Bless, H. (1992). Constructing reality and its alternatives: Assimilation and contrast effects in social judgment. In L. L. Martin & A. Tesser (Eds.), *The construction of social judgment* (pp. 217–245). Hillsdale, NJ: Erlbaum. A comprehensive model of the emergence of context effects in attitude measurement.

Schwarz, N., & Sudman, S. (Eds.). (1992). *Context effects in social and psychological research.* New York: Springer-Verlag. The contributors review different approaches to context effects in attitude measurement, focusing mostly on representative sample surveys.

Schwarz, N., & Sudman, S. (Eds.). (1996). *Answering questions: Methodology for determining cognitive and communicative processes in survey research.* San Francisco: Jossey-Bass. The contributors review different methodologies for assessing how respondents answer attitude questions.

Sudman, S., Bradburn, N. M., & Schwarz, N. (1996). *Thinking about answers: The application of cognitive processes to survey methodology.* San Francisco, CA: Jossey-Bass. A comprehensive review of the cognitive and communicative processes involved in answering attitude questions.

Tourangeau, R., & Rasinski, K. A. (1988). Cognitive processes underlying context effects in attitude measurement. *Psychological Bulletin, 103,* 299–314. A comprehensive review of context effects in attitude measurement.

Norbert Schwarz

ATTRACTION. Humans are among the most social creatures in the animal kingdom, a reflection of the fact that from birth to death each individual's welfare and survival depend on the actions of other people. The answer to the question "Who likes whom and why?" thus has special import for people, and positive or negative sentiment for others is a central theme of the human condition.

Although attempts to identify the laws governing interpersonal attraction have been evident at least since Aristotle, the first empirical investigations date from J. L. Moreno's development of "sociometry." In *Who Shall Survive?* (1934/1953), Moreno presented his method for assessing interpersonal "attractions and repulsions" as reflected in people's preferences for interacting with, or avoiding, certain members of their group. Sociometry became integral to the emerging discipline of social psychology, but subsequent investigation revealed that questions of "affiliation," or who *interacts* with whom and why, are different from questions of "attraction," or who *likes* whom and why. Attraction has been shown to be neither a necessary nor a sufficient condition for affiliation; people often interact with those they do not like and attraction to another does not always lead to interaction.

Fear is one condition that often leads people to interact with others, especially others who are experiencing the same fearful situation (Schachter, 1959). Other determinants of affiliation now are described by large bodies of research addressed to such topics as people's need for social comparison, and there is also now strong evidence that the company of others promotes the individual's survival, reducing morbidity and premature mortality.

Social psychological investigations of attraction rapidly increased in the 1960s (Berscheid & Walster [Hatfield], 1969). Attraction has been defined as a positive "attitude" toward another, or a relatively stable predisposition to respond to another individual in positive ways, including: attributions of positive characteristics to the other; the experience of positive emotions and feelings in association with the other; and positive actions, including those which maintain proximity to the other or enhance the other's welfare (Berscheid, 1985). Beyond defining attraction as an attitude, a hypothetical construct inferred from observable behavior, attraction theorists have done little to explicate the concept. Little effort, for example, has been devoted to explicating the different varieties of attraction (e.g., respect, affection).

Love, the strongest variety of attraction, constitutes an important exception to the rule of conceptual neglect. Several theories of love have been offered in recent years (Sternberg & Barnes, 1988) and many taxonomies of varieties of love have been proposed. Virtually all love taxonomies include "romantic love," which has been of special interest in part because this variety of love is generally regarded as a prerequisite for marriage in Western culture. The antecedents of romantic love were initially believed to be the same in kind, but present in higher strength, as those producing such mild forms of attraction as liking. However, romantic love and liking (sometimes termed *companionate love*) are now viewed as qualitatively different phenomena (e.g., compared to liking, romantic love is relatively short-lived). Empirical investigations of romantic love continue to increase (e.g., Hendrick & Hendrick, 1992). In addition to qualities characteristic of all forms of attraction, especially a concern for the other's welfare, romantic love also importantly includes sexual desire. Recent evidence suggests that this form of love is pancultural.

Although many nonverbal measures of attraction have been explored over the years (e.g., eye gaze, attention), most have been found to be contaminated by factors extraneous to attraction. As a consequence, the most frequently used measure of attraction remains the simple question, How much do you like or dislike X?—usually answered on a bipolar scale ranging from extreme dislike to extreme like. Recent studies of the structure of affective space suggest, however, that positive and negative affect are relatively independent di-

mensions and, thus, bipolar scales conceal such important phenomena as ambivalence (e.g., Cacioppo & Bernstein, 1994). Attention to both the positive and negative affective dimensions has become important as investigators have shifted their focus from attraction between individuals who are strangers to one another to people engaged in ongoing close relationships (Berscheid, 1985; Berscheid & Reis, 1998).

Myriad motives may underlie an individual's attraction for another, reflecting the fact that people rely on others for the satisfaction of many different needs throughout their lives. Nevertheless, social psychologists have identified several "laws" of attraction. These general principles describe conditions that tend to elicit attraction because they signal that the other is likely to satisfy many commonly experienced needs and, at the least, is unlikely to cause the individual harm.

Perhaps the most basic principle of attraction is familiarity; familiar people usually are judged to be safe. Familiarity grows with repeated exposure to the other or to people who are similar to that other. Many investigations of the "mere exposure" hypothesis have confirmed that under most conditions, repeated exposure to a person or object enhances attraction to it (Bornstein, 1989).

Familiarity is at least partially responsible for the well-established finding that people are more likely to be attracted to, and initiate relationships with, others who are in close physical proximity than they are with people only a short distance away. Physical proximity to another not only makes an interaction attempt less costly in time and effort, but it often increases familiarity with the other which itself increases the probability of interaction initiation. For example, investigators have found that the more strangers have seen but not interacted with another, the more likely they are to choose to interact with that person over others less familiar. However, the effect of increasing familiarity may not be as beneficial in long-term relationships as it is between strangers. Familiar people gradually lose their ability to capture the individual's attention and may become neglected, and there also is suggestive evidence that familiarity in romantic relationships may reduce the partners' sexual desire for each other.

Reciprocity is another venerable law of attraction; people like people who like them. Another's expression of esteem and approbation, in fact, is regarded as a "universal reinforcer" of social behavior. Another's esteem is a valuable commodity because it signals that the other not only is unlikely to harm the individual, but may act in ways that promote the individual's well-being. The reciprocity of attraction effect has been demonstrated experimentally, as well as in more naturalistic interaction situations, providing validation for the accepted dictum that "attraction breeds attraction."

One possible exception to the attraction reciprocity

effect that has received attention concerns people who possess low self-esteem; for such individuals, incongruent expressions of high esteem from others may cause cognitive dissonance and discomfort. Investigations of the "positivity versus congruency" hypothesis indicate that, regardless of their self-esteem, most people prefer positivity in first encounters with strangers; preference in long-term relationships is less clear (Berscheid & Reis, 1998). Similarity is yet another well-established principle of attraction; similarity along virtually every dimension yet examined has been shown to be associated with attraction. Many types of similarity have been shown to be causal determinants of attraction and attitudinal dissimilarity appears to produce affective "repulsion" (Rosenbaum, 1986). Although one form of dissimilarity, personality "complementarity" (e.g., a "dominant" individual paired with a "submissive person"), was initially hypothesized to produce attraction, there is little evidence to support the hypothesis. For example, Caspi and Herbener (1990) found evidence of assortative mating (like marrying like) along personality dimensions.

But as is true of the other principles of attraction, the similarity rule has been shown to have exceptions as well as moderators. Certain personality dispositions have been shown to heighten or decrease the impact of similarity on attraction, for example, and the closeness of the relationship appears to interact with the nature of the similarity to enhance or reduce attraction (Tesser, 1988). Moreover, recent studies continue to confirm that at least part of the association between similarity and attraction is produced by people's assumption that similar others will like them more than dissimilar others will, thereby inducing attraction reciprocity.

A principle of attraction that has captured much interest in recent years concerns the other's physical appearance; people tend to like those who are physically attractive more than those who are not (see Hatfield & Sprecher, 1986). This effect holds true in a wide range of situations, from the dating and mating arena to schooling and employment settings, and from infancy through old age, and it has been demonstrated with all ethnic, national, and cultural groups examined.

One explanation of the effect has been the "what is beautiful is good" stereotype associated with physically attractive people. Meta-analyses of studies of the stereotype have shown that people ascribe more favorable personality traits and more successful life outcomes to the physically attractive. Differential inferences appear to be largest on social competence dimensions, intermediate on personal adjustment and intellectual competence dimensions, but nonexistent with respect to integrity and concern for others (Eagly, Ashmore, Makhijani, & Longo, 1991). The content of the stereotype may differ across cultures, however. Wheeler and Kim (in press) found that what is "good" in collectivist cultures, and thus what is perceived to be characteristic of physically attractive people, may be different from what is "good" in an individualistic culture such as the United States. For example, Koreans perceived attractive people to be higher in integrity and concern for others but North Americans did not.

Researchers have almost exclusively focused on facial attractiveness. Facially attractive individuals are usually identified through the consensus of many judges, and there appears to be high agreement, even across cultural groups, about who is attractive. Interest in identifying the factors associated with such judgments has increased. Some investigators have examined the size and arrangement of facial features in order to identify those configurations associated with judgments of attractiveness (e.g., Cunningham, 1986). Others, inspired by evolutionary theory, have hypothesized that faces representing the mathematical average of faces in a population should be perceived as attractive.

Evidence in support of the "attractive is average" hypothesis has been provided by Langlois and her associates (e.g., Langlois & Roggman, 1990). Both male and female computer-generated composites, or "averaged," faces are judged to be more attractive than the individual faces that contribute to the composite. A number of explanations have been offered for the finding, including the preferred evolutionary explanation that average faces are more familiar and familiarity is itself associated with judgments of attractiveness. Indeed, Langlois finds that the association between perceived attractiveness and perceived familiarity in male and female individual faces is strong and positive and, moreover, averaged faces are perceived as more familiar than individual faces contributing to the composite.

The role of physical attractiveness and of other attributes in mate selection continues to be extensively investigated. The basic rule of mate selection is homogamy, or assortative mating, along virtually every dimension examined (except biological sex, reflecting the fact that men and women tend to prefer each other). Only some of the homogamy effect is due to preference, however; a larger proportion is probably due to the fact that the pool of an individual's available partners is overwhelmingly similar on numerous dimensions and thus if the individual is to mate at all, it will be with someone similar.

In addition to other similarities, similarity in the physical attractiveness level of mates, as expressed by the "matching hypothesis," has been found as well; people who progress in courtship and who ultimately marry tend to be more matched in physical attractiveness than chance would predict. Although the matching hypothesis was originally derived from the supposition that people would be more comfortable and thus prefer others of their own social desirability level (physical attractiveness being one component of desirability), it is now clear that given a choice, most people prefer the most physically attractive person available to them. De facto matching in physical attractiveness probably occurs because the most physically attractive tend to pair off, leaving those of lesser attractiveness to pair off among themselves.

The characteristics desired in a potential mate also have been repeatedly examined, with differences between men and women receiving special scrutiny because evolutionary theorists posit that the differential biology of reproduction should result in gender differences in sexual strategy and mate preference (Buss, 1996). The evidence indicates that, overall, men and woman tend to desire the same characteristics in a mate (e.g., kind). Within this general effect, however, many studies conducted across age, racial, and cultural groups have found that although physical attractiveness is an important factor in both men's and women's choices, men more strongly prefer physically attractive mates than women do and women more than men prefer mates who have good earning potential. The extent to which these gender differences reflect the lower socioeconomic status of women as opposed to genetically determined sexual strategy is the subject of debate.

Each of the well-documented principles of attraction—familiarity, proximity, similarity, attraction reciprocity, and physical attractiveness—tend to be confounded in naturalistic situations. For example, similar people are generally arrayed in close proximity to each other and thus, for this reason alone, similar people are also more familiar; people expect similar others to like them which induces attraction reciprocity even before actual interaction and, as discussed, physically attractive people also seem more familiar than the unattractive. It has been demonstrated that people prefer to like others rather than dislike them even when there are countervailing pressures. Mother Nature appears to have cooperated with the human wish to feel positive sentiment toward fellow humans by putting together in time and space people who are more likely than not to like each other.

Bibliography

Berscheid, E. (1985). Interpersonal attraction. In G. Lindzey & E. Aronson (Eds.), *Handbook of social psychology* (3rd ed., pp. 413–484). New York: Random House.

Berscheid, E., & Reis, H. T. (1998). Attraction and close relationships. In S. Fiske, D. Gilbert, & G. Lindzey (Eds.), *Handbook of social psychology* (4th ed., pp. 193–281). New York: McGraw-Hill.

Berscheid, E., & Walster [Hatfield], E. (1969). *Interpersonal attraction*. Reading, MA: Addison-Wesley.

Bornstein, R. F. (1989). Exposure and affect: Overview and meta-analysis of research, 1968–1987. *Psychological Bulletin, 106,* 265–289.

Buss, D. M. (1996). The evolutionary psychology of human social strategies. In E. T. Higgins & A. W. Kruglanski (Eds.), *Social psychology: Handbook of basic principles* (pp. 3–38). New York: Guilford Press.

Cacioppo, J. T., & Berntson, G. C. (1994). Relationship between attitudes and evaluative space: A critical review, with emphasis on the separability of positive and negative substrates. *Psychological Bulletin, 115,* 401–423.

Caspi, A., & Herbener, E. S. (1990). Continuity and change: Assortative marriage and the consistency of personality in adulthood. *Journal of Personality and Social Psychology, 58,* 250–258.

Cunningham, M. R. (1986). Measuring the physical in physical attractiveness: Quasi experiments on the sociobiology of female facial beauty. *Journal of Personality and Social Psychology, 50,* 925–935.

Eagly, A. H., Ashmore, R. D., Makhijani, M. G., & Longo, L. C. (1991). What is beautiful is good, but . . . : A meta analytic review of research on the physical attractiveness stereotype. *Psychological Bulletin, 110,* 109–128.

Hatfield, E., & Sprecher, S. (1986). *Mirror, mirror: The importance of looks in everyday life.* Albany, NY: State University of New York Press.

Hendrick, S. S., & Hendrick, C. (1992) *Romantic love.* Newbury Park, CA: Sage.

Langlois, J. H., & Roggman, L. A. (1990). Attractive faces are only average. *Psychological Science, 5,* 214–220.

Moreno, J. L. (1953). *Who shall survive?* (2nd ed.). Beacon, NY: Beacon House. (Original work published 1934)

Rosenbaum, M. E. (1986). The repulsion hypothesis: On the nondevelopment of relationships. *Journal of Personality and Social Psychology, 51,* 1156–1166.

Schachter, S. (1959). *The psychology of affiliation.* Stanford, CA: Stanford University Press.

Sternberg, R. J., & Barnes, M. L. (Eds.). (1988). *The psychology of love.* New Haven, CT: Yale University Press.

Tesser, A. (1988). Toward a self evaluation maintenance model of social behavior. *Advances in Experimental Social Psychology, 21,* 181–227.

Wheeler, L., & Kim, Y. (1997). What is beautiful is culturally good: The physical attractiveness stereotype has different content in collectivist cultures. *Personality and Social Psychology Bulletin, 23,* 795–800.

Ellen Berscheid

ATTRIBUTION THEORIES. "Why is she constantly provoking her boss?" "Why do all my intimate relationships turn out to be so abusive?" In both of these examples, the inquirer is attempting to discover why he or she or another person behaved in a certain way, or why a certain interpersonal event or series of events occurred. The person is attempting to form an attribution that will explain a behavior or an event. Although there is no single, dominant theory of attribution, several prominent theories have guided much of the research in this domain. In general, all of these theories describe the kinds and combinations of information people typically consider when trying to arrive at explanations of events, the kinds of inferences that follow, and their consequences for our mental, emotional, and social lives.

The "Why," "When," and "What" of Attribution Processes

Why do we, as perceivers, attempt to discern the underlying causes of our own or others' behaviors? According to all of the major theorists, people engage in attributional analyses because of their functional needs to understand, predict, and control what goes on around them. That is, by searching for the stable structures and invariant processes underlying observable behaviors and events, people come to know, predict, and to some degree, control their social worlds (Heider, 1958).

These needs to understand, predict, and control are, of course, not always strongly activated. Indeed, many types of attributional analyses require considerable cognitive effort, and we cannot expect busy social perceivers always to be engaged in causal analyses of their social worlds. When can we expect them to ask "why" questions? Research indicates that they will be most likely to engage in attributional analyses when the available evidence calls into question their understanding of reality. Unexpected events are, perhaps, the prototypical example of situational factors that instigate causal inference processes. Similarly, information indicating a current or potential threat to control tends to engender greater interest in and a more careful, detailed manner of processing relevant attributional information. Perceiver characteristics also have been associated with more frequent or more extensive attributional activity. For example, the chronic feelings of control deprivation often characteristic of depressed perceivers have been shown to be related to more attributional activity (Weary & Edwards, 1996).

What kinds of attributions might result from observation of some behavior or event? A number of underlying dimensions of specific attributions have been identified in the literature. Causal attributions are inferences that explain why an event occurred. Just as scientists attempt to understand complex phenomena by discovering stable, universal laws, so too does the naive attributor attempt to understand the social world by referring transient events to stable, underlying factors. This search for the underlying causes of events is thought to focus on either the enduring aspects of the person involved in the event or to various structural properties of the situation. Consequently, causal attributions often are categorized as internal or as external

to the target person. Examples of internal causes would include the actor's characteristics, such as his or her traits, abilities, or effort expenditure; external attributions would include various factors external to the target, such as task characteristics, other people's actions, or inherent properties of some external entity (e.g., a comedy can be said to be inherently funny). Causal attributions also may be categorized as involving stable or unstable factors, global or specific factors, and controllable or uncontrollable factors. Such underlying categories or dimensions of attributions carry with them important implications for perceivers' subsequent motivations, expectations, affect, and behavior.

It is important to note that although internal, dispositional factors may be invoked as explanations for why a behavior or event occurred, several theorists have argued that dispositional attributions are not the same as causal attributions, which seek to explain why an event occurred. Dispositional attributions involve a kind of impression formation or updating process whereby we learn more about the characteristics of some target person. In this article, our focus on dispositional attributions will be restricted to their use as explanations for why a behavior or event might have occurred.

The "How" of Attribution Processes: Major Theories

There are three major theories of attribution processes.

Heider's Naive Analysis of Action. In his seminal book, Heider (1958) examined action from the point of view of the layperson and as revealed through everyday language. His analysis suggested that perceivers search for the causal structure underlying observed events by attending to potential personal and environmental causal forces. Personal force was viewed as a multiplicative combination of the actor's power or ability ("can" in Heider's terminology) and motivation ("trying"), which was further broken down into both a directional (intention) and a quantitative (effort) component. Environmental force consisted of relevant external factors, primarily task difficulty. In his naive analysis of action, Heider posited that the actor's exertion varies directly with task difficulty and inversely with his or her power or ability.

How do social perceivers extract information about personal and environmental forces from their observations of often complex interpersonal events? This was the explicit focus of Jones's correspondent inference theory.

Jones's Correspondent Inference Theory. According to Jones (Jones & Davis, 1965; Jones & McGillis, 1976), a correspondent inference is a dispositional inference that follows directly from or corresponds to another's observed behavior. How do perceivers make inferences about the correspondence of observed behaviors and dispositions? Correspondent inference theory posited that every action is a choice between alternative actions or between action and inaction. It further postulated that perceivers analyze the chosen behavior in terms of the number of noncommon, or nonoverlapping effects of the chosen and the alternative, unchosen behaviors. Perceivers also consider the degree to which the behavior fits their prior expectations about the outcomes that most people desire (category-based expectancies) and the target person desires (target-based expectancies).

For example, if a person observed a politician advocate the use of products containing chlorofluorocarbons, he or she might infer that the politician is personally antienvironment. What if the perceiver then learned that the talk was given to an audience of scientists concerned about global warming? He or she would be likely to conclude that there would have been few common consequences for the politician of having chosen to give an anti- versus a proenvironment speech for this particular audience. Moreover, the assumed desirability or expected nature of the speech would likely depart from what most perceivers would have expected to hear, given this audience. A confident inference that the politician's personal beliefs correspond to his or her behavior would be very likely.

Currently, several prominent stage models of the dispositional inference process have been advanced (Gilbert, 1989; Trope, 1986). These models owe an intellectual debt to correspondent inference theory. They generally propose that the dispositional inference process involves a relatively automatic behavior identification or characterization stage, wherein an observed behavior is characterized in terms of a disposition, followed by a more effortful, resource-demanding correction stage, wherein the attributed disposition is adjusted for any circumstance or situational factors that might have constrained the actor's behavior. Many studies have provided support for these stage models and have indicated that the correction stage can be impaired by concurrent activities that deplete cognitive resources or by insufficient motivation. Returning to our politician, these stage models would suggest that, as social perceivers, we quickly and effortlessly arrive at an inference that the politician is antienvironment. We then adjust this inference in light of plausible situational factors (audience characteristics inconsistent with the politician's espoused position), if we have the requisite resources and motivation. In this instance, our corrected inference that the politician holds antienvironment beliefs would be stronger after the adjustment process.

Kelley's Models of Attribution Processes. Kelley also built his theory of attribution on the work of Heider. He proposed (1967, 1972) two general classes of

models of the causal inference process: one of these addressed how perceivers arrive at causal inferences by analyzing in a careful and complex fashion the available information; and the other focused on how perceivers arrive at such inferences when they have neither the time, motivation, nor information necessary for such effortful, cognitive analyses. We describe first how, according to Kelley, perceivers infer causality through the use of complex, inductive reasoning.

Kelley proposed that perceivers use the principle of covariation to link potential causes with effects. They attribute the cause of an observed event to that factor which is present when the effect is present and absent when the effect is absent. Kelley considered three classes of potential causes: persons, entities, and time-modality. For example, if the perceiver is trying to explain a person's hostile behavior toward another, he or she might consider whether it is due to something about the person; something about the target, or recipient, of the hostile behavior; or something about the time or circumstance under which the behavior occurred.

According to Kelley, social perceivers use three kinds of information in analyzing the covariation of potential causes and effects: consensus over persons, consistency over time and modality, and distinctiveness over other entities. In essence, perceivers ask three questions: Is everyone behaving in a hostile fashion toward the target, or is the hostile behavior particular to this person? Does the person always behave in a hostile fashion toward the target, or is the hostility particular to a certain time or setting? Is the person hostile toward all other targets, or is there something distinctive about this particular one? Generally, effects that are low in consensus, high in consistency, and low in distinctiveness will be attributed to persons; and effects that are high in consensus, high in consistency, and high in distinctiveness will be attributed to the entity.

The bulk of empirical evidence in the field indicates that perceivers frequently base causal attributions on the covariation principle (for recent extension refinements of Kelley's covariation-based model, see Hewstone & Jaspars, 1987; Hilton & Slugoski, 1986). They sometimes, however, employ a principle of generative force instead of covariation. This principle holds that perceivers' estimations of the causal importance of a disposition or motive would be determined by perceivers' beliefs about its strength. Such is particularly likely to be the case for common events.

What happens when perceivers are unable or unmotivated to invest the cognitive effort necessary to engage in the complex analysis of information described above? Kelley proposed that in such circumstances perceivers rely on their past experience and knowledge of interaction of causal forces. He identified a number of causal schemata based on such information that when activated may allow perceivers to make quick causal inferences. These include the multiple sufficient and the multiple necessary cause schemata, the compensatory schema, and the graded effects schema.

Attributional Errors

Just as visual illusions reveal a great deal about the way our visual system processes information, attributional errors reveal how we think about the causes of our own and others' behavior. Often, these errors are a byproduct of our generally adaptive cognitive strategies for simplifying complex information.

The Fundamental Attribution Error. Both Jones's and Kelley's theories argue that when people do just what the situation ordered, dispositional inferences should logically be discounted. However, people often fail to recognize the extent to which the situation impacts behavior and overestimate the extent to which behavior reflects enduring traits and attitudes. This error has been referred to as the "correspondence bias" or the "fundamental attribution error."

Why does this error occur? Heider (1958) proposed that "behavior tends to engulf the field" and that perceivers tend to attribute behavior to whatever grabs their attention. Since a person's actions are more likely to grab an observer's attention than are subtle situational factors, internal attributions are facilitated. Researchers have provided additional theoretical explanations for this error (Gilbert & Malone, 1995). They have noted that, since situations, especially as perceived by the actor, are relatively "invisible" to observers, the latter may misunderstand the situation facing an actor. Observers also may have unrealistic expectations about how a situation should affect an actor's behaviors, or may categorize the behavior as more extreme than it truly is. Any of these errors would lead perceivers to overestimate the influence of dispositional relative to situational factors. Finally, perceivers may lack the motivation or the ability to correct their spontaneous, effortless dispositional attributions.

What are the consequences of such an error? On a positive note, besides serving as a useful heuristic which saves time and energy, this "error" can engender a sense of control over the social environment and can actually lead to better behavioral predictions in natural settings. Thus, it is an error that does not always lead to mistakes. However, the fundamental attribution error also can have negative consequences. Believing that the main causes of people's behavior reside internally can lead perceivers to be indifferent to the situations faced by the homeless, acquired immune deficiency syndrome (AIDS) patients, and other underprivileged groups. Fortunately, despite its name, the fundamental attribution error is not without limits. Perceivers are less likely to commit the fundamental attribution error if they are suspicious of an ulterior motive, feeling accountable for their judgments, or highly motivated to process information carefully and accurately.

The Actor-Observer Bias. Perceptions of the causes of behavior can depend largely on perspective. Specifically, observers tend to explain others' behavior with dispositional causes, while actors tend to emphasize situational causes for their own behavior. Thus, actors view their own behavior as more variable than do observers.

The explanations for this actor-observer bias are varied. According to the attentional explanation, an observer's attention is drawn to the actor as the source of behavior, while an actor's attention is focused on the environmental context within which a behavior occurred. A more cognitive analysis suggests that actors have more knowledge of their past behaviors and the variation of these behaviors across situations than do observers. The motivation to view themselves as responsive to the demands of the current situation and in control of their behavior also may contribute to the lesser dispositional attributions made by actors.

The generality of this bias has recently been questioned, as has the true nature of the actor-observer differences. Recent research suggests that the difference may lie in the types of behaviors explained; actors tend to explain experiences, which generally elicit situational explanations, whereas observers explain actions, which tend to be explained by dispositional factors.

The Self-Serving Bias. People tend to take credit for their own successes, but deny responsibility for their failures. The self-serving bias involves making internal attributions to ability and effort for one's own favorable outcomes, but external attributions to difficulty and luck for one's unfavorable outcomes. This bias is functionally important because it serves to maintain positive affect and self esteem.

Motivational and cognitive processes have been posited to account for this bias. Both self-esteem and impression management concerns may motivate self-serving attributions. Alternatively, the bias could result from a rational cognitive process in which knowledge of past success and expectations of future success lead individuals to perceive a success as attributable to internal factors; it is consistent with the past and with intentions. Failure, being inconsistent with past outcomes and current intentions, engenders external attributions.

Special Topics and Applications

Subjects under discussion in this category include culture and attribution, achievement, and emotional problems.

Culture and Attribution. Cultural groups differ in

their theories of personhood, and these differences appear to be associated with different understandings of social causation (Markus, Kitayama, & Heiman, 1997). Western cultural groups perceive the person as an independent and autonomous entity with internal attributes that lead him or her to act. Non-Western cultural groups, on the other hand, view the person as fundamentally interdependent, intertwined in a social fabric involving roles, expectations, and interpersonal relationships that lead him or her to act. These cultural beliefs may focus attention on different causal factors for social behavior. Western cultural beliefs may predispose perceivers to see the person as the source of behavior, while non-Western beliefs may lead perceivers to see contextual or relational factors as the source of behavior.

As a result of these cultural differences in attentional focus and theories of personhood, the fundamental attribution error may be much less fundamental than Western researchers originally thought. People in non-Western cultures, particularly in Asian groups, tend to attribute behavior more to situational and relational factors than to dispositional ones. Interestingly, patterns of attributions seem to show a developmental shift within each type of culture; for example, the attributions of American children become more dispositional with age, while those of Hindu children become more situational.

More fundamentally, cultures also may differ in the extent to which they emphasize causality itself. Non-Western cultures may not share the Western emphasis on causality and its link to behavior, partially because they view causality as multidirectional, rather than unidirectional. Causal attributions may thus be less frequent among non-Western people.

Application to the Achievement Domain. While success and failure outcomes have their own affective consequences, the attributions people make about *why* those outcomes occurred can have profound effects on emotions, expectations, and persistence (Weiner, 1985). Weiner has suggested that happiness and disappointment are outcome-related affects that occur immediately upon knowledge of the outcome. However, more specific affective reactions, such as pride and shame, are the result of performance attributions.

The outcome-related affects of frustration and disappointment are likely to accompany a failure, but the type of attribution made for the failure is especially consequential. If failure is attributed to lack of effort, a person will often respond positively to the failure, experiencing an increase in motivation and expectations for future success, along with attribution-related emotions like guilt. Such results are presumably due to the nature of an effort attribution as unstable and controllable, and therefore possible to purposefully change. However, attributing failure to a more stable, uncon-

trollable cause, such as lack of ability, has deleterious consequences for motivation, future expectations of success, persistence and self-esteem, and can lead to the attribution-related affects of shame and humiliation.

Emotional Problems in Living. Since attributions have emotional and motivational consequences, it is not surprising that differences in attributional style and frequency are associated with various emotional problems in living. In contrast to the self-serving attributional style of nondepressed individuals, depressed individuals see their failures or negative outcomes as due to something internal, uncontrollable, stable, and global. Positive outcomes are often attributed to external, unstable, and specific factors. Thus, depressives appear to lack an important mechanism for maintaining and protecting self-esteem.

Depression also is related to the amount of attributional processing in which perceivers engage. Mild to moderately depressed individuals report more motivation to think effortfully about the causes of social events. Evidence suggests that this motivation may result from expectations of the uncontrollability of life events and feelings of causal uncertainty. The attributions that depressed people make for various outcomes also tend to be more complex than those of nondepressed people.

Conclusion

Causal inference processes are central to people's attempts to construct cognitive representations of the external world and, thus, to survival. Although the particular foci of basic research or applications may change, interest in attributional processes is not likely to abate.

Bibliography

Gilbert, D. T. (1989). Thinking lightly about others: Automatic components of the social inference process. In J. S. Uleman & J. A. Bargh (Eds.), *Unintended thought: Limits of awareness, intention, and control.* New York: Guilford Press. Discusses a stage model of the attribution process and proposes that the early stages, during which a perceiver characterizes the actor in dispositional terms, occur effortlessly and require few cognitive resources.

Gilbert, D. T., & Malone, P. S. (1995). The correspondence bias. *Psychological Bulletin, 117,* 21–38. Outlines the history of the correspondence bias within social psychology, postulates mechanisms that may produce the bias, and discusses how the consequences of the bias act to perpetuate it.

Heider, F. (1958). *The psychology of interpersonal relations.* New York: Wiley. Seminal book that laid the foundations for attribution theory.

Hewstone, M., & Jaspars, J. (1987). Covariation and causal attribution: A logical model of the intuitive analysis of variance. *Journal of Personality and Social Psychology, 53,* 663–672. Presents a logical model which specifies how information is encoded and how causality is determined by considering which causal factors are necessary and sufficient for an effect to occur.

Hilton, D. J., & Slugoski, B. R. (1986). Knowledge-based causal attribution: The abnormal conditions focus model. *Journal of Personality and Social Psychology, 93,* 75–88. Presents an extension of Kelley's (1967) covariation-based model of attribution.

Jones, E. E., & Davis, K. E. (1965). From acts to dispositions: The attribution process in person perception. In L. Berkowitz (Ed.), *Advances in experimental social psychology* (Vol. 2, pp. 219–266). New York: Academic Press. Outlines an early and very influential theory concerning causal attributions and the "constraintedness" of human behavior. Described several factors that influence the nature of a perceiver's attributions.

Jones, E. E., & McGillis, D. (1976). Correspondent inferences and the attribution cube: A comparative reappraisal. In J. Harvey, W. J. Ickes, & R. F. Kidd (Eds.), *New directions in attribution research* (Vol. 1, pp. 389–420). Hillsdale, NJ: Erlbaum. Revises the correspondent inference theory presented in Jones and Davis (1965), extending the model to multiple behavioral episodes and discussing the impact of target- and category-based expectancies on the correspondence of inferences.

Kelley, H. H. (1967). Attribution theory in social psychology. In D. Levine (Ed.), *Nebraska symposium on motivation* (Vol. 15, pp. 192–238). Lincoln, NE: University of Nebraska Press. Outlines a very influential model in attribution theory, the covariation model, which discusses how perceivers make attributions when they have information from multiple observations.

Kelley. H. H. (1972). Causal schemata and the attribution process. In E. E. Jones, D. E. Kanouse, H. H. Kelley, R. E. Nisbett, S. Valins, & B. Weiner (Eds.), *Attribution: Perceiving the causes of behavior* (pp. 151–174). Morristown, NJ: General Learning Press. Discusses the causal schemas that perceivers use to make attributions when they have information from only a single observation.

Markus, H. R., Kitayama, S., & Heiman, R. (1997). Culture and basic psychological principles. In E. T. Higgins & A. W. Kruglanski (Eds.), *Social psychology: Handbook of basic principles* (pp. 857–913). New York: Guilford Press.

Trope, Y. (1986). Identification and inferential processes in dispositional attribution. *Psychological Review, 93,* 239–257. Presents a stage model of the dispositional attribution process.

Weary, G., & Edwards, J. A. (1996). Causal uncertainty beliefs and related goal structures. In R. M. Sorrentino & E. T. Higgins (Eds.), *Handbook of motivation and cognition: Vol. 3. The interpersonal context* (pp. 148–181). New York: Guilford Press. Summarizes work on depression and attribution processes, and describes the development of the model of causal uncertainty and of the Causal Uncertainty scale (CUS) as a measure of chronic individual differences in uncertainty about the causes of events in the social environment.

Weary, G., Stanley, M. A., & Harvey, J. H. (1989). *Attribution.* New York: Springer-Verlag. Survey of major foundation work, early qualifications, and more recent extensions and applications of attribution theories.

Weiner, B. (1985). Attributional theory of achievement motivation and emotion. *Psychological Review, 92,* 548–573. Presents an analysis of the emotional and motivational consequences of different types of attributions for success and failure.

Gifford Weary and Darcy A. Reich

AUDITION. *See* Hearing, *article on* Behavioral and Functional Aspects.

AUDITORY DEFECTS. *See* Hearing, *article on* Behavioral and Functional Aspects.

AUDITORY IMPAIRMENT. The effects of hearing loss on human communication and subsequent social interaction are devastating. Verbal communication is at the root of what we learn and how we think, and it is also at the root of most social interactions. Hearing is an essential part of that communication. Unfortunately, many things can go wrong with the auditory system.

The outer ear, made up of the visible auricle (pinna), directs sounds into the external auditory canal (EAC). A thin tissue known as the tympanic membrane covers the medial end of the EAC and separates the outer and middle ear system. The middle ear houses the ossicles (malleus, incus, and stapes) which transmit the sound from the tympanic membrane medially to the inner ear (cochlea). From the cochlea neural fibers pass through several levels of nuclei within the brain stem, terminating predominantly at the primary auditory cortex. These fibers also terminate, though less abundantly, at numerous additional sites within the brain stem and cortex.

The mechanism is made up not only of the peripheral outer, middle, and inner ear, but also a complex neurologic system that parses the acoustic signal into functional units such as pitch and timing information. The neural signals are processed in parallel through the brain stem and then distributed through cortical channels to be resolved into complex meaningful messages. Abnormal function at any point in the system can distort or reduce the clarity of the message. Fortunately, both the repetitive acoustic signal of speech and the redundant neural encoding help protect the system from minor disruptions or distortions.

In general, pathologies have different effects on the auditory system depending on the site of the disruption. Dysfunction of the outer and middle ear tends to result in conductive hearing problems, characterized by a loss of sensitivity without distortion of the acoustic message. Conductive hearing losses can be fluctuating, as in cases of otitis media (inflammation of the middle ear), or fixed, as in congenital or acquired ossicular abnormalities.

Nearly 90% of all children experience one or more episodes of otitis media. Half of the children who experience otitis media before one year of age will have six or more episodes before age 2. Treatment regimens include antibiotic therapy and may require one or more myringotomies with placement of middle ear ventilating tubes. The prevalence of otitis media in early childhood appears to be related, in many cases, to Eustachian tube dysfunction as a result of either an enlarged adenoid blocking the tube orifice into the nasal cavity, and/or the angle of the tube creating an inefficient vector for the muscles which open the tube. Significant change in both of these structures by adolescence makes otitis media a rare event in adults. In addition, the Eustachian tube is actively opened to equalize air pressure, using the same muscle group that lifts the soft palate located in the oral cavity. Therefore, any disruption of this muscle activity may be accompanied by chronic otitis media. Common pathologies associated with otitis media include clefts of the palate, congenital palatopharyngeal incompetence, Pierre Robin sequence, and Mobius syndrome.

Nonfluctuating conductive hearing losses are often observed in children with mandibular malformations and in adults with otosclerosis. They also can result from head trauma that break or dislocate the ossicles.

Most hearing loss in childhood is conductive and related to middle ear dysfunction. The effects of conductive loss are complex and vary according to the degree of loss, length of time the loss is present, time between episodes of loss, age of onset, and amount of stimulation while the loss is present. Repeated episodes of otitis media in children may lead to reduced rates of language acquisition and result in lower verbal performance measures. Otitis media with hearing loss during the school years can lead to distractibility and inattention in class. Moreover, it is difficult to fit children with amplification in cases where medical and surgical intervention is unsuccessful. The fluctuating nature of the loss requires constant readjusting of the hearing aid. Moreover, if the ear is actively draining, occluding the external auditory meatus may be inadvisable. In cases with ossicular or middle ear malformation, where hearing loss is stable, amplification using hearing aids is typically successful in cases that are not surgically amenable. Early fitting of infants, coupled with language stimulation, often results in excellent prognosis for verbal performance.

Cochlear hearing loss is much less common than middle ear conductive loss in childhood. However, it is relatively common in adulthood, particularly in the elderly and those exposed to excessive noise levels. The cochlea functions by stimulating small hair cells that rest on a moveable membrane (basilar membrane) in the inner ear. There is one row of inner hair cells and three to four outer rows. The inner hair cells are receptor cells connected to the afferent auditory nervous system. The outer hair cells are different in shape and function from the inner hair cells and serve to modify basilar membrane movement to enhance stimulation of the inner hair cells. Most cochlear loss is associated with disruption of outer hair cell function.

Noise induced hearing loss can result either from small cumulative insult to the outer hair cells over time or from a single intense noise exposure. Such hearing loss has a characteristic drop in hearing sensitivity in the 3 to 6 kHz region, but recovers in the higher audiometric frequencies. With repeated exposure the area of loss will spread to higher and lower frequencies and likely disrupt speech communication ability.

Presbycusis is a cochlear loss typically related to the natural aging process as well as environmental factors such as noise. The loss, typically seen beginning in the sixth or seventh decade of life, starts as a change in the higher frequency regions of the cochlea, above 8 kHz, and progresses with age to lower frequency regions.

In children, cochlear hearing loss appears in isolation as both genetic dominant and genetic recessive traits and in relation to a number of syndromes (e.g., Crouzon, Waardenburg, Alport, and achondroplasia). Degree of loss can vary from mild to profound. As with other cochlear losses, high-frequency regions are typically more affected than low-frequency regions, though flat losses are not uncommon. In cases of profound deafness, where traditional hearing aids are ineffective, a cochlear implant may be considered, whereby electrical current is sent to a series of electrodes placed in the cochlea in order to stimulate the acoustic nerve.

Recruitment and tinnitus are two common characteristics of cochlear loss. Recruitment is an abnormal growth in the loudness of a sound and often results in a significantly compressed dynamic range, whereby soft sounds are not heard and loud sounds cause discomfort. Traditionally, recruitment was a significant problem in the fitting of hearing aids. However, newer technology makes "nerve deafness" treatable through amplification.

Tinnitus is a spontaneous sound that occurs in the auditory system and can take many forms, ranging from tones and chirps to general noise. Tinnitus is most often noticed in quiet situations and can become disruptive to daily activity. Treatment for tinnitus includes psychological counseling, noise maskers, and sectioning the auditory-vestibular nerve (VIIIth Cranial N.), each of which has been tried with varying degrees of success.

Cochlear hearing loss has a significant impact on speech communication ability, particularly in noisy situations. In the typical cochlear hearing loss, high-frequency information is lost before low-frequency information. This creates a problem in everyday communication where noise is characterized by low-frequency signals and speech intelligibility is characterized by high-frequency information. The low-frequency background noise competes with the speech information and degrades intelligibility. This situation makes communication in crowds or with competing background noise a very tiring function for the person with cochlear impairment and may lead to withdrawal from group activities and even isolation.

In contrast to conductive and cochlear hearing disorders, which result in loss of auditory sensitivity, disorders of the central auditory system often reflect only minor changes in sensitivity. However, such disorders typically evidence changes in ability to decode the acoustic message into meaningful information, resulting in significant discrepancies between auditory sensitivity level and the ability to discriminate speech.

In adults, central losses are typically associated with space occupying lesions, stroke, and neurodegenerative diseases such as multiple sclerosis. Losses of function for cortical lesions typically are observed in the ear contralateral to the lesion due to the crossing nature of the auditory pathway. Lesions of the brain stem and auditory-vestibular nerve, however, typically produce loss of function in the ear ipsilateral to the site of the lesion.

In children, central auditory processing disorders (CAPd) are most often associated with microscopic pathologies and maturational delays. Children with CAPd may have problems in language learning, reading and spelling, auditory figure-ground discriminations, short-term auditory memory, and a host of other related auditory processing difficulties. Moreover, because test protocols normally require speech and language skills, children may not be suspected of having auditory processing problems before educational difficulties in reading, spelling, and language appear. Problems with the central auditory system are difficult to differentially diagnose from specific language impairment and attention deficit disorders.

Many of the measures used for CAPd diagnoses are based on adult site of lesion testing designed to identify macroscopic lesions. Applying these measures to children requires extensive renorming as the auditory system matures over the first two decades of life. For instance, on the pitch pattern test, response accuracy improves from ages five to twelve, when an adult performance level is achieved. However, children below age 5 cannot perform the test.

Children with otitis media may be at risk for central auditory processing problems if the otitis media is present during critical periods of development, typically the first 2 years of life. The argument is that reduced and fluctuating hearing levels may affect formation of synaptic connections in the auditory system.

Pure-tone stimuli presented across several frequency regions have traditionally been used to assess the outer, middle, and inner ear. Pure tones are presented by way of earphones and then by a bone conduction oscillator, which is an accelerometer coupled by pressure to the head. Differences in the response level for a given ear can be attributed to losses in the outer and middle ear. Masking, usually in the form of noise presented to the nontest ear, is used in situations where the contralateral ear could respond. Speech reception thresholds (SRT) are obtained using spondee words, whereby equal stress is placed on the two syllables of each word. The threshold for the pure-tone average (.5 kHz + 1 kHz + 2 kHz/3) should be within 8 dBHL of the SRT value. Threshold variations greater than this suggest the possibility of pseudohypoacousis. In addition, a speech recognition score is used to estimate the difficulty a person will have receiving speech. Speech recognition scores are typically obtained from phonetically balanced word lists (e.g., the W-22 and NU-6).

Assessing central auditory dysfunction is difficult in that most acoustic signals contain highly redundant information, allowing the auditory system multiple opportunities to extract required information. The central auditory system too is highly redundant, with multiple pathways from the cochlea to the cortex. Because of this neural redundancy a degraded acoustic signal can still be received and processed by a normal system. Similarly a normal acoustic signal can often be processed by an impaired central system. Thus measures that increased the complexity of the signal were developed to stress the auditory system. The most popular of these measures are based on speech materials.

Dichotic listening tests (e.g., SSW, Competing Words, Binaural Fusion) present words simultaneously to both ears in an attempt to overload the auditory system. Degraded performance will appear at lower levels of overload if pathology exists.

Other tests, such as compressed speech and filtered speech, remove portions of the signal to reduce the number of redundant acoustic cues. Time compressed speech signals extract small segments of the acoustic signal, reabutting the remaining portions. This maintains essential pitch information but increases the rate of presentation. Normal individuals can process the signal with up to 60% of the information removed. Individuals with lesions of the central nervous system exhibit intelligibility degradation at approximately 40% compression. Filtered speech cuts off high and/or low frequency information, again reducing the redundancy of the acoustic message to stress the system.

Physiological measurements have been developed to differentially diagnose cochlear losses from lesions affecting the VIIIth nerve. The auditory brain-stem response (ABR) is an evoked potential measure used for threshold assessment and determination of VIIIth nerve and brain-stem lesions. Using click stimuli for threshold assessment, the ABR reflects functioning in the higher frequency region of the cochlea (2–4 kHz). Tone pips also have been used for threshold assessment, but cochlear physiology and spectral spread bias the results to the high-frequency region. The use of ABR for determination of VIIIth nerve lesions has given way in recent years to magnetic resonance imaging (MRI). However, the ABR is still a valuable measure in cases of microscopic rather than macroscopic pathologies.

Otoacoustic emissions (OAE) testing assesses the integrity of the outer hair cell (OHC) system. When an OHC is stimulated, it enters a positive feedback situation and imparts motion onto the basilar membrane. This motion is back propagated through the cochlea and ossicular chain and is emitted into the external auditory meatus as a low-level sound. When OHCs are damaged (hearing loss poorer than 30 dBHL), otoacoustic emission is typically not observed.

Combining ABR and OAE evaluations has led to the study of auditory neuropathy, whereby otoacoustic emission is present and larger than normal, and the ABR is absent. This indicates that the outer hair cells are working, but the signal is not reaching the VIIIth nerve, suggesting a problem with the inner hair cells, or with the inner hair cell/VIIIth nerve synapse. In cases of auditory neuropathy, amplification may be detrimental, because hearing aids are designed to amplify low-level signals that normally would be enhanced by outer hair cell activity. It has been suggested that auditory neuropathy may be prevalent in high-risk neonates, thereby requiring the use of both OAE and ABR in screening protocols in the neonatal intensive care unit.

The auditory pathway above the brain stem is assessed with the middle latency response (MLR) evoked potential and several late auditory responses. The MLR is most likely generated in the primary auditory cortex and possibly in the thalamus. The MLR is subject to the same cochlear mechanics that affect the ABR, whereby the response to click stimuli stems from the basal, high-frequency end of the cochlea. In assessing some individuals with mental handicaps, ABR is not recorded because of a lack of neural synchrony. Because the MLR is a longer latency response, neural synchrony is

not as critical in obtaining the response and may be useful with this population.

Auditory late responses are evoked potentials that arise from several distinct cortical areas in response to both external stimulus and to cognitive activity associated with processing the stimuli. It currently is rarely used for auditory assessment, having been replaced by first the MLR and then ABR recording. Other waves in the late auditory response are influenced by cognitive factors and are currently being researched as a method for identifying central auditory processing disorders.

[*See also* Deafness and Hearing Loss.]

Bibliography

Durrant, J. D., & Lovrinic, J. H. (1995). *Bases of hearing sciences* (3rd ed.) Baltimore: Williams & Wilkins. A readily understandable basic description of the neural auditory pathways.

Gerber, S. E. (1996). *The handbook of pediatric audiology*. Washington, DC: Gallaudet University Press.

Gorlin, R. J., Toriello, H. V., & Cohen, Jr., M. M. (1995). *Hereditary hearing loss and its syndromes*. New York: Oxford University Press.

Hall, III, J. W. (1992). *Handbook of auditory evoked responses*. Boston, MA: Allyn & Bacon.

Katz, J. (1994). *Handbook of clinical audiology* (4th ed.). Baltimore: Williams & Wilkins.

Konigsmark, B. W., & Gorlin, R. J. (1976). *Genetic and metabolic deafness*. Philadelphia: W. B. Saunders. Contains excellent discussions on the genetic bases of hearing losses in children.

Lipscomb, D. M. (1985). *Hearing conservation in industry, schools, and the military*. Boston: College Hill/Little, Brown. A primary source of information on noise-induced hearing loss.

Northern, J. L., & Downs, M. P. (1991). *Hearing in children* (4th ed.) Baltimore: Williams & Wilkins. An excellent source on pediatric audiology and particularly the vagaries of otitis media.

Schow, R. L., & Nerbonne, M. A. (1989). *Introduction to aural rehabilitation* (2nd ed.). Austin, TX: Pro Ed.

Herbert Jay Gould and Daniel S. Beasley

AUDITORY PATTERN RECOGNITION. Auditory perception is similar to visual perception in many important ways. Both occur in a context based on the physical properties of the source, other ongoing events in the environment, the person's expectations, and attentional and memory constraints, as well as the nature of task. One critical factor that differs between the two is the transparency of the sound waves coming from two or more sound-producing sources. The pressure waves from every source (e.g., lawn mower, radio, and speaker) add together at each time point, so that the individual pressure wave from each source is lost in the composite. For this reason, the unique problem for auditory perception is to untangle this composite to recover the individual waves that lead to the perception of each separate source. We do hear each of the sources easily without conscious calculations, but this effortlessness belies the difficulty of the segregation into sources. In contrast, nearly all visual objects are opaque, so that the light ray from each point in space invariably comes from light reflecting off only one object. A second difference is that each inner ear (i.e., cochlea) is laid out in terms of frequency, not space. Thus, to localize events outside the head requires the listener to compare the signal at the two ears.

Due to the wide diversity of sound events, no single rule exists that can invariably split the composite sound wave correctly. Instead, it seems that the auditory system simultaneously uses several heuristics about sound events. It tries out different ways of allocating parts of the sound wave into events, and settles on the partition that appears to be most plausible. A heuristic is a rule that usually works, but that may lead to the wrong outcome in some instances so that a strategy of "majority rules" most likely leads to the correct sound sources. Our perceptual systems have evolved in a world that contains regularities among the vibrations creating sounds, so that we would expect that these systems should be tuned to extract those regularities. We know that the first step in processing the composite signal occurs in the inner ear, where the signal is analyzed into a set of frequency components. The heuristics, therefore, are based on the normal regularities among the physical properties of the frequency components and sound events. To see how this works, first we will consider a single sound.

Partitioning a Single Sound

The perceptual problem is to decide if the single sound comes from one source or comes from the mixture of two or more sources. If we analyze the acoustic signal generated by a single source, there are many regularities that could be the basis for heuristics to segregate a complex signal: (1) Nearly all sound sources generate a harmonic sound wave; the frequency of the components are multiples of the frequency of the fundamental (e.g., the frequencies are in the ratios 1:2:3:4:5). (2) Frequency components from the same source usually begin and end at the same time. (3) Sounds from one source probably come from a single point in space. (4) Natural sources change over time for several reasons. First, the physical vibrations producing sounds will decay due to friction and speakers will produce unwitting frequency and intensity changes (termed *jitter*) due to variations in the air pressure creating the sounds. Sec-

ond, performers will vary the frequency (vibrato) and intensity of the sound to produce esthetic effects. For these two reasons, the frequency components from a single source usually change in the same way, increasing or decreasing in frequency or amplitude.

Research has shown that all the above physical properties influence the partitioning of the composite sound wave, but that the harmonic relationships and onset/offset timing are the most important. The harmonic relationships among the frequency components create the first predominant cue. If all the frequency components are harmonically related, the obvious decision would be that all the components come from a single source and the percept is that of one complex tone. If one of the components is mistuned so that its harmonic relationship is lost (e.g., 200, 415, 600, 800 Hz), the percept is divided: the mistuned component is heard as one emergent tone and the remaining components are heard as a second tone that has changed in sound quality because the mistuned harmonic has been segregated out. If the frequency components are inharmonic (e.g., 100, 125, 200, 250, 300, 375 Hz . . .) the auditory system partitions the components so that each set is harmonically related: one complex tone based on a fundamental frequency of 100 Hz and a second based on a fundamental of 125 Hz. For speech, differences between fundamental frequencies as small as 2% are sufficient to lead to the perception of two vowels or syllables, each spoken by a different voice.

Differences in onset and offset create the second predominant cue. Normally, the minimum difference in the onset of the components that leads to hearing more than one sound is about 50ms. In nearly all conditions, a difference in the onset time is a more important cue for segregation than a difference in offset time. Listeners do not report that they hear two sounds starting at different time points. Instead, they simply report hearing two sounds and are unable to report the order. Thus, curiously, short-time asynchronies are converted into source information and not order information.

Surprisingly, spatial position is not a strong cue for partitioning the components. Suppose we create a conflict between organization by harmonics and organization by spatial position by presenting a complex tone like 200, 600, 800, and 1,000 Hz to the left ear and a simple tone of 400 Hz to the right ear. In such a case, listeners hear the complex tone localized correctly to the left ear. However, they do not hear the 400 Hz tone correctly localized in the right ear. Instead, that tone shifts to the left ear. Thus, the harmonic heuristic dominates the position heuristic and causes the 400 Hz tone to be heard as a part of the complex tone in the left ear. This might occur because the position cues can be ambiguous. Spatial position must be derived from the difference in the sound wave between ears. There are two major cues: (1) the time difference between the sounds arriving at each ear; and (2) the difference in amplitude of the components due to the head shadowing and attenuating the sound wave arriving at the far ear. However, in an enclosed space the sound waves can bounce off several surfaces before reaching the listener and therefore both the timing and intensity cues to position can be distorted.

It is important to note that the spatial position and sound quality or timbre of a sound emerges *after* the components have been allocated to each source. We do not hear a clarinet and a violin as separate instruments even when they are playing at the same time because the two instruments have a different quality or because they are located at different positions. Instead, we hear two because the heuristics have allocated the simultaneous components to two harmonic sources. The perceived quality and location of each instrument is the consequence of that allocation.

Partitioning a Sequence of Sounds

For a sequence of sounds, the segregation problem is to decide if all of the sounds come from one source or from two or more sources. Following the same logic used for single sounds, we can identify several physical properties that might underlie segregation. Single sources are more likely to produce sounds that (1) tend to vary gradually and smoothly; (2) occur at equal time intervals, i.e., are rhythmical; and (3) tend to come from the same location.

To simplify the problem somewhat, assume that two strictly harmonic sounds, one high and one low, alternate. Moreover, assume that we can vary the frequency separation between the sounds and vary the time interval between the onsets of two adjacent sounds. Listeners report whether they hear a coherent alternation between the two tones representing one source (i.e., a trill), or whether they hear two sequences, one of the lower tones and one of the higher tones each representing a different source. Data indicate that there are two regions defined by combinations of the interval between onsets and frequency separation: (1) For short intervals and/or large frequency separations, listeners invariably heard the two tones as representing separate sources or streams. The interval and frequency separation can be traded off; that is, at larger frequency separations the interval can be increased and yet still yield separate streams. The gradual change heuristic determines that the frequency change occurred so rapidly that it is likely that the two sounds represent different sources. The split into sources is involuntary, it occurs even if the listener is actively trying to keep the sequence coherent. (2) Conversely, for long intervals and/or small frequency separations listeners invaria-

bly hear the two tones as one coherent whole, representing one source. Listeners can hear each tone separately by means of voluntary attention.

We can make the sequence more complex by interleaving several low-pitch tones (A,B,C) with several high-pitch tones (X,Y,Z) to create a recycling sequence such as CXBYAZCXBYCX . . . If the time interval is short enough so that the low- and high-pitch tones segregate, listeners are unable to identify the whole sequence. They can tell that the low-pitch tones form a CBA pattern and not an ABC pattern and, similarly, that the high-pitch elements form an XYZ pattern and not a ZYX pattern. But, they cannot distinguish between CXBYAZ, XCYBZA, and XAYCZB. In other words, when sounds become allocated to two or more sources, it becomes impossible to integrate them in time. Phenomenally, it appears that the sounds overlap; you can pay attention to one source or the other, but not to both simultaneously.

There is an interesting variant of the gradual change heuristic that has been named the old + new heuristic. Consider a simple sound that quickly increases and then decreases in loudness. Instead of hearing one sound undergoing a rapid change, listeners hear one continuous sound and a second short equivalent sound that is added to the former one. The old + new heuristic assumes that because the original sound continues beyond the loudness change, and the increase and decrease in loudness is so rapid that it "violates" the normal rate of change of a single tone, that the change was most probably due to the occurrence of a second source. If the loudness change is more gradual, then the percept is one tone that undergoes a change in loudness. Another example of the operation of the gradual change heuristic is the continuity illusion. If a long, soft tone alternates with a short, louder noise, the tone is heard as continuing through the loud noise (if the noise is removed the correct perception occurs, as a series of tones separated by silence). The auditory system incorrectly assumes that the noise has masked one continuous tone because the tone reappears after the noise, and uses the appropriate frequency component of the noise to simulate the tone. The auditory system strips a part of the noise signal (i.e., captures a part of the noise) to create a continuous tone.

Normally segregation based on these heuristics is automatic; if the components are inharmonic or asynchronous, or if a sequence of tones undergoes rapid frequency changes, the signal breaks into different sources even when the listener is trying to maintain a single percept. It is important to note that initially the sounds are heard as coherent, and that segregation takes a few seconds to emerge and to dissipate. The evidence for segregation is cumulative, and that avoids switching back and forth among the competing organizations. Furthermore, this time course suggests that segregation is not merely cognitive because if it were, we would expect the segregation to disappear as soon as the listener switched attention. It suggests instead that segregation is accomplished by linking some physiological units and attenuating others.

Conclusions

Many of the auditory heuristics have parallels in the laws of visual organization proposed by the Gestalt psychologists. For the Gestalt psychologists, the two basic laws are those of similarity and proximity. Visually, elements that are similar in color, brightness, or other characteristics and that are close spatially join to create one object. In similar fashion, sounds that are similar in frequency or loudness and are close in time join into one sound source. A third Gestalt law is that of good continuation. Visually, elements that create a smooth trajectory are joined together, and similarly sounds that have smooth frequency glides or trajectories are assigned to the same stream. The frequency glides in normal speech are assumed to tie together the physically different parts of speech. A fourth Gestalt law is common fate; a set of points that undergo the same spatial movements are joined together to form one object. In similar fashion, a set of frequency components that have the same onset and offset, or that have the identical pattern of loudness or frequency variation are joined into one source.

There are also laws or heuristics that have no parallel form. In vision, bilateral symmetry often leads to the formation of an enclosed figure. In contrast, there is no evidence that temporal symmetry of sounds leads to source organization. In audition, a harmonic relationship among the components leads to the fusion of the components into one source. There seems to be no parallel in vision. There are complementary hues (red/green, blue/yellow), but there is no priority for organization based on these opposites.

Finally, for both vision and audition there is the distinction between preattentive and attentive organization. Preattentive processes operate automatically to organize and segregate the visual and auditory stimulus into sources. These processes are thought to be the result of evolution, matched to the invariant properties of visual objects and auditory events. Attentive processes operate voluntarily, and allow the perceiver's intention and knowledge to influence the outcome. These processes become tuned to the cultural properties of the environment (e.g., one's own name). For example, we can attend to one conversation at a party, even if the voices are very similar, based on our knowledge of the topic. There is always an interaction between these processes, and it is difficult to explain perception without considering both.

[*See also* Pattern Recognition.]

Bibliography

Bregman, A. S. (1993). Auditory scene analysis: Hearing in complex environments. In S. McAdams & E. Bigand (Eds.), *Thinking in sound: The cognitive psychology of human audition* (pp. 10–36). Oxford: Oxford University Press. A good general introduction to the issues underlying sound segregation.

Bregman, A. S. (1990). *Auditory scene analysis: The perceptual organization of sound.* Cambridge, MA: MIT Press. A comprehensive, continuously interesting treatment of all issues in segregation.

Darwin, C. J., & Carlyon, R. P. (1995). Auditory grouping. In B. C. J. Moore (Ed.), *Handbook of perception and cognition: Hearing* (2nd ed., 387–424). San Diego, CA: Academic Press. An update on research emphasizing psychoacoustic factors.

Handel, S. (1995). Timbre perception and auditory object identification. In B. C. J. Moore (Ed.), *Handbook of perception and cognition: Hearing* (2nd ed., pp. 425–461). San Diego, CA: Academic Press. A summary of the factors affecting the perception of instrumental timbre and voice quality.

Handel, S. (1989). *Listening: An introduction to the perception of auditory events.* Cambridge, MA: MIT Press.

Moore, B. C. J. (1997). *An introduction to the psychology of hearing* (4th ed.). San Diego, CA: Academic Press. Provides a general introduction to auditory perception, along with Handel's (1989) *Listening*.

Yost, W. A., & Sheft, S. (1993). Auditory perception. In W. A. Yost, A. N. Popper, & R. R. Fay (Eds.), *Human psychophysics* (pp. 193–236). New York: Springer-Verlag. This chapter, along with others in the same book, provides a psychoacoustic treatment of many topics in auditory sensitivity, discrimination, and identification.

Stephen Handel

AUDITORY PERCEPTION. *See* Hearing, *article on* Behavioral and Functional Aspects; *and* Pitch Perception.

AUSTRALIA. Psychology was *globalized* long before that term came into vogue, in terms of what is taught and practiced, how it is organized, and where its intellectual roots lie. As Lunt and Poortinga (1996) noted, most of the world's psychologists have lived and worked in North America. Virtually all of the leading journals and textbooks are published in the United States, with a few British contributions making up the rest. In an earlier empirical study, Lonner and Adams (1972) gave the Strong Vocational Interest Test (SVIT) to psychologists in eight countries including Australia. The results were compared with data from 1,045 U.S. psychologists. They found no differences, concluding that worldwide, psychologists tend to have similar interests. An equally likely inference is that North American theories and practices provided a global reference point for most non-American psychologists at the time, and that Australian psychology did not escape that influence. Nevertheless, throughout its brief history Australian psychology has exhibited some unique characteristics, and some of the traffic in ideas and procedures has been two-way. Evidence to be reviewed later will show that Australia's contribution to the discipline has been disproportionate to the size of the Australian population in general, and its psychological community in particular.

Historical Context

The derived nature of Australian psychology, both with respect to its organizational structures, as well as its intellectual origins, is not surprising given Australia's history as a very young country. Captain Cook stumbled on the east coast of the continent in 1770. His description of what he had discovered inspired various prominent English politicians, including Lord Sydney, to declare the place an ideal location for a penal colony. The First Fleet under the command of Captain Arthur Phillip, made up of six convict transport ships, three store ships, and two ships of war, arrived in Sydney Cove on 26 January 1788, the day that Australians celebrate as the birthdate of the nation in what was then called the colony of New South Wales. During the next century further colonies were established, and in 1901 these were joined into a federal system called the Commonwealth of Australia. The strong legal and emotional ties to Britain, customarily referred to as the mother country up to the 1950s without any sense of irony, gradually weakened over the years. About the only vestige of the influence of the once mighty British Empire was that the Australian head of state was still the Queen of England at the end of the twentieth century. But Australia has long been moving toward changing its status from a constitutional monarchy to a republic.

The History of Australian Psychology

Australian psychology was conceived in three universities: Sydney, Western Australia, and Melbourne. Fortunately for the development of the discipline, the three departments were quite different from each other, providing a foundation that had breadth and diversity. At the University of Sydney, psychology grew out of philosophy, with many of its senior academics having been students or colleagues of the charismatic John Anderson, a highly influential logical positivist. Western Aus-

tralia's first departmental head was Hugh Fowler, an educational psychologist. The foundation professor at Melbourne was Oscar Oeser, who had strong interests in intergroup relations.

By world standards, Australian higher education is very young. The University of Sydney was the first to be established in 1850. The first lecturer in psychology was appointed in 1890 to a part-time job teaching medical students. As other universities came into being, psychology courses were offered in various departments, usually philosophy, by lecturers who had become exposed to and interested in what was then a new and exciting field. However, the first fully independent department of psychology was not established until 1928 at the University of Sydney, with H. Tasman Lovell as foundation professor (Turtle, 1997).

Most of the early psychology pioneers arrived in Australia from Britain at the turn of the century, and included W. Boyce-Gibson in Melbourne, and Francis Anderson in Sydney. In the main, these scholars were steeped in the philosophical discipline of British empiricism, which insisted that knowledge should be derived from and tested against experience rather than arrived at by deduction. They tended to believe that the human condition could be improved by education. However, they were basically still philosophers, albeit with an empirical bent.

The next wave, in the twenties, consisted of scholars whose *social identity* (to use a contemporary term) increasingly derived from the discipline of psychology. The majority were Australians who had received some of their training abroad. The career of the first professor of psychology in Australia, H. Tasman Lovell at the University of Sydney, provides a good illustration of how Australian psychology developed. He graduated with a bachelor's degree in philosophy and French and a master's degree in philosophy from Sydney University. In 1907 he obtained a scholarship to study for a doctorate at Jena in Germany. While abroad, he was exposed to Wundtian experimental psychology, Alfred Binet's work on mental measurement, Freudian theory, and the British functionalists. He returned in 1913 to a lectureship in philosophy, which he interpreted as an assignment to develop courses in psychology. With the assistance of colleagues holding similar interests, these courses gradually became a full honors degree option, leading ultimately to the establishment of an independent psychology department, of which he became the foundation professor in 1928.

John Smyth became principal of the Melbourne Teachers College in 1903. There he set up a Wundtian laboratory, and later became professor of education. He too had been abroad, studying in Germany and Scotland. Other pioneers included Gilbert Phillips, who had trained in London under Charles Edward Spearman, returning in 1919 to join the Sydney Teachers College, later becoming its principal; H. L. Fowler, also a Spearman graduate, who founded the second Australian department of psychology in the University of Western Australia in 1930; and K. S. Cunningham, who had trained at Columbia University under Thorndike and became the first director of the Australian Council for Educational Research in the twenties.

Three other pioneers stand out. Bernard Muscio, a Sydney graduate in philosophy, went to Cambridge and then to the (British) First World War Industrial Fatigue Research Board, experiences that led to his writing a seminal book on industrial psychology in the early 1920s. Elton Mayo was professor of philosophy at the University of Queensland until 1923, when he departed for the Harvard Business School to make his name on the international scene, particularly as coauthor with Roethlisberger in the Hawthorne studies. Stanley Porteus, whose first job was as a teacher in Melbourne in 1913 in a special school for handicapped children, developed an instrument to measure the intelligence of his students, which later became the Porteus Maze, an original contribution in the area of mental testing. This thumbnail sketch of some of the founders illustrates the two main antecedents of Australian psychology: It grew out of the logical positivist stream in philosophy; and its theoretical models and empirical procedures had their origins in Europe, Britain, and the United States. Both sets of influences are evident in contemporary Australian psychology. However, what made these pioneers distinctive was an explicit interest in the application of their knowledge to Australian social issues, particularly in the field of education.

The Contemporary Sociocultural Scene

At the end of World War II, about 95% of the population came from British stock. By contrast, in 1998 one in three of the population of about 20 million were either born overseas or are the offspring of parents who were born overseas in non-English-speaking countries (McLennan, 1996). The population also includes substantial numbers of non-European settlers, particularly from Southeast Asia. There are also about 300,000 descendants of the aboriginal inhabitants of Australia, who are currently emerging as a potent political force in their attempts to achieve restitution for past exploitation.

Despite some ethnocentric opposition to these changes, in the brief period of the second half of the twentieth century Australia had begun to transform itself from an Anglo-dominated monocultural nation into a successful multicultural society characterized by a substantial degree of mutual tolerance. The ethnic composition of university students and staff reflects this wider national heterogeneity.

Australian constitutional arrangements resemble those of the United States. There are six states (going clockwise round the continent, Queensland, New South Wales, Victoria, Tasmania, South Australia, and Western Australia) and two territories: the Northern Territory and the Australian Capital Territory (ACT). Like the District of Columbia in the United States, the ACT is a small enclave that contains Canberra, the national capital, created because the founders of the Commonwealth could not agree on whether to locate the capital in Sydney or Melbourne. Each state and territory has its own government and public service, with inevitable overlaps and duplication of responsibilities, particularly in education. Psychologists who have to deal with this maze have been heard to rail against it. Still, by and large Australians are willing to put up with the inefficiencies of the system, in the interest of denying too much power to any single authority.

Growth in Australian Psychology

Growth in Australian psychology coincided with the expansion of the Australian university system during the post–World War II period. In 1972, there were 14 departments of psychology in the 17 universities in existence then (compared to two departments prior to 1945). In 1997 there were 38 universities, all of them with psychology departments, or psychology sections as part of a wider behavioral science organizational unit. Most, but not all, offer the full bachelor's, master's, and doctoral degrees.

Teaching Psychology: The Contemporary Scene

Psychology in Australia is taught almost exclusively in its 38 universities. Students tend to fall into two distinct categories: those who wish to learn *about* psychology and those who intend to *become* psychologists and practice it as a profession. The former may take several courses as part of a general arts or science degree. Many will do up to three years of psychology and then use this knowledge to enhance their effectiveness in a variety of occupations, such as school teaching, journalism, or advertising. However, these graduates are restricted by law from calling themselves psychologists. Students who intend to become practitioners must first complete a 4-year honors degree accredited by the Australian Psychological Society (APS) and by the respective State Psychologist Registration Boards. Such degrees provide rigorous training in research methods and statistical analysis, and the fourth year includes an empirical thesis.

Although many students learn about psychology, only relatively few undertake the professional course. For instance, in the University of New South Wales, Sydney, where I teach, we typically enroll 1,000 students in our first year, 300 in our second year, and about 200 in the third year, but only about 60 in the fourth-year honors course. To put these figures into a wider context, the standing of students completing an Australian 4-year bachelor's degree would be comparable to the levels achieved by North American master's graduates. This is one reason why Australians tend to do rather well in postgraduate psychology courses overseas.

Australian psychology has developed a very strong research tradition, reflected in the growing number of doctoral graduates being produced. Most university departments now offer Ph.D. degree programs, which are modeled on the British system of emphasizing the thesis as its core element rather than requiring students to do course work, as is the case in most North American programs.

Another feature of Australian psychology is its tendency to promote a synthesis of British and American research. We tend to read both the British and the American literature and spend our sabbaticals alternating between those two countries. My own experience can provide an illustration. One of my research interests is social skills training, on which there is a substantial British literature, dominated by the work of Michael Argyle and his students at Oxford (e.g., Argyle, 1981). Not surprisingly, the Americans have also done significant work in this area (e.g., LaFromboise & Rowe, 1983). However, when I was reviewing the social skills literature for a book I was writing at the time (Furnham & Bochner, 1986), I was surprised to find that the two research streams did not cite each other's work. As outsiders, we tend to escape the insularity that characterizes some of North American and British psychology.

Growth in Applied and Clinical Psychology

As mentioned earlier, a major characteristic of Australian psychology has been its close relationship between theory and practice, a link that goes back to the early days. The first Vocational Guidance Bureau was set up in 1926 by the New South Wales Department of Education, and has continued providing its services to this day. In 1927 A. H. Martin established in Sydney the Australian Institute of Industrial Psychology, which is also still active.

The Effect of World War II. As was the case in the United States and elsewhere, World War II provided a major impetus to psychology, because of the urgent need to develop procedures to select and train large numbers of recruits for the Army, Navy, and Air Force, as well as for workers in the munitions industries. Australian applied psychology flourished under these circumstances, particularly in New South Wales, leading to the establishment of institutions such as the Industrial Welfare Division (1941), and the Manpower Directorate (1942) with P. H. Cook as Senior Industrial Psychologist. Despite its name, the major function of the Manpower Directorate was to select, place, and train women to work in factories to replace the male workers who had been called up to serve in the military. Since the war effort required a more efficient industrial system, the Directorate embarked on the conduct of pioneering research into employee morale and job satisfaction, supervisor-subordinate relations, teamwork, and the need to include unions in the productivity equation. Their work provided the foundation for a vibrant and influential Australian applied psychology movement which persists to this day.

The Post–World War II Period. Probably the Australian psychologist who is best known overseas is Fred Emery, for his work on industrial democracy, semiautonomous work groups, and sociotechnical and open systems. Because he did not suffer fools gladly, he had difficulty in adjusting to conventional academic life, and his most significant contributions were made during his tenure at the Tavistock Institute in London and on his many projects worldwide, particularly in Scandinavia and later in the United States.

Donald McElwain, foundation professor of psychology (1955) at the University of Queensland, played a major role in introducing the systematic consideration of cross-cultural issues into the Australian psychological curriculum. On the practical side, his team developed the Queensland Test, a nonverbal culture fair procedure measuring the intelligence of Australian Aboriginal and Papua-New Guinean children. Other Australian psychologists also worked in the South-Pacific region. For instance, I. G. Ord set up psychological services units in Papua New Guinea and Fiji to recruit and train local public servants and members of the armed services. Many of the tests that Ord used had to be developed from scratch, and they constitute a major contribution to the cross-cultural assessment literature (e.g., Brislin, Lonner, & Thorndike, 1973; Ord, 1977).

Another pioneer in the cross-cultural domain was Ron Taft, for many years professor of social psychology in the Faculty of Education at Monash University, whose seminal work on the psychology of Australian immigration has provided the foundation for most of the work being done in this area to this day.

Clinical and counseling psychology are also very actively professed, going back to the formation of the Mental Health Research Institute in Melbourne in 1955. Research and practice have followed the traditional path, concentrating on the diagnosis and treatment of clinical disorders. Earlier practitioners tended to favor a psychodynamic framework, including the use of projective tests in diagnosis, but more recent work has been influenced by advances in behavior modification and rational-cognitive therapeutic procedures.

A particular feature of current Australian clinical psychology is its practical response to contemporary social problems such as drug and alcohol abuse and acquired immune deficiency syndrome (AIDS). Several research institutes and programs have been established, in the main funded by government. They include the National Drug and Alcohol Research Centre (NDARC) at the University of New South Wales, and the National Centre in HIV Social Research also at UNSW.

Practicing Psychology: The Contemporary Scene

In most Australian states, psychologists must be registered by the relevant statutory government body (for instance, in the state of New South Wales, it is the Psychologists' Registration Board, under the aegis of the Department of Health). These bodies set out and enforce codes of ethics and professional conduct, with powers to deregister individuals found to be in breach of the code. The universities also emphasize ethics in their professional courses. Practitioners, particularly those engaged in clinical and industrial psychology, are encouraged to belong to the relevant College of the Australian Psychological Society, where membership is to some extent contingent on workers keeping themselves up to date by attending continuing education courses.

From the year 2000, intending practitioners, after completing a 4 year degree, undertake a further 2 years of formal course work (usually leading to a master's degree), plus 1,000 hours of supervised professional practice, if they wish to be registered. This merely formalizes a trend that is already widespread in the profession. In 1995, there were 52 APS accredited course work master's degree programs (i.e., professionally oriented programs). While all this may seem like a lot of regulation, it does ensure high standards in ethics and the professional conduct of psychology in Australia.

The universities have from the beginning exerted a major influence on the substance and organizational structures of Australian psychology, a legacy that persists to the present, despite some inevitable tensions between town and gown. The progress of Australian professional psychology has been closely linked to developments in the university sector. One reason is that, as was mentioned previously, several of the founders of Australian academic psychology had strong applied interests, reflecting a pragmatic streak in Australian culture. Indeed, Australian pioneers who achieved prominence on the international scene, such as Elton Mayo, Stanley Porteus, and Fred Emery, were all applied psychologists. This does not mean that theory is ignored, but that the usefulness of the discipline is given due emphasis. From its inception, Australian psychology has followed the scientist-practitioner model.

Organizational Structures. The Australasian Association of Psychology and Philosophy was established in 1923, and produced a journal with that title. Its first meeting was held in Sydney on 19 May 1923, the subject for discussion being recent trends in psychoanalysis. In 1946 the two strands formally separated, as did the journal. The philosophers formed the Australasian Association of Philosophy, and produced the first edition of the *Australasian Journal of Philosophy* in 1947, maintaining continuity with the past by numbering it volume 25. The psychologists formed an Australian Branch of the British Psychological Society (BPS), an entirely reasonable development, bearing in mind the pull of the mother country, and volume 1 of the *Australian Journal of Psychology* appeared in 1949. It took until 1966 to sever the British connection, when the erstwhile branch became the Australian Psychological Society (APS). The APS has evolved into a national structure, with branches in every state, and as of 1998, two divisions (Scientific Affairs, Independent Practice) and eight colleges (Neuropsychology, Clinical, Community, Counselling, Educational, Forensic, Organizational, and Sport). These bodies, too, have formal or informal sections in most of the states. Many of these groups meet on a regular basis, undoubtedly supported by another great Australian institution, an excuse to have a "quiet little drink." Whatever the motivation, this network of associations gives Australian psychology much of its grassroots strength.

In addition to the *Australian Journal of Psychology*, which is an outlet for reporting theory-driven research, the APS publishes the *Australian Psychologist*, which is modeled on the *American Psychologist*, containing more practically oriented research reports and organizational announcements. It also provides a forum for practitioners who wish to draw attention to current professional issues. Both journals regularly attract contributions from overseas scholars and practitioners. The APS also publishes a newsletter called *In-Psych*. In addition, the APS runs general as well as special interest conferences and meetings on an annual basis. All these publications and activities further add to the cohesiveness of Australian psychology, give it a distinctive voice, and often lead to international exposure and influence.

In 1988, the APS was host, on behalf of the International Union of Psychological Science, to the twenty-fourth International Congress of Psychology. This Congress was held in Sydney, and provided the opportunity for large numbers of overseas visitors to acquire first-hand knowledge of Australian psychology.

Women in Australian Psychology

The first chair (in 1946) of the Australian Branch of the BPS was H. Tasman Lovell. Not until 1972 did a woman (Mary Nixon) occupy that position (in the APS). Although the status of women in Australian society in general and in higher education in particular has improved, women are still underrepresented in senior positions. In university departments of psychology, in the period between 1987 and 1995, the proportion of lecturers and above who were women increased from 25 to 39%. However, most women were in lower positions, whereas the majority of the men were employed at higher levels.

Funding the Australian University System

All but 2 of Australia's 38 universities are public institutions. Of the two private universities, one is supported by the Roman Catholic Church. The other is Bond University, which depends on student fees and investments, exposing it to the vagaries of the economy. The funds for the public universities are provided primarily by the Commonwealth (Federal) Government, using an arcane formula based on a fictional creature called an Equivalent Full Time Student Unit (EFTSU). In theory, the more of these a university, or for that matter a department can say that it owns, the more money it gets. Although even that is not strictly true, because different real students are given different EFTSU loadings depending on their discipline, year, and several other characteristics. Apart from providing endless scope for high-level bureaucratic machinations, the system creates competition among universities and departments, which in my view is a mixed blessing.

The history of Australian tuition fees mirrors social change in this country. In the 1950s, students were required to pay tuition fees, reflecting the elitism of higher education in those days. When university education came to be regarded as a universal right in the seventies, tuition fees were abolished and tertiary education was free. With the advent of economic rationalism and the user-pay doctrine, Australia developed a unique fee paying system known in the vernacular as being hexed, after its official name, the Higher Education Contribution Scheme (HECS). Students can defer payment of their tuition fees until they earn an annual salary set by the government, in 1998 A$28,495, calculated as a complex function of average weekly wages. The "hecs" is then paid off through the income tax system annually on a graduated basis, depending on the person's taxable income. Repayments continue until the liability is discharged, with discounts available to those willing and able to pay more than the minimum each year. Despite the inevitable grumbling, most people, including those who are paying, regard this as an equitable scheme, because it is related to the person's ability to pay, which in turn is enhanced by the skills the person acquired at university.

It should be noted that Australia does not have a tradition of benefactors supporting higher education. Additional funds come from two sources. The first are international students, who are charged the full cost of their education. It is estimated that such students, drawn mainly from the emerging middle classes in English-speaking Southeast Asia (Hong Kong, Singapore, Malaysia, the Philippines), contribute about A$2 billion a year, directly and indirectly, to the Australian economy. In the larger and more prestigious universities, full fee-paying international students may comprise up to 20% of the overall student body, and many universities have developed a financial dependence on overseas students. However, because Southeast Asian psychology has not yet taken off, only relatively few overseas students are enrolled in Australian psychology departments, and then usually only at the postgraduate level.

The other substantial source of funds for Australian universities comes from upfront fees paid by students undertaking professional courses, which have recently been dehexed to much noisy but ineffective protest. In psychology, this may have a direct bearing on the number of students able and willing to do such courses in the future, and ultimately have an effect on the profession, both in terms of the number entering, and the level of their qualifications.

Research Funding

Up to the end of the 1960s, university research in psychology was basically unfunded. This did not deter many of us from doing significant work, assisted by our students, and in the case of field research, anyone we could talk into helping. One of my early published studies on race relations (Bochner, 1971) consisted of an Australian Aboriginal and a blonde European woman walking a dog through a public place, with observers recording the responses of passers-by. The Aboriginal confederate was one of my students. The rest of the cast, including Snowy the dog and the observers, were members of my family, friends, and neighbors. We used to marvel at the tales of returned travelers from the United States, regaling us with what we thought must be fabricated stories of "research factories," like Cattell's laboratory in Illinois. Well, for better or worse, times have changed. In the 1970s the Commonwealth Government established the Australian Research Grants Committee, today called the Australian Research Council (ARC), which annually injects money into all Australian research, including psychology. The quantity, complexity, and probably the quality of basic as well as applied research has increased dramatically.

Psychologists doing research at the medical end of the spectrum have access to grants distributed by the National Health and Medical Research Council (NHMRC). Grants are also available for the purchase of major equipment. Applied and clinical psychologists can secure funds from a variety of specialized government and in some cases industry sources, ranging from the Department of Immigration, to companies in the coal and steel industries, to private bodies and organizations.

All grants are peer reviewed, the Matthew principle being much in evidence ("For whosoever hath, to him shall be given, and he shall have more abundance," Matthew 13:12). This is not surprising, since the guidelines to reviewers ask that the track record of the applicant should be taken into account, but it does constitute somewhat of a Catch-22 for beginners.

Research Output

A major study conducted in 1996 for the Australian Academy of Science found that Australia produced 2.5% of the world research in psychology and 2.8% of the papers published in the world's major journals. These figures indicate that the outward influence of Australian psychology, compared to other countries similar in population and economic development, is relatively high.

The Role and Status of Psychology in Australian Society

Australia, relative to its population, has always had a large number of psychologists. In a study reported in Taylor and Taft (1977), the number of psychologists as a proportion of the Australian population was larger than in Britain but smaller than in the United States probably because of a lower demand for personal clinical services in Australia.

In 1994 the APS commissioned an independent study of the economic and social value of psychology in Australia. This study came up with an annual figure of $A1.43 billion. Skeptics (including myself) may have their doubts about the methodology and underlying assumptions of such econometric studies, but even if we were to heavily discount the dollar value reported, the results do confirm anecdotal evidence that Australian psychology is making a positive contribution.

Employment Opportunities

Graduates in psychology have good employment prospects. The Australian (federal) government, as well as each of the states, employs qualified psychologists in a variety of areas, the main ones being mental health, education, immigration, welfare, vocational guidance, prisons, the Army, Navy, and Air Force, occupational health and safety, special education, and organizational change and development. The private sector is also a major source of employment, mainly in the applied, organizational, and clinical fields. Salaries, although not inordinately high, are reasonable, with psychologists in the private sector doing a little better on average.

Several studies conducted over the past few years have consistently shown that psychology is one of the fastest growing professions in Australia. Forecasts by various government departments indicate that in the next twenty years, the profession of psychology will grow faster than employment in one hundred and twenty comparable occupations, with most of the growth occurring in the private sector.

Conclusion

The origins, growth, and special characteristics of Australian psychology were linked to developments in the Australian university system during the past century, which in turn were related to changing sociocultural patterns in Australian society. Fred Emery, referred to earlier in this article, would have approved of this open-systems treatment. Although British and North American influences are evident at all three systemic levels, Australian psychology does exhibit some unique and positive characteristics. Due to the egalitarian nature of Australian society, the university system is fairly cost effective, because so far we have been able to avoid the excessive salary structures evident in some American and European universities, as well as the restrictive work practices that characterize the British system. We have also been successful in providing access to minority groups, without having to resort to formal processes such as affirmative action or quotas based on ethnicity, both with respect to student and staff participation. This has been particularly the case in psychology and also has influenced the content of the curriculum, with most departments now routinely offering courses dealing with the psychology of intercultural contact.

There is evidence that the Australian community regards psychology as a useful discipline that can make a positive contribution to the quality of life and increase the productivity and efficiency of industry and commerce. The universities produce well-trained, ethically minded professionals in the scientist-practitioner mold, whose remuneration reflects the value that is placed on their work. Basic research is also being actively pursued and attracts well-qualified and motivated young people into its ranks. The organizational infrastructure is now well established, supports both basic and applied work, and represents the interests of the profession to government and the public. Finally, the outward influence of Australian psychology is continuing to make a modest but nevertheless significant contribution to world psychology, as indicated by the number of Australian-generated publications in overseas journals and books, the strong Australian presence routinely evident at international conferences, and the number of expatriate Australians who can be found in psychology departments in major universities around the world.

Bibliography

Argyle, M. (Ed.). (1981). *Social skills and health.* London: Methuen.

Australian Academy of Science. (1996). *Psychological science in Australia.* Canberra: Australian Government Publishing Service.

Bochner, S. (1971). The use of unobtrusive measures in cross-cultural attitudes research. In R. M. Berndt (Ed.), *A question of choice: An Australian Aboriginal dilemma.* Nedlands, WA: University of Western Australia Press.

Boreham, P., Pemberton, A., & Wilson, P. (Eds.). (1976). *The professions in Australia: A critical appraisal.* St. Lucia, Queensland: University of Queensland Press.

Brislin, R. W., Lonner, W. J., & Thorndike, R. M. (1973). *Cross-cultural research methods.* New York: Wiley.

Cumming, G., Siddle, D., & Hyslop, W. (1997). Psychological science in Australia. *International Journal of Psychology, 32,* 409–424.

Furnham, A., & Bochner, S. (1994). *Culture shock: Psychological reactions to unfamiliar environments.* London: Methuen. (Original work published 1986.)

LaFromboise, T. D., & Rowe, W. (1983). Skills training for bicultural competence: Rational and application. *Journal of Counselling Psychology, 30,* 589–595.

Lonner, W. J., & Adams, H. L. (1972). Interest patterns of psychologists in nine western nations. *Journal of Applied Psychology, 56,* 146–151.

Lunt, I., & Poortinga, Y. H. (1996). Internationalizing psychology: The case of Europe. *American Psychologist, 51,* 504–508.

McConkey, K. M., Wilton, H., Barnier, A. J., & Bennett, A. (Eds.). (1994). *Australian psychology: Selected applications and initiatives.* Carlton, Victoria: Australian Psychological Society.

McLennan, W. (1996). *Year book Australia: Number 78.* Canberra: Australian Bureau of Statistics.

Nixon, M., & Taft, R. (Eds.). (1977). *Psychology in Australia: Achievements and prospects.* Sydney: Pergamon.

Ord, I. G. (1977). Australian psychology and Australia's neighbours. In M. Nixon & R. Taft (Eds.), *Psychology in Australia: Achievements and prospects.* Sydney: Pergamon.

Taylor, K. F., & Taft, R. Psychology and the Australian zeitgeist. In M. Nixon & R. Taft (Eds.), *Psychology in Australia: Achievements and prospects.* Sydney: Pergamon.

Turtle, A. M. (1997). Institution, ideology, icon: Psychology at Sydney 1921–1996. *Australian Journal of Psychology, 49,* 121–127.

Walker, K. F., O'Neil, W. M., & Clark, J. F. (Eds.). (1958). In honour of H. Tasman Lovell. *Australian Journal of Psychology* [Special Issue], *10*(1).

Stephen Bochner

AUSTRIA is a land-locked mountainous country in southern-central Europe with an area of 83,858 square kilometers (32,369 square miles). The Austrian Alps cover 64% of the country, farmland 18%, pastures 27%, and forests 47%. Notwithstanding the mainly mountainous and rural landscape, Austria also has a highly developed industrial and service sector. The 1997 statistics showed that agriculture and forestry accounted for only 3% of Austria's GDP, while manufacturing, energy, and mining accounted for 35%, and the service sector 63%. Austria's population of slightly more than 8 million is highly urbanized. Vienna, the federal capital, is a commercial and political center of international significance, with 1.6 million inhabitants. Its urban sophistication is not matched by other Austrian cities. The second largest city is Graz (240,000 inhabitants) followed by Linz (200,000), Salzburg (150,000), Innsbruck, and Klagenfurt (100,000 each). In terms of language, culture, and religion, Austrian society is relatively homogeneous. Seventy-eight percent of the population is Catholic, 5% Lutheran Protestant, 3% Muslim, 9% no religious affiliation, 5% others, and Catholic traditions still prevail in rural areas. Surrounded by eight other countries, ethnic minorities (Croats, Slovaks, Hungarians, and mainly Slovenes) coexist with the German majority along the border regions. In addition to naturalized guest workers from Turkey and the former Yugoslavia, there has been an increase in the number of political and economic refugees from European countries that were formerly client states of the Soviet Union, and from Third World countries.

Political and Social-Economic System

The Republic of Austria (Republik Österreich) is a parliamentary democracy with a federal structure comprising nine states (Bundesländer), Burgenland, Carinthia, Lower Austria, Upper Austria, Salzburg, Styria, Tyrol, Vienna, and Vorarlberg. Its social-economic system can be classified as "social market economy." Central business sectors such as postal service, public transport, energy, and even television are monopolized by semigovernmental agencies. Another key feature is the Economic and Social Partnership (Sozialpartnerschaft) which includes quasi-governmental "chambers" (e.g., for commerce, labor, and agriculture) and the Austrian Federation of Unions in addition to governmental agencies. Economic measures are negotiated by representatives of employers and employees of the partner organizations, and implemented through their spheres of influence. An elaborate social security and welfare system accompanies Austrians throughout life. Mandatory social security payments cover sick leave, unemployment compensation, and retirement benefits. Free education, child benefits, and parental leave for two years are also provided by the state.

Bureaucratic System. After joining the European Union in 1995, Austria's political and administrative structure increased from four to five layers (European, federal, state, county, and local village). The highly complex and somewhat inconsistent functioning of governmental and semigovernmental agencies creates an overregulated bureaucracy. One often needs persistence and creativity to get things done within the framework of systems, controls, and procedures. This red tape is a maze for business sojourners and immigrants who are not familiar with the system. However, the European Union's requirement for social, economic, and legal harmony amongst its states will inevitably reform the system.

A Hierarchical and Formal Society. The usual form of address between adults is the formal "Sie." The informal "Du" is reserved for family, close friends, and children. It is not unusual for long-time colleagues to address each other as "Sie." A transition from "Sie" to "Du" and from last name to first name is a sign of intimacy, and is at the "invitation" of the older or senior person. Academic titles become part of the name, and are indicated in abbreviated form on all official documents.

The Construction of an Austrian Identity

A brief journey through history shows that Austrian identity was formed in the wake of the twentieth-century's major political events.

Medieval Austria. During the Babenberg dynasty (976–1246 CE), the region of Lower and Upper Austria called Ostarrîchi (the ancient form of *Österreich*) at the southeastern border of the German Holy Roman Empire became a hereditary duchy. In the late Middle Ages, the succeeding Habsburg dynasty (1273–1918 CE) established their rule over the "Austrian Core Lands" (*Dominium Austriae*) of Lower and Upper Austria, Styria, Carinthia, Tyrol, and Vorarlberg.

Imperial Austria. From the early fifteenth century, the Habsburg dynasty consolidated their territories in Austria (which was still part of the German Holy Roman Empire), and also gained control over Bohemia (the modern Czech Republic) and Hungary. Throughout the centuries, they expanded their empire toward eastern and southeastern Europe, including Slovakia, Slovenia, Croatia, Yugoslavia, northern Italy, southern Poland, northern Romania, and Bosnia-Herzegovina. In the course of the Napoleonic wars, the German Holy Roman Empire ceased to exist and the Habsburg dynasty proclaimed the Empire of Austria (1808–1867). Salzburg, an independent ecclesiastical state until 1805, also became part of Austria.

The Austro-Hungarian Dual Monarchy. In 1870, Prussia unified the numerous German states and formed a new German empire which excluded Austria. Upon losing their century-long supremacy in Germany, the Habsburg dynasty shifted its focus to the south-central and southeastern European territories, and established the Austro-Hungarian Monarchy (Österreichisch-Ungarische Doppelmonarchie, 1867–1918). Formally, this dual monarchy consisted of (1) the kingdom of Hungary, and (2) the "rest of the Habsburg lands" (incorrectly known as the "Austrian empire"). In reality, it was an assembly of culturally and ethnically diverse regions united by a few common denominators (mainly foreign, defense, and economic policies) that faced growing nationalist movements.

". . . and the remnant is Austria": The First Republic of Austria. After World War I, centrifugal national tendencies broke up the Austro-Hungarian monarchy into different nation-states. In the Saint-Germain peace treaty, the (first) Republic of Austria (1919–1938 CE) was defined as the German-speaking parts of the former Austrian empire (excluding Bohemia and South Tyrol), and the German-speaking part of western Hungary (Burgenland). Without a national identity, many Austrians had no faith in this "German-Austria" and wanted reunification with the "German motherland." More drastically, the industry which was developed in the nineteenth century to cater to the needs of the Austro-Hungarian Empire's huge and closed economic market was cut off from its previous suppliers and customers. In addition, the western provinces, Vorarlberg and Tyrol, wanted independence. Vienna was perceived as a liability. After a civil war with the Social Democrats in 1934, the ruling Christian Democrats formed an authoritarian regime (Austro-Facism) which faced increasing political pressure from Hitler's Nazi Germany. Despite these political and economic difficulties, the Jewish-influenced German-speaking bourgeoisie maintained strong connections with the new states across the borders and, especially, between Vienna and Prague. This "Austro-German culture" was destroyed in the Holocaust during 1938 to 1945 when Nazi Germany annexed Austria as the East March (*Ostmark*) of the Third Reich.

Modern Austria: The Second Republic of Austria. After World War II ended in 1945, Austria was occupied by the Allied forces until 1955. Those ten long years were filled with the ever imminent fear of being "sliced up" into a Soviet and a Western zone, as was the case with Germany. Austria finally became independent in 1955. It declared its "perpetual neutrality," a cornerstone of Austrian politics and a key element of the new Austrian identity. Although Austrians are friendly toward "Big Brother" Germany, they do not appreciate being mistaken for Germans.

History of Empirical Psychology as an Academic Discipline

The shared history and language of Austria and Germany resulted in a German-language psychology rather than an Austrian psychology, and is reflected by the large number of Austrian scientific psychologists who belong to the German Psychological Society. Three of its congresses (1929, 1964, and 1984) were held in Vienna. German-language psychology started by separating slowly from philosophy. The forefathers of empirical psychology, who held chairs in philosophy, emancipated themselves from traditions such as the phenomenological and speculative-rational approach advocated by Johann Friedrich Herbart (*Lehrbuch zur Psychologie*, 1816) and his disciples (see also Boring, 1929).

The Graz School of Psychology. Austria's first experimental psychology center is associated with Vittorio Benussi, Alexius von Meinong, and Stephan Witasek (cf. Antonelli, 1994; Mittenecker & Schulter, 1994). Meinong, a student of Franz Brentano in Vienna, held a chair of philosophy at the University of Graz from 1889 to 1920. The first Austrian laboratory for human experimental psychology (Psychologisches Laboratorium) was officially founded in January 1895, a few years after Wilhelm Wundt's laboratory in Germany (Leipzig, 1879). The remains of the more than 200 instruments are on display in the department's historical apparatus collection (cf. Huber, Dorfer, & Hohenester, 1994). The early Gestalt psychology's concepts of Meinong's first scholar, Christian von Ehrenfels (*Über Gestaltqualitäten*, 1890), stimulated the department's and, especially, Benussi's experimental research on optical illusions and time perception. Benussi's experimental work on respiratory symptoms of lying is of note. Fritz Heider was also one of Meinong's doctoral students. After the death of Meinong (1920) and Witasek (1915), and the "forced" return of the "Italian" Benussi to Italy (1918), the empirical research tradition faded out, and was only revitalized in 1968 when Erich Mittenecker, a scholar of Hubert Rohracher, was appointed to the chair of psychology.

The First Viennese School of Psychology. The Vienna Institute of Psychology, created in 1923 as a "joint venture" between the Viennese School Board and the University of Vienna (cf. Asch, 1987; Benetka, 1995), was the center of Austrian scientific psychology until the Nazi invasion in 1938. A ten-year grant from the Rockefeller Foundation enabled the institute, led by Karl Bühler and his wife Charlotte Bühler, to pursue internationally recognized research in experimental, cognitive, child, developmental, and educational psychology which included teacher training (cf. Albert, 1985; Benetka, 1995; Rollett, 1994). Together with Marie Jahoda and Hans Zeisl, the statistician and sociologist Paul F. Lazarsfeld, who was a part-time assistant at the Institute of Psychology, conducted the famous 120-day field study (*Die Arbeitslosen von Marienthal*, 1933) on the social and psychological consequences of long-term unemployment. In order to finance their research, Lazarsfeld established the Institute of Empirical Market Research (Wirtschaftspsychologische Forschungsstelle) which worked in close cooperation with the Institute of Psychology. After immigrating to the United States in 1936, this form of cooperation served as a model for his Bureau of Applied Social Research at Columbia University. Egon Brunswick and Sir Karl Popper were also Bühler's students.

Freud and the Psychoanalytic School. The establishment of psychology as an empirical science by the Graz and First Viennese Schools coincided with Sigmund Freud's development of psychoanalysis as a psychodynamic theory and as a psychotherapy in Vienna (cf. Penguin Freud Library). He evolved his structural model of the id, ego, and superego (*The Ego and the Id*, 1923) from his earlier work on the unconscious (e.g., *The Interpretation of Dreams*, 1900; "The Unconscious," 1915). The International Psychoanalytic Association was founded in 1910 and the English *International Journal of Psycho-Analysis* in 1920. Anna Freud, his daughter, was one of his disciples, and contributed to psychoanalytic theory (e.g., *The Ego and the Mechanisms of Defense*, New York, 1936/1966), and was known especially for her work on child analysis. Although Freud, who taught at the Medical Faculty of the University of Vienna, received international recognition for his work (e.g., honorary member of the British Royal Society of Medicine in 1935), leading figures of the Viennese School of Psychology shunned him and his psychoanalytic school. René Spitz and Erik Erikson were two of the few students who frequented both circles. Charlotte Bühler indicated in her autobiography (Pongratz, Traxel, & Wehner, 1972, p. 29) that Karl Bühler's attitude to psychoanalysis was predominantly negative. Even after World War II, Hubert Rohracher (see below) wrote that Freud was considered a physician, and that his ideas were never mentioned in psychology circles (Pongratz, et al., 1972, p. 266; see also Guttmann, 1987). Even today, psychoanalysis can only be studied outside the university (e.g., at the Vienna Psychoanalytic Society). In psychology, it is only offered as an optional introductory course given by external lecturers or by members of the medical faculty.

Explanations for the Antagonism. One commonly cited reason for this antagonism is that experiment-oriented psychology studied "normal" people (clinical psychology did not exist then) while psychoanalysis, originated and dominated by physicians, worked with patients (other than self-analysis). This is not completely correct because both Sigmund Freud (1881) and Karl Bühler (1903) were medical doctors, although the latter also received a Ph.D. degree in 1904. Moreover, Bühler's famous theory of language (*Sprachtheorie*, 1934) was significantly influenced by his research on soldiers suffering from aphasia. What was probably more important was the substantial difference in the paradigms used by the two schools. "Free associations," the central psychoanalytic technique, contrasted starkly to the experimental paradigm pursued by the Graz and Viennese Schools of Psychology. Furthermore, Freud, who collected Greek, Roman, and Egyptian antiquities, referred extensively to philology (the Oedipus complex is named after a figure from classical Greek literature) and cultural anthropology (e.g., *Totem and Taboo*, 1919) in his writings. This was probably seen as threatening by the young science of empirical psychology, which had just been emancipated from philosophy. Further explanations are discussed in Benetka (1995).

The Second Viennese School of Psychology. The revitalization of Austrian psychology after Nazi psychology during the war (cf. Benetka, 1992; Mittenecker & Schulter, 1994) is strongly associated with Hubert Rohracher (cf. Albert, 1985; Pongratz, et al., 1972). An assistant of the experimental psychologist Theodor Erismann in Innsbruck, he headed the Department of Psychology at the University of Vienna from 1943 to 1972. Rohracher's experimental and biological research orientation included early electroencephalograph research and muscular microvibration. The significance of his school is reflected in the number of scholars who received professorships in Germany (more than twenty) and Austria (about ten). Paul Watzlawick from Palo Alto was also one of his students. In Vienna, two of Rohracher's disciples continue with his strong empirical orientation: Giselher Guttmann, a neuropsychologist, is the only psychologist elected to the Austrian Academy of Sciences. Gerhard H. Fischer, a psychometrician and a student of Georg Rasch, received international recognition for his work on Linear Logistic Test Models (LLTM).

University of Innsbruck. Although not as prominent as Vienna and Graz, the University of Innsbruck in Tyrol has an equally long tradition in experimental psychology. It was started by Franz Hillebrand in 1897 (cf. Goller, 1989), continued by Theodor Erismann between the wars, and by Ivo Kohler (known for his experiments on human perception; cf. Spillmann, 1984) after World War II.

The Current Situation of
Psychology in Austria

Since 1990, psychology (especially clinical and health psychology) and psychotherapy have been regulated by two federal laws (BGB 360 and 361). The proportion of psychologists to the population is about 1 to 2,700 (cf. Jirasko, Glück, & Rollett, 1996). About two thirds of the practitioners work as clinical, counseling, or school psychologists in governmental or semigovernmental institutions. Other than the Traffic Psychology Section at the Austrian Road Safety Board, research is mainly conducted in academic institutions. Except for *Psychologie in Österreich*, a psychological bulletin, Austria has no psychological journals. There are also no book publishers for psychology. The only major Austrian company in the field of psychology is the Dr. G. Schuhfried Ges.m.b.H which specializes in computer-assisted testing and training (their *Vienna Test System* was translated into almost 20 languages).

Psychological Organizations. The two Austrian psychological organizations are organized into a fed-

eration (*Föderation Österreichischer Psychologenvereinigungen*) which represents Austria in international metaorganizations such as the International Union of Psychological Societies and the International Test Commission. The Association of Austrian Psychologists (Berufsverband Österreichischer Psychologen; BÖP) is primarily interested in psychology as a profession. The Austrian Psychological Society (Österreichische Gesellschaft für Psychologie; ÖGP), which is also the Austrian regional group of the German Psychological Society, focuses on research and the teaching of psychology.

Study of Psychology. There is no minimum grade point average for admission into university, so even the most mediocre student who passed his or her Higher School Certificate (*Matura*) examination can enroll in a master's degree program. Master's and Ph.D. degree programs are offered by the departments of psychology at the University of Vienna (6,500 students), the University of Graz (2,000), the University of Innsbruck (2,000), and the University of Salzburg (1,200). As compared to international standards, the student-faculty ratio is extremely high in all four locations (about 200 to 1). The psychology sections at the universities of Linz and Klagenfurt only offer psychology courses to other disciplines. Further details can be found in Rollett (1999) and in the annual German *Psychologen-Kalender* published by Hogrefe, Göttingen, Germany. The first part of the 5-year master's degree program in psychology takes 2 years and is roughly equivalent to a bachelor degree, although no formal degree is awarded. The second part takes 3 years and requires an empirical thesis (*Diplomarbeit*). Graduates who completed their master's degree are awarded the academic title of "Magister" of Philosophy (Mag. phil.) or of Natural Sciences (Mag. rer.nat.) and can enroll in the predominantly research-oriented Ph.D. degree programs.

Bicameral Faculty System. There are two levels of faculty positions: university professors and university assistants (Akademischer Mittelbau). The number of positions in each chamber is regulated by federal budget law (Austrian universities are federal agencies), and a promotion from assistant to professor is not possible. The minimum qualification for a tenure-track position of university assistant is a master's degree. The first contract is for 4 years. Upon completion of his or her Ph.D. degree and a few publications within this period, a prolongation for another 6 years is usually granted. Within these 6 years, the assistant can apply for tenure. Granting of tenure is based on publication, quality of teaching, and the department's needs. Tenured assistants are given the title of assistant professor but are not allowed to supervise or evaluate master's or doctoral theses. They also cannot apply for vacant professorships unless they have successfully passed another evaluation, the *habilitation*. Since 1997, habilitated assistants have been given the title of associate professor (Ao.Univ.Prof.) but, structurally, they still remain at the assistant level.

The Habilitation. The monographic habilitation, a remnant from the nineteenth-century Germanic university system which was dominated by nonempirical humanities, necessitates a major research monograph (usually in German) in addition to a substantial (but unspecified) number of articles or book chapters. The average habilitation age of Germanic psychologists is 42 years (Meinong habilitated in 1878 at 25, Benussi in 1905 at 27, Rohracher in 1932 at 29, and Fischer in 1968 at 30). Since 1998, the German Psychological Association has been advocating a "publication-oriented" habilitation that requires only a number of articles published in peer-reviewed international journals on a common theme. Given the strong connections between German and Austrian scientific psychology, it is only a matter of time before Austrian universities follow suit.

Academic Research. Although individual faculty members work on a broad range of research topics (cf. Jirasko, Glück, & Rollett, 1996), the departments are broadly structured according to the nationwide curriculum which covers general, human experimental, developmental educational, social, differential (including personality and psychometrics), biological (including psychophysiology and neuroscience), and applied (including industrial-organizational and environmental) psychology. Unless habilitated, assistants are usually perceived as "belonging" to a professor (cf. Rollett, 1997), and are expected to do research in the same field ("hereditary lines"). Thus, it is not uncommon to find a whole section of a department working in just one research field such as depression. This may also be one of the reasons why Austrian psychology is slow in responding to new challenges such as affirmative action, the global environment, and cultural diversity.

Being Austrian Means Being European: A New Challenge for Austrian Psychology

Despite the homogeneous appearance of present-day Austria, its cultural roots are diverse and manifold. Given Austria's geopolitical position and historical role in Europe, Austrian psychology could yield a significant contribution to the ambitious project of integrating all Eastern European countries into the European Union. The international conference on Cultural Diversity and European Integration held at the University of Graz in 1999 was a first step toward this role.

[*Many of the people mentioned in this article are the subjects of independent biographical entries.*]

Bibliography

Albert, D. (Ed.). (1985). *Bericht über den 34. Kongreß der Deutschen Gesellschaft für Psychologie in Wien 1984. Band 1* [Proceedings of the 34th Congress of the German Psychological Society in Vienna, 1984, Vol. 1]. Göttingen, Germany: Hogrefe.

Antonelli, M. (1994). *Die experimentelle Analyse des Bewußtsein bei Vittorio Benussi* [Benussi's experimental approaches to consciousness]. Amsterdam, the Netherlands: Rodopi.

Asch, M. G. (1987). Psychology and politics in interwar Vienna: The Vienna Psychological Institute, 1922–1942. In M. G. Ash & W. R. Woodward (Eds.), *Psychology in twentieth-century thought and society* (pp. 143–164). London: Cambridge University Press.

Benetka, G. (1992). "Dienstbare Psychologie:" Besetzungspolitik, Arbeitsschwerpunkte und Studienbedingungen in der "Ostmark" [Austrian psychology during the annexation]. *Psychologie und Gesellschaftskritik, 16*, 43–81.

Benetka, G. (1995). *Psychologie in Wien. Sozial- und Theoriegeschichte des Wiener Psychologischen Instituts 1922–1938* [The history of the Department of Psychology, University of Vienna between 1922 and 1938]. Vienna, Austria: Wiener Universitätsverlag.

Boring, E. G. (1929). *History of experimental psychology.* New York: Century.

Goller, P. (1989). *Die Lehrkanzeln für Philosophie an der Philosophischen Fakultät der Universität Innsbruck* [Chairs in philosophy and the philosophy faculty, University of Innsbruck]. Innsbruck, Austria: Wagnersche Kommissionsbuchhandlung.

Guttmann, G. (1987). Austria. In A. R. Gilgen & C. K. Gilgen (Eds.), *International handbook of psychology* (pp. 67–78). London: Aldwych Press.

Huber, H. P., Dorfer, A. J., & Hohenester, A. (1994). *Das erste "Experimentalpsychologische Labor" in Österreich—die Anfänge der apparativen Psychologie* [The first Austrian Laboratory of Experimental Psychology]. Graz, Austria: University of Graz.

Jirasko, M., Glück, J., & Rollett, B. (Eds.). (1996). *Perspektiven psychologischer Forschung in Österreich* [Psychological Research in Austria]. Vienna, Austria: Wiener Universitätsverlag.

Mittenecker, E., & Schulter, G. (Eds.). (1994). *100 Jahre Psychologie an der Universität Graz* [100 years of psychology at the University of Graz]. Graz, Austria: Akademische Druck- und Verlagsanstalt.

Pongratz, L. J., Traxel, W., & Wehner, E. G. (Eds.). (1972). *Psychologie in Selbstdarstellungen* [Psychology in self-portrayals]. Bern, Switzerland: Huber.

Rollett, B. (1994). Siebzig Jahre Institut für Psychologie an der Universität Wien [Seventy years of the Institute of Psychology, University of Vienna]. In G. Gittler, M. Jirasko, U. Kastner-Koller, C. Korunka, & A. Al-Roubaie (Eds.), *Die Seele ist ein weites Land* [The soul is a vast place] (pp. 11–16). Vienna, Austria: Wiener Universitätsverlag.

Rollett, B. (1997). Psychology in Austria. *World Psychology, 3*, 289–309.

Rollett, B. (1999). Psychology in Austria. *European Psychologist, 4*, 115–118.

Spillmann, L. (Ed.). (1984). *Sensory experience, adaptation, and perception: Festschrift for Ivo Kohler.* Hillsdale, NJ: Erlbaum.

Norbert K. Tanzer and Catherine Q. E. Sim

AUTHORITARIANISM refers to a complex of attitudes, opinions, and personality processes that constitute a psychological basis of prejudice, discrimination, and oppression. The concept first appears in the psychoanalytic writings of Wilhelm Reich and Erich Fromm, as well as the "critical theory" of T. W. Adorno and others at the Frankfurt Institut für Sozialforschung (Institute for Social Research) in the 1930s (see the historical review in Stone, Lederer, & Christie [1993, chaps. 1–2]). In the 1940s, in an effort to explain anti-Semitism, the rise of fascism in Germany, and the Holocaust, these perspectives were further elaborated and combined with an extensive program of empirical research by Adorno, Frenkel-Brunswik, Levinson, and Sanford (1950). The result was *The Authoritarian Personality*, a landmark study that contributed a general psychological theory of authoritarianism as well as the F scale measure of "antidemocratic" or prefascist tendencies. A sample questionnaire item is, "Obedience and respect for authority are the most important virtues children should learn."

According to the theory of Adorno et al., the authoritarian is characterized by intolerance of ambiguity, which leads to anti-intraception and splitting of impulses, feelings, and perceptions of people. Whatever is "good" is idealized (especially conventional authority, which is enthusiastically obeyed). In contrast, whatever is "bad" (especially sexual thoughts and wishes) is projected onto deviant out-groups, which then become targets for prejudice, discrimination, and aggression. Such a portrait fits with the results of independently carried out personality studies of actual Nazi supporters.

After 1950, the F scale was widely used in personality research. Results showed that members of extreme antidemocratic groups tended to have high scores. The F scale and related measures correlate with prejudice against a wide variety of racial, ethnic, political, gender, life style, and sexual orientation out-groups. High scorers support aggressive government policies and harsh punishment for offenders. They administer higher levels of shock in the Milgram experiment and show perceptual rigidity, especially under stress (Winter, 1996, chap. 7).

At the same time, the work of Adorno et al. drew strong criticism (see Christie & Jahoda, 1954). Methodological problems included a confusion of authoritarianism with acquiescence (all F scale items are keyed in the "agree" direction), and the lack of blind coding of interviews and projective tests. Some critics proposed alternatives to the psychoanalytic theoretical framework Adorno used. Others (perhaps affected by the rise of McCarthyism in the United States and the Cold War) suggested that authoritarianism theory and the F scale focused only on right-wing (conservative) authoritarians, while neglecting left-wing authoritarianism. Extensive studies, however, failed to show any relationship between left-wing politics and high F scale scores (see Altemeyer, 1996, chap. 9; Stone, Lederer, & Christie, 1993, pp. 144–156; Winter, 1996, chap. 7). Still others argued that the F scale simply tapped common working-class beliefs, thus reflecting the prejudices of middle-class psychologists. For all these reasons, research on authoritarianism declined somewhat during the 1960s.

Beginning in the 1980s, however, interest in authoritarianism increased. Altemeyer (1981, 1996) developed a new, balanced scale of *right-wing authoritarianism* (RWA), based on social learning theory and with excellent psychometric credentials. (A sample, negatively keyed item is, "It is wonderful that young people today have greater freedom to protest against things they don't like, and to make their own 'rules' to govern their behavior.") Summarizing many studies, Altemeyer (1996) concluded that authoritarianism consisted of *authoritarian submission* (obedience to "established" or status quo authorities), *authoritarian aggression* (supported by self-righteousness and vindictiveness), and *conventionalism*.

Researchers have found strong relationships between RWA and attitudes on a wide variety of important social issues of the 1980s and 1990s: for example, favoring harsh treatment of people with AIDS and harsh drug policies; opposition to environmentalism, abortion, and educational diversity; viewing homeless people as basically lazy; endorsing traditional gender roles and sexual orientation; and supporting the Gulf War (see the references in Altemeyer, 1996; also Duncan, Peterson, & Winter, 1997).

Studies using innovative social indicator measures as well as laboratory experiments have demonstrated that *threat* increased authoritarian sentiments and behaviors (Doty, Peterson, & Winter, 1991). Taken together with Altemeyer's (1988) results on family backgrounds, this suggests an overall theory of origins of authoritarianism: sustained high levels of societal or personal threat creates *dispositional authoritarianism*, perhaps by "setting" people's characteristic level of ambiguity tolerance at a low level. Thus people from more stressed (and punitive) family and social-class backgrounds tend to score high. Transitory increases in threat (e.g., economic-social crises, as in early-1930s

Germany) can temporarily increase people's *situational authoritarianism* scores, again by affecting their tolerance for ambiguity.

With the collapse of communist governments and the breakup of the Soviet Union, researchers have at last directly studied authoritarianism in Russia, and appear thereby to have resolved the "left-wing authoritarianism" controversy. Research by McFarland and his colleagues (summarized in Stone, Lederer, & Christie, 1993, chap. 10; see also Winter, 1996, pp. 244–247) shows that, like their Western counterparts, Russian high scorers are prejudiced against Jews, women, and people of "other" nationalities, as well as holding strongly negative attitudes about environmentalism and people with AIDS. Unlike their Western counterparts, however, high scorers favored strict equality and were against a market economy and laissez-faire individualism. They are also against "youth," "democracy," and a free press. They support hard-line communist leaders against political and economic reforms, regret the breakup of the Soviet Union, are nostalgic for communism, and support various quasi-fascist national front organizations.

Taken together, these findings suggest that in both Russia and the West, authoritarianism is consistently associated with support for and willingness to use force on behalf of established status quo systems of authority and morality, and prejudice against "different" or "threatening" groups (labels such as "right-wing" and "left-wing," being saturated with ideology, may only obscure these consistent findings). At the most fundamental level, then, authoritarianism represents an *identification with hegemonic authority*. This further suggests that the array of terms reflecting the contrast or opposite of authoritarianism ("democratic," "egalitarian," and according to Reich, "revolutionary") should also include *reactance, rebellion, escape,* and even *transcendence.*

Two variables somewhat conceptually and empirically related to authoritarianism can be mentioned briefly: (1) *Left-right orientation* reflects the contrast between humanistic and normative ideologies (see Stone & Schaffner, 1988, chap. 4 and pp. 289–298). (2) *Social dominance orientation* (Pratto, Sidanius, Stallworth, & Malle, 1994) reflects beliefs that social groups are inherently unequal and group relations are inherently zero-sum, and a corresponding preference for in-group status.

Bibliography

Adorno, T. W., Frenkel-Brunswik, E., Levinson, D. J., & Sanford, R. N. (1950). *The authoritarian personality.* New York: Harper & Row. Classic original presentation of authoritarianism theory and empirical results with the F scale.

Altemeyer, B. (1981). *Right-wing authoritarianism.* Winnipeg, Canada: University of Manitoba Press. Introduced psychometrically improved version of F scale and suggested an alternative social learning theory interpretation of authoritarianism.

Altemeyer, B. (1996). *The authoritarian specter.* Cambridge, MA: Harvard University Press. Reports extensive original research program on right-wing authoritarianism, as well as a full bibliography of others' research.

Christie, R., & Jahoda, M. (Eds.). (1954). *Studies in the scope and method of "The authoritarian personality."* Glencoe, IL: Free Press. Introduced the main theoretical issues and empirical criticisms of *The Authoritarian Personality.*

Doty, R. M., Peterson, B. E., & Winter, D. G. (1991). Threat and authoritarianism in the United States, 1978–1987. *Journal of Personality and Social Psychology, 61,* 629–640. Uses social indicators to measure authoritarianism at the collective level, and relates authoritarianism to measures of social, political, and economic threat.

Duncan, L. E., Peterson, B. E., & Winter, D. G. (1997). Authoritarianism and gender roles: Toward a psychological analysis of hegemonic relationships. *Personality and Social Psychology Bulletin, 21,* 914–924. Argues that authoritarianism involves identification of hegemonic authority, especially in the domain of gender relationships.

Pratto, F., Sidanius, J., Stallworth, L. M., & Malle, B. F. (1994). Social dominance orientation: A personality variable predicting social and political attitudes. *Journal of Personality and Social Psychology, 67,* 741–763.

Stone, W. F., Lederer, G., & Christie, R. (Eds.). (1993). *Strength and weakness: The authoritarian personality today.* New York: Springer-Verlag. Reviews the history and current status of authoritarianism theory and research, discussing specifically the issues of the antecedents of authoritarianism and left-wing authoritarianism.

Stone, W. F., & Schaffner, P. E. *The psychology of politics* (2nd ed.). New York: Springer-Verlag. Presents theory and data on "left-right orientation," a construct related to authoritarianism.

Winter, D. G. (1996). *Personality: Analysis and interpretation of lives.* New York: McGraw-Hill. Chapter 7 presents research and references on authoritarianism.

David G. Winter

AUTISTIC DISORDER. Initially described as an emotional disorder caused by inadequate mothering (Bettelheim, 1967), autism is now well established as having a biological basis and is classified as the most severe of the developmental disabilities (Mesibov, Adams, & Klinger, 1998). The primary problems of people with autism are related to how their brains process, organize, integrate, and retrieve information, resulting in difficulties with social relationships, communication, and repetitive behaviors plus narrow interests (Schopler & Mesibov, 1988). Factors contributing to the causes of autism are continually being identified, and it is believed that a variety of neurological mechanisms are involved. Although autism is a severely handicapping condition, effective treatments are being developed that enable these people to have full, productive, and meaningful lives.

Autism begins early in life, with clear indications of difficulties almost always present before the age of three. Although signs of autism are typically present from birth, there are a significant number of cases in which normal development is followed by a loss of skills and period of deterioration in cognitive, behavioral, and communicative functioning (Gillberg & Coleman, 1992).

Primary Characteristics

Autism is currently described as a triad of impairments including problems with reciprocal social interaction, verbal and nonverbal communication, and a restricted repertoire of activities and interests (*DSM-IV*, American Psychiatric Association, 1994). During the development of the current diagnostic system, researchers investigated the predictability of specific criteria for making a diagnosis of autism. The individual criteria with the greatest predictive power included a lack of awareness of the feelings of others, impaired ability to imitate, absence of social play, impaired nonverbal communication, and abnormal speech. Recent studies suggest that problems with joint attention or not sharing interests with other people and not looking at others' faces or meeting their gaze are among the earliest indications of autism (Osterling & Dawson, 1994).

Associated characteristics, often present in people with autism but not included in most diagnostic criteria, include uneven cognitive patterns, hyperactivity, attention problems, impulsivity, aggression, self-injury, and temper tantrums (American Psychiatric Association, 1994). Some people with autism have unusual or extreme responses to sensory stimuli, abnormal eating and sleeping behaviors, flat affect, and extreme fearfulness.

Self-injurious behaviors, such as hand biting and head banging, are the most severe and difficult behaviors observed in autism. They are also the most difficult to remediate or control. When they occur, self-injurious behaviors can be frightening and intense. Fortunately they occur in less than 10% of people with autism (Schopler & Mesibov, 1994).

Epidemiological Data

According to the *Diagnostic and Statistical Manual of Mental Disorders* (*DSM–IV*) the prevalence of autism is 2 to 5 cases per 10,000 people (American Psychiatric Association, 1994). Epidemiological studies, however, report a wide range of figures with some as low as 2 cases per 10,000 and others as high as 1 per 750

(Hando, Shimizu, Misumi, Kiimi, & Ohashi, 1996). Autism occurs more frequently in males than females; the sex ratio is approximately 4 to 1. Although most learning disorders affect more boys than girls, the size of this discrepancy is larger in autism than in other learning problems. Despite a higher incidence in males, autism seems to be more severe in females.

Although autism was once thought to be diagnosed more frequently among the higher social classes, recent studies have demonstrated equal distribution among social classes, ethnic groups, racial minorities, and nationalities. The only population difference identified at this point, therefore, seems to be the gender distribution.

Some investigators postulate that recent estimates of the prevalence of autism are increasing due to an actual rise in the number of cases of autism (Hando et al., 1996). It has been suggested that improved medical technology might be saving more people with autism prenatally, at birth, or at very young ages. Roland Ciaranello proposed an anticipation genetic model for autism, in which the genetic disorder intensifies over generations. Others postulate that environmental pollutants might be causing a higher incidence today, although there is not yet strong supporting evidence for this hypothesis (Mesibov, Adams, & Klunger, 1998).

Treatments

Historically there have been three major approaches to treatment for children with autism: psychodynamic, medical, and behavioral. When autism was first identified, it was viewed as an emotional disorder. Psychodynamically oriented group and individual therapy were the most common approaches to treatment for both children and their parents. Bruno Bettelheim (1967) was the most visible of the analysts who blamed parents, especially mothers, and suggested that their inadequate parenting was the cause of their children's autism. He described them as "refrigerator mothers" because of their cold and rejecting style. Pioneering work by Bernie Rimland, Eric Schopler, Bob Reichler, and Mike Rutter contradicted Bettelheim's theory as they identified the organic basis of the disorder and led the field to consider medical and behavioral approaches to intervention.

Many autistic children are unpredictable responders to medication and are not helped by this type of medical intervention. However, a significant percentage do benefit from pharmacological interventions, 30% of whom have seizures and are clearly helped with anticonvulsant medications (Deykin & MacMahon, 1979). There is no single drug or biological intervention designed specifically for autism. Instead medications are prescribed based on the most intrusive symptoms observed in the individual with autism. For example, Ritalin might be prescribed for a child with autism whose hyperactivity is significantly interfering with classroom functioning, Anafranil might be used when obsessive behaviors preclude successful classroom placement, or Clonidine might be prescribed to control anxiety. Medications alone rarely improve behavior significantly; most professionals advise that they be combined with educational and behavioral interventions (Schopler & Mesibov, 1994).

Behavioral interventions, generated from learning theory, have strongly influenced treatments for children with autism. Operant behavioral approaches, emphasizing increasing behaviors through rewards and decreasing them through punishments, have been incorporated into many treatment regimens. Operant approaches have been effective in facilitating improved communication and initiating functional social behaviors. They have also been used to decrease some of the most severe and troublesome behaviors that are observed in autistic youngsters, such as severe self-injury and aggression (Favell, 1983). Many proponents of the behavioral approaches are advocating for early and very intensive applications of these techniques (Lovaas, 1987).

Cognitive behavioral approaches are similar to operant behavioral techniques in that they are derived from learning theory and emphasize observable behavior as a treatment focus. Unlike operant behavioral techniques, however, cognitive approaches view unobservable thoughts as suitable for study and as a legitimate focus of intervention. Although unobservable cognitions might be difficult to measure, thoughts and ideas are central constructs that follow the basic rules of learning and behavior and can help guide intervention techniques. Structured teaching approaches, based on cognitive techniques, have been widely implemented and demonstrated to be effective (Mesibov, Schopler, & Hearsey, 1995).

Individuals with autism exhibit significant deficits in interpersonal functioning. Many behavioral programs incorporate social skills training into their intervention programs to address the social needs and skills deficits of autistic children. Classroom approaches for young children with autism often utilize nonhandicapped peers as major teachers and models of appropriate social interaction.

Basic behavioral educational practices have also affected the field of autism. Although most professionals argue that traditional special education approaches require specific modifications to meet the needs of children with autism, the influence of these general practices has been significant and important. Community-based instruction helps children with autism who otherwise have problems with generalization. Inclusion and integration into regular education programs is another important advance, although the extent to which children with autism can benefit from regular instruction is variable and needs further investigation. The current emphasis on vocational rather than academic training to prepare individuals with autism for life after school is significant and has had an important impact on positive outcomes for this population.

In summary, since autism was first identified by Leo Kanner (1943), research on the etiology, diagnosis, and treatment of this disorder has evolved continuously and productively. Professionals now have a much better understanding of the problems autism creates in communication, social relationships, and repetitive behaviors. The definition of autism is more reliably and consistently applied, and effective treatment strategies are evolving. Although there is still much to learn about this puzzling neurological condition, the promise of continued progress and development is most encouraging.

[See also Developmental Disorders.]

Bibliography

American Psychiatric Association. (1994). Diagnostic and statistical manual of mental disorders (4th ed.). Washington, DC: Author.

Bettelheim, B. (1967). The empty fortress. New York: Free Press.

Deykin, E. Y., & MacMahon, G. (1979). The incidence of seizures among children with autism. American Journal of Psychiatry, 136, 1310–1312.

Favell, J. E. (1983). The management of aggressive behavior. In E. Schopler & G. B. Mesibov (Eds.), Autism in adolescents and adults (pp 187–222). New York: Plenum Press.

Gillberg, C., & Coleman, M. (1992). The biology of the autistic syndromes (2nd ed.). London: Mac Keith.

Hando, H., Shimizu, Y., Misumi, K., Niimi, M., & Ohashi (1996). Cumulative incidents and prevalence of childhood autism in children in Japan. British Journal of Psychiatry, 169, 228–235.

Kanner, L. (1943). Autistic disturbances of affective contact. Nervous Child, 2, 217–250.

Lovaas, O. I. (1987). Behavioral treatment and normal educational and intellectual functioning in young autistic children. Journal of Consulting and Clinical Psychology, 55, 3–9.

Mesibov, G. B., Adams, L., & Klinger, L. (1998). Autism: Understanding the Disorder. New York: Plenum Press.

Mesibov, G. B., Schopler, E., & Hearsey, K. (1994). Structured teaching. In E. Schopler & G. B. Mesibov (Eds.), Behavioral issues in autism (pp 195–207). New York: Plenum Press.

Osterling, J., & Dawson, G. (1994). Early recognition of children with autism: A study of first birthday home videotapes. Journal of Autism and Developmental Disorders, 24, 247–257.

Schopler, E., & Mesibov, G. B. (Eds.). (1988). Diagnosis and assessment in autism. New York: Plenum Press.

Schopler, E., & Mesibov, G. B. (Eds.). (1994). *Behavioral issues in autism*. New York: Plenum Press.

Gary B. Mesibov

AUTOMATICITY. There has long been consensus on the qualities of conscious information processing: it is characterized by its intentionality and controllability; the individual is generally aware of conscious processes; and they are highly consumptive of attentional resources and so can occur only serially, one at a time in sequence. Historically, automatic information processing has been defined as that which is "not conscious"; that is, in contradistinction to conscious or controlled information processing. Thus, automatic processes were described as being unintentional, uncontrollable, efficient, and to occur outside of awareness.

Intentionality refers to whether an act of conscious will is a necessary condition to put the process in motion. Many automatic processes occur as a direct result of perceiving objects, people, or events in the environment, with no conscious choice intervening. Whereas intentionality of a process refers to the conditions needed to start it, *controllability* refers to one's ability to stop a process once it is operating. One may laugh spontaneously at something and then quickly stifle the laugh if it is inappropriate to the situation or moment. A *lack of awareness* of a process is the quality that sets an automatic process in most dramatic contrast to conscious processing. Being unaware of the operation of a process—say, stereotyping a member of a certain group—is important for its controllability as well. One cannot control a process if one is unaware of its occurrence. *Efficiency* is primarily important as a process quality because it means that the process is not constrained by limits on or the current focus of attention. This means that the process occurs regardless of the concurrent demands on attention, a situation that is very common in the busy, complex environments in which there are many things to attend to at the same time.

Historically two different forms of "not conscious" or automatic processes have been studied—those that follow immediately upon the perception of a person, object, or event in the environment (*preconscious* automaticity), and those that do not require conscious guidance once started intentionally (*goal-dependent* automaticity).

Preconscious Automaticity

These two basic varieties of automatic processing evolved from distinct and separate lines of research. The phenomenon of preconscious automaticity has its roots in *selective attention* research dating back to Donald Broadbent's seminal work *Perception and Communication* (London, 1958). Broadbent postulated an "early selection" theory of attention, in that what information was to be selected was determined very early in the "stages" of information processing, prior to any complex analysis of the input for meaning or importance or relevance. Nonselected information was said to be not processed at all. However, Ulric Neisser (*Cognitive Psychology*, New York, 1968) marshaled the accumulating evidence that preconscious processing for meaning was a pervasive and constant feature of mental life, but limited it to "figural synthesis"—the segmentation of the environment into basic objects (buildings, cars, people, trees). Conscious, deliberate thought was said to take these preattentively produced objects as its starting point.

Recent automaticity research, however, has shown that these immediate, preconscious reactions to one's environment extend beyond figural synthesis to the production of evaluative, emotional, motivational, and even behavioral responses to the environment. For example, clinical psychologists such as Aaron Beck (*Cognitive Therapy and the Emotional Disorders*, New York, 1976) have argued that complex sequences of reasoning can be put into motion by a seemingly innocuous event, running off automatically to their conclusion (for example, "I'm worthless"), so that a negative emotion is produced and experienced, without awareness of the thought process that produced it. Similarly, researchers of prejudice have shown that racial and ethnic stereotyping can occur automatically at a preconscious level (i.e., triggered by the mere presence of the associated racial or ethnic group features in an individual) and result in biased judgments and behavior without conscious awareness of the stereotype's effect, and often despite the individual's intentions not to be prejudiced.

Goal-Dependent Automaticity

Researchers of intergroup prejudice have also found that stereotypes influence deliberate, consciously made judgments and interpretations in ways of which the individual is not aware. Because such effects occur only when the person is consciously and intentionally forming an impression or a causal interpretation of another's behavior, they have been termed *implicit* effects, and are an example of the second major form of automaticity, that which is *goal dependent*. These are autonomous processes that require the intention that the process occur in the first place (and thus awareness that it is occurring) but once started, need no conscious guidance.

It has long been recognized that thought and behavior patterns that were repeated frequently come to require less and less conscious attention; they become more "efficient" and eventually require no conscious attention at all. Joseph Jastrow, a student of William James, was the first to argue (in *The Subconscious*, New York, 1906) that with experience, mental processes gradually recede from conscious awareness and guidance into the subconscious, where they operate autonomously. From these roots, a second stream of automaticity research emerged that focused on how mental and motor skills are acquired. These are well-practiced processes that subside into the subconscious over time. When one first learns to drive an automobile, or play chess, one is overwhelmed by the very many aspects of the task to which one must pay attention, and about which one must make decisions. Over time, many of the components of the skill are taken over by goal-dependent automatic processes, freeing limited attention to be used to anticipate one's opponents' moves, plan strategy, or mull over the day's events or plan dinner while threading through heavy traffic.

Automatic processes develop out of one's frequent and consistent experience and so come to reflect the regularities of the world. They relieve limited conscious processing of much of the information processing workload, and this is essential for successful adaptation to the world. But at the same time, when automatic processes develop out of sources other than one's own direct experience—as the automatic negative thoughts of depression, or stereotypes propagated by the culture—they can be maladaptive.

Bibliography

Ansfield, M. E., & Wegner, D. M. (1996). The feeling of doing. In P. M. Gollwitzer & J. A. Bargh (Eds.), *The psychology of action* (pp. 482–506). New York: Guilford Press.

Bargh, J. A. (1994). The four horsemen of automaticity: Awareness, intention, efficiency, and control in social cognition. In R. S. Wyer, Jr., & T. K. Srull (Eds.), *Handbook of social cognition* (2nd ed., pp. 1–40). Hillsdale, NJ: Erlbaum.

Devine, P. G. (1989). Stereotypes and prejudice: Their automatic and controlled components. *Journal of Personality and Social Psychology, 56,* 680–690.

Erdelyi, M. (1974). A new look at the New Look: Perceptual defense and vigilance. *Psychological Review, 81,* 1–25.

Greenwald, A. G., & Banaji, M. R. (1995). Implicit social cognition: Attitudes, self-esteem, and stereotypes. *Psychological Review, 102,* 4–27.

Logan, G. D. (1988). Toward an instance theory of automaticity. *Psychological Review, 95,* 492–527.

Nisbett, R. E., & Wilson, T. D. (1977). Telling more than we can know: Verbal reports on mental processes. *Psychological Review, 84,* 231–259.

Posner, M. I., & Snyder, C. R. R. (1975). Attention and cognitive control. In R. L. Solso (Ed.), *Information processing and cognition: The Loyola symposium* (pp. 55–85). Hillsdale, NJ: Erlbaum.

Shiffrin, R. M., & Schneider, W. (1977). Controlled and automatic human information processing: II. Perceptual learning, automatic attending, and a general theory. *Psychological Review, 84,* 127–190.

John A Bargh

AVERSION THERAPY. The most common form of aversive control from an operant conditioning perspective is punishment. Defined functionally, punishment is the presentation (positive punishment) or removal (negative punishment) of a stimulus (e.g., electric shock, money) contingent upon the occurrence of a target behavior that suppresses the future occurrence of that behavior. When punishment is arranged correctly, the target behavior may still produce a desired consequence (e.g., the child may stay out all night before getting grounded), but the punishing consequences arranged for the target behavior outweigh the desired consequences and prevent future occurrence of the target behavior. A second form of aversive control is negative reinforcement, which is the removal of a stimulus (e.g., electric shock), contingent on a particular behavior, to increase the future occurrence of that target behavior. For example, a child may clean her room to avoid being scolded.

In addition to punishment and negative reinforcement, a third form of aversion control is aversion therapy. Based on respondent conditioning principles, aversion therapy involves the pairing of a stimulus that elicits an undesirable target behavior (e.g., sight of drug) with a noxious stimulus such as a nausea-inducing drug or electric shock. Eventually, presentations of the original stimulus begin to elicit immediate unpleasant bodily consequences (e.g., nausea or pain). Consequently, individuals may avoid these stimuli, thereby reducing or eliminating the occurrence of the target behavior (cf. Lejuez, Schaal, & O'Donnell, 1998).

Although aversive conditioning procedures frequently are characterized as either operant or respondent, most incorporate both types of conditioning. Before reviewing various forms of psychological treatment using aversive control, we provide an overview of basic research support. We also discuss the potential drawbacks and ethical concerns associated with aversive control. Our conclusions apply only to the judicious data-based implementation of aversive control by psychologists rather than penalizing procedures imposed and executed by other social agents (e.g., courts, prisons).

Basic Research Support

Laboratory work with rats in the 1950s by B. F. Skinner, arguably the most influential American psychologist of the twentieth century, suggested that although punishment temporarily suppresses behavior, the behavior frequently returns to its previous level following the removal of the punishing stimulus (Skinner, 1953). Later work by N. A. Azrin, a student of Skinner's, obtained different results in an extensive set of studies examining punishment and its parameters (cf. Azrin & Holz, 1966). Azrin and his associates showed that the frequency and magnitude of the punisher were crucial variables, and when the appropriate parameters were used, punishment could produce long-term changes in behavior of a degree comparable to changes produced by reinforcement. In addition to punishment, negative reinforcement is another effective form of aversive control. For example, both rats and humans will engage in a particular task (e.g., lever pressing) to prevent the delivery of an aversive stimulus (e.g., shock). The long-term effectiveness of negative reinforcement is supported by the fact that organisms will engage in avoidance behavior despite few, if any, presentations of the aversive stimulus.

Basic research provides ample data on the effects of noxious stimuli within a respondent conditioning framework. Estes and Skinner (1941) presented rats with unavoidable presentations of shock that were reliably preceded by a presentation of an auditory stimulus, such that the tone served as a warning signal for the shock. After several pairings of the tone and shock, tone presentations produced a "conditioned emotional response" that prevented the rats from engaging in other behavior (e.g., lever pressing). In a related "classic" study, Garcia, Ervin, and Koelling (1966) demonstrated that the efficacy of a particular noxious stimulus is not universal but is affected by factors such as biological similarity ("belongingness") between paired stimuli.

Applications and Efficacy

The beneficial effects of operant-based aversive control procedures have been most clearly shown in the area of self-injury. One example, the Self-Injurious Behavior Inhibiting System (SIBIS), is a lightweight device worn by the client that delivers brief electric shock contingent on instances of self-injurious behavior. Advantages include precise monitoring of self-injury and the immediate delivery of shock contingent upon instances of self-injury that may cause bodily harm. Although research is limited, SIBIS produces a rapid and profound decrease in the frequency of self-injurious behavior in most patients (Linscheid, Iwata, Ricketts, Williams, & Griffin, 1990). Nevertheless, long-term benefits of SIBIS vary widely from individual to individual, and may depend on contextual factors such as parental support and developmental functioning.

From a respondent conditioning framework, aversive conditioning procedures have been used most frequently to treat substance abuse and sexually deviant behavior. When using an aversive counterconditioning procedure to treat substance abuse, stimulus properties of an abused substance (e.g., presentation of a powder substance or a drug-related odor) are paired with unpleasant bodily sensations (e.g., chemical-induced nausea or shock-induced pain). Using this procedure, it is hoped that future exposure to those or related stimuli also will elicit unpleasant bodily sensations, thereby decreasing or terminating future cravings for the actual substance in question. Although this type of aversive counterconditioning has been shown to have considerable effects in the laboratory (e.g., Garcia et al., 1966), support in the natural environment is equivocal (for a review, see Heather, 1990). In response to mixed support for aversive counterconditioning, and rising ethical concerns about the use of aversive control in general, nonaversive methods have been advocated and used increasingly more often (Evans & Meyer, 1985; Meyer & Evans, 1989; Miltenberger, 1997).

Two issues must be considered to maximize the therapeutic efficacy of aversive control procedures. First, when a particular type of behavior has been punished, a functionally equivalent behavior may replace the punished behavior. Although this replacement behavior may be more appropriate, it also may be inappropriate. For example, if contingencies are arranged to punish head banging, it is imperative to determine what functions were served by head banging (e.g., attention) so that a more adaptive replacement behavior can be established (cf. Meyer & Evans, 1989). This treatment component is crucial to produce behavior that meets the functional need served by the original target behavior, in a more socially appropriate and safe manner. This issue also is relevant to eliminating behavior with respondent conditioning procedures. For example, an aversive counterconditioning procedure for an individual who has molested children may primarily involve the pairing of electric shock or nausea-inducing drugs with pictures of young children. In addition, treatment should include a component in which more appropriate stimuli such as pictures of consenting adults are paired with pleasant bodily sensations.

Second, the removal of a problem behavior and the shaping of more appropriate behavior that occurs in the context of therapy must be generalizable to the patient's natural environment. If aversive counterconditioning is used with contrived stimuli in the lab (e.g., pictures of generic drug paraphernalia), the conditioned aversive response may not generalize to the natural environment. Instead, if stimuli used in therapy are more related to the patient's natural environment (e.g., sight of the patient's own drug paraphernalia), it is more likely that the effects of therapy will generalize and treatment gains will persist after therapy has ended.

Ethical Concerns

The use of aversive control has produced passionate debate among psychologists and educators. Although both basic and applied support has been provided for aversive-control procedures, many individuals have questioned their use because of potential side effects (LaVigna & Donellan, 1986). Empirical evidence from the basic laboratory (for a review, see Newsom, Favell, & Rincover, 1983) as well as from clinical and other applied settings (Kazdin, 1989) attests to some serious negative side effects of punishment (e.g., aggression or avoidance). As behavior is punished in particular situations, the frequency of other related behavior either may increase (contrast) or decrease (induction). Applied to the natural environment, a child scolded for talking out of turn may increase the frequency or intensity of other attention-maintained inappropriate behavior such as making noises (contrast), or the child may stop talking altogether (induction). On the other hand, positive side effects may be produced in the same manner as negative effects. For example, the same child may increase the frequency or intensity of other attention-maintained appropriate behavior such as turning in more homework assignments (contrast), or the child may decrease the number of aggressive acts against classmates (induction). In such cases, beneficial contrast and induction effects are especially likely if contingencies have been rearranged so that these more appropriate responses are reinforced.

Proponents of aversive-control procedures have argued that the failure to use aversive control is itself unethical (1) in the case of problems for which aversive procedures have been shown to be more effective than nonaversive procedures (e.g., self-injury) and (2) in situations in which the frequency of a particular behavior must be decreased faster than is typically possible with nonaversive procedures (e.g., head banging or self-mutilation by a severely retarded child). In any event, Miltenberger (1997) rightly pointed out that less restrictive nonaversive treatments are typically used before punishment is considered as a last resort. In many cases, severe problem behaviors can be eliminated with nonaversive procedures (e.g., positive reinforcement) after conducting a careful functional problem analysis.

[*See also* Avoidance Learning; *and* Taste Aversion Learning.]

Bibliography

Azrin, N. H., & Holz, W. C. (1966) Punishment. In W. K. Honig (Ed.), *Operant behavior: Areas of research and application* (pp. 380–447). New York: Appleton-Century-Crofts. Possibly the seminal paper on punishment and its procedures.

Estes, W. K., & Skinner, B. F. (1941). Some quantitative properties of anxiety. *Journal of Experimental Psychology, 29,* 390–400.

Evans, I. M., & Meyer, L. H. (1985). *An educative approach to behavior problems: A practical decision model for intervention with severely handicapped learners.* Baltimore: Paul H. Brookes. A manual for treating children and youth with severe behavior problems in school and other educational settings using only nonaversive interventions.

Garcia, J., Ervin, F. R., & Koelling, R. A. (1966). Learning with prolonged delay of reinforcement. *Psychonomic Science, 5,* 121–122.

Heather, N. (1990). Treatment of alcohol problems: With special reference to the behavioral approach. In D. J. K. Balfour (Ed.). *Psychotropic drugs of abuse. International encyclopedia of pharmacology and therapeutics* (pp. 283–312). Elmsford, NY: Pergamon.

Kazdin, A. E. (1989). *Behavior modification in applied settings* (4th ed.). Pacific Grove, CA: Brooks/Cole. Detailed descriptions and critical evaluation of specific aversive control procedures and their alternatives in a variety of applied and educational settings.

LaVigna, G. W., & Donellan, A. M. (1986). *Alternatives to punishment: Solving problems with nonaversive strategies.* New York: Irvington. A spirited debate of the efficacy and ethical concerns regarding the use of aversive control procedures and their alternatives.

Lejuez, C. W., Schaal, D. W., & O'Donnell, J. (1998). Behavioral pharmacology and the treatment of substance abuse. In J. J. Plaud & G. H. Eifert (Eds.). *From behavior theory to behavior therapy* (pp. 116–135). Boston: Allyn & Bacon.

Linscheid, T., Iwata, B. A., Ricketts, R., Williams, D., & Griffin, J. (1990). Clinical evaluation of the self-injurious behavior inhibiting system (SIBIS). *Journal of Applied Behavior Analysis, 23,* 53–78. A detailed description of SIBIS and critical evaluation of its results with individual patients.

Meyer, L. H., & Evans, I. M. (1989). *Nonaversive interventions for behavior problems: A manual for home and community.* Baltimore: Paul H. Brookes. Detailed descriptions of community and home-based nonaversive interventions for individuals with developmental disabilities. Contains many practical suggestions and forms for assessing and treating severe behavior problems.

Miltenberger, R. (1997). *Behavior modification: Principles and procedures.* Pacific Grove, CA: Brooks/Cole. Detailed descriptions and critical evaluation of the most frequently employed aversive control procedures. This book also presents the full array of nonaversive interventions.

Newsom, C., Favell, J. E., & Rincover, A. (1983). The side effects of punishment. In S. Axelrod & J. Apsche (Eds.), *The effects of punishment on human behavior* (pp. 285–316). New York: Academic Press.

Skinner, B. F. (1953). *Science and human behavior.* New York: Macmillan. A "classic" text outlining behavioral principles and their bold application to many facets of everyday life.

Georg H. Eifert and Carl W. Lejuez

AVIATION PSYCHOLOGY. The discipline of aviation psychology studies all aspects of the psychology of the pilot, air traffic controller, and maintainer that influence the safety and efficiency of flight. The discipline may also be characterized by content and methods.

Content

A combination of four features make the aviation task somewhat different from the tasks in other complex domains to which psychology has been applied. (1) The target system—the airplane—is primarily *spatial* and analog, involving the translation and rotation of the aircraft in space, adhering to the constraints of Newtonian physics. (2) Flying has multiple tasks and multiple goals, at least three of which are to *stabilize* the aircraft (i.e., prevent it from stalling and falling out of the air), to *navigate* to points in 3D space, and to carry out some *mission* (e.g., transport passengers). (3) Flying requires interacting and communicating with multiple agents, both human (copilots, air traffic controllers) and inanimate (the aircraft controls, automation). (4) Very high risks are involved, since human error can easily lead to fatalities.

Perception and Attention. During visual contact flight, when the pilot can see the ground below, knowledge of where the aircraft is in space is gained, in part, from a variety of perceptual cues related to movement across and orientation relative to the surface of the earth, and to other aircraft. These processes are well captured by the pioneering work of James Gibson on ecological perception. [*See the biography of Gibson.*] Of particular relevance in aviation are the sorts of visual illusions of size, distance, and motion that are induced by the somewhat unnatural viewing conditions from high above the earth's surface, often with impoverished depth cues. These illusions may be compounded by illusions of motion and orientation signaled by the vestibular senses as the aircraft proceeds through accelerations and orientations that are not natural aspects of human movement (Hawkins, 1993; O'Hare & Roscoe, 1990).

An important issue that underlies just about all aspects of perception in aviation is the powerful role of expectancy-driven "top-down" processing of both visual and auditory material, which is often impoverished or degraded in its quality.

Because of the distortions of visual perception, and the need to fly at night and in poor weather, aircraft have been equipped with flight instruments designed to convey information regarding position and motion. Since World War II, aviation psychologists have addressed the principles of attention and perception that will reduce the costs of integrating and interpreting this information. Some steps have been taken to improve the layout of flight instruments or displays; for example, by positioning related displays close together and the most important ones in the central viewing region. Other steps have been directed to changing the format of displays (their motion and orientation) in ways that are more compatible with the pilot's mental representation of spatial orientation and location. Display designers are considering more integrated perspective displays and electronic maps made possible by computer graphics capabilities. Recent advances have exploited head-up displays in which cockpit instruments are projected on the windshield in a way that reduces the costs of dividing attention between cockpit information and the view of the world. In combat aircraft, helmet-mounted displays allow head motion while viewing cockpit instrumentation. New computer-generated displays, whether presented head-up or head-down, continue to make relevant the important psychological process of visual search, and the manner in which display clutter hinders the acquisition of and the focus of attention on relevant material.

Consideration of the *perceptual motor skills* involved in flying, has enabled researchers to both understand and apply principles of tracking performance, and how such performance can be supported by the design of displays that better integrate information and offer prediction and preview.

Cognitive Processes. As with perception, so a wide variety of cognitive processes are involved in flying, and define the relevance of corresponding psychological research. Understanding pilots' mental representations of space has helped to explain the circumstances when spatial awareness is lost, and support the design of controls that are spatially compatible with displayed information. Much of flying is also characterized by following an extensive set of *procedures* that must be carried out in a precise order at precise times. Hence, the study of procedural knowledge and memory is relevant. Because such memory is highly fallible, pilots are supported by extensive *checklists*, and other memory aids, whose design and organization should be driven in part by the pilot's mental representation of tasks to be performed (Seamster, Redding, & Kaempf, 1997). While many procedural tasks are fairly routine and automatic, others depend upon carefully considered decisions and judgments made in the face of uncertainty (e.g., whether to fly on during bad weather, or turn around). Hence, the study of *aeronautical decision making* has represented an emerging focus of the cognitive aspects of aviation psychology (Wiener & Nagel, 1988).

Working memory is a construct that is relevant to many aspects of aviation psychology. For example, the pilot must rely on such memory to retain instructions from the air traffic controller; the controller must employ spatial working memory to visualize future trajectories of aircraft, and the maintenance technician must often use working memory to diagnose the source of failures. Various forms of computer-based automation have been proposed to alleviate some of these working memory demands (Billings, 1996; Wickens, Mavor, Parasuraman, & McGee, 1998).

Finally, two important and related cognitive constructs, *mental workload* and *situation awareness* have emerged from the study of aviation psychology. Mental workload defines the demands imposed by the multiple and often heterogeneous tasks confronting the pilot. The study of mental workload helps predict its sources, and the consequences to cockpit task management when that workload is excessive (e.g., which tasks are postponed or poorly performed and which ones are protected from degradation). Situation awareness refers to the pilot's current understanding and future projection of the evolving, changing characteristics of the airspace, the aircraft systems, and the tasks that must be performed. Situation awareness is often lost when workload is high, and may be supported by effective displays and by training of attention control skills (Endsley, 1999).

Communications and the Social Context. The pilot is typically a part of at least two, and often three "groups" or teams: one includes the air traffic controller, one includes other members of the flight deck (e.g., the copilot), and often one includes the "mission crew" (e.g., the flight attendants on a commercial airliner). The social interactions among these members can be examined on two levels. First, the study of voice perception is critical to understanding the causes of breakdowns in pilot-air traffic control communications that are the sources of many accidents and incidents. Expectancy-driven processing causes errors of hearing, and long messages can exceed the limits of working memory. Second, venturing into the realm of social psychology, aviation psychologists have learned much about the causes of failures of these teams to operate effectively because of poor group dynamics (e.g., ambiguous messages, authoritative unidirectional communications). This research area is labeled *cockpit resource management* (Wiener, Kanki, & Helmreich, 1993), and also incorporates some consideration of pilot personality differences and cultural differences that support or inhibit good teamwork.

Remediations and Supports. Pilot error in any of the above areas has led to pursuit of one of four types of remediations. (1) As noted above, modern *design* concepts (e.g., integrated electronic displays) can assist in preventing many breakdowns of perception, attention, and situation awareness. Of particular interest are the sources of positive or negative transfer of performance between aircraft with similar or different design features. Positive transfer will reduce retraining on the new aircraft. Negative transfer will invite pilot error. (2) Pilot *selection* research attempts to identify those skills necessary for good piloting, such that they can be pre-

dicted on the basis of tests. (3) Pilot *training* research has applied principles from learning theory in an effort to train pilots more efficiently in the safer "risk-free" environment of the classroom or flight simulator, rather than the aircraft (Hawkins, 1993; O'Hare & Roscoe, 1993). At issue are the appropriate training strategies to use for teaching flight skills, and the study of *transfer of training* from lessons and skills learned on the ground (classroom, computer, or flight simulator), to those demonstrated in the air. Such training programs have recently been broadened from those involving perceptual motor and procedural aspects of flight, to those addressing aeronautical decision making and cockpit resources management (Wiener et al., 1993; Garland, Wise & Hopkin, 1999). (4) Many aviation safety problems have been addressed by introduction of *computer automation*, to remediate or replace error-prone aspects of pilot performance as well as to improve the efficiency of some aspects of flight. These include features like autopilots, automatic checklists, electronic databases, fault diagnosis assistance, computer-mediated communications, and automatic collision warnings. Lessons learned in the early introduction of cockpit automation have revealed a host of cognitive issues or problems related to trust and mistrust of automation, lowered situation awareness, and increased complacency. Such issues have important implications for the design of automation on the flight deck and for air traffic control. The concept of human-centered automation is one that offers principles for implementing automation that are sensitive to these problems (Billings, 1996; Wickens et al., 1998).

Air Traffic Control and Maintenance

Air traffic controllers and aircraft maintenance technicians have received less attention by aviation psychologists, although their tasks are every bit as critical to flight safety as those of the pilot. For air traffic controllers, critical task components involve visual monitoring, an accurate deployment of attention across the radar-generated display, maintaining situation awareness of present position and future trajectories of the aircraft under supervision. They must also implement a series of decisions to either allow the aircraft to continue on a scheduled flight path, or to alter heading, airspeed, and/or altitude, in order to balance the goals of safety (protect separation between planes) and efficiency (maximize the rate of movement across the skies) (Wickens, Mavor, & McGee, 1997; Hopkin, 1995). To execute these decisions, controllers are heavily engaged in communications with pilots and with other controllers. Their task is supported by extensive knowledge of procedures, by an elaborate mental model of the airspace characteristics of the area in which they work (Seamster, Redding, & Kaempf, 1997), and by various forms of automation (Wickens et al., 1998).

The psychological process underlying the aircraft maintenance often involves maintaining vigilance during lengthy inspections with a low probability of a defect. Diagnostic and troubleshooting skills are critical for understanding more complex failures, and so is an accurate procedural memory for carrying out many maintenance activities.

Research Methodologies

Knowledge of how pilots, controllers, and maintainers interact with the aircraft and its supporting elements has been gained by a variety of research techniques (Wickens et al., 1997). Accident investigations reveal the contributions of human error in a majority of aircraft accidents. However, the frequency of aircraft accidents is so low, and their causes so multiply determined, that statistically valid causal inferences are very difficult to draw. In contrast, incident analyses, based upon a much larger sample of anonymously reported pilot, controller, and maintainer errors, provide more reliable inferences regarding error causes, but, as with accidents, the circumstances under which incidents occur also lack experimental control. Such control can be imposed in aircraft simulation and laboratory studies, but these may sometimes fall short of generalizability to the complexity and stressfulness of the cockpit environment. Pilot or air traffic controller surveys can reflect important issues such as attitudes toward automation, but their results may be biased by low response rates, and by other factors associated with the uncertain validity of subjective ratings. Finally, computational human (pilot) performance models are beginning to provide useful research results in certain well-understood areas, like cockpit visibility, visual search, or manual control, in which the models have been clearly validated. While each research technique has its own strengths and weaknesses, relatively firm conclusions about many aspects of aviation psychology are best drawn from the use of multiple methodologies in consort.

Conclusion

Aviation psychology has, in many ways, been a pioneering field in demonstrating the relevance of psychological principles and theory to other aspects of human interaction with complex systems, the domain of engineering psychology. Hence researchers in this area helped to establish engineering psychology as a discipline. Correspondingly, the rapid automatization of many aspects of the flight deck is leading aviation psychologists to seek guidance from the field of human-computer interaction.

[*See also* Psychology; *and* Transportation Systems Design.]

Bibliography

Billings, C. E. (1996). *Aviation automation: The search for a human-centered approach.* Mahwah, NJ: Erlbaum. A comprehensive treatment of human factors issues in aircraft automation, presenting the concept of human-centered automation.

Endsley, M. (1999). Situation awareness. In D. Garland, J. Wise, & V. D. Hopkin (Eds)., *Handbook of aviation human factors.* Mahwah, NJ: Erlbaum.

Garland, D., Wise, J. & Hopkin, V. D. (Eds). (1999). *Handbook of aviation human factors.* Mahwah, NJ: Erlbaum.

Hawkins, F. H. (1993). *Human factors in flight* (H. W. Orlady, Ed.). (2nd ed.) Brookfield, VT: Ashgate.

Hopkin, V. D. (1995). *Human factors in air-traffic control.* London: Taylor & Francis.

Jensen, R. (Ed.). (1991–1999). *International Journal of Aviation Psychology.* Best source of research results in this area.

O'Hare, D., & Roscoe, S. (1990). *Flightdeck performance: The human factor.* Ames, IA: Iowa State University Press.

Seamster, T. L., Redding, R. E., & Kaempf, G. L. (1997). *Applied cognitive task analysis in aviation.* Brookfield, VT: Ashgate. Offers insight into many of the cognitive factors involved in aviation tasks.

Wickens, C. D., Mavor, A. S., & McGee, J. P. (Eds.). (1997). *Flight to the future: Human factors in air traffic control.* Washington, DC: National Academy Press.

Wickens, C. D., Mavor, A. S., Parasuraman, R., & McGee, J. P. (Eds.). (1998). *The future of air traffic control: Human operators and automation.* Washington, DC: National Academy Press. An examination of human factors issues in automation in general, and air traffic control automation in particular.

Wiener, E. L., Kanki, B. G., & Helmreich, R. L. (Eds.). (1993). *Cockpit resource management.* San Diego, CA: Academic Press. An edited volume of chapters focusing on the social and team interaction factors involved in aviation psychology.

Wiener, E. L., & Nagel, D. C. (Eds.). (1988). *Human factors in aviation.* San Diego, CA: Academic Press. An edited volume of chapters by experts in the field.

Christopher D. Wickens

AVOIDANCE LEARNING is a form of instrumental conditioning that occurs in situations where an aversive stimulus is likely to occur. The instrumental avoidance response prevents the presentation of the aversive stimulus.

Historical Antecedents

The first systematic study of avoidance learning was published in 1913 by the Russian psychologist Vladimir

Bechterev who studied Pavlovian conditioning in human participants. Bechterev developed the finger withdrawal conditioning task in which participants were required to place a finger on a metal plate. A conditioning trial consisted of presentation of a warning stimulus or signal just before a mild electric shock was applied to the metal plate. The participants quickly lifted their finger when they were shocked. After a few trials, they also came to lift their finger when the warning stimulus was presented. By withdrawing their finger from the metal plate during the warning stimulus, the participants avoided getting shocked.

Bechterev's work had important theoretical and methodological consequences for the study of avoidance learning. Methodologically, Bechterev established the *discriminated avoidance procedure*. In this procedure, discrete learning trials are arranged by the experimenter. Each trial begins with a warning stimulus or conditioned stimulus (CS). A few seconds later, an aversive event, the unconditioned stimulus (US), is delivered if the participant does not perform the specified avoidance response. If the instrumental response occurs during the warning stimulus, delivery of the aversive event is canceled on that trial. Delivery of the aversive stimulus is blocked only if the instrumental response occurs during the warning stimulus. Responses at other times have no effect in a discriminated avoidance procedure.

Bechterev's work established a strong Pavlovian tradition in the analysis of avoidance learning. In this tradition, explanations of behavior are sought in relationships between conditioned and unconditioned stimuli, rather than in the relationship between an instrumental response and its outcome. In fact, Bechterev considered the finger-withdrawal behavior that developed in his procedure to be due entirely to pairings of the warning stimulus with shock. He did not think it was important that the finger-withdrawal response also protected the participants from encountering the US. Not until a couple of decades later did investigators begin to seriously entertain the possibility that prevention of an aversive stimulus may be an important component of avoidance conditioning procedures.

The importance of the avoidance contingency in a discriminated avoidance procedure was evaluated in several experiments, including a famous study by Brogden, Lipman, and Culler ("The Role of Incentive in Conditioning and Extinction," *American Journal of Psychology*, 1938, 51, 109–117). They tested two groups of guinea pigs in a running wheel apparatus. One group received a pure Pavlovian conditioning procedure in which a two-second tone ended with brief shock on every trial regardless of the behavior of the subjects. For the other group, the shock was omitted after the warning stimulus if the subjects rotated the running wheel during the CS. The addition of this avoidance contingency dramatically elevated responding. This outcome indicated that discriminated avoidance learning could not be explained just in terms of Pavlovian mechanisms.

Two-Process Theory of Avoidance Learning

Instrumental processes were integrated with Pavlovian conditioning in the analysis of avoidance learning in the two-process theory that was developed by O. H. Mowrer (1947) and others. According to this theory, avoidance learning first requires the Pavlovian conditioning of fear to the CS or warning stimulus. This Pavlovian conditioning occurs on trials when the subject fails to perform the avoidance response and the CS is paired with the aversive US. Once the CS has come to elicit conditioned fear, termination of the CS provides instrumental reinforcement of the avoidance response. According to two-process theory, the avoidance response occurs because it is instrumental in terminating the warning stimulus and producing a reduction in conditioned fear. This negative reinforcement through reduction of conditioned fear is assumed to be critical for instrumental conditioning of the avoidance response. The omission of the US on avoidance trials is viewed as incidental to the fear-reduction reinforcement.

Although two-factor theory dominated studies of avoidance learning for several decades after its introduction in the 1940s, the theory came under increasing challenge. One problematic finding was that avoidance learning was difficult to extinguish by discontinuing presentations of the US. Contrary to two-process theory, responding persisted when USs were discontinued if the avoidance response was still permitted to terminate the CS. Another troublesome finding was that once the avoidance response was well established, it became dissociated from conditioned fear elicited by the CS. During the initial stages of the acquisition of avoidance behavior, both conditioned fear and avoidance behavior increase. However, conditioned fear declines after avoidance responding is well established. Thus, contrary to two-process theory, avoidance behavior is not correlated with conditioned fear throughout acquisition of the avoidance response.

Nondiscriminated or Free-Operant Avoidance

Another finding that initially challenged two-factor theory was that avoidance behavior can be acquired with a free-operant procedure that does not include an explicit warning signal. In the free-operant or nondiscriminated avoidance procedure, devised by Murray Sidman, an aversive stimulus is scheduled to occur periodically (as set by the S-S interval) if the organism does not perform the avoidance response. Whenever the avoidance response occurs, a period of safety (as set by the R-S interval) is created. The R-S interval is reset each time the avoidance response occurs. Therefore, by always responding before the safe period is over, the organism can effectively avoid ever getting the aversive stimulus.

The free-operant avoidance procedure encouraged the formulation of an alternative to two-process theory—shock frequency reduction theory (also known as the "negative law of effect"). According to this theory, avoidance responses occur because they are effective in reducing the frequency of aversive stimuli. However, empirical tests have indicated that shock frequency reduction is not necessary to produce avoidance learning. Avoidance learning can occur even if the total number of shocks is not reduced, provided shocks are postponed after each avoidance response.

Although the free-operant avoidance procedure was initially presented as requiring a drastic overhaul of two-process theory, ways have been found to extend the theory to accommodate the new findings. In these reformulations, temporal cues associated with periodic presentations of the aversive stimulus are assumed to elicit conditioned fear. These temporal cues are terminated by the avoidance response, which resets the R-S interval. In addition, proprioceptive or other feedback cues that accompany an avoidance response are assumed to become safety signals or conditioned inhibitors of fear because these cues are always followed by a period without aversive stimulation. Conditioned inhibitory safety signals are assumed to serve as positive reinforcers that can reinforce instrumental avoidance responses in aversive situations. The safety signal mechanism complements two-factor theory by adding a positive instrumental reinforcement mechanism to the fear conditioning and negative reinforcement processes assumed by two-process theory.

Neural Mechanisms of Avoidance Learning

The neural systems that underlie avoidance learning have attracted increasing attention. In a typical study by Gabriel, one of the major investigators in this area, rabbits have to learn to rotate a large running wheel to avoid signaled foot shock (Gabriel & Schmajuk, 1990). The signal (the CS+) is provided by a tone that is presented 5 seconds before each shock. A different tone (the CS−) is presented an equal number of times but is never paired with shock. The rabbits quickly learn to avoid shock and rotate the wheel more vigorously during the CS+ than the CS−.

Through a combination of electrophysiological recordings and selective lesions, Gabriel's research team has shown that avoidance learning depends on components of the limbic system. The limbic system is generally characterized as the most primitive portion of the forebrain, the first to have evolved. Anatomically, the limbic system lies above the brain stem at the core of

the forebrain. Functionally, evidence suggests that components of this system are involved in learning, memory, and emotion.

Acquisition of discriminated avoidance appears to depend on three mechanisms: a GO system which initiates responding during the CS+, a STOP system that generally inhibits behavior, and a discriminative system that differentiates the CS+ from the CS−. Two limbic structures, the cingulate cortex and limbic thalamus, represent the core of the GO system. Volleys of thalamic activity elicited by the CS stimulate neurons in the cingulate cortex. This in turn triggers the locomotor reflex, which is organized by neural systems within the brain stem and spinal cord.

The STOP system generally opposes the production of locomotor behavior. This inhibitory effect emerges early in training when the organism associates the contextual cues of the experimental chamber with the aversive US (shock). This context-shock association produces a state of immobility (freezing) that inhibits the avoidance response. At a neural level, the STOP system depends on the subicular complex of the hippocampus, which regulates locomotor behavior through a projection to the cingulate cortex and limbic thalamic nuclei. Removing this source of inhibition during the CS+ allows the surge in thalamic neuronal activity to generate the avoidance response. Thus, an active avoidance response depends on two competing processes, the thalamomotor GO system and the hippocampal STOP system. In essence, the hippocampus, which integrates information from a variety of sources, maintains veto power over the production of the avoidance response by the less well-informed thalamomotor system.

Electrophysiological studies have shown that discriminated avoidance training causes differential neuronal activity to develop within the limbic thalamus. Specifically, the CS+ comes to elicit a stronger response than the CS−. This discriminative electrophysiological activity does not depend on the hippocampal STOP system. Indeed, lesioning the hippocampus can enhance the development of thalamic plasticity. Discriminative activity does, however, depend on another limbic structure, the amygdala. Lesioning the amygdala blocks the development of both discriminative thalamic activity and avoidance learning. Amygdala lesions are also known to disrupt the acquisition of conditioned fear. The fact that amygdala lesions block avoidance learning as well as the conditioning of fear provides further support that fear conditioning mediates the acquisition of avoidance behavior.

SSDRs and Predatory Imminence

The mechanisms involved in two-process theory and its extensions take numerous trials to develop. In an influential paper published in 1970 ("Species Specific Defense Reactions and Avoidance Learning," *Psychological*

Review, 71, 32–48), Robert Bolles argued that to be adaptive, avoidance behavior has to occur rapidly. An animal that fails to defend itself the first time it encounters a predator is apt to be severely injured, if not killed. Because of this, Bolles suggested that much of defensive behavior is set by the genetic rather than learning history of the organism. Bolles proposed that animals are equipped with *species specific defense reactions* (SSDRs) that they do not have to learn. These include responses such as freezing, fleeing, and fighting. According to Bolles, these SSDRs predominate during the first few encounters with an aversive stimulus. If an SSDR is not successful in providing safety, the aversive stimulus will occur and serve to punish that SSDR. As ineffective SSDRs become suppressed by punishment, other SSDRs will take their place until one is found that is effective in preventing the aversive stimulation.

SSDR theory was important in drawing attention to unconditioned aspects of defensive behavior, but its emphasis on punishment as the only learning mechanism turned out to be inaccurate. SSDRs have been shown to be remarkably resistant to the effects of punishment. Instead of relying on punishment mechanisms, subsequent conceptualizations of defensive behavior have assumed that selection among instinctive defensive responses is determined by the perceived likelihood of being attacked by a predator. This perception is called predatory imminence (Fanselow, 1997).

Different defensive behaviors are assumed to be activated at different levels of predatory imminence. For rats that live in underground burrows, for example, a low level of predatory imminence is experienced when the rat leaves its nest to forage for food and enters an area where a predator may appear. Predatory imminence increases when the rat becomes fearful either because it actually encounters a predator or encounters a signal that has become associated with a predator. This postencounter state elicits immobility or freezing and an analgesic response mediated by the release of an endogenous opioid (endorphin). Predatory imminence is greatest when contact with the predator occurs or is inevitable. At this point the rat may flee, exhibit a threat display, or engage in circa-strike aggressive responses. During this highest level of predatory imminence, a nonopioid system inhibits responses that might interfere with effective defense.

Postencounter and circa-strike defensive behaviors appear to be organized by a neural system within the brain stem known as the periaqueductal gray (PAG). The PAG is a region that wraps around the aqueduct. The ventral (abdominal) side of this structure plays a critical role in organizing postencounter defensive behavior, such as freezing and opioid analgesia. These behaviors are elicited when the ventral region is artificially activated, and lesioning this structure eliminates these defensive responses. Under natural conditions, the activation of the ventral PAG is controlled by the amygdala, a forebrain system known to be involved in emotion and fear.

Circa-strike behavior appears to depend on portions of the PAG that lie above (dorsal), and to the sides (lateral), of the ventral zone, an area collectively referred to as the dorsolateral PAG. Artificially activating this region elicits fighting, escape behavior, threat displays, and the inhibition of protective reflexes by means of a nonopioid system. Interestingly, the type of behavior elicited depends on the region stimulated. Stimulating rats in the rostral (toward the nose) portion causes backward defense (fight) while caudal sites (toward the tail) generate forward avoidance (flight). Under natural conditions, these behaviors may be directly engaged by incoming (afferent) pain signals and by contact-related stimuli through a projection from the superior colliculus.

SSDR theory and the concept of predatory imminence are useful in characterizing what occurs during the first few trials of avoidance training. However, these concepts cannot explain various other results that have been found after extensive training on both discriminated and free-operant avoidance procedures. These considerations suggest that a comprehensive account of avoidance learning will require concepts from several different theoretical perspectives.

[*See also* Aversion Therapy; *and* Learning.]

Bibliography

Bolles, R. C. (1972). The avoidance learning problem. In G. H. Bower (Ed.), *The psychology of learning and motivation* (Vol. 6, pp. 97–145). New York: Academic Press. Describes the history of empirical and theoretical approaches to the study of avoidance learning.

Denny, M. R. (Ed.). (1991). *Fear, avoidance, and phobias.* Hillsdale, NJ: Erlbaum. A comprehensive modern account of avoidance learning and related issues.

Depaulis, A., & Bandler, R. (1991). The midbrain periaqueductal gray matter: Functional, anatomical, and neurochemical organization. *NATO ASI Series A: Vol. 213.* New York: Plenum. Describes research on the organization and function of the periaqueductal gray.

Fanselow, M. S. (1994). Neural organization of the defensive behavior system responsible for fear. *Psychonomic Bulletin & Review, 1,* 429–438. Discusses the role of the periaqueductal gray in species-specific defense reactions.

Fanselow, M. S. (1997). Species specific defense reactions: Retrospect and prospect. In M. E. Bouton & M. S. Fanselow (Eds.), *Learning, motivation, and cognition* (pp. 321–341). Washington, DC: American Psychological Association. Describes the status of current research on species specific defense reactions and the role of predatory imminence.

Gabriel, M., & Schmajuk, N. (1990). Neural and computational models of avoidance learning. In M. Gabriel & J. Moore (Eds.), *Learning and computational neuroscience: Foundations of adaptive network* (pp. 143–171). Cambridge, MA: MIT Press. Describes neurobiological studies of discriminated avoidance behavior in rabbits.

Hineline, P. N. (1997). Negative reinforcement and avoidance. In W. K. Honig & J. E. R. Staddon (Eds.), *Handbook of operant behavior* (pp. 364–414). Englewood Cliffs, NJ: Prentice Hall. Describes research and theory on avoidance learning, with emphasis on free-operant avoidance.

Mowrer, O. H. (1947). On the dual nature of learning: A reinterpretation of "conditioning" and "problem solving." *Harvard Educational Review, 17,* 102–148.

Poremba, A., & Gabriel, M. (1997). Amygdalar lesions block discriminative avoidance learning and cingulothalamic training-induced neuronal plasticity in rabbits. *Journal of Neuroscience, 17,* 5237–5244. Provides evidence that amygdalar neurons are involved in learning to avoid dangerous situations.

Michael Domjan and James W. Grau

B

BACK-TRANSLATION. Cross-cultural studies often involve the need to communicate with people in languages other than the researchers' own (Brislin, 1993). Back-translation is one tool in the arsenal of methods for cross-cultural research (Van de Vijver & Leung, 1997). It is used to prepare research materials such as tests, interview schedules, and instructions to research participants that will be used in different cultures. Back-translation also allows researchers to have some control over the preparation of the research materials even if they are not fluent in other languages.

In its most basic form, a back-translation procedure begins with materials that have been prepared in one language, usually the researcher's own. Such materials can be standardized, as in a published test such as the Minnesota Multiphasic Personality Inventory (MMPI), or they can be prepared by the researcher according to the goals of a particular study. Assume that the materials are prepared in English. These materials are given to a bilingual person who then translates them to another language called the "target." A second bilingual person, working independently of the first, translates from the target back into English. The researcher can then compare the two English versions and begin to make assessments of the translation's quality.

This basic form of back-translation is not perfect since some bilingual people are so skilled that they can make sense out of a mangled target language version and present it in good English. This situation is similar to what many people have experienced: they meet international visitors who present their request in imperfect English. The native speaker listeners, with the proper application of social skills, can often make sense of the request and respond in a helpful manner. One way to overcome this potential problem is to add another step to the procedure. After the target version is prepared, another bilingual person (whose skills can be much stronger in the target language) prepares a second target version.

The instructions to this person would be to rewrite the target version so that it is clear and easily understandable to the study's eventual participants. If the back-translated version of this "target rewrite" is clear, this represents another piece of evidence that the translators have been doing quality work.

Other methodological tools can be added. In *decentering*, researchers attempt to avoid imposing a point of view from one culture on others. This has long been a possibility with standardized tests and leads to a critical question: Are standardized tests of concepts such as intelligence or personality, prepared and validated in one country, usable in another or are they just impositions of the concepts? In decentering, there is no unmodifiable standard. Rather, items are changed, added, and deleted so that the concepts are meaningful and valid in all the cultures that are part of a study. Often, good information for decentering decisions will come from the back-translation process. Researchers should keep careful notes concerning what aspects of their work translators find easy, difficult, unfamiliar, and impossible. For instance, assume that a study deals with relations among family members. If the original English phrase is "interactions with my brother," this cannot be translated into Japanese or Chinese. These languages have different terms for "older brother" and "younger brother," but no term that encompasses both. With decentering as a goal, researchers would then change the original English and ask about relations with younger and older brothers in all cultures that are part of the research project.

[*See also* Cross-Cultural Test Adaptation.]

Bibliography

Brislin, R. (2000). *Understanding culture's influence on behavior* (2nd ed.). Fort Worth, TX: Harcourt Brace Jovanovich.

Van de Vijver, F., & Leung, K. (1997). Methods and data analysis of comparative research. In J. Berry, Y. Poortinga, & J. Pandey (Eds.), *Handbook of cross-cultural psychology: Vol. 1, Theory and method* (2nd ed., pp. 257–300). Boston: Allyn & Bacon.

Richard W. Brislin

BACON, FRANCIS (1561–1626), English philosopher. The son of Nicholas Bacon, a statesman, and Anne Cooke, a scholar and translator, Bacon was sent to Cambridge University at the age of 12 and graduated in 1575, having acquired a distaste for the sterility of Aristotelian scholasticism. Following a successful career in law, he entered a turbulent life in politics, serving as a member of Parliament and, later, as Lord Chancellor under James I. During these years, Bacon began publishing on philosophical topics, but it was not until after his banishment from public office on bribery charges in 1621 that he devoted full attention to the work that brought him lasting fame.

An older contemporary of Galileo and Descartes, Bacon shared with them the role of heralding the Scientific Revolution, discerning its implications for society, and ushering in the modern age. Unlike Galileo and Descartes, who represented the revolution's rational-mathematical side, Bacon extolled the value of empiricism in modern science. Against the medieval view that human knowledge was static and circumscribed, he argued that careful use of the inductive method would produce a vast expansion of knowledge that could be applied to the betterment of humankind. Bacon's views on the prospects for science-based human progress made him a key source for Enlightenment thinkers in the following century, and his forceful writing style did much to enhance the reception of his otherwise controversial and visionary ideas.

In the *Novum Organum* (1620), Bacon expressed his empiricism in three ways. First, he urged that the language of science be divorced from the languages of common sense and speculative metaphysics. Using the metaphor of "idols" to characterize preconceptions that block the road to scientific truth, he warned against the idols of the marketplace—the use of vernacular concepts that draw unreal distinctions—and the idols of the theater—systems of philosophical speculation that, like stage sets, create coherent but unreal worlds. Bacon's attention to the perils of misleading language would become a theme of much subsequent philosophy, beginning with Thomas Hobbes (who, for a time, served as Bacon's secretary) and extending through David Hume to the logical positivism and operationism of the twentieth century.

Second, Bacon championed a method of inductive inference by which scientists could rise by a "gradual and unbroken ascent" from particular observations to progressively more general "axioms." His famous tables of induction involved assembling cases in which a specified property (say, heat) was present, absent, or varying in degrees. Although criticized for neglecting the role of hypotheses in science, Bacon's inductive method underscored the value of particular observations in confirming or ruling out generalizations, and was later refined by John Stuart Mill as a means for ascertaining the necessary and sufficient conditions for the occurrence of phenomena.

The third expression of Bacon's empiricism was his advocacy of the experimental method, a method relatively unknown to the scientists of his day. However useful the tables of induction were for extracting a "first vintage" of provisional truths, the search for underlying causes, according to Bacon, was best pursued through diligent experimentation, a procedure characterized by him as the forcing of nature out of its usual ways in order to extract its secrets. Such discovery of causes was seen as crucial for the command of nature.

Bacon's experimentalism was linked to his reverence for the technological developments of his time. Citing such advances as the compass and the printing press, he recommended the tradition of Renaissance crafts as the surest model for the growth of science. Under the motto that knowledge is power, Bacon's scientific utopia *New Atlantis* (1627) depicted a technologically advanced society governed by the scientists of Salomon's House, an institution that became the model for the Royal Society of London and presaged the advent of state-supported science and the modern research university.

In both its intellectual and social aspects, Baconism became the favored ideology of science in England, endorsed by such scientists as Robert Boyle and Isaac Newton. Its utilitarian bent and utopian promise of progress also gained it a favorable reception in America, where it was embraced by leaders of the American Enlightenment. Baconian ideals helped shape the emergence of American science, especially in the empirically oriented biological and social sciences, including psychology. Reinforced by America's indigenous pragmatism, these ideals inspired psychologists as diverse as G. Stanley Hall, James McKeen Cattell, and B. F. Skinner, and set the context for the widespread definition of psychology's goal as the prediction and control of human behavior.

The practical and empiricist tenor of Anglo-American science—as contrasted with the more theoretical style of Continental science—owes much to the Baconian aversion to abstract theorizing and focus on experimentation and application. Bacon's death in 1626 was emblematic of these themes. Not content to speculate on the beneficial preservative effects of cold on meat, Bacon conducted an experiment by stuffing a chicken carcass with snow, succumbing a few days later to bronchitis brought on by the episode.

[*Many of the people mentioned in this article are the subjects of independent biographical entries.*]

Bibliography

Works by Bacon

Bacon, F. (1857–1874). *The works of Francis Bacon* (J. Spedding, R. L. Ellis, & D. D. Heath, Eds.). London: Longmans. The standard edition of Bacon's writings, in fourteen volumes, with commentaries.

Bacon, F. (1942). *New Atlantis*. In G. S. Haight (Ed.), *Essays and New Atlantis* (pp. 243–302). New York: Black. (Original work published 1627)

Bacon, F. (1994). *Novum organum* (P. Urbach & J. Gibson, Eds. & Trans.). La Salle, IL: Open Court. (Original work published 1620.) A new translation of Bacon's masterwork from the Latin, with a useful introduction by the editors.

Works about Bacon

Anderson, F. H. (1962). *Francis Bacon: His career and his thought*. Los Angeles: University of Southern California Press. The best concise biography of Bacon, eloquent and accessible.

Bowen, C. D. (1994). *Francis Bacon: The temper of a man*. New York: Fordham University Press. Reissue of a classic biography. (Original work published 1963)

Morawski, J. G. (1982). Assessing psychology's moral heritage through our neglected utopias. *American Psychologist, 37,* 1082–1095. On the Baconian heritage in psychologists' utopias, including those of G. Stanley Hall and John B. Watson.

Pauly, P. J. (1987). *Controlling life: Jacques Loeb and the engineering ideal in biology*. New York: Oxford University Press. An account of the Baconian technological tradition in American biology and psychology, as transmitted through European positivism.

Perez-Ramos, A. (1988). *Francis Bacon's idea of science and the maker's knowledge tradition*. Oxford: Oxford University Press. Places Bacon in the epistemological tradition of "maker's knowledge," stressing Bacon's admiration for the craft tradition and hands-on manipulation of nature.

Skinner, B. F. (1983). *A matter of consequences*. New York: Knopf. Contains discussion of Skinner's debt to Bacon, including his inductive method, utopianism, and philosophy of control.

Urbach, P. (1987). *Francis Bacon's philosophy of science: An account and a reappraisal*. La Salle, IL: Open Court. A sympathetic exposition of Bacon's philosophy of science, defending it against charges of naive inductivism.

Vickers, B. (Ed.). (1968). *Essential articles for the study of Francis Bacon*. Hamden, CT: Archon Books. Useful essays on Bacon's life and work, including a classic assessment of his philosophy of science by the philosopher Mary Hesse.

Wallace, K. R. (1967). *Francis Bacon on the nature of man:*

The faculties of man's soul: Understanding, reason, imagination, will, and appetite. Urbana: University of Illinois Press. Treats Bacon's views on psychology, which, though largely unoriginal and only implicit in his writings, underlay his philosophy of science in interesting ways.

Laurence D. Smith

BAIN, ALEXANDER (1818–1903), Scottish moral philosopher/psychologist. Bain contributed to modern psychology a convincing naturalistic reorientation of moral philosophy in the form of a two-volume treatise, *The Senses and the Intellect* (1855) and *The Emotions and the Will* (1859). His trenchant illustrations and theoretical discussions long influenced diverse thinkers who were considering how mental life was based on the functional organization of the nervous system.

Bain's reorientation was closely intertwined with the educational opportunities that nineteenth-century liberal Scotland provided him as the son of an impoverished handloom weaver. Bain rejected unconditionally the attribution of inherently different psychological characteristics to members of different classes. For example, he objected to restricting decision-making ability to the upper classes and sheer physical effort to the lower classes. He sought above all, however, to overturn the Calvinist doctrine of predestination which placed the determination of the origins and consequences of moral actions outside of a naturalistic, temporal framework. One consequence of this was that Bain obtained only a professorship of English and rhetoric in Scotland and not the one he sought in moral philosophy/psychology.

Learning was not only crucial to Bain's highly successful academic career and to his political activity as a second-generation philosophical radical formulating and promoting democratic liberalism, it was also central to his psychology. To achieve full human potential, individuals required both the knowledge and the respite to maintain a healthy constitution and to develop vocationally. Therefore, access by all to the cultural inheritance of society was to be politically mandated. To this end, adult authority figures played a significant pragmatic, psychological, and moral role in development from early childhood on. Thus, Bain expanded the concept of learning beyond the classroom to the motor movements of infancy and provided intellectual credence for the skilled movements of craftsmen.

Bain's natural history of differentiated mental development expressed the Victorian self-understanding of individual achievement through personal effort. In devising a temporal framework of human development characterized by goal-directed behavior, Bain drew upon the naturalist Georges Cuvier's study of animal pursuit, on human locomotion research, but also on the literary concept of plot-interest. Bain utilized the image of the working scientist as a model for the mature citizen, who in whatever station in life adaptively constructs a better future through the critical assessment of experience.

Whereas the development of character, that is, the ability to persevere against odds, provided a regularity in human behavior, it did not for Bain fit easily within the simple cause-effect schema of the physical sciences. Bain's original concept of "constructive association" was based on the mind's ability to meet practical environmental challenges through an imaginative application of memory. Creative solutions expanded both the psychological and practical future, as human nature "surpassed itself."

Bain's natural history reorientation of the human mind wedded motor phenomena and association psychology. Thereby, he laid the psychological foundations in the English tradition for a thoroughgoing sensorimotor physiology. Bain's contribution, however, stands in a decisively complementary relationship to that of Darwin. This is due to Bain's primary interest in ontogeny rather than phylogeny, in cultural rather than genetic transmission, and in intentional volition and innovative production rather than in environmental influences on species adaptation.

Bain critiqued phrenology in *On the Study of Character* (London, 1861). He illustrated the importance of a psychological approach to rhetoric in his *English Composition and Rhetoric* (London, 1866) and to education in his *Education as a Science* (London, 1879). He also produced biographies of *James Mill* (London, 1882) and *John Stuart Mill* (London, 1882), the latter a significant colleague. Bain's founding and early financial support of the journal *Mind* (1876) created a significant English-language venue for philosophical and psychological discussion of the rapidly growing international body of experimental psychophysiological research. Moreover, Bain made formidable contributions to this literature.

Bain's works were translated into German, French, Russian, and Italian and were widely influential. In Great Britain, for example, the physiologist Hughlings Jackson learned from Bain that "the anatomical substrata of words are motor (articulatory) processes" (quoted in Young, 1970, p. 110). In America, Bain's interpretation of belief as a willingness to act influenced social psychology through the Princeton moral philosopher James Mark Baldwin and also pragmatism. William James considered Bain the foremost classical psychologist, critically developing Bain's ideas about habit, ideomotor phenomena, volition, and belief. Bain was also an important transitional figure pointing the way toward behaviorism, setting a precedent for later notions of instrumental learning and operant behavior

with his treatment of spontaneous motor activity as the source of trial-and-error learning.

[*Many of the people mentioned in this article are the subjects of independent biographical entries.*]

Bibliography

Works by Bain

Bain, A. (1894). *The senses and the intellect* (Rev. ed.). London: J. W. Parker. (Original work published 1855.) Revised editions also appeared in 1864 and 1868.

Bain, A. (1899). *The emotions and the will* (Rev. ed.). London: J. W. Parker. (Original work published 1859). Revised editions also appeared in 1865 and 1875. The first editions of Bain's two-volume text have been reprinted in *Significant contributions in the history of psychology, 1750–1920* (Vols. 4 & 5), prefaces by D. N. Robinson, Ed. (Washington, DC: University Publications of America, 1977). Robinson critiques Bain's contributions from an idealist perspective.

Bain, A. (1904). *Autobiography.* (W. L. Davidson, Ed.). London: Longmans, Green. Clear, factual, extensive, with a supplemental chapter. Bibliography by J. P. Anderson.

Works about Bain

Davidson, W. L. (1910–1922). Alexander Bain. *Encyclopaedia Britannica*, 11th ed. New York: Encyclopedia Britannica, Inc. The best concise biographical record.

Flesher, M. M. (1986). *Human nature surpassing itself: An intellectual biography of the early life and work of Alexander Bain (1818–1903).* Unpublished doctoral dissertation, Lehigh University (Michigan Microfilm #86-28593). The only full-length study of Bain, but restricted to his early life and thought through 1860. Emphasis on his education, important friendships, politics, and the originality of his early ideas.

Greenway, A. P. (1973). The incorporation of action into associationism: The psychology of Alexander Bain. *Journal of the History of the Behavioral Sciences*, 9, 42–52. Evaluates in detail the impact of Bain's concepts of spontaneity of action, primitive credulity, and motor association on subsequent psychological theories.

Mischel, T. (1966). "Emotion" and "motivation" in the development of English psychology: D. Hartley, James Mill, and A. Bain. *Journal of the History of the Behavioral Sciences*, 2, 123–144. Places Bain's application of association of ideas to actions within the earlier associationist tradition as its proponents interpreted emotion. (Bain is considered by many inadequate on the concept of emotion in contrast to those of intellect and will. W. L. Davidson, however, suggests that Bain's mature work on the emotions appears in his later rhetorical writings.)

Young, R. M. (1970). *Mind, brain and adaptation in the nineteenth century: Cerebral localization and its biological context from Gall to Ferrier.* Oxford: Clarendon Press. Chapter 3 traces the influence on British views of sensorimotor physiology of Bain's view of action (based, according to Young, on the German physiologist

Johannes Müller's motor theory). By interpreting evolutionary thought within the broader category of adaptive change, Young manages to include Bain's depiction of modifiable habits within its framework.

Mary Mosher Flesher

BALANCE THEORY. *See* Cognitive Consistency Theories.

BALDWIN, JAMES MARK (1861–1934), American psychologist. A year before Baldwin was born, his parents had moved from Connecticut to Columbia, South Carolina, where his father became involved with the Reconstruction administration after the Civil War. Following an undergraduate education at Princeton, Baldwin spent a year in Germany, where he studied with Wilhelm Wundt in Leipzig and the philosopher Friedrich Paulsen in Berlin. Baldwin then returned to Princeton where from 1885 to 1887 he completed his doctoral work with the president of the college, the Scottish philosopher and Presbyterian minister James McCosh. At Princeton he attended courses in the Divinity School before committing himself to philosophy and psychology. After finishing his dissertation, Baldwin taught philosophy and psychology at Lake Forest University in Illinois, a Presbyterian college, for 2 years (1887–1889). In 1889, he was appointed to the Chair of Metaphysics and Logic at the University of Toronto, where he founded a laboratory. In 1893, he was appointed to the Stuart Chair in Psychology at Princeton University, where he founded his second laboratory. In 1894, he and James McKeen Cattell founded and subsequently coedited the *Psychological Review* and the adjunct journals *Psychological Index* and *Psychological Monographs*. In 1897, Baldwin served as president of the American Psychological Association. In 1903, he was appointed Professor of Philosophy and Psychology and Chair of the Psychology Department at Johns Hopkins University. There he reestablished the laboratory founded earlier by G. Stanley Hall and founded the *Psychological Bulletin*. Because of a scandal, he left Johns Hopkins in 1908. For the next few years he was associated with the National University of Mexico in Mexico City, where he aided the organization of the faculties of philosophy and the social sciences. From 1913 until his death in 1934, he was professor at L'École des Hautes Études Sociales in Paris.

The early career of James Mark Baldwin was typical of many first-generation psychologists in the United States. As a result of his visit to Wilhelm Wundt's psychological laboratory in the fall of 1884, Baldwin became enthusiastic about the possibilities the new psychology offered for answering primarily philosophical questions. After completing his philosophy degree at Princeton, his founding of three psychological laboratories in North America provided a significant impulse to the institutionalization of experimental psychology. Nevertheless, his interest in experimentation decreased when, in the 1880s, he became involved in developmental psychology, for which Wundtian experimental practices were largely irrelevant. Baldwin's developmental psychology was strongly influenced by his adherence to a functionalist psychology based on his interpretation of Darwin's evolutionary theories. As well as introducing evolutionary ideas to psychology, Baldwin contributed his conception of organic evolution to evolutionary biology, later to be called the Baldwin-effect, by proposing a mechanism that explained how characteristics acquired through individual learning could be inherited by the species without resorting to Lamarckian arguments.

Before 1889, Baldwin's work can best be characterized as mental philosophy. After that date, Baldwin became an evolutionary psychologist. Inspired by Darwin's evolutionary theories and Herbert Spencer's writings, he emphasized the need for a functional instead of a faculty psychology focusing on development rather than intuition and introspection. As a consequence, he broke with Wilhelm Wundt and Edward B. Titchener's structuralist psychology. In his works on developmental psychology, Baldwin attempted to integrate Darwin's evolutionary theory and Hegel's philosophy. In Baldwin's view, the development of the child's mind is closely related to the evolution of humankind as well as to the evolution of the species. Baldwin (1895) discerned a prelogical phase (based on imagination and memory), a logical phase (based on reasoning; concurrent with language acquisition), and a hyperlogical phase (based on flexible processes of problem solving transcending syllogistic reasoning) in the development of the child's mind. Baldwin (1897) provided a complementary overview of the social development of the child's personality. The child passes through a projective stage (in which the child recognizes the differences between people and inanimate objects); a subjective stage (in which the child becomes aware of his or her own body as distinct from the bodies of others); and an ejective stage (in which the child infers that people have experiences in their bodies similar to his or her own). The child's development is propelled by imitation, assimilation, and activity.

Baldwin's developmental theories only became influential in American psychology after his death. In Paris, Baldwin maintained close contacts with the French psychologists Pierre Janet and Edouard Claparède and the philosopher Henri Bergson. He was also in contact with the young Jean Piaget, whom he strongly influenced. Piaget's stage theory of cognitive development bears strong similarities to Baldwin's own developmental theories. Since Piaget's reception in American psychology, Baldwin's contributions have been reassessed (see, for example, the many contributions in Broughton and Freeman-Moir, 1982). His conception of organic evolution has recently become influential in cognitive psychology (Turney, Whitley, & Anderson 1996).

Bibliography

Baldwin, J. M. (1889–1891). *Handbook of psychology: Vol. 1. Senses and intellect; Vol. 2. Feeling and will.* New York: Holt. The first volume was written during Baldwin's tenure at Lake Forest University because there were hardly any textbooks in psychology available for teaching; it discusses Wundt's physiological psychology. The second volume discusses feeling, emotion, and voluntary action; in it, Baldwin abandons associationism and structuralism for functionalism and a genetic (i.e., evoionary and developmental) approach.

Baldwin, J. M. (1895). *Mental development in the child and in the race.* New York: Macmillan. Synthetic work on developmental psychology based on observations on his two daughters. Discusses issues such as the origins of right- and left-handedness, color-perception, suggestion, imitation, and the development of language. The third edition, published in 1911, contains the original 1896 formulation of Baldwin's conception of organic evolution, later to be called the Baldwin effect.

Baldwin, J. M. (1897). *Social and ethical interpretations in mental development: A study in social psychology.* New York: Macmillan. Presents Baldwin's ideas on personality development and social psychology, which in his perspective were closely related. It outlines how the individual acquires his personality though social interaction.

Baldwin, J. M. (Ed.). (1901–1902). *Dictionary of philosophy and psychology.* New York: Macmillan. An immense collaborative effort to provide clarity in psychological terminology in which over 60 psychologists and philosophers participated.

Baldwin, J. M. (1909). *Darwin and the humanities.* Baltimore: Review. Provides an overview of the place of evolutionary theory in psychology, sociology, ethics, and religion. Argues for the principles of natural selection as well as Baldwin's original formulation of organic selection (the "Baldwin effect") in these subjects.

Baldwin, J. M. (1926). *Between two wars (1861–1921), being memories, opinions and letters received* (Vols. 1–2). Boston: Stratford. Extensive and informal autobiography.

Baldwin, J. M. (1930). James Mark Baldwin. In C. Murchison, (Ed.), *A history of psychology in autobiography* (Vol. 1, pp. 1–30). Worcester, MA: Clark University Press. Short autobiographical entry in the famous series initially edited by Carl Murchison. Emphasizes Baldwin's ideas while in France: genetic logic, aesthetic theory, and his philosophy of pancalism, in which the dichot-

omies of mind and body, subject and object, and reality and appearance are overcome in aesthetic experience.

Broughton, J. M., & Freeman-Moir, D. J. (Eds.). (1982). *The cognitive developmental psychology of James Mark Baldwin: Current theory and research in genetic epistemology.* Norwood, NJ: Ablex. Discussion of the relevance of Baldwin's work in cognitive development by a number of modern researchers in the area. The historical essay by Robert H. Wozniak provides an excellent intellectual biography of Baldwin.

Turney, P., Whitley, D., & Anderson, R. W. (1996). Evolution, learning, and instinct: 100 years of the Baldwin effect. *Evolutionary Computation, 4,* iv–viii. Editorial of the special issue of this journal devoted to the Baldwin effect. Contains several references to discussions of the Baldwin thesis within computer science and cognitive psychology.

Hans Pols

BALTIC COUNTRIES. Estonia, Latvia, and Lithuania (the Baltic countries) are usually differentiated from Finland, Sweden, Norway, and Denmark (the Nordic countries), but all seven countries are on the shores of the Baltic Sea. While different cultural factors have influenced psychology in each of the Baltic countries, they share a common fate of 50 years of Soviet occupation from 1940 to 1991.

Estonia

The beginnings of Estonian psychology may be found in the first Estonian university, established in 1632, when Academia Gustaviana was founded in Tartu (then known by its German name, Dorpat) by decree of the Swedish king, Gustavus II Adolphus. The university functioned in Tartu until 1656, and then in Pärnu (1690–1710) under the name Academia Gustavo-Carolina until Estonia was incorporated into the Russian Empire in 1721. Several dissertations and other works dealing with the problems of the senses, sense illusions, and character date from this period (e.g., L. Emzelius, 1645; J. Oern, 1695; F. Uraelius, 1645; A. Westerman, 1692).

In 1802 the university reopened in Tartu as Universitas Dorpatensis (K. Ramul, *Iz istorii psikhologii,* Tartu, 1974, pp. 98–113). Since that time, Tartu University has an almost unbroken record of providing psychology courses, mainly taught by German philosophers. The first professor, Gottlob Benjamin Jäsche (1762–1842), taught psychology courses between 1802 and 1838. He was a student of Immanuel Kant and publisher of Kant's lectures on logic. He was followed by Moriz Conrad Posselt (1805–1875), a follower of Hegelian philosophy, and Ludwig A. H. Strümpell (1812–1899), a student of the German psychologist and educator, Johann Friedrich Herbart, who established the study of childhood disabilities as a discipline and also developed a theory of dreams. Strümpell taught psychology between 1845 and 1870. Parallel courses in psychology were also taught by the professor of theology, Pavel Alekseyev, from 1850 to 1859. After Strümpell, psychology was taught by one of the most original philosophical thinkers from Tartu, Gustav Teichmüller (1832–1888), whose views were closer to those of the German philosophers Leibniz and Lotze. Teichmüller opposed Darwin's evolutionary theory, supporting a theory of the immortality of the soul (Berlin, 1878). His students, who continued his work, were Jekabs Osis (Jakob Ohse; 1867–1920), a Latvian who taught psychology from 1889 to 1918, and Yevgeni A. Bobrov (1867–1933), a Russian who was interested in art and literature and lectured in Tartu between 1894 and 1896. Ohse left Tartu when the university was transferred to Voronezh (Russia) in 1918. Most of the courses taught by philosophers were speculative in nature.

Experimental psychology at Tartu University was more related to physiology and psychiatry. Alfred Wilhelm Volkmann (1800–1877), who taught at Tartu University from 1837 to 1842, was the founder of experimental physiology in Estonia. He contributed a chapter on vision to Rudolph Wagner's *Handwörterbuch der Physiologie* (Manual of physiology; 1846) and contributed to experiments which were the basis of Gustav Theodor Fechner's *Elemente der Psychophysik* (Elements of psychophysics; 1860).

In 1886, Emil Kraepelin (1856–1926), a student of Wilhelm Wundt and the founder of modern psychiatry, accepted a professorship in psychiatry at Tartu University and taught there until 1891. He founded an experimental psychology laboratory at the university and was the advisor for several medical dissertations dealing with psychological problems and based on experimental data, including amongst other subjects, the influence of caffeine on the speed of mental processes. Kraepelin's own work was concerned with fatigue, and at Tartu he also initiated word association experiments which were later developed by C. G. Jung.

Opposing the Russification of Estonia, Kraepelin returned to Germany, and his laboratory was taken over by Vladimir Chizh (1855–1922) who remained as professor of psychiatry at Tartu University until 1918. Chizh, a Russian nobelman, was the first non-German to have worked in Wundt's Leipzig laboratory (1884). Chizh translated Wundt's textbook on physiological psychology into Russian (1893). Chizh continued Kraepelin's experimental tradition, acting as advisor for doctoral candidates preparing medical dissertations on psychological topics like memory of movements (F. Schneider, 1894), experimental studies of skin sensitiv-

ity (H. Hildebrandt, 1899). By the end of the nineteenth century, graduates of Tartu University had written 14 dissertations on psychological topics. Chizh himself studied mental disorders among Russian prostitutes, concluding that they were more stable mentally than the general population.

The Tartu University theologian, Alexander von Oettingen, is one of the pioneers of the use of statistical social indicators for the empirical study of values. In his book *Moralstatistik* (Moral statistics; 1881) he systematically incorporates such indicators as suicide and divorce rates in order to explore the moral issues and their resolution at a particular place and time (F. G. Wimmer, *Die Relevanz von Werthaltungen im internationalen Vergleich* (The relevance of value orientations in international comparison; Frankfurt am Main, 1991).

In the nineteenth century, the majority of students at Tartu University were non-Estonians. Rudolf Kallas (1851–1913) was the first Estonian to write a book on a psychological topic. He was a theologian and student of Teichmüller who discussed the system of sound mnemonics used in folklore (Dorpat/Tartu, 1897).

Tartu University was also home to the Dorpat school of religious psychology, founded by Karl Gustav Girgensohn (1875–1925), a student of Oswald Külpe. Girgensohn graduated from Tartu University in 1903, and after getting advanced degrees in Germany, returned to Tartu in 1911. Using the experimental introspection method, he distinguished feelings, images, and will as components of religious experience. His work was continued by Werner Gruehn (1887–1961) who worked at the University of Tartu during Estonia's first period of independence (1918–1940). Eduard Tennmann (1878–1936), a student of Teichmüller, who wrote some popular interpretations of his mentor's ideas, was also a member of this school.

In 1919, after Estonia had gained independence, a national university was opened in Tartu. Courses were taught primarily in Estonian and psychology became a discipline in its own right. Aleksander Kaelas (1880–1920) is the first Estonian professional psychologist. From 1914 to 1919 he worked at Moscow University and published several Russian-language experimental studies on emotions that were critical of Wundt's theory of emotion. Later Kaelas worked at the University of Irkutsk (Russia), and in 1919 was invited to be professor of psychology at Tartu University. However, he was unable to reach Tartu because of the Russian Civil War, and he died in Irkutsk in 1920 from an acute illness. Konstantin Ramul (1879–1975) became professor of psychology and established a psychological laboratory at the university in 1922. He was assisted by Eduard Bakis (1900–1970) who was the first exponent of applied psychology in Estonia. Some foreign lecturers were invited to work in Tartu. Andreas Bjerre (Bjärre;

1879–1925) from Sweden taught at Tartu University from 1919 to 1925. His *Zur Psychologie des Mordes* (On the psychology of murder; Stockholm, 1910) is still relevant to forensic psychology today.

Psychology became a standard subject at the university level. Nine master's degrees were granted in psychology between 1919 and 1940 and four doctoral dissertations were written (K. Ramul, R. Hippius, J. Tork, and A. Kuks). The study by Juhan Tork (1889–1980) in 1940 on the intelligence of Estonian children (*Acta et Commentationes Universitatis Tartuensis*, 47) is generally considered the most remarkable publication in Estonian psychology between the two world wars. It analyzes the mental aptitude of about 6,000 Estonian children aged between 10 and 15 years and relates these to their parents' socioeconomic background and to geographical and regional variables. Ramul is the author of several well-known textbooks and popular books on psychology, but his lasting contribution is to the history of psychology (K. Ramul, The problem of measurement in the psychology of the 18th century, *American Psychologist*, 1960, 15, 256 265). The organizational activities of Ramul's 50-year career were essential for keeping psychology alive in Estonia following World War II when the country was under Soviet domination.

Between 1943 and 1944 several Estonian psychologists left Estonia to avoid the Soviet occupation. Among them were Tork, Bakis, and Theodor Künnapas (1902–1994) who established successful careers at Stockholm University. Of the younger generation who got their education after leaving Estonia, Vello Sermat, Endel Tulving, Jaak Panksepp, and Aita Salasoo have become well-known psychologists in Canada and the United States.

After World War II the department of logic and psychology was established at Tartu University; a full-time undergraduate program in psychology has existed since 1968. In 1973 a department of education and psychology was established at the Tallinn Pedagogical University (then Tallinn Teachers' College) by Heino Liimets (1928–1989) which became a full-time undergraduate program in 1993. With the educational reforms in 1991, after Estonia regained its independence, master's and doctoral degree programs were reintroduced in both departments. The first undergraduate psychology students from Tallinn graduated in 1997. By the late 1990s there were about 900 Estonians with an undergraduate degree in psychology (B.Sc. or a university diploma).

Two groups of Estonian researchers have gained attention at the international level, both of them in the mid-1970s. One group has been affiliated with the University of Tartu (J. Allik, A. Luuk, T. Bachmann, M. Rauk, A. Pulver, T. Tuulmets, and others) and has been involved in the psychophysiological and psychophysical research of sensory and cognitive processes. The other group, the Environmental Psychology Research Unit (M. Heidmets, J. Kruusvall, T. Niit, M. Raudsepp, K. Liik, and others), has been affiliated with Tallinn Pedagogical University since 1979, and has studied a wide range of psychological problems related to the environment. For example, they have studied the effects of living in high-rise apartment buildings, privacy and crowding, postoccupancy evaluation, and urban spaces. The third notable tradition in Estonian psychology is the historical-cultural approach and its application to both cognitive and developmental psychology (P. Tulviste and J. Valsiner).

Latvia

Prior to 1919, no full-fledged university existed in Latvia, and little is known about psychology in Latvia before the twentieth century. The first Latvian textbook, *Fundamental Problems of Psychology* by Kārlis Ašmanis, appeared in 1908. It emphasized the biological foundations of psychology and eschewed philosophical speculation. Also in 1908, a small psychological laboratory was established by a high-school teacher, Z. Lancmanis. Initially oriented toward providing vocational guidance, it quickly outgrew its mission. Prodigious amounts of data were collected at the annual nationwide school fairs on children's attention, memory, and other cognitive variables. Innovative semiprojective techniques involving story and drawing completion were also introduced. These promising efforts were cut short by the upheaval during and after World War I.

The University of Latvia was inaugurated less than a year after the proclamation of independence in 1919. Psychology was accorded a prominent place in the curriculum; however, many senior faculty members were philosophers first and psychologists second. For this reason, experimentation languished and faculty members were slow to apply quantitative and objective methods. Initially, introspection was the method of choice, but gradually a wider range of approaches came into being, and there were noteworthy contributions to the field. *The Psychology of Artistic Creation* by Pēteris Birkerts, published in 1922, may be the first psychological monograph on creativity in any language. On the same subject, Pauls Dāle studied 250 Latvian writers, painters, and actors and compared them with an equal number of university students. Other areas of research emphasis included child and adolescent development, personality motivation, and volition. Milda Liepiņa anticipated negative findings elsewhere in finding only slight correlations between Kretschmer's three principal body types and their hypothesized corresponding personality variables. Similarly, L. Cenne reported low test-retest reliability for most adolescents' Rorschach scores, thereby calling into question the clinical usefulness of this test, but also raising the possibility of complete person-by-situation interactions over time.

During the first period of Latvian independence (1918–1940) psychology existed mainly within the disciplines of philosophy and education. Psychology was included in both the university and grammar school curricula of the period. Some of the works of Freud, Adler, and Spranger were translated into Latvian; the Adlerian Society was founded in the late 1920s.

Empirical research received greater emphasis during this period at the Municipal Youth and Vocational Research Institute in Rīga. Along with vocational guidance, the Institute's activities included the validation of intelligence and aptitude tests, the development of a standardized test battery for adolescents, plotting age curves for sensory acuity and motor reactivity for people ages 12 to 75, and innovative human subject research. Rudolfs Drillis improved the design of agricultural hand tools and thereby achieved a marked gain in productivity. This direction was continued in a comprehensive project, under the auspices of the U.N. Food and Agriculture Organization, for improving the efficiency of hand tools throughout the developing world after World War II.

Activities at the institute came to a halt at the onset of World War II. The institute was plundered and vandalized during the German occupation and closed entirely by the Soviets. At the University of Latvia, everything that was done prior to the imposition of Soviet rule was dismissed as idealistic. Less continuity was preserved within psychology in Latvia than in Estonia or Lithuania. During World War II several thousand Latvians emigrated to the West and many of them became psychologists. Leonards Zuzne and Juris Draguns are probably the best known among them. From the younger generation, J. Daugman and J. Goldberg have done significant work. Even in the early 1980s there were more psychologists of Latvian origin abroad than in Latvia. Most of the middle-aged psychologists in Latvia today were trained at Moscow or Leningrad (St. Petersburg) universities.

In the post–World War II era, Kārlis Volmers investigated the role of attentional, motivational, and volitional factors involved in increasing the efficiency of classroom learning. I. Plotnieks studied the emergence of initiative and independence in the school context. As ideological restrictions were relaxed in the 1960s, research expanded into social, industrial, clinical, sports, and environmental psychology. A. Līvmane analyzed the development of gymnasts' powers of concentration just prior to a performance. R. Bebre conducted psychobiographical studies of the creative process, notably by the Latvian poet Rainis. V. Renģe focused on cognitive variables in schizophrenia, and V. Avotiņš compared the thought processes of normal and retarded children.

When Latvia regained its independence in 1991, political control of psychology was swept away and chaotic growth ensued. Unresolved problems included inadequate funding, incomplete professional regulation, and gradually evolving standards of professional training. Recent research projects include styles of performance and self-expression (A. Karpova), retroactive distortion of recall of significant biographical events (S. Sebre), adolescents' self-concept and its relationship to future orientation (G. Breslavs), integrative conception of personality over time and its relationship to teacher–student interaction (A. Vorobjovs). Latvian psychologists have also addressed some of the current pressing issues in the country, such as the relations between Latvian and Russian ethnic groups, tense after decades of Soviet domination. Latvian psychologists have also addressed serious social problems, systematically investigating such issues as child abuse, suicide, depression in adults and children, and the psychological impact of unemployment.

In 1989 a full-time undergraduate program in psychology was initiated at the University of Latvia (Riga). By the late 1990s master's and doctoral degree programs had been introduced and there were around 150 psychology students. It is now possible to get an undergraduate degree in psychology at several teachers' colleges. Dozens of Latvians study psychology abroad, the majority in Sweden. Independent (nonstate) institutions offering training in psychology emerged in the mid-1990s. There were approximately 300 psychologists in Latvia in the late 1990s and the number continues to grow.

Lithuania

Psychology had its beginnings in Lithuania in the sixteenth century. In 1507 psychology was first introduced into the curriculum of the Dominican Monastery School in Lithuania. In 1571, a Scotsman, Ioannes Hay, taught psychology at the Vilnius Jesuit College and later it was also taught in other schools. Lithuanian scholastic psychology (animastica) was mainly engaged with developing commentaries on Aristotle's De anima and was eclectic in approach. The most prominent representatives of scholastic psychology at the time were J. Kimbaras, who wrote a dissertation, Philosophical Theorems of the World and Its Parts (1600); J. Markvartas, who taught philosophy from 1613 to 1616; J. Drevsas, who taught at Kražiai from 1676 to 1679 and at the Vilnius Academy from 1680 to 1683; and S. Losevskis who taught from 1690 to 1693.

By the mid-eighteenth century animastica (scholastic psychology) had faded away and psychology became devoted entirely to metaphysics. The works of Ch. von Wolff (Psychologia empirica, Frankfurt 1732; Psychologia rationalis, Frankfurt, 1734) were used as textbooks. The theories of René Descartes and John Locke were also taught. In 1773 Vilnius Academy came under the control of the Educational Commission. The latter reformed the educational system, separating scientific subjects from philosophy, and it was not until 1803 that philosophy was once again taught at Vilnius University (formerly Academy). J. H. Abicht (1762–1816), who came from Erlangen, Bavaria, headed the department of philosophy from 1804. In his *Philosophical Encyclopedia* he discussed the problems of soul and imagination and defined the field of psychology. Further development of psychology was curbed by the closing of Vilnius University in 1832. The ban on the Lithuanian press, which continued for four decades (1864–1904) during a period of Russian rule, also had a negative effect on the dissemination of psychological knowledge. Nevertheless, such progressive Lithuanian intellectuals as J. Adomaitis-Sernas, St. Matulaitis, J. Sliupas, and others continued to write popular pamphlets on psychological topics. A monograph by A. Gučas published in Lithuanian, *Psichologijos raida Lietuvoje (19a. pabaiga–20a. pradzia* (Vilnius, 1968) gives the most exhaustive picture of Lithuanian psychology at the turn of the century.

Vydunas (1868–1953) and R. Bytautas (1886–1915) were the central figures in Lithuanian psychology during the first two decades of the twentieth century. His interpretation of consciousness lies at the heart of Vydunas's philosophical psychology, and he treats it in a manner reminiscent of Hindu thought, distinguishing several levels of consciousness. R. Bytautas worked at Moscow University and his work centered around national consciousness. Although Vydunas attended W. Wundt's lectures and Bytautas attended G. Chelpanov's lectures, neither of them was interested in empirical research. In the second decade of the twentieth century educational psychology became a popular topic and through publications primarily addressed to the academic world psychological knowledge reached a wider audience.

Interest in experimental psychology was most evident in the work of Jonas Steponavičius (1881–1947) and Jonas Vabalas-Gudaitis (1881–1955). Steponavičius studied at several German universities and wrote his doctoral dissertation under Wundt's guidance in 1912. Later in his career he abandoned experimental psychology and devoted himself to the study of parapsychological phenomena. Vabalas-Guidaitis, who had studied at the St. Petersburg and Moscow universities, founded a laboratory of experimental psychology in Lithuania in 1921, and in 1931, together with Vladimiras Lazersonas (1889–1945) and others, he founded the Lithuanian Society of Psychotechnics and Professional Guidance (LSPPG). Later he became head of the psychology departments at both Kaunas and Vilnius universities. By 1929 he had published works on education, the history of psychology, and an original theory of interaction (*synergasia*). Two departments of psychology existed at Vilnius University during Lithuania's independence, one was a part of the faculty of theological philosophy, headed by Bishop Mecislovas Reinys (1884–1953) and the other was a part of the faculty of the humanities. Reinys translated G. Chelpanov's textbook on psychology into Lithuanian in 1921, and it was widely used until 1940. The LSPPG established a laboratory in 1932, and psychotechnical laboratories also functioned at the Military Hospital, Military School, and the Railway Administration.

World War II thinned out the ranks of Lithuanian psychologists, as it had in Estonia. According to Bagdonas (1996), "Some of them found themselves in Siberia, some in the West, some, though they did not leave Lithuania [this was during the Soviet occupation], resigned from active scientific activities for political reasons or because of advanced age." After the war only three psychologists continued to pursue psychological activities: J. Vabalas-Gudaitis, J. Lauzikas (1903–1980), and A. Gučas (1907–1988). They passed on the prewar psychological traditions to a younger generation in Lithuania. Vilnius Pedagogical University began training professional psychologists in 1946, and by 1955 there were 83 graduates. In 1954, when the teaching of psychology was eliminated in secondary schools, many psychologists had to be retrained so they could find other work, but several are still engaged in university teaching and research (S. Kregždė, J. Lapė, L. Jovaiėa, and others). In 1969, full-time study in psychology again became possible at Vilnius University, and in 1973 the Laboratory of Special Psychology was created, and at its height it had about 30 full-time staff members and 20 part-time workers. In the mid-1990s there were about 600 Lithuanians with bachelor's, master's, or doctoral degrees.

From 1954 to 1974, when no professional psychologists graduated from the university, several academics entered psychology from linguistics, mathematics, physiology, biology, and other disciplines. E. Rimkutė (psychodiagnostics and clinical psychology), A. Gostautas (clinical psychology), F. Laugalis (psychophysiology), A. Suslavičius (social psychology), and A. Bagdonas (cognitive, special, and animal psychology), are still actively engaged in research.

The training of professional psychologists became more readily available in the final third of the twentieth century. Psychologists are now trained at Kaunas Vitautas Didysis University, Šiauliai Pedagogical University, and Klaipėda University. Two psychological centers offer doctoral degrees. The Institute of Humanistic and Existential Psychology and the Vilnius Institute of Psychotherapy have been established. Around 50 psychologists of Lithuanian origin live in exile, mainly in the United States. Many of them, including I. Užgirienė, L.

Bieliauskas, D. Katiliutė, V. Černius, and others developed close contacts with Lithuanian universities in the 1980s and 1990s.

Societies and Associations

Branches of the Soviet Psychological Society (SPS) were established in the Baltic countries in the late 1950s and early 1960s and continued to function until between 1988 and 1991. In Estonia, the Union of Estonian Psychologists (UEP) was founded in May 1988. The requirements for membership are a degree in psychology and three recommendations from current members. The UEP became a member of the International Union of Psychological Studies (IUPsyS) and the European Federation of Professional Psychologists' Association (EFPPA) in 1992. The other relevant organizations include the Association of Cognitive-Behavioral Therapy, the Association of School Psychologists, the Association of Child Psychologists, the Association of Gestalt Therapy, and the Psychodrama Society.

In Latvia the branch of SPS became the Latvian Psychological Society in 1990. It was more of a "club" for those with similar interests than a professional organization for psychologists. In 1991 a small group of enthusiasts founded the Latvian Association of Professional Psychologists (LAPP) where the membership requirements are 5 or 6 years of university-level training in psychology and at least two years of practical experience in the field. LAPP has grown to about 150 full and associate members. The other psychological associations in Latvia are the Latvian Association of School Psychologists and the Latvian Adlerian Society. The Latvian Psychoanalytic Society has also been established by a small group of young psychiatrists and psychologists who have received psychoanalytic training abroad.

The Lithuanian Branch of the SPS was founded in 1958. In 1988 it resolved to establish an independent organization, and in January 1989 the Union of Lithuanian Psychologists was founded, which applied for membership in EFPPA in the late 1990s. Several more specialized organizations were founded in the 1990s, including the Association of Humanistic Psychology, the Association of Psychoanalysis, the C. G. Jung Association, the Association of Psychotherapy, the Association of Transactional Analysis, the Association of Suicidology, the Association of Group Psychotherapy, and the Association of School Psychologists.

Significant Publications

In Estonia a collection of articles by researchers at the University of Tartu, *Studies in Psychology*, was published on an almost annual basis in the series *Acta et Commentationes Universitatis Tartuensis* from the early 1970s until 1991 (there were 17 issues in all). The papers were in Russian for the most part, but some issues were published in English and Estonian. Since 1997 an English-language social science journal, *Trames*, has been published four times a year. Scientific papers in Estonian are sometimes published in the monthly journal *Akadeemia* (Academy). The UEP published 30 issues of its newsletter in Estonian between 1988 and 1998. A series of books and conference proceedings has been published by the Environmental Psychology Research Unit at Tallinn Pedagogical University since 1976. Only a couple of books by Estonian psychologists have been published in English.

Pedagogika ir psichologija (Education and psychology; *Psichologija* since 1980) is published in Lithuanian. A popular magazine, *Psichologija tau* (Psychology for you) was founded in 1991. Nowadays it appears six times a year and has a circulation of 10,000. Probably the most prominent psychological publication in Lithuanian is the *Dictionary of Psychology*, and a collection of papers by J. Vabalas-Gudaitis is also significant (*Psichologijos ir pedagogikos straipsniai*, Vilnius, 1983).

Joint Activities

Although the Baltic countries are geographically close, there are few joint efforts either in research or publishing on psychology. The reason is evident: The only languages the Baltic psychologists have had in common are Russian, during the Soviet period, and, following independence, English. Despite these difficulties, a series of joint conferences were organized over the years, the first of which took place in May 1960 in Vilnius, and thereafter every 2 years until 1972, with locations rotating between Tartu, Riga, and Vilnius. In 1975, the eighth conference took place in Tartu, and there was then a break until 1991 when a conference was held in Vilnius. From 1994 onward the conferences took place on a biannual basis again (see J. Lape, Conferences of psychologists of the Baltic states and related problems, In B. Pociūtė, & A. Bagdonas (Eds.), *Multidimensionality of Contemporary Psychology: Social, Political and Cultural Influences* (pp. 67–70), Vilnius, 1998).

Bibliography

Allik, J. (1992). Psychology in Estonia. *News from EFPPA*, 6(1), 7–10. (Available Web site: http://sys130.psych.ut.ee/uk/phistory.html) Includes a critical review of the Soviet period in Estonian psychology.

Anspaks, J., & Plotnieks, I. (1972). *Razvitiye psikhologicheskoi nauki v Latvii.* [The development of psychological science in Latvia]. Riga: Latvijas Valsts Universitate. A review of Latvian psychology.

Bachmann, T. (1994). *Psychophysiology of visual masking: The fine structure of conscious experience.* Commack, NY:

Nova Science. One of the few books by an Estonian cognitive psychologist available in English.

Bagdonas, A. (Ed.). (1990). *Psichologija Baltijos respublikose: 1990* [Psychology in Baltic republics: 1990]. Vilnius: Vilnius University Press. Proceedings of a conference in Russian and English which gives a picture of areas of interest of Baltic psychologists on the eve of independence.

Bagdonas, A. (1996). Lithuanian psychology or psychology in Lithuania? In T. Niit & A. Baltin (Eds.), *Identity, freedom, values and memory: Proceedings of the 2nd International Baltic Psychology Conference* (pp. 18–33). Tallinn: Union of Estonian Psychologists. A thorough review of Lithuanian psychology from the Middle Ages to the 1990s.

Niit, T. (1996). Estonian psychology 1976–1996: Has anybody noticed? In T. Niit & A. Baltin (Eds.), *Identity, freedom, values and memory: Proceedings of the 2nd International Baltic Psychology Conference* (pp. 72–91). Tallinn: Union of Estonian Psychologists. A digest of papers and books published by Estonian psychologists. Includes a list of all Estonian publications in psychology cited in the journals included in Social Sciences Citation Index (SSCI) between 1976 and 1996.

Niit, T., & Baltin, A. (Eds.). (1996). *Identity, freedom, values and memory: Proceedings of the 2nd International Baltic Psychology Conference*. Tallinn: Union of Estonian Psychologists. Proceedings of a conference which includes full texts of several keynote speakers (A. Bagdonas, J. Draguns, L.-G. Nilsson) and a list of addresses of all participants.

Niit, T., Heidmets, M., & Kruusvall, J. (1987). Environmental psychology in the Soviet Union. In D. Stokols & I. Altman (Eds.), *Handbook of environmental psychology* (Vol.2, pp. 1311–1335). New York: Wiley. Describes the theoretical approaches to environmental psychology developed by the authors who are all Estonian psychologists.

Niit, T., Heidmets, M., & Kruusvall, J. (1994). Environmental psychology in Estonia. *Journal of Russian and East European Psychology, 32*(3), 5–40. Gives a thorough review of Estonian environmental psychology between 1972 and 1989 with a full list of publications. It was translated from a paper published in Russian and unfortunately many names are incorrectly spelled.

Pociūtė, B., & Bagdonas, A. (Eds.). (1998). *Multidimensionality of contemporary psychology: Social, political and cultural influences*. Vilnius: Vilnius University Press, 1998. Proceedings of the twelfth conference of Baltic psychologists reflecting changing emphases.

Renge, V. (1995). Psychology in Latvia. *News from EFPPA, 9*(3), 19–21. A review of the status of Latvian psychology from 1918 to the mid-1990s.

Tulviste, P. (1991). *Cultural-historical development of verbal thinking: A psychological study*. Commack, NY: Nova. A book by an Estonian psychologist advocating the cultural approach in psychology.

Wulff, D. M. (1985). Experimental introspection and religious experience: The Dorpat school of religious psychology. *Journal for the History of Behavioral Science, 21*, 131–150.

Zuzne, L. (1976). Development of psychology in Latvia. *Catalog of Selected Documents in Psychology, 6* (17 pp.).

Toomas Niit and Juris Draguns

BARGAINING. *See* Negotiation.

BARKER, ROGER G. (1903–1990), American developmental psychologist. Although educated in a traditional psychology program (Stanford University, Ph.D. degree, 1934), Barker described himself as "a naturalist, investigating relations between persons, environments, and behavior as they occur, without input from me as investigator." He was troubled by the fact that psychologists, despite a century of research and theory, knew little more than laypeople about the naturally occurring frequency and distribution of psychological phenomena, about behavior outside psychological laboratories, clinics, testing rooms, and interview sites. Psychologists knew even less about the kinds of environments that communities provide for behavior and how behavior and environments are related in unconstrained, investigator-free contexts.

To address these problems, Barker inaugurated the research program that subsequently dominated his life. In 1947, while chair of the Psychology Department at the University of Kansas, Barker, with Herbert F. Wright, established the Midwest Psychological Field Station as a locus for continuing, naturalistic studies of behavior and environments in Oskaloosa, Kansas, a small town near the University.

Over the next 25 years, the mainly observational studies of children's behavior in ordinary, everyday life situations that Barker, Wright, and their colleagues and students carried out from the Field Station produced pioneering works in *ecological psychology*. With Paul V. Gump, Barker conducted an influential study of the effects of high school size on student behavior. Their report, *Big School, Small School* (Stanford, CA, 1964), showed that students in small schools participate much more actively and responsibly in the voluntary, extracurricular activities of the school than students in large schools, a finding that has been confirmed in studies of churches, business organizations, and experimental groups.

Barker increasingly concentrated on the *ecological* (objective, nonpsychological) environment and its relation to behavior. A National Institute of Mental Health (NIMH) Career Research Award (1963–1972) enabled him to spend most of his time in research, thinking, and writing. He discovered that the ecological environment consists of highly structured, well-organized phenomena that require serious investigation on their own merit quite apart from their connections with behavior. He also found that the laws that govern the ecological environment are different from and utterly incommensurate with the psychological laws governing individual behavior. Yet there are mutual causal relations between the ecological environment and behavior, not merely probabilistic or statistical relations. He identified the *behavior setting*, an objective entity, as the basic unit of analysis of the ecological environment.

Barker concluded that important questions about environments and their relations to human behavior and experience could not be answered by the traditional methods of psychological science. A new *ecobehavioral* science is required. With his biologist wife, Louise Shedd Barker, other colleagues and students, he developed and applied technical operations for conducting empirical surveys of all behavior settings in small towns and institutions.

Barker's honors include the Distinguished Scientific Contribution Award of the American Psychological Association (1963), the Kurt Lewin Award of the Society for the Psychological Study of Social Issues (1963), and the G. Stanley Hall Award from Division 7 of the APA (1969).

Bibliography

Barker, R. G. (1968). *Ecological psychology: Concepts and methods for studying the environment of human behavior*. Stanford, CA. Stanford University Press. The most complete presentation of Barker's theory and methods, but see 1989 revision by Schoggen, below.

Barker, R. G., & Schoggen, P. H. (1973). *Qualities of community life: Methods of measuring environment and behavior applied to an American and an English town*. San Francisco: Jossey-Bass. A detailed report of the most extensive empirical application of Barker's theory and behavior setting survey methods to the study of whole towns as environments for human behavior.

Barker, R. G., & Associates. (1978). *Habitats, environments, and human behavior: Studies in ecological psychology and eco-behavioral science from the Midwest Psychological Field Station, 1947–1972*. San Francisco: Jossey-Bass. Includes analyses of observational records of children's behavior in natural, everyday life situations.

Barker, R. G. (1989). Roger G. Barker. In G. Lindzey (Ed.), *A history of psychology in autobiography* (Vol. 8, pp. 4–35). Stanford, CA: Stanford University Press. Includes selected references to his primary and other related works.

Schoggen, P. (1989). *Behavior settings: A revision and extension of Roger G. Barker's "Ecological psychology."* Stanford, CA: Stanford University Press. Preserves the original except for changes required by advances since 1968.

Phil Schoggen

BARTLETT, FREDERIC CHARLES (1886–1969), British experimental and applied psychologist. Bartlett was born in Stow-on-the-Wold, England. Partly self-taught prior to his university education, he earned an undergraduate degree in 1909 from the University of London, concentrating on philosophy, especially logic, and achieving first class honors. Then came a master's degree in 1911, also from London, with an emphasis on sociology and ethics. His introduction to psychology was through the writings of G. F. Stout, James Ward, and C. S. Myers.

In 1912, Bartlett began work on a second undergraduate degree at the University of Cambridge, entering St. John's College to study anthropology with W. H. R. Rivers. He read moral science first, which required four hours a week doing experimental research in the Cambridge Psychological Laboratory, then under the direction of C. S. Myers. Graduating in 1914, again with first class honors, Bartlett was hired to teach at the laboratory in experimental psychology. With the onset of World War I, Rivers and Myers took leave to serve in the Army. Bartlett, unfit for military service because of his health, remained at Cambridge in charge of the laboratory.

After the war both Rivers and Myers returned to Cambridge though not for long. In 1922 Rivers died and Myers left to pursue a career in industrial psychology in London. Bartlett was appointed director of the laboratory, and as Cambridge's senior psychologist, he set about building the department of psychology. This he steadily accomplished and in 1931 he became the university's first professor of experimental psychology. He retired in 1952 and was professor emeritus until his death in 1969.

Bartlett's psychological legacy consists of his contributions to cognitive psychology, applied psychological research, and the development of psychology in Britain. His importance to cognitive psychology lies in his 1932 book, *Remembering: A Study in Experimental and Social Psychology*. The research reported therein was actually begun and largely completed by 1916. What developed during the intervening 16 years was Bartlett's interpretation of his findings. In this he was profoundly influenced by Sir Henry Head's concept of the schema.

In *Remembering*, Bartlett argued that perceiving, imagining, thinking, and remembering are interdependent. Moreover, all are affected by one's social and cultural context. He believed that artificial materials in the vein of those used by Ebbinghaus were likely to produce excessive variability in their encoding. So in his investigations of perception and memory, Bartlett employed materials that he considered more representative of those encountered in everyday life: folk stories, newspaper reports, pictures of faces, and the like. The book contained no experiments or statistics. Instead, Bartlett drew on qualitative observations and protocols of participants' repeated or serial reproductions of materials to support the points that he was intent on making. He summarily rejected a trace theory of memory: "Remembering is not the re-excitation of innumerable fixed, lifeless and fragmentary traces" (*Remembering*, p. 213). Such a conception was too passive and utterly incapable of accounting for the numerous inventions, omissions, and distortions that Bartlett observed in his subjects' reports. He argued instead that a perception was first constructed, often involving "an effort after meaning." Then came recollection, which was an active and imaginative reconstruction based on a general impression of what is to be remembered, on a few outstanding details, but mostly on a schema. This was the application of Head's concept and by it Bartlett meant that remembering is guided by an active organization of past reactions or experiences.

The ideas set forth in *Remembering* have had substantial appeal, although it was delayed in coming. It was only with the advent of cognitive psychology in the 1970s, and especially Ulric Neisser's book, *Cognitive Psychology* (New York, 1967), which embraced Bartlett's constructivist approach, that his views achieved wide currency. Since then they have been part and parcel of thinking about memory and cognition.

Applied psychology is the second area in which Bartlett played a prominent role. During World War I, he initiated research on psychoacoustics, in particular, on listening to signals from antisubmarine equipment. Bartlett's second book, *Psychology and the Soldier* (Cambridge, 1927), was the outgrowth of a course on the psychology of military problems that he was responsible for after World War I. Subsequent applied interests included but were not restricted to intelligence testing, the psychological effects of noise, personnel selection and training, and the psychological effects of aging. What engaged him most, however, was the nature of human skills (e.g., their timing) and how they were affected by fatigue and adverse environmental conditions. Such problems were paramount in the research performed at the time of World War II under Bartlett's aegis at the Cambridge Psychological Laboratory. It is worth noting that he saw applied and pure psychological research as equally important foundations for the advance of psychology as a science. This attitude has traditionally characterized British psychology and it is due as much to Bartlett as anyone.

His third major contribution has been to the development of psychology in Britain as an independent discipline. Bartlett arrived on the scene at a time when for all practical purposes British psychology did not exist. His efforts helped change all that. He was the editor of the *British Journal of Psychology* from 1924 to 1948. The Medical Research Council's Applied Psychology Unit was established in 1944 at the University of Cambridge largely as the result of his efforts, and he himself served as its Honorary Director from 1945 until his retirement in 1952. Psychology at Cambridge, as already noted, was Bartlett's creation, but its growth from a single laboratory assistant in 1922 to over 70 staff and research workers by the time of his retirement merits special note. His influence has been felt especially through his students, many of whom went on to hold distinguished academic positions in Britain and other countries.

Bartlett's retirement in 1952 did not mean that he gave up psychological endeavors. *Thinking: An Experimental and Social Study* was published in 1958. It was an attempt to complete what he believed remained undone from his earlier work on remembering. But it may also be seen as an extension of his interest in human skill, in this instance, thinking. Bartlett differentiated between thinking within closed systems, the task being to fill in the gaps in the required information, and adventurous thinking, the task being to extrapolate beyond what is known. The book met with only modest success, however, and it is best seen as a coda of the two prominent themes of Bartlett's science: remembering and skill.

[*Many of the people mentioned in this article are the subjects of independent biographical entries.*]

Bibliography

Works by Bartlett

Bartlett, F. C. (1923). *Psychology and primitive culture*. Cambridge, UK: Cambridge University Press. Bartlett's first book, it reflects his early interest in anthropology and cross-cultural psychology.

Bartlett, F. C. (1932). *Remembering: A study in experimental and social psychology*. Cambridge, UK: Cambridge University Press. Bartlett's most enduring legacy to basic psychology. It emphasized the centrality of construction, the schema, and an individual's social and cultural context to perception, memory, and recollection.

Bartlett, F. C. (1936). Autobiography. In C. Murchison (Ed.), *A history of psychology in autobiography* (Vol. 3, pp. 39–52). Worcester, MA: Clark University Press. Written when Bartlett was approximately 50 years old, it is less an account of his life and more an articulation of the approach of a Cambridge psychologist.

Bartlett, F. C. (1943). Fatigue following highly skilled work. *Proceedings of the Royal Society of London* B, *131*, 247–257. Bartlett's Ferrier lecture to the Royal Society in 1941 in which he draws on the results of wartime research conducted at the Cambridge Psychological Laboratory.

Bartlett, F. C. (1958). *Thinking*. London: Allen & Unwin.

Works about Bartlett

Harris, A. D., & Zangwill, O. L. (1973). The writings of Sir Frederic Bartlett, C. B. E., F. R. S.: An annotated handlist. *British Journal of Psychology*, *64*, 493–510.

Roediger, H. L. (1997). Remembering [Retrospective review of the book *Remembering: A study in experimental and social psychology*]. *Contemporary Psychology, 42,* 488–492. A scholarly and authoritative review of Bartlett's classic work written from the perspective of 65 years of hindsight.

There are a dozen or so obituaries, memoirs, and accounts of Bartlett's life and science. The more significant of them are the following:

Broadbent, D. E. (1970). Frederic Charles Bartlett 1886–1969. *Biographical Memoirs of Fellows of the Royal Society, 16,* 1–13.

Broadbent, D. E. (1970). Sir Frederic Bartlett: An appreciation. *Bulletin of the British Psychological Society, 23,* 1–3.

Conrad, R. (1979). Sir Frederic Bartlett: 1886–1969. A personal homage. *Ergonomics, 13,* 159–161.

Hearnshaw, L. (1964). Sir Frederic Bartlett (b. 1886). In *A short history of British psychology, 1840–1940* (pp. 216–219). London: Methuen.

Oldfield, R. C. (1972). Frederic Charles Bartlett: 1886–1969. *American Journal of Psychology, 85,* 132–140.

Zangwill, O. L. (1970). Obituary notice. Sir Frederic Bartlett (1886–1969). *Quarterly Journal of Experimental Psychology, 22,* 77–81.

Darryl Bruce

BATTERED WOMEN. *See* Domestic Violence.

BAYES THEORUM. *See* Data Analysis.

BAYLEY, NANCY (1899–1994), American developmental psychologist. The very model of a developmental psychologist, Nancy Bayley followed development of many kinds over time and anticipated many current topics of concern and views about them. She was the first woman to receive the Distinguished Scientific Contribution Award of the American Psychological Association (APA) in 1966. Her citation read in part: "For the enterprise, pertinacity and insight with which she has studied human growth over long segments of the life cycle. . . . with respect and sensitiveness for her subjects, she has rigorously recorded their physical, intellectual, emotional and social development. . . ." She was President of APA's Division on Developmental Psychology (1953–1954) and of the Society for Research in Child Development (1961–1963).

After completing her doctorate at the University of Iowa in 1926 and spending 2 years as an instructor at the University of Wyoming from 1926 to 1928, Bayley went to the University of California at Berkeley as a research associate in the Institute of Child Welfare (now the Institute of Human Development). There she remained for the rest of her career, except for 1954 to 1964, when she was Chief of the Section on Child Development at the National Institute of Mental Health (NIMH). Her publications (1926 to 1968, for both professional and lay audiences) cover a broad range of developmental characteristics. She developed a number of useful measurement tools—but always stressed the importance of noting individual differences, following change over time, following the development of any psychological process from its earliest appearance, and studying the child in a normal environment (thus antedating today's ecological psychology).

Best known for her infant tests, her contributions went far beyond them. Bayley pioneered the study of physical growth with contributions described as classic in their penetration and simplicity. She developed accurate predictions of adult height, and pioneered in studying androgyny and sex differences in physical and psychological characteristics of adolescent boys and girls. Concerned with testing from the beginning of her career, Bayley received a citation for this work in the 1930s. She antedated current findings and trends in noting (1) the relation between sitting erect and mental achievements; (2) an increasing influence of both environmental pressures and complex hereditary potentialities on mental development, and showing that under normal conditions environmental factors had minimal influence on intelligence; and (3) types of changes in intellectual performance in adulthood. At NIMH, Bayley collaborated with E. S. Schaeffer on studies that included maternal behaviors. Among the findings: social patterns are not fixed in infancy, activity-passivity is largely biological (relatively independent of parent-child relationships)—both precursors to current views. She cautioned against generalizations about the long-term effects of "mothering" because outcomes are additionally determined by the child's behaviors and sex, and a multitude of other genetic and environmental factors.

Bayley believed that the ultimate value of scientific research lies in its application to enhance human welfare and happiness. She was immensely respected as a scientist and as a person of great integrity and warmth.

Bibliography

Works by Bayley

Bayley, N. (1955). On the growth of intelligence. *American Psychologist, 10,* 805–818. One of her classic papers showing individual differences in development of intelligence and pointing to the long-term growth of intelligence; requires some statistical sophistication to follow.

Bayley, N. (1956). Implicit and explicit values in science as related to human growth and development. *Merrill-Palmer Quarterly*, *2*, 121–126. A very good but brief view of Bayley's humane and questing values.

Bayley, N. (1962). The accurate prediction of growth and adult height. *Modern Problems in Paediatrics*, *7*, 234–255. An example of her important work in this field that is so important for decisions about the need for growth hormone.

Bayley, N. (1965). Research in child development: A longitudinal perspective. *Merrill-Palmer Quarterly*, *11*, 183–208. A good overview of the Berkeley Growth Study with lots of data.

Bayley, N. (1968). Behavioral correlates of mental growth: Birth to thirty-six years. *American Psychologist*, *23*, 1–17. The crucial paper on relations between personality factors and intelligence; very data loaded, however.

Works about Bayley

Lipsitt, L. P., & Eichorn, D. H. (1990). Nancy Bayley. In A. N. O'Connell & N. F. Russo (Eds.), *Women in psychology: A bio-bibliographic sourcebook* (pp. 23–29). New York: Greenwood Press.

Rosenblith, J. F. (1992). A singular career: Nancy Bayley. *Developmental Psychology*, *28*, 747–758.

Judy F. Rosenblith

BEACH, FRANK A. (1911–1988), American psychologist. Beach was among the leading psychobiologists of his time, especially known for his contributions to behavioral endocrinology and comparative psychology. Beach's psychobiology was integrative, in that he was concerned with both the physiological analysis of behavior and the role of behavior in the adaptation of animals to their environments. This led him to study instinctive behavioral patterns, such as sexual and parental behavior, rather that patterns that were largely learned. He advocated careful description and analysis of a variety of behavioral patterns. Although Beach devoted much effort to studying physiological factors, he opposed reductionism. He was an ardent experimentalist, but his experimentalism was of an old-fashioned, follow-your-nose variety, rather than one based on complex mathematical operations or equipment, both of which he mistrusted.

Beach was born in Emporia, Kansas on 13 April 1911, the son of a homemaker and a professor of music at what was then called the Kansas State Teachers College at Emporia. Beach completed his bachelor's degree in education at the Teachers College in 1932, intending to become a high school English teacher. Difficulty in finding such employment during the Depression led him to graduate school in psychology first at the Teachers College and later at the University of Chicago, where he studied with Karl Lashley and Harvey Carr,

among others. In 1936 he married Anna Beth Odenweller, with whom he had two children. After her death in 1971 Beach married Noel Gaustad.

In 1936 Beach moved to Lashley's laboratory, then located at Harvard University, and he accepted a position as an assistant curator in the department of experimental biology of the American Museum of Natural History in New York City the next year. In 1940 Beach completed his language requirements at Chicago and received his Ph.D. degree.

Beach accepted a professorship at Yale University in 1946 and was named a Sterling Professor there in 1952. After a year as a Fellow at the Center for Advanced Study in the Behavioral Sciences at Stanford University, California, Beach moved to the University of California in 1958. There he founded the Field Station for Behavioral Research in 1963. Beach formally retired in 1978, but continued active in the field until his death in Berkeley on 15 June 1988.

In his early research, Beach explored the various determinants of instinctive behavior, primarily in rats. His earliest work was with brain lesions, but he soon became interested in effects of hormones, in stimulus control, and in factors influencing the development of various patterns of behavior, especially sexual behavior.

For all of his emphasis on research, it was Beach's synthetic reviews that created his greatest impact on the field. He was a gifted writer, with a feel for the important questions that emerged as psychobiology evolved and with a great sense of timing. Beach thus helped crystallize and influence the development of various trends. His first review of central nervous mechanisms involved in copulation appeared in 1942.

When he realized the importance of hormones in the control of behavior, and the lack of research on their effects, he explored the area and wrote his first book (*Hormones and Behavior*, New York, 1948). Together with William C. Young, he established and shaped the field of behavioral endocrinology. Beach believed that hormone-behavior interactions were two-way, with behavioral effects on hormones as important as effects of hormones on behavior. In 1979 Beach, along with Julian Davidson and Richard Whalen, founded the field's primary journal, *Hormones and Behavior*.

Beach has been called "the conscience of comparative psychology." In his famous article, "The Snark Was a Boojum" (1950), he called for an expansion of both the range of species and the range of problems studied by comparative psychologists. He advocated careful description of behavioral patterns and caution in assigning functional significance to motor patterns. Beach was a leader in bringing recognition in North America to the work of European ethologists, including Konrad Lorenz and Nikolaas Tinbergen.

An interest in human sexual behavior was apparent throughout much of Beach's career, but he was cautious in applying results from nonhuman species to humans, believing that there were many differences in complexity of such phenomena as homosexuality when studied in humans and nonhumans.

Among his honors were honorary doctorates from McGill University, Williams College, and Emporia State University, the Warren Medal of the Society of Experimental Psychologists, the Distinguished Scientific Contribution Award of the American Psychological Association, the American Psychological Foundation's award for distinguished teaching in biopsychology, and membership in the National Academy of Sciences, the American Philosophical Society, and the American Academy of Arts and Sciences.

[*Many of the people mentioned in this article are the subjects of independent biographical entries.*]

Bibliography

Works by Beach

Beach, F. A. (1942). Central nervous mechanisms involved in the reproductive behavior of vertebrates. *Psychological Bulletin, 39*, 200–226. Beach's early review of physiological mechanisms.

Beach, F. A. (1948). *Hormones and behavior*. New York: Hoeber.

Beach, F. A. (1950). The snark was a boojum. *American Psychologist, 5*, 115–124. A key article in the history of comparative psychology, containing Beach's plea for greater breadth in the field.

Beach, F. A. (1967). Cerebral and hormonal control of reflexive mechanisms involved in copulatory behavior. *Physiological Reviews, 47*, 289–316.

Beach, F. A. (1975). Behavioral endocrinology: An emerging discipline. *American Scientist, 63*, 178–187. A key synthesis of the then-emerging discipline.

Beach, F. A. (1976). Sexual attractivity, proceptivity, and receptivity in female mammals. *Hormones and Behavior, 7*, 105–138. An important article differentiating various components of female sexual behavior.

Beach, F. A. (1981). Historical origins of modern research on hormones and behavior. *Hormones and Behavior, 15*, 325–376.

Beach, F. A. (1969). Locks and beagles. *American Psychologist, 24*, 971–989. A summary of some of Beach's research on sexual behavior in dogs.

Ford, C. S., & Beach, F. A. (1951). *Patterns of sexual behavior*. New York: Harper. An early comprehensive survey of information on sexual behavior oriented toward human sexuality.

Works about Beach

Beach, F. A. (1974). Frank A. Beach. In G. Lindzey (Ed.), *A history of psychology in autobiography* (Vol. 7, pp. 31–58). Englewood Cliffs, NJ: Prentice Hall.

Dewsbury, D. A. (1989). Frank Ambrose Beach: 1911–1988. *American Journal of Psychology, 102*, 414–420.

Glickman, S. E., & Zucker, I. (1989). Frank A. Beach (1911–1988). *American Psychologist, 44*, 1234–1235.

Donald A. Dewsbury

BECK DEPRESSION INVENTORY. Depression is a widespread disorder, and depressive symptoms are common across a broad range of psychological problems. In order to identify and treat people who have depressive symptomatology, it is helpful to have a method of quantifying depression. The original Beck Depression Inventory was developed in 1961 by Beck, Ward, Mendelson, Mock, and Erbaugh (*Archives of General Psychiatry, 4*, 561–571). Beck and his associates were interested in developing an inventory measuring depression for clinical and research purposes. A revised version was introduced into routine use at the Center for Cognitive Therapy at the University of Pennsylvania Medical School in 1971. In 1972, the revised Beck Depression Inventory (BDI) was published and has become the most widely used instrument for assessing severity of depression symptomatology in adults and adolescents. As Beck and Steer (*Journal of Clinical Psychology, 1984, 40*, 1365–1367) pointed out, the revised and original versions are comparable in psychiatric patients. A brief form of the BDI consisting of 13 items is also mentioned in the literature, although it failed to become widely used (Reynolds, W. M., & Gould, J. W., *Psychology, 1981, 49*, 306–307).

The BDI is a 21-item instrument that uses a four-point scale ranging from 0 to 3 (3 is the most severe symptom). The items were chosen to assess the severity of depression and were not selected to reflect any particular theory of depression or to provide a differential diagnosis (Beck & Steer, 1987). The symptoms assessed by the BDI include the following content areas: mood, pessimism, sense of failure, self-dissatisfaction, guilt, punishment, self-dislike, self-accusations, suicidal ideas, crying, irritability, social withdrawal, indecisiveness, body image, work difficulty, insomnia, fatigability, loss of appetite, weight loss, somatic preoccupation, and loss of libido.

The BDI is designed for quick and easy administration. It can be read to the client by a trained interviewer, but it is usually self-administered. The BDI is written at an eighth-grade reading level so that it may be used for adult and late adolescent patients from a wide variety of educational backgrounds. Its consistency with psychiatric ratings of depression, as well as its simplicity and brevity, has made the BDI a popular screening instrument for detecting the presence of depressive symptoms, and alerting clinicians to the presence of suicidal thoughts. In addition, it is a frequently used measure of improvement following psychotherapy and pharmacological interventions in studies of depression as well as a variety of other disorders.

The BDI has been used with a wide variety of populations: psychiatric inpatients, psychiatric outpatients, university populations, adolescents, and the elderly. Results of reliability and validity studies suggest that the BDI is a useful measure for assessing depression. Beck and his colleagues (Beck, Steer, & Garbin, 1988) presented a number of studies that reported reliability based on test-retest administrations. Depending upon time intervals, the Pearson Product-Moment correlations for psychiatric patients ranged from 0.48 to 0.86. For nonpsychiatric patients, the test-retest coefficients ranged from 0.60 to 0.90. There has been an extensive review of the literature regarding the assessment of the internal consistency of the BDI. In 1961, Beck and colleagues presented the first psychometric studies based on 606 outpatient and inpatient psychiatric subjects. The Pearson Product-Moment correlation yielded a reliability coefficient of 0.86 and with a Spearman-Brown corrected correlation this number increased to 0.93.

Content validity of the BDI appears to be adequate. It is important to note that the questions were derived through a professional consensus of the definition of depression and since the creation of the BDI, there have been a number of significant refinements to this definition. Moran and Lambert (Moran & Lambert, 1983, in M. J. Lambert, E. R. Christensen, & S. S. DeJulio, Eds., *The Assessment of Psychotherapy Outcome*, New York, pp. 263–303), concluded that the BDI reflected six out of the nine criteria for DSM-based depression (American Psychiatric Association, *Diagnostic and Statistical Manual of Mental Disorders*, Washington, D.C. 1980). Individual BDI items help the therapist to focus on particular symptoms while also providing information about the patient's negative mood and thoughts.

Concerning discriminant validity, studies on the BDI have indicated that the test can differentiate psychiatric patients from a normal sample (Steer, Beck, Riskind, & Brown, *Journal of Clinical Psychology*, 1986, *40*, 475–478). As mentioned in the *Beck Depression Inventory Manual*, when comparing the BDI and selected concurrent measures of depression across a variety of studies, a mean correlation of 0.72 was discovered. Studies centering around the validity of the BDI have been generally positive. Instruments that are comparable to the Beck Depression Inventory are the Zung Self-rating Depression Scale (Zung, *Archives of General Psychiatry*, 1965, *12*, 63–70), the Hamilton Psychiatric Rating Scale for Depression (*Journal of Neurology, Neurosurgery, and Psychiatry*, 1960, *23*, 56–62), the Depression-Dejection scale of the SCL-90-R (L. R. Derogatis, *SCL-90-R Administration, Scoring and Procedures Manual*, Baltimore, MD, 1977) and the Depression scale of the MMPI.

Using a mathematical formula for identifying separate samples, Seggar (L. B. Seggar and M. J. Lambert, *Paper presented at the Society for Psychotherapy Research*, York, U.K., 1996) established cutoff points and confidence levels for the BDI. A cutoff of 3.69 for asymptomatic normal controls was found with a lower confidence band of 0.68 and an upper confidence band of 6.71. Regarding normal controls versus clinical groups, a cutoff of 14.29 was discovered with a lower confidence band of 8.98 and an upper confidence band of 19.60. These cutoff scores can be used to decide which population (patient, nonpatient, or asymptomatic) a person belonged to when he or she began treatment. By tracking the patient's score over the course of treatment, the clinician can compare the patient's progress in relation to normative samples. This can help to alert the clinician to the need for additional treatment; referral for more intensive, less intensive, or alternative therapy; or to consider ending therapy. In this way, the BDI is playing an important role in both managing treatment and in identifying patients who are not being helped by treatment efforts.

The BDI can be criticized for being too transparent to patients and thus easily faked by those wishing to present themselves in a favorable or unfavorable light. Fortunately this is not a widespread problem. In most situations in which it is used, the persons taking it have no reason to intentionally distort their mental or emotional state. In routine clinical use with voluntary patients, it seems to provide an accurate index of depressive psychological distress. The BDI tends to correlate with measures of other negative psychological states such as anxiety. Rather than just measuring depression, the BDI appears to measure the presence and degree of negative emotional states.

Bibliography

American Psychiatric Association. (1980). *Diagnostic and statistical manual of mental disorders* (3rd ed.). Washington, DC: Author.

Beck, A. T. (1972). *Depression: Causes and treatment*. Philadelphia: University of Pennsylvania Press.

Beck, A. T., & Beamesderger, A. (1974). Assessment of depression: The Depression Inventory. In P. Pichot (Ed.), *Psychological measurements in psychopharmacology: Modern problems in pharmacopsychiatry* (Vol. 7, pp. 151–169). Basel, Switzerland: Karger.

Beck, A. T., & Steer, R. A. (1987). *Beck Depression Inventory manual*. San Antonio, TX: Psychological Corporation/Harcourt Brace Jovanovich.

Beck, A. T., Steer, R. A., & Garbin, M. G. (1988). Psychometric properties of the Beck Depression Inventory: Twenty-five years of evaluation. *Clinical Psychology Review, 8*, 77–100.

Edwards, B. C., Lambert, M. J., Moran, P. W., McCully, T., Smith, K. C., & Ellington, A. G. (1984). A meta-analytic comparison of the Beck Depression Inventory and the Hamilton Rating Scale for Depression as measures of treatment of outcome. *British Journal of Clinical Psychology, 23*, 93–99.

Gallagher, D. (1986). The Beck Depression Inventory and older adults: Review of its development and utility. *Clinical Gerontologist, 5*, 149–163.

Michael J. Lambert and Annette Stephenson

BEDWETTING. *See* Enuresis.

BEEBE-CENTER, JOHN GILBERT (1897–1958), American experimental psychologist. Beebe-Center was born the son of Cyrus Gilbert Beebe (president of a bank) and Janet Ingliss Hogg in Boston on 19 March 1897. After his father died when John was 4, his mother married Edward Chester Center; during John's schooling in France as well as America he was known as Beebe Center, but when he entered Harvard in 1915 he registered under the name Beebe-Center, the name by which he is now known.

When he entered university, he could speak English, French, and German, thanks to having been sent by his wealthy parents to various schools in Europe (listed by Boring, 1959). Following experience as an interpreter in the U.S. Armed Forces (various sections, also listed by Boring, 1959), he returned to Harvard and obtained his A.B. degree in 1921 and his Ph.D. degree in 1926. He then spent a year at the psychology department at the University of Berlin, the heartland of the Gestalt movement. On returning to Harvard, he was appointed as instructor (1927–1935), then lecturer (1935–1958) on psychology. In the presence of his wife, Roxanna Smiley Murphy, whom he had married in 1925, and of his son, he died suddenly of a coronary thrombosis on 6 December 1958.

He was led early in life to focus on feeling and emotion as his main research area. His Ph.D. degree research (Beebe-Center, 1929) indicated that, if a series of unpleasant odors was presented before a given test series, three subjects rated the test series as more "pleasant" (on average) on a paired-comparisons task than was the case when the same test series was preceded by a series of pleasant odors. This demonstration of a contrast effect was condensed by Beebe-Center into a "law of affective equilibrium"; this stated that "the affective value of the experiential correlate of a stimulus varies conversely with the sum of the affective values of those experiences preceding this correlate which constitute with it a unitary temporal group"

(Beebe-Center, 1929, p. 69). This law anticipated Harry Helson's demonstrations of the effects of context on subjective judgments (*Adaptation Level Theory*, New York, 1964), but it was not entirely novel because Lillien J. Martin (1851–1943) had put forward three similar laws about the role of contrast in determining aesthetic feelings (Martin, 1906).

Beebe-Center wrote a scholarly and very complete book entitled *The Psychology of Pleasantness and Unpleasantness* (New York, 1932), which included chapters on hedonic tone, particularly as it related to our physiological needs and to learning. Early twentieth-century research on the localization of emotional and hedonic feelings in the thalamus and neighboring areas was also reviewed, as were a number of theories (both physiological and psychological) of hedonic tone current in the early twentieth century. He later completed a book entitled *Feeling and Emotion: A History of Theories* (New York, 1937). H. M. Gardiner, a philosopher at Smith College, had written the first eight chapters, covering the period from the Greeks to the eighteenth century; Beebe-Center wrote the final two chapters, covering the nineteenth and twentieth centuries.

Bibliography

Beebe-Center, J. G. (1929). The law of affective equilibrium. *American Journal of Psychology, 41*, 54–69. Beebe-Center's research is notable for the care taken to eliminate sources of unwanted variability.

Boring, E. G. (1959). John Gilbert Beebe-Center: 1897–1958. *American Journal of Psychology, 72*, 311–315. An obituary by one of Beebe-Center's colleagues at Harvard.

Martin, L. J. (1906). An experimental study of Fechner's principles of aesthetics. *Psychological Review, 13*, 142–219. Lillien Martin wrote a detailed paper in German on the psychophysical method of right and wrong cases with G. E. Müller (1850–1934) before returning to California; the present paper is one of the few sources in English on Fechner's aesthetics.

Young, P. T. (1934). [Review of the book *The psychology of pleasantness and unpleasantness*]. *American Journal of Psychology, 46*, 343–347. This favorable review includes a detailed summary of the book's contents.

Young, P. T. (1938). [Review of the book *Feeling and emotion: A history of theories*]. *American Journal of Psychology, 51*, 594–595. Young calls this work "a permanent contribution to the history of psychology" (p. 595).

David J. Murray

BEERS, CLIFFORD WHITTINGHAM (1876–1943), founder of the National Committee for Mental Hygiene, philanthropist. Clifford W. Beers received his bachelor of arts degree from the Yale University Sheffield Scientific School in 1897. In the years following, he suffered from a variety of mental problems, including depression, delusions of persecution, and hypochondria. In 1900, after a failed suicide attempt, he was institutionalized. During the following 3 years, he was committed to three different mental institutions. Here, Beers was able to witness the lack of adequate provisions for the mentally ill as well as the existence of widespread abuse. He vowed to start a movement that would improve the conditions of the insane. His autobiography, *A Mind That Found Itself* (1908), describing his own institutionalization, would be the movement's founding document. The book was positively received. In the meantime, Beers had been active organizing the leadership of the movement that would realize his ideals. Through his contacts at Yale, Beers built a powerful network of psychiatrists, academics, and philanthropists to lead the movement. The influential psychiatrist Adolf Meyer, the psychologist William James, Johns Hopkins physician William H. Welch, and former Harvard University president Charles W. Eliot were among his earliest supporters.

In 1909, the National Committee for Mental Hygiene was founded in New York City. Beers was appointed secretary, a position he held until 1939. During the four decades of its existence, the Committee was instrumental in the professionalization and expansion of the discipline of psychiatry, receiving generous funds from several foundations. The National Committee fueled a movement typical of the progressive era in its interest in the application of science to the solution of social problems. The committee popularized a psychological perspective on personal and social problems, which aided the development of psychology as a discipline by promoting its applications.

One of the consequences of the activities of the National Committee for Mental Hygiene with respect to the discipline of psychology was its encouragement of the use of mental tests during the 1910s and 1920s. Initially, mental tests were used in the diagnosis of mentally handicapped people. Later, psychologists associated with the mental hygiene movement used mental tests to diagnose children referred to child guidance clinics and used them within the educational system. The child guidance clinics, which were established on the initiative of the National Committee throughout the 1920s and 1930s, were led by a team consisting of a psychiatrist, a psychologist, and a social worker. Initially, the psychologist was only involved in the diagnostic process but, over time, became increasingly involved in treatment as well. The second contribution the National Committee made to psychology was related to the rise of clinical psychology after World War II. Many veterans were in need of psychotherapy and psychologists were invited to help meet this need. Third, by supporting rational business practices in industry with regard to the management of personnel, the mental hygiene movement encouraged the application of mental tests in the selection of employees and later the development of personnel psychology.

Bibliography

Beers, C. W. (1981). *A mind that found itself: An autobiography*. Pittsburgh, PA: Pittsburgh University Press. (Original work published 1908)

Dain, N. (1980). *Clifford W. Beers: Advocate for the insane*. Pittsburgh, PA: Pittsburgh University Press.

Hans Pols

BEHAVIORAL GENETICS. An understanding of the relations between the actions of an individual organism and molecules transmitted from its parents is the subject of behavioral genetics. This is sometimes expressed as the relation between the set of genes that is inherited (the genotype) and the measured characteristic of the individual (the phenotype) that develops. Unlike disciplines that examine connections between adjacent levels of reality, such as social psychology and physiological psychology, behavioral genetics strives to span several levels (Figure 1). How this is to be achieved depends on which of two major questions is asked. Some investigators focus on the roles of heredity and environment in the development of the individual from embryo to adult, whereas others are interested mainly in the causes of differences between individuals in a population. Despite the obvious connection between these two questions, their methodologies and limitations are distinct.

Heredity and Development

To comprehend how a one-cell embryo is transformed into an organism capable of marvelously complex and adaptive behaviors requires that we investigate all levels of the system between the genes and behavior. If a gene influences foraging behavior or appetite, for example, it is important to find out what the gene does in what kinds of cells and when; how the actions of the gene are regulated; how the cells are organized into a nervous system; and how that system results in behavior. This immense task brings behavior genetics into close contact with molecular and developmental biology as well as neurophysiology and developmental psychology, and the multidisciplinary enterprise is sometimes termed neurobehavioral genetics or neurogenetics (Figure 1). Although work on all levels of the system may

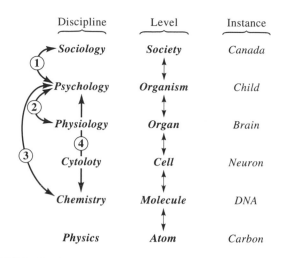

Discipline	Level	Instance
Sociology	Society	Canada
Psychology	Organism	Child
Physiology	Organ	Brain
Cytoloty	Cell	Neuron
Chemistry	Molecule	DNA
Physics	Atom	Carbon

BEHAVIORAL GENETICS. Figure 1. Living things are analyzed at different levels by different disciplines. Some interdisciplinary research examines the interface of adjacent levels, such as social psychology (1) and physiological psychology (2), whereas the statistical approach to behavior genetics (3) spans several levels. Neurobehavioral genetics (4) explores the pathways between genes and behavior.

be done in one laboratory, especially when working with invertebrates, the research often involves collaboration among scientists specializing in each level. Because of its emphasis on detecting and comprehending the actions of specific genes, this approach applied to humans has much in common with medical and psychiatric genetics.

Discovery of a new gene often begins with an observation of grossly aberrant behavior or an anatomical brain defect, and then the researcher asks whether the hypothetical gene is inherited according to Mendel's laws. Once the reality of the gene is confirmed, the mutation becomes available for research at the molecular and neural levels. On the other hand, molecular biologists working with experimental animals can now create mutations deliberately in specific genes that code for known proteins, and then behavioral geneticists can explore the consequences for brain and behavior. The mutant gene in question is often disabled entirely, and in some cases the animal is so grossly deficient that it cannot survive or reproduce without special aids. The new biotechnology vastly enhances the study of development but has had little impact to date on the study of more subtle individual differences in the normal range of behavior.

Individual Differences

Psychologists have always been keenly interested in differences between people in intelligence, personality, and social behaviors. The disciplines of differential psychology, developmental psychology, and psychological testing from their earliest beginnings debated the relative importance of differences in heredity and environment. Behavioral genetics attempts to separate these influences with a variety of methods. Two things are characteristic of most behavior genetic studies of individual differences in viable populations. First, statistical models are used when there is no information about how many or what kinds of genes may be important. Second, the methods are sensitive only to those genetically encoded proteins that happen to differ markedly among members of the population, and they are completely oblivious to proteins where almost everyone has essentially the same kind. Because the numbers of the latter greatly exceed the former in most species, the study of individual differences, while relevant to the question of organismic development, can never provide a comprehensive account of development or brain function.

Theoretical Perspectives

Three major views of heredity (H), environment (E), and behavior can be discerned in behavioral genetics (Figure 2). In theories where all heredity is thought to consist of Mendelian genes, the symbol G (genes) is more appropriate than H, which may involve nongenetic inheritance. The terse symbols attached to them here convey only the essence of well-elaborated doctrines. Although the doctrines are conceptually distinct, more than one view is sometimes espoused in different places by the same writer; this is a classification of theories, not necessarily theorists. (1) G versus E: A behavior is specified either genetically or by experience, and a genetically determined behavior may be regarded as instinctive. A variant espoused by Konrad Lorenz in classical ethology maintains that a complex behavior consists of components, each of which derives exclusively from either G or E, resulting in learning-instinct intercalation. This view is rare in behavior genetics and is regarded as a relic by many modern ethologists as well. (2) G + E: Virtually every behavior is generated by both G and E, although the strength of the two influences need not be equal. An individual's score on a test consists of two additive components, and the proportion of variance in test scores in a population that is attributable to variation in genotype is the heritability of the characteristic. The influence of G on a behavior occurs independently of the organism's environment, and the effects of a change in E should be the same for all individuals, regardless of their genotypes. This perspective is commonplace among those studying individual differences in human mental abilities. (3) H ↔ E: Both H and E must be considered when trying to understand the origin of any behavior, but their effects are neither separate during development nor separable

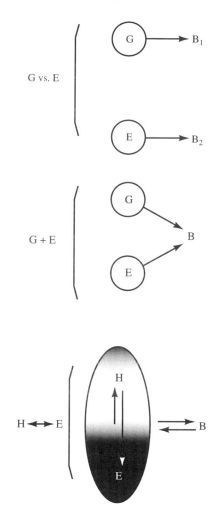

BEHAVIORAL GENETICS. Figure 2. Three theoretical perspectives on the relations between genes (G), environment (E) and behavior (B). G vs. E asserts that some behaviors are genetically encoded, whereas others are products of experience. G + E claims both factors are important but they may differ in strength, and it views G and E as acting separately. H ⇄ E considers heredity (H) to be more than just genes, and it recognizes that the distinction between the two is not maintained sharply as development proceeds. Interactions between H and E are crucial, and behavior can itself influence these processes.

statistically. The distinction between H and E is clear at conception, but as development proceeds, it becomes less distinct. Unlike G + E, which portrays the causal effects of genes as proceeding only upward from molecule to brain to behavior, this view emphasizes bidirectional causation and heredity-environment coaction. According to the well-established principles of molecular and developmental genetics, the actions of genes are regulated by their surroundings, whereas psychological processes can initiate changes at the molecular

level (although they do not change the structure of the DNA). Known variously as interactionism, developmental systems theory, or developmental contextualism, this approach employs the ubiquitous, generic statistical methods so familiar to psychologists to analyze data but rejects additivity and heritability analysis as biologically unrealistic. It is favored by many researchers doing rigorously controlled experiments with animals.

Two of these perspectives are sometimes joined in chimeric theories. For example, Sandra Scarr (*Child Development*, 1992, 63, 1–19) asserts that within the range of environments commonly encountered in society, individual variation arises mainly from genetic variation (the G + E view), whereas in extremely poor environments the expression of genetic individuality may be suppressed (interactionism). The hardware/software or computer model argues that genes provide a code or program for brain development (G versus E) and hard-wired neural structures then determine the sensitivity of the individual to variations in the environment or the ease of modifying behavior by experience (a form of interactionism termed the norm of reaction).

History

Early research on Mendelian inheritance in relation to brain and behavior was mainly conducted by biologists specializing in genetics and working with fruit flies and mice. Geneticists preferred to study genes that had obvious effects on stable characteristics such as color and morphology, but in the course of this work they noted that behavior was often modified as well. Geneticists also attended to distinct human syndromes of medical importance, many of which involved mental deficiency. Gradually the number of discrete mutations proven to affect the behavior of flies, mice, and humans accumulated (e.g., R. L. Sidman, M. C. Green, and S. H. Appel, *Catalog of the Neurological Mutants of the Mouse*, Cambridge, Mass., 1965; V. A. McKusick, *Mendelian Inheritance in Man*, Baltimore, 1966). Those working with single genes found little value in the heritability (G + E) approach, and several of the founders of behavior genetics, such as Benson Ginsburg, John Paul Scott, and Anne Anastasi saw genetic effects as interactive and context dependent (H ↔ E). Their principal interest from the outset was to learn *how* genes influence brain development and behavior.

In the 1950s and 1960s, molecular geneticists discovered that genes are contained in DNA molecules, that the genetic code is transcribed into RNA and then translated into a protein, and that this process is often regulated by environmental stimuli. These findings were soon exploited by neurobiologists to study in great detail the roles of identified genes in brain development and function. This research was often presented at the annual meetings of the Society for Neuroscience, founded in 1971, and published prominently in a wide range of journals. In the 1980s techniques to visualize the time and anatomical location of gene action became widely available, and in the 1990s new tools to alter specific genes gave added impetus to the growth of experimental behavior genetics. Thanks to the new molecular methods, many genetic variants known in the past only by their adherence to Mendel's laws have now had their DNA sequenced and their protein products identified. The full impact of these remarkable advances has yet to be felt in psychology.

Pioneers of the psychological study of individual differences, including Francis Galton and Karl Pearson, were not geneticists; instead, they rejected Mendelian inheritance, and their biometrical or correlational methods of comparing relatives presumed blending inheritance. Ronald Fisher later showed that particulate inheritance and biometrical methods can be reconciled when numerous genes, each with small effect, are involved. Psychologists working in the biometrical tradition typically applied their art to normal humans and tried to assess the relative strengths of hereditary and environmental sources of variation. Twin and family studies done in the 1920s and 1930s usually reported simple correlations of test scores of the different classes of relatives. Holzinger and others devised a crude heritability ratio for use with twins, and elaborate analysis of variance methods were later imported for this purpose from agricultural genetics. More recent techniques allow evidence from several kinds of relatives to be combined into one large multivariate model using path analysis or linear structural equation models (LISREL). The research designs employed with humans living beyond experimental control have of necessity changed little over the decades, whereas statistical methods have become more complex and capable of partitioning variance and even covariance into more components. Within this tradition, there has been a long and heated debate about the true magnitude of the heritability of intelligence in particular.

Behavioral genetics emerged as a self-designated discipline primarily within psychology following World War II. The Division of Behavior Studies was established in 1948 at the Jackson Laboratory by John L. Fuller and John Paul Scott, and several comprehensive reviews of the field were published from 1947 to 1954. Articles defining this area first appeared in the *Annual Review of Psychology* in 1955 (F. J. Kallmann and G. S. Baroff, 6, 297–326) and 1960 (J. L. Fuller, 11, 41–70); a book-length treatment appeared in 1960 (J. L. Fuller and R. Thompson, *Behavior Genetics*, New York, 1960); and the comprehensive collection of chapters edited by Jerry Hirsch appeared in 1967 (*Behavior-Genetic Analysis*, New York, 1967). The Institute for Behavioral Genetics was established by Gerald McClearn and John DeFries at the University of Colorado in 1967, the Behavior Genetics Association was founded at the University of Illinois in 1970, and the first issue of the journal *Behavior Genetics* appeared in 1970. In 1997 the International Behavioural and Neural Genetics Society was established.

Methods

For ethical and legal reasons, when studying the role of nonspecific heredity (no genes identified or mapped), radically different techniques are employed in the study of humans and nonhuman animals. However, the methods for detecting specific genes and assigning them to chromosomes are substantially the same in most species that reproduce sexually.

Heredity in laboratory animals is rigorously controlled by breeding in closed colonies protected from introgression of foreign genes. Over 60 generations of brother by sister inbreeding, commonly practiced with mice, yields a genetically pure strain where every animal has the same genotype. Over 100 such inbred strains are now widely available for research, and many interesting behavioral and neural differences among them have been documented. Rearing genetically identical animals in different environments provides a good test of heredity-environment interaction. Selective breeding involves mating of males and females that both have high or both have low scores on a test of behavior. This is best done without inbreeding, and it often yields selected lines that differ greatly on the chosen characteristics. The difference between behaviors of two strains or lines can then be analyzed with reciprocal cross-breeding to determine whether it arises from nonsex chromosomes, sex chromosomes, organelles in the cytoplasm (e.g., mitochondria), the maternal environment, or a complex combination of two or more factors. The influences of genotype and the global maternal environment can be surgically separated by ovarian grafting (inbred ovaries into a hybrid mother) or fertilized embryo transfer done shortly after conception. Prenatal and postnatal aspects of maternal environment can then be analyzed with fostering shortly after birth. Several inbred strains can be mated in a diallel cross to determine whether genetic effects combine additively or there is dominance plus maternal effects.

In human family studies, the correlations of first-degree relatives (parent-child, siblings) are expected to be greater than second-degree relatives (grandparent-grandchild, uncle-niece, etc.) if genetic variation is important, but similar patterns of correlations can occur because of shared environments. The adoption method seeks to uncouple the close association of heredity and environment in a nuclear family, but it cannot exclude the influences of prenatal or early postnatal environments, and there is often a correlation between characteristics of the birth mother and the adopting families because of policies of selective rather than random placement in homes by adoption agencies. The twin method compares genetically identical, one-egg or monozygotic (MZ) twins with two-egg or dizygotic (DZ) twins, but interpretation is clouded by the generally greater similarity of experiences of MZ twins. Evidence from all three methods can be combined into a multivariate statistical model to assign percentages of total phenotypic variance to additive and dominance genetic influences, environmental factors common to relatives, and things that are unique to the individual, including test unreliability. The validity of this partitioning of variance remains in dispute because no one method cleanly separates the influences of heredity and environment, and because advocates of the systems view (H ↔ E) consider the assumption that heredity and environment act additively (G + E) to be flawed in principle.

The adoption and twin methods have valuable applications in the study of nongenetic effects. Comparing children from similar backgrounds adopted into poor or superior homes can provide unambiguous evidence for the importance of family circumstances. The offspring of male MZ twins may be less similar than those of female MZ twins if cytoplasmic or maternal environment effects are important for mental development. Discordant MZ twins can be employed very effectively to study environmental influences, as can comparisons of MZ twins derived from one versus two chorions. Likewise, comparisons of DZ twins with nontwin siblings can detect environmental cohort effects because the two classes of relatives are equally dissimilar genetically but differ in shared experiences. Same-sex DZ versus opposite-sex DZ comparisons are sensitive to gender-related environments and even the prenatal hormonal environment.

The influence of a single gene on behavior can be demonstrated by *genetic linkage analysis*. This requires that we already know the location of DNA markers on a specific chromosome and that there are different forms (alleles) of the markers in the population. Ideally, a marker itself should be neutral and have no direct effect on the phenotype. If differences in behavior tend to be associated with different marker alleles in a family, then there must be a behaviorally important gene nearby. Chromosome mapping has been done for hundreds of genes that influence behavior of fruit flies, mice, and humans. More than 10,000 neutral DNA markers have been identified recently in mice and humans (see Figure 3), making it feasible to locate a quantitative trait locus (QTL) that exerts only modest effects, rather than the devastating effects common among the rarer neurological mutations.

Once a gene has been identified, it becomes possible to learn when and where it is expressed in messenger RNA during development using *in situ* hybridization or in protein using immunocytochemistry.

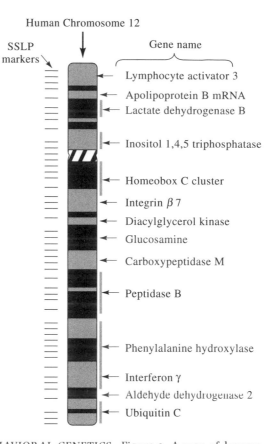

BEHAVIORAL GENETICS. Figure 3. A map of human chromosome 12, showing the locations of several DNA markers known as simple sequence length polymorphisms (SSLP) on the left side and a few of the genes known to reside nearby. The closer a gene is to a particular marker, the more likely the two are to be transmitted together to offspring. PAH is the gene coding for the liver enzyme phenylalanine hydroxylase which is defective in phenylketonuria. A gene is usually named for the enzyme or protein for which it codes. No gene codes for a behavior or component of a behavioral trait.

Powerful molecular methods also give the experimenter new tools to manipulate an animal's genotype. A known gene can be transferred from one species to another to create a transgenic animal and see how the new gene influences development. If the DNA sequence of a gene is known, molecular probes can be constructed to disable the normal gene, and these targeted mutations (knockouts) can then be examined for a wide range of phenotypic effects. A recent innovation enables the experimenter to turn a specific gene off or on in the adult animal by exposing it to dietary or other factors that control gene action (inducible mutations). These methods are doubly important because they provide information about the roles of genes that do not normally vary in laboratory populations. These methods are not likely to be useful with humans, but the great similarity of humans, mice, and flies at the molecular level renders the new knowledge highly relevant for understanding human development.

Applications and Public Policy

Despite impressive progress, animal behavioral and neural genetics is largely basic research with few practical applications to date. If anything, this knowledge has resulted in an appreciation of the daunting complexity at the molecular level and the great difficulties in making useful predictions. The genome of most mammals contains upwards of 50,000 distinct genes, only a minority of which have been identified. Well-documented single genetic effects on behavior often result from molecules expressed ubiquitously in many kinds of tissue throughout the body or do not involve specifically psychological processes such as memory. Behavior genetics has had surprisingly little impact on research in the psychology of animal learning, where poorly standardized stocks of rats and mice of unknown genetic composition are commonly employed. This neglect may reflect a pervasive belief that the laws of behavior will be the same in all organisms, despite quantitative differences in rates of learning or intensity of emotions and motives, a belief eloquently professed by Clark Hull (*Psychological Review*, 1945, 52, 55–60).

The study of heredity and human behavior, on the other hand, was conceived in political intercourse and nurtured by concerns about state policy. Arguments that nature predominates over nurture were invoked to justify eugenic sterilization, restrict immigration, and deny aid to the poor in the era before genetic principles were introduced into psychology. Eugenics lost support among geneticists when it was realized that few socially significant behavior problems have a simple genetic basis, that children with recessive genetic disorders usually have phenotypically normal parents, and that many chromosome defects arise *de novo* from normal parents (e.g., Down syndrome and the sex chromosome anomalies XXX, XXY, and XYY). As the corpus of knowledge grew, it became apparent that genetic disorders such as phenylketonuria can often be treated and negative symptoms prevented. It is now widely recognized by geneticists that a characteristic that appears heritable may also be substantially modifiable in a new environment. Nevertheless, two nongeneticists, Richard Herrnstein and Charles Murray (*The Bell Curve*, New York, 1994) resurrected the discredited claim that high heritability of IQ makes aid to the poor futile, and they proposed instead that eugenic measures be implemented to enhance national intelligence. Behavior genetics thus continues to find itself at the podium of political debate.

Application of behavioral genetic research is possible when genes with major effects are discovered. When solid scientific evidence of a specific genetic effect is lacking, on the other hand, behavior genetics has no valid policy implications. Genetic knowledge may aid the search for treatments and thereby help to rescue victims from an unpleasant fate. In the case of Huntington's disease, where effective treatment remains elusive, knowing the DNA sequence of the gene now allows reliable identification of carriers long before neurological disease is apparent. Whether this knowledge is then used to decide if carriers may reproduce, if they may purchase medical insurance, or if embryos with the bad gene may be aborted has become a serious ethical, legal, and political issue. Most behavioral geneticists support voluntary genetic counseling where prospective parents are provided with facts needed to make an informed choice, but compulsory eugenic measures dictated by the state have little sympathy in this profession.

Future Directions

Given the large number of genes that has already been documented in fruit flies, mice, and other experimental animals, the challenge for the future is to understand how these function as part of an integrated nervous system that subserves behavior. It is essential that we learn how many interacting molecular parts are pertinent to a neural or psychological process. It is already apparent that several hundred genes are involved in the operation of merely one synapse between two neurons, and it seems likely that several thousand genes at the very minimum are active in a moderately complex tissue such as the hippocampus or cerebellum.

The Human Genome project aims to determine the nucleotide base sequence for the DNA of all 22 chromosomes plus the X and Y (see http://www.ncbi.nlm.nih.gov/genemap99/), and parallel enterprises will sequence the fruit fly and mouse genomes. Once the full DNA sequences are known, all functional genes can then be identified. Work already completed with a one-celled organism (yeast) indicates that thousands of previously unheralded genes will present themselves in flies, mice, and humans, too. Targeted mutations in animals will facilitate a rapid evaluation of newly discovered genes, and *in situ* hybridization will readily reveal where and when they act.

Understanding the principles regulating networks of components will require a new phase of research that assesses variations in two or more genes simultaneously in one experiment (e.g., double mutants afflicted by two genetic defects), which in turn will require larger sample sizes to detect interaction effects. Provided that sophisticated molecular techniques are united with similarly advanced psychological testing procedures and a nonreductionistic conceptual scheme, a comprehensive picture of the neural bases of the simpler learning and memory processes becomes a realistic goal not too far over the horizon.

Research on the normal range of human behavior is still at the threshold of gene discovery, and many preliminary claims have turned out to be false positives. To date, no gene influencing intelligence, personality, sexual orientation, alcoholism, or schizophrenia has been rigorously verified. At the same time, many mutations are known that lead to relatively rare and gross deficits. Now the big question is whether genes with moderate effects of greater interest to the psychology of individual differences will be detectable.

Fortunately, the thousands of new DNA markers make it possible to answer this question. Methods now allow one to prove conclusively that a particular region of a chromosome does *not* contain a gene with noteworthy effect on a specific behavior. For example, long stretches of DNA have been "swept" and found to have no gene of major importance for bipolar disorder (see www-srb.nimh.nih.gov/gi.html). Thus, powerful genetic techniques could eventually prove that there is no gene anywhere in the human genome relevant to homosexuality, for example, if this happens to be the case. If, on the other hand, such a gene exists, it should be found before too long. The future direction of human behavior genetics will be dictated by the findings of this odyssey.

Principal Figures

Founders have been mentioned earlier. Several of the next generation of leading authorities are as follows. The fruit fly *Drosophila* is the focus of work by Ralph Greenspan at New York University, Jeff Hall at Brandeis University, Tim Tully at the Cold Spring Harbor Laboratory, and Marla Sokolowski at the University of Toronto in Canada. Lab mice are utilized by Michèle Carlier, Wim Crusio, and Pierre Roubertoux at the CNRS center in Orléans, France, Hans-Peter Lipp at the University of Zürich in Switzerland, John Crabbe at the Oregon Health Sciences University, Jeanne Wehner at the University of Colorado, and Robert Gerlai at GENENTECH, Inc. Experts on human behavior genetics include Kenneth Kidd at Yale University, Kenneth Kendler, and Michael Neale at the Virginia Commonwealth University, Robert Plomin at King's College London, England, and Dorret Boomsma at Vrije Universiteit in Amsterdam.

Training Requirements

To pursue research in behavioral genetics, the student typically earns a Ph.D. degree in psychology or biology and then spends 1 to 3 years as a postdoctoral fellow working closely with a leading investigator. Several centers offer training specifically in behavior genetics at the Ph.D. degree level, but people from diverse backgrounds enter the field during their postdoctoral studies. It is expected that the aspiring researcher will have a solid foundation in the behavioral and natural sciences at the undergraduate level, and that he or she will acquire a high level of knowledge of psychological testing, statistical data analysis, transmission genetics, and, to an increasing extent, neuroscience and molecular genetics. The Institute for Behavioral Genetics, University of Colorado (ibgwww.colorado.edu/), offers training in both human and mouse behavioral genetics. The CNRS group in Genetics, Neurogenetics and Behavior in Orléans, France (rosalie.cnrs-orleans.fr/~webgnc/page1.html), specializes in lab mice, whereas the Virginia Institute for Psychiatric and Behavioral Genetics (electro.psi.vcu.edu/~vipbg) specializes in human disorders. The Jackson Laboratory at Bar Harbor, Maine (www.jax.org) no longer sponsors a group working on behavior but is an excellent source of information on mice and offers valuable courses of short duration. Many centers working with invertebrates can be located via the Web sites for the fruit fly (flybase.bio.indiana.edu) and nematode worm (elegans.swmed.edu).

Professional Organizations

The three major organizations are Behavior Genetics Association (www.bga.org); International Behavioural and Neural Genetics Society (www.ibngs.org); and International Society for Twin Studies (kate.pc.helsinki.fi/twin/ists.html)

Specialty Journals

The three major journals in the field are *Behavior Genetics* (www.plenum.com/title.cgi?2068); *Journal of Neurogenetics* (e-mail: hall@binah.cc.brandeis.edu); and *Twin Research* (kate.pc.helsinki.fi/twin/ists.html).

[*Many of the people mentioned in this article are the subjects of independent biographical entries.*]

Bibliography

Landmark Papers

Fisher, R. A. (1918). The correlation between relatives on the supposition of Mendelian inheritance. *Transactions of the Royal Society of Edinburgh, 52,* 399–433. A landmark paper reconciling Mendelism and biometry.

Johannsen, W. (1911). The genotype conception of heredity. *American Naturalist, 45,* 129–159. The first clear distinction between genes that are inherited and phenotypes that develop.

Osborne, K. A., Robichon, A., Burgess, E., Butland, S., Shaw, R. A., Coulthard, A., Periera, H. S., Greenspan, R. J., & Sokolowski, M. B. (1997). Natural behavior polymorphism due to a cGMP-dependent protein kinase of *Drosophila. Science, 277,* 834–836. Relates a viable difference found in wild fruit fly larval foraging behavior to a genetic difference in one enzyme. Culmination of a classic series of experiments.

Recent Reviews of the Field

Plomin, R., Defries, J. C., McClearn, G. E., & Rutter, M. (1997). *Behavioral genetics* (3rd ed.). New York: Freeman. A leading textbook for undergraduate instruction, emphasizing the G + E approach.

Sternberg, R. J., & Grigorenko, E. (Eds.). (1997). *Intelligence, heredity, and environment.* New York: Cambridge University Press. Presents 20 chapters with a wide range of perspectives on the topic.

Discussions of Methods and Theory

Devlin, B., Daniels, M., & Roeder, K. (1997). The heritability of IQ. *Nature, 388,* 468–470. Reports a Bayesian meta-analysis of models with and without maternal effects, and finds that heritability estimates are considerably lower when maternal effects are included.

Kidd, K. K. (1997). Can we find genes for schizophrenia? *American Journal of Medical Genetics (Neuropsychiatric Genetics), 74,* 104–111.

Lander, E. S., & Schork, N. J. (1994). Genetic dissection of complex traits. *Science, 265,* 2037–2048. Discusses methods of detecting genes with small effects and argues that criteria for significance commonly used in behavioral genetics yield too many false positives.

Neale, M. C., & Cardon, L. R. (1992). *Methodology for genetic studies of twins and families.* Dordrecht: Kluwer Academic.

Strohman, R. C. (1997). The coming Kuhnian revolution in biology. *Nature Biotechnology, 15,* 194–200. Proposes replacement of genetic reductionism by an epigenetic, developmental approach to understanding complex living systems.

Wahlsten, D. (1990). Insensitivity of the analysis of variance to heredity-environment interaction. *Behavioral and Brain Sciences, 13,* 109–161. Discusses the meaning of interaction and shows that common statistical methods are not likely to detect real interaction effects.

Douglas Wahlsten

BEHAVIORAL MEDICINE. *See* Health Psychology; *and* Psychiatry.

BEHAVIORAL TERATOLOGY. In 1963, Werboff and Gottlieb coined the term *behavioral teratology* to refer to the study of postnatal behavioral effects resulting from prenatal drug exposure (*Obstetric and Gynecologic Survey, 18,* 420–423). However, it was not until a decade later that behavioral teratology began to emerge as a distinct field of study. In the interim, several key papers were published examining the effects of prenatal exposure to drugs and chemicals on postnatal behavioral development. For example, Spyker and colleagues published an article showing deviant swimming behavior in mice exposed to methyl mercury during gestation (*Science,* 1972, *177,* 621). They pointed out that methyl mercury–exposed mice were indistinguishable from unexposed mice until their behavior was quantified under experimental conditions. This paper, and others published in the early 1970s, led to the growing realization that teratogenicity encompassed a wide range of effects including subtle behavioral changes.

As the field progressed, researchers became aware of a number of factors which make the developing nervous system uniquely vulnerable to toxic insult. In mature organisms, many drugs and chemicals are excluded from the brain by the blood-brain barrier that exists at the level of the capillary wall. In other tissues, there are gaps between capillary endothelial cells which allow free exchange of molecules between the blood and adjacent tissue. In the brain, however, the outer membranes of the capillary endothelial cells are fused together, preventing diffusion of substances from the blood into the brain. These capillary-tight junctions do not begin to form until the middle of gestation, and the blood-brain barrier is not completely functional until sometime after birth. Thus, drugs and chemicals that are excluded from the adult brain can enter and damage the fetal brain. The developing organism also does not have the same capacity to metabolize and excrete foreign substances. Slower excretion acts in concert with the incomplete blood-brain barrier to result in higher concentrations of foreign substances in the brain.

Probably the single most important factor contributing to the susceptibility of the brain to toxic insult is its lengthy developmental period. The brain is different from other organs in that it develops over a very long period of time, beginning early in gestation and extending well into the postnatal period. This creates a wide "window of vulnerability" to toxic exposures. The brain is also a structurally diverse organ, with different cell groups forming at distinct periods during development. Because of the structural diversity of the brain and its long developmental trajectory, the same agent can have very different effects, depending on the time at which exposure occurs. For example, exposure to antimitotic agents during the middle of gestation has been shown to produce hyperactivity in mice. This coincides with the period of time when the striatum, a structure important in controlling motor activity, is developing. The same exposure either very early or very late in brain development has just the opposite effect, producing hypoactivity. These time periods coincide with development of specific cell groups associated with another motor center, the cerebellum. Both the chronology of neuron development and the timing of exposure are discussed in an excellent review by Patricia Rodier (1980).

The importance of the timing of exposure in determining the behavioral outcome is straightforward. Perhaps less obvious is the importance of the time at which behavioral assessments are made. Brain injuries that occur during fetal or early neonatal development are not necessarily expressed consistently throughout the lifespan. The most obvious examples are transient effects that resolve as the drug or chemical is cleared from the body, or as the organism matures. However, sometimes the converse is true, and the effects of a toxic exposure are not obvious until after the organism has matured. A now classic set of experiments by Patricia Goldman and colleagues provides a dramatic example of this (reviewed by Rodier, 1986).

Goldman and colleagues examined the role of the dorsolateral prefrontal cortex in delayed response performance of monkeys, and found that bilateral ablations severely impaired performance in adult monkeys. In contrast, monkeys lesioned neonatally performed much like controls. Initially it was assumed that the plasticity of the developing brain allowed the neonatally lesioned animals to recover more completely. However, later experiments demonstrated that it was the relatively late development of the dorsolateral prefrontal cortex that actually explained the finding. The performance of the control monkeys on delayed response tasks was quite poor in the first two years after birth. Neonatally lesioned animals did not differ much from controls at this stage. However, as the controls matured, their performance improved dramatically, whereas the performance of the lesioned animals remained poor. These results highlighted the importance of repeated behavioral assessments across the lifespan.

About the same time that behavioral teratology was becoming established as a field of study, a groundbreaking paper identified a specific pattern of congenital malformations in offspring of alcoholic mothers (K. L. Jones, D. W. Smith, C. N. Vileland, and A. P. Streissguth, *Lancet*, 1973, *1*, 1267–1271). It was not long before scientists recognized that the effects of fetal alcohol exposure occurred along a dose-response continuum. Physical malformations occurred only with high, chronic maternal alcohol consumption, but behavioral dysfunction was present at much lower exposure levels. This observation lead to an explosion of research on the behavioral effects of fetal alcohol exposure in animal models, and that research helped to shape the field of behavioral teratology by bringing several important methodological issues, including the nutritional status of the mother during gestation, to the forefront.

From the perspective of environmental chemicals, none has had a larger impact than lead. Although lead has been recognized as a central nervous system poison since antiquity, it is only since the advent of behavioral teratology as a field of study that the impact of low-level environmental lead exposure on childhood intellectual functioning has been recognized. As our sophistication in assessing subtle behavioral sequelae of chemical exposures has increased over the last 20 to 30 years, the level of lead exposure considered safe for children has steadily declined.

Bibliography

Neurotoxicology and Teratology. New York: Elsevier. This journal is jointly sponsored by the Neurobehavioral Teratology Society and the Behavioral Toxicology Society and is one of the primary places where scientists publish original research in the field of behavioral teratology. The journal includes research in animals and humans, and articles on prenatal exposure to therapeutic agents, drugs of abuse, and environmental chemicals.

Riley, E. P. & Vorhees, C. V. (Eds.). (1986). *Handbook of behavioral teratology*. New York: Plenum Press. This book includes works by a number of authors who were influential in the development of behavioral teratology as a field of study. It includes chapters on the origins of behavioral teratology, and on the principles and methods of behavioral teratology, as well as chapters reviewing the behavioral teratology of various drugs and chemicals. The later, while now somewhat out of date, will give readers an overview of much of the early work in the field.

Risau, W., & Wolburg, H. (1990). Development of the blood-brain barrier. *Trends in Neuroscience, 13*, 174–178. This review article provides an excellent overview of the blood-brain barrier and its development during the embryonic period.

Rodier, P. (1980). Chronology of neuron development: Animal studies and their implications. *Developmental Medicine and Child Neurology, 22*, 525–545. This classic article reviews the chronology of neuron development in various brain regions and discusses how timing of exposure to drugs and chemicals can impact on the behavioral outcome.

Rodier, P. (1986). Time of exposure and time of testing in developmental neurotoxicology, *Neurotoxicology, 7*, 69–76. This succinct paper gives several nice examples of the importance of timing of exposure and timing of assessment in behavioral teratology.

Susan L. Schantz

BEHAVIOR ANALYSIS. The decomposition of behavior into its component parts or processes is known as behavior analysis. For example, a child may cry because of some painful stimulus, or because crying reliably produces important consequences such as a caregiver's attention, or for both reasons in some combination. A behavior analysis of the child's crying is concerned with identifying the relative contributions of these and other possible sources. The analysis will be effective only if there exists a sound taxonomy of types of behavior and behavioral processes.

The main features of the contemporary experimental analysis of behavior grew out of the research of the American psychologist, B. F. Skinner (1904–1990). [*See the biography of Skinner.*] The philosophy of science upon which it is based is sometimes called radical behaviorism. One of its special features is that it takes behavior itself as fundamental rather than treating behavior as a derivative or index of something else such as cognition or mind: behavior, as the interaction between the organism and its environment, is worthy of study in its own right.

Another distinctive feature of the experimental analysis of behavior is its emphasis on the behavior of the individual. Procedures that generate large and reliable effects can be conducted with only a few subjects, and the results of one experiment can be confirmed in later research that extends the original findings. Experimental analyses are cumulative, in the sense that successive procedures depend on what has gone before. If experiments produce variable results, solutions are sought not by averaging over an increased number of subjects but by refining details of procedure to identify sources of variability. These characteristics make behavior analysis particularly useful in applications to important practical aspects of human behavior, as in education and behavioral medicine. The applied analysis of behavior is notable for both effectiveness and accountability.

Some behavior is instinctive or innate and other behavior is acquired or learned during the organism's lifetime. One task of an experimental analysis is to distinguish behavior that arises from the organism's evolutionary history, its phylogeny, from behavior that originates from the organism's experience, its ontogeny. Imprinting in ducklings provides an example of behavior analysis that involves distinguishing between phylogenic and ontogenic sources of behavior. Imprinting occurs when a duckling sees its mother or some other moving object shortly after hatching. The moving stimulus acquires special significance for the ducking, which then follows the mother (or object) wherever she (or it) goes. Early accounts of imprinting treated the phenomenon as one in which the imprinted stimulus elicits or releases the behavior of following. But the duckling's environment can be arranged so that following does not inevitably keep the duckling close to the imprinted stimulus, as in natural environments. Instead, the duckling may have to stand still on a platform or peck on a disk on the wall to keep the imprinted stimulus visible. Ducklings learn to do whatever keeps the imprinted stimulus available.

The analysis shows that what is given phylogenically in imprinting is not a special relation between the imprinted stimulus and the following. Instead, it is the capacity of a moving stimulus seen early in the duckling's life to acquire special significance. Once that has happened, the relation between the imprinted stimulus and the following comes about as an ontogenic contribution, in that the duckling learns which behavior has the consequences of keeping this significant stimulus visible. In the natural world, following typically keeps ducklings close to mother ducks, but the experimental analysis shows that what ducklings do is determined by the consequences of their behavior.

Another example of behavior analysis is provided by the organization of behavior in time. Some behavior sequences can be divided into components such that each response produces an opportunity to engage in the next. For instance, in moving through a doorway, turning the knob permits the opening of the door, which in turn allows the stepping through. The sequence is called a response chain, and some behavior sequences are reasonably reducible to smaller units in this way. But some sequences cannot be reduced to such chains. For example, the keystrokes of a skilled typist cannot be discriminative stimuli for later strokes, because each stroke is executed even before the typist could have been affected by the previous letter. Some behavior sequences can be put together so that each response produces stimulus conditions that occasion the next, whereas others must be integrated so that responses appear in the proper order without depending on stimuli produced by earlier responses. It takes a behavior analysis to determine which type any given sequence is.

Behavior analyses have been applied to a vast range of phenomena, including the relative contributions of verbal and nonverbal processes to complex human behavior. Experimental analyses of behavior involve taking complex behavior apart to find out what it is made of. Once behavior analyses have teased apart the components, they can be validated by seeing whether the parts can be put back together again. The reversal of an analysis is a synthesis (as when, in chemistry, a compound is synthesized after an analysis has determined its elements and its structure). For example, the interpretation of complex behavior in a natural habitat can be tested by trying to assemble its components in a laboratory setting, and this depends on making explicit all assumptions about the behavior to be synthesized. Failures of synthesis are usually more informative than successes, because they force the reexamination of assumptions.

[*See also* Applied Behavior Analysis; Association for Behavior Analysis; *and* Behavior Therapy.]

Bibliography

Lashley, K. S. (1951). The problem of serial order in behavior. In L. A. Jeffress (Ed.), *Cerebral mechanisms in behavior* (pp. 112–146). New York: Wiley. A classic account of some sequential properties of behavior.

Peterson, N. (1960). Control of behavior by presentation of an imprinted stimulus. *Science, 132,* 1395–1396. An example of the behavior analysis of imprinting.

Sidman, M. (1960). *Tactics of scientific research.* New York: Basic Books. A survey of experimental methods as specifically applied to behavior analysis.

Skinner, B. F. (1938). *The behavior of organisms.* New York: Appleton-Century-Crofts. The classic experimental work that provided the foundation concepts for the experimental analysis of behavior.

Skinner, B. F. (1966). The phylogy and ontogeny of behavior. *Science, 153,* 1204–1213. A treatment of the phylogenic and ontogenic sources of behavior.

A. Charles Catania

BEHAVIORISM AND NEOBEHAVIORISM.

While the status of behaviorism as the dominant twentieth-century program for experimental psychology began to wane in the 1950s, its lasting impact was secured by the institutionalization of its methods and concepts into psychological science and practice. Behaviorism's influence today ranges from the philosophy and history of science, including theoretical work in epistemology and the social construction of knowledge, to the experimental and applied sciences of psychology, including, among others, organizational behavior, psychotherapy, psychopharmacology, neuroscience, medicine, education, economics, and behavior analysis. The continued vitality of psychology's most controversial school was documented in a special issue of the *American Psychologist* (1992), which focused on the relationship between contemporary psychology and the work of B. F. Skinner (1904–1990). In a century in which the American public would come to expect little from psychology as a science, Skinner's concept of reinforcement came to rank alongside Freud's concept of the unconscious as having attained the status of widespread public familiarity, acceptability, and applicability.

Origins of Behaviorism

While behaviorism has never existed as a single set of ideas or practices, it can be distinguished from other movements in the history of psychology by its adherence to a specific principle: the possibility of a *natural science* of human behavior. Rather than a *mental science*, which treats unobservable mental events as ultimate causes of behavior, behaviorism placed the causes of action in local and historical environmental contingencies. John B. Watson (1878–1958) was among the first to eschew all of psychology's attachments to mentalism, calling for psychology to be a wholly objective science. His 1913 *Psychological Review* manifesto, "Psychology as the Behaviorist Views It," and later his book, *Psychology from the Standpoint of a Behaviorist* (1919),

secured his place in history as the founder of behaviorism.

Watson argued vehemently that a natural science of behavior must have a scientifically accessible subject matter that can be linked to manipulable and measurable aspects of the environment. His goal was to use the powers of a natural science approach, already realized in disciplines such as physics and physiology, to understand the forces that govern human action and how these forces could be manipulated to alter its course. The influence of early experimental work by E. L. Thorndike and Ivan Pavlov notwithstanding, Watson's behaviorism was a philosophy of science first and a science of behavior second. Even as Watson's heir to behaviorism, B. F. Skinner, began to articulate general principles of learning, behaviorism continued to be defined broadly as a philosophy of science. Indeed, only when behaviorism as a philosophy of science was coupled with its empirical branch—the radical-empiricist epistemology of B. F. Skinner—did it begin to reveal the full implications of behaviorism's thoroughly empirical approach to psychology.

Watson's science of behavior dismissed consciousness as a pseudoscientific variable with no relevance to experimental psychology. In the early years of American psychology, introspective investigations into mental life seemed for many to be too theoretical, too unreliable, and too great a luxury for an emerging psychological science. As an infant science striving for its own autonomy, American psychology had all the pressures on it that one might expect for a new entrepreneurial venture. In other words, psychology would have to get on with the business of producing practical results. Born under these pressures, it is hardly surprising that behaviorism remained a distinctly American affair throughout twentieth-century psychology, driven by the character of a nation that was clearly more pragmatic, practical, and industrious than it was philosophical and reflective. It was partly for this reason that the mental sciences of Wilhelm Wundt and William James were permitted only a brief opportunity to win the favor of their American investors—primarily colleges and universities and the federal government.

Despite James's mentalistic approach to psychology as set forth in his *Principles of Psychology* (1890), one finds there several themes that would also figure prominently in Watson's behaviorism. For example, James drew the connection between consciousness and human action in clearly functionalist terms. The classical structuralist/functionalist distinction in the history of experimental psychology stresses the role James played in the transition from psychology as a science of consciousness to psychology as a science of behavior. Wundt in Germany and Titchener in the United States sought general structural laws describing the mental organization of a detached consciousness. James's functionalism, on the other hand, reflected the practical spirit of American progressivism, where consciousness was framed in functionalist terms as an aid in the advance of humankind. As historian John M. O'Donnell writes, "While Titchener viewed psychology in terms of a systematic theory of logic, both philosophers and practically oriented psychologists were looking at mind in the light of Darwin's theory of adaptation. . . . William James had treated mind not as an entity, as had Titchener, but as a functional activity of the organism" (p. 11).

As a bridge between the existing science of mind and the developing science of behaviorism, James's functionalism represented the impact Darwinism would have on making psychology a natural science. Although James articulated a phenomenology of mind and worked to avoid a reductionism of human experience, he nevertheless agreed that human action was, like all organized systems in nature, the product of external forces that could be measured, described, and ultimately manipulated. Thus James's move to eliminate the study of consciousness as an independent, causal realm was quickly followed in turn by Watson's move to eliminate the study of consciousness from psychology altogether. As Watson (1913) noted, "Psychology as the behaviorist views it is a purely objective experimental branch of natural science. . . . Introspection forms no essential part of its methods, nor is the scientific value of its data dependent upon the readiness with which they lend themselves to interpretation in terms of consciousness" (p. 158).

The impact of Darwin's naturalism on American psychology took its most organized form as *comparative psychology*. The influence of comparative psychology in the origins of behaviorism was obvious in Watson's successful use of animals in his 1903 dissertation at the University of Chicago entitled *Animal Education*, and in his first book, *Behavior: An Introduction to Comparative Psychology* (1914). Comparative psychology, with its stress on continuity of species and on parsimony in the explanation of complex behavior, had both philosophical and methodological relevance for the possibility of a natural science of behavior. Its philosophical import is clear in James's functionalism, for example, in which humans are seen as being subject to the same natural laws governing the behavior of other organisms. Its methodological import concerns the question of how to derive scientific principles that accurately describe nature's governance of human action. To be sure, a natural science must have experimental control over its subject matter, and thus the prospect of isolating general laws of human behavior would be greatly enhanced if these principles could be observed first in animals.

The comparative approach nevertheless remained unpopular during Watson's reign over psychology, be-

ing viewed as too restrictive an analogue of human behavior. Indeed, this is among the reasons why Watson went on to champion a new school of psychology in 1913, which relied on the main assumptions of comparative psychology but also departed from it by stressing the contributions experimental psychology would make in the realm of everyday human affairs. The rise of Watsonian behaviorism, as it would be called, was about more than placing psychology on a sound scientific footing. Behaviorism promised to be practical and relevant to producing outcomes of obvious public utility. Watson's later success in advertising reflects not only the skills of persuasion that made him the pioneer of behaviorism, but also his commitment to psychology as an applied discipline.

From the Conditioned Response to the Free Operant

Watsonian behaviorism, which has also been called eliminative behaviorism or metaphysical behaviorism, can be differentiated from the *methodological behaviorism* of many experimentalists at the time. Methodological behaviorism involves a reliance on Watson's methodological principles, but holds that consciousness is also causally related to behavior. As B. F. Skinner wrote (1974), "Most of the psychologists at the time [of Watson] believed they were studying mental processes in a mental world of consciousness, and they were naturally not inclined to agree with Watson" (p. 3).

An even more divergent break from Watsonian behaviorism was Tolman's *molar behaviorism*, which was an experimental analysis of animal behavior that emphasized the causal role of intervening variables, such as purpose and insight. Meanwhile, with the rise of logical positivism in the 1920s and 1930s, currents of behaviorism were also being felt in philosophy. Most important was the development of *analytical* or *logical behaviorism*, which derives from the eliminative philosophies put forward in Gilbert Ryle's *The Concept of Mind* (1949) and, to a lesser extent, Ludwig Wittgenstein's *Philosophical Investigations* (1953).

Because the vast majority of work undertaken in the name of behaviorism in the first half of the twentieth century was in fact of a methodological sort, B. F. Skinner eventually defined all variants of Watsonian behaviorism as methodological behaviorism, which he then distinguished from his own *radical behaviorism*. Radical behaviorism was distinguishable in part because it gave greater attention to "private events," a category into which Skinner collapsed consciousness, feelings, states of mind, purpose, and thought. Skinner "behavioralized" private events by treating them as natural phenomena, products of our biogenetic and personal history, with the same functional attributes as public stimuli and responses.

The thrust of Watson's experimental work centered

on his application of the conditioned response, as developed earlier by Russians Ivan Petrovich Pavlov and Vladimir Mihailovich Bekhterev, to the formation of habit. Watson conceptualized learning in terms of the strengthening of habits, which could be studied experimentally by conditioning responses through associative pairing. Most notable here was Watson's study of conditioned emotion, where a basic emotion such as fear is transferred to a neutral or positively meaningful stimulus. In the famous case of little Albert, this consisted of pairing a loud noise that frightened Albert, with a white rat that initially did not frighten him; following this pairing, Albert reacted fearfully to the presence of the white rat, even when presented alone (Watson & Rayner, 1920). Watson believed a conditioning process of this sort was necessary and therefore responsible for the development of an individual's emotional life.

Also influenced by Pavlov's early associative conditioning and the notion of habit strength, as employed by Watson, was Yale University professor Clark L. Hull (1884–1952). Hull's contribution to the emerging science of psychology was the concept of drive reduction, which stated that the learning of habit occurs when a response that produces a stimulus results in drive reduction, at which time the significance of the stimulus changes. Apart from his theory of drive reduction, Hull's behaviorism is best known for its highly deductive approach—the hypotheticodeductive approach—which represented the hope at the time that scientific psychology could produce a grand quantitative theory of behavior. The immense popularity and influence of Hull's work in experimental psychology during the 1940s showed that this hope was shared throughout much of the psychological community. Ultimately, however, the complexity of Hull's theory was found to greatly outweigh its explanatory power, and the theory gradually faded into the annals of history.

By 1959, all the great learning theorists had died, including Watson and neobehaviorists Tolman, Guthrie, and Hull. The one chief exception was B. F. Skinner, who at the time of Hull's death in 1952 was only midway through a career that would span more than 60 years.

As much as one might assume the different schools of behaviorism to have more in common than not, the differences between Hullian and Skinnerian behaviorism were considerable. The influences of Francis Bacon and physicists Earnst Mach and P. W. Bridgman on Skinner's philosophy of science were not shared by Hull, for example, and they led Skinner to develop a highly inductive approach to studying behavior. While Hull's hypotheticodeductive approach put theory in a position of driving science, Skinner's inductive approach put science in the position of driving theory. Psychology historian Laurence D. Smith (1986) writes, "Because of Skinner's inductivist, radical empiricist approach, his work enjoyed little popularity during psychology's Age of Theory; but once the elaborate theoretical systems began to fall from favor in the fifties, Skinner's approach made him well suited to succeed Hull as the dominant figure in behaviorism" (p. 259).

The inductive approach also meant a shift away from the classical unit of study in behaviorism, the conditioned response. In Thorndike's early studies of trial-and-error learning, the behavior under study was instrumental rather than reflexive or respondent. This meant that behavior was not derived from unconditioned responses already existing in the animal's repertoire (e.g., a fear response), but rather from its function, as defined by the context in which behavior occurred. Skinner returned to this instrumental approach with the free operant, which he defined in his 1935 article, as "type R" conditioning (as opposed to "type S" or respondent conditioning; Skinner defined the "operant" in 1938 in The Behavior of Organisms). In Hull's research, as in earlier studies of respondent conditioning, the experimenter controlled the presentation of the reinforcer. In the free operant arrangement, however, it was the behaving organism that determined when the reinforcer or punisher was presented, by responding or not responding.

This shift to operational responses allowed Skinner to move away from the Hull's mechanistic approach to behavior to an approach that emphasized contingency in learning. The notion of contingency refers to the environmental contingencies that define an existing relationship between behavior and reinforcing or punishing stimuli. By building such a contingency into the experimental setting, Skinner made a crucial move away from the study of a circumscribed set of evolutionarily specified responses (i.e., unconditioned, elicited responses) to the kinds of stimuli and responses that have a local function, defined by the contingencies of the prevailing environment. Using arbitrarily defined reinforcement schedules and operant responses (e.g., lever presses or key pecks), for example, Skinner and others were able to study the "natural lines of fracture" that constitute different units of behavior, rather than dictating them via the use of eliciting stimuli. Indeed, this set of procedures revealed that orderly relations emerge between behavior and the prevailing contingencies of reinforcement. Such discoveries were seen as important (1) because they demonstrated the possibility of identifying lawful relations between behavior and the local environment, and (2) they allowed for an experimental analysis into the origins of complex and diverse behavioral repertoires that such environments produce.

Operant Psychology and Behavior Analysis

Skinner's influence in psychology began with his philosophy of science, radical behaviorism, and his study of the operant as the basic unit of experimental analysis. This work quickly led to a number of empirical generalizations and conceptual developments that together formed the empirical and philosophical foundations of Skinner's neobehaviorist enterprise. Most influential here has been the empirical branch, which is referred to today as *behavior analysis*. As an organized group of teachers, scientists, and practitioners, behavior analysis has become the most prominent organization of behaviorism. Behavior analysis includes the basic science of operant psychology—the experimental analysis of behavior—and specific applied sciences, including applied behavior analysis, behavioral therapy, behavioral pharmacology and toxicology, and organizational behavior management. Journals serving these areas of research include, among others, *Behavior Analysis, Journal of the Experimental Analysis of Behavior, Journal of Applied Behavior Analysis, Behavior Therapy, Behavioural Pharmacology,* and *Journal of Organizational Behavior Management.*

Skinner believed, however, that his discoveries went well beyond the psychology of the individual to include the philosophy of science and the study of society and culture. Social psychologist Robert Lana (1991) notes, for example, that "most of the questions [Skinner] raises and attempts to answer are epistemological to a greater degree than almost any other psychological theorist of this century." Skinner's popularization of these ideas in books (1948, 1971, and 1974) represent this ambition to apply behavioral principles to larger world issues. And while it is clear that these efforts succeeded in making Skinner a wealthy, known, and often controversial figure, it also seems clear that this vulgarization of behaviorism kept him from earning the kind of careful study from scholars outside of behavior analysis that his earlier radical ideas required. Instead, these ideas have become simplified in the course of popularization, both within and outside of psychology, which has made for considerable misunderstanding and often superficial discussion.

Radical Behaviorism Misunderstood

The misunderstandings that have persisted for radical behaviorism began early with its most fundamental empirical principle, *reinforcement*. As widely recognized as this concept has become, there appears to be a considerable gap between what has been developed within radical-behaviorist theory and what is known, understood, and taught within the larger field of psychology. For example, most psychologists, by focusing on the

functionalism of the operant, interpret reinforcement in terms of how consequences of behavior, reinforcers and punishers, alter the future strength of behavior—as would be defined, not by Skinner's principle of reinforcement, but by Thorndike's *law of effect*. For example, introductory and learning texts often define a "reinforcer [as] anything that strengthens the behavior that leads to it" (Leahy & Harris, Englewood Cliffs, NJ, 1997). Consequently, the notion of operant conditioning is often thought only to mean that behavior occurs because of its stimulus consequences, when in fact, according to radical behaviorists, no instance of operant behavior can be explained in this way. According to Skinner's *three-term contingency*, consequences do not alter the strength of the response, but rather alter the strength of a relationship; i.e., a relationship between antecedent stimuli and the behavior that these stimuli come to occasion. Thus, for radical behaviorism, while the consequences of responding are enormously influential, they are influential only because they alter the significance (i.e., the meaning) of antecedent stimuli that come before behavior and guide it into effective action.

One implication of Skinner's three-term contingency that has been missed as a result of its popularization concerns the battle against the role of *teleology* in psychological theory. The notion that reinforcers strengthen behavior and that punishers weaken it has encouraged the idea that behavior is motivated toward reinforcers and away from punishers, implying that present actions are somehow governed by future events. Psychological textbooks often use teleological examples of reinforcement, such as "a rat jumping over a barrier to escape an electric shock" or "a pigeon . . . trained to hop on a treadle to get some grain." Radical behaviorists note, however, that if reinforcement is to be a scientific principle that adheres to traditional notions of causality, reinforcers and punishers must be defined in terms of how they alter the *future* probability of behavior, which they do only indirectly by altering the significance of stimuli, both public and private, that come before behavior.

Rather than explaining behavior by the immediate consequences that the behavior produces, Skinner argued that behavior can be explained only by taking into account the discriminative control exerted by the environment, which in turn can be explained only by the organism's history of reinforcement. The environmental selection of behavior by reinforcement shapes the individual organism's behavior to adapt to the significant aspects of its environment, just as the selection of morphological traits by natural selection shapes organisms over time to adapt to particular aspects of their ecological niche. Defining stimuli and responses in this way—in generic terms—helps explain how they acquire functions appropriate to the prevailing environment, especially with regard to the highly variable, socially constructed environments that define human cultures. Hence Skinner's (1935) conclusion that "an infinitely large number of stimuli may . . . be made to evoke the same response, but there need be no common property among them except that of being a stimulus . . . and no distinction is, as we have said, possible when we do not know the history of the organism" (Skinner, 1972, p. 462).

A related aspect of reinforcement theory that has been important for radical behaviorism, and that also appears to be poorly understood outside of this community, concerns the question of whether reinforcement can account for more abstract forms of learning, such as concept learning and novel behavior. Consider the case of modeling, as when a young child imitates something seen on television. Psychologists have often pointed to phenomena of this sort as an example of novel behavior that cannot be explained by the concept of reinforcement. Radical behaviorists have responded, however, that this criticism follows only when one conceptualizes reinforcement as a two-term process in which consequences strengthen behavior. When reinforcement is defined instead in terms of the relationship between behavior and the environment (outlined above), the possibility of a more molar process taking place is said to arise.

Behavior analysts have researched this notion by creating contingencies that specify a more conceptual relationship between behavior and the environment, rather than reinforcing a specific, topographically defined behavior. For example, studies have set up contingencies that reinforce behavior that differs in its topography from all other recent behaviors, such as when a pigeon must make a sequence of three responses on a nine-panel grid that differs from all recent sequences. If what is reinforced and punished here are the responses correlated with the presentation of the reinforcer, the organism would never succeed in learning, since any behavior that met the requirement of novelty would be reinforced and thus strengthened; i.e., it would become more likely to occur, but since it is not novel, it would no longer meet the specified contingency.

Such studies are now thought to have demonstrated that both animals and humans are indeed sensitive to molar contingencies, confirming the view of radical behaviorists that the process of reinforcement describes more than just the rewarding of, say, a specific act of imitation or modeling. What appears to be learned instead is the nature of the relationship between the act and the environment in which it has been reinforced (or punished). This means that if the environmental contingency is a simple one, a simple environment-behavior relationship is learned; if the contingency is a more complex or abstract one, a more conceptual environment-behavior relationship may be learned (i.e., with enough experience, the child learns the more molar contingency of "imitation," rather than specific acts that we call imitation).

The Death of Behaviorism

The oversimplification of reinforcement theory by researchers, scholars, and the public has contributed, behaviorists believe, to the rise of other explanatory concepts that are thought to explain much the same behavioral phenomena. Radical behaviorists also believe that the vulgarization of behavioral principles underlies the waning influence of behaviorism and the claim that behaviorism is for all intents and purposes dead. To understand these claims one must also consider the relationship between behaviorism and the philosophical movement of logical positivism.

The rise of logical positivism as a philosophy of natural science was linked with the rise of Watsonian (and logical) behaviorism, such that the fate of one appeared to be inexorably tied to the other. The tendency for critics of behaviorism, especially in the philosophy of science and the philosophy of mind, to draw a connection between these two schools stemmed from the fact that both jettisoned metaphysical explanations in science and gave a central role to the practices of operationalism or verificationism. As historian Laurence D. Smith notes, "Edwin G. Boring, America's most eminent historian of psychology, treated behaviorism, behavioristics, operational psychology, and logical positivism as though they were but aspects of a single movement" (p. 6). The significance of this connection between logical positivism and behaviorism is important in that it has allowed the inadequacies and eventual collapse of logical positivism in the philosophy of science to prove, or at least to imply, the inadequacies of behaviorism as a psychological system.

The link between the philosophy of logical positivism and the science of behaviorism is, however, a more tenuous one. In the case of Skinner, this relationship was almost exclusively a critical one, a fact that appears to have been overlooked inside and outside psychology, despite Skinner's well-known (1945) paper on the subject. Challenging the operational assumptions of logical positivism, Skinner argued that the question of truth in science has less to do with logical agreement about observable events and more to do with developing a set of empirical principals that, when applied, bring law and order to the subject matter. Thus, contrary to logical positivism's commitment to a logical analysis, Skinner's approach was much more empirical and inductive, stating that description and control will bring people into agreement about what should be considered true and false, not an *a priori* operationalizing of scientific terms. As in the case of defining stimuli and responses in generic terms, where the ecology of the working environment determines the particular categories of stimuli and responses, Skinner believed that the behavior of the scientist should be governed primarily by experiences with the subject matter, not primarily by experiences between scientists. Thus, relying on the empirical epistemology of Skinner, some scholars have concluded that the failings of logical positivism do not imply the end of behaviorism, at least not the behaviorist philosophy of science Skinner called radical behaviorism.

Conclusions

There can be little doubt that behaviorism is no longer the driving force in psychological science it once was. Watson's and Skinner's hopes for a science of behavior based on observable relations between behavior and environment have been thwarted by psychology's, and to a large extent the lay public's, desire for more cognitive explanations of human action. However, the philosophy of radical behaviorism and the practice of behavior analysis still appear to be vital in and outside of psychology. Although no single behaviorist has emerged to don Skinner's robes as champion of the behaviorist cause, the areas of behavioral epistemology, the experimental analysis of behavior, and applied behavior analysis remain active, even vibrant, fields of study. In fact, the application of behavior-analytic principles to solving applied problems in fields such as child development, business, education, and drug abuse continues to expand at ever-increasing rates. Perhaps this, more than anything else, is testimony to the utility of behaviorism in advancing psychology's role in understanding and changing, for better or worse, human thought and action.

[See also Applied Behavior Analysis; Behavior Analysis; Behavior Therapy; Cognitive-Behavioral Therapy; Psychology, articles on Early Twentieth Century and Post–World War II; and the biographies of Pavlov and Skinner.]

Bibliography

Donahoe, J. W., & Palmer, D. C. (1994). Learning and complex behavior. New York: Allyn & Bacon.

Freeman, M., & Locurto, C. (1994). In Skinner's wake: Behaviorism, poststructuralism, and the ironies of intellectual discourse. New Ideas in Psychology, 12, 39–56.

Guthrie, E. R. (1935). The psychology of learning. New York: Harper & Row.

Hilgard, E. R. (1987). Psychology in America: A historical survey. New York: Harcourt Brace Jovanovich.

Hull, C. L. (1943). Principles of behavior. New York: Appleton-Century-Crofts.

James, W. (1890). Principles of psychology (Vols. 1–2). New York: Holt.

Lana, R. E. (1991). Assumptions of social psychology: A reexamination. Hillsdale, NJ: Erlbaum.

O'Donnell, J. M. (1985). The origins of behaviorism: American psychology, 1870–1920. New York: New York University Press.

Page, S., & Neuringer, A. (1985). Variability as an operant. Journal of Experimental Psychology: Animal Behavior Processes, 11, 429–452.

Palmer, D. C., & Donahoe, J. W. (1992). Essentialism and selectionism in cognitive science and behavior analysis. American Psychologist, 47, 1344–1358.

Ringen, J. D. (1993). Critical naturalism and the philosophy of psychology. New Ideas in Psychology, 11, 153–177.

Ryle, G. (1949). The concept of mind. New York: Barnes & Noble.

Skinner, B. F. (1935). The generic nature of the concepts of stimulus and response. The Journal of General Psychology, 12, 40–65.

Skinner, B. F. (1938). The behavior of organisms: An experimental analysis. New York: Appleton-Century-Crofts.

Skinner, B. F. (1945). The operational analysis of psychological terms. Psychological Review, 52, 270–277, 291–294.

Skinner, B. F. (1948). Walden two. New York: Macmillan.

Skinner, B. F. (1950). Are theories of learning necessary? Psychological Review, 57, 193–216.

Skinner, B. F. (1953). Science and human behavior. New York: Free Press.

Skinner, B. F. (1966). The phylogeny and ontogeny of behavior. Science, 153, 1205–1213.

Skinner, B. F. (1971). Beyond freedom and dignity. New York: Knopf.

Skinner, B. F. (1972). Cumulative record: A selection of papers. New York: Appleton-Century-Crofts.

Skinner, B. F. (1974). About behaviorism. New York: Knopf.

Skinner, B. F. (1981). Selection by consequences. Science, 213, 501–504.

Skinner, B. F. (1987). Upon further reflection. Englewood Cliffs, NJ: Prentice-Hall.

Smith, L. D. (1986). Behaviorism and logical positivism: A reassessment of the alliance. Stanford, CA: Stanford University Press.

Todd, J. T., & Morris, E. K. (1992). Case histories in the great power of steady misrepresentation. American Psychologist, 47, 1441–1453.

Tolman, E. C. (1949). There is more than one kind of learning. Psychological Review, 56, 144–155.

Watson, J. B., & Rayner, R. (1920). Conditioned emotional reactions. Journal of Experimental Psychology, 3, 1–14.

Wittgenstein, L. (1953). Philosophical investigations. Oxford, UK: Basil Blackwell.

Zuriff, B. E. (1979). Ten inner causes. Behaviorism, 7, 1–8.

Richard J. DeGrandpré and William Buskist

BEHAVIOR MODIFICATION. See Cognitive-Behavioral Therapy.

BEHAVIOR THERAPY. From 1940 through the 1960s, there were many concerns in the mental health field about the dominant views of abnormal behavior that held sway in both psychiatry and clinical psychology. The two main objections were that the dominant views presented a disease model of psychopathology and that they lacked a scientific basis for practice and research, particularly as typified by the psychodynamic and humanistic approaches. Behavior therapy, or behavior modification, emerged as a reaction to these views. It must be emphasized, however, that both the psychodynamic and humanistic approaches now have effective psychological techniques of assessment and treatment, many of which have been well documented by research data on outcome. The introduction of behavior therapy has stimulated a wealth of research and theories into the causes, course, and characteristics of various types of abnormal behavior. Its impact has changed the whole face of psychiatry, clinical psychology, and our thinking about aberrant behavior.

A popular definition of behavior therapy said that it applied the principle of learning theory to abnormal behavior. This definition was not universally accepted, and there was considerable debate on what constituted an acceptable definition. It is usually agreed that behavior therapy is a scientific approach to the assessment and modification of abnormal behavior, a definition broad enough to include development of cognitive approaches.

The History of Behavior Therapy

It has been said that behavior therapy has a "long past but a short history" (Franks & Wilson, 1973). For example, Pliny the Elder used aversion strategies such as placing dead spiders in the bottom of the cup of the unfortunate person he was attempting to "cure" of alcoholism. The best known example in modern times, however, is the famous case of Peter by Mary Cover Jones (1924). Jones used performance of responses incompatible with anxiety (eating) while the feared stimulus (a rabbit) was gradually brought closer to the client. This was a forerunner of systematic desensitization, an effective and popular treatment procedure developed by Joseph Wolpe (Wolpe & Lazarus, 1966). Dunlap (1932) used "negative practice" in the 1930s where an undesirable motor habit was repeated over and over in order to eliminate it. Guthrie (1935) also drew attention to the use of a counterconditioning method as a tool to change behavior.

The three key figures in the development of behavior therapy were Ivan P. Pavlov, John B. Watson, and B. F. Skinner. Although other individuals contributed to the growth and development of behavior therapy, these three people initiated the philosophy and research base of the movement. It was Pavlov's work with classical conditioning that energized the behavioral movement and his study on experimental neuroses that demonstrated that these principles were applicable to abnormal behavior. Watson was the spokesperson for "behaviorism" and a critic of the internal or unobservable causes of behavior. Skinner contributed the techniques of operant conditioning as development of the single case or N = 1 designs. In single-case designs, where the individual serves as his or her own control, some guesses about cause-and-effect relationships are allowed. These designs were used frequently in feasibility studies of various behavioral techniques, although they have faded in popularity. These pioneers stimulated the second generation of innovators such as Wolpe, Bandura, Kanfer, and many others who began to develop the techniques which became the arsenal of behavior therapy. It is worth mentioning that most of these early techniques were derived from animal research.

In the last two decades of the twentieth century, behavior therapy has been contaminated by cognitive theorists and practitioners such as Aaron Beck, Albert Ellis, and others. Although behavior therapy has always had cognitive theorists, the tremendous influence of the cognitive movement has caused some concern among some of its exponents because they viewed the movement as a regression to "mentalism" or, even worse, to the "talk" therapies so foreign to the basic assumptions of behavior therapy. These fears have been largely groundless, and the majority of therapists now refer to themselves as cognitive-behavioral therapists. Thus there are three rather broad overlapping camps in behavior therapy: the Skinnerians who refer to themselves as behavior modifiers; the cognizance experts, who refer to themselves as cognitive-behavioral therapists; and the classic behavior therapists.

The new movement in the 1960s was associated with the initiation of a new Association for the Advancement of Behavior Therapy (ABBT), which was open to all professionals with an interest in behavior therapy. The Association of Applied Behavioral Analysis, which catered to people with a Skinnerian orientation, began at a similar time. New journals were developed, such as *Behavior Therapy* and *Experimental Psychiatry*. Reflecting this renewed interest in cognitive factors, ABBT started its own journal entitled *Cognitive Research and Therapy*.

Techniques of Behavior Therapy

Eysenck's famous article (1952) on the effect of psychotherapy called for behavior therapists to develop treatment techniques that were short-term and effective. One of the first of these procedures was presented in Meyer's classic article (1957) on the treatment of two phobia patients using learning principles. From the 1950s through the 1970s a large number of publications described a variety of treatment techniques with various disorders.

Anxiety and Phobic Disorders. Phobias were the "bread and butter" cases for behavior therapists because they were amenable to a variety of learning techniques. Simple phobias were very successfully treated with systematic desensitization, flooding, exposure, shaping, assertiveness training, modeling and/or guided participation, and even cognitive restructuring. A number of analog and clinical studies consistently demonstrated the effectiveness of these techniques with anxiety disorders, particularly the simple phobias.

In 1988, Barlow developed a very comprehensive program to treat panic disorder and panic disorders cum agoraphobia. This program requires 12 to 15 sessions and is highly effective with these disorders. Similar techniques have worked effectively on children suffering from similar anxiety disorders such as school phobias. The behavior programs are more effective typically than are drug therapies, with less chance for relapses. Behavior therapy has had splendid success with the anxiety disorders and is or should be considered the treatment of choice.

Obsessive-Compulsive Disorders. "Washers and checkers" have been considered notoriously resistant to psychological or psychiatric intervention. The usual techniques of anxiety reduction did not seem to work even though obsessive-compulsive disorders are considered to be an anxiety disorder. In his classic 1966 article Vic Meyer first described the use of response prevention and flooding as treatment techniques for compulsive rituals, which proved to be effective methods for stopping or decreasing these repetitions. Later works by Edna Foa and Samuel Turner demonstrated the value of these procedures. Obsessions without rituals, however, proved to be more difficult to treat effectively. While a number of behavioral techniques such as "thought stopping" have been used, no technique has proved to be completely satisfactory with that disorder.

Sexual Inadequacy and Deviance. The treatment of sexual inadequacy by behavior therapists has been consistent with the work of Masters and Johnson (1970), using sensate focus, relaxation, and a helpful partner for impotence and female inorgasmic disorder and the "squeeze" technique for premature ejaculation. While Masters and Johnson (1970) and Wolpe and Lazarus (1966) have reported high rates of success with these techniques, it has become increasingly obvious that many of these disorders have biological etiology, and the psychological basis has been overestimated, particularly with male impotence. Nevertheless, these techniques have become useful procedures in the armory of sex therapists.

A major contribution of behavior therapy was the treatment of sexual deviations where traditional psychological techniques had little to offer. At first, the focus was on reducing deviant sexual arousal in voy-

euristic individuals, exposers, pedophiles, and patients with similar disorders through the use of aversion techniques such as electric shock, ammonia, and covert sensitization. However, it soon became obvious that unless the development of a satisfactory sexual life was included in these programs, relapse would be likely to occur. Later programs included techniques similar to those used to treat impotence as part of the treatment package. These often included a sex partner who was willing to reorient the individual to a normal sexual activity. An innovation has been to include relapse prevention in the package (Laws, 1989). Stimulus satiation, ammonia aversion, sensate focus, cognitive restructuring, and relapse prevention have been the typical treatment programs offered for these disorders by most behavioral therapists. In general, these programs appear to be effective. For instance, in the Vermont Treatment Programs for Sexual Aggressors (a prison program), Pithers and Cumming (1989) reported only a 4% relapse (reoffense) rate for 167 patients over a 6-year period.

Alcoholism and Drug Addiction. The treatment of addictions, like sexual deviations, has been dominated by the use of aversion techniques. This idea was made popular in the 1930s by Voeglin and his colleagues (Voeglin, 1940). The patient is administered a nausea-inducing drug, either orally or by injection, and asked to drink alcohol. This procedure was fairly successful, with an abstinence rate in the 50% range. This procedure, however, is rarely used anymore, although Anabuse, a drug causing nausea if alcohol is ingested, is common in many treatment programs. Although some behavior therapists have used electric shock, covert sensitization—where drinking is paired with unpleasant imagery—has received much attention.

With the recognition that some alcoholics return to normal drinking and the belief that "one drink then drunk" was probably false, some behavior therapists, including the Sobells, attempted to train problem drinkers to drink modestly. This social drinking program caused outrage among members of Alcoholics Anonymous (AA), who insisted that alcoholism was a disease and that alcoholics could never drink at all. The result was a political and perhaps scientific war with claims of "faking data" that were investigated by the Canadian government and the U.S. Congress. Perhaps the best outcome of this situation was a recognition that there may be some alcoholics who are not suitable for social drinking programs, but many are. However, such claims do elicit a very strong negative response from AA. Another major advance in this area has been the development and implementation of a relapse prevention component to various treatment programs. This relapse prevention aspect increases the efficiency of alcohol treatment programs. The behavioral treatment of other drug addictions are very similar to the alcohol program with some modifications. [*See* Alcoholics Anonymous; *and* Alcoholism.]

Psychoses. The modification of psychotic behavior, particularly schizophrenia, has been of interest to most behavior therapists from the beginning of the movement. Ayllon and Michael's classic article (1959), describing the use of operant principles to eliminate psychotic talk, how to approach self-feeding, and similar problems with hospitalized schizophrenic patients was followed by the development of "token economies" to shape appropriate behavior in hospitalized patients. Perhaps the most comprehensive and best designed clinical study in psychology is the Paul and Lentz (1977) comparison of social learning programs (token economy programs), milieu therapy, and standard hospital treatment of chronic schizophrenic patients. The results were quite clear. Even in the absence of psychotropic drugs, social learning was the treatment of choice by far, and it was even more cost effective than the other two. It is particularly important that this program included training manuals for staff and a variety of assessment tools both to evaluate the patients and monitor staff compliance with the program. While this program is the treatment of choice for patients hospitalized in clinics, it is no longer available in state hospitals with large numbers of chronic patients.

Other Populations. Behavior therapy has also been successful with a variety of other populations, such as children suffering from enuresis, encopresis, autism, fear and phobias, and mental retardation. Behavior therapy has had a strong impact in behavioral medicine for various problems, from pain control to stress management. Behavioral approaches have been applied in education and industry with good success.

The Future

Is behavior therapy a passing fad that will eventually fade from the scene? Although there is no sure answer to this question, I feel it will continue to be a viable treatment option. When behavioral therapy began to become popular, most people thought of it as the application of learning principles to abnormal behavior. Actually it was much more than this. It was the first application of the basic research in psychology to clinical problems, and this trend has continued. If one looks closely at the behavioral literature, one can see examples of the basic research data in a number of areas—not only learning—being applied to clinical problems from social to cognitive psychology. Behavioral therapy has become like clinical medicine. Even though the term *behavior therapy* may disappear, the application of basic scientific knowledge to psychopathology, which began with behavioral therapy, will continue. The field of assessment and treatment will progress along with the basic research.

[*See also* Applied Behavior Analysis; Behavior Analysis; and Cognitive-Behavioral Therapy.]

Bibliography

Ayllon, T., & Michael, J. (1959). The psychiatric nurse as a behavioral engineer. *Journal of the Experimental Analysis of Behavior, 2,* 323–334.

Barlow, D. H. (1998). *Anxiety and its disorders.* New York: Guilford Press.

Dunlap, K. A. (1932). *Habits: Their making and unmaking.* New York: Liveright.

Eysenck, H. J. (1952). The effects of psychotherapy: An evaluation. *Journal of Consulting Psychology, 16,* 319–324.

Franks, C. M., & Wilson, G. T. (1973). *Annual review of behavioral therapy: Theory and practice, 1973.* New York: Brunner/Mazel.

Guthrie, E. R. (1935). *The psychology of human learning.* New York: Harper Press.

Jones, M. C. (1924). The elimination of children's fears. *Journal of Experimental Psychology, 7,* 382–390.

Laws, D. R. (Ed.). (1989). *Relapse prevention with sexual offenders.* New York: Guilford Press.

Masters, W. H., & Johnson, V. E. (1970). *Human sexual inadequacy.* Boston: Little, Brown.

Meyer, V. (1957). The treatment of two phobic patients on the basis of learning principles. *Journal of Abnormal and Social Psychology, 55,* 261–266.

Paul, G. L., & Lentz, R. J. (1977). *Psychosocial treatment of chronic mental patients.* Cambridge, MA.: Harvard University Press.

Pithers, W. D., & Cumming, G. F. (1989). Can relapses be prevented? Initial data from the Vermont Treatment Program for Sexual Aggressors. In D. R. Laws (Ed.), *Relapse prevention with sexual aggressors.* New York: Guilford Press.

Voegtlin, W. L. (1940). The treatment of alcoholism by establishing a conditioned reflex. *American Journal of Mental Science, 199,* 802–810.

Wolpe, J., & Lazarus, A. A. (1966). *Behavior therapy techniques.* New York: Pergamon Press.

Henry E. Adams

BÉKÉSY, GEORG VON (1899–1972), Hungarian sensory scientist. Born in Budapest on 3 June 1899, to Alexander and Paula von Békésy, the former a diplomat, Georg graduated in chemistry from the University of Bern (Switzerland) in 1916 and obtained his doctorate in physics with a thesis on interference microscopy from the University of Budapest in 1923. The best-equipped laboratory in Hungary after World War I belonged to the Hungarian Post and Telegraph service. Békésy worked there until 1946 apart from one year spent in Berlin (1926–1927). He also had an appointment at the University of Budapest from 1932 to 1946. Being psychologically traumatized by the Nazi occupation of Budapest in 1944, followed by the Communist occupation in 1945, he was relieved to be invited the following year to work at the Karolinska Institute in Stockholm, Sweden, where he might have stayed indefinitely had it not been that in 1947 S. S. Stevens (1906–1973) arranged a nonfaculty research position for him at the Psycho-Acoustic Laboratory at Harvard University. Békésy was awarded the Nobel Prize in Physiology or Medicine in 1961. Békésy stayed at Harvard until 1966, when he accepted a Professorship of Sensory Sciences that had been offered to him initially in 1963 by the University of Hawaii. A lifelong bachelor, he died on 13 June 1972 in Honolulu. He bequeathed his extensive collection of works of art to the Nobel Foundation in Stockholm in gratitude for their having given him the prize.

His most important papers, including some translated from German, are included in his *Experiments in Hearing* (New York, 1960). This book documents his achievements in microsurgery, audiometry, comparative anatomy, and biophysics. But it also documents much research that is of special interest to psychologists; the page numbers below refer to that book.

In 1930 he reasoned that Fechner's Law of 1860, concerning the way *sensations* increase in intensity more slowly than the corresponding *stimuli* increase in intensity, might rest upon the fact that increasing the intensity of a stimulus brings into play an increasing number of sensory receptors, yielding sensations that change in a quantumlike manner (pp. 238–257).

In 1931 he utilized the concept of a "conscious present" of 0.8 to 1.2 seconds, a concept analogous to William James's "specious present" of 1890, to explain why, if the *physical* intensity of a tone faded continuously over a second or more, the apparent loudness (*psychological* intensity) of the tone faded continuously for up to about 0.8 to 1.2 seconds, at which point the loudness dropped unexpectedly before recovering to resume its continuous decrease. Békésy also asserted that optimal acoustics could be obtained in concert halls if sounds reflected off the walls and ceilings "met" the sounds directed outward by the musicians toward the audience within the time frame of the average duration of the "conscious present" of the members of the audience (pp. 369–392).

In 1928 he began a series of studies in which he showed, both by observing the cochleas from fresh cadavers of various species, and by building mechanical models designed to behave like the cochlea, that, when a sound causes the stapes (the stirrup-bone) indirectly to agitate the fluid in the coiled cochlea, a certain region of the basilar membrane is displaced downward then upward, forming a sinusoidal vibration extending over that region. This movement may also be modeled as being the result of a "traveling wave" that causes a maximum displacement at that region; the location of the region depends on the frequency of the tone, the width of the basilar membrane (which widens toward the apex of the cochlea, the narrower part near the stapes being joined to the cochlea wall by bone), and the elasticity of the membrane (which decreases in stiffness, the farther the region is from the stapes).

Békésy also suggested in 1928 that the sensation of the tone might be sharpened by lateral inhibition, which Ernst Mach (1838–1916) postulated might account for Mach bands in visual sensation and which Békésy himself demonstrated might explain the two-point threshold on the skin. But about 40 years later, both in his *Sensory Inhibition* (Princeton, NJ, 1967), and in his article entitled "Similarities of Inhibition in the Different Sense Organs" (*American Psychologist*, 1969, 24, 707–719), even though he himself had shown how lateral inhibition might also sharpen sensations of taste and smell, he scarcely mentioned the question of whether lateral inhibition in the cochlea served to sharpen pitch sensations.

In 1942 he showed that the presence of Reissner's membrane did dampen the upward movement of the basilar membrane when it was stimulated by a tone, but the dampening was small except for tones whose frequencies exceeded 3,000 cps (pp. 429–469).

In 1958 he wrote a general article on how neural summation and inhibition at the periphery could "funnel" information to the brain, presumably to reduce sensory overload. But he added that, at a higher level in the nervous system, neural interactions took place that determined how the subject *localized* the sources of sensations. It had been known since the 1920s that the localization of a sound depends on slight differences in the arrival times at the two ears of the sound waves from that source. But Békésy extended this finding to the two fingers, the two nostrils, and two regions of the tongue; *where* a touch, smell, or taste appeared to originate depended on time-differences in the moment at which each of the two fingers, nostrils, or tongue regions was stimulated (pp. 609–634).

Békésy therefore proved the general truth that our abilities to discriminate stimuli of the same sensory modality from each other and to localize them in space depend on neural interactions in the periphery as well as in the brain. But his Nobel Prize was awarded for his more specialized theory of how a traveling wave in the cochlea can yield discrete sensations of pitch.

Bibliography

Bernhard, C. G., (1986). Georg von Békésy and the Karolinska Institute. *Hearing Research, 22,* 13–17. This article discusses Békésy's stay in Stockholm in the 1940s, his receipt of the Nobel Prize in 1961, and his donation of his art collection to the Foundation in 1972.

Moore, B. C. J. (1997). *An introduction to the psychology of hearing* (4th ed.). New York: Academic Press. Discusses how, using new techniques, researchers since Békésy's time have been able to demonstrate that, even though his theory of the traveling wave in the basilar membrane is correct in general, the surgical techniques he used led him to underestimate the degree to which individual neurons responded specifically to individual frequencies.

Newman, E. B. (1973). Georg von Békésy: 1899–1972. *American Journal of Psychology, 86*, 855–857. Obituary by a psychologist who was a colleague of Békésy's during his Harvard years.

Ratliff, F. (1976). Georg von Békésy, June 3, 1899–June 13, 1972. *Biographical memoirs. National Academy of Sciences of the United States of America, 48*, 25–49. This biography is particularly useful for its discussion of Békésy's early research on telephone systems as well as his later research on hearing, and for a list of his academic honors; it also contains a complete bibliography.

Tonndorf, J. (1986). Georg von Békésy and his work. *Hearing Research, 22*, 3–10. This biography stresses Békésy's elegant experimental methods in the context of his contributions to auditory science.

David J. Murray

BEKHTEREV, VLADIMIR MIKHAILOVICH

(1857–1927), Russian neuroanatomist, neuropathologist, psychiatrist, psychologist/reflexologist. Although he has received far less recognition than Ivan Pavlov, Bekhterev probably had more influence than Pavlov on the early, general acceptance of conditioning by psychologists. Bekhterev and his students introduced motor conditioning using animals and humans, which he believed provided a better methodological foundation for psychology than Pavlov's salivary conditioning. Bekhterev's "objective psychology," a sophisticated "behaviorism," influenced John B. Watson's development of behaviorism. Watson devoted his 1914–1915 winter seminar at Johns Hopkins to the 1913 French translation of Bekhterev's *Objective Psychology*, and before World War I prevented it, Watson's protégé, Karl Lashley who had participated in the seminar, was to have worked and studied with Bekhterev in Russia. Watson emphasized Bekhterev's methods, but instead of Bekhterev's term *association reflex* used Pavlov's term *conditioned reflex*, which stamped the latter into the vocabulary of behaviorism and obscured Bekhterev's influence. Further reducing Bekhterev's influence were the suppression of his views and those of his followers in the Soviet Union after his "mysterious" death (see below). However, with glastnost in the former Soviet Union, Bekhterev gained renewed international recognition, especially in social psychology. His textbook in social psychology, *Collective Reflexology, Part I*, received its first English translation in 1994, only the second of Bekhterev's psychological texts ever to be translated into English.

Bekhterev earned a medical doctorate at age 24 from the Military Medical Academy in St. Petersburg. He then studied with leading European scientists such as Jean-Martin Charcot (psychiatry/hypnosis), Emil duBois-Reymond (neurophysiology), Paul Emil Flechsig (neuroanatomy/neuropsychiatry), and Wilhelm Wundt (psychology). Bekhterev accepted the chair in Psychiatry at the University of Kazan in 1885 where he founded Russia's first psychophysiological laboratory and first institute for brain research addressing mental diseases. During his career, he published significant work in neuroanatomy, neurology, and psychology, resulting in more than six hundred articles and books. Several neurological conditions or symptoms and several brain structures were given his name (e.g., "Bekhterev's disease," a spinal cord disability, and "Bekhterev's nucleus," now known as the superior vestibular nucleus). He also founded numerous laboratories, hospitals, clinics, academic institutes, and journals.

Basic research and clinical application were equally important to Bekhterev. His conditioning procedures were used to investigate behavioral and organic abnormalities. His knowledge of hypnosis and skill as a practitioner influenced his theoretical views about social behavior. For example, he compared social suggestion to "psychological infection" which he related to infectious disease, "every personality . . . inoculates others with the peculiarities of his own psychological nature, and . . . takes from them one or another kind of psychological trait" (see Jaan Valsiner's "Introductory Commentary" to *Collective Reflexology*, p. xx).

In 1893, Bekhterev accepted a position at the Military Medical Academy in St. Petersburg where in 1896, he founded the first journal with the term *experimental psychology* in its title, *Review of Psychiatry, Neuropathology, and Experimental Psychology*. In 1907, he founded the Psychoneurological Institute, an independent, highly progressive academic institution with a diverse faculty and a mission to study scientifically all aspects of being human. The institute was exceptionally successful in attracting students, and, notably, women and Jews were admitted, not a common practice at that time.

Bekhterev was in and out of favor with both the tsarist and the postrevolutionary governments. For example, his role in a tsarist-rigged, anti-Semitic trial (the Beilis case, 1911–1912) resulted in Beilis's acquittal but Bekhterev's loss of the Psychoneurological Institute. However, Bekhterev's importance and value were such that by 1917, he was allowed to found the Reflexological Institute for Brain Research. As an expert in neuropathology, he served twice as medical consultant to Vladimir Lenin and once to Joseph Stalin. The latter consultation may have caused Bekhterev's death and the suppression of his influence in Russia (see below).

Like I. M. Sechenov, Russia's "father of physiology," who influenced him, Bekhterev believed that psychology must be methodologically objective and philosophically mechanistic and materialistic (e.g., "mind" reduced to actions of the brain). By 1912, Bekhterev replaced the term *psychology* with the term *reflexology*, because much of psychology was too subjective for him. However, the objectivity of reflexology did not mean a narrower scope. Reflexology was constructed with equal foundations in biology and sociology.

According to Alexander Schneirman ("Bekhterev's Reflexological School" in Murchison's *Psychologies of 1930*, Worcester, MA, 1930, p. 225.) the Reflexological Institute had five divisions, all addressing normal and abnormal behavior. To indicate the breadth of the institute, consider its five divisions: (1) *General reflexology* was the basic science division which was said to be almost physiological; (2) *Individual reflexology* addressed individual variations, personality types, etc.; (3) *Age reflexology* addressed physical and psychological abnormalities associated with child development; (4) *Collective reflexology* was social psychology from a standpoint that included the study of evolutionary and genetic influences; and (5) *Genetic reflexology* was developmental psychology considered from ontogenetic and phylogenetic perspectives.

With glasnost has emerged a strong but perhaps unprovable circumstantial case that Bekhterev's death resulted from poisoning at the direction of Stalin. Despite apparently excellent health, Bekhterev died late the same day he examined Stalin for neuropathology associated with stroke and a dysfunctional arm. Soon after the examination, Bekhterev was overheard to refer to Stalin as a "paranoic with a withered arm." That evening Bekhterev attended the Bolshoi Theater and later became ill. Accounts vary regarding food eaten and with whom he interacted at the Bolshoi, as well as how he was examined and treated by an attending government physician, but there is consensus that there was gastrointestinal involvement and that poisoning was possible. An autopsy hastily arranged by government authorities under highly suspicious circumstances examined only the brain and, then, without cutting it or taking tissue samples. The remainder of the body was cremated without examination.

[*Many of the people mentioned in this article are the subjects of independent biographical entries.*]

Bibliography

Bauer, R. A. (1952). *The new man in Soviet psychology*. Cambridge, MA: Harvard University Press. Addresses issues connecting Bekhterev's and Marxist-Leninist philosophies.

Bekhterev, V. M. (1973). *General principles of human reflexology* (4th ed.). (E. & W. Murphy, Trans.). New York: International. (Original work published 1928; original translation published 1932) This is an abbreviated, updated version of Bekhterev's earlier three-volume work, *Objective Psychology* (1907–1910) which has never been translated into English.

Bekhterev, V. M. (2000). *Collective reflexology: The complete edition*. L. H. Strickland (Ed.) E. Lockwood & A. Lockwood (Trans.). New Brunswick, NJ: Transaction.

Joravsky, D. (1989). *Russian psychology: A critical history*. Oxford, UK: Basil Blackwell. Includes useful information about Bekhterev and about his rivalry with Pavlov.

Kozulin, A. (1984). *Psychology in Utopia: Toward a social history of Soviet psychology*. Cambridge, MA: MIT Press. Includes a useful comparison of the personalities and legacies of Bekhterev and Pavlov.

Misiak, H., & Sexton, V. S. (1966). *History of psychology: An overview*. New York: Grune & Stratton. The chapter "Psychology in the Soviet Union" may be the best of its kind for a general history of psychology textbook in English.

Moroz, O. (1989). The last diagnosis: A plausible account that needs further verification. *Journal of Russian and East European Psychology* (formerly *Soviet Psychology*), 27, 71–91. (E. Lockwood, Trans.) Appeared first in Russian in 1988 in *Literaturnaia Gazeta*, and see Shereshevskii below.

Razran, G. (1965). Russian physiologists' psychology and American experimental psychology: A historical and systematic collation and a look into the future. *Psychological Bulletin*, 63, 42–64. A frequently cited and useful source that examined the contributions of Bekhterev, Sechenov, and Pavlov to American and Russian psychology.

Shereshevskii, A. M. (1991). The mystery of the death of V. M. Bekhterev. *The Bekhterev Review of Psychiatry and Medical Psychology*, 2, 102–111. Contains information possibly inconsistent with and details not seen in Moroz above. Shereshevskii, who is currently associated with the Bekhterev Psychoneurological Institute in St. Petersburg, acknowledged that the evidence is incomplete, suggested that more could be forthcoming, and offered his opinion that Bekhterev was poisoned.

Strickland, L. H. (1991). Russian and Soviet social psychology. *Canadian Psychology*, 32, 580–593. An examination of Russian and Soviet social psychology with considerable emphasis on Bekhterev by the leading contemporary Western authority. Strickland edited the translation of Bekhterev's *Collective reflexology*.

Roger K. Thomas

BELGIUM. From a European perspective, the Kingdom of Belgium is both a small and a young country. It was formed in 1830 when it separated from the Netherlands (after the battle of Waterloo in 1815 the two countries had been rather artificially brought together). Considering its size, Belgium is an overpopulated country (10 million inhabitants). Belgium has three language communities: Dutch (about 60% of the population), French (about 38% of the population), and German (about 2% of the population), which is geographically close to Germany. Generally, French is spoken in the south of the country, Flemish (a dialect of Dutch) in the north, and German in a small territory (annexed from Germany to Belgium after World War I) in the east. The capital, Brussels, is largely French-speaking although it is geographically situated in the middle of the Flemish part of the country, and is also capital of the European Union and headquarters of NATO. In the late twentieth century the country changed its governing structure to a federation, reflecting more appropriately the existence of separate communities, each one with its own culture, language, and history.

Soon after founding scientific psychology in Leipzig in 1879, Wilhelm Wundt regularly received visits from several Belgian scientists, some even preparing Ph.D. dissertations under his supervision. Although the first Laboratory of Experimental Psychology was established at the University of Ghent in 1891, the first full research program in psychology was founded in 1892 at the University of Louvain/Leuven by Désiré Mercier (1851–1926), who was one of Wundt's visitors from Belgium, then the head of a recently created Institute of Philosophy and later to become a cardinal of the Catholic Church. The Louvain/Leuven Laboratory of Experimental Psychology received its major impetus through the work of Albert Michotte van den Berck (1881–1965; he also visited Wundt). Michotte's impact through his extensive international contacts, research work, and initiatives to improve our science in Belgium has been profound. Beyond Ghent and Louvain/Leuven, outstanding research was carried out as well at the universities of Brussels (e.g., Quételet, 1796–1874) and Liège (e.g., Delboeuf, 1831–1896).

While the research work from Belgian psychologists received acknowledgment abroad, it took a long time to establish full-fledged teaching programs in psychology. In almost all universities such programs gradually but slowly developed from psychological applications, typically within institutes of educational sciences. With the huge increase in the number of psychology students in the late 1960s and early 1970s, the psychology programs became more independent. Today at most universities there is a faculty of psychology (but also including educational sciences).

Following the upsurge of politicolinguistic clashes and problems in the late 1960s (which were started at the University of Louvain/Leuven where the two linguistic communities of students had to share the same teaching and research facilities), both the University of Brussels and Louvain/Leuven were each split into two universities, one for French-speaking and the other for Flemish students. The French-speaking University of Louvain moved to a new campus, Louvain-la-Neuve, about at twenty miles from the Dutch-speaking Leuven. There is now also a psychology program at the University of Mons, which brings to seven the number of psychology programs in the country (Ghent, Dutch-speaking and French-speaking Brussels, Leuven, Louvain-la-Neuve, Liège, and Mons). The universities of Leuven and Louvain-la-Neuve as well as the two universities of Brussels are private institutions, the first two dependent on Catholic religious authorities and the other two originally dependent on secular sources. For most practical purposes, all seven universities are now almost completely financially supported by governmental sources, and they share equal access to research funding. Compared with most other countries, student registration fees in Belgian universities are very low.

While all universities are free to define the training program of psychologists for themselves, the programs at the seven Belgian universities are in fact quite similar. It is also fair to state that the quality and outcome of the programs and training are all about at the same level, although some aspects are sometimes more distinctive at some universities. Typically, a 2-year psychology program leads to the title of "candidate in psychology," but this title has no career value. Those 2 years cover the major fields of psychology and also introductions to other disciplines which are important for psychology (e.g., philosophy, advanced statistics, biology, psychophysiology, anthropology, logic, sociology). Any student successfully finishing secondary school may study psychology at the university; therefore, the candidates' years can be considered as a way to select students for further study in the field. Approximately 60 percent of first-year students in the university psychology programs drop out of the 2-year training course for the candidate degree. They then typically choose another discipline or leave the university to enter a vocational school ("higher nonuniversity education").

The first two years are followed by three years during which the student specializes in one or another field of psychology and must write a master's thesis to earn the degree of licentiate. The three years also include an internship in the student's selected field of specialization. The degree of licentiate is the major requisite to start a career. Only a very few continue on to a doctoral degree, which takes 4 to 7 years. In most universities, the doctoral program only includes the preparation of a doctoral thesis, covering the research done during the doctoral years. At some universities, a full-fledged program has been worked out including lectures and seminars to be attended beyond the research for the thesis. Some universities require that the doctoral dissertation be published before the degree is officially conferred.

At the level of candidature and license, there are only a few foreigners in the psychology programs; the bulk of foreigners can be found in doctoral programs. However, since the European Union launched the university credit system, students are allowed to obtain class credits at other universities within the countries of the European Union. Therefore, the number of foreign students at the level of candidature and license is expected to grow significantly in coming years. As yet, it is rather unusual to begin training at one university and to continue at another one; Belgian students typically complete all their training (candidature, license, and doctoral program) at the same university.

With almost 1,000 students obtaining a degree of licentiate each year in a country with about 10 million inhabitants, the prospect of finding a job immediately is a major problem. The job prospects for industrial-organizational psychologists are currently somewhat encouraging. There are very few openings in school psychology but there are also very few students selecting school psychology as a specialty. The same is true for students in research psychology: few openings but also few students. The major employment problem is in clinical psychology, the specialty chosen by a majority of students. In this area job prospects are rather poor. However, the job situation for clinical psychology is not necessarily much worse than in many other academic fields. After earning their licentiate, many students in clinical psychology receive special training in one or more other psychotherapeutic techniques. Clinical employment is critically dependent on government health care policies: a single governmental decision may immediately change the employment prospects in clinical psychology in one or another direction. Although their number is still small, more and more clinical psychologists are in private practice.

Outside the universities, some schools have programs of three-year courses that prepare the student for the position of "assistant in psychology"; their function consists mainly of testing subjects under the supervision of a university-trained psychologist or medical personnel. A recent law regulating use of the title of "psychologist" means they may not call themselves psychologists.

There are a large number of psychological organizations in the country, and these serve both the clinical orientation and the linguistic community. Most of the organization agreed in 1979 to establish an umbrella organization, the Belgian Federation of Psychologists. Within the federation, the federating organizations are working smoothly together as a function of common professional interests. To become a member of the federation, one must belong to at least one of the member associations (the reciprocity rule). The federation is a founding member of the European Federation of Professional Psychologists Association (EFPPA). The first and major task of the Belgian Federation of Psychologists was to obtain the legal recognition and protection of the title of "psychologist"; since that was achieved a few years ago, the main focus of the federation is now on professional aspects of the practice of psychology. Currently, it is considering a change that would reflect more accurately the linguistic structure of the country as well as the several domains of psychological practice. The reciprocity rule is currently also under discussion. One major problem is that most Belgian psychologists don't feel the need to become members of the federation through peripheral or affiliated associations. Of 10,000 psychologists in Belgium, only one tenth belong to the federation. With the small number of members and repeated complaints of excessive registration fees, the federation lacks a sound financial basis to support new initiatives in defending the professional interests of its members.

In the Belgian Federation of Psychologists, two federating organizations have the largest number of members: the Flemish Society for Clinical Psychology (Vlaamse Vereniging voor Klinische Psychologie) and the Belgian Psychological Society (BPS). The latter is one of the oldest psychological organizations in the country and was established in 1947. Initially, BPS activities were mainly academic, with active researchers regularly presenting their newest findings at meetings. Gradually, and as defined in its original statutes, the society became more involved in the professional aspects of psychology; in the late 1970s, the society pushed forward the idea of a professional umbrella federation. Once the federation was established, the society returned to its original goal of being a learned society where research findings are presented and communicated to all psychologists in the country. The Belgian Psychological Society is a founding member of the International Union of Psychological Science (IUPsyS). Three Presidents of the Society (Albert Michotte van den Berck, Joseph Nuttin, and Géry van Outryve d'Ydewalle) also became President of the IUPsyS. In 1957 and 1992, the society organized the International Congress of Psychology under the auspices of IUPsyS, striking achievements for a society in a small country.

Both the Belgian Federation of Psychologists and the Belgian Psychological Society have organizational structures that reflect the splitting of the country into two large language communities. For example, the Belgian Psychological Society has two secretaries general and two deputy secretaries, one for the Flemish-speaking section of the country and one for the French-speaking part.

Despite structural and organizational problems, it can be stated that psychology flourishes in Belgium. Good Belgian research is published in the major international scientific journals. Compared with several years ago, the discipline and its practice have recently gained much more visibility in the country. Although the social status of the discipline can still be improved and its contribution to the well-being of the society still be better acknowledged, recent developments allow Belgian psychologists to be optimistic for the near future.

Géry d'Ydewalle

BELIEFS. *See* Philosophy, *article on* Philosophy of Mind.

BENDER-GESTALT VISUAL MOTOR TEST. The original *Bender Visual Motor Gestalt Test Design Cards* were published in 1938 by the American Orthopsychiatric Association, as a maturational test of the visual-motor-gestalt function in children between the ages of four and eleven (VMGT; *American Orthopsychiatric Association Research Monographs, 1938, 3*). The test was originally designed to measure ability of the perceptual system to organize visual stimuli into "Gestalten" or configurational wholes. Original VMGT test stimuli were a set of nine black designs each on a white card consecutively labeled A, then 1 through 8. The designs were selected by Bender from a longer series originally employed by Max Wertheimer, one of the founders of the Gestalt school. The cards are presented to subjects one at a time and they are required to copy the designs exactly as they see them. Total test time is about ten minutes. Bender formulated test results based on subjective evaluation of drawings by experienced clinicians. The test is commonly referred to as the *Bender-Gestalt*.

Since the original test development in 1938, the VMGT has undergone approximately 10 revisions, most of which centered on changes in scoring procedures and interpretation. Suited for children ages 10 and over, the *Hutt Adaptation of the Bender Gestalt Test* (HABGT; M. L. Hutt, New York, 1944) and its three subsequent revisions turned the focus away from visual-motor difficulties and more toward interpretation of personality problems. Koppitz was the first to carry out extensive standardization of the test for young children. Termed the *Bender Gestalt Test for Young Children*, Koppitz's version included an objective developmental scoring system designed to assess the level of maturity in visual-motor perception acquired by age 12 (Koppitz, New York, 1964).

The original VMGT and its subsequent versions have been variously reported to measure visual-motor integration skills, organic impairment, and personality problems. Test scores have been used to predict school achievement and learning disabilities. There is mixed support for the test as an accurate predictor of school achievement or neurological impairment. It has been supported that Bender-Gestalt test results should be optimally used to generate hypotheses, rather than form absolute conclusions regarding neurological function or school achievement. Reliability estimates have been reported as $r = 0.74$ (criterion-related validity), 0.70 (24-hour interval retest), and 0.90 (interrater). Reliability estimates were reported as $r = 0.88$ and 0.96 (interrater), 0.55 to 0.66 (four-month interval retest), and 0.48 to 0.79 (criterion-related validity). Internal consistency estimates have been reported as $r = 0.84$ (Caucasians), 0.81 (African Americans), 0.72 (Mexican Americans), 0.81 (males), and 0.80 (females). Survey data indicate that, despite occasional criticism, the Bender-Gestalt test continues to be ranked among the top 10 assessment instruments in current use.

[*See also* Testing.]

Linda D. Nelson

BENTLEY, MADISON (1870 1955), American psychologist. Bentley studied psychology at the University of Nebraska under H. K. Wolfe, who had received his doctorate at Leipzig under Wilhelm Wundt in 1887. Graduating in 1895, Bentley continued at Cornell University under Edward B. Titchener, completing his doctorate in 1899. He remained at Cornell to teach, was promoted to assistant professor in 1902, and became chairman of the undergraduate division in 1910. In 1912 Bentley was called to the University of Illinois as professor and head of department. Volunteering for military service in 1917, he conducted research on the nonacoustical organs of the ear for the Air Corps until his discharge at the end of 1918. In 1928 Bentley returned to Cornell to succeed Titchener as Sage Professor of Psychology and chair of the department.

Over the span of his career, Bentley made significant research and scholarly contributions on a wide range of topics. These included work on the memory image (*American Journal of Psychology*, 1899, 11, 1–48), the design of a technique for analyzing and synthesizing complex sensations such as "wetness" (*American Journal of Psychology*, 1900, 11, 405–425), a controversial demonstration of learning in Paramecia (with L. M. Day, *Journal of Animal Behavior*, 1911, 1, 67–73), a major study with E. V. Cowdry of mental disorders (*The Problem of Mental Disorders*, New York, 1934), and several articles on anthropological psychology (e.g., *American Journal of Psychology*, 1947, 60, 479–501).

Theoretically, Bentley opposed both behaviorism and mentalism. His own position was intended to overcome metaphysical dualism and to establish a distinctly psychological science that was not merely secondary to biology. He proposed a disciplinarily neutral organism whose functions could be classified as either biological or psychological. Psychological functions were distinguished in that they overcame the separation of organism and environment through "absorption" of the latter by the former, as when one imaginatively plans to rebuild an object that no longer exists. Research, in Bentley's view, ought to be less concerned with measuring results of tasks completed by psychological functions than with describing their modes and derivations.

Bentley's most widely recognized contribution to psychology by far was in the field of editing. He became cooperating editor of the *American Journal of Psychology* in 1903, holding that position until 1926 when he became coeditor with Karl Dallenbach, in which position he remained active until 1950. He was editor of the *Psychological Index* (1916–1925), associate editor of the *Journal of Comparative Psychology* (1921–1935), editor of the *Journal of Experimental Psychology* (1926–1929), and editor of three issues of *Psychological Monographs* in 1916, 1921, and 1926. Karl Dallenbach (1956) described Bentley as an editor of the old school. He was known to completely rewrite contributors' articles that he thought promising but poorly written. According to Dallenbach, "no manuscript ever passed under his editorial pen without being the better for it. . . . The debt that psychology and various psychologists owe Bentley for his editorial services is great" (*American Journal of Psychology*, 1956, 69, 185).

Bibliography

Bentley, M. (1926). The major categories of psychology. *Psychological Review*, 33, 71–105. Bentley's APA presidential address of 1925. A sometimes whimsical but always penetrating critique of the dominant psychologies and psychological practices of the time.

Bentley, M. (1930). A psychology for psychologists. In C. Murchison (Ed.), *Psychologies of 1930* (pp. 95–114). Worcester, MA: Clark University Press. The most accessible of Bentley's systematic statements of his own theoretical ideas about psychology as a distinctly *psychological* discipline.

Bentley, M. (1936). Autobiography. In C. Murchison (Ed.), *A history of psychology in autobiography* (Vol. 3, pp 53–67). Worcester, MA: Clark University Press. Bentley's own account of his career. Biographical details are scarce, but the thoughts leading to his own theoretical position are vividly portrayed.

Dallenbach, K. M. (1956). Madison Bentley: 1870–1955. *American Journal of Psychology*, 69, 169–193. The most complete account of Bentley's life and career.

Charles W. Tolman

BENUSSI, VITTORIO (1878–1927), Italian psychologist. Benussi was born in Triest and studied in Graz under the head of the phenomenological school, Alexius Meinong. In Graz, he also directed the psychology laboratory until 1918, distinguishing himself for his experimental research on "forms" and "time."

At the end of World War I, Benussi, with the full support of the eminent psychologist Sante de Sanctis, was appointed professor of experimental psychology at the University of Padua. From 1919 to 1927, he applied himself incessantly to the experimental activity that would lead to his being recognized, by E. G. Boring for instance (1950), as one of the most original and creative psychologists of the period.

Continuing the work he had begun in 1902 with his doctoral dissertation, Benussi, in 1904, conducted experimental investigations on optical-geometric illusions, obtaining results that would later be used by Gestalt psychologists. In particular, he proposed an original theoretical solution to the classic nativism-empiricism antinomy by underscoring the complementary relationship between representations of sensorial and asensorial origin. With the publication of his volume *Psychologie der Zeitauffassung* (1913), Benussi gave rise to the field of experimental psychology of time perception, and he demonstrated that the subjective distortions of our perceptions of the flow of time always consist of temporal contractions and not of dilations.

In 1914, at the International Conference of Göttingen, Benussi described 23 general laws relative to the inadequate perception of forms, resuming a line of research initiated by Alfred Binet and William Stern. In the same year, he also published a study in which he discussed the psychology of courtroom testimony in experimental terms. By employing respiratory analysis in an innovative and original manner, Benussi observed that when a subject bears witness in the presence of a large audience, the respiratory correlates—obtained by calculating the inhalation-exhalation time ratio—would differ considerably according to whether the subject was aware of lying or aware of stating the truth.

In Padua, Benussi dedicated himself primarily to research on "states of consciousness" and "affective states," referring to his own experimental results obtained in Graz, and adopted suggestion and hypnosis as methods of experimental psychic analysis. He rejected the traditional introspective method and adopted hypnotic-suggestive procedures as "material tools capable of performing an analysis or decomposition of psychic life, which, far from being purely mental or metaphorical in nature, can be considered as real as the analysis and decomposition that physicists or chemists perform on matter" (1925, p. 248). Moreover, in 1927 Benussi advocated the functional autonomy of emotion, namely, the complete independence of the emotional and affective functions from the intellectual functions, on both conscious and unconscious levels.

In the mid-1920s, Benussi, favorably inclined to

psychoanalysis, became one of the first to recognize the need for experimental control of Freudian psychoanalytic concepts. He therefore initiated an extensive experimental research program on the posthypnotic actions of subjects under conflict-inducing conditions, induced amnesia, and dreams guided by peripheral stimulation. In this context, he coined the term *negative hallucination* to describe a phenomenon he observed in hypnotized subjects—namely, that they "annulled" or failed to perceive objects in their visual fields—considering this to be a sensorial equivalent of the psychoanalytic mechanism of repression.

Bibliography

Benussi, V. (1904). Zur Psychologie des Gestalterfassens. In A. Meinong (Ed.), *Untersuchungen zur Gegenstandstheorie und Psychologie* (pp. 304–448). Leipzig, Germany: Barth.

Benussi, V. (1913). *Psychologie der Zeitauffassung.* Heidelberg, Germany: Winter.

Benussi, V. (1914). Die Atmungssymptome der Lüge. *Archiv für die gesamte Psychologie, 31,* 244–273.

Benussi, V. (1914). Gezetze der inadäquäten Gestaltauffassung. *Archiv für die gesamte Psychologie, 32,* 396–419.

Benussi, V. (1925). *La suggestione e l'ipnosi come mezzi di analisi psichica reale.* Bologna, Italy: Zanichelli.

Benussi, V. (1927). Sur l'autonomie fonctionnelle émotive. *Journal de Psychologie Normale et Pathologique, 24,* 341–344.

Benussi, V. (1932). Suggestione e psicanalisi (S. Musatti de Marchi, Ed.). Messina-Milano, Italy: Principato.

Boring, E. G. (1950). *A history of experimental psychology* (2nd ed.). New York: Appleton-Century-Crofts.

Mucciarelli, G. (Ed.). (1987). *Vittorio Benussi nella storia della psicologia Italiana.* Bologna, Italy: Pitagora.

Stucchi, N. (1991). Seeing and thinking: Vittorio Benussi and the Graz School. In P. Simons (Ed.), *Essays on Meinong* (pp. 98–113). Munich: Philosophia.

Nino Dazzi

BEREAVEMENT. *See* Death and Dying; *and* Grief and Loss.

BEREAVEMENT PROGRAMS. Bereavement can be defined as the reaction to a loss of something or someone important in our lives. There are many kinds of losses that people experience for which they will grieve. These can range, for example, from the sense of loss that follows after an actual death or the loss of a job, to the loss of a home, to the loss experienced by women who place children for adoption and by adoptive parents for the child they could not conceive (Marris, 1974; Miller-Havens, 1996; Nickman, 1996; Silverman, 1981). This entry primarily focuses on programs that respond to an actual death.

There are programs for the bereaved being developed in many settings that range from mutual help programs staffed and directed by volunteers who are bereaved themselves, to church sponsored support groups, to clinical programs run by trained mental health professionals. Over the past 30 years the numbers of programs have increased more than a hundred fold from a time when there was almost nothing available to a time when the bereaved may have choices in where to turn for guidance and assistance. However, there are still many parts of the country where little or no formal assistance is available outside of friends and family.

Where to turn in part may be a function of what is available, but it also may relate to how bereavement is viewed. There are several views of grief that dominate contemporary thinking (Silverman, 2000; Silverman and Klass, 1996; Stroebe, Gergen, Gergen, Stroebe, 1996). While all these views overlap, there are enough differences to influence how and what services a particular program provides. The most prevalent view looks at people's reaction to a death in the family in what can be labeled a medical model. In this view the focus is largely on the mourners' feelings, on the need to give appropriate expression to these feelings, so that with time the mourner can recover. Mourners are expected to sever their connection to the deceased so that they can then reinvest in new relationships. If the mourner does not follow a prescribed path of mourning, in a prescribed period of time, then there is danger of their developing what is being now called complicated mourning (Rando, 1993). The help offered then is designed to guide people through prescribed steps, to complete the prescribed tasks (Rando, 1993; Worden, 1991).

A contrasting view sees the death as opening a period of transition in the mourner's life. This is a process that changes people, the way they live, and the way they see themselves in the world. They do not recover, they accommodate (Silverman, 1966, 1978, 1981, 1986, 2000). This is a process that extends over time; life is ongoing and people negotiate and renegotiate their accommodation to this loss for the rest of their lives. They learn to live in the world in a different way, they view themselves from a new perspective, and often feel empowered by this new sense of self that has emerged (Attig, 1996; Silverman, 1988, 2000). As part of this process of accommodation, they construct a new relationship to the deceased which provides them with solace (Silverman and Klass, 1996). What the mourner needs is an understanding of this process, a language for helping the individual talk about the changes in feelings, in self, and in their lives that they must deal with. They need a language without the phrases *recover*, *closure*, or *being over it*, or *getting on with your life*. There is typically no single mourner; every death impacts on the family and the community of which the deceased was a part (Shapiro, 1994; Silverman, 2000). Since death is a universal event all of us will experience and is not a respecter of age, then all of us need to be expert in dealing with loss. All of us need to find a place for death in our understanding of life, and in how we make meaning in this world (Neimeyer, 1997; Silverman, 1988, 2000). The goal of any helping program should be to promote competent coping and to enhance participants' ability to accommodate to such losses. In some ways this type of education has to begin in early childhood as we teach children about loss, and continue from there. It begins in the family and in community institutions such as churches and synagogues and in our schools. We also need to recognize that no one can get through their grief without support and help from family and friends. But often people need something else. They need to know how other mourners have dealt with a particular loss. They need role models, they need perspective, and they need to learn tricks of the trade (Silverman, 1978). These include tips on what to do when well-meaning friends will not allow the bereaved to talk about the deceased, or (in the case of the loss of a child) what to say when people ask how many children you have. These suggestions expand the mourner's coping repertoire and resources (Silverman, 1995).

The setting in which this kind of assistance is most likely to be available is in organizations run by and for the bereaved (Silverman, 1978, 1980). Mothers Against Drunk Driving, Widowed Person's Service, Compassionate Friends, and Motherless Daughters are examples of such organizations (Madara, 1995). Members are all bereaved parents, widowed persons, or bereaved children and siblings, as are the people who run the organization. They provide their members with educational seminars, outreach to the newly bereaved, newsletters, group discussions and support, and social activities. Each group has its designated helpers who have participated in training or orientation seminars to provide them with the skills to use their own experience to help others (Silverman, 2000).

The Dougy Center (1997a, 1997b) in Portland, Oregon has become the model for programs for bereaved children throughout the United States. The model is for the open-ended play groups for children from ages four through late adolescence. Children meet in groups on a biweekly basis and stay in the group as long as they wish. Groups are organized by age and types of death: suicide, violence, natural causes, or ac-

cidents. Parents meet at the same time. While a professional staff runs the organization—most staff members have experienced deaths in their lives—each group is facilitated by trained volunteers. Those who have experienced personal losses are considered more effective as helpers. Many hospices in the United States have adopted programs modeled after the Dougy program. These serve the bereaved children and their families from the larger community, not simply those families served by the hospice. In some cities, there are freestanding programs such as Bereaved Parents of Ontario in Toronto, Canada. A list of programs throughout the United States and Canada and training opportunities are available from the Dougy Center. Variations on this model are found in many places and are proliferating. For the most part support and guidance is provided and the goal is to help children and their parents integrate their feelings and the changes associated with the death into their ongoing lives.

Another source of information and support is the Internet. This is a new phenomenon but widely used, as more people avail themselves of its resources. People can be in touch with other bereaved people, have access to professional information, and even take courses related to bereavement on-line. Most of the support groups listed above have Web pages. One way to begin exploring the subject on the Web is by logging onto the mental health resource listing http://www/cmhc.com/guide/grief/htm. The Widowed Person's Service of the AARP has a Web site with information about programs and resources for people dealing with different types of death: http://www.aarp.org/griefandloss.

Professionally led support groups are important sources of information and support (Buell, 1989; Hughes, 1992; Jordon & Ware, in press; Levy, 1992). These are often time-limited and are run by experienced facilitators who have worked for many years with the bereaved. Effective facilitators recognize the value of the mutual support available in these groups and the knowledge that the members have accrued from their experience. These groups provide educational opportunities for their members and often continue long after the facilitator has ended his or her relationship with the group. These groups are sponsored by religious organizations as well as independent agencies. Mutual help organizations sometimes hire professional facilitators to offer an intense group experience to their members focusing on the different issues people face at different points in the bereavement process.

Finally counseling or therapy can also be an effective resource. This is not what mourners typically need. However, very often the death can trigger old problems that can now be revisited and looked at from a different perspective. In addition, mourners for whom the support and help available in other settings is inadequate for helping them find a way through their pain and disarray may need other assistance as well (Cook and Dworkin, 1992). In choosing a therapist it may be wise to interview several and choose one who has experience and understanding of the grieving process.

There is no right way to mourn, there is no one help that will meet all of any one person's or family's needs. Mourners may need to orchestrate many kinds of help from mutual help organizations, support groups, the Internet, and professional counselors as they deal with their grief over their lifetime and the many changes with which they must cope.

Bibliography

Attig, T. (1996). *How we grieve: Relearning the world.* New York: Oxford University Press.

Buell, J. S. (1989). Bereavement groups in the hospice program. [Special Issue] *Hospice Journal, 5,* 107–118.

Cook, A. S., & Dworkin, D. S. (1992). *Helping the bereaved: Therapeutic interventions for children, adolescents and adults.* New York: Basic Books.

Dougy Center. (1997a). *National directory of children's grief services.* The National Center for Grieving Children and Families, 3909 S.E. 52nd St., Box 36852, Portland, OR 97286.

Dougy Center. (1997b). *An activity manual for children in grief.* The National Center for Grieving Children and Families, 3909 S.E. 52nd St., Box 36852, Portland, OR 97286.

Hughes, M. (1992). *Bereavement and support: Healing in a group environment.* Washington, DC: Taylor & Francis.

Jordon, J. R., & Ware, E. S. (1997). Feeling like a motherless child: A support group model for adults grieving the death of a parent. *Omega: Journal of Death and Dying, 35,* 361–376.

Levy, L. H. (1992). Bereavement support groups: Who joins; who does not; and why. *American Journal of Community Psychology, 20,* 649–662.

Madara, E. (1995). *The self help sources book: The comprehensive reference of self-help group resources.* Denville, NJ: American Self Help Clearinghouse, Northwest Covenant Medical Center.

Marris, P. (1974). *Loss and change.* New York: Pantheon.

Miller-Havens, S. (1996). Grief and the birth origin fantasies of adopted women. In D. Klass, P. R. Silverman, & S. L. Nickman (Eds.), *Continuing bonds: A new understanding of grief.* Washington, DC: Taylor & Francis.

Neimeyer, R. (1997). Meaning reconstruction and the experience of chronic loss. In K. Doka with J. Davidson (Ed.), *Living with grief: When illness is prolonged.* Washington, DC: Taylor & Francis.

Nickman, S. L. (1996). Retroactive loss in adoptive persons. In D. Klass, P. R. Silverman, & S. L. Nickman (Eds), *Continuing bonds: A new understanding of grief.* Washington, DC: Taylor & Francis.

Rando, T. (1993). *Treatment of complicated mourning.* Champaign, IL: Research Press.

Shapiro, E. (1994). *Grief as a family process.* New York: Guilford Press.

Silverman, P. R. (1966). Services for the widowed during the period of bereavement. *Social Work Practice.* New York: Columbia University Press.

Silverman, P. R. (1980). *Mutual help groups and the role of the mental health professional.* Washington, DC: U.S. Government Printing Office, NIMH, DHEW Publication No. (ADM) 78–646.

Silverman, P. R. (1980). *Mutual help groups: Organization and development.* Beverly Hills, CA: Sage.

Silverman, P. R. (1981). *Helping women cope with grief.* Beverly Hills, CA: Sage.

Silverman, P. R. (1986). *Widow to widow.* New York: Springer Press.

Silverman, P. R. (1988). In search of selves: Accommodating to widowhood. In L. A. Bond (Ed.), *Families in transition: Primary prevention programs that work.* Beverly Hills, CA: Sage.

Silverman, P. R. (1995). Helping the bereaved through social support and mutual help. In I. Corless, B. Germino, & M. Pittman (Eds.), *A challenge for living: Dying, death and bereavement.* Boston: Jones & Bartlett.

Silverman, P. R. (2000). *Never too young to know: Death in children's lives.* New York: Oxford University Press.

Silverman, P. R., & Klass, D. (1996). Introduction: What's the problem? In D. Klass. P. R. Silverman, & S. L. Nickman (Eds.), *Continuing bonds: A new understanding of grief.* Washington, DC: Taylor & Francis.

Stroebe, M., Gergen, M., Gergen, K., & Stroebe, W. (1996). Broken hearts or broken bonds. In D. Klass, P. R. Silverman, & S. L. Nickman (Eds), *Continuing bonds: A new understanding of grief.* Washington, DC: Taylor & Francis.

Worden, J. W. (1991). *Grief counselling and grief therapy.* New York: Springer.

Phyllis Rolfe Silverman

BERKELEY, GEORGE (1685–1753), Irish philosopher. Berkeley was born in Kilkenny, Ireland, whose college he entered in 1696, later enrolling in Trinity College, Dublin (1700). There he earned the baccalaureate degree (1704), becoming a junior fellow (1707) with a master's degree. After travels in England and on the Continent, he returned to Dublin, receiving the doctorate of divinity degree. He was appointed divinity lecturer in the university (1721), senior proctor in 1722, and lecturer in Hebrew in 1723. Berkeley resigned his university post in 1724 to become dean of Derry. At this time he began to prosecute his interest in founding a college in Bermuda, successfully earning a modest grant for the project from the House of Commons (1726). Two years later Berkeley married Anne Foster and set sail for America where his first child was born in Newport, Rhode Island, in a house that still stands.

Berkeley's plans for the Bermuda college did not bear fruit. Back in Ireland he was named Bishop of Cloyne in 1734, later declining the offered Vice Chancellor's position at Dublin University and the Bishopric of Clogher. The final 2 years of his life were spent at the University of Oxford, where he is buried in Christ Church chapel.

With Francis Bacon, John Locke, David Hume, and John Stuart Mill, George Berkeley is one of the major architects of British empiricistic philosophy and psychology. It is chiefly on two grounds that his prolific and original contributions recommend themselves to contemporary students of psychology. First, he examined closely the monocular and binocular cues to depth perception within the larger context of optics and projective geometry. In keeping with the *Dioptrics* (1692) of William Molyneux, Berkeley reasoned that points in space projected on the retinal surface cannot convey information of distance and that accordingly knowledge of distance must be "suggested" by other cues: binocular convergence, the tension of the muscles associated with eye movement, interposition, size, and, significantly, inferences from the sense of touch. Apart from the delineation of depth cues, Berkeley's efforts here were foundational for theories of sensory interaction and of the role of learning in perception.

Second, Berkeley wrote tellingly against the materialistic psychological treatises that arose in the wake of the scientific achievements of the seventeenth century. The most influential of these in the English-speaking world was John Locke's *Essay Concerning Human Understanding* (1690). In that work Locke applied the Newtonian corpuscular theory to mind, asserting that the ultimate constituents of mind are elementary sensations. By a process of association (akin to gravitation), these sensations are held together to form simple and then ever more complex ideas. As all knowledge of the external world is by way of sensation, there are some elements of knowledge that bear the impress of the senses themselves, though some elements of knowledge faithfully record the actual properties of things. The latter come under the heading of *primary* qualities: The extension and hardness of an object are not only perceived, but it is actually the extension and the hardness that are perceived. Other qualities, however, such as the color of an object, are not in the object but arise from the effects certain unperceived properties have on the organs of perception. These are the *secondary* qualities of things.

Taking Locke's theory of primary and secondary qualities to its logical limit, Berkeley insisted that all of the so-called qualities of bodies are, in Locke's sense, *secondary* in that all must subsist in the conscious awareness of the percipient. Indeed, there is nothing that can truthfully be said of any (allegedly) material entity except by way of perceived attributes. Berkeley's famous conclusion was *Esse est percipi*: To be is to be perceived. The allegedly material world of being is instead one in which only ideas and spirits have actual independent being; thus, Berkeley's immaterialism. Its echo is audible in J. S. Mill's definition of matter as "the permanent possibility of sensations," as it is in all phenomenalistic theories of knowledge.

[*Many of the people mentioned in this article are the subjects of independent biographical entries.*]

Bibliography

Foster, J., & Robinson, H. (1985). *Essays on Berkeley: A tercentennial celebration.* Oxford: Clarendon Press.

Berkeley, G. (1985). *A treatise concerning the principles of human knowledge.* London: Fontana. (Original work published 1710)

Locke, J. (1959). *An Essay Concerning Human Understanding.* New York: Dover. (Original work published 1690)

Luce, A. A. (1968). *The life of George Berkeley, Bishop of Cloyne.* New York: Greenwood.

Luce, A. A., & Jessop, T. E. (Eds.). (1934). *The works of George Berkeley.* London: Oxford University Press. Bishop of Cloyne (Vols. 1–9). New York: Routledge and Kegan Paul.

Pitcher, G. W. (1977). *Berkeley.* London: Routledge and Kegan Paul.

Robinson, D. N. (1995). Empiricism. In *An intellectual history of psychology* (3rd ed., pp. 149–196). Madison: University of Wisconsin Press.

Daniel N. Robinson

BERNARD, CLAUDE (1813–1878), French physiologist. Born on 12 July 1813, at Saint Julien near Villefranche, a department of the Rhone, Claude Bernard was a student of François Magendie. Bernard laid the foundation for modern physiology, providing the cynosure for modern inductive scientific thought, including in psychology. Bernard's *An Introduction to the Study of Experimental Medicine* (1949)/1865) was published a few years after Darwin's *Origin of the Species* (1859). Bernard was an early champion of animal models of human anatomy, physiology, and disease. The concepts of mechanism and site of drug action grew out of Bernard's research on the effects of curare on striped muscle, and his research on carbon monoxide asphyxiation by competition with oxygen on the hemoglobin molecule. He introduced the concept of internal environment.

Bernard generated physiological knowledge at a startling rate. It was said of him that "he discovered as others breathed." Bernard argued that it was the task of physiology to discover the circumstances under which biological phenomena occur, and the relation between values of causal and consequential variables, a radical concept in mid-nineteenth-century Europe which was steeped in hypotheticodeductive theory. Anticipating the schism in American psychology 73 years later with publication of Skinner's *The Behavior of Organisms*, Bernard rejected hypothetical constructs in medicine. He wrote that such terms as "force of attraction" in physics were merely words to abbreviate speech, and the moment they are granted scientific status "we abandon experience and fall into scholasticism" (Bernard, 1865, p. 187), leading to "blind faith in theories which is only scientific superstition" (p. 37.)

Despite his deep commitment to reductionism, paradoxically, there are strong links between Bernard's work and modern behavior analytic theory in psychology. Bernard argued that physiological processes were the only subject matter of his science, not the nonobservable theoretical events which most of his colleagues focused on. Bernard said the goal of his science was "foreseeing and directing phenomena" (Bernard, 1865, p. 57), while Skinner stated, "We need to establish laws by virtue of which we may predict behavior, and we may do this only by finding variables of which behavior is a function" (Skinner, 1938, p. 8). Bernard introduced the ABA single subject reversal experimental design. Like Skinner, Bernard eschewed averaging data across individuals. "In physiology, we must never make average descriptions of experiments, because the true relations of phenomena disappear in the average" (Bernard, 1865, p. 135). "If based on statistics, medicine can never be anything but conjectural science; only by basing itself on experimental determinism can it become a true science" (Bernard, 1865, p. 139).

Bernard jousted with vitalism as part of the deterministic battle over free will. The battlefield was the laboratory, and the instrument of combat was the inductive experimental method. Bernard's writing and thought profoundly influenced modern medicine and modern psychology, leading to the conclusion that the experimenter is, indeed, "the examining magistrate for nature," a thought with which Claude Bernard introduced his masterpiece, *Experimental Medicine*. When Bernard died in Paris in 1878 it was said "The light, which has just been extinguished, cannot be replaced" (Paul Bert, in his introduction to *Experimental Medicine* 1878, p. xix).

Bibliography

Bernard, C. (1949). *An introduction to the study of experimental medicine* (Henry Copely Greene, Trans.) New York: Henry Schuman. (Original work published 1865)

Olmstead, J. M. D., & Olmstead, E. M. (1952). *Claude Bernard and the experimental method in medicine.* New York: Henry Schuman.

Skinner, B. F. (1938). *The behavior of organisms.* New York: Appleton.

Tarshis, J. (1968). *Claude Bernard: Father of experimental medicine.* New York: Dial Press.

Thompson, T. (1984). The examining magistrate for nature: A retrospective review of Claude Bernard's *An introduction to the study of experimental medicine. Journal of the Experimental Analysis of Behavior 41*, 211–216.

Virtanen, R. (1960). *Claude Bernard and his place in the history of ideas.* Lincoln, NE: University of Nebraska Press.

Travis Thompson

BIAS. *See* Artifact.

BIAS AND EQUIVALENCE. Much psychological research involves the comparison of groups to which members have not been randomly assigned, such as gender and culture. Comparisons of scores across nonequivalent groups require the existence of a common standard (*tertium comparationis*), but various factors may challenge this standard. If a cognitive test is administered to literates and illiterates, it is likely that the former group will be more familiar with the test stimuli and assessment procedures. Inferences about group differences in cognitive aptitudes are incorrect when familiarity is not taken into account. Bias is the generic name for such nuisance factors. It is a common problem in the assessment of nonequivalent groups that occurs when the psychological meaning of the assessment outcome, such as test scores or grades, differs across groups, and also when group differences are to be accounted for (at least to some extent) by auxiliary psychological constructs or measurement artifacts. A closely related concept is equivalence, which refers to the absence of bias, and hence to the similarity of meaning across groups. Historically speaking, the concepts of bias and equivalence have different roots and became associated with somewhat different aspects of group comparisons. Whereas bias usually refers to nuisance factors, equivalence has become the generic term for the implications of bias on the comparability of scores.

Bias and equivalence are characteristics of a particular score comparison; they are not inherent properties of a measurement instrument (e.g., test or inventory), but arise in a group comparison with a particular instrument. Score comparisons of groups that differ in more test-relevant aspects will be more susceptible to bias.

Bias

Different types of bias can be envisaged. The first is construct bias, which occurs when the construct measured is not identical across groups. An example comes from Ho's work (1996) on filial piety in China. The concept refers to the behaviors associated with being a good son or daughter. In Western countries the core of the concept is made up of immaterial aspects such as love and respect; the Chinese concept is broader. In China it is more commonly expected that children play an active role in taking care of their parents once they are unable to support themselves. A Western-based measure of filial piety will insufficiently cover the Chinese concept, while a Chinese questionnaire will be too broad according to Western standards.

Method bias refers to all sources of assessment problems emanating from an instrument or its administration, such as the influence of the person of the tester on the best outcome. Finally, item bias (or differential item functioning) refers to anomalies at item level, such as a poor translation of words or difference in connotations in multilingual studies. For instance, the word *aggression* can be translated into various languages, but in most translations it will be impossible to maintain the combined American meaning of violence ("an aggressive predator") and enterprising energy ("an aggressive salesperson").

Sophisticated psychometric techniques are available to identify item bias.

Equivalence

As an elaboration of categorizations proposed in the literature (e.g., Lonner & Berry, 1986), four different types of equivalence are proposed here (cf. Van de Vijver & Leung, 1997). The first type involves construct inequivalence ("comparing apples and oranges"). The second and best known is called structural, or functional, equivalence. Measures show structural equivalence if they assess the same construct in each group at hand, but the measures may use different stimuli across groups. In the case of nonidentical instruments, the construct validity is often examined by means of a comparison of nomological networks across groups. [*See* Construct Validity.] If identical measures have been applied, exploratory factor analyses, followed by target rotations, may be applied to examine construct validity (Van de Vijver & Leung, 1997). There is no sound rationale for the common practice of comparing scores across cultures after factoral similarity has been established. Despite this practice, the identity of factor solutions across groups does not yet warrant numerical score comparisons. Such a comparison is only allowed when construct and method bias (e.g., social desirability or stimulus familiarity) are absent.

The third type of equivalence is called measurement unit equivalence. Two measures show this type of equivalence if their measurement scales have the same unit and a different origin. For example, suppose that a Western intelligence test has been administered to literate and illiterate subjects. Group differences in performance may be due to a mixture of valid group differences and measurement artifacts (method bias). Without evidence of the relative contributions of both sources, it is prudent to refrain from direct score comparisons. Structural equation modeling of covariance structures and multigroup comparisons of confirmatory factor analytic models have become a popular tool to examine measurement unit equivalence (Van de Vijver & Leung, 1997).

Only in the fourth type, scalar equivalence or full scale equivalence, can direct score comparisons be made, enabling statements such as "Group A scores higher on propensity X than group B." This type of equivalence assumes equal interval or ratio scales across groups. Decisions about which of the latter two types of equivalence apply are often difficult to make and controversial. Racial differences in intelligence test scores have been interpreted as due to valid differences (scalar equivalence) and as reflecting measurement artifacts (measurement unit equivalence).

Linguistic Equivalence

Linguistic equivalence arises in the context of multilingual studies. Two language versions of an instrument show linguistic equivalence if the versions have the same characteristics that are relevant for the measurement outcome, such as meaning, connotations of words, comprehensibility, and readability. Some lexical features may jeopardize linguistic equivalence, such as the use of idiom and metaphors (e.g., "feeling blue") or words that are hard to translate because of the absence of an equivalent word in the target language (e.g., the English word *distress* does not have an equivalent in many languages).

Bibliography

Berry, J. W., Poortinga, Y. H., & Pandey, J. (Eds.). (1997). *Handbook of cross-cultural psychology.* Boston: Allyn & Bacon. Bias and equivalence are discussed in various chapters, particularly in the first of the three volumes.

Hambleton, R. K. (1994). Guidelines for adapting educational and psychological tests: A progress report. *European Journal of Psychological Assessment 10,* 229–244. Presents an elaborate set of recommended practices in multilingual studies prepared by an international committee of psychologists. The combined efforts of psychologists and experts in the language and culture of target populations are proposed as a powerful means to safeguard accurate translations and adaptations.

Inkeles, A., & Sasaki, M. (Eds.). (1996). *Comparing nations and cultures*. Englewood Cliffs, NJ: Prentice Hall. Contains reprinted material of nonpsychological comparative studies. The first two sections contain contributions by eminent comparative sociologists.

Lonner, W. J., & Berry, J. W. (Eds.). (1986). *Field methods in cross-cultural research*. Newbury Park, CA: Sage. A practical guide for cross-cultural researchers.

Naroll, R., & Cohen, R. (Eds.). (1970). *A handbook of method in cultural anthropology*. New York: Natural History Press. A classical text on the methodological aspects of cultural anthropology. The chapter by Werner and Campbell deals with linguistic equivalence (decentering).

Van de Vijver, F. J. R., and Leung, K. (1997). *Methods and data analysis for cross-cultural research*. Newbury Park, CA: Sage. Provides a rather comprehensive overview of the methodological issues of nonequivalent studies.

Fons J. R. van de Vijver

BIBLIOTHERAPHY. *See* Self-Help Therapy.

BICULTURALISM. *See* Cultural Pluralism.

BILINGUALISM. A large proportion of the world's population knows and uses more than one language on a regular basis. These individuals are functionally bilingual, although their range in proficiency and use may vary considerably. According to the 1990 U.S. census, an estimated 32 million people live in households where a language other than English is spoken. In many other societies, most of the populace is bilingual, with different languages being used in separate parts of the social system. For example, in Tanzania, the local vernacular language is used in everyday conversations and in local courts, a lingua franca known as Swahili is used as the broader language of communication and commerce, and English occupies the space of higher education and certain official business. English continues to play a substantial role in many parts of the world as "the other language," initially as part of British colonialism, and more recently as a de facto standard of the world. Although many North Americans continue to insist that the monolingual native speaker is the pure idealized individual, sociolinguists such as Charles Ferguson have observed that "the whole mystique of native speaker and mother tongue should probably be quietly dropped from the linguists' set of professional myths about language" (Ferguson, 1982, p. vii).

Common Typologies

Bilingualism is a complex phenomenon, involving variation at both the individual and social levels. A number of characterizations have been offered to capture some of the complexities of bilingualism, deriving from the various disciplines that have taken an interest in the phenomenon, particularly sociology, psychology, and linguistics.

Joshua Fishman (1977) focused on the social status of the group that becomes bilingual, and distinguished between elite and folk bilingualism. The *elite* bilingual develops a second language by choice, often in order to enhance social status. For example, many English-speaking parents in Canada send their children to programs that immerse them in French so that their children develop high proficiency in both French and English. By contrast, *folk* bilinguals develop second-language capacity under circumstances that are not often of their own choosing, and in conditions where society does not value their native language. Folk bilingualism characterizes the situation of many immigrant groups in the United States, a situation that usually results in a shift to English monolingualism within one or two generations. Bilingualism in elite groups is celebrated by society, whereas bilingualism of the folk variety is kept private. Elite bilingualism is accompanied by literacy in both languages, whereas in folk bilingualism, literacy in the native language is haphazard. Society holds different expectations for the educational attainment of elite and folk bilinguals.

Another consideration is the relative proficiency in one language versus the other, for example, as measured through tests of verbal intelligence. Bilinguals are not expected to be completely equivalent in their two language capacities, but those who approach this are said to be *balanced* bilinguals. By contrast, those still in the early stages of second-language acquisition or with incomplete development are said to be *dominant* in their native language. The term *semilingualism* is often used to describe the language situation of immigrant and language-minority populations whose native language may be different from the standards of their native country, yet whose second language is also considered substandard. As a cognitive construct, this concept should be viewed with considerable suspicion because psychometric tests of language proficiency have questionable validity for nonstandard varieties of the language (Romaine, 1995).

Other approaches have looked at the cognitive organization of bilinguals. Particularly influential is a classic distinction by Uriel Weinreich (1953/1974) in how concepts and words are organized in the two languages depending on the conditions under which the two languages are learned. In a *compound* bilingual, the two languages are learned in the same context, such that the equivalent words in the two languages are associated with the same concept. In a *coordinate* bilingual, the languages are learned in different environments (e.g., home vs. school), such that the two words are associated with distinct concepts. A considerable number of studies have asked whether these different experiences lead to different psychological outcomes. The answer seems to be a mild "yes," but it is also difficult to separate this from the fact that compound bilinguals typically become bilingual at an earlier age than coordinate bilinguals. Other studies asked whether the verbal memory systems of bilinguals are independent or interdependent. A wide variety of cognitive measures using memory and psycholinguistic processing tasks have been applied to these questions, especially with bilinguals who are considered relatively balanced in their proficiencies in the two languages. Generally, these studies suggest that bilinguals are able to keep their two languages functionally separate, but that much depends on the particular demands of the cognitive task (Hamers & Blanc, 1989).

Another useful distinction is the age at which one becomes bilingual. A *simultaneous* bilingual is one who is exposed to both languages from birth. If exposure to the second language occurs after age 3, the term *sequential* bilingual is used. Among sequential bilinguals, it is common to distinguish between whether the second-language acquisition took place in childhood, adolescence, or adulthood, since age of learning is related to the extent of second-language development.

The research literature does not address what many laypersons would consider to be a possibly important typology: the degree of linguistic similarity or difference between the two languages. For example, all other factors being equal, are Chinese English bilinguals cognitively different from Spanish English bilinguals? Lack of attention to this question is primarily due to the tradition of second-language acquisition research that has paid more attention to the commonality between languages than their differences.

Second-Language Acquisition

Understanding the process of becoming bilingual (second-language acquisition) draws significantly from the study of first-language acquisition in children. The learner approaches the task equipped with considerable a priori knowledge about linguistic structure, the connections between linguistic and cognitive categories, and the social conditions of language use. Acquisition is best described as a learner-driven, selective process that is relatively robust to environmental variation (Bialystok & Hakuta, 1994).

Studies of second-language acquisition can be divided into those of children and adults, and those in conditions of formal and informal learning environments. Generally, they demonstrate a surprising amount of similarity across different conditions of learning in the observable patterns of development and in the types of errors that can be found. For example, the order of acquisition of certain English grammatical function words is very similar across learners of different native language backgrounds and across different ages of learners. Errors of overregularization (e.g., "comed" for "came") and simplification ("Peter like ice cream"), commonly found in children learning English as a first language, are also commonly found in second-language learners. Second-language learners are also capable of mastering highly complex and abstract rule systems described by generative linguists, which are considered unlearnable from experience (White, 1989).

The nature and extent to which the native language plays a role in second-language acquisition have been under investigation for some time. Early researchers believed that most of second-language acquisition could be accounted for by transfer from the native language, and that areas of difficulty in learning could be predicted from a contrastive analysis of the structures of the two languages. The evidence supported only a modest version of this view, and it is now generally accepted that the structural aspects of second-language acquisition are primarily driven by characteristics of the target language rather than by those of the native language.

Another dimension of the relationship between the first and second language is a quantitative one: Is the proficiency level in the native language related to the speed and extent to which the second language develops? This is an important question for bilingual education programs. In general, studies suggest that there is a positive relationship between the development of the two languages, especially on measures of language proficiency that resemble school related verbal aptitude rather than conversational proficiency (National Research Council, 1997).

Age of the learner is clearly an important predictor of the ultimate level of second-language acquisition, and is amply documented. Some have gone further and hypothesized a biologically determined critical period for this capacity that ends at puberty (Johnson & Newport, 1989). The hypothesis would predict both quantitative and qualitative differences in learning when it occurs within and outside the period. This does not appear to be the case. The probability of success in acquisition is a linear function of age, decreasing from early childhood and well into adulthood, and there are no marked discontinuities at puberty. There are no major qualitative differences in patterns of second-language acquisition among learners before and after puberty, such as in types of grammatical errors. And there is ample evidence of successful second-language acquisition by individuals past the critical period, even in aspects of the language considered to require specialized a priori knowledge of language in order to be learnable.

Outcomes of Bilingualism

The early American literature on bilingualism pointed to its negative consequences (Hakuta, 1986). In most of the studies, IQ tests were administered to immigrant students, and bilingual children scored lower than native English monolinguals. They concluded that bilingualism confused the child and should be avoided. This led to the common advice offered to immigrant parents: use English in the home even if the parents could not speak it proficiently. Critics of this work pointed out that many of these students were probably not bilingual at all and were handicapped in taking the test because they were not proficient in English. More recent research, which has selected participants carefully, such as choosing only balanced bilinguals, has shown advantages for bilinguals on a variety of verbal and nonverbal tasks (Romaine, 1995). In general, negative findings tend to appear when bilingualism is a characteristic of low social status, and thus it is more properly understood through sociological rather than psychological analysis.

Studies of bilingual language use are primarily descriptive. Many studies have described *code-switching*, the many meanings and functions that are conveyed in conversation when bilinguals switch from one language to the other. Earlier literature would have treated the phenomenon as a sign of linguistic confusion, whereas modern sociolinguistics interprets code-switching as a rhetorical device that is part of the linguistic repertoire available to bilinguals (Zentella, 1997). Other studies have looked at the various social spaces occupied by the two languages, such as in homes, schools, and community institutions. They portray an ecological picture of community bilingualism that defies simple stereotypes (Vasquez, Pease-Alvarez, & Shannon, 1994).

A strong interest of the sociolinguistic literature on bilingualism is in the stability of bilingualism over generations, a field known as *language maintenance and shift*. Bilingualism tends to be more stable when the languages occupy clear institutional space and pockets of social identity, for example, Hebrew for religious services, Spanish at home. Bilingualism among immigrant groups is especially characterized by a shift to monolingualism in the societal language. It is useful to remember that language shift occurs over generations much more than over the course of an individual life span. Psycholinguistic evidence suggests that once acquired, individuals do not forget the language. However, it is common for individuals to shift their usage of language such that they become functionally monolingual, rarely using their native language or only on restricted occasions.

Bilingual Education

In the United States, bilingual education commonly refers to programs that have been developed for students of non-English home backgrounds whose English proficiency is limited (the commonly used acronym is L.E.P. for limited English proficient). These programs help L.E.P. students learn English and develop academic skills, using the native language as part of the medium of instruction. Most programs have a transitional goal, in which the use of the native language is reduced as the students acquire English. Students are transitioned out of such programs into English-only mainstream classes within two to five years. A smaller number of bilingual programs have maintenance of the native language and balanced bilingualism as an explicit goal. It is important to note that, although a large variety of languages are represented within the L.E.P. population, approximately 75% are from Spanish language background. Poverty level is also disproportionately represented among Spanish speakers, with about 80% of the L.E.P. students from homes below the poverty level. Most bilingual education programs are located in population centers with high concentrations of Spanish speakers (National Research Council, 1997).

For those not receiving bilingual education, a number of other approaches are commonly used. In an English-as-a-second-language (ESL) approach, the student is placed in regular mainstream classes but is pulled out by a specialist teacher several times a week and given special instruction aimed at the development of English skills, with a primary focus on grammar, vocabulary, and communication rather than academic content areas. In a structured immersion program, the student is placed in a class consisting only of L.E.P. students, and instruction is given in English only, but with teachers making special modifications to simplify their English in order to be more comprehensible to students. The "sink-or-swim" approach offers no special assistance of L.E.P. students, and is also often called "the old-fashioned method" experienced by previous generations of immigrants.

These methods (with the exception of sink or swim) came about in response to federal and state laws requiring local school districts to provide special support for L.E.P. students, especially after a U.S. Supreme Court decision ruled that "There is no equality of treatment merely by providing students with the same facilities, textbooks, teachers, and curriculum; for students who do not understand English are effectively foreclosed from any meaningful education" (*Lau v. Nichols*, 1974).

The ruling, widely referred to as *Lau*, mandates that special assistance be given L.E.P. students to overcome their handicap. Sink-or-swim methods violate *Lau*.

Research on second-language acquisition and the outcomes of bilingualism have provided a theoretical base for bilingual programs (Baker, 1993). The native language is seen as providing a base for English-language acquisition, and strengthening the native language is seen to enhance, rather than detract from, the goal of second-language acquisition. The ideal program also emphasizes the development of the whole child, rather than just English-language skills (Genesee, 1994). Programs based on sound educational and psychological theory are considered optimal, but their full implementation has obstacles, both practical and political.

The practical obstacles include a shortage of teachers who can teach bilingually, and a complex set of legal, administrative, and funding issues in urban school districts that balance the needs of school desegregation and the needs for specialized, and often segregated, instruction. The political obstacles are wariness and lack of support among substantial portions of the population. The reasons for this are threefold. First, bilingual education is a product of the civil rights movement and represents the politics of group identity and recognition by a new wave of immigrants, especially Latinos. Second, it is a form of official U.S. language policy, and is seen by some to threaten the status of English. And third, it is seen as government intervention in the affairs of education, which is considered a local responsibility.

Evaluation of the effectiveness of bilingual education and other programs serving L.E.P. students has been frustrated by the narrowness of the outcome measures being used and by the inherent variation that exists in a highly decentralized educational system such as in the United States. Demonstrating the effectiveness of the programs is also limited by the fact that the overwhelming majority of the students are poor, and the disadvantages of poverty are known to have large effects on educational outcomes independent of language status. Evaluation designs that emphasize strategies to improve the whole school climate and balance formative evaluation with more traditional modes of summative evaluation are needed (National Research Council, 1997)

Foreign language programs in the United States present an opportunity for the development of bilingualism as well, but for the English-speaking population. Foreign language immersion programs for English-speaking students have been motivated by the poor success of traditional foreign language education programs in attaining anything close to bilingual proficiency among American students. They were modeled after Canadian French immersion programs, which were developed to help Canadian Anglophone students attain strong proficiency in French. Since these programs were begun for middle-class students and at the demand of parents who saw value in promoting bilingualism in their children, they can safely be considered a case of elite bilingualism. In these programs, the target language is used as the medium of instruction from kindergarten, and instruction in the native language (the majority language of the society) is gradually introduced as the students develop proficiency in the target language. Immersion programs are considered to be very effective in promoting strong bilingual ability for the language-majority group, and have been successfully replicated in the United States.

Two-way (dual) immersion programs are a hybrid of maintenance bilingual education programs for language-minority students and foreign language immersion programs for English-speaking students. Native speakers of English are placed in programs with native speakers of the target language, and the goal is to develop balanced bilingualism for both groups, with each group serving as native language models for the other. The programs begin with an emphasis on the non-English language and gradually move to equal proportions of each language. Such programs are growing in popularity as a way of counteracting the stigma of bilingualism in the United States (National Research Council, 1997).

Conclusion

Bilingualism is a widespread phenomenon of substantial individual and societal consequence. Although cognitive and linguistic representations of bilingualism in individuals may be relatively stable across sociological variations, the long-term prospects for the development of bilingualism in the population depend on societal and political factors. Broad public acknowledgment of bilingualism as an asset for all segments of society would be an important step in improving education programs along with other efforts to stimulate language capacity in the nation.

[*See also* Language, *article on* Language Acquisition; *and* Psycholinguistics.]

Bibliography

Baker, C. (1993). *Foundations of bilingual education and bilingualism.* Clevedon, England: Multilingual Matters.

Bialystok, E., & Hakuta, K. (1994). *In other words: The science and psychology of second-language acquisition.* New York: Basic Books.

Crawford, J. (1992). *Hold your tongue: Bilingualism and the politics of "English only."* Reading, MA: Addison-Wesley.

Extra, G., & Verhoeven, L. (Eds.). (1993). *Immigrant lan-*

guages in Europe. Clevedon, England: Multilingual Matters.

Ferguson, C. (1982). Foreword. In B. Kachru (Ed.), *The other tongue: English across cultures* (pp. vii–xi). Urbana: University of Illinois Press.

Fishman, J. (1977). The social science perspective. In *Bilingual education: Current perspectives* (Vol 1). Arlington, VA: Center for Applied Linguistics.

Genesee, F. (Ed.). (1994). *Educating second-language children: The whole child, the whole curriculum, the whole community*. Cambridge, England: Cambridge University Press.

Hakuta, K. (1986). *Mirror of language*. New York: Basic Books.

Hamers, J., & Blanc, M. (1989). *Bilinguality and bilingualism*. Cambridge, England: Cambridge University Press.

Johnson, J. S., & Newport, E. L. (1989). Critical periods effects in second-language learning: The influence of maturational state on the acquisition of English as a second language. *Cognitive Psychology, 21*, 60–99.

Lau v. Nichols, 414 U.S. 563 (1974).

National Research Council. (1997). *Improving schooling for language minority children: A research agenda*. Washington, DC: National Academy Press.

Romaine, S. (1995). *Bilingualism* (2nd ed.). Oxford: Blackwell.

Vasquez, O., Pease-Alvarez, L., & Shannon, S. (1994). *Pushing boundaries: Language and culture in a Mexicano community*. Cambridge: Cambridge University Press.

Weinreich, U. (1974). *Languages in contact: Findings and problems*. The Hague: Mouton. (Original work published 1953)

White, L. (1989). *Universal grammar and second language acquisition*. Philadelphia: John Benjamins.

Zentella, A. C. (1997). *Growing up bilingual: Puerto Rican children in New York*. Williston, VT: Blackwell.

Kenji Hakuta

BINET, ALFRED (1857–1911), French psychologist. Binet is best known to psychologists for initiating the modern approach to intelligence testing. Although the idea of an intelligence test had been proposed by Francis Galton (1822–1911) as early as 1865, attempts by Galton and successors such as James McKeen Cattell (1860–1944) to implement the idea with neurophysiologically based measures had met with little success. In 1905 Binet, with his younger colleague Théodore Simon (1873–1961), developed a series of test items (revised and expanded in 1908 and 1911) that were graded in terms of the age at which normal French children were first able to pass them. Requiring a general knowledge of French language and culture but no specific school learning, these items served as norms according to which a mental level, or *mental age*, could be calculated for any child, based on the most difficult items he or she could pass. Binet and Simon's principal goal was to identify subnormal children who would be unable to prosper in an ordinary school curriculum. As a rule of thumb (but with the proviso that test results should never be the sole criterion for diagnosing subnormality), Binet suggested that children whose mental ages lagged more than 2 years behind their actual ages should be targeted for further investigation. Implicit here was the notion that mental deficiency in children can be conceptualized as a *retardation* in the normal rate of intellectual development. Although originally intended for the relatively restricted purpose of assessing the lower end of the intelligence distribution in children, the Binet–Simon method was soon adapted by others in attempts to measure the full range of mental ability, in adults as well as children.

Binet's Early Career

Although the intelligence tests introduced by Binet between 1905 and 1911 were the most famous of his contributions, they were actually just the capstone of a career as a versatile and prolific general psychologist. Previously he had done significant work in psychophysics, hypnosis, abnormal psychology, social psychology, cognition, developmental psychology, and personality assessment. He made his multifaceted contributions without benefit of formal training in psychology, and never held a paid position in the field.

The only child of wealthy parents, Binet took an unsatisfying first degree in law before a brief experience in medical school precipitated a severe emotional breakdown. Near the end of his convalescence he acquired a reader's ticket for Paris's great Bibliothèque Nationale and—following some vague inclination—began browsing the literature in psychology. He quickly realized that he had found his vocation and impulsively began writing articles about his new interests. His first published article, on the two-point threshold, contained numerous beginner's errors and elicited a stinging critique from the Belgian physiologist Joseph L. R. Delboeuf (1831–1921). A second publication incautiously asserted that the major operations of the mind are nothing but diverse forms of the three classical laws of association. Then, seeking some firsthand experience in the emerging field of dynamic psychology, Binet volunteered in 1884 to work as an unpaid assistant for the eminent neurologist, Jean-Martin Charcot (1825–1893), at Paris's Salpêtrière Hospital.

During 6 years at the Salpêtrière, Binet produced 3 books and 20 articles on such topics as hypnotism, illusions of movement, alterations of personality, attention and reasoning, and sexual *fetishism* (a term Binet himself coined). Besides broadening his knowledge of psychology, he benefited from exposure to Charcot's "clinical" method of intensively studying individual cases, and consequent appreciation of the individuality and complexity of each person. These positive developments were ultimately overshadowed, however, by his overly enthusiastic advocacy of Charcot's controversial theory of *grand hypnotisme*: the notion that hypnotic susceptibility occurs in a particularly pure or "major" form in a very small minority of individuals who demonstrate spectacular symptoms while entering a hypnotic trance in a sequence of stereotyped stages. This theory was challenged by the Nancy school of hypnotists, who interpreted hypnotic susceptibility as akin to ordinary suggestibility. It also aroused the skepticism of Binet's old nemesis Delboeuf, who visited the Salpêtrière and then published a devastating critique of the manner in which Binet had blatantly conveyed his expectations to the hypnotized participant. In due course Binet himself conceded that his hypnotic experiments had been fatally tainted by the effects of unintended suggestion, which he referred to as the "cholera of psychology."

The chastened Binet left the Salpêtrière, and for a year confined his psychological research to home experiments on his two young daughters, to whom he administered a wide variety of puzzles and mental tests, some of which anticipated the later conservation tasks of Piaget. The experience left Binet skeptical about the potential of sensory or neurophysiologically based tests for discriminating intellectual differences in children. Then in 1891 he volunteered to serve as an unpaid assistant in France's first Laboratory of Experimental Psychology, just established at the Sorbonne. There, Binet quickly proved himself invaluable and was named associate director in 1892 and director (although still without pay) in 1895. In 1894 he established *L'Année Psychologique* as a publication outlet for the laboratory's research findings, a journal that continues today as France's best known psychology periodical.

Psychologist at the Sorbonne

From his Sorbonne base, Binet became a prolific and versatile experimenter. He conducted influential case studies of a small number of chess and calculating prodigies, as well as some of France's leading authors. With his student Victor Henri (1872–1940), he studied visual memory in groups of young children and then—in an experiment that clearly anticipated Solomon E. Asch's conformity studies of the 1950s—showed how their reported memories could be influenced by various suggestive pressures, including "leading questions" and the hearing of false reports from fellow participants. Binet's 1900 book, *La Suggestibilité*, elaborated by demonstrating how sensitive children are to the style as well as the content of questions put to them. This work is now recognized as a pioneering and still valid warning about the potential unreliability of children's eyewitness testimony.

In 1896, Binet and Henri proposed a program called "Individual Psychology" with the goal of developing a series of short tests that would yield a profile of an individual comparable in richness and complexity to Binet's laboriously conducted case studies. Although that specific goal proved elusive, Binet continued to experiment usefully with his growing daughters. His 1903 book, *L'Étude Expérimentale de l'Intelligence*, described the results of more than 20 exercises that today would be called projective tests, including sentence-completion items, imaginative storytelling in response to neutral stimuli, or (a decade before Herman Rorschach) responding to ink blots. The book also reported some observations suggesting the existence of imageless thought, four years before that concept became well known through the publications of the so-called Würzburg school. In still other studies from his Sorbonne base, Binet and his collaborators investigated correlations between psychological and physiological variables such as blood pressure, physical strength, or head measurements. He conducted exhaustive experiments on the two-point threshold, more than compensating for the limitations of his first publication. He studied intellectual fatigue and the influence of the scholarly life on the consumption of bread.

Intelligence Tests

Around the turn of the nineteenth century, Binet joined and became a leader of La Société Libre pour l'Étude Psychologique de l'Enfant (The Free Society for the Psychological Study of the Child), a group of teachers and school administrators interested in practical educational issues. In 1904, he led a commission to investigate the problem of diagnosing mental deficiency, an issue that had gained visibility with the enactment of universal education laws, dictating that all children had to be provided with publicly funded education. It became crucial to identify children who were genuinely subnormal and could not hope to prosper in a normal academic curriculum. Simon, a young physician who had contacts with some schools for mentally deficient children, came to work with Binet at the Sorbonne at about the same time. Working together, the two soon had their insight about the age-related nature of intellectual growth, and the famous test of 1905 duly appeared, followed by the revisions of 1908 and 1911.

Ironically, given future developments with his testing method, Binet always retained a belief in the necessity of regarding people as individuals, and he cautioned against the dangers of excessive quantification. Mere numbers, he argued, can never capture the real essence of any individual's reactions. Binet himself never quantified the results of his intelligence tests beyond the calculation of a mental age, which could be approximately compared to a child's actual age. Furthermore, he firmly believed that the intelligence measured by his tests was not a fixed entity, but could be enhanced by appropriate training, which he called *mental orthopedics*. Unfortunately, he died in 1911 before he could defend these views against the work of other investigators who eagerly adopted his testing technique but interpreted the results very differently. The German psychologist Louis William Stern (1871–1938) proposed computing an "intelligence quotient" for each child by taking the ratio of mental age over chronological age, and the American Lewis M. Terman (1877–1956) multiplied Stern's quotient by 100 and abbreviated the result as the now famous "IQ." Terman also argued strongly that IQs significantly higher than 100 represented valid indications of superior intelligence or even genius. The Englishman Charles E. Spearman (1863–1945) argued for IQ scores as representative of a unitary and primarily hereditary "general intelligence." These ideas have remained controversial as well as highly influential, and would undoubtedly have been opposed by Binet had he lived longer. [*See also* Stanford–Binet Intelligence Scale.]

[*Many of the people mentioned in this article are the subjects of independent biographical entries.*]

Bibliography

Works by Binet

Binet, A. (1900). *La suggestibilité* [Suggestibility]. Paris: Schleicher. Describes Binet's pioneering but seldom cited work on conformity, suggestibility, and eyewitness testimony in children.

Binet, A. (1903). *L'Étude expérimental de l'intelligence* [The experimental study of intelligence]. Paris: Schleicher. Documents Binet's use of projective methods to study his two daughters; also contains a chapter on imageless thought.

Binet, A. (1973). *Les idées modernes sur les enfants* [Modern ideas about children]. Paris: Flammarion. (Original work published 1909) Expresses Binet's belief in the plasticity of intelligence, and describes his program of mental orthopedics.

Binet, A., & Henri, V. (1896). La psychologie individuelle [Individual psychology]. *L'Année Psychologique, 2,* 411–465. Outlines Binet and Henri's ultimately unsuccessful program of individual psychology.

Binet, A., & Simon, T. (1973). *The development of intelligence in children (The Binet–Simon Scale)*. New York: Arno Press. English translations of the famous 1905, 1908, and 1911 Binet–Simon tests with their original introductions by the authors.

Works about Binet

Fancher, R. E. (1985). *The intelligence men: Makers of the IQ controversy*. New York: Norton. A general history of intelligence testing, with Binet featured in Chapter 2.

Pollack, R. H., & Brenner, M. W. (Eds.). (1969). *The experimental psychology of Alfred Binet: Selected papers*. New York: Springer. English translations of several of Binet's shorter articles on a variety of topics.

Siegler, R. S. (1992). The other Alfred Binet. *Developmental Psychology, 28,* 179–190. An appreciative account of Binet's diverse contributions, apart from intelligence testing.

Wolf, T. (1973). *Alfred Binet*. Chicago: University of Chicago Press. The definitive biography.

Raymond E. Fancher

BINGHAM, WALTER VAN DYKE (1880–1952), American psychologist and founder of industrial/organizational psychology. Bingham, who was born in Swan Lake City, Iowa, discovered psychology at Beloit College in a course taught by Guy Allen Tawney, a student of Wilhelm Wundt. After graduating and teaching high school, Bingham began doctoral work at the University of Chicago. His dissertation (1908) on the perception of melody reflected the early professional sway of Wundtian psychophysics; Bingham soon joined the American disciples of Wundt, the "Experimentalists," whose leader, E. B. Titchener, defended laboratory standards against the corrupting influence of practical applications.

Yet Chicago's functionalist psychology had a greater impact on Bingham's career than might be suggested by his membership in the Experimentalists. He was influenced by John Dewey's "reflex arc" critique. In a letter to E. G. Boring dated 6 March 1948 (Bingham Papers), Bingham wrote that James R. Angell "committed" him "to the [William] Jamesian position and the incurable habit of asking 'What good is this mental process? What function has it in the cycle of on-going biological adjustments? What use can we put it to outside the laboratory?' "

When Bingham became an instructor at Columbia University, another functionalist mentor led him to applied psychology. E. L. Thorndike, America's leading educational psychologist, guided Bingham in developing mental tests that aimed to help students adapt to school environments. Thorndike encouraged him to take a position at Dartmouth University, where Bingham created a psychological laboratory and wrote mental tests for Dartmouth's individualized advisement system.

After presenting data on tests of Dartmouth freshmen to the American Psychological Association in 1914, Bingham was approached by the president of the Carnegie Institute of Technology, Arthur Hamerschlag, who wondered what role psychology might play in the administration of his 10-year-old school. Bingham developed a comprehensive plan for psychological assistance: in predicting prospective students' performance, in improving teaching in the diverse colleges, and in counseling current students on appropriate employment. Carnegie Tech hired Bingham in September 1915 to create the first American "division" of applied psychology, which was both an administrative unit and an academic department.

The division demonstrated how the administrative and educational functions of higher education could vertically integrate the extraction, processing, and distribution of student materials. Several local corporate leaders immediately developed a consortium to sponsor a Bureau of Salesmanship Research in the division in 1916. Bingham hired Walter Dill Scott to direct the bureau and named him the first American professor of applied psychology. He eschewed such designation for himself in order to maintain his Experimentalist standing while promoting psychology as a (Baconian) science that experimented in socially useful contexts. Creation of several other practical bureaus followed, but the remarkable extra-academic success of psychological management spoiled the original purpose of Bingham's program, which was to manage students. The Division of Applied Psychology disbanded in 1924, when a liberal arts oriented president succeeded Hamerschlag. Bingham resigned from academia for a career of private consulting.

The expansion of practical programs followed largely upon the success of Bingham and other psychologists in World War I. Consistent with his efforts to balance practical and Experimentalist concerns, Bingham served as top assistant to both Scott and Robert M. Yerkes, who failed to reconcile these differences and established separate psychological organizations in the U.S. Army. After helping Yerkes write the first group test of intelligence, Bingham took charge of validating the new test against Scott's subjective Rating Scale for Selecting Captains. Mediating experimentalist interests in "general intelligence" and the Army's concern for the special abilities of their personnel, Bingham initiated and led the Trade Test Division, which constructed the first paper-and-pencil achievement tests. The Army commissioned Bingham as a lieutenant colonel at the end of the war, and, in World War II, as its chief psychologist.

Bingham was executive director of the Personnel Research Federation (1924–1934), an early director of the Psychological Corporation (1921–1947; president, 1926–1928), and president of the American Association of Applied Psychology (1942) as it merged with the American Psychological Association. He was a founder and president of the National Research Council Division on Anthropology and Psychology. He wrote *Procedures in Employment Psychology* (with Max Freyd, Chicago, 1926), *How to Interview* (with Bruce V. Moore, New York, 1931), and *Aptitudes and Aptitude Testing* (New York, 1938). He was editor in chief of *Journal of Personnel Research* (1923–1933) and was a consulting editor of the *Journal of Applied Psychology* and *Journal of Consulting Psychology*.

More an impresario than an innovator, Bingham represents the cautious transition of professional psychology into industrial settings. Bingham married Mil-

licent Todd, a naturalist. They had no children. Bingham died in Washington, D.C., in 1952.

[*Many of the people mentioned in this article are the subjects of independent biographical entries.*]

Bibliography

Bingham, W. V. (1923). Psychology applied. *Scientific Monthly*, *16*, 141–159. Describes mission at Carnegie Institute of Technology.

Bingham, W. V. Papers. Hunt Library, Carnegie-Mellon University, Pittsburgh, PA. Bingham's papers were collected largely by Leonard Ferguson, whose own (complementary) papers are at the same location.

Bingham, W. V. (1952). Walter Van Dyke Bingham. In E. G. Boring, H. S. Langfeld, H. Werner, & R. M. Yerkes, (Eds.), *A history of psychology in autobiography* (Vol. 4, pp. 1–26). Worcester, MA: Clark University Press.

Ferguson, L. (1963). *The heritage of industrial psychology*. Hartford, CT: Finlay Press. Ferguson first called Bingham an "impresario," although Bingham's wife asked him to use the term "dean" instead.

von Mayrhauser, R. T. (1987). The manager, the medic, and the mediator: The clash of professional psychological styles and the wartime origins of group mental testing. In M. M. Sokal (Ed.), *Psychological testing and American society: 1890–1930* (pp. 128–157). New Brunswick, NJ: Rutgers University Press.

Richard T. von Mayrhauser

BIOFEEDBACK has been defined as "a process in which a person learns to reliably influence physiological responses of two kinds: either responses which are not ordinarily under voluntary control or responses which are ordinarily easily regulated but for which regulation has broken down due to trauma or disease" (Blanchard & Epstein, 1978). Three processes, all of which are handled electronically, are involved in biofeedback: (1) the detection and amplification of various *bio*logical or *bio*electrical signals present in an individual's body; (2) the conversion of these amplified signals into information which is easy to process (usually visual or auditory); and (3) *feeding back* this information to the individual on a relatively immediate basis.

Historical Overview

The term *biofeedback* emerged in 1969 after a meeting in Santa Monica, California, of more than 100 researchers interested in various aspects of feedback influences, basic and applied, on physiology. At this meeting, the Biofeedback Research Society was formed as a vehicle for sharing information and support for this line of inquiry. Its early interests encompassed, among other topics, working with curarized rats and brain stimulation as a reward for controlling autonomically mediated responses such as heart rate and vasodilation, controlling aspects of the human electroencephalogram (EEG), and retraining stroke victims by use of peripherally measured changes in electromyogram (EMG).

The organization continued to grow and began publishing its own journal, *Biofeedback and Self-Regulation*, in 1976. Also in 1976, reflecting the growing interests in the clinical application of biofeedback within the organization, its name was changed to the Biofeedback Society of America. It underwent another change of name, to the Association of Applied Psychophysiology and Biofeedback, in 1989. Also, reflecting the interests of biofeedback practitioners and third-party payers, the Biofeedback Certification Institute of America, a certification institution, was founded in 1983. This organization conducts regular certification examinations and training programs for those interested in the clinical applications of biofeedback. In 1997, the name of its journal was changed to *Applied Psychophysiology and Biofeedback*. Thus, over the 30-plus years of its formal existence, *biofeedback* has evolved from a term which encompassed the interests of diverse researchers investigating the role of external feedback in the control of physiological responses, to a set of clinical procedures routinely used in the care of certain types of patients, and widely, but unevenly, used with a wide array of other clinical conditions.

Research and development in biofeedback has gone through at least three phases: the early, or basic science, phase saw research demonstrating the phenomenon that various physiological responses not normally thought of as being under voluntary control could apparently be brought under control with the assistance of feedback. Responses included aspects of the EEG, heart rate, blood pressure, degree of peripheral vasodilation or constriction (skin surface temperature), electrodermal (GSR), and various aspects of striated muscle, especially those for which control seemed as impaired as the extremities of the stroke victim or the scalp muscles of the chronic tension-type headache sufferer. The parameters of feedback control, such as whether visual or auditory feedback was more efficacious, were also studied. During this time isolated reports of the clinically beneficial effects of biofeedback appeared.

The second phase, which could be termed the early clinical application phase, saw ever increasing reports on the clinical uses of biofeedback to a wide array of problems and also the beginnings of controlled evaluations of biofeedback for the treatment of headaches, Raynaud's disease, as well as its use in neuromuscular rehabilitation.

The third phase, which could be termed the late clinical application phase, or professional acceptance phase, witnessed a number of controlled clinical trials evaluating biofeedback's contribution to the treatment of certain disorders, and its acceptance as a standard treatment alternative or a standard adjunct to total care for certain disorders. It was also recognized that biofeedback was one of several nonpharmacological procedures which had value in treating medical populations.

The two chief forms of biofeedback used on a clinical basis are biofeedback from surface electrodes to measure aspects of the EMG (so-called EMG biofeedback) and biofeedback from a skin surface temperature probe to measure surface temperature (usually from the finger tips), which relates to degree of peripheral vasodilation and vasoconstriction (so-called thermal biofeedback). Three other forms of biofeedback found in clinical practice are biofeedback of electrodermal activity (typically the electrical resistance between two electrodes attached to the hand), biofeedback of various aspects of the electroencephalogram, and biofeedback of cardiac rate (the rate at which the heart is beating). Most agencies providing clinical biofeedback would have the first three routinely available. A good overall text describing the clinical practice of biofeedback is *Biofeedback: A Practitioner's Guide*, by Mark Schwartz.

In this phase there also appeared a new term, *neurofeedback*, which involves biofeedback training of certain aspects of the EEG to benefit attention-deficit/hyperactivity disorder (ADHD) and other problems. This form of biofeedback is still in the second developmental phase, although its proponents probably claim a higher status for it.

Current Issues in Biofeedback

In most clinical applications of biofeedback, the biofeedback training is, per se, one part of a total treatment package that usually includes other procedures, such as various forms of relaxation training, instruction in both regular home practice and application of the new control skills, education about the disorder and organ system(s) involved, and perhaps some cognitive-specific forms of therapy. A topic of some debate and research controversy is what role biofeedback training plays in all of this: Is it necessary or sufficient for clinical improvement, or merely facilitative?

A second topic of debate and research is what role cognitive factors, such as changed expectations, play in the clinical benefits derived from biofeedback training as opposed to the actual physiological changes. Successful biofeedback training inherently carries with it a series of "success experiences" for the participant: he or she can see, moment by moment, that they are controlling some aspect of their physiology. Could it be that these success experiences change expectations and other cognitive factors, which in turn are the prime vehicles for clinical improvement and symptom relief?

In a brilliant study by Holroyd and others (1984), physiological responses and patient expectations were independently manipulated among young tension-type headache sufferers by means of bogus end-of-session computerized feedback. Individuals who believed they were highly successful at the EMG biofeedback task experienced significantly greater headache relief than those who believed they were only modestly successful, regardless of whether muscle tension level was increased or decreased. Blanchard and colleagues replicated this finding with vascular headache patients receiving thermal biofeedback (Blanchard et al., 1994). Thus, the mechanisms by which biofeedback brings about beneficial effects remains a topic of controversy and investigation, especially since a strong dose-response relationship between the degree of biofeedback-trained physical change and the degree of clinical symptom improvement have not been found.

Well-Established Clinical Applications of Biofeedback

Arguably, there is strong evidence for the efficacy of biofeedback training for the following disorders: tension-type HA, migraine HA, low back pain, temperomandibular joint (TMJ) pain, primary Raynaud's disease, fecal incontinence, and as an adjunct in neuromuscular rehabilitation (Blanchard, 1995). It is also clear that biofeedback training can assist an individual to learn to relax deeply and rapidly. Thus, all of the problems for which relaxation training is beneficial are potential areas of biofeedback application, although it is not clearly established that biofeedback training adds to other forms of relaxation training (such as for anxiety disorders).

Other More Controversial Clinical Applications of Biofeedback

A second list could include essential hypertension, epilepsy, ADHD, anxiety disorders, and alcohol and substance abuse. For these diverse disorders, other than hypertension, the problem is the lack of controlled clinical trials demonstrating the superiority or equivalence of biofeedback to standard therapy.

Probably the strongest evidence for the clinical efficacy of biofeedback exists in the application of EMG biofeedback in the form of a frontal placement (active sensors over the eyes with a ground sensor in the middle of the forehead) for tension-type headaches. As early as 1973 there was evidence from a controlled trial (Budzynski et al., 1973) that frontal EMG biofeedback was superior to either attention-placebo control or symptom-monitoring control. This form of biofeedback has been shown repeatedly to be equivalent to various forms of relaxation training and superior to standard physical therapy. For tension-type headaches, relaxation training and cognitive therapy appear to be useful

adjuncts to frontal EMG biofeedback. The beneficial results hold up for at least five years (Blanchard et al., 1987). EMG biofeedback using a trapezius placement seems equally effective.

Another clinical problem for which EMG biofeedback has been proved useful is temperomandibular joint syndrome, or TMJ, a functional disorder of the muscles operating the lower jaw. EMG biofeedback is superior to waiting list controls and equivalent or superior to standard occlusal splint therapy (Dahlstrom et al., 1982) and to cognitive behavioral therapy (Flor & Birbaumer, 1993). EMG biofeedback has also been shown to be effective in the treatment of lower back pain. Flor and Birbaumer (1993) showed it to be superior to cognitive behavioral therapy for this problem. Frontal EMG biofeedback was also shown to be of use in treating generalized anxiety disorder (Rice et al., 1993) and to be helpful in teaching overall relaxation.

The second strongest evidence for the clinical efficacy of biofeedback is the application of thermal biofeedback to Raynaud's disease, a functional disorder involving painful vasospastic episodes in the hands and feet in response to cold and to emotional stress. Freedman and colleagues (Freedman, et al., 1983) have shown that thermal biofeedback is superior to other forms of relaxation (frontal EMG biofeedback and autogenic training) in reducing vasospastic episodes; beneficial results hold up for several years (Freedman et al., 1985). Thermal biofeedback might be preferable to standard medical therapy (nifedipine).

By far the most widespread use of thermal biofeedback for hand warming is in the treatment of migraine headaches, either alone or combined migraine and tension-type headaches. This nonintrusive use of biofeedback was initially described by Sargent and colleagues (Sargent et al., 1973). It has been shown to be equivalent to relaxation training, though superior to a psychological placebo (Blanchard et al., 1990). Comparisons with the standard prophylactic medication propranolol have yielded mixed results, with biofeedback being equivalent (Sovak et al., 1981) or inferior. Beneficial effects hold up for at least five years (Blanchard et al., *Headache*, 1987). There is reason to believe that with migraine headaches in a child or adolescent, thermal biofeedback might be the treatment of choice (Hermann et al., 1995).

A more controversial use of thermal biofeedback is in the treatment of essential hypertension, where first hand warming and then foot warming are taught. Fahrion and colleagues (1986) described good results in a large uncontrolled trial; Blanchard and colleagues (1993) demonstrated good initial results in controlled comparisons to relaxation and autogenic training but were unable to replicate the level of efficacy in a second round of studies. Direct feedback of blood pressure has had a similar history of initial successes (Benson et al.,

1971; Goldstein et al., 1982) but was followed by failures at replication. Thermal biofeedback has been used as part of a multicomponent treatment regimen with irritable bowel syndrome and rheumatoid arthritis. Although there is reasonable support for the value and efficacy of the total treatment package, the necessity of including thermal biofeedback has not been demonstrated. Chronic fecal incontinence is a very debilitating condition. It has been shown that brief biofeedback treatment involving a pressure transducer to detect anal sphincter tone and the coordination of the internal and external anal sphincter can be highly effective (Cerulli et al., 1979). [*See* Irritable Bowel Syndrome and Functional Disorders; *and* Arthritis.]

Another area of biofeedback application has been in the rehabilitation of neuromuscular disorders (spasticity or flaccidity) following stroke. EMG biofeedback from the appropriate placements is used as an adjunct to standard rehabilitation and shows a distinct advantage when it is added (Basmajian et al., 1975). It is routinely incorporated into rehabilitation efforts.

Biofeedback has emerged as a well-recognized alternative therapy for many medical disorders and as a useful adjunct to many others.

Bibliography

Basmajian, J. V. (1975). Biofeedback treatment of food-drop compared with standard rehabilitation techniques: Effects on voluntary control and strength. *Archives of Physical Medicine and Rehabilitation, 56*, 231–236.

Benson, H. (1971). Decreased systolic blood pressure through operant conditioning techniques in patients with essential hypertension. *Science, 173*, 740–742.

Blanchard, E. B. (1995). Biofeedback and its role in the treatment of pain. In proceedings of the NIH Technology Assessment Conference: Integration of behavioral and relaxation approaches into the treatment of chronic pain and insomnia. Washington, DC: National Institutes of Health, pp. 33–38.

Blanchard, E. B., & Epstein, L. H. (1978). *A biofeedback primer.* Reading MA: Addison-Wesley.

Blanchard, E. B. (1987). Five-year prospective follow-up on the treatment of chronic headache with biofeedback and/or relaxation. *Headache, 27*, 580–583.

Blanchard, E. B. (1990). A controlled evolution of thermal biofeedback combined with cognitive therapy in the treatment of vascular headache. *Journal of Consulting and Clinical Psychology, 58*, 216–224.

Blanchard, E. B. (1993). Thermal biofeedback as an effective substitute for sympathetic medication in moderate hypertension: A failure to replicate. *Biofeedback and Self-Regulation, 11*, 237–253.

Budzynski, T. H. (1973). EMG Biofeedback and tension headache: A controlled outcome study. *Psychosomatic Medicine, 6*, 509–514.

Cerulli, M. A. (1979). Progress in biofeedback conditioning for fecal incontinence. *Gastroenterology, 76*, 742–746.

Dahlstrom, L. (1982). Comparison of effects of electromyographic biofeedback and occlusal splint on mandibular function. *Scandanavian Journal of Dental Research, 90*, 151.

Fahrion, S. (1986). Behavioral treatment of essential hypertension: A group outcome study. *Biofeedback and Self-Regulation, 11*, 257–278.

Flor, H. & Birbaumer, N. (1993). Comparison of the efficacy of electromyographic behavioral cognitive therapy, and conservative medical interventions in the treatment of chronic musculoskeletal pain. *Journal of Consulting and Clinical Psychology, 61*, 653–658.

Freedman, R. R. (1983). Behavioral treatment of Raynaud's disease. *Journal of Consulting and Clinical Psychology, 51*, 539–549.

Freedman, R. R. (1985). Behavioral treatment of Raynaud's disease: Long-term follow-up. *Journal of Consulting and Clinical Psychology, 53*, 136.

Goldstein, I. B. (1982). Comparison of drug and behavioral treatments of essential hypertension. *Health Psychology, 1*, 7–26.

Hermann, C. (1995). Behavioral and prophylactic pharmacological intervention studies of pediatric migraine: An exploratory meta-analysis. *Pain, 60*, 239–256.

Holroyd, K. A. (1984). Change mechanisms in EMG biofeedback training: Cognitive changes underlying improvements in tension headache. *Journal of Consulting and Clinical Psychology, 52*, 1039–1053.

Rice, K. (1993). Biofeedback treatments of generalized anxiety disorder: Preliminary results. *Biofeedback and Self-Regulation, 18*, 93–105.

Sargent, J. D. (1973). Preliminary report on the use of autogenic biofeedback training in the treatment of migraine and tension headache. *Psychosomatic Medicine, 35*, 129–135.

Sovak, M. (1981). Mechanism of biofeedback therapy of migraine: Volitional manipulation of the psychophysiological background. *Headache, 21*, 216–224.

Edward B. Blanchard

BIOGRAPHY. *See* Psychobiography.

BIOLOGICAL PSYCHOLOGY. The history of biological psychology—the study of psychology in terms of bodily mechanisms—is a major part of the history of modern scientific psychology. It has been a prominent field of psychology from the start in Europe and North America and remains a major area of research and instruction in many countries. Over one and one half centuries, biological psychology has found new ways to answer old questions, has tackled important new questions, and has abandoned some problems as poorly defined. Carefully designed behavioral experiments and innovative biomedical techniques have been essential to its progress. Biological psychology has been a site of exchange of concepts, information, and techniques between psychology and the biological sciences.

The current scope of biological psychology is broad, including the following topics: evolution of brain and behavior; development of the nervous system and behavior over the life span; psychopharmacology; sensory and perceptual processes; control and coordination of movements and actions; control of behavioral states (motivation), including sex and reproductive behavior, and regulation of internal states; biological rhythms and sleep; emotions and mental disorders; neural mechanisms of learning and memory, language and cognition; and recovery of function after damage to the nervous system. Developing from biological psychology and overlapping with parts of it are such fields as behavior genetics and hormones and behavior.

Origins of Biological Psychology

During much of its history, biological psychology was known as "physiological psychology," but we should note two meanings of this term. First, *physiological psychology* was the name Wilhelm Wundt and his contemporaries used for the new, scientific psychology. The preface to Wundt's most important book, *Grundzüge der physiologischen Psychologie* (*Principles of Physiological Psychology*, 1873–1874), stated his purpose:

> The work which I here present to the public is an attempt to mark out a new domain of science. . . . The question may be raised, whether the time is yet ripe for such an undertaking. The new discipline rests upon anatomical and physiological foundations which, in certain respects, are themselves very far from solid; while the experimental treatment of psychological problems . . . [is] still at its first beginnings. (1948, p. 248)

Wundt's book treated general experimental psychology, which he hoped to demonstrate could be as scientific as physiology. Physiology itself was one of the streams of investigation and theory that joined to form the new psychology. Other lines that led to psychology included human and comparative neuroanatomy, study of sensation, and sociomedical studies.

By the 1920s, *physiological psychology* was acquiring its second, more restricted meaning: the study of behavior in terms of its biological mechanisms. Textbooks on physiological psychology in this sense began to appear in the 1930s. The discipline of physiology also became more restricted during the twentieth century as new sciences split from it—sciences such as endocrinology, genetics, and biochemistry. Thus the term *biological psychology* arose as being more appropriate to designate the relations of psychology to the life sciences. Textbooks entitled *Biological Psychology* began to appear in the 1980s. Other terms sometimes used as alternatives to biological psychology or "biopsychology"

include *physiology of behavior* and *behavioral neuroscience*. Currently, biological psychology encompasses four main aspects: biological mechanisms of behavior; the development of behavior and its biological mechanisms over the life span; the evolution of behavior and its biological mechanisms; and applications, which entail both tests of the adequacy of formulations and use of findings to benefit health and quality of life (Rosenzweig, Leiman, & Breedlove, 1999).

Persistent Themes in Biological Psychology

Biological psychology continues some of the main lines of theorizing and research that led to the development of psychology as an independent discipline. These lines include the explanation and interpretation of behavior in terms of the physiology of the nervous system; the development of psychology on the basis of evolution; the localization of function in the nervous system; and the plasticity of the nervous system.

Physiological Explanations of Behavior. René Descartes (1596–1650) was an important forerunner of modern psychology who sought to locate mental functions in the nervous system and to explain aspects of behavior in terms of physiological mechanisms. Another pioneer was the physician David Hartley (1705–1757), a philosopher by avocation. In his *Observations on Man* (1749), Hartley attempted to integrate the current facts and theories of anatomy and physiology with concepts of associationistic philosophy. Apparently the first to use the term *physiological psychology* in a book title was English physician Robert Dunn (1858). The philosopher and psychologist Alexander Bain (1818–1903) sought to establish solid connections between psychology and physiological knowledge in his textbooks of the 1850s, *The Senses and the Intellect* and *The Emotions and the Will*. Combined and abridged as *Mental and Moral Science* (1868), this was the major textbook of psychology in Great Britain for almost 50 years. Among other anticipations of later work, Bain suggested that memory formation involves growth of what we now call synaptic junctions:

> for every act of memory, every exercise of bodily aptitude, every habit, recollection, train of ideas, there is a specific grouping or coordination of sensations and movements, by virtue of specific growths in the cell junctions. (1872, p. 91)

Evolution. Herbert Spencer espoused the concept that evolution of mind is central to psychology in his influential book, *Principles of Psychology* (1855). This was shortly before Charles Darwin and Alfred Russel Wallace formally proposed the theory of evolution by natural selection. Darwin also envisaged the importance of evolution for psychology. In *On the Origin of Species*, Darwin, who had not yet read Spencer's *Prin-*

ciples of Psychology, looked forward to the time when "Psychology will be based on a new foundation, that of the necessary acquirement of each mental power and capacity by gradation" (1859, p. 113). Darwin contributed directly to psychology in later writings: *The Descent of Man* (1871), *The Expression of Emotions in Man and Animals* (1872), and the first detailed case study of child development, "A Biographical Sketch of an Infant" (1877). He has been credited with "overwhelming importance in the development of psychology as a branch of evolutionary biology in the three separable areas of comparative psychology, functional psychology, and the study of the nervous system" (Young, 1970, p. 191). Once the laws of heredity were recognized at the beginning of the twentieth century and the mechanisms of heredity were worked out later in the century, evolution of aspects of behavior became a fruitful subject of investigation, and behavior genetics became a productive field.

Some vestiges of older thinking persisted into the twentieth century, however, such as the Aristotelian concept that animals can be arranged in a *scala naturae*, a single ladderlike progression from the simplest to the most complex and perfected, with humans at the pinnacle. Thinkers in the nineteenth century referred to this as the *phylogenetic scale*, and this concept was still reflected in Clifford Morgan's influential textbook, *Physiological Psychology* (1943). In the twentieth century, evolutionary biologists developed the concept of a widely branching *phylogenetic tree* that replaced the phylogenetic scale. Current textbooks in biological psychology and related fields refrain from suggesting that evolution necessarily means an increase in complexity and avoid such terms as *primitive species* or *advanced species* (Butler & Hodos, 1996; Rosenzweig et al., 1999).

Localization of Function. A critical advance was the discovery of the difference between sensory and motor nerves, made independently by Charles Bell in 1811 and François Magendie in 1822. Bell and Magendie showed that cutting dorsal spinal roots made a limb insensitive but did not prevent motion, whereas cutting the ventral roots made the limb immobile. Previously, many physiologists had believed that spinal nerves carried sensory and motor messages in both directions at once. Bell also argued for further subdivision among the nerves, claiming that the five senses are mediated by different nerves, thus anticipating Johannes Müller's 1826 doctrine of "specific energies of nerves" of the different senses. This doctrine was later extended by Müller's student Hermann Helmholtz and others to account for differences within a sensory modality (e.g., hues, tones, and different skin sensations such as touch, warmth, and cold).

The "law of spinal roots" can be considered a special case of the more general idea of localization of function in the nervous system that gained much attention in scientific circles early in the nineteenth century. The first formal proponent of the concept of localization was the physician and anatomist Franz Joseph Gall, who called his system "organology" because he believed the brain to be composed of a number of different organs with different functions (1810–1819). Johann Spurzheim, who was associated for several years with Gall, popularized the term "phrenology," which Gall refused to use. Gall believed he could identify and localize 27 faculties or abilities in different parts of the human cerebral cortex. On the basis of comparative studies of other mammals, he believed he could demonstrate and localize nineteen of these faculties in animals. Both Gall and Spurzheim attempted to locate the organs of the brain by studying the protuberances in the skulls of people who had particular talents or striking characteristics or by assessing individuals with unusually shaped skulls.

A prominent anatomist-physiologist, Marie Jean Pierre Flourens, attacked the claims of Gall and Spurzheim. Making experimental lesions in the brains of a variety of species, especially birds, and stimulating parts of the brain, he found only limited evidence for localization of function (Flourens, 1824). Flourens found that each sense organ has its own representation in the cerebrum, and he also noted that, following localized brain lesions, animals would lose certain functions but could recover them completely. He therefore concluded that the cerebral cortex functions as a whole and that all of its parts are responsible for intelligence, the will, and perception. As one neurohistorian notes: "it is possible to think of Gall as the visionary who had the right idea but the wrong method, and of Flourens as the laboratory scientist with the better method but the wrong theory" (Finger, 1994, p. 36).

Paul Broca's evidence for localization of speech function in the left frontal cortex (1865) gained wide acceptance for the concept of localization of function in the cortex and initiated a long period of fruitful studies. Further developments, associated with names such as Eduard Hitzig and David Ferrier, led to a concept of the brain as being composed of fixed compartments. Thus anatomist Korbidian Brodmann (1909) divided the human cerebral cortex into 52 regions based on cytoarchitectonic criteria and suggested that each region has a special function. Further anatomical research indicated even finer subdivisions, with some investigators claiming as many as 200 separate cortical fields. Among the skeptics about functional mapping and diagramming was Karl Lashley, who showed that considerable variation existed among the primary visual cortices of monkeys (Lashley & Clark, 1946).

Research by Roger Sperry, a student of Lashley's, on development of brain connections in amphibians was understood by many neurobiologists to mean that connections in the brain are formed independently of activity or experience and are programmed by a set of recognition molecules on each neuron (Sperry, 1963). Sperry, however, limited inflexibility to the basic neural projection systems and believed that learning could alter connections in higher brain regions (Sperry, 1951).

Much current research on localization of function in the human brain utilizes methods of noninvasive brain imaging. Brain imaging, done either when a person is at rest or performing a mental task, shows activity over much of the brain. It is only when brain activity recorded under a "baseline" condition is subtracted from activity during the task that certain brain regions are seen to have heightened or depressed levels of activity. Psychologists contribute to this research in part by designing specific tasks to study particular functions.

Plasticity of the Nervous System. Early in the nineteenth century theorists differed about whether plasticity was a property of the nervous system. Thus Gall emphasized the innate development of the different "organs" of the cortex, each of which he hypothesized to correspond to a different mental faculty. Gall rejected Spurzheim's idea that humankind is almost indefinitely perfectible and that exercise or education could influence the development of the faculties or the organs of the brain (Gall, vol. 4, 1819, pp. 252–256). Jean-Baptiste Lamarck, the originator of the ill-fated doctrine of evolution through inheritance of acquired characteristics, held that the brain and each of its special regions develops through appropriate use of the related faculties, and he criticized Gall's belief that brain development is determined innately (1809/1914).

Hermann Ebbinghaus's (1885) demonstration that learning and memory can be measured encouraged psychologists and neurobiologists to speculate further about neural mechanisms of learning and memory. Thus William James (1890) speculated that learning is related to anatomical changes at neural junctions, as did neurobiologists Eugenio Tanzi (1893), Santiago Ramon y Cajal (Cajal, 1894), and Charles Sherrington (Foster & Sherrington, 1897). In the same publication, Sherrington proposed the term "synapses" for these junctions (Foster & Sherrington, 1897, p. 929).

Initial publications about learning in animals by Edward Thorndike (1898) and Ivan P. Pavlov (1906) encouraged research on neural mechanisms of learning. Psychologist Shepard I. Franz was the first to seek to determine the site of learning in the brain by combining Thorndike's methods of training and testing animals with the technique of inducing localized brain lesions. Franz later inducted Karl Lashley, and through Lashley many others, into research on this topic. Franz also worked on rehabilitation of brain-injured soldiers, claiming success in obtaining functional recovery even

in cases of long-standing paralysis: "we should probably not speak of permanent paralysis, or of residual paralysis, but of uncared for paralysis" (Franz, Sheetz, & Wilson, 1915).

By the mid-twentieth century, the study of brain plasticity and neural mechanisms of learning and memory seemed to have stalled. Lashley published a pessimistic review in 1950. Hans-Lukas Teuber stated that

the absence of any convincing physiological correlate of learning is the greatest gap in physiological psychology. Apparently, the best we can do with learning is to prevent it from occurring, by intercurrent stimulation through implanted electrodes . . . , by cerebral ablation . . . , or by depriving otherwise intact organisms, early in life, of normal sensory influx. (1955, p. 267)

In fact, around the middle of the twentieth century, major advances were beginning to occur in research on the neural mechanisms of learning and memory. Some of these resulted from recently developed techniques, such as single-cell electrophysiological recording, electron microscopy, and use of new neurochemical methods. Another major influence encouraging research on neural mechanisms of learning and memory was Donald O. Hebb's 1949 monograph, *The Organization of Behavior*. Hebb was more optimistic about possible synaptic changes in learning than Lashley was. Hebb noted some indirect evidence for neural changes and did not let the absence of conclusive evidence deter him from reviving hypotheses about the conditions that could lead to formation of new synaptic junctions and underlie memory. In essence, Hebb's hypothesis of synaptic change underlying learning resembled James's formulation: "When two elementary brain-processes have been active together or in immediate succession, one of them, on recurring, tends to propagate its excitement into the other" (James, 1890, p. 566). Hebb's "dual trace hypothesis" also resembles the "consolidation-perseveration" hypothesis formulated in 1900 by Georg Müller and Alois Pilzecker. Much current neuroscience research concerns properties of what are now known as Hebbian synapses.

In the early 1960s two experimental programs announced findings demonstrating that the brain can be altered measurably by training or differential experience. First was the demonstration by an interdisciplinary group at Berkeley that both formal training and informal experience in varied environments led to measurable changes in neurochemistry and neuroanatomy of the rodent brain (Krech, Rosenzweig, & Bennett, 1960; Rosenzweig, Krech, & Bennett, 1961; Rosenzweig, Krech, Bennett, & Diamond, 1962). Soon after came the report of David Hubel and Torsten Wiesel that occluding one eye of a kitten led to reduction in the number of cortical cells responding to that eye (Hubel & Wiesel, 1965; Wiesel & Hubel, 1963, 1965). Later reports of the Berkeley group and others demonstrated specific changes in anatomy of neurons and synapses as a result of training or enriched experience, and such changes were induced in adults as well as in young animals.

In spite of initial skepticism, by the early 1970s some neurobiologists began to accept the reports that significant changes in the brain can be caused by training or exposure of animals to differential experience. Other neurobiologists continued into the 1980s to believe that neural connections in the adult brain remained fixed. The report of Wiesel and Hubel (1965) that changes can be induced in the visual system only during a critical period early in life served to solidify the belief of many neurobiologists that neural connections in the adult brain are fixed and do not vary as a result of training. Later, however, investigators found that modifying sensory experience in adult animals could alter both receptive fields of cells and cortical maps (see reviews by Kaas, 1991; Weinberger, 1995).

In the current synthesis, localization of function and brain plasticity are not incompatible. For example, knowing the modal location of somatosensory representation in the cortex helps investigators to study in detail how the "cortical map" in that region changes as a result of specific training of the fingers.

Training, Professional Organizations, and Journals

Professional positions in biological psychology are mainly in academic and research institutions. Training for most of these positions requires a doctorate, and many departments of psychology that offer doctorates have programs in biological psychology or behavioral or cognitive neuroscience. The number of doctoral programs in physiological and/or biological psychology in the United States and Canada almost doubled from 1973 to 1992. The National Research Council lists more than 100 research doctorate programs in neuroscience in the United States. Some of these programs are located in departments of psychology. In fact, psychology departments were mentioned as sites of neuroscience programs more frequently than any other specific departments. A plurality of the neuroscience programs were listed as interdisciplinary or multidisciplinary, and many of these mentioned psychology as one of the disciplines involved. Overall, it appears that psychology is participating in the growth of neuroscience rather than being overshadowed by it. (See Rosenzweig, 1998, for a discussion of relations between psychology and neuroscience.)

Among the scholarly and professional organizations and journals related to biological psychology are the following: Division 6 of the American Psychological Association (APA), founded in 1945, when the APA reorganized, as the Division of Physiological and Comparative Psychology and renamed the Division of Behavioral Neuroscience and Comparative Psychology in 1995. The APA publishes the journal *Behavioral Neuroscience*, known from 1921–1982 as the *Journal of Comparative and Physiological Psychology*. Other organizations and publications in which biological psychologists participate include the Society for Neuroscience and its *Journal of Neuroscience*, the European Brain and Behaviour Society and its journal *Behavioural Brain Research*, the Forum of European Neuroscience Societies and its *European Journal of Neuroscience*, and the International Brain Research Organization (IBRO).

There are several current textbooks in the field. Reviews of research in biological psychology appear regularly in *Annual Review of Neuroscience*, *Annual Review of Psychology*, and *Trends in Neurosciences*.

[*See also* Psychology.]

Bibliography

Bain, A. (1868). *Mental and moral science*. London: Longmans.

Bain, A. (1872). *Mind and body: The theories of their relation*. London: King.

Broca, P. (1865). Sur le siège de la faculté du langage articulé [On the site of the faculty of speech]. *Bulletin de la Societé d'Anthropologie, 6*, 337–393.

Brodmann, K. (1909). *Vergleichende Lokalisationslehre der Grosshirnrinde in ihren Prinzipien dargestellt auf Grund des Zellenbaues* [Comparative study of localization in the cerebral cortex in terms of principles based on cytoarchitectonics]. Leipzig, Germany: Barth

Butler, A. B., & Hodos, W. (1996). *Comparative vertebrate neuroanatomy: Evolution and adaptation*. New York: Wiley-Wiss.

Cajal, R. S. (1894). La fine structure des centres nerveux [The microscopic structure of the central nervous system]. *Proceedings of the Royal Society, London, 55*, 444–468.

Darwin, C. (1859). *On the origin of the species by means of natural selection, or the preservation of favoured races in the struggle for life*. London: Murray.

Darwin, C. (1871). *The descent of man and selection in relation to sex*. London: Murray.

Darwin, C. (1872). *The expression of the emotions in man and animals*. London: Murray.

Darwin, C. (1877). A biographical sketch of an infant. *Mind: Quarterly Review of Psychology and Philosophy, 2*, 285–294.

Dennis, W. (Ed.) (1948). *Readings in the history of psychology*. New York: Appleton-Century-Crofts.

Dunn, R. (1858). *An essay on physiological psychology*. London: Churchill.

Ebbinghaus, H. (1885). *Ueber das Gedächtnis* [On memory]. Leipzig, Germany: Dunker & Humbolt.

Finger, S. (1994). *Origins of neuroscience: A history of explorations into brain function.* New York: Oxford University Press.

Flourens, P. (1824).*Recherches expérimentales sur les propriétés et les fonctions du système nerveux dans les animaux vertébrés* [Experimental research on the properties and the functions of the nervous system in vertebrate animals]. Paris: Ballière.

Foster, M., & Sherrington, C. S. (1897). Part III. *The central nervous system: A text-book of physiology* (pp. 915-1252). London: Macmillan.

Franz, S. I., Sheetz, M. E., & Wilson, A. A. (1915). The possibility of recovery of motor functions in long-standing hemiplegia. *Journal of the American Medical Association, 65,* 2150-2154.

Gall, J. F. (1810–1819). *Anatomie et physiologie du système nerveux en général, et du cerveau en particulier, avec des observations sur la possibilité de reconnoitre plusieurs dispositions intellectuelles et morales de l'homme et des animaux par la configuration de leurs têtes* [The anatomy and physiology of the nervous system in general, and of the brain in particular, with some observations on the possibility of recognizing several intellectual and moral dispositions of man and animals by the configuration of their heads]. (Vols. 1–4). Paris: Maze.

Hartley, D. (1749). *Observations on man, his frame, his duty, and his expectations.* London: Leake & Frederick.

Hebb, D. O. (1949). *The organization of behavior: A neuropsychological theory.* New York: Wiley.

Hubel, D. H., & Wiesel, T. N. (1965). Binocular interaction in striate cortex of kittens reared with artificial squint. *Journal of Neurophysiology, 28,* 1041–1059

James, W. (1890). *Principles of psychology.* New York: Holt.

Kaas, J. H. (1991). Plasticity of sensory and motor maps in adult animals. *Annual Review of Neuroscience, 14,* 137–167.

Krech, D., Rosenzweig, M. R., & Bennett, E. L. (1960). Effects of environmental complexity and training on brain chemistry *Journal of Comparative and Physiological Psychology, 53,* 509–519.

Lamarck, J. B. (1914). Zoological philosophy. (H. Elliott, Trans.). London: Macmillan. (Original work published 1809)

Lashley, K. S. (1950). In search of the engram. *Symposia of the Society for Experimental Biology, 4,* 454–482.

Lashley, K. S. & Clark, G. (1946). The cytoarchitecture of the cerebral cortex of Ateles: A critical examination of architectonic studies. *Journal of comparative neurology, 85,* 223–305.

Morgan, C. T. (1943). *Physiological psychology.* New York: McGraw-Hill.

Pavlov, I. P. (1906). The scientific investigation of the psychical faculties or processes in the higher animals. *Science, 24,* 613–619. The same article also appeared in *Lancet, 2,* 911–915.

Rosenzweig, M. R. (1998). Reciprocal relations between psychology and neuroscience. In M. Sabourin, F. Craik, & M. Robert (Eds.), *Proceedings of the Twenty-sixth International Congress of Psychology: Vol. 2. Advances in psychological science: Biological and cognitive aspects* (pp. 215–236). Hove, England: Psychology Press.

Rosenzweig, M. R., Krech, D., & Bennett, E. L. (1961). Heredity, environment, brain biochemistry, and learning. In *Current trends in psychological theory* (pp. 87–110). Pittsburgh, PA: University of Pittsburgh Press.

Rosenzweig, M. R., Krech, D., Bennett, E. L., & Diamond, M. C. (1962). Effects of environmental complexity and training on brain chemistry and anatomy: A replication and extension. *Journal of Comparative and Physiological Psychology, 55,* 429–437.

Rosenzweig, M. R., Leiman, A. L., & Breedlove, S. M. (1999). *Biological psychology: An introduction to behavioral, cognitive, and clinical neuroscience* (2nd ed.). Sunderland, MA: Sinauer.

Spencer, H. (1855). *The principles of psychology.* London: Longmans.

Sperry, R. W. (1951). Mechanisms of neural maturation. In S. S. Stevens (Ed.), *Handbook of experimental psychology* (pp. 236–280). New York: Wiley.

Sperry, R. W. (1963). Chemoaffinity in the orderly growth of nerve fiber patterns and connections. *Proceedings of the National Academy of Sciences USA, 50,* 703–710.

Tanzi, E. (1893). I fatti e le induzioni nell'odierna istologia del sistema nervoso [Facts and conclusions from present-day history of the nervous system]. *Revista Sperimentale di Freniatria e di Medicina Legale, 19,* 419–472.

Teuber, H.-L. (1955). Physiological psychology. *Annual Review of Psychology, 6,* 267–296.

Thorndike, E. L. (1898). Animal intelligence: An experimental study of the associative processes in animals. *Psychological Monographs, 8,* 1–109.

Weinberger, N. M. (1995). Dynamic regulation of receptive fields and maps in the adult sensory cortex. *Annual Review of Neuroscience, 18,* 129–158.

Wiesel, T. N., & Hubel, D. H. (1963). Single-cell responses in striate cortex of kittens deprived of vision in one eye. *Journal of Neurophysiology, 26,* 1003–1017.

Wiesel, T N., & Hubel, D. H. (1965). Comparison of the effects of unilateral and bilateral eye closure on cortical unit responses in kittens. *Journal of Neurophysiology, 28,* 1029–1040.

Wundt, W. (1873–1874). *Grundzüge der physiologischen Psychologie* [Principles of physiological psychology]. Leipzig, Germany: Engelmann. [Part of the author's preface, translated by Edward B. Titchener, appears on p. 248 in W. Dennis (Ed.) (1948). *Readings in the history of psychology.* New York: Appleton-Century-Crofts.]

Young, R. M. (1970). *Mind, brain, and adaptation in the nineteenth century.* New York: Oxford University Press.

Mark R. Rosenzweig

BIOMECHANICS AND KINEMATICS. The remarkably complex musculoskeletal system of the human being may be considered, with increasing levels of validity, to be amenable to engineering analysis. This approach includes the expectation that mechanical overstressing of the structure will lead to injury and that repetitive overuse may overwhelm the adaptive and repair capabilities of the biological components of the system. Biomechanics is a discipline directed at understanding the stresses and strains on the biological organism, and it is a widely applied approach to reducing injury and disease. Occupational biomechanics is used to examine the physical interaction of workers with their tools, machines, and materials so as to maximize a worker's performance while minimizing the risk of musculoskeletal disorders.

The establishment of precise and quantitative criteria for ensuring safe exposures remains controversial. In particular, the relationship between multiple assaults and single, high-peak assaults is epidemiologically difficult to determine. However, the biomechanical approach can successfully be used to compare the relative stresses at a particular joint or joints. Combining the study of *kinematics*—the movement patterns and characteristics of the limbs—and of *kinetics*—the particular forces that result in these movements—with *anthropometrics*—the dimensions of the human body—allows various interventions to be taken to minimize strains on the musculoskeletal system. Three questions are frequently asked of biomechanics: (1) Can the stress caused by load, speed, or the combination of the two be consistently reduced? (2) Can the mechanical advantages be reliably maximized by the use of mechanical assistance? (3) Can the stability of the whole body or certain joints be restored following misjudgment of weight, size, or balance due to unexpected situations?

Because of its prevalence, low back pain is a major interest of biomechanics. The need for effective approaches to this musculoskeletal strain is socially very significant—a large proportion of people suffer from low back pain during their adult lives, and the occupational disabilities produced by low back pain are the most significant source of workplace injuries and disorders. The majority of such cases are idiopathic and hitherto have not been shown to be the result of observable physical damage. Nevertheless, an approach based on reducing stresses on the musculoskeletal system appears *a priori* to offer benefits for the design of workplaces to avoid such losses of time and productivity.

Initial approaches involved calculating peak stresses in the region of discs L_5/S_1 in the lower back and attempting to relate these to injuries. Increasingly, dynamic approaches with three-dimensional models are refining our understanding of the coactivation muscular activities of the torso that produce high stresses at the susceptible point between the lumbar and sacral spines. Additionally, the approach of examining a single exposure or event believed to lead to low back pain is being complemented by an approach based on the consideration of the mechanical effects of cumulative assaults and the associated concept of dose.

The development of high-speed 3D instrumentation (e.g., electromagnetic, acoustic, cinematographic sensors) to investigate kinematics allows movement patterns to be determined. The effects of rapid accelerations in mechanical systems are well understood, and the significance of sudden changes of direction, jerks, and snatches in movement, which produce very high forces in the lower back, has been determined and has implications for training approaches. Typically, earlier studies of training have shown that so-called back schools have had little effect on injury rates, as they were largely based on artificial approaches that were often not practical in real workplaces. However, the biomechanical demonstration of loading effects suggests that an understanding by the worker of the excessive demands of jerking movements and the benefits of reducing load, rate, and moments may lead to lifting training that is more productive than previous efforts have been.

The second major source of musculoskeletal injuries is the very large number of upper extremity and upper spinal disabilities that result from activities of daily living, from occupational exposures, and from accidents. The proportion of these injuries that are idiopathic is probably lower than for low back pain. Noxious conditions, such as compromised blood flow to muscles or nerves, may be more readily identifiable and traceable to physical conditions that have resulted from the inappropriate biomechanical activity of a particular joint. With the more readily determined pathology of the upper extremity, consideration of the anatomical processes coupled with an understanding of the biomechanical stresses enable neutral postures of the upper extremity to be determined and recommended.

Specific workplace demands on a person's physical structure result from equipment and task design, as well as from functional demands to complete the task. Thus, by creating appropriate designs for the workplace and comparing the physical demands of alternative approaches to the task, the function can often be achieved at a lower biomechanical cost. Storing parts and tools closer to the body to minimize reaching and bending; positioning heavy loads close to the edge of a rack so a person can lift them in such a way as to reduce the moment arm of the load about the lower spine; designing storage bins of appropriate heights so that heavy weights can be positioned at a level above the floor, preventing awkward lifting positions; and designing jobs to avoid repetitively picking pieces of work from awkward locations are all simple ways to reduce biomechanical stresses. The current models also identify the role of twists and asymmetric loading of the spine in increasing the stresses on the back, compared with the same task performed in a workplace designed to provide symmetrical and nonrotational access to all components.

An additional source of high stresses results from so-called static work. One common form is adopting certain postures, particularly forward-leaning postures or arm-raised postures, for long periods. Even if there is little movement of the work piece, excessive muscular and physiological cost may be involved in maintaining that posture. A large proportion of such exposures results from designing a workplace without regard to the anthropometry of the worker. Another form of static work is the use of a limb as a static clamp or vise. Frequently much attention is paid to the activities of the preferred hand while ignoring the long-term demands of the nonpreferred hand that is required to hold the work piece and provide a reaction to the tool being used.

Workplaces that capitalize on biomechanical knowledge are likely to produce benefits in the form of reduction of widely prevalent injuries in both occupational and nonoccupational situations. Additionally, the performance of a person-process system that has been redesigned to minimize biomechanical demands is often significantly improved.

Tom B. Leamon and Simon M. Hsiang

BIPOLAR DISORDER. For people with bipolar disorder, common human emotions become intensely magnified and often unpredictable. Individuals can quickly alternate between extreme exaggerations of sadness and happiness, of fatigue and energy. Feelings of omnipotence, euphoria, boundless energy, and clarity can abruptly transform into a lack of self-confidence, fear, and overwhelming confusion. The impact of these emotional swings can be so painful that suicide is chosen as a means for escape. Sadly, one in five people with untreated bipolar disorder successfully takes his or her life (Goodwin & Jamison, 1990). This statistic is quite alarming given that not even one third of people with bipolar disorder receive care despite the existence of effective treatments such as lithium and other medications.

Definition of the Disorder and Clinical Presentation

According to the *Diagnostic and Statistical Manual of Mental Disorders* (*DSM–IV*, American Psychiatric Association, 1994), the critical defining feature of the bipolar disorder is a clinical course characterized by the occurrence of one or more manic or mixed episodes. Although most people also experience one or more episodes of major depression, this is not a requirement

for the diagnosis. A recurrence of the disorder is indicated by either a shift in the polarity of the episode (e.g., major depression evolves into mania) or an interval between episodes of at least 2 months without manic symptoms.

The distinctive nature of mania makes this disorder one of the most consistently identifiable of all the mental disorders (Goodwin & Jamison, 1990). Mania is characterized by abnormally and persistently elevated, expansive, or irritable mood lasting at least one week (*DSM–IV*, 1994). Elevated moods are distinguished by excessive euphoria, and expansiveness is demarcated by unrelenting and indiscriminate enthusiasm for interpersonal, sexual, or occupational interactions. Diagnostic criteria also require three or more of the following symptoms to be present: grandiosity, decreased need for sleep, more and faster speech, flight of ideas, distractibility, increased goal-directed behaviors, psychomotor agitation, and/or excessive involvement in pleasurable activities that have potential negative consequences (e.g., sexual indiscretions). If the mood is primarily irritable, then four of these symptoms must exist. The impairment caused by the disturbance must be severe enough to result in marked impairment in functioning or to require hospitalization. Hypomania, which is the less severe form of mania, has a symptom duration of four days or less and may or may not result in serious problems for the person, such as huge debts or hospitalization. When an individual suffers from full depressive symptoms in conjunction with hypomanic episodes, the diagnosis is bipolar II disorder.

Although the euphoria and boundless energy may feel good initially, these feelings can quickly change into deep depression. Research suggests that the depressive syndrome in bipolar disorder is more oppressive and disruptive than that in unipolar depression and much more likely to lead to rehospitalization (Goldberg, Harrow, & Grossman, 1995). People typically suffer from a slowing or decrease in rate of thought and speech, in energy, in sexuality, and in ability to experience pleasure. Symptoms can vary from mild physical and mental slowing with very little distortion in cognition and perception to profound and pervasive depressive stupors, delusions, hallucinations, and clouding of consciousness.

People with bipolar disorder can also experience mixed states, which involve the simultaneous presence of both manic and depressive symptoms for at least one week. Although mixed states are often conceived as a transition from one phase of the illness to another, an episode may last for months.

There are several features associated with bipolar-disorder mood states. Although thought disorder is typically linked with schizophrenia, approximately 70% of acutely manic bipolar patients have psychotic symptoms (Sands & Harrow, in press). During mania, thinking becomes fluid and productive to the point of causing a loosening of normal patterns of association, racing thoughts, and flight of ideas. Traditional psychotic features such as paranoid ideation, delusions, and hallucinations can also occur. Obviously, for patients with both psychosis and mania, making the differential diagnosis between bipolar disorder and schizoaffective disorder can be difficult. The *DSM–IV* requires that psychotic features co-occur with affective symptoms for a diagnosis of bipolar disorder.

The development of *DSM–IV* provided a greater nosological complexity for bipolar disorder and its variations. Of particular importance is the inclusion of criteria for bipolar II and the specifications of subgroups of individuals with seasonal variants, postpartum onset, and rapid cycling (*DSM–IV*, 1994). The *DSM–IV* classification system also allows clinicians to code according to whether the person is experiencing a first episode or has a recurrent disorder.

Etiology and Pathogenesis

Although the underlying cause of bipolar disorder has yet to be conclusively identified, there are a few empirically established theories concerning its etiology and pathogenesis. For example, it appears that bipolar disorder has a significant genetic transmission. Research consistently demonstrates significantly higher rates of family history of mental illness among bipolar patients, with estimates ranging as high as 48% (Alexander et al., 1995). Genetic research is currently focusing on identifying a possible genetic locus for the disorder, as well as attempting to determine whether it is due to a single major gene, a smaller number of genes, or multifactorial polygenic inheritance (Sands & Harrow, in press). Research involving the examination of bipolar patients and their relatives has tentatively identified several possible locations, including chromosomes 18 and 11 and the X chromosome (Marshal, 1994).

Technological advances in brain imaging and related technologies have provided the opportunity to investigate possible structural brain abnormalities in people with bipolar disorder. Interestingly, neuroimaging studies suggest neurodevelopmental similarities between schizophrenia and bipolar disorder. Both populations appear to have enlarged ventricles. However, the enlargement is greater for people with schizophrenia, and the pathogenesis of the two disorders may be quite different. Nevertheless, a neurodevelopmental model remains useful for understanding the pathogenesis of both disorders.

Post (1990) proposes that behavioral sensitization and electrophysiological kindling could be the possible mechanisms underlying the disorder. Specifically, he hypothesizes that frequent early episodes of the illness predispose an individual to more frequent future episodes. Thus pathophysiological changes in the individual neuron, which occur as a result of stress during the early stages of the illness, result in increased morbidity over subsequent years.

Although the well-established genetic vulnerability studies suggest that psychosocial factors cannot be a single cause of bipolar disorder, research does indicate that they may play a potential role in relapse rate (Pichot, 1995). Although longitudinal studies have found significant relationships between life events and relapse rates of the disorder independent of level of compliance with medication or treatment, other studies have found no such association (Sands & Harrow, in press).

Course and Outcome

By definition, bipolar disorder is recurrent. Research shows that more than 90% of people who have a single manic episode go on to have future ones (*DSM–IV*, 1994). The age of onset is usually younger than 30 (Fogarty, Russell, Newman, & Bland, 1994), with a median age of 18 years (Goodwin & Jamison, 1990). Research conducted prior to the advent of lithium treatment revealed that on average a person experiences four episodes in 10 years. When multiple (four or more) episodes occur within a year, then the disorder can be described as rapid cycling. This occurs in about 5 to 15% of people with the disorder and is associated with a poorer outcome. Although the majority of people return to a completely functional level between episodes, approximately 20 to 30% continue to exhibit mood lability and interpersonal or occupational difficulties.

Poor outcome is related to a number of factors. Negative affective style in the family, such as attitudes of criticism and overinvolvement, and the behavioral expression of these attitudes have been linked with relapse and outcome over a nine-month follow-up (Miklowitz et al. 1988). Age of onset can also indicate a poor outcome. For individuals experiencing their first episode during adolescence, the disruption caused by the illness makes it difficult to develop an identity, establish peer relationships, or develop adult social skills (Young & Harrow, 1993). Finally, psychotic symptoms and rapid cycling are linked with higher relapse rates and poorer social outcomes.

Treatment

For approximately 80% of bipolar patients, lithium effectively controls symptoms, thus enabling them to live normally (Goodwin & Jamison, 1990). For nonresponders, high levels of social and occupational difficulties may exist, and anticonvulsant medications (e.g., valproic acid and carbamazepine) may be used either alone or in conjunction with lithium. The use of antidepressants, however, is controversial due to evidence indicating that they may induce manic episodes, as well as produce a treatment-resistant mixed state in those patients with psychotic depression. When people are in acute manic states, antipsychotics are frequently used in conjunction with mood stabilizers because they have a more rapid onset of action, thus greatly facilitating initial stabilization. Finally, research has indicated that systemic family therapy aimed at reducing environmental stress or increasing support for patients was effective at reducing relapse rates among people with bipolar disorder (Miklowitz et al., 1988).

Conclusion

Bipolar disorder is a complex illness requiring both cross-sectional information on symptom patterns and longitudinal information on course. It disrupts the lives of 1% of the population and has been estimated to cost society up to $7 billion in inpatient and outpatient care. Consequently, it remains imperative that we continue to improve our understanding of its underlying pathology and the mechanisms that result in its observed psychopathology.

Bibliography

American Psychiatric Association. (1994). *Diagnostic and statistical manual of mental disorders* (4th ed.). Washington, DC: Author.

Alexander, J. R., Benjamin, J., Lerer, B., Baron, M., & Belmaker, R. H. (1995). Frequency of positive family history in bipolar patients in a catchment-area population. *Progress in Neuro-Psychopharmacology & Biological Psychiatry, 19,* 367–373.

Fogarty, F., Russell, J. M., Newman, S. C., and Bland, R. C. (1994). Mania. *Acta Psychiatrica Scandinavica, 89,* 16–23.

Goldberg, J. F., Harrow, M., & Grossman, L. S. (1995). Course and outcome in bipolar affective disorder: A longitudinal follow-up study. *American Journal of Psychiatry, 152,* 379–384.

Goodwin, F. K., & Jamison, K. R. (1990). *Manic-depressive illness.* New York: Oxford University Press.

Marshal, E. (1994). Highs and lows on the research roller coaster. *Science, 264,* 1693–1695.

Miklowitz, D. J., Goldstein, M. J., Nuechterlein, K. H., Snyder, K. S., & Mintz, J. (1988). Family factors and the course of bipolar affective disorder. *Archives of General Psychiatry, 45,* 225–231.

Pichot, P. (1995). The birth of bipolar disorder. *European Psychiatry, 10,* 1–10.

Post, R. M. (1990). Sensitization and kindling perspectives for the course of affective illness: Toward a new treatment with the anticonvulsant carbamazepine. *Pharmacopsychiatry, 23,* 3–17.

Sands, J. R., & Harrow, M. (in press). *Bipolar disorder: Psychopathology, biology and diagnosis.*

Young, M. A., & Harrow, M. (1993). Bipolar disorders. In A. S. Bellack & M. Hersen (Eds.), *Psychopathology in adulthood* (pp. 234–251). Boston: Allyn & Bacon.

Jean S. Gearon and Alan S. Bellack

BIRAN, MAINE DE (1766–1824), French philosopher. Maine de Biran (born Marie-François-Pierre Gonthier or Gontier) was descended from a prominent Bergerac family. As a member of Louis XVI's body guard, he participated in the October 1789 defense of Versailles. Surviving the revolution by retiring to the country, Biran devoted himself to intellectual pursuits, passing as he commented in one leap "from frivolity to philosophy." Returning to Paris, he combined the life of bureaucrat and politician with that of his preferred avocation, mental and moral philosophy.

Biran's complete writings comprise 14 volumes, although most were published posthumously. He also presented papers to the Institut de France and the Academies of Berlin and Copenhagen and he associated with the leading intellectuals of the day. Biran's early views are exemplified in *Sur L'Influence de l'habitude sur la faculté de penser* (1802–1803), those of his mature middle period in the *Essais sur les fondements de la psychologie* (1859), and his final mystical ideas in *Nouveau essais d'anthropogie* (1859). Perhaps his most interesting book is the *Journal intime*, the intellectual diary he kept for most of his adult life. A masterpiece of introspective writing, its pages document the author's intellectual development.

Initially an adherent of Étienne Bonnot de Condillac's sensationalist and mechanistic epistemology, Biran quickly adopted some of that theory's revisions, particularly those focusing on active mental processes, proposed by Pierre Cabanis and his fellow Ideologues. One of Biran's first signs of intellectual independence was a call for a psychology of will.

Biran argued for the need for a pure science of psychology based on the facts of consciousness derived from careful introspection. His observations revealed that, in addition to the passive habits Condillac described, there are other active habits that are conscious and willed. These give us the experience of self and the perception of willed endeavor. The awareness of the effort (will) needed to overcome external resistance leads in early infancy to consciousness of self. In later years, Biran rejected his early scepticism and adopted a form of mysticism, arguing that above the "properly human life of voluntary effort" there is a divine force and a spiritual life.

The assessment of Biran's influence is complex. The delay in publication of most of his works limited his immediate impact; the *Essais,* his most important psychological work, was not published until 1859. Similarly, his eventual drift to a mystical spiritualism diminished his influence in scientific circles. More positively, however, younger scholars such as Laromiguière, Ampère, Royer-Collard and, particularly, Victor Cousin were all personally influenced by him. Biran was aware that Cousin "poached on his preserves" but thought Cousin's success as a teacher would prove useful when the *Essais* should finally appear. In Cousin, Biran's mental activism and voluntarism were combined with the doctrines of the Scottish Common Sense and Faculty School. The call for a psychology of will was finally answered and that concept assumed a place at the heart of nineteenth-century French psychology. Mid-century alienists were also impressed by Biran's emphasis on the contrast between the conscious and the unconscious, the active and the passive; such views influenced both Pierre Janet and Sigmund Freud. However, other scholars such as Hippolyte Taine, concerned that Germany had superseded France as the center of psychology, placed the blame for this development on Biran's evolution toward spiritualism.

[*Many of the people mentioned in this article are the subjects of independent biographical entries.*]

Bibliography

Biran, Maine de. (c.1803/1929; repr. 1971). *The influence of habit on the faculty of thinking* (M. D. Boehm, Trans.). Baltimore, MD: Williams & Wilkins. This is the only one of Biran's works available in its entirety in English translation. Unfortunately, at the point when it was written, he had not yet developed his distinctive and influential views.

Biran, Maine de. (1912/1966). "Essay upon the foundations of psychology, chapters 1 and 2." In B. Rand (Ed. & Trans.), *The classical psychologists* (pp. 448–462). Gloucester, MA: Peter Smith. These brief chapters represent the only English translation of Biran's mature thought.

Biran, Maine de. (1920–1942). *Oeuvres de Maine de Biran* (P. Tisserand & H. Gouhier, Eds.). Paris: Presses Universitaires de France. This edition was reprinted in Geneva in 1982.

Cousin, V. (1852). *Course of the history of modern philosophy* (Vol. 2). (O. W. Wright, Trans.).

Hallie, P. P. (1959). *Maine de Biran: Reformer of empiricism.* Cambridge, MA: Harvard University Press.

Höffding, H. (1900). *A history of modern philosophy* (Vol. 2) (B. E. Meyer, Trans.). London: Macmillan.

Biran, Maine de. (1954–1957). *Journal* (3 vols.) (H. Gouhier, Ed.). Neuchâtel: Editions de la Baconnière.

Moore, F. C. T. (1970). *The psychology of Maine de Biran.* Oxford: Clarendon.

Trueman, N. E. (1904). *Maine de Biran's philosophy of will.* New York: Macmillan

Gary Brooks

BIRTH ORDER. The idea that birth order has important relationships to various psychological characteristics dates back over a century to Sir Francis Galton's book, *English Men of Science* (London, 1874), which noted an overrepresentation of early-born men among great British scientists. Since then, there have been literally thousands of research articles and books published on birth order. A few social scientists have proposed birth-order theories. But most birth-order research has been almost completely empirical, meaning that interesting birth-order patterns have been noted in empirical data and then interpreted in a post hoc fashion. Both empirical patterns and theories will be reviewed here.

Birth order refers to the ordinal position that a child occupies within a family. Often, birth-order researchers distinguish between first- or early-borns, middle-borns, and later- or last-borns. Birth order is the most popular of a whole range of structural measures of the family environment experienced by a child, including measures of family size, age spacing between children, gender composition, and number of parents in the family. These family-structure characteristics are salient to both parents and researchers, a fact that provides at least partial explanation for their popularity as research variables. It is much easier to observe a child's birth order than it is to directly observe parental discipline, sibling interaction, genes, or hormones. These latter influences are more important determinants of child outcomes such as intelligence or personality than are structural measures such as birth order. Nevertheless, research on birth order and family structure continues apace.

Empirical Research

A great deal of the birth-order literature is atheoretical. The most widely published birth-order research follows the basic methodology begun by Galton, defining the distribution of birth order within a group that shares an interesting common characteristic. Using this approach, researchers have found birth-order patterns among alcoholics, artists, authors, assassins, delinquents, dentists, heroin addicts, hockey players, presidents, risk takers, scientists, smokers, soldiers, strippers, thumb suckers, and unwed mothers, among many others. Even the birth order of birth-order researchers has been studied. The atheoretical nature of such work, combined with a lack of coherence across many of these studies, has led a number of scholars to publish criticisms of birth order as a meaningful research variable. Notable among these critiques are Schooler's (1972) article, "Birth Order Effects: Not Here, Not Now!" and Ernst and Angst's (1983) book, *Birth Order*.

Another methodology that has been used is the study of birth-order patterns in large cross-sectional samples. In such samples, there has been a consistent negative relation observed between birth order and intelligence, educational outcome, and emotional health. The consistency of such findings has led to some important theoretical developments.

Both of these approaches have well-documented methodological problems. Using intact-family data provides a much stronger basis for the study of birth-order effects. Such data allow a direct comparison between children within the same family and avoid several threats to both internal and external validity that are present in the other two methodologies.

Theories of Birth Order

Birth order played a role in Sigmund Freud's theories, and Alfred Adler used birth order as one of the cornerstones of his theories of personality. It is notable, though, that neither Freud nor Adler subjected their birth-order theories to empirical evaluation. Birth-order "experts" still assert birth-order causes and effects without proper evaluation of their size and importance.

An important theoretical proposition to emerge from Adler's work was the "conservators of tradition" hypothesis, which suggested that early-born children are more likely than later-born children to adopt a traditional family orientation. Another important theoretical perspective was "family resource theory" (or "dilution theory"), which suggested that each additional child in a family further stretches the available household resources, including money, household space, and parental attention. The confluence model (Zajonc & Markus, 1975) suggested that each new child in a family reduces the intellectual richness of the family in a way that inhibits intellectual growth for all children in the family. The confluence model also suggested that there is a "tutoring effect" that is intellectually facilitating for children who have younger siblings to teach. These theories have not held up consistently to empirical evaluation, however.

A recent birth-order theory was published in Frank Sulloway's 1996 book, *Born to Rebel*. Sulloway blended the "conservators of tradition" hypothesis with evolutionary theory to suggest that early-born children have an adaptive advantage if they build and maintain strong parental and family ties, whereas later-born children will be more successful if they have rebellious tendencies. Sulloway offered empirical evidence in support of his theory by examining the birth order of scholars who have led scientific, intellectual, and political rebellions.

The "Birth Order Artifact"

A challenge to all within-family theories is the proposal that birth order and family size are not the important process variables that they appear to be. Rather, birth order and family size can act as proxy measures of other more important processes. For example, it is documented across a number of cultures that, on average, parents with lower levels of education have larger families. As a result, seventh-born children are more likely than first-born children to have come from households headed by parents with low levels of education. This fact may make seventh-born children appear to have lower achievement outcomes than firstborn children. In this case, birth order is not the causal variable but an indirect measure of parental education. Even Sulloway noted that "Birth order is not the *real* cause of radical thinking, even though it is strongly correlated with it. But birth order can be seen as a proxy. . . . Common sense tells us that causation probably lies in those other variables, not in birth order per se" (1996, p. 373). Birth order can act as a proxy for many different processes, including parental education, parental intelligence, family socioeconomic status, birth weight, and prematurity. The type of cross-sectional data that have been used in many previous studies completely confound these within- and between-family explanations.

For this reason, most sophisticated family-structure scholars emphasize the importance of using data that explicitly account for interrelations among children in a family (so that actual brothers and sisters are compared to one another). Studies that have used intact-family data have generally cast a great deal of doubt on the existence of powerful birth-order effects (e.g., Retherford & Sewell, 1991). Small birth-order effects probably do exist and can be measured and studied. These effects appear to be somewhat stronger for personality than for intelligence, and social conservatism appears to be an area that shows bigger birth-order effects than most others. But the effect sizes directly attributable to birth order are small and virtually disappear next to the importance of more process oriented measures. The ways parents treat their children are much more important determinants of behavioral outcomes than the order of the child's birth. The genes with which a child is born will ultimately account for much more variance in the child's personality and intelligence than birth order or family size.

Birth order is easy to observe and inherently interesting, and researchers and parents will undoubtedly continue to study how birth order influences behavior. But methodological problems in studying birth order have led to an inflated appearance of its importance. Birth order does appear to have small and subtle influences that are real, and these are worth studying. But the popular belief that birth order has strong and consistent effects on psychological outcomes is not supported by well-designed research.

[*See also* Sibling Relationships.]

Bibliography

Adler, A. (1959). *The practice and theory of individual psychology.* Paterson, NJ: Littlefield, Adams. Shows how birth order is accounted for by one of the original birth-order theorists.

Altus, W. D. (1966). Birth order and its sequelae. *Science, 151,* 44–49. Excellent review article of early birth-order research.

Ernst, C., & Angst, J. (1983). *Birth order.* New York:

Springer-Verlag. Still the most complete review of birth-order research.

Galton, F. (1874). *English men of science*. London: Macmillan. The original treatment of birth order.

Retherford, R. D., & Sewell, W. H. (1991). Birth order and intelligence: Further tests of the confluence model. *American Sociological Review, 56*, 141–158. Demonstrates sophisticated methods applied to study of birth order, with typical results.

Rodgers, J. L. & Thompson, V. (1985/86). Toward a general framework of family structure research: A review of theory-based empirical research. *Population and Environment, 8*, 143–172. Shows the important interplay between theories and data and discusses birth-order methodological problems in detail.

Schooler, C. (1972). Birth order effects: Not here, not now! *Psychological Bulletin, 78*, 161–175. Much-cited criticism of birth-order research.

Sulloway, F. J. (1996). *Born to rebel: Birth order, family dynamics, and creative lives*. New York: Vintage. Popular blending of family systems and evolutionary theory.

Warren, J. R. (1966). Birth order and social behavior. *Psychological Bulletin, 65*, 38–49. Treatment of birth order in social domains.

Zajonc, R. B., & Markus, G. B. (1975). Birth order and intellectual development. *Psychological Review, 82*, 74–88. Presents the confluence model, a popular birth-order theory.

Joseph Lee Rodgers

BISEXUALITY is sexual attraction toward, or sexual behavior with, both men and women. The concept was introduced into psychoanalytic theory when the German physician Richard von Krafft-Ebing used the term *psychical hermaphroditism* to explain homosexuality in terms of evolutionary theory. Sigmund Freud then applied the evolutionary view of bisexuality to the realm of psychosexual development. While Freud interpreted homosexuality as arrested psychosexual development, he simultaneously stressed that all individuals experience some homosexual feelings. Others, such as the Austrian psychiatrist Wilhelm Stekel, viewed bisexuality as an integral stage of childhood development that is eventually repressed to yield an adult heterosexual or homosexual orientation (Fox, 1995).

The pioneering sex researcher Alfred Kinsey considered human sexuality from a descriptive rather than a clinical perspective, focusing primarily on sexual behavior for his analyses. He emphasized that bisexuality is merely the middle position on a seven-point continuum, between heterosexuality and homosexuality, not a specific identity nor a discrete category of sexual functioning. More elaborate models have since been forwarded to account for factors overlooked by Kinsey. The multidimensional measurement instruments developed independently by American researchers Klein and Coleman assess emotional and social preferences, lifestyle, self-identification, sexual attraction, fantasy, and behavior, as well as changes in these factors over time. Australian psychologists Paul and Ross developed a continuum of gender-linked sexuality with heterosexuality and homosexuality at one end (highly gender linked) and bisexuality at the other end (nongender linked). Their research suggests that personality factors unrelated to gender are important in romantic partner choice for bisexuals (Mondimore, 1996). Canadian psychologist Blackford and colleagues (1996) have also found that bisexual women differ from lesbian and heterosexual women in measures of subjective sexual arousal to video stimuli. Taken together, data derived from these models have resulted in a recognition of bisexuality as a distinct sexual orientation.

Equal sexual responsiveness to both sexes over the lifespan is rare but appears to be more common in women than in men. Same-sex attractions and behavior generally occur after those to the opposite sex for bisexual women, whereas bisexual men typically experience their first homosexual attractions and behavior before, or at approximately the same age as, their first heterosexual experience. Nonetheless, bisexual women tend to move from their first homosexual attractions to a bisexual identity more quickly than bisexual men (Fox, 1996).

Freud conceived of two bisexual categories: the first, "contingent," was dependent upon external conditions, such as prison confinement, and the second "amphigenic," was inborn or established so early in psychosexual development that it could be considered inborn (Fox, 1995). Employing the seven-point Kinsey scale, Weinberg and colleagues (1994) identify five categories of bisexuals. These are: the "pure type," which scores a Kinsey 3 on all dimensions; the "mid-type," which yields an average score of 3 on the dimensions assessed; the "heterosexual-leaning type," which scores more heterosexual than homosexual on all dimensions; the "homosexual-leaning type," which scores more homosexual than heterosexual on all dimensions; and the "varied type," which is substantially heterosexual on one dimension while much more homosexual on another. Psychiatrist Fritz Klein (1993) elaborates four typologies of bisexuality based upon the extent and timing of past and present sexual behavior. "Concurrent bisexuality" refers to relationships with both women and men during the same time period. "Sequential bisexuality" denotes a pattern of relationships with both sexes, but with only one person during a particular period of time. "Historical bisexuality" refers to sexual attractions or behavior experienced with both sexes in the past, but current exclusive homosexuality or heterosexuality. "Transitional bisexuality" represents a stage in the process of coming out as homosexual. While population estimates of bisexuality vary, a representative survey conducted by Laumann and his colleagues (1994) in the United States found that 3.9% of men and 4.1% of women report attractions to both sexes, whereas 0.8% of men and 0.5% of women self-identify as bisexual.

Several models of bisexual identity formation have been proposed. The four-stage model developed by Weinberg and colleagues (1994) begins with "initial confusion." This can be of extended duration and stems largely from being disoriented and unsettled about experiencing attractions to both sexes. The second stage, "finding and applying the label," denotes assigning meaning to feelings and behaviors. This is followed by "settling into the identity," which involves an ongoing process of self-acceptance. The last stage, "continued uncertainty," relates to a lack of closure often surrounding bisexual identities due to deficits in social support and validation. American Sociologists Blumstein and Schwartz (1977) argue that adopting a bisexual identity is a continuous, nonlinear process that is characterized by several possible sequences in which sexual behavior and lifestyle may not necessarily be congruent with self-identification. Educational psychologist Twining developed a task model for bisexual development that identifies issues that must be faced in the coming out process: self-acceptance, resolving societal homophobia, building a support network, self-disclosure to family and friends, and coping with professional matters (Fox, 1996).

Anthropologist Herdt (1990) noted that bisexuality is present in many cultures. In ancient Greece and Rome, as well as certain modern societies in Africa, Melanesia, Australia, China, and Japan, homosexual relationships between persons of different ages occur during a specified period in adolescence for the younger partner. Following this phase, marriage and the onset of heterosexual activity are typically expected. Transformation to the gender role opposite of one's biological sex with accompanying bisexual or homosexual behavior is a pattern found among Native American Two-Spirit People, Siberian Chukchee and Koryak Shamans, the Hijras of India, and the Tahitian Mahu. Bisexuality is also common in Mediterranean and Latin American cultures where for men it is structured according to active and passive roles. The active partner has sexual encounters with both women and men and is neither considered bisexual nor homosexual. The receptive partner usually has sexual encounters exclusively with men and is considered homosexual. Egalitarian same-sex relationships for both adult men and women that often occur concurrently with heterosexual marriage have been described in the Near East, China, and Australia, and among the Azande, Hottentot, Nyakyusa, Nandi, Akan, Nupe, Hausa, and !Kung in Africa, as well as the Akuna, Asmat, and Santa Cruz Islanders in Melanesia.

Bibliography

Blackford, L., Doty, S., & Pollack, R. (1996). Differences in subjective sexual arousal in heterosexual, bisexual, and lesbian women. *Canadian Journal of Human Sexuality, 5(3)*, 157–167.

Blumstein, P. W., & Schwartz, P. (1977). Bisexuality: Some social psychological issues. *Journal of Social Issues, 33(2)*, 30–45.

Fox, R. C. (1995). Bisexual identities. In A. R. D'Augelli & C. J. Patterson (Eds.), *Lesbian, gay, and bisexual identities over the lifespan: Psychological perspectives* (pp. 48–86). New York: Oxford University Press. An in-depth analysis of sexual identities, including concepts, personal development over the lifespan, relationships and families, and community and contextual issues.

Fox, R. C. (1996). Bisexuality in perspective: A review of theory and research. In B. A. Firestein (Ed.), *Bisexuality: The psychology and politics of an invisible minority* (pp. 3–50). Thousand Oaks, CA: Sage. A particularly strong examination of counseling issues, identity formation, lifestyle, and issues surrounding stigmatization.

Garber, M. (1995). *Vice versa: Bisexuality and the eroticism of everyday life.* New York: Simon and Schuster. Explores the nature and influence of bisexuality in American culture, gathering evidence from art, literature, history, pop culture, science, and psychology.

Herdt, G. (1990). Developmental discontinuities and sexual orientation across cultures. In D. P. McWhirter, S. A. Sanders, & J. M. Reinisch (Eds.), *Homosexuality/heterosexuality: Concepts of sexual orientation* (pp. 208–236). New York: Oxford University Press.

Klein, F. (1993). *The bisexual option* (2nd ed.). New York: Harrington Park. Explains the concept of bisexuality, the variables of sexual orientation, and where bisexuality fits.

Laumann, E. O., Gagnon, J. H., Michael, R. T., & Michaels, S. (1994). *The social organization of sexuality: Sexual practices in the United States.* Chicago: University of Chicago Press. A report on the most comprehensive representative survey of sexual behavior in the general population of the United States.

Mondimore, F. M. (1996). *A natural history of homosexuality.* Baltimore, MD: The Johns Hopkins University Press. Examines the nature of homosexuality and bisexuality with a particular emphasis on the effects of stigmatization.

Weinberg, M. S., Williams, C. J., & Pryor, D. W. (1994). *Dual attraction: Understanding bisexuality.* New York: Oxford University Press. A report based upon ten years of in-depth interviews and surveys that presents a comprehensive examination of bisexuality, including theories of identity formation, typologies, sexual activities, and strategies used to balance same- and opposite-sex relationships.

Ángela Pattatucci Aragón

BLEULER, EUGEN (1856–1939), Swiss psychiatrist. Eugen Bleuler was an exponent of the more psychologically minded psychiatry, which gathered momentum in the late nineteenth and early twentieth centuries. He was born in the small village of Zollikon at a time when many psychiatrists came from Germany and did not understand Swiss German dialects, or appreciate the needs of the local population. This schism seems to have impressed Bleuler and he decided to study medicine and psychiatry in Zurich. He also traveled internationally and spent time at Charcot's clinic in Paris where he was exposed to psychological treatments like hypnosis and suggestion. In 1885 Bleuler became August Forel's assistant at the Burghoelzli psychiatric clinic in Zurich. A year later he was appointed director of the psychiatric hospital in Rheinau, Switzerland, a position he held until 1898 when he took over the Burghoelzli directorship from his former teacher. Bleuler retired from this directorship at the age of 70. His son Manfred also became a psychiatrist and followed in his father's footsteps, directing the clinic from 1940 to 1969.

Bleuler was distinguished by a receptive stance toward new ideas and gradually broke with the custodial and descriptive traditions of nineteenth-century psychiatry. As a teacher and professor of psychiatry at the University of Zurich he supported the early development of psychiatrists Carl Jung and Ernest Jones, among others. He was a dedicated clinician, and skeptical about existing psychiatric treatments like water therapy and chloral hydrate. This led him to introduce new elements, including occupational therapy, into psychiatry. He helped pioneer psychiatric treatment programs for alcoholism. In addition, he was one of the first psychiatrists to believe in the value of psychosocial and psychotherapeutic intervention for people with serious mental illness. For a brief time he maintained a formal association with Sigmund Freud and the psychoanalytic movement. Bleuler valued psychoanalysis but maintained a critical distance from the new field. He resigned from the International Psychoanalytic Association in 1910 because of his discomfort with Freud's apparent dogmatism and intolerance for dissenting viewpoints on psychoanalytic theory.

As a scholar and researcher, Bleuler wrote more than 150 articles and papers that reflected his broad interests, ranging from endocrinology to addictions to psychosis. He is best known for his book on schizophrenia, *Dementia Praecox* (New York, 1950) and his *Textbook of Psychiatry* (New York, 1924), which were used in medical schools in German-speaking Europe and elsewhere in translation for many years.

In approaching the puzzle of psychotic disorder Bleuler departed from the prevailing view represented by Emil Kraepelin (1856–1926). Kraepelin (*Psychiatrie*, Leipzig, Germany, 1898) had distinguished dementia praecox, an adolescent-onset mental deterioration and psychosis, from affective psychosis. Bleuler disagreed with the characterization of the disorder as a precocious dementing process and introduced the term *schizophrenia*. The new term was meant to reflect the splitting of psychological functions that underpinned the illness. He also recognized that schizophrenic symptoms like delusions, hallucinations, and withdrawal occurred in other disorders. Moreover, such symptoms were heterogeneous and variable even in schizophrenia. Therefore, he considered these more obvious psychotic phenomena as "accessory" and proposed a more basic underlying symptomatology for the illness. This core disturbance encompassed dissociations, splitting, fragmentation, and the coexistence of contradictory impulses in the patient's mental life. Thus speech became disconnected from a unifying thought, emotional expression became incongruent with speech content, desire competed with disgust, and thought contradicted action. More formally, Bleuler defined simple and compound fundamental symptoms of schizophrenia. These included associative and affective disturbances and ambivalence (simple functions), along with autism, attention and personality-related, volitional, intellectual, and behavioral disturbances (compound functions). Although Bleuler believed in a root cause for schizophrenia that was biological in nature, he theorized extensively about the mental processes giving rise to fundamental and accessory symptoms.

Bleuler's most obvious legacy is the use of the term *schizophrenia* itself, which quickly superseded *dementia praecox*. More substantially, his description of the illness was influential in European and North American psychiatry and clinical psychology until the advent of more explicit diagnostic criteria. Yet his concept of schizophrenia, with its abstract and convoluted fundamental and accessory symptoms, is now regarded as excessively broad, more akin to a spectrum of disorders that includes schizoaffective, schizoid, and schizotypal personality disorder, than to the narrow concept of schizophrenia as described in the *Diagnostic and Statistical Manual of Mental Disorders* (American Psychiatric Association, 1994). Similarly, although he encouraged psychodynamic theorizing and psychotherapeutic approaches to the illness, such ideas and approaches have declined in the face of evidence from biological psychiatry and psychopharmacology that schizophrenia is mediated by neurochemical events. Perhaps the most contemporary echo of Bleulerian thinking can be seen in efforts by psychologists like Richard Bentall (1994) and Christopher Frith (1992) to articulate the cognitive processes that underpin psychotic symptoms, and in psychologist Paul Meehl's (1990) theory of schizophrenia, which acknowledges a debt to the work of this innovative psychiatrist.

[*Many of the people mentioned in this article are the subjects of independent biographical entries.*]

Bibliography

American Psychiatric Association. (1994). *Diagnostic and statistical manual of mental disorders* (4th ed.). Washington, DC: Author.

Berrios, G. E. (1987). The fundamental symptoms in dementia praecox or the group of schizophrenias. 1911: Eugen Bleuler. In C. Thompson (Ed.), *The origins of modern psychiatry* (pp. 165–209). Chichester, England: Wiley.

Bentall, R. P. (1994). Cognitive biases and abnormal beliefs. Towards a model of persecutory delusions. In A. S. Davis & J. Cutting (Eds.), *The neuropsychology of schizophrenia* (pp. 337–360). London: Erlbaum.

Bleuler, M. (1984). Eugen Bleuler and schizophrenia. *British Journal of Psychiatry, 144*, 327–328. An assessment of Bleuler's life and work by his son.

Brill, A. A. (1939). In memoriam: Eugen Bleuler. *American Journal of Psychiatry, 96*, 513–516. An evaluation of Bleuler's life and work from a psychoanalytically oriented psychiatrist.

Frith, C. D. (1992). *The cognitive neuropsychology of schizophrenia.* Hillsdale, NJ: Erlbaum.

Hoenig, J. (1983). The concept of schizophrenia Kraepelin Bleuler–Schneider. *British Journal of Psychiatry, 142*, 547–556.

Meehl, P. E. (1990). Toward an integrated theory of schizotaxia, schizotypy, and schizophrenia. *Journal of Personality Disorders, 4*, 1–99. Provides an example of contemporary theory on schizophrenia that is influenced by Bleuler's views.

R. Walter Heinrichs

BOAS, FRANZ (1858–1942), German American anthropologist. Born in Minden, Germany, Boas was educated at Heidelberg, Bonn, and Kiel universities. As a liberal and a Jew, Boas took up anthropology to address the problem of group or racial differences. In the United States, Boas taught at Columbia University where he trained many leading American anthropologists.

His main contribution to psychology was the study of racial differences. Unlike Sir Francis Galton, who argued that biological phenomena were distributed according to the normal curve of probability, Boas wished to understand biological and developmental *processes*, not mere *structures*. Simply put, Boas rejected

Galton's reification of numbers as if they were psychobiological reality. He wanted to know about race mixture, growth, development, spurts and slowdowns, the interaction of biology and environment, and all other events that might produce asymmetries in the distribution of traits. Thus, in a study of White–Native American hybrids, he found, contrary to conventional wisdom, that hybrids were more, not less, fertile, and that they were taller than pure Native American stock, thus suggesting that race mixtures yielded healthy, not degenerate, offspring. In his famous study done for the United States Immigration Commission, completed in 1911, about the adaptation of two generations of eastern European immigrants to America, he argued that changes in head forms (cephalic index) of 18,000 individuals showed that if such "hard" or permanent physical traits could change in a new environment, then so could the "soft" cultural traits. Boas also insisted that nature and culture were dynamic, not static, in historical time—an assumption basic to the behavioral sciences as they were crystallizing in that decade in psychology—as did John B. Watson and other social scientists.

After 1910, the Boasians (Boas and his doctoral graduates) took the next step in opposing the idea that some races were superior to other races. They advanced the idea of culture. Defining culture as all the capabilities and habits that people acquire as the consequence of living in society, they insisted that cultural phenomena were of a different order than physical or biological phenomena; none could be explained as the consequence of any of the others. Culture was essentially a mental, not a physical, construction. They argued that every people had a cultural history, which was specific to time and place, and, borrowing from German idealist philosophy, they insisted that the facts of culture were essentially mental, not material, that they were unique, and that there could be no easy, grand, determinist syntheses, whether Marxian or racist in character. Culture history came from cultural facts. Cultural facts were mental pictures of the external world that drove human behavior because they defined and shaped human perception. In this way they battled biological determinism and reductionism in the American natural sciences. In the 1910s and 1920s, psychologists interested in mental testing tried to show that intelligence was innate and varied according to specific classes and castes: a model of a social hierarchy of class, race, and gender, symptomatic of larger patterns of thought of that era. The Boasians attacked the view that Army tests showed a racial hierarchy, with the Nordic types at the pyramid's apex, and "lesser" groups, especially immigrants from southern and eastern Europe and non-Whites, at or near the bottom. Thus, a young psychologist, Otto Klineberg (1935), began a long-term study under Boas's supervision of selective migration of Blacks from the plantation south to northern cities. As in Boas's study of the head forms of immigrants, racial IQ was related to length of residence in the new environment. Thus, races were not permanent or essential, but changing entities that fluctuated in adaptation to new situations and forces. By taking on such typological thinking, the Boasians undermined much of the racist thinking of the era.

With Melville J. Herskovits's *The American Negro: A Study in Race Crossing* (New York, Knopf) and Margaret Mead's *Coming of Age in Samoa* (New York, Morrow), both published in 1928, the Boasians again contributed a dynamic concept to psychology: group theory, which, of course, was related to racial psychology and anthropology. Thus, Herskovits linked population genetics to anthropology and psychology by insisting that American Blacks were the product of an American environment, and were thus a group distinct from African Blacks. Mead argued that even sexual morality had a different meaning in a different culture. They linked physical and cultural anthropology and the new group psychology of such giants as Kurt Lewin, John Dollard, and Robert R. Sears, thus enriching psychological theory, especially group theory, until then notably absent from psychology. Thus Boas's ultimate contribution to psychology was to assist its transit from the static world of late nineteenth- and early twentieth-century social science to the dynamic world of mid-twentieth-century behavioral science.

[*Many of the people mentioned in this article are the subjects of independent biographical entries.*]

Bibliography

Works by Boas

Boas, F. (1911). *The mind of primitive man*. New York: Macmillan. A seminal statement.

Boas, F. (1972). *The professional correspondence of Franz Boas* (microfilm edition). Wilmington, DE: Scholarly Resources.

Works about Boas

Cravens, H. (1988). *The triumph of evolution: The heredity–environment controversy, 1900–1941*. Baltimore: Johns Hopkins University Press. (Original work published 1978.) Places the issues that Boas and others raised in a broader scientific and social and cultural historical context.

Klineberg, O. (1935). *Negro intelligence and selective migration*. New York: Columbia University Press.

Stocking, G. W., Jr. (1968). *Race, culture, and evolution: Essays in the history of anthropology*. New York: Free Press. A nuanced series of articles, centering on the work of Boas and his associates, or work that they challenged.

Stocking, G. W., Jr. (Ed.). (1974). *The shaping of American anthropology, 1883–1911. A Franz Boas reader*. New York: Basic Books. An excellent edition of some of Boas's most important early papers.

Hamilton Cravens

BODY IMAGE is a psychological concept that refers to an individual's mental representation of his or her own body. The earliest view of body image was as a neurological construct—the brain's registration of the body's sensory and motor activities. One important impetus for this perspective was an attempt to understand the "phantom limb phenomenon," whereby patients still felt pain or other sensations from amputated limbs.

Later, influenced by the psychoanalytic theorizing of Paul Schilder and Seymour Fisher, body image came to be seen as the complex experience of one's physical being at varying levels of consciousness. This view regards the body as the boundary between the self and everything outside the self, and one's experience of the body is a projective representation of early emotional learning. Thus, body image has less to do with feelings about the body itself than about unconscious events and feelings about the self. Projective methods (e.g., inkblots and drawings) have typically been used, albeit with dubious success, to assess this psychoanalytic conception of body image.

The third more recent viewpoint considers body image as a perceptual representation of the body, particularly its size and shape. This narrower perspective was greatly influenced by clinical researchers trying to understand the distorted perceptions held by patients with eating disorders, such as anorexia nervosa and bulimia nervosa. Assessment of perceptual body image uses various body size estimation techniques to measure the accuracy or distortion of one's judgments.

The fourth contemporary perspective defines body image as a psychological attitude toward one's own physical characteristics, especially one's appearance, though it may incorporate physical competence and somatic health illness as well. Body-image attitudes are evident in people's mostly conscious, body-related cognitions, emotions, and behaviors. Researchers typically use self-report questionnaires to measure specific components of body-image attitudes, such as evaluations of physical attributes, beliefs, and emotional feelings about the importance of one's appearance, and behaviors to manage one's appearance or one's own reactions to it. Frequently used measures are the Body Cathexis Scale, the Body Shape Questionnaire, the Multidimensional Body-Self Relations Questionnaire, and the Situational Inventory of Body Image Dysphoria.

Body-Image Development

A person's sense of self is rooted, in part, in the experience of embodiment. By the age of two years, most children can recognize their bodily self in the mirror. Increasingly, this image becomes one representation of personal identity. The process of socialization about the meaning and significance of physical appearance is influenced by the norms and expectations of one's culture, family, and peers. Cognitive and social learning entail the acquisition of emotion-laden attitudes about one's own body. Largely as the result of explicit and implicit social feedback, people develop evaluative concepts about the acceptability and attractiveness of their physical attributes—such as their height, weight, facial features, and overall appearance. Children not only acquire beliefs about what they look like, but they also internalize personal standards or ideals about what they *should* look like. According to self-discrepancy theory, a positive or satisfying body image emerges to the extent that one's self-perceived physical attributes and one's ideals are congruent. A "negative body image" results from self-appraisals that these attributes fall short of one's ideals, especially if the ideals are strongly held self-expectations.

Researchers have identified several factors that influence the course of body-image development during childhood, at least in Western culture. While appearance-related teasing by peers is not uncommon, such taunting experiences, if recurrent and distressing, have been associated with developing a less favorable body image in adolescence and adulthood. Obese children develop a more negative body image, which may persist into adulthood even after excess weight has been lost. Parents' modeling of body dissatisfaction may teach children critical scrutiny of their own looks. Furthermore, having a more attractive sibling may engender familial and personal social comparisons that adversely affect one's body image development.

An understanding of body image must recognize that the body and its appearance change over the lifespan. For example, the nature and timing of pubescent changes can be quite influential. Adolescence is a period that involves increased personal and social emphasis on physical appearance. Premature puberty among girls and delayed puberty among boys can adversely affect body-image development. Prevalent appearance-altering conditions such as facial acne can diminish teenagers' body satisfaction and their sense of interpersonal acceptability.

During adulthood, the normal physical changes that come with aging can lead some appearance-invested people to worry about losing their youthful looks. For example, the onset of androgenetic alopecia, or common genetic pattern balding, can provoke body-image discontent among many men. Nonetheless, cross-sectional research reveals that older adults do not necessarily have a more negative body image than younger adults. One explanation is that aging tempers one's investment in physical appearance relative to other sources of self-evaluation, such as success in family and career roles.

Whereas some physical changes are the expected result of aging, other changes are precipitated by unforeseen illness or injury. Body image difficulties may follow traumatic events, such as facial disfigurement, mastectomy, or limb amputation. These conditions are a challenge to body-image adaptation, whereby individuals must integrate their altered appearance into their self-view and must manage unwanted social consequences of "looking different." Acutely acquired disfigurements are generally more disruptive of body image than congenital deformities that are incorporated into one's early body-image development.

Body Image, Gender, and Culture

National research surveys from the 1970s through the 1990s point to Americans' growing body dissatisfaction. Moreover, the data indicate that regardless of respondents' age or when the survey was conducted, women consistently report less favorable body-image evaluations than do men. For both genders, body weight, shape, and muscle tone have been found to be the foci of greatest dissatisfaction. The vast majority of weight-dissatisfied women believe that they are too heavy, even if average in weight. On the other hand, men who are unhappy with their weight are fairly equally divided into those who believe they are overweight versus those who believe they are underweight. Moreover, compared to men, women appear to be more psychologically invested in their appearance and engage in more appearance-management behaviors. These gender differences likely reflect Western society's greater emphasis on women's attractiveness and the current "thin-and-fit" cultural standards defining feminine beauty. Considerable evidence points to the role that the media play in defining physical ideals, which if internalized can produce overinvestment in appearance and increased personal body dissatisfaction.

There are also cultural differences in body image. For example, African American women appear to have a more positive body image than European American women, and this is especially apparent at higher body weights. Like various black African cultures, African Americans view a more full-figured female shape as feminine and attractive. Individual differences in body image may also depend on sexual orientation. Relative to heterosexual men, gay men are more invested in and less satisfied with their physical appearance. Perhaps this difference reflects the fact that they must please men who, to a greater extent than women, stress physical attractiveness as a criterion of sexual or romantic desirability. Though less clear, some research has found that lesbians are less appearance invested and more body satisfied than are heterosexual women.

Body-Image Disturbances and Disorders

Body dissatisfaction can lead to a variety of psychosocial problems. Evidence indicates that body image and overall self-esteem are moderately correlated for both genders. Moreover, persons who are discontented with their physical appearance are at risk for self-conscious social anxiety, depression, sexual difficulties, and eating disturbances.

Substantial research attests to the central role of body-image disturbances in anorexia nervosa and bulimia nervosa. Sufferers from these two eating disorders are principally young women who hold extremely disparaging views of their body weight and shape, including distorted perceptions (i.e., overestimations) of their actual size. In addition, their physical appearance is a criterion of self-worth. Longitudinal studies suggest that body-image disturbances are precursors to the disordered eating behavior per se and serve to maintain the maladaptive behavior once it has begun. Treatment studies further indicate that recovery from an eating disorder may require body-image change; without such improvement, relapse of the disorder is much more likely.

Another severe body-image disorder is body dysmorphic disorder. Although long recognized by Asian and European professionals, this disorder was only recently recognized in the *Diagnostic and Statistical Manual of mental disorders* (4th ed.) by the American Psychiatric Association (Washington, DC, 1994). Classified as a somatoform disorder, body dysmorphic disorder refers to an excessive preoccupation with a nonexistent or very minor physical defect. Individuals with this disorder believe that their "defect" is quite socially noticeable. They spend inordinate time compulsively inspecting themselves in the mirror and often self-protectively avoid ordinary social events where they might experience intense self-consciousness and anxiety. Although they are usually able to recognize that their perceptions are distorted, rather than seek mental-health assistance they are more likely to consult with medical–surgical professionals to "fix" the perceived physical flaw.

Body-Image Change

There are two basic approaches to changing body image. The first and more prevalent approach is to alter the body so that it will conform to the person's body-image ideals. Thus, many body-dissatisfied people pursue weight loss, physical exercise, plastic surgery, medical treatments, as well as aesthetic grooming changes, in attempts to create a more satisfying appearance. Scientific studies confirm that such body-modifying methods can improve body image. However, critics of this approach, especially feminists and other advocates of societal change, argue that many of these "remedies" have inherent health risks and that all ultimately reinforce conformity to unrealistic social expectations of physical attractiveness.

Alternatively, psychotherapeutic interventions can promote body acceptance without bodily change. The most thoroughly researched of these interventions is cognitive-behavioral body-image therapy, principally developed by American psychologists Thomas F. Cash and James C. Rosen. Cognitive-behavioral therapy is based on the premise that people can overcome problems by learning more adaptive patterns of thought and action and by eliminating self-defeating thoughts and behaviors. Its application to body-image change typically entails systematically teaching people: (a) to become more objectively cognizant of the personal causes and effects of their body-image experiences; (b) to monitor and reduce self-denigrating thoughts about their physical appearances; (c) to decrease avoidant or compulsive behaviors that are motivated by anxious or self-conscious reactions to their bodies; (d) to increase positive, self-affirming experiences about their bodies; and (e) to prevent "relapses" of previous body-image difficulties. The published research on this approach supports its effectiveness with various populations, including moderately body-dissatisfied college students, chronically obese persons, and individuals diagnosed with body dysmorphic disorder. The data also show that body-image improvement leads to gains in self-esteem and other aspects of psychosocial well-being. Moreover, for some people, cognitive-behavioral programs can be carried out successfully as structured self-help, without a professional therapist.

Bibliography

American Psychiatric Association. (1994). *The diagnostic and statistical manual of mental disorders* (4th ed.). Washington, DC: Author.

Cash, T. F. (1995). *What do you see when you look in the mirror?* New York: Bantam Books.

Cash, T. F. (1997). *The body image workbook: An 8-step program for learning to like your looks.* Oakland, CA: New Harbinger. A cognitive-behavioral self-help program for body-image change.

Cash, T. F., & Deagle, E. A. (1997). The nature and extent of body-image disturbances in anorexia nervosa and bulimia nervosa: A meta-analysis. *International Journal of Eating Disorders, 21,* 2–19. A quantitative review of published research on how eating disordered patients and normal controls differ in body perceptions and attitudes.

Cash, T. F., & Grant, J. (1996). The cognitive-behavioral treatment of body-image disturbances. In V. Van Hasselt & M. Hersen (Eds.), *Sourcebook of psychological treatment manuals for adult disorders* (pp. 567–614). New

York: Plenum. A practitioner-oriented presentation of cognitive-behavioral body-image therapy—its rationale, procedures, and efficacy.

Cash, T. F., & Henry, P. E. (1995). Women's body images: The results of a national survey in the U.S.A. *Sex Roles,* 33, 19–28.

Cash, T. F., & Pruzinsky, T. (Eds.). (1990). *Body images: Development, deviance, and change.* New York: Guilford Press. An edited volume of theory and research on body-image concepts and their assessment, normal and dysfunctional body-image development, and the psychological and surgical treatment of body-image disorders.

Fisher, S. (1986). *Development and structure of the body image.* Hillsdale, NJ: Erlbaum. A two-volume compendium of theory and research on body image, especially from a psychodynamic perspective.

Jackson, L. A. (1992). *Physical appearance and gender: Socio biological and sociocultural perspectives.* Albany, NY: SUNY Press. A scholarly review of theory and research on the influences of physical attractiveness and self-perceived attractiveness (or body image) that focuses on gender differences.

Phillips, K. A. (1996). *The broken mirror.* New York: Oxford University Press. A leading psychiatrist's presentation of clinical and research information on body dysmorphic disorder and its treatment.

Rodin, J. (1992). *Body traps.* New York: Morrow. A very readable yet research-based discussion of the body-image consequences of vanity, shame, food and dieting, compulsive exercise, competition, and perfectionism.

Rosen, J. C. (1995). The nature of body dysmorphic disorder and treatment with cognitive behavior therapy. *Cognitive and Behavioral Practice, 2,* 143–166.

Thompson, J. K. (Ed.). (1996). *Body image, eating disorders, and obesity: An integrative guide for assessment and treatment.* Washington, DC: American Psychological Association.

Thomas F. Cash

BODY LANGUAGE. *See* Nonverbal Communication; *and* Sign Language.

BOLIVIA. The first formal course on psychology in Bolivia was taught at the Faculty of Law of the Universidad Mayor de San Andrés, La Paz, in 1912. It focused on developmental psychology and was part of the study of criminology. From this beginning the study of psychology evolved as a very important professional discipline.

In 1938, the Institute of Social Science of the Universidad Mayor de San Andrés began to develop programs based on the theories of Pavlov, which had influenced many studies related to psychology carried out in other Latin American countries during this period. In 1944, the Institute issued a series of publications based on the work carried out by Mira y Lopez (1896–1964), an important pioneer in Latin American psychology, who was a great influence in other South American countries, notably Brazil and Argentina.

René Calderón Soria was the first Bolivian psychologist to reach national and international importance. In 1950, Calderón founded the Center of Psychology in La Paz, and a year later he taught a course of "Psychosomatic Psychology" for students of nursing. In 1956, he introduced the course "Medical Psychology" for medical students. His influence is seen in areas such as psychological research, the formation of professional psychologists, and the general development of the discipline in Bolivia. He can be regarded as the true founder of psychology in his country. Also, his importance can be observed in the fact that his son, René Calderón Jemio, has been the most significant psychologist in Bolivia during the last decades of the twentieth century. He has been dean of faculties of psychology, has written important research papers, and has been president of the Latin American Association of Behavior Analysis and Modification (ALAMOC).

The first center for professional training was formed in 1971 in the Universidad Católica Boliviana. Other departments of psychology were later created in the Universidad de San Simon (a state university in Cochabamba), the Universidad de San Andrés in La Paz (the main state university in Bolivia), and others both in the public and private sectors. At the present time there are eight departments of psychology in various universities in the country.

The College of Psychologists was founded in 1977; its first president was Enrique Cervantes. There are 17 professional and scientific associations that cover the principal fields and approaches of psychology. The main areas in which psychologists are active in Bolivia are related to social psychology, community psychology, health, and education. This is a response to the social problems that Bolivia faces in its socioeconomic development as a multicultural, multilingual society.

As in many other countries, clinical psychology is another area of rapid growth. There has not been the friction between the disciplines of psychiatry and psychology, often found in other countries, because many psychiatrists have been the teachers of psychologists. They provide an emphasis on the biological and pharmaceutical aspects of treatment of psychological disorders. On the other hand, the majority of clinical psychologists are young women. They work in both hospitals and private practice using an eclectic approach. It is possible to say that approaches such as behavior therapy, existential psychotherapy, psychoanalysis, Gestalt theory, and Rogerian psychotherapy coexist in Bolivia.

In Bolivia there is another form of philosophy alongside the western scientific approaches to philosophy and psychology: shamanism, or the ancestral philosophy of the indigenous people such as the Aymara Indians and other groups. The acceptance of these beliefs spreads wider than the indigenous Bolivian tribes; many people will consult nonorthodox sources (for example, a fortuneteller or a witch), for advice or help, as well as a psychiatrist or psychologist. Equally, they may visit a person well experienced in human behavior, such as a priest or an astrologer.

The acceptance of such "pseudosciences" probably explains why Bolivian psychologists insist on the importance of studying their real social situation. The Bolivian identity is based on a multicultural, multilinguistic society that requires heterogeneity in the systems of education and health care. There is a multidisciplinary approach in which anthropologists, psychologists, linguists, and other professionals involved in the behavioral sciences contribute from each of their disciplines to develop an approach to the study of psychology and formation of professional psychologists that will create a better quality of life for Bolivia and its society.

Bibliography

Calderón Soria, R., & Calderón Jemio, R. (in press). *Historia de la psicología en Bolivia* [A history of psychology in Bolivia].

Rubén Ardila

BONDING. *See* Attachment.

BORDERLINE PERSONALITY DISORDER (BPD) is a recent addition to mental disorder nosology, added to the *Diagnostic and Statistical Manual* (*DSM*) of the American Psychiatric Association in 1980. Many aspects of the disorder are still a matter of controversy, discussion, and research. Perhaps most controversial was the decision to use the term "borderline" in the official designation of the disorder. It was first used by Adolf Stern in 1938 to describe a group of outpatients who did not profit from classical psychoanalysis and who did not seem to fit into the then standard neurotic or psychotic psychiatric categories. Depending on the theorist, borderline patients have been viewed as on the borderline between neurosis and psychosis, schizophrenia and nonschizophrenia, the normal and the abnor-

mal, and sanity and insanity. Over the years, the term borderline generally evolved in the psychoanalytic community to refer to both a particular structure of personality organization as well as to an intermediate level of severity of personality functioning.

Current criteria for BPD are defined in both the *Diagnostic and Statistical Manual* (*DSM–IV*, APA, 1994) and the *International Classification of Diseases* (Version 10 of the World Health Organization). The disorder is characterized by a pervasive instability in five functional domains: affect regulation, impulse control, self-image and experiencing, interpersonal relationships, and reality testing. Dysregulation of emotions includes marked lability of mood, including intense, episodic dysphoria, anxiety, fear, anger, and irritability. Impulsive behavior is common, especially behaviors associated with intense emotions such as violence or "behavioral explosions" associated with anger and recurrent avoidance of tasks or precipitous quitting of jobs or school associated with fear and anxiety. A tendency to become involved in intense, chaotic, and unstable relationships may be associated with repeated interpersonal crises and with excessive efforts to avoid abandonment. Chronic feelings of emptiness are frequent, and change, particularly in the interpersonal sphere, may be extremely painful. Self-image, goals, and preferences (including sexual) are often unclear, unstable, or disturbed, making pursuit of long-term goals difficult. Transient, stress-related severe paranoid ideation or dissociative experiences have been reported in 30 to 75% of BPD patients. Suicide attempts and other nonfatal self-injurious behaviors have been said to be the hallmark of BPD. From 70 to 75% of BPD patients have a history of at least one self-injurious act (Clarkin, Widiger, Frances, Hurt, & Gilmore, 1983). These acts can vary in intensity from slight scratches, head banging, and cigarette burns requiring no medical treatment to overdoses, self-stabbings, and asphyxiations requiring care in an intensive care unit. Nor is the suicidal behavior of BPD individuals always nonfatal. Suicide rates are estimated at 8 to 10%. In a series of BPD inpatients followed from 10 to 23 years after hospital discharge, patients exhibiting eight of the BPD criteria when admitted had a suicide rate of 36%, compared to a rate of 7% for individuals who met five to seven criteria (Stone, Hurt, & Stone, 1987).

Reliability and Validity of Diagnosis

The expert consensus is that BPD is best diagnosed using semistructured clinical interviews. Interrater reliability of the major interviews tends to be high and comparable to interviews for other major mental disorders (Loranger, 1992). The correspondence between diagnoses based on semistructured interviews and self-administered inventories is poor with self-report inventories tending more often to be overinclusive. Self-report inventories, however, rarely miss anyone and thus may be quite appropriate for initial screening. Comorbidity of BPD with other mental disorders (primarily depression and anxiety but also high rates of eating disorders and substance abuse disorders) and personality disorders (primarily avoidant, narcissistic, and schizotypal) is more the norm than the exception (Widiger & Weissman, 1991). Major depression is diagnosed in 24 to 74% of BPD patients, while dysthymia is observed in approximately 3 to 14%. Bipolar disorder is estimated to occur in 4 to 20% of this population. The most common comorbid anxiety disorder is panic disorder, found in 10 to 25% of BPD patients (Stein & Skodol, 1993). Posttraumatic stress disorder can also be high, especially in those BPD patients with histories of suicide attempts.

The high prevalence of BPD, especially among patients in mental health treatment, the high comorbidity of the disorder, and an association of BPD with reports of severe childhood trauma (Paris, Zweig-Frank, & Guzder, 1994) have caused many to question the validity of the diagnoses. These individuals have suggested instead that BPD is best considered a marker of severity and comorbidity, a specific type of mood disorder, or a variation of posttraumatic stress disorder. Others have argued convincingly that the relationship between BPD and both mood and posttraumatic stress disorders is nonspecific at best (Gunderson & Phillips, 1991). Although association with childhood events suggests a possible etiological factor, it does not in itself negate the specific construct validity of the disorder. Biologically oriented theorists have conceptualized BPD as a set of clinical syndromes, each with its own etiology, course, and outcome based on respective types of biological trauma or disorder associated with the specific syndrome.

Prevalence

BPD is diagnosed more frequently than any other personality disorder. Epidemiological estimates range from 0.2 to 1.8% meeting criteria in the general population (Widiger & Weissman, 1991). Prevalence increases to 8% in outpatient settings, 15% among inpatients and, among all patients with personality disorders, to 27% of outpatients and 51% of inpatients. Increases in the prevalence of the disorder over time cannot be disentangled from changes in diagnostic criteria. Females constitute approximately 75% of all diagnosed cases (Widiger & Weissman, 1991), although this may be due to the overlap between BPD and depression and the higher prevalence of depression among women.

Follow-up studies consistently indicate that BPD is chronic. Two to three years after index assessment, 60 to 70% of patients continued to meet criteria. Other follow-up studies found little change in level of func-

tioning and consistently high rates of psychiatric hospitalization over two to five years. Four to seven years after index assessment, 57 to 67% of patients continued to meet criteria. An average of 15 years after index assessment, 25 to 44% continued to meet criteria (McGlashan, 1986).

Treatment Approaches

BPD has been associated with worse outcome in treatments of Axis I disorders such as major depression, obsessive-compulsive disorder, bulimia, and substance abuse. Follow-up studies of BPD individuals who have received inpatient and outpatient mental health treatment-as-usual suggest that traditional treatments in the community are marginally effective at best when outcomes are measured two to three years following treatment (Tucker, Bauer, Wagner, Harlam, & Shear, 1987; Perry & Cooper, 1985). There is a vast body of literature on treatment of BPD, but there is very little systematic study of various treatment approaches.

No one medication has been found to be effective for the wide variety of symptoms with which the BPD patient will present. Low-dose neuroleptics (e.g., haloperidol, thiothixene) have demonstrated some positive effects on many of these symptoms. However, there is some indication that low-dose neuroleptics may be indicated only for severely cognitively disturbed individuals and that patients who are less so and/or more affectively ill may experience little benefit and perhaps more distress. Tricylics generally have not proven to be effective with BPD patients. Any improvements in mood symptoms that have been shown have been only slight. In one study, half the patients treated with amitriptyline showed an increase in paranoid ideation, aggression, and suicidality, and these effects were not related to the side effects profile. Moreover, the presence of comorbid major depression did not predict treatment response.

Monamine oxidase inhibitors (MAOIs) have received some attention because of the commonly observed atypical depression seen in BPD patients. Like haloperidol, the effects of MAOIs are not specific to depressive symptoms; improvements have been shown on anger and hostility, but efficacy for depressive symptoms has been equivocal. Fluoxetine has shown efficacy for borderline symptomatology, though again these effects have not been specific to depression. Its greatest efficacy may be in the reduction of anger. There is also some evidence that carbamazepine and lithium carbonate may be helpful for the impulsivity and lability of the borderline patient (Cowdry & Gardner, 1988). Results with anxiolytic medications have been mixed. For example, reports suggested improvements in hostility, cognitive dysregulations, and sleep, but others have reported increases in serious behavioral dyscontrol in a majority of patients (Cowdry & Gardner, 1988; Soloff,

1994). Dropout rates in pharmacotherapy treatments have been very high (Cowdry & Gardner, 1988) and medication compliance has been problematic, with upwards of 50% of patients reporting misuse of their medications and 87% of therapists reporting medication misuse, including taking other than prescribed dosages or taking an overdose (Waldinger & Frank, 1989). It is commonly assumed that some form of ancillary behavioral treatment is necessary for BPD clients.

The dominant psychosocial intervention for BPD patients has been psychodynamically oriented psychotherapy. The most influential of these has been the object/relations psychotherapy developed by Kernberg (Kernberg, Selzer, Koenigsberg, Carr, & Appelbaum, 1989). This approach is widely applied in both inpatient and outpatient settings. Interpersonal psychotherapies, exemplified by the work of Benjamin, are also widely used (Benjamin, 1993). In one of the very few randomized clinical trials of any psychosocial treatment for BPD, researchers found that structured, interpersonal group therapy is more effective than treatment-as-usual in the community at keeping patients in the treatment (Marziali & Munroe-Blum, 1994). This is no small feat given the very high dropout rates of BPD patients. Cognitive-behavioral treatments have also been developed for this disorder. The best known of these is dialectical behavior therapy (Linehan, 1993). DBT explicitly targets the highly dysfunctional behaviors in which these patients engage. Originally, this treatment was targeted for the treatment of the most severely parasuicidal patient in an outpatient setting. In clinical trials, it has been shown effective in reducing suicidal behaviors, treatment dropout, psychiatric inpatient days, use of illicit drugs, and anger and increasing general, and particularly social, functioning.

[See also Personality Disorders.]

Bibliography

American Psychiatric Association. (1994). *Diagnostic and statistical manual of mental disorders* (4th ed.). Washington, DC: Author.

Benjamin, L. S. (1993) *Interpersonal diagnosis and treatment of personality disorder.* New York: Guilford Press.

Clarkin, J. F., Widiger, T. A., Frances, A. J., Hurt, F. W., & Gilmore, M. (1983). Prototypic typology and the borderline personality disorder. *Journal of Abnormal Psychology, 92,* 263–275.

Cowdry, R. W., & Gardner, D. L. (1988). Pharmacotherapy of borderline personality disorder: Alprazolam, carbamazepine, trifluoperazine, and tranylcypromine. *Archives of General Psychiatry, 45,* 111–119.

Gunderson, J. G., & Phillips, K. A. (1991). A current view of the interface between borderline personality disorder and depression. *American Journal of Psychiatry, 148,* 870–874.

Kernberg, O. F., Selzer, M. A., Koenigsberg, H. W., Carr A. C., & Appelbaum, A. H. (1989). *Psychodynamic psychotherapy of borderline patients.* New York: Basic Books.

Linehan, M. M. (1993). *Cognitive behavioral therapy of borderline personality disorder.* New York: Guilford Press.

Loranger, A. W. (1992). Are current self-report and interview measures adequate for epidemiological studies of personality disorders? *Journal of Personality Disorders, 6,* 313–325.

Marziali, E., & Monroe-Blum, H. (1994) *Interpersonal group psychotherapy for borderline personality disorder.* New York: Basic Books.

McGlashan, T. H. (1986). The Chestnut Lodge follow-up study, III: Long-term outcome of borderline personality disorder. *Archives of General Psychiatry, 43,* 20–30.

Paris, J., Zweig-Frank, H., & Guzder, J. (1994). Psychological risk factors for borderline personality disorder in female patients. *Comprehensive Psychiatry, 35,* 301–305.

Perry, J. C., & Cooper, S. H. (1985). Psychodynamics, symptoms, and outcome in borderline and antisocial personality disorders and bipolar type II affective disorder. In T. H. McGlashan (Ed.), *The borderline: Current empirical research* (pp. 19–41). Washington, DC: American Psychiatric Press.

Soloff, P. H. (1994). Is there any drug treatment of choice for the borderline patient? *Acta Psychiatrica Scandinavica, 379,* 50–55.

Stein, Hollander, E., & Skodol, A. E. (1993). Anxiety disorders and personality disorders: A review. *Journal of Personality Disorders, 7,* 87–104.

Stern, A. (1938). Psychoanalytic investigation and therapy in the borderline group of neuroses. *Psychoanalytical Quarterly, 7,* 467–489.

Stone, M. H., Hurt, S. W., & Stone, D. K. (1987a). The PI 500: Long-term follow-up of borderline inpatients meeting DSM-III criteria. I: Global outcome. *Journal of Personality Disorders, 1,* 291–298.

Tucker, L., Bauer, S. F., Wagner, S., Harlam, D., & Shear, I. (1987). Long-term hospital treatment of borderline patients: A descriptive outcome study. *American Journal of Psychiatry, 144* (11), 1443–1448.

Waldinger, R. J., & Frank, A. F. (1989). Clinicians' experiences in combining medication and psychotherapy in the treatment of borderline patients. *Hospital and Community Psychiatry, 40,* 712–718.

Widiger, T. A., & Weissman, M. M. (1991). Epidemiology of borderline personality disorder. *Hospital and Community Psychiatry, 42,* 1015–1021.

Marsha M. Linehan

BOREDOM refers to a general state of listlessness or apathy that pervades consciousness when a person feels that there is nothing interesting or meaningful to do. It is generally considered to be one of the least desirable conditions of daily life and is often associated with psychopathology. When people in our culture are asked to identify what makes them feel depressed, boredom is one of the three most often mentioned causes—the others being a letdown after having accomplished something important, and a feeling of not having control over one's life (Riperre, 1977).

Although it is not among the group of basic emotions generally recognized by psychologists (Izard, 1977), boredom can be seen as involving the opposite of two of them: *interest* and *surprise*. Early studies of boredom focused on the cognitive aspects of this state and assumed it to be the result of redundant stimulation. When the central nervous system processes stimuli that are very familiar because they resemble previous inputs, attention ceases to be directed to such stimuli (Berlyne, 1960), and the organism reduces its cognitive and emotional activity.

This rather mechanistic view has been found to give too simple an explanation for the origins of boredom because it ignores the fact that familiar stimuli might not necessarily cause a person to be bored. Listening over and over to a favorite song, looking out a window at a familiar landscape, rereading a story known by heart to one's child, are often enjoyable rather than boring. More recent conceptualizations, therefore, focus on the meaning that the stimuli have in relation to the goals of the individual (Campos & Barrett, 1984). These approaches assume that information acquires a negative valence only if it is perceived as hindering persons from reaching their goals. Thus, for instance, if a person wishes to sort out ideas or emotions without being disturbed, familiar stimuli will not be experienced as boring.

Boredom as a Personal Trait

These considerations suggest that boredom is not caused so much by outside circumstances, such as the greater or lesser familiarity of incoming stimuli, but rather depends on the quality of the interaction between the person and the environment. If a person is able to actively process thoughts, emotions, and memories in a purposeful way, then boredom is unlikely to result. For instance, accounts of prisoners in solitary confinement or explorers marooned in isolated outposts show that, despite the extreme monotony of the surroundings, it is possible to avoid boredom and even enjoy the objectively barren situation.

Therefore, boredom should be seen as having both traitlike and statelike components. However, very little is known of boredom as a trait. Even though it is part of our tacit knowledge that some individuals are often bored and others never are—and that some people *are* boring, whereas others are interesting and stimulating—there has been little research on this topic. It seems, however, that by adolescence some children develop structures of attention and activity that allow them to be excited and involved in whatever they are doing, whereas others develop habits of low involvment that lead to patterns of thought and action characterized by boredom and apathy. In a study of talented teenagers, for instance, Csikszentmihalyi, Rathunde, and Whalen (1993) found that those who tended to be more excited when working in their area of talent (mathematics, science, art, or music) continued throughout high school to take advanced courses and increased their commitment to their talent; however, their equally gifted peers who felt bored while studying decreased their involvment throughout high school and ended up taking less advanced courses.

At the highest levels of human functioning, creative individuals rarely experience boredom. Such individuals are nearly always involved mentally and emotionally and have no time to be bored. In fact, many of them suggest that it is a low threshold for boredom that drives them to do creative work. Whether at the situational level or at the level of a personality trait, the ability to self-regulate mood and avoid boredom is one of the most important skills to learn in order to achieve a satisfying life (Hamilton, 1981).

Boredom in the Context of Consciousness

In the full context of everyday phenomenology, boredom can be seen as the outcome of a specific ratio between the opportunities for action (or challenges) that a person is aware of at any moment in time, and the abilities to act (or skills) that the person perceives as having. When the challenges are higher than the skills, one experiences anxiety; when the skills are higher, boredom ensues; when they are both high, one experiences flow, or enjoyment (Csikszentmihalyi, 1997). These relationships have been found in a great variety of samples in many different cultures. [*See* Flow.]

Typically, people report boredom when doing maintenance work such as cleaning the house; when engaged in passive leisure such as watching television; and when studying or working on a repetitive job that is not under the person's own control. In such states, a great number of other negative experiences are also reported; when bored, people tend to feel dissatisfied, passive, lonely, sad, and low in self-esteem. Therefore, we might think of boredom as one aspect of *psychic entropy*, or the state of mind in which consciousness is disordered and unable to accomplish work. Instead of being engaged productively, attention is diffused and ruminates on its own internal states.

Hence, the ability to avoid boredom is an essential component of well-being. Whether at the level of momentary experience, or in terms of habits developed over the entire life span, a person who is able to remain involved and excited will be able to extract more rewards from life. In this sense the issue of boredom is of central importance to parents, educators, clinicians, researchers, and laypersons interested in enhancing the quality of life.

Bibliography

Berlyne, D. (1960). *Conflict, arousal, and curiosity.* New York: McGraw-Hill.

Campos, J. J. & Barrett, K. C. (1984). Toward a new understanding of emotions and their development. In C. E. Izard, J. Kagan, & R. B. Zajonc (Eds.), *Emotions, cognition, and behavior* (pp. 229–263). Cambridge, England: Cambridge University Press.

Csikszentmihalyi, M. (1996). *Creativity: Flow and the psychology of discovery and invention.* New York: Harper-Collins.

Csikszentmihalyi, M. (1997). *Finding flow: The psychology of engagement with everyday life.* New York: Basic Books.

Csikszentmihalyi, M., Rathunde, K., & Whalen, S. (1993). *Talented teenagers: The roots of success and failure.* Cambridge, England: Cambridge University Press.

Hamilton, J. A. (1981). Attention, personality, and self-regulation of mood: Absorbing interest and boredom. *Progress in Experimental Personality Research, 10,* 282–315.

Izard, C. E. (1977). *Human emotions.* New York: Plenum Press.

Riperre, V. (1977). Commonsense beliefs about depression and antidepressive behaviour: A study of social consensus. *Behaviour Research and Therapy, 15,* 465–473.

Mihaly Csikszentmihalyi

BORING, EDWIN GARRIGUES (1886–1968), American psychologist. One of the most influential leaders of the discipline from the 1920s to the 1960s, Boring was born in Philadelphia, Pennsylvania, and grew up in a matriarchal Quaker household. In childhood he was fascinated by electricity and decided to study electrical engineering at Cornell University, where he received a master's degree in electrical engineering in 1908. For one of the few electives in the engineering program, he selected E. B. Titchener's psychology course. Boring found Titchener's lectures "magic" and was motivated by Titchener's praise for his examination paper. After a year of factory work at Bethlehem Steel and another year teaching science in a Moravian Church school, Boring returned to Cornell in 1910 for an A.M. degree to augment his teaching credentials. He was soon drawn to psychology by Madison Bentley's course. He became a devoted student and lifelong admirer of Titchener and a member of Titchener's laboratory group, as was his future wife, Lucy Day. Boring's dissertation

topic, assigned to him by Titchener, was on sensory processes in the alimentary tract, but he also carried out work on schizophrenia and other problems during his graduate student career.

After receiving a doctorate in 1914, he spent 4 additional years as an instructor at Cornell. In 1918, Robert M. Yerkes asked Boring to assist with the U.S. Army's intelligence testing work, and Boring became chief psychological examiner at Camp Upton, Long Island. Later he worked directly under Yerkes and played a major role in preparing the massive report on the Army testing. Boring remained cautious about the interpretation of intelligence tests for the rest of his career. In 1919, G. Stanley Hall offered Boring the position of professor of experimental psychology at Clark University. Three years later, in the midst of political controversies at Clark, he was invited to Harvard. He became the director of the psychological laboratory from 1924 to 1949 and the *de facto* chair of the psychology department, which was not formally separated from the philosophy department until 1934. He was named Edgar Pierce Professor of Psychology in 1956, and remained at Harvard until his retirement in 1957.

Boring is best known as the foremost historian of the discipline through his *History of Experimental Psychology* (New York, 1929) and its 1950 revision. Although heavily criticized in recent years for presenting Wundt through a Titchenerian lens, Boring's *History* was the classic in the field. Used by nearly all graduate students through the 1960s, it shaped the way in which psychologists viewed their emergence as a science and helped define the scope and goals of experimental psychology. In addition to the text, Boring published on the history of psychology throughout his career. Many of these widely read papers dealt with the psychology of science, with social and cultural factors in scientific development, with the history of method, and with problems of scientific communication. He introduced psychologists to Goethe and Herder's concept of *Zeitgeist* and used it as an organizing theme for his discussions of creativity, "Great Man" approaches to history, scientific change, and historiography. Boring's work on the nature of scientific activity was wide ranging and included papers written with Alice Bryant on the status and career difficulties of women in psychology that were published in the 1940s.

His other contributions were primarily his systematic and critical works. His *Physical Dimensions of Consciousness* (New York, 1933) moved beyond Titchener's dualism and bridged structuralism and behaviorism using monistic physicalism as a guiding principle. This physicalism was conceptually related to Percy Bridgman's operationism, which Boring had not yet read. Of his many students at Harvard, the most influential of all was undoubtedly S. S. Stevens. Together, they promoted operationism and thereby changed the vocabulary of American psychology. Stevens and other students collaborated with Boring on studies of sensation and perception, and Boring's best known series of experiments dealt with the moon illusion. Working with A. H. Holway, he showed that the illusion depends on the position of the eyes in the skull. Boring's heavy administrative responsibilities left him little time for experimental work; nevertheless, he managed to write a summary of the field, *Sensation and Perception in the History of Experimental Psychology* (New York, 1942).

Boring worked tirelessly for the organization and promotion of psychology and served as the president of the American Psychological Association in 1928, the secretary of the Ninth International Congress of Psychology in 1929, and honorary president of the Seventeenth International Congress of Psychology in 1963. He was a founder and the first editor of the highly influential journal of book reviews, *Contemporary Psychology*. Presenting psychology to the general audience was also important to Boring. With Herbert Langfeld and Harry Weld, he authored a series of widely used introductory textbooks, and Boring was one of the first to present a psychology course on public television as the 1957 Harvard Lowell Television Lecturer. In 1959, the American Psychological Foundation awarded him a gold medal for his achievements as an experimentalist, teacher, critic, theorist, administrator, popularizer, and editor. So respected and influential was Boring that Robert Yerkes once dubbed him "Mr. Psychology."

Bibliography

Boring, E. G. (1940). Was this analysis a success? *Journal of Abnormal and Social Psychology, 35*, 4–16.

Boring, E. G. (1961). *Psychologist at large: An autobiography and selected essays.* New York: Basic Books. This is an autobiographical sketch expanded from *History of Psychology in Autobiography,* 1952 (Vol. 4, pp. 27–52).

Campbell, D. T., & Watson, R. I. (Eds.). (1963). *History, psychology, and science: Selected papers of E. G. Boring.* New York: Wiley.

Cerullo, J. J. (1988). E. G. Boring: Reflections on a discipline builder. *American Journal of Psychology, 101*, 561–575.

Furumoto, L. (1998). Lucy May Boring (1886–1996). *American Psychologist, 53*, 59.

Jaynes, J. (1969). Edwin Garrigues Boring: 1889–1968. *Journal of the History of the Behavioral Sciences, 5*, 99–112.

Kelly, B. (1981). Inventing psychology's past: E. G. Boring's historiography in relation to the psychology of his time. *Journal of Mind and Behavior, 2*, 229–241.

O'Donnell, J. M. (1979). The crisis of experimentalism in the 1920s: E. G. Boring and his uses of history. *American Psychologist, 34*, 289–295.

Rosenzweig, S. (1970). E. G. Boring and the Zeitgeist: *Eruditione gesta beavit. Journal of Psychology, 75*, 59–71.

Winston, A. S. (1998). "The defects of his race . . .": E. G. Boring and antisemitism in American psychology, 1923–1953. *History of Psychology, 1*, 27–51.

Andrew S. Winston

BOULDER CONFERENCE. *See* Training.

BOWLBY, EDWARD JOHN MOSTYN (1907–1990), British psychiatrist and psychoanalyst. John Bowlby is best known for the development of attachment theory, which emphasizes the importance of early emotional attachments for later personality development and adjustment.

The son of a distinguished surgeon, Bowlby began his psychoanalytic training before graduating medical school in 1933 from University College Hospital in London. He trained in the Kleinian tradition of British psychoanalysis, based on the theorizing of Melanie Klein. She had somewhat different ideas about development than Freud did and believed that even very young infants harbor deeply ambivalent unconscious fantasies about their mothers.

After qualifying in psychiatry, Bowlby worked in a child guidance clinic from 1936 to 1940, then became an army psychiatrist. In 1946, following his discharge from the army, he took a position at the Tavistock Clinic in London, where he remained throughout his subsequent career.

Based on earlier work Bowlby had done on the causes of juvenile delinquency, the World Health Organization commissioned him in 1950 to investigate the mental health of homeless children. Bowlby's 1951 report, *Maternal Care and Mental Health* (republished as *Child Care and the Growth of Maternal Love*, 1953), in which he argued for the harmful effects of "maternal deprivation" on the child, established Bowlby's reputation.

Fueled by his discovery of Lorenz's concept of imprinting, Bowlby began to conceive of attachment as an evolutionary adaptation. A child's attachment to the mother insures proximity to her in dangerous conditions, enhancing childhood (and species) survival. For individuals, early attachment experiences serve as prototypes for later relationships, with secure ones leading to emotional stability and insecure (anxious) ones to later difficulties. This is the core of attachment theory as it developed over the years. The standard version of the theory is contained in *Attachment and Loss*, a three-volume work published between 1969 and 1980. It represented Bowlby's attempt to integrate psychoanalysis with evolutionary biology and cognitive psychology.

Although writing that his "frame of reference" was psychoanalytic, Bowlby rejected the Freudian view that the child's attachment toward the mother was based on the mother's association with physiological drive reduction. Despite his Kleinian background, he also criticized Klein for overemphasizing unconscious childhood fantasy, thereby minimizing the importance of the child's actual experience.

More generally, Bowlby believed that psychoanalysts needed to make more use of traditional scientific methods and to rely less on inferences from case histories. Although critical, however, Bowlby remained a psychoanalyst, and his emphases on early emotional relationships and the importance of trauma and loss continued important themes in psychoanalytic theorizing.

Despite this, Bowlby's theory was initially rejected by most psychoanalysts. Jeremy Holmes (1993) has written that this rejection was partly due to conflicts between the culture of psychoanalysis and the scientific culture represented by Bowlby. Holmes suggests that the psychoanalytic world was too closed and narrow to accept Bowlby's ideas and criticisms, whereas Bowlby largely ignored the internal mediating world of unconscious meanings and fantasy in his stress on the child's environment.

In the 1960s, Mary Ainsworth, Bowlby's major theoretical collaborator, developed the Strange Situation procedure. This provided a powerful research tool and popularized attachment theory among developmental psychologists (Ainsworth & Marvin, 1995). In this procedure, mothers and children engage in a brief series of standardized interactions, enabling researchers to identify different patterns of childhood attachment.

Attachment research has burgeoned since the 1970s, although the focus has shifted from major disruptions such as death or desertion (whose consequences are not as automatic as Bowlby assumed) to styles of parent-child interaction (Holmes, 1993). Insecure attachment has been found to relate to a variety of difficulties, and the study of early attachment has now been extended to adults. Attachment concepts are also being incorporated into efforts at treating and preventing psychological difficulties. (For a general review of current attachment research, see the work by Holmes in the Bibliography.)

These developments, coming at a time when psychoanalysis has become more open to outside influences, has led to a growing acceptance of Bowlby's ideas by analysts. Bowlby's work is now often seen as supporting the "object relations" tradition in psychoanalysis, which emphasizes early emotional relationships. If the separate worlds of psychoanalysis and developmental psychology have moved closer to one another, it is a development that owes much to Bowlby.

Bowlby's final major work was a well-received psychobiography of Darwin published in 1990, which stressed the importance of early childhood loss in understanding Darwin's later life. Bowlby had earlier brought an evolutionary perspective to psychoanalysis and child development; he now brought a developmental and psychoanalytic one to the history of evolutionary theory.

[See also Attachment Theory; Object Relations Theories; and the biography of Klein.]

Bibliography

Ainsworth, M. D. S., & Marvin, R. S. (1995). On the shaping of attachment theory and research. In E. Waters, B. E. Vaughn, G. Posada, & K. Kiyoma (Eds.), New growing points of attachment theory and research. *Monographs of the Society for Research in Child Development*, 60, (2–3, Serial No. 244). An interview with Mary Ainsworth on the history of attachment theory. The remainder of the monograph consists of articles exploring new directions in theory and research.

Bowlby, J. (1951). *Maternal care and the growth of maternal love* (World Health Organization Monograph Series No. 2). Geneva, Switzerland: World Health Organization. Reprinted in 1966 (New York: Shocken Books), this review established Bowlby's reputation. Bowlby argues that the mental health of infants and young children depends on adequate relationships with their mothers or mother substitutes. For Bowlby's later comments on this work, see the preface to the second edition of *Attachment and Loss: Vol. 1, Attachment*.

Bowlby, J. (1965). *Child care and the growth of maternal love* (2nd ed.). Harmondsworth, England: Penguin Books. (Original work published 1953.) The 1953 book is an abridged edition of *Maternal care and mental health*. The second edition is a revised and enlarged edition of the first, with additional material provided by Mary Ainsworth.

Bowlby, J. (1975). *Attachment and loss: Vol. 2. Separation: Anxiety and anger*. New York: Basic Books. (Original work published 1973.) Reprinted with corrections in 1981.

Bowlby J. (1981). *Attachment and loss: Vol. 3. Loss: Sadness and depression*. New York: Basic Books. (Original work published 1980.) These three volumes provide the standard version of Bowlby's theory and are easily available. References to the theory in this article refer to the later printings and editions.

Bowlby, J. (1982). *Attachment and loss: Vol. 1, Attachment*. (2nd ed.). New York: Basic Books. (Original work published 1969)

Bowlby, J. (1990). *Charles Darwin: A new biography*. London: Hutchinson.

Greenberg, J. R., & Mitchell, S. A. (1983). *Object relations in psychoanalytic theory*. Cambridge, MA: Harvard University Press. Provides an excellent discussion of current psychoanalytic approaches to "object relations." It includes a section on attachment theory and discusses Bowlby's place within the object relations tradition.

Holmes, J. (1993). *John Bowlby and attachment theory*. New

York: Routledge. The best single source for those wishing a general overview of Bowlby and attachment theory. It provides an excellent bibliography as well.

Fredric Weizmann

BRAID, JAMES (1795–1860), British physician. Born in 1795 in Fifeshire, James Braid earned a medical degree at the University of Edinburgh and practiced among the miners in Lanarkshire, Dumfries, and later Manchester, where he lived until his death in 1860. Braid first became known to the medical world for his work with clubfoot, strabismus, curvature of the spine, and stammering, but his greatest achievement was his investigation of the phenomenon of animal magnetism and his development of the theory and nomenclature of hypnotism.

In 1841 Braid attended a demonstration of animal magnetism in Manchester given by the well-known Swiss magnetizer Charles Lafontaine (1803–1888). Braid saw, to his surprise, that the phenomenon was genuine. He was unwilling, however, to accept the explanation given by Lafontaine. Instead, he did his own experiments and developed his own theory. Braid concluded that the phenomenon of animal magnetism was due to a "derangement of the state of the cerebrospinal centres, and of the circulatory, and respiratory, and muscular systems" (*Neurypnology*, p. 101). He insisted that no magnetic fluid was involved and that an individual could go into a somnambulistic state simply by staring at a fixed object. Braid called his new approach *neurohypnotism*, a term he first used in a pamphlet entitled *Satanic Agency and Mesmerism Reviewed* (Manchester, 1842). Braid developed his ideas more fully in his magnum opus *Neurypnology or The Rationale of Nervous Sleep*; here he shortened the name to "hypnotism."

As Braid challenged the magnetizers, his new theory began to attract attention. Using his fixed-stare method of induction, Braid successfully employed hypnotism to treat people for the very illnesses with which magnetizers had been successful. At the same time, he augmented his theory, claiming that the powers of the imagination were at work in many other phenomena that had been attributed to magnetic fluid by the animal magnetizers.

Braid observed something else already remarked upon by magnetizers: that hypnotic subjects were able to vividly recall incidents from the distant past that they formerly had been unable to remember, calling this phenomenon *revivification*. He also noted what the magnetizers had called *double consciousness*, the fact that the hypnotized state was very different from the ordinary waking state and that amnesia for events in the hypnotic state created a chain of hypnotic memories parallel to waking memories but unknown to the waking subject.

In his later writings, Braid moved toward a more psychological description of hypnotism, describing it essentially as concentrated attention and emphasizing the role played by suggestion, an "expectant idea in the mind." He pointed out that people can be taken over by a "dominant idea" that powerfully affects their psychological and physiological state. Thus an individual can be made ill by a negative dominant idea that becomes fixed in the mind. On the other hand, that illness can be cured by a physician who, through suggestion, induces a dominant idea of the opposite kind. Braid came to believe that the main task of the hypnotic physician was to treat illnesses through suggestions of this kind.

Bibliography

Braid, J. (1843). *Neurypnology or the rationale of nervous sleep considered in relation with animal magnetism. Illustrated by numerous cases of its successful application in the relief and cure of disease.* London: Churchill.

Braid, J. (1960). *Braid on hypnotism. The beginnings of modern hypnosis. Revised edition by Arthus Edward Waite. Edited with an introduction biographical and bibliographical embodying the author's later views and further evidence on the subject.* New York: Julian Press.

Crabtree, A. (1993). *From Mesmer to Freud: Magnetic sleep and the roots of psychological healing.* New Haven, CT: Yale University Press.

Gauld, A. (1992). *A history of hypnotism.* Cambridge, UK: Cambridge University Press.

Kravis, N. M. (1988). James Braid's psychophysiology: A turning point in the history of dynamic psychiatry *American Journal of Psychiatry, 145,* 1191–1206.

Adam Crabtree

BRAIN. With many distinct structures associated in separable but interlocking subsystems, the brain is a complex organ. Most of the basic component parts are known, but their modes of interaction and the neural substrates underlying specific functions and behaviors are areas of active research. A special difficulty in understanding the organization of the brain is that it is a multifunctional organ—unlike the liver, lung, heart, or other organs—and it is highly plastic. With the exception of reflexes, brain functions can be, and frequently are, implemented in several different ways.

Historically, there has been a strong tendency to analyze brain design in terms of localization of function. This approach, phrenology in its stronger manifestations, is largely discredited, but it is not clear that there is any compelling unifying framework to replace it. As shown from any number of functional imaging studies (PET or fMRI), most stimuli to the brain produce multiple foci of activation in what appears to be a "distributed" pattern. What this means, and even the best way to describe the results, remains controversial.

Experimental Approaches

The organization of brain components and how these interact are analyzed through complementary research in humans and animals. In humans, experimental and clinical neuropsychology can address questions of behavior and cognition, but acquiring precise anatomical and physiological data, which depends on invasive procedures, is more feasible using animal models. The variety and effectiveness of technical tools for investigating the nervous system have increased remarkably over the last decade. These range from sophisticated neurogenetic or "knock-out" experiments in rodents to complex imaging studies of brain activity patterns in humans during specific stimulus conditions. Imaging experiments (PET or fMRI) are a particularly exciting development with the potential to bridge studies of brain function at the physiological level and studies of psychological processes at the cognitive level (Frackowiak et al., 1997).

Traditionally, investigations of the nervous system and the neural bases of behavior have drawn on techniques from anatomy, psychology, physiology, and pharmacology (Feldman et al., 1997; Frackowiak et al., 1997). Neuroanatomical investigations aim to define functionally relevant structures (aggregates of nerve cells called nuclei, or areas) and their interconnections (circuits). In order to analyze connections, dyes or tracer substances are placed in a particular structure and are then transported along axons to interconnected structures (the source or target). Connections, for want of a better notation, are often depicted as little tubes or literal pathways between several regions. This graphically captures their physical reality as more or less definite bundles of axons, but only hints at their real complexity—having the unfortunate connotation of a point-to-point relay (or "bucket brigade"). In reality, connectional systems are part of a complex divergent-convergent architecture: One structure sends divergent connections to several others and receives multiple convergent connections. This is an important distinction with implications for the neural substrates of behavior. In the shorthand jargon of connections-as-relays (structure A projects to B, which projects to C and D), it is easy to think of behavior as progressively built up from simple components. But the more realistic network architecture suggests a more intricately textured substrate.

Microelectrode electrophysiology permits the analysis of the biophysical and response properties of individual neurons. These can be highly specific, and populations of neurons have been identified that respond to psychophysical features, such as color, shape, or motion (in the visual system), or even to more complex stimuli, such as faces. It is still a matter of controversy whether behavior can best be described in terms of single neurons or network populations (Parker & Newsome, 1998). In one experimental paradigm, investigators compared the psychophysical sensitivity of monkeys trained to observe and respond to a visual stimulus with the sensitivity of single neurons in one of the visual areas. They found that the response of a typical neuron could provide an accurate account of the monkey's psychophysical performance. Moreover, when the neural responses were manipulated through microstimulation of the visual cortex, the psychophysical judgments of the animal were altered in a predictable fashion. The pool of neurons necessary to influence behavioral performance has been calculated to be relatively small—about 25.

Lesion or stimulation experiments have been important probes of neural function at the level of circuits and systems. These can result in striking behavioral changes (see below), although there are also instances of mild or seemingly negligible effects. Also, both inactivation and stimulation techniques have serious limitations and need to be interpreted with caution. A structure may be involved in or necessary for a particular function, but it can rarely be proved to be sufficient. Eye movements, for example, absolutely depend on contacts between the ocular muscles and the controlling motoneurons in the oculomotor nuclei of the brainstem. Damage to the oculomotor nuclei results in partial or complete paralysis, but normal movements require, in addition, complex inputs from many other cortical and subcortical structures. To give another example, language ability depends on several cortical centers (the classically described Broca's area and Wernicke's area), but normal performance requires a more widely distributed constellation of structures.

Pharmacological studies provide a dynamic probe of mental states as these are affected by altered brain states, and the combination of psychopharmacology and brain imaging further allows the visualization of where the drug may be having an effect. Different drugs have been associated with particular behavioral profiles, but the evidence of any one-to-one mapping of a single transmitter system with a given cognitive process is less supportive (see below for further discussion of psychopharmacological systems).

Brain Regions

The brain is customarily divided into five regions (figure 1) on the basis of gross anatomical, functional, and embryological criteria. [*See* Brain Development.] These are the medulla, pons and cerebellum, midbrain, thalamus, and forebrain. (The equivalent Greek terms are

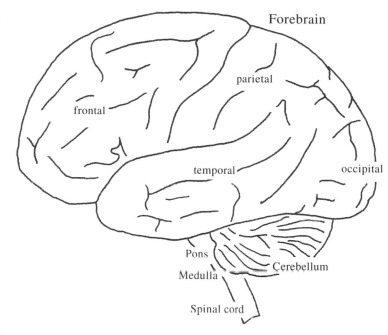

(a)

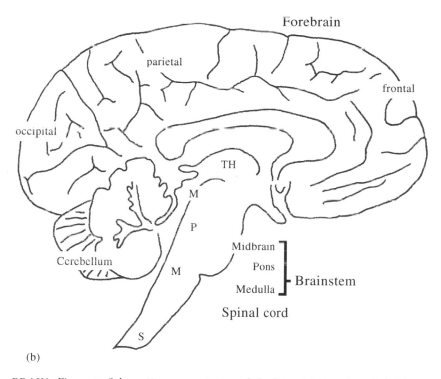

(b)

BRAIN. Figure 1. Schematic representation of the lateral (A) and medial (B) surfaces of the human brain to indicate the five major brain regions (forebrain, thalamus, midbrain, pons and cerebellum, and medulla). The four main lobes of the cerebral cortex (frontal, parietal, temporal, and occipital) are also indicated. TH = thalamus.

myelencephalon, metencephalon, mesencephalon, diencephalon, and *telencephalon,* where *encephalon* means "head"). The three caudal subdivisions are often considered together as the brain stem; or, in another grouping, the caudal four subdivisions along with some parts of the forebrain are classified together as subcortical, as distinguished from the large cortical mass of the forebrain.

Brain Stem. The brain stem can be viewed as the rostral continuation of the spinal cord, and therefore can be partly described in terms of sensory and motor territories. Ten of the twelve cranial nerves enter or exit the brain stem (sensory or motor nerves, respectively; the olfactory nerve enters the forebrain, and the optic nerve terminates directly in the thalamus), and their associated nuclei are a major component of the brain stem parenchyma. Unlike the spinal cord, which receives some direct cortical connections but does not project back to the cortex, some brain stem structures also send projections to cortical regions. There are massive indirect connections from the brain stem, through the thalamus, to the cortical areas.

Other brain stem structures are the reticular formation, which is somewhat analogous to the interneuronal networks of the spinal cord; several structures concerned with the autonomic control of visceral activity, such as salivation, respiration, heartbeat, and digestion; the cerebellum; and nuclei whose cells release biogenic amines. Because of their widespread connections, these cell groups (in the locus coeruleus, raphe, and ventral tegmentum) are often termed modulatory, although they are known to play a role in important mental and neurological dysfunctions, such as depression, schizophrenia, drug addiction, and Parkinson's disease.

Many brain stem structures mediate reflex behavior (the pupillary light response, the gag or startle reflex) or behavioral repertoires (smell and facial expressions; interactions of the tongue, jaw, and facial musculature; auditory and oculomotor reactions, among others). The reticular formation, which is widely connected to the cerebellum, spinal cord, thalamus, and cortex, is implicated in alertness and sleep-and-wake cycles. Stimulating the reticular formation of a deeply anesthetized animal changes the animal's EEG from a sleeping pattern to one of wakefulness.

An interesting example of brain stem structures is the periaqueductal gray (PAG). The PAG is a cell-dense region surrounding the midbrain aqueduct (i.e., the connecting part of the ventricular system between the third ventricle in the thalamus and the fourth ventricle in the caudal brain stem). The PAG is one of the more striking examples of localization of function in the form of defined behavioral repertoires ("fight or flight," defensive, analgesic, or cardiovascular reactions). The analgesic and behavioral responses elicited from the PAG

can be conceptualized as components of coordinated reactions important for survival (Bandler & Shipley, 1994). They evolve in association with dense inputs from several cortical regions that, as a simplification, might be thought to exert control over functions that would otherwise be automatic or unconscious.

Microinjections of excitatory amino acids or electrical stimulation of different sectors of the PAG result in several responses: a confrontational stance, an avoidance or flight reaction, a cessation of ongoing spontaneous activity (quiescence) and profound hyporeactivity similar to the reactions of an animal after injury or defeat in a social encounter, or heightened defensive reactivity ("changed a normally calm, placid cat into a highly defensive animal," Bandler & Shipley, 1994, p. 380). Opposite patterns of cardiovascular changes are also evoked by stimulating different zones of the PAG, that is, either increased arterial pressure and tachycardia or decreased arterial pressure and bradycardia.

Another example of the complexity of brain stem structures is the cerebellum. Traditionally, the cerebellum has been associated with the subconscious coordination of movement. Various ascending and descending inputs (e.g., from the spinal cord and cerebral cortex) impinge on the cerebellum, and one of its major outputs is to motor cortices via the thalamus (see Shepherd, 1998, for a more detailed discussion of cerebellar circuitry). More recently, the cerebellum has been implicated in higher cognitive processes as well. ("Intact cerebellar function facilitates actions harmonious with the goal, appropriate to context, and judged accurately and reliably according to the strategies mapped out prior to and during behavior" Schmahmann, 1996, p. 190.)

Thalamus. The thalamus is a collection of sensory, motor, autonomic, and associational nuclei. It has sometimes been described as the "gateway" to the neocortex, because its sensory nuclei receive direct and indirect input from the peripheral receptors for the visual, auditory, and somatosensory modalities and project to primary sensory cortices. Connections between the thalamus and cortex are largely reciprocal, and current thinking emphasizes the importance of the thalamus in filtering and transforming information, both from the periphery to the cortex and among several cortical areas (Steriade et al., 1997). Incoming sensory signals, in addition to information content, may contribute to a tonic excitatory background important in brain excitability.

The lateral geniculate nucleus, for example, receives input from the retina and is often thought to be a sensory relay in the visual pathway. However, it also receives input ("feedback") from primary visual cortex and several brainstem nuclei. Together, the cortical and brain stem inputs numerically outweigh those from the retina, although their precise functional importance is still under investigation (see Shepherd, 1998, for further detail).

The thalamus is implicated in a variety of functions (Steriade et al., 1997). Pathological dysfunction can result in pain, tremor, and amnesia. Structures within the thalamus may contribute significantly to language. The disruption of attentional gating by certain thalamic lesions has been suggested to impair the operation of neuronal networks in temporal and parietal cortical areas that serve as the substrate of lexical-semantic functions. Thalamic networks are closely involved in states of brain arousal, waking, and REM sleep. The thalamus may be critical for cognition and awareness and, as a major structure integrating inputs involved in emotion and cognitive functions, has been suggested to contribute to dysfunction in schizophrenia. The thalamic architecture has been summarized as "crucial for shifting the functional mode of the brain in a continuous way between an adaptive behavioral state, open to the outside world, and a disconnected state when thalamic gates are closed" (Steriade et al., 1997, p. 1).

The ventral subdivision, or hypothalamus, is more concerned with visceral and autonomic functions. It contributes to the constancy of the internal environment (homeostasis) and to behavior that contributes to the survival of the individual and the species. As with the PAG, experimental manipulations of the hypothalamic nuclei (lesions or stimulation) can result in dramatically specific symptoms, such as excessive eating or fasting.

Forebrain. The forebrain consists of the cerebral hemispheres, the basal ganglia, hippocampus, and amygdula. Ontogenetically and phylogenetically, the forebrain is distinct from brain stem structures. Functionally, the cerebral cortex in particular has been associated with higher cognitive functions, such as language, learning, memory, perception, and planning.

The basal ganglia are part of a widespread system involved in the generation of goal-directed voluntary movement (see Shepherd, 1998). Dysfunction of the basal ganglia, as in Parkinson's and Huntington's disease, results in motor deficits that are distinctive if not entirely easy to describe: tremor and involuntary movements, changes in posture and muscle tone, poverty and slowness of movement, and cognitive and affective disorders. In contrast with the cerebellum, which has many connections to brain stem nuclei and receives direct connections from the spinal cord, the basal ganglia have no direct connections with the spinal cord and only a few with brain stem nuclei. They are, however, heavily connected to most areas of the cerebral cortex. This differential connectivity correlates with the involvement of the basal ganglia in the planning, timing, and execution of complex motor sequences—the higher-order aspects of motor control. Unlike the neo-

cortex, the basal ganglia are associated with routines that have become automatic.

The hippocampus, a small, sea-horse-shaped structure within the core of the temporal lobe, participates in several functional circuits. One major circuit is the connectional loop formed by the hippocampus, the mamillary bodies of the hypothalamus, the anterior thalamic nucleus, the cingulate cortex, and cingulo-hippocampal connections (Gloor, 1997). This is the classical circuit formulated by James Papez in 1937 and proposed to form an anatomical substrate for central emotions. Another major circuit is made up of reciprocal connections between the subdivisions of the hippocampus and the adjoining entorhinal cortex, through which the hippocampus communicates with large sectors of neocortex. Interruptions of this pathway result in profound deficits in declarative (but not procedural) memory.

The amygdala is another temporal lobe structure with widespread connections and multiple functions, including viscerosensory, autonomic, affective, perceptual, and mnemonic (Gloor, 1997). Of these, the clearest and most dramatic association may be with emotional function. Stimulation of the amygdala, either by electrodes or during an epileptic seizure, commonly results in fear, as evidenced by a rising epigastric sensation, palpitation, mydriasis, pallor, fearful hallucinations, or a frightening memory flashback (Frackowiak et al., 1997; Gloor, 1997). Concordantly, lesions or ablations of the amygdala result in affective changes. In monkeys, bilateral removal of the temporal lobes results in a Klüver–Bucy syndrome (first described by these investigators in 1937). The lesioned animals, described as suffering from "psychic blindness," approached inanimate and animate objects without hesitation or fear, engaged in hyperorality as if they could no longer rely on their visual sense, and exhibited profound changes (in the direction of placidity) in emotional, sexual, and attentive behavior. Patients with long-standing lesions of the amygdala have selective difficulty in recognizing fear in the faces of others (Adolphs et al., 1994; Frackowiak et al., 1997).

A comparative study of patients with bilateral damage to the amygdala or hippocampus was able to demonstrate, by double dissociation, the distinctive functions associated with these two structures (Bechara et al., 1995). Selective damage to the amygdala resulted in the inability to acquire conditional autonomic responses to visual or auditory stimuli, but did not impair the acquisition of declarative facts about which visual or auditory stimuli were paired with the unconditioned stimulus. Selective bilateral damage to the hippocampus resulted in the inability to acquire the facts but did not impair conditioning.

The cerebral hemispheres envelop the thalamus and brain stem and, in humans, constitute about 40% of the brain's weight. The hemispheres are themselves subdivided into four lobes: the occipital lobe, concerned with visual functions; the temporal lobe, concerned with auditory function, higher order visual function, and cortico-hippocampal systems; the parietal lobe, concerned with somesthetic and visuospatial functions; and the frontal lobe, concerned with motor and higher order executive functions. The limbic lobe, comprised of the cingulate gyrus, hippocampal formation, and parahippocampal gyrus, is often distinguished as a fifth major subdivision, concerned with autonomic, visceral, and emotive processes.

Within the large lobar territories, the cortex is further organized into distinct areas. In older studies (e.g., the "architectonic" studies of Brodmann, which identified subtle distinctions in cell density and cell size), 52 areas had been established, but further work with modern techniques have allowed for a much finer subdivision (i.e., nine areas within the occipital lobe alone, as opposed to Brodmann's three).

The cortical areas can be classified as primary sensory, early and intermediate sensory, or motor, and higher order or associational. This grouping implies a hierarchical progression, from primary sensory areas, which are relatively directly connected with peripheral sense organs, to higher order areas. As a simplification, primary sensory areas might be conceived to carry out and elaborate on simpler, sensation-related operations, while higher order areas are involved with perceptual, mnemonic, or other cognitive processes. Thus, lesions or stimulation of the primary somatosensory cortex result in the loss of sensation in a topographically delimited body surface. However, lesions in the posterior parietal cortex cause a condition known as astereognosis (the loss of the ability to name an object held in the hand), even though somatosensory sensations and the ability to perceive the existence of the object are intact. Frontal lobe lesions result in profound changes in personality and behavior.

Other data raise the possibility of alternative interpretations (Rockland et al., 1997) and stress the importance of internally driven ("top-down") phenomena. For example, imaging studies demonstrate that the primary visual cortex is activated not only by external visual stimuli routed through the retina and thalamus, but also by imagined stimuli evoked in response to a verbal direction (the "eyes-closed" condition). Some other areas may be less concerned with information processing than with specifying operational rules or encoding ("brain syntax"). Needless to say, the demonstration of more abstract functions may be difficult, just as it was initially difficult to assign particular functions to the intrahemispheric system of connections through the corpus callosum.

Distinct substrates of cortical function—what makes the cortex, cortex, and what might distinguish one area from another—are still under investigation. Key aspects are likely to include the dense reciprocal connections between thalamic nuclei and cortical areas (the intricate web of corticothalamocortical connections), and the dense set of inter- and intracortical connections. It is significant that the single densest source of input to any cortical locus (constituting about 80% of the total) is intrinsic, from neighboring neurons within the surrounding 25 mm² area.

Brain-Behavioral Correlations

Behavior depends on and evolves from neural substrates and interactions. The correlation can sometimes be direct, as if a given reaction can be localized to a particular structure or circuit. More typically, several structures and circuits are involved, although the individual contributions and sequences (which must be at least as complex as those in metabolic cycles) are only sketchily understood. Pharmacological interactions are an integral part of these interactions.

Drug Manipulations

Connections between brain structures have excitatory or inhibitory effects. These are achieved by two basic types of synaptic contacts, which use different neurotransmitter chemicals. [*See* Synapse.] Most long-distance connections are excitatory and use either the amino acids glutamate or aspartate as neurotransmitters. A few long-distance connections (from the cerebellum and basal ganglia) and most local, interneuronal connections are inhibitory and use GABA. "Modulatory" effects are achieved through the colocalization of GABA with one of several neuropeptides (for inhibitory connections), or through interactions with acetylcholine, catecholamine, or serotonin pathways (Feldman et al., 1997, and the literature reviewed therein). For each neurotransmitter, there are several chemically distinct membrane receptors. These can be targeted by drug agonists and antagonists that selectively mimic or block a specific subset of responses to a particular transmitter. As briefly presented below, drug manipulations provide an important and versatile tool for investigating neural substrates of behavior (see Feldman et al., 1997, and Frackowiak et al., 1997, for more detailed descriptions).

Acetylcholine. Cholinergic neurons are located in each of the five brain regions, with one important group of cholinergic projection neurons located in the basal forebrain. These cells project widely to the cerebral cortex and hippocampus and are thought to be involved in aspects of learning, memory, and attention. Loss of these neurons results in significant reduction of the cholinergic innervation of the cortex and has been implicated in the cognitive deficits of Alzheimer's pathology. The cognitive effects of acetylcholine are probably brought about by its interaction with other transmitter systems.

There are two broad subtypes of cholinergic receptors: muscarinic and nicotinic (named, respectively, for muscarine, an alkaloid found in the fly agaric mushroom, and nicotine, an alkaloid from the tobacco plant; these substances, by interacting with receptors, mimic some of the effects of peripherally administered ACh). Blockade of muscarinic receptors by atropine or scopolamine interferes with the acquisition and maintenance of many learning tasks in animals. Low dosages of scopolamine in human subjects result in deficits in memory and attention.

Acetylcholine also plays an important role in sleep and arousal. The transition from sleep to waking is associated with the heightened activity of cholinergic neurons in the basal forebrain and brainstem, and numerous studies show that cortical arousal can be increased by cholinergic agonists or decreased by cholinergic antagonists.

Norepinephrine. Noradrenergic cell groups are distributed in the pons and medulla. The most important noradrenergic nucleus is the locus coeruleus, whose neurons project widely throughout the forebrain and thalamus, among other structures. Noradrenergic neurons contribute to several behavioral processes, for example, hunger and satiety, attention, arousal, and vigilance.

Dopamine. Dopamine-containing neurons are situated rostrally in the brain, in the midbrain and hypothalamus. Dopaminergic pathways have been dramatically implicated in motor functions, and depletion of dopaminergic neurons in the substantia nigra is a direct cause of the motor and psychological syndromes of Parkinson's disease. Dopamine is also thought to play a role in motivational processes of reward and reinforcement and is believed to contribute to psychomotor effects and the etiology of schizophrenia.

The dopamine imbalance hypothesis suggests that schizophrenia results from lowered levels of dopamine in the prefrontal cortex coupled with heightened levels in limbic cortices. The reduced mesocortical function is postulated to result in the negative symptoms of schizophrenia as well as in the removal of inhibitory control from limbic structures. The subsequent excess of subcortical dopamine activity may be a source of the positive symptoms of the disorder. Acetylcholine, GABA, endorphins, and serotonin all interact with dopaminergic transmission and may have potential roles in schizophrenia.

Serotonin. Serotonergic neurons are clustered mainly in the raphe nucleus in the brainstem and project widely, in their ascending component, to the thalamus, basal ganglia, and cortex. Selective agonist and antagonist experiments have demonstrated a role for serotonin in eating behavior and body weight regulation, aggression, and the regulation of impulsivity. Treatment with serotonin agonists (tryptophan or fluoxetine) promotes the attainment of high social rank in primate colonies, and accords with the observation of high serotonin levels in the blood of dominant male primates. Antagonist drugs (fenfluramine) block serotonin effects and are reported to increase the incidence of aggression. Thus, abnormally low serotonin activity correlates with pathological aggression as well as suicidality.

While transmitter interactions are notably complex, as a general principle, dopamine and serotonin operate in an opposing relationship. Serotonin, in particular, constrains the emotional and motor behaviors on which dopamine has a facilitory influence. In animal models, hyperlocomotion, exploratory behavior, and intracranial self-stimulation are enhanced following either increases of dopamine or decreases of serotonin transmission. In human volunteers, the administration of dopamine and serotonin agonists (respectively, bromocriptine and fenfluramine) demonstrates similar opposing effects in a working memory task; that is, bromocriptine facilitated spatial delayed memory performance while fenfluramine resulted in impaired performance (Luciana et al., 1998).

[See also Brain Injury and Recovery; Neuron; and Synapse.]

Bibliography

Adolphs, R., Tranel, D., Damasio, H., & Damasio, A. (1994). Impaired recognition of emotion in facial expressions following bilateral damage to the human amygdala. Nature, 372, 669–672. One of several research reports investigating the role of the amygdala in humans. The neuropsychological testing of a patient with bilateral destruction of the amygdala as a result of Urbach-Wiethe disease suggests specific recognition impairments. These include deficits in the ability to recognize fear in facial expressions.

Bandler, R. & Shipley, M. T. (1994). Columnar organization in the midbrain periaqueductal gray: Modules for emotional expression? Trends in Neuroscience, 17, 379–389. A mini-review of the structure and functional organization of the midbrain PAG from the perspective both of historical traditions and recent results. The article emphasizes recent evidence for functionally specialized longitudinal columnar circuits, which have specialized roles in coordinating distinct strategies for coping with different types of stress, threat, and pain.

Bechara, A., Tranel, D., Damasio, H., Adolphs, R., Rockland, C., & Damasio, A. R. (1995). Double dissociation of conditioning and declarative knowledge relative to the amygdala and hippocampus in humans. Science,

269, 1115–1118. This study uses conditioning experiments to investigate the distinctive roles of the amygdala and hippocampus in emotional and declarative learning. Results are similar to those in previous studies in animal models and demonstrate the applicability of these to humans.

Feldman, R. S., Meyer, J. S., & Quenzer, L. F. (1997). *Principles of neuropsychopharmacology*. Sunderland, MA: Sinauer Associates. This is a broad-scope textbook intended for advanced undergraduates or beginning graduate students in psycho- or neuropharmacology. The book attempts to incorporate the latest technical developments in molecular neuropharmacology and brain imaging techniques while addressing all levels of psychotropic drug assessment: from molecular and biochemical characterization, to behavioral effects in animal test paradigms, to clinical applications. The emphasis on drugs, neural systems, and behavior sets this apart from other excellent textbooks in neuroscience (for example, Kandel & Schwartz, or Zigmond, M. J. et al.) that tend to adopt a more cellular and molecular approach.

Frackowiak, R. S. J., Friston, K. J., Frith, C. D., Dolan, R. J., and Mazziotta, J. C. (1997). *Human brain function*. San Diego: Academic Press. This nineteen-chapter volume, written by members of a multidisciplinary collaborative group, addresses the functional organization of the human brain. The relationship of brain function and anatomy is treated mainly at the level of the cerebral cortex, with discussion of the neural substrates of perception, cognition, action, and other higher processes. The emphasis is on neuroimaging in human subjects as a natural successor and complement to clinical neuropsychology, but there is also a thorough account of relevant studies in animals.

Gloor, P. (1997). *The temporal lobe and limbic system*. New York: Oxford University Press. This scholarly monograph provides an exhaustive treatment of the anatomy, development, physiology, and pathophysiology of cortical and subcortical temporal lobe structures. Pierre Gloor, writing from a background that combined neurophysiological research and clinical involvement with epileptic patients, takes a vantage point that integrates basic neuroscience and clinical experience. The book is timely because of widespread current interest in the temporal lobe and limbic system in relation to epilepsy and Alzheimer's disease; memory, learning, and emotional and visceral aspects of behavior; and the pathophysiology of schizophrenia.

Luciana, M., Collins, P. F., and Dupue, R. A. (1998). Opposing roles for dopamine and serotonin in the modulation of human spatial working memory functions. *Cerebral Cortex, 8*, 218–226. This is a specialized research report in which the authors use pharmacological manipulations to investigate monoaminergic influences in working memory tasks. The article has an excellent discussion of the proposed roles of dopamine and serotonin in cognitive behaviors, and includes an up-to-date survey of related work.

Parker, A. J. and Newsome, W. T. (1998). Sense and the single neuron: Probing the physiology of perception. *Annual Review of Neuroscience, 21*, 227–277. This article reviews studies designed to explore the links between neural activity at the level of individual neurons and perception at the level of a behaving animal subject. Included are considerations of psychophysical detection thresholds in different sensory modalities, technical factors, and comparable approaches in human and animal subjects.

Rockland, K. S., Kaas, J. H., & Peters, A. (Eds.). (1997). *Cerebral cortex: Extrastriate cortex in primates* (Vol. 12). New York: Plenum. This is a specialized monograph devoted to the extrastriate visual cortex, but with applicability to general problems of cortical organization. Seventeen chapters include a historical perspective, critical evaluations of single-unit physiological and mapping techniques, exegeses of current work on individual cortical areas, comparisons of visual cortical organization in monkeys and humans, and considerations of higher cortical function, including the contribution of individual areas to conscious vision.

Schmahmann, J. D. (1996). From movement to thought: Anatomic substrates of the cerebellar contribution to cognitive processing. *Human Brain Mapping, 4*, 174–198. This paper reviews the connectional circuitry of the cerebellum and attempts to relate this to functional processes. Evidence is incorporated from human neurological cases, and these and functional imaging studies are thoughtfully compared with data from animal experiments.

Shepherd, G. M. (Ed.). (1998). *The synaptic organization of the brain*. New York: Oxford University Press. An authoritative synthesis of the synaptic organization of ten selected structures (the ventral horn of the spinal cord, cochlear nucleus, olfactory bulb, retina, cerebellum, thalamus, basal ganglia, olfactory cortex, hippocampus, and neocortex). This book emphasizes dendritic properties and aims to incorporate them into concepts of neuronal and circuit organization. The approach is thus heavily toward the cellular level. Each chapter considers the same topics: neural elements, synaptic connections, a basic circuit for the particular structure under review, synaptic physiology, neurotransmitters and neuromodulators, membrane and dendritic properties, and a synthesis of specific information-processing tasks of that region. This is an excellent source for further readings of specialized monographs, surveys, and research reports.

Steriade, M., Jones, E. G., & McCormick, D. A. (1997). *Thalamus, organization and function* (Vol. 1). New York: Elsevier. This is an up-to-date compendium (959 pages in volume 1) on thalamic structure, microstructure, chemical anatomy, cellular physiology, and connectivity. Function is lengthily discussed in the context of thalamocortical activating systems and physiological oscillations during sleep-and-wake cycles. An explicit attempt is made to relate isolated circuits to brain function as a whole and to the behaving animal. The treatment includes both a scholarly review and a critique of relevant contemporary and historical papers.

Kathleen S. Rockland

BRAIN DAMAGE. *See* Alzheimer's Disease; *and* Brain Injury and Recovery.

BRAIN DEVELOPMENT. One reason for studying brain development is its role in psychopathology. Autism and schizophrenia, for example, are now widely considered to be neurodevelopmental disorders, and there is increasing evidence that early neglect or trauma can affect children's brain development and function. It is not surprising that brain development can go awry, as building a human brain is an especially difficult process. The primary sources of information for the brain blueprint are many millions of years old, and it is this genetic information that allows for the foundation and building blocks of the human brain to proceed. It is important to realize that many of the genes for brain chemicals or structures in humans are nearly identical to those of jellyfish and fruit flies. Thus, although humans are understandably proud of their specialized and refined intellectual capacities, underlying them are genetic processes common to nearly all vertebrates (and many other animals as well). Yet, human brain evolution has pushed some developmental processes to an extreme that makes its ultimate product unique among mammals. One clear adaptation has been the substantial expansion in size of cerebral cortex, cerebellum, and related brain structures, which has greatly enhanced their complexity and altered their function. Another modification relatively unique to humans is the greatly prolonged period of brain development; at birth, the human brain is less than one third of its adult size. Another evolutionary strategy has been to co-opt older structures for new purposes. The language areas of cortex, for example, are expanded and modified homologues of similar areas in the cerebral cortex of other primates. Another example of this strategy is the cerebellum, which typically serves a motor function in most mammals, but which has been expanded and modified in humans for use in language, emotion, and other complex cognition.

Early Embryogenesis

Human brain development starts from a humble beginning, shared in many respects with numerous species, with formation of the vertebrate neural plate on the primitive shell of the embryo (*ectoderm*). This plate of cells is initially uncommitted, that is, any cell in it might become any part of the brain if repositioned during early development. As development proceeds, these cells become progressively more defined and their ultimate developmental fate becomes more constrained. After the embryo builds the neural plate through patterned cell division, it folds into a neural "tube." *Homeobox* genes regulate differentiation along the length of this neural tube on the anterior-posterior axis, resulting in swellings along the neural tube (*neuromeres*) that will ultimately become the forebrain, midbrain, and hindbrain. Although many aspects of neural tube formation are controlled by gene activity of cells in the plate itself, some of the patterning arises from gene activity in the tissue just below it (*mesoderm*). At this embryonic stage, the parts of the human brain greatly resemble homologous structures of many other developing vertebrates, and many cells may be proliferating dramatically but not yet committed to becoming neurons.

Much of early brain development is tightly regulated by genetic constraints and is relatively insensitive to the environment. Clearly, it is advantageous for early brain development not to be very sensitive to changes in chemical concentrations, body temperature, or nutrition. Indeed, the concept of *canalization* is highly useful: under most circumstances, the embryo will develop a normal brain in spite of prenatal environmental variation, and it even has "self-righting" capacities that can correct for minor developmental deviations. Nevertheless, a few subtle alterations in the timing or effect of genes controlling neural tube development can produce profound disturbances of brain development. A notorious neural tube defect is spina bifida, in which the posterior spinal cord fails to close completely. Like many neurodevelopmental problems, it can have many causes, but spina bifida in particular can result from a simple deficiency of folate, a vitamin that is sometimes deficient in the diet. Metaphorically, the ordinarily successful progression of brain development has a number of small Achilles' heels.

Becoming a Neuron. After the basic plan of the brain is laid down in neuromeres, neurons and other cells must continue their differentiation. The cells in the neuromeres have several principal tasks: multiplying in number or dying off in a controlled manner in specific locations, determining cell identity (e.g., becoming a particular type of neuron), migrating to their predesignated location, and ultimately, forming functional synaptic connections. During these middle and later stages of brain development, structure and patterns of change become more specific to a species and to the genes that have been modified during its evolution. Although we often focus on neurons, some non-neuronal cell types are extremely important. Glial cells play important roles in the development, sustenance, and functional regulation of the neurons; they also shield the brain from toxins and provide immune system responses.

Whereas vertebrate species may differ in the timing and location of neuron formation, some relatively ubiquitous features of neuron formation are becoming understood at a molecular level. Genes such as *notch* and its homologues set cells on the path of becoming neurons (i.e., *neuroblasts*), and other genes regulate their duplication in a manner highly determined by their "birth date" and regional location. In humans, for example, neuron proliferation ordinarily occurs throughout most of gestation. Neurons for a particular cranial nerve nucleus may all be formed early and within days of each other, but neurons forming layered structures, such as the cerebral cortex, typically have birth dates spread out more broadly and later in brain development. It is somewhat surprising, but normal, for the brain to produce an overabundance of primitive cells and then have them die in a programmed, genetically controlled fashion (*apoptosis*). This species-specific program of cell death presumably reflects the evolutionary modification of preexisting programs, changing the developmental path toward a species-specific brain. In classic experiments with chick embryos, half or more of motor neurons from the spinal cord will die in the period during which those neurons form connections with muscle. Adding or deleting target muscle before that period will correspondingly increase or decrease the number of surviving motor neurons. Other factors also affect apoptosis, including a number of neurochemicals (e.g., nerve growth factor) and neural activity itself. Of course, this process of cell multiplication and apoptosis is sensitive to disruption, and excesses, deficits, or maldistributions of different cell types can occur in the mature brain. Early fetal exposure to intense X-rays or methyl mercury, for example, can kill neurons and result in a brain that is relatively normal but smaller with fewer neurons than normal. Depending on the timing and amount, alcohol consumption during pregnancy can kill or impair specific neuron types with resulting specific alterations in cognition and behavior.

Finding the Way. Once formed, neurons must typically migrate to their designated location. In the development of cerebral cortex, for example, the neuroblasts are formed on the inner surface of the neural tube and must travel a substantial distance, a process that continues for months after birth in humans. Just as neurogenesis is often precisely timed, neuron migration often proceeds in tightly coordinated "waves" of movement, sometimes with neurons having similar birth dates all arriving in a similar location. Classic studies of layered structures like the cerebellar cortex have demonstrated cooperative interaction between neurons and other cells. For example, radial glial cells form a stringlike shape spanning the cerebellar cortex that neuroblasts use as a guide to "climb" down from their birth place to their ultimate destination in the granule cell layer. In addition to physical constraints on migration, nearby cells are covered with molecular markers that signal some neurons to stop and others to pass by, and soluble factors are also released that mark target locations.

Making Connections. The next important developmental task for migrating neurons is to make functional connections with other neurons (i.e., *synapses*) and to differentiate. The neuron determines which *neurotransmitters* it will use and which *receptors* it will express at the synapse. Neurotransmitters further affect differentiation through various receptors. We will focus here on synapse formation. During development, neurons continuously extend thin strands called *filopodia*, most of which do not result in any permanent connection. Numerous soluble and membranous factors can influence the direction of filopodia growth, the speed of growth, and which ones are retracted. A classic idea about guiding growth is *chemotaxis*, that is, that diffusible chemical gradients guide the processes. Some growth factors specifically target certain neurons, others act more generally, and some play a continuing role in adult neural plasticity. Another important guide for making neural connections is neural activity itself.

Nature and Nurture

Given this staggeringly complex orchestration of molecular mechanisms in brain development, it has sometimes been difficult to resist the lure of genetic determinism. A different but equally unfounded position likens the human brain to a blank slate of unlimited neural plasticity upon which experience simply imprints information. A much more useful synthesis has been to view brain development in terms of *self-organizing, dynamic systems*. This acknowledges the necessity of preexisting structures (e.g., genetic codes and basic neural units) that constrain and organize experiential information used in brain development (i.e., the hard wiring provides the structure upon which experience is written). Biology is inherently fluid, responsive, and nonlinear in its properties, such that complex structures can self-organize without any rigid blueprints or programmed instructions. From a dynamic systems perspective, each brain follows a unique path influenced by a constellation of genetically based structures and constraints, which are in turn influenced by both chance and regularities inherent in the environment.

Experience and the Brain

Many species have evolved neural systems that take advantage of experiences that are predictable in timing and quality for all juveniles, such as the early visual experience of kittens or the first foraging experience of honeybees. We have previously termed such developmental processes *experience-expectant* neural plasticity, because the developmental programs have evolved to expect certain types of experience at specific times. One of the best-studied examples is visual development in the cat. The cortical neurons that will process visual information overproduce axonal and dendritic processes prior to eye opening. If both eyes receive normal visual stimulation at eye opening, synaptic connections will be pruned back so that axonal input is neatly organized into cortical columns. If one eye is deprived of visual stimulation, then the axons that would have carried that information to cortex are more severely pruned back, leading to narrow columns for the deprived eye and wider columns for the other. This overproduction and systematic elimination of synaptic connections ("blooming and pruning") is common in mammalian nervous systems. Experience-expectant processes appear to be staggered in their timing, much as if one structure could help organize or provide information later needed for another. Humans also appear to have a staggered and protracted pattern of cortical development, such that visual cortex matures early, whereas some aspects of prefrontal cortex are not completed until adolescence.

Some systems have evolved to benefit from experience that is unpredictable and idiosyncratic, but that is, nevertheless, useful for survival. Such open-ended neural plasticity captures experience regardless of its timing or programming, and we previously termed it *experience dependent*. One example of this can be illustrated in a motor learning paradigm, in which rats learn difficult visuomotor tasks such as climbing rope ladders or traversing narrow beams. Many new synaptic connections are formed in brain areas associated with the tasks learned. This occurs independent of age, and animals with severe brain damage from prenatal alcohol exposure can also learn these tasks and show nearly equivalent brain responses. Experience-dependent mechanisms might store information about the location of food or the characteristics of predators, and in humans these mechanisms may be used to store tremendous amounts of information, such as many particulars of language, a college education, social relationships, emotional skills, and perhaps even culture itself.

Some Clinical Conjectures

Brain development can account for much of the enormous variation in human abilities and behavior. Children with different brains may need different experiences to put them back on a more functional developmental path. Some early promise has been shown in matching the characteristics of experience to specific learning disabilities of children. Relatively subtle prenatal neurologic variations may manifest themselves later as autism or schizophrenia, with symptoms that interfere with experience-dependent storing and processing of information. What are the neuroanatomical consequences of hearing auditory hallucinations for years? What happens to experience-expectant or experience-dependent mechanisms presumably involved in language and social development if experience is severely disrupted by autism? Can illiteracy, emotional neglect, or psychological trauma affect synaptic connec-

tivity through these mechanisms? These questions suggest the importance of early recognition and intervention for some disorders, as well as expanding our understanding of the principles of brain development.

Bibliography

Black, J. E., & Greenough, W. T. (1998). Developmental approaches to the memory process. In J. L. Martinez & R. P. Kesner (Eds.), *Neurobiology of learning and memory* (pp. 55–88). San Diego: Academic Press. A review detailing the concepts of experience-expectant and experience-dependent neural plasticity; a number of other chapters in the book are accessible and recommended.

Feess-Higgins, A., & Larroche, J. C. (Eds.). (1987). *Development of the human fetal brain: An anatomical atlas.* Paris, France: Masson Editeur, CNRS/INSERM. Although somewhat difficult to find, this book is highly recommended for its ability to amaze the reader with its photographic representation of human brain development.

Gazzaniga, M. S. (1998). *The mind's past.* Berkeley: University of California Press. This is an accessible survey of cognitive neuroscience, with special emphasis on evolutionary features of brain development that constrain and shape cognitive development.

Meisami, E., & Timiras, P. S. (Eds.). (1988). *Handbook of human growth and developmental biology: Vol. 1. Neural, sensory-motor and integrative development* Pt A (developmental neurobiology), Pt B (sensory, motor and integrative development), Pt C (factors influencing brain development). Boca Raton, FL: CRC Press. An older but encyclopedic reference to brain development.

Merzenich, M. M., Jenkins, W. M., Johnston, P., Schreiner, C., Miller, S. L., & Tallal, P. (1996). Temporal processing deficits of language-learning impaired children ameliorated by training. *Science, 271*, 77–81. This article demonstrates the clinical utility of matching the quality of experience to the specific neurologic impairments of children. It is also one of the first clinical interventions to be based on experimental studies of neural plasticity.

Purves, D., & Lichtman, J. W. (1985). *Principles of neural development.* Sunderland, MA: Sinauer. A classic, graduate-level textbook.

Thelen, E., & Smith, N. B. (1995). *A dynamic systems approach to the development of cognition and action.* Cambridge, MA: MIT Press. Although the neuroscience is somewhat thin, this is an excellent introduction to dynamic systems theory applied to developmental psychology.

James E. Black and William T. Greenough

BRAIN IMAGING TECHNIQUES allow indirect measurement of brain activity in awake, human volunteers. Their application can inform questions about normal brain function, as well as questions surrounding brain dysfunction (e.g., after stroke, in Alzheimer's disease, during schizophrenic episodes). These techniques cause minimal risk to volunteers and are used in a large number of human laboratories and clinical environments around the world. Functional brain imaging techniques are not a single entity, but rather comprise a set of methods based on different engineering principles that measure brain activity through distinct, indirect, physiologic mechanisms. As a result of their different origins, certain techniques are more amenable to questions about determining the locations of activity change within the brain (high spatial resolution), whereas others are better for determining the precise timing of activity change (high temporal resolution). Four commonly used techniques are described in the following.

Blood Flow Based Techniques

Positron emission tomography (PET) and functional magnetic resonance imaging (fMRI) are based on the observation that changes in brain activity correlate with local changes in blood flow in the brain. Measurement of changes in blood flow (or properties of blood related to blood flow) thus enables an estimate of local brain activity. However, blood flow change does not correlate closely in time with brain activity. If an area of the brain becomes active, blood flow changes take several seconds to begin and do not dissipate for tens of seconds or even longer. For this reason, PET and fMRI have relatively poor temporal resolution and achieve estimates of brain activity on the order of seconds.

PET. PET relies on positron-emitting tracers to measure blood flow. Typically, a volunteer lies with his or her head inserted into a PET scanner. The scanner is a large, donut-shaped device with detectors surrounding the volunteer's head. An extremely low dosage of a positron-emitting tracer, such as radiolabeled water, is safely injected into the blood stream of the volunteer. While the tracer is present in the blood stream, the PET scanner can estimate the amount of cerebral blood flow, and does so locally: a single injection of a tracer will allow a complete brain image of local cerebral blood flow in less than a minute. Importantly, additional images can be acquired by repeating the process after the radiolabeled tracer has decayed—about 10 minutes for radiolabeled water.

Local changes in brain activity are measured by changing information processing or sensory stimulation across sequentially acquired PET images and then examining those images for changes in local blood flow. For example, to identify changes related to visual stimulation, a volunteer might view nothing while one PET image is acquired and then view a flashing light while a second image is acquired. Contrasting the two images would reveal increased blood flow in visual cortex for the image acquired during the flashing light stimulus because such stimuli increase net neuronal activity in visual cortex. More complex and subtle brain activity changes can be examined in a similar fashion as long as they can be manipulated across sequential PET image acquisitions. PET images have low temporal resolution (about one minute) and relatively high spatial resolution (about 10 millimeters, or 0.39 inch).

fMRI. FMRI enables measurement of blood property changes linked to blood flow using high-field magnets. FMRI is performed using standard (or slightly modified to be faster) MRI scanners available in most large hospitals and many research settings. Volunteers lie with their heads inserted into the bore of a high-field magnet (the central component of the MRI scanner). Brain images are then repeatedly generated such that the images are highly sensitive to changes in blood properties. In this way, brain activity change can be localized by identifying regions of the brain in which blood properties change in concert with changes in information processing or sensory stimulation.

PET and fMRI methods are highly analogous. However, fMRI has several advantages: higher spatial resolution and better temporal resolution. Increased spatial resolution translates to better localization and resolution for brain activity measurements, although the limits of these improvements are currently unknown. Current estimates are that fMRI provides resolution of about 3 to 6 millimeters (0.117 to 0.234 inch) and can localize activity changes within about 1 millimeter (0.039 inch) of their sources. Whole-brain images can be repeatedly acquired with fMRI every 2 seconds, such that the temporal limits of the method are imposed by the temporally blurred blood flow response.

Techniques Based on Electrical Activity

Cell activity within the brain causes electrical fields that can be measured outside the brain. By measuring the electrical field potentials at or near the scalp, these methods can make indirect measurements of brain activity. Two available techniques are electroencephalogram (EEG) and magnetoencephalograph (MEG). Unlike PET and fMRI, electrical activity based techniques derive their signal directly from the activity of cells and are thus tightly time-locked to this activity (on the order of tens of milliseconds). EEG and MEG can be applied to questions about brain function by examining how different kinds of sensory or processing events evoke temporally locked changes in brain activity (called *event-related potentials* or ERP). However, because EEG and MEG base their measurements on electrical potentials near the scalp, their ability to determine the locations of activity change within the brain is limited.

EEG. EEG measures brain activity by directly attaching arrays of electrodes on the scalp of a volunteer. These electrodes are sensitive to the small fluctuations in the spontaneous electrical activity of the brain. By connecting these electrodes to an amplifier and to a digital computer, the field potentials on the scalp can be reconstructed and used to make inferences about brain activity.

MEG. MEG is based on the measurement of local magnetic fields produced by electrical activity in the brain. MEG scanners are typically positioned upright above the volunteer's head where magnetic field sensitive detectors (called *superconducting quantum interference devices* or SQUID) are positioned. Much like EEG, measurement of brain activity with MEG is based on the detection of transient evoked neuronal events measured on a time scale of tens of milliseconds.

Bibliography

Binder, J. R., & Rao, S. M. (1994). Human brain mapping with functional magnetic resonance imaging. In A. Kertesz (Ed.), *Localization and neuroimaging in neuropsychology* (pp 185–308). San Diego: Academic Press.

Frackowiak, R. S. J., & Friston, K. J. (1995). Methodology of activation paradigms. In F. Boller & J. Grafman (Eds.), *Handbook of neuropsychology* (Vol. 10, pp. 369–282). Amsterdam: Elsevier.

Picton, T. W., Lins, O. G., & Scherg, M. (1995). The recording and analysis of event related potentials. In F. Boller & J. Grafman (Eds.), *Handbook of neuropsychology* (Vol. 10, pp. 3–73). Amsterdam: Elsevier.

Posner, M. I., & Raichle, M. E. (1994). *Images of mind.* New York: Scientific American Books.

Raichle, M. E. (1987). Circulatory and metabolic correlates of brain function in normal humans. In F. Plum & V. Mountcastle (Eds.), *The handbook of physiology: Section 1. The nervous system. Vol. 5: Higher functions of the brain* (Pt. 1, pp. 643–674). Bethesda, MD: American Physiological Association.

Rosen, B. R., Buckner, R. L., & Dale, A. M. (1998). Event-related fMRI: Past, present, and future. *Proceedings of the National Academy of Sciences USA, 95,* 773–780.

Rugg, M. D. (1995). ERP studies of memory. In M. D. Rugg & M. G. H. Coles (Eds.), *Electrophysiology of mind: Event-related brain potentials and cognition.* New York: Oxford University Press.

Randy Buckner

BRAIN INJURY AND RECOVERY. From a behavioral perspective "recovery of function" can be taken to mean that the cognitive, sensory, or motor deficits following brain injury are reduced or eliminated. In a clinical setting, it is difficult to determine exactly what constitutes specific "restitution of function" because there are rarely any behavioral or physiological measures of preinjury performance that could be used to evaluate the extent of postinjury recovery. When laboratory animals are used in experimental preparations it is easier to define what is meant by recovery because pre- and postinjury measures of behavior can be examined and quantified. For example, rats are routinely examined in maze tasks, and their performance is used to define spatial function(s) and, after brain damage, which structures "mediate" the function. After an initial functional deficit is observed, any subsequent improvement can be taken as a measure of recovery of function. If no training or special handling is provided, then the recovery is said to be spontaneous; however, if training or pharmacological manipulations are employed, then the improvement is attributed to the treatments under study. Thus, in the laboratory, investigators can define recovery when their subjects achieve a particular goal in a maze, regardless of how the task is accomplished.

Unfortunately, there is no single definition of functional recovery that appeals to everyone who has an interest in the subject. Trauma and emergency room surgeons may define recovery when their patients emerge from coma. Rehabilitation specialists or nurses report recovery when patients no longer require constant monitoring or other personal attentions. Managed care representatives may define recovery in terms of how long a patient has received therapy while the patients themselves might only be content to define recovery by when they can comfortably return to their previous jobs.

Is Substitution of Function the Same as Recovery of Function?

Because until recently, many clinicians held belief the that the adult nervous system cannot undergo physiological/anatomical restructuring, they rejected the idea that true recovery from serious brain injury was possible. Opponents of the concept of cerebral plasticity argued instead that recovery need not be identical to the function(s) lost as a result of the injury. In this view recovery is the result of substituting new behavioral strategies for those that were lost following brain injury. Sometimes the tricks are said to be so subtle that they could mask underlying deficits. Under such conditions, impairments would only be revealed under very careful scrutiny or by sophisticated testing techniques. Simply observing the achievement of a goal (ends) rather than how that goal is achieved (means), can lead to false conclusions about whether recovery occurs at all. This is often the position that has been used by people who argue that brain damage always results in permanent and irreversible loss of functions. It is an argument difficult to refute because proponents can always claim that tests used to show recovery in human subjects are just not sensitive enough to reveal the true underlying deficits.

Recovery in the Context of Localization of Functions

Recovery from brain damage is hard to reconcile with the long-held doctrine of cerebral localization of function when the doctrine is taken in its most literal sense. If the adult brain is considered to be parcellated anatomically with respect to behavioral functions, extensive removal or significant damage to an area should result in the unequivocal loss of that particular function. In this context, Pöppel (1989) has defined central nervous system (CNS) functions "as those that, in principle, can be lost after circumscribed injuries of the brain."

Some investigators of cerebral plasticity are now using computer assisted tomography (CAT), cerebral blood flow techniques, or magnetic resonance imaging variety to examine the changes in activation of CNS areas following brain injury. These techniques do not measure behavioral functions per se but, instead, are assumed to represent complex cognitive processes. Despite these new methods, Patricia Churchland (1986) argues that the concept of localization of function is not quite as straightforward as it seems. "If A is the lesioned (sic) area and the patient can no longer do Y, then A is the center for Y? For many reasons, the answer must be no" (p. 163). Churchland also states that:

> Breezy use of the [concept of localization] will yield a bizarre catalogue of centers—including, for example, a center for inhibiting religious fanaticism, since lesions in certain areas of the temporal lobe sometimes result in a patient's acquiring a besotted religious zeal . . . the willy-nilly nature of Gall's phrenological catalogue comes back to haunt us. (p. 164)

Until very recently the strict localization perspective was the prevailing paradigm in the field of clinical neuropsychology, and indeed its acceptance served as a very useful diagnostic and simplified didactic tool for developing concepts about how the brain works. Localization theory also served as the basis for most of the diagnostic testing of patients with brain lesions, i.e., determination of the locus of the lesion and the behavioral symptoms that were likely to ensue from the loss of that specific tissue. In the laboratory, lesion research was concerned with the experimental creation of injury, the precise measurement of the lesion parameters (e.g., locus and extent of the damage, tracing of neural degeneration, and alterations of pathways), and the careful description of behavioral deficits caused by the damage to provide support for the clinical observations.

Contextual Factors Play a Role in Brain Injury Outcome

There is now a growing body of literature demonstrating that functional recovery in the adult mammalian central nervous system depends upon a number of contextual factors operating at the time of the injury. One example of how context can influence the functional outcome of traumatic brain damage is provided by the work of Anderson, Demasio, and Tranel (1990). The investigators compared patients with slow-growing tumors localized to the anterior left hemisphere to those who had stroke-induced lesions of the same area. In other words, the tumor injury to cerebral tissue occurred slowly while following stroke, the injury occurred rapidly. After careful matching of lesion size the patients were tested to evaluate verbal and nonverbal intellect, verbal and visual memory, speech, and language. The patients with cerebral tumors had different outcomes than those with the same locus and extent of damage caused by stroke. The left hemisphere stroke patients had more severe language deficits than the patients with tumors, and some of the tumor patients had no impairments at all on any of the tests, despite the extensive brain damage.

The Anderson et al. data (1990) represent an example of the "serial lesion effect" in which slowly inflicted brain lesions in frontal cortex, hippocampus, visual cortex, hypothalamus, and the reticular formation, to name a few, result in the elimination or reduction of impairments compared to subjects with identical damage created in a single stage (see Finger & Stein, 1982). In the animal literature the context is simply the momentum of the lesion since all damage is inflicted using the same technique. With respect to the clinical data, the "contexts" of the injuries are twofold: the type of injury (tumor versus stroke) and the momentum of the damage (slow versus rapid onset). For a more detailed discussion of the role of context in determining the outcome of brain damage and its relation to localization of function see Stein (1988, pp. 15–28).

Sex Hormones Influence the Outcome of Brain Damage

Another example of a "contextual factor" influencing recovery is the sex of the subject. Although there is a growing awareness that there are sexually dimorphic structures in the brain (e.g., Juraska, 1991; Kimura, 1987), little is known about whether there are systematic sex differences in response to brain damage. Recently, Stein, Fulop, and Roof (in press) reviewed research showing that the timing of injury with respect to hormonal cycling can affect the outcome of bilateral frontal cortex injury in laboratory animals. These investigators found that progesterone significantly reduces injury-induced cerebral edema, and consequently enhances the recovery of the animal's ability to solve a spatial learning task. The authors suggested that the circulating levels of this hormone at the time of injury may account for why normally cycling female rats given contusion injuries of the frontal cortex have less edema than males. Surprisingly, edema and behavioral deficits can also be dramatically reduced in male rats given injections of progesterone at the time of injury. Aside from the therapeutic implications, considered together, the different studies discussed here can be taken to indicate that the outcome of traumatic brain damage is not just a question of which area is damaged, but depends upon "contextual factors" present at the time the injury occurs. In other words, age at time of injury, momentum of the lesions, and hormonal status represent several of the contextual factors that can alter the prognosis and outcome of traumatic brain damage.

Recovery of Function Involves Multiple and Distributed Changes Throughout the Brain

As evidence showing that functional recovery could occur under appropriate conditions, the localization doctrine has been modified by introducing the concept of "serial and parallel processing circuits" (and areas). Instead of a single structure or a small aggregate of areas mediating function, it is now argued that complex functions may require the simultaneous integration of a network of structures acting in unison to produce the behavior. Using positron emission tomography to examine stroke patients, Weiller and colleagues (1992) showed that there were widespread changes in cerebral blood flow patterns in the brain ipsilateral and contralateral to the injured side. As recovery of hand use proceeded, changes in cerebral blood flow were seen in both hemispheres. Instead of localized changes in blood flow, there was a very complex pattern of functional reorganization (as measured by cerebral blood flow) concomitant with the behavioral recovery. The authors suggested that "major mechanisms for the restoration of function may include bilateral activation of the motor system with use of ipsilateral pathways and recruitment of additional motor areas" (p. 471). Nonetheless, the addition of more neural structures to account for reorganization and recovery still does not address the question of how the new functions emerge or how the different parts work together or how "compensatory takeover" occurs following injury.

Although considerable progress is being made, we do not yet understand all of the conditions that prevent repair of brain damage. When recovery is observed, we do not know whether it is permanent or whether with aging or other systemic changes, the deficits might return. While there is no general agreement on what is meant by "function" or "recovery," we do know that brain damage itself is not a monolithic event limited to a highly focalized region. Instead, it is now thought that injury causes a cascade of biochemical and structural changes beginning immediately after damage and progressing for days, weeks and perhaps even years after the initial trauma.

The effects of localized damage need to be viewed in the context of how the injury alters cerebral organization. Although local events may trigger the process, functional recovery is likely to be the result of multiple events distributed throughout the central nervous system rather than coming about through local changes in small neural networks near the site of the injury. New and refined technologies including PET, MRI, and SPECT provide the opportunity to examine these complex processes in living beings so that correlations between behavioral functions and some physiological processes can be quantified and evaluated systematically. From these technologies we can perhaps gain some insight into the patterns of neural disruption leading to the expression of symptoms, as well as the potential mechanisms underlying recovery. Just as bricks alone are not a building, the anatomical substrates are not the behavioral recovery itself but rather just components of it.

Bibliography

Anderson, S. W., Damasio, H., & Tranel, D. (1990). Neuropsychological impairments caused by tumor or stroke. *Archives of Neurology, 47,* 397–405.

Churchland, P. S. (1986). *Neurophilosophy: Toward a science of the mind/brain.* Cambridge, MA: MIT Press.

Finger, S., & Stein, D. G. (1982). *Brain damage and recovery: Research and clinical perspectives.* New York: Academic Press.

Juraska, J. M. (1991). Sex differences in "cognitive" regions of the rat brain. *Psychoneuroendocrinology, 16,* 105–119.

Kimura, D. (1987). Are men's and women's brains really different? *Canadian Psychology, 28,* 133–147.

Pöppel, E. (1989) Taxonomy of the subjective: An evolutionary perspective. In J. W. Brown (Ed.), *Neuropsychology of visual perception* (pp. 219–232). Hillsdale, NJ: Erlbaum.

Stein, D. G. (1988). In pursuit of new strategies for understanding recovery from brain damage: Problems and perspectives. In T. Boll & B. K. Bryant (Eds.), *Clinical neuropsychology and brain function: Research, measurement, and practice* (pp. 9–56). Washington, DC: American Psychological Association.

Stein, D. G., Roof, R. L., & Fulop, Z. L. (in press). Brain damage, sex hormones and recovery. In D. T. Stuss, G. Winocur, & I. H. Robertson (Eds.), *Cognitive neurorehabilitation: A comprehensive approach.* Cambridge: Cambridge University Press.

Weiller, C., Chollet, F., Friston, K. J., Wise, R. J. S., & Frackowiak, R. S. J. (1992). Functional reorganization of the brain in recovery from striatocapsular infarction in man. *Annals of Neurology, 31,* 463–472.

Donald G. Stein

BRAINSTORMING. Group brainstorming is a technique for generating creative ideas in groups. It was developed and popularized in the 1950s and 1960s by Alex Osborn in a series of editions of his book, *Applied Imagination.* Osborn was an executive in a marketing firm who felt that groups often inhibited their creative potential by premature judgement or evaluation of ideas as they were being shared. He proposed that groups should defer judgment during the idea-generation stage and focus on generating as many ideas as possible. He suggested four general rules for effective brainstorming. Group members should not evaluate or criticize each others' ideas as they are being generated. They should focus on generating as many ideas as possible. Group members should express all ideas that come to mind no matter how unusual or strange the ideas might be. They are encouraged to attend to the ideas of others and combine or improve them.

Osborn and his colleagues used the brainstorming technique with hundreds of organizations and cited evidence for its effectiveness in generating large numbers of useful ideas. His most controversial statement was contained in his 1957 book, in which he suggested that group brainstorming would double the production of ideas. He believed that group members would have positive motivational and cognitive stimulation effects on one another. A 1959 study by two of Osborn's disciples, Parnes and Meadow, in the *Journal of Educational Psychology,* demonstrated that the brainstorming rules were useful in increasing the number of ideas generated in groups. However, another group of academic researchers (Taylor, Berry, & Clifford, 1958) compared the performance of a group of four brainstormers to that of four individual brainstormers. That comparison revealed that the group brainstormers actually generated only about half as many ideas as the sets of four individuals (generally labeled as nominal groups). Much subsequent research has demonstrated similar loss of productivity in brainstorming groups. Groups not only produce fewer ideas, they also produce fewer good ideas.

One focus of research has been to understand the basis for the relatively poor productivity of group brainstormers. Social psychologists Michael Diehl and Wolfgang Stroebe (1987) evaluated various possible interpretations and suggested that the major problem in brainstorming groups is production blocking. Group members can express ideas only when others are not talking, but solitary brainstormers can express their ideas as they come to mind. Social anxiety or apprehension about being evaluated by other group members also inhibits productivity. A lack of individual accountability in groups may lower the level of task motivation. As a result of these factors, groups often experience relatively low levels of productivity in the initial phases. This low level of performance may become a group norm or standard that is maintained in later group sessions. Interestingly, group brainstormers typically feel that they have performed at a higher level than do individual brainstormers (Paulus et al., 1993). This fact may help explain the continuing popularity of the brainstorming technique.

To overcome these limitations of group brainstorming, some scholars have suggested the use of computer-based brainstorming in which individuals can share ideas simultaneously and anonymously. In these sessions, group members type ideas into individual computers, and during this process they can have access to the ideas being generated by other group members. Electronic brainstorming is often part of a computer-based group decision-making system that allows groups to subsequently evaluate the ideas generated and come to a consensus about an issue. The electronic brainstorming phase minimizes the production blocking and evaluation apprehension that may be present in typical group brainstorming. Computer-based brainstorming is more effective than typical group brainstorming but not necessarily better than different forms of solitary brainstorming. When the size of electronic groups increases to eight or more, there is sometimes evidence for increased productivity. However, thus far the basis for this performance enhancement with larger groups is not well understood.

One major limitation of research on group brainstorming is that it has mostly involved the use of untrained strangers. In traditional practice, group brainstorming involves some degree of training and the use of trained facilitators to aid the group in the effective use of brainstorming rules and other strategies (Rawlinson, 1981). When facilitators are employed, group brainstorming can be significantly improved. Groups may also be beneficial in stimulating ideas that come to mind after the group session. In fact, Osborn recommended that some alternation between individual and group brainstorming would be most beneficial. Although there are no published demonstrations of the effectiveness of this procedure, it would seem likely that the creative stimulation from group interaction might be most evident afterward. Idea exchange in groups is also more likely to be beneficial when there is some degree of diversity in the background or expertise of the group members.

Group brainstorming may be more suitable for some individuals than for others. Individuals who enjoy group activities, have low social interaction anxiety, and are able to process information while generating their own ideas may benefit most from group interaction.

Robert Sutton, an organizational psychologist, has argued that the utility of group brainstorming is not adequately measured by the efficiency in production of ideas (1996). It may have a number of advantages in corporations that focus on creativity. Group members can share their knowledge and expertise and can practice and display a variety of intellectual skills. In addition, clients or observers may be impressed with the results of brainstorming sessions. However, strong evidence for the overall utility of group brainstorming as part of the corporate culture is lacking.

Bibliography

Diehl, M., & Stroebe, W. (1987). Productivity loss in brainstorming groups: Toward the solution of a riddle. *Journal of Personality and Social Psychology, 53,* 497–509.

Offner, A. K., Kramer, T. J., & Winter, J. P. (1996). The effects of facilitation, recording, and pauses on group brainstorming. *Small Group Research, 27,* 283–298.

Osborn, A. F. (1957, 1963). *Applied imagination* (1st and 2nd eds.). New York: Scribner.

Parnes, S. J., & Meadow, A. (1959). Effect of "brainstorming" instructions on creative problem-solving by trained and untrained subjects. *Journal of Educational Psychology, 50,* 171–176.

Paulus, P. B., Brown, V., & Ortega, A. H. (1999). Group creativity. In R. E. Purser & A. Montuori (Eds.), *Social creativity in organizations* (Vol. 2, pp. 151–176). Cresskill, NJ: Hampton. An overview of the group creativity literature that suggests a theoretical basis for enhanced creativity in groups.

Paulus, P. B., & Dzindolet, M. T. (1993). Social influence processes in group brainstorming. *Journal of Personality and Social Psychology, 64,* 575–586. Provides a social influence perspective that contrasts with the blocking perspective of Diehl and Stroebe (1987).

Paulus, P. B., Dzindolet, M. T., Poletes, G., & Camacho, L. M. (1993). Perception of performance in group brainstorming: The illusion of group productivity. *Personality and Social Psychology Bulletin, 19,* 78–89. Provides evidence that group members rate their performance more highly than do solitary brainstormers.

Rawlinson, J. G. (1981). *Creative thinking and brainstorming.* New York: Wiley. Provides practical guidelines for group brainstorming consistent with the Osborn perspective.

Sutton, R. I. (1996). Brainstorming groups in context: Effectiveness in a product design firm. *Administrative Science Quarterly, 41,* 685–718.

Taylor, D. W., Berry, P. C., & Block, C. H. (1958). Does group participation when using brainstorming facilitate or inhibit creative thinking? *Administrative Science Quarterly, 3,* 23–47.

Valacich, J. S., Dennis, A. R., & Connolly, T. (1994). Idea generation in computer-based groups: A new ending to an old story. *Organizational Behavior and Human Decision Processes, 57,* 448–467. Provides evidence that idea generation improves with group size for computer brainstorming.

Paul B. Paulus

BRAINWASHING is a technique that has been used for centuries and is no mystery to psychologists in the military. Edward Hunter, a British journalist stationed in China, used the term "brainwashing" to describe the process he saw being applied in China to coerce conformity among its citizens. The concept was used again during the Korean War to explain the defections of American soldiers. Hunter alleged that these persuasive techniques were so powerful as to be irresistible and irreversible. This view received added credibility following the release of the novel *The Manchurian Candidate* (Condon, 1959). Little research, however, has been conducted to support Hunter's claims for the power of brainwashing.

Brainwashing can be a powerful tool of persuasion, especially effective if a systematic set of conditions and procedures are utilized. The result of this indoctrination process is an impairment of autonomy, an inability to think independently, and a disruption of beliefs and affiliations. In this context, brainwashing refers to the involuntary reeducation of basic beliefs and values in a population of captured civilians or soldiers. However, in the bigger sense, all people are being reeducated continually. The experience of the brainwashed individual differs in that the inconsistent information is forced upon him under controlled conditions after his capacity for critical judgment has been reduced. Anyone can be broken psychologically by someone with persistence, patience, and the use of techniques outlined below and the desire to incapacitate the critical capacity of an individual.

After the Korean War, the U.S. government commissioned several independent studies of brainwashing. The two published studies were by Lifton (1961) and Schein (1961). One secret study was conducted by the CIA in 1956 and declassified in 1984 under the moniker MKULTRA (Winn, 1984).

If we accept the definition of brainwashing as stated, it implies force, but the "effects" of forcible brainwashing—profound changes in beliefs and attitudes—can be achieved without the use of physical coercion. If applied systematically, brainwashing will result in the disruption of critical judgment, changes in behavior, personality disintegration, and the adoption of a different set of values and beliefs. Some techniques of brainwashing are as follows:

- Instilling a complete loss of control or hope of rescue.
- Creating a total dependency on captors for basic biological functions.

- Creating an environment of uncertainty.
- Threatening the use of torture; since brainwashing thrives on inner conflict, the threat of torture works much better than actual torture itself.
- Introducing the presence of informants to discourage communication between captives.
- Inducing extreme fatigue and exhaustion; for example, sleep deprivation alternating with heavy physical labor and blocks of interrogation, as well as the administration of stimulants and depressants to hasten the process of deterioration and produce radical "mood swings."
- Using isolation or solitary confinement equivocally. Some victims have tremendous difficulty coping while others do not.
- Using intense interrogation to break down the integrity of the captive's personality and belief system.

These interrogation sessions are designed to create internal conflict and strong feelings of guilt associated with the victim's behavior. It is not at all difficult to create such feelings in military personnel or civilians, as terrorists have demonstrated. Every moral vulnerability is exploited by incessant questioning until the individual begins to question his own value system. The captive constantly fights his fear of "going insane." He finds his mind "going blank" for longer and longer periods of time. He can no longer think clearly or constructively. Eventually, he concludes that if he is to maintain any semblance of sanity or personal integrity, he must capitulate to the request to write a confession.

Captives who have undergone brainwashing report that the decision to confess produces an overwhelming sense of relief. They realize that by confessing, their inner conflict ceases and they will not be driven insane. It is at this point that they are prepared to make major concessions in their value system. This is the result of a systematic, progressive, conditioned response, not one based on a rational decision-making process. They have lost their ability to think or process information critically as a result of the brainwashing techniques.

If this were all there was to the process, brainwashing would not have occurred. The captive would simply have been coerced to comply with his captor's demands. Actually, the brainwashing process has just begun. No matter what the prisoner writes in his confession, the captor is not satisfied. The captor questions every sentence and edits it with the prisoner. The prisoner is forced to argue against every change. This is the real essence of brainwashing. Every time the prisoner gives in on a point, he must rewrite his whole confession. In a desperate attempt to maintain some semblance of personality integration and to avoid further interrogation, the prisoner begins to argue that what he had confessed to was the truth. This results in his accepting as his own the statements he has written. He ends up using many of the captor's arguments to buttress his position. Through this process, his identification with the captor's value system becomes complete. It is in this last phase that the captive's personality is reintegrated and an over-identification with the captor's value system occurs. His new value system, along with his manner of perceiving, organizing, and interpreting events, has been totally altered, and the brainwashing process is complete. He is no longer capable of thinking or speaking in ways other than those that he has adopted as a result of the brainwashing.

However, recently developed techniques of self-discipline and awareness may allow someone to combat and possibly overcome the effects of these manipulative procedures.

Bibliography

Hunter, E. (1951). *Brainwashing in red China.* New York: Vanguard.

Lifton, R. J. (1956). "Thought reform" of western civilians in Chinese communist prisons. *Psychiatry, 19,* 173–195.

Lifton, R. J. (1961). *Thought reform and the psychology of totalism.* New York: Norton.

Schein, E. H. (1956). The Chinese indoctrination for prisoners of war: A study of attempted brainwashing. *Psychiatry, 19,* 149–156.

Schein, E. H. (1961). *Coercive persuasion.* New York: Norton.

Winn, D. (1984). *The manipulated mind: Brainwashing, conditioning and indoctrination.* Ishk Book Service.

Dennis M. Kowal

BRAZIL. Psychology in Brazil had its origins in philosophy education and the medical sciences. From these three fields, Brazilian psychology inherited a humanistic, clinically oriented psychology, and in the earlier times, test oriented. Main cultural influences came from France, rather than from the United States and Great Britain. In the first half of the twentieth century, psychologists were mostly philosophers, educators, and medical doctors who specialized in psychology through independent reading or who underwent training abroad.

Psychology in Brazil was mostly associated with clinical psychology and psychoanalysis. Among the most distinguished medical doctors who were responsible for the development of clinical psychology in Brazil were Durval Marcondes, André Ombredane, Decio de Souza, and Manoel Lyra. At the same time, educational psychology developed in Brazil with the contribution of Lourenço Filho (who was influenced by John Dewey) and Helena Antipoff, the latter having made an integration between clinical and educational psychology. Antipoff was noted for her work with the mentally retarded in Belo Horizonte. Cuban-born Mira y Lopez gave strength to the applied testing movement, and Nilton Campos followed a Gestalt and phenomenological approach at the University of Brazil (now the Federal University of Rio de Janeiro).

Some of the pioneer psychologists in São Paulo were Noemi Rudolfer, who studied at Columbia University Teachers College in New York City; Betti Katzenstein; Annita Cabral, who received her degree from the University of Hamburg; and Aniela Ginsberg, who had studied at the University of Cracow. In Rio de Janeiro, leaders in developing psychology programs were Hans Lippman from Germany; Rev. Antonius Benko, S. J., a Catholic Jesuit priest from Hungary, who had studied at the University of Louvain (Belgium) and at the Pontifical Catholic University of Rio de Janeiro; and Antonio Gomes Penna of the Federal University of Rio de Janeiro. Otto Klineberg was at the University of São Paulo between 1945 and 1947. Arrigo Angelini studied with David McClelland and Roy D'Andrade. During the 1950s, they did research on achievement motivation.

Other influential psychologists were Fred Keller and Robert Berryman, who introduced B. F. Skinner's work to Brazil. Carolina M. Bori distinguished herself as a researcher and served as president of the Brazilian Society for the Advancement of Science. Other major figures include Maria Helena Novaes Mira in the field of educational psychology, Maria Clotilde Rossetti Ferreira in developmental psychology, and Aroldo Rodrigues, probably the best internationally known Brazilian social psychologist.

Except for a few isolated efforts such as those of W. Radecki, as early as 1928, and more recent ones in São Paulo, Ribeirao Preto, and Brasilia, Brazil has never been a stronghold for experimental psychology or basic research. As Ruben Ardila (a former president of the Interamerican Society of Psychology) wrote his 1982 essay titled "Psychology in Latin America Today": "science is not a cultural value in Latin America. Literature, art, and the humanities are very positively evaluated . . . but science and technology do not receive much esteem." In Brazil, according to Hutz and Adair, "psychology is thought of as an art rather than a science by many of its Brazilian practitioners" (Hutz & Adair, 1994, p. 145). They further state:

> psychology has developed in peculiar ways in Brazil. . . . Brazilian psychology started as a speculative discipline. The emphasis on reflective thought and interpretation, the belief that practical or clinical skills depend mostly on personal experience, and the rejection of empirical research as a valid procedure to investigate psychological events or social problems is reflected in the citation patterns observed in the journal *Arquivos Brasileiros de*

Psicologia. The data from another journal, *Psicologia: Teoria e Pesquisa*, show the beginning of a shift toward a research-oriented psychology. (p. 148)

Hutz and Adair add that although the country had over 80,000 registered psychologists in 1992, "there were only some 200 active researchers who publish regularly in scientific journals" (p. 146).

The Training of Psychologists

The 1960s were a major turning point for Brazilian psychology. Federal law No. 4119, in 1962, regulated the profession, and Resolution 403 of the Federal Council of Education established the required curriculum for psychology programs. Psychology began to "formally exist" as a regular profession. The core curriculum for a degree in psychology in the 1960s consisted of courses in physiology, statistics, general and experimental psychology, developmental and social psychology, and psychopathology. The professional degree of psychologists also required courses in techniques for psychological diagnosis and psychotherapy, professional ethics, as well as three subjects chosen from among a list of seven: exceptional group dynamics and human relations; therapeutic pedagogy; school psychology and learning problems; theories and techniques of psychotherapy; personnel selection and vocational guidance; and industrial psychology. In addition to that, each university could require additional courses, thus constituting the "full curriculum." Practicums in the areas of clinical, school, or organizational psychology were also required.

In 1996, a new law did away with the "minimum curriculum." Universities were allowed to establish their own curriculums.

Professional Associations

Another major step for the profession of psychology in Brazil was the establishment of the Federal Council of Psychologists and the Regional Councils of Psychology in 1974, which are licensing boards and serve also as ethical committees. In 1984, the National Association for Graduate Work and Research was founded. ANPEPP is the association of the 27 graduate programs in psychology and organizes biennial meetings. Other organizations include the Brazilian Association of Applied Psychology, with headquarters at the Foundation Getulio Vargas in Rio de Janeiro, the Brazilian Association of Psychology in São Paulo, as well as the Brazilian Society of Psychology. Many Brazilian researchers and professionals belong to the Interamerican Society of Psychology, which comprises psychologists from North, Central, and South America and holds biennial meetings, each time in a different country. It was founded in 1995. Two Brazilian psychologists have been presidents of this organization: Angela M. B. Biaggio and Arnoldo Rodrigues, both APA fellows.

Theory and Research Trends

The great spur of research in Brazil began in the late 1960s when the military regime expanded university education and sent many university teachers or candidates to the United States and a few other countries to study for advanced degrees. The first graduate programs (credits plus thesis) started in 1966, and many faculty members pursued master and doctoral degrees. With the gradual return to democracy in the 1980s, governmental scholarships were granted in larger proportions for studies in France, England, Belgium, and other countries. Tensions arose initially between psychoanalytically oriented psychologists and experimental psychologists. Later, strained relations developed between those interested in quantitative methodologies and those committed to qualitative approaches. The field of social psychology also reflects these conflicting approaches. Experimental social psychologists represent the American tradition, while Marxist social psychologists represent the European traditions. The field of developmental psychology has been influenced by Freud, Melanie Klein, Bowlby, Bandura, Piaget, and Vygotsky.

Since the 1960s the number of psychologists has increased greatly. In 1962, there were only 15 psychologists registered in the Ministry of Education; as of 1999, there were over 90,000 psychologists registered with the Regional Councils, with the vast majority in Rio de Janeiro and São Paulo. There are over 100 psychology programs and 27 master's programs in Brazil, with the majority of programs in Rio de Janeiro and São Paulo. Doctoral programs, however, are available in the country's capital, Brasilia, as well as in the southeast and south, in Rio de Janeiro, São Paulo, and Porto Alegre.

Major Journals

The most important psychology journals are *Psicologia: Teoria e Pesquisa* (Psychology: Theory and Research), published by the University of Brasilia; *Psicologia: Reflexao e Crítica* (Psychology: Reflection and Criticism), published by the Federal University of Rio Grande do Sul; *Arquivos Brasileiros de Psicologia Aplicada* (Brazilian Archives of Applied Psychology), the oldest journal in the country, published by the Federal University of Rio de Janeiro; and *Estudos de Psicologia* (Studies in Psychology), published by the Pontifical Catholic University of Campinas. All of the journals use peer reviews. The first two are indexed in *Psychological Abstracts/Psych Lit.*

Psychology in Brazil is a thriving, progressive field, with many different nuances, dealing with the issues facing Brazilian society, such as street children, the poor, and drugs. Community and institutional programs continue to be implemented, in addition to the individual psychotherapy for the wealthy, which dominated earlier times.

Bibliography

Ardilla, R. (1982). Psychology in Latin America. *American Psychologist, 23,* 567–574.

Biaggio, A. (1983). Note: Historical aspects of psychology in Brazil—with special emphasis on clinical psychology. *Interdisciplinaria* (Buenos Aires), 3, 207–213.

Biaggio, A., & Grinder, R. E. (1992). Brazil. In V. Sexton & J. Hogan (Eds.), *International psychology: Views from around the world* (pp. 54–62). Lincoln, NE.

CFE (Conselho Federal de Educação). (1976). *Psicologia— Legislação.* Série A. N° 1.

Hutz, C., & Adair, J. (1996). The use of references in Brazilian psychology journals reveals trends in thought and research. *International Platform for Psychologists.* International Union of Psychological Sciences.

Mattos, M. A. (1996). Psicologia: Descrição da Área. Ministério da Educação e do Desporto. Brasilia, D. F.

Velloso, E. (1979). *Psicologia Clínica no Brasil.* Paper presented at the II Seminar on the History of Different Areas of Psychology, Institute of Psychology, University of Sao Paulo.

Angela M. B. Biaggio

BRENTANO, FRANZ (1838–1917), German philosopher and psychologist. Brentano was born on 16 January 1838 at Marienberg-am-Rhein into a distinguished German intellectual family; his grandfather, aunt, uncle, and father were all noted authors on various literary, philosophical, or theological topics. Young Brentano studied philosophy at Munich, Würzburg, and Berlin before completing his doctoral dissertation on Aristotle at the University of Tübingen in 1862. He then studied for the priesthood and was ordained at Würzburg in 1864. Returning to academics, he completed a highly praised habilitation thesis on Aristotelian psychology for the University of Würzburg in 1866, qualifying him to become a *Dozent*, or officially sanctioned lecturer there. In 1869 he wrote an influential but ultimately unsuccessful critique of the doctrine of papal infallibility, then being debated at Vatican Council I. When the church officially adopted that doctrine, Brentano resigned from the priesthood and left Würzburg, accepting a professorship at the University of Vienna in early 1874.

Brentano's arrival at Vienna coincided with the publication in 1874 of his most famous book, *Psychology from an Empirical Standpoint.* Appearing in the same year as Wundt's *Principles of Physiological Psychology,* this landmark work helped establish psychology as a distinct academic and scientific discipline. It presented what has become known as an "act psychology," based in part on the Aristotelian concept of "intentionality." Brentano argued that although the analytical methods of the physical sciences and scientific psychology are similar, their subject matters differ qualitatively. Physical scientists always study objects of some kind (stars, falling bodies, etc.), which are held immediately and directly in consciousness. Psychologists, by contrast, analyze experiences (Greek *empieria*) or mental acts that always "contain" or "intend" objects. The act of thinking, for example, must the always be about something that is its contained or intended object. Further, the "inner perception" of one's own mental acts is not immediate (as is the astronomer's direct observation of a star) but is inevitably retrospective to one degree or another. For example, when I think about a star, the star itself, pure and simple, is the object of my consciousness. If I turn my attention from astronomy to psychology and introspect, "I have been thinking about a star," the direct object of my thought is no longer something immediately present but rather my memory of the previous mental activity.

In *Psychology* and its 1911 elaboration, *The Classification of Mental Phenomena*, Brentano argued that there are just three different kinds of mental act. First and most fundamental are acts of "presentation" or "representation" (German *Vorstellung*)– the simple bringing of some object to conscious awareness. Second are acts of "judgment"—the attachment of varying degrees of belief or unbelief in the reality or truth of presented objects. And third are acts of "desire"—the assumption of attitudes of attraction or aversion to the presented objects. Acts or attitudes of desire may vary dramatically over time to the same object and thus override the simple effects of the laws of association. For example, one's associations to thoughts of food will vary tremendously depending on whether one is feeling hungry or nauseated. Brentano's insistence on the importance of temporally varying acts of desire lent his psychology a "dynamic" quality, enabling it to account for the ever-varying, motivated nature of thought; he was explicitly critical of purely associational psychologies, such as that of his friend John Stuart Mill, which he argued were highly limited in that respect.

In 1880, Brentano married, a breach of his priestly vow, which in Catholic Austria caused him to lose his title as professor and much of his salary. In 1895, he retired to Florence, Italy, as a private scholar. After Italy entered World War I, the pacifist Brentano moved to Zurich where he died on 17 March 1917. Never a prolific author, Brentano's importance derives largely from the numerous able students whom he influenced and inspired, and who in their varying ways disseminated and elaborated upon aspects of his thought. At Würzburg, for example, he taught and befriended the young Carl Stumpf (1848–1936), the future leader of the "Berlin School" of Gestalt psychology. At Vienna, his prominent students included Alexius Meinong (1853–

1920), Sigmund Freud (1856–1939), Christian von Ehrenfels (1859–1932), and Edmund Husserl (1859–1938). One modern context in which Brentano's thought has reemerged is the field of artificial intelligence, where the question has been debated as to whether or not purely mechanical processes can ever take on the capacity for intentionality or "aboutness" that he emphasized as the defining characteristic of all genuinely mental acts.

Bibliography

Brentano, F. (1995). *Psychology from an empirical standpoint.* O. Kraus & L. L. McAlister (Eds.). New York: Routledge. This edition includes translations of both the 1874 *Psychology* and its 1911 sequel, *The classification of mental acts.*

Fancher, R. E. (1977). Brentano's *Psychology from an empirical standpoint* and Freud's early metapsychology. *Journal of the History of the Behavioral Sciences 13*, 207–227. Discusses the influence of Brentano on one of his most famous students.

McAlister, L. L. (Ed.), (1976). *The philosophy of Brentano.* London: Duckworth. Reprints interpretations and appreciations of Brentano by his students Husserl and Stumpf, among others.

Rancurello, A. C. (1968). *A study of Franz Brentano: His psychological standpoint and his significance in the history of psychology.* New York: Academic Press.

Raymond E. Fancher

BRETT, GEORGE S. (1879–1944), British philosopher and psychologist. Brett graduated from Oxford University in 1902 with a master of arts degree. After a period spent as a professor of philosophy in the Indian Educational Service, Brett joined Trinity College of the university of Toronto in 1908. He rose through various positions to become full-time professor of philosophy in the university itself (1921) and later dean of the School of Graduate Studies (1932).

Brett's scholarly interests were broad, and he published widely in areas ranging from the history of psychology to Indian culture. However, most of his work can be characterized as that of an Oxford-trained philosopher who, after paying his professional dues with the *Philosophy of Gassendi* (London, 1908), applied the conceptual and historical insights afforded by this grounding to the history of science, especially to that most conceptually reflexive of subjects, psychology. Thus Brett's monumental and highly successful three-volume *History of Psychology* (1912–1921) explicitly equates the development of psychology with the development of philosophy. Although initially reflecting something of his early training in anthropology under E. B. Taylor at Oxford, this work demonstrates Brett's fundamental belief that psychology, from the pre-Socratic Greeks to Freud and the animal psychologists of the twentieth century, is the product (and beneficiary) of philosophy (with additional support for the thesis provided by Indian, Arabic, and Jewish writings on the soul).

In Brett's hands, ideas became the paramount driving force behind all progress in psychology, whether in cognition, psychophysiology, the emotions and the will, or morality and ethics. Moreover, although psychology can be loosely defined as "the science of the soul," its detailed operations are invariably determined by the prevailing historical context, thus yielding a highly tempting prospect, for the historically minded psychologist, of a subject for which one can make both relative and absolute conceptual claims. This tendency to see the present as little more than an extension of the distant past (an approach used with some historiographic delicacy in the *History of Psychology*) became a more strident and less convincing *leitmotif* in *Psychology, Ancient and Modern* (1928), Brett's last contribution of any significance to the history of psychology. Here he argued that much of modern psychology seems to have been anticipated by either Aristotle or Plato, the justification being that, as all scientific knowledge is cumulative, so early ideas necessarily tend to dictate the subsequent progress of the subject.

Clearly, the alternative, more empirically oriented and historically compact account of the history of psychology by E. G. Boring (*History of Experimental Psychology*, New York, 1929) can be viewed as a reaction to Brett's grand philosophical vision. Nevertheless, until very recently, most post–World War II historians of psychology followed the Brett line both historically and ideologically, albeit allotting proportionately more space to the rapidly burgeoning field of twentieth-century psychology. Finally, equally significant in Brett's *oeuvre* is his steadfast commitment to a historical method for understanding science, perhaps best illustrated by one of his last papers, which contextualized the discovery of the barometer in the seventeenth century within the science and culture of that period ("The Effect of the Discovery of the Barometer on Contemporary Thought," 1943).

Bibliography

Works by Brett

Brett, G. S. (1912–1921). *History of psychology* (Vols. 1–3). London: Allen & Unwin. This is the most influential of Brett's writings in the history of psychology. An abridged version with a supplement on twentieth-century theories in psychology was produced by the philosopher R. S. Peters in 1953, also published by Allen & Unwin.

Brett, G. S. (1928). *Psychology, ancient and modern*. New York: Longmans.

Brett, G. S. (1930). Assocationism and "act" psychology: A historical retrospect. In C. Murchison (Ed.), *Psychologies of 1930* (pp. 39–55). Worcester, MA.: Clark University Press.

Works about Brett

Brown, H. (1945–1946). George Sidney Brett. *Isis, 36,* 110–114. This obituary considers Brett's contributions to the history of science rather than to psychology but provides biographical material and personal reminiscences.

Gauvreau, M. (1988). Philosophy, psychology and history: George Sidney Brett and the quest for a social science at the University of Toronto 1910–1940. *Historical Papers-Communications Historiques, 45,* 209–236.

Irving, J. A. (1947). George Sidney Brett (1879–1944). *Psychological Review, 54,* 52–58. This obituary by a colleague at Toronto assesses Brett's work on the history of psychology.

A. D. Lovie and P. Lovie

BREUER, JOSEF (1842–1925), Austrian physician and physiologist. The founder of the "cathartic method," Josef Breuer was born in Vienna, Austria, the son of Leopold Breuer, a Jewish religion teacher and educator, and Bertha Semler, a lover of art and literature. He enrolled at the University of Vienna in 1858, where he first joined the faculty of philosophy for one year of general studies prior to initiating his education in medicine. As the Viennese medical school was in its heyday, Breuer had opportunity to study with the pathologist Carl Rokitansky (1804–1878), the diagnostician Josef Skoda (1805–1881), the anatomist Josef Hyrtl (1810–1894), the physiologist Ernst Brücke (1819–1892), and the internist Johann Oppolzer (1808–1871). He married Mathilde Altmann in 1868 and had five children.

Breuer first embarked on his clinical career in 1867, when he became assistant to Johann Oppolzer, who was then regarded as the leading Viennese specialist in internal medicine. His clinical practice included the treatment of internal diseases, as well as otorhinolaryngological, gynecological, and psychiatric cases. In 1871, following Oppolzer's unexpected death from a typhus epidemic, Breuer left the clinic and established himself as a medical practitioner. He quickly became recognized by the Viennese elite as a diagnostician, outstanding physician, and productive researcher.

Breuer conducted his first individual research program, a study of respiratory regulation, under the supervision of Ewald Hering (1834–1918). In it he elaborated the idea that respiration rests on an automatic control mechanism and successfully showed the existence of a regulatory reflexive system, underscoring the notion of biological feedback. This mechanism is still known today as the Hering-Breuer reflex (1868). Early in his career, he discovered the function of the semicircular canals in the labyrinth of the ear (1873–1874), delineating the aural labyrinth as a site in balance regulation, and the involvement of the vestibular apparatus in sensing static movement. This work earned him the position of *Dozent* in internal medicine and brought him under the tutelage of Ernst Brücke, the father of Austrian physiology. Further work in this area culminated in the Mach-Breuer endolymph flow theory (1874), a credit he shares with Ernst Mach (1838–1916), who reached similar conclusions while working independently.

Physiology spanned Breuer's entire life, whereas his collaboration with Sigmund Freud (1856–1939) was limited to the years 1882–1895. Nonetheless, Breuer figures most significantly in the history of psychoanalysis. Breuer became acquainted with Freud in 1877 at the Physiological Institute, beginning a friendship in which Breuer was at first a financial patron and adviser and later a collaborator in the publishing of the book *Studies on Hysteria* in 1895. It was the famous case of "Anna O." (Bertha Pappenheim), a patient of Breuer's, that led to the development of the "talking cure." This method, originally termed *cathartic* in 1893, involved the concept of abreaction of affects, whereby neurotic symptoms (somatic conversions) were removed individually by being traced to earlier traumatic experiences that had remained repressed and out of conscious awareness. The physical symptoms were thus viewed as substitutes for the conscious recollection of painful memories. This original formulation helped lead Freud to his later technique of free association, recognizing the importance of fantasy and associations.

In explaining how affect becomes "strangulated" in hysterical patients, Breuer and Freud argued for three types of hysteria. The first, retention hysteria, was viewed as stemming from external circumstances (such as combat) that conspire to prevent the expression of affect. The second, Breuer's notion of hypnoid hysteria, viewed some individuals as more prone to hypnoidlike states due to monotonous activities, thus potentially explaining why women were more prone to these states than men. More important, it implied the notion of a pathogenic idea, a strictly mental entity (memory) capable of exerting a direct influence on the physical processes of the body. The third type, defense hysteria, was ultimately the only one to be retained in Freud's work and elaborated in his theory of defense mechanisms and the sexual etiology of neurosis. The disagreement between Breuer and Freud regarding the etiology of hysteria ultimately led to the final dissolution of their friendship and partnership in 1896. Although Breuer was not averse to recognizing the role of sexuality in the genesis of neurosis, he disagreed with Freud's early notion that hysteria was caused by childhood seduction.

The notion of the biological regulation of body functions in the service of meaningful and necessary capacities to the organism as a whole is central to Breuer's work. For him, structure and function were inseparable. Breuer's dynamic views of biological regulating mechanisms combined with his philosophical background and medical training translated easily to his work on hysteria and led him to the development of the cathartic method, or "talking cure." Breuer significantly advanced psychoanalytic theory and practice by insuring that greater prominence was given to psychogenic rather than hereditary components in hysteria. He also underscored the importance of psychic trauma caused by the conflation of an incompatible thought and affect and, most important, offered the possibility of effecting a cure by tracing the pathogenic idea back to consciousness and releasing the isolated affect (catharsis). Despite their differences, Freud secured Breuer's place in psychoanalytic history by representing him as the founder of psychoanalysis in his famous lectures delivered at Clark University in 1909.

Bibliography

Bernfield, S. (1944). Freud's earliest theories and the school of Helmholtz. *Psychoanalytic Quarterly, 13,* 341–362.

Breuer, J. (1953). Autobiographical sketch. *International Journal of Psycho-Analysis, 34,* 64–67.

Cranefield, P. F. (1958). Josef Breuer's evaluation of his contribution to psycho-analysis. *International Journal of Psycho-Analysis, 39,* 319–322.

Ellenberger, H. F. (1972). The story of Anna O. A critical review with new data. *Journal of the History of the Behavioral Sciences, 8,* 267–279.

Freud, S. (1961). Josef Breuer. In J. Strachey (Ed. and Trans.), *The standard edition of the complete psychological works of Sigmund Freud* (Vol. 19, pp. 279–208). London: Hogarth Press. (Original work published 1925)

Hirschmuller, A. (1989). *The life and work of Josef Breuer: Physiology and psychoanalysis.* New York: New York University Press.

Muller, J. P. (1992). A re-reading of "Studies on Hysteria": The Freud-Breuer break revisited. *Psychoanalytic Psychology, 9,* 129–156.

Velleda C. Ceccoli

BRIDGMAN, PERCY WILLIAMS (1882–1961), American physicist. Bridgman's lifelong experimental work at Harvard in the field of high pressure physics earned him the Nobel Prize in 1946. In psychology, he is credited with the original enunciation of the methodological precept that became known as operationism or, alternatively, operationalism. The seminal statement appeared in his book *The Logic of Modern Physics*, in which he stated, "In general we mean by any concept nothing more than a set of operations; the concept is synonymous with the corresponding set of operations" (1927, p. 5).

The basis of what Bridgman called his operational method can be found in a subtle misreading of Einstein's physical insights as expressed in his 1905 paper on special relativity, together with Bridgman's interpretation of dimensional analysis, a technique used by physicists to infer the form of a physical equation from assumptions made about how its elementary terms must combine. For Bridgman, an operation referred primarily to the physical act of measurement and, as an afterthought, to a mathematical procedure. Bridgman intended his operational method, called operational analysis, to be used to purify physics of any unsuspected metaphysical ideas that might be hidden within its corpus. Upon operational analysis, any concept that did not correspond to a measurement was to be declared meaningless.

Bridgman's operational method was brought to the attention of Harvard psychologists by the logical positivist philosopher Herbert Feigl, who had come to Harvard to study scientific philosophy under Bridgman. While the introductory papers on what became transformed from Bridgman's operational analysis to the psychologists' operationism were published by the psychology doctoral student S. S. Stevens, it was Stevens's senior mentor, Harvard psychologist E. G. Boring, whose enthusiasm and influence on Stevens provided the momentum that supported the operational movement among behavioral psychologists in America during the 1930s. In margin notes to a draft of Stevens's first paper, Boring advised him to say that "operationism consists simply in referring any concept for definition to the operations by which knowledge of the thing in question is had." By means of the operational definition, psychologists believed that they could establish the scientific objectivity of psychological concepts.

However, without entirely repudiating operationalism, critics soon began to discover in operationalism the classical difficulties inherent in every empiricist philosophy of science. Given that experience is by its very nature subjective, by what pathway does it become objective and public? How do you and I know we are observing the same thing? Furthermore, since experience is individual and unique, how is it possible to form general categories? Strictly speaking, each operation should refer to a unique entity that has its own name. Finally, an operational definition is circular; there is no outside standard to verify that a measurement measures what it is thought to measure.

Although psychologists and philosophers struggled with these difficulties, Bridgman himself came to accept the idea that all knowledge, including scientific knowledge, is private, existing only in the mind of the understanding knower. He also asserted that there is no method that can uniquely be called the scientific method.

Bibliography

Boring, E. G. (1950). *A history of experimental psychology* (2nd ed.). New York: Appleton-Century-Crofts.

Bridgman, P. W. (1927). *The logic of modern physics.* New York: Macmillan.

Bridgman, P. W. (1961). The present state of operationalism. In P. G. Frank (Ed.), *The validation of scientific theories* (pp. 74–80). New York: Collier Books.

Stevens, S. S. (1939). Psychology and the science of science. *Psychological Bulletin, 36,* 221–262.

Symposium on Operationism. (1945). *Psychological Review, 52,* 241–294. Organized by E. G. Boring. Papers by Boring, Bridgman, Israel, Pratt, Feigl, and Skinner.

Walter, M. L. (1990). *Science and cultural crisis: An intellectual biography of Percy Williams Bridgman (1882–1961).* Stanford, CA: Stanford University Press.

Maila L. Walter

BRIEF THERAPY. Since various approaches to psychotherapy define brevity differently, it is difficult to identify any single duration of treatment as "brief." (See Koss & Shiang, 1994, and Steenbarger, 1992, for overviews.) For instance, there are several short-term models of psychodynamic therapy that can extend for twenty sessions or more. Alternatively, in managed care systems, it is not unusual to find capitation or case rate formulas based upon a five-session average duration of solution-focused or behavioral treatment.

It is perhaps best to think of brief therapy as any helping modality that actively addresses the issue of time in treatment planning. Such therapy is time effective by design rather than default, focusing change efforts and maximizing the use of time between sessions. It is thus possible to conduct time-effective therapy with populations experiencing severe and chronic disorders, even though the treatment might not fit all definitions of brevity. This is quite different from "time-limited" approaches to care, which administratively define a fixed number of sessions for all clients and attempt to fit treatment into these. In the presentation below, we will be focusing on time effectiveness as a hallmark of brevity: purposeful planning to address the identified needs of patients in as efficient a manner as possible.

A Brief History of Brief Therapy

It is often overlooked that Freud's initial case studies described short-term treatments, in which insight and abreaction led to rapid cures. As psychoanalysis became a method for studying mind as well as a therapeutic modality, and as it wrestled with the intransigence of character pathologies, its duration expanded meaningfully. While some in the early movement pursued treatment of shorter duration—most notably Rank—the topic of brevity did not take center stage until the publication of Alexander and French's (1946) volume on psychoanalytic therapy. That then controversial and now surprisingly contemporary text proposed that the duration of therapy could be shortened by deemphasizing insight as a treatment goal and focusing instead upon the achievement of powerful "corrective emotional experiences." Subsequent theory in short-term dynamic psychotherapy, including the efforts of Luborsky, Strupp, Sifneos, and Davanloo, have built upon this framework, emphasizing techniques for achieving an interpersonal treatment focus and providing powerful relationship experiences through the therapeutic alliance.

With the ascendance of behavioral treatments in the 1950s and cognitive restructuring therapies in the 1960s and 1970s, treatment became less exploratory and more closely grounded in learning methodologies. This framework lent itself to active, skills-based approaches to helping and short-term care (see Barlow, 1993, for an overview of cognitive-behavioral treatments). Indeed, most behavioral therapies reported in the literature were completed within seven sessions, and most cognitive treatments fell within a 15-session parameter. In both cases, brevity could be achieved by defining a narrow treatment focus and relying upon active in-session and out-of-session rehearsals for facilitating change.

The 1950s and 1960s work of Milton Erickson, combined with the initial family systems research into schizophrenia conducted by Gregory Bateson and colleagues, inspired a third strain of short-term psychotherapy. These strategic-systems approaches tended to view presenting complaints as artifacts of problem-solving behavior that unwittingly reinforce maladaptive patterns. The goal of helping, therefore, was less to cure illness than to interrupt self-reinforcing problem patterns and allow individuals to establish new action modes. This has most recently found expression in solution-focused approaches to treatment, which search for exceptions to presenting problem patterns and encourage the conscious enactment of these pattern-breaking, exceptional behaviors. As with the cognitive-

behavioral approaches, the focus upon directive action, rather than exploration and insight, contributes to the time effectiveness of the strategic modalities.

The Common Ingredients of Brief Therapy

A number of authors have pointed to underlying similarities among the short-term approaches to psychotherapy. These include the maintenance of a treatment focus, flexible strategies aimed at heightening client involvement in treatment, and sensitivity to client strengths as well as deficits.

Unlike therapies that seek a restructuring of basic character structure, time-effective treatments focus upon specific problem patterns that interfere with life functioning. Such work is typically goal oriented, undertaken with the understanding that broader change can occur through normal developmental processes once focal stumbling blocks are overcome. Client and therapist share responsibility for maintaining this focus, giving many of the briefer therapies an instrumental, as opposed to a purely exploratory, quality. Of particular help in maintaining the focus are homework assignments and tasks to be performed between sessions. This work maximizes the use of time during the change process, allowing for a concentrated rehearsal and application of skills and insights.

Another characteristic ingredient of brief therapy is the effort to maximize client involvement in change efforts. The aforementioned homework assignments are one example of such involvement. Within sessions as well, however, time-effective therapists employ strategies that will enhance client experiencing and openness to change. These include such interventions as the use of metaphor, guided imagery, role playing, direct confrontation, exposure to feared stimuli, and prescribed tasks. The planned employment of such strategies helps to account for the high level of therapist activity in the briefer therapies. Rather than serve as a nondirective, reflective "blank screen," time-effective therapists typically assume a hands on posture in catalyzing change.

This level of activity also requires that short term therapists work flexibly. Unlike longer term modalities, which place emphasis upon the working through of client resistances, time-effective treatments seek to accelerate the pace of change efforts by avoiding such resistances altogether. This requires a nimbleness on the part of the therapist, who may have to quickly abandon one unfruitful line of approach for one that is more productive. This flexibility extends to the selection of treatment goals, as well. Rather than attempt changes that the client may not have yet contemplated, the time-effective therapist will assess the client's readiness for change, focus limited treatment resources on those problems most likely to prove open to change efforts, and advance the readiness for change with respect to other issues.

Yet another common ingredient to the short-term therapies is an emphasis of client strengths and explicit attempts to build on these as a way of addressing focal concerns. Clients are seen as possessing considerable adaptive and coping abilities in spheres of their lives that are relatively symptom free. Many times these adaptive capacities can be mobilized within and between sessions to help clients modify problematic patterns. In systematic desensitization, for example, the client begins by mastering relatively nonthreatening stressful situations and gradually applying coping skills to situations of increasing threat. Solution-focused therapies, alternatively, identify exceptions to problem patterns that reveal adaptive capacities and help clients recruit these into problematic life areas.

An especially noteworthy aspect of brief therapy technique is the rapid introduction of novelty by therapists, including the active reframing of presenting problems and introduction of new insights, skills, and experiences. Very often this novelty is introduced in the context of enhanced states of client experiencing, during periods of imagery induction, introspection, role playing, task fulfillment, and/or confrontation. It would appear that the active, focused introduction of new patterns in the context of heightened client experiencing is a major facilitative ingredient of the short-term therapies.

Is Brief Therapy Effective?

Reviews of the effectiveness of brief therapy point out that the vast majority of studies in the outcome literature have investigated treatments of short duration, making the outcome literature a virtual testimonial to the effectiveness of brief work.

Studies that have examined the outcome of therapy as a function of duration (see Steenbarger, 1994, for an overview) suggest that much of the observed changes that occur in therapy tend to occur relatively early in treatment, with positive, but diminishing returns thereafter. It appears, however, that this relationship is highly sensitive to the severity of the patient's presenting complaints. Hence, while clients with situational anxiety disorders may achieve the bulk of their gains within five sessions, those with more severe and chronic concerns—such as psychotic disorders or borderline conditions—continue to achieve (albeit comparatively modest) gains beyond session 20.

There are also indications that the effectiveness of brief treatments may be partly dependent upon the outcome measures employed. Measures of emotional well-being and psychiatric symptomotology appear to be most sensitive to change efforts, and are thus likely to show change after a short number of visits. More trait-based measures and those emphasizing psychosocial functional status are less sensitive to the remoralization effects of meeting with a helping professional and thus may yield more conservative estimates of outcome efficacy.

Finally, the issue of the effectiveness of brief therapy is complicated by the issue of relapse. It is not uncommon for patients to show changes on symptom-based measures within several sessions. Whether those changes persist beyond treatment is another matter. Interestingly, estimates for relapse among patients with anxiety disorders tend to be lower than those among patients with major depression, suggesting that the chronicity of the disorder being treated may be a factor in the long-term effectiveness of treatment.

Overall, there is a sense among practitioners that highly abbreviated treatments are most appropriate to situational concerns of relatively low severity and less appropriate to long-standing disorders that significantly impair multiple life domains. Research further suggests that client readiness to change—the ability to identify a focal concern requiring immediate action—may be an important mediator of whether or not treatment can be brief. Clients who have vaguely articulated concerns and/or a lack of clarity regarding the need to change may require a greater number of sessions to reach the point of taking corrective action. Similarly, patients with a favorable interpersonal history may be able to form a ready alliance with a therapist, greatly speeding the change process. Those with histories of interpersonal trauma may require lengthy periods of security- and trust-building, extending the course of treatment.

The Future of Brief Therapy

The heightened demand for cost effectiveness on the part of insurers and purchasers of health benefits guarantees that therapists will continue to experience mandates for time-effectiveness. Even when clients are not appropriate for classically brief therapies, ongoing, time-unlimited individual psychotherapy may not be the preferred alternative. Rather, clinicians may engage clients in a modular series of intermittent brief therapies, addressing focal components of more general syndromes. This is most clearly illustrated in the work of Linehan (1993), whose cognitive-behavioral work with borderline personality disorder replaces time-unlimited treatment with sequential brief therapies.

Also, given the favorable outcomes observed among short-term group therapies, it is likely that group work will continue to accompany individual services for populations needing greater degrees of treatment intensity and structure. This is especially evident among intensive outpatient and psychosocial rehabilitation programs designed to keep patients out of life-interrupting, expensive inpatient settings. For the most vulnerable clients in the public sector, the blending of time-effective individual and group therapeutic modalities—and the linkage of these services to ongoing vocational, residential, juvenile justice, and case management interventions—are emerging as important tools in creating cost-effective, integrated systems of service delivery.

Bibliography

Alexander, F., & French, T. M. (1946). *Psychoanalytic therapy: Principles and applications.* Lincoln: University of Nebraska Press. First introduced the concept of "corrective emotional experiences" in time-sensitive treatment.

Barlow, D. H. (Ed.). (1993). *Clinical handbook of psychological disorders: A step-by-step treatment manual* (2nd ed.). New York: Guilford Press. Excellent overview of empirically validated therapies and their applications.

Budman, S. H., & Gurman, A. S. (1988). *Theory and practice of brief therapy.* New York: Guilford Press. Classic work on time effective treatment.

Budman, S. H., & Steenbarger, B. N. (1997). *The essential guide to group practice in mental health: Clinical, legal, and financial fundamentals.* New York: Guilford Press. Comprehensive overview of managed care issues and new, time-effective delivery systems.

Budman, S. H., Hoyt, M. F., & Friedman, S. (Eds.). (1992). *The first session in brief therapy.* New York: Guilford Press. Interesting comparisons among brief therapy models.

Crits-Christoph, P., & Barber, J. P. (Eds.). (1991). *Handbook of short-term dynamic psychotherapy.* New York: Basic Books. Excellent overview of brief dynamic models of psychotherapy.

Cummings, N. A., & Sayama, M. (1995). *Focused psychotherapy: A casebook of brief intermittent psychotherapy throughout the life cycle.* New York: Brunner/Mazel. Comprehensive presentation of sequential brief treatments as an alternative to time-unlimited therapies.

Koss, M. P., & Shiang, J. (1994). Research on brief psychotherapy. In A. E. Bergin & S. L. Garfield (Eds.), *Handbook of psychotherapy and behavior change* (4th ed., pp. 664–700). New York: Wiley. Comprehensive overview of brief therapy issues and research.

Linehan, M. M. (1993). *Cognitive-behavioral treatment of borderline personality disorder.* New York: Guilford Press. Innovative, time-sensitive model of treatment for a difficult population.

Roth, A., & Fonagy, P. (1996). *What works for whom? A critical review of psychotherapy research.* New York: Guilford Press. Stimulating integration of outcome research.

Steenbarger, B. N. (1992). Toward science-practice integration in brief counseling and therapy. *Counseling Psychologist, 20,* 403–450. Comprehensive overview of research and practice in brief therapy.

Steenbarger, B. N. (1994). Duration and outcome in psychotherapy: An integrative review. *Professional Psychology: Research and Practice, 25,* 111–119. Thorough survey of factors mediating the relationship between the duration of therapy and its effectiveness.

Wells, R. A., & Giannetti, V. J. (Eds.) (1990). *Handbook of the brief psychotherapies.* New York: Plenum. Thorough overview of models and applications of brief therapy.

Brett N. Steenbarger and Simon H. Budman

BRITISH ASSOCIATION FOR THE ADVANCEMENT OF SCIENCE. Founded in 1831, the British Association for the Advancement of Science (BA) held its first meeting in York. Sir David Brewster, chief founder of the BA, stated in a letter to the secretary of the York Philosophical Society that "the principal objects of the society would be to make the cultivators of science acquainted with each other; to stimulate one another to new exertions; to bring the objects of science before the public eye, and to take measures for advancing its interests and accelerating its progress." The aims of the BA are still to promote the public understanding of science by raising awareness and understanding of the importance of science by enhancing the contribution of science to cultural, economic, and social life and by improving the communication of science to the general public and the scientific community.

The BA encompasses all branches and aspects of science, encouraging and developing links between scientists, technologists, and nonscientists of all ages. Sixteen sections represent different fields of science, social science, engineering, and medicine and provide access to national and international professional communities in these fields. There are also a number of regional groups, a network of science clubs for young people, and national and international networks for the advancement and understanding of science. The work of a section includes the preparation of a program of activities for the annual meeting of the BA. Now known as the Annual Festival of Science, this meeting is the primary scientific meeting of its type in the United Kingdom and has been held every year since 1831 excepting some war years. The officers of each section committee include a president, who is appointed each year, and a recorder, who is responsible for the activities of the section, including the program at the Annual Festival of Science and other events such as the National Week of Science, Engineering, and Technology.

The psychology section, formerly known as Section J in the rather quaint early terminology of the BA, was founded in 1921, although it was 15 years earlier that psychology first made an impact on the BA audience. Sir Edwin Ray Lankester, then director of the Natural

History Museum and president of the BA in 1906, included a section on psychology in his presidential address. He said:

> I have given a special heading to this subject because its emergence as a definite line of experimental research seems to me one of the most important features in the progress of science in the past quarter of a century. . . . The science is still in an early phase—that of the collection of accurate observations and measurements—awaiting the development of great guiding hypotheses and theories. But much has been done. (Lankester, 1906)

A period followed in which psychology was a subsection of the physiology section, since subsumed by the medical sciences and biological sciences sections. A separate psychology section was eventually established in 1921, with C. Lloyd Morgan as president, Charles S. Myers, W. H. R. Rivers, George M. Robertson, and James Seth as vice-presidents, and Cyril Burt as recorder. Lloyd Morgan, who was also the first person to be elected to a Fellowship of the Royal Society for psychological work, addressed the Edinburgh meeting that year on the topic of consciousness and unconsciousness. Rivers was due to be the next president, but, sadly, he died three months before the meeting. Charles S. Myers took his place and presented an appreciation of the work of Rivers in his address. The early presidents included the major figures in the development of psychology in Britain in the first half of the 1900s: Cyril Burt, William McDougall, Charles Spearman, James Drever, William Brown, T. H. Pear, and Frederic C. Bartlett. Postwar presidents have included Hans J. Eysenck, Donald Broadbent, Lawrence Weiskrantz, Richard Gregory, and Alan Baddeley. Notable foreign contributors to BA meetings include B. F. Skinner and George A. Miller. It was Broadbent, in fact, who invited Skinner to speak to the BA. He has stated that he disagreed with what Skinner actually said but wanted him to say it. Miller presented a Granada Lecture (one of a series of BA special lectures) in 1964 on computers, communication, and cognition. Each year at the annual festival, around 25 prominent psychologists, including academic researchers and practitioners, present high-quality and accessible papers to a general audience, as well as to a much wider audience through the media.

It is probably fair to say that in the mid-1900s the activities of the psychology section were seen by the professional psychological societies in the United Kingdom as popularizing and, sometimes, trivializing psychology. However, for the past 30 years a very healthy and fruitful relationship has existed between the BA and the British Psychological Society (BPS). Closer links have been developed, with the BPS sponsoring a special lecture for young people each year.

The BA has provided a forum for debate and the presentation of new and exciting developments in psychology, as well as the promotion of research. The BA first awarded grants for primarily psychological topics in 1909–1911 for research on mental and muscular fatigue, an enduring research topic in British psychology in the first part of the 1900s; in 1917 it awarded grants for an influential program of work on psychological war research. The grant was for only £10 but covered work on mental tests of industrial fatigue, alcoholism, evidence and rumor, the efficacy of thrift posters, and other issues. The activities of the psychology section have played a major role in gaining prominence and recognition for the discipline among the scientific community.

For many years the BA published *The Advancement of Science*, which included details of many of the influential presentations at the annual meetings. It now produces *Science and Public Affairs*, a quarterly magazine published by the BA and the Royal Society, and *SCAN*, a monthly science awareness newsletter.

[*Many of the people mentioned in this article are the subjects of independent biographical entries.*]

Bibliography

Harrison, W. H. (1881). *The founding of the British Association for the Advancement of Science.* London: Harrison.

Hearnshaw, L. S. (1964). *A short history of British psychology, 1840–1940.* London: Methuen. Provides a thorough and accessible history of the early development of psychology in Britain.

Howarth, O. J. R. (1922). *The British Association for the Advancement of Science: A retrospect, 1831–1921.* London: British Association.

Andrew J. Tattersall

BRITISH PSYCHOLOGICAL SOCIETY. In 1901, ten people met at University College at the University of London to form a psychological society. A library was started, and scientific meetings began to be held. From these small beginnings, the British Psychological Society (BPS) grew into what it is today, a thriving scientific society but also a professional body concerned with the standards of training, practice, and conduct of psychologists in the United Kingdom.

Purpose

In 1941, the BPS was registered under the United Kingdom Companies Act, and in 1965 it was granted a Royal Charter. Within the United Kingdom, Royal Charters are granted sparingly to organizations that are constituted to act in the public interest. Certain privileges are conferred on chartered bodies. For instance, it is through their Royal Charters that the universities in the United Kingdom are authorized to grant degrees. In 1987, amendments to the Royal Charter were agreed upon by the government that authorized the BPS to maintain a public Register of Chartered Psychologists. In essence, chartered psychologists are those members of the BPS who are judged by the Council "to have reached a standard sufficient for professional practice in psychology without supervision." Training to become a chartered psychologist takes at least 6 years.

By its Royal Charter of 1965, the BPS is charged with national responsibility for the development, promotion, and application of psychology for the public good. This mission is delivered through three major aims: encouraging the development of psychology as a scientific discipline; raising standards of training and practice in the application of psychology; and raising public awareness of psychology and increasing the influence of psychological practice in society, industry, and the economy. In recent years the BPS has made a major effort to promote psychology and the services that psychologists offer. The BPS is increasingly effective at influencing both the public at large and decision makers in British society. On average, the society's press office receives over 40 inquiries each day from journalists. Special presentations are prepared for Members of Parliament. The BPS is consulted by government departments on its plans for legislation on about sixty different issues each year.

The Members

The BPS is the only national psychology association in the United Kingdom that all psychology graduates in the country may join if they wish. Some graduate members are taking postgraduate degree courses aiming to qualify as chartered psychologists. Others are primarily interested in belonging to the BPS as a scientific "club" that publishes several prestigious scientific journals, holds several meetings and conferences, and owns a major research library. By the end of December 1996, the BPS had 21,239 full members with at least bachelor's degrees or equivalent qualifications in psychology, of which 8,459 were chartered psychologists, a designation for which postgraduate qualifications are also required. A further 6,369 contributors were also shown on the society's list of members. These include student members; affiliates, a category of membership open to anyone interested in participating in the society's affairs who does not have formal qualifications in psychology; and affiliates from overseas.

Publications

As a learned society, the BPS now publishes several scholarly journals of international repute: *The British Journal of Psychology, The British Journal of Medical Psychology, The British Journal of Mathematical and Statistical Psychology, The British Journal of Social Psychology, The British Journal of Clinical Psychology, The British Journal of Occupational and Organizational Psychology, The British Journal of Developmental Psychology, The British Journal of Educational Psychology, The British Journal of Health Psychology,* and *Legal and Criminological Psychology. The Psychologist: The Bulletin of the British Psychological Society* is the house organ, which is sent monthly to all members, accompanied by the *Appointments Memorandum* broadsheet in which job vacancies for psychologists in the United Kingdom are advertised. The BPS also publishes books in psychology. It has more than 100 titles in its catalog of publications and has sold more than three quarters of a million books worldwide.

Conferences

Each year the BPS holds a four-day conference at which several hundred papers are presented in up to seven parallel sessions. A second nonresidential two-day conference is held each year in London just before Christmas. At these conferences, papers and symposia are devoted to a wide range of topics in psychology, from specialist academic papers to matters of practical concern to professional applied psychologists. Several plenary session lectures for honored invited speakers are given at these conferences, including the presidential address.

Academic Specialties

Academic specialties within psychology are represented by 12 separate sections, specializing in such areas as cognitive psychology, social psychology, psychobiology, and mathematical, statistical and computing psychology. Nearly all sections hold annual conferences, seminars, and workshops, sometimes in conjunction with the annual conference of the BPS. The BPS has six branches covering those geographical areas of the United Kingdom in which there is demand for a branch. The branches in Wales, Northern Ireland, and Scotland run further separate programs of conferences and other events, some of which are planned to appeal to an international audience. The BPS owns an extensive collection of psychological journals, and these periodicals, most of which are in the English language, are housed with those of the University of London.

Professional Psychology and Divisions

The BPS has divisions representing the interests of professional psychologists working in the fields of clinical, counseling, educational, occupational, forensic, health, neuropsychology, and teaching and research. Most divisions publish regular newsletters for their members and occasional papers on current issues in professional applied psychology. The divisions all appoint training committees, which are responsible for reviewing and recommending approval of postgraduate degree courses for recognition by the BPS as appropriate training in their fields of applied professional psychology. Approval of the degree courses is important, as the major employers of psychologists in the United Kingdom will not employ psychologists who do not have a society-approved qualification. Since 1987, the same qualifications have led to registration as a chartered psychologist.

The BPS has a further category, special groups, for psychologists who are providing a service, tuition, or advice in areas in which, unlike the divisions, there may not necessarily be specific work qualifications. Currently, there is one special group for psychologists and social services.

The BPS is an examining body offering its own qualifying examination for membership. It also offers postgraduate qualifications that give access to registration as a chartered psychologist in the areas of clinical psychology, educational psychology, the applied psychology of teaching for lecturers and teachers of psychology, and counseling psychology. A postgraduate certificate in occupational psychology is also offered. Within the United Kingdom, it is usual for chartered professional bodies, as an alternative to the universities, to examine candidates who are to enter practice in a professional field as "chartered" members of the profession.

Further information is available from the British Psychological Society in Leicester, England, or at http://www.bps.org.uk.

[*See also* England.]

Colin V. Newman

BROADBENT, DONALD E. (1926–1993), British experimental psychologist. Broadbent's work on attention and memory in the 1950s contributed significantly to the rise of the cognitive movement. He was one of the first theorists to view the human organism as an information processor. That insight led him to bring a number of concepts from communications engineering and mathematical decision theory to bear on problems of perception, attention, and learning. His most influential publication was his 1958 book *Perception and Communication*, in which he laid out his ideas on the structure of the cognitive system. To capture the observation that people are consciously aware of only a limited amount of information at any given time, Broadbent proposed that the structural correlate of awareness was a limited-capacity channel, dealing with bits of information in the information-theory sense. This central channel was preceded by a selective filter that could be tuned to one of many competing input channels: a particular voice, for example, or a page of text. Unattended information was held briefly in an appropriate sensory memory store preceding the filter, but this information decayed rapidly and was lost unless it was selected in time. Finally, the central channel interacted quickly and easily with long-term memory, a relatively permanent store of knowledge and contingencies. This model immediately suggested a program of experiments, and the experimental results influenced Broadbent and other researchers to modify and improve his theoretical proposals of 1958.

Broadbent's 1958 model placed selective attention early in the flow of information through the organism; the filter was tuned to one channel or another in an all-or-none manner. He was forced to change this aspect, however, in response to the finding that a semantically relevant or highly meaningful stimulus on an unattended channel (the person's own name, for example) was fully processed and consciously perceived. His revised ideas on the interplay of social, emotional, and cognitive factors, and their effects on aspects of human performance were published in *Decision and Stress*, published in 1971. Now the early selection device of filtering was modulated by a further top-down process in which currently relevant categorical representations could be activated (and thus perceived) by sensory "evidence," even if the evidence was attenuated by its arrival on an unattended channel. Broadbent's theoretical and empirical work was also presented in two other books, *Behaviour* (1961) and *In Defence of Empirical Psychology* (1973), and in over 200 journal articles.

Broadbent originally developed his model as a way of integrating his theoretical ideas about mind with very practical concerns stemming from engineering and other real-life situations. He was born in 1926, grew up in Wales, and was educated at Winchester College, an English public school. He served in the Royal Air Force from 1944 to 1947, and during that time made the observation that communication difficulties were often caused by inefficiencies of attention, perception, and memory, rather than by failures of hearing or technical equipment. Broadbent's interests thus turned from engineering to psychology, and on leaving the Air Force he studied psychology at Cambridge University under Sir Frederic Bartlett. After graduating in 1949 he joined the Medical Research Council's Applied Psychology Unit in Cambridge where he remained for 25 years, serving as director from 1958 to 1974. In that capacity he was a major influence on the development of theoretical and applied cognitive psychology in Britain, Europe, and internationally. His 1958 model was an important precursor of the information-flow theories of the 1960s, yet he continually stressed the additional need for societal relevance in research. His emphasis on the useful interplay between theory and practice influenced a generation of experimental psychologists and contributed to the lasting value of his work. In 1974 Broadbent moved to the University of Oxford to concentrate on his own research. With his wife Margaret and a series of students and colleagues, he continued to study the problems that interested him: the effects of stress on performance and decision making; mechanisms of perception, attention, and memory; and the role of social factors in affecting workplace performance.

Apart from his major contributions to theoretical and empirical work in cognitive and engineering psychology, Donald Broadbent was influential in two other ways. First, he gave his time generously to the development of psychology as a science by serving on a multitude of committees and advisory bodies; and second, his commitment as a scientist and as a member of society served to make him a commendable role model for young researchers. His achievements were honored in many ways: He was elected as a Fellow of the Royal Society in 1968, and as a Foreign Associate of the U.S. National Academy of Sciences in 1971, and he received the Distinguished Scientific Contribution Award of the American Psychological Association in 1975. After a short retirement in Oxford, he died on 10 April 1993.

Bibliography

Works by Broadbent

Broadbent, D. E. (1958). *Perception and communication.* London: Pergamon Press.

Broadbent, D. E. (1961). *Behaviour.* London: Eyre & Spottiswoode.

Broadbent, D. E. (1971). *Decision and stress.* London: Academic Press. Summarizes the evidence on attention, perception, memory, stress, and decision making that led Broadbent to revise his 1958 theory.

Broadbent, D. E. (1973). *In defence of empirical psychology.* London: Methuen. Contains the 1971 William James Lectures given at Harvard by Broadbent. The essays emphasize his approach to the study of mind and human performance.

Works about Broadbent

Baddeley, A. D., & Weiskrantz, L. (Eds.). (1993). *Attention: Selection, awareness, and control. A tribute to Donald Broadbent.* Oxford, England: Clarendon Press. An excellent set of chapters on topics relating to Broadbent's ideas by his former students and colleagues.

Craik, F. I. M., & Baddeley, A. D. (1995). Donald E. Broadbent (1926–1993). *American Psychologist, 50,* 302–303. An obituary notice giving further details of Broadbent's life and ideas.

Fergus I. M. Craik

BROCA, PAUL (1824–1880), best remembered for his pioneering research on speech and cortical localization of function, was born in Sainte-Foy-la-Grande, a town east of Bordeaux. As noted by his biographer, Francis Schiller (1979), Broca attended medical school in Paris, graduated in 1848, and remained in the French capital for the rest of his life.

Broca, a Protestant in Catholic France, kept his mind open to different ideas and gave careful consideration to all sides of an issue before voicing his opinion. He was highly respected for his intellect and his sincerity, and his contributions spanned an impressive array of disciplines, including neurology, neuroanatomy, comparative anatomy, human evolution, pathology, statistics, oncology, and therapeutics. He published more than 500 scientific articles, founded the Parisian Société d' Anthropologie, and was instrumental in merging laboratory science with medicine.

Broca began his distinguished scientific career by using the microscope to show that cancer cells can be spread through the blood. He also studied muscular dystrophy and rickets. He became much better known, however, in 1861, when he openly supported the cortical localizationist movement. Prior to this year, most "respectable" scientists had steered away from the notion that different parts of the cerebral cortex could serve different functions. These individuals looked upon cortical localization as no more than phrenology and a throwback to the discredited ideas of Franz Joseph Gall. Nevertheless, the situation had changed since the opening decades of the nineteenth century, and the promoters of the "new" localizationist movement, notably J. B. Bouillaud and S. Aubertin, were now guided by neurological case studies, not cranial features.

Broca became convinced that Bouillaud and Aubertin were right about localization after he examined a dying man by the name of Leborgne in his surgical ward at the Bicêtre. This patient, who later became known as "Tan" because this was one of the few sounds he uttered, had lost his ability to speak voluntarily. In his famous report of 1861 in the *Bulletin de la Société Anatomique* (Paris), Broca took great care in identifying Leborgne's brain damage and deficits. He associated Tan's speech impairment (motor aphasia, or Broca's aphasia) with the third frontal convolution of the cerebral cortex.

Later in the same year, Broca presented another case study to support his contention that fluent speech is dependent upon the third frontal convolution. This report, on a man named Lelong, further established him as the leader of the cortical localizationist movement.

In 1865, Broca went a giant step further by writing that speech is probably not controlled equally by both frontal lobes; that is, damage to the left frontal lobe is more likely to cause a loss of fluent speech. Broca, however, was not the first person to recognize what we now call cerebral dominance. Marc Dax, a doctor from southern France, had written a paper on speech and the left hemisphere for presentation at a regional congress in 1836. But, as Broca found out after making his own inquiries, there was no concrete evidence to prove that Dax actually presented his paper in public. In fact, his short but insightful paper remained unknown until it was sent to Paris in 1863 by his son Gustave. It arrived at about the same time as Broca was recognizing something remarkable about the lesions in his own patients, and it was eventually published in 1865, the same year as Broca's paper on cerebral dominance.

In addition to arguing for a cortical center for articulate language in the frontal lobes, Paul Broca raised the possibility that the frontal lobes may serve other executive or intellectual functions, including judgment, reflection, and abstraction. The broader role for the frontal lobes, based on neurology, neuroanatomy, and comparative anatomy, was welcomed by the localizationists, who were trying to explain why some people with very large skulls could still be deficient in intellect, whereas others with merely average-sized skulls could be geniuses. In the 1870s, Broca noted that many recently unearthed Cro-Magnon specimens had cranial capacities that far exceeded those of the nineteenth-century Parisians who were studying them. The great size of the Cro-Magnon craniums, he pointed out, is due to the excessive development of the posterior brain, which is not a reliable indicator of intelligence.

By this time, Broca was considered one of the world's leading authorities on the family of man. He had developed many instruments for measuring skulls and was instrumental in introducing statistical standardization to the young science of anthropology. He was also among the first to recognize manmade (trepan) openings in ancient skulls for what they were. In 1867, he had argued that an opening in an old skull given to him by Ephraim George Squire, an American cultural attaché to Peru, was made deliberately several days before the "patient" died. This skull convinced him that "advanced surgery" had been performed in the New World well before the European conquest, although the exact motivation for the operation was not clear. Broca then searched for even older skulls with trepan openings in his own country, and in this endeavor he was successful.

In 1877, Broca gave the limbic convolution its name. He recognized that it surrounds the lower edge of the cerebral hemispheres somewhat like a rim or an edge (limbus means "border" in Latin). The callosal (cingulate) and hippocampal gyri formed the two major components of Broca's limbic lobe and, on the basis of comparative studies, he concluded that it is probably involved with smell. In the twentieth century, James Papez and his followers developed the limbic system concept more fully and associated it with the emotions.

In addition to his scientific accomplishments, Broca was a great humanist and political activist. Although he lived in a society with extreme racial prejudices, he tended to be a moderate-to-liberal for the times and viewed education as the best way to improve humankind. He was elected to the French senate in 1879 but died from heart disease one year later. There he was responsible for only one memorandum, and in it he argued for opening the public high schools to women.

Bibliography

Some Papers by Broca

Broca, P. (1861). Remarques sur le siège de la faculté du langage articulé; suivies d'une observation d'aphémie (perte de la parole). *Bulletin de la Société Anatomique, 6,* 330–357, 398–407. Translated as "Remarks on the seat of the faculty of articulate language, followed by an observation of aphemia." In G. von Bonin (Ed. and Trans.). (1960). *Some papers on the cerebral cortex* (pp. 49–72). Springfield, IL: Charles C. Thomas.

Broca, P. (1865). Sur le siège de la faculté du langage articulé. *Bulletin de la Société d'Anthropologie, 6,* 337–393. Translated as "Localization of speech in the third left frontal convolution" by Berker, E. A., Berker, A. H., & Smith, A. (1986). *Archives of Neurology, 43,* 1065–1072.

Broca, P. (1873). Sur les crânes de la caverne de l'Homme Mort (Lozère). *Revue d'Anthropologie, 2,* 1–53.

Broca, P. (1877). Sur la circonvolution limbique et la scissure limbique. *Bulletin de la Société d'Anthropologie, 12,* 646–657.

Broca, P. (1878). Anatomie comparée des circonvolutions cérébrales. Le grand lobe limbique et la scissure limbique dans la série des mammifères. *Revue d'Anthropologie, sér. 2, 1,* 385–498.

Books about Broca

Finger, S. (1994). *Origins of neuroscience.* New York: Oxford University Press.

Schiller, F. (1979). *Paul Broca: Founder of French anthropology, explorer of the brain.* Berkeley, CA: University of California Press.

Stanley Finger and Daniel Roe

BRONFENBRENNER, URIE (1917–), American psychologist. Although born in Moscow in 1917, at the age of 6 Bronfenbrenner came to the United States with his mother to join his father, a physician who was a research pathologist at Letchworth Village, a state institution for the feebleminded in New York. A precocious student, Bronfenbrenner graduated from high school in Haverstraw, New York, in 1934 and entered Cornell University that same year where he completed a double major in psychology and music in 1938. Following graduation from Cornell, Bronfenbrenner went to Harvard where he finished his master's degree in developmental psychology, then went to the University of Michigan where he completed his doctorate in 1942. The day after completing his degree, Bronfenbrenner was inducted into the Army.

World War II was an important experience for Bronfenbrenner, as it was for many of those who later went on to lead American psychology. During the war, Bronfenbrenner had the opportunity to work with Edward C. Tolman, Neal Miller, John Dollard, Kurt Lewin, Nicholas Hobbs, and John Murray, to name a few who went on to eminence.

Following demobilization and a 2-year stint as assistant professor of psychology at the University of Michigan, Bronfenbrenner returned to his undergraduate alma mater as professor of psychology and human development and family studies. He remained at Cornell thereafter, teaching, advising, and doing research for half a century. Bronfenbrenner is best known for his seminal research contributions. It was written of him that approximately every 10 years he has published an article that has become a catalyst for a new field of inquiry. For example, Bronfenbrenner's chapter in Maccoby (1953) was the first to show the importance of historical and social change on child rearing practices. His interviews in the Soviet Union in the 1960s provided the raw material for his book, *Two Worlds of Childhood*, widely regarded as a classic in the field of cross-cultural studies. His intimate knowledge of the Soviet Union led to a series of reports on Soviet perceptions of the United States, which led to his appointment on the scientific advisory committee of the U.S. Arms Control Agency. In 1979 Bronfenbrenner published his most influential work, *The Ecology of Human Development*, which has continued to influence developmental science worldwide.

Throughout his lifetime, Bronfenbrenner has pursued three interrelated themes: (a) developing theory and research paradigms at the frontiers of developmental science; (b) laying out the implications of developmental theory for public policy (an example is his role in creating the Head Start program); and (c) communicating the findings of developmental science through lectures to students, the public, and decision makers.

One of the most decorated psychologists in America and abroad, Bronfenbrenner has been the recipient of numerous prestigious awards around the world. A short list includes the James McKeen Cattell award, a prestigious honor bestowed annually by the American Psychological Society, several lifetime career contribution awards given by the American Psychological Association, six honorary doctorates around the world, and a lifetime career award established in his own name by the Division of Developmental Psychology of the American Psychological Association, "The Urie Bronfenbrenner Award for a Lifetime Contribution to

Developmental Psychology in the Service of Science and Society." Author of over 300 articles, books, and chapters, several of which have become citation classics, Bronfenbrenner continued to maintain a vigorous schedule of writing, public speaking, and teaching well into his eighth decade. [*For a description of Bronfenbrenner's theoretical contributions, see his own entry on* Ecological Systems Theory.]

Bibliography

Bronfenbrenner, U. (1970). *Two worlds of childhood: The United States and the U.S.S.R.* New York: Russell Sage Foundation.

Bronfenbrenner, U. (1979). *The ecology of human development.* Cambridge, MA: Harvard University Press.

Bronfenbrenner, U. (1989). Ecological systems theory. In R. Vasta (Ed.), *Annals of child development* (Vol. 6). Greenwich, CT: JAI Press.

Bronfenbrenner, U., & Ceci, S. J. (1994). Nature–nurture in developmental perspective: A bioecological theory. *Psychological Review, 101,* 141–166.

Bronfenbrenner, U., McClelland, P., Wethington, E., Moen, P., & Ceci, S. J. (1996). *The state of Americans.* New York: Free Press.

Stephen J. Ceci

BROWN, ROGER WILLIAM (1925–1997), American psychologist. Born and raised in Detroit, Michigan, Brown received his undergraduate and graduate education at the University of Michigan. Except for a 5-year interlude at the Massachusetts Institute of Technology, he spent his professional career at Harvard University.

Brown's contributions to psychology fall primarily within psycholinguistics and social psychology. When he began teaching at Harvard in 1952, he was assigned to teach the courses "The Psychology of Language" and "Introduction to Social Psychology." These serendipitous teaching assignments ultimately led Brown to publish some of his most significant works, and set his career path into the field of psycholinguistics, where he would make his greatest research contributions on the acquisition of language.

Brown's approach to research was to take exciting questions, often abandoned in frustration by other serious researchers as beyond investigation, and develop new approaches to them. For example, he characterized the topics covered in *Words and Things*—from phonetic symbolism and metaphor to linguistic relativity and determinism—as "a real set of chestnuts, most of them either given up for dead, or demonstrated to be pseudo questions, or officially proscribed by scholarly societies" (Brown, 1958, p. 16).

Perhaps Brown's most lasting contribution to psycholinguistics is *A First Language: The Early Stages* (1973), in which he set out to map the acquisition of language by examining a near-exhaustive corpus of utterances from three young children. In this work he combined complex elements of grammar and semantics to describe the first stages of language acquisition.

Brown may also be credited with writing one of the most engaging and successful textbooks within the field of social psychology. Like *Words and Things, Social Psychology* (1965) was not a traditional textbook, but rather a collection of "real chestnuts" from the social psychological literature—chestnuts that Brown examined through exegesis of how the research questions came to be, why they were interesting, how they had been studied, and with what results.

Brown's other works include a collection of his papers on psycholinguistics, published in 1970. Among the 14 papers in this volume are "The First Sentences of Child and Chimpanzee," a paper comparing the linguistic capabilities of human children with those of chimpanzees, primarily the chimpanzee Washoe, who was taught the rudiments of American Sign Language. "The 'Tip of the Tongue' Phenomenon," written with David McNeill, was also in this collection. Brown and McNeill were able to induce the "tip of the tongue" state, and then discover some of the principles of what has since come to be called networks in memory storage. In "The Pronouns of Power and Solidarity," coauthored with Albert Gilman, Brown examined the phenomenon of nonreciprocal pronominal address, in which a person with greater social status is allowed to use a more familiar mode of address than a person of lesser social status. This collection also includes Brown's wonderful review of Vladimir Nabokov's *Lolita*. Although not in this collection, his 1977 paper "Flashbulb Memories," coauthored with James Kulik, has also been enormously influential in psychology.

Brown's final book came as a surprise to many of his colleagues and students. In *Against My Better Judgment*, Brown described his reaction to his companion Albert Gilman's death from cancer, and his own descent into the illusory world of young male escorts and prostitutes. Although in some ways a self-indictment, this book had a deeper message as well, about the intensity of loneliness among older gay men and the need for love that is part of the human experience.

Bibliography

Brown, R. (1958). *Words and things.* New York: Free Press. Brown's "textbook" in psycholinguistics, a work that infused many of the philosophical topics in language with a more sophisticated psychological analysis.

Brown, R. (1965). *Social psychology.* New York: Free Press. Brown's seminal textbook in social psychology, perhaps the most influential published in that field.

Brown, R. (1970). *Psycholinguistics: Selected papers.* New York: Free Press. A collection of fourteen papers, most previously published in psychological journals, divided into sections on development of a first language and psycholinguistic processes in adulthood.

Brown, R. (1973). *A first language: The early stages.* Cambridge, MA: Harvard University Press. Based on Brown's groundbreaking research in developmental psycholinguistics, this book details the early stages of language acquisition in three children, dubbed Adam, Eve, and Sarah.

Brown, R. (1989). Roger Brown. In G. Lindzey (Ed.), *A history of psychology in autobiography* (Vol. 8, pp. 37–60). Stanford, CA: Stanford University Press.

Brown, R. (1996). *Against my better judgment: An intimate memoir of an eminent gay psychologist.* Binghampton, NY: Haworth Press. Brown's sometimes shocking, but also poignant, memoir about his sexuality and his tremendous need to be loved. The memoir also sheds important light on the development of his psychological thinking, and particularly his love of psycholinguistics.

Brown, R., & Kulik, J. (1977). Flashbulb memories. *Cognition, 5,* 73–99.

J. Roy Hopkins

BRUNSWIK, EGON (1903–1955), Austrian and American psychologist. Brunswik stood at the nexus of several philosophical and psychological traditions, created his own distinctive psychology, and died without foreseeing the influence of his concepts and methods. Yet more than forty years after his death by suicide, certain of his ideas and techniques are still being explored and used.

Brunswik was born in Budapest, Hungary, on 18 March 1903. In 1923, he undertook the study of psychology under Karl Bühler at the University of Vienna. In the same period, he participated in a discussion group (led by Moritz Schlick) that gave birth to logical positivism. He was also aware of contemporary developments in psychoanalysis, especially through his future wife, Else Frenkel-Brunswik. After earning his Ph.D. in 1927, Brunswik remained in Bühler's Psychological Institute in order to continue his research in perception. Then, soon after the publication of his seminal work, *Wahrnehmung und Gegenstandswelt* (Leipzig, 1934), Brunswik met Edward C. Tolman, who was on sabbatical in Vienna, and the two of them produced an important theoretical article on "The Organism and the Causal Texture of the Environment" (*Psychological Review*, 1935, *42*, 43–77), which provided a suggestive synthesis of European cognitivism and American behaviorism. As a result, Brunswik spent much of 1935 and 1936 at the University of California, Berkeley, and moved permanently to Berkeley in 1937. He remained there until his death in 1955.

Brunswik's early perceptual research led him to develop a "lens model," positing that "distal objects" emanate energy which creates "proximal cues" on the surface, or "lens," of the organism. This "lens" transduces multiple cues into a central focus, or unified perception. In the United States, Brunswik adopted statistics to express the probabilistic implications of his thinking. (He was aware that any single cue is at best an approximate index of the object to which it refers.) After publishing "Probability as a Determiner of Rat Behavior" (*Journal of Experimental Psychology*, 1939, *25*, 175-197), he applied his new-found approach to "Thing Constancy as Measured by Correlation Coefficients" (*Psychological Review*, 1940, *47*, 69–78). This study showed that subjects can attain veridical perception, even when cues are unreliable.

An important feature of these studies was Brunswik's growing realization that behavior and perception had to be studied in more realistic ways. His next, radical step, definitive of his "probabilistic functionalism," was to study the perceptions of *one subject* within *multiple settings* in the *natural environment* (rather than many subjects in a single experimental situation). Thereafter, Brunswik advocated this new approach to psychological research, emphasizing "functional" and "ecological" validity.

"Distal Focusing of Perception" (*Psychological Monographs*, 1944, *56*, 1–49) illustrated what could come from this exacting approach. For the rest of his life, Brunswik tried to convince others of its efficacy, while further elaborating its implications. Sadly, poor health, combined with pessimism about the acceptance of his ideas, brought about the ending of his life. In a vindication of his efforts, however, the concepts of ecological validity and of the perceptual system as an intuitive statistician have inspired subsequent developments in the discipline that seemed initially to ignore his radical innovations.

Bibliography

Gigerenzer, G. (1987). Survival of the fittest probabilist: Brunswik, Thurstone, and the two disciplines of psychology. In L. Krüger, G. Gigerenzer, & M. S. Morgan (Eds.), *The probabilistic revolution* (Vol. 2, pp. 49–72). Cambridge, MA: MIT Press. An historical and conceptual study of Brunswik's place in psychology.

Gigerenzer, G. & Murray, D. J. (1987). *Cognition as intuitive statistics*. Hillsdale, NJ: Erlbaum. An extrapolation of Brunswik's notion of the perceptual system as an intuitive statistician.

Hammond, K. R. (Ed.) (1966). *The psychology of Egon Brunswik*. New York: Holt, Rinehart and Winston. The best selection of Brunswik's work, plus examples of its historical influence, edited by one of his major followers.

Leary, D. E. (1987). From act psychology to probabilistic functionalism: The place of Egon Brunswik in the history of psychology. In M. G. Ash, & W. R. Woodward (Eds.), *Psychology in twentieth-century thought and society* (pp. 115–142). Cambridge: Cambridge University Press. A historical and conceptual analysis of the basic dimensions and legacy of Brunswik's psychology.

David E. Leary

BUCCOLA, GABRIELE (1854–1885), Italian psychologist. At an early age, Buccola distinguished himself for his cultural interests. In 1873, he enrolled in the Faculty of Medicine of the University of Palermo, and during his university studies he was deeply influenced by the thought of Charles Darwin, Herbert Spencer, and Ernst Heinrich Häckel, as his volume *La dottrina e le leggi dell'ereditarietà* (1879) indicates. In particular, he believed that evolutionary theory could provide a unifying perspective for biology and psychology.

After obtaining his medical degree, Buccola dedicated himself to the study of mental illness. In 1879, he joined the Institute of Psychiatry of Reggio Emilia under the direction of Alberto Tamburini, who strongly asserted that psychiatry should be based on experimental psychology. In his work *La psicologia fisiologica in Italia* (1880), he briefly described the characteristics, methods, and problems of current psychology as well as its ties to biology and physiology. In particular, he emphasized that in order to investigate psychological phenomena empirically, the speculative obscurity of the "dreamers of transcendental philosophy" must be abandoned. The main thesis advanced by Buccola in this study, in strict adherence to the position of the French physiologist Claude Bernard, is that a theoretical distinction between normal and pathological physiological phenomena does not exist. An understanding of normal functioning allows for pathological disorders to be explained as particular instances of the very same laws operating in particular circumstances. Conversely, the study and analysis of certain disorders allows functions and phenomena to be identified that would otherwise not be as evident during their pathological intensification.

In his first psychiatric writings, *Sulle idee fisse e le loro condizioni fisiopatologiche* (1880) and *La legge fisica della coscienza dell'uomo sano e dell'uomo alienato* (1881), Buccola was inspired by English biological doctrines and the thought of Alessondro Herzen. He considered consciousness to be a function of the neuro-physiological substrate and therefore subject to the same physical laws that govern neuro-physiological processes. In his view, these considerations constituted the theoretical foundation of the necessarily complementary relationship between psychiatry and psychology.

Between 1880 and 1881, employing Hipp's chronoscope and other devices of his own invention, Buccola began a methodical series of psychochronometric experiments on normal and mentally ill subjects. In 1881, he was invited to the Psychiatric Institute of the University of Turin by Enrico Morselli, one of the first to endorse the relevance of experimental psychology research to the field of psychiatry. Here he continued his research, publishing the results in *Rivista di filosofia scientifica*, a journal founded with Morselli, which was to become an official organ of Italian positivism.

In Turin, Buccola resumed and extended the studies of the German physiologist Robert Schiff, who had introduced psychochronometric research and experimentation into Italy. He began to consider that the "temporal law"—a general principle stating that every psychic process has a certain measurable temporal duration—constitutes a fundamental principle underlying all psychic activity. He therefore initiated a rigorously systematic series of psychometric experiments that consisted of thousands of trials divided into coordinated groups of experimental themes. The importance of these experiments was that they encouraged research and experimental studies in the field of psychology, thus ensuring a rigorous and scientifically promising experimental analysis of psychological processes. This approach was incompatible with the propensity for speculation peculiar to the philosophic discipline, from which psychology sought to differentiate itself.

In the span of a few short years, Buccola had published a number of experimental papers that were collected in his main work, *La legge del tempo nei fenomeni di pensiero* (1883), as well as several studies in psychiatry. As a result of disappointing academic circumstances, however, he left for specialized training in a psychiatric clinic directed by von Gudden in Munich. He returned to Turin in order to finish several research projects and, in 1884, published a short psychometric study on color perception. Bernard Buccola had begun a paper on catatonia, as well as some experimental research on the electrostimulation of the acoustic nerve in the mentally ill, when he died on 5 March 1885, at only 31 years of age.

Bibliography

Buccola, G. (1936). *Scritti di Gabriele Buccola*. Palermo, Italy: Arti Grafiche G. Castiglia.
Buccola, G. (1984). *La legge del tempo nei fenomeni del pensiero*. Bologna, Italy: Pitagora.

Nino Dazzi

BUDDHIST PSYCHOLOGY. *See* Eastern Religions and Philosophies.

BÜHLER, CHARLOTTE M. (1893–1974), German-born psychologist. Charlotte Malachowski Bühler, a pioneer in life-span development and humanistic psychology, grappled early with questions about God that led her to study thought processes with Oswald Kulpe at the University of Munich. After his untimely death, she met and married Kulpe's associate, Karl Bühler. Charlotte Bühler completed her Ph.D. in 1918 at the University of Munich, then conducted research in Dresden on adolescent thought processes. In 1923, she moved to Vienna. The Vienna Psychological Institute, a research center concerned with practical applications, became her intellectual base for the next 15 years. There she observed infants, children, and their families; expanded her investigations of adolescent thought processes by pioneering the autobiographical method (using diaries); integrated experimental research with application; wrote for publication; and forged her major thesis: that people develop throughout the life span. She determined that infants are not simply reactive, but directed, intentional individuals who reach out to people and things and set personally selected goals as they mature. She also affirmed that developmental (maturational) age is more significant psychologically than "mental age" or "intelligence quotient." This productive period ended abruptly in 1938 when the Nazis invaded Austria, closed the Vienna Psychological Institute, destroyed research records, and imprisoned Karl Bühler for his involvement with socialist politics. Fortunately, Charlotte Bühler, who was away from Austria at that time, contacted a sympathetic Norwegian diplomat, whose negotiations led to Karl Bühler's release from prison.

In 1940, Charlotte and Karl Bühler emigrated to the United States. Here Charlotte Bühler became known for theoretical and clinical work that helped launch the Third Force and, within it, humanistic psychology. She, Abraham Maslow, and others addressed what they considered to be deficiencies in behaviorism and psychoanalysis. They lamented, for instance, the emphasis on homeostasis. Instead, Bühler and like-minded colleagues viewed homeostasis simply as a transitory state from which healthy human beings actively move, as they direct themselves toward fulfilling, self-chosen accomplishments. By mid-century, Bühler's major thesis, that people develop throughout life, became a creative point of view in developmental psychology.

Charlotte Bühler's study of flawed, yet "essentially healthy" people led her to refine her theory of lifelong development and direct its practical ramifications. According to Bühler, essentially healthy people face challenge continually as they attempt to integrate four basic tendencies: satisfying one's needs (for love, sex, ego recognition); making self-limiting adaptations (by fitting in, belonging, and remaining secure); moving toward creative expansion (through self-expression and creative accomplishments); and upholding and restoring the inner order (by being true to one's conscience and values.) Although competing tendencies may at times be difficult to reconcile, people who meet Bühler's challenge of developing lifelong tend to look beyond self and self-comfort. They opt instead for dedication to chosen values. Late in her career, Bühler honed techniques that she felt would help "essentially healthy" people make progress toward self-realization and fulfillment. She leaves a legacy in life-span development that finds echoes especially in the recent upsurge of interest in interiority and spirituality.

Bibliography

Bühler, C. (1954). The reality principle. *American Journal of Psychotherapy, 8*, 626–647. Clarifies Bühler's misgivings regarding psychoanalysis.

Bühler, C. (1959). Theoretical observations about life's basic tendencies. *American Journal of Psychotherapy, 13*(3), 561–581.

Bühler, C. (1971). Basic theoretical concepts of humanistic psychology. *American Psychologist, 26*, 378–386. Bühler's theoretical stand towards the end of her career.

Bühler, C., & Massarik, F. (Eds.). (1968). *The course of human life: A study of goals in the humanistic perspective.* New York: Springer. Contains key writings by Bühler and other humanistically oriented psychologists.

Eileen A. Gavin

BÜHLER, KARL (1879–1963), German psychologist. Trained in medicine at Freiburg and in philosophy at Strasbourg, Bühler first came to prominence as a controversial representative of the "Würzburg School" of imageless thought. His most productive years, however, were at the University of Vienna which were cut short in 1939 by his forced emigration to America following the Nazi absorption of Austria. He later taught briefly at Fordham University and the College of Saint Thomas and had a private psychological practice in California. Bühler's early work focused on perceptual and developmental problems and had a fundamentally Gestalt theoretical orientation. While never repudiating this orientation, Bühler gradually exploited and developed further a semiotic (sign-based) approach to psychology. This approach culminated in three masterful books, a veritable semiotic trilogy, written in the late 1920s and early 1930s dealing with the dialectic of methods in psychology, the nature of a philosophically and semiotically sophisticated language theory, and the scope and nature of the phenomenon of expression.

In *Die Krise der Psychologie* (The Crisis of Psychology) Bühler used the distinction between *signals, indices,* and *symbols* to thematize and relate what he considered the three autonomous object-domains and methodologies of psychological theory. Signals and signaling as a steering activity became the key to behavioral psychology, whose American analogue was the symbolic behaviorism of G. H. Mead, with whom Bühler has a deep, if unacknowledged, intellectual affinity. Indices, the key to the analysis of perception, justified a refined introspective psychology of the manifold of sensations and of the experiential phenomena of consciousness quite generally. Symbols, by which Bühler meant ideal sense-bearing structures, became the key to the historical and cultural psychology developed initially by Wilhelm Dilthey, Georg Simmel, Eduard Spranger, and others. Following Saussure's lead, Bühler taught that it was not the material reality of the sign that mattered but its sense-function or role. Bühler's approach was accordingly pluralistic and antireductionist.

The fertile semiotic distinction between indices, signals, and symbols grounded Bühler's trichotomy of irreducible language functions, schematized in his organon-model of language: the *expressive*, revealing the interiority of the speaker; the *appellative* (or conative), directed toward the behavior of the addressee; and the *representational*, whose distinctive function is to articulate in objective fashion "things and states of affairs." These functions were abstract moments, differentially weighted, read off from a concrete speech-event, the focal point of Bühler's investigations into language's many dimensionalities. Bühler was most concerned with delineating the distinctively human nature of the full-fledged representational function. This became the organizing focus of his *Theory of Language*, in which he developed his two-field theory, built around the fundamental and irreducible distinction between *deixis* (pointing) and *symbolization*. Symbolization involved a creative and selective act of abstraction. Using phonology as a heuristic clue, Bühler explored the various ways in which symbolization articulates and mediates distinctive features or relations of pertinence, including the powerful semantic engine of metaphor, which exemplifies the emergent, nonsummative nature of perception and language together. This reliance on distinctive features arrayed in fields which Bühler used to analyze expression in *Ausdruckstheorie* (Theory of Expression) foregrounds the essentially social nature of meaning-making and the exchange of signs.

For Bühler, language and other sign systems were not a form of abstract algebra, but an independent system of signifiers. It was a species of social action bound to the knowledge structures of the language users. His work is marked by an attempt to balance the psychological, the abstract, and the social dimensions of language and sign use quite generally. It is this breadth and methodological sophistication that grounds his continuing heuristic fertility for psychology and the philosophy of psychology.

Bibliography

Bühler, K. (1927). *Die Krise der Psychologie.* Reprinted with an introduction by Hubert Rohracher. Stuttgart: Gustav Fischer, Verlag,1965.

Bühler, K. (1933). *Ausdruckstheorie. Das System an der Geschichte aufgezeigt.* Reprinted with an introduction by Albert Wellek. Stuttgart: Gustav Fischer, Verlag, 1968.

Bühler, K. (1934). *Theory of language: The representational function of language.* Translated by D. Goodwin. Amsterdam: John Benjamins. Original publication: Jena: Gustav Fischer, Verlag.

Eschbach, A. (1988). *Karl Bühler's theory of language.* Amsterdam: John Benjamins.

Innis, R. E. (1982). *Karl Bühler: Semiotic foundations of language theory.* New York: Plenum Press.

Innis, R. E. (1988). The thread of subjectivity: Philosophical remarks on Bühler's language theory. In Eschbach (1988).

Robert E. Innis

BUILT ENVIRONMENTS. *See* Environment Research Design.

BULIMIA is derived from the Greek word *boulimos,* which can be translated into English as "ravenous hunger," or binge eating (Stunkard, 1993). The symptom of binge eating is referred to as bulimia, whereas the syndrome of binge eating followed by some type of compensatory behavior to prevent weight gain is referred to as bulimia nervosa. Gerald Russell (1979) is generally credited with the "discovery" of the syndrome of bulimia nervosa. Prior to 1979, there were case reports of binge eating and binge eating and purging, but Russell was the first to describe bulimia nervosa as a syndrome which was distinctly different from anorexia nervosa. Anorexia nervosa, in its modern form (American Psychiatric Association, 1994), was first described by Gull (1874) and Lesegue (1873) over a century ago. In contrast, bulimia nervosa must be considered a "modern" eating disorder.

The incidence of bulimia nervosa has increased significantly over the past thirty years (Stunkard, 1993). During the 1980s and 1990s, there was considerable controversy over the best description of clinical problems related to binge eating. In the *Diagnostic and Statistical Manual of Mental Disorders* (*DSM–III*, 1980), the American Psychiatric Association included, for the first time, an eating-disorder syndrome by the name bu-

limia. This syndrome included persons who were purely binge eaters and those who binged and purged (Williamson, 1990). The outcry of dissatisfaction with this diagnostic category led to a significant revision in *DSM–III–R* (American Psychiatric Association, 1987), and the name of the syndrome was changed to bulimia nervosa. This new eating disorder category reflected Russell's original description of bulimia nervosa, which is overconcern with body size, binge eating, and compensatory behaviors to prevent weight gain, all viewed as the central features of the disorder. The *DSM–III–R* definition did not include persons who engaged in binge eating but did not engage in compensatory behaviors, such as self-induced vomiting or laxative abuse, to control body weight.

Current Clinical Description

In response to this omission, *DSM–IV* (American Psychiatric Association, 1994) again revised the category to include two subtypes of bulimia nervosa: purging and nonpurging. As defined by *DSM–IV*, the essential features of bulimia nervosa are: (1) recurrent episodes of binge eating; (2) compensatory behaviors to prevent weight gain, which might include self-induced vomiting, misuse of laxatives, diuretics, enemas, or other medications; fasting, or excessive exercise; and (3) overconcern with body size. As an index of severity, *DSM–IV* requires that the person engage in binge eating and compensatory behaviors at least twice per week for three months to receive a diagnosis of bulimia nervosa. Furthermore, episodes of bulimia nervosa must be distinct from anorexia nervosa.

Another syndrome called binge eating disorder was considered for inclusion in *DSM–IV*. Binge eating disorder is similar to the nonpurging type of bulimia nervosa, in that it involves episodes of binge eating without compensatory behavior. Persons with binge-eating disorder do not express overconcern with body size; however, they are generally overweight. There was considerable controversy over the inclusion of binge eating disorder in *DSM–IV*, and experts in the field ultimately decided that it should be included as a "diagnostic category in need of further study."

Studies of the prevalence of bulimia nervosa have found it to affect about 1 to 2% of adolescent girls and young women (Stunkard, 1993), although less severe forms of binge eating and purging may affect another 2 to 3% of the same population. About 90% of bulimia nervosa cases occur in females, although bulimia (binge eating), as a symptom, is found equally across genders. Bulimia has been viewed as predominantly occurring in Caucasian women (American Psychiatric Association, 1994), although recent research has questioned this viewpoint (Fitzgibbons et al., 1998).

Most experts agree that bulimia nervosa is most reliably diagnosed using semistructured interviews that are specifically designed for this purpose (Kutlesic, Williamson, Gleaves, Barbin, & Murphy-Eberenz, 1998). There are a number of questionnaires that have been validated as measures of the symptoms of bulimia nervosa (Williamson, 1990), and these are often used in research studies of bulimia nervosa.

Other psychopathological conditions are often comorbid with bulimia nervosa. Common comorbid conditions include depression, anxiety, obsessive-compulsive disorder, personality disorders, and substance abuse (Wonderlich & Mitchell, 1997; Williamson, 1990). Common medical problems secondary to bulimia nervosa include: erosion of dental enamel by frequent vomiting, electrolyte imbalances, hypotension, and fainting. Diagnostic evaluations of bulimia nervosa should include psychological and medical assessments.

Etiology of Bulimia Nervosa

Binge eating is believed to be motivated by: (1) hunger stemming from dieting to lose body weight; (2) efforts to cope with stress and negative emotions; and (3) the hedonic effects of food (Williamson, 1990). Compensatory behaviors to prevent weight gain are motivated by fear of fatness. Bulimia nervosa typically has its onset during adolescence or young adulthood. The most common etiology is that the person becomes concerned about weight gain and begins to diet. Eventually, the person finds that dieting cannot be maintained, and when efforts to restrain eating are broken, binge eating ensues. Since weight gain is to be avoided at all costs, dieting is reinitiated but again broken with binge eating. This cycle persists until the person becomes obsessed with the loss of control of eating and weight gain. With fear of fatness, body image disturbances typically develop in that the person feels fat and desires to be exceedingly thin. Ultimately, the person begins to feel very fat despite being normal in body weight. Once body image disturbances and fear of weight gain develop, the person begins to interpret information related to body size in a distorted manner. Yet, because this interpretation is automatic, the person is unaware that his or her thinking is biased in favor of a fatness interpretation (Williamson, Muller, Reas, & Thaw, in press). This bias is then believed in order to maintain disturbed eating patterns, e.g., restrictive eating, binge eating, and purging.

Prevention of Bulimia Nervosa

Since eating disorders commonly begin after puberty, primary prevention programs have typically targeted young female adolescents in school-based programs (Taylor & Altman, 1997). The content of these programs has varied from lectures on the symptoms of eating disorders to discussions on the social pressures for thinness. Controlled outcome studies have generally found that prevention programs enhance knowledge of eating disorders but result in little actual change in behaviors or attitudes related to dieting and weight control. Also, there is some evidence to suggest that prevention programs which provide "how-to-do-it" information about eating disorders may actually increase the prevalence of disturbed patterns of eating.

Considering the enormous cost and human agony that is often associated with the treatment of chronic bulimia nervosa, there is considerable interest in whether early interventions might prevent the occurrence of a chronic problem. Early interventions can be viewed as a form of secondary prevention. Recent research has suggested that treatment of bulimia nervosa within the first few years of its onset may be a very effective means of preventing a chronic eating disorder (Taylor & Altman, 1997). There have been very few studies that directly targeted "recent onset" cases to test whether they could be treated at low cost with lasting effectiveness.

Psychotherapy

Two types of psychological treatment have been validated as effective therapeutic methods for bulimia nervosa: cognitive-behavioral therapy (CBT) and interpersonal therapy (IPT). CBT is based on a cognitive model that postulates that overconcern with body size is a central motivational feature of the compensatory behaviors of bulimia nervosa (Williamson, 1990). Dieting and purging are negatively reinforced by the reduction of anxiety about weight gain that is associated with these compensatory behaviors. Efforts to restrict eating and purging after binge eating are assumed to produce hunger, which in turn motivates binge eating. Also, these compensatory behaviors are believed to disrupt learned satiety, which regulates food intake. Thus, binge eating and purging result in disturbed patterns of eating, which is experienced as being "out of control." The main goals of CBT are: (1) modification of the binge-purge cycle; (2) modification of faulty attitudes and beliefs about dieting, weight regulation, body image, and social pressures related to thinness as an ideal body shape; and (3) prevention of relapse and the maintenance of behavioral and attitudinal changes. The efficacy of CBT for bulimia nervosa was established in a number of early controlled trials (e.g., Agras et al., 1983). Since these early studies, there have been many other controlled trials which have found that CBT is more effective than no treatment, behavior therapy, nondirective psychotherapy, and psychodynamically-oriented psychotherapy (Wilfley & Cohen, 1997). CBT is generally administered in outpatient therapy of about 15 to 20 sessions over a 4- to 5-month period.

IPT is based on a theoretical model which postulates that bulimia nervosa stems from disturbances in social functioning. The foci of treatment using IPT are: (1) resolution of grief; (2) modification of interpersonal disputes; (3) management of role transitions common in adolescence and young adulthood; and (4) improvement of interpersonal skill deficits. Only a few controlled tests of the efficacy of IPT have been reported (e.g., Fairburn, Kirk, O'Connor, & Cooper, 1986), but these studies have yielded support for the effectiveness of IPT for bulimia nervosa (Wilfley & Cohen, 1997). IPT is typically administered in outpatient therapy of the same duration and intensity as CBT. Studies comparing the efficacy of CBT and IPT have found that they yield comparable success rates at 6-month and 12-month assessments (Fairburn et al., 1995). An interesting feature of IPT is that it does not directly address eating or weight concerns as a part of therapy, which suggests that IPT and CBT may be affecting behavioral and attitudinal changes via very different mechanisms.

Pharmacotherapy

In many double-blind placebo-controlled studies, antidepressant medications have been validated as effective drugs for the reduction of binge eating and other symptoms of bulimia nervosa (Agras, 1997). The duration of these trials has generally been quite short, i.e., 6 to 16 weeks, and long term follow-up has not been commonly reported. Many different types of antidepressant medications, including tricyclics, monoamine oxidase inhibitors, and selective serotonin reuptake inhibitors, have been tested and found to be effective in these short-term studies. Administration of any one of these antidepressants leads to recovery in about 25% of the bulimia nervosa patients who are treated (Agras, 1997). It is common for many patients to develop intolerable side effects or to not respond to the first antidepressant medication prescribed. If the first medication is not tolerated or is ineffective, prescription of a second, different type of antidepressant can increase the rate of recovery to approximately 50%, which is comparable to the success rates reported for CBT. Many patients, however, relapse after discontinuing the short-term use of an antidepressant medication. Current evidence suggests that 6 months should be the shortest duration of an antidepressant medication trial for bulimia nervosa if lasting effects are to be realistically achieved (Agras, 1997).

Combining Psychotherapy and Pharmacotherapy

Several controlled studies have compared the efficacy of CBT and antidepressant medications as treatments for bulimia nervosa. These studies (e.g., Mitchell et al., 1990) have generally found that antidepressant medications are not as effective as CBT for reducing binge eating and purging (Wilfley & Cohen, 1997). Several studies have also addressed the question of whether the addition of an antidepressant medication enhances the efficacy of CBT, and there is some evidence that adding medication to CBT may yield some advantages, such as a greater reduction in the depression that often accompanies bulimia nervosa (Agras, 1997). Current evidence also suggests that adding CBT to a medication trial may reduce the probability of relapse after withdrawal of the medication. Thus, there is a growing consensus that CBT and antidepressant medications may be combined to yield the best overall success rates with bulimia nervosa, though there are still some questions about the optimal sequencing of these two types of treatment (Agras, 1997).

Treatment of Comorbid Problems

As noted earlier, other psychological disorders are often associated with bulimia nervosa. Common comorbid problems are: mood disorders, anxiety disorders, personality disorders, and substance abuse (Wonderlich & Mitchell, 1997). Treatment studies have often excluded persons with various comorbid disorders. If one assumes that the presence of comorbid problems might inhibit therapeutic success, then it is possible that controlled trials may overestimate the efficacy of psychotherapy. When these studies have reported changes in conditions such as depression and anxiety, they have typically reported that improvement of these symptoms covary with improvement of bulimic symptoms. Studies of the impact of comorbid psychological problems on the successful treatment of bulimia nervosa have generally failed to find that these problems significantly reduce the success rates of CBT. The one primary exception to this finding is the presence of borderline personality disorder. Several studies have found this disorder to be associated with poorer outcome in trials of CBT and antidepressant medications (Wonderlich & Mitchell, 1997). These findings suggest that if optimal results are to be expected, specialized therapy for bulimia nervosa with borderline personality disorder may be required. It is unclear whether the personality disorder should be treated first or concurrently with the eating disorder.

Treatment of Chronic Cases

Current research evidence suggests that the general course of bulimia nervosa is one of improvement, even in the absence of treatment. There are some patients, however, who have persistent problems that do not improve, even with considerable treatment. These patients often have many comorbid problems, including substance abuse, depression, and personality disorders. It is often difficult to determine which of these problems is the "primary" problem and thus the focus of treatment. These chronic patients are often treated in psychiatric inpatient settings and may have many hospitalizations, some for bulimia nervosa and others for the various comorbid conditions, e.g., suicide attempts or substance abuse. There has been very little research on this small group of patients, but current evidence suggests that health-care providers should continue to try different treatment approaches because many persons eventually respond to long-term efforts.

Summary

Bulimia nervosa was identified as a distinct eating disorder syndrome in 1979. Over the past twenty years, research studies have found that overconcern with body size is a central feature of bulimia nervosa and that dieting often leads to binge eating. Compensatory behaviors such as self-induced vomiting are motivated by fear of weight gain. Also, the pattern of binge eating and purging is believed to disturb the regulation of eating behavior. Psychological treatment research has found that CBT and IPT are effective approaches. Antidepressant medications have also been validated as an effective short-term treatment, with the combination of CBT and antidepressant medication possibly being the most effective approach for bulimia nervosa.

[*See also* Eating Disorders.]

Bibliography

Agras, W. S. (1997). Pharmacotherapy of bulimia nervosa and binge eating disorder: Longer-term outcomes. *Psychopharmacology Bulletin, 33,* 433–436.

Agras, W. S., Schneider, J. A., Arnow, B., Raeburn, S. D., & Telch, C. F. (1989). Cognitive-behavioral and response-prevention treatments for bulimia nervosa. *Journal of Consulting and Clinical Psychology, 57,* 215–221.

American Psychiatric Association. (1980). *Diagnostic and statistical manual of mental disorders* (3rd ed.). Washington, DC: Author.

American Psychiatric Association. (1987). *Diagnostic and statistical manual of mental disorders* (3rd ed., revised.). Washington, DC: Author.

American Psychiatric Association. (1994). *Diagnostic and statistical manual of mental disorders* (4th ed.). Washington, DC: Author.

Fairburn, C. G., Kirk, J., O'Connor, M., and Cooper, P. J. (1986). A comparison of two psychological treatments for bulimia nervosa. *Behaviour Research and Therapy, 24,* 629–643.

Fairburn, C. G., Norman, P. A., Welch, S. L., O'Connor, M. E., Doll, H. A., & Peveler, R. C. (1995). A prospective study of outcome in bulimia nervosa and the long-term effects of three psychological treatments. *Archives of General Psychiatry, 52,* 304–312.

Fitzgibbons, M. L., Spring, B., Avellone, M. E., Blackman, L. R., Pingitore, R., & Stolley, M. R. (1998). Correlates of binge eating in Hispanic, Black, and White women. *International Journal of Eating Disorders, 24,* 43–52.

Gull, W. W. (1874). Anorexia nervosa. *Transactions of the clinical society of London, 7,* 22–28.

Kutlesic, V., Williamson, D. A., Gleaves, D. H., Barbin, J. M., & Eberenz-Murphy, K. P. (1998). The interview for diagnosis of eating disorders IV: Application of DSM-IV diagnostic criteria. *Psychological Assessment, 10,* 41–48.

Lacey, J. H. (1983). Bulimia nervosa, binge eating, and psychogenic vomiting: A controlled treatment study and long-term outcome. *British Medical Journal, 286,* 1609–1613.

Lesegue, E. C. (1873). De l'anorexie hysterique. *Archives of General Medicine, 21,* 385–403.

Mitchell, J. E., Pyle, R. L., Eckert, E. D., Hatsukami, D., Pomeroy, C., & Zimmerman, R. (1990). A comparison study of antidepressants and structured intensive group psychotherapy in the treatment of bulimia nervosa. *Archives of General Psychiatry, 47,* 149–157.

Russell, G. F. M. (1979). Bulimia nervosa: An ominous variant of anorexia nervosa. *Psychological Medicine, 9,* 429–448.

Stunkard, A. J. (1993). A history of binge eating. In C. G. Fairburn & G. T. Wilson (Eds.), *Binge eating: Nature, assessment, and treatment* (pp. 15–34). New York: Guilford Press.

Taylor, C. B., & Altman, T. (1997). Priorities in prevention research for eating disorders. *Psychopharmacology Bulletin, 33,* 413–417.

Wilfley, D. E. and Cohen, L. R. (1997). Psychological treatment of bulimia nervosa and binge eating disorder. *Psychopharmacology Bulletin, 33,* 437–454.

Williamson, D. A. (1990). *Assessment of eating disorders: Obesity, anorexia, and bulimia nervosa.* New York: Pergamon Press.

Williamson, D. A., Muller, S. L., Reas, D. L., & Thaw, J. E. (in press). Cognitive bias in eating disorders: Implications for theory and treatment.

Wonderlich, A. and Mitchell, J. E. (1997). Eating disorders and comorbidity: Empirical, conceptual, and clinical implications. *Psychopharmacology Bulletin, 33,* 381–390.

Donald A. Williamson

BULLYING. An individual is being bullied or victimized when he or she is exposed, repeatedly and over time, to negative actions on the part of one or more other individuals (Olweus, 1993). It is a negative action by which someone intentionally inflicts or attempts to inflict injury or discomfort upon another individual (by physical contact, by words, or in more indirect and subtle ways); bullying is thus a form of aggressive behavior. The term *bullying* also assumes an imbalance in strength, an asymmetric power relationship: The individual who is exposed to the negative actions has difficulty defending himself or herself. Further, bullying often occurs without apparent provocation. This definition makes it clear that bullying, at least in more serious cases, can be considered a form of abuse by peers. What sets it apart from other forms of abuse, such as child abuse and wife or partner abuse, is chiefly the context in which it occurs and the relationship characteristics of the interacting parties. Here the focus is on bullying among schoolchildren—the kind of bullying that has been researched most extensively so far.

Prevalence

Large-scale surveys in Scandinavia have found that at least 15% of the students in elementary and junior high schools have been involved in bully/victim problems with some regularity—either as bullies, victims, or both. Some 9% were victims, and approximately 7% bullied other students, whereas less than 2% were both victim and bully. Some 5% of the students were involved in more serious bullying (as bully, victim, or both), occurring once a week or more.

Most of the bullying occurred among students at the same grade level, but many children and adolescents were bullied by students in higher grades. In the majority of cases, the victim was harassed by a group of two or three students, but a considerable proportion of victims reported being bullied by a single student. More boys than girls bullied others, and a relatively large percentage of girls reported that they were mainly bullied by boys. Also, a somewhat higher percentage of boys were victims of bullying. Bullying with physical means was less common among girls; girls typically used more subtle and indirect ways of bullying, such as slandering, spreading of rumors, and intentional exclusion from the group.

Similar data collected in other countries, including the United States, Canada, England, Japan, and Australia, indicate that bully/victim problems also exist outside Scandinavia and with similar or usually somewhat higher prevalence rates.

Common Myths

Several common conceptions about the causes of bullying have failed to receive support in empirical studies. Two such myths are, first, that the prevalence of bully/victim problems increases in proportion to class size or school size; and, second, that students with some form of external deviation, such as overweight, red hair, or glasses, are more likely to become victims. Accordingly, one must search for other factors to find the origins of these problems. The available research evidence suggests that personality characteristics and typical reaction patterns, in combination with physical strength or weakness in the case of boys, are important for the development of these problems in individual students. At the same time, other factors, such as teachers' attitudes and behavior, play a major role in determining the extent to which the problems will manifest themselves in a larger unit such as a classroom or a school.

Characteristics of Victims and Bullies

The typical passive and submissive victims are more anxious, insecure, and sensitive than students in general and tend to suffer from low self-esteem. They are not aggressive or teasing in their behavior, however, and one cannot explain the bullying as a consequence of the victims themselves being provocative to their peers. If the victims are boys, they are likely to be physically weaker than boys in general. In summary, the typical victims are characterized by an anxious and submissive reaction pattern combined (in the case of boys) with physical weakness. There are good reasons to believe that characteristics of this kind are both a cause and a consequence of the victimization. Negative long-term effects of persistent victimization in the form of increased depression and poor self-esteem have also been documented in a follow-up study of former school victims and their nonvictimized peers in young adulthood. Another smaller group of victims, the provocative victims, are characterized by a combination of both anxious and aggressive reaction patterns.

Besides being aggressive toward their peers, Typical bullies, also tend to be aggressive toward adults, both teachers and parents, They are often characterized by impulsivity and a strong need to dominate others in a negative way. They have little empathy with victims of bullying. If they are boys, they are likely to be physically stronger than boys in general and then the victims in particular. Little or no empirical support has been found for the common assumption that bullies are basically insecure individuals under a tough surface. In summary, the typical bully can be described as having an aggressive reaction pattern combined, in the case of boys, with physical strength.

Bullying can also be viewed as a component of a more generally antisocial and rule-breaking (conduct-disordered) behavior pattern. As would be expected from such a view, follow-up data have shown that former school bullies tended to be more involved in various externalizing problem behaviors such as criminality and alcohol abuse in young adulthood (age 24).

Group Mechanisms

When several students jointly engage in bullying another student, certain group mechanisms are likely to be at work. Several such mechanisms have been discussed, for example, social contagion and diffusion of responsibility.

Intervention

The first large-scale intervention project was initiated as part of a nationwide campaign against bullying in Norwegian schools in 1983. A school-based intervention program was implemented in 42 primary and junior high schools in the city of Bergen (Olweus, 1993). The 2,500 students involved in the project were followed over a period of 2½ years. The results were quite positive, indicating a 50 to 70% reduction in bully/victim problems. There were also reductions in general antisocial behavior such as vandalism, fighting, and truancy and positive effects with regard to the social climate of the schools. The intervention program is built on a limited set of key principles that have been been "translated" into a number of specific measures to be used at the school, class, and individual levels. Explanations of the positive results of the program have focused on a change of the opportunity and reward structures for bullying behavior (resulting in fewer opportunities and rewards for bullying), among other factors.

The basic approach implied in this project was evaluated in another large-scale study conducted in England (Smith & Sharp, 1994). In this project, comprising 23 schools, the results were quite positive. The Norwegian antibullying program is now in use or in the process of being implemented in a considerable number of schools in Europe and North America.

A Historical Glimpse

Although bullying among schoolchildren is a very old and well-known phenomenon, only recently was it made the object of more systematic research. The first large-scale study of the problem was conducted in the early 1970s on a Swedish sample of 900 boys and published as a book in 1973; a slightly modified English version of this book appeared in 1978 under the title *Aggression in the Schools: Bullies and Whipping Boys* (Olweus, 1978). For many years, the interest in bullying problems was largely confined to Scandinavia. In the 1980s and early 1990s, however, bullying among schoolchildren has attracted considerable attention and has become a pressing social issue in countries such as Scotland, England, Ireland, Japan, and the Netherlands. The late 1990s, saw clear indications of an increasing societal, as well as research, interest into bully/victim problems in several parts of the world, including the United States.

Bibliography

Farrington, D. (1993). Understanding and preventing bullying. In M. Tonry (Ed.), *Crime and justice: A review of research* (Vol. 17, pp. 348–458). Chicago: University of Chicago Press. This is a comprehensive research-oriented review of the area.

Journal of Emotional and Behavioral Problems (1996), 5 (1). This special issue on bullying features nontechnical and relatively "popular" articles focusing on the bullying experience, research on bullying, and building positive youth cultures.

Olweus, D. (1978). *Aggression in the schools: Bullies and whipping boys.* Washington, DC: Hemisphere Press. Based on Olweus, D. (1973). *Hackkycklingar och översittare. Forskning om skolmobbning.* Stockholm: Almqvist & Wicksell.

Olweus, D. (1993). *Bullying at school: What we know and what we can do.* Oxford, England: Cambridge, Blackwell. This book has been published in some fifteen different languages. It gives an overview of the research-based knowledge about bullying and describes in some detail the intervention program mentioned in the article.

Olweus, D. (1994). Annotation: Bullying at school: Basic facts and effects of a school based intervention program. *Journal of Child Psychology and Psychiatry, 35,* 1171–1190.

Olweus, D. (1996). *The Olweus Bully/Victim Questionnaire* (Rev ed.) University of Bergen, Norway. This questionnaire (originally created in 1983) for the measurement of various aspects of bullying among schoolchildren has been used in a number of international studies and is available in several different languages. It can be ordered from the author at the Research Center for Health Promotion (HEMIL), Christies gate 13, N-5015 Bergen, Norway.

Perry, D. G., Kusel, S. J., & Perry, L. C. (1988). Victims of peer aggression. *Developmental Psychology, 24,* 807–814. One of the first systematic studies of victimization problems in the United States, this study uses a peer nomination technique for the identification of victims and aggressors.

Ross, D. M. (1996). *Childhood bullying and teasing: What school personnel, other professionals, and parents can do.* Alexandria, VA: American Counseling Association. This gives a detailed overview of the problem and various measures of intervention and contains an annotated bibliography of resource materials (mainly books and videos).

Skinner, A. (1992). *Bullying: An annotated bibliography of literature and resources.* London: Youth Work Press.

Smith, P. K., & Sharp, S. (Eds.). (1994). *School bullying: Insights and perspectives.* London: Routledge. This book describes in some detail the English intervention project mentioned in the article.

South Carolina Educational Television. (1995). *Bullying* [Videotape]. (Available from South Carolina Educational Television, P. O. Box 11000, SC 29211). This videotape portrays scenes from the everyday lives of four bullied children. It is modeled on the video used in the Norwegian intervention program described in the article.

Dan Olweus

BURN-OUT. *See* Job Stress.

BUROS MENTAL MEASUREMENTS YEARBOOK.

First published in 1938 by its founder, Oscar Krisen Buros (1905–1978), the *Buros Mental Measurements Yearbook* is recognized internationally as the premier resource for independent scholarly evaluations of all commercially published psychological and educational tests. The series is now in its thirteenth edition and is published by the Buros Institute of Mental Measurements, housed in the Department of Educational Psychology at the University of Nebraska–Lincoln. James C. Impara and Barbara S. Plake edited the thirteenth edition.

Dubbed "the *Consumer Reports* of the testing industry," the central mission of the *Mental Measurements Yearbook* series is to provide its readers with comprehensive and objective information pertaining to assessment instruments. The centerpiece of each test entry in the yearbook is one or more scholarly reviews of the instrument, written by a scholar with specialized expertise in the area or areas addressed by each test. Test reviewers are completely independent of the test publisher for the instrument they are reviewing and thus are in a position to provide unbiased evaluations. Reviews typically examine the psychometric quality of a test, including its norming sample, reliability, validity, research history, and professional usage. Information is also given on the test's title, authors, publisher, price, populations for which the test is intended, stated purposes of the test, publication data, any acronyms by which the test is known (e.g., the third edition of the Wechsler Intelligence Scale for Children is referred to as the WISC-III), descriptions of scores produced by the test, whether any alternate forms or special editions are available, and how long it typically takes to administer the test.

Each edition of the *Mental Measurements Yearbook* reviews instruments and editions of tests that have come on the market since the publication of the prior yearbook. As such, each edition of the yearbook builds on the prior editions but does not duplicate them. To help bridge the multiyear time gaps between the publication of each new yearbook, the Buros Institute of Mental Measurements also publishes a supplement that includes reviews of tests published since the last yearbook. Cumulatively, thousands of reviews have been published in the yearbook series since its inception, with the latest edition including over 350.

Test reviews and entries can be located in the yearbook by using a variety of indices, including those arranged according to the test's title, acronym, authors, reviewers, scores, and subject matter. The latter index is divided into 18 different subject areas: achievement, behavior assessment, development, education, English, fine arts, foreign languages, intelligence and scholastic aptitude, mathematics, miscellaneous, neuropsychological, personality, reading, science, sensory-motor, social studies, speech and hearing, and vocations. Electronic access to yearbook test reviews, beginning with the ninth edition, can also be obtained on a CD-ROM SilverPlatter titled *The Mental Measurements Yearbook* (updated semi-annually), available from SilverPlatter (Norwood, MA).

Since the *Buros Mental Measurements Yearbook* was moved to the Department of Educational Psychology at the University of Nebraska–Lincoln in 1979, the Buros Institute of Mental Measurements has expanded dramatically. The result has been both the continuation of existing publications and the creation of new ones.

Among the most important of the continuing volumes has been *Tests in Print*, which is now in its fifth edition and contains detailed information on more than 4,000 tests currently in print. A typical entry includes a brief description of an instrument and its intended use, information detailing those populations for whom the instrument was developed, administration and scoring procedures, a reference list of professional literature citing articles relevant to the instrument, which versions of the instrument are available and their respective prices, and the name of the test publisher. Among the most important characteristics of *Tests in Print* is that it is cumulative, with the fifth edition providing a cross-referencing system that allows users to locate test reviews for instruments published in the *Mental Measurements Yearbook*.

Beginning in the early 1980s, the Buros Institute began offering the Buros-Nebraska Symposium on Measurement and Testing, a national forum addressing a broad variety of important contemporary issues relating to assessment. The proceedings of each symposium were subsequently published in a series of Buros volumes. Among the topics addressed by the Buros-Nebraska Symposium have been family assessment, curriculum-based measurement, multicultural assessment, computer-based testing and the decision-making process, the influence of cognitive psychology on testing, teacher training in measurement and assessment skills, and licensure testing. Most recently, the Buros Institute has added the *Buros Desk Reference* series to its collection. Each volume in this series highlights a specialized area of assessment and the instruments used most frequently by practitioners and researchers in that area. Generally encompassing between 100 and 125 tests, *Desk Reference* volumes feature descriptive information and the most recent reviews from the *Mental Measurements Yearbook* for each instrument identified. Thus far, two publications have been produced in this series. One addresses psychological assessment in the schools and the other the assessment of substance abuse.

In 1994, the Buros Institute of Mental Measurements was subsumed by the Oscar and Luella Buros Center for Testing. This testing center extended the traditional Buros mission of publishing assessment-related books to include a more service-oriented focus. Specifically, the Buros Institute for Assessment Consultation was created to add an outreach function to the center. Through this addition to the Buros Center, outside agencies and individuals can contract with Buros faculty and staff for professional assistance with complex and pressing assessment problems. To date, consultation services have been offered to schools, state education and certification agencies, and private industry.

Bibliography

Conoley, J. C., & Werth, E. (Eds.). (1995). *Family assessment*. Lincoln, NE: Buros Institute of Mental Measurements. One of the volumes to emerge from the Buros-Nebraska Symposium on Measurement and Testing.

Impara, J. C., Murphy, L. L., & Conoley, J. C. (Eds.). (1994). *Buros desk reference: Psychological assessment in the schools*. Lincoln, NE: Buros Institute of Mental Measurements. A good example of the *Desk Reference* publication produced by Buros.

Impara, J. C., & Plake, B. S. (Eds.). (1998). *Thirteenth mental measurements yearbook*. Lincoln, NE: Buros Institute of Mental Measurements. Latest edition of the *Mental Measurements Yearbook*.

Izard, J. (1995). *Tests in print IV*: An index to tests, test reviews, and the literature on specific tests. *Journal of Educational Measurement, 32*, 320–322. Details the purpose and history of the *Tests in Print* series.

Jordan, R. P. (1996, March). *Searching for information on tests: Reference sources and a search strategy*. (Iowa Testing Programs Occasional Papers No. 38). Iowa City, IA: University of Iowa Testing Programs. Provides an illustration of how to use a variety of sources, including products from the Buros Institute of Mental Measurements, to locate published and unpublished tests.

Murphy, L. L., Impara, J. C., & Plake, B. S. (Eds.). (1999). *Tests in print V*. Lincoln, NE: Buros Institute of Mental Measurements. Latest edition of the *Tests in Print* series.

Plake, B. S., Conoley, J. C., Kramer, J. J., & Murphy, L. L. (1991). The Buros Institute of Mental Measurements: Commitment to the tradition of excellence. *Journal of Counseling and Development, 69*, 449–455. Describes the expanded mission of the Buros Institute of Mental Measurements and provides an overview of its history.

Sireci, S. G. (1997). The Twelfth Mental Measurements Yearbook. *Journal of Educational Measurement, 34*, 187–190. Provides a review of the twelfth edition of the *Mental Measurements Yearbook*, which was published in 1995.

Sodowsky, G. R., & Impara, J. C. (Eds.). (1996). *Multicultural assessment in counseling and clinical psychology*. Lincoln, NE: Buros Institute of Mental Measurements. One of the volumes to emerge from the Buros-Nebraska Symposium on Measurement and Testing.

Terry B. Gutkin

BURT, CYRIL LODOWIC (1883–1971), English psychologist. Burt was the preeminent British professional psychologist from 1930 to 1950. He was renowned for his use of factor analysis in psychological testing and for studying the effect of heredity on intelligence and behavior. He taught at Liverpool University and worked for the London County Council as Great Britain's first educational psychologist, before becoming the Endowed Professor of Psychology at University College, London, in 1932. Conferred Knight of the Royal Garter in 1946, he was the first psychologist so recognized.

Considerable research has since been amassed to support Burt's central thesis that cognitive ability is the result of genetic endowment. During Burt's lifetime, few dissented from his view that general cognitive ability is the major determiner of social status; he identified social class of origin as a simple outcome of intelligence rather than being subject to a mediating influence of educational opportunity. His published "calculations" paralleled the findings of others.

A member of the Eugenics Society, Burt, after his death, was characterized as fascist, racist, and elitist. A newspaper reporter's exposé led to wholesale rejection of Burt's work and reputation. Leslie Hearnshaw persuasively documented how Burt's analyses relied on fabricated data "collected by non-existent research-assistants. . . . [N]either Burt nor any of his alleged assistants carried out any field work after 1955 and it is probably that all his data [were] collected prior to his retirement in 1950 [or] prior to the second World War" (Hearnshaw, 1979, p. 239). Burt falsely claimed that he had measured the intelligence of 53 pairs of monozygotic twins, separated in infancy and reared apart, reporting correlations among these twins demonstrating that intelligence was largely under genetic control. He also asserted himself to be the originator of several cornerstone equations in correlational statistics, as well as foundational principles in factor analysis (supplanting the contribution of his former teacher and senior colleague, Charles Spearman). The British Psychological Society General Council (BPS) accepted Hearnshaw's finding that Burt was a "scientific fraud."

Joynson (1989) and Fletcher (1987, 1991)—apologists campaigning for Burt's rehabilitation—posited Hearnshaw and "other enemies" (for example, Leon Kamin and Donald D. Dorfman) as "guilty of selective reporting." In 1992, the BPS determined that BPS no longer had "a corporate view on the truth of allegations concerning Burt . . . despite [not having] looked at the evidence and come up with a different conclusion" (BPS, 1992, p. 147). Essentially, BPS stated that since they had not conducted a formal inquiry, their charter did not allow them to issue a finding.

To understand Cyril Burt is difficult without recognizing the social and political conditions that shaped Great Britain in the mid-twentieth century. Both before and after World War II, one of the chief arguments of eugenicists was that national intelligence was declining because of poor breeding-control—an explanation supported by Burt's linking of intelligence and genetic inheritance. Stratification of educational opportunities (and, consequently, eventual employment and economic independence) was driven by powerful political and economic pressures. Postwar Great Britain's educational infrastructure was reeling from economic stringency and constraints; policymakers leaned on the status quo as a means for maintaining the very social security threatened by the recent hostilities of World War II. At the time, secondary educational opportunity was determined solely by the highly selective Eleven-Plus Examination—a consequence of the 1944 Education Act (which would not have been adopted but for Burt's influence). This led to a disproportionate number of children from Great Britain's working class being placed in vocational education tracks, with middle-class children attending academic grammar schools or being privately educated. Thus, social stratification became institutionalized as educational stratification, with a bifurcation of life's opportunities into what was called the "haves" and the "have-nots." Burt insisted that social inequality reflected a meritocracy based on cognitive ability.

Burt speculated on the relationship of social class variables—and, thus, by implication, innate ability—to poverty and undesirable behaviors, including delinquency, social maladjustment, idleness, illegitimacy, incivility, welfare dependency, inadequate parenting, and poor citizenship. He concluded that economic and social behavior were due to IQ, not socioeconomic status; he made no corrections (neither did his contemporaries) for genotype-environment interaction and the high colinearity between these variables.

Burt displayed an aristocratic demeanor in mannerism and etiquette; he used arcane language peppered with classical references regardless of his audience's understanding. He was an unapologetic elitist and a defender of all forms of status-quo stratification then practiced by "polite society." He dismissed claims that if educational opportunities were equalized, then identifiable differences between children would dissipate. An intensely private man, he maintained contact with his university colleagues, including his research assistants, through memoranda rather than personal contact.

Excepting for the crucial distinction of his fabrications, Burt's scientific rigor was comparable to his contemporaries. He was the editor/coeditor (1947–1963) of the *British Journal of Statistical Psychology*; he published at least 63 articles over 17 years in *BJSP* under his own name, with nom-de-plumes, and with imaginary collaborators, all absent independent review. At the time his statistical skills were seen as preeminent. There were few, if any, contemporaries with sufficient renown, interest, or research background to check the veracity of Burt's pronouncements. As a Fellow of the British Academy, an American Psychological Association award recipient, president of MENSA, the Charter

Patron of the Association of Educational Psychologists (1964, UK), and the holder of an endowed chair in psychology, his conclusions were fervently sought and widely accepted. Resulting from almost universal deference, his "findings" became established "truth."

While Burt was among educational psychology's forerunners in Great Britain, he was never an innovator of a significant scientific rationale. Rather, in tune with his times, he was an explanatory thinker and speculator, albeit with the reservation that his pronouncements were scaffolded upon manufactured empirical foundations. He used his role as a social scientist to formulate and justify social policy. Burt egregiously erred by dressing his beliefs with the garb of an empirically unsound database.

Bibliography

British Psychological Society. (1992). The late Sir Cyril Burt. *The Psychologist, 5* (4), 147.

Fletcher, R. (1987). The doubtful case of Cyril Burt. *Social policy and administration, 21,* 40–57.

Fletcher, R. (1991). *Science, ideology, and the media: The Cyril Burt scandal.* Transaction Publishers.

Hearnshaw, L. S. (1979). *Cyril Burt, psychologist.* Hodder & Stoughton.

Joynson, R. B. (1989). *The Burt affair.* Routledge.

Caven S. Mcloughlin

BUYTENDIJK, FREDERIK J. J. (1887–1974), Dutch psychologist. A physician by training, and a philosophical anthropologist and biologist by interest, after World War II Buytendijk became the leader of the Utrecht School of existential-phenomenological psychology in the Netherlands. During and after his medical training at the University of Amsterdam, Buytendijk specialized in physiology and biology at various European laboratories. In 1914 he was appointed lecturer and in 1919 professor of both biology and physiology at the Protestant Free University, Amsterdam. The books on animal psychology he wrote in the 1920s were translated into several languages. His interest in philosophical anthropology, physical education, and mental health resulted from his contacts with members of the psychiatric clinic of his university. His acquaintance with the German philosophical anthropologists Max Scheler and Helmuth Plessner during this period was a decisive influence. During his professorship at Groningen University (1925–1946) these contacts broadened to the whole West European community of biologically oriented philosophers and psychiatrists. He contributed several books and numerous papers to the vitalistic biophysiological ideas during this period. He kept up a lively correspondence with many of its international representatives, part of which was published after his death (e.g., he corresponded with Ludwig Binswanger, Romano Guardini, Helmuth Plessner, Erwin Straus, Erich Wasmann, and Victor von Weizsäcker).

Buytendijk's fame as a psychologist is chiefly based on his role in the existential-phenomenological movement that originated after his appointment in 1946 to the chair of psychology at Utrecht University. Some of the other members of this Utrecht School were pedagogue and child psychologist M. J. Langeveld, psychiatrists H. C. Rümke and J. H. van den Berg, applied psychologist D. J. van Lennep, personality psychologist B. J. Kouwer, and Buytendijk's most famous student and successor Johannes Linschoten (1925–1964). Typical of the new Utrecht thinking is its rejection of Cartesian dualism and the implied reductionistic natural science approach in the human and life sciences. The phenomena of human behavior and experience, and of life in general, should be understood not mechanistically but in their essence, and in the context of the life-world of the persons involved. Genuine human cognizance can only be attained in the *loving* person-to-person encounter with the other's being-in-the-world. Buytendijk's phenomenology is closer to Binswanger and Merleau Ponty's existentialism than to the transcendentalism of Edmund Husserl. As a Christian (baptized Protestant, converted to Roman Catholicism in 1937) Buytendijk rejected the nihilistic existentialism of Martin Heidegger and Jean-Paul Sartre, and felt more affinity to the Christian existentialism of the French philosopher, dramatist, and critic, Gabriel Marcel. He was deeply involved in problems of education and mental health. In his long-standing position as president of the Catholic Center for Mental Health he had a profound influence on the renewal of moral attitudes in the Catholic segment of the Dutch population. Buytendijk's most important later work includes *On Pain* (1943), his *General Theory of Human Posture and Movement* (1948), and his book *Woman* (1951), in which, as a rejoinder to Simone de Beauvoir's *The Second Sex*, he developed a phenomenology of "feminine existence." Buytendijk remained productive well into his 80s, receiving honors from many European institutions. The Utrecht School, however, disbanded soon after his retirement and the subsequent renunciation by his pupil Linschoten of phenomenological psychology.

Bibliography

Buytendijk, F. J. J. (1928). *Psychologie des animaux* [The psychology of animals]. Paris: Payot.

Buytendijk, F. J. J. (1935). *The mind of the dog*. London: Allen & Unwin.

Buytendijk, F. J. J. (1938). *Wege zum Verständnis der Tiere* [Ways of understanding animals]. Zürich: Niehans.

Buytendijk, F. J. J. (1943). *On Pain*. Chicago: University of Chicago Press.

Buytendijk, F. J. J. (1952). *Phénoménologie de la rencontre* [The phenomenology of the encounter]. Paris: Desclée de Brouwer.

Buytendijk, F. J. J. (1956). *Allgemeine theorie der menschlichen Haltung und Bewegung* [A general theory of human posture and movement]. Heidelbert: Springer.

Buytendijk, F. J. J. (1968). *Women*. Glen Rock, NJ: Newman Press.

Buytendijk, F. J. J. [Festschrift] (1957). *Rencontre/encounter/Begegnung: Contributions toward a human psychology* Utrecht: Spectrum. Contains a complete bibliography up to 1957.

Dehue, T. (1995). *Changing the rules: Psychology in the Netherlands, 1900–1985* (pp. 62–91). New York: Cambridge University Press.

Spiegelberg, H. (1972). Frederik Jacobus Johanne Buytendijk: Phenomenology in biology. In *Phenomenology in psychology and psychiatry* (pp. 281–300). Evanston, IL: Northwestern University Press.

Pieter J. van Strien

BYSTANDER PHENOMENON. Some years ago, a young woman was stabbed to death in New York City while 38 of her neighbors watched and did nothing. Shocked, the *New York Times* found that there had been numerous other incidents in which people died because bystanders failed to intervene. Bystander apathy became a national issue. The first explanations were personalistic in nature, postulating alienation or frustration-produced hostility as characteristics of those who failed to respond. Latane and Darley (1970) suggested that the real explanation for bystander inaction might exist in the social forces that acted on the crowds of bystanders. The very fact that so shocked people—that not one, but 38 people all witnessed the event and failed to help—might provide the key to understanding the phenomenon.

They suggested that three psychological processes were critical for producing bystander inaction. First was the definition of the situation effect. Many emergencies start as ambiguous events. The reactions of other people then provide evidence about how the event is to be defined. If the other witnesses do not respond to the event as if it were an emergency, then the witness takes this as evidence that they do not define the event as an emergency and adopts their interpretation. This prediction was confirmed experimentally. An individual who sees smoke leaking into a room responds to the possibility of danger by finding a building occupant and reporting the incident. However, the same incident is not reported when an individual sees the smoke in the presence of two confederates who calmly continue to work on their tasks (Latane & Darley, 1968). During interviews, the nonresponders did not seem sure how to define the situation that the smoke signaled, but seemed quite sure that it did not signal danger.

The nonresponsive confederates were intended to simulate the natural reactions of bystanders when confronted with an ambiguous event that might be an emergency. Given that in our culture it is common to display an unperturbed exterior until one interprets the meaning of unexpected events, each person who witnesses an event that might signal an emergency also views other bystanders, whose apparently unperturbed facial expressions and demeanors are read as signaling that they think, or perhaps know, that nothing really wrong is happening. Confirming this, the three ordinary respondents facing the smoke tended to fail to respond. Miller and McFarland (1987) pointed out an interesting aspect of this effect, which they called *pluralistic ignorance*: A bystander is aware that he fails to respond out of confusion, but does not realize that the others are failing to respond out of confusion, that is, does not realize that the others are failing to respond for exactly the same reason that he or she is failing to respond.

Persons writing about panic mobs have observed a similar definition of the situation effect: Initially, the crowd sits frozen in place as smoke begins to billow into the theater, then someone yells "fire." The crowd's definition of the situation shifts rapidly, and the panicked exit begins.

In a particularly interesting replication and extension of the definition of the situation effect, Ross and Braband (1973) created two possible emergencies, one signaled by a loud crash, the other by the sight of smoke. They then conceptually replicated the initial effect; they demonstrated that for either the smoke or the crash, a confederate who did not act, thus signaling a definition of the incident as no emergency, lowered the likelihood of the other participants responding. The researchers then paired the participant with a confederate whom the participant believed was unsighted. The inaction of the unsighted confederate inhibited response rates in the situation signaled by the crash, which could be heard, but not by the smoke, which could only be seen. This means that in interpreting the meaning of the confederate's responses, the respondents were carrying out quite complex calculations about what the confederate could know; specifically, because the confederate could not see the smoke, his inaction provided no information about the meaning of the smoke.

The tendency for others' actions or inactions to affect the way that an individual defines the meaning of jointly witnessed physical events is called *the definition of the situation effect*. It is highly similar to Asch's (1940) interpretation of conformity as not so much involving a change in the judgment of an object as a change in the categorization of the object, "a change in the object of judgment."

The second psychological process accounting for bystander effect occurs even when it is clear that the witnessed event is an emergency. When one knows that many other individuals are also witnessing an emergency, the felt responsibility for any one individual to intervene is lessened. This is known as the *diffusion of responsibility effect*. Testing for this effect, Darley and Latane (1968) created a situation within a group of two to six people communicating with each other over an intercom system, in which one participant, a confederate, slipped into a fit or seizure and called for help. They found that 85% of the respondents who thought they were the only one to overhear an emergency intervened, whereas less than one third of those who thought the emergency was overheard by four other people intervened. Others have replicated this effect and extended it. Bickman (1971) demonstrated that it was not simply the number of other witnesses to the emergency that determined helping rates, but the number of witnesses who were available to help.

Either when deciding on the meaning of an ambiguous event or in deciding on whether to intervene, the presence of other people generally raises the costs of the possible intervention behaviors. Displaying uncertainty or confusion to others is embarrassing, and similar feelings of embarrassment or inadequacy are risked when a person intervenes in an emergency in front of a witnessing crowd. These *audience inhibition effects* are the third psychological process relevant to bystander intervention, and illustrate how all three processes can cascade to produce inhibition of responding. The postulated processes have generally been confirmed as causes of bystander interaction in other studies (for a review, see Latane & Nida, 1981).

Bystander-intervention research studies the reactions of individuals to suddenly arising, unexpected events that may be or are emergencies. It is, therefore, a subset of what psychologists now call *prosocial behavior*, which also includes more considered acts of helping, such as donating to charities or volunteering for good causes. Psychologists have examined the motives for such prosocial behaviors, and a lively experimental exchange has developed about the existence of genuinely altruistic motives. Developmental psychologists have also studied the emergence of empathic concern and prosocial behavior in children.

[*See also* Intergroup Relations.]

Bibliography

Asch, S. (1940). Studies in the principles of judgments and attitudes: II. Determinations of judgments by group and by ego standards. *Journal of Social Psychology, 12,* 433–465.

Bickman, L. (1971). The effect of another bystander's ability to help on bystander intervention in an emergency. *Journal of Experimental Social Psychology, 1,* 367–379.

Darley, J. M., & Latane, B. (1968). Bystander intervention in emergencies: Diffusion of responsibility. *Journal of Personality and Social Psychology, 8,* 279–287.

Latane, B., & Darley. J. M. (1968). Group inhibition of bystander intervention. *Journal of Personality and Social Psychology, 10,* 215–221.

Latane, B., & Darley. J. M. (1970). *The unresponsive bystander: Why doesn't he help?* New York: Appleton-Century-Crofts.

Latane, B., & Nida, S. (1981). Ten years of research on group size and helping. *Psychological Bulletin, 89,* 308–324.

Miller, D., & McFarland, C. (1987). Pluralistic ignorance: When similarity is interpreted as dissimilarity. *Journal of Social and Personality Psychology, 53,* 298–305.

Ross, A. S., & Braband, J. (1973). Effect of increased responsibility on bystander intervention: II. The cue value of a blind person. *Journal of Personality and Social Psychology, 25,* 254–258.

John M. Darley